Fodor's 91
Caribbean

Fodor's Travel Publications, Inc.
New York and London

ISBN 0-679-01891-3

Fodor's Caribbean

Editors: Larry Peterson
Editorial Contributors: Carmen Anthony, Pamela Bloom, Trisha Cambron, John DeMers, Dan Dignam, John English, Nigel Fisher, Ian Glass, David Grambs, Robert Grodé, Sandra Hart, Joan Iaconetti, Lisa Kagel, Glenn Mangel, Regina McGee, Erica Meltzer, Honey Naylor, Carolyn Price, Mark Rowland, Jacqueline Russell
Research: Todd Whitley
Art Director: Fabrizio La Rocca
Cartographer: David Lindroth
Illustrator: Karl Tanner
Cover Photograph: T. Nakamura/Four by Five

Design: Vignelli Associates

Special Sales

Contents

Maps and Plans

Foreword

We would like to thank the Caribbean Toruism Association, all the island tourist boards, Jose DeJesus at American Airlines, and the people at British West Indies Airlines, and Leeward Island Air Transport for their help and support.

While every care has been taken to assure the accuracy of the information in this guide, the passage of time will always bring change, and consequently, the publisher cannot accept responsibility for errors that may occur.

All prices and opening times quoted here are based on information supplied to us at press time. Hours and admission fees may change, however, and the prudent traveler will avoid inconvenience by calling ahead.

Fodor's wants to hear about your travel experiences, both pleasant and unpleasant. When a hotel or restaurant fails to live up to its billing, let us know and we will investigate the complaint and revise our entries where the facts warrant it.

Send your letters to the editors of Fodor's Travel Publications, 201 E. 50th Street, New York, NY 10022.

Highlights'91 and Fodor's Choice

Highlights '91

The destruction brought about by **Hurricane Hugo** in September 1989 is now past history for most of the Caribbean islands that were in its path. The British Virgin Islands and French and Dutch islands survived relatively intact. The exceptions were Guadeloupe, Dominica, and—especially—Montserrat. Also hard hit were the U.S. Virgin Islands of St. Thomas, St. John, and St. Croix, along with Puerto Rico.

All the islands began an immediate cleanup and rebuilding campaign. As often happens following such a disaster, once the shock wore off, residents found themselves presented with an opportunity for a fresh start. Hoteliers, shopkeepers, and restaurateurs took advantage of the insurance monies to not only rebuild but also improve their businesses. Luckily, the historic buildings on the various islands—forts, churches, and great houses—survived quite well.

Today, a visitor to most of the effected islands will be hard pressed to find much evidence of the hurricane. The sea grapes are bushy and green, actually benefitting from the serious pruning that Mother Nature gave them, and most of the beaches are back to their beautiful selves.

Northwest Airlines now has daily service to Montego Bay, Jamaica, and Grand Cayman from New York's LaGuardia Airport. **Eastern Airlines** cancelled its Miami–Montego Bay flights in May 1990. At press time (May 1990) there are Eastern flights from LaGuardia to Montego Bay and St. Thomas. **BWIA International** stepped up its operations with 51 weekly flights to several islands from the United States and eight from Toronto. It also added service to three new BWIA destinations: Aruba, Curaçao, and Martinique.

Antigua Antigua's **Divi Anchorage,** formerly the Anchorage Hotel, will soon get much-needed renovations.

The tiny island of **Barbuda,** 30 miles north of Antigua, is set to become the new in spot for the chic international set with the opening of Italian designer Mariuccia Mandelli's **K's Place.** The 368-acre property has 24 bungalows and a rich-and-famous-only price tag of about $1,000 per night. Those of more modest means head for the **Sunset View Hotel** for about $75 per night. Day-trippers can hop on the daily LIAT morning flight over from Antigua and return on the evening flight.

Aruba The news from Aruba is hotels, hotels, and more hotels. By 1991 the number of hotel rooms on Aruba will be just about double what it was in 1989. The **Americana Aruba Beach**

Resort & Casino, on Palm Beach on the island's southwest shore, completed a $25 million renovation and expansion project in mid-1990 that refurbished the tennis courts and existing meeting space, expanded the casino and swimming pool, and added a nine-story tower with 213 new rooms and 4,500 square feet of meeting space, with squash and racquetball courts to be finished later in the year.

The **Sonesta Hotel, Beach Club & Casino,** a new 300-room, five-story atrium property overlooking the harbor from its own private 40-acre island at water's edge in Oranjestad, opened in February 1990. The hotel is the centerpiece of **Seaport Village,** a new shopping and entertainment complex that includes 85 shops and restaurants. Other hotels opening in time for the 1990–91 season include the 360-room **Hyatt Regency Aruba Resort & Casino** on Palm Beach, the **Carnicon,** the **Amsterdam Manor Beach Resort, La Cabana Beach & Racquet Club,** the **Plantation Bay Beach Resort, Ramada Renaissance, The Mill Resort,** and **Paradise Beach Villas.**

While all of this is good news for the local economy and visitors alike, inquire about construction going on around the hotel you plan to stay at. Jackhammers and bulldozers next door can shatter the tranquil mood of even the finest hotel.

Barbados   All phases of Barbados's **ABC Highway** are now complete, speeding travel from the airport to the west coast hotels and restaurants. The highway is named in honor of Barbados's most respected politicians: Tom **Adams,** Erroll **Barrow,** and Dr. H. G. **Cummings.**

In downtown Bridgetown, the new **City Centre** opened its doors, with a cluster of shops, with plenty of parking in a multilevel garage.

Bonaire   The Sonesta Hotels group took their first of two plunges into the Caribbean here (the second is in Aruba) with the 150-room **Sonesta Beach Resort Bonaire.** Completed in January 1990, the hotel has two restaurants, a private beach, a marina, a pool, tennis courts, a dive shop, and a lab.

British Virgin Islands   By mid-1990, in the wake of Hurricane Hugo, life on the British Virgin Islands was pretty much back to normal, and nearly all hotels had reopened for the remainder of the season, even as rebuilding and repair were still under way and damaged roads were being patched up.

Cayman Islands   The **Gerrard-Smith International Airport** on Cayman Brac, 69 miles from Grand Cayman, added a new terminal and a restaurant in 1990. **Cayman Airways** now has year-round service three days a week from New York's **JFK Airport** to **Owen Roberts International Airport** on Grand Cayman, with continuing service to Cayman Brac.

The newest hotel on Grand Cayman is the 306-room **Radisson Resort Grand Cayman,** which opened in the spring of 1990. The hotel, on Seven Mile Beach, has two restaurants, a swimming pool, and tennis courts. Another hotel, the 68-room **Cayman Islander,** also on Grand Cayman, underwent a total rehaul in 1990.

Curacao Among the many travelers in Curaçao in 1990 was **Pope John Paul II,** making the first-ever papal visit to the island.

The **Otrobanda** area of Willemstad, near the Cruise Line Terminal, is undergoing a renovation designed to restore its historic buildings and create more tourist facilities. The recently completed **Koral Agostini,** for one, is an 18th-century building across from the terminal and now houses restaurants, bars, a nightclub, and three shops.

Dominica The destruction by Hurricane Hugo of some 70% of the island's banana crop put a dent in Dominica's economy, but damaged roads and property have been repaired.

Dominican A major expansion underway at **Las American Internation-**
Republic **al Airport** in Santo Domingo will double the airport's ticketing, check-in, and baggage-handling facilities. At **Puerto Plata Airport** the customs and immigration clearance area is being upgraded. The international airport at **Barahona,** on the southwest coast, is expected to open this year. **American Eagle** (a subsidiary of American Airlines) now has service from Miami to Santo Domingo and Puerto Plata, and may begin service to Samana from Puerto Rico by 1991. **Victoria Air** (tel. 809/538-2541) offers scheduled flights to Samana from Santo Domingo's Herrera Airport, making four round-trips weekly, and two round-trip flights to Samana every Wednesday.

The 320-room **Flamenco Beach,** Occidental Hotels' newest Puerto Plata property, opened in 1990. The **Punta Cana Beach Resort,** on the east coast, doubled its capacity by adding 250 rooms last year. The property features an 18-hole golf course, 10 tennis courts, and a marina. Also in 1990, an 18-hole golf course was opened at the nearby **Bavaro Beach Resort.** Occidental Hotels has taken over management of the **Bahia Beach, Cayo Levantado,** and **Cayacoa** resorts in Samana, though the properties probably won't come up to international standards until 1993 or so. Previous management—the national government—had grappled with a number of operational problems. The 90-bungalow **Cacao Beach Resort & Hotel** opened in 1990 on the Samana Peninsula, west of Las Terrenas.

Like many of its Caribbean neighbors, the Dominican Republic is gearing up for celebrations of the 500th anniversary of Columbus's first voyages to America (Columbus landed on the Dominican Republic in December 1492). In honor of that event, a **Lighthouse Monument** dedicated to Columbus is under construction in the eastern end of Santo Domingo on a hill overlooking the sea. When finished it will house five museums and the marble sarcophagus containing the remains of the Great Navigator (though Cuba and Spain also claim the famous remains). The building of the $80 million lighthouse has been controversial, with opponents saying that the funds would be better used to improve the country's badly outdated infrastructure and to feed and house the poor.

Grenada In June 1990, **American Airlines** initiated daily flights from San Juan, Puerto Rico. Previously, all flights connected via Barbados. While still an option on **BWIA** (and a good one from Miami), for other areas of the United States, the American alternative is a blessing.

Elections in March 1990 brought a continuation of the National Democratic Congress (NDC) rule of the government, with Nicholas Braithwaite as prime minister. Partly because of this continuity of public officials, and a pattern of small, but consistent growth of the infrastructure, Grenada has a steady and impressive record of increased tourism. A new 14-member tourist board has been created to take charge of developing the tourism industry in the three-island nation of Grenada, Carriacou, and Petit Martinique.

It is now possible to reserve a hotel room by calling the islands' hotel reservations system from the United States and Canada (tel. 800/322–1753).

Guadeloupe A mammoth post–Hurricane Hugo cleanup effort has restored all the tourist facilities that were so badly battered by the vicious storm. As on other islands hit by Hugo, many of Guadeloupe's damaged hotels used the opportunity to not only rebuild but to remodel, spruce up, and improve their facilities. Most of the flora is lush again, and the main attraction on Guadeloupe remains the lack of commercialism and the locals' friendliness—with the exception of those who work in Pointe-à-Pitre and serve the cruise ship passenger trade.

Club Med 1, the $100 million, 617-foot sailing vessel, made its maiden voyage in February 1990. The ship, which can accommodate 425 passengers, is the largest and most technologically advanced sailing ship in the world. It offers seven-day winter cruises from Guadelopu and calls at Antigua, St. Martin/St. Maarten, Virgin Gorda, Puerto Rico, St. Thomas, and St. Barts. The **Caribbean Express** ferry service stays in waters closer to Guadeloupe, shuttling five days a week to St. Lucia, Dominica, and Martinique. The cost is some 30% less than air travel.

Jamaica The ownership of **Trident Villas** in Port Antonio is spearheading a group planning a new luxury property at San San, as well as the renovation of some of Jamaica's neglected grand dames: **Frenchman's Cove, Coblin Hill,** and the **Club Marbella** at Dragon Bay. (The pièce de résistance will be the introduction of helicopter service to these resorts from Kingston airport.)

Trident Villas is also one of the properties clustering under the banner of **The Elegant Resorts of Jamaica,** a cooperative venture of "elegant" resorts, namely **Round Hill Hotel and Villas; Tryall Golf, Tennis and Beach Club; Half Moon Golf, Tennis and Beach Club; San Souci Hotel, Club and Spa;** and the **Plantation Inn.** Under the group's **Platinum Plan,** guests pay one (hefty) price, which includes all taxes and gratuities, and then can freely go from one hotel to any of the other allied properties for a meal or a night on another part of the island.

Here in the birthplace of the all-inclusive resort are two more entries, newly minted for the '90s: **Swept Away** in Negril and **Sandals Dunn's River.** Both provide an upscale environment and offer health-conscious meals and a variety of sports activities.

The new decade is also bringing a new style to the historic Rose Hall Plantation, 11 miles east of Montego Bay. The Wyndham Hotel & Resorts purchased the plantation from the Jamaican government, spent $10 million renovating, then reopened the property in January 1990 as **Wyndham Rose Hall.** Set on 1,000 feet of private shoreline, the resort's sports facilities include an 18-hole golf course and six lighted tennis courts.

Martinique A new airline called **Key Airlines** (in cooperation with Club Med's weekly charters) began weekly direct flights from New York's JFK Airport in 1990, giving U.S. travelers an option to the usual air routes through Miami or San Juan. It is hoped that this service will become a permanent fixture.

Montserrat Hurricane Hugo did some of its worst work on Montserrat, ripping the roofs off 95% of the island's residences and leaving nearly half the population without shelter. After the storm, rebuilding began immediately. Some of the island's hotels managed to clean up the wind and water damage and limp through the 1990 season, amid occasional blackouts and fewer-than-usual visitors. Relief efforts were remarkably swift and effective, and by the spring of 1990, most hotel properties were up to full speed and anxiously awaiting the 1990–91 high season. Among those offering help was George Martin of **Air Studios'** all-star album *Songs for Montserrat,* featuring the music of some of the international rock superstars (Paul McCartney, Stevie Wonder) who have recorded in Martin's Montserrat studio since it opened in 1979. Profits from the record went to a fund to help the island's recovery. Whether because of Hugo, or other reasons, Martin has put Air Studios up for sale, so if you're in the market for a state-of-the-art recording studio in an idyllic island setting, look no further.

Puerto Rico Although Hurricane Hugo caused extensive damage to all but 11 hotels on the island, repairs were made swiftly. All of the hotels opened for the 1989–90 season, including the hard-hit **Parador Villa Esperanza** on the offshore island of Vieques.

The **Horned Dorset Primavera Hotel** opened in Rincon on the west coast in 1989. The Mediterranean-style villa complex has 26 suites overlooking the sea. The 122-room **Days Inn Ponce** opened in late 1989, a 250-room **Holiday Inn** opened in Isla Verde in late 1990, and construction began on a 150-room Holiday Inn in Mayaguez.

The $350 million **Puerto del Rey Marina and Beach Resort** is under development near Fajardo, on the east coast. The marina is the largest in the Caribbean and can accommodate 750 boats. Trafalgar PLC (parent company of Cunard Hotels) is developing the property, which will include a 325-room hotel, more than 1,000 condominium units, a golf course, tennis facilities, and beach clubs. Construction began in 1990 and will continue over a seven-year period. Also in Fajardo, the **El Conquistador Hotel** is under new ownership and in the midst of a $200 million overhaul and expansion.

In San Juan, the **Caribe Hilton International** is undergoing a $10 million improvement program. Unveiled for 1990 were a free-form pool with waterfalls and slides and a Jacuzzi big enough for 30 people. Also in San Juan, the **El San Juan Hotel** added a free-form "fantasy pool," replete with waterfalls and grottos, and surrounded by deck space for 300 people and modular tents for banquets.

Saba The pier at Fort Bay was damaged by Hurricane Hugo, but repairs were completed by the end of 1989.

St Eustatius Though "Statia" was badly buffeted by Hurricane Hugo, the island rebounded quickly. The **La Maison sur la Plage** hotel, the **Old Gin House,** and the **Golden Era,** all damaged by the Hurricane, were back to normal by mid-1990.

St. Kitts Considerable development is under way in the southeast section of the island. **Banana Bay** and **Cockleshell Bay,** which have the island's best beaches, were previously accessible only by boat but can now be reached via the **South East Peninsula Road,** which was completed in late 1989. **Sandals Resorts** of Jamaica purchased the 20-room **OTI Banana Bay Beach Hotel** and turned it into a 250-room luxury resort; it is scheduled to open in December 1990. At Cockleshell Bay, the **Casablanca Hotel** is under construction. Located on 150 acres, the hotel will eventually have 600 rooms. Phase one—275 rooms and a casino—is scheduled to open for the 1990–91 season.

The Frigate Bay area has a new hotel and condo complex, the **St. Christopher Club,** which became fully operational in March 1990. The hotel has a casino, a restaurant, and rooms with views of the Caribbean on one side and the Atlantic on the other. The **Royal St. Kitts Golf Course** adjoins the property. Also in Frigate Bay is **Leeward Cove,** a six-building hotel and condominium complex that opened in late 1989. The property fronts the Atlantic and is across the road from the golf course.

Ottley's Plantation Inn, near the village of Ottley on the Atlantic coast, opened 15 rooms in early 1990. Set on 35 acres, 520 feet above sea level, the inn occupies the great house and cottages of a former sugar plantation.

On the nearby island of **Nevis,** damage from Hurricane Hugo was severe, and though rebuilding is proceeding apace, the **Four Seasons** will not be ready to reopen until 1991. The **Cliff Dwellers Hotel** may not be rebuilt at all.

St. Lucia The waterfront town of Soufrière opened the **Soufrière Heritage Center** and launched the **Historical Architectural Walk** in January 1990. The Heritage Center, which helps preserve and restore select houses and churches, provides visitors with a self-guided walking tour of historic sites. Soufrière, near the Pitons and Sulphur Springs "drive-in" volcano, began its restoration project in 1988. The project involved restoring many of the 200-year-old gingerbread houses and buildings in the old section of town. The jetty was reconstructed for improved cruise ship and yacht mooring facilities. Construction is now under way on a marine boardwalk, extending from the jetty. Future plans include a permanent market where arts, crafts, and local food will be sold daily.

St. Martin/ St. Maarten The building boom has started in earnest on the French side of this island that never seems to tire of putting up condo hotels. One of the newest is **Alizéa,** which has already established itself as having some of the finest food on the island. Less appealing are some of the huge hotel complexes that have spoiled the view of Orient Bay.

On the Dutch side, two major projects are under way. A large docking facility at **Philipsburg** will accommodate more cruise ships coming to the island. The **Sheraton Port de Plaisance Resort & Casino** on Simpson Bay (halfway between Philipsburg and Marigot), scheduled to open in late 1990, will contain the island's largest casino, 15 restaurants and lounges, banquet and meeting facilities for up to 800 people, three swimming pools, a private marina and beach, and an 18-hole golf course.

St. Martin/St. Maarten's ever-growing popularity has brought with it the usual pitfalls of a paradise found, namely huge throngs of visitors. Traffic on the island's main roads has become what people come here trying to escape (it can take an hour to drive the 10 miles from Philipsburg to Juliana Airport during rush hour), and secluded beaches are harder and harder to find. Fortunately, there are relatively secluded beaches at the western end of the island that are still reachable only by gravel roads.

St. Vincent and Grenadines The island of Bequia, the closest of the Grenadines to St. Vincent, is building an airport big enough to handle 19-seat aircraft. Construction is scheduled for completion by the end of 1990.

Trinidad and Tobago At press time (August 1990), the U.S. State Department was advising caution to visitors to Trinidad and Tobago, following a hostage crisis in Port-of-Spain, during which several government officials were held prisoner. Although the hostages were released, the government is intact, and conditions are on the way back to normal, a nighttime curfew is still in effect, and scheduled flights out of Trinidad are erratic. U.S. citizens are urged to seek the latest information before visiting, and to register with the U.S. embassy, (15 Queen's Park West, Port-of-Spain, tel. 809/622–6372).

Turks and Caicos The Turks and Caicos remain relatively unspoiled, and the recent opening of the posh 8-room **Windmills Plantation** on Salt Cay has done nothing to disturb the even temper of the islands. The ambience is in perfect keeping with the island's understated style. Longtime T&C aficionados hope that the islands can retain their simplicity and warmth while becoming as better known as they deserve to be.

U.S. Virgin Islands The visitor to the U.S. Virgin Islands in 1991 will still find evidence of damage from Hurricane Hugo, especially on St. Croix. Although some hotels and resorts throughout the three islands had reopened by early 1990, several others stayed closed for the season, in order to rebuild, refurbish, and, in some cases, expand and improve. At press time, however, there were still a number of properties that didn't know when, or even if, they would be able to rebuild or reopen at all. Check with your travel agent, the U.S. Virgin Islands Government Tourist Office, and the U.S. Virgin Island Division of Tourism for up-to-the-minute information.

St. Thomas One of this island's elegant new properties is the **Elysian Hotel,** and its **Palm Court Restaurant,** which opened in 1990. The hotel is a complex of two-story pink buildings set on Cowpet Bay and surrounded by lush vegetation.

Two hotels scheduled for completion for the 1991 season are the 150-unit **Glitter Bay** (from Pemberton Resorts of Glitter Bay and Royal Pavilion in Barbados) and **Sugar Bay Plantation,** a 300-room property with a 1,000-seat convention center being built by Krish Hotels.

St. John In April 1990, Hyatt Hotels took over operation of the 264-room beachfront Virgin Grand Beach Hotel on Great Cruz Bay. It has been renamed **Hyatt Regency St. John.** Hyatt plans a $6 million refurbishing of the property.

Construction began last year for **Estate Concordia,** a luxury resort community owned by Stanley Selengut, developer of St. John's Maho Bay Campgrounds. Selengut intends this new resort to be a prototype of man in harmony with nature. He says he is working with the National Park Service to develop environmental guidelines of the highest caliber.

St. Croix Hurricane Hugo scored a direct hit on St. Croix, leaving
the island isolated and cut off from even its closest neighbors for several days. Few properties—commercial or
private—escaped unscathed, and even by the spring of
1990, it was questionable whether some of them would reopen at all. The cruise ship dock, which was destroyed, has
been rebuilt and will be fully operational in plenty of time
for the 1990–91 season. The rest of the island is slowly on
the mend, with a few hotels having reopened in early 1990,
and most others set to open for 1990–91.

St. Croix's **Divi Hotels** has shut down to completely renovate and rebuild. **Carambola Resorts** reopened in 1990,
with its award-winning golf course back in pristine condition. The **Tamarind Reef** has no plans to reopen. The much-
debated **Virgin Grand,** planned for construction at Salt River on land of archaeological and historical significance, has
been delayed indefinitely.

Fodor's Choice

No two people will agree on what makes a perfect vacation, but it's fun and helpful to know what others think. We hope you'll have the chance to experience some of Fodor's Choices yourself while visiting the Caribbean. For detailed information about each entry, refer to the appropriate chapter in this guidebook.

Scenic Views

El Yunque Rain Forest, Puerto Rico

Grand Etang, Grenada

The Pitons (Petit and Gros), St. Lucia

Brimstone Hill, St. Kitts

Mountain Top, St. Thomas

Governor's Coach ride (on the Catadupa Choo Choo) out of Montego Bay into the Jamaica mountains

Beaches

Magens Bay, St. Thomas, U.S. Virgin Islands

Negril, Jamaica

Las Terrenas, Dominican Republic

Seven Mile Beach, Grand Cayman

Shoal Bay, Anguilla

Petite Anse, Diamant, Martinique

Trunk Bay, St. John, U.S. Virgin Islands

Most of Antigua's 366 beaches

Diving/Snorkeling

Palm Beach, Aruba

Buck Island Reef, St. Croix, U.S. Virgin Islands

Cayman Islands (all three of them)

St. Vincent and Bequia for diving; Tobago Cays for snorkeling

Virgin Gorda, British Virgin Islands

Turks and Caicos Islands' reefs

Golf

Tryall Golf, Tennis and Beach Club, Jamaica

Mahogany Run, St. Thomas, U.S. Virgin Islands

Casa de Campo, Dominican Republic

Hyatt Dorado Beach, Puerto Rico

Mount Irvine, Tobago

Britannia Golf Course, Grand Cayman (played with a Jack Nicklaus–designed ball that goes half the normal distance)

Fishing

The waters around . . .

Little Cayman

La Romana, Dominican Republic

Puerto Rico

Caicos Island

Port Antonio, Jamaica

U.S. Virgin Islands

Parks and Gardens

St. John, U.S. Virgin Islands, national park

Parc Naturel, Basse-Terre, Guadeloupe

Washington/Slagbaai National Park, Bonaire

Andromeda Gardens, Barbados

Carinosa Gardens, Ocho Rios, Jamaica

Morne Trois Pitons National Park, Dominica

Shopping

Willemstad, Curaçao

Charlotte Amalie, St. Thomas, U.S. Virgin Islands

Philipsburg, St. Maarten

George Town, Grand Cayman

St. George's, Grenada (if just for those incredible spices)

Old San Juan, Puerto Rico

Casinos

The Alhambra, Aruba

Curaçao Caribbean Hotel and Casino, Curaçao

El Embajador, Santo Domingo, Dominican Republic

Treasure Island Hotel and Casino, St. Maarten

Cerromar Beach, Dorado, San Juan, Puerto Rico

St. James Club, Antigua

Nightlife and Bars

Mas Camp Pub, Trinidad

Silver's Country and Western, Treasure Island Beach Hotel, Grand Cayman

Hedonism II, Negril, Jamaica

Condado Beach Hotel, San Juan, Puerto Rico

Le Club disco, Mullet Bay, St. Maarten

Yesterdays, St. Thomas, U.S. Virgin Islands

Hotels

Castelets, St. Barthélemy *(Very Expensive)*

Malliouhana, Mead's Bay, Anguilla *(Very Expensive)*

Sandy Lane, Barbados *(Very Expensive)*

Trident Villas and Hotel, Port Antonio, Jamaica *(Very Expensive)*

Hotel Santo Domingo, Santo Domingo, Dominican Republic *(Expensive)*

La Belle Creole, St. Martin *(Expensive)*

Ramada Hotel El Convento, San Juan, Puerto Rico *(Expensive)*

Stouffer Grand Beach Resort, St. Thomas, U.S. Virgin Islands *(Expensive)*

Restaurants

Admiral's Inn, Antigua *(Expensive)*

Alizéa, St. Martin *(Expensive)*

Bistro Le Clochard, Curaçao *(Expensive)*

Château de Feuilles, near Le Moule, Guadeloupe *(Expensive)*

Grand Old House, Grand Cayman *(Expensive)*

La Bèlle France, Anse Marcel, St. Martin *(Expensive)*

La Cage aux Folles, St. James, Barbados *(Expensive)*

La Canne à Sucre, Point-à-Pitre, Guadeloupe *(Expensive)*

Le Lafayette, Fort-de-France, Martinique *(Expensive)*

Getaways

Mustique, The Grenadines (where you can rent Princess Margaret's house)

Southern Cross Club, Little Cayman

Captain's Quarters, Saba

Peter Island Hotel and Yacht Harbour, British Virgin Islands

Jumby Bay, Long Island, off Antigua

Golden Lemon, Dieppe Bay, St. Kitts

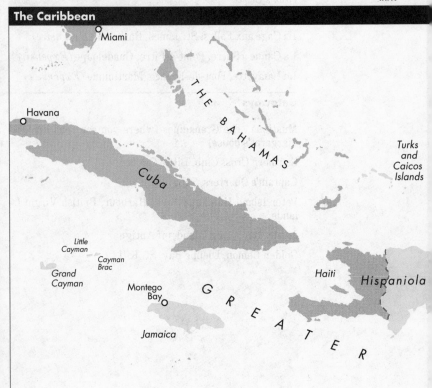
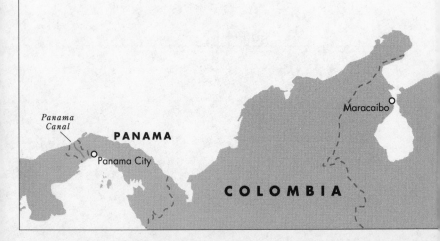

The Caribbean

Miami

Havana

Cuba

THE BAHAMAS

Turks and Caicos Islands

Little Cayman

Cayman Brac

Grand Cayman

Montego Bay

Haiti

Hispaniola

G R E A T E R

Jamaica

Caribbean

Panama Canal

PANAMA

Panama City

Maracaibo

COLOMBIA

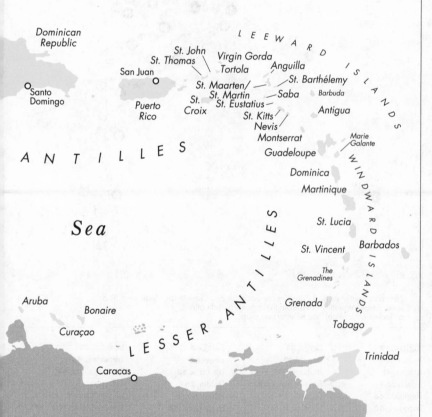

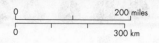

ATLANTIC OCEAN

N

Dominican
Republic

LEEWARD ISLANDS

St. John
St. Thomas
Virgin Gorda
Tortola
Anguilla
San Juan
St. Barthélemy
Santo
Domingo
St. Maarten/
St. Martin
Saba
Barbuda
St.
Croix
Puerto
Rico
St. Eustatius
St. Kitts
Antigua
Nevis
Montserrat
Marie
Galante
Guadeloupe
ANTILLES

WINDWARD ISLANDS

Dominica
Martinique
Sea
St. Lucia
St. Vincent
Barbados
LESSER ANTILLES
The
Grenadines
Aruba
Bonaire
Grenada
Curaçao
Tobago
LESSER ANTILLES
Trinidad
Caracas

VENEZUELA

World Time Zones

MONDAY
SUNDAY

International Date Line

+12 +13

-9

-10

-11

-10

+11

+12

-4

-3

25

-5 -4

-7

-6

-5 -4

-5

-4 -3

-3

-4

-3

+11   +12 -   -11   -10   -9   -8   -7   -6   -5   -4   -3   -2

Numbers below vertical bands relate each zone to Greenwich Mean Time (0 hrs.).
Local times frequently differ from these general indications,
as indicated by light-face numbers on map.

Algiers, **29**	Berlin, **34**	Delhi, **48**	Istanbul, **40**
Anchorage, **3**	Bogotá, **19**	Denver, **8**	Jerusalem, **42**
Athens, **41**	Budapest, **37**	Djakarta, **53**	Johannesburg, **44**
Auckland, **1**	Buenos Aires, **24**	Dublin, **26**	Lima, **20**
Baghdad, **46**	Caracas, **22**	Edmonton, **7**	Lisbon, **28**
Bangkok, **50**	Chicago, **9**	Hong Kong, **56**	London (Greenwich), **27**
Beijing, **54**	Copenhagen, **33**	Honolulu, **2**	Los Angeles, **6**
	Dallas, **10**		Madrid, **38**
			Manila, **57**

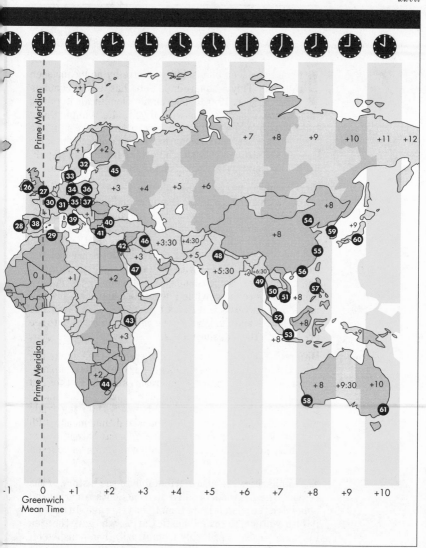

Introduction

I f you have seen one island you have by no means seen them all. Tiny 5-square-mile Saba has less in common with the vast 19,000-square-mile Dominican Republic than Butte, Montana, has with Biloxi, Mississippi. Butte and Biloxi, however different in terrain and traits, sit in the same country and the citizenry speak more or less the same language. Saba, which is Dutch, and the Dominican Republic, whose roots are in Spain, simply sit in the same sea.

The Caribbean has towering volcanic islands, such as Saba; islands with forests, such as Dominica and Guadeloupe; and some islands, notably Puerto Rico, that boast both rain forests and deserts. Glittering discos, casinos, and dazzling nightlife can be found on islands like Aruba and the Dominican Republic, and throughout the region there are isolated cays (pronounced *keys*) with only sand, sea, sun, lizards, and mosquitoes. Some islands, St. Kitts among them, have ancient forts to view, while Puerto Rico and the Caicos islands have caverns and caves to explore. There are also places like Grand Turk where the only notable sights to see are beneath the translucent sea.

Different though they are in many ways, the islands are stylistically similar. The style-setter is the tropical climate. Year-round summertime temperatures and a plethora of beaches on which to bask produce a pace that's known throughout the region as "island time." Only the trade winds move swiftly. Operating on island time means, "I'll get to it when the spirit moves me." You may hate it, or you may become addicted to it and not be able to peel yourself off the beach and return home.

The similarities are also attributable to the history of the region. The Arawaks paddled up from South America and populated the islands more than 1,000 years ago. In the early 14th century, the cannibalistic Caribs, who gave the area its name, probably from Brazil, then polished off the peaceful Arawaks and managed, for a time at least, to scare the living daylights out of the Europeans who sailed through in search of gold. (The original name of the Caribs was Galibi, a word the Spanish corrupted to *Canibal*—the origin of the word "cannibal.") Christopher Columbus made four voyages through the region between 1492 and 1503, christening the islands while dodging the Carib arrows. He landed on or sailed past all of the Greater Antilles and virtually all of the eastern Caribbean islands.

From the 16th century until the early 19th century, the Dutch, Danes, Swedes, English, French, Irish, and Spanish fought bitterly for control of the islands. Some islands have almost as many battle sites as sand flies. Having gained control of the islands and annihilated the Caribs, the Europeans established vast sugar plantations and brought in Africans to work the fields. With the abolition of slavery in the mid-19th century, Asians were imported as indentured laborers. Today, the Caribbean population is a rich gumbo of numerous nationalities, including Americans and Canadians who have retired to and invested in the islands.

It must be remembered that the Caribbean, like the European continent, is made up of individual countries, replete with customs, immigration officials, and, in some instances, political difficulties. Most of the islands/nations have opted for independence; others retain their ties to the mother country. They are developing nations, and many have severe economic and unemployment problems.

Virtually all of the islands depend upon tourism, which is an industry that moves on island time. Human nature being such as it is, many islanders are resentful of their dependency on tourist dollars. Like as not, the person who serves you has stood in a long line, vying with other anxious applicants for the few available jobs. After serving your meals and cleaning your luxurious room, he or she returns to a tiny shack knowing full well that in less than a week you will have shelled out more than an islander makes in a month. If you encounter fewer smiling faces than you anticipated, consider chalking it up to your perceived great wealth and life of leisure.

Mother Nature has endowed most of these islands with the proverbial sun-kissed beaches, swaying palms, and year-round summer. These pleasures notwithstanding, there are some who deem it overrated. They object to encountering resentment when all they seek is a pleasant vacation for which they have paid dearly. Some feel rather keenly that they'd always like hot water—or at least *some* water—when they turn on the shower; in even the most luxurious resorts there are times when things simply don't work, and that's a fact of Caribbean life. And other visitors simply have no patience for island time.

On the other hand, there are those who travel to the Caribbean year after year. Some return to the same familiar hotel on the same familiar beach on the same familiar island, while the more adventurous try to sample as much as this smorgasbord has to offer.

Defining the Caribbean

The Caribbean Sea, an area of more than a million square miles, stretches south of Florida down to the coast of Venezuela. In the northern Caribbean are the **Greater Antilles**—the islands closest to the United States—comprised of Cuba, the Cayman Islands, Jamaica, Haiti, the Dominican Republic, and Puerto Rico. (Due to the political unrest in Haiti and Cuba, they are not included in this book.) The

Lesser Antilles—greater in number but smaller in size than the Greater Antilles—are divided into three groups: The Leewards and the Windwards in the eastern Caribbean, and the islands in the southern Caribbean. The eastern Caribbean islands, from the Virgin Islands in the north all the way south to Grenada, form an arc between the Atlantic Ocean and the Caribbean Sea. Islands in the Leeward chain in order of appearance are the U.S. and British Virgin Islands, Anguilla, St. Maarten/St. Martin, St. Barthélemy, Saba, St. Eustatius, St. Kitts, Nevis, Antigua, Barbuda, Montserrat, and Guadeloupe; the Windwards are comprised of Dominica, Martinique, St. Lucia, Barbados, St. Vincent and the Grenadines, and Grenada. In the southern Caribbean, off the coast of Venezuela, Trinidad and Tobago are anchored in the east, while Aruba, Bonaire, and Curaçao (known as the ABC islands) bathe in the western waters. The Turks and Caicos Islands, which lie in the Atlantic Ocean between Florida and the north coast of Hispaniola (Haiti and the Dominican Republic), are part of the Bahamas but are included in this book because of their proximity to and affinity with the Caribbean islands.

When to Go?

"The Season" in the Caribbean traditionally coincides with winter in North America—that is, roughly, from mid-December till mid-April. But, contrary to common North American belief, the islands are not completely deserted during the summer. That's the time when the islanders themselves and many Europeans travel in the region. While the climate varies less than 10° between summer and winter, many hotels slash prices 30% or more in the summer. And Mother Nature is at her glamourous best then, with brilliant flamboyant trees, as well as other spectacular tropical plants that bloom from summer till fall.

You will find it easier to rent a car and to make hotel and restaurant reservations in summer; easier, that is, if the facilities are open. Many hotels and restaurants close during August and September or have limited facilities; some are also closed in October. They close to renovate, to rest . . . and to wait out the season for hurricanes and tropical depressions, which are most likely to occur between June and October. Storms such as Hurricane Gilbert in 1988 and the even nastier Hugo in 1989 can wreak great havoc.

Finding Your Own Place in the Sun

The glory of the Caribbean, aside from the guaranteed qualities of warm sun and warm sea, is that no one island is exactly like another, so that they cater to a variety of tastes. What follows is a list of the Caribbean islands broken down by their specialties. The French islands, for example, have in common fine wine and cuisine, but each has its own special appeal.

Luxury Resorts A wealth of posh resorts await those who seek comfort in the lap of luxury. **Anguilla,** rapidly becoming one of the Caribbean's most popular destinations, has the dazzling Malliouhana, the Coccoloba, and the Moroccan-style Cap Juluca. **Antigua's** elegant Curtain Bluff has a long list of well-heeled repeat guests. On **St. Lucia,** the deluxe lodgings are Cunard La Toc and La Toc Villas. On French St. Martin, La Samanna is a favorite hideaway of the rich and/or famous, and La Belle Creole is a re-creation of a Mediterranean village, replete with a village square and opulent villas. For the ultimate in luxurious privacy, the **British Virgin Islands** has the Peter Island Resort and Yacht Club on its own 1,300-acre private island. Castelets on **St. Barts** draws worldly personalities to its intimate setting. And Caneel Bay Resort on **St. John, U.S. Virgin Islands,** which has six beaches, takes up 170 acres of the Virgin Islands National Park.

Casinos and Nightlife You can flirt with Lady Luck until the wee small hours in the dazzling casinos of Santo Domingo, **Dominican Republic;** San Juan, **Puerto Rico; St. Maarten;** and **Curaçao. Aruba** is loaded with lively night places, and San Juan's glittering floor shows are legendary. The merengue, born in the **Dominican Republic,** is exuberantly danced everywhere on the island. Both **Guadeloupe** and **Martinique** claim to have begun the beguine, and on both islands it is danced with great gusto.

Getting Away from It All If you're looking to back out of the fast lane, you can park at one of the secluded, Spartan mountain lodges on **Dominica,** which is one of the friendliest islands in the Caribbean. Or opt for the quiet grandeur of a renovated sugar plantation on **Nevis,** where you can feast in an elegant dining room or enjoy a barbecue on the beach. Tranquil **Anguilla,** with soft white beaches nudged by gin-clear water, offers posh resorts as well as small, inexpensive, locally owned lodgings. From the low-key **Turks and Caicos Islands,** which lie in stunning blue-green waters, you can boat to more than a score of isolated cays where the term "low key" sounds too fast-paced. **St. Kitts** is another peaceful green oasis with lovely beaches and upscale accommodations in the bargain. **St. Lucia** offers a plethora of places, from the simple to the simply elegant, for "liming" (we call it "hanging out"), the local favorite pastime. On tiny **Saba** there is little to do but tuck into a small guest house, admire the lush beauty of the island, and chat with the friendly Sabans. Nearby **St. Eustatius** is another friendly, laid-back island, as is **Montserrat.**

Foreign Culture

African   **Trinidad** moves with the rhythm of Calypso and is the stomping ground of a flatout, freewheeling Carnival that rivals the pre-Lenten celebrations in Rio and New Orleans. The Trinidadians, whose African heritage has been augmented by many Asian races, have built up the most prosperous commercial center in the Caribbean. Politically volatile Haiti is not included in this book, but exotic and unique Haitian artwork is prominently displayed throughout the Caribbean.

British   **St. Kitts** is known as the Mother Colony of the West Indies; it was from here that British colonists were dispatched in the 17th century to settle Antigua, Barbuda, Tortola, and Montserrat. If you're a history buff, you won't want to miss Nelson's Dockyard at **Antigua's** English Harbour or the hunkering fortress of Brimstone Hill on St. Kitts. Sports fans who understand the intricacies of cricket can watch matches between **Nevis** and St. Kitts teams. And the waters around Antigua and the **British Virgin Islands** are a mecca for serious sailors.

Dutch   **Saba, St. Eustatius, St. Maarten, Bonaire,** and **Curaçao** all fly the Dutch flag, but there the similarity ends. Saba is a tiny volcanic island known for its beauty, its friendly inhabitants, and its gingerbread-trimmed houses. Curaçao's colorful waterfront shops and restaurants are reminiscent of Amsterdam. Quiet St. Eustatius—affectionately called Statia—has well-preserved historical sites and is famed for being the first foreign nation to salute the new American flag in 1776. The main streets of Philipsburg, the capital of St. Maarten, are lined with colorful Dutch colonial buildings replete with fretwork and verandas. It's also popular for its duty-free shops. Bonaire is best known for its excellent scuba diving.

French   **Martinique, Guadeloupe, St. Martin,** and **St. Barthélemy** (often called St. Barts or St. Barths) comprise the French West Indies. The language, the currency, the cuisine (the most imaginative in the Caribbean), the culture, and the style are *très* French. St. Barts is the quietest, Martinique the liveliest, St. Martin the friendliest, and Guadeloupe the lushest. And as an extra added attraction, you can wing over from Guadeloupe to see what life is like on the offshore islands of Les Saintes, Marie Galante, or Désirade.

Spanish   In the **Dominican Republic,** which occupies the eastern two-thirds of the island of Hispaniola, the language and culture are decidedly Spanish. The Colonial Zone of Santo Domingo is site of the oldest city in the Western Hemisphere, and its restored buildings reflect the 15th-century Columbus period. One also gets a sense of the past in **Puerto Rico's** Old San Juan, with its narrow cobblestone streets and filigreed iron balconies. The well-preserved town was founded by Ponce de León in the 16th century.

The Beauties of Nature
Dominica, laced with rivers and streams, is a ruggedly beautiful island with arguably the lushest, most untamed vegetation in the Caribbean. **Puerto Rico's** luxuriant 28,000-acre El Yunque is the largest rain forest in the U.S. Forestry system. Little **Saba** is awash with giant vegetation, and the island's Mt. Scenery is justly named. **Guadeloupe's** 74,000-square-mile Natural Park boasts dramatic waterfalls, cool pools, and miles of hiking trails. Majestic Mt. Pelée, a not entirely dormant volcano, towers over **Martinique's** rain forest; on **St. Eustatius,** adventurers can crawl down into a jungle cradled within a volcanic crater; and on **St. Lucia** you can drive right through a volcano.

The Lure of History
Antigua's well-preserved Nelson's Dockyard is a must for history aficionados. The ancient colonial zones of both Santo Domingo, **Dominican Republic,** and Old San Juan, **Puerto Rico,** should also be high on your "history" list. The Historical Society in **St. Eustatius** (Statia) publishes an excellent walking tour of sites to be seen. Brimstone Hill on **St. Kitts** is a well-maintained fortress with several museums full of military memorabilia. **Nevis** has many sugar mills restored as comfortable hotels. Port Royal, outside Kingston, **Jamaica,** was a pirates' stronghold until an earthquake shook things up in 1692.

Cuisine
The cuisine on **Martinique** and **Guadeloupe** is a marvelous marriage of Creole cooking and classic French dishes; you'll find much of the same on the other French islands of **St. Martin** and **St. Barts.** You'll also find a fine selection of French wines in the French West Indies. **Grenada,** the spice island, has an abundance of seafood available and an incredible variety of vegetables.

Music
Calypso was born in **Trinidad; Jamaica** is the home of reggae; the **Dominican Republic** gave the world the merengue; and both **Martinique** and **Guadeloupe** claim to be the cradle of the beguine. The music of **Barbados** ranges from the Crop Over Festival (late June—early August) to the hottest jazz. Steel drums, limbo dancers, and jump-ups are ubiquitous in the Caribbean. Jump-up? Simple. You hear the music, jump up, and begin to dance.

Diving
Jacques Cousteau named Pigeon Island, off the west coast of **Guadeloupe,** one of the 10 best dive sites in the world. The Wall off Grand Turks in the **Turks and Caicos Islands** is a sheer drop of 7,000 feet and has long been known by scuba divers. The eruption of Mt. Pelée at 8 AM on May 8, 1902, on **Martinique** resulted in the sinking of several ships. **St. Eustatius** boasts an undersea "supermarket" of ships, as well as entire 18th-century warehouses, somewhat the worse for wear, below the surface of Orange Bay. The wa-

ters surrounding all three of the **Cayman Islands** are acclaimed by experts, who make similar pilgrimages to **Bonaire**'s 50 spectacular sites.

Boating **Guadeloupe**'s Port de Plaisance and the marinas on Tortola in the **British Virgin Islands, St. Vincent and the Grenadines,** and St. Thomas in the **U. S. Virgin Islands** are the starting points for some of the Caribbean's finest sailing. Yachtsmen also favor the waters around **Antigua** and put in regularly at Nelson's Dockyard, which hosts a colorful regatta in late April or early May.

Golfing According to those who have played it, the course at Casa de Campo in the **Dominican Republic** is one of the best in the Caribbean. That island also has a Robert Trent Jones course on the Amber Coast at Playa Dorada. Golfers on St. Thomas, **U. S. Virgin Islands,** play the spectacular Mahogany Run. There are superb courses in **Puerto Rico,** including four shared by the Hyatt Dorado and the Hyatt Regency Cerromar. **Jamaica** has nine courses, with Tryall west of Montego Bay rated among the top.

Day Trips There are many day trips from St. Martin/St. Maarten. **Saba** is just 28 miles away; **St. Eustatius** is another 10 miles south; and **Anguilla,** the new "in" place in the Caribbean, is just a 15-minute boat ride away from St. Martin/St. Maarten. **Nevis** is a mere 2 miles south of **St. Kitts,** while **Dominica** sits about halfway between **Martinique** and **Guadeloupe. Barbuda,** 30 miles from **Antigua,** is noted for hunting and diving. **Les Saintes, Désirade,** and **Marie Galante** are easily accessible from Guadeloupe. Islands like these are small enough to explore in a day, and so seductive that you'll probably insist upon returning.

Water Sports

Sunbathing

Before abandoning yourself to the pleasures of the tropics, you would be well advised to take precautions against the ravages of its equatorial sun. Be sure to use a sunscreen with a high sun-protection factor, or SPF (an SPF of under 15 offers little protection); if you're engaging in water sports, be sure the sunscreen is waterproof. At this latitude, the safest hours for sunbathing are 4–6 PM, but even during these hours it is wise to limit exposure during your first few days to short intervals of 15–20 minutes. Keep your system plied with fruit juices and water; avoid coffee, tea, and alcohol, which have a dehydrating effect on the body.

Touring the island in an open Jeep or dangling an arm out of a car window can also expose you to sunburn, so be sure to use sunscreen. If you have permed or color-treated hair, you may wish to use a sun-protective gel to keep it from becoming brittle; if you have a bald head, apply sunscreen. While snorkeling, *always* wear a T-shirt and apply sunscreen to protect the top and backs of your thighs from "duck burn."

Swimming

Any resort you visit is likely to offer a variety of swimming experiences, depending on which side of the island you choose.

The calm, leeward Caribbean side of most islands has the safest and most popular beaches for swimming. There are no big waves, there is little undertow, and the saltwater—which buoys the swimmer or snorkeler—makes staying afloat almost effortless.

The windward, or Atlantic, side of the islands, however, is a different story: Even strong, experienced swimmers should exercise caution here. The ocean waves are tremendously powerful and can be rough to the point of being dangerous; unseen currents, strong undertows, and uneven, rocky bottoms may scuttle the novice. Some beaches post signs or flags daily to alert swimmers to the water conditions. Pay attention to them! Where there are no flags, limit your water sports to wading and sunbathing.

Swimmers on these islands must also be aware of underwater rocks, reefs, shells, and sea urchins—small, spike-covered creatures whose spines, while not fatal, can cause very painful punctures if you step on them, even through snorkel fins. Moray eels, which are harmless unless provoked, almost never leave the crevices they live in. But don't *ever* poke at one, or even point closely at them—they're lightning-fast and may mistake your finger for a predator. It's possible to receive a minor cut while swimming and not feel it until you're out of the water, so make a habit of checking yourself over after leaving the beach. If you do get a small cut from a broken glass or shell, clean it immediately with soap and water.

Nike, Inc. now manufactures an athletic shoe for wear in water sports. The Aqua Sock, a lightweight slip-on shoe with a waffle rubber outsole and Spandex mesh upper, offers protection from rocky beaches and underwater hazards such as coral and broken shells, and cushions the foot against the impact of windsurfing. It floats, is unaffected by salt and chlorine, and dries quickly.

How much truth is there to the old saw that you should wait an hour after eating before going for a swim? According to Mark Pitman, MD, Chief of Sports Medicine at the Hospital for Joint Diseases in New York City, blood travels from the muscles to the intestines after a meal to absorb the digesting food. This leaves the muscles "cold" and more likely to cramp. It is safe to float or dogpaddle after a light lunch, but save the Olympic lap-swimming for later. *Never* dive, particularly from a boat or cliff, without checking the depth of the water and the bottom conditions. And even when the Caribbean is mirror-calm, never run blindly into the water, even if the beach is familiar. Changes in the tide can turn what was a sandy bottom yesterday into a collection of broken shells today.

Few beaches or pools in the Caribbean—even those at the best hotels—are protected by lifeguards, so you and your children swim at your own risk.

Sharks More than a decade after the release of the film *Jaws*, shark phobia endures. Sharks *are* among the fish that populate Caribbean waters; they can swim in water as shallow as three feet and are attracted by the splashing of swimmers. But there are only about a dozen shark attacks reported each year worldwide, and most of these take place off the coasts of California and Florida. You are unlikely to see a shark while swimming or diving in the Caribbean, especially if you spot dolphins nearby. The dolphin is a natural enemy of the shark, and will attack its most vulnerable points—the gills and the tip of the nose—so sharks steer clear of them.

Snorkeling

Snorkeling requires no special skills, and most hotels that rent equipment have a staff member or, at the very least, a booklet offering instruction in snorkeling basics.

As with any water sport, it's never a good idea to snorkel alone, especially if you're out of shape. You don't have to be a great swimmer to snorkel, but occasionally currents come up that require stamina.

The four dimensions as we know them seem altered underwater. Time seems to slow and stand still, so wear a water-resistant watch and let someone on land know when to expect you back. Your sense of direction may also fail you when you're submerged. Many a vacationer has ended up half a mile or more from shore—which isn't a disaster unless you're already tired, chilly, and it's starting to get dark.

Remember that taking souvenirs—shells, pieces of coral, interesting rocks—is forbidden. Many reefs are legally protected marine parks, where removal of living shells is prohibited because it upsets the ecology. Because it is impossible to tell a living shell from a dead one, the wisest course is simply not to remove any. Needless to say, underwater is also not the place to discard your cigarette packs, gum wrappers, or any other litter.

Good snorkel equipment isn't cheap, and you may not like the sport once you've tried it, so get some experience with rented equipment, which is always inexpensive, before investing in quality mask, fins, and snorkel. The best prices for gear, as you might imagine, are not to be found at seaside resorts.

Scuba Diving

Diving is America's fastest-growing sport. While scuba (which stands for self-contained underwater breathing apparatus) looks and is surprisingly simple, *phone your physician before your vacation and make sure that you have no condition that should prevent you from diving!* Possibilities include common colds and other nasal infections, which can be worsened by diving, and ear infections, which can be worsened and cause underwater vertigo as well. Asthmatics can usually dive safely but must have their doctor's okay. A full checkup is an excellent idea, especially if you're over 30. Since it can be dangerous to travel on a plane after diving, you should schedule both your diving courses and travel plans accordingly.

At depths of below 30 feet, all sorts of physiological and chemical changes take place in the body in response to an increase in water pressure, so learning to dive with a reputable instructor is a must. Nitrogen, for example, which ordinarily escapes from the body through respiration, forms bubbles in the diver's bloodstream. If the diver resurfaces at a rate of more than one foot per second, these nitrogen bubbles may accumulate; the severe joint pains caused by this process are known as "the bends." If the nitrogen bubbles travel to your heart or brain, the result can be fatal.

In addition to training you how to resurface slowly enough, a qualified instructor can teach you to read "dive tables," the charts that calculate how long you can safely stay at certain depths. Many instructors supplement these charts with underwater computers that continuously monitor nitrogen, depth, and other information.

The ideal way to learn this sport is to take a resort course once you've arrived at your Caribbean destination. The course will usually consist of two to three hours of instruction on land, with time spent in a swimming pool or waist-deep water to get used to the mouthpiece and hose (known as the regulator) and the mask. A shallow 20-foot dive from a boat or beach, closely supervised by the instructor, follows.

Successful completion of this introductory course may prompt you to earn a certification card—often called a C-card—from one of the major accredited diving organizations: NADI (National Association of Diving Instructors), CMAS (Confederation Mondiale des Activities Subaquatiques, which translates into World Underwater Federation), NASE (National Association of Scuba Educators), or PADI (Professional Association of Diving Instructors).

PADI offers a free list of training facilities; write PADI for information (Box 24011, Santa Ana, CA 92799).

The more advanced Openwater I certification course takes five or six sessions—once a day at a beach hotel, or once a week at a YMCA or school pool back home. You must be able to swim a certain distance to qualify, even if it's dog-paddling. The course requires about 20 hours of classroom work, followed by a written test covering use of dive gear, basic skills and safety measures, and basic rescue techniques. Underwater skills are also practiced and tested.

A certification course will keep you very busy and pleasantly tired for most of your vacation. If your travel plans include a great deal of sightseeing as well, you'll have little time left to relax. You may wish to complete the classroom instruction and basic skills training at your hometown YMCA, for example, then do your five required open-water dives on vacation.

Unfortunately, there are a few disreputable individuals who may try to assure you that they can teach you everything you need to know about diving even though they aren't certified instructors. DON'T BELIEVE IT! Reputable diving shops proudly display their association with the organizations mentioned above. If you have any doubt, ask to see evidence of accreditation. Legitimate instructors will happily show you their credentials and will insist on seeing *your* C-card before a dive.

Keep in mind that your presence can easily damage the delicate underwater ecology. By standing on the bottom you can break fragile coral that took centuries to grow. Many reefs are legally protected marine parks; spearfishing or taking living shells and coral is rude and destructive, and often strictly prohibited. When in doubt, remember the diver's caveat: "Take only pictures, leave only bubbles."

Snuba

Not quite ready for scuba diving? Not to worry. For those kept from diving by poor health or claustrophobia, there is snuba, a combination of snorkeling and scuba diving. The snuba system consists of an inflatable raft that supports a tank of compressed air and a 20-foot air hose for one or two persons. The raft not only warns boats of your presence, but also provides a convenient resting place when you're tired. (There is even a clear window in the raft so you can still have an underwater view while taking a break.) The rental cost is approximately $25 an hour, and it takes only about an hour to become a certified snuba user.

Caribbean snuba outlets include **Virgin Island Diving Schools,** St. Thomas (tel. 809/774-8687); **SNUBA of St. Thomas** (tel. 800/524-7389 or 809/774-2775); **Pineapple Beach Club Resort,** Antigua (tel. 809/463-2006); and

SNUBA of St. John, U.S. Virgin Islands (tel. 809/776–6922). At press time, eight additional Caribbean islands were slated to get snuba equipment: Aruba, Barbados, Curaçao, Grand Cayman, Saba, St. Croix, St. Maarten, and Tortola. Check with your travel agent or the tourism board of the island you plan to visit for availability and information.

Waterskiing

Some large hotels have their own waterskiing concessions, with special boats, equipment, and instructors. Many beaches (especially those in Barbados), however, are patrolled by private individuals who own boats and several sizes of skis; they will offer their services through a hotel or directly to vacationers, or can be hailed like taxis. Ask your hotel staff or other guests about their experiences with these entrepreneurs. Be *sure* they provide life vests and at least two people in the boat: one to drive and one to watch the skier at all times.

Windsurfing

Windsurfing is as strenuous as it is exciting, so it is perhaps not the sport to try on your first day out, unless you're already in excellent shape. As with most water sports, it is essential to windsurf with someone else around who can watch you and go for help if necessary.

Always wear a life vest and preferably a diveskin to protect your own skin from the sun. Avoid suntan oil that could make your feet slippery and interfere with your ability to stand on the board. Nike, Inc. now makes athletic shoes specifically for wear in water sports (*see* Swimming, above).

Sailing

Whether you charter a yacht with crew or captain a boat yourself, the waters of the Caribbean—especially those around the Virgin Islands and the Grenadines—are excellent for sailing, and the many secluded bays and inlets provide ideal spots to drop anchor and picnic or explore. Like hotel rates, charter prices are lower during the offseason.

The Sailing School (tel. 800/447–4700), sponsored by the National Sailing Industry Association, can provide you with information about sailing schools in resort areas throughout the world. The service, which is free of charge, can steer you to schools offering basic sailing, board sailing, or advanced courses to sharpen old skills for chartering or racing.

St. Thomas, U.S. Virgin Islands, and Tortola and Virgin Gorda in the British Virgin Islands do most of the charter and marina business. In St. Thomas, contact the **Virgin Island Charter Yacht League** (tel. 809/774–3944). In Tortola, **The Moorings** (tel. 809/494–2332); in Virgin Gorda, **North South Yacht Charters** (tel. 809/495–5421). The cost of chartering a yacht ranges from $100 to $250 a day per person (all-inclusive, with meals and drinks).

Sailing out of Grenada through the Grenadines is also recommended and many charters are available. From Guadeloupe, you can sail to Dominica and Antigua and anchor at the Isles of Marie Galante and Les Saintes.

1 Essential Information

Before You Go

Government Tourist Offices

Each of the various tourist boards listed below is a good source of general information on the particular island (or islands) it represents. Call or write for free brochures with histories, listings of hotels, restaurants, sights and stores, and up-to-date calendars of events. The **Caribbean Tourism Association** (20 E. 46th St., New York, NY 10017, tel. 212/682–0435) is another resource, especially for information on the islands that don't have tourist offices in the United States. In addition, the names and addresses of tourist boards located on the islands themselves appear under *Tourist Information Services* in each individual island chapter.

Anguilla **Anguilla Tourist Information & Reservations. In the United States.** 271 Main St., Northport, NY 11768, tel. 516/261–1234 or 800/553–4939.
In the United Kingdom: 3 Epirus Rd., London SW6 7UJ, tel. 071/937–7725.

Antigua and Barbuda **Antigua and Barbuda Department of Tourism. In the United States:** 610 5th Avenue, Suite 311, New York, NY 10020, tel. 212/541–4117; 121 SE 1st Street, Suite 508, Miami, FL 33131, tel. 305/381–6762.
In Canada: 60 St. Clair Avenue E, Suite 205, Toronto, Ont. M4T 1N5, tel. 416/961–3085.
In the United Kingdom: 15 Thayer Street, London W1M 5LD, tel. 071/486–7073.

Aruba **Aruba Tourist Authority. In the United States:** 1270 Avenue of the Americas, Suite 2212, New York, NY 10020, tel. 212/246–3030; Box 776, Streamwood, IL 60107, tel. 312/337–1716; Box 012348, Miami, FL 33101, tel. 305/326–7280.
In Canada: 1801 Eglinton Avenue W, Suite 109, Toronto, Ont. M6E 2H7, tel. 416/782–9954.

Barbados **Barbados Board of Tourism. In the United States:** 800 2nd Avenue, New York, NY 10017, tel. 212/986–6516; 3440 Wilshire Boulevard, Suite 1215, Los Angeles, CA 90010, tel. 213/380–2199 or 800/221–9831.
In Canada: 20 Queen Street W, Suite 1508, Toronto, Ont. M5H 3R3, tel. 416/979–2137; 615 Dorchester West Boulevard, Suite 960, Montreal, P.Q. H3B 1P5, tel. 514/861–0085.
In the United Kingdom: 263 Tottenham Court Road, London W1P 9AA, tel. 071/636–9448 or 071/636–9449.

Bonaire **Bonaire Government Tourist Office. In the United States:** 275 7th Avenue, New York, NY 10001, tel. 212/242–7707.
In Canada: 815 A Queen Street E, Toronto, Ont. M4M 1H8, tel. 416/465–2958.

British Virgin Islands **British Virgin Islands Tourist Board. In the United States:** 370 Lexington Avenue, New York, NY 10017, tel. 212/696–0400.
In Canada: (no mailing address), tel. 416/283–2235.
In the United Kingdom: c/o Wingjet Ltd., 26 Hockerill Street, Bishop's Stortford, Hertfordshire CM23 2DW, tel. 279/506747.

Cayman Islands **Cayman Islands Tourist Board. In the United States:** 420 Lexington Avenue, Suite 2733, New York, NY 10170, tel. 212/682–5582; c/o One Magnificent Mile, 980 North Michigan Avenue,

Suite 1260, Chicago, IL 60611, tel. 312/944–5602; 9794 Forest Lane, Suite 569, Dallas, TX 75243, tel. 214/823–3838; Two Memorial City Plaza, 820 Gessner, Suite 170, Houston, TX 77024, tel. 713/461–1317; 3440 Wilshire Boulevard, Suite 1202, Los Angeles, CA 90010, tel. 213/738–1968; 250 Catalonia Avenue, Suite 401, Coral Cables, FL 33134, tel. 305/444–6551.
In Canada: 234 Eglinton Avenue E, Suite 306, Toronto, Ont. M4P 1K5, tel. 416/485–1550.
In the United Kingdom: Trevor House, 100 Brompton Road, London SW3 1EX, tel. 071/581–9960.

Curaçao **Curaçao Tourist Board. In the United States:** 400 Madison Avenue, Suite 311, New York, NY 10017, tel. 212/751–8266.

Dominica **Caribbean Tourism Organization. In the United States:** 20 East 46th Street, 4th floor, New York, NY 10017, tel. 212/682–0435.
In the United Kingdom: c/o Dominica High Commission, 1 Collingham Gardens, London SW5 0HW, tel. 01/370–5194 or 071/373–8743.

Dominican **Dominican Republic Tourist Office. In the United States:** 485
Republic Madison Avenue, New York, NY 10022, tel. 212/826–0750.
In Canada: 29 Bellair Street, Toronto, Ont. M5R 2C8, tel. 416/928–9188.

Grenada **Grenada Tourist Office. In the United States:** 141 East 44th Street, New York, NY 10017, tel. 212/687–9554 or 800/638–0852.
In Canada: 439 University Avenue, Suite 820, Toronto, Ont. M5G 1Y8, tel. 416/595–1339.
In the United Kingdom: c/o Grenada High Commission, 1 Collingham Gardens, Earls Court, London SW5 0HW, tel. 071/370–5164.

Guadeloupe **French West Indies Tourist Board. In the United States:** 610 5th Avenue, New York, NY 10020, tel. 212/757–1125; French Government Tourist Office, 9454 Wilshire Boulevard, Beverly Hills, CA 90212, tel. 213/272–2661; French Government Tourist Office, 645 North Michigan Avenue, Chicago, IL 60611, tel. 312/337–6301; French Government Tourist Office, 103 World Trade Center, Dallas, TX 75258, tel. 214/720–4010; 1 Hallidie Plaza, Suite 250, San Francisco, CA 94102, tel. 415/986–4161.
In Canada: French Government Tourist Office, 1981 Avenue, McGill College, Suite 490, Montreal, P.Q. H3A 2W9, tel. 514/288–4264; French Government Tourist Office, 1 Dundas Street W, Suite 2405, Toronto, Ont. M5G 1Z3, tel. 416/593–4717.
In the United Kingdom: c/o French Government Tourist Office, 178 Piccadilly, London W1V 0AL, tel. 071/499–6911.

Jamaica **Jamaica Tourist Board. In the United States:** 866 2nd Avenue, New York, NY 10017, tel. 212/688–7650 or 800/223–5225; 36 South Wabash Avenue, Suite 1210, Chicago, IL 60603, tel. 312/346–1546; 1320 South Dixie Highway, Coral Gables, FL 33146, tel. 305/665–0557; 8235 Douglas Avenue, LB18, Dallas, TX 75225, tel. 214/361–8778; 3440 Wilshire Boulevard, Suite 1207, Los Angeles, CA 90010, tel. 213/384–1123.
In Canada: 1 Eglinton Avenue E, Suite 616, Toronto, Ont. M4P 3A1, tel. 416/482–7850.
In the United Kingdom: Jamaica House, 63 St. James's Street, London SW1A 1LY, tel. 071/493–3647.

Martinique **French West Indies Tourist Board. In the United States:** 610 5th Avenue, New York, NY 10020, tel. 212/757–1125; French Government Tourist Office, 9454 Wilshire Boulevard, Beverly

Hills, CA 90212, tel. 213/272–2661; French Government Tourist Office, 645 North Michigan Avenue, Chicago, IL 60611, tel. 312/337–6301; French Government Tourist Office, 103 World Trade Center, Dallas, TX 75258, tel. 214/720–4010; 1 Hallidie Plaza, Suite 250, San Francisco, CA 94102, tel. 415/986–4161.

In Canada: French Government Tourist Office, 1981 Avenue, McGill College, Suite 490, Montreal, P.Q. H3A 2W9, tel. 514/288–4264; French Government Tourist Office, 1 Dundas Street W, Suite 2405, Toronto, Ont. M5G 1Z3, tel. 416/593–4717.

In the United Kingdom: c/o French Government Tourist Office, 178 Piccadilly, London W1V 0AL, tel. 071/499–6911.

Montserrat **Montserrat Tourist Board. In the United States:** 110 East 59th Street, New York, NY 10022, tel. 212/752–8660.

Nevis **St. Kitts-Nevis Tourist Board. In the United States:** 414 East 75th Street, New York, NY 10021, tel. 212/535–1234.

In Canada: 11 Yorkville Avenue, Suite 508, Toronto, Ont. M4W 1L3, tel. 416/921–7717.

Puerto Rico **Puerto Rico Tourism Company. In the United States:** 575 5th Avenue, 23rd floor, New York, NY 10017, tel. 212/599–6262 or 800/223–6530.

In Canada: c/o Puerto Rico Tourism Information Company, 11 Yorkville Avenue, Suite 1003, Toronto, Ont. M4W 1L3, tel. 416/925–5587.

Saba **Saba & Statia Information Office. In the United States:** c/o Medhurst & Associates, 271 Main St., Northport, NY 11768, tel. 516/261–7474 or 800/344–4606.

St. Barthélemy **French West Indies Tourist Board. In the United States:** 610 5th Ave., New York, NY 10020, tel. 212/757–1125; French Government Tourist Office, 9454 Wilshire Boulevard, Beverly Hills, CA 90212, tel. 213/272–2661; French Government Tourist Office, 645 North Michigan Avenue, Chicago, IL 60611, tel. 312/337–6301; French Government Tourist Office, 103 World Trade Center, Dallas, TX 75258, tel. 214/720–4010; 1 Hallidie Plaza, Suite 250, San Francisco, CA 94102, tel. 415/986–4161.

In Canada: French Government Tourist Office, 1981 Avenue, McGill College, Suite 490, Montreal, P.Q. H3A 2W9, tel. 514/288–4264; French Government Tourist Office, 1 Dundas Street W, Suite 2405, Toronto, Ont. M5G 1Z3, tel. 416/593–4717.

In the United Kingdom: c/o French Government Tourist Office, 178 Piccadilly, London W1V 0AL, 071/499–6911.

St. Eustatius **Saba & Statia Information Office. In the United States:** c/o Medhurst & Associates, 271 Main St., Northport, NY 11768, tel. 516/261–7474 or 800/344–4606.

St. Kitts **St. Kitts-Nevis Tourist Board. In the United States:** 414 East 75th Street, New York, NY 10021, tel. 212/535–1234.

In Canada: 11 Yorkville Avenue, Suite 508, Toronto, Ont. M4W 1L3, tel. 416/921–7717.

St. Lucia **St. Lucia Tourist Board. In the United States:** 820 2nd Ave., 9th floor, New York, NY 10017, tel. 212/867–2950 or 800/456–3984.

In Canada: 151 Bloor Street W, Suite 425, Toronto, Ont. M5S 1S4, tel. 416/961–5606.

In the United Kingdom: 10 Kensington Court, London W8 5DL, tel. 071/937–1969.

St. Maarten **French West Indies Tourist Board. In the United States:** 610 5th Ave., New York, NY 10020, tel. 212/757–1125; French Government Tourist Office, 9454 Wilshire Boulevard, Beverly Hills,

CA 90212, tel. 213/272–2661; French Government Tourist Office, 645 North Michigan Avenue, Chicago, IL 60611, tel. 312/337–6301; French Government Tourist Office, 103 World Trade Center, Dallas, TX 75258, tel. 214/720–4010; 1 Hallidie Plaza, Suite 250, San Francisco, CA 94102, tel. 415/986–4161.

In Canada: French Government Tourist Office, 1981 Avenue, McGill College, Suite 490, Montreal, P.Q. H3A 2W9, tel. 514/288–4264; French Government Tourist Office, 1 Dundas Street W, Suite 2405, Toronto, Ont. M5G 1Z3, tel. 416/593–4717.

In the United Kingdom: c/o French Government Tourist Office, 178 Piccadilly, London W1V 0AL, 071/499–6911.

St. Maarten **St. Maarten Tourist Office. In the United States:** c/o Mallory Factor, 275 7th Avenue, 19th floor, New York, NY 10001, tel. 212/989–0000.

In Canada: 243 Ellerslie Avenue, Willowdale, Ont. M2N 1Y5, tel. 416/223–3501.

St. Vincent and **St. Vincent and the Grenadines Tourist Office. In the United**
the Grenadines **States:** 801 2nd Avenue, New York, NY 10017, tel. 212/687–4981; 14347 Hay Meadow Circle, Dallas, TX 75240, tel. 214/239–6451.

In Canada: 100 University Avenue, Suite 504, Toronto, Ont. M5J 1V6, tel. 416/971–9666 or 416/971–9667.

In the United Kingdom: 10 Kensington Court, London W8 5DL, tel. 071/937–6570.

Trinidad **Trinidad and Tobago Tourist Board. In the United States:** 118-35
and Tobago Queens Boulevard, 15th floor, Forest Hills, NY 11375, tel. 718/575–3909; 330 Biscayne Boulevard, Miami, FL 33132, tel. 305/370–2056.

In Canada: c/o Trinidad and Tobago Tourism Development Authority, 40 Holly Street, Suite 102, Toronto, Ont. M4S 3C3, tel. 416/367–0390 or 800/268–8986.

In the United Kingdom: 48 Leicester Square, London WC2 H7LT, tel. 071/839–7155.

Turks and Caicos **In the United States:** For general information contact Medhurst & Associates, 271 Main St., Northport, NY 11768, tel. 516/261–9600. On Grand Turk, 800/441–4419.

In the United Kingdom: c/o West India Committee, 48 Albermarle Street, London W1X 4AR, tel. 071/629–6353.

U.S. Virgin Islands **U.S. Virgin Islands Tourist Information Office. In the United States:** 1270 Avenue of the Americas, New York, NY 10020, tel. 212/582–4520.

In the United Kingdom: 25 Bedford Square, London WC1B 3JA, tel. 071/637–8481.

Tour Groups

A good number of the islands are little more than a few miles wide, so there is little call for traditional escorted tours in the Caribbean. The primary options here are air/hotel packages (*see* Package Deals for Independent Travelers, below) and cruise tours (*see* Cruises, below). Cruise tours function somewhat like escorted programs, shuttling groups from island to island and arranging transportation when the sights are far apart. Both types of package mix and match Caribbean Islands in seemingly infinite varieties. If you don't see the particular itinerary you had your heart set on, tell your travel agent or tour operator to keep looking; odds are it exists somewhere.

When considering a tour, be sure to find out (1) exactly what expenses are included—particularly tips, taxes, side trips, additional meals, and entertainment; (2) ratings of all hotels on the itinerary and the facilities they offer; (3) cancellation policies for both you and the tour operator; (4) the number of travelers in your group; and (5) if you are traveling alone, the cost of the single supplement. Most tour operators request that bookings be made through a travel agent—in most cases there is no additional charge for doing so.

General-Interest Tours **American Express Vacations** (Box 5014, Atlanta, GA, 30302, tel. 800/241–1700) offers a host of both escorted and independent packages. Trips range anywhere from 3 to 21 days in length to any one island location in the Caribbean. **Horizon Tours** (1010 Vermont Ave., Suite 202, Washington, DC 20005, tel. 202/393–8390 or 800/525–7760) serves as many as 45 different Caribbean locations while smaller operations like **Bonaire Enterprises** (Box 775, Morgan, NJ 08879, tel. 201/566–8866 or 800/526–2370) provide a welcome alternative: The company confines all business to Bonaire alone.

Vacation packages need not drain your bank account—**Tour-Scan, Inc.** (Box 2367, Darien, Connecticut 06820, tel. 203/655–8091 or 800/962–2080) gathers and computerizes up to 12,000 deals each season, and boasts an average $300–$400 savings per traveler, while exacting no club fee.

Other major operators include **Certified Tours** (Box 1525, Fort Lauderdale, FL, 33302, tel. 800/872–7786), **GWV International** (300 1st Ave., Needham, MA 02194, tel. 800/225–5498), and **Cavalcade Tours** (450 Harmon Meadow Blvd., Secaucus, NJ 07096, tel. 201/617–7100 or 800/521–2319).

Special-Interest Tours The **Smithsonian Associates Travel Program** (1100 Jefferson Dr., SW, Washington, DC 20560, tel. 202/357–4700) offers many educational and research programs around the world, including a close look at the culture and customs of Jamaica.
Culture/Arts

Diving **Aqua Adventures** (114 E. 32nd St., Suite 501, New York, NY 10016, tel. 212/686–6210 or 800/654–7537) offers scuba packages at some 68 or so diving resorts in the Caribbean. **Sea Safaris Travel** (3770 Highland Ave., Suite 102, Manhattan Beach, CA 90266, tel. 213/546–2464, 800/821–6670, or 800/262–6670 in CA) specializes in Cayman Islands dive packages.

Environmentalist **Oceanic Society Expeditions** (Fort Mason Center, Bldg. E, San Francisco, CA 94123, tel. 415/441–1106) is a nonprofit environmental group with a variety of research and preservation projects open to public participation. One program charts sections of coral reef and takes a census of underwater life in the West Indies; in another, participants swim with dolphins. No special skills are necessary, just good swimming ability.

Equestrian **Fits Equestrian** (2011 Alamo Pintado Rd., Solvang, CA 93463, tel. 805/688–9494) offers horseback riding in Jamaica, polo lessons and instructions for beginners and experienced riders.

Honeymoon Many hotels and most Caribbean tour operators (*see* Package Deals for Independent Travelers, below) offer honeymoon packages, with special suites and other options.

Natural History **Questers Worldwide Nature Tours** (257 Park Ave. S, New York, NY 10010, tel. 212/673–3120) focuses on the flora and fauna of Trinidad and Tobago. Rain-forest, beach, and swamp environments are explored with an experienced naturalist. **Oceanic Society Expeditions** (*see* above) explores the island and marine ecology of St. Vincent and St. Lucia. Day trips include opportunities to search for whales and dolphins.

Singles **Singleworld** (Box 1999, Rye, NY 10580, tel. 914/967–3334 or 800/223–6490) offers packages strictly for singles, organized by two age groups: "under 35" and "all ages."

Club Med (tel. 800/258–2633) offers a number of all-inclusive packages at several locations throughout the Caribbean.

Package Deals for Independent Travelers

Most packages include air transportation, accommodations, and transfers to and from your hotel. Some add meals and sightseeing, and make local representatives available to answer questions. The travel section of a local newspaper and a good travel agent are your best resources.

The number of Caribbean packages is truly overwhelming; the following is a small sampling of typically reliable packagers. **American Airlines Fly AAway Vacations** (tel. 800/854–TOUR), **American Express Vacations** (tel. 800/241–1700), **Cayman Airtours** (tel. 800/247–2966), **Continental Airlines' Grand Destinations** (tel. 800/634–5555), and **GoGo Tours** (68 offices across the country; if you can't find one near you, call GoGo's headquarters at tel. 201/934–3500). **Thomson Vacations** and **Travel Impressions** only work through travel agents; your agent should have information on their deals.

Leeward Islands Air Transport (LIAT, tel. 809/462–0700), which has its headquarters at Antigua's V. C. Bird International Airport, offers a *21-day Explorer* ticket and a *30-day Super Caribbean Explorer* ticket, both of which allow unlimited onward stopovers (no backtracking except to transfer). The Explorer is valid only from July 1 through August 31 and December 15 through January 31. The cost is $169 in summer, $199 in winter. This ticket is sold worldwide, *except in the Caribbean*. The 30-day Super Caribbean Explorer is available year-round for $357 and is sold worldwide. There are no refunds; a $20 charge is assessed for a change in routing; and the tickets are valid only on LIAT flights. Both tickets are very good options if you plan to do extensive island-hopping.

Tips for British Travelers

Tourist There is no general office for the Caribbean in the United King-
Information dom, but a number of different islands have their own tourist information offices (*see* Government Tourist Offices, above).

Passports *See* the Before You Go section in each island chapter for specific
and Visas passport and visa requirements. Some islands require passports, others do not but may require a "British Visitor's" passport, generally available from the post office.

Customs Exact customs regulations vary slightly from island to island, but in general, the restrictions apply to alcohol and cigarettes only. Travelers are allowed to bring in 200 cigarettes, 1 liter of alcohol over 22% by volume (most spirits), or 2 bottles of wine.

Returning to the United Kingdom, if you are 17 or over, you may take home: (1) 200 cigarettes or 100 cigarillos or 50 cigars or 250 grams of tobacco; (2) 2 liters of table wine and (a) 1 liter of alcohol over 22% by volume (most spirits), or (b) 2 liters of alcohol under 22% by volume (fortified or sparkling wine); (3) 60 milliliters of perfume and ¼ liter of toilet water; and (4) other goods up to a value of £32.

Insurance We recommend that to cover health and motoring mishaps, you insure yourself with **Europ Assistance** (252 High St., Croydon, Surrey CR0 1NF, tel. 081/680–1234).

It is also wise to take out insurance to cover the loss of luggage (although check that such loss isn't already covered in any existing homeowner's policies you may have). Trip-cancellation insurance is another wise buy. **The Association of British Insurers** (Aldermary House, Queen St., London EC4N 1TT, tel. 071/248–4477) will give comprehensive advice on all aspects of vacation insurance.

Tour Operators Here is just a selection of companies offering packages to the Caribbean. Also, contact your travel agent for the latest information:

Caribbean Connection (Concorde House, Forest St., Chester CH1 1QR, tel. 0244/41131) has a 70-page catalogue devoted to Caribbean Holidays, with a number of special deals, including Supersavers, and Second Week Free offers. A separate brochure describes all-inclusive resort holidays.

Kuoni Travel (Kuoni House, Dorking, Surrey RH5 4AZ, tel. 0306/740500) specializes in "Caribbean Multi-Centre Holidays," which allow you to mix and match your stays on different islands. Prices start at £1119 for 14 days.

Sovereign Holidays (Groundstar House, London Rd., Crawley, West Sussex, RH10 2TB, tel. 0293/561444) offers a variety of packages with special offers, including "2 Centre" vacations, combining stays on two separate islands, and special "2 for 1" and "3 for 2" offers, giving you an extra week or two for free. Prices range from £511 to £2,724 for one week.

Tradewinds Faraway Holidays (Station House, 81/83 Fulham High St., London SW6 3JP, tel. 071/731–8000) has trips to a number of islands, ranging from £648 to £1692 for seven nights.

Airlines and Airfares **British Airways** and **British West Indian Airways** are the only airlines with direct flights from London to the Caribbean. APEX fares range from £497 low season to £584 high season. It is always worth checking the small ads in *Time Out* magazine or the Sunday papers for cheaper charter flights. You may be able to pick up something for rock-bottom prices, but you should be prepared to be flexible about your dates of travel, and you should book as early as possible.

Festivals and Seasonal Events

January **Antigua:** The first week in January brings international tennis tournaments, clinics, and friendly and not-so-friendly matches for an official Tennis Week.

Aruba: The New Year takes off with midnight fireworks, and, on earth, groups of singers stroll from house to house with musical greetings.

Curaçao: Marking the first of the Carnival seasons to hit the Caribbean, the Curaçao Carnival creates its own blend of music, dance, and costumed parade from January to February.

Dominican Republic: Duarte's Birthday is held on January 26 in celebration of the founding father.

Grenada: There's a New Year Fiesta and yacht race, highlighted by the "Around Grenada" sailing contest. An annual Game Fishing Tournament is held in mid-January, with serious fishermen vying for sailfish, marlin, yellowfin, and tuna.

Guadeloupe: Carnival celebrations begin on a Sunday in January and continue until Lent.

St. Barthélemy: The Annual St. Bart's Music Festival, held from January 30 to February 5, imports an international collection of soloists and musicians. Artists perform four musical concerts at L'Orient; and there are additional dance performances in Gustavia.

St. Lucia: Food vendors sell local delicacies, bands play, and masqueraders come down from the countryside to show off their dancing skills during New Year's Fiesta on January 1 and 2.

February **Aruba:** From mid- to late February, Carnival hits Aruba. The entire island participates in dancing street parades, musical contests, and the election of Carnival Queen. The culmination is a Grand Parade that begins at noon on the Sunday preceding Lent.

Barbados: The Holetown Festival commemorates the first settlement of Barbados on February 17, 1627, with a week of fairs, street markets, and medieval revelry. Fifteenth- and 16th-century religious chorales echo throughout the village churches against the backdrop of an unmistakably modern beat resounding across the fairgrounds.

Bonaire: Bonaire drinks and feasts its way through Carnival in the month of February.

Dominican Republic: A nationwide Carnival takes place during the third week of the month, followed by National Independence Day on February 27.

Guadeloupe: Carnival continues in Guadeloupe as a pre-Lenten fantasy culminating on Ash Wednesday. On Shrove Tuesday, or "Mardi Gras," the peak of Carnival frenzy, a parade of floats and costumed red devils and diablesses flood the streets of Pointe-à-Pitre. Last but not least, Ash Wednesday arrives and commands an all black-and-white dress code for the revelers. "King Carnival" burns on his funeral pyre, rum flows, and the dancing climbs to a fevered pitch.

Martinique: One of the biggest and best Carnivals offers six weeks of *zouks* (all-night revelries). Wheeled carnival floats, ranging from the grotesque and the extravagant to the naive, sometimes carry more than 50 revelers, an orchestra with massive amplification, and a delirious multitude of costumed dancers at its heels. When the processions break up at sunset, the revelers split into small groups and dance until dawn. Burlesque marriages, burning effigies, and devils in red with tridents in tow are all part of the Mardi Gras scene.

St. Barthélemy: A smaller-scale Mardi Gras takes to the streets of St. Barthélemy.

St. Lucia: This island's riotous version of Carnival merrymaking precedes Independence Day on February 22, which itself remains the biggest celebration of the year. The Carnival features a Kiddies Carnival where schools and children's groups compete against one another in costumed themes. Also, a predawn jump-up called *J'Ouvert* winds through the streets of Castries, then climaxes with the "Last Lap"—a parade renowned for its magnificent array of colorful dress.

St. Martin/St. Maarten: During Carnival, which continues until

Ash Wednesday, all business stops for five days. The celebration peaks on Shrove Tuesday, when dancing fills the streets of Marigot and Grand Case. The Dutch version of Carnival comes at Eastertime. Also, look for the St. Maarten/Heineken Regatta, an annual weekend of yacht races and soirees, in the early part of the month.

Trinidad and Tobago: During Carnival, adults and children alike are swept up in the excitement of "Playing Mas"—the state of surrendering completely to the rapture of fantastic spectacle, parades, music, and dancing. For those who feel the urge, places in a genuine "mas' band" can be purchased (long in advance) for fees that vary according to the prestige of the group and the intricacy of the costumes.

March   **Curaçao:** The Curaçao Regatta is an open race for all types of boats.

Montserrat: St. Patrick's Day (March 17) is celebrated here on the "Emerald Isle" with great gusto; Montserrat claims a substantial citizenry of Irish descent.

St. Barthélemy: The St. Barts Cooking School manages three one-week cooking courses sponsored by Chef Hubert, the owner of a restaurant at the Hotel Manapany in Paris.

Trinidad and Tobago: Usually observed on a Sunday in March or April (consult the island tourist office for confirmation of dates), Phaguah celebrates the triumph of good over evil. Hindus observe a daylong agenda of prayer and fasting as well as singing, dancing, drumming, and a fair share of good-natured dousing of your neighbor with *aheer*, a vermillion dye.

April   **Antigua:** In mid-month, Windsurfing Antigua Week takes off with nine days of sailing and endless parties. Immediately following comes International Sailing Week, when over 300 yachts from the four corners of the globe converge in Antigua for the Caribbean's greatest regatta and nonstop parties.

Barbados: The Oistins Fish Festival is a two-day affair held every Easter to honor the local fishing industry: Fishing competitions, boat races, street entertainment, and open-air bazaars abound. Steel bands and food stalls make the events all the more lively, and spectators can mingle with the thronging crowds of Bajans on the beaches, in the marketplace, and in the quaint rum shops that line the roadside. An exhibition by the Coast Guard rounds out the activities.

Bonaire: The Queen's Birthday on April 30 is an annual open-to-all celebration of Her Royal Majesty's "official birthday," and the lieutenant governor invites everyone on the island (including visitors) to his home for a cocktail reception.

British Virgin Islands: Virgin Gorda Festival and the Spring Regatta.

Cayman Islands: Grand Cayman Carnival comes first to Grand Cayman (Batabano) and then to Cayman Brac a week later (Brachanal).

Grenada: The Grenada Easter Regatta includes a week of both interisland and local races.

Guadeloupe: Easter Monday is a public holiday here. Families picnic on beaches and riverbanks. Soccer games between Guadeloupe and Martinique remain the year's classic sports events.

Jamaica: Negril Reggae Festival is a popular musical event.

Puerto Rico: Citron Harvest Festival.

St. Barthélemy: Local handicrafts are put on display and sold during St. Barts Arts, Crafts, and Products Week.

St. Martin/St. Maarten: For 15 days around Easter, the Dutch side celebrates its Carnival when "King Moumou" and "Queen of the Carnival" are elected. Visitors can count on numerous beauty contests, food competitions, musical concerts including calypso, parades, "jump-ups," floats, steel bands, string bands, and bright, fanciful costumes.

U.S. Virgin Islands: At Carnival time residents compete for the title of Calypso King. In addition, St. Thomas holds the International Rolex Cup Regatta—a three-day schedule of yacht racing and social events.

May
Anguilla: Boat racing is the national sport in Anguilla, and the most important competitions take place on Anguilla Day (May 30).

Barbados: The Barbados Jazz Festival is a two-day event held at the end of the month. Performances of original compositions and traditional jazz take place in several locations in Bridgetown.

Puerto Rico: A 16th-century Dominican convent in San Juan is the setting for a week of music and dance performances known as *Semana de la Danza.*

St. Lucia: Just about every type of competition that can be held on or in water constitutes the week-long "Aqua Action" festival on Whitsun (Pentecost) weekend—canoe racing, Sunfish sailing, windsurfing, sport fishing, waterskiing, and a non-mariners race. At the end of the month, local fishermen decorate their boats and the whole island feasts on St. Peter's Day.

St. Martin/St. Maarten: The Historical and Cultural foundations organize the St. Martin Food Festival in May. All segments of society take part, contributing many of the dishes, desserts, liquors, and crafts; older citizens dress in their traditional garb. Entertainment includes steel bands and "old-time" band music.

Turks and Caicos Islands: At the end of May, the Annual South Caicos Regatta features local catboat and powerboat races, dances, and entertainment.

June
Aruba: The Aruba High Winds Windsurfing Tournament features half a dozen different races, including one to Venezuela and back. But the real highlight of the season is the Aruba Jazz and Latin Music Festival, held in Oranjestad early in the month. Well-known entertainers offer Latin, pop, jazz, and salsa music at Mansur stadium. Soloists have included Ruben Blades, Wynton Marsalis, Wilfrido Vargas, and Diane Schuur.

Bonaire: Dia de San Juan (June 24) and Dia de San Pedro (June 28) recall folkloric traditions of music and dance in the villages of Bonaire.

British Virgin Islands: The U.S. and British Virgin Islands share the Hook In & Hold On Boardsailing Regatta in June and July.

Cayman Islands: The Cayman Islands host Million Dollar Month, a series of saltwater fishing contests with huge cash prizes.

Dominican Republic: Puerto Plata presents a Windsurfing International Tournament the second week in June.

Puerto Rico: From all over the world, orchestras, choruses, and choirs converge on San Juan for Festival Casals.

U.S. Virgin Islands: From June to July, the Hook In & Hold On Boardsailing Regatta challenges competitors from around the world to a race between the U.S. and British Virgin Islands.

July **Antigua:** Antigua's Carnival in late July lasts 10 days, during which a queen is crowned, calypso and steel bands compete, and the streets are full of floats and dancing celebrants in colorful costume.

Barbados: Cutting across July and August, the Crop Over Festival is a month-long cheer for the end of the sugarcane harvest. Tents ring with the fierce battle of Calypsonians for the coveted Calypso Monarch award, and the air is redolent with smells of Bajan cooking during the massive "Bridgetown Market" street fair. The "Cohobblopot" blends drama, dance, and music with the crowning of the king and queen of costume bands, and both the King of Calypso and the Clown Prince are crowned on the night of "Pic-O-de-Crop Show." Finally, "Kadooment Day"—a national holiday—closes the show, but not before fireworks fill the sky and costumed bands fill the streets with pulsating Caribbean rhythms.

Dominican Republic: In the third week in July Santo Domingo cuts loose with the immensely popular Merengue Festival. During this 10-day party that rivals the best of the Caribbean Carnivals in overall gaiety and gastronomic splendor, outdoor bands and orchestras play on the Malecón, and all the hotel chefs proudly present their best.

French West Indies: Bastille Day (July 14).

Martinique: The Festival of Fort-de-France, which lasts the entire month, features theater, art, music, and dance performances from all over the world. Look for the Tour de la Martinique in mid-month—an annual island bike race registering international contestants.

Saba: Carnival is celebrated with picnics, sporting events, entertainment, and various recreational activities.

St. Martin/St. Maarten: Schoelcher Day honors Victor Schoelcher, the French parliamentarian who led the campaign against slavery. Look for boat races in Grand Case featuring the beautiful Anguillan sailing boats.

U.S. Virgin Islands: Besides a Fourth of July celebration, the islands mark the anniversary of the July 3, 1848, abolition of slavery.

August **Anguilla:** The beginning of August is Carnival time in Anguilla. Street dancing, Calypso competitions, Carnival Queen Coronation, the Prince and Princess Show, and nightly entertainment are all featured alongside sumptious beach barbecues serving local lobster, chicken, and a vast array of fresh grilled fish.

Barbados: Once an end-of-August celebration, Crop Over has expanded into a whole month's worth of folk fests. With the sugarcane harvest complete, the islanders party with total abandon. Kadooment Day, the first Monday in August, tops it all off with dance jams and, for the children, a costume parade christened Kiddies Kadooment.

Grenada: Catch the ample street selections of food and craft exhibits during Rainbow City Festival on August 4 and 5. The first weekend in August is the annual Carriacou Regatta, which takes place on this offshore island some 16 miles to the north, a week of racing and partying. Then in mid-August the official Carnival takes off with steel-band and calypso music galore.

Guadeloupe: In imitation of the celebrated French "Tour de France," Guadeloupe has its own "Tour de la Guadeloupe": an exciting 10-day race in early August featuring teams from many countries. Nine grueling itineraries cover the whole island. The famous Fête des Cuisinières (Festival of Cooks) held on August 11 is a true Guadeloupe original. This is both a religious and gastronomic occasion, with some 100 women chefs in Creole dress honoring St. Laurent, the patron saint of cooks. Each chef carries her finest dishes, decorated with flowers, to the Pointe-à-Pitre Cathedral to celebrate High Mass. Following the Mass, there's an all-day feast at the Ecole Amédée Fengarol with feasting, singing, and dancing. Tickets are in great demand; a limited number are available from the Tourist Office.

Jamaica: The August Reggae Sunsplash International Music Festival is getting hotter every year. The best, brightest, and newest of the Caribbean reggae stars gather to perform in open-air concerts in Kingston and MoBay.

Martinique: The annual Tour de Yoles Rontes is a point-to-point race for yawls held in early August.

St. Barthélemy: The Festival de la Saint Barthélemy on August 24 marks the feast day of the patron saint of St. Barts. The feast of St. Louis on August 25 is commemorated in Corrossol by a fishing festival with dances and windsurfing contests.

St. Lucia: Members of La Rose Flower Society parade the streets dressed as kings and queens, princes and princesses, even doctors and nurses, for the Feast of St. Rose de Lima.

Turks and Caicos Islands: In early August, Provo Days gear up with a slew of activities: sailing races, regattas, parties, parades, dances, and a Miss Inter-Island/Miss Universe representative beauty contest. The Turks and Caicos Billfish Tournament is held at Turtle Cove Marina on Provo.

September **Martinique:** Bridge devotees enjoy the Bridge Tournament in mid-September.

St. Barthélemy: The Fête du Vent on September 1 and 2, is celebrated with fishing contests and dances in L'Orient.

Trinidad and Tobago: Hosein is a Muslim religious festival, which, though solemn, is never lacking in color or imagination. Celebrants parade through the streets singing, beating drums, and carrying *tadgeahs* (large, exquisitely colored mosquelike models).

October **Bonaire:** The annual Sailing Regatta is mid-October, with much ado about boats.

Cayman Islands: Pirate's Week finds Caymanians dressed as rogues and wenches and out to capture first a local galleon, and then the local governor. There's a mock battle, and the day ends in parties and parades.

Curaçao: One of the more uncommon musical events is the World Troubador Festival.

Dominican Republic: Puerto Plata has started its own Merengue Festival in the second week of October.

St. Vincent and the Grenadines: Independence Day is October 27.

Trinidad and Tobago: In October or November of each year, the Hindus create a Festival of Lights to pay tribute to the goddess Lakshmi. The devout scatter thousands of little earthenware lamps all over the cities and villages, in their homes and temples alike. At night, the result is an enchanted spectacle. Another highlight of the month is Trinidad's Pan Jazz Festival, during which leading pannists (players of metal drums, called *pans*) from North and South America converge in Port of Spain.

U.S. Virgin Islands: Hurricane Thanksgiving Day is the day when islanders give thanks for what they *didn't* get.

November   **Aruba:** In addition to the International Theatre Festival this month, Aruba sponsors the International Fishing Tournament on the first weekend in November.

Barbados: Residents show off their music, singing, dancing, acting, and writing talents during National Independence Festival of the Creative Arts. Shows lead all the way up to Independence Day on November 30.

Martinique: If you want to try a Semi-Marathon, Martinique invites you to a 22-kilometer race starting in Fort-de-France on November 25.

St. Martin/St. Maarten: On Concordia Day, parades and a joint ceremony by French and Dutch officials at the obelisk Border Monument commemorate the long-standing peaceful coexistence between both countries. This is also "St. Martin's Day" and the official beginning of "the season."

December   **Anguilla:** Separation Day is a day of patriotic festivities.

Barbados: The first weekend of December marks the annual Run Barbados International Road Race Series. The 26-mile, 385-yard marathon course (42,195 meters) over paved roads alongside the seashore and the 10K in and around Bridgetown attracts competitors from around the world. Among the top prizes for overseas entrants are airfare and hotel accommodations for the next year's race!

French West Indies: From Christmas to New Year's is Reveillon season, marked by special menus and dances at hotels and restaurants.

Guadeloupe: On Young Saints Day costumed children parade through the streets carrying toys.

Martinique: The town of Robert on the Atlantic coast (about a half-hour drive from Fort-de-France) holds the annual Nautique du Robert, a festival of the sea. On alternate years, Fort-de-France hosts either an International Jazz Festival or an International Guitar Festival, the latter with classes and concerts from world-famous guitarists. This is always held the first two weeks in December.

Nevis-St. Kitts: Carnival Week.

Puerto Rico: Although they hold a White Christmas Festival in Puerto Rico, you have little reason to fear snow in the Caribbean.

St. Barthélemy: The Route du Rose, a transatlantic regatta of Tall Ships that sets sail from St-Tropez in early November, arrives at St. Barts and there are many festivities to celebrate the finale.

St. Lucia: St. Lucia National Day is an island-wide celebration in honor of the island's patron saint.

When to Go

The Caribbean "season" has traditionally been a winter one, usually extending from December 15 to April 14. The winter months are the most fashionable, the most expensive, and the most popular for cruising or lazing on the beaches, far from the icy north, and most hotels are heavily booked at this time. You have to make your reservations at least two or three months in advance for the very best places. Hotel prices are at their highest during the winter months; the 20–40% drop in rates for "summer" (after April 15) is one of the chief advantages of off-season summer travel. Cruise prices also rise and fall with the seasons. Saving money isn't the only reason to visit the Caribbean during the off-season. Temperatures in summer are virtually the same as in winter. Some restaurants close and many hotels offer limited facilities, but reservations are easy to get, even at top establishments, and you'll have the beaches virtually to yourselves. Couples will enjoy relative solitude off-season, but singles in search of partners should visit during the high season, or choose a resort that enjoys a high occupancy rate year-round.

The flamboyant flowering trees are at their height of glory in summer, and so are most of the flowers and shrubs of the West Indies. The water is clearer for snorkeling and smoother in May, June, and July for sailing in the Virgin Islands and the Grenadines.

The Caribbean climate approaches the ideal of perpetual June. Average year-round temperature for the region is 78° to 85°. The extremes of temperature are 65° low, 95° high, but as everyone knows, it's the humidity, not the heat, that makes you suffer, especially when the two go hand in hand. You can count on downtown shopping areas being hot at midday any time of the year, but air-conditioning provides some respite. Stay near beaches, where water and trade winds can keep you cool, and shop early or late in the day.

High places can be cool, particularly when the Christmas winds hit Caribbean peaks (they come in late November and last through January), but a sweater is sufficient for protection from the trade winds.

Since most Caribbean islands are mountainous (notable exceptions being the Caymans, Aruba, Bonaire, and Curaçao), the altitude always offers an escape from the latitude. Kingston (Jamaica), Port of Spain (Trinidad), and Fort-de-France (Martinique) are three cities that swelter in summer, but climb 1,000 feet or so and everything is fine.

Hurricanes occasionally sweep through the Caribbean, and officials on many islands are unfortunately not well equipped to provide locals, much less tourists, with much warning. It's best to check the news daily and try to keep abreast of brewing tropical storms by reading stateside papers when available. The rainy season, which usually refers to the fall months, consists mostly of brief showers interspersed with sunshine. You can watch the clouds come over, feel the rain, and remain on your lounge chair for the sun to dry you off. A spell of overcast days is "unusual weather," as everyone will tell you.

Generally speaking, there's more planned entertainment in the winter months. The peak of local excitement on many islands, most notably Trinidad, St. Vincent, and the French West Indies, is Carnival.

Climate What follows are the average daily maximum and minimum temperatures for the Caribbean islands.

Current weather information on 750 cities in the United States and around the world is only a phone call away. To obtain the **WeatherTrak** telephone number for your area, call 900/370-8725. The number plays a taped message that tells you to dial the three-digit access code for the destination you're interested in. The code is either the area code (in the United States)

Caribbean Temperature Chart

ISLAND	JANUARY / FEBRUARY	MARCH / APRIL	MAY / JUNE	JULY / AUGUST	SEPTEMBER / OCTOBER	NOVEMBER / DECEMBER
Anguilla	26.5°C – 21.5°C	29.0°C – 25°C	30.5°C – 26.0°C	31.5°C – 27.0°C	30.5°C – 26.0°C	29.5°C – 25.0°C
	79.7°F – 70.7°F	84.2°F – 86.0°F	87.0°F – 78.8°F	89.0°F – 80.6°F	87.0°F – 78.8°F	85.1°F – 86.0°F
Antigua	27.0°C – 22.0°C	28.0°C – 22.5°C	29.0°C – 24.5°C	30.0°C – 25.0°C	30.0°C – 24.0°C	28.5°C –23.5°C
	81.0°F – 72.0°F	83.0°F – 73.0°F	85.0°F – 76.5°F	86.0°F – 77.0°F	86.0°F – 76.0°F	84.0°F – 75.0°F
Aruba	29.0°C – 23.0°C	30.5°C – 23.0°C	31.0°C – 24.0°C	32.0°C – 25.5°C	32.5°C – 26.5°C	30.5°C – 24.0°C
	85.0°F – 74.0°F	87.0°F – 74.0°F	88.0°F – 76.0°F	90.0°F – 78.0°F	91.0°F – 79.5°F	87.0°F – 76.0°F
Barbados	28.0°C – 21.0°C	29.5°C – 21.5°C	31.0°C – 23.0°C	30.5°C – 23.0°C	30.5°C – 23.0°C	31.0°C – 21.5°C
	83.0°F – 70.0°F	85.5°F – 71.0°F	88.0°F – 74.0°F	87.0°F – 74.0°F	87.0°F – 74.0°F	88.0°F – 74.0°F
Bonaire			specific monthly temperatures not available (25.5°C – 32.0°C year round)			
			specific monthly temperatures not available (78.0°F – 90.0°F year round)			
British Virgin Islands			specific monthly temperatures not available (24.0°C – 30.0°C year round)			
			specific monthly temperatures not available (76.0°F – 86.0°F year round)			
Cayman Islands	30.5°C – 18.5°C	31.5°C – 16.0°C	32.5°C – 21.0°C	32.5°C – 22.5°C	33.0°C – 22.0°C	31.0°C – 17.0°C
	87.0°F – 66.0°F	89.0°F – 61.0°F	91.0°F – 70.0°F	91.0°F – 73.0°F	92.0°F – 72.0°F	88.0°F – 63.0°F
Curaçao	28.5°C – 23.5°C	29.5°C – 23.5°C	30.5°C – 25.5°C	31.0°C – 25.5°C	31.5°C – 26.0°C	29.5°C – 24.0°C
	84.0°F – 75.0°F	85.5°F – 75.0°F	87.0°F – 78.0°F	88.0°F – 78.0°F	89.0°F – 79.0°F	85.5°F – 76.0°F
Dominica			specific monthly temperatures not available (23.5°C – 32.0°C year round)			
			specific monthly temperatures not available (75.0°F – 90.0°F year round)			
Dominican Republic	29.0°C – 19.0°C	29.0°C – 20.0°C	30.5°C – 22.0°C	31.0°C – 22.5°C	31.0°C – 22.0°C	29.5°C – 20.5°C
	85.0°F – 67.0°F	85.0°F – 68.5°F	87.0°F – 72.0°F	88.0°F – 73.0°F	88.0°F – 72.0°F	85.5°F – 69.0°F
Grenada	29.0°C – 24.0°C	29.0°C – 24.5°C	30.0°C – 25.5°C	30.0°C – 25.0°C	29.0°C – 24.5°C	29.5°C – 24.5°C
	85.0°F – 76.0°F	85.0°F – 76.5°F	86.0°F – 78.0°F	86.0°F – 77.0°F	87.0°F – 76.5°F	85.5°F – 76.5°F
Guadeloupe	28.0°C – 19.0°C	29.0°C – 20.0°C	30.5°C – 22.5°C	31.0°C – 23.0°C	31.0°C – 22.0°C	29.0°C – 20.5°C
	83.0°F – 67.0°F	85.0°F – 68.5°F	87.0°F – 73.0°F	88.0°F – 74.0°F	88.0°F – 72.0°F	85.0°F – 69.0°F
Haiti	29.0°C – 17.5°C	30.0°C – 18.5°C	30.5°C – 20.0°C	32.0°C – 21.0°C	30.5°C – 20.5°C	28.5°C – 18.5°C
	85.0°F – 64.0°F	86.0°F – 66.0°F	87.0°F – 68.0°F	90.0°F – 70.0°F	87.0°F – 69.0°F	84.0°F – 66.0°F

Jamaica	30.0°C – 19.0°C 86.0°F – 67.0°F	30.5°C – 20.5°C 87.0°F – 69.0°F	31.5°C – 22.5°C 89.0°F – 73.0°F	32.0°C – 23.0°C 90.0°F – 74.0°F	31.5°C – 23.0°C 89.0°F – 73.0°F	31.0°C – 21.5°C 88.0°F – 71.0°F
Martinique	28.5°C – 21.0°C 84.0°F – 70.0°F	29.5°C – 21.5°C 85.5°F – 71.0°F	30.5°C – 23.0°C 87.0°F – 74.0°F	30.5°C – 23.0°C 87.0°F – 74.0°F	31.0°C – 23.0°C 88.0°F – 74.0°F	29.5°C – 22.0°C 88.5°F – 72.0°F
Montserrat	28.0°C – 21.0°C 83.0°F – 70.0°F	29.5°C – 21.5°C 85.5°F – 71.0°F	31.0°C – 23.5°C 88.0°F – 75.0°F	31.0°C – 24.0°C 88.0°F – 76.0°F	31.5°C – 23.0°C 89.0°F – 74.0°F	28.5°C – 22.5°C 84.0°F – 73.0°F
Nevis	27.0°C – 21.5°C 81.0°F – 71.0°F	28.0°C – 22.5°C 83.0°F – 73.0°F	29.0°C – 24.0°C 85.0°F – 76.0°F	30.0°C – 24.0°C 86.0°F – 76.0°F	29.5°C – 24.0°C 88.5°F – 76.0°F	28.5°C – 23.0°C 84.0°F – 74.0°F
Puerto Rico	28.0°C – 22.0°C 83.0°F – 72.0°F	28.5°C – 22.5°C 84.0°F – 73.0°F	31.5°C – 24.5°C 87.0°F – 76.5°F	31.0°C – 25.5°C 88.0°F – 78.0°F	31.0°C – 24.0°C 88.0°F – 76.0°F	29.5°C – 23.0°C 85.5°F – 74.0°F
Saba	specific monthly temperatures not available (24.0°C – 28.5°C year round) specific monthly temperatures not available (76.0°F – 84.0°F year round)					
St. Barthelemy	25.0°C 77.0°F	26.0°C 78.0°F	27.0°C 80.0°F	27.0°C 80.0°F	27.0°C 80.0°F	26.0°C 78.0°F
St. Eustatius	29.0°C – 22.5°C 85.0°F – 73.0°F	30.0°C – 23.0°C 86.0°F – 74.0°F	31.0°C – 23.5°C 88.0°F – 75.0°F	32.0°C – 24.0°C 90.0°F – 76.0°F	32.0°C – 24.0°C 90.0°F – 76.0°F	30.0°C – 23.5°C 86.5°F – 75.0°F
St. Kitts	27.0°C – 21.5°C 81.0°F – 68.0°F	28.0°C – 23.0°C 83.0°F – 74.0°F	29.0°C – 24.0°C 85.0°F – 76.0°F	25.0°C – 24.0°C 86.0°F – 76.0°F	29.5°C – 24.0°C 85.5°F – 76.0°F	28.5°C – 24.0°C 84.0°F – 75.5°F
St. Lucia	27.0°C – 20.0°C 81.0°F – 68.0°F	28.0°C – 21.0°C 83.0°F – 70.0°F	29.0°C – 22.0°C 85.0°F – 72.0°F	29.5°C – 22.0°C 85.5°F – 72.0°F	29.5°C – 22.0°C 85.5°F – 72.0°F	28.0°C – 21.5°C 83.0°F – 71.0°F
St. Martin / St. Maarten	27.5°C – 22.0°C 82.0°F – 72.0°F	29.0°C – 22.5°C 85.0°F – 73.0°F	29.5°C – 23.5°C 85.5°F – 75.0°F	30.5°C – 24.0°C 87.0°F – 75.0°F	30.5°C – 24.0°C 87.0°F – 75.0°F	28.0°C – 22.0°C 83.0°F – 72.0°F
St. Vincent and the Grenadines	29.0°C – 22.0°C 85.0°F – 72.0°F	29.5°C – 23.5°C 85.5°F – 75.0°F	29.5°C – 23.0°C 85.5°F – 74.0°F	25.0°C – 24.0°C 86.0°F – 76.0°F	30.5°C – 24.0°C 87.0°F – 76.0°F	29.5°C – 23.5°C 85.5°F – 75.0°F
Trinidad and Tobago	31.0°C – 20.0°C 88.0°F – 69.0°F	32.0°C – 20.5°C 90.0°F – 69.0°F	32.0°C – 22.0°C 90.0°F – 72.0°F	31.0°C – 22.0°C 88.0°F – 72.0°F	32.0°C – 22.0°C 90.0°F – 72.0°F	31.5°C – 21.5°C 89.0°F – 71.0°F
Turks and Caicos Islands	27.0°C – 21.0°C 81.0°F – 70.0°F	28.5°C – 22.5°C 84.0°F – 73.0°F	30.5°C – 24.5°C 87.0°F – 76.5°F	31.5°C – 24.5°C 89.0°F – 78.0°F	31.0°C – 24.5°C 88.0°F – 76.5°F	28.5°C – 23.5°C 84.0°F – 73.0°F
U.S. Virgin Islands	25.0°C – 23.0°C 86.0°F – 74.0°F	30.5°C – 21.5°C 87.0°F – 71.0°F	31.0°C – 24.0°C 88.0°F – 75.0°F	35.0°C – 25.0°C 95.0°F – 77.0°F	33.0°C – 25.0°C 92.0°F – 76.0°F	25.0°C – 22.0°C 86.0°F – 72.0°F

or the first three letters of the foreign city. For a list of all access codes, send a stamped, self-addressed envelope to Cities, Box 7000, Dallas, TX 75209. For further information, phone 214/869–3035 or 800/247–3282.

What to Pack

Pack light because baggage carts are scarce at airports and luggage restrictions are tight.

Clothing Dress on the islands is light and casual. Bring loose-fitting clothes made of natural fabrics to see you through days of heat and high humidity. Take a coverup for the beaches, not only to protect you from the sun, but also to wear to and from your hotel room. Bathing suits and immodest attire are frowned upon off the beach on many islands. A sun hat is advisable, but there's no need to pack one because inexpensive straw hats are available everywhere. For shopping and sightseeing, bring walking shorts, jeans, T-shirts, long-sleeve cotton shirts, slacks, and sundresses. Air-conditioning in hotels and restaurants often borders on the glacial, so bring a sweater or jacket for dining out. Evening wear is casual; jacket and tie is rarely required.

Miscellaneous It's advisable to wear a hat and sun-block lotion while sightseeing. Bring a spare pair of eyeglasses and sunglasses and an adequate supply of any prescription drugs you may need. You can probably find what you need in the pharmacies, but you may need a local doctor's prescription. Although you'll want an umbrella during the rainy season, you can pick up inexpensive ones locally. Leave the plastic or nylon raincoats at home; the high humidity makes them extremely uncomfortable. Bring suntan lotions and film from home in abundant supply; they're much more expensive on the islands. It's wise, too, to bring insect repellent, especially if you plan to walk through rain forests or visit during the rainy season.

Carry-on Luggage Passengers on U.S. airlines are limited to two carry-on bags. For a bag you wish to store under the seat, the maximum dimensions are 9″ × 14″ × 22″. For bags that can be hung in a closet or on a luggage rack, the maximum dimensions are 4″ × 23″ × 45″. For bags you wish to store in an overhead bin, the maximum dimensions are 10″ × 14″ × 36″. Any item that exceeds the specified dimensions may be rejected as a carryon and taken as checked baggage. Keep in mind that an airline can adapt the rules to circumstances, so on an especially crowded flight don't be surprised if you are allowed only one carry-on bag.

In addition to the two carryons, you may bring aboard a handbag (pocketbook or purse); an overcoat or wrap; an umbrella; a camera; a reasonable amount of reading material; an infant bag; crutches, cane, braces, or other prosthetic device; and an infant/child safety seat (depending upon space availability).

Foreign airlines have slightly different policies. They generally allow only one piece of carry-on luggage in tourist class, in addition to handbags and bags filled with duty-free goods. Passengers in first and business class may also be allowed to carry on one garment bag. It is best to call your airline to find out its current policy.

Checked Luggage Luggage allowances vary slightly from airline to airline. Many carriers allow three checked pieces; some allow only two. It is best to check before you go. In all cases, check-in luggage cannot weigh more than 70 pounds per piece or be larger than 62 inches (length + width + height).

Taking Money Abroad

Traveler's checks and all major U.S. credit cards are widely accepted in the Caribbean. U.S. dollars are also widely accepted on most of the islands. The large hotels, restaurants, and department stores accept credit cards readily, but some of the smaller restaurants and shops operate on a cash-only basis. There may even be some room for bargaining when paying with U.S. dollars.

Although you won't get as good an exchange rate at home as abroad, it's wise to change a small amount of money into the local currency before you go to avoid long lines at airport currency-exchange booths. Some U.S. banks will change your money. If your local bank can't provide this service, you can exchange money through **Deak International.** To find the office nearest you, contact Deak (630 5th Ave., New York, NY 10011, tel. 212/635–0515).

For safety, it's always wise to carry traveler's checks. The most widely recognized are **American Express, Barclays, Thomas Cook,** and those issued through such major commercial banks as **Citibank** and **Bank of America.** Some banks will issue the checks free to established customers, but most charge a 1% commission fee. Buy some of the traveler's checks in small denominations to cash toward the end of your trip. This will save your having to cash a large check and ending up with more foreign currency than you need. You can also buy traveler's checks in the currency of some of the islands, a good idea if the dollar is dropping in relation to the local currency. The value of some currencies changes with great frequency and very radically; some are subject to inflation, others to devaluation, while still others float with the U.S. dollar. Remember to take the addresses of offices in the islands where you can get refunds for lost or stolen traveler's checks.

Banks and government-approved exchange houses give the best rates; hotels will also change currency, but generally at lower rates.

Getting Money from Home

There are at least three ways to get money from home:

1) Have it sent through a large commercial bank with a branch on the island where you're staying. The only drawback is that you must have an account with the bank; if not, you will have to go through your own bank and the process will be slower and more expensive.

2) Have it sent through **American Express.** If you are a cardholder, you can cash a personal check or a counter check at an American Express office for up to $1,000; $200 will be in cash and $800 in traveler's checks. There is a 1% commission on the traveler's checks. You can also get money through **American Express MoneyGram.** Through this service, you can receive up

to $5,000 cash. It works this way: You call home and ask some-one to go to an American Express office or an American Express MoneyGram agent located in a retail outlet and fill out an American Express MoneyGram. It can be paid for with cash or any major credit card. The person making the payment is given a reference number and telephones you with that number. The American Express MoneyGram agent calls an 800 number and authorizes the transfer of funds to an American Express office or participating agency on the islands. (MoneyGram is not available on *all* islands; find out before you go whether your destination has this service.) In most cases, the money is avail-able immediately on a 24-hour basis. You pick it up by showing identification and giving the reference number. Fees vary ac-cording to the amount of money sent. For sending $300, the fee is $30; for $5,000, $175. For the American Express MoneyGram location nearest your home, and to find out where the service is available on the islands, call 800/543-4080. You do not have to be a cardholder to use this service.

3) Have it sent through **Western Union** (tel. 800/325-6000). If you have a MasterCard or Visa, you can have money sent for any amount up to your credit limit. If not, have someone take cash or a certified cashier's check to a Western Union office. The money will be delivered in two business days to a bank near where you're staying. Fees vary with the amount of money sent and its destination. For Puerto Rico and the U.S. Virgin Is-lands, the rate is $47 for $1,000 and $37 for $500. For other destinations in the Caribbean, the fees average $69 for $1,000 and $59 for $500. Add $10 if you use credit cards.

Cash Machines Virtually all U.S. banks now belong to a network of Automatic Teller Machines (ATMs) that dispense cash 24 hours a day. There are eight major networks in the United States, and some banks belong to more than one. In the past year, two of the larg-est systems, Cirrus, which is owned by MasterCard, and Plus, which is affiliated with Visa, have extended their service to U.S. territories and to foreign cities that attract large num-bers of tourist and business travelers. The Plus system, for example, already has outlets in Puerto Rico and the U.S. Vir-gin Islands and may be expanding to other islands in the Caribbean. Each network has a toll-free number you can call to locate its machines in a given city. The Cirrus number is 800/424-7787; the Plus number is 800/843-7587. Note that these cash cards are not issued automatically; they must be re-quested at your specific branch.

Cards issued by Visa, American Express, and MasterCard can also be used in ATMs, but the fees are usually higher than the fees on bank cards (and there is a daily interest charge on the loan). All three companies issue directories that list the nation-al and international outlets that accept their cards. You can pick up a Visa or MasterCard directory at your local bank. For an American Express directory, call 800/CASH-NOW (this number can also be used for general inquiries). Contact your bank for information on fees and the amount of cash you can withdraw on any given day. Although each bank individually charges for taking money with the card, using your American Express, Visa, or MasterCard at an ATM can be cheaper than exchanging money in a bank because of variations in exchange rates.

Traveling with Film

If your camera is new, shoot and develop a few rolls of film before you leave home. Pack some lens tissue and an extra battery for your built-in light meter. Invest about $10 in a skylight filter and screw it onto the front of your lens. It will protect the lens and also reduce haze.

Film doesn't like hot weather. If you're driving in summer, don't store film in the glove compartment or on the shelf under the rear window. Put it behind the front seat on the floor, on the side opposite the exhaust pipe.

On a plane trip, never pack unprocessed film in check-in luggage; if your bags get X-rayed, you can say good-bye to your pictures. Always carry undeveloped film with you through security, and ask to have it inspected by hand. (It helps to isolate your film in a plastic bag, ready for quick inspection.) Inspectors at American airports are required by law to honor requests for hand inspection; abroad, you'll have to depend on the kindness of strangers.

The old airport scanning machines—still in use in some countries—use heavy doses of radiation that can turn a family portrait into an early morning fog. The newer models—used in all U.S. airports—are safe for anything from five to 500 scans, depending on the speed of your film. The effects are cumulative; you can put the same roll of film through several scans without worry. After five scans, though, you're asking for trouble.

If your film gets fogged and you want an explanation, send it to the **National Association of Photographic Manufacturers** (550 Mamaroneck Ave., Harrison, NY 10528). They will try to determine what went wrong. The service is free.

Staying Healthy

Few real hazards threaten the health of a visitor to the Caribbean. Poisonous snakes are hard to find, and the small lizards that seem to have overrun the islands are harmless. The worst problem may well be a tiny predator, the "no see'um," a small sand fly that tends to appear after a rain, near wet or swampy ground, and around sunset. If you feel particularly vulnerable to insect bites, bring along a good repellent.

The worst problem tends to be sunburn or sunstroke. Even people who are not normally bothered by strong sun should head into this area with a long-sleeve shirt, a hat, and long pants or a beach wrap. These are essential for a day on a boat but are also advisable for midday at the beach. Also carry some sun-block lotion for nose, ears, and other sensitive areas such as eyelids, ankles, etc. Be sure to drink enough liquids. Above all, limit your sun time for the first few days until you become used to the heat.

Since health standards vary from island to island, it's best to inquire about the island you plan to visit before you go. No special shots are required for most destinations in the Caribbean; where they are, we have made note of it in the individual chapters. If you have a health problem that might require purchasing prescription drugs while in the Caribbean, have your doctor write a prescription using the drug's generic name; brand names can vary widely from island to island.

The International Association for Medical Assistance to Travelers (IAMAT) is a worldwide organization offering a list of approved English-speaking doctors whose training meets British and American standards. Contact IAMAT for a list of physicians and clinics in the Caribbean that belong to this network. **In the United States:** 417 Center Street, Lewiston, NY 14092, tel. 716/754–4883. **In Canada:** 40 Regal Road, Guelph, Ontario N1K 1B5. **In Europe:** 57 Voirets, 1212 Grand–Lancy, Geneva, Switzerland. Membership is free.

Insurance

Travelers may seek insurance coverage in three areas: health and accident, lost luggage, and trip cancellation. Your first step is to review your existing health and home-owner policies. Some health insurance plans cover health expenses incurred while traveling, some home-owner policies cover luggage theft, and some major medical plans cover emergency transportation.

Health and Accident
Several companies offer coverage designed to supplement existing health insurance for travelers:

Carefree Travel Insurance (Box 310, 120 Mineola Blvd., Mineola, NY 11501, tel. 516/294–0220 or 800/343–3553) provides coverage for medical evacuation. It also offers 24-hour medical advice by phone, will help find English-speaking medical and legal assistance anywhere in the world, and offers direct payment to hospitals for emergency medical care.

Wallach and Company, Inc. (243 Church St., NW, Suite 100D, Vienna, VA 22180, tel. 703/281–9500 or 800/237–6615) offers comprehensive medical coverage, including emergency evacuation for trips of 10–90 days.

International SOS Assistance (Box 11568, Philadelphia, PA 19116, tel. 215/244–1500 or 800/523–8930) does not offer medical insurance but provides medical evacuation and repatriation services.

Travel Guard International, underwritten by Transamerica Occidental Life Companies (1100 Centerpoint Dr., Stevens Point, WI 54481, tel. 715/345–0505 or 800/782–5151), offers reimbursement for medical expenses with no deductibles or daily limits, and emergency evacuation services.

Lost Luggage
Luggage loss is usually covered as part of a comprehensive travel insurance package that includes personal accident, trip cancellation, and sometimes default and bankruptcy insurance. Several companies offer comprehensive policies:

Access America, Inc., a subsidiary of Blue Cross–Blue Shield (600 3rd Ave., Box 807, New York, NY 10163, tel. 212/490–5345 or 800/284–8300).

Near Services (1900 N. MacArthur Blvd., Suite 210, Oklahoma City, OK 73127, tel. 800/654–6700 or in Oklahoma City, 405/949–2500).

Travel Guard International (*see* Health and Accident Insurance, above).

Carefree Travel Insurance (*see* Health and Accident Insurance, above).

Luggage Insurance
Airlines are responsible for lost or damaged property only up to $1,250 per passenger on domestic flights, and $9.07 per

pound ($20 per kilo) for checked baggage on international flights, and up to $400 per passenger for unchecked baggage on international flights. If you're carrying valuables, either take them with you on the airplane or purchase additional insurance for lost luggage. Some airlines will issue additional insurance when you check in, but many do not. One that does is American Airlines. Rates for both domestic and international flights are $1 for every $100 valuation, with a maximum of $400 valuation per passenger. Hand luggage is not included.

Insurance for lost, damaged, or stolen luggage is available through travel agents or directly through various insurance companies. Two companies that issue luggage insurance are **Tele-Trip** (P.O. Box 31685, 3201 Farnam St., Omaha, NE 68131, tel. 800/228–9792), a subsidiary of Mutual of Omaha, and **The Travelers Insurance Co.** (Ticket and Travel Dept., 1 Tower Square, Hartford, CT 06183, tel. 203/277–0111 or 800/243–3174). Tele-Trip, which operates sales booths at airports and also issues policies through travel agents, insures checked luggage for up to 180 days and for $500–$3,000 valuation. For one-three days, the rate for a $500 valuation is $8.25; for 180 days, $100. The Travelers Insurance Co. insures checked or hand luggage for $500–$2,000 valuation per person, also for a maximum of 180 days. Rates for up to five days for $500 valuation are $10; for 180 days, $85. Both companies offer the same rates on domestic and international flights. Check the travel pages of your local newspaper for the names of other companies that insure luggage.

Before you go, itemize the contents of each bag in case you need to file an insurance claim. Be certain to put your home address on each piece of luggage, including carry-on bags. If your luggage is stolen and later recovered, the airline must deliver the luggage to your home free of charge.

Trip Cancellation Flight insurance is often included in the price of a ticket when paid for with an American Express, Visa, or other major credit and charge cards. It is usually included in combination travel insurance packages available from most tour operators, travel agents, and insurance agents.

Student and Youth Travel

The **International Student Identity Card** (ISIC) entitles students to special fares on local transportation and discounts at museums, theaters, sports events, and many other attractions. If purchased in the United States, the $10 ISIC also includes $2,000 in emergency medical insurance, plus $100 a day for up to 60 days of hospital coverage and a collect-call phone number to use for emergencies. Apply to the **Council on International Educational Exchange (CIEE)** (205 E. 42nd St., New York, NY 10017, tel. 212/661–1450). In Canada, the ISIC is available for C$7.50 from the Federation of Students–Services (171 College St., Toronto, Ont. M5T 1P7).

Council Travel, a CIEE subsidiary, is the foremost U.S. student travel agency, specializing in low-cost charters and serving as the exclusive U.S. agent for many student airfare bargains and student tours. (CIEE's 80-page *Student Travel Catalog* and "Council Charter" brochure are available free from any Council Travel office in the United States; enclose $1 postage if ordering by mail.) In addition to the CIEE headquarters at 205 East 42nd Street and a branch office at 35 West 8th Street in New York City (tel. 212/254–2525), there are Council Travel offices in Berkeley, La Jolla, Long Beach, Los Angeles, San Diego, San Francisco, and Sherman Oaks, CA; New Haven, CT; Washington, DC; Atlanta, GA; Chicago and Evanston, IL; New Orleans, LA; Amherst, Boston, and Cambridge, MA; Minneapolis, MN; Portland, OR; Providence, RI; Austin and Dallas, TX; Seattle, WA; and Milwaukee, WI.

The **Educational Travel Center** (438 N. Frances St., Madison, WI 55703, tel. 608/256–5551) is another student travel specialist worth contacting for information on student tours, bargain fares, and bookings.

Students who would like to work abroad should contact **CIEE's Work Abroad Department** (205 E. 42nd St., New York, NY 10017) tel. 212/661–1414, ext. 1130. The council arranges various types of paid and voluntary work experiences overseas for up to six months. CIEE also sponsors study programs in Latin America and publishes many books of interest to the student traveler: these include *Work, Study, Travel Abroad; The Whole World Handbook* ($9.95 plus $1.00 book-rate postage or $2.50 first-class postage) and *Volunteer! The Comprehensive Guide to Voluntary Service in the U.S. and Abroad* ($6.95 plus $1.00 book-rate postage or $2.50 first-class postage).

The Information Center at the **Institute of International Education** (809 UN Plaza, New York, NY 10017, tel. 212/984–5413) has reference books, foreign university catalogues, study-abroad brochures, and other materials that may be consulted by students and nonstudents alike, free of charge. The Information Center is open weekdays 10–4. For a current list of IIE publications, prices, and ordering information, write to Institute of International Education Books at the above address. Books must be purchased by mail or in person; telephone orders are not accepted. General information on IIE programs and services is available from the institute's regional offices in Atlanta, Chicago, Denver, Houston, San Francisco, and Washington, DC.

Traveling with Children

Publications *Family Travel Times* is an 8- to 12-page newsletter published 10 times a year by **TWYCH** (Travel with Your Children, 80 8th Ave., New York, NY 10011, tel. 212/206–0688). The $35 yearly subscription includes access to back issues and twice-weekly opportunities to call in for specific information. Send $1 for a sample issue. The September issue is always devoted entirely to the Caribbean.

Great Vacations with Your Kids, (second edition) by Dorothy Jordan (founder of TWYCH) and Marjorie Cohen, offers complete advice on planning a trip with children (toddlers to teens) and details everything from city vacations to adventure vacations to child-care resources ($12.95, E.P. Dutton, 2 Park Ave., New York, NY 10016).

"Kids and Teens in Flight" and **"Fly Rights"** are U.S. Department of Transportation brochures with information on special services for young travelers. To order free copies, call 202/366–2220.

Accommodations
Hotels

In addition to offering family discounts and special rates for children (for example, some large hotel chains do not charge extra for children under 12 if they stay in their parents' room), many hotels and resorts arrange for baby-sitting services and run a variety of special children's programs. The following list is representative of the kinds of services and activities offered by some of the major chains and resorts. It is by no means exhaustive. If you are going to be traveling with your children, be sure to check with your travel agent for more information or ask hotel representatives about children's programs when you are making reservations.

In **Puerto Rico,** the **Hyatt Regency Cerromar Beach** and the **Hyatt Dorado Beach Hotel** operate a complimentary camp for children age 5–12 all summer, at Christmastime and at Easter. One of the camp's main attractions is a meandering, free-form freshwater pool with waterfalls, bridges, and a 187-foot water slide. The camp's staff includes bilingual college-age counselors. For more information, call 800/233–1234. The **El San Juan** in Puerto Rico (tel. 800/468–2818) has a program for children in the same age group that features swimnastics, treasure hunts, beach walks, exercise classes, tennis, and an always-open game room.

Superclub's Boscobel Beach in **Jamaica** (tel. 800/858–8009) is an all-inclusive resort that specializes in traveling families. Seven-night packages are in the $1,000-per-person range, and two children under 14 are allowed to stay free if they occupy the same room as their parents. A small army of SuperNannies is on hand to take charge. The activities are scheduled in half-hour periods so that children can drop in and out. For younger children there are morning "Mousercises," a petting zoo, shell hunts, and craft classes; for teens, "Coke-tail" parties at a disco and "No-Talent" shows. The classes in the Jamaican patois are popular with all ages.

Casa de Campo in the **Dominican Republic** (tel. 800/223–6620) has a fully operational summer camp that children can attend on a day-by-day basis. The program includes lessons in sailing, tennis, golf, painting, and pottery as well as bike races, donkey polo, and softball and soccer games. "Campers" are divided into two groups—age 5–8 and 9–12. On **St. Thomas** in the U.S. Virgin Islands the **Stouffer Grand Resort** (tel. 800/233–4935) has half-day and full-day programs for children age 3–12. In addition to supervising volleyball matches, arts and crafts classes, water games, and iguana hunts, the staff arranges outings to the Coral World Marine Life Park and Observatory. **Club Med** has recently added Mini Club programs for children to their regular roster of activities at resorts in the **Dominican Republic** and **St. Lucia.** Designed for children age 2–11 and scheduled from 9 AM to 9 PM, the fully supervised Mini Club activities include tennis, waterskiing, sailing, scuba diving in a pool, costume parties, and painting and pottery classes. For more information, call 800/CLUB–MED.

Villa Rentals

At Home Abroad, Inc. (405 E. 56th St., Suite 6H, New York, NY 10022, tel. 212/421–9165).
Villas International (71 W. 23rd St., Suite 1402, New York, NY 10010, tel. 212/929–7585 or 800/221–2260).
Hideaway International (Box 1270, Littleton, MA 01460, tel. 508/486–8955).

Villas and Apartments Abroad (420 Madison Ave., Room 305, New York, NY 10017, tel. 212/759–1025).

Home Exchange Exchanging homes is a surprisingly low-cost way to enjoy a vacation abroad, especially a long one. The largest home-exchange service, **International Home Exchange Service** (Box 3975, San Francisco, CA 94119, tel. 415/435–3497) publishes three directories a year. Membership, which costs $35, entitles you to one listing and all three directories. Photos of your property cost an additional $8.50, and listing a second home costs $10. A good choice for domestic home exchange, **Vacation Exchange Club, Inc.** (12006 111th Ave., Unit 12, Youngstown, AZ 85363, tel. 602/972–2186), publishes one directory in February and a supplement in April. Membership is $24.70 per year, for which you receive one listing. Photos cost another $9; listing a second home costs $6. **Loan-a-Home** (2 Park La., Mount Vernon, NY 10552) is popular with the academic community on sabbatical and with businesspeople on temporary assignment. There's no annual membership fee or charge for listing your home, however one directory and a supplement costs $30. Loan-a-Home publishes two directories (in December and June) and two supplements (in March and September) each year. All four books cost $40 per year.

Getting There All children, including infants, must have a passport for foreign travel; family passports are no longer issued. (For more information, *see* the Passports and Visas sections in the individual chapters.)

On international flights, children under age 2 not occupying a seat pay 10% of adult fare; on domestic flights, they travel free. Various discounts apply to children age 2–12. Reserve a seat behind the bulkhead of the plane, which offers more legroom and can usually fit a bassinet (supplied by the airline). At the same time, inquire about special children's meals or snacks, which are offered by most airlines. (See "TWYCH's Airline Guide" in the February 1990 issue of *Family Travel Times* for a rundown on children's services furnished by 46 airlines; an update is planned for February 1992.) Ask your airline in advance if you can bring aboard your child's car seat. (For the pamphlet *Child/Infant Safety Seats Acceptable for Use in Aircraft*, contact the Community and Consumer Liaison Division, APA-200, Federal Aviation Administration, Washington, DC 20591, tel. 202/267–3479.)

Hints for Disabled Travelers

The **Information Center for Individuals with Disabilities** (Fort Point Place, 1st floor, 27–43 Wormwood St., Boston, MA 02210, tel. 617/727–5540) offers useful problem-solving assistance, including lists of travel agents who specialize in tours for the disabled.

Moss Rehabilitation Hospital Travel Information Service (12th St. and Tabor Rd., Philadelphia, PA 19141, tel. 215/329–5715) provides information on tourist sights, transportation, and accommodations in destinations around the world. There is a small fee.

Mobility International U.S.A. (Box 3551, Eugene, OR 97403, tel. 503/343–1284) is a membership organization with a $20 annual fee offering information on accommodations, organized study, and so forth around the world.

The **Society for the Advancement of Travel for the Handicapped** (26 Court St., Penthouse Suite, Brooklyn, NY 11242, tel. 718/858–5483) offers access information. Annual membership costs $40, $25 for senior travelers and students. Send $2 and a stamped, self-addressed envelope for a list of tour operators who arrange travel for the disabled.

Travel Industry and Disabled Exchange (TIDE, 5435 Donna Ave., Tarzana, CA 91356, tel. 818/343–6339) is an industry-based organization with a $15-per-person annual membership fee. Members receive a quarterly newsletter and a directory of travel agencies for the disabled.

Publications Twin Peaks Press publishes a number of useful resources: *Travel for the Disabled* ($9.95), *Directory of Travel Agencies for the Disabled* ($12.95), and *Wheelchair Vagabond* ($9.95 paperback, $14.95 hardcover). Order through your local bookstore or directly from the publisher (Twin Peaks Press, Box 129, Vancouver, WA 98666, tel. 206/694–2462). Add $2 per book postage and $1 for each additional book.

Access to the World: A Travel Guide for the Handicapped, by Louise Weiss, is a well-known and trusted guidebook that has recently been updated (Henry Holt & Co., $12.95 plus $2 shipping (tel. 800/247–3912 to order; include order number 0805001417).

"Fly Rights," a free U.S. Department of Transportation brochure, offers airline access information for the handicapped. To order, call 202/366–2220.

Accommodations In the more popular destinations throughout the Caribbean, the specific needs of the disabled are now often being taken into consideration when new hotels are built or existing properties are renovated. A number of cruise ships, such as the *QE II* and the Norwegian Caribbean Line's *Seward*, have also recently adapted some of their cabins to meet the needs of disabled passengers. To make sure that a given establishment provides adequate access, ask about specific facilities when making a reservation or consider booking through a travel agent who specializes in travel for the disabled (*see* above).

The **Divi Hotel** company, which has nine properties throughout the Caribbean, runs one of the best dive programs for the disabled at its resort in **Bonaire.** The facility is equipped with ramps, guest rooms and bathrooms can accommodate wheelchairs, and the staff is specially trained to assist disabled divers. For more information, call 800/367–3484.

Hints for Older Travelers

The **American Association of Retired Persons** (AARP, 1990 K St., NW, Washington, DC 20049, tel. 202/872–4700) has two programs for independent travelers: (1) *The Purchase Privilege Program,* which offers discounts on hotels, airfare, car rentals, TV rentals, and sightseeing; and (2) the *AARP Motoring Plan,* which furnishes emergency aid (road service) and trip-routing information for an annual fee of $33.95 per person or married couple. The AARP also arranges group tours through **Olson-Travelworld** (100 N. Sepulveda Blvd., 10th Floor, El Segundo, CA 90245, tel. 213/615–0711 or 800/421–2255). As of 1991, group tours will be arranged by **American Express Vacations** (*see* Tour Groups, above). AARP members must be at least 50 years old. Annual dues are $5 per person or per couple.

If you're planning to use an AARP or other senior-citizen identification card to obtain a reduced hotel rate, mention it at the time you make your reservation rather than when you check out. At restaurants, show your card to the maître d' before you're seated; discounts may be limited to certain set menus, days, or hours. Your AARP card will identify you as a retired person but will not ensure a discount in all hotels and restaurants. When renting a car, remember that economy cars, priced at promotional rates, may cost less than the cars that are available with your ID card.

The **National Council of Senior Citizens** (925 15th St., NW, Washington, DC 20005, tel. 202/347–8800) is a nonprofit advocacy group with some 5,000 local clubs across the country. Annual membership is $12 per person or per couple. Members receive a monthly newspaper with travel information and an ID for reduced rates on hotels and car rentals.

Mature Outlook (6001 N. Clark St., Chicago, IL 60660, tel. 800/336–6330), a subsidiary of Sears, Roebuck, & Co., is a travel club for people over 50 years of age, offering hotel discounts and a bimonthly newsletter to its 800,000 members. Annual membership is $9.95 per person or couple. Instant membership is available at participating Holiday Inns.

Elderhostel (80 Boylston St., Suite 400, Boston, MA 02116, tel. 617/426–7788) is an innovative educational program for people 60 or over (only one member of a traveling couple has to qualify). Participants live in dormitories on some 1,200 campuses around the world. Mornings are devoted to lectures and seminars, afternoons to sightseeing and field trips. The fee for a trip includes room, board, tuition (in the United States and Canada) and round-trip transportation (overseas). Special scholarships in the United States and Canada are available for those who qualify financially. A catalogue of courses is free for a year *and* if you participate in a course; $10 a year after that if you don't.

Publications *The International Health Guide for Senior Citizen Travelers,* by Dr. W. Robert Lange, MD, is available for $4.95, and *The Senior Citizens Guide to Budget Travel in the United States and Canada,* by Paige Palmer, is available for $4.95, plus $1 for shipping from Pilot Books (103 Cooper St., Babylon, NY 11702, tel. 516/422–2225).

The Discount Guide for Travelers over 55, by Caroline and Walter Weintz, lists helpful addresses, package tours, reduced rate car rentals, etc., in the United States and abroad. To order, send $7.95 plus $1.50 for shipping to Penguin USA/NAL, Cash Sales (Bergenfield Order Department, 120 Woodbine St., Bergenfield, NJ 07621, tel. 800/526–0275; include order number ISBN 0-525-483-58-6).

"Fly Rights" (tel. 202/366–2220), a free brochure published by the U.S. Department of Transportation, offers information on airline services available to elderly passengers.

Further Reading

Caribbean Style (Crown Publishers) is a coffee-table book with magnificent photographs of the interiors and exteriors of homes and buildings in the Caribbean. The collection runs the gamut from splendid plantations to ramshackle shanties.

Don't Stop the Carnival, by Herman Wouk, is a hilarious novel about a New York press agent who left his old life behind and bought a resort hotel in the Caribbean. The novel is slightly dated, but the vicissitudes of the hero are acknowledged by everyone who has ever tried to run a hotel in the islands. It is a marvelous romp through the region.

If you want to familiarize yourself with the sights, smells, and sounds of the West Indies, pick up Jamaica Kincaid's *Annie John,* a richly textured, coming-of-age novel about a girl growing up on the island of Antigua. *At The Bottom Of The River,* also by Kincaid, is a collection of short stories that depicts the mysteries and manners of a world replete with merengue music, bay rum, and blooming red hibiscus in the dreams and reminiscences of a young adult.

Michelle Cliff is the author of *The Land of Look Behind, Claiming an Identity They Taught Me to Despise,* and, most recently, *No Telephone to Heaven,* a structurally daring, often violent novel set in Jamaica—a landscape of wild bamboo and jasmine, populated by refugees moving through the outskirts of Kingston.

Another notable chronicle of Caribbean life and customs is the provocative *Wide Sargasso Sea,* by Jean Rhys. Published in 1968, its imaginative construction still entices the reader into a world of exotic, haunting beauty that Rhys herself encountered growing up on the Windward Islands of the West Indies.

James Michener's islands saga, titled *Caribbean,* was published in 1989. Michener headquartered himself in Coral Gables, Florida, to facilitate his 10 extensive research expeditions through the Caribbean region, and he has publicly expressed both the dramatic assets and liabilities inherent to a culture so rich in diversity.

If you're interested in probing this very issue more deeply, head for V. S. Naipaul. *Guerrillas, The Loss of El Dorado,* and *The Enigma of Arrival* all examine the multicultural origins of Caribbean society, and the complexities of colonization, enslavement, and economic dispossession.

Staying in the Caribbean

Dining

For the longest time, cuisine in the Caribbean was thought the weakest part of many an island vacation. In recent years, however, island visitors have come to realize that most of what they had been eating and complaining about was not Caribbean at all—just poorly prepared Continental fare with a papaya slice or banana leaf for garnish.

The cuisine of the islands is difficult to pin down because of the region's history as a colonial battleground and ethnic melting pot. The gracefully sauced French presentations of Martinique, for example, are far removed from the hearty Spanish casseroles of Puerto Rico, and even farther removed from the pungent curries of Trinidad.

The one quality that best defines Caribbean-style cooking has to be its essential spiciness. While reminiscent of Tex-Mex and Cajun, Caribbean cuisine is more varied and more subtle than its love of peppers implies. There is also the seafood that is unique and abundant to the region. Caribbean lobster, closer in comparison to crawfish than to Maine lobster, have no claws and tend to be much tougher than the New England variety.

Another local favorite is conch, biologically quite close to land-loving escargots. Conch chowder, conch fritters, conch salad, conch cocktail—no island menu would be complete without at least a half dozen conch dishes.

For many vacationers, much of the Caribbean experience has to do with the consumption of frothy blended fruit drinks, whose main and potent ingredient is Caribbean rum. Whether you are staying in a super-deluxe resort or a small locally operated guest house, you will find that rum flows as freely as water.

After each restaurant review, we have indicated only when reservations are necessary or suggested. Since dining is usually casual throughout the region, we have mentioned attire only when formal wear is needed.

Lodging

Plan ahead and reserve a room well before you travel to the Caribbean. If you have reservations but expect to arrive later than 5 or 6 PM, advise the hotel, inn, or guest house in advance. Some places will not, unless so advised, hold your reservations after 6 PM. Also, during high season be sure to find out what the rate quoted includes—European Plan (EP: no meals), American Plan (AP: three meals), or Modified American Plan (MAP: two meals); use of sporting facilities and equipment; airport transfers; and the like. Be sure to bring your deposit receipt with you in case any questions arise when you arrive at your hotel.

An American Plan may be ideal for travelers on a budget who don't want to worry about additional expenses; but travelers who enjoy a different dining experience each night will prefer to book rooms on a European Plan. Since many hotels insist on a Modified American Plan (breakfast and dinner), particularly during the high season, find out whether you can exchange dinners for lunch.

Decide whether you want a hotel on the leeward (calm water, good for snorkeling) or windward (waves, good for surfing) side of the island. Decide, too, whether you want to pay the extra price for a room overlooking the ocean or pool. Beachcombers will want to know how close the property is to a beach; at some hotels you can walk barefoot from your room onto the sand; others are across a road or a 10-minute drive away.

Nighttime entertainment is alfresco in the Caribbean, so if you go to sleep early or are a light sleeper, ask for a room that doesn't overlook the dance floor.

Air-conditioning is not a necessity on all islands, most of which are cooled by trade winds; but an air conditioner can be a plus if you enjoy an afternoon snooze. Breezes are stronger in second-floor rooms, particularly corner rooms, which enjoy cross ventilation.

Given the vast differences in standards and accommodations in the various islands covered in this book, it would be impossible (and misleading) to establish uniform categories such as deluxe, first class, etc. Instead, we have used categories to indicate price rather than quality. Prices are intended as a guideline only. The larger resort hotels with the greater number of facilities are, naturally, going to be more expensive, but the Caribbean is full of smaller places that make up in charm, individuality, and price for what they lack in activities—and the activity is generally available on a pay-per-use basis everywhere.

Credit Cards

The following credit card abbreviations have been used: AE, American Express; CB, Carte Blanche; DC, Diners Club; MC, MasterCard; V, Visa. It's a good idea to call ahead to check current credit card policies.

Electrical Current

110 and 120 volts A.C. is the general rule throughout the Caribbean, but there are a number of exceptions. To be sure, check with your hotel when making reservations.

Cruises

Cruising the Caribbean is perhaps the most relaxed and convenient way to tour this beautiful part of the world. A cruise offers all the benefits of island-hopping without the inconvenience. For example, a cruise passenger packs and unpacks only once and is not bound by flight schedules, tour-bus schedules, and "non schedules" of fellow travelers.

Cruise ships usually call at several Caribbean ports on a single voyage. Thus, a cruise passenger experiences and savors the mix of nationalities and cultures of the Caribbean, as well as the variety of sightseeing opportunities, the geographic and topographic characteristics, and the ambience of each of the islands. A cruise passenger tries out each island on his or her cruise itinerary and has the opportunity to select favorites for in-depth discovery on a later visit.

As a vacation, a cruise offers total peace of mind. All important decisions are made long before boarding the ship. For example, the itinerary is set in advance, and the costs are known ahead of time and are all-inclusive. There is no additional charge for accommodations, entertainment, or recreational activities. All meals are included, and (surprise!) there are no prices on the menu. A cruise ship is a floating Caribbean resort; each passen-

Caribbean Cruises

Class/Ship	Number of passengers	Length (days)	Alternate lengths (segments) available	Departs from	Anguilla	Antigua	Aruba	Barbados	Bonaire	BVI	Cayman Islands
CELEBRITY CRUISES											
M.V. Horizon	1354	7	6	San Juan		●		●			
S.S. Meridian	1,106	7	6	Ft. Lauderdale		●					
CHANDRIS FANTASY CRUISES											
Amerikanis	614	7	6, 8	San Juan		●		●			
Azur	648	7	6, 8	San Juan				●			
Britanis	960		5, 2	San Juan							
Victoria	550	7	6, 8, 14	San Juan							
COMMODORE CRUISE LINE											
The Caribe	1,100	7		Miami							●
COSTA CRUISES											
CarlaCosta	800	7		San Juan							
CostaRiviera	1,000	7		Ft. Lauderdale							
CUNARD											
Countess	750	7	14	San Juan		●		●		●	
Queen Elizabeth II	1,900	10	11, 15	NYC				●			
Sagafjord	588	12	10,11,12,13,16	Ft. Lauderdale		●		●		●	
Vistafjord	736	13	16	NYC				●		●	
HOLLAND AMERICA											
M.S. Westerdam	1,100	7		Ft. Lauderdale							
Neeuw Amsterdam	1,200	7		Tampa							●
Noordam	1,200	7		Ft. Lauderdale						●	
Rotterdam	1,114	10		Ft. Lauderdale							
NORWEGIAN CRUISE LINE											
Norway	2,044	7		Miami							
Skyward	730	7		San Juan			●				
Starward	758	7		San Juan		●		●			
Seaward	1,534	7		Miami							
PRINCESS CRUISES											
Dawn Princess	925	7		San Juan				●			
Crown Princess	626	7		Ft. Lauderdale							●
Sky Princess	1,202	10		Ft. Lauderdale				●			●
Star Princess	1,470	7		San Juan				●			
ROYAL CARIBBEAN CRUISE LINE											
Nordic Prince	1,012		8,10	Miami		●		●			
Song of America Western	1,390	7		Miami							●
Song of Norway	1,022	7		San Juan		●		●			
Sovereign of the Seas	2,280	7		Miami							
Sun Viking	726	7	8,10	San Juan				●			
SUN LINE CRUISES											
Stella Solaris	620	10	14	Ft. Lauderdale				●			

Curaçao	Dominica	Dominican Rep.	Grenada	Guadeloupe	Jamaica	Martinique	Montserrat	Nevis	Puerto Rico	Saba	St. Barthelemy	St. Eustatius	St. Kitts	St. Lucia	St. Martin	St. Vincent & the Grenadines	Trinidad/Tobago	Turks & Caicos	USVI		Bermuda	Mexico
						•								•					•			
																			•			
•			•	•		•			•					•	•				•			
				•					•	•			•	•		•			•			
									•					•					•			•
•			•			•			•					•					•			•
		•			•				•										•			•
•			•			•		•											•			
																			•			
			•	•		•			•					•	•		•		•			
•			•			•									•				•			
•				•			•		•						•				•			
			•			•									•				•		•	
									•										•			
					•														•			•
									•										•			
•			•	•		•													•			
															•				•			
•									•										•			
						•			•						•				•			
				•																		•
						•									•	•			•			
				•		•			•								•		•			•
				•		•											•	•	•			•
						•			•										•			
						•			•						•				•			
				•																		•
						•									•				•			
									•										•			
			•						•				•						•			
			•						•			•		•			•	•	•			•

ger gets to know the cruise staff and sits back and relaxes while he or she enjoys the consistency of service and experience.

Fly-and-Cruise

Several cruise lines offer attractive fly-and-cruise options, which give passengers the option of flying first to a warm-weather port like Miami or San Juan and boarding the ship there. The airfare is built into the rate, so the cost of the total package is usually higher than the cost of cruise-only packages that cover comparable distances at sea. In most cases, however, the air-plus-cruise rate will be lower than round-trip airfare to the ship's pier.

When to Go

Cruise ships sail the Caribbean year-round—the waters are almost always calm, and the prevailing breezes keep temperatures fairly steady. Tropical storms are most likely in September, October, and November, but modern navigational equipment warns ships of impending foul weather, and, if necessary, cruise lines vary their itineraries to avoid storms.

Cruises are in high demand—and therefore also higher priced —during the standard vacation times in midsummer to early fall and around Easter. Some very good bargains are usually available during the immediate post-vacation periods such as fall to mid-December, early spring, and the first few weeks after the Christmas and New Year's holidays. Christmas sailings are usually quite full and are priced at a premium.

Choosing a Cabin

Write to the cruise line or ask your travel agent for a ship's plan. This elaborate layout, with all cabin numbers noted, may seem overwhelming at first, but closer inspection will show you all facilities available on all decks (the higher the deck, the higher the prices). Outside cabins have dramatic portholes that contribute to the romance of cruising, but even if they aren't sealed shut, most provide no more than a view of the surrounding deck. Inside cabins are less expensive, but check the plan—you don't want to be over the kitchen, over the engine room, or next to the elevators if you want quiet. Then check on the facilities offered. Those prone to motion sickness would do best in a cabin at midship, on one of the lower decks. Cabins in the center of the ship are the most stable, and the higher you go, the more motion you'll experience. Look over the less-expensive cabins that have upper and lower berths, those that have bathtubs in addition to showers, and the luxury suites, which can still provide all the accoutrements of a voyage across the sea.

Tipping

Even though some of the liners advertise a no-tipping policy, be aware that most of the ship's service personnel depend on tips for their livelihood. There is no hard-and-fast rule about who gets what, but if you think of services rendered on board as you would at resort hotels, bars, and restaurants, you'll come close. It is customary to tip the cabin steward, the dining-room waiter, the maître d', the wine steward, and the bartender. Gratuities to other ship's personnel are usually given the night before the voyage ends.

Shore Excursions

Tour options are typically posted on the bulletin board near the purser's office a day before arrival at your port of call. If the ship is in port for a full day, you might choose to join a tour offered by one of the local tour companies or to rent a car and explore on your own (*see* Guided Tours and Getting Around sections of the individual island chapters).

Cruise Lines

To find out which ships are sailing where and when they depart, contact the **Caribbean Tourism Association** (20 E. 46th St., New York, NY 10017, tel. 212/682–0435). The CTA carries up-to-date information about cruise lines that sail to its member nations. Travel agencies are also a good source; they stock brochures and catalogues issued by most of the major lines and usually have the latest information about prices, departure dates, and itineraries. The **Cruise Lines International Association** publishes a useful pamphlet entitled *Answers to the Most Asked Questions about Cruising;* to order a copy send a stamped, self-addressed envelope to CLIA (17 Battery Pl., Suite 631, New York, NY 10004).

The accompanying chart gives the names and ports of call of all of the individual cruise ships run by the companies given in the following list. Use the addresses and phone numbers listed below to contact the individual lines for more information.

American Canadian Caribbean Line (Box 368, Warren, RI 02885, tel. 800/556–7450).
Bermuda Star Line (1086 Teaneck Rd., Teaneck, NJ 07666, tel. 800/237–5361).
Carnival Cruise Lines (5225 N.W. 87th Ave., Miami, FL 33178, tel. 800/327–9501; in FL, 800/432–5424).
Chandris Fantasy Cruises (900 3rd Ave., New York, NY 10022, tel. 212/750–0044, 800/621–3446, or 800/432–4132 in FL).
Clipper Cruise Line (7711 Bonhomme Ave., St. Louis, MO 63105, tel. 800/325–0010; in MO, 314/727–2929).
Commodore Cruise Line (1007 North America Way, Miami, FL 33132, tel. 800/327–5617 or 800/432–6793 in FL).
Costa Cruises (World Trade Center, 80 S.W. 8th St., Miami, FL 33130, tel. 305/358–7325 or 800/462–6782).
Cunard (555 5th Ave., New York, NY 10017, tel. 800/5–CUNARD).
Holland America (300 Elliot Ave. W, Seattle, WA 98119, tel. 206/281–3535 or 800/426–0327).
Norwegian Cruise Lines (95 Merrick Way, Coral Gables, FL 33134, tel. 305/447–9660 or 800/327–3090).
Ocean Cruise Lines (1510 S.E. 17th St., Ft. Lauderdale, FL 33316, tel. 305/764–3500, 800/556–8850 on the East Coast, or 800/338–1700 on the West Coast).
Ocean Quest International (512 S. Peters St., New Orleans, LA 70130, tel. 800/338–3483).
Princess Cruises (10100 Santa Monica Blvd., Los Angeles, CA 90067, tel. 213/553–1666, 800/421–0522).

Royal Caribbean Cruise Line (903 South America Way, Miami, FL 33132, tel. 305/379–2601 or 800/327–6700).

Royal Viking Line (95 Merrick Way, Coral Gables, FL 33134, tel. 305/447–9660 or 800/422–8000).

Seabourn Cruise Line (55 Francisco St., San Francisco, CA 94133, tel. 415/391–7444 or 800/351–9595; 800/527–0999 in Canada).

Sun Line Cruises (1 Rockefeller Plaza, New York, NY 10020, tel. 212/397–6400 or 800/445–6400).

Windjammer Barefoot Cruises (Box 120, Miami Beach, FL 33119, tel. 305/672–6453 or 800/327–2601; in Canada 800/233–2603).

2 Anguilla

by Honey Naylor

The author of Fodor's Pocket New Orleans, *Honey Naylor has contributed to various other Fodor's guides. Her featured articles have appeared in* Travel & Leisure, USA Today, New Orleans Magazine, Travel-Holiday, *and other national publications.*

At first glance, Anguilla's (which rhymes with vanilla) charms may be difficult to detect. It is not a particularly pretty island. There are no lush rain forests or majestic mountains. The highest point on the island rises a dizzying 213 feet above sea level. It's a dry limestone isle with a thin covering of soil over the rock and has neither streams nor rivers, only saline ponds used for salt production. And there isn't a whole lot to do here. You won't find glittering casinos, dance-till-dawn discos, knock-your-socks-off nightclubs, world-famous historic sites, or duty-free shops stuffed with irresistible buys. Nevertheless, this long, skinny, eel-shape island just 20 minutes from the bustle of St. Martin-Sint Maarten's resorts and casinos has debuted and become a very popular, and so far unspoiled, princess at the Caribbean ball.

Anguilla's beauty is apt to be found in its 30 beaches surrounded by gin-clear waters and coral reefs. Peace, quiet, and pampering account for the island's growing popularity among travelers searching for a Caribbean getaway. You can swim, do some diving, practice your backhand, catch up on your reading, compare the relative merits of the beaches, or just find one that suits you and sink down on it to worship the sun.

This is the most northerly of the Leeward Islands, lying between the Caribbean Sea and the Atlantic Ocean. Stretching from northeast to southwest, it's about 16 miles long and only 3 miles across at its widest point. The keen eye of Christopher Columbus seems not to have spotted this island. Anguilla means eel in Italian, but the Spanish *anguila* or French *anguille* (both of which also mean eel) may have been the original name. New archaeological evidence shows that the island was inhabited as many as 2,000 years ago by Indians who named the island Malliouhana, a more mellifluous title that's been adopted by some of the island's shops and resorts.

In 1631, the Dutch built a fort here and maintained it for several years, but no one has been able to locate it today. English settlers from St. Kitts colonized the island in 1650. And, despite a brief period of independence with St. Kitts-Nevis in the 1960s, Anguilla has remained a British colony ever since the 17th century.

There were the obligatory Caribbean battles between the English and the French, and in 1688 the island was attacked by a party of "wild Irishmen," some of whom settled on the island. But Anguilla's primary discontent was over its status vis-à-vis the other British colonies, particularly St. Kitts. In the 18th century, Anguilla, as part of the Leeward Islands, was administered by British officials in Antigua. In 1816, Britain split the Leeward Islands into two groups, one of them comprised of Anguilla, St. Kitts, Nevis, and the British Virgin Islands administered by a magistrate in St. Kitts. For more than 150 years thereafter various island units and federations were formed and disbanded, with Anguilla all the while simmering over its subordinate status and enforced union with St. Kitts. Anguillans twice petitioned for direct rule from Britain, and twice were ignored. In 1967, when St. Kitts, Nevis, and Anguilla became an Associated State, the mouse roared, kicked St. Kitts policemen off the island, held a self-rule referendum, and for two years conducted its own affairs. In 1968, a senior British official arrived and remained for a year working with the Anguilla Council. A second referendum in 1969 confirmed the desire of the Anguillans to remain apart from St. Kitts-Nevis and the following month a British "peacekeeping force" parachuted down to the island, where it was greeted with flowers, fluttering Union Jacks, and friendly smiles. When the paratroopers were not working on their tans, they helped a team of royal engineers improve the port and build roads and schools. Today Anguilla elects a House of Assembly and its own leader to handle internal affairs, while a British governor is responsible for public service, the police, and judiciary and external affairs.

The territory of Anguilla includes a few offshore islets or cays, such as Scrub Island to the east, Dog Island, Prickly Pear Cays, Sandy Island, and Sombrero Island. The island's population numbers about 7,500, predominantly of African descent but also including descendants of Europeans, especially Irish. Historically, because the limestone land was hardly fit for agriculture, Anguillans have had to seek work on neighboring islands. Until recently, the primary means of employment were fishing and boat building. Today, tourism has become the growth industry of the island's stable economy. But the government is determined to keep Anguilla's tourism growing at a slow and cautious pace to protect the island's natural resources and beauty. New hotels, scattered throughout the islands, are being kept small, select, and casino-free, and promotion of the island emphasizes its quality service, serene surroundings, and friendly people.

Before You Go

Tourist Information Contact the **Anguilla Tourist Information and Reservation Office** (c/o Medhurst & Assoc., Inc., 271 Main St., Northport, NY 11768, tel. 212/869–0402, 516/261–1234, or 800/553–4939). In the United Kingdom, contact the **Anguilla Tourist Office** (3 Epirus Rd., London SW6 7UJ, tel. 01/937–7725). You can also get information directly from the island by writing or calling the **Anguilla Tourist Office** (The Valley, Anguilla, British West Indies, tel. 809/497–2759). Reservations can be made through **Medhurst & Associates, Inc.** (271 Main St., Northport, NY 11768, tel. 800/553–4939).

Arriving and Departing By Plane **American Airlines** (tel. 800/433–7300) has nonstop flights from the United States to its hub in San Juan. The airline's **American Eagle** flies twice daily to Anguilla, the first flight connecting with East Coast and Canadian flights, the second with those from the Midwest and West. **Windward Islands Airways** (Winair) (tel. 809/775–0183) wings in daily from St. Thomas and four times a day from St. Maarten's Juliana Airport. **Air BVI** (tel. 809/774–6500) flies in five times daily from St. Thomas and from San Juan three times a week, and **LIAT** (tel. 809/465–2286) comes in from St. Kitts and Antigua. **Air Anguilla** (tel. 809/497–2643) has regularly scheduled daily flights from St. Thomas, St. Maarten, and Tortola. It also provides air-taxi service on request from neighboring islands, as does **Tyden Air** (tel. 809/497–2719).

From the Airport At **Wallblake Airport** you'll find taxis lined up to meet the planes. A trip from the airport to Sandy Ground will cost about $7. Fares, which are government-regulated, should be listed in brochures the drivers carry. If you are traveling in a group, the

Anguilla

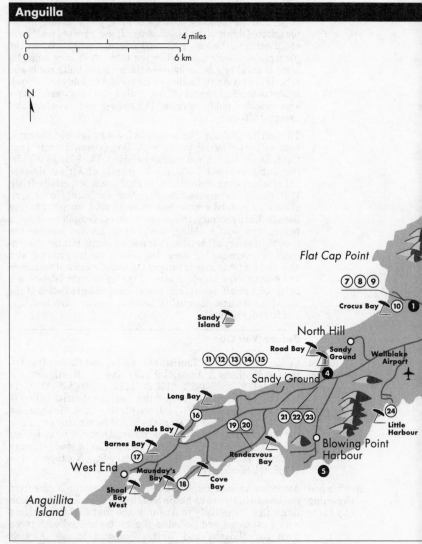

0   4 miles

0   6 km

N

Flat Cap Point

⑦ ⑧ ⑨

⑩ ①

Crocus Bay

Sandy Island

North Hill

Road Bay ⬤ Sandy Ground

Wallblake Airport

⑪ ⑫ ⑬ ⑭ ⑮

Sandy Ground ④

Long Bay

⑯

⑲ ⑳

㉑ ㉒ ㉓

㉔

Little Harbour

Meads Bay

Barnes Bay

⑰

Rendezvous Bay

Blowing Point Harbour

West End

Maunday's Bay

⑱

Cove Bay

⑤

Shoal Bay West

Anguillita Island

Exploring

Blowing Point
Harbour, **5**

The Fountain, **2**

Sandy Ground, **4**

Sandy Hill Bay, **3**

Wallblake House, **1**

Dining

Anguilla Great
House, **19**

Aquarium, **21**

Arlo's, **22**

The Barrel Stay, **11**

Cinnamon Reef Beach
Club, **24**

Coccoloba
Plantation, **17**

Cross Roads, **7**

Hibernia, **12**

Johnno's, **14**

Lucy's Harbour View
Restaurant, **23**

Malliouhana, **16**

Pepper Pot, **8**

Pimm's, **18**

Riviera Bar &
Restaurant, **13**

Roy's, **10**

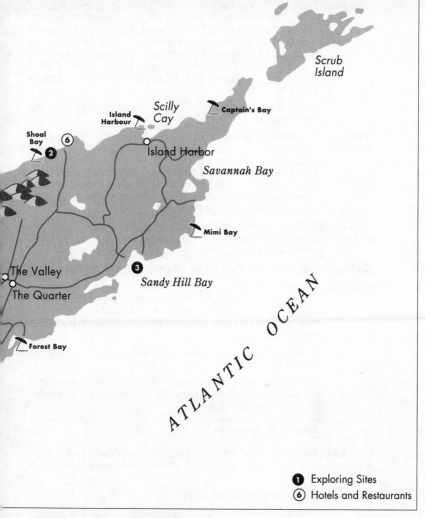

Scrub
Island

Scilly
Cay

Island
Harbour

Captain's Bay

Shoal
Bay

②

⑥

Island Harbor

Savannah Bay

Mimi Bay

The Valley

③

The Quarter

Sandy Hill Bay

Forest Bay

ATLANTIC OCEAN

① Exploring Sites
⑥ Hotels and Restaurants

Lodging

Anguilla Great
House, **19**
Cap Juluca, **18**
Cinnamon Reef Beach
Club, **24**
Coccoloba
Plantation, **17**
Inter-Island Hotel, **9**

Malliouhana, **16**
The Mariners, **15**
Rendezvous Bay
Hotel, **20**
Shoal Bay Villas, **6**

fares apply to the first two people; each additional passenger adds $2 to the total.

By Boat   There are ferry-boat journeys across the water from Marigot on St. Martin several times a day between 7:30 AM and 5:30 PM. You pay the $8 one-way fare on board. Don't buy a round-trip ticket, which restricts you to the boat on which you bought the ticket. In the evenings, the boats leave at 7 PM and 10:45 PM. The trip takes about 15–20 minutes, and if you're inclined toward seasickness, it's a good idea to take motion-sickness medication before boarding.

Taxis are always waiting to pick passengers up at the Blowing Point landing.

Passports   U.S. and Canadian citizens need proof of identity. A passport is
and Visas   preferred (even one that's expired, but not more than five years ago). A photo ID, along with a birth certificate (original with raised seal), a voter registration card, or a driver's license is also acceptable. Visitor's passes are valid for stays of up to three months. British citizens must have a passport. All visitors must also have a return or ongoing ticket.

Customs   You may bring in duty-free one carton of cigarettes or cigars, a
and Duties   reasonable personal supply of tobacco, one bottle of liquor, and perfume for personal use.

Language   English, with a West Indian lilt, is spoken on Anguilla.

Precautions   The manchineel tree, which resembles an apple tree, shades many beaches. The tree bears poisonous fruit and the sap from the tree causes painful blisters, so avoid sitting beneath the tree, because even dew or raindrops falling from the leaves can blister your skin.

Be *sure* to take along a can of insect repellent—mosquitoes are all over the place.

Anguilla is a quiet, relatively safe island, but there's no point in tempting fate by leaving your valuables unattended in your hotel room or on the beach.

Staying in Anguilla

Important   **Tourist Information:** The **Anguilla Tourist Office** (The Secretar-
Addresses   iat, The Valley, tel. 809/497–2759) is open weekdays 8–noon and 1–4.

Emergencies   **Police** and **Fire:** 809/497–2333.

Hospital: There is a 24-hour emergency room at **The Cottage Hospital** (The Valley, tel. 809/497–2551).

Ambulance: 809/497–2551.

Pharmacies: The **Government Pharmacy** (The Valley, tel. 809/497–2551) is located in the Cottage Hospital. The **Paramount Pharmacy** (Waterswamp, tel. 809/497–2366) is open Monday–Saturday 8:30 AM–8:30 PM and has a 24-hour emergency service.

Currency   Legal tender here is the Eastern Caribbean dollar (E.C.), but U.S. dollars are widely accepted. (You'll usually get change in E.C.s.) The E.C. is fairly stable relative to the dollar, hovering between E.C.$2.60 and $2.70 to U.S.$1. Credit cards are not widely accepted, but some places accept personal and traveler's checks. Be sure to carry lots of small bills; change for a $20 bill is often difficult to obtain.

Taxes and The government imposes an 8% tax on accommodations. The
Service Charges departure tax is $5 at the airport, $1.15 by boat.

A 10% service charge is added to all hotel bills and most restaurant bills. If you're not certain about the restaurant service charge, ask. If you are particularly pleased with the service, you can certainly leave a little extra. Tip taxi drivers 10% of the fare.

Guided Tours A round-the-island tour by taxi will take about 2½ hours and will cost $40 for one or two people, $5 for each additional passenger.

Bennie Tours (Blowing Point, tel. 809/497–2788), **Bertram's Tour and Taxi Service** (The Valley, tel. 809/497–2256), and **Malliouhana Travel and Tours** (The Valley, tel. 809/497–2431) all put together personalized package tours on and around the island.

Getting Around Taxi rates are regulated by the government and there are fixed
Taxis fares from point to point. Posted rates are for one to two people; each additional person pays $2. The fare from the airport to hotels ranges from $8 to $15, from Blowing Point Landing $11 to $12.50.

Rental Cars This is your best bet for maximum mobility if you're comfortable driving on the left. For the most part, Anguilla's roads are narrow paved two-laners, and some of the ritziest hotels are only reachable on ghastly dirt roads. Watch out for the four-legged critters that amble across the road, and observe the 30 mph speed limit. To rent a car you'll need a valid driver's license and a local license, which can be obtained for $10 at any of the car rental agencies. Among the agencies are **Bennie & Sons (Avis)** (tel. 809/497–2221 or 800/331–2112), **Budget** (tel. 809/497–2217 or 800/527–0700), **Connors (National)** (tel. 809/497–6433 or 800/328–4567), and **Island Car Rental** (tel. 809/497–2804).

Telephones To call Anguilla from the United States, dial area code 809 +
and Mail 497 + the local four-digit number. International direct-dial is available on the island. **Cable & Wireless** (Wallblake Rd., tel. 809/497–2210) is open weekdays 8–6, Saturday 9–1, Sunday and holidays 10–2. A pay phone is accessible 24 hours a day for credit card and collect calls. To make a local call on the island, dial the four-digit number.

Airmail letters to the United States cost E.C. .60; postcards E.C. .25.

Opening and Banks are open Monday–Thursday 8–1; Friday 8–1 and 3–5.
Closing Times Shopping hours are variable. No two shops seem to have the same hours. Your best bet is to call the shop you're interested in, or ask at the tourist office for opening and closing times.

Beaches

The island's big attractions are its beaches. All are free to the public and all are white sand. Nude bathing is a no-no, but is nevertheless not uncommon. Most of the island's beaches are on coral reefs that are great for snorkeling.

One of the prettiest beaches in the Caribbean, **Shoal Bay** is a 2-mile L-shape beach of talcum-powder-soft white sand. There are beach chairs, umbrellas, a backdrop of seagrape and coconut trees, and for seafood and tropical drinks there's Trader Vic's, Uncle Ernie, and the Round Rock. Souvenir shops for T-shirts, suntan lotion, and the like abound. Head to Shoal Bay for good snorkeling in the offshore coral reefs, and visit the water-sports center to arrange diving, sailing, and fishing trips.

Rendezvous Bay is 1½ miles of pearl-white sand. Here the water is calm, and there's a great view of St. Martin. The Anguilla Great House's open-air beach bar is handy for snacks and Happy Jacks (rum punches).

One of the most popular beaches, wide, mile-long **Maunday's Bay** is known for good swimming and snorkeling. Rent water-sport gear at Tropical Watersports. Try Pimm's at Cap Juluca for fine food and drink (*see* Dining, below).

Adjacent to Maunday's Bay, **Shoal Bay West** is a pleasant beach with a backdrop of Cove Castles, a set of futuristic villas where Chuck Norris has a home. The snorkeling is best in the area of the Oasis restaurant. Comb this beach for lovely conch shells as well.

Barnes Bay is a superb spot for windsurfing and snorkeling. The elegant Coccoloba Plantation perches above and offers a poolside bar. In high season this beach can get a bit crowded with day-trippers from St. Martin.

The clear blue waters of **Road Bay** beach are usually dotted with yachts. The Mariners Hotel, several restaurants (*see* Lodging, below), a water-sports center, and lots of windsurfing and waterskiing activity make this an active commercial area. The snorkeling is not very good here, but do visit this bay for its glorious sunsets.

Sandy Island, nestled in coral reefs about 2 miles offshore from Road Bay, is a tiny speck of sand and sea, equipped with a beach boutique, beach bar and restaurant, and free use of snorkeling gear and underwater cameras. The *Shauna* (tel. 809/497–6395 or 809/497–6845) will ferry you there from Sandy Ground.

Island Harbor, another busy beach, is shaded by coconut trees and lined with colorful fishing boats. Depart from here for **Scilly Cay,** a three-minute motorboat ride away. You can get snorkeling equipment on the ferrying motorboat, but at times the waters are too rough to see much. On Scilly Cay there is a beach bar that serves drinks and grilled lobster and seafood.

The good news and the bad news about **Cove Bay** is the same—it's virtually deserted. There are no restaurants or bars, just calm waters, coconut trees, and a talcum-powder-soft sand that stretches down to Maunday's Bay.

Mimi Bay is a difficult-to-reach, isolated, half-mile beach east of Sea Feathers. But the trip is worth it. When the surf is not too rough the barrier reef makes for great snorkeling.

Also not far from Sea Feathers is **Sandy Hill,** a base for fishermen. Here you can buy fresh fish and lobster right off the boats and snorkel in the warm waters. Don't plan to sunbathe—the beach is quite narrow here.

The reward for traveling along an inhospitable dirt road via four-wheel drive is complete isolation at **Captain's Bay** on the northeastern end of the island. The surf slaps the sands with a vengeance and the undertow is quite strong here. Wading is the safest water sport.

Exploring Anguilla

Numbers in the margin correspond with points of interest on the Anguilla map.

Make the Tourist Office in the Valley your first stop on the island. Here you can pick up a large, colorful map of the island with splashy pictures of Anguilla's beaches. The island is sprinkled with salt ponds and small villages, the most important of which is The Valley, where administrative offices, banks, a few boutiques, guest houses, eateries, and markets are located. But there is little to see in Anguilla except for the beaches and the resorts. Take a look at the island's historic house, and then go beachcombing.

❶ Wallblake House is a plantation house that was built around 1787 by Will Blake (Wallblake is probably a corruption of his name). Legends of murders, invasions by the French in 1796, and high living surround the house. Now owned and actively used by the Catholic Church, the plantation has spacious rooms, some with tray ceilings edged with handsome carving. The long, narrow pantry with red and black baked brick tiles is now being converted to a kitchen. On the grounds there is an ancient vaulted stone cistern and an outbuilding called the Bakery (which wasn't used for breadmaking but for baking turkeys and hams). The oven measures 12 feet across and rises 3 feet up through a stepped chimney. *Cross Roads. Call Father John, tel. 809/497–2405, to make an appointment to tour the plantation.*

If you follow the road west toward the Cottage Hospital, you'll come to a dirt road that leads to **Crocus Bay** and several strips of white-sand beaches.

❷ Four miles northeast of The Valley on the main road, as you approach the coast at **Shoal Bay,** you'll pass near **The Fountain,** where Arawak petroglyphs have been discovered. Presently closed to the public, the area is being researched by the Anguilla Archaeological and Historical Society. The AAHS (tel. 809/497–2767) plans to open a museum in the former Customs House in The Valley.

Two miles farther east, the fishing village of **Island Harbour** nestles in its sheltered cove.

Follow rutted dirt roads from Island Harbour to the easternmost tip of the island. On the way to the aptly named **Scrub Island** and **Little Scrub Island** off the eastern tip of the island, you'll pass Captain's Bay, with its isolated beach, on the north coast.

❸ You can also choose to bypass the east end of the island because there isn't much to see there. From Island Harbour, a paved road leads south, skirts Savannah Bay on the southeast coast, and continues to **Sandy Hill Bay.** If you're an aficionado of ruined forts, there's one here you might want to explore.

Four miles down the coast, beyond the Long Salt Pond, is **Forest Bay,** a fit place for scuba diving. South of Forest Bay lies **Little Harbour,** with a lovely horseshoe-shape bay and the splendid **Cinnamon Reef Beach Club.**

From Forest Bay, follow the paved road past Wallblake Airport, just outside The Valley, and turn left on the main road. **4** In 4 miles you'll come to **Sandy Ground,** one of the most active and most developed of the island's beaches. It is home to the **Mariners Hotel, Tamariain Watersports,** dive shop, a commercial pier, and several small guest houses and restaurants. The *Shauna* departs from here for Sandy Island 2 miles offshore.

5 Farther down the south coast is **Blowing Point Harbour,** where you'll have docked if you arrived by ferry from Marigot in St. Martin.

Time Out If you plan to picnic (on the beach or in your room), try the **Fat Cat** (George Hill, tel. 809/497–2307) for escargots to go, as well as take-out quiche, soups, chili, chicken, and conch dishes. **Amy's Bakery** (Blowing Point, tel. 809/497–6775) turns out homemade pies, cakes, tarts, cookies, and breads.

The main paved road travels down more or less the center of the island, which at this northwest end is quite narrow. Teeth-jarring dirt roads lead to the coasts, the beaches, and some of the best resorts on the island.

On the south coast, west of Blowing Point, is the crescent-shape home of **Rendezvous Bay,** the island's first hotel, built in 1959. The white sand drifts down the coastline to **Cove Bay,** a pretty coconut palm-fringed beach.

Maunday's Bay, on the extreme southwest coast, is the home of **Cap Juluca,** a stunning resort that looks as if it was plucked out of Marrakech.

On the opposite side of the island is **Coccoloba Plantation,** one of the most dazzling resorts in the Caribbean, overlooking the white sands of **Barnes Bay.** A five-minute walk from Barnes Bay is **Meads Bay,** and **Long Bay** is farther to the north.

Participant Sports

Bicycling There are plenty of flat stretches, making wheeling pretty easy. Bikes can be rented at **Island Car Rental** (Airport Rd., tel. 809/497–2723).

Boating Sunfish and Hobie Cats are available at **Tropical Watersports** (tel. 809/497–6666 or 809/497–6779). *Sundancer,* a 30-foot powerboat, is available for charters at **Tamariain Watersports.** (809/497–2020). Sailboats and speedboats can be rented at **Sandy Island Enterprises** (tel. 809/497–6395).

Deep-Sea Fishing Albacore, dolphin, and kingfish are among the sea creatures angled after off Anguilla's shores. Trips can be arranged through **Tropical Watersports.** Fishing tackle, diving gear, and other sports equipment are available at the **Tackle Box Sports Center** (The Valley, tel. 809/497–2896).

Fitness Lest you go flabby lolling around on the beach, you'll find exercise equipment, aerobics, and martial arts instruction at **Island Gym** (Long Ground, tel. 809/497–2363).

Jogging There are miles and miles of broad, flat beaches. Just pick one out and jog away.

Tennis For professional instruction, contact Carl Gavine at **Coccoloba** (tel. 809/497–6871), where there are two lighted courts. There are two courts at the **Carimar Beach Club** (tel. 809/497–6881), three championship courts at **Malliouhana** (tel. 809/497–6111), two Deco Turf tournament courts at **Cinnamon Reef** (tel. 809/ 497–2727), and six courts at **Fountain Beach and Tennis Club** (tel. 809/497–6395). Tennis is also available at **Cap Juluca** (tel. 809/497–6666), **Cove Castles** (tel. 809/497–6801), **Mariners** (tel. 809/497–2671), **Masara** (tel. 809/497–3200), **Rendezvous Bay** (tel. 809/497–6549), **Pelicans** (tel. 809/497–6593), **Sea Grapes** (tel. 809/497–6433), and **Spindrift Apts.** (tel. 809/497–4164).

Sea Excursions Picnic, swimming, and diving excursions to Prickly Pear, Sandy Island, and Scilly Cay are available through **Sandy Island Enterprises** (tel. 809/497–6395) and **Tropical Watersports** (tel. 809/497–6666 or 809/497–6779).

Water Sports The major resorts offer complimentary Windsurfers, paddle-boats, and waterskis to their guests. If your hotel has no water-sports facilities, you can get in gear at **Tropical Watersports** (Maunday's Bay, tel. 809/497–6666 or 809/497–6779) or **Tamariain Watersports** (Sandy Ground, tel. 809/497–2020).

Tamariain Watersports has PADI instructors, short resort courses, and more than a dozen dive sites.

Shopping

Shopping tips are readily available in *Anguilla Life* and *What to Do in Anguilla*, but you have to be a really dedicated shopper to peel yourself off the beach and poke around in Anguilla's few shops.

Good Buys
Resort Wear and
Jewelry
Head for **La Romana** (Malliouhana, tel. 809/497–6111), cloned from the St. Martin and St. Barts boutiques; **Whispers** (Cap Juluca, tel. 809/497–6666); and **Sunshine Shop** (South Hill, tel. 809/497–2149) for island cotton pareos (polynesian-style wraps), silkscreened items, cotton resort wear, and hand-painted wood items from Haiti.

Native Crafts **Lismaca Boutique** (The Valley, no phone) carries locally designed and made embroidered and crocheted dresses, shawls, separates, and even men's suits. **The Valley Gap** (Shoal Bay Beach, tel. 809/497–2754) has local crafts, T-shirts, and swimwear. **Vanhelle Boutique** (Sandy Ground, tel. 809/497–2965) carries gift items, as well as Brazilian swimsuits for men and women. The **Anguilla Arts and Crafts Center** (The Valley, no phone) has a wide selection of island crafts. The **Local Gift Shop** (The Quarter, no phone) has shells, handmade baskets, wood dolls, hand-crocheted mats, lace tablecloths and bed-spreads.

Dining

Anguilla's eateries range from the exotic to down-home seaside shacks. Call ahead—in the winter to make a reservation, and in the summer to see if it's open.

The most highly recommended restaurants are indicated by a star ★.

Category	Cost*
Expensive	over $30
Moderate	$20–$30
Inexpensive	under $20

per person, excluding drinks, service, and sales tax (8%)

The Barrel Stay. The eclectic menu in this thatched-roof beachside eatery includes Hawaiian ham steak, red snapper Portuguese (in a sauce of tomatoes, onions, and green peppers), and French ice cream. Dinner is by candlelight. *Sandy Ground, tel. 809/497-2831. Reservations suggested in season. AE. Expensive.*

★ **Cinnamon Reef Beach Club.** Out on the stylish terra-cotta-tile terrace, begin with snails served in their shells in light garlic butter or chilled jumbo shrimp with cocktail sauce. You can order a soup sampler, which is a serving of two of the soups: black bean, chilled cream of pumpkin, or Anguillan goat soups. Shrimp baked with garlic butter and stuffed with homemade breadcrumbs and herbs, steak au poivre, and chicken Florentine are among the main dishes. Try the banana pudding cream pie or hot butterscotch sundae for dessert. On Friday nights enjoy a "jump-up" with steel band and barbecue. *Little Harbour, tel. 809/497-2727. Reservations advised. AE, MC, V. Expensive.*

Coccoloba Plantation. Dining is either indoors or on a lovely terrace overlooking the sea. Executive Chef Eric Scuiller, who trained at the Ecole Hôtellerie Chaptal in Brittany, presents an à la carte menu of Continental cuisine with a focus on fish. Main dishes include monkfish pan-fried with Virginia bacon and braised cabbage, grilled swordfish with diced tomato and sweet basil, breast of chicken with orange-ginger sauce, and duckling broiled with lime sauce. Don't miss the lobster Coccoloba. Lunch is a poolside buffet of salads, sandwiches, burgers, fish, cold meats, and homemade desserts. *Barnes Bay, tel. 809/497-6871. Reservations required in high season. AE, DC, MC, V. Expensive.*

Malliouhana. Sparkling crystal, fine china, romantic lighting, and sterling-silver domed platters make even a lowly hamburger seem elegant. Jo Rostang, owner-chef of La Bonne Auberge in Antibes, created the menu and is still the consulting chef. Not surprisingly, the cuisine is haute French. Fresh salmon in a croissant pastry and spit-roasted duck or chicken are among the choices. The wine cellar contains about 35,000 bottles. During high season the restaurant is reserved for guests. *Mead's Bay, tel. 809/497-2731. Reservations imperative. No credit cards. Expensive.*

Pimm's. More dramatic than this there isn't. You expect Rudolph Valentino to sweep in beneath the domes, arches, and billowing canvas of this Arabian Nights tent. For starters, try the fresh lobster gazpacho soup chilled with avocado mousse. For the main course there is fish pot-au-feu, fresh local fish cooked in its own juices with white wine; Pimm's grouper with leeks in a light vermouth sauce; Juluca Conch, slices of conch in a puff pastry with banana and curry sauce. You can end things

lightly with lemon mousse, or succumb to the Devil Made Me
Do It white and dark chocolate in mint sauce. *Cap Juluca,
Maunday's Bay, tel. 809/497-6666. Reservations required.
AE, MC, V. Expensive.*

Anguilla Great House. At lunch, this open-air beach bar serves
light fare: salads, burgers, and sandwiches. Dinner is more serious, with veal cordon bleu, curried lamb, curried goat, West
Indian-style snapper, pepper steak, ginger chicken, and lobster topped with cream sauce. *Rendezvous Bay, tel. 809/497-
6061. Reservations accepted. AE, MC, V. Moderate.*

Arlo's. Pasta, pizza, and other simple fare are served in this
Italian-American restaurant beside the sea. The large bar is a
popular gathering place, with animated conversation lasting
long into the evening. *South Hill, tel. 809/497-6810. Reservations suggested. No credit cards. Moderate.*

★ **Hibernia.** A French restaurant in the flower-fringed courtyard
of Syd-An's Apartments. Nouvelle cuisine is beautifully presented at the six tables covered with black-and-white checked
cloths. Begin with cream of vegetable soup and warm salad
with chicken liver and grapefruit. For entrées, try the medallions of beef in red mustard sauce, breast of chicken with
tomato and basil, and grilled lobster. Check out the T-shirts for
sale; they're probably the best on the island. *Sandy Ground,
tel. 809/497-3180. Reservations suggested in high season. No
credit cards. Closed Tues. in high season. Moderate.*

★ **Lucy's Harbour View Restaurant.** Passing through a swinging
wood gate you'll step up to a terrace restaurant with a splendid
sea view. The specialty is "Lucy's delicious whole red snapper," but there is a wide selection here, including several
curried and Creole dishes, such as conch and goat. Be sure to
try Lucy's sautéed potatoes. Live music Wednesdays and Fridays. *South Hill, tel. 809/497-6253. Reservations accepted. No
credit cards. Closed Sun. Moderate.*

Riviera Bar & Restaurant. A beachside bistro serving French
and Creole specialties with an Oriental accent. A four-course
lobster meal is featured, and the fish soup à la Provençale is
highly recommended. Sushi, sashimi, and oysters sautéed in
soy sauce and sake are also among the eclectic offerings.
There's a very happy Happy Hour from 6 to 7 daily. Live entertainment is featured frequently in season. *Sandy Ground, tel.
809/497-2833. Reservations accepted. AE, V. Moderate.*

★ **Aquarium.** An upstairs terrace all gussied up with gingerbread
trim, bright blue walls, and red cloths. The lunch menu lists
sandwiches and burgers. Stewed lobster, curried chicken, barbecued chicken, and mutton stew are offered at night. This is a
popular spot with locals. *South Hill, tel. 809/497-2720. Reservations accepted. No credit cards. Closed Sun. Inexpensive.*

Cross Roads. Millie Philip's roadside bar features hearty breakfasts and, at lunch, seafood salads, fish, and chicken. Hearty
fare at low prices. *Wallblake, tel. 809/497-2581. Reservations
accepted. No credit cards. Inexpensive.*

Johnno's. This is *the* place to be on Sunday afternoons for barbecue and music by the island band AngVibes, but grilled or
barbecued lobster, chicken, and fish are good anytime. *Sandy
Ground, tel. 809/497-2728. No reservations. No credit cards.
Inexpensive.*

Pepper Pot. Cora Richardson's small eatery in the center of
town offers roti aficionados their favorite dish, made of boneless chicken, *tanias* (poi), celery, pepper, onion, garlic, and
local peas—a full meal in itself—for E.C. $5. Dumpling din-

ners, lobster, whelk, and conch are also good choices. *The Valley, tel. 809/497–2328. Reservations accepted. No credit cards. Inexpensive.*

★ **Roy's.** An Anguillan mainstay, Roy and Mandy Bosson's pub is a spacious covered deck. One of the island's best buys, it features Roy's fish and chips, cold English beer, pork fricassee, and a wonderful chocolate rum cake. Sunday lunch special is roast beef and Yorkshire pudding. A faithful clientele gathers in the lively bar. *Crocus Bay, tel. 809/497–2470. Reservations accepted. No credit cards. Closed Mon. and Sat. lunch. Inexpensive.*

Lodging

Anguilla has a wide range of accommodations. There are grand and glorious resorts; apartments and villas from the deluxe to the simple; and small locally owned guest houses where you can get a real taste of life on Anguilla. When you call to reserve a room in a resort, be sure to inquire about special packages.

The most highly recommended lodgings are indicated by a star ★.

Category	Cost*
Very Expensive	over $250
Expensive	$180–$250
Moderate	$80–$180
Inexpensive	under $80

* *All prices are for a standard double room for two, excluding 8% tax and a 10% service charge.*

Hotels **Cap Juluca.** Once you get past the potholed road leading to this luxurious, whitewashed Moorish resort with its domes, arches, low walls, and private courtyards, you'll be rewarded with a pampering touch. The still-developing property, situated on 179 acres and a lovely white beach, has four villas with such luxe touches as huge marble baths and sunken double tubs in walled gardens, private pools, rooftop solariums with refrigerators and built-in barbecues, and Continental breakfast brought to your terrace. Ceiling fans whir over spacious rooms and suites with king-size platform beds. (All rooms are also fully air-conditioned.) The resort will eventually have 66 rooms, a free-form pool, more tennis courts with a clubhouse, and a section of private villas, each with its own pool. *Box 240, Maunday's Bay, tel. 809/497–6666/6779 or 800/235–3505. 25 rooms, plus 5 suites. Facilities: restaurant, bar, boutique, room service, laundry service, library, VCRs and cassettes for rent, 3 tennis courts, water-sports center. No credit cards (personal checks accepted upon prior arrangement). Very Expensive.*

★ **Cinnamon Reef Beach Club.** Low-key luxury in these recently redecorated villas with vast expanses of terra-cotta tile, polished wood, and handsome upholstered bamboo furniture. Each villa is split-level, with living room, raised bedroom (two double beds), dressing room, sunken shower, patio, and hammock. Each has a built-in hairdryer and minibar. Most of the villas are beachfront; five are tucked up on a bluff. Two villas, each with two beachfront and two garden suites (the latter with kitchenettes), can be converted into two-bedroom houses for families. (During the winter, children under 12 are not allowed.) This is a fun, friendly place with a gracious staff and lots of repeat guests. A calypso combo plays nightly, and the Friday night barbecue is an island favorite. Meal plans and packages are available. *Box 141, Little Harbour, tel. 809/497–2727, 800/223–1108, or 416/485–8724 in Canada. 22 rooms. Facilities: restaurant, lounge, pool, 2 tennis courts, room service, turndown service, all water sports. AE, MC, V. Very Expensive.*

★ **Coccoloba Plantation.** E. David Brewer, who has been at the helm of Jumby Bay and some of the Rockresorts, is now the managing director of this stunning property. The reception area in the great house is an enormous room with soaring ceiling, sofas upholstered in vivid fabrics, and handsome artwork. Guests stay in oceanfront villas, done in orange or magenta, each with a step-up bedroom, oversize marble bath, and gingerbread-trim patio. All rooms and suites are air-conditioned, with ceiling fans, glass-top coffee tables, personal safe-deposit box, built-in hair dryer, amenity packages, and one-time complimentary fully stocked refrigerator and minibar. Some suites have Jacuzzis, but most baths have showers only. Complimentary early-morning coffee and afternoon tea are served. The tennis program is directed by Peter Burwash International Pro Carl Gavine. A tennis package is one of several special packages available. *Box 332, Barnes Bay, tel. 809/497–6871, 800/351–5656, or 800/468–0023 in Canada. 51 units. Facilities: restaurant, 2 bars, concierge, boutique, 2 tennis courts, 2 pools, Jacuzzi, TV/reading room, sauna, massage, exercise rooms, water-sports center. AE, DC, MC, V. Very Expensive.*

★ **Malliouhana.** Brick steps lead to a broad, airy reception area with high ceilings, splashing fountain, and Haitian prints. Accommodations range from deluxe double rooms to super-deluxe suites. All are stunning, with miles of white tile, king-size platform beds or canopied king-size or twin beds, balconies, Haitian prints, minibars, oversize tubs in marble baths, ceiling fans (as well as air-conditioning). The hotel sits on a bluff overlooking the beach and a secluded cove. The resort also provides excursions to Sandy Island, which is excellent for snorkeling. It is necessary to reserve well in advance. *Box 173, Meads Bay, tel. 809/497–6111 or 212/696–1323. 52 rooms and suites. Facilities: restaurant, bar, boutique, beauty salon, concierge, 3 pools, 4 lighted tennis courts, Nautilus-equipped exercise room, massage room, water-sports center. No credit cards. Very Expensive.*

Anguilla Great House. On Rendezvous Bay, these five one-story white West Indian bungalows feature chaise longues on verandas with vine-covered trellises. Each of the five units has five rooms with connecting doors to make up two-bedroom suites. Lush fabrics, antique reproductions, and marble baths with enormous showers evoke an earlier era. When complete, the hotel will have 65 rooms and a great house with a formal dining room. *Box 157, Rendezvous Bay, tel. 809/497–6061 or 800/223–0079. 25 rooms. Facilities: restaurant, pool, gym. AE. Expensive–Very Expensive.*

The Mariners. West Indian–style cottages are set in lush landscaped gardens overlooking the harbor at Road Bay. Accommodations vary considerably, ranging from deluxe two-bedroom, two-bath cottages with full kitchens to small rooms with twin beds, minibars, and minuscule shower baths. Charter the Mariner's Boston whaler for picnics, snorkeling, and fishing trips. The Thursday night barbecue and Saturday West Indian night in the beachfront restaurant are popular island events. *Box 139, Sandy Ground, tel. 809/497-2671, 809/497-2815, or 800/223-0079. 50 rooms and suites. Facilities: restaurant, bar, boutique, pool, lighted tennis court, water-sports center. AE, MC, V. Expensive-Very Expensive.*

Shoal Bay Villas. On 2 splendid miles of sand, these fan-cooled units include studio, one-bedroom, and two-bedroom suites, all with modern Italian furnishings and kitchens. Happy Jack's Beach Bar and open-air restaurant is a pleasant spot for breakfast, lunch, and dinner. All water sports can be arranged. Children are not allowed during the winter. *Box 61, Shoal Bay, tel. 809/497-2051; 212/535-9530 in NY; 416/283-2621 in Canada. 13 units. Facilities: restaurant, bar. AE, MC, V. Expensive-Very Expensive.*

Rendezvous Bay Hotel. Anguilla's first hotel sits amid 60 acres of coconut groves and fine white sand. The water here is as clear as Perrier. The main building is low and rose-colored, with a broad front patio, tile floors, and wicker chairs. The rooms are clean and simple, with one double and one single bed and a private shower bath. Ask for room No. 1 if you're traveling with your family—a king-bed room adjoins a twin-bed room with a connecting marble bath. Two deluxe villas have recently been completed, one with two bedrooms and a studio, the other with three bedrooms and a studio. *Box 31, Rendezvous Bay, tel. 809/497-6549; 201/738-0246 or 800/223-9815 in USA; 800/468-0023 in Canada. 20 rooms. Facilities: restaurant, lounge, game and TV room, 2 tennis courts, water-sports center. No credit cards. Moderate.*

Inter-Island Hotel. The West Indian cottage is modestly furnished (no air-conditioning) with wicker and rattan, and the hotel has some rooms with balconies. Most rooms have refrigerators and shower baths. There are also two small one-bedroom apartments, each with a separate entrance on the ground floor. A homey dining room serves hearty breakfasts and fine West Indian dinners. *Box 194, The Valley, tel. 809/497-6259 or 800/ 223-9815; 800/468-0023 in Canada. 12 rooms. Facilities: restaurant, bar/nightclub, TV lounge, transportation to beach ½ mi away. No credit cards. Inexpensive.*

Home and Apartment Rentals

The Tourist Office has a complete listing of vacation rentals. You can also contact **Sunshine Villas** (Box 142, Blowing Point, tel. 809/497-6149) or **Property Real Estate Management Services** (Box 256, George Hill, tel. 809/497-2596). Housekeeping accommodations are plentiful and well organized. The following are recommended:

Cove Castles Villa Resort. A sumptuously decorated, well-equipped, and very private compound along the beach of Shoal Bay West. Very elegant. *Shoal Bay West, Box 248, tel. 809/497-6801 or 800/223-9815; in Canada, 800/468-0023. 4 3-bedroom villas. Facilities: restaurant. No credit cards. Very Expensive.*

★ **Carimar Beach Club.** This is the place for travelers seeking a quiet beach retreat. To ensure privacy, each villa is in a separate building. The location is sparkling Meads Bay, adjacent to the Malliouhana. There's one three-bedroom apartment, all others are two-bedrooms; accommodations are sumptuous but not air-conditioned. *Box 327, The Valley, tel. 809/497-6881 or*

800/223–5581. 24 rooms. Facilities: laundry, 2 tennis courts, water-sports center. AE, MC, V. Very Expensive.

Sea Grape Beach Club. Also on Meads Bay, these luxurious 2,000-square-foot two-bedroom condos are laid out on five levels. Each unit features acres of glass affording spectacular views, enormous closets, three baths, king-size beds, elegant furnishings, and spacious, very private decks. *Box 65, The Valley, tel. 809/497–6433, 809/497–6541, or 800/223–9815. 10 condos. Facilities: restaurant, bar, 2 tennis courts, satellite TV, water-sports center. No credit cards. Very Expensive.*

★ **Easy Corner Villas.** These one-, two-, and three-bedroom apartments with kitchens are furnished right down to microwaves. Only three of the units are air-conditioned; all have only shower baths. No. 10 is a deluxe two-bedroom villa. Not located on the beach but on a bluff overlooking Road Bay, this is a good buy for families. *Box 65, South Hill, tel. 809/497–6433, 809/497–6541, or 800/223–8815. 17 units. AE, MC, V. Moderate.*

Rainbow Reef. David and Charlotte Berglund's secluded units are set on three dramatic seaside acres. A gazebo, with beach furniture and barbecue facilities, perches right over the beach. Each self-contained villa has two bedrooms, fully equipped kitchen, spacious dining and living area, and a large gallery overlooking the sea. *Box 130, Sea Feather Bay, tel. 809/497–2817 or 312/325–2299. 4 units. No credit cards. Moderate.*

★ **La Sirena.** Overlooking busy Meads Bay, this secluded complex has two- and three-bedroom apartments done in handsome upholstered rattan furnishings with queen-size beds, terra-cotta tile floors, and modern, fully equipped kitchens. Each unit is fan-cooled. A good buy, but children under 12 are not welcome. *Box 200, The Valley, tel. 809/497–6827 or 800/223–9815; 800/468–0023 in Canada. 5 units. Facilities: pool, restaurant, picnic and snorkeling equipment. No credit cards. Moderate.*

★ **Skiffles Villas.** These self-catering villas, perched on a hill overlooking Road Bay, are usually booked a year in advance. The one-, two-, and three-bedroom apartments have fully equipped kitchens, floor-to-ceiling windows, and pleasant porches. *Box 82, Lower South Hill, tel. 809/497–6110, 219/642–4855, or 219/642–4445. 5 units. Facilities: pool. No credit cards. Moderate.*

Nightlife

The **Mayoumba Folkloric Group** performs song-and-dance skits depicting Antillean and Caribbean culture, replete with African drums and a string band. They entertain every Thursday at the Cul de Sac's **Pappagallo** restaurant (tel. 809/497–6461). Be on the lookout for Bankie Banx, Anguilla's own reggae superstar. He has his own group called New Generations. Other local groups include Keith Gumbs and The Mellow Tones; Spracker, an excellent guitarist; and Dumpa, who plays a steel pan. Steel Vibrations, a pan band, often entertains at barbecues and West Indian evenings. The big beat of North Sound Brass International is popular for dancing.

The **Cinnamon Reef** (tel. 809/497–2850) has popular Friday evening poolside barbecues and nightly live entertainment. The **Mariners** (tel. 809/497–2671) has regularly scheduled Thursday night barbecues and Saturday night West Indian parties, both with live entertainment by local groups.

During high season, **Pimm's** (Cap Juluca, tel. 809/497–6666) has soothing dance music after dinner. Things are pretty loose

and lively at **Johnno's** (tel. 809/497–2728), with alfresco dancing on weekends. The **Dragon's Disco** (no phone) is a hot spot on
weekends. On Sunday evenings you can find Sleepy and the All
Stars, a popular string and scratch band, waking things up at
the **Round Rock** (tel. 809/497–2076). The **Coconut Paradise** restaurant (Island Harbour, tel. 809/497–4454) has nightly
entertainment ranging from disco to limbo.

3 Antigua

One could spend an entire year—and a leap year, at that—exploring Antigua's (An-tee-ga) beaches; the island has 366 of them, many with snow-white sand. All the beaches are public, and many are backed by lavish resorts offering sailing, diving, windsurfing, and snorkeling.

Antigua, largest of the British Leeward Islands, is where Lord Horatio Nelson headquartered for his forays into the Caribbean to do battle with the French and pirates in the late 18th century. (Nelson was also in Antigua to enforce the British Navigation Act, which prohibited trade with the newly independent "Americans," a position that made him rather unpopular with the island's would-be tradesmen.) There is still a decidedly British atmosphere on the island, with Olde-English public houses that will raise the spirits of Anglophiles.

Visitors with a taste for history will enjoy exploring English Harbour and its carefully restored Nelson's Dockyard, as well as an 18th-century Royal Naval base, old forts, historic churches, and tiny villages. Hikers will want to spend hours viewing a tropical rain forest, lush with pineapples, banana trees, and mangoes. Those of an archaeological bent will head for the megaliths of Greencastle to seek out some 30 excavations of ancient Indian sites.

About 4,000 years ago, Antigua was home to a people called Siboney. They disappeared mysteriously, and the island remained uninhabited for about 1,000 years. When Columbus happened on the 108-square-mile island in 1493, the Arawaks had set up housekeeping. The English took up residence 139 years later in 1632. Then a sequence of bloody battles involving the Caribs, the Dutch, the French, and the English began. Slaves had been imported from Africa to work the sugar plantations by the time the French ceded the island to the English in 1667. On November 1, 1981, Antigua, with its sister island Barbuda (30 miles to the north), achieved full independence.

The combined population of the two islands is about 80,000, only 1,200 of whom live on Barbuda. Having survived a battered childhood, Antigua and Barbuda are currently experiencing the growing pains typical of a newly created nation. Tourism is the main industry here—there has been a recent building boom in tourism properties, with the construction of condominiums and the extensive renovation and expansion of the major hotels—and the government is seeking to broaden its monetary resources by reintroducing agriculture and manufacturing into the economy.

Before You Go

Tourist Information Contact the **Antigua and Barbuda Tourist Offices** in the United States (610 5th Ave., Suite 311, New York, NY 10020, tel. 212/541–4117), in Canada (60 St. Clair Ave., Suite 205, Toronto, Ont. MT4 1N5, Canada, tel. 416/961–3085), and in the United Kingdom (Antigua House, 15 Thayer St., London WI, England, tel. 01/486–7073).

You could try to contact the island directly (Box 373, St. John's, Antigua, tel. 809/463–0480); however, letters have been known to float around for three months before delivery, and the phone system is maddening.

Arriving and Departing

By Plane American Airlines (tel. 800/433–7300) has daily direct service from New York; Eastern Airlines (tel. 800/EAS–TERN) offers daily service via Miami or San Juan; and Pan Am (tel. 800/221–1111) provides daily service from New York and Miami. BWIA (tel. 800/327–7401) has direct service from New York, Miami, Toronto, and San Juan; Air Canada (tel. 800/422–6232) from Toronto, British Airways (tel. 800/247–9297) from London, and Lufthansa (tel. 800/645–3880) from Frankfurt. LIAT (tel. 809/462–0701) has daily flights from Antigua to Barbuda, 15 minutes away, as well as to down-island destinations.

V. C. Bird International Airport is, on a much smaller scale, to the Caribbean what O'Hare is to the Midwest. When several wide-bodies are sitting on the runway at the same time, all waiting to be cleared for takeoff, things can get a bit congested.

From the Airport Taxis meet every flight, and drivers will offer to guide you around the island. The taxis are unmetered, but rates are posted at the airport and drivers are required to carry a rate card with them. The fixed rate from the airport to St. John's is $8 in U.S. currency (although drivers often *quote* beewee dollars); from the airport to English Harbour, $18.75; and from St. John's to the Dockyard, $33 round-trip, with "reasonable" time allocated for waiting while you wander.

Passports and Visas U.S. and Canadian citizens need only proof of identity. A passport is best, but a birth certificate (an original, not a photocopy) or a voter registration card will do. A driver's license is *not* sufficient. British citizens need a passport. All visitors must present a return or ongoing ticket.

Customs and Duties Visitors may bring in 200 cigarettes, one quart of liquor, and six ounces of perfume, plus any personal items.

Language Antigua's official language is English.

Precautions Some beaches are shaded by manchineel trees, whose leaves and applelike fruit are poisonous to touch. Most of the trees are posted with warning signs and should be avoided; even raindrops falling from them can cause painful blisters. If you should come in contact with one, rinse the affected area and contact a doctor.

Incidents of petty theft here are increasing. Leave your valuables in the hotel safe-deposit box; don't leave them unattended in your room or on the beach. Also, the streets of St. John's are fairly deserted at night, so it's not a good idea to wander out alone.

Staying in Antigua

Important Addresses Tourist Information: The Antigua and Barbuda Department of Tourism (Thames and Long Sts., St. John's, tel. 809/462–0480) is open Monday–Thursday 8–4:30, Friday 8–3. The Antigua Hotels Association (Long St., St. John's, tel. 809/462–3702) can also provide assistance.

Emergencies Police (tel. 809/462–0125), Fire (tel. 809/462–0044), and Ambulance (tel. 809/462–0251).

Hospital: There is a 24-hour emergency room at the 210-bed Holberton Hospital (Hospital Rd., St. John's, tel. 809/462–0251/2/3).

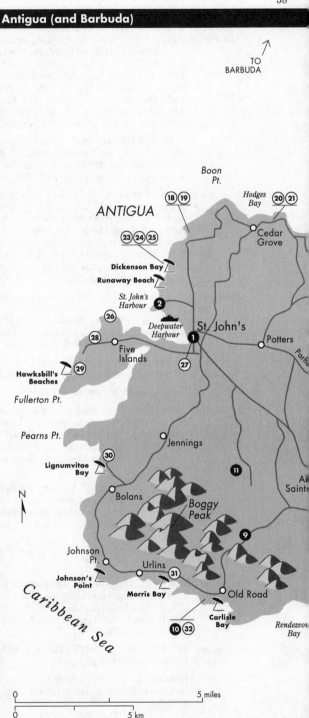

Antigua (and Barbuda)

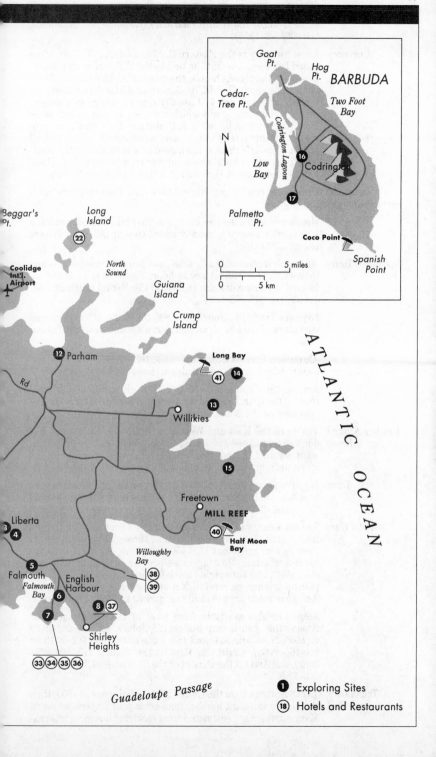

BARBUDA

Goat Pt.

Hog Pt.

Cedar-Tree Pt.

Two Foot Bay

Codrington Lagoon

Low Bay

16 Codrington

17

Palmetto Pt.

Coco Point

Spanish Point

N

0   5 miles

0   5 km

Beggar's Pt.

Long Island

22

Coolidge Int'l. Airport ✈

North Sound

Guiana Island

Crump Island

A T L A N T I C   O C E A N

12 Parham

Rd

Long Bay

41 **14**

13

Willikies ○

15

Freetown ○

MILL REEF

40

Half Moon Bay

Liberta

3

4

5

Falmouth

Falmouth Bay

English Harbour

6

Willoughby Bay

38

39

7

8 **37**

Shirley Heights ○

33 34 35 36

Guadeloupe Passage

1 Exploring Sites

18 Hotels and Restaurants

Pharmacies: Joseph's Pharmacy (Redcliffe St., St. John's, tel. 809/462–1025) and **Health Pharmacy** (Redcliffe St., St. John's, tel. 809/462–1255).

Currency Local currency is the Eastern Caribbean dollar (E.C.$), often called beewees. The E.C. is tied to the U.S. dollar and fluctuates only slightly. At hotels, the rate is E.C.$2.60 to U.S.$1; at banks, it's about E.C.$2.70. American dollars are readily accepted, although you will usually receive change in beewees. Be sure you understand which currency is being used, since most places quote prices in E.C. dollars. Most hotels, restaurants, and duty-free shops take major credit cards, and all accept traveler's checks. It's a good idea to inquire at the Tourist Office or your hotel about current credit-card policy. Note: Prices quoted are in U.S. dollars unless indicated otherwise.

Taxes and Service Charges Hotels collect a 7% government room tax. The departure tax is $8.

Hotels add a 10% service charge to your bill. In restaurants, a 10% service charge is usually added to your bill. Taxi drivers expect a 10% tip.

Guided Tours All **taxi** drivers double as guides, and you can arrange an island tour with one for about $20 an hour. The most reliable and informed driver/guides are at **Capital Car Rental** (High St., St. John's, tel. 809/462–0863).

Bryson's Travel (St. John's, tel. 809/462–0223) offers personalized tours of the island, as well as cruises and deep-sea fishing trips.

Alexander, Parrish Ltd. (St. John's, tel. 809/462–0387) specializes in island tours and can also arrange overnight stays.

Antours (St. John's, tel. 809/462–4788) gives half- and full-day tours of the island. Antours is also the **American Express** representative on the island.

Getting Around Buses You'll see the East and West Bus Stations in St. John's, but don't expect to see many buses. Bus schedules here epitomize what is called "island time," which is to say they roll when the spirit (infrequently) moves them.

Taxis If you're uncomfortable about driving on the left, a taxi is your best bet. Taxis are unmetered, but rates are fixed from here to there, and drivers are required to carry a rate card at all times.

Rental Cars To rent a car, you'll need a valid driver's license and a temporary permit ($12), which is available through the rental agent. Rentals average about U.S.$50, in-season, per day, with unlimited mileage. Most agencies provide both automatic and stick shift, and both right- and left-hand-drive vehicles. If you plan on driving, be careful! Not only is driving on the left, but Antiguan roads are generally unmarked and full of potholes.

Jeeps are also available from most of the rental agencies. Among the agencies are **Budget** (St. John's, tel. 809/462–3009 or 800/527–0700), **National** (St. John's, tel. 809/462–2113 or 800/468–0008), **Carib Car Rentals** (St. John's, tel. 809/462–2062), and **Avis** (at the airport or the St. James's Club, tel. 809/462–2840).

Telephones and Mail To call Antigua from the United States, dial area code 809, then the local seven-digit number (and cross your fingers for luck). Many numbers are restricted from receiving incoming international calls. In addition, the telephone system is primitive, and even local connections crackle.

To place a call in the United States, dial 1, the appropriate area code, and the seven-digit number. To place an intraisland call, dial the local seven-digit number.

In an emergency, you can make calls from Cable & Wireless (WI) Ltd. (42–44 St. Mary's St., St. John's, tel. 809/462–9840, and Nelson's Dockyard, English Harbour, tel. 809/463–1517).

Airmail letters to North America cost E.C.60¢; postcards, E.C.40¢. The post office is at the foot of High Street in St. John's.

Opening and Closing Times In general, shops are open Monday–Saturday 8:30 AM–noon and 1–4 PM. Some close at noon on Thursdays and Saturdays. Duty-free shops that cater to tourists often have flexible hours. Banks are open Monday–Wednesday 8 AM–2 PM, Thursday 8 AM–1 PM, Friday 8 AM–1 PM and 3–5 PM.

Beaches

All of Antigua's beaches are public, and many are dotted with resorts that provide water-sports equipment rentals and a place to grab a cool drink.

Hurricane Hugo did minimal damage to Antigua when it whipped through in September 1989, but it did chop away at some of the superb beaches on the southern coast. Time and tides should have more than replaced them by this reading, however. For more information regarding beachfront hotels, *see* Lodging, below.

Antigua A large coconut grove adds to the tropical beauty of **Carlisle Bay,** a long snow-white beach over which the estimable Curtain Bluff resort sits. Standing on the bluff of this peninsula, you can see the almost blinding blue waters of the Atlantic Ocean drifting into the Caribbean Sea.

Dickenson Bay has a lengthy stretch of powder-soft white sand and a host of hotels (the Siboney, the Divi Anchorage, Antigua Beach Village, and Halcyon Cove) that cater to water-sports enthusiasts.

Five Islands has four secluded beaches of fine tan sand and coral reefs for snorkeling. The Hawksbill Hotel is nearby.

Half Moon Bay (home of Half Moon Bay Hotel) was a ¾-mile crescent of sand that Hugo struck, but by now it should be back as a prime area for snorkeling and windsurfing. The hotel will let you borrow gear with a refundable deposit.

Johnson's Point is a deliciously deserted beach of bleached white sand on the southwest coast.

Lignumvitae Bay, south of the Jolly Beach Hotel on the west coast, is a beautiful beach at the edge of a saltwater swamp.

Long Bay, on the far eastern coast, has coral reefs in water so shallow that you can actually walk out to them. Here is a lovely beach, and the Long Bay Hotel, along with the rambling Pineapple Beach Club.

The white sand of **Runaway Beach** is home to the Barrymore Beach Hotel and the Runaway Beach Hotel, so things can get crowded. Refresh yourself with hot dogs and beer at the Barry-more's Satay Hut.

Barbuda   **Coco Point,** on Barbuda, is an uncrowded 8-mile stretch of white sand. Barbuda is great for scuba-diving, with dozens of shipwrecks off its coasts.

Exploring Antigua

Numbers in the margin correspond with points of interest on the Antigua map.

St. John's   The capital city of **St. John's,** home to some 35,000 people
❶   (nearly half the island's population), lies at sea level on the northwest coast of the island. The city has seen better days, but it is in the midst of a face-lift and there are some notable sights.

All major hotels provide free maps and island brochures, or, if you happen to be in St. John's, stop in at the Tourist Bureau, at the corner of Long and Thames streets.

Cross Long Street and walk one block to Church Street. The **Museum of Antigua and Barbuda** is a "hands-on history" oppor-tunity. Signs say Please Touch, with the hope of welcoming both citizens and visitors into Antigua's past. Exhibits inter-pret the history of the nation from its geological birth to political independence in 1981. There are fossil and coral re-mains from some 34 million years ago, a life-size Arawak house, models of a sugar plantation, a wattle and daub house, and a minishop with handicrafts, books, historical prints, and paint-ings. The colonial building that houses the museum is the former courthouse, which dates from 1750. *Church and Market sts., tel. 809/463–1060 or 809/462–3946. Admission free. Open weekdays 10–4, Sat. 10–1.*

Walk two blocks east on Church Street to **St. John's Cathedral.** The Anglican church sits on a hilltop, surrounded by its church-yard. At the south gate, there are figures of St. John the Baptist and St. John the Divine, said to have been taken from one of Napoleon's ships and brought to Antigua. The original church on this site was built in 1681 and replaced by a stone building in 1745. An earthquake destroyed that church in 1843, and the present building dates from 1845. With an eye to future earthquakes, the parishioners had the interior completely en-cased in pitch pine, hoping to forestall heavy damage. The church was elevated to the status of cathedral in 1848. *Between Long and Newcastle Sts., tel. 809/461–0082. Admission free.*

Recross Long Street, walk one block, and turn left on High Street. At the end of High Street, you'll see the **Cenotaph,** which honors Antiguans who lost their lives in World Wars I and II.

Trek seven blocks to the **Westerby Memorial,** which was erected in 1888 in memory of the Moravian Bishop George Westerby. One block south of the memorial is **Heritage Quay** (pronounced Key), a new multimillion-dollar complex, which opened some of its 40 shops in summer 1988. The complex, when completed, will include a 28-unit condominium/hotel, casino, supper club, 200-seat theater, shopping arcade, and food court. As soon as the construction of a new 500-foot pier and 200-foot causeway is completed, cruise-ship passengers will be able to disembark in the middle of Heritage Quay.

Redcliffe Quay, just south of Heritage Quay, is an attractive waterfront marketplace with more of an upscale feel to its shops, restaurants, and boutiques. This is the shopping area favored by both residents and return guests. Long ago on this site, slaves were held captive prior to being sold.

Time Out   There's a choice of over 20 crepes at the **Tutti Frutti Cafe** (High St., St. John's, tel. 809/462–0295), and a fresh juice bar offering the day's pick of papaya, pineapple, grapefruit, melon, and passion fruit.

At the far south end of town, where Market Street forks into Valley Road and All Saints Road, a whole lot of haggling goes on every Friday and Saturday during the day when locals jam the public **marketplace** to buy and sell fruits, vegetables, fish, and spices. Be sure to ask before you aim a camera, and expect the subject of your shot to ask for a tip.

Elsewhere on the Island   After touring Fort James, we will divide the island into two more tours. First, we'll take in English Harbour and Nelson's Dockyard on the south coast, returning to St. John's along the Caribbean (western) coast. Then we'll travel to the eastern side of the island for sights ranging from historical churches to Devil's Bridge.

It's a good idea to wear a swimsuit under your clothes while you're sightseeing—one of the sights to strike your fancy may be an enticing, secluded beach. Be sure to bring your camera along. There are some picture-perfect spots around the island.

Fort James   Follow Fort Road northwest out of town. In 2 miles, you'll come ❷ to **Fort James,** named after King James II. The fort was constructed between 1704 and 1739 as a lookout point for the city and St. John's Harbour. The ramparts overlooking the small islands in the bay are in ruins, but 10 cannons still point out to sea. If you continue on this road, you'll come to Dickenson Bay, with its string of smart, expensive resorts.

English Harbour   Take All Saints Road south out of St. John's. Eight miles out of ❸ town—almost to the south coast—is **Liberta,** one of the first settlements founded by freed slaves. East of the village, on ❹ Monk's Hill, is the site of **Fort George,** built from 1689 to 1720. The fort wouldn't be of much help to anybody these days, but among the ruins, you can make out the sites for its 32 cannons, its water cisterns, the base of the old flagstaff, and some of the original buildings.

❺ **Falmouth,** 1½ miles farther south, sits on a lovely bay, backed by former sugar plantations and sugar mills. **St. Paul's Church** was rebuilt on the site of a church once used by troops during the Nelson period.

❻ **English Harbour** lies on the coast, just south of Falmouth. This is the most famous of Antigua's attractions. In 1671, the governor of the Leeward Islands wrote to the Council for Foreign Plantations in London pointing out the advantages of this landlocked harbor, and by 1704, English Harbour was in regular use as a garrisoned station.

In 1784, 26-year-old Horatio Nelson sailed in on HMS *Boreas* to serve as captain and second in command of the Leeward Island

Station; he made frequent stops there for a period of three years. Under his command was the captain of HMS *Pegasus*, Prince William Henry, Duke of Clarence, who was to ascend the throne of England as William IV. The prince was Nelson's close friend and acted as best man when Nelson married the young widow Fannie Nisbet on Nevis in 1787.

The Royal Navy abandoned the station in 1889, and it fell into a state of decay. The Society of the Friends of English Harbour began restoring it in 1951, and on Dockyard Day, November 14, **7** 1961, **Nelson's Dockyard** was opened with much fanfare.

Nelson's Dockyard is to the Caribbean very much what Williamsburg, Virginia, is to the United States. Within the compound there are crafts shops, hotels, and restaurants. It is a hub for oceangoing yachts, and there is an abundance of activity here. (It serves as headquarters for the annual Sailing Week Regatta.) One of the Dockyard's former storehouses is now the beautifully restored and very British **Copper and Lumber Store Hotel.** Another fine hostelry, the **Admiral's Inn,** started out as a pitch and tar store, built of bricks that had been used as ballast in British ships.

The **Admiral's House Museum** has several rooms displaying ship models, a model of English Harbour, silver trophies, maps, prints, and Nelson's very own telescope and tea caddy. *English Harbour, tel. 809/463–1053 or 809/463–1379. Admission: $1.60 per person. Open daily 8–6.*

On a ridge overlooking the dockyard is **Clarence House** (tel. 809/463–1026), built in 1787 and once the home of the Duke of Clarence. Princess Margaret and Lord Snowdon spent part of their honeymoon here in 1960, and Queen Elizabeth and Prince Philip have dined here. It is now used by the governor-general; visits are possible when he is not in residence. Slip a tip to the caretaker, who'll give you a fascinating tour; the place is worth a visit.

As you leave the dockyard, turn right at the crossroads in English Harbour and drive to **Shirley Heights** for a spectacular **8** view of English Harbour. The heights are named for Sir Thomas Shirley, the governor, who fortified the harbour in 1787.

Time Out Cool off with the yachting crowd on the terrace of the **Admiral's Inn** (English Harbour, tel. 809/463–1027), where the deeply tanned crews can keep an eye on their multimillion dollar babies offshore, and on each other. The people-watching is first-rate, and so are the banana daiquiris (with or without Antiguan rum).

Drive back up to Liberta. Four and a half miles north of town, opposite the Catholic church, turn left and head southwest on **9** **Fig Tree Drive.** (Forget about plucking figs; *fig* is the Antiguan word for banana.) This drive takes you through the rain forest, which is rich in mangoes, pineapples, and banana trees. This is also the hilliest part of the island—**Boggy Peak,** to the west, is the highest point, rising to 1,319 feet. Fig Tree Drive runs into **10** Old Road, which leads down to **Curtain Bluff,** an unforgettable sight. On this peninsula, between Carlisle Bay and Morris Bay, the Atlantic Ocean meets the Caribbean Sea, resulting in wonderful color contrasts in the water.

From here, the main road sweeps along the southwest coast, where there are lovely beaches and spectacular views. The road then veers off to the northeast and goes through the villages of Bolans and Jennings.

⑪ From Jennings, a road turns right to the **Megaliths of Greencastle Hill,** an arduous climb away. Some say the megaliths were set up by humans for the worship of the sun and moon; others believe they are nothing more than unusual geological formations.

The East End St. John's is 6 miles northeast of Jennings. To explore the other half of the island, take Parham Road east out of St. John's. Three and a half miles to the east, you'll see on your left the now-defunct sugar refinery. Drive 2 miles farther and turn left on the side road that leads 1¼ miles to the settlement of **⑫** **Parham. St. Peter's Church,** built in 1840 by Thomas Weekes, an English architect, is an octagonal Italianate building whose facade was once richly decorated with stucco, though it suffered considerable damage during the earthquake of 1843.

Backtrack and continue east for about three-quarters of a mile, to a fork in the road. One branch veers in a southeasterly direction toward Half Moon Bay and the other continues toward the northeast coast. The latter route runs through the villages of **⑬** Pares and Willikies to **Indian Town,** a national park, where archaeological digs have revealed evidence of Carib occupation.

⑭ Less than a mile farther south along the coast is **Devil's Bridge,** a natural formation sculpted by the crashing breakers of the Atlantic at Indian Creek. The bluffs took their name from the slaves who committed suicide there in the 18th century because they believed they had the devil in them. Surf gushes out through blowholes that were carved by the breakers.

If you take the southeast fork outside of Parham, you'll travel 9 miles to Half Moon Bay. Just before the coast is the village of **Freetown** and the **Mill Reef area,** where many pre-Columbian discoveries have been made.

⑮ **Harmony Hall,** northeast of Freetown, is an interesting art gallery. A sister to the Jamaican gallery near Ocho Rios, Harmony Hall is built on the foundation of a 17th-century sugar-plantation great house. Artist Graham Davis and Peter and Annabella Proudlock, who founded the Jamaican gallery, teamed up with local entrepreneur Geoffrey Pidduck to create an Antiguan art gallery specializing in high-quality West Indian art. A large gallery is used for one-man shows, and another exhibition hall displays watercolors. A small bar and an outside restaurant under the trees are open in-season. *Brown's Mill Bay, tel. 809/463–2057. Open daily 10–6.*

Barbuda Thirty miles due north of Antigua is Barbuda—all 62 square **⑯** miles of it. Almost all the island's 1,200 people live in **Codrington.** Barbuda's 8-mile **Coco Point** lures beachcombers, and the island is ringed by wrecks and reef, which makes it a great draw for divers and snorkelers.

⑰ The sole historic ruin here is **Martello Tower,** which is believed to have been a lighthouse built by the Spaniards before the English occupied the island. LIAT (*see* Before You Go, above) has regularly scheduled daily flights from Antigua; air and boat charters are also available (contact the Tourist Board).

Participant Sports

Almost all the resort hotels can come up with fins and masks, Windsurfers, Sunfish, glass-bottom boats, catamarans, and other water-related gear (*see* Lodging, below).

Boating **Wadadli Watersports** (tel. 809/462–4101 or 4100) rents catamarans and other crafts. **Shorty's** at Dickenson Bay has some of the best water sports on the island, if a somewhat hectic pace (tel. 809/462–2393). Check yacht charters through **Nicholson Yacht Charters** (tel. 800/662–6066).

Fitness Center The **Benair Fitness Club** (Country Club Rd., Hodges Bay, tel. 809/462–1540) has fitness equipment, Jacuzzi, aerobic classes, and a juice bar.

Golf There is an 18-hole course at **Cedar Valley Golf Club** (tel. 809/462–0161), and a nine-hole course at **Half Moon Bay Hotel** (tel. 809/463–2101).

Hiking There are no organized hiking trips, but you can trek up 687-foot Monk's Hill, tackle Boggy Peak's slopes, or climb up Greencastle Hill to see the megaliths (*see* Exploring Antigua, above).

Horseback Riding First-rate Texas quarter horses and former racehorses are found at the **St. James Stables**, attached to the St. James's Club (tel. 809/463–1430 or 809/463–1113). Guided trail rides can be arranged through **Wadadli Stables** (tel. 809/462–2721).

Sailing The **Antigua School of Sailing** (tel. 809/462–2026) offers short resort courses.

Scuba Diving With all the wrecks and reefs, there are lots of undersea sights to see. Contact **Dive Antigua** (tel. 809/462–0256) or **Aquanaut Dive Center**, which offers certification courses and day and night dives from three separate locations: the St. James's Club (tel. 809/463–1113), Galleon Beach Club (tel. 809/463–1024), and the Royal Antiguan (tel. 809/462–3733). Dive packages are offered by the **Runaway Beach Club** (tel. 809/462–2626).

Sea Excursions The 50-foot catamaran *Cariba* offers full-day sails (10–4) with lunch or half-day sails (9:30–12:30 or 1:30–4:30) that include an on-board picnic. There are swim and snorkel stops on all trips, but the *Cariba* also has underwater viewing windows for those who prefer to stay dry. **Wadadli Watersports** (tel. 809/462–4101 or 4100) makes trips to Bird Island and Barbuda that include soft drinks and barbecue on the beach. The *Jolly Roger* (tel. 809/462–2064) has a "fun cruise," complete with "pirate" crew, limbo dancing, walking the plank, and other pranks. *Paradise I* (tel. 809/462–4158) is a 45-foot Beneteau yacht that offers lunch or sunset cruises. The *Falcon* (tel. 809/462–4792) is a catamaran schooner that cruises to Bird Island and Barbuda for snorkeling and barbecue; it also makes sunset cruises.

Tennis The **Temo Sports Complex** (Falmouth Bay, tel. 809/463–1781) has floodlit courts, glass-backed squash courts, showers, sports shop, and snack bars. There are also seven courts at the St. James's Club (five are lighted for night play), five courts at the **Half Moon Club**, four Har-Tru and one grass court at **Curtain Bluff**.

Waterskiing Rentals are available at **Wadadli Watersports** (tel. 809/462–4101 or 4100).

Windsurfing The **High Wind Centre** at the Lord Nelson Hotel is *the* spot for serious board sailors. Run by expert Patrick Scales (tel. 809/462–3094). Rentals are also available at **Wadadli Watersports** (tel. 809/462–4101 or 4100) and **Hodges Bay Club** (tel. 809/462–2300); most major hotels offer boardsailing equipment.

Spectator Sports

For information about sports events, contact **Antigua Sports and Games** (tel. 809/462–1925).

Cricket Practically the only thing most Americans know about this game is that there's something called a "sticky wicket." Here, as in Britain and all the West Indies, the game is a national passion. Youngsters play on makeshift pitches, which apparently compare to sandlots, and international matches are fought out in the stadium on Independence Avenue, St. John's (*see* Exploring Antigua, above).

Shopping

Antigua's duty-free shops are the reason so many cruise ships call here. Bargains can be found in perfumes, liqueurs and liquor (including, of course, Antiguan rum), jewelry, china, and crystal. As for local items, look for straw hats, baskets, batik, pottery, and hand-printed cotton clothing.

Shopping Areas The 30-odd boutiques, plus restaurants and nightclub, at **Redcliffe Quay** are generally interesting and upscale, all housed in a restored "barracoon," once a slave-holding compound and auction site. The newer **Heritage Quay** (also in St. John's) has some 35 shops that cater primarily to the cruise crowd that docks almost at its doorstep. The main tourist shops in St. John's are along **St. Mary's, High,** and **Long streets.**

Good Buys **Specialty Shoppe** (St. Mary's St., tel. 809/462–1198), **The Scent**
China and Crystal **Shop** (High St., tel. 809/462–0303), and **Norma's Duty-Free Shop** (Heritage Quay Shopping Center and Halcyon Cove Hotel, tel. 809/462–0172) have wares that make impressive presents. **Little Switzerland** (Heritage Quay, tel. 809/462–3108) houses pricey buys in a luxurious, and air-conditioned, setting. Stop by, if only to browse and cool off!

Jewelry Hans Smit is **The Goldsmitty** (Redcliffe Quay, tel. 809/462–4601), a European-trained expert goldsmith who turns gold, black coral, precious and semiprecious stones into one-of-a-kind works of art that adorn the wrists and necks of the rich and famous. **Colombian Emeralds** (Heritage Quay, tel. 809/462–2086) is the largest retailer of Colombian emeralds in the world. Jewelry bargains are also at **Norma's Duty-Free Shop** (Heritage Quay Shopping Center and the Halcyon Cove Hotel, tel. 809/462–0172).

Liquor and **The Warehouse** (St. Mary's St., tel. 809/462–0495) and **Manuel**
Liqueurs **Diaz Liquor Store** (Long and Market Sts., tel. 809/462–0440) should whet your appetite.

Native Crafts Janie Easton designs many of the original finds in her two **Galley Boutiques** (the main shop in a historic building in English Harbour, tel. 809/462–1525; another at the upscale **St. James's Club** tel. 809/463–1333) with pizzaz and reasonable prices. Trinidadian Natalie White sells her sculptured cushions and wall hangings, all hand-painted on silk, and signed, from her home-studio (tel. 809/463–2519), but she is expanding to a larger **Craft Originals Studio** on the Coast Road. Artist-filmmaker Nick Maley, with his wife Gloria, have turned the **Island Arts Galleries** (three locations: their home-studio, Alton Place, on Sandy Lane, behind the Hodges Bay Club, tel. 809/461–3332; Heritage Quay, tel. 809/462–2787; and the St. James's Club, tel. 809/463–1113) into a melting pot for Caribbean artists, with prices ranging from $10 to $15,000. **Harmony Hall** the bookstore (at Brown's Bay Mill, near Freetown) is the Antiguan sister to the original Jamaica location. In addition to "Annabella Boxes," books and cards, there is pottery and ceramic pieces, carved wooden fantasy birds, and an ever-changing roster of exhibits (tel. 809/460–4120). John and Katie Shears have opened **Seahorse Studios** (at Cobbs Cross, en route to English Harbour, tel. 809/463–1417), presenting the works of good artists in a good setting. **Bona,** (Redcliffe Quay, tel. 809/462–2036) presents antiques, select crystal and porcelain, leaf-of-lettice pottery from Italy, and "wedding frogs" from Thailand, collected during the world travels of owners Bona and Martin Macy. The **CoCo Shop** (St. Mary's St., tel. 809/462–1128) is a favorite haunt for Sea Island cotton designs, and Daks, or Liberty of London fabrics, along with their own designs for the country-club set. **A Thousand Flowers** (Redcliffe Quay, tel. 809/462–4264) uses only natural fibers and is also the place for Java wraps. A "must" buy at the **Map Shop** (St. Mary's St., tel. 809/462–3993) for those interested in Antiguan life, is the paperback *To Shoot Hard Labour (The Life and Times of Samuel Smith, an Antiguan Workingman)*. This is $12 you won't regret spending. Also check out any of the three books of Jamaica Kincaid, whose works on her native Antigua have caused international, albeit controversial, acclaim.

Perfume **CoCo Shop** (St. Mary's St., tel. 809/462–1128), **The Scent Shop** (High St., tel. 809/462–0303). In Heritage Quay, two shops, **La Parfumerie** (tel. 809/462–2601) and **Little Switzerland** (tel. 809/ 462–3108), have extensive selections of European scents for men and women.

Dining

The focus, naturally, is on fresh-caught fish and lobster, but Antigua offers sophisticated Continental and American dining as well. Because of its British heritage, Antigua tends to be a bit more formal in dressing for dinner. There are a few places, which will be noted, that require both jacket and tie.

Most menu prices are listed in E.C. dollars; some are listed in both E.C. and U.S. dollars. Be sure to check in advance if credit cards are accepted and ask in which currency the prices are quoted. Dinner reservations are needed during high season.

The most highly recommended restaurants are indicated by a star ★ .

Category	Cost*
Very Expensive	over $45
Expensive	$25–$45

Moderate	$15–$25
Inexpensive	under $15

per person, excluding drinks, service, and sales tax (7%)

★ **Jumby Bay,** a private 300-acre island resort that's just a 15-minute launch ride from Antigua's shores, accepts a limited number of outside guests for lunch or dinner when advance reservations are made. For a set price of $45 (plus government tax), guests board the noon boat for a nonstop buffet, after several sips of Woody's (the infamous bar director's) famed fruit punches. The management will also give an informal tour of their special island on request. A dinner reservation means catching the 6 or 7 PM launch and, for $60, a choice of five entrées. While the menu changes nightly, a few of the favored dishes are sautéed breast of chicken filled with wild mushrooms, Mediterranean seafood terrine with sprinkled saffron, and soufflé of scallops with basil puree. *Tel. 809/462-6000. Closed Sept. and Oct. No outside dinner reservations for Wed. or Sun. nights. AE, MC, V. Very Expensive.*

★ **Le Bistro** is the elegant creation of Raffaele and Philippa Esposito, who offer two sittings for dinner in-season (7–7:30 or 9–9:30). Sip one of the wines from the extensive wine cellar, then move on to tables tucked inside this renovated country house. An extensive menu offers some 18 main dishes—from fresh local fish (langouste, grilled, or fondue, poached fillet of snapper) to imported Dover sole, salmon garnished with caviar, prime ribs of beef, roast Long Island duck, and roast quail in a passionfruit sauce. Desserts are divine and decadent. *Hodges Bay, tel. 809/462-3881. AE, DC, MC, V. Closed Mon., and early May–early Apr. Very Expensive.*

Admiral's Inn. In-season, the Ad's is a yachting "in" spot, where the owners dine on pumpkin soup, curried conch, fresh snapper with equally fresh limes or maybe lobster Thermidor, at crisply set tables covered in linen. Their crews are usually on the outside terrace, where a steel band often plays, or clustered around the bar that dates from 1788. *Nelson's Dockyard, tel. 809/463-1027. Reservations required. AE, MC, V. Expensive.*

Cacubi Room. Candlelight and crisp white napery enhance the elegant mood in the Blue Waters Hotel's air-conditioned restaurant. For openers, try the homemade liver pâté marinated in brandy and flavored with herbs. The chef's special creation in Flying Fish Cavelier (two fillets cooked in white wine and herbs, served in a cream sauce flavored with Cavalier rum and sprinkled with butter-fried coconut). This restaurant is famed for its flambéed desserts—try the pineapple flambé or crepes Suzette. Liqueurs and cigars are brought to your table after your meal. *Blue Waters Hotel, Boon Pt., tel. 809/462-0290. Jackets required. Reservations suggested. AE, MC, V. Expensive.*

Casuarina. The limited (but excellent) French-inspired menu starts with a choice of escargot, pâté, lobster feuillete, and stuffed crab back, and continues with blackened steak of marlin, grilled jumbo shrimp, local langouste, filet mignon, veal cutlet flambé, and duck in a homemade raspberry vinegar—all served in an elegant, restored West Indian house. *Anchorage Rd., tel. 809/462-3751, AE, DC, MC, V. Expensive.*

★ **Clouds.** The elegantly decorated terrace sits high on a hill, overlooking Halcyon Cove and Dickenson Bay. Chef Julian Waters turns out starters such as melon glazed with ginger and honey, accompanied by grape and red wine sorbet. Soups include chilled zucchini and carrot. Among the entrées are panfried medallions of venison, noisettes of lamb, and breast of chicken filled with duck and pistachio-nut mousse, accompanied by herb butter and avocado. For dessert, try the fresh strawberry parfait. *Halcyon Cove Beach Resort, tel. 809/462–0256. Jacket and tie required. Reservations required. AE, MC, V. Closed Sun. Expensive.*

The Wardroom Restaurant, on the ground floor of the beautifully restored Copper and Lumber Store, offers an international menu, mixing an interesting vegetarian casserole with steak and veal dishes or fresh-fish creations. It's a place for lingering over unusual desserts (kiwi and white-wine syllabub) and a choice of five coffees with liqueurs. *Nelson's Dockyard, tel. 809/463–1058. Reservations advised. Moderate–Expensive.*

Alberto's. Owners Alberto and Vanessa Ravanello, who once held sway at the Yacht Club, now wow the English Harbour crowd with local seafood with an Italian accent. Try eggplant parmiggiana veal pizzaiola, linguini with clams, fresh langouste, or Alberto's creation for the evening. *Red Hill, near the St. James's Club. Reservations required via VHF 68. AE, DC, MC, V. Closed Mon. in-season; Mon. and Tues. off-season. Dinner only. Moderate.*

Colombo's. The Sardinians who run this restaurant make every effort to please, and they do. The thatch-roof patio is evocative of the South Seas, and the full Italian menu includes homemade pastas, veal scalloppine, tournedos, and lobster Mornay. *Galleon Beach Club, English Harbour, tel. 809/463–1081. Reservations suggested. No credit cards. Closed Sept. Expensive.*

Lemon Tree is an air-conditioned, art deco oasis on the second floor of a freshly painted St. John's building. Open for breakfast, lunch and dinner, it fast became *the* in-town spot, offering an eclectic menu that mixes minipizzas and ribs, potato skins and nachos, with beef Wellington, cornish hen, lobster or vegetarian crepes, Cajun garlic shrimp, and pasta dishes. There's always a smattering of Mexican dishes (burritos, chili, nachos, or fajitas). Owners Jerry and Janet Ferrara offer different live entertainment every night, from soft classical piano to upbeat reggae. Officially, the closing time is 11 PM, but few pay attention, especially on weekends! *Long and Church Sts., St. John's, tel. 809/461–2507. AE, DC, MC, V. Open 10 AM–11 PM. Moderate.*

Shirley Heights Lookout. This restaurant is in part of an 18th-century fortification, and the view of English Harbour below is breathtaking. There's a breezy pub downstairs that opens onto the lookout point, and upstairs, a cozy, windowed room with hardwood floors and beamed ceilings. Pub offerings include burgers, sandwiches, and barbecue, while the upstairs room serves the likes of pumpkin soup and lobster in lime sauce. There's a barbecue livened by island music from a steel band every Sunday. *Shirley Heights, tel. 809/463–1785. Reservations required in season. AE, MC, V. Moderate.*

Lodging

Antigua's beaches are decorated with an assortment of resorts, ranging from the spectacular to small and self-catering homes away from home. Those seeking active nightlife and opportunities for meeting other island guests will want to stay in one of the hotels in Dickenson Bay, where properties are close together, which makes for lots of beach action, and St. John's is just a five-minute cab ride away. The resorts scattered elsewhere on the island tend to cater more to honeymooners and to those who seek some seclusion. Most hotels offer the MAP, and due to distances to town, most guests take advantage of it. Therefore, unless otherwise noted, our price categories include breakfast and dinner.

The most highly recommended lodgings are indicated by a star ★.

Category	Cost*
Very Expensive	over $350
Expensive	$250–$350
Moderate	$150–$250
Inexpensive	under $150

All prices are for a standard double room for two, excluding 7% tax and a 10% service charge.

★ **Blue Waters Beach Hotel.** Luscious lime-colored buildings, set in a tropical garden along two white-sand beaches, draw a European clientele to this casually elegant property, where the staff speaks 10 different languages. Accommodations are in air-conditioned rooms or two- and three-bedroom villas, all of which are beachfront with balconies or patios. *Box 256, St. John's, tel. 809/462–0290 or 800/372–1323; in UK 01/367–5175. 67 rooms. MAP or EP available. Facilities: 2 restaurants, 2 bars, pool, 1 lighted tennis court, gift shop, water-sports center. AE, MC, V. Very Expensive.*

★ **Curtain Bluff.** It's difficult not to go overboard about this resort. A long avenue of trees leads out onto the peninsula where the hotel is bordered by the Atlantic Ocean on one side, the Caribbean Sea on the other; two white-sand beaches beckon below the bluff. Deluxe beachfront rooms and suites have cedar ceilings with whirring fans, marble baths, private balconies, and chaises longues. Owner Howard Hulford is a connoisseur of wine, and his collection makes up the hotel's 50,000-bottle wine cellar. His villa overlooking the waters is the ritzy locale of weekly cocktail parties and anniversary parties honoring guests who are visiting the hotel for the 10th or 20th time. The hotel has a dive boat, sailboats, Windsurfers, and facilities for a host of water-related activities. Curtain Bluff is not for the budget conscious. *Box 288, St. John's, tel. 809/463–1115 or in NY, 212/289–8888. 60 rooms and suites. Facilities: restaurant, lounge, 4 tennis courts, pro shop, croquet, putting green, water-sports center. No credit cards. Closed Sept. Very Expensive.*

Halcyon Cove Beach Resort and Casino. Days and nights are activity-packed in this government-owned Dickenson Bay hotel. Luxury accommodations, all with air-conditioning and private balcony or patio, are scattered around the courtyard pool or on the beach. A water-sports center offers excursions on a glass-bottom boat and waterskiing, in addition to the other usual water sports. In the evening, you can go for a spin in the casino or around the dance floor. *Box 251, St. John's, tel. 809/ 462–0256 or 800/223–1588. 135 rooms. Facilities: 4 restaurants, 3 bars, room service, pool, 4 lighted tennis courts, casino, boutiques, water-sports center. AE, DC, MC, V. Very Expensive.*

Half Moon Bay. This two-story hotel sits on a lovely horseshoe bay on the southeastern tip of the island. Its reception area is an open breezeway with tile floors and wood rafters. All the rooms are oceanfront; the white sand beach, lined with tall palms, is literally a step away. Each room has either a balcony or a patio; standard rooms have half-tubs with showers. Suites have minifridges and lounge areas, and there is a two-bedroom cottage with a kitchen. There are no air-conditioning, phones, or TVs. Lunch is served by the free-form pool, and tea is served each afternoon. All water sports are free to guests. The hotel hosts annual tennis tournaments in January, April, and October. *Box 144, St. John's, tel. 809/460–4300 or 800/223–6510. 100 rooms. Facilities: 2 restaurants, 2 bars, pool, 5 tennis courts (1 lighted) with a pro, 9-hole golf course, water-sports center. AE. Very Expensive.*

Hawksbill Beach Hotel. The Hawksbill, on 37 acres on the Five Islands peninsula, boasts no fewer than four beaches of fine tan sand. Best accommodations are in a luxurious two-story, three-bedroom West Indian Great House, with king-size beds, tile floors, wicker furniture, and kitchenette/bar. Also good are the new deluxe cottages that face the sea. Gentlemen are requested not to wear short sleeves into the dining room after 7 PM; children under age 8 are not welcome here. Water sports are complimentary except for a small charge for waterskiing. *Box 108, St. John's, tel. 809/462–0301 or 800/327–6511; in Canada, 416/622–8813). 75 rooms. Facilities: 2 restaurants, 2 bars, pool, tennis court, boutique, water-sports center. AE, DC, MC, V. Very Expensive.*

★ **Hodges Bay Club.** Opposite Prickly Pear Island, on a great snorkeling beach, are Hodges Bay's luxury one- and two-bedroom condominium villas. All villas have fully equipped kitchens, king-size beds, two balconies, and daily maid service. All bedrooms are air-conditioned and each has a private bath. *Box 1237, St. John's, tel. 809/462–2300 or 800/223–5581; in NY 212/535–9530). 26 suites. Facilities: restaurant, pool, 2 tennis courts, water-sports center. AE, DC, MC, V. Very Expensive.*

★ **Jumby Bay.** Fifteen minutes by launch from Antigua is this 300-acre private island retreat where the feeling among guests and long-serving staff is like that of an extended family. Accommodations are in junior suites located either in a multiunit facility or in cottages, both set amid quiet, sandy beaches and miles of walking trails. All meals are included in the rates, along with bar drinks, house wines, bicycles, tennis, water sports, and the ferry to and from Antigua. The management believes that children under age 8 would not be comfortable here. *Box 243, St. John's, tel. 809/462–6000 or 800/437–0049. 38 suites. Facilities: 2 restaurants, 3 bars, tennis, bicycles, sailboats, water-sports center. No credit cards. Very Expensive.*

Pineapple Beach Club (formerly the New Horizons). A broad stone walk leads directly from the reception area to the beach of this all-inclusive (meals, drinks, gratuities, sports, you name it) resort. The fan-cooled beachfront doubles have private terraces and shower-baths. There are no phones or TVs. Garden-view rooms are air-conditioned. The pool and the windsurfing school are located on Long Bay's white-sand beach. Live entertainment is offered nightly. *Box 54, St. John's, tel. 809/463-2006 or 800/223-9815; in Canada, 800/468-0023. 97 rooms. Facilities: restaurant, bar, pool, 2 tennis courts. AE, DC, MC, V. Very Expensive.*

★ **Ramada Renaissance Royal Antiguan Resort.** This is the largest hotel in Antigua. Ramada took over and redecorated this long-standing Antiguan belle at Deep Bay on the northwest coast in 1989. The results are a crisper tone and such expanded amenities as three restaurants (the premiere room is La Regence), three bars, and a 5,500-square-foot casino with the games (blackjack, roulette, craps, baccarat, and 130 slot machines) played by Atlantic City rules. *Deep Bay, St. John's (tel. 809/462-3733 or 800/228-9898). 300 air-conditioned rooms. Facilities: 3 restaurants, 3 bars, casino, swimming pool with swim-up bar, full water sports (snorkeling, Sunfish sailing, windsurfing, waterskiing, fishing), a certified dive master, 5 tennis courts, golf arranged at nearby 18-hole Cedar Valley course, a minicrafts market on site. All major credit cards. Expensive.*

★ **St. James's Club.** Set on a 100-acre split of land at Mamora Bay, this location is both dramatic and desirable. A redecoration of the rooms and suites was under way in 1990, with the villas soon to follow. The club clings to the side of a hill, with cobblestone paths for both people and the vans needed for transport. In-season, there's a hum of international guests, with lots of on-site activities. *Box 63, St. John's, tel. 809/463-1430 or 809/463-1113; in NY, 212/486-2575 or 800/274-0008. 105 total accommodations. Facilities: 3 restaurants, 5 bars, 24-hour room service, 3 swimming pools, Jacuzzi, minigym, 5 boutiques, beauty salon and masseuse, disco and nightclub, European-style casino, 7 tennis courts (4 are lighted), waterskiing, snorkeling, scuba-diving certification school, sailboating, windsurfing, Aqua Bikes, peddleboats, deep-sea fishing, lawn croquet, golf at the 18-hole Cedar Valley Golf club, horseback riding. AE, MC, V. Very Expensive.*

★ **Galley Bay Surf Club.** This is a quiet and peaceful getaway in a tropical setting between a white beach and a blue lagoon. Beachfront villas have king-size beds, ceiling fans, showers, upscale tropical decor, and, of course, the beach. Rooms in Gauguin Village, a group of thatch-roof Tahitian-style cottages on the lagoon, are simply furnished (twin beds), and while each has a private patio, you have to walk across it to get to the bath. *Box 305, St. John's, tel. 809/462-0302 or 800/223-5581; in NY, 212/535-9530. 30 rooms. Facilities: restaurant, bar, tennis court, horseback riding, water-sports center. AE, MC, V. Expensive-Very Expensive.*

★ **Siboney Beach Club.** Ann and Tony Johnson's all-suites beach club on Dickenson Bay is a gem that's set in a tropical garden smack on the beach. Each suite is done in tropical decor, with rattan furnishings and colorful island prints. Guests can choose between air-conditioned or fan-cooled bedrooms and king-size or twin beds. Just off the living area, there's a private balcony or patio, each framed by palm fronds and tropical plants. There are fully equipped Pullman kitchens, which you can either use or seal off behind louvered panels and forget about while you dine at the Coconut Grove adjacent to the reception area. The staff here is especially friendly and helpful. *Box 222, St. John's, tel. 809/462–0806 or 800/533–0234. 12 suites. Facilities: restaurant, bar, pool. AE, MC, V. Expensive–Very Expensive.*

★ **Copper and Lumber Store Hotel.** The former supply store in Nelson's Dockyard has been transformed into a very British inn, with old brick, hardwood floors, Oriental rugs, and old English prints and maps. Stairs lead up to Old World suites with kitchens, each decorated differently but all with period furnishings, antique washstands, secretaries, and four-poster and canopy beds. If you're an Anglophile, you won't want to go home. *Box 184, St. John's, tel. 809/463–1058. 14 suites. Facilities: restaurant/pub. AE, MC, V. Moderate–Expensive.*

Callaloo Beach Hotel. Nick Fuller's place on Morris Bay is set on 37 acres with 1,600 feet of white-gold sand. Each of the twin-bedded rooms has Spanish tile floors, beamed ceilings, rattan furnishings, private bath, and veranda. The atmosphere is very laid back. *Box 676, St. John's, tel. 809/463–1110. 16 rooms. Facilities: restaurant, bar. AE, MC, V. Moderate.*

Jolly Beach Resort. This sprawling, Spanish-style stucco hotel is the largest in the eastern Caribbean. It's set on 38 tropical acres, with 1½ miles of beach at Lignumvitae Bay. The accommodations range from tiny functional rooms to villas. There's free waterskiing, windsurfing, and paddle- or sailboats. This is the place for jolly, energetic folks. *Box 744, St. John's, tel. 809/462–0061 or 800/321–1055; in FL, 800/432–6083; in Canada, 800/368–6669. 500 rooms. Facilities: 3 restaurants, 4 bars, disco, pool, 8 tennis courts, movie room, shops, car rental desk, water-sports center. AE, MC, V. Moderate.*

★ **Admiral's Inn.** Built in the 18th century of old brick that had been used as ballast for sailing vessels, this English inn in Nelson's Dockyard once housed engineers' offices and a warehouse. If you're looking for glitz and glamour, head for Dickenson Bay. The rooms here are simple (some are air-conditioned, some have ceiling fans), and bathrooms have only showers. A complimentary boat runs you to the beach at Freeman's Bay, where you have free use of sailboats. *Box 713, St. John's, tel. 809/463–1027 or 800/223–5695; in NY, 914/833–3303; in Canada, 416/447–2335; in the United Kingdom, 01/387–1555. 14 rooms. Facilities: restaurant, pub. No credit cards. Inexpensive.*

Nightlife

Most of Antigua's evening entertainment centers on the resort hotels, which feature calypso singers, steel bands, limbo dancers, and folkloric groups on a regular basis. Check with the Tourist Board for up-to-date information.

Shirley Heights Lookout (Shirley Heights, tel. 809/463–1785) does Sunday-afternoon barbecues that continue into the night with music and dancing. It's a favorite local spot on Sunday night for residents, visitors, and the ever-changing yachting crowd. (Best gossip on the island!)

Casinos There are five hotel casinos open from early evening until 4 AM. The newest gaming addition is the **King's Casino** at Heritage Quay. Slot machines and gaming tables attract gamblers to the **Halcyon Cove Resort** (Dickenson Bay, tel. 809/462–0256), and the **Flamingo** (Michaels Mount, tel. 809/462–1266). The **St.**

James Club (Mamora Bay, tel. 809/463–1113) has a private casino with a European ambience. Ramada has turned their Maiones Casino, at the Ramada Renaissance Royal Antiguan Resort, into an Atlantic City–style casino.

Discos **Tropix** (Redcliffe Quay, St. John's, tel. 809/462–2317) is a hot spot in Redcliffe Quay. Open Wednesday through Saturday, from 9 PM till whenever, it draws locals, residents, and energetic visitors; **Chips** (Halcyon Cove Beach Resort, tel. 809/462–0256) is a hot spot that attracts tourists. An insider's favorite remains **Peter Scott's Cafe** (St. John's). Owner Scott is his own best entertainment, playing the guitar and mixing songs from reggae to ballads. On Wednesday nights, **Columbo's** (Galleon Beach Club, English Harbour, tel. 809/463–1081) is the place to be for live reggae, and the **Lemon Tree Restaurant** (Long and Church Sts., St. John's, tel. 809/461–2507) swings every night in-season until at least 11 PM.

4 Aruba

by Pamela Bloom

Pamela Bloom writes on pop music and the cabaret scene in New York. She also writes about travel for a number of magazines.

Imagine Aruba as one big Love Boat cruise. Most of its 20 hotels sit side by side down one major strip along the southwestern shore, with restaurants, exotic boutiques, fiery floor shows, and glitzy casinos right on their premises so you don't even have to step outside. Nearly every night there are wild theme parties, Carnival blasts, treasure hunts, beachside barbecues, and fish fries with steel bands and limbo dancers. Every Tuesday evening year-round, Arubans celebrate the Bonbini ("Welcome" in the Native Papiamento dialect) with arts and crafts and musical and dancing shows in the courtyard of Oranjestad's Fort Zoutman.

The "A" in the ABC Islands, Aruba is a small island—12 miles long and approximately 70 square miles. The national anthem proclaims, "the greatness of our people is their great cordiality," and this is no exaggeration. Once a member of the Netherlands Antilles, Aruba became an independent entity within the Netherlands in 1986, with its own royally appointed governor, a democratic government, and a 21-member elected parliament. Long secure in a solid economy, with good education, housing, and health care, the island's population of about 65,000 actually regards tourists as welcome guests. Waiters serve you with smiles and solid eye contact, English is spoken everywhere, and hotel hospitality directors appear delighted to serve your special needs. Good direct air service from the United States *(see* Arriving and Departing, below) makes Aruba an excellent choice for even a short vacation.

The island's distinctive beauty lies in its countryside—an almost extraterrestrial landscape full of rocky deserts, cactus jungles, secluded coves, and aquamarine vistas with crashing waves. With its low humidity and average temperatures of 82° F, Aruba has the climate of a paradise; rain comes mostly during November. Many of the same tourists return year after year, and many hotels honor longtime customers with special plaques and presentations.

Before You Go

Tourist Information Contact the **Aruba Tourism Authority,** 521 5th Ave., 12th Floor, New York, NY 10175, tel. 212/246-3030 or 800/TO–ARUBA, telex 668–688; in Miami, 85 Grand Canal Dr., Suite 200, Miami, FL 33144, tel. 305/267–0404; in Canada, 1801 Englinton W. Street, 3118, Toronto, Ontario, M6E2H7, tel. 416/782–9954.

Arriving and Departing
By Plane Flights leave daily to Aruba from both New York's JFK International and Miami's International airports, with easy connections from most American cities. From New York, **American Airlines** (tel. 800/433–7300) has one nonstop daily flight to Aruba. From Miami, **ALM** (tel. 800/327–7230) flies nonstop to Aruba. **Continental Airlines** (tel. 800/525–0280) flies nonstop daily from Newark, NJ, in winter; off-season, less frequently. From Toronto and Montreal, you can fly to Aruba on American Airlines via San Juan. American also has connecting flights from several U.S. cities via San Juan. **VIASA** (tel. 800/327–5454) has Monday and Thursday nonstop flights out of Houston. **BWIA** (tel. 800/327–7401) has a daily flight from Miami.

Passports and Visas U.S. and Canadian residents need show proof only of identity—a valid passport, birth certificate, naturalization certificate, green card, valid nonquota immigration visa, or a valid

Aruba

Exploring

Bushiribana Gold Mine, **4**

California Lighthouse, **9**

Frenchman's Pass, **3**

Guadirikiri/Fontein Caves, **7**

Hooiberg (Haystack Hill), **2**

Natural Bridge, **8**

Oranjestad, **1**

Savaneta, **6**

Spanish Lagoon, **5**

Dining

Bali Floating Restaurant, **31**

Bon Appetit, **15**

Boonoonoonoos, **33**

Brisas del Mar, **37**

Buccaneer Restaurant, **34**

Chez Mathilde, **28**

La Dolce Vita, **29**

Mi Cushina, **38**

Old Cunucu House, **16**

The Old Mill, **14**

La Paloma, **11**

Papagayo, **35**

Papiamento, **30**

Talk of the Town Restaurant, **32**

Twinklebone's House of Roastbeef, **12**

Valentino's, **13**

Lodging

Americana Aruba Hotel & Casino, **17**

Aruba Beach Club, **24**

Aruba Concorde Hotel & Casino, **18**

Aruba Palm Beach Hotel & Casino, **19**

Atlantis Hotel & Villas, **10**

The Best Western Talk of the Town Resort, **32**

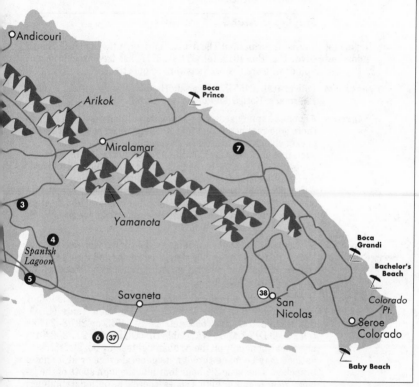

● Exploring Sites

⑩ Hotels and Restaurants

Caribbean Sea

○ Andicouri

Arikok

Boca Prince

○ Miralamar

❼

❸

Yamanota

❹

Spanish Lagoon

❺

Boca Grandi

Bachelor's Beach

Savaneta

㊳ San Nicolas

Colorado Pt.

❻ ㊲

○ Seroe Colorado

Baby Beach

Bushiri Beach Resort, **27**

Casa del Mar Beach Resort, **26**

Divi Divi Beach Resort, **23**

Golden Tulip Aruba Caribbean Resort & Casino, **20**

La Quinta Beach Resort, **22**

Playa Linda Beach Resort, **21**

Sonesta Hotel Beach Club & Casino, **36**

Tamarijn Beach Resort, **25**

voter registration card. All other nationalities must submit a valid passport.

Customs and Duties Besides articles for personal use, persons over 18 are allowed one-fifth of liquor and 200 cigarettes, 50 cigars, 250 grams of tobacco, and 2 liters each of alcohol and wine.

Precautions Aruba is a party island, but only up to a point. A police dog sniffs for drugs at the airport.

The strong trade winds are a relief in the subtropical climate, but don't hang your bathing suit on a balcony—it will probably blow away. And help Arubans conserve water and energy. Turn off air-conditioning when you leave your room and keep your faucets turned off.

Staying in Aruba

Important Addresses **Tourist Information:** The **Aruba Tourism Authority** (L.G. Smith Blvd. 172, Box 1019, tel. 297/8–23777) has free brochures and guides who are ready to answer any questions.

Emergencies **Police:** (tel. 24555). **Hospital:** Horaceo Oduber (tel. 24300). **Pharmacy:** Botica del Pueblo (tel. 21253).

Currency Arubans happily accept U.S. dollars virtually everywhere, so there's no real need to exchange money, except for necessary pocket change (cigarettes, soda machines, or pay phones). The currency used, however, is the Aruban florin (AFl), which at press time exchanged to the U.S. dollar at AFl for 1.68 for cash, AFl 1.79 for traveler's checks, and to the Canadian dollar at AFl 1.30. Major credit cards and traveler's checks are widely accepted, but you will probably be asked to show identification when cashing a traveler's check. Prices quoted here are in U.S. dollars unless otherwise noted.

Taxes and Service Charges Hotels collect a 5% government tax. The departure tax is $9.50. Hotels add an 11% service charge on rooms and a 15% service charge on food and beverages; restaurants usually add a 15% service charge to your bill.

Guided Tours *Orientation* Most of Aruba's highways are in excellent condition, but guided tours save time and energy. **De Palm Tours** (L. G. Smith Blvd. 142, Box 656, tel. 297/8–24545 or 297/8–24400; telex 5049 DPALM B+NA; Cable DPTOURS; fax 297/8–23012) has a nearmonopoly on the Aruban sightseeing business; reservations may be made through its general office or at its hotel branches. The basic 2½-hour tour hits the high spots of the island. Wear tennis or hiking shoes (there'll be optional climbing) and note that the air-conditioned bus can get cold. The tour, which begins at 9:30 AM, picks you up in your lobby and costs $12.50 per person.

Special-Interest **Corvalou Tours** offers unusual excursions for specialized interests. The Archeological/Geological Tour involves a four- to six-hour field trip through Aruba's past, including the huge monoliths and rugged, desolate north coast. Also available are architectural, bird-watching, and botanical tours. The fee for all tours is $40 per person, $70 per couple, with special prices for parties of five or more. Contact the Aruba Tourism Authority *(see* Important Addresses, above) for arrangements.

For a three-in-one tour of prehistoric Indian cultures, volcanic formations, and natural wildlife, contact archaeologist E.

Boerstra of **Marlin Booster Tracking, Inc.** at Charlie's Bar (tel. 297/8–45086). The fee for a six-hour tour is $30 per person, including cold picnic lunch and beverages. Tours can be given in English, Dutch, German, and French.

Hikers will enjoy a guided three-hour trip to remote sites of unusual natural beauty, accessible only on foot. The fee is $25 per person, including refreshments and transportation; a minimum of four people is required. Contact **Windsurfing Aruba** (tel. 297/8–33472) or **De Palm Tours** (tel. 297/8–24545).

Boat Cruises   If you try a cruise around the island, know that trimarans are much smoother than three-sail boats; people with queasy stomachs will be helped by lemon or lime candy, but avoid going on an empty stomach.

Midnight cruises, though stunning, are appreciated most by honeymooners. Prices run about $20 per person. Contact **Pelican Watersports** (tel. 297/8–24739) or De Palm Tours (tel. 297/8–24545).

Three-hour trimaran cruises with an hour's stop for swimming and snorkeling run daily; fee is $17.50 per person. On Monday, Wednesday, Friday, and Saturday, enjoy two-hour sunset cruises, including snacks and drinks, for $20 per person. Pelican Watersports (tel. 297/8–24739).

You can swim, sunbathe, and snorkel on a Fun Cruise on a 51-foot catamaran to the west coast of Oranjestad and to De Palm's privately owned coral island. The fee of $38.50 per person includes games and a treasure hunt. Contact De Palm Tours (tel. 297/8–24545).

On a sunset cruise to the soft white sands of Surfside Beach, you can eat barbecue and dance to the tropical sounds of a steel band. Fee of $40 per person includes all the food you can eat. Contact De Palm Tours (tel. 297/8–24545).

Catamaran cruises, sunset sails, and a romantic dinner cruise are among the on-the-water delights offered at prices that range from $25 to $45 per person. Contact **Red Sails Sports** (tel. 297/8–31603).

Take a 97-foot luxury cruiser to dine at the Marina Pirata. A four-hour round-trip jaunt on the *Maria Monica* will cost $38 per person, which includes dinner. Contact **Ronald de Cuba** (tel. 297/8–34424).

Explore the floor of the sea through a cruise on a glass-bottom boat for $15 per person, from either De Palm Tours (tel. 297/8–24545) or Pelican Watersports (tel. 297/8–24739).

Getting Around   A dispatch office is located at Alhambra Bazaar and Boulevard
Taxis   Center; you can also flag down taxis on the street. Since taxis do not have meters, rates are fixed and should be confirmed before you take your ride. All Aruba's taxi drivers have participated in the government's Tourism Awareness Programs and have received their Tourism Guide Certificate. An hour's tour of the island by taxi will run you between $20 and $22, for a maximum of five persons.

Rental Cars   You'll need a valid U.S. or Canadian driver's license to rent a car, and you must be able to meet the age requirements of each rental service, instigated for insurance reasons. **Budget** (tel. 800/527–0700) requires drivers to be between 23 and 65, **Avis** (tel. 800/331–2112) requires drivers to be between 25 and 60, and **Hertz** (tel. 800/654–3131) requires drivers to be older than 21. Insurance is available starting at $6 per day, and all companies offer unlimited mileage. Budget and Avis generally have lower rates, but fees, which may range from $25 to $50 a day, are generally determined by the make of the vehicle.

Avis (Kolibristraat 14, tel. 297/8–28787; airport tel. 297/8–25496), **Budget Rent-A-Car** (Kolibristraat 1, tel. 297/8–28600), **Hertz, De Palm Car Rental** (L. G. Smith Blvd. 142, Box 656, tel. 297/8–24545), **Dollar Rent-a-Car** (Grebedaweg 15, tel. 297/8–22783; airport tel. 297/8–25651; Manchebo tel. 297/8–26696), and **National** (Tank Leendert 170, tel. 297/8–21967; airport tel. 297/8–25451).

Motorcycle and Bike Rentals
Rates vary according to the make of the vehicle. For a Honda 450cc, ($35 per day), call **Donasine Cycle Car Rental** (Soledad 3, Tank Leendert, tel. 297/8–27041). For Suzuki scooters ($23 day, $100 week), contact **George Cycle Center** (Morgenster 27, Box 434, tel. 297/8–25975). For a fully automatic Moped ($22.50 per day), contact **Aruba Scooters and Mopeds Rentals** (1 Kolibristraat, tel. 297/8–28600).

Buses
For inexpensive trips between the beach hotels and Oranjestad, buses run hourly. The round-trip fare is $1.50, and exact change is preferred. Contact the Aruba Tourist Bureau for a bus schedule or inquire at your front desk.

Telephones and Mail
Local and international calls can be made via hotel operators or from the Government Long Distance Telephone Office, which is in the Post Office in Oranjestad. To dial direct to Aruba, dial 011–297–8, followed by the number in Aruba. When dialing locally in Aruba, simply dial the five-digit number.

Telegrams and telexes can be sent through the Government Telegraph and Radio Office at the Post Office Building in Oranjestad or via your hotel. There is also an ITT office located on Boecoetiweg 33 (tel. 297/8–21458).

You can send an airmail letter from Aruba to the United States for AFl 1.00, a postcard for AFl .60.

Opening and Closing Times
Shops are generally open between 8 AM and 6:30 PM. Most stores open through the lunch hour of noon–2 PM, Monday through Saturday. Store hours vary at each hotel. Many stores open when cruise ships are in port on Sunday and holidays. Nighttime shopping at the Alahambra Bazaar runs 5 PM–midnight.

Beaches

Beaches in Aruba are legendary in the Caribbean: white sand, turquoise waters, and virtually no garbage, for everyone takes the "no littering" sign—"No Tira Sushi"—very seriously. The influx of tourists in the past decade, however, has crowded the major beaches, which back up to the hotels along the southwestern strip. These beaches are public, and you can make the one-hour hike from the Holiday Inn to the Bushiri Beach Hotel free of charge and without ever leaving sand. If you go strolling during the day, make sure you are well protected from the sun —it scorches fast. Luckily, there's at least one covered bar (and often an ice cream stand) at virtually every hotel you pass. If you take the stroll at night, you can literally hotel-hop for dinner, dancing, gambling, and late-night entertainment. On the northern side of the island, heavy trade winds make the waters too choppy for swimming, but the vistas are great and the terrain is wonderfully suited to sunbathing and geological explorations. Among the finer beaches are these:

B.A. Beach. On the north of San Nicolas, this gorgeous beach is perfect for windsurfing. The view from the highway is dramatic, with huge sloping dunes dotted with cacti and blue-green crashing waves.

Baby Beach. On the island's eastern tip, this tiny strip is as placid as a wading pool and only four to five feet deep—perfect for tots and terrible swimmers. Thatched shaded areas are good for cooling off.

Boca Grandi. Just west of Bachelor's Beach, on the northwest coast (near the Seagrape Grove and the Aruba Golf Club), Boca Grandi is excellent for wave jumping and windsurfing.

Boca Prince. Near the Fontein Cave and Blue Lagoon, this beach is about as large as a Brazilian bikini, but with two rocky cliffs and tumultuously crashing waves, it's as romantic as you get in Aruba.

Eagle Beach. Across the highway from La Quinta Resort, Eagle Beach is one of the last undiscovered stretches on the southern coast. Not long ago, early one morning, it was a nearly deserted isle, with only one or two joggers in sight.

Fishermans' Hut. Next to the Holiday Inn, this beach is a windsurfer's haven. Take a picnic lunch (tables are available) and watch the elegant purple, aqua, and orange Windsurfer sails struggle in the wind.

Manchebo Beach. In front of the Manchebo Beach Resort, this impressively wide stretch of white powder is Aruba's "topless" beach. Most of the sunbathers, though, tend to remain horizontal, so feel free to stroll by.

Palm Beach. Called one of the 10 best beaches in the world by the *Miami Herald*, this is the stretch behind the Americana Aruba, Concorde, Aruba Palm Beach, and Holiday Inn hotels. It's the center of Aruban tourism, offering the best in swimming, sailing, snorkeling, fishing, and scuba diving. During high season, however, it's a sardine can.

Exploring Aruba

Numbers in the margin correspond with points of interest on the Aruba map.

Oranjestad
❶
Aruba's charming Dutch capital is best explored on foot. Take a taxi or bus from your hotel to the corner of L.G. Smith Boulevard and Arnold Shuttestraat. Cruise ships dock very close to here, and if you arrive early enough, you may find a Venezuelan trade ship selling fruits, vegetables, and other goods right on the dock. At the corner of Shuttestraat is the **Bali Floating Restaurant,** where you can enjoy fine *rijstaffel* (an Indonesian rice dish) or a cool drink on the outdoor terrace *(see* Dining, below).

To reach the main shopping district, turn left onto Shuttestraat, bear left to the plaza, and take the second right. You're now on **Nassaustraat,** the main shopping district of Aruba, offering a variety of clothes, curios, electronic equipment, perfume, and jewelry stores.

If you're interested in Dutch architecture, walk back to the corner of Olde School Straat and go three blocks south (toward the harbor) to **Wilheminastraat.** The oldest and most interesting buildings are located here, some dating back to 1790 when Oranjestad was founded. Walk west, and you'll pass old homes, the library, and the Protestant church.

When you reach Shuttestraat again, turn left and go one block south to Zoutmanstraat. The small **Archeology Museum** is here, with two rooms of Indian artifacts, farm and domestic utensils, and skeletons. *Zoutmanstraat 1, tel. 297/8–28979. Admission free. Open weekdays 8–noon, 1:30–4:30.*

One block to the east lies **Fort Zoutman,** the island's oldest building, constructed in 1796 and used as a major fortress in the skirmishes between British and Curaçao troops. The Willem III tower, named for the Dutch monarch of that time, was added in 1868. The fort's Historical Museum displays centuries' worth of Aruba relics and artifacts in an 18th-century lighthouse. *Willem III Toren, tel. 297/8–26099. Admission: 50¢. Open weekdays 9–4.*

Walk one block south and you'll chance upon **Wilhelmina Park,** a small grove of palm trees and flowers overlooking the sea. Head back to Nassaustraat and turn north to the corner of Hendrikstraat to see the **Saint Francis Roman Catholic Church.**

Just behind the church is the **Numismatic Museum,** displaying coins and paper money from more than 400 countries. *Iraussquinplein 2-A, tel. 297/8–28831. Admission free. Open weekdays 7:30–noon and 1–4:30.*

Time Out The motto at **Le Petit Café** (at Mainstreet, corner of Schlepstraat, tel. 297/8-26577) is "Romancing the Stone"—referring to tasty cuisine cooked on hot stones. The low ceiling and hanging plants make this an intimate lunch spot for shoppers. Jumbo shrimps, sandwiches, ice cream, and fresh fruit dishes are light delights.

The Countryside The "real Aruba"—what's left of a wild, untamed beauty—can be found only in the countryside. Before you rent a car and dash off, consider hiring a cab for $10 an hour. Although most of the main highways are well paved, some of the more interesting sights are difficult to find because there are few clear road signs. If you do decide to go it alone, rent a Jeep. And get specific instructions. Traffic is sparse, but you'll need to keep a sharp eye out for cars that dart out of driveways unexpectedly. After a rainfall, the dirt roads turn to mush and are dangerous.

Few beaches outside the hotel strip have refreshment stands, so take your own food and drink. And one more caution: Note that there are *no* public bathrooms—anywhere—once you leave Oranjestad, except in the infrequent restaurant.

East to San Nicolas For a shimmering vista of blue-green sea, drive east on L. G. Smith Boulevard toward San Nicolas. Past the airport, you'll
2 soon see the towering 54-foot peak of **Hooiberg** (Haystack Hill). If you have the energy, climb the 580 steps up to the top for an impressive view of the city.

Just past the drive-in theater (a popular hangout for Arubans),
3 a road on your left will take you to **Frenchman's Pass:** a dark,

luscious stretch of highway arbored by overhanging trees. Local legend claims the French and native Indians warred here during the 17th century for control of the island. Nearby are
4 the cement ruins of the **Bushiribana Gold Mine** (take the dirt road veering to the right)—a lovely place to picnic, listen to the parakeets, and contemplate the towering cacti. A magnificent gnarled divi-divi tree guards the entrance.

Returning to the main road, drive through the area called
5 **Spanish Lagoon,** where pirates once hid to repair their ships.

6 Back on the main highway, pay a visit to **Savaneta,** Aruba's oldest village, also known as the Aruba Sunrise Side. During the heyday of the Exxon refineries, the town was a bustling port; now it's dedicated to tourism, with the main street promenade full of interesting kiosks. The **China Clipper Bar** on Main Street used to be a famous "whore" bar frequented by sailors docked in port. These days, the promenade features folkloric shows held at 6 PM on the first Thursday of every month.

Time Out   Now an institution, **Charlie's Bar** (Zeppenfeldstraat 56, San Nicolas, tel. 297/8–45086) has been a San Nicolas hangout for artists, writers, and musicians for more than 50 years. During the oil-refinery days, it was a hopping bar for all kinds of rough-and-scrufs. Folks touring San Nicolas stop here for lunch and many leave mementos behind—witness the bras, panties, shirts, shoes, and helmets hanging from the ceiling. The specialty is "shrimps—jumbo and dumbo." The bus to San Nicolas stops right at the door.

Anyone looking for geological exotica should head for the northern coast, driving northwest from San Nicolas. Stop at
7 the two old Indian caves **Guadirikiri** and **Fontein.** Both were used by the native Indians centuries ago, but you'll have to decide for yourself whether the "ancient Indian inscriptions" are genuine—rumor has it they were added by a European film company that made a movie here years ago. You may enter the caves, but there are no guides available, and bats are known to make appearances. Take your flashlights.

8 A few miles up the coast is the **Natural Bridge,** sculpted out of coral rock by centuries of raging wind and sea. Nearby is a café overlooking the water and a souvenir shop stuffed with trinkets, T-shirts, and postcards for reasonable prices.

West of Palm Beach   Drive or take a taxi west from the hotel strip to Malmok, where Aruba's wealthiest families reside. Open to the public, **Malmok Beach** is considered one of the finest spots for shelling and snorkeling. Right off the coast here is the wreck of the German ship *Antilla,* which was scuttled in 1940—a favorite haunt for
9 divers. At the very end of the island stands the **California Lighthouse,** now closed, which is surrounded by huge boulders that look like extraterrestrial monsters; in this stark landscape, you'll feel as though you've just landed on the moon.

What to See and Do with Children

The **children's playground** on L. G. Smith Boulevard across the street from the Talk of the Town Hotel is open Tuesday–Saturday 3:30–6:30, Sundays 11–6:30. Admission: AFl 1 or about U.S. 60¢. For parties, call Mrs. Wekker (tel. 297/8–21059).

The Waterslide at Indian Rock Garden (Hoolberg 77, tel. 297/8–34030) is open on Saturday and Sunday 10–6 (phone during the week for special times). Fees are $1 per hour for pool use and $2 per hour for waterslide use.

Off the Beaten Track

Near the Fontein and Guadirikiri caves lies the **Tunnel of Love.** Marco Marlin, a local artist with a quirky sense of humor, will lead you on a 20-minute climb through the heart-shape tunnel past naturally sculpted rocks that look just like the Madonna, Abe Lincoln, and even a jaguar. Depending on your state of mind, the tour and Marco's jokes are either very scary or hysterically funny—and Marco just might call out his bats for you. Afterward, calm your nerves with a beer at his bar without walls. Warning: The actual climb is difficult for anyone not in average physical condition, and it's definitely not recommended for elderly people or young children who lack coordination. The fee is $3 per person; no reservations are necessary.

Participant Sports

Deep-Sea Fishing With catches ranging from barracuda to kingfish, bonito, and black and yellow tuna, deep-sea fishing is great sport on Aruba, and many charter boats are available. Sail for a half day or a full day. **De Palm Tours** (L.G. Smith Blvd. 142, Box 656, Box 656, tel. 297/8–24400) can arrange parties for up to six people, in boats that range from 24 to 27 feet. Half-day tours, including all equipment, can be arranged for $125–$160 for two people, with special rates for up to six people. Private yachts, manned by independent sea captains, can also be arranged. Check with the Aruba Tourism Authority.

Golf The **Aruba Golf Club** (Golfweg 82, near San Nicolas, tel. 297/8–93485) features a nine-hole course with 20 sand traps, five water hazards, roaming goats, and lots of cacti. There are 11 oiled sand greens, enabling 18-hole tournaments. The clubhouse contains a bar, storage rooms, workshop, and separate men's and women's locker rooms. The course's official U.S. Golf Association rating is 67; greens fees are $4 and a caddy costs $5. Complete golf bags are available for $5.

Horseback Riding One-hour jaunts arranged through **Rancho El Paso** (tel. 297/8–23310) or **De Palm Tours** (tel. 297/8–24400) will take you through countryside flanked by cacti, divi-divi trees, and aloe vera plants; two-hour trips also go to the beach. Remember to wear headgear and take lots of suntan lotion.

Snorkeling and Scuba Diving With visibility up to 90 feet, Aruban waters are excellent for snorkeling in shallow waters, and scuba divers will discover exotic marine life and coral. The *Antilla* shipwreck—a German freighter sunk off the northwest coast of Aruba near Palm Beach—is a favorite spot with divers.

De Palm Tours (L.G. Smith Blvd. 142, Box 656, tel. 297/8–24545 or 297/8–24400; telex 5049 DPALM B+NA; Cable DPTOURS; fax 297/8–23012) has a near-monopoly on all water sports in Aruba; the company maintains a registration desk in the lobby of most of the large hotels, or you can make arrangements directly through its main office. Equipment for both snorkeling and scuba diving is available, as is certified instruction.

Pelican Watersports (Box 1193,, Oranjested, tel. 297/8–24739 or 297/8–23600, ext. 511 or ext. 329) also offers water-sports packages, including snorkeling, scuba diving, sailing, windsurfing, and deep-sea fishing.

Windsurfing **Pelican Watersports** (Box 1193, tel. 297/8–24739) rents equipment and offers instruction with a certified Mistral instructor. Stock boards and custom boards rent for $10 hour, $30 per day, $150 per week, with $100 deposit.

Roger's Windsurf Place (L.G. Smith Blvd. 472, tel. 297/8–21918) offers high-performance lessons with Kiepper and custom boards. Packages available include one complete sailboard plus hotel room for a week, double occupancy; cost is $295 per person during off-season, $399 during high season.

Windsurfing is also available through **Windsurfing Aruba** (Boliviastraat 14, Box 256, tel. 297/8–21036), **Windward Leeward Watersports** (Beatrixstraat 29, tel. 297/8–22690), and **De Palm Tours** (L.G. Smith Blvd. 142, Box 656, tel. 297/8–24545).

Shopping

Nassaustraat—Aruba's chief shopping street—makes for a pleasant diversion from the beach and casino life. *Duty-free* is a magic word here. Major credit cards are welcome virtually everywhere, U.S. dollars are accepted almost as often as local currency, and traveler's checks can be cashed with proof of identity.

Aruba's souvenir and crafts stores are full of Dutch porcelains and figurines, as befits the island's Netherlands heritage. Dutch cheese is a good buy (you are allowed to bring up to one pound of hard cheese through U.S. customs), as are hand-embroidered linens and any products made from the native plant aloe vera—sunburn cream, face masks, and skin refresheners. Since there is no sales tax, the price you see on the tag is the price you pay. But one word of warning: Don't pull any bargaining tricks. Arubans consider it rude to haggle.

Native Crafts **Artesania Arubiano** (L.G. Smith Blvd. 78, next to the Aruba Tourism Authority, tel. 297/8–25311). Charming home-crafted pottery and folklore objets d'art.

Good Buys **Artistic Boutique** (Nassaustraat 25, tel. 297/8–23142). Lively enough to have branches at the Aruba Concorde and the Holiday Inn, this chain features Aruba hand-embroidered linens, gold and silver jewelry, Persian carpets and dhurries, porcelain and pottery from Spain, and lots of antiques.

Aruba Trading Company (Nassaustraat 12, tel. 297/8–22600). A name synonymous with old-fashioned reliability, ATC offers internationally known brand names, at 30% discounts, but you have to hunt for them. Perfumes and cosmetics are on the first floor, jewelry on the second. Both men's and women's clothes are sold. Low-priced liqueurs are a good buy.

Aquarius (Nassaustraat 9, tel. 297/8–24871). This store features the trendiest names in both apparel and decor; men, women, and children can stock up on Maud Frizon, Gianfranco Ferre, Valentino, Fiorucci, and Fendi merchandise. Chrome trim, track lighting, and ever-present rock music set a fast-track mood.

La Bonbonniere (Nassaustraat 75-AB, tel. 297/8–22375). This dollhouse-size gourmet shop is stocked with chocolates, rum cakes, caviar, and Cuban cigars.

El Globo Aruba (Nassaustraat 70, tel. 297/8–22900). Electronics, cameras, and souvenirs are sold here.

Gandelman's Jewelers (Nassaustraat 5-A, tel. 297/8–29143). A name of distinction in the Caribbean offers Gucci and Swatch watches at reasonable prices, gold bracelets, and pink and red coral. It carries a full line of Gucci accessories, from key chains to handbags.

Little Switzerland (Nassaustraat 14, tel. 2297/8–4360). The Curaçao-based giant in china, crystal, and fine tableware offers good buys on Omega and Rado watches, Swarovski silver, Baccarat crystal, and Lladro figurines. If you don't see what you want, ask and they ship it to you.

Palais Oriental (Nassaustraat 8, tel. 297/8–21510). One of the best stores for Lladro figurines, Delft hand-painted porcelain, jewel-beaded blouses made in India, Vuitton luggage, and Cristofle silver and assorted crystal.

J.L. Penha & Son's (Nassaustraat 11, tel. 297/8–24161). One of the most venerated names in Aruban merchandising, this clothes-and-cosmetics store features Pringle, Lanvin, Dior, and Castoni for women and Givenchy, Pierre Cardin, and Papillon for men.

Wulfsen's (Nassaustraat 51, tel. 297/8–23823). For 18 years one of the highest rated stores in the Netherlands Antilles, Wulfsen's offers Italian, French, German, and Dutch fashions for both sexes. The Dutch-line Mexx is a favorite of hip teens; Betty Buckley and Mondo are popular for women.

Shopping Malls **The Boulevard Shopping Center** (located on L. G. Smith Blvd., tel. 297/8–23754) is a wood-raftered covered mall that's a pleasure to stroll through, with more than 60 shops, including boutiques, restaurants, and perfumeries. The arcade is lined with tropical plants and caged birds. Shops are open daily 9–6.

Two new shopping areas in Oranjestad are the **Holland Aruba Mall,** a collection of smart shops and eateries, and, on Swain Wharf, **Harbortown,** a blue-and-white postmodern version of a seaside village. The on-the-water setting is lovely, the boutiques and bistros enormously appealing.

Dining

Aruba's restaurants serve a cosmopolitan variety of cuisines, although most menus are specifically designed to please American palates—you can get fresh surf and New York turf almost anywhere. Make the effort to try Aruban specialties—*pan bati* is a delicious beaten bread that resembles a pancake, and plantains are similar to cooked bananas.

Dress ranges from casual to elegant, but even the finest restaurants require at the most only a jacket for men and a sundress for women. The air-conditioning does get cold, so don't go bare-armed. And anytime you plan to eat in the open air, remember to douse yourself first with insect repellent—the mosquitos can get unruly.

On Sunday, it may be difficult to find a restaurant outside of the hotels that's open for lunch. One of the best bets is the extensive buffet at the Holiday Inn.

The most highly recommended restaurants are indicated by a star ★ .

Category	Cost*
Expensive	over $15
Moderate	$8–$15
Inexpensive	under $8

per person, excluding drinks, service, and sales tax (15%)

★ **Chez Mathilde.** This elegant restaurant is in a renovated private home, one of the last surviving 19th-century dwellings in Aruba. The chef is Swiss, the owner is the honorary counsel of Germany, and the French-style menu is constantly being re-created. To the tune of Strauss waltzes, dine on frogs' legs or escargots Dijonaise, or try the *emincée à boeuf*—paper-thin slices of fillet beef spiked with horseradish. The wine list is one of the best on the island. *Havenstraat 23, Oranjestad, tel. 297/8–34968. Reservations required. AE, MC, V. Expensive.*

La Dolce Vita. At one of the most critically acclaimed restaurants in Aruba, start with antipasto (the antipasto bar is free with a coupon from the *Aruba Visitor's Guide*, available at your hotel), then progress to stuffed calamari, bartolucci (fried veal with cheeses and herbs), fettuccine, and zuppa de pesce. *Nassaustraat 164, Oranjested, tel. 297/8–25675. Reservations advised. AE, MC, V. Expensive.*

The Old Mill (Die Olde Molen). A gift from the queen of Holland, this real Dutch mill was shipped brick by brick to Aruba and reassembled here. The present owner, Bill Waldron, is a native Virginian but has maintained the excellence of the international cuisine. For starters, try the seafood crepe Neptune, nestled in a delicate cheese bed. Also excellent is the shrimp with spinach and cream sauce, or the dutch fries—crunchy little nuggets of potato. Order the ice cream with chocolate liqueur and take the bottle home as a souvenir. A time-sharing condominium complex, including tennis courts, is now being added to the estate. *Palm Beach, tel. 297/8–22060. Reservations required. 2 dinner seatings: 6:30 and 9 PM. AE, MC, V. Expensive.*

★ **Papiamento.** Take Papiamento's winding staircase up 20 steps and enjoy French cuisine in the island's most elegant tropicalia, with massive brass chandeliers, an exquisite garden built into a wall of rock, and a beautiful mahogany floor. A private room with a circular glass window has an eight-seat table. The salad bar is luscious, and entrée specialties include rack of lamb and mixed seafood cooked on a stone. The prize, though, goes to the *poulet grand-mère*, which comes in a clay pot you break with a hammer and then take home. *Wilhelminastraat 7, Oranjestad, tel. 297/8–4544. Reservations required. AE, MC, V. Expensive.*

Talk of the Town Restaurant. Here you'll find candlelight dining and some of the best steaks in town—the owner comes from a family of Dutch butchers. Located in the Best Western Talk of the Town Resort, between the airport and Palm Beach, this fine restaurant is now a member of the elite honorary restaurant society, Chaine de Rotisseurs. Saturday night is prime-rib-as-much-as-you-can-eat night, but seafood specialties are popular, too—such as the crabmeat crepes and the *escargots à la bourguignonne*. *L. G. Smith Blvd., Oranjestad, tel. 297/8–23380. AE, DC, MC, V. Expensive.*

Valentino's. The airy, two-level dining room here is inviting with its rose and sparkling-white color scheme. The tables are placed comfortably far apart, and the service is attentive without being overbearing. The menu is Italian and the *Gamberoni zi Teresa* (shrimps sautéed in garlic and fresh tomatoes) a knockout. The atmosphere is festive since the restaurant is popular with celebrating Arubans. You'll find their gaiety infectious. *Caribbean Palm Village, Noord, tel. 297/8–32700. Reservations requested. AE, MC, V, DC. Expensive.*

Bali Floating Restaurant. Floating in its own Oriental houseboat and anchored in Oranjestad's harbor, the Bali is considered to have the best Indonesian food on the island. Bamboo rooftops and Indonesian antiques add charm. Sunday buffets are good for quantity and variety; full *rijstaffel* dinners (rice table with 21 different meat, chicken, shrimp, vegetable, fruit, and relish dishes) run about $22 per person. Service is terminally slow but well-meaning. Happy hour 6–8 PM. *L.G. Smith Blvd., Oranjestad, tel. 297/8–22131. AE, MC, V. Moderate. .*

Bon Appetit. With its yellow tablecloths, clay-potted plants, and burnt-orange beams, this restaurant glows like a beautiful tan—but it's the savory smells that hook you. Prepared by the Curaçaoan chef Robert Volkerts, the international cuisine wins acclaim—*Gourmet* magazine once requested the recipe for his *keshi yena*, baked cheese stuffed with meat and condiments. The roast rack of lamb is a winner. *Palm Beach 29, tel. 297/8–25241. Reservations required. AE, DC, V. Moderate.*

★ **Boonoonoonoos.** The name—say it just like it looks!—means extraordinary, and that's no hyperbole for this Austrian-owned Caribbean bistroquet in the heart of town. Orchids and aloe veras bloom on the tables and the waitresses wear folkloric ruffled dresses. The roast chicken Barbados is sweet and tangy, marinated in pineapple and cinnamon and simmered in fruit juices. The Jamaican jerk ribs (a 300-year-old recipe) are tiny but spicy, and the satin-smooth hot pumpkin soup drizzled with cheese and served in a pumpkin shell might as well be dessert. *Wilhelminastraat 18A, Oranjestad, tel. 297/8–31888. Reservations advised. AE, V. Closed Sun. Moderate.*

Buccaneer Restaurant. Imagine you're in a sunken ship—fish nets and turtle shells hang from the ceiling, and through the portholes you see live sharks, barracudas, and groupers swimming by. That's the Buccaneer, snug in an old stone building flanked by heavy black chains and boasting a fantastic 5,000-gallon saltwater aquarium, plus 12 more porthole-size tanks. The surf-and-turf cuisine is prepared by the chef-owners with European élan, and the tables are always full. Order the fresh catch of the day, or more exotic fare such as shrimps with Pernod; smoked pork cutlets with sausage, sauerkraut, and potatoes; or the turtle steak with a light cream sauce. Go early (around 5:45 PM) to get a booth next to the aquariums. *Gasparito 11-C., Oranjestad, tel. 297/8–26172. Reservations not accepted. AE, MC, V. Closed Sun. Moderate.*

Old Cunucu House. Situated on a small estate in a residential neighborhood three minutes from the high rises, this 70-year-old Aruban home has been renovated into a restaurant of casual élan. Dine on local recipes for red snapper, coconut-fried shrimp, Cornish hen, and New York sirloins, or beef fondue à deux. Private dining rooms hold groups up to 20. Happy hour 5–6 PM. *Palm Beach 150, tel. 297/8–31666. Reservations suggested. AE, DC, MC. Closed Mon. Moderate.*

★ **La Paloma.** "The Dove" has an air of low-key loveliness with no gimmicks, and it's usually packed. The restaurant has its own fishing boat, so the fish is always fresh. There's conch stew with *pan bati* and fried bananas for exotic tastes. Minestrone soup is a house specialty. *Noord 39, tel. 297/8–24611. AE, MC, V. Closed Tues. Moderate.*

Mi Cushina. The names means "My Kitchen," and the menu lists such Aruban specialties as *Sopi di mariscos* (seafood soup) and *Kreeft Stoba* (lobster stew). The walls are hung with antique farm tools and there's a small museum devoted to the aloe verde plant. *Cura Cabai 24, San Nicholas, tel. 297/8–48335. Reservations advised. AE, MC, V. Moderate.*

Papagayo. This is a noisy restaurant crazy with the sound of cawing parrots and squeaking parakeets; it's even moist from the tropical plants that hang everywhere. Waitresses are dressed in tight muumuus with flowers in their hair. The view of the harbor is superb and the northern Italian kitchen has a fine reputation for linguine with lobster, chicken Papagayo (stuffed breast), and prime cuts of meat. *Boulevard Shopping Center, Oranjestad, tel. 297/8–24140. Reservations required. AE, MC, V. Moderate.*

Twinklebone's House of Roastbeef. Prime rib with Yorkshire pudding is the kitchen's pride, but there's a full international menu with dishes named after local friends and residents. The chef is known to leave the stove and sing Aruban tunes with the maitre d'. *Turibana Plaza, Noord 124, tel. 297/8–26806. Reservations advised. AE, MC, V. Closed Sun. Moderate.*

★ **Brisas del Mar.** A cozy, friendly 10-table place that is popular with tourists because you'll feel as if you're dining in an Aruban home overlooking the sea. The menu features mostly fried fish with spicy sauces of tomatoes and onions served with loads of *funchi* (cornmeal squares) and *pan bati*. To find it, drive east in Oranjestad on L. G. Smith Boulevard to the town of Savaneta, 10 miles away. *Savaneta 22A, tel. 297/8–47718. Reservations suggested. No credit cards. Closed Mon. Inexpensive.*

Lodging

Most of the hotels in Aruba are located west of Oranjestad along L. G. Smith Boulevard, and there are several new properties—including the **Ramada Renaissance Hotel and Casino** and the **Hyatt Regency Aruba**—that are scheduled to open for the winter 1990/1991 season. You may want to check with the Aruba Tourism Authority (tel. 212/246–3030 or 800/TO ARUBA) about the status of these. They generally include a host of facilities—drugstores, boutiques, health spas, beauty parlors, casinos, restaurants, pool bars, and gourmet delis. Do not arrive in Aruba without a reservation; many hotels are booked seasons in advance. The restaurants and clubs, however, are open to all guests on the island, so you can visit other properties no matter where you're staying. Look out for Charlie, the island's coconut expert, who makes constant rounds of the hotels demonstrating his special talent: devastating a coconut samurai style in three seconds.

The most highly recommended lodgings are indicated by a star
★.

Category	Cost*
Very Expensive	over $115
Expensive	$90–$115
Moderate	$60–$90
Inexpensive	under $60

*All prices are for a standard double room for two, excluding
5% tax and a 10% service charge.*

Casa del Mar Beach Resort. This beachfront low rise featuring
completely furnished suites is one of Aruba's most expensive
time-shares. The two-bedroom suites each have a dining table
seating six; the full kitchen comes stocked with an eight-piece
table service. Baby-sitters are on call, and a social hostess provides children's programs. *L. G. Smith Blvd. 53, Punta Brabo
Beach, tel. 297/8–27000; in NY 212/563–6940. 32 2-bedroom
suites, 75 2-bedroom suites. Facilities: restaurant (2 restaurants and pool bar at sister property), lobby bar, TVs with in-
room movie satellite, fitness center, sauna and massage, pool,
2 Jacuzzis, 2 lighted tennis courts, children's playground,
shops. AE, DC, MC, V. Very Expensive.*
Americana Aruba Hotel & Casino. This luxurious high rise located on Palm Beach is a haven for Americans, with most of the
social activity centered around the large pool area and casino.
A shopping mall with seven boutiques makes trips into town
nearly irrelevant. Guests at the spectacular Stellaris Gourmet
Dinner Club enjoy nightly cabaret shows at 9:15 PM, with full-
course dinners running about $25–$30. *L. G. Smith Blvd. 83,
Palm Beach, tel. 297/8–24500 or 800/223–1588; in NY, 212/661
–4540. 406 rooms. Facilities: restaurants, coffee shop, ice
cream parlor, swimming pool with pool bar, TV, tennis,
ground tour/water-sports center, laundry/valet, car rentals,
telex/xerox/typewriters, boutiques, beauty parlor/barbershop.
AE, DC, MC, V. Expensive.*
Aruba Concorde Hotel & Casino. At 18 stories, the Concorde
rates as Aruba's highest building. The terraced guest rooms
are all air-conditioned; the marble-and-chrome lobby feels like
a Four Seasons's, only slightly downscaled. It's not a lobby to
traipse through in your bikini, but during happy hour, the piano bar and surrounding couches make an elegant place to
relax (and meet rich South Americans). The boutique row offers luxurious items, such as gold jewelry, designer clothes,
fine perfumes, and leather bags. The Olympic-size pool and
day-and-night tennis make fine alternatives to the omnipresent
ocean sports. Dining possibilities befit the cosmopolitan ambience: from northern Italian (Adriana's) to the elegant Continental cuisine of Le Serre to intimate late-night suppering at
Rendez-Vous Gourmet. Club Arubesque, off the main lobby, is
a nightclub, complete with showgirls, and the casino competes
with that of the Aruba Caribbean for biggest on the island.
*L. G. Smith Blvd. 77, Palm Beach, tel. 297/8–24466 or 800/
223–7944; in NY 212/757–8989. 500 rooms. Facilities: 6
restaurants, nightclub, casino, 3 cocktail lounges, pool, 2
lighted tennis courts, massage room, game room, car rental,
ground tours and water sports, ballroom with meeting and*

banquet rooms, shops, beauty parlor, deli, children's corner. AE, DC, MC, V. Expensive.

Aruba Palm Beach Hotel & Casino. Formerly a Sheraton and now government-owned, this pink-blue-and-white Moorish palazzo even has pink-swaddled palm trees dotting its drive. The lobby, with its impressive grand piano, is a haze of pink and purple, underlaid with cool marble. The large backyard sunning grounds are a well-manicured tropical garden, with a fleet of pesky parrots guarding the entrance. Guest rooms are air-conditioned, roomy, and cheerful, with tiny balconies, baths with separate dressing areas, and large walk-in closets. All overlook either the ocean, the pool, or the gardens. For entertainment, try the chrome-glitzed disco Galactica Lounge or the dinner-cum-floor-show (about $30 per person) at the elegant Rembrandt Room. *L. G. Smith Blvd. 79, Palm Beach, tel. 297/8-23900 or 800/344-1212; in NY 212/832-2277. 200 rooms. Facilities: 2 restaurants, pool, coffee shop, disco, TV, shops, beauty shop. AE, DC, MC, V. Expensive.*

★ **Divi Divi Beach Resort.** One of the more popular low rises, the Divi Divi's motto is "barefoot elegance," which means you can streak through the lobby in your bikini. The main section has 90 standard guest rooms, 20 lanai rooms, and 40 casitas (garden bungalows) that look out onto individual courtyards. A newer section, Divi Dos, contains 49 luxury rooms and 1 suite, all with ocean view and Jacuzzi bathtubs. All rooms are air-conditioned. Divi Divi has the reputation of being a honeymoon hotel —special packages that include champagne breakfast, "just married" signs, photo albums, and fruit baskets are available. The free-form pool includes a small island with a teahouse at the center, accessible by a bridge. A breakfast buffet is served on the Pelican Terrace, just steps away from the sea ($8.75 plus 15% service). Special theme nights include Tuesday's Carnival and Saturday's Beach barbecue, with folkloric show and steel band. *L. G. Smith Blvd. 45, Punta Brabo Beach, tel. 297/8-23300 or 800/367-DIVI. 200 rooms. Facilities: 4 restaurants, TV, radio, ceiling fan, free-form pool, swimming pool, Jacuzzis, tennis courts, shuffleboard, shops, ground tours and water sports. AE, MC, V. Expensive.*

Sonesta Hotel, Beach Club & Casino. At this recently opened caravansary, a canal bisects the spacious atrium/lobby. From here, guests board boats for a 10-minute trip to the hotel's 40-acre private Sonesta Island, located in the harbor. Two beaches, water sports, whirlpools, a restaurant, and a bar are among the "on-island" delights. The airy guest rooms come complete with color TVs, safes, minibars, and even hair dryers. The 10,000-square-foot Crystal Casino adds to the glamour. *L. G. Smith Blvd. 82, Oranjestad, tel. 297/8-24622. 300 rooms. Facilities: restaurant, bar, pool, minispa, casino, conference facilities. All major credit cards. Expensive.*

Tamarijn Beach Resort. A sprawling melange of two-story white stucco town houses opens onto one of the longest beachfronts (1 mile) in Aruba. The ambience is barefoot casual: the staff even discourages jackets. All rooms have a beachfront view and are air-conditioned. Guests can ride to the Alhambra Casino and the Divi Divi Beach Hotel in free carts, and exchange privileges have been arranged with the Divi Divi Beach resort, including nightly entertainment. The poolside bar stays open till 1 AM. *L. G. Smith Blvd. 64, Punta Brabo Beach, tel. 297/8-24150 or 800/367-DIVI. 236 rooms. Facilities: 1 res-*

taurant, 2 bars, radio, pool, tennis courts, 2 Jacuzzis, shops, activities center. AE, MC, V. Expensive.

Golden Tulip Aruba Caribbean Resort & Casino. Called La Grand Dame of the Caribbean, the Golden Tulip was the first high rise on the island and still lives up to its stylish standards, having been renovated in 1984–86. Liz Taylor used to stay here when she was married to Eddie Fisher, and the queen of Holland still stays in the Royal Suite (available on request), so the staff is used to filling special needs. The turquoise-and-white tiled lobby gives the feeling of an Art Deco tropical palazzo, and even the hallways are lined with trees. The sunny air-conditioned rooms, all with some ocean view, are scattered among four buildings, with added balconies for private sunning. The fitness center on the top floor offers a Universal weight system, squash and racquetball courts, rowing machine, and aerobics classes. French and American wine tastings are held on Monday night; nightly shows are held in the blue-and-gold Fandango Nightclub. *L. G. Smith Blvd. 81, Palm Beach, tel. 297/8–33555. 400 rooms. Facilities: 4 restaurants, 4 bars, nightclub, meeting and banquet rooms, casino, pool, 4 lighted tennis courts, fitness center, ground tours and water sports, putting green, videogame room, laundry and dry cleaning, shops, beauty parlor, deli. AE, MC, V. Expensive.*

Playa Linda Beach Resort. Designed in a ziggurat of receding balconies, this time-share complex sits on an enticing stretch of white sandy beach sheathed in a facade of terra-cotta and cream. Accommodations are stylishly comfortable, outfitted with private kitchens, verandas, and air-conditioning. Units (all of which are suites) sleep four to six persons. Rates vary according to season. All three meals heartily served at the open-air Palapa Restaurant. Water sports and tennis can be arranged. *L. G. Smith Blvd. 87, Palm Beach, tel. 297/8–31000; in NJ 201/617–8877. 192 1-bedroom and 12 2-bedroom suites. Facilities: restaurant, bar, TV, radio, activity center, adults' and children's pools, tennis courts, minimarket/gift shop. AE, MC, V. Expensive.*

Aruba Beach Club. This attractive low-rise resort on Druif Beach also doubles as a time-share. The open-air lobby leads to a patio, gardens, and pool, with the beach only a few steps beyond. Action settles around the pool bar, with a clientele that's mostly American, mostly young-to-middle-aged marrieds. The rooms are air-conditioned and tastefully designed with balconies and kitchenettes. *L. G. Smith Blvd. 53, Punta Brabo Beach, tel. 297/8–23000. 133 suites. Facilities: 2 restaurants, cocktail lounge, pool bar, ice cream parlor, satellite TV, radio, pool (adults' and children's), 2 lighted tennis courts, children's playground, baby-sitting service. AE, MC, V. Moderate.*

Atlantis Hotel & Villas. Set on the island side of Palm Beach, north of the high-rise hotels and near Malmok, this property offers fully furnished air-conditioned apartments that sleep five and have full kitchens. You'll have to cross the street to get to the beach, however. Weekly and monthly rates are available. *Salina Cerca 51, Noord, tel. 297/8–24343 fax 297/8–24145. 76 apartments. Facilities: restaurant, nightclub, satellite TV, pool, laundry service, game room, arrangements with water sports and tour operators, baby-sitting. AE, MC, V. Moderate.*

★ **Best Western Talk of the Town Resort.** Originally a run-down chemical plant, Talk of the Town was transformed by two Floridians into a first-class resort. It gets its name from the excellent on-premises restaurant (*see* Dining, above). A huge pool is at the center of this two-story motel-like structure, with all the guest rooms overlooking the charming Spanish-style court-yard. Some accommodations have kitchens and all offer TVs, air-conditioning, and minifridges. There's also a heated hydro-therapy whirlpool bath. The tropical café/cabaret Temptations on the beach is one of Aruba's jumpiest night spots, and add-on packages for dinner and entertainment elsewhere on the island can be bought at the hotel at a 20% discount. The beach is just 200 yards from your door and Oranjestad's shopping center is a 15-minute stroll away. *L. G. Smith Blvd. 2, Oranjestad, tel. 297/8–23380; in NY 212/628–3319; or 800/233–1108. 63 rooms. Facilities: 3 restaurants, nightclub, cable TV, free scheduled transportation, facilities exchange with Manchebo Beach Hotel, gift shop, beach across the road. AE, MC, V. Moderate.*

Bushiri Beach Resort. This long, low attractive building is the first beach hotel you encounter driving out of Oranjestad. Associated with a hotel school and the only all-inclusive hotel on the island, it's a real bargain and has an enthusiastic staff. All rooms are air-conditioned and have ocean views. The Flamboyan Restaurant makes for good dining. Due to its proximity to town, the Bushiri attracts businessmen. *L. G. Smith Blvd. 35, Oranjestad, tel. 297/8–25216 or 800/622–7836. 150 rooms. Facilities: 2 restaurants, pool bar, cocktail lounge, piano bar, pool, satellite TV, tennis courts, night entertainment, beach, water-sports center, drugstore. AE, DC, MC, V. Moderate.*

★ **La Quinta Beach Resort.** This new resort designed by a Venezuelan architect is in the middle of several phases of construction, but the work has been planned so as not to disturb guests. La Quinta is a low rise with the sophistication of a high rise; the one- and two-bedroom suites are spacious, with full cooking facilities, two TVs (including a VCR), and a shower/bath combo. The hotel is across the street from Eagle Beach and only a five-minute walk to the casino at Alhambra (*see* Nightlife, below). *Eagle Beach, tel. 297/8–35010. Facilities: restaurant, bar, cocktail lounge, pool, cable TV, VCR with cassette rentals, fitness center, tennis courts, racquetball courts. AE, DC, MC, V. Moderate.*

Nightlife

Casinos   The hottest casino action on the island can be found in the **Alhambra Casino** (L. G. Smith Blvd. 93, Oranjestad, tel. 297/8–25434), where a "Moorish slave" gives every gambler a hearty handshake upon entering. The Alhambra is decorated like a Moroccan bazaar, complete with numerous restaurants and more than 30 boutiques—including the New York Deli, which is open 24 hours. If you're staying at any of the three Divi Divi Hotels, you'll enjoy free transportation to and from your lobby.

There's also action along the Oranjestad "strip" in the casinos at the **Aruba Concorde Hotel** (L. G. Smith Blvd. 77, tel. 297/8–24466) and the **Golden Tulip Caribbean** (L. G. Smith Blvd. 81, tel. 297/8–33555). The **Holiday Inn's** casino (L. G. Smith Blvd. 230, tel. 297/8–23600) is open 22 hours a day, with an adjacent New York–style deli open until 5 AM. The **Americana Hotel Casino** (L. G. Smith Blvd. 83, tel. 297/8–24500) opens daily at 1 PM for slots, 9 PM for all games. The **Aruba Palm Beach Hotel Casino** (L. G. Smith Blvd. 79, tel. 297/8–23900) opens at 9 PM. You can also woo Lady Luck at the new Sonesta Hotel's **Crystal Casino**

(L. G. Smith Blvd. 82, tel. 297/8–24622), where the action is
nonstop from 10 AM to 5 AM for slots; 1 PM to 5 AM for the gaming
tables.

Disco and Dancing **Alhambra's Roseland Night Club/Disco** (Alhambra Complex, L.
G. Smith Blvd. 93, tel. 297/8–25434). Originally a bandstand,
Roseland in the Alhambra complex looks dark and scary from
the outside, but only lacks intimacy once you're inside. Mostly a
disco for teens 16–18.

Le Visage (L. G. Smith Blvd. 93, tel. 297/8–35000). Almost like
an adult amusement park, Le Visage is an in-spot disco for both
Arubans and tourists. Arubans usually start partying late,
and action doesn't start till around midnight, mostly on the
weekends. Besides dancing, there are three slot machines, video games, two wide-screen TVs, two bars, five pool tables, ping
pong, and pinball—and even condom machines in the bathroom. The Sirena Cocktail Lounge offers light snacks; the
specialty is deep-fried chicken wings.

Contempo Disco (Talk of the Town Hotel, L. G. Smith Blvd. 2,
Oranjestad, tel. 297/8–23380). This is a convenient place to
dance after a festive meal at the Talk of the Town restaurant
next door.

Temptations on the Beach (L. G. Smith Blvd. 2, across from,
and owned by Talk of the Town hotel, tel. 297/8–23380). This
beach-bum-café-cum-cabaret is so casual that you mix your own
drinks between 6 and 10:30 PM. Munch on tapas as you listen to
jazz, disco, steel bands, and native merengues and tumbas.

Hotels with lounges that feature live bands include the **Aruba
Concorde Hotel** (L. G. Smith Blvd. 77, Palm Beach, tel. 297/8–
24466), the **Aruba Beach Club** (L. G. Smith Blvd. 53, Punta
Brabu Beach, tel. 297/8–23000), the **Golden Tulip Aruba Carib-
bean Hotel** (L. G. Smith Blvd. 81, tel. 297/8–33555), the
Holiday Inn (L. G. Smith Blvd. 230, tel. 297/8–23600), the **Best
Western Manchebo Beach Resort Hotel** (L. G. Smith Blvd. 55,
Punta Brabu Beach, tel. 297/8–23444), **Divi Divi Beach Resort**
(L. G. Smith Blvd. 93, Punta Brabu Beach, tel. 297/8–23300),
the **Bushiri Beach Resort** (L. G. Smith Blvd. 35, tel. 297/8–
25216), the **Americana Hotel** (L. G. Smith Blvd. 83, tel. 297/8–
24500), and the **Tamarijn Beach Resort** (L. G. Smith Blvd. 64,
Punta Brabo Beach, tel. 297/8–24150).

Theater **Aruba Dance Theater** (L. G. Smith Blvd. 81, tel. 297/8–33555).
Held at the Golden Tulip Hotel's Pelican Terrace, Saturday's
Aruban night features native dancers in bright folkloric costumes in an open-air pavilion. Children will love the rooster
dance and the maypole ribbons. Dine during the shows.

Aladdin Theater (L. G. Smith Blvd. 93, tel. 297/8–25434). This
cabaret theater tucked into the Alhambra Bazaar features a variety of shows—the last one seen was unabashedly American,
with film clips from *That's Entertainment* and skits out of *Gone
with the Wind.* Go only if you're homesick. There's free popcorn.

5 Barbados

by Joan Iaconetti

A writer, photographer, and communications consultant based in New York, Joan Iaconetti is an avid scuba diver who spends winters on the island of Bequia. Her articles have appeared in Travel & Leisure, Travel-Holiday, Cosmopolitan, and Self.

Barbados has a life of its own that goes on after the tourists have packed their sun oils and returned home. Since the government is stable and unemployment relatively low, the difference between haves and have-nots is less marked—or at least less visible—than on other islands, and visitors are neither fawned upon nor resented for their assumed wealth. Genuinely proud of their country, the quarter million Bajans welcome visitors as privileged guests. Barbados is fine for people who want nothing more than to offer their bodies to the sun; yet the island, unlike many in the Caribbean, is also ideal for travelers who want to discover another life and culture.

Because the beaches of Barbados are open to the public, they lack the privacy that some visitors seek; but the beaches themselves are lovely, and many along the tranquil west coast—in the lee of the northwest trade winds—are backed by first-class resorts. Most of the hotels are situated along the beaches on the southern and southwestern coasts. The British and Canadians often favor the hotels of St. James Parish; Americans (couples more often than singles) tend to prefer the large south coast resorts.

To the northeast are rolling hills and valleys covered by acres of impenetrable sugarcane. The Atlantic surf pounds the gigantic boulders along the rugged east coast, where the Bajans themselves have their vacation homes. Elsewhere on the island, linked by almost 900 miles of good roads, are historic plantation houses, stalactite-studded caves, a wildlife preserve, and the Andromeda Gardens, one of the most attractive small tropical gardens in the world.

No one is sure whether the name *los Barbadoes* ("the bearded ones") refers to the beardlike root that hangs from the island's fig trees or to the bearded natives who greeted the Portuguese "discoverer" of the island in 1536. The name Los Barbados was still current almost a century later when the British landed— by accident—in what is now Holetown in St. James Parish. They colonized the island in 1627 and remained until it achieved independence in 1966.

Barbadians retain a British accent. Afternoon tea is habitual at numerous hotels. Cricket is still the national sport, producing some of the world's top cricket players. Polo is played in winter. The British tradition of dressing for dinner is firmly entrenched; a few luxury hotels require tie and jacket at dinner, and in good restaurants most women will consider themselves inappropriately dressed in anything less formal than a sundress. (A daytime stroll in a swimsuit is as inappropriate in Bridgetown as it would be on New York's 5th Avenue.) Yet the island's atmosphere is hardly stuffy. When the boat you ordered for noon doesn't arrive until 12:30, you can expect a cheerful response, "He okay, mon, he just on Caribbean time." Translation: No one, including you, needs to be in a hurry here.

Before You Go

Tourist Information Contact the **Barbados Board of Tourism** (800 2nd Ave., New York, NY 10017, tel. 212/986–6516); additional offices are in Los Angeles and in Winter Park, Florida. Barbados is also represented by Peter Rotholtz Assoc., Inc. (380 Lexington Ave., New York, NY 10017, tel. 212/687–6565).

Arriving and Departing By Plane Grantley Adams Airport in Barbados is a Caribbean hub. There are daily flights from New York (via San Juan); however, **American Airlines** (tel. 800/433–7300), **Pan Am** (tel. 800/221–1111), and **BWIA** (tel. 800/327–7401) all have nonstop flights from New York; there are direct flights from Washington, DC, on Pan Am; from Miami on **Eastern Airlines** (800/327–8376), Pan Am and BWIA. From Canada, **Air Canada** (tel. 800/422–6232) connects from Montreal through New York or Miami and flies nonstop from Toronto. From London, **British Airways** (tel. 800/247–9297) has nonstop service and BWIA connects through Trinidad.

Flights to St. Vincent, St. Lucia, Trinidad, and other islands are scheduled on LIAT and BWIA; Air St. Vincent/Air Mustique links Barbados with St. Vincent and the Grenadines.

From the Airport Airport taxis are not metered. A large sign at the airport announces the fixed rate to each hotel or area, stated in both Barbados and U.S. dollars (about $20 to the west coast hotels, $13 to the south coast). The new highway around Bridgetown saves time and trouble in getting up the western coast.

By Boat A popular cruise port, Barbados has room for eight ships (which is some indication of how crowded the Bridgetown shops can be). Bridgetown Harbour is located on the northwest side of Carlisle Bay, and most cruise ships organize transportation to and from the new **Carlisle Bay Centre,** a "hotel without rooms" for passengers on shore excursions. The CBC provides changing facilities, a restaurant, gift shops, and water-sports facilities—including floats, snorkel equipment, Sunfish sailboats, waterskiing, Windsurfers—for a nominal fee.

Passports and Visas U.S. and Canadian citizens need proof of citizenship plus a return or ongoing ticket to enter the country. Acceptable proof of citizenship is a valid passport or an original birth certificate and a photo ID; a voter registration card is not acceptable. British citizens need a valid passport.

Customs and Duties Barbados is a noted free port where most duty-free items can be bought over the counter when you show your passport or air/sea ticket. Items that must be delivered to your point of departure are tobacco, wines, and video/stereo/computer equipment.

Language English is spoken everywhere, sometimes accented with the phrases and lilt of a Bajan dialect.

Precautions Beach vendors of coral jewelry and beachwear will not hesitate to offer you their wares. The degree of persistence varies, and some of their jewelry offerings are good; sharp bargaining is expected on both sides. One hotel's brochure gives sound advice: "Please realize that encouraging the beach musicians means you may find yourself listening to the same three tunes over and over for the duration of your stay."

Water The water on the island, both in hotels and in restaurants, has been treated and is safe to drink.

Insects Insects aren't much of a problem on Barbados, but if you plan to hike or spend time on secluded beaches, it's wise to use insect repellent.

Toxic Tree Little green apples that fall from the large branches of the manchineel tree may look tempting, but they are poisonous to eat and toxic to the touch. Even taking shelter under the tree when it rains can give you blisters. Most manchineels are iden-

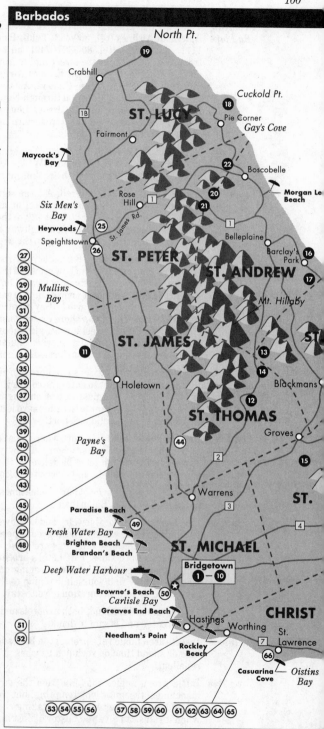

Barbados

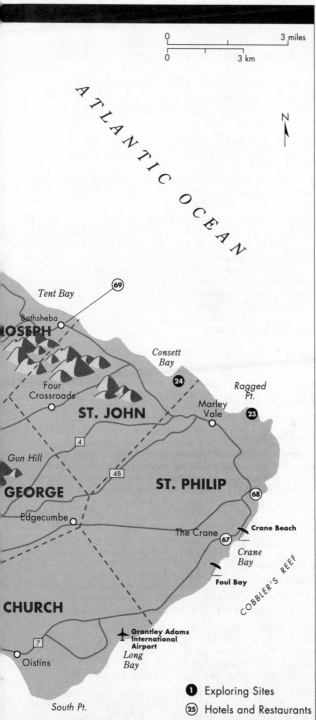

ATLANTIC OCEAN

N

Tent Bay

Bathsheba

JOSEPH

Consett Bay

Four Crossroads

ST. JOHN

Ragged Pt.

Marley Vale

Gun Hill

GEORGE

Edgecumbe

ST. PHILIP

The Crane

Crane Beach

Crane Bay

Foul Bay

COBBLER'S REEF

CHURCH

Grantley Adams International Airport

Long Bay

Oistins

South Pt.

1 Exploring Sites

25 Hotels and Restaurants

tified with signs; if you do come in contact with one, go to the nearest hotel and have someone there phone for a physician.

Crime Don't invite trouble by leaving valuables unattended on the beach or in plain sight in your room, and don't pick up hitchhikers.

Further Reading *In the Castle of My Skin*, an autobiographical novel by George Lamming (who lives part of each year in the Atlantis Hotel), is a lyrical remembrance of growing up in the West Indies, told from a young boy's point of view.

Louis Lynch's *The Barbados Book* uses anecdotes to recount the social history of Barbados and to describe the island way of life, past and present.

Barbados: A to Z, is an excellent new book that covers things Barbadian from the architectural to the zoological, by Carrington, Frazer, and Gilmore.

Local News The daily newspapers include *The Barbados Advocate* and *The Nation* (which appears on Sunday as *The Sun*). They publish, respectively, *The Sun Seeker* and *The Visitor*. The Board of Tourism prepares the free "Official Guide to Barbados" and the "Things You Should Know" brochures, but the bible for residents and visitors alike is *The Ins and Outs of Barbados*, now in its eighth year of publication, which is distributed free at most hotels and is sold at the larger shops.

Staying in Barbados

Important Addresses **Tourist Information: The Barbados Board of Tourism** is on Harbour Road in Bridgetown (tel. 809/427–2623).

Emergencies **Emergency:** tel. 119.

Ambulance: tel. 809/426–1113.

Police: tel. 112.

Fire department: tel. 113.

Scuba diving accidents: Divers' Alert Network (DAN) (tel. 919/684–8762 or 919/684–2948). Barbados decompression chamber, Barbados Defense Force, St. Ann's Fort, Garrison, St. Michael Parish (tel. 809/427–8819).

Currency One Barbados dollar (BDS\$1) equals about U.S.50¢. Because the value of the Barbados dollar is pegged to that of the U.S. dollar, the ratio remains constant. Both currencies and the Canadian dollar are accepted everywhere on the island, but changing your money to Barbados dollars will get you slightly better value. Prices quoted throughout this chapter are in U.S. dollars unless noted otherwise.

Taxes and Service Charges At the airport you must pay a departure tax of BDS\$20 (about U.S.\$10) in either currency before leaving Barbados.

A 10% service charge is added to your hotel bill and to most restaurant checks; any additional tip recognizes extraordinary service. When no service charge is added, tip maids \$1 per room per day, waiters 10% to 15%, taxi drivers 10%. Airport porters and bellboys expect BDS\$2 (U.S.\$1) per bag.

Guided Tours For an island of its size (14 miles by 21 miles), Barbados has a lot to see. A bus or taxi tour, which can be arranged by your hotel, is a good way to get your bearings. **L. E. Williams Tour Co.** (tel.

809/427–1043) offers an 80-mile island tour for about $40; a bus picks you up at 10 AM and takes you through Bridgetown, the St. James beach area, past the Animal Flower Cave, Farley Hill, Cherry Tree Hill, Morgan Lewis Mill, the east coast, St. John's Church, Sam Lord's Castle, Oistin's fishing village, and to St. Michael Parish, with drinks along the way and a West Indian lunch at the Atlantis Hotel in Bathsheba.

Sally Shern operates **VIP Tours** (Hillcrest Villa, Upton, St. Michael, tel. 809/429–4617), custom-tailored to each client, whom she picks up in an air-conditioned Mercedes-Benz. Bajan-born Ms. Shern knows her island well and provides the unusual and unique: a champagne lunch at Sunbury Plantation House, a swim at her favorite beach. Helicopter Tours offer an eagle's-eye view of Barbados (The Wharf, Bridgetown, tel. 809/425–0688). Depending upon the time spent aloft, prices range from $30 (U.S.) to $125 (U.S.) a person.

Custom Tours (tel. 809/425–0099 or 809/424–3516) arranges personalized tours for one to four persons. Staff members determine your particular interests (such as gardens, plantation houses, swimming at secluded beaches), pack a picnic lunch, and drive you in their own cars. They offer a familiarization tour for first-time visitors, and often they can take you to places that aren't normally open to the public.

Getting Around
Taxis Taxis operate at a fixed rate (BDS$30 for the first hour, less after that); settle the rate before you start off, and be sure you agree on whether it's in U.S. or Barbados dollars. Most drivers will cheerfully narrate a tour, though the noise of the car may make it difficult for you to follow a rambling commentary colored with Bajan inflections.

Buses Public buses along Highway 1, St. James Road, are cheap (BDS$1, exact change appreciated), plentiful, reliable, and usually packed. The buses provide a great opportunity to experience local color, and your fellow passengers will be eager to share their knowledge.

Rental Cars It's a pleasure to explore Barbados by car, provided you take the time to study a good map and you don't mind asking directions frequently. The more remote roads are in good repair, yet few are well lighted at night, and night falls quickly—at about 6 PM. Even in full daylight, the tall sugarcane fields lining a road can create near-zero visibility. Yet local residents are used to pointing travelers in the right direction, and some confused but intelligent drivers have been known to flag a passing taxi and pay to follow it back to a city area. Use caution: Pedestrians are everywhere. And remember, traffic keeps to the left throughout the island.

To rent a car you must have an international driver's license, obtainable at the airport and major car-rental firms for $5 if you have a valid driver's license. More than 40 offices rent minimokes for upwards of $35 a day (about U.S. $200 a week), usually with a three-day or four-day minimum; cars with automatic shift are $45–$55 a day, or U.S. $180–$260 a week. Gas costs just over BDS$1 a liter (about $2 a gallon) and is extra. The speed limit, in keeping with the pace of life, is 37 miles per hour (60 kilometers per hour) in the country, 21 miles per hour in town. Operating a motorbike also requires an international driver's license—and some skill and daring.

The principal car-rental firms are **National** (tel. 809/426–0603), **Dear's Garage** on the south coast (tel. 809/429–9277 or 809/427–7853), **Sunny Isle** in Worthing (809/428–8009 or 809/428–2965), and **Sunset Crest Rentals** in St. James (tel. 809/432–1482). **P&S Car Rentals** (Spring Garden Hwy., tel. 809/424–2052) offers air-conditioned cars with free customer delivery; they also arrange visitor driving permits.

Telephones and Mail The area code for Barbados (and the entire Caribbean is 809. Except for emergency numbers, all phone numbers have seven digits and begin with 42 or 43.

To send an airmail letter to the United States or Canada costs BDS75¢ per half ounce; an airmail postcard costs 45¢.

Opening and Closing Times Stores are open weekdays 8–4, Saturday 8–1. Some supermarkets remain open daily 8–6. Banks are open Monday to Thursday 9–3, Friday 9–1 and 3–5.

Beaches

Barbados is blessed with some of the Caribbean's most beautiful beaches, all of them open to the public. (Access to hotel beaches may not always be public, but you can walk onto almost any beach from another one.)

West Coast Beaches The west coast has the stunning coves and white-sand beaches that are dear to postcard publishers—plus calm, clear water for snorkeling, scuba diving, and swimming. The afternoon clouds and sunsets may seem to be right out of a Turner painting; because there is nothing but ocean between Barbados and Africa, the sunsets are rendered even more spectacular by the fine red sand that sometimes blows in from the Sahara.

While beaches here are seldom crowded, the west coast is not the place to find isolation. Owners of private boats stroll by, offering waterskiing, parasailing, and snorkel cruises. There are no concession stands per se, but hotels welcome nonguests for terrace lunches (wear a cover-up). Picnic items and necessities can be bought at the Sunset Crest shopping center in Holetown.

Beaches begin in the north at **Heywoods** (about a mile of sand) and continue almost unbroken to Bridgetown at **Brighton Beach,** a popular spot with locals. There is public access through the Barbados Beach Club and the Barbados Pizza House (both good for casual lunches), south of the Discovery Bay Hotel.

Good spots for swimming include **Paradise Beach,** just off the Paradise Beach Hotel; **Brandon's Beach,** a 10-minute walk south; **Browne's Beach,** in Bridgetown; and **Greaves End Beach,** south of Bridgetown at Aquatic Gap, between the Holiday Inn and the Hilton in St. Michael Parish.

The west coast is the area for scuba diving, sailing, lunch-and-rum cruises on the red-sailed *Jolly Roger* **"pirate" party ship** (tel. 809/426–0767). Somewhat more sedate sea experiences can be had on the ***Bajan Queen*** (tel. 809/436–2149 or 809/436–2150), a Mississippi-style riverboat that offers day and night cruises, each with buffet or dinner, and local musicians.

The *Atlantis* **Submarine** (tel. 809/436–8929 or 809/436–8932) goes to depths of 150 feet off wrecks and reefs in a Canadian-built 50-foot submarine that seats 28 passengers at a time, each at his or her own porthole. Classical music plays while an oceanography specialist informs.

South Coast Beaches The heavily traveled south coast of Christ Church Parish is much more built up than the St. James Parish coast in the west; here you'll find condos, high-rise hotels, many places to eat and shop, and the traffic (including public transportation) that serves them. These busier beaches generally draw a younger, more active crowd. The quality of the beach itself is consistently good, the reef-protected waters safe for swimming and snorkeling. Two of the best are in the St. Lawrence Gap area, near **Casuarina Cove.** The **Barbados Windsurfing Club Hotel** in Maxwell caters specifically to windsurfing aficionados, and most hotels and resorts provide boards or rent them for a nominal fee.

Crane Beach has for years been a popular swimming beach. As you move toward the Atlantic side of the island, the waves roll in bigger and faster; the waves at the nearby Crane Hotel are a favorite with bodysurfers. (But remember that this is the ocean, not the Caribbean, and exercise caution.)

Nearby **Foul Bay** lives up to its name only for sailboats; for swimmers and alfresco lunches, it's lovely. **Needham's Point,** with its lighthouse, is one of Barbados's best beaches, crowded with locals on weekends and holidays.

North Coast Beaches Those who love wild natural beauty will want to head north up the east coast highway. With secluded beaches and crashing ocean waves on one side, rocky cliffs and verdant landscape on the other, the windward side of Barbados won't disappoint anyone who seeks dramatic views. But be cautioned: Swimming here is treacherous and *not* recommended. The waves are high, the bottom tends to be rocky, and the currents are unpredictable. Limit yourself to enjoying the view and watching the surfers—who have been at it since they were kids.

A worthwhile little-visited beach for the adventurous who don't mind trekking about a mile off the beaten track is **Morgan Lewis Beach,** on the coast east of Morgan Lewis Mill, the oldest intact windmill on the island. Turn east on the small road that goes to the town of Boscobelle (between Cherry Tree Hill and Morgan Lewis Mill), but instead of going to the town, take the even less traveled road (unmarked on most maps; you will have to ask for directions) that goes down the cliff to the beach. What awaits is more than 2 miles of unspoiled, uninhabited white sand and sweeping views of the Atlantic coastline. You might see a few Barbadians swimming or sunning or fishing, but for the most part you'll have privacy.

Return to your car, cross the island's north point on the secondary roads until you reach the west coast. About a mile west from the end of Highway 1B is **Maycock's Bay,** an isolated area in St. Lucy Parish about 2 miles north of Heywoods, the west coast's northernmost resort complex.

Exploring Barbados

Numbers in the margin correspond with points of interest on the Bridgetown map.

The island's most popular sights and attractions can be seen comfortably in four or five excursions, each lasting one day or less. The five tours described here begin with Bridgetown and then cover central Barbados, the eastern shore, north-central Barbados, and the south shore. Before you set out in a car, minimoke, or taxi, ask at your hotel or the Board of Tourism for a free copy of the detailed Barbados Holiday Map and check performance or opening times.

Bridgetown

❶ **Bridgetown** is a bustling city complete with rush hours and traffic congestion; you'll avoid hassle by taking the bus or a taxi. Sightseeing will take only an hour or so, and the shopping areas are within walking distance.

❷ In the center of town, overlooking the picturesque harbor known as the Careenage, is **Trafalgar Square** with its impressive monument to Horatio, Lord Nelson. It predates the Nelson's Column in London's Trafalgar Square by about two decades (and for more than a century Bajans have petitioned to replace it with a statue of a Bajan). Here are also a war memorial and a three-dolphin fountain commemorating the advent of running water in Barbados in 1865.

❸ Bridgetown is a major Caribbean free port. The principal shopping area is **Broad Street,** which leads northwest from Trafalgar Square past the House of Assembly and Parliament Buildings. These Victorian Gothic structures, like so many smaller buildings in Bridgetown, stand beside a growing number of modern office buildings and shops. Small colonial buildings, their balconies trimmed with wrought iron, reward the visitor who has patience and an appreciative eye.

❹ The water that bounds Trafalgar Square is called the **Careenage,** a finger of sea that made early Bridgetown a natural harbor and a gathering place. Here working schooners were careened (turned on their sides) to be scraped of barnacles and repainted. Today the Careenage serves mainly as a berth for fiberglass pleasure yachts.

❺ While no one has proved it conclusively, George Washington, on his only visit outside the United States, is said to have worshiped at **St. Michael's Cathedral** south of Trafalgar Square. The structure was nearly a century old when he visited in 1751, and it has since been destroyed by hurricanes and rebuilt twice, in 1780 and 1831.

❻
❼ The two bridges over the Careenage are the Chamberlain Bridge and the Charles O'Neal Bridge, both of which lead to Highway 7 and south to the **Fairchild Market.** On Saturdays the activity there and at the **Cheapside Market** (on the north end of Lower Broad Street, across from St. Mary's Church Square) recall the lively days before the coming of the supermarket and the mall, when the outdoor markets of Barbados were the daily heart and soul of shopping and socializing.

❽ About a mile south of Bridgetown on Highway 7, the unusually interesting **Barbados Museum** has artifacts and mementos of military history and everyday life in the 19th century. Here you'll see cane-harvesting implements, lace wedding dresses, ancient (and frightening) dentistry instruments, and slave sale accounts kept in a spidery copperplate handwriting. Wildlife and natural history exhibits, a well-stocked gift shop, and a good café are also here, in what used to be the military prison.

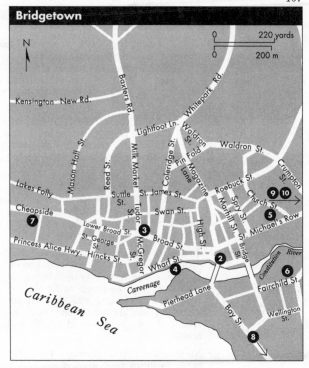

Bridgetown

Hwy. 7, Garrison Savannah, tel. 809/435–6900. Admission: BDS$4. Open Mon.–Sat. 9–6.

9 East of Bridgetown, **Queen's Park,** now being restored to its original splendor, is home to one of the largest trees in Barbados: an immense baobab more than 10 centuries old. The **10** historic **Queen's Park House,** former home of the commander of the British troops, has been converted into a theater—with an exhibition room on the lower floor—and a restaurant. Queen's Park is a long walk from Trafalgar Square or the museum; you may want to take a taxi. *Open daily 9–5.*

Central Barbados *Numbers in the margin correspond with points of interest on the Barbados map.*

The most interesting place for getting into the water is the **11** **Folkestone Underwater Park** (809/422–2814), north of Holetown. While Folkestone has a land museum of marine life, the real draw is the underwater snorkeling trail around Dottin's Reef, with glass-bottom boats available for use by nonswimmers. A dredge barge sunk in shallow water is the home to myriad fish, and it and the reef are popular with scuba divers. Huge sea fans, soft coral, and the occasional giant turtle are sights to see.

12 Highway 2 will take you to **Harrison's Caves.** These pale-gold limestone caverns, complete with subterranean streams and waterfalls, are entirely organic and said to be unique in the Caribbean. Open since 1981, the caves are so extensive that tours are made by electric tram (hard hats are provided, but all that may fall on you is a little dripping water). *Admission: BDS$10. Open daily 9–4. Reservations are recommended.*

⑬ Continue along Highway 2 to reach the **Flower Forest,** 8 acres of fragrant flowering bushes, canna and ginger lilies, and puffball trees. Another hundred species of flora combine with the tranquil views of Mt. Hillaby to induce in visitors what may be a relaxing and very pleasant light-headedness. *Admission: BDS$6. Open daily.*

⑭ The nearby **Welchman's Hall Gully,** a part of the National Trust in St. Thomas, affords another ideal opportunity to commune with nature. Here are acres of labeled flowers and trees, the occasional green monkey, and great peace and quiet.

⑮ Take Highway 4 and smaller roads to **Gun Hill** for a view so pretty it seems almost unreal: Shades of green and gold cover the fields all the way to the horizon, the picturesque gun tower is surrounded by brilliant flowers, and the white limestone lion behind the garrison is a famous landmark. Military invalids were once sent here to convalesce.

The Eastern Shore Take Highway 3 across the island to Bathsheba and the phenomenal view from the **Atlantis,** one of the oldest hotels in Barbados, where you may need help getting up from the table after sampling the lunch buffet. In the nearby **Andromeda Gardens,** a fascinating small garden set into the cliffs overlooking the sea, are unusual and beautiful plant specimens from around the world, collected by the horticulturist Iris Bannochie.

⑯ North of Bathsheba, **Barclay's Park** offers a similar view and picnic facilities in a wooded seafront area. At the nearby
⑰ **Chalky Mount Potteries,** you'll find craftspersons making and selling their wares.

A drive north to the isolated Morgan Lewis Beach (*see* Beaches, above) or to Gay's Cove, which every Bajan calls Cove Bay,
⑱ will put you in reach of the town of **Pie Corner.** Pie Corner is known not for baked goods but for artifacts left by the Caribe and Arawak tribes who once lived here.

⑲ The **Animal Flower Cave** at North Point, reached by Highway 1, displays small sea anemones, or seaworms, that resemble jewel-like flowers as they open their tiny tentacles. For a small fee you can explore inside the cavern and see the waves breaking just outside it. *Admission: BDS$2. Open daily.*

North-Central The attractions of north-central Barbados might well be com-
Barbados bined with the tour of the eastern shore.

⑳ The **Barbados Wildlife Reserve** can be reached on Highway 1 from Speightstown on the west coast. Here are herons, land turtles, a kangaroo, screeching peacocks, innumerable green monkeys and their babies doing all manner of things, geese, brilliantly colored parrots, and a friendly otter. The fauna are not in cages, so step carefully and keep your hands to yourself. The preserve has been much improved in recent years with the addition of a giant walk-in aviary and natural-history exhibits. Terrific photo opportunities are everywhere. *Admission: BDS$6. Open daily 10–5.*

㉑ Just to the south, **Farley Hill Mansion** is a national park in northern St. Peter Parish; the rugged landscape explains why they call this the Scotland area. Gardens, lawns, gigantic mahogany, whitewood, and casuarina trees, and an avenue of towering royal palms surround the imposing ruins of a once magnificent plantation great house. Partially rebuilt for the filming of *Island in the Sun*, the structure was later destroyed by fire. *Admission free. Open daily until dusk.*

㉒ St. Nicholas Abbey near Cherry Tree Hill, named for a former owner and the oldest (c. 1650) great house in Barbados, is well worth visiting for its stone an wood architecture in the Jacobean style. Fascinating home movies, made by the present owner's father, record scenes of Bajan town and plantation life in the 1920s and 1930s. There are no set showing times; you need only ask to see them. *Admission: $2.50. Open weekdays 10–3:30.*

The South Shore Driving east on Highways 4 and 4B, you'll note the many **chattel houses** along the route; the property of tenant farmers, these ever-expandable houses were built to be dismantled and moved when necessary. On the coast, the appropriately named **㉓ Ragged Point Lighthouse** is where the sun first shines on Barbados and its dramatic Atlantic seascape. About 4 miles to the northwest, in the eastern corner of St. John Parish, the coralstone buildings and serenely beautiful grounds of **㉔ Codrington Theological College,** founded in 1748, stand on a cliff overlooking Consett Bay.

Take the smaller roads southeast to reach Marriott's **Sam Lord's Castle** (*see* Lodging, below), the Regency house built by the buccaneer. Most of the rooms are furnished with the fine antiques he is said to have acquired from passing ships (note the mahogany four-poster), but he had to hire Italian artisans to create the elaborate plaster ceilings. The tour is free to guests; others pay a small fee.

Participant Sports

Barbados offers a comprehensive variety of sports activity.

Golfing The newest 18-hole course is at the Royal Westmoreland Golf and Country Club, where the first Barbados Open Golf Championship is being held. Repeat golfers favor the seasoned 9-hole course at the **Sandy Lane Club** (tel. 809/422–1405), 9 holes at the **Rockley Resort** (tel. 809/427–5890), and another 9-hole course at **Heywoods** (tel. 800/223–9815). All are open (for various fees) to nonguests.

Hiking Hilly but not mountainous, the interior of Barbados is ideal for hiking. The **Outdoor Club of Barbados** organizes escorted treks weekly. *Sturdee House, Bank Hall, St. Michael Parish, tel. 809/426–6739 or 809/426–0024. Cost: $15–$25.*

Less serious (but great fun) is the **Hash House Harriers,** an international running group with relaxed jogging at different points each week. Contact **Barry Johnson** (tel. 809/437–0827).

The **Barbados National Trust** (tel. 809/426–2421) sponsors free walks on Sunday, from 5 or 6 AM to about 9 AM, during the winter. Newspapers announce the time and meeting place (or you can call the Trust).

Horseback Riding Reasonable prices ($17–$22) for one-hour trots, including hotel pickup, come from **Valley Hill Stables** (Christ Church, tel. 809/423–0033), and **Ye Old Congo Road Stables** (St. Philip, tel. 809/423–6180), which take riders through sugar plantations. On the west coast, **Brighton Stables** (tel. 809/425–9381) offers sunrise and sunset walks along beaches and palm groves.

Parasailing Parasailing, where you wear a parachute harness and take off from a raft as you're towed by a speedboat, is available, wind conditions permitting, on the beaches of St. James and Christ Church. Just ask at any hotel, then flag down a speedboat (though it may have found you first).

Sailing and Fishing Sailing and deep-sea fishing charters can be arranged through **Jolly Roger Watersports** (tel. 809/426–0767). **Blue Jay Charters** (tel. 809/422–2098) has a 45-foot, fully equipped fishing boat, with a crew that knows the waters where blue marlin, sailfish, barracuda, and kingfish play. Two new entries are **Sail Barbados** (tel. 809/436–5725) and *Carie-Dee,* a 36-foot private yacht (tel. 809/422–2319) that takes guests by the day or half day. For day-long sails and party cruises, consult the **Barbados Cruising Club** (tel. 809/426–4434) or the **Barbados Yacht Club** (tel. 809/427–1125).

Scuba Diving Barbados is a rich and varied underwater destination, one of the few in the Caribbean that offer activity for both divers and nondivers. Many dive shops provide instruction (the three-hour beginner's "resort courses" and the week-long certification courses) followed by a shallow dive, usually on Dottin's Reef. Trained divers can explore reefs, wrecks, and the walls of "blue holes," the huge circular depressions in the ocean floor. Not to be missed by certified, guided divers is the *Stavronikita*, a 368-foot Greek freighter that was deliberately sunk at about 125 feet; hundreds of butterfly fish hang out around its mast, and the thin rays of sunlight that filter down through the water make exploring the huge ship a wonderfully eerie experience.

Dive Barbados (Jolly Roger Watersports, Sunset Crest Beach, near Holetown, St. James Parish, tel. 809/432–7090 or 703/893–4704) provides beginner's instruction (resort course) and reef and wreck dives with a friendly, knowledgeable staff.

The **Coral Reef Club** (St. James Beach, tel. 809/422–3215) has its own dive facility and school, available to nonguests. The dive boat leaves daily at 10:30 and 2:30.

At **The Dive Shop, Ltd.** (on the beach, St. Michael Parish, tel. 809/426–9947), Paquia Diega leads experienced divers on deep dives to old wrecks to look for bottles and other artifacts (and you can usually keep what you find). Don't be put off by the grubby shop; the instructor knows his stuff.

Willie's Watersports (Cunard Paradise Beach Hotel, tel. 809/424–0888, ext. 7429, and Heywoods Hotel, tel. 809/422–4900, ext. 2831) offers instruction and a range of diving excursions.

Underwater Barbados (Sand Acres Beach Club, Maxwell, tel. 809/428–9739) operates a full range of daily dives and unusual finders-keepers bottle dives.

Dive Boat Safari (Hilton Hotel, tel. 809/427–4350) offers full diving and instruction services.

Snorkeling Snorkeling gear can be rented for a small charge from nearly every hotel.

Squash Squash courts can be reserved at the **Rockley Resort** (tel. 809/427–5890) and the **Barbados Squash Club** (tel. 809/427–7193).

Submarining	Submarines are enormously popular with families and those who enjoy watching fish without getting wet, and the 28-passenger *Atlantis* turns the Caribbean into a giant aquarium. The 45-minute trip takes you as much as 150 feet below the surface for a look at what even sport divers rarely see. The nighttime dives, using high-power searchlights, are spectacular. *Tel. 809/436–8929. Cost: about $45.*
Tennis	The **Paragon Tennis Club** (tel. 809/427–2054) is one possibility, but most hotels have tennis courts that can be reserved day and night. Be sure to bring your whites; appropriate dress is expected on the court.
Waterskiing	Waterskiing is widely available, often provided along St. James and Christ Church by the private speedboat owners. Inquire at your hotel, which can direct you to the nearest Sunfish sailing and Hobie Cat rentals as well.
Windsurfing	Windsurfing boards and equipment are often guest amenities at the larger hotels and can be rented by nonguests. The best place to learn and to practice is on the south coast at the **Barbados Windsurfing Club Hotel** (Maxwell, Christ Church Parish, tel. 809/428–9095).

Spectator Sports

Cricket	The island is mad for cricket, and you can sample a match at almost any time of year. While the season is June through late December, test matches are played in the first half of the year. The newspapers give the details of time and place.
Horse Racing	Horse racing takes place on alternate Saturdays, from January to May and from July to November, at the **Garrison Savannah,** about 3 miles south of Bridgetown. Appropriate dress might be described as "casual elegance." *Tel. 809/426–3980. Admission: about $6.*
Polo	Polo, the sport of kings, is played seriously in Barbados. Matches are held at the **Polo Club** in St. James on Wednesday and Saturday from September to March. Hang around the club room after the match. That's where the lies, the legends, and the invitations happen. *Admission: about $2.50.*
Rugby	The rough-and-tumble game of rugby is played at the Garrison Savannah; schedules are available from the **Barbados Rugby Association** (tel. 809/435–6455).
Soccer	The football, or soccer, season runs from January through June; game schedules are available from the **Barbados Football Association** (tel. 809/424–4413).

Shopping

Traditionally, Broad Street and its side streets in Bridgetown have been the center for shopping action. Hours are generally weekdays 8–4, Saturday 8–1. Many stores have an in-bound (duty-free) department where you must show your travel tickets or a passport to buy duty-free goods.

Recently, several new areas opened their freshly painted doors. The mall-like **Sheraton Centre** (at Sargeant's Village in Christ Church) has toys for tots, togs for teens, and temptations for all. (Adjacent movie theaters and video arcades are coming soon.) The **Quayside Shopping Center** (at Rockley in

Christ Church) is smaller and more select, with frozen yogurt at **Toppings** and a look at **Artwork** in Shop 5, where everything is handmade in Barbados, Trinidad, St. Lucia, or Guyana.

Best 'N The Bunch is both a wildly colored chattel house at The Chattel House Village (at St. Lawrence Gap) and its own best advertisement. Here the expert jewelry of Bajan David Trottman sells for that rarity—reasonable prices. **Perfections** also has good finds—all from Bajan artists—for men, women, and children, and **Beach Bum** offers teens "barely" bikinis.

Luxury Goods Bridgetown stores have values on fine bone china, crystal, cameras, stereo and video equipment, jewelry, perfumes, and clothing. **Cave Shepherd** and **Harrison's** department stores offer wide selections of goods at many locations and at the airport. **De Lima's** and **Da Costa's Ltd.** stock quality imports. Among the specialty stores are **Louis I. Bayley** (gold watches), **J. Baldini** (Brazilian jewelry and Danish silver), and **Correia's** (diamonds, pearls, semiprecious stones). The 20 small shops of **Mall 34** in Bridgetown's central district sell everything from luxury goods to crafts.

Handicrafts Island handicrafts are everywhere: woven mats and placemats, dresses, dolls, handbags, shell jewelry. The **Best of Barbados** shops, at the airport, the Sandpiper Inn, Mall 34 in Bridgetown (tel. 809/436–1416), and three other locations, offer the highest quality artwork and crafts, both "native style" and modern designs. A resident artist, Jill Walker, sells her watercolors and prints here and at **Walker's World** shops (tel. 809/428–1183) near the south shore hotels in St. Lawrence Gap.

At the **Pelican Village Handicrafts Center** (tel. 809/426–1966) on the Princess Alice Highway near the Cheapside Market in Bridgetown, in a cluster of conical shops, you can watch goods and crafts being made before you purchase them. Rugs and mats made from pandanus grass and khuskhus are good buys.

Antiques Antiques and fine memorabilia are the stock of **Greenwich House Antiques** (tel. 809/432–1169) in Greenwich Village, Trents Hill, St. James Parish, and at **Antiquaria** (tel. 809/426–0635) on St. Michael's Row next to the Anglican cathedral in Bridgetown.

Chic Shops Hidden in separate corners of Barbados are some very upscale, little-known shops that can hold their own in New York or London. Carol Cadogan's **Cotton Days Designs** at Rose Cottage (Lower Bay St., tel. 809/427–7191) and her **Petticoat Lane** on the Wharf in Bridgetown (tel. 809/427–9037) set the international pace with all-cotton, collage creations that have been declared "wearable art." These are fantasy designs, with prices that begin at U.S. $250. Fortunately, she takes credit cards.

Corrie (Scott), owner of **Corrie's** (Bay St. in Hastings, tel. 809/427–9184) designs hand-knit cotton sweaters and dresses that begin at U.S. $75; she also carries jewelry by David Trottman, as well as the exotic dress designs of Derek Went.

Simon Foster of **Simon's** (Paynes Bay, St. James, tel. 809/432–6242) creates jazzy scene stealers, usually some with a tie-dye theme, although his collections vary from season to season. Very occasionally, he has a sale.

Dining

The better hotels and restaurants of Barbados have employed chefs trained in New York and Europe to attract and keep their sophisticated clientele. Gourmet dining here usually means fresh seafood, beef, or veal with finely blended sauces.

The native West Indian cuisine offers an entirely different dining experience. The island's West African heritage brought rice, peas, beans, and okra to its table, the staples that make a perfect base for slowly cooked meat and fish dishes. Many side dishes are cooked in oil (the pumpkin fritters can be addictive). And be cautious at first with the West Indian seasonings; like the sun, they are hotter than you think.

Every menu features dolphin (the fish, not the mammal), kingfish, snapper, and flying fish prepared every way imaginable. Shellfish abound; so does steak. Everywhere for breakfast and dessert you'll find mangoes, soursop, papaya (called pawpaw), and, in season, mammyapples, a basketball-size, thick-skinned fruit with giant seeds.

Cou-cou is a mix of corn meal and okra with a spicy Creole sauce made from tomatoes, onions, and sweet peppers; steamed flying fish is often served over it. A version served by the Brown Sugar restaurant, called "red herring," is smoked herring and breadfruit in Creole sauce.

Pepperpot stew, a hearty mix of oxtail, beef chunks, and "any other meat you may have," simmered overnight, is flavored with *casareep,* an ancient preservative and seasoning that gives the stew its dark, rich color.

Christophines and **eddoes** are tasty, potatolike vegetables that are often served with curried shrimp, chicken, or goat.

Buljol is a cold salad of codfish, tomatoes, onions, sweet peppers, and celery, marinated and served raw.

Callaloo is a soup made from okra, crabmeat, a spinachlike vegetable that gives the dish its name, and seasonings.

Among the liquid refreshments of Barbados, in addition to the omnipresent Banks Beer and Mount Gay rum, there are **falernum,** a liqueur concocted of rum, sugar, lime juice, and almond essence and **mauby,** a refreshing nonalcoholic beerlike drink made by boiling bitter bark and spices, straining the mixture, and sweetening it.

The most highly recommended restaurants are indicated by a star ★.

Category	Cost*
Expensive	over $40
Moderate	$25–$40
Inexpensive	under $25

Per person, excluding drinks and service charge. There is no sales tax on Barbados.

The following credit-card abbreviations are used: AE, American Express; CB, Carte Blanche; DC, Diners Club; MC, MasterCard; and V, Visa.

Expensive **Bagatelle Great House.** Occupying a converted plantation house in a hill area, Bagatelle Great House gives diners an impression of colonial life. The terrace allows intimate dining at tables for two, while inside the castlelike walls are much larger round tables. The superb ambience is somewhat more memorable than the expensive Continental dishes. *St. Thomas Parish, tel. 809/425–0666. Reservations necessary. Jacket and tie required. AE, MC, V.*

★ **Carambola.** Brian Ward of the Treasure Beach Hotel ownership family took over Carambola in 1990 and brought his favorite chef, Paul Owens, with him. This highly skilled duo now operate from a spectacular setting on a cliff overlooking the Caribbean in St. James Parish, with tables scattered over manicured lawns. Quite possibly the best restaurant in Barbados. *Derricks, St. James, tel. 809/432–0832, 809/432–8091, or 809/432–6182. Reservations necessary. AE, MC, V.*

★ **Fathoms.** Veteran restaurateurs Stephen and Sandra Toppin have opened their newest property seven days a week, for lunch and dinner, with 22 well-dressed tables scattered from the inside dining rooms to the patio's ocean edge. Dinner might bring a grilled lobster, flamed bonito tuna, sautéed cutlets of conch, or tangerine ginger ribs. *Paines Place, St. James, tel. 809/432–2568. Reservations necessary. AE, MC, V.*

La Cage aux Folles. Acclaimed as the island's true gourmet French restaurant, the intimate La Cage aux Folles seats only 22. The tropical French decor includes a cage of colorful parrots and macaws and lots of fresh flowers; soft music throughout the evening further sets the mood. The menu is simple, the lobster and beef are exceptional, the wine list is good. *Payne Bay, St. James Parish, tel. 809/432–1203. Reservations necessary. Jacket and tie required. AE, MC, V. Dinner only.*

Noelle's. Noelle's, a family-run restaurant, has an Old World inn atmosphere and a menu that is strong on local seafood and Continental fare. The service is excellent, but the prices are exceptionally high. *Holetown, St. James Parish, tel. 809/432–6159. Reservations necessary. AE, MC, V.*

★ **Raffles.** Young, international owners have made this one of Barbados's top restaurants. Forty guests can be seated at beautifully decorated tables featuring a tropical safari theme. Main dishes might be shrimp saki, blackened fish, steak served in a wine-and-lime sauce, basil-curry chicken, and sweet-and-sour pork. The desserts are both delicious and decadent. *1st St., Holetown, St. James, tel. 809/432–6557 or 809/432–1280. Reservations necessary. AE, MC.*

Moderate **Balmore House Restaurant.** New on the beach in St. James Par-
★ ish, the elegant Balmore House features English country-home furnishings in a colonial-style house with a paneled bar that opens onto a seaside terrace dining area. There are candles on the tables, and the service is attentive. Pepper steak and shrimp mousseline are featured. *Holetown, St. James Parish, tel. 809/432–1156. Reservations recommended. AE, MC, V. Closed Sun. and Mon.*

Brown Sugar. A special-occasion atmosphere prevails at Brown Sugar, located just behind the Island Inn outside Bridgetown. Dozens of ferns and hanging plants decorate the breezy multilevel restaurant. The extensive and authentic West Indian lunch buffets, popular with local businessmen, include cou-cou, pepperpot stew, Creole orange chicken, and such homemade desserts as angelfood chocolate mousse cake and passionfruit and nutmeg ice cream. *Aquatic Gap, St. Michael Parish, tel. 809/426-7684. Reservations recommended. AE, MC, V. Closed Sun. No lunch Sat.*

★ **David's Place.** Here you'll be served first-rate dishes in a first-rate location—a black-and-white Bajan cottage overlooking St. Lawrence Bay. Specialties include Baxters Road chicken, local flying fish, pepperpot (salt pork, beef, and chicken boiled and bubbling in a spicy casareep stock), and curried shrimp. Homemade cheesebread is served with all dishes. Desserts might be banana pudding, coconut-cream pie, carrot cake with rum sauce, or cassava pone. *St. Lawrence Main Road, Worthing, Christ Church, tel. 809/428-2708 or 809/428-4537. All major credit cards. Reservations necessary.*

Flamboyant. Local residents who look forward to dining in a cozy old Barbadian home favor Flamboyant and its generous portions of West Indian and European dishes, some of them with a German influence. *Worthing, Christ Church Parish, tel. 809/427-5588. AE, MC, V. Dinner only.*

★ **Ile De France.** French owners Martine and Michel Granalia have adapted the pool and garden areas of the Windsor Arms Hotel and turned them into an island "in" spot. White latticework opens to the night sounds, soft taped French music plays, and a single, perfect hibiscus dresses each table. Just a few of their specialties: foie gras, tournedos Rossini, lobster-and-crepe flambé, and filet mignon with a choice of pepper, béarnaise, or champignon sauce. *Windsor Arms Hotel, Hastings, Christ Church, tel. 809/436-2967. Reservations required. No credit cards. Dinner only. Closed Mon.*

Koko's. For a dramatic beach setting, drive up Highway 1 to Koko's in Prospect, where the ocean view from the terrace is stunning. The "nu-Bajan" menu offers an imaginative West Indian twist on nouvelle cuisine. The *kohoblopot* soup recalls the all-in-one-pot the Awawak Indians are said to have kept going for a week, using casareep as a preservative; the shrimp Kristo is simmered in red gravy with christophines. *Prospect, St. James Parish, tel. 809/424-4557. Reservations recommended. AE, MC, V. Dinner only.*

★ **Ocean View Hotel.** This elegant pink grande dame of a hotel is dressed in fresh fabrics, with great bunches of equally fresh flowers and sparkling crystal chandeliers. Bajan dishes are featured for lunch and dinner, and the Sunday-only Planter's Luncheon Buffet in the downstairs Club Xanadu (which fronts the beach) offers course after course of traditional dishes. Pianist Jean Emerson plays Hoagy Carmichael tunes and sings in dusky tones. *Hastings, Christ Church Parish, tel. 809/427-7821. Reservations recommended. AE, MC, V.*

Plantation. Wednesday's Bajan buffet and Tuesday's entertainment are big attractions here. The Plantation is set in a renovated Barbadian residence surrounded by spacious grounds above the Southwinds Resort; its cuisine combines French and Barbadian influences, and you can eat indoors or on the terrace. *St. Lawrence, Christ Church Parish, tel. 809/428-5048. Reservations suggested. AE, MC, V. Dinner only.*

Rose and Crown. The casual Rose and Crown serves a variety of fresh seafood, but it's the local lobster that's high on diners' lists. Indoors is a paneled bar, outdoors are tables on a wraparound porch. *Prospect, St. James Parish, tel. 809/425–1074. Reservations suggested. AE, MC, V.*

The Virginian. The locally popular Virginian offers intimate surroundings and some of the island's best dining values. The specialties are seafood, shrimp, and steaks. *Sea View Hotel, Hastings, Christ Church Parish, tel. 809/427–7963. Reservations suggested. AE, MC, V. Dinner only.*

Witch Doctor. The interior of the Witch Doctor is a cascade of tropical plants; the menu features traditional Barbadian dishes and local seafood. *St. Lawrence Gap, Christ Church Parish, tel. 809/428–7856. Reservations recommended. AE, MC, V. Dinner only.*

Inexpensive **Atlantis Hotel.** While the surroundings may be simple and the rest room could use a coat of paint, the nonstop food and the magnificent ocean view at the Atlantis Hotel in Bathsheba on the east coast make it a real find. Owner-chef Enid Maxwell serves up an enormous Bajan buffet daily, where you're likely to find pickled souse (marinated pig parts and vegetables), pumpkin fritters, spinach balls, pickled breadfruit, fried "fline" (flying) fish, roast chicken, pepperpot stew, and West Indian-style okra and eggplant. Among the homemade pies are an apple and a dense coconut. *Bathsheba, St. Joseph Parish, tel. 809/423–1526. Reservations suggested. No credit cards.*

Lodging

The southern and western shores of Barbados are lined with hotels and resorts of every size and price, offering a variety of accommodations from private villas to modest but comfortable rooms in simple inns. At the same time, apartment and home rentals and time-share condominiums have become widely available and are growing increasingly popular among visitors to the island; information about these arrangements follows the hotel listings below.

Hotels are grouped here by parish, beginning with St. James in the west and St. Peter to the north, then St. Michael, Christ Church, St. Philip, and St. Joseph.

The most highly recommended lodgings are indicated by a star ★.

Category	Cost*
Very Expensive	over $350
Expensive	$250–$350
Moderate	$150–$300
Inexpensive	under $150

All prices are for a standard double room, excluding 10% service charge.

Hotels **Glitter Bay.** Once the estate of Sir Edward Cunard, the former
St. James Parish beach house has been transformed into five garden suites
★ (there are four new suites with Jacuzzis), and the 85 one- to three-bedroom accommodations (each with full kitchen) have recently been refurbished. Manicured grounds connect this property to an adjacent sister resort, The Royal Pavilion, via 27 acres of gardens and a half mile of crunchy beach. Comple-

mentary water-sports facilities are shared, along with dining privileges at either resort. *Porters, St. James Parish, tel. 809/ 422-4111. 94 rooms. Facilities: pool, restaurant, water sports, 2 lighted tennis courts, golf course nearby. AE, DC, MC, V. Very Expensive.*

Coconut Creek Club. A luxury cottage colony, the Coconut Creek Club is set on handsomely landscaped grounds with a private beach and a bar pavilion for entertainment and dancing. MAP (breakfast and dinner) available. *Reservations: Box 249, Bridgetown; Hwy. 1, St. James Parish, tel. 809/432-0803. 53 rooms. Facilities: pool, dining room, pub. AE, DC, MC, V. Expensive.*

Colony Club. The seven-acre Colony Club a cottage colony on the beach, is a "residential club." All rooms have private patios. There is a dining room and cocktail terrace, and there are water sports on the beach. *Reservations: Box 429, Bridgetown; Hwy. 1, St. James Parish, tel. 809/422-2335. 76 rooms. Facilities: pool, dining room. AE, MC, V. Expensive.*

★ **Coral Reef Club.** The cottages of the Coral Reef Club are scattered over 12 flower-filled acres. Extensive water-sports activities include a scuba-diving school. Luncheon on a terrace, dining, dancing, and beach barbecues make you feel pampered. *Reservations: St. James Beach; Hwy. 1, St. James Parish, tel. 809/422-2372 or 800/223-1108. 70 rooms. Facilities: pool, entertainment. AE, MC, V. Very Expensive.*

Discovery Bay Hotel. The rooms of the quiet, white-columned recently renovated Discovery Bay Hotel open onto a central lawn and a pool. Some rooms have ocean views. Beach activities include windsurfing, Sunfish, Hobie Cats. *Hwy. 1, Holetown, St. James Parish, tel. 809/432-1301. 85 rooms. Facilities: pool, table tennis, terrace restaurant, boutique. AE, DC, MC, V. Expensive.*

Divi St. James Beach Resort. The Divi St. James, formerly the Club St. James, is the island's only all-inclusive property; week-long packages include accommodations, meals, beverages, and water sports. An exchange program allows the use of sports and recreation facilities of the Divi Southwinds, a sister property. Regular rates are available, too, as well as dive packages. *Holetown, St. James Parish, tel. 809/432-7840. 316 rooms. Facilities: golf, pool, Nautilus fitness center, sauna. No guests under age 16. AE, DC, MC, V. Very Expensive.*

★ **The Royal Pavilion.** Seventy-two of the 75 rooms here are oceanfront suites, the remaining three nestled in a garden villa. This is the sister property to adjacent Glitter Bay, and the combination is glamorous knockout. The Palm Restaurant is open-air with diners protected by floor-to-ceiling arches and indoor palms. A half mile of beach and 27 acres of tropical gardens connect the two properties. *St. James, Barbados, tel. 809/ 422-5555; fax 809/422-3940. 75 rooms. Facilities: 2 restaurants, 2 bars, 2 lighted tennis courts, supper-club entertainment, water-sports center, golf course nearby. AE, DC, MC, V. Very Expensive.*

★ **Sandy Lane.** One of the Caribbean's most famous hotels is now a Trusthouse Forte Ltd. property, and has undergone redecoration. Public areas still have ornate mirrors and crystal chandeliers to offset the thick, coral-stone walls, and of course, the white Rolls-Royce is at the door, but now suites have increased to 30, and the additional 82 double rooms are California-style comfy. Amenities include bathrobes, fine toiletries, and careful service. All water sports are available on the 1,000 feet of beach. *Hwy. 1, Sunset Crest, St. James Parish, tel. 809/432–1311 or 800/223–5672. 112 rooms. Facilities: pool, 5 tennis courts, golf course, 2 restaurants, 2 cocktail lounges, entertainment. AE, DC, MC, V. Very Expensive.*

Settlers' Beach. The accommodations at Settlers' Beach are two-story, two-bedroom homes with full kitchen and dining room (or one-story villas with atrium), arranged asymmetrically around a large courtyard filled with towering palms and a pool. The outdoor pool and bar area has just been renovated, and the new chef is from the Parker Meridien Hotel in Manhattan. Your neighbors may turn out to be British film stars. *Hwy. 1, St. James Parish, tel. 809/422–3052. 22 villas. Facilities: pool, restaurant. AE, MC, V. Very Expensive.*

★ **Treasure Beach.** Indeed a treasure, this flawlessly run property has just changed hands. There are twenty-five spacious suites that include private patios with views of the spectacular gardens or sea on Barbados's west coast. There's a clublike atmosphere here, with many repeat guests. *Payne's Bay, St. James, tel. 809/432–1346; fax 809/432–1094. 24 one-bedroom, air-conditioned suites; 1 two-bedroom penthouse suite. Facilities: restaurant, water sports. Closed Sept.–mid-Oct. AE, MC, V. Expensive.*

Barbados Beach Village. Vacationers choose from twin-bedded rooms, studios, apartments, and duplexes at the Barbados Beach Village. The beach has a terrace bar, and the restaurant is seaside. *Hwy. 1, St. James Parish, tel. 809/425–1440. 88 rooms. Facilities: pool, restaurant, disco nightclub. AE, DC, MC, V. Moderate.*

Golden Palms. With one-, two-, and three-bedroom villas set around a shopping center with a supermarket, a deli, a beauty shop, a bank, and a department store, Sunset Crest resembles a small village. The resort is very popular with families (especially Canadians), who find here the ingredients of a reasonable self-catering holiday. The recreation area has a clubhouse, two pools, a pitch-and-putt golf course, and tennis courts. Across the road, the Beach Club has two pools, two restaurants, a bar and games room, and a fine stretch of beach. The calypso group Merrymen often entertains here. *Hwy. 1, St. James Parish, tel. 809/432–1290. 111 rooms. Facilities: 2 pools, tennis courts, shops, entertainment. AE, DC, MC, V. Moderate.*

St. Peter Parish **Cobblers Cove Hotel.** The comfortable, unpretentious Cobblers
★ Cove Hotel, about 11 miles up the coast from Bridgetown, offers luxury efficiency units with kitchenettes and balconies or patios. Water sports are available on the beach. *Hwy. 1, Road View, St. Peter Parish, tel. 809/422–2291. 38 rooms, 1 suite. Facilities: pool, dining terrace, bar. AE, MC, V. Very Expensive.*

Heywoods Barbados. Everything is on a grand scale here: The seven buildings of the Heywoods Barbados, each with its own theme and decor, house hundreds of luxury rooms. The mile-long beach has space for all water sports. Owned by the Barbados government, the property is worth a visit just for a look at the landscaping and the layout. *Hwy. 1, St. Peter Parish, tel. 809/422–4900. 306 rooms. Facilities: 3 pools, 5 lighted tennis courts, squash courts, 9-hole golf course, restaurants, bars, boutiques, entertainment. AE, DC, MC, V. Expensive.*

King's Beach Hotel. The newly opened King's Beach, a property of Tropical Resort Ltd., has a two-story, semicircular design and draws a European clientele. *Hwy. 1, Road View, St. Peter*

Parish, tel. 809/422–1690. 57 rooms. Facilities: pool, restaurant, bar, shops, library, games room. AE, MC, V. Moderate.

St. Michael Parish **Grand Barbados Beach Resort.** Once a Holiday Inn, the Grand Barbados Beach Resort at Carlisle Bay is convenient to Bridgetown. Its renovated rooms have minibars, and refrigerators, hair dryers, and satellite TVs; 100 rooms have ocean views. "Executive floors" have a hospitality suite and secretarial services. Box 639, Bridgetown; on Carlisle Bay, St. Michael Parish, tel. 809/426–0890 or 800/223–9815. 133 rooms. Facilities: restaurant, secretarial services. AE, DC, MC, V. Expensive.

Cunard Paradise Beach Hotel. A recently completed renovation added a conference center and upgraded the rooms and public areas of the Cunard Paradise Beach Hotel, convenient to Bridgetown and popular with younger Canadians and Americans. The beach offers rental boats, water sports, and nocturnal goings-on for those who want constant activity. Hwy. 1, St. Michael Parish, tel. 809/424–0888. 172 rooms. Facilities: dining rooms, bar, entertainment. AE, DC, MC, V. Expensive.

Barbados Hilton International. A large resort just five minutes from Bridgetown, the Hilton International is for those who like activity and having plenty of other people around. Its attractions include an atrium lobby, a man-made beach 1,000 feet wide with full water sports, and lots of shops. The cuisine is "Hilton international." All rooms and suites have balconies. Needhams Point, St. Michael Parish, tel. 809/426–0200. 185 rooms. Facilities: pool, tennis courts, coffee shop, lounge. AE, CB, DC, MC, V. Moderate–Expensive.

Christ Church **Divi Southwinds Beach Hotel.** Situated on 20 lush acres, the
Parish Divi Southwinds offers rooms and luxury suites with private terraces or balconies, and the suites have fully equipped kitchens. The beach is fine white sand; complete scuba and water-sports activities are available. St. Lawrence, Christ Church Parish, tel. 800/367–3484. 160 rooms. Facilities: 3 pools, 2 lighted tennis courts, putting green, shopping arcade, beauty salon. AE, DC, MC, V. Very Expensive.

Sandy Beach Resort. All rooms face the sea at Sandy Beach, where there are drinks and entertainment poolside and the Green House Restaurant serves a weekly West Indian buffet. Water-sports activities include scuba-diving certification, deep-sea fishing, and harbor cruises. Worthing, Christ Church Parish, tel. 809/435–8000. 139 rooms. Facilities: pool, restaurant, bar, entertainment. AE, CB, DC, MC, V. Expensive.

Southern Palms. A plantation-style hotel on a 1,000-foot stretch of pink sand near the Dover Convention Center, Southern Palms is a convenient businessperson's hotel. You may choose from standard bedrooms, deluxe oceanfront suites with kitchenettes, and a four-bedroom penthouse. Other attractions are a full water-sports center, Le Petit Flambe dining room, and the Unicorn I disco. St. Lawrence, Christ Church Parish, tel. 809/428–7171. 93 rooms. Facilities: pool, tennis court, dining room, disco. AE, DC, MC, V. Expensive.

Barbados Windsurfing Club Hotel. A small hotel that began as a gathering place for windsurfing enthusiasts, the Barbados Windsurfing Club is now a complete school and center for the sport. The spacious and comfortable yet unpretentious rooms overlook the fishing village of Oistins on the south coast. The bar and restaurant overlook the water and offer weekly jazz nights. All sports can be arranged, but windsurfing (learning, practicing, and perfecting it) is king. *Maxwell, Christ Church Parish, tel. 809/428–9095. 15 rooms. Facilities: restaurant, bar, entertainment. AE, MC, V. Moderate.*

Casuarina Beach Club. This luxury apartment hotel on 900 feet of pink sand takes its name from the towering casuarina pines that surround it, and the quiet setting provides a dramatic contrast to that of the platinum-coast resorts. The bar and restaurant are on the beach. Scuba diving, golf, and other activities can be arranged. The Casuarina Beach is popular with those who prefer self-catering holidays in a secluded setting, convenient to nightlife and shopping. *St. Lawrence Gap, Christ Church Parish, tel. 809/428–3600. 100 rooms. Facilities: pool, tennis courts, squash courts, restaurant, bar. AE, MC, V. Moderate.*

★ **Ocean View.** Possibly the best-kept secret in the Caribbean, the 40 rooms and suites of this individualistic hideaway, house celebrities on their commute to private villas in Mustique and savvy travelers who know a good thing when they find it. Owner John Chandler places his personal antiques throughout his three-story grande dame nestled against the sea, adds great bouquets of tropical flowers everywhere, and calls it home. In-season, the downstairs Xanadu Club presents very good, off-off-Broadway reviews. *Hastings, Christ Church Parish, tel. 809/427–7821. 40 rooms. Facilities: restaurant and bar; supper club. AE, MC, V. Moderate.*

Sichris Hotel. The Sichris is a "discovery," more attractive inside than seen from the road, a comfortable and convenient self-contained resort that can be ideal for businesspeople who need a quiet place in which to work. Just minutes from the city, the air-conditioned one-bedroom suites all have kitchenettes and private balconies or patios. It's a walk of two or three minutes to the beach. *Worthing, Christ Church Parish, tel. 809/435–7930. 24 rooms. Facilities: pool, restaurant, bar. AE, MC, V. Moderate.*

Accra Beach Hotel. The Accra Beach offers neatly furnished housekeeping suites with dining rooms, cocktail lounges, beach bars, and water sports. *Rockley Beach, Christ Church Parish, tel. 809/427–7866 or 800/223–9815. 52 rooms. Facilities: dining room, lounge, beach bar, water-sports center. AE, MC, V. Inexpensive.*

St. Philip Parish **Crane Beach Hotel.** Although it has changed hands with alarming regularity, this remote hilltop property on a cliff overlooking the dramatic Atlantic coast remains one of the special places of Barbados. The Crane Beach has suites and one-bedroom apartments in the main building and additional bedrooms at the beach club next door. *Crane's Bay, St. Philip Parish, tel. 809/423–6220. 18 rooms. Facilities: 2 pools, restaurant, 2 bars. AE, DC, MC, V. Expensive.*

Marriott's Sam Lord's Castle. Set on the Atlantic coast about 14 miles east of Bridgetown, Sam Lord's Castle is not a castle with moat and towers but a sprawling great house surrounded by 71 acres of grounds, gardens, and beach. The seven rooms in the main house have canopied beds; downstairs, the public rooms have furniture by Sheraton, Hepplewhite, and Chippendale. Additional guest rooms in surrounding cottages have more conventional hotel furnishings. The beach is a mile long, the Wanderer Restaurant offers Continental cuisine, and there are even a few slot machines, as befits a pirate's lair. *Long Bay, St.*

Philip Parish, tel. 809/423-7350. 256 rooms. Facilities: 2 pools, lighted tennis courts, restaurant, entertainment. AE, DC, MC, V. Very Expensive.

St. Joseph Parish **Atlantis Hotel.** The Atlantis provides a warm, pleasant atmosphere in a pastoral location overlooking a majestically rocky Atlantic coast. The hotel is modest and in need of a bit of paint, yet the congeniality and the Bajan food more than make up for that. *Bathsheba, St. Joseph Parish, tel. 809/433-9445. 16 rooms. Facilities: dining room. No credit cards. Inexpensive.*

Rental Homes and Apartments Private homes are available for rental south of Bridgetown in the Hastings–Worthing area, along the St. James Parish coast, and in St. Peter Parish. The **Barbados Board of Tourism** (tel. 809/427-2623) has a listing of rental properties and prices.

Beyond the Blue. Two one-bedroom villas and a three-bedroom (three baths) villa with maid service and access to the beach and facilities of the Cunard Paradise Beach Resort are available year-round. *Willie Hassell, Black Rock, St. Michael Parish, tel. 809/424-1808. No credit cards.*

Caribbean Home Rentals. Cook, maid, gardener, airport pickup, and the delivery of rental cars are available with the 125 properties listed here. Rates range from $150 a night in the off-season for a one-bedroom cottage to $2,600 a week for a six-bedroom villa in high season. *Box 710, Palm Beach, FL 33480, tel. 407/833-4454. No credit cards.*

Time-Share Condominiums **Rockley Resort and Beach Club.** The Rockley Resort's air-conditioned one- and two-bedroom accommodations, with a balcony or a patio, are located about 5 miles from Bridgetown. On the grounds are a health club, six swimming pools, five tennis courts, a nine-hole golf course, squash courts, and volleyball and croquet facilities. A special playground for children, a free shuttle bus to the beach (five minutes), a dining room, and a cocktail lounge are further amenities. *Rockley Resort, Suite 512, Christ Church Parish, tel. 800/223-9815. 288 rooms. AE, CB, DC, MC, V.*

The Arts and Nightlife

The Arts **Barbados Art Council.** The gallery shows drawings, paintings, and other art, with a new show about every two weeks. *2 Pelican Village, Bridgetown, tel. 809/426-4385. Admission free. Open Mon.–Sat.*

Barbados Museum. Theater and a buffet dinner are the major attraction here twice a week in the courtyard. The professional Barbados Dance Theatre performs a show of history and folklore with terrific calypso, limbo, and stilt dancing. The costumes alone are worth a visit. The West Indian buffet is tasty, but don't arrive ravenous, for the line is long and slow (yet the desserts are worth waiting for). Stroll the museum exhibits before or after the performance. *Hwy. 7, Garrison Savannah, tel. 809/435-6900. Show and dinner, Sun. and Thurs., about $30. Reservations recommended.*

A selection of private art galleries offer Bajan and West Indian art at collectible prices. **Coffee and Cream** (Paradise Village, St. Lawrence Gap, Christ Church, tel. 809/428-2708) is dedicated to showing the work of local artists, paintings and mixed media, jewelry, wall hangings, sculptures, and prints. **The Stu-**

dio **Art Gallery** (Fairchild St., Bridgetown, tel. 809/427–5463), also exhibits local work (particularly that of Rachael Altman) and will frame purchases. The **Queen's Park Gallery** (Queen's Park, Bridgetown, tel. 809/427–2345) is run by the National Culture Foundation and is the island's largest gallery, presenting month-long exhibits. **Wild Feathers** (Edgecumbe Plantation, St. Philip, tel. 809/423–2346), owned by artists Joan and Jeff Skeet, is both a studio and an aviary, with the birds the Skeets lovingly care for depicted in intricate wood pieces (delivery can take up to a year). **Artwork** (Shop 5, Quayside Centre, Rockley, tel. 809/435–8112) is the most recent entry, selling only handmade items from carved wooden trains, pottery, and ceramic jewelry to watercolors and prints.

Nightlife When the sun goes down, the musicians come out, and folks go limin' in Barbados (anything from hanging out to a chat-up or jump-up). Competitions between reggae groups, steel bands, and calypso singers are major events, and tickets can be hard to come by, but give it a try.

Most of the large resorts have weekend shows aimed at visitors, and there is a selection of dinner shows that are a Barbados-only occasion. **1627 And All That** is a cultural folkloric dinner show held at the Barbados Museum on Thursdays and Sundays. There's transportation to and from your hotel, hot hors d'oeuvres, a buffet dinner (with a l-o-n-g line), an open bar, and a good show put on by the Barbados Dance Theatre that combines history and folklore with calypso, limbo, and stilt dancing. *Hwy. 7, Garrison Savannah, tel. 809/435–6900. Show and dinner, Sun. and Thurs., about $35. Reservations recommended. AE, DC, MC, V.*

If it's Tuesday, it must be the **Plantation Tropical Spectacular** at the Plantation and Garden Theatre, with the internationally known Merrymen making the music and dance. It's a high-energy calypso show with fire-eaters, flaming limbo dancers, steel bands, and calypso, preceded by dinner and drinks, for about $35. (Show and drinks only, about $17). *St. Lawrence Road, Christ Church Parish, tel. 809/428–5048. Reservations recommended. AE, DC, MC, V.*

The Xanadu is a December through April cabaret, and on Thursday and Friday nights, that's the hottest ticket in town. David McCarty, who danced on Broadway and with the New York City Ballet, has joined forces with chanteuse Jean Emerson, and, along with local strutters, they put on the best show in town. Dinner in the upstairs flower-decked dining room is $40 (with show); cabaret admission only, approximately, $12.50. *Ocean View Hotel, Hastings, tel. 809/427–7821. Reservations required.*

Island residents have their own favorite night spots that change with the seasons. High on the list this year is **After Dark** (St. Lawrence Gap, Christ Church, tel. 809/435–6547), with the longest bar on the island and a jazz-club annex.

Harbour Lights claims to be the the "home of the party animal," and most any night features live music with dancing under the stars. *On the Bay, Marine Villa, Bay St., St. Michael, tel. 809/436–7225.*

Disco moves are made on the floor at the **Hippo Disco** at the Barbados Beach Village Hotel *(St. James, tel. 809/425–1440)*, and above it, where dancers girate in an overhead cage.

Another dusky disco, **Club Miliki,** (tel. 809/422–4900) takes center stage at the Heywoods Resort in St. Peter.

A late-night (after 11) excursion to **Baxter Road** is de rigueur for midnight Bajan street snacks, local rum, great gossip, and good lie-telling. **Enid & Livy's** and **Collins** are just two of the many long-standing favorites. The later, the better.

Bars and Inns Barbados supports the rum industry in more than 1,600 "rum shops," simple bars where men congregate to discuss the world's ills, and in more sophisticated inns, where you'll find world-class rum drinks and the island's renowned Mount Gay and Cockspur rums. The following offer welcoming spirits: **The Ship Inn** (St. Lawrence Gap, Christ Church Parish, tel. 809/428–9605), **The Coach House** (Paynes Bay, St. James Parish, tel. 809/432–1163), **Harry's Oasis** (St. Lawrence, Christ Church, no phone), **Bert's Bar** at the Abbeville (Rockley, Christ Church Parish, tel. 809/427–7524), serve the best daiqueries in town . . . any town. **The Boat Yard** (Bay Street, Bridgetown, tel. 809/429–4806), **Barbados Windsurfing Club** (Maxwell, Christ Church Parish, tel. 809/428–9095), and **TGI Boomers** (St. Lawrence Gap, Christ Church Parish, tel. 809/428–8439).

6 Bonaire

by Pamela Bloom Bonaire is a stark desert island, perfect for the rugged individualist who is turned off by the overcommercialized high life of the other Antillean islands. The island boasts a spectacular array of exotic wildlife—from fish to fowl to flowers—that will keep nature-watchers awestruck for days. It's the kind of place where you'll want to rent a Jeep and go dashing off madly in search of the wild flamingo, the wild iguana, or even the wild yellow-winged parrot named the Bonairian lora.

A mecca for divers, Bonaire offers one of the most unspoiled reef systems in the world. The water is so clear that you can lean over the dock and look the fish straight in the eye.

Kudos for the preservation of the 112-square-mile isle go to the people and government of Bonaire, who in 1970, with the help of the World Wildlife Fund, developed the Bonaire Marine Park—a model of ecological conservation. The underwater park includes, roughly, the entire coastline, from the high-water tidemark to a depth of 200 feet, all of which is protected by strict laws. Because the Bonairians desperately want to keep their paradise intact, any diver with a reckless streak is firmly requested to go elsewhere.

This is not the island for connoisseurs of fine cuisine, shopping maniacs, or those who prefer hobnobbing with society. The island itself may be lacking in splendor, but what lies off its shores keeps divers enthralled.

Before You Go

Tourist Information Contact the **Bonaire Government Tourist** Office (275 7th Ave., 19th Floor, New York, NY 10001, tel. 212/242–7707) for advice and information on planning your trip.

Arriving and Departing
By Plane **American** (tel. 800/433–7300) and **ALM** (tel. 800/327–7230) will get you to Bonaire. ALM flies nonstop to Bonaire from New York once a week and from Miami twice a week. American offers daily flights from New York to Curaçao and Aruba, but you must connect to Bonaire through ALM. ALM also has daily flights to Curaçao from Miami, with a connecting flight to Bonaire.

From the Airport Bonaire's airport is tiny, but you'll appreciate its welcoming ambience. The customs check is perfunctory if you are arriving from another Dutch isle; otherwise you will have to show proof of citizenship, plus a return or ongoing ticket. Rental cars and taxis are available at the airport, but try to arrange the pickup through your hotel.

Passports and Visas U.S. and Canadian citizens need only offer proof of identity, so a passport, notarized birth certificate, or voter registration card will suffice. British subjects may carry a British Visitor's Passport, available from any post office. All other visitors must carry an official passport. In addition, any visitor who steps onto the island must have a return or ongoing ticket and must confirm that reservation 48 hours before departure.

Customs and Duties U.S. residents returning to the United States may bring $400 worth of duty-free articles. Included may be one carton of cigarettes as well as one quart of liquor per person over 21. Articles in excess of $400 up to $1,000 are assessed at a flat rate of 10%.

Language The official language is Dutch, but few speak it, and even then only on official occasions. The street language is Papiamento, a

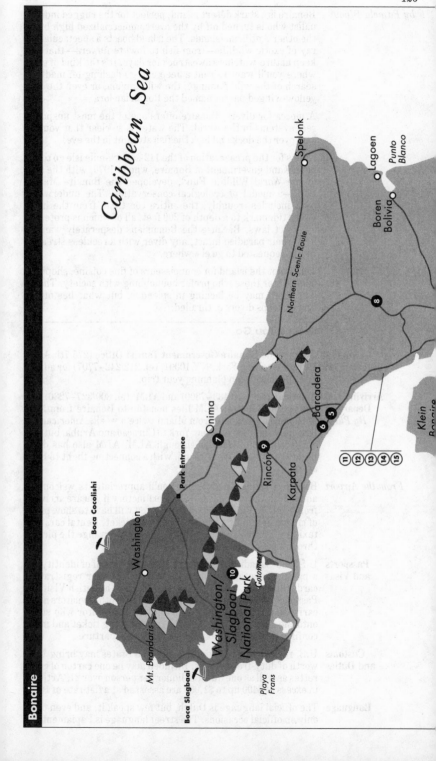

Bonaire

Caribbean Sea

Spelonk

Lagoen

Punto Blanco

Boren

Bolivia

Northern Scenic Route

8

Barcadera

5

6

Klein Bonaire

⑪ ⑫ ⑬ ⑭ ⑮

9

Rincón

Karpata

Onima

7

Park Entrance

Boca Cocolishi

Washington

Mt. Brandaris

Washington/ Slagbaai National Park

10

Cotomeer

Playa Frans

Boca Slagbaai

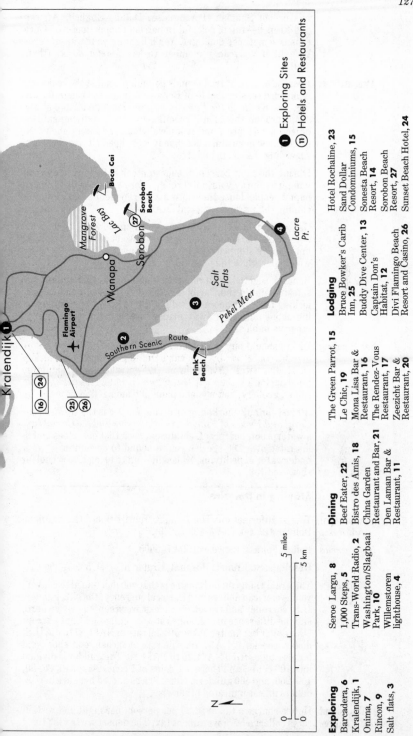

● Exploring Sites

⑪ Hotels and Restaurants

Exploring

Barcadera, **6**
Kralendijk, **1**
Onima, **7**
Rincon, **9**
Salt flats, **3**

Seroe Largu, **8**
1,000 Steps, **5**
Trans-World Radio, **2**
Washington/Slagbaai
Park, **10**
Willemstoren
lighthouse, **4**

Dining

Beef Eater, **22**
Bistro des Amis, **18**
China Garden
Restaurant and Bar, **21**
Den Laman Bar &
Restaurant, **11**

The Green Parrot, **15**
Le Chic, **19**
Mona Lisa Bar &
Restaurant, **16**
The Rendez-Vous
Restaurant, **17**
Zeezicht Bar &
Restaurant, **20**

Lodging

Bruce Bowker's Carib
Inn, **25**
Buddy Dive Center, **13**
Captain Don's
Habitat, **12**
Divi Flamingo Beach
Resort and Casino, **26**

Hotel Rochaline, **23**
Sand Dollar
Condominiums, **15**
Sonesta Beach
Resort, **14**
Sorobon Beach
Resort, **27**
Sunset Beach Hotel, **24**

mixture of Spanish, Portuguese, Dutch, English, African, and French—full of colorful Bonairian idioms that even Curaçaoans sometimes don't get. You'll light up your waiter's eyes, though, if you can remember to say *Masha danki* (thank you).

Precautions Because of violent trade winds pounding against the rocks, the windward (eastern) side of Bonaire is much too rough for diving. The *Guide to the Bonaire Marine Park* (available at dive shops around the island) specifies the level of diving skill required for 44 sites, and it knows what it's talking about. No matter how beautiful a beach may look, heed all warning signs regarding the rough undertow.

During the rainy season, the mosquitoes in Bonaire are nearly vampiric. Spray your hotel room before you go to bed. Smart, happy people douse themselves with repellent all day long, including their arms, legs, and face.

Get an orientation on what stings underwater and what doesn't. As the island's joke goes, you won't appreciate Bonaire until you've stepped on a long-spined urchin, but by then, you won't appreciate the joke.

Bonaire used to have a reputation for being the friendliest and safest island in the Caribbean, but lately, even residents are locking their car doors for safety. Don't leave your camera lying about, and tuck away money, credit cards, jewelry, and other valuables.

Further Reading Divers should buy the island's diving bible, *Guide to the Bonaire Marine Park*, by Tom van t'Hof, for in-depth descriptions of 44 dive sites. Available at the entrance to Washington/Slagbaai Park is the *Field Guide*, which details the park's geography, geology, history, and plant and animal life.

A must for any snorkeling or diving fanatic is the *Guide to the Coral and Fishes of Florida, the Bahamas and the Caribbean*, a waterproof, boatproof, childproof book that describes and illustrates over 260 species you're bound to encounter on your underwater expeditions. Kids will want to bring it to school for show-and-tell.

Staying in Bonaire

Important Addresses **Tourist Information:** The **Bonaire Tourist Board** (Kaya Simon Bolivar #12, tel. 599/7–8322/8649).

Emergencies **Police:** For assistance call 599/7–8000.

Hospitals: St. Francis Hospital, Kralendijk (tel. 599/7–8900).

Currency The great thing about Bonaire is that you don't need to convert your American dollars into the local currency, the NAf guilder. U.S. currency and traveler's checks are accepted everywhere, and the difference in exchange rates is negligible. Banks accept U.S. dollar banknotes at the official rate of NAf 1.77 to the U.S. dollar, checks at NAf 1.79. The rate of exchange at shops and hotels ranges from NAf 1.75 to NAf 1.80. The guilder is divided into 100 cents, and there are coins of 1 cent, 2½, 5, 10, 25, 50, 100, 250, and 500 guilders. Note: Prices quoted here are in U.S. dollars unless indicated otherwise.

Taxes and Service Charges Hotels charge a tax of $2.30 per person, per night and restaurants collect a 5% government tax. The departure tax is $10.

Hotels usually add a 10%–15% service charge to your bill; most restaurants add 15%.

Guided Tours If you don't like to drive, **Bonaire Sightseeing Tours** (tel. 599/7–8300, ext. 225) will chauffeur you around the island (about $10 per person) on two different two-hour tours, north and south. A complete three-hour expedition of the island goes for $15 per person, and parties of four may spend up to four hours exploring Washington National Park at a cost of $17 per person.

Getting Around You can zip about the island in a Suzuki Jeep. Scooters and bicycles, which are also available, are less practical but can be fun, too. Just remember that there are at least 20 miles of unpaved road; the roller-coaster hills at the national park require strong stomachs; and during the rainy season, mud—called Bonairian snow—is unpleasant. All traffic stays to the right.

Rental Cars **Budget** has jeeps available from its three locations: Head Office (tel. 599/7–8300, ext. 25/242), at the airport (tel. 599/7–8315), and the Flamingo Beach Resort & Casino (tel. 599/7–830, ext. 234). It's always a good idea to wire in advance: Cable BUDGET BONAIRE; telex 1280 BTC NA.

Scooters For scooters and two-seater 80-cc Yamahas, try **Happy Chappy Rentals** (tel. 599/7–8761) or the **Bonaire Trading Company** (tel. 599/7–8300, ext. 225). Rates are approximately $15 per day.

Bicycles The **Sunset Beach Hotel** (tel. 599/7–8448) and the **Divi Flamingo Beach Resort** (tel. 599/7–8285) rent bicycles by the half hour.

Taxis Taxis are unmetered; they have fixed rates. A trip from the airport to your hotel will cost about $4; from Sunset Beach Hotel to the Flamingo Beach Resort, $5. Fares increase from 8 PM to midnight by 25% and from midnight to 6 AM by 50%. Taxi drivers are usually knowledgeable enough about the island to conduct half-day tours; they charge about $25–$30. Inquire at your hotel.

Telephones and Mail It's difficult for visitors to Bonaire to get involved in dramatic, heart-wrenching phone conversations or *any* phone discussions requiring a degree of privacy: There are no telephones in any hotel rooms on the island. All calls must be made from hotel front desks or from the central telephone company office in Kralendijk. To call Bonaire from the United States, dial 011–599–7 + the local four-digit number.

Airmail postage rates to the United States are NAf1.00 for letters and NAf.65 for postcards; to Canada, NAf1.10 for letters and NAf.70 for postcards; to Britain, NAf1.25 for letters and NAf.80 for postcards.

Opening and Closing Times Stores in the Kralendijk area are generally open Monday through Saturday 8–noon and 2–6 PM. On Sundays and holidays, when cruise ships arrive, most shops open for a few extra hours. Few restaurants besides those affiliated to hotels are open for lunch.

Beaches

In general, beaches in Bonaire are not runways for voyeurs—anybody with a roving eye is usually underwater looking at the fish. Consequently, figure-shy sunbathers will find Bonaire a pleasant, private place in which to relax. Don't come expecting Aruba-length stretches of glorious white sand. Bonaire's beaches are smaller, and though the water is indeed blue (several shades of it, in fact), the sand is not always white. You can have your pick of beach in Bonaire according to color: pink, black, or the more familiar white.

Hermit crabs can be found along the shore at **Boca Cocolishi,** a black-sand beach in Washington/Slagbaai Park on the northeast coast. Tiny bits of dried coral and shells form the basin and beach, their dark hues giving the sand an unusual look. Virtually free of current, the spot is perfect for a nontaxing swim or an intimate picnic *à deux.* To get there, take the Northern Scenic Route to the park, then ask for directions at the gate.

Also inside Washington Park is **Boca Slagbaai,** a stretch of fine white powder that is totally free of coral at some points. The gentle surf makes it an ideal place for swimming, especially for children.

As the name suggests, the sand at **Pink Beach** boasts a pinkish tint that takes on a magical shimmer in the late-afternoon sun. The water is suitable for swimming, snorkeling, and scuba diving. Take the South Scenic Route on the western side of the island, past the Trans-World Radio station, close to the slave huts. A favorite hang-10 site for Bonairians on the weekend, it is virtually deserted during the week.

For uninhibited sun worshipers who'd rather enjoy the rays in the altogether, the private, "clothes-optional" beach at the **Sorobon Beach Resort** offers calm water and clean sand. Nonguests are welcome for a small fee.

If you enjoy water sports, find out which beaches are best for a specific sport: *See* Participant Sports, below.

Exploring Bonaire

Numbers in the margin correspond with points of interest on the Bonaire map.

Kralendijk
① Bonaire's capital city of **Kralendijk** (population: 2,500) is five minutes from the airport and a short walk from the Carib Inn and the Flamingo Beach Resort. There's really not much to explore here, but there are a few sights worth noting in this small, very tidy city.

Kralendijk has one main drag, J. A. Abraham Boulevard, which turns into **Breedestraat** (Broad Street) in the center of town. Along it are most of the island's major department stores, boutiques, restaurants, duty-free shops, and jewelry stores (*see* Shopping, below).

Crossing Breedestraat, opposite the Spritzer & Fuhrmann jewelry store, is **Kerkweg Street,** with several small supermarkets, the ALM office, a handful of snack shops, and some of the better restaurants, including Bistro des Amis and Rendez Vous (*see* Dining, below). Walk down the narrow waterfront avenue called C. F. B. Hellmundweg, which leads straight to the **North** and **South piers.** Along this route you will see **Fort Oranje,** with cannons pointing to the sea. Throughout the week, many seagoing vessels dock in the harbor, including the *Aquanaut Holiday,* a diver's cruise ship, and the *Freewinds,* owned by the Scientology Church. The elegant white structure that looks like a tiny Greek temple is the **Fish Market,** where local fishermen sell their early-morning haul.

Time Out | **Rendez Vous Restaurant** (3 Kaya L. D. Gerharts, tel. 599/7–8454) is a bistrolike café that serves soups, salads, and terrific vegetable entrées for lunch. The restaurant's terrace is an ideal locale for people watching.

Elsewhere on the Island | A complete tour around the 24-mile-long island is essential to really "do" Bonaire. Two tours, north and south, are possible; both will take from a few hours to a full day, depending upon whether you stop to snorkel, swim, dive, or lounge.

South Bonaire | The trail south from Kralendijk is chock-full of icons—both natural and man-made—that tell the minisaga of Bonaire. Rent a Jeep (a heavy-treaded car will do, but during the rainy months this place becomes a virtual mudslide) and head south along the South Scenic Route.

❷ The first icon you'll come to is the unexpected symbol of modernism—the towering 500-foot antennas of **Trans-World Radio,** one of the most powerful stations in Christian broadcasting. From here, evangelical programs and gospel music are transmitted daily in 20 languages to countries worldwide, including those of the Eastern bloc.

❸ Keep on cruising about three more miles to the **salt flats,** voluptuous white drifts that look something like huge mounds of vanilla ice cream. Harvested twice a year, the "ponds" are owned by the Antilles International Salt Company, which has reactivated the 19th-century salt industry with great success. (One reason for that success is that the ocean on this part of the island is higher than the land—which makes irrigation a snap.) Keep a lookout for the three 30-foot obelisks—white, blue, and pink—which were used to guide the trade boats coming to pick up the salt. On this stark landscape, these obelisks look decidedly phallic; today, the blue one is used as a point of reference to direct traffic.

The gritty history of the salt industry is revealed down the road in **Rode Pan,** the site of two groups of tiny slave huts. During the 19th century the salt workers, imported slaves from Africa, worked the fields by day, then crawled into these huts at night to sleep, returning to their homes in Rincon for the weekend. In recent years, the government has restored the huts to their original simplicity, complete with cane-thatch roofs.

❹ Regain your bearings and head south to **Willemstoren,** Bonaire's first lighthouse, built in 1837 and still in use. Check out the shipwreck near the shore here—legend has it that the skipper just didn't take directions well.

Rounding the tip of the island, head north and notice how the waves, driven by the trade winds, play a crashing symphony against the rocks. Locals make a habit of stopping here to collect pieces of driftwood in spectacular shapes. To the north are two of the most picturesque beaches in Bonaire—**Sorobon Beach** and **Boca Cai** at Lac Bay. The road here winds through otherworldly desert terrain, full of organ-pipe cacti and spiny-trunk mangroves—huge stumps of saltwater trees that rise out of the marshes like witches. At Boca Cai, you'll be impressed by the huge piles of conch shells discarded by local fishermen. (Sift through them; they make great gifts—but pack them carefully.) On the weekends at Cai, live bands play daily from 10 to 4, and there's beer and food available at the local restaurant. When the mosquitoes arrive in late afternoon, it's time to hightail it home.

North Bonaire The northern tour takes you right into the heart of Bonaire's natural wonders—desert gardens of towering cacti, tiny coastal coves, dramatically shaped coral grottoes, and plenty of fantastic panoramas. A snappy excursion with the requisite photo stops will take about 2½ hours, but if you pack your swimsuit and a hefty picnic basket (forget finding a Burger King or any other restaurant outside Kralendijk), you could spend the entire day exploring this northern sector, including a few hours snorkeling in Washington Park.

Head out from Kralendijk on the Breedestraat until it turns into the Northern Scenic Route on the outskirts of town. Fifteen minutes north of the Sunset Beach Hotel is a site called **❺ 1,000 Steps,** a limestone staircase carved right out of the cliff on the left side of the road. Actually, there are only 67 steps, but if you take the trek down them, you'll discover a great place to snorkel and scuba dive.

Following the route northward, look closely for a turnoff marked Vista Al Mar Restaurant. A few yards ahead, you'll discover some stone steps that lead down into a cave full of stalactites and vegetation. Once used to trap goats, this cave, **❻** called **Barcadera,** is one of the oldest in Bonaire; there's even a tunnel that looks intriguingly spooky.

Note that once you pass the antennas of the Radio Nederland, you cannot turn back to Kralendijk. The road becomes one-way, and you will have to follow the cross-island road to Rincon and return via the main road through the center of the island.

If you continue toward the northern curve of the island, the green storage tanks of the **Bonaire Petroleum Corporation** become visible. The road to Rincon and Washington Park is clearly marked. The route to the left will carry you along the **❼** east coast to **Onima.** Small signposts direct the way to a three-foot limestone ledge that juts out like a partially formed cave entrance. Inside you'll find red-stained designs and symbols inscribed on the limestone, said to have been the handiwork of the Arawak Indians when they inhabited the island centuries ago.

❽ Follow that same fork and you'll come to **Seroe Largu,** the highest point on the southern part of the isle. During the day, a winding path leads to a magnificent view of Kralendijk's rooftops; at night, the twinkling city lights below make this a romantic stop. If you've got some time, sit on one of the stone benches and watch the friendly turquoise-footed lizards slithering about. They rely on tourists for their main source of crumbs, but if they should happen to ignore you, throw a pebble near them and they'll trot right over.

If you bear right at the fork south of the park you'll pass **❾** through **Rincon**—a well-kept cluster of pastel cottages and century-old buildings that constitute Bonaire's oldest village. Watch your driving—herds of goats often sit right in the middle of the main drag.

Washington/ Once a plantation producing divi divi trees (whose pods were *Slagbaai Park* used for tanning animal skins), aloe (used for medicinal lo-**❿** tions), charcoal, and goats, **Washington/Slagbaai Park** is now a model of conservation, designed to maintain fauna, flora, and geological treasures in their natural state. Visitors may easily tour the 15,000-acre tropical desert terrain along the dirt roads. Although well marked, the roads sometimes rise and fall like a roller-coaster, consequently four-wheel drive is a must. (Think twice about coming here if it rained the day before—the mud you may encounter will be more than inconvenient.) There are two different routes: The long one (21 miles) is marked by yellow arrows; the short one (15 miles) is marked by green arrows. Goats and donkeys may dart across the road, and if you keep your eyes peeled, you may catch sight of large, camouflaged iguanas in the shrubbery. Some folks even look out for shooting cacti.

Bird-watchers are really in their element here. Right inside the park's gate, flamingos roost on the salt pad known as **Salina Mathijs,** and exotic parakeets dot the foot of **Mt. Brandaris,** Bonaire's highest peak at 746 feet. Some 130 species of colorful birds fly in and out of the shrubbery in the park. Keep your eyes open and your binoculars at hand. (For choice beach sites in the park *see* Beaches, above.) *The park is open daily 8–5. Admission: $2 adults, children under 15 free. Swimming, snorkeling, and scuba diving are permitted, but visitors are requested not to frighten the animals or remove anything from the grounds. There is absolutely no hunting, fishing, or camping allowed. A useful guidebook to the park is available at the entrance to the park for about $4.*

What to See and Do with Children

Captain Don's Habitat offers a **See Under Sea** program, in which children 5–16 can learn to snorkel. They also have a **Family Week** in August, with packages that provide a variety of activities, in and out of the water, for children (*see* Lodging, below).

The Sand Dollar condominiums have the **Sand Penny Club** for the children of guests, where children can learn to snorkel, and participate in a number of activites and games (*see* Lodging, below).

The **Sunset Beach Hotel, Divi Flamingo Beach Resort,** and the **Sonesta Beach Resort** also offer family packages and programs for children (*see* Lodging, below).

Off the Beaten Track

Spiny-legged wild flamingos—affectionately called "pink clouds"—at first look like swizzlesticks. But they're magnificent birds to observe—and there are about 15,000 of them in Bonaire. The best time to catch them at home is March–May, when they tend to their blue-plumed young. One of their favorite hangouts is in **Gotomeer,** a saltwater lagoon on the north coast, easily reached by the Northern Scenic Route. At **Playa Frans,** on the northwest curve of the island, you're also sure to make a sighting, with a few turkeys, chickens, and ducks thrown in for good measure. Right inside the gate of **Washington/Slagbaai Park** is another flamingo haunt. And in the south, the birds camp out at the salt ponds, site of their largest breeding grounds.

Participant Sports

Horseback Riding   Guided trips may be arranged at the **Tinis Stable** through the Sunset Beach Hotel or Captain Don's Habitat (*see* Lodging, below).

Scuba Diving   Bonaire has the best reef diving this side of Australia's Great Barrier Reef. The island is unique primarily for its incredible dive sites; it takes only 5–25 minutes to reach your site, and many of the reefs have very sudden, steep drops. General visibility runs 60 to 100 feet, except during surges in November. An enormous range of coral can be seen, from knobby brain and giant brain coral to elkhorn, staghorn, mountainous star, and gorgonian, as well as the black coral that locals use to handcraft jewelry. You're also likely to encounter schools of parrotfish, surgeonfish, angelfish, eels, snappers, and groupers.

The well-policed Bonaire Marine Park, roughly the entire coastline around Bonaire and Klein Bonaire, remains an underwater wonder because visitors take the rules here seriously. Do not even think about (1) spearfishing, (2) dropping anchor, or (3) touching, stepping on, or collecting coral.

Dive Operations   All the hotels listed in this guide, with the exception of the Hotel Rochaline, have dive centers. The competition for quality and variety is fierce. Before making a room reservation, inquire about specific dive/room packages that are available. Many of the dive shops also have boutiques where you can purchase T-shirts, color slides showing underwater views, postcards, and tropical jewelry. Some of the larger centers include **Bonaire Scuba Center** (Sunset Beach Hotel; write Box 775, Morgan, NJ 08879, or call tel. 201/566–8866 or 800/526–2370), **Buddy Dive Resort** (tel. 599/7–8647/8065), **Habitat Dive Center** (Captain Don's Habitat; write Maduro Travel, 1080 Port Blvd., Miami, FL 33132, or call 800/327–6709), and **Peter Hughes Dive Bonaire** (Flamingo Beach Resort; contact Divi Hotels, tel. 800/367–3484 or 607/277–3484).

Dive Sites   The *Guide to the Bonaire Marine Park* lists 44 sites that have been identified and marked by moorings. In the past year, dive expert Don Stewart has added several sites through a conservation program called Sea Tether. Guides associated with the various dive centers can give you more complete directions. The following are a few popular sites to whet your appetite; these and selected other sites are pinpointed on our Bonaire Diving map.

Take the track down to the shore just behind Trans-World Radio station; dive in and swim south to **Angel City,** one of the shallowest and most popular sites in the reef complex called **Alice in Wonderland.** The boulders and green and tan coral are home to black margates, spanish hogfish, gray snappers, and the large purple sponge tube.

Calabas Reef, located off the Flamingo Beach Hotel, is the island's most frequently dived site. All divers using the hotel's facilities take their warm-up dive here where they can inspect the wreck sunk by Don Stewart for just this purpose. The site is replete with Christmas-tree sponges and fire coral adhering to the ship's hull. Fish life is frenzied, with the occasional octopus putting in an appearance.

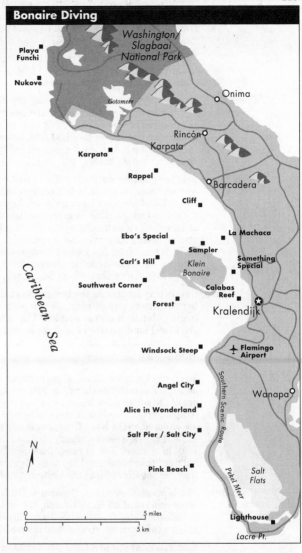

Bonaire Diving

Playa Funchi

Nukove

Washington/ Slagbaai National Park

Gotomeer

Onima

Rincón

Karpata

Karpata

Rappel

Barcadera

Cliff

Ebo's Special

La Machaca

Sampler

Carl's Hill

Klein Bonaire

Something Special

Southwest Corner

Calabas Reef

Forest

Kralendijk

Windsock Steep

Flamingo Airport

Angel City

Wanapa

Southern Scenic Route

Alice in Wonderland

Salt Pier / Salt City

Caribbean Sea

N

Pink Beach

Salt Flats

Pekel Meer

0   5 miles

0   5 km

Lighthouse

Lacre Pt.

You'll need to catch a boat to reach **Forest,** a dive site off the coast of Klein Bonaire, so named for the abundant black-coral forest found there. Responsible for occasional currents, this site gets a lot of fish action, including what's been described as a "friendly" spotted eel who lives in a cave.

Rappel is one of the most spectacular dives, right near the Karpata Ecological Center. The shore is a sheer cliff and the lush coral growth is home to an unusual variety of marine life, including orange seahorses, squid, spiny lobsters, and a spotted trunkfish named Sir Timothy, who will befriend you for a banana or a piece of cheese.

Something Special, just south of the entrance of the marina, is famous for its garden eels that slither around the relatively shallow sand terrace.

Windsock Steep, situated in front of the small beach opposite the airport runway, is an excellent first-dive spot and a popular place for snorkeling close to town.

Snorkeling Don't consider snorkeling the cowardly diver's sport; in Bonaire the experience is anything but elementary. For only $4–$8 per day, you can rent a mask, fins, and snorkel at any hotel with a water-sports center (*see* Lodging, below). The better spots for snorkeling are on the leeward side of the island, where you have access to the reefs.

Swimming Beaches good for swimming can be found anywhere along the western coast of the island. Excellent sites are by the **Sunset Beach Hotel** and the **Flamingo Beach Resort,** where there is no undertow and the slope from the beach to deep water is gradual. Or hitch a ride on a diving expedition to **Klein Bonaire,** a tiny stretch of land where you can spend the day playing king of the dune. Except for a few forgotten sneakers, there is absolutely *nothing* on Klein Bonaire, so remember to take some food along. And don't miss the boat back home.

Tennis Guests play for free on the two courts at the **Sunset Beach Hotel;** nonguests pay to play, $5 per hour (day), $15 per hour (night). Tennis is also available at the **Sand Dollar Beach Club** and **Club Flamingo** (Divi Flamingo Resort and Casino).

Shopping

You can get to know all the shops in Bonaire in a matter of a few hours, but sometimes there's no better way to enjoy some time out of the sun and sea than to go shopping, particularly if your companion is a dive fanatic and you're not. Almost all the shops are situated on the Kaya Grandi or in adjacent streets and tiny malls. There are several snazzy boutiques worth a browse. One word of caution: Buy as many flamingo T-shirts as you want, but don't take home anything made of goatskin or tortoiseshell; they are not allowed into the United States.

Good Buys The hippest boutique in Bonaire is **Birds of Paradise** (in the small courtyard off Kaya Grandi, tel. 599/7–8998), with merchandise ranging from flamingo earrings and other desert-chic jewelry to Esprit sportswear and stylish swimsuits.

Kibracha Souvenir and Gifts (33 Kaya Corsow, no phone) features wall hangings, exotic shells and driftwood, embroidered dresses, and Dutch curios.

Home Collection Shop (Kaya Grandi, tel. 599/7–8460) specializes in decorations for the home, including locally made *chibichibi* (sugar birds), tile paintings, Dutch souvenirs, and unusual stuffed fish and cloth parrots.

Spritzer & Fuhrmann (29 Kaya Grandi, tel. 599/7–8466) is the duty-free source for Baccarat, Lalique, Royal Doulton, Minton china, silver souvenir spoons, gold jewelry and watches.

Aries Boutique (33 Kaya Grandi, tel. 599/7–8901) is good for a browse in casual men's and women's fashions. It's also the place to pick up picnicking goods, such as Dutch cheeses, crackers, chocolates, and fine wines.

One shop that's sure to inspire a purchase is the **Ki Bo Ke Pakus,** or **What Do You Want?** (Flamingo Beach Hotel, tel. 599/7–8285), with an exquisite line of batiks, dashikis, and island-made jewelry. Swimsuits and beach cover-ups are very chi-chi, with prices to match.

Things Bonaire (Sunset Beach Hotel, no phone) offers T-shirts, souvenirs, and guidebooks.

A government-funded crafts center, **Fundashon Arte Industri Bonairiano** (J. A. Abraham Blvd., Kralendijk), offers locally made necklaces of coral in a variety of colors, hand-painted shirts and dresses, and the "fresh craft of the day."

Other locally made ceramics can be found at **MOR-ANG Ceramics** (J. A. Abraham Blvd., just north of Flamingo Beach).

Dining

Gourmets have not been sneaking off to Bonaire for five-star cuisine, but with a healthy variety of dining experiences, visitors should not go home hungry.

The most highly recommended restaurants are indicated by a star ★ .

Category	Cost*
Expensive	over $25
Moderate	$15–$25
Inexpensive	under $15

per person, excluding drinks, service, and sales tax (5%)

Beef Eater. This is a Bonairian-run restaurant with old-English decor, but don't let the name mislead you into thinking it's a steak-'n'-aler. The amiable service and the likes of shrimp thermidor, pepper steaks, and fresh catch of the day make for adequate dining. A bar in the back sometimes features rowdy Bonairians—feel free to join in. *12 Kralendijk, Kaya Grandi, tel. 599/7–8081. Reservations required. AE, DC, MC, V. Expensive.*

★ **Bistro des Amis.** Expensive but worth every guilder. The Bistro's creative French menu and the sensual Folies Bergère ambience have all been designed by chef-owner Jan Van Tilburg. Try to get this engaging Dutchman to talk about his specialties (though he's usually frantic in the kitchen), then savor his unforgettable red-pepper soup, duck with red-wine sauce, mousse of smoked eel, and red snapper steamed in fish stock. Or just have a drink around the mahogany bar. *1 Kaya L. D. Gerharts, tel. 599/7–8003. Reservations required. AE, MC, V. Closed Sun. Expensive.*

Den Laman Bar & Restaurant. The 9,000-foot aquarium that once enlivened a visit to this open-air seafood restaurant is no more, and it's a shame. Without the distractions of the "ocean-floor" show, the service seems even more lethargic and the marinated conch Kralendijk even tougher. The red snapper Creole is still a winner, though. *77 Gouverneur Debrotweg, next to the Sunset Beach Hotel, tel. 599/ 7–8955. Reservations required. AE, MC, V. Closed Mon. Expensive.*

★ **Le Chic.** A renovated 80-year-old home in town, Le Chic, with its French menu and pale-green decor, is leagues away from snorkels and wetsuits, so don't go grubby. A Dutch-schooled Aruban chef prepares specialties, such as *Le Pateau*, a meat-fish combo with two sauces, and interesting desserts. *Kaya C. E. B. Hellmund, tel. 599/7–8617. Reservations suggested. AE, DC, MC, V. Expensive.*

The Green Parrot. This restaurant, which is located on the dock of the Sand Dollar Beach Club premises, features the biggest hamburgers and the best dacquiris on the island. The view of the setting sun from this casual eatery is spectacular. *Kaya Grandi, tel. 599/7–8738. Reservations accepted. AE, MC, V. Moderate.*

★ **Mona Lisa Bar & Restaurant.** The restaurant offers local, Dutch, and Indonesian dishes at unbeatable prices. Its most famous plate is the pork tenderloin drizzled with a special peanut-butter sauce. Somehow, Mona Lisa has become renowned for fresh vegetables, though God knows where they come from since nearly everything in Bonaire has to be imported. This is a late-night hangout for local shmoozing, and its bar can make light snacks until about 2 AM. *15 Kaya Grandi, tel. 599/7–8718. No reservations. AE, MC, V. Moderate.*

The Rendez-Vous Restaurant. From the shaded terrace of this bistrolike café, watch the world of Bonaire go by as you fill up on warm bread, hearty soups, seafood, steaks, and vegetarian specialties. Or munch on light pastries accompanied by steamy espresso. Those in the know swear the Rendez Vous is the place to go to recover from disco-burnout. *3 Kaya L. D. Gerharts, tel. 599/7–8454. No reservations. AE. Closed Sun. morning and Tues. Moderate.*

Zeezicht Bar & Restaurant. Zeezicht (pronounced zay-zeekt and meaning sea view) is one of the better restaurants open for lunch in town. Dining is on the terrace overlooking the harbor or upstairs inside an air-conditioned enclave. Local fishermen are dedicated to this hangout, especially for the ceviche, conch sandwiches, local snails in hot sauce, and the Zeezicht special soup with conch, fish, shrimp, and oysters. *Kaya Corsow, across from the old fish market, tel. 599/7–8434. No reservations. AE, MC, V. Moderate.*

China Garden Restaurant and Bar. Despite its name, this place has an everything-you-could-ever-want menu, from American sandwiches to shark's fin soup, steaks, lobster, even omelets. The sweet-and-sour dishes are not bad. The cable TV at the large bar can be handy, but in general the decor is somewhat sleazy. *47 Kaya Grandi, tel. 599/7–8480. No reservations. No credit cards. Closed Tues. Inexpensive.*

Lodging

The most highly recommended lodgings are indicated by a star ★.

Category	Cost*
Expensive	$95–$150
Moderate	$55–$95
Inexpensive	under $55

* All prices are for a standard double room for two, excluding a $2.30 per person, per night tax and a 15% service charge.

Hotels **Sunset Beach Hotel.** The island's largest hotel, the Sunset Beach complex recently underwent extensive renovation. The property is spread across 12 acres and encompasses the 600-foot beach Playa Leche. For divers, the Dive Inn offers a complete scuba and underwater photography center plus special packages that include diving and the free use of all watersports equipment. Nondivers can rent Sunfish, Windsurfers, and snorkeling gear. *Gouverneur Debrotweg 75, Box 34, tel. 599/7–8448. U.S. rep.: ITR, tel. 800/223–9815. 148 rooms. Facilities: dining room, cocktail lounge, coffee shop, tennis courts, beach bar, dive and water-sports center. AE, MC, V. Expensive.*

★ **Captain Don's Habitat.** With its recent expansion and massive renovation, the Habitat can no longer pass itself off as a mere guest house for divers, once a sort of extended home of Captain Don Stewart, the island's wildest sharpshooting personality. New management has added a fabulous set of private villas that rank among the island's best: all with ocean-view verandas, full kitchens, and spacious, stylish arrangements. For entertainment, look up Captain Don, who lives on the premises and whose uninhibited presence on Tex-Mex night can throw an entire room of diners into a roaring brawl. Visit his unusual rock garden and nursery on the grounds and ask him about his novels and the night he shot a mosquito with a shotgun. A full dive center, complete with PADI certification, rounds out the picture. *Kaya Gouverneur Debrotweg 103, Box 88, tel. 599/7–8290. U.S. reps: Habitat North American, tel. 800/327–6709. 11 cottages, 9 villas, 16 rooms. Facilities: bar, restaurant, gift shop, dive center, photo labs. AE, MC, V. Expensive.*

Divi Flamingo Beach Resort and Casino. Flamingo is the closest thing you'll find to a small village on Bonaire—a plantation-style resort that will serve your every need. No matter which hotel you're staying at, reserve a table at the Chibi Restaurant, one of the most sought-after dining spots on the island, where you can see ocean waves pounding beneath the open floorboards. The dive facility, called Dive Bonaire, was founded by world-class expert Peter Hughes and features some of the best photo labs in the Caribbean. A special one-hour class in "Zen Diving" will help make divers more comfortable underwater and teach them how to preserve the reef. For those who need it, there's even the world's first barefoot casino. *J. A. Abraham Blvd., tel. 599/7–8285. U.S. rep.: Divi Hotels, tel. 800/367–3484. 110 rooms, 40 time-sharing units. Facilities: casino, 2 restaurants, 2 pools, dive shop, boutique. AE, MC, V. Expensive.*

Sorobon Beach Resort. Here's the perfect place for acting out all your *Swept Away* fantasies. Avidly trying to outgrow its previous reputation as a sleazy nudist colony, the Sorobon is an intimate, family-style cluster of cottages on a private beach at Lac Bay, on the southeast shore. Today, about a quarter of the upscale, mostly European guests are not "naturalists," as the other guests prefer to be called—that is, no one will force you to disrobe and no one will force you to look. New Agers will like the natural look of the Scandinavian wood furniture. The heady windsurfing here, a result of the unbeatable combo of shallow bay and strong trade winds, draws raves. And who could hate massage and shiatsu right on the beach? Restaurant, bar, volleyball, nature-oriented book and video library, even a telescope to view the stunning night skies are all for the asking. But act blasé when the manager arrives wrapped in a towel.

Box 14, tel. 599/7–8738. 25 cottages. Facilities: kitchenettes, restaurant, bar, library, water-sports center. AE, MC, V. Expensive.

Sand Dollar Condominiums. Studios, one-, two-, and three-bedroom rental units are available in this well-maintained condominium complex set on a low bluff next to the Sunset Beach Hotel. Accommodations are spacious and include everything from fridge to flatware. Private balconies and terraces look out to the sea and the low silhouette of Klein Bonaire. The Green Parrot restaurant on the property serves breakfast, lunch, and dinner. *Kaya Grandi, tel. 599/7–8760. 75 units and 10 town houses. Facilities: restaurant, bar, dive center, photo lab, tennis, pool. AE, V. Expensive.*

Sonesta Beach Resort Bonaire. The newest addition to the Bonaire vacation scene is set on a point of land jutting into the Caribbean. The cluster of eight low-rise buildings barely breaks the shimmering line of the horizon. Well-appointed guest rooms and suites with balconies or patios overlook the private beach or the marina, which can accommodate 60 yachts. *Kaya Gobernador Debrot, tel. 599/7–7500. 150 units. Facilities: two restaurants, bar, pool, tennis, marina, dive center, photo lab, water sports. AE, MC, V. Expensive.*

★ **Bruce Bowker's Carib Inn.** Fifteen years ago, American diver Bruce Bowker started his small diving lodge out of a private home, continually adding on and refurbishing. Serious divers who like unpretentious digs get a kick out of the intimate college-dorm feel; Bowker knows everybody by name and loves to fill special requests. The two units with no kitchen have a refrigerator and electric kettle, but for more involved dining, you'll have to escape to town because there's no restaurant on the premises. Nervous virgin divers will enjoy Bowker's small scuba classes (one or two people); PADI certification is available. *Box 68, tel. 599/7–8819. U.S. rep: ITR, tel. 800/223–9815 or 212/545–8649. 9 units. Facilities: pool, scuba classes, cable TV. AE, MC, V. Moderate.*

Buddy Dive Center. Europeans who tend to eschew luxury and require only basic amenities with matching rates enjoy this growing complex situated on the beach. In keeping with its no-frills style, this hotel advertises "every day only one clean towel per person." *Box 231, Marina area, tel. 599/7–8647/8065. 10 apartments and 10 bungalows. Facilities: pool with bar; restaurant under construction. AE, MC, V. Moderate.*

Hotel Rochaline. Stay in the Rochaline only as a last resort in Bonaire. It has gained a reputation for seediness, but check first: Renovations could have taken place. *Box 27, Kralendijk, tel. 599/7–8286. 20 rooms. Facilities: restaurant. AE, MC, V. Inexpensive.*

Home and Apartment Rentals The **Bonaire Government Tourist Office** (tel. 212/242–7707) can help you locate suitable housing in Bonaire.

The Arts and Nightlife

The Arts Slide shows of underwater scenes keep both divers and nondivers fascinated in the evenings. The best is Dee Scarr, a dive guide whose show "Touch the Sea" is presented Monday night at 8:45 PM at **Captain Don's Habitat** (tel. 599/7–8290). Check with the Habitat for other shows throughout the week. **Flamingo Beach Resort** (tel. 599/7–8285) offers a free underwater video, "Discover the Caribbean," on Sunday night at 9:30 PM.

The best singer on the island is guitarist **Cai-Cai Cecelia,** who performs with his duo Thursday night at **Flamingo Beach Resort** and Monday at **Habitat.** He sings his own compositions, as well as Harry Belafonte classics.

Nightlife Most divers are exhausted after they finish their third, fourth, or fifth dive of the day, which probably explains why there's only one disco in Bonaire. Nevertheless, **E Wowo** (Kralendijk, at the corner of Kaya Grandi and Kaya L. D. Gerharts) is usually packed in high season, so get there early. The name E Wowo means "eye" in Papiamento, illustrated with two flashing opart eyes on the wall. Recorded music is loud, and the large circular bar seats a lot of action. The entrance fee varies according to the season.

For late-night conversations, **The Rendez-Vous Restaurant** is open late, with light pastries and espresso, as is the **Mona Lisa Bar & Restaurant** (*see* Dining, above).

The popular bar **Karel's** (no phone), on the waterfront across from the Zeezicht Restaurant, sits on stilts above the sea and is *the* place to flirt with diving pros. Closed Monday.

Bonaire has only one casino, the **Flamingo Beach Hotel Casino,** which opens at 4 PM.

7 The British Virgin Islands

by David L.
Grambs

*A freelance writer
and editor from
New York City,
David L. Grambs
is the author of
two books—*
Dimboxes, Epopts,
and Other
Quidams: Words to
Describe Life's
Indescribable
People *and* Words
About Words—
*and a contributing
editor to the*
Random House
Dictionary of the
English Language.

There's no gambling, no golf, no lavish nightly entertainment.
Don Rickles has never cracked a joke here. Nassau hats and
Hawaiian shirts look slightly gauche on Main Street, where
there's little to buy, none of it duty-free. On all the islands
there are fewer beds than in the Caribe Hilton in San Juan. Hotels are by law no more than two stories high, and few have air-
conditioning—just ceiling fans and a steady breeze brushed
with the scent of frangipani blossoms, jasmine, and sage.

There are three crucial facts you might want to know right off.
One, you won't hear a great many Oxbridge accents; this is still
the West Indies. Two, your American money is not only good
here, it's the official currency. Three, many of the better resorts are rather expensive, even for the Caribbean.

On the map you'll find this destination 60 miles east of Puerto
Rico, where you'll get your connecting flight if you don't choose
as your stop-off the much closer island of St. Thomas. Tortola
(not to be confused with various Tortugas) is the largest island,
with a population of 9,200. Off Tortola's northern shores are
the islands of Jost Van Dyke, Guana, and Great Camanoe,
among others.

Tortola's sister in size and beauty is smaller, spindly Virgin
Gorda to the east, which has a population of about 1,400 and
geographically seems to leave a trail of jigsaw pieces parallel to
(west to east) and south of Tortola: Norman, Peter, Salt, Cooper, and Ginger islands.

But the glory of this archipelago is less the islands themselves
than the 5-mile-wide Sir Francis Drake Channel. It sparkles
like a vast turquoise river in the sunlight as you careen along
Tortola's curving Waterfront Drive (perhaps the only road in
the BVI on which you'll hear cars whoosh by). It makes you
want to visit one of the islands over there, or to just sail up and
down its length; you're not sure which. Maybe to anchor over
the wreck of the R.M.S. *Rhone*— off Salt Island, which, with
Virgin Gorda's bouldered grotto called T⊦ ᴿaths, is the prime
tourist attraction in the BVI.

The British Virgin Islands are in fact ⟨ ailor's heaven. To
"bareboat" here is not to go skinny-shippiⁿ but to be your own
captain. From old yacht club members t ⟩ young couples who
hire a crew and captain, many BVI visitorⱫ ⱬail happily from anchorage to anchorage, from Prickly Pea⥾ ⥾o Great Dog, from
Sandy Cay to Scrub Island, from Pelican Island to Dead Chest
—if not to mysterious Anegada, the unique coral island north
of Virgin Gorda's North Sound. Hundreds ⊃f wrecks lie in these
waters, and most of them lie around Anegada—its highest
point is only 28 feet above sea level—and unlucky Horseshoe
Reef.

Driving on the British Virgin Islands is never dull. On Tortola
go as slowly as you can along the beautiful stretch from Long
Bay to Cane Garden Bay or up the roller-coaster switchback
from Road Town called Joe's Hill. On Virgin Gorda yᵒu can
drive to the haunting and ruggedly beautiful place calleʮ Copper Mine Point or get to the highest point you can find
overlooking Leverick Bay and North Sound for a view that will
become a freeze-frame in your memory.

In the British Virgins, you won't find high-rise hotels, marble lobbies, shopping arcades, cruise-ship hordes, groaningly

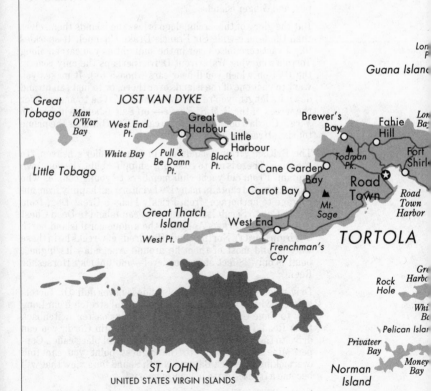

A T L A N T I C

Lon
P

Guana Island

Great
Tobago

Man
O'War
Bay

JOST VAN DYKE

West End
Pt.

Great
Harbour

Little
Harbour

Pull &
Be Damn
Pt.

White Bay

Black
Pt.

Little Tobago

Brewer's
Bay

Fahie
Hill

Lon
Ba

Fort
Shirl

Cane Garden
Bay

Carrot Bay

Todman
Pk.

Road
Town

Road
Town
Harbor

Great Thatch
Island

West End

Mt.
Sage

West Pt.

Frenchman's
Cay

TORTOLA

Rock
Hole

Gre
Harbo

Whi
Bo

Pelican Islan

Privateer
Bay

Money
Bay

ST. JOHN
UNITED STATES VIRGIN ISLANDS

Norman
Island

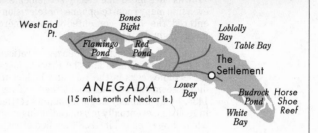

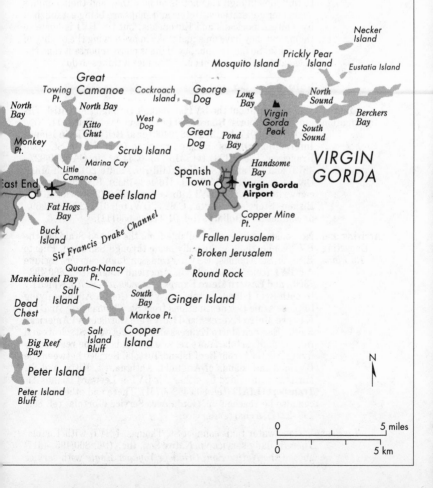

West End Pt.

Bones Bight

Flamingo Pond

Red Pond

Loblolly Bay

Table Bay

The Settlement

ANEGADA
(15 miles north of Neckar Is.)

Lower Bay

Budrock Pond

Horse Shoe Reef

White Bay

OCEAN

Anegada Passage

Necker Island

Prickly Pear Island

Mosquito Island

Eustatia Island

Great Camanoe

Cockroach Island

George Dog

Long Bay

North Sound

Towing Pt.

North Bay

Virgin Gorda Peak

Berchers Bay

North Bay

Kitto Ghut

West Dog

South Sound

Monkey Pt.

Scrub Island

Great Dog

Pond Bay

VIRGIN GORDA

Marina Cay

Little Camanoe

Spanish Town

Handsome Bay

East End

Beef Island

Virgin Gorda Airport

Fat Hogs Bay

Buck Island

Copper Mine Pt.

Sir Francis Drake Channel

Fallen Jerusalem

Broken Jerusalem

Quart-a-Nancy Pt.

Round Rock

Manchioneel Bay

Salt Island

South Bay

Ginger Island

Dead Chest

Markoe Pt.

Salt Island Bluff

Cooper Island

Big Reef Bay

Peter Island

Peter Island Bluff

N

0   5 miles

0   5 km

packed safari buses, traffic jams, or honeymoon-package hype. "Towns" are more like sleepy settlements. In fact, you won't even find many room telephones or television sets. The BVI has entered the 1990s contentedly uncommercialized—still the more virginal Virgins.

It must be the British influence, or reticence. The English, along with the Dutch and the French, began sniffing around these Indies cays in the 16th and 17th centuries when Spain didn't seem too serious about them. (They were sighted, in 1493, by Columbus.) English planters settled on Virgin Gorda in 1680, and eventually prospered on sugarcane and cotton, but when slavery ended in 1833 they fled elsewhere, leaving their lands in the hands of their former slaves. In 1893 there were only two whites on the islands, the deputy governor and the doctor. Until tourism began in the late 1960s, the BVI was a society of small farmers and fishermen.

Today most islanders own their own land and can afford to treat visitors as welcome guests. What will happen when hotel chains rattle at their doors is anyone's guess; but for now they're avoiding the plight of other West Indians, who are lucky to find jobs in high-rise hotels on land they and their families owned for generations. Hotels and shops are being established by white Americans and Europeans, but the BVI is home to them, and they have an equal stake in preserving the quality of island life. So far, the quality of life is more important than the pace, and nothing is still one of the nicest things to do.

Before You Go

Tourist Information Information about the BVI is available through the **British Virgin Islands Tourist Board** (370 Lexington Ave., Suite 511, New York, NY 10017, tel. 212/696–0400) or at **British Virgin Islands Information Offices** in San Francisco (1686 Union St., San Francisco, CA 94123, tel. 415/775–0344 or, in CA, 800/922–4873) and Ontario (801 York Mill Rd., Suite 201, Don Mills, Ont., Canada MCB 1X7, tel. 416/443–1859). British travelers can write or visit the **BVI Information Office** (26 Hockerill St., Bishops Stortford, Herts., CM23 2DW, tel. 01/44279–654969), or contact **BVI Holidays** (tel. 01/44279–656111).

Arriving and Departing
By Plane No nonstop service is available from the United States to the BVI; connections are usually made through San Juan, Puerto Rico, or St. Thomas, USVI. From San Juan, carriers include **Air BVI** (tel. 800/468–2485), **American Eagle** (tel. 800/433–7300), and **Eastern Metro Express** (tel. 800/327–8376), which fly to both Beef Island/Tortola and Virgin Gorda. Airlines flying to those same two destinations from St. Thomas are Air BVI, Eastern Metro Express, and (to Virgin Gorda only) American Eagle. Eastern Metro Express also flies between St. Croix and Beef Island/Tortola. More remote Anegada can be reached by flying Air BVI from Beef Island/Tortola. Service between the BVI and the islands of Anguilla, Antigua, St. Kitts, and St. Maarten is provided by either Air BVI or **Leeward Islands Air Transport (LIAT)** (tel. 809/462–0701). These and other islands can also be reached via **Gorda Aero Service** (Tortola, tel. 809/495–2271), a charter service.

By Boat Various water taxis connect St. Thomas, USVI, with Tortola. There is daily service via **Native Son, Inc.,** (tel. 800/495–4617) aboard the *Native Son, Oriole* or *Voyager Eagle* with service between St. Thomas and Virgin Gorda on Wednesdays and Sundays. **Smiths Ferry Services** (tel. 809/494–4430 or 809/494–2355) carries passengers between St. Thomas and Tortola Mondays through Saturdays and travels between St. Thomas and Virgin Gorda on Tuesday, Thursday, and Saturday. **Speedy's Fantasy** (tel. 809/495–5240) makes the run between Virgin Gorda and Road Town daily.

Speedy's connects Tortola and Virgin Gorda with Anegada on Tuesdays and Sundays. Speedy's also goes from both Tortola and Virgin Gorda to St. John and back on Thursdays. **Varlack Ventures** (tel. 809/776–6412 or 809/776–6695) has daily ferries between St. Thomas, St. John, and Tortola, and **Inter-Island Boat Services'** *Sundance II* (tel. 809/776–6282) connects St. John and Tortola daily. Running daily between Virgin Gorda's North Sound (Bitter End Yacht Club) and Beef Island are **North Sound Express** boats (tel. 809/494–2746). There are also daily boats between Tortola's CSY Dock and Peter Island. **Jost Van Dyke Ferry Service** (tel. 809/495–2775) services the Jost Van Dyke/Tortola route daily via the *Argus* and *Wen* ferries, and *Reel World* also makes daily trips between Jost and Tortola (tel. 809/494–3450).

Passports and Visas U.S. and Canadian citizens must present proof of citizenship upon entering the BVI in the form of a passport, birth certificate, or voter registration card.

Customs and Duties A $400 duty-free exemption on purchased goods is allowed by U.S. Customs as long as you have been out of the United States at least 48 hours. Such limits can be "pooled" by family members into a joint or collective duty-free allowance; thus a husband and wife are allowed $800 in duty-free exemption regardless of who bought what. For an article costing up to $1,000, the duty is 10% of the remainder or excess over the exempt amount; for example, for a $1,000 necklace, spouses traveling together will pay 10% duty on $200. Unlimited gifts may be mailed back home duty-free as long as the gift's value doesn't exceed $50 per day to any single address. The allowance on items classified as island crafts, art, or antiques is unlimited. The cigarette allowance is one carton duty-free (80¢ tax on additional cartons), and the liquor allowance one liter per person over 21. If you are traveling to St. Thomas, you may buy $400 worth of goods in the BVI and another $400 worth in St. Thomas.

Language British English, with a West Indian inflection, is the language of the BVI.

Precautions There are no perils from drinking the water in these islands. Insects, notably mosquitoes, are not usually a problem in these breeze-blessed isles, but it is always a good idea to bring some repellent along. Animals in the BVI are not dangerous but they can be road hazards, if shy ones. Give goats, sheep, horses, and cows the right of way.

Beware of the little varmints called "no-see 'ums." They're for real and are especially pesky at twilight near the water. So if you're going for an evening stroll on the beach, apply some type of repellent liberally. No-see 'um bites itch worse than mosquito bites and take a lot longer to go away. Prevention is the best cure, but witch hazel offers *some* relief if they get you.

Further Reading   Robb White's *Our Virgin Island* is about Marina Cay a couple of decades ago (it became the Sidney Poitier and John Cassavetes movie *Virgin Island);* you might still be able to find a copy in a library.

Lito Valls's *What a Pistarckle!*, published in 1981 on St. John, USVI, is an entertaining paperback dictionary of Virgin Islands' English Creole. If you can't find a copy in Road Town, you will at the Sugar Mill hotel's little gift shop.

Margaret Truman's *Murder in the CIA* has a British Virgin Islands setting.

Once you've arrived in the BVI, the place to find numerous local books and pamphlets about these islands is **The Cockle Shop** (Main St., Road Town, near the post office, tel. 809/494–2525) or nearby **Past and Presents** (tel. 809/494–2747).

Staying in the British Virgin Islands

Important Addresses   **Tourist Information:** On Tortola there is a **BVI Tourist Board Office** at the center of Road Town near the ferry dock, just south of Wickhams Cay I (Box 134, Road Town, Tortola, BVI, tel. 809/494–3134). For all kinds of useful information about these islands, including rates and phone numbers, get a free copy of *The Welcome Tourist Guide*, available at hotels and other places.

Emergencies   **Police:** Dial 999.

Hospitals: Dial 998 for a medical emergency. On Tortola there is **Peebles Hospital** in Road Town (tel. 809/494–3497). Virgin Gorda has two clinics, one in Spanish Town or The Valley (tel. 809/495–5337) and one at North Sound (tel. 809/495–7310).

Pharmacies: Pharmacies in Road Town include **BVI Drug Center** (tel. 809/494–2702) and **Lagoon Plaza Drug Store** (tel. 809/494–2498). On Virgin Gorda, in Spanish Town, there is **J. R. O'Neal Marketing Associates** (tel. 809/495–5325).

Currency   British though they are, the BVI have the U.S. dollar as the standard currency.

Taxes and Service Charges   Hotels collect a 7% accommodations tax. For those leaving the BVI by air, the departure tax is $5; by sea it is $4. A tourist information card must also be filled out by visitors.

Guided Tours   If you'd like to do some chauffeured sightseeing on Tortola, get in touch with **B.V.I. Taxi Association** ($12 per person, minimum three persons, tel. 809/494–2875, 809/494–2322, or 809/495–2378), **Style's Taxi Service** (tel. 809/494–2260 during the day or 809/494–3341 at night), or **Travel Plan Tours** (tel. 809/494–2872). An inclusive tour program is also offered by **Rancal Rent-a-Car** (tel. 809/494–4534, 809/494–4535, or 809/495–4330). **Scato's Bus Service** in Road Town (tel. 809/494–2365) provides public transportation, special tours with group rates, and beach outings.

Guided tours on Virgin Gorda can be arranged through **Andy's Taxi and Jeep Rental** (tel. 809/495–5252 or 809/495–5353).

Getting Around   Whether you're behind the wheel yourself or not, motoring about on Tortola or Virgin Gorda is pleasurable, scenic, and sometimes exciting. Roads tend to have simple names rather than highway numbers. If there is a traffic light anywhere in the BVI, only a secret society knows where it is. Ascents and descents can be thrilling, particularly when the views to the side are so astoundingly lovely as to be distracting. If chugging up Joe's Hill from Road Town doesn't have you holding your breath a bit, the roll down to the northern coast—or the view of Cane Garden Bay—on the other side of the ridge, will. The same holds for the main road on Virgin Gorda from Spanish Town to Gun Creek and North Sound.

Driving is *à l'Anglais*, on the left side of the road. You can get used to this by driving slowly. This is easily done since the speed limit is 30 mph, 10 to 15 mph in residential areas.

Taxis Your hotel will be happy to summon a taxi for you when you want one. There is a taxi stand in Road Town near the ferry dock (tel. 809/494–2322) and one on Beef Island, where the airport is (tel. 809/495–2378). You can also usually find a taxi at Sopers Hole, West End, where water taxis or ferries come in from St. Thomas.

Buses For information about rates and schedules, call **Scato's Bus Service** (tel. 809/494–2365).

Mopeds Scooters can be rented on Tortola from **Hero's Bicycle Rental** (tel. 809/494–3536 or 809/494–3746).

Rental Cars You must have a valid driver's license and you must pay $10 for a temporary BVI driver's license, valid for three months. You can pick up the license at a police station or purchase it as part of the paperwork when you are renting a car.

Car-rental agents on Tortola are **Alphonso Car Rentals** (tel. 809/494–3137 or 809/494–4886), **Anytime Car Rental** (tel. 809/494–2875 or 809/494–3107), **Avis** (tel. 809/494–3322 or 809/494–2193), **Budget** (tel. 809/494–2639), **Caribbean** (tel. 809/494–2595), **Inner Harbour Marina Car Rentals** (tel. 809/494–4502/3/4/5), **International** (tel. 809/494–2516 or 809/494–2517), **Island Suzuki** (tel. 809/494–3666), **National** (tel. 809/494–3197), and **Rancal** (tel. 809/494–4534, 809/494–4545, or 809/495–4330).

On Virgin Gorda you can lease a vehicle from **Speedy's** (tel. 809/495–5235 or 809/495–5240). **Mahogany Rentals** (tel. 809/495–5542 or 809/494–5322) does not accept credit cards but has lower rates and *especially* courteous and helpful service.

Telephones and Mail The area code for the BVI is 809, which, of course, needn't be dialed for a local call. Furthermore, only the last five digits of a number have to be dialed here: Instead of dialing 494–1234, just dial 4–1234. A local call from a public pay phone costs 25¢. For long-distance calls, the best place to hook up with public phones on Tortola is **Cable & Wireless,** in Road Town; on Virgin Gorda, at the Yacht Harbour.

There are post offices in Road Town on Tortola and in Spanish Town on Virgin Gorda. Postage for a first-class letter to the United States is 40¢ and for a postcard 30¢. (It might be noted that postal efficiency is not first-class in the BVI.)

Opening and Closing Times Stores are generally open from 9 to 5 Monday through Saturday. Bank hours are Monday through Thursday 9–2:30 and Friday 9–2:30 and 4:30–6.

Beaches

Beaches here are less developed than, say, on St. Thomas or St. Croix. You'll also find fewer people. Try to get out on a boat at least one day during your stay in these islands, whether a dive-snorkeling boat or a day-trip sailing vessel. It's sometimes the best way to get to the most virgin Virgin beaches (some have no road access). The beaches mentioned below can be reached by car or Jeep, possibly with a little walking involved, too. Rent a Jeep if you're a seeker of remote beaches and want to be able to handle the worst kind of terrain to get there. If you explore numerous beaches in a single drive, know that most of the best ones on both Tortola and Virgin Gorda are on the northern coasts.

Are you welcome at a beach that seems to belong to a particular resort? Technically, yes, and technically, no: You're welcome on the beach, but not always welcome on the private property you have to cross in order to get to it. While welcoming your use of their beach, most resorts also hope to safeguard the prerogatives and privacy of their own guests. (Little Dix Bay Resort on Virgin Gorda is particularly concerned with privacy.) In short, it's a gray area. Feel free to hit the sand anywhere, but don't leave your manners at home.

Tortola If you want to surf, **Apple Bay** (Cappoons Bay) is the spot. Sebastians, the very casual hotel here, caters especially to those in search of the perfect wave. Good waves are never a sure thing, but January and February are usually high times here.

The water at **Brewers Bay** is good for either snorkeling (calm) or surfing (swells). There's a campground here, but in the summer you'll find almost nobody around. The beach and its old sugar mill and rum distillery ruins are just north of Cane Garden Bay on the road near Luck Hill.

Cane Garden Bay rivals St. Thomas's Magens Bay in majesty but is besieged by visiting hordes. It's a grand beach for jogging if you can resist veering into that translucent water. You can rent sailboards and such, and for noshing or sipping there is Stanley's Welcome Bar, Rhymer's, and Quito's Gazebo. From Road Town you'll drive a steep uphill and a steep downhill to get here, and you'll feel as if you've landed in Paradise.

Long Bay on Beef Island is gorgeous and visited only by a knowledgeable few. The view of Little Camanoe and Great Camanoe islands is appealing, and if you walk around the bend to the right, you can see little Marina Cay and Scrub Island. Take the Queen Elizabeth Bridge to Beef Island and watch for a small dirt turnoff before the airport. Drive across that dried-up marsh flat—there really is a beach (with interesting seashells) on the other side.

At **Smuggler's Cove** (Lower Belmont Bay) you'll really feel as if you've found a hidden place and will hardly notice the has-seen-better-days hotel back in the overgrowth. There is a fine view of the island of Jost Van Dyke. The snorkeling is good.

About the only thing you'll find moving at **Trunk Bay** is the surf. It's directly north of Road Town, midway between Cane Garden Bay and Beef Island, and you'll have to hike down a *ghut* (defile) from the high Ridge Road.

Virgin Gorda Anybody going to Virgin Gorda must experience swimming or snorkeling among its unique boulder formations. But why go to The Baths—usually crowded—when you can get your rocks next door—just north—at **The Crawl?** And right next to it is **Guavaberry's Spring Bay** beach, which is a gem.

Leverick Bay is a small, busy beach-cum-marina that fronts a resort restaurant and pool. Don't come here to be alone or to jog. But if you want a lively little place and a break from the island's noble quiet, take the road north and turn left before Gun Creek. The view of Prickly Pear Island is an added plus, and there's a dive facility right here to motor you out to beautiful Eustatia Reef just across North Sound.

It's worth going out to **Long Bay** (near Virgin Gorda's northern tip, past the Diamond Beach Club) for the snorkeling (Little Dix Bay resort has outings here). Going north from Spanish Town, go left at the fork near Pond Bay. Part of the route there is dirt road.

Savannah Bay is a lovely place, and though it may not be deserted it seems wonderfully private for a beach just north of Spanish Town (on the north side of where the island narrows, at Black Rock). From town it's only 15 minutes or so on foot.

Other Islands Beaches on other islands, reachable only by boat, include Jost Van Dyke's **Little Harbour** and **White Bay; Marina Cay;** Peter Island's **Big Reef Bay, White Bay,** and **Dead Man's Bay;** Mosquito Island's **Limetree Beach, Long Beach,** and **Honeymoon Beach;** Cooper Island's **Manchioneel Bay;** and farther-off, reef-laced **Anegada.**

Exploring Tortola

Numbers in the margins correspond with points of interest on the Tortola map.

❶ This outing begins at the populous indentation in the middle of Tortola called **Road Town.** The route will acquaint you with this mountainous island's western half, where its more popular beaches and views are to be found. You will drive along both the southern and northern coasts with chances to stop at lovely bays, and there will be some heady mountain roads, a misty rain forest, and one of the best panoramic views in all the Caribbean. Be sure to bring your swimsuit!

We'll start at **Wickhams Cay.** This is the center of the action in Road Town and the place from which to enjoy a broad view of the wide harbor, home to countless sailing vessels and yachts and a base for the well-known yacht-chartering enterprise called The Moorings. You'll find a **BVI Tourist Board** office to serve you right here as well as banks, a post office, and most of Tortola's stores and boutiques. If you walk about to do a little shopping, don't miss **The Pusser's Co. Store and Pub.** This handsome emporium has a nautical theme, and its sporty knickknacks, Pusser's rum mugs, and all-cotton clothes make attractive purchases. Outside the store, along the main harborfront sidewalk, you'll also find some good clothing buys from street vendors. Check out some of the unusual BVI T-shirts (seconds), some of which cost only a couple of dollars.

Hitting the road, head west on the one and only main street, which hugs the island's southern coast. The turretlike building

---

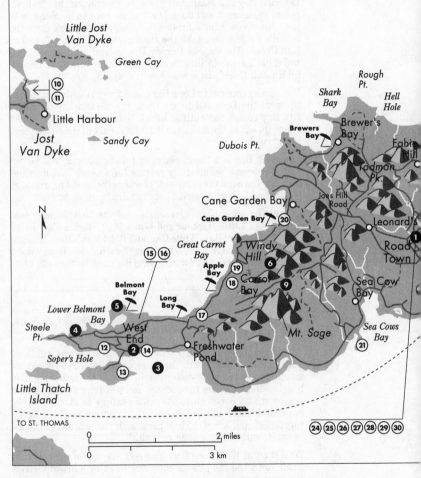

ATLANTIC OCEAN

Tortola

Exploring
Beef Island, **7**
Belmont Pond/Belmont Point, **5**
Callwood Distillery, **6**
Frenchman's Cay, **3**
Marina Cay, **8**
Road Town, **1**
Sage Mountain National Park, **9**

Smuggler's Cove, **4**
West End, **2**

Dining
The Apple, **19**
Cell 5 Lounge, **25**
The Cloud Room, **24**
Fort Burt Restaurant, **31**

Long Bay Beach Resort, **15**
The Pusser's Deli, **27**
Spaghetti Junction, **26**
Sugar Mill, **17**

Lodging
Anegada Reef Hotel (Anegada Island), **34**
Cane Garden Bay Beach Hotel, **20**
Fort Burt, **31**
Fort Recovery, **14**
Frenchman's Cay Resort Hotel, **13**
Guana Island Club (Guana Island), **32**

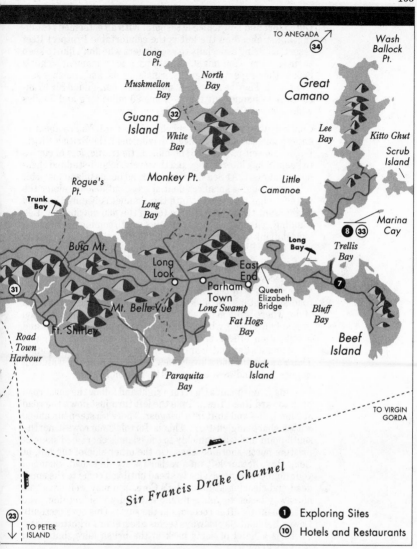

Exploring Sites ①

Hotels and Restaurants ⑩

Hotel Castle Maria, **29**
Jolly Roger Inn, **12**
Long Bay Beach Resort, **16**
Maria's by the Sea, **28**
Marina Cay Hotel (Marina Cay), **33**
Nanny Cay Resort and Marina, **21**

Peter Island Hotel and Yacht Club (Peter Island), **23**
Prospect Reef, **22**
Rudy's Marina Inn (Jost Van Dyke), **10**
Sandcastle (Jost Van Dyke) **11**
Sebastion's on the Beach, **18**

Sugar Mill, **17**
Treasure Isle Hotel, **30**

perched on that little hill to your right is **Fort Burt,** once an old Dutch fort and now a nice little hotel with an esteemed restaurant. Just ahead on the left is the comfortable **Prospect Reef** resort, catering especially to vacationers who don't like to keep their feet dry. You might want to park for a moment to get a look at the property's lagoons, canals, pools, and amazing seafront pool. They're all man-made, but the sun-gilded **Sir Francis Drake Channel** out there—some 20 miles long and 5 miles wide—was definitely made by higher powers.

Continue west on the ever-curving shore road. You're about to enjoy 5 miles or so of the nicest driving in all the British Virgin Islands: a well-paved road, no hills, little traffic, lots of curves to keep things interesting, and the lovely, island-studded channel on your left. At Sea Cow Bay the road bends inland just a bit to pass through a small residential area, but it soon rejoins the water's edge. Jutting out into the channel is **Nanny Cay.** You might want to swing left here to see the marina and Peg Leg Landing, a lively restaurant on stilts worth coming back to for a sunset drink or a moonlight dinner. The hotel here has recently come under Ramada management.

After Nanny Cay this pleasant, wide-open coastal road passes **Fort Recovery.** There are now vacation villas here, but the ruins of the 17th-century Dutch fort are still to be seen. The
❷ road straightens out and brings you to **West End** and **Sopers Hole,** where—if you didn't fly in to Beef Island Airport—you probably arrived by boat. The boat terminal and customs and immigration offices are here. Turn left over the bridge to
❸ **Frenchman's Cay** and bear right on the other side of the bridge. There's a marina and a lovely view across the peaceful waters of Sopers Hole and west toward Little Thatch Island.

Leaving Frenchman's Cay, turn right and follow the coast road back toward Road Town. Take the left turn just down the road at Zion Hill—and shift into low gear. There's a steep hill ahead with a sharp-angled turn. This is Tortola's narrowest north–south point and leads quickly to the island's cherished skein of pristine north-shore beaches. On the other side of the hill, at Long Bay, detour left up a rather twisty dirt road. Suspend your doubts and drive slowly ahead until you come to the small
❹ dead-end clearing at **Smuggler's Cove.** You may well have this hideaway beach to yourself (and a friendly resident dog, who loves sprinting after coconuts in the surf). This cove (actually Lower Belmont Bay) always seems a secret or forgotten place. There is a hotel of sorts back in the brush here, but you'd scarcely know it.

The rocky road back will give you a brief but stunning prospect
❺ of **Belmont Pond** and pyramidal **Belmont Point** to your left. Ahead—returning, thankfully, to a paved road—you'll pass Long Bay and, again, at a curve on the hill just past this resort, there is a car-halting view of Long Bay's brilliant white beach extending down to the seemingly carved green hump of Belmont Point (somehow a little reminiscent of Rio de Janeiro's Sugar Loaf Mountain). The road levels out now as you pass Little Apple Bay, Apple Bay, Little Carrot Bay, and Great Carrot Bay, all presenting equally enticing vistas to the northwest of **Jost Van Dyke** and smaller **Sandy Cay.** These waters draw many avid surfers to Tortola. Just past Sebastians on the Beach, a casual hostelry for the hang-five set, you'll notice a curiously decorated—or graffitoed—ramshackle beach hut on the left,

Bomba Shack. It may look like a giant semicollapsed wooden wind chime, but it's actually a bar of sorts run by an unconventional local gentleman. Just ahead is Sugar Mill, one of Tortola's nicest places to dine in if you're game for some truly intimate, candlelight ambience.

So many of Tortola's best sights seem to be preceded by a hill or two, and **Cane Garden Bay** is no exception. After zigzagging up and down Windy Hill you glide down to this long and curved beach justly celebrated as one of the most beautiful in all the Caribbean. Its sparkling calm waters attract many boats seeking an idyllic place to drop anchor. You'll want to walk at least part of its length, maybe even rent a Windsurfer and do a little stand-up sailing.

Time Out Have a snack and cooling soda or beer at **Stanley's Welcome Bar** (Cane Garden Bay, tel. 809/495–4520) right on Cane Garden's beach, which will give you a place out of the sun.

6 Before leaving the area, stop at the **Callwood Distillery** nearby, sort of a Tortolan version of a backwoods still, but a legal one. If you're interested, venturesome, and not a brand-name-only type, you can purchase a bottle of Callwood's potent moonshine rum for very little.

You'll roll over a little bridge as you proceed east from Cane Garden Bay. Don't relax. You have a long thrill of a hill to drive up here—even Tortolans don't seem to be sure of its official name, but some call it Soldiers Hill. Drive along the high central ridge of the island and down Joe's Hill back to Road Town. If you want to continue exploring, don't return to Road Town but continue along the central ridge east past the communities of Wesley Will and Long Swamp to the modestly slender **Queen Elizabeth Bridge.** Over the bridge is quite flat **Beef Island** and its airport. If you like interesting seashells, **Long Bay** is a find.

8 Also worth a visit is **Marina Cay,** a tiny reef-fringed island resort and marina that can be reached by boat (a short ride) from a dock near the airport.

You have another option at this point before returning to Road Town. The area at the top of the Cane Garden Bay hill (called Meyers) is where four different roads more or less converge. If you bear to the right at the top of the hill and go straight (don't turn off toward the radio tower on your right), you'll come to the parking lot for **Sage Mountain National Park.** Sage Mountain, at 1,716 feet, is the highest peak in the Virgin Islands.

Your best unobstructed views up here are actually from the parking area. From here a trail will lead you around in a loop not only to the peak itself but also to the island's rain forest, sometimes shrouded in mist. Most of the island's forest was cut down over the centuries to clear land for sugarcane, cotton, other crops, pastureland, and timber. But in 1964 this park was established to preserve the remaining rain forest, which not only has exotic trees and plants but also serves an important function in preserving water for Tortola's aquifer. Up here you can see mahogany trees, white cedars, mountain guavas, elephant-ear vines, mamey trees, and giant bulletwoods, to say nothing of such birds as mountain doves and thrushes. As you walk the trail to the main gate, you'll also have good views on your right of the Sir Francis Drake Channel.

If you're not feeling like a naturalist or hiker, from Meyers you can bear left instead of right at the top of the Cane Garden Bay incline and shoot up that steep, drivewaylike hill to Skyworld restaurant. The panoramic vista from here is a marvel. There are telescopes on the highest terrace, but even your naked eye will appreciate that this is one of the best views in the Leeward seas—particularly at sunset. Islands, islands everywhere. From here it's a short, gravity-assisted drive back down to Road Town.

Exploring Virgin Gorda

Numbers in the margin correspond with points of interest on the Virgin Gorda map.

Virgin Gorda, with its mountainous central portion connected by skinny necks to southern and northern appendages—on a map they look like they might break away—is quite different from Tortola. Paved roads are few, alternate routes are limited, and there are few places where you can actually drive right along the coast. Yet it has a simple and primitive beauty and is small enough that you can easily get a good fix on most areas of the island in a single day.

❶ From **Spanish Town,** or **The Valley,** as it's sometimes called, drive south past Fischer's Cove Hotel, which is on your right. Continue south until you see a road to the left. Take the left and then the next right. Notice how distinctively dry and desert-like the terrain and plant life are at this end of Virgin Gorda, as evidenced by cactus growth. The road bends east toward the coast. There's an abrupt hill, some badly paved spots, and then no paving at all. But in minutes the rocky dirt road brings you **❷** to spectacular **Copper Mine Point.** A tall, chimney-like stone tower stands amid broken walls and rubble at this windswept promontory, those being the ruins of a 400-year-old Spanish copper mine. You are at the southeastern tip of Virgin Gorda, a rugged, seemingly unvisited place that has something haunting about it. There is a special vividness about the greenish blues of the sea here and the jagged coast it washes against. This is also one of the few places in the British Virgin Islands where you won't see islands dotting the horizon.

Follow the road back north but turn left at the first intersection and then left again. Driving south, you will pass the **Guavaberry Spring Bay** resort, where guests stay in elevated-deck cottages nestled up against huge boulders—the singular feature of Virgin Gorda's southern end. At the end of the road **❸** you'll reach the island's most famous attraction, **The Baths,** where clusters of behemoth prehistoric rocks form cool grottoes. Walk—squeeze—into this cave-like formation to see the shallow pools and the play of sunlight slanting in through crevices. Outside you can enjoy some unusual boulder snorkeling, though you may bump into more people than boulders. The Baths tend to be a little crowded, and many of its visitors come from all those boats you see anchored just offshore. The less besieged beaches just north of here also have majestic boulders.

Drive north from The Baths to **Spanish Town.** At the **Virgin Gorda Yacht Harbour** you can enjoy a stroll along the dock front or do a little browsing in the shops there, such as the Virgin Gorda Craft Shop, Pelican's Pouch Boutique, Island Woman, or The Wine Cellar.

Time Out | Settle down by the fountain on the cool patio of the **Bath and Turtle** (Virgin Gorda Yacht Harbour, tel. 809/495–5239), an English-style pub off the marina mall courtyard, and have a burger or fish sandwich with a mug of Courage or your favorite rum drink.

Having seen a bit of the island's arid and relatively flat southern leg, we can look forward to some very different scenery north of Spanish Town. On the way out of town you'll pass the extensive, beautifully cared-for property of **Little Dix Bay,** the Rockresort retreat that is the grandmother of all British Virgin Islands resorts. Much of its sloping 400 acres of verdant grounds looks like a golf course invaded by beautiful tropical trees.

Past Little Dix the road takes you quickly out of town and downhill to the island's thin neck at Savannah Bay. The view— the Sir Francis Drake Channel to the north and the mainstream Caribbean to the south—might make you want to pull over to

❹ be sure it's real. It is, and this scenic elbow is called **Black Rock.** The road forks as it goes uphill. The left prong winds past the Mango Beach and Diamond Beach Club resorts (and not much else) to Long Bay and not quite to Mountain Point. To continue exploring, take the road on the right, which winds uphill and looks down on beautiful South Sound. You'll notice that you see nary a dwelling or sign of mundane civilization up here, only a green mountain slope on your left and a spectacular view down to South Sound on the right. From here, too, you can also look back and get a wonderful, living sense of Virgin Gorda's stringy, crooked shape: Back there, looking flat and almost like a separate island, is Spanish Town, which you've just left. Because of this shape, Virgin Gorda is one of those places where you can get a bird's-eye (or map's-eye) view of things from right inside your car.

❺ You'll see a small sign on the left for the trail up to **Virgin Gorda Peak,** the island's summit at 1,359 feet. It's about a 15-minute hike up to a small clearing, where you can climb a ladder to the platform of a wood observation tower. If you're keen for some woodsy exercise or just stretching your legs, go for it. But the view at the top is somewhat tree-obstructed and may not be as good as the one you have right here at roadside.

No trip to Virgin Gorda would be complete without seeing

❻ some of its **North Sound** area. This is a yachtsman's paradise, but you can appreciate its isolated beauty from a car as well. The route ahead will lead you merely to a view—but what a view!

This corniche comes to a hilly little settlement—there's a clinic, church, and school—just above Gun Creek. Go left, or north, and you'll come out at **Leverick Bay.** There is a resort here, with a cozy beach and marina area and some luxurious hillside villas to rent, all a little like a tucked-away tropical suburb. Low-gear your way up one of the narrow hillside roads (you're not on a driveway, it only seems that way) to one of those topmost Leverick dwellings, where you can park for a moment. (Three of the highest, if you can find them, are called Seaview, Tamarind, and Double Sunrise.)

Out to the left, across Blunder Bay, you'll see **Mosquito Island;** the hunk of land straight ahead is **Prickly Pear,** which has just

Virgin Gorda

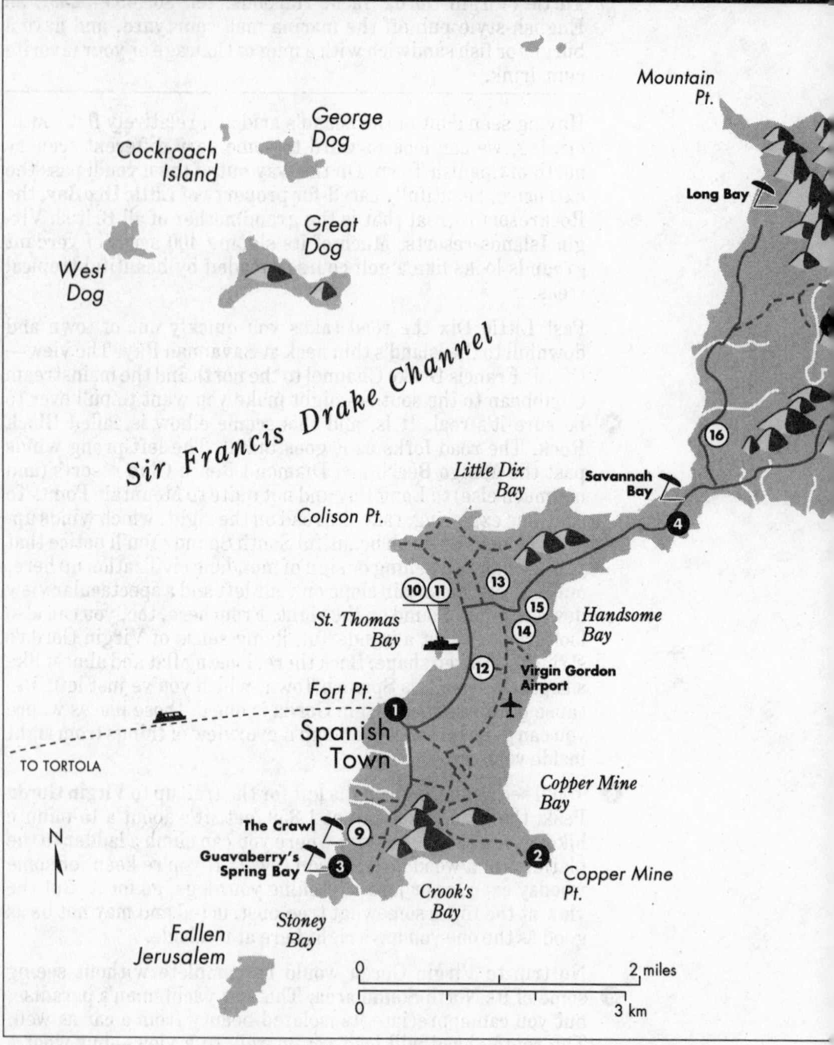

Mountain Pt.
George Dog
Cockroach Island
Great Dog
West Dog
Long Bay
Sir Francis Drake Channel
16
Little Dix Bay
Savannah Bay
Colison Pt.
4
13
10
11
15
St. Thomas Bay
Handsome Bay
14
12
Virgin Gordon Airport
Fort Pt.
1
Spanish Town
TO TORTOLA
Copper Mine Bay
The Crawl
9
N
Guavaberry's Spring Bay
3
2
Copper Mine Pt.
Crook's Bay
Stoney Bay
Fallen Jerusalem
0
2 miles
0
3 km

Exploring
The Baths, **3**
Black Rock, **4**
Copper Mine Point, **2**
Eustatia Sound, **8**
North Sound, **6**
Saba Rock, **7**
Spanish Town, **1**
Virgin Gorda Peak, **5**

Dining
Biras Creek, **21**
Chez Michelle, **10**
Olde Yard Inn, **14**
Salty Whale Pub & Eatery, **19**

Lodging
Biras Creek, **22**
Bitter End Yacht Club, **18**
Drakes Anchorage (Mosquito Island), **17**
Fischer's Cove Beach Hotel, **11**
Guavaberry Spring Bay Vacation Homes, **9**
Leverick Bay Resort and Marina, **20**
Little Dix Bay, **13**
Mango Beach Resort, **16**
Ocean View Hotel, **12**
Olde Yard Inn, **15**

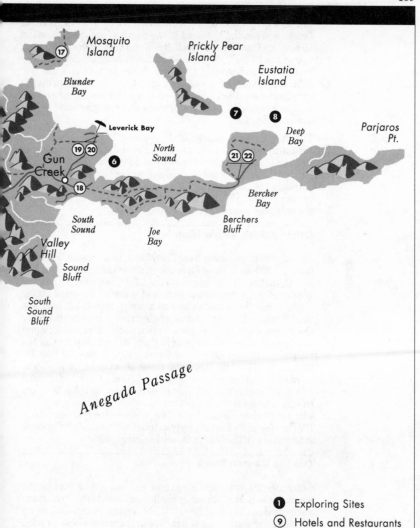

Mosquito Island

Prickly Pear Island

Eustatia Island

Blunder Bay

Leverick Bay

North Sound

Deep Bay

Parjaros Pt.

Gun Creek

Bercher Bay

South Sound

Joe Bay

Berchers Bluff

Valley Hill

Sound Bluff

South Sound Bluff

Anegada Passage

1 Exploring Sites

9 Hotels and Restaurants

been named a National Park to protect it from development. At the neck of land to your right, across from Gun Creek, is **Biras Creek,** and around the bend to the north of that you'll see the Danish-roof buildings of the **Bitter End Yacht Club,** these being two of the British Virgin Islands' finest resorts. Between the Bitter End and Prickly Pear you should be able to make out **7** **Saba Rock,** home of one of the Caribbean's best-known diving entrepreneurs, Bert Kilbride—a man who knows where all the wrecks are buried and is recognized and commissioned by the Queen of England.

That magical color change in the sea near Prickly Pear reveals **8** **Eustatia Sound** and its valued reef. Beyond that are Horseshoe Reef and the flat coral island of Anegada. Out there is where most of those wrecks *are* buried and where bareboaters are not permitted to sail because of the perilous reefs. But you can easily take a boat to Biras Creek or the Bitter End. In fact, that's the only way you can get there.

Other British Virgin Islands

Just across the channel from Road Town on Tortola is **Peter Island,** a 1,000-acre island known for its hotel and yacht club. **Jost Van Dyke,** the sizable island north of Tortola's western tip, is a good choice for travelers in search of isolation and good hiking trails; it has three hostelries and a campground, but only one small town and no cars, roads, or electricity. Hikers also enjoy the nature trails and wildlife sanctuary on **Guana Island,** a private island just above the eastern tip of Tortola. **Marina Cay** is a snug six-acre islet near Great Camanoe, just north of Beef Island, east of Tortola. **Anegada,** about 20 miles north of Virgin Gorda's North Sound, is a flat mass of coral 11 miles long and 3 miles wide with a population of only about 250. Visitors are chiefly scuba divers and fishermen, some of whom are interested in the bonefishing here. The island can be reached by Air BVI as well as by boat (Speedy's, tel. 809/495–5240). (For more information on these islands, *see* Lodging, below.)

Off the Beaten Track

Get yourself some snorkeling gear and hop a dive boat to the **wreck of the R.M.S.** *Rhone,* off Salt Island (just across the channel from Road Town on Tortola). This is your chance to float on crystal-clear water over or near one of the world's best wrecks: a royal mail steamer 310 feet long that sank here in a hurricane in 1867. It was used in the movie *The Deep.* Its four parts are at various depths of from 20 to 80 feet. Even if you can't see down to the main part of the wreck, you'll definitely be fascinated watching the moves and bubbles of scuba divers below you. Nearby Rhone Reef is only 20 to 50 feet down. Simple and safe flotation devices are available, and the scuba supervisors will keep an eye on you. Call **Baskin in the Sun** (tel. 809/494–2858), **Underwater Safaris** (tel. 809/494–3235), **Blue Water Divers** (tel. 809/494–2847), **Island Diver, Ltd.** (tel. 809/494–3878), or **Caribbean Images** (tel. 809/495–2563).

Participant Sports

Horseback Riding On Tortola, equestrians should get in touch with **Tamarind Country Club Hotel** (East End, tel. 809/495–2477) or **Mr. Ellis**

Thomas (Sea Cows Bay, tel. 809/494–4442). On Virgin Gorda call **Little Dix Bay** (The Valley, tel. 809/495–5555).

Sailboarding   **Boardsailing B.V.I.** (Long Look, Tortola, tel. 809/495–2447) has private lessons for $45 per hour and cheaper group rates. **The Nick Trotter Sailing School** (Bitter End Yacht Club, North Sound, Virgin Gorda, tel. 800/872–2392) has both beginner's and advanced courses.

Sailing/Boating   The BVI has been a charter boat paradise for the past 20 years, and the flagship of charter operators has all along been **The Moorings,** at The Moorings-Mariner Inn in Road Town's harbor, Tortola (tel. 809/494–2331 or 800/535–7289; AE, MC, V). About 25 other sailing enterprises offer crewed or bareboat charters or both, and some also have arrangements for cruise trips or day sails.

Tortola   **B.V.I. Bareboats** (Road Town, tel. 809/494–4289) offers both bareboat and skippered charters. **Go Vacations** (East End, tel. 809/495–2379) has cat boats, sloops, ketches, and trawlers for bareboat or crewed hire. **Patsy Lady/Foxy Lady** (Road Town, tel. 809/494–3540) will rent you a 24′ or 43′ twin-engine motorcruiser.

Virgin Gorda   **The Bitter End Yacht Club** (North Sound, tel. 809/494–2746 or 800/872–2392, AE, DC, MC, V) is island headquarters for most sailing activity and offers Cal; 27 charters **Malcolm & Niki** (Yacht Harbor, tel. 809/495–5555) rents the *Beruthiel,* a 35′ ocean-going catamaran.

Scuba Diving and Snorkeling   The famed wreck of the R.M.S. *Rhone,* off Salt Island, is reason enough to do some diving before your BVI stay is over. Except for wall diving, there is a great variety of dive sites along the channel and north of Tortola, including an underwater pinnacle called Blonde Rock. **Baskin in the Sun** (Prospect Reef Hotel; Road Town, tel. 800/233–7938, 809/494–2858, or 809/494–2859, AE, MC, V), the successor to Aquatic Centres, offers resort courses and packages as well as day and night dives and works with six hotels on the island. **Caribbean Images** (Road Town, tel. 809/495–2563 or 809/494–3311) specializes in snorkeling tours and also has glass-bottom boats and photo and video services. **Dive B.V.I.** (tel. 809/495–5513; AE, MC, V), with shops at both the Yacht Harbour and Leverick Bay in Virgin Gorda, has both three- and five-day packages.

Sportfishing   A number of companies can transport and outfit you for a few hours of reel fun; try **Charter Fishing Virgin Islands** (Prospect Reef, Tortola, tel. 809/494–3311), **Harrigan's Rent-A-Boat** (Yacht Harbour, Virgin Gorda, tel. 809/495–5542), or **Kingfisher** (Yacht Harbour, Virgin Gorda, tel. 809/495–5230 or 809/495–5336).

Tennis   Resorts on Tortola that have tennis courts are **Frenchman's Cay, The Moorings-Mariner Inn, Long Bay Hotel, Prospect Reef,** and **Treasure Isle Hotel.** You may reserve court time at **Prospect Reef** without being a guest there (Road Town, tel. 809/494–3311). There is also the **Tortola Tennis Club,** in Road Town (tel. 809/494–3733). On Virgin Gorda **Biras Creek** at North Sound (tel. 809/494–3555) and **Little Dix Bay** in The Valley (tel. 809/495–5555) have courts.

Shopping

Unlike the U.S. Virgin Islands, the British Virgins are not known as a shopping haven. There isn't a lot to choose from on these tranquil isles, but what is there is select and sophisticated.

Shopping Districts Most of the shops and boutiques on Tortola are clustered on and off Road Town's Main Street. The Wickhams Cay shopping area adjacent to the Marina has a number of new shops that have an upscale feel, and upscale prices. On Tortola's resort-crested sister isles most boutiques are located within the individual hotel complexes. One of the best is the one in the Little Dix Bay Rockresort on Virgin Gorda. Other properties on the same island—Biras Creek, the Bitter End, and Leverick Bay—have small but equally select boutiques, and there's a more than respectable and diverse scattering of shops in the minimall adjacent to the bustling yacht harbor in Spanish Town.

Drake's Anchorage on Mosquito Island has one of the best resort shops; American owner Jamy Faust stocks both maillots and basic bikinis, T-shirts, shell jewelry, pareos, and straw hats, as well as sun lotions and other sundries. Other resorts with on-site shops include the Peter Island Hotel and Yacht Club on Peter Island, the Marina Cay and the Anegada Reef on Anegada, and the Sandcastle on Jost Van Dyke.

Specialty Stores
Art **Collector's Corner** (Columbus Centre, Wickhams Cay, Tortola, tel. 809/494–3550) has serious Caribbean art at serious prices. They also carry antique maps and a collection of eelskin wallets, bags, and belts.
The Courtyard Gallery (Main St., Road Town, Tortola) shows its exclusive Carinia Collection, delicate crushed-coral sculptures depicting darting hummingbirds, angelfish, nesting pelicans, and flowers.
Naucraft Galleries (Wickhams Cay II, Road Town, Tortola, tel. 809/494–4790) has a wide range of Caribbean art (and prices); its offerings include original watercolors, oils, and acrylics, as well as signed prints, limited-edition serigraphs, and turn-of-the-century sepia photographs.
Sunny Caribbee Skyworld Boutique and Art Gallery (Skyworld Restaurant, Ridge Rd., Tortola, tel. 809/494–3567) has one of the largest displays of paintings throughout the Caribbean; the collection is hung in the restaurant's dining room and is heavy on Haitian primitive. They also sell their own line of spices, soaps, and sun-protection creams.

Clothing **Island Woman** (The Valley, Virgin Gorda, tel. 809/495–5237) offers an array of cotton Java Wraps and belts, beads, bracelets, and other accessories from Indonesia.
Sally Bell's (Main St., Road Town, Tortola, tel. 809/494–4670) has a sophisticated selection of British and French fashions (some trendy, some classic) for men and women.
Sea Urchin (Columbus Centre, Road Town, Tortola, tel. 809/494–3129) has a good selection of island-living designs: print shirts and shorts, slinky swimsuits, sandals, and, of course, T-shirts.
Turtle Dove Boutique (Flemming St., Road Town, Tortola, tel. 809/494–3611) is among the best of the best in the BVI for French perfume, international swimwear, and premium cotton batiks from Thailand.

Food and Drink **The Ample Hamper** (Village Cay Marina, Wickhams Cay, Tortola, tel. 809/494–2494), the leader in gourmet foods in Tortola, offers serious take-home packages that can serve as the foundation for an elegant picnic.

The Pusser's Company Store & Pub (Main St. and Waterfront Rd., Road Town, Tortola, tel. 809/494–2467) is a find for both rum lovers and teetotalers. Those who drink appreciate the free rum tastings and the assortment of handsome bottles of this renowned brew (available here for about half of what they cost elsewhere). Those who don't shop for nautical memorabilia, ship models, marine paintings, and an entire line of clothes and gift items bearing the Pusser's logo.

The Sunny Caribbee Herb & Spice Company (Main St., Road Town, Tortola, tel. 809/494–2178), located in a brightly painted West Indian house, packages its own herbs, teas, coffees, herb vinegars, hot sauces, and natural soaps and skin lotions.

Gifts **Carousel Gift Shop** (Tropic Aisle, Wickhams Cay, Tortola, tel. 809/494–2442) carries fine crystal and china, embroidered table and bed covers, and French perfume.

Past and Presents (Main St., Road Town, Tortola, tel. 809/494–2747 or 809/494–2163), now in its 20th year of operation, has quality books from the British Isles, United States, and Canada, as well as a good selection of paperbacks for the beach. They also have a very good (if small) selection of antique silver and china.

Jewelry **Flaxcraft Jewellers** (Main St., Road Town, Tortola, tel. 809/494–2892) carries fine gold and silver jewelry; many of the pieces are one-of-a-kind creations incorporating shells and fragments of coral.

Little Denmark (Main St., Road Town, Tortola, tel. 809/494–2455) stocks handsome, streamlined designs from Scandinavia as well as brand-name china.

Local Crafts **The Basket Case** (Cell 5 Complex, The Rufus L. deCastro Centre, Tortola, tel. 809/494–4608) has the best selection of hand-woven baskets from islands throughout the Caribbean as well as a sampling of other local crafts.

Delightfully Yours (opposite the Post Office in Road Town, Tortola) is a yellow-and-cream century-old shop that houses a choice selection of ceramics, wood carvings, woven fabrics, and pewter and sandstone pieces made by BVI craftsmen.

The Shipwreck Shop (Main St., Road Town, Tortola, tel. 809/494–2567) is one of a chain of Shipwreck Shops scattered throughout the Caribbean, all of which offer distinctive items at very reasonable prices: woven baskets, hammocks, shell and coral jewelry, hand-blocked pareos, painted T-shirts (long and short), and wood plates and bowls. If you enjoy a challenge, consider the Arawak Indian game of *warri;* the sets here come with a carved wood board and beans that are used as markers.

Textiles **Bonker's Gallery** (Main St., Road Town, Tortola, tel. 809/494–2535) features designs created by the owner along with the muted-color sarongs from Java Wraps. There's also a swimwear and T-shirt corner as well as a selection of miscellaneous gifts and trendy ties for the hair or waist.

Zenaida (Cutlass House, Wickhams Cay, Road Town, Tortola, tel. 809/494–2113) displays the fabric finds of Argentinian Vivian Helm, who travels through South America, Africa, and India in search of batiks, hand-painted and hand-blocked fabrics, and interesting weaves that can be made into pareos or wall hangings. The shop also offers a selection of unusual bags, belts, and beads.

Dining

The most popular choices in BVI restaurants are seafood dishes. Almost everything else has to be imported and thus tends to be more expensive. Most restaurants offer varied fare, including seafood and an array of Continental dishes.

The most highly recommended restaurants are indicated by a star ★.

Category	Cost*
Very Expensive	over $35
Expensive	$25–$35
Moderate	$15–$25
Inexpensive	under $15

per person, excluding drinks and service; there is no sales tax in the BVI

Tortola
★ **Sugar Mill.** Low candles, low breezes, and low music complement an ever-creative menu and ample wine list. The tenderloin cooked in red-wine sauce is excellent, and a typical potage is curried banana soup. Owners/chefs Jeff and Jinx Morgan somehow also find time to write for *Bon Appetit* magazine. *West End (North Shore), Apple Bay, tel. 809/495–4355. Reservations advised. AE, MC, V. Very Expensive.*

The Cloud Room. Not only do you have a mountaintop view, but the roof moves to make things alfresco. The proprietors pick up guests from local hotels, then return them after dinner. The menu is varied. *Ridge Rd., above Road Harbour, tel. 809/494–2821. Reservations required. AE, MC, V. Dinner only. Expensive.*

Fort Burt Restaurant. This respected restaurant is situated on the site of a 17th-century Dutch fort on a roadside hill overlooking the harbor. Its entrées range from pan-fried dolphin and lobster Thermidor to tournedos of beef, mixed grill, and beefsteak-oyster-ale pie. *Fort Burt, Road Town, tel. 809/494–2587. Reservations advised. AE, MC, V. Expensive.*

★ **Long Bay Beach Resort.** Recent renovation here has involved only the building, not the menu, which needs none. From a chicken-and-melon salad or pâté appetizer you can go on to West Indian curry with rice and peas or pork, duck, or filet mignon. *West End (North Shore), Long Bay, tel. 809/495–4252. Reservations advised. AE, MC, V. Expensive.*

Cell 5 Lounge. Relax with the local folks at this casual bar-and-burger joint looking out on Road Harbor. *Rufus L. de Castrol Center, Road Town, tel. 809/494–4629. Inexpensive.*

The Apple. This inviting restaurant is located in a small West Indian house not far from the cooling breezes of Little Apple Bay. Soft candlelight complements local seafood dishes such as conch in garlic and wine sauce and fish steamed in lime butter. Sunday nights feature a barbecue buffet with all the trimmings for $16. *Little Apple Bay, tel. 809/495–4437. No credit cards. Moderate.*

★ **Spaghetti Junction.** At this merry, airy little upstairs box of a restaurant, unbeatable selections are stuffed mushrooms, Caesar salad with sun-dried tomatoes, artichoke linguini, and the tortellini. The salads are as fresh as you'll ever have. *Road Town, across from Wickhams Cay I, tel. 809/494–4880. Reservations advised. No credit cards. Moderate.*

The Pusser's Deli. This publike eatery is a good place to know, whether your budget is limited or strained. You'll find English shepherd's pie and chicken-and-asparagus pie, roast beef and other deli sandwiches, and even some Mexican dishes. You can also get a Key lime pie or a milk shake. *Main St., Road Town, tel. 809/494–2467. No credit cards. Inexpensive.*

Virgin Gorda **Biras Creek.** You come by boat (provided free) to this serene
★ restaurant on a turretlike terrace with the sea on one side and a beautiful North Sound marina on the other. The excellent dishes are never heavy, and the wine list is considerable. There is a prix fixe dinner of five courses. *North Sound, tel. 809/494–3555 or 809/495–4356. Reservations advised. AE, MC, V. Expensive.*

Chez Michelle. The restaurant is simply decorated and the building is nondescript—cuisine is the thing. Entrées include broiled lobster, seafood fettuccine Alfredo, rack of lamb, and Chicken Cordon Chic (slices of banana and Black Forest ham encased in chicken breast, roasted and served with curry sauce). A favorite here is the Caesar salad with garlic walnuts. *The Valley, near the Yacht Harbour, tel. 809/495–5510. Reservations requested. MC, V. Dinner only, 6:30–9:30. Expensive.*

★ **Olde Yard Inn.** The high thatch ceiling, background classical music, and sofas and chess set near the bar are thoroughly enticing—and the dishes equally so. The pasta and breads are all homemade. Entrées include Caribbean lobster and sirloin steak; the breast of chicken is prepared with rum, cream, and nuts. *The Valley, tel. 809/495–5544. Reservations requested. MC, V. Moderate.*

Salty Whale Pub & Eatery. Out North Sound way, this outdoor terrace faces a small, covelike marina and offers chicken, ribs, or local fish dishes at modest prices, as well as Continental entrées and fiery chicken wings. *Leverick Bay, tel. 809/495–7421 or 809/495–5433. AE, MC, V. Moderate.*

Lodging

The number of rooms available in the BVI is small compared with other destinations in the Caribbean; what is available is also often in great demand, and the prices are not low. The top-of-the-line resorts here are among the most expensive in the Caribbean and are sometimes difficult to book even off-season. Even the more moderately priced hotels command top dollar during the season; off-season, however, they are legitimate bargains at about half the price. There are some inexpensive hotels, but their accommodations are often Spartan; their locations, however, sometimes more than make up for that.

The most highly recommended lodgings are indicated by a star ★.

Category	Cost*
Very Expensive	over $200
Expensive	$125–$200

Moderate	$65–$125
Inexpensive	under $65

*All prices are for a standard double room, excluding 7% accommodation tax.

Tortola **Nanny Cay Resort and Marina.** This new Ramada marina resort has its own nub of land, just off Tortola's south coast road between Road Town and West End. All rooms have a kitchenette, cable TV, telephone, air-conditioning and ceiling fans, and a patio or balcony. Peg Leg Landing restaurant, on stilts, is perfect for viewing sunsets. *Box 281, Road Town, tel. 809/494–2512. 41 rooms. Facilities: beach, 2 pools (1 saltwater), restaurant, bar, marina. AE, MC, V. Expensive.*

Fort Recovery. The simple, air-conditioned beachfront villas have garden patios, full kitchens, and an ideal view of the Sir Francis Drake Channel. On the grounds stands part of a Dutch fort built in 1600. A small commissary sells home-cooked entrées for quick reheating. The resort is located close to Frenchman's Cay and West End. *Box 239, Road Town, tel. 809/495–4354, 212/929–7929, or 518/377–7216. 7 1-bedroom villas, 1 2-bedroom villa, and 1 4-bedroom luxury house. Facilities: beach, snorkeling, commissary. AE. Expensive.*

Frenchman's Cay Resort Hotel. The breezes blow strong at this finely situated 12-acre resort connected to Tortola's coastal road by a small bridge. The one- and two-bedroom villas have full kitchens and shaded terraces. *Box 1054, West End, tel. 809/494–4844 or 800/223–9832. 23 rooms. Facilities: beach, restaurant, bar, tennis courts, pool, water sports. AE, MC, V. Expensive.*

★ **Long Bay Beach Resort.** Set along one of the longest sweeps of white-sand beach on Tortola, the Long Bay offers hillside units, beachfront cabanas, and deluxe new beachfront rooms that share a large porch. Most rooms have kitchenettes. The excellent Garden restaurant has been totally renovated, and a new Modified American Plan (MAP) allows you to have breakfast late into the afternoon. An additional 18 units should be completed by late 1990. *Box 433, Road Town, tel. 809/495–4252. 44 rooms. Facilities: beach, 2 restaurants, 2 bars, pool, tennis court, commissary. AE, MC, V. Expensive.*

★ **Prospect Reef.** This large resort is a paradise for water-sports enthusiasts. It has its own harbor inlet, bridges, lagoon, and craggy, rock-terraced sea pool. Every room overlooks the water. Garden rooms have air-conditioning, and superior and deluxe studios have kitchens. The panoramic channel view of islands to the south is never less than irresistible. *Box 104, Road Town, tel. 809/494–3311 or 800/356–8937. 131 rooms. Facilities: man-made beach area, 3 pools (2 freshwater: 1 Olympic-size and 1 for diving), children's splash pool, 6 tennis courts, pitch-and-putt golf course, water sports, restaurant and bars, shopping arcade. AE, MC, V. Expensive.*

★ **Sugar Mill.** Dine at night here, where candles flicker within old walls hung with Haitian paintings and voices are never too loud against the roll of the Apple Bay surf, and you'll know the magic of Tortola. Owners Jeff and Jinx Morgan are also writers and gourmet cooks and know all the ingredients of innlike peacefulness and romance; with manager Patrick Conway they are ever personable and helpful hosts. Buildings are on a snug hillside property, and deluxe accommodations have kitchenettes and balconies. *Box 425, Road Town, tel. 809/495-4355. 20 rooms. Facilities: beach, restaurant, 2 bars, pool. AE, DC, MC, V. Expensive.*

Fort Burt. This well-run small hotel is perched neatly by itself on a small hill—site of a 1666 Dutch fort—overlooking Road Harbour. All rooms face the water. The restaurant is one of Tortola's best, and the cool, well-like bar area is an interesting place to quaff. A boat takes guests to a private beach. *Box 187, Road Town, tel. 809/494-2587. 7 rooms. Facilities: bar, restaurant, pool. AE, MC, V. Moderate.*

★ **Sebastians on the Beach.** This casual north-shore outpost, at Little Apple Bay, is a favorite of surfers and Europeans. (Surfboards can be rented.) All rooms have refrigerators, and most have a queen-size and a twin bed. The restaurant fare is simple, mainly grilled fish or meat. A homey atmosphere prevails. *Box 441, Road Town, tel. 809/495-4212. 26 rooms. Facilities: beach, restaurant, bar, water sports, and commissary. AE. Moderate.*

Treasure Isle Hotel. Renovation is ongoing at this lively hillside hotel recently purchased by The Moorings, a yacht-charter company. All rooms have telephones, are air-conditioned, and some even have rattan double swings. Daily transportation is provided to two beaches, and you can be brought by boat to the hotel's own beach club on Cooper Island. *Box 68, Road Town, tel. 809/494-2501 or 800/526-4789. 40 rooms. Facilities: restaurant, bar, pool, 2 tennis courts, squash court, water sports, marina. AE, MC, V. Moderate.*

Cane Garden Bay Beach Hotel. Beautiful Cane Garden Bay and the stunning white beach cradled by steep mountain greenery are the main attractions here. The simple hotel rooms have beach-view balconies, ceiling fans, and screened windows. Snorkeling equipment, Windsurfers, Sunfish, and other paraphernalia for water activities can be rented on the beach. The hotel is only a 15-minute drive from Road Town. *Box 570 CGB, tel. 809/495-4639 or 809/495-4215. 27 rooms. Facilities: beach, restaurant, bar, water sports. AE, MC, V. Inexpensive.*

Hotel Castle Maria. This clean hotel gets lovely breezes through its balconies, which have wide, cushioned chairs. The many island-scene paintings give the place a friendly West Indian atmosphere. Some rooms have air-conditioning and cable TV and all have small refrigerators. *Box 206, Road Town, tel. 809/494-2553. 30 rooms. Facilities: restaurant, bar, pool. AE, MC, V. Inexpensive.*

Jolly Roger Inn. A money-saver just west of the ferry dock at the sunset end of Tortola, this very unfancy place has just a few rooms with shared bath and a few with private bath: stay six nights and the seventh is free. The turnoff to north-shore beaches is conveniently just down the road. *West End, Sopers Hole, tel. 809/495-4559. 6 rooms. Facilities: restaurant, bar, harborside bar, dinghy dock. No credit cards. Inexpensive.*

Maria's by the Sea. The sea here is Road Harbour, as this simple two-story building is situated on a flat patch of land at Wickhams Cay I. The rooms are cooled by ceiling fans and have balconies, kitchenettes, and rattan furniture. Local food is served at the restaurant. Don't look for shade here on this sandy spit of waterfront. *Box 206, Wickhams Cay I, Road Town, tel. 809/494-2595. 14 rooms. Facilities: restaurant, pool. AE, MC, V. Inexpensive.*

Campgrounds **Brewers Bay Campground.** This campground, which opened in 1976 as the BVI's first, is at a beautiful location. Bare sites are in a grove 150 feet from the beach. Tent sites come with floor, beds and linens, propane-gas stove and lantern, ice chest, cooking and eating utensils, and picnic table and bench. Toilets and showers are in a separate building. *Box 185, Road Town, tel. 809/494–3463. 15 beds. Facilities: beach, beach bar. Babysitters available. No credit cards or personal checks.*

Virgin Gorda **Biras Creek.** A turretlike stone building (clubhouse and dining ★ room) quietly watches over this magically private resort, which is neatly fit into a North Sound isthmus and can be reached only by boat. From your two-unit modern cottage— with bedroom, living room, and elegant open-air walled shower —you can bicycle (provided free) down a desert-garden path to the ocean-view pool, tennis courts, a salt-pond bird sanctuary, or the Deep Bay swimming beach, which has an honor bar, raft, and water-sports equipment. A few super-deluxe suites are also available. There are no roads, only miles of hiking trails (and one Iguana Crossing). The restaurant and wine list are first-rate. British hosts Brian and Judith Connelly might allow you to guess which one of them is the former Yorkshire mayor and which the sometime singer and impersonator. There is not a dram of pretention in them. *Box 54, tel. 809/494–3555 or 809/494–3556. 32 rooms. Facilities: beach, restaurant, bar, tennis courts, marina, pool, water sports, hiking trails. AE, MC, V. Very Expensive.*

Bitter End Yacht Club. When the Caribbean yachting set want to get their feet dry or whistles wet, this sporty village-length North Sound resort is a favorite anchorage. Guests stay in hillside or beachfront villas or chalets—or on a live-aboard yacht. Pick your boat, your restaurant, your bar, your sailing-instruction course, or your dive package. You will be taxied around on People Mover carts, a Hillevator, or pontoon shuttle boats. For maximum peace and quiet, the topmost hillside chalets or endmost beachfronts are your best bet. *Box 46, North Sound, tel. 809/494–2746. 100 rooms. Facilities: beach, 3 restaurants, bar, marina, pool. AE, DC, MC, V. Very Expensive.*

★ **Little Dix Bay.** Set on 400 verdant acres along the Sir Francis Drake Channel, this quiet Rockresort property is possibly the most famous resort in the BVI. The curving beach is magnificent, and a broad, sheltering reef completes its circle. Cone-roof guest cottages, some on stilts, are furnished with elegant understatement in a Caribbean way, and all have a terrace or balcony. *Box 70, tel. 809/495–5555. 102 rooms. Facilities: beach, restaurant, bar, water sports, marina, 7 tennis courts. AE, DC, MC, V. Very Expensive.*

Fischer's Cove Beach Hotel. A short walk from the Virgin Gorda Marina, this casual beachfront hotel with unmanicured grounds is West Indian in atmosphere and gets good breezes. The 11 buildings each have two guest units; there are also two two-bedroom cottages with kitchens. The rooms are oddly shaped but spacious and cool. *Box 60, The Valley, tel. 809/495–5252 or 809/495–5253. 22 rooms. Facilities: beach, restaurant, bar, water sports, discotheque. AE, MC, V. Expensive.*

★ **Olde Yard Inn.** You'll find beach chairs under physic nut trees, hammocks, and a few Virgin Gordan boulders on these peaceful grounds. There are private patios, and upstairs rooms look out to sea. But most special about this homey oasis is its octagonal library pavilion, with handsome books, a chess set, and a

George Steck spinet kept in perfect tune. (It could be a gentleman's club room in 19th-century Kenya.) It's all enough to make you forget about the beach, which is a 20-minute walk away. *Box 26, Spanish Town, tel. 809/495-5544. 14 rooms. Facilities: restaurant and bar, library, horseback riding. AE, MC, V. Expensive.*

Leverick Bay Resort and Marina. Nestled on a picturesque, steep bend of Gorda Sound, this resort is centered on a clustered beach area, marina dock, and pool. Its luxury villas at various levels of the hillside are rentable by the week and have one, two, or three bedrooms. Only the studio apartments have air-conditioning. Prickly Pear Island and some excellent reefs are part of the resort's view. *North Sound Yacht Charter, Ltd., Box 1077, tel. 809/495-7421 or 809/495-5433. 41 rooms. Facilities: 2 beaches, beach restaurant and bar, marina, pool, water sports. AE, MC, V. Moderate-Expensive.*

Mango Beach Resort. The Italians have landed at Mahoe Bay and built this array of modern white duplex villas, tucked privately downhill from the north-coast road winding out of Spanish Town. Everything is very new, spacious, and airy, including the terraces. Each villa is divided into separate one- and two-bedroom units with full kitchens. The lagoonlike waters are tranquil, and there is a small dock. *Box 1062, tel. 809/495-5672 or 809/495-5673. 21 rooms. Facilities: beach, dock, snorkeling. No credit cards. Moderate-Expensive.*

Guavaberry Spring Bay Vacation Homes. From the exquisite tamarind-shaded beach you can swim to the mammoth boulders and shaded basins of the famed Baths, which adjoin this property. The one- and two-bedroom cottages, all with kitchen facilities, have curved decks and are a bit like tree houses. You'll hear twittering birds and branches swaying in the breeze. Guests emphatically do not miss telephones. *Box 20, tel. 809/495-5227. 16 rooms. Facilities: beach, commissary. No credit cards. Moderate.*

Ocean View Hotel. You can save money here, but management also saves with 25-watt lightbulbs, loud ceiling fans, and velvet wall art. On the other hand, it's cheap and right across the road from the marina shops of Spanish Town. Special rates for groups or stays over 14 days. *Box 66, tel. 809/495-5230. 12 rooms. Facilities: restaurant and bar. AE, MC, V. Inexpensive.*

Peter Island **Peter Island Hotel and Yacht Club.** This resort is close to the last word in luxury in all the Caribbean. There are 52 rooms and five villas and every imaginable living, dining, or recreational amenity, including a gourmet restaurant, saltwater pool, tennis, and horseback riding. *Box 211, Road Town, Tortola, BVI, tel. 809/494-2561 or 800/346-4451. AE, MC, V. Very Expensive.*

Anegada **Anegada Reef Hotel.** The only hotel on Anegada, this resort has 12 rooms, a beach, beach bar, restaurant, dive shop, gift shop, anchorage with moorings, and taxi service. *Lowell Wheatley, Anegada Reef Hotel, Anegada, BVI, tel. 809/494-3111 (marine operator), 809/495-8002 in Tortola and 809/776-8282 in St. Thomas. Fishing and diving packages available. No credit cards. Expensive.*

Jost Van Dyke **Sandcastle,** at White Bay, has four beach cottages and a restaurant and bar. *Box 540, Pawley's Island, SC 29585, tel. 803/237-8999. No credit cards. Very Expensive.*

Rudy's Mariner Inn, at Great Harbour, has three rooms with kitchenettes and dining areas. There is a restaurant and beach bar. *Great Harbour, Jost Van Dyke, BVI, tel. 809/775–3558 (USVI). No credit cards. Expensive.*

Tula's N & N Campground offers bare sites and 8 × 10 or 9 × 12 tents. *Reservations: Box 8364, St. Thomas, USVI 00801, tel. 809/775–3073 or 809/774–0774.*

Guana Island   **Guana Island Club.** This luxurious hideaway has 15 rooms, terrace dining, tennis, nature trails, and water sports for its guests. *Box 32, Road Town, Tortola, BVI, tel. 809/494–2354 or 800/54GUANA. No credit cards. Very Expensive.*

Mosquito Island   **Drake's Anchorage.** The bungalows at this secluded getaway are West Indian in style. Besides the 12 oceanfront rooms (two of them suites), there are two fully equipped villas. There is a restaurant, hiking trails, and water-sports facilities. *Box 2510, North Sound, Virgin Gorda, BVI, tel. 809/494–2254 or 800/624–6651. AE, MC, V. Very Expensive.*

Marina Cay   **Marina Cay Hotel.** A favorite spot for sailing visitors, this resort has 12 colorful rooms, two restaurants and bars, and water-sports facilities. *Box 76, Road Town, Tortola, BVI, tel. 809/494–2174. AE, MC, V. Very Expensive.*

Nightlife

If going out on the town is to be a big part of your Caribbean vacation, well, you won't find much in the way even of towns in the British Virgin Islands. Most BVI guests are content to find their nightlife at the resort (or boat) where they're staying.

Tortola   But on the evening when you just have to drive somewhere to hear some music, clinking glasses, and conversational din, one spot on Tortola that might fit the bill is **The Pub** (Fort Burt Marina, tel. 809/494–2608), which has a buzzing bar and live bands (rock, reggae, or calypso) on Friday and Saturday nights. Another playroom, built on stilts at a marina, is **Peg Leg Landing** (Nanny Cay, tel. 809/494–2512). Down at Sopers Hole, West End, are **Pusser's Landing** (tel. 809/495–4554 or 809/495–4553), which has a steel band Thursday nights and, with a slightly more raw and hard-drinking ambience, **The Jolly Roger** (tel. 809/495–4559). For West Indian entertainment try **Skylight** (Fat Hog's Bay, tel. 809/495–2584).

Virgin Gorda   The biggest noise, literally, on Virgin Gorda is in The Valley at **Andy's Chateau de Pirate** (tel. 809/595–5253), a disco that pumps at full volume at Fischer's Cove Hotel, where the crowd is mostly young local residents. But for setting, conviviality, and a sporty atmosphere, you can't do much better than to join the yachting crowd—who will not be in formal dress—and guests from the States at the **Bitter End Yacht Club** on beautiful North Sound (tel. 809/494–2746).

8 Cayman Islands

by John English

The venerable old *Saturday Evening Post* dubbed them "the islands that time forgot." The paper did not survive long enough to see the Cayman Islands, a British Crown colony comprising Grand Cayman, Cayman Brac, and Little Cayman, become one of the Caribbean's hottest tourist destinations.

Why do metropolis-weary visitors continue to trek to these islands 480 miles south of Miami? Why do they fill the hotels and condominiums that line Grand Cayman's famed Seven Mile Beach, even during the traditionally slow summer season? Their dollars certainly go farther in other Caribbean destinations, for in Cayman—which positively reeks of prosperity, bulging as it does with some 500 offshore banks located in George Town, the capital, on Grand Cayman—the U.S. dollar is worth 80 Cayman cents, and the cost of living is 20% higher than in the United States.

Certainly it is not because of overwhelming advertising in the United States. The Department of Tourism's ad budget is small compared with the budgets of tourist rivals like the Bahamas and Jamaica.

The secret is word-of-mouth testimonials. The Cayman Islanders—the population is 18,000, almost all of it residents of Grand Cayman—are renowned for the courteous and civil manners befitting their British heritage. If they sometimes appear to be slightly aloof, truth is the attitude is born of innate shyness. Visitors will find no hasslers or panhandlers, and no need to look apprehensively over their shoulder on dark evenings, for the colony is virtually crime-free. Add to that permanent political and economic stability, and you have a fairly rosy picture.

The Caymans are a paradise for divers: Translucent waters and a colorful variety of marine life are protected by the government, which has designated various marine parks.

Columbus is said to have sighted the islands in 1503, but he didn't stop off to explore. He did note that the surrounding sea was alive with turtles, so the islands were named Las Tortugas. The name was later changed to Cayman.

The islands stayed largely uninhabited until the latter part of the 1600s, when Britain took over the Cayman Islands and Jamaica from Spain under the Treaty of Madrid. Cayman attracted a mixed bag of settlers, pirates, refugees from the Spanish Inquisition, shipwrecked sailors, and deserters from Oliver Cromwell's army in Jamaica. Today's Caymanians are the descendants of those nationalities.

The caves and coves of the islands were a perfect hideout for pirates of the ilk of Blackbeard and Sir Henry Morgan, who plundered Spanish galleons that were hauling riches from the New World of South America to Spain. Many a ship also fell afoul of the reefs surrounding the islands, often with the help of the Caymanians, who lured the vessels to shore with beacon fires. Some of the old pioneer homes on the islands were made from the remains of those galleons.

The legend of the Wreck of the Ten Sails was to have a lasting effect on the Caymanians. In 1788, a convoy of 10 Jamaican ships bound for England foundered on the reefs, but the islanders managed to rescue everyone. Royalty was purportedly aboard, and a grateful George III decreed that Caymanians should forever be exempt from conscription and never have to pay taxes.

The islands were a dependency of Jamaica until the 1961 formation of the West Indies Federation. Jamaica opted for independence from Britain, but Cayman chose to remain a colony, and it has since remained loyal to the Crown.

Queen Elizabeth II is represented in the Cayman Islands by a governor—at present, H.E. (for His Excellency) Alan Scott—who appoints three official members to the Legislative Assembly. Twelve other members are elected every four years. The governor has to accept the advice of the Executive Council in all matters except foreign affairs, defense, internal security, and civil service appointments.

Before You Go

Tourist Information For the latest information on activities and lodging, write or call any of the following offices of the **Cayman Islands Department of Tourism:** 250 Catalonia Ave., Suite 401, Coral Gables, FL 33134, tel. 305/444–6551; 2 Memorial City Plaza, 820 Gessner, Suite 170, Houston, TX 77024, tel. 713/461–1317; 420 Lexington Ave., Suite 2733, New York, NY 10170, tel. 212/682–5582; 1 Magnificent Mile, 980 N. Michigan Ave., Suite 1260, Chicago, IL 60611, tel. 312/944–5602; 3440 Wilshire Blvd., Suite 1202, Los Angeles, CA 90010, tel. 213/738–1968; 234 Eglinton Ave. E., Suite 306, Toronto, Ont. M4P 1K5, tel. 416/485–1550; Trevor House, 100 Brompton Rd., Knightsbridge, London SW3 1EX, tel. 071/584–4463.

Arriving and Departing
By Plane Grand Cayman is serviced by **Northwest** (tel. 800/447–4747), **Cayman Airways** (tel. 800/422–9626), **Air Jamaica** (tel. 800/523–5585), **Pan American** (tel. 800/221–1111), and **American Airlines** (tel. 800/433–7300). Cayman Airways flies nonstop from Miami and Tampa; nonstop service from New York leaves Friday–Sunday and returns to New York Thursday–Saturday. **Cayman Airtours** (tel. 800/247–2966) offers package deals. Cayman Airways also operates daily flights to Cayman Brac and provides service to Little Cayman every day except Tuesday. Flights land at Owen Roberts Airport, Gerrard Smith Airport, or Edward Bodden Airport.

Upon arrival, some hotels offer free pickup at the airport. Taxi service and car rentals are also available.

Passports and Visas Passports are not required for American and Canadian citizens, but they must show some proof of citizenship, such as a birth certificate or voter registration card, plus a return ticket. British and Commonwealth subjects do not need a visa but must carry a passport. Visitors to the islands cannot be employed without a work permit.

Customs and Duties You may bring into the United States $400 worth of merchandise duty-free if you've been out of the country more than 48 hours, provided that you've not used any part of it during the preceding 30 days. In addition, you may send $50 worth of gifts to friends daily and take back one liter of liquor and five cartons of cigarettes duty-free. U.S. taxes beyond the limit are 10% on the first $1,000 above the $400 quota.

Turtle products are banned in the United States and will be seized upon importation.

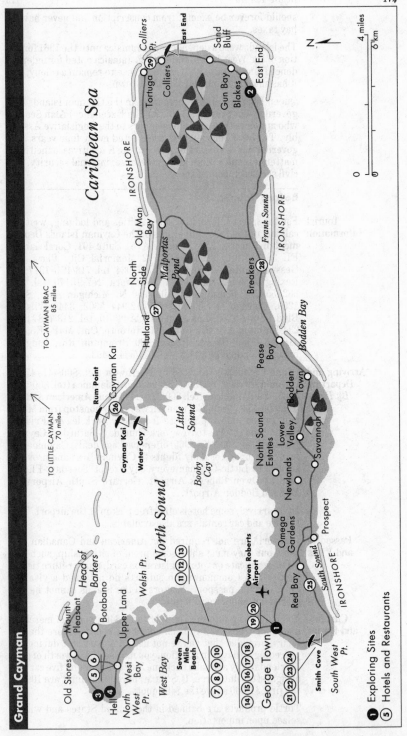

Cayman Brac and Little Cayman

Caribbean Sea

CAYMAN BRAC

North East Pt.
Spot Bay
Booby Pt.
Pollard Bay
North East Bay
Cat Head Bay
Tibbetts Turn
Tom Jennett's Bay
Mallarb's Pt.
Sea Feather Bay
Stake Bay Pt.
Deadman's Pt.
Cedar Pt.
Frenchman's Fort
West End
Tiara Beach
Brac Reef Beach
Gerrard-Smith Airport
West End Pt.

N

0   2 miles
0   3 km

Caribbean Sea

East Pt.
Sandy Point

Crawl Bay

LITTLE CAYMAN

Lower Spot Bay
Charles Bight
Jacksons Pt.
Bloody Bay
Smith Hole Sound
South Town
Anchorage Bay
West End Pt.
Owen Island
Edward Bodden Airfield

Exploring
East End, **2**
George Town, **1**
Hell, **4**
Turtle Farm, **3**

Dining
Caribbean Club, **7**
Chef Tell's Grand Old House, **21**
The Cook Rum, **17**
Corita's Copper Kettle, **20**
The Cracked Conch, **12**
Crow's Nest, **25**
Garden Loggia Cafe, **9**
Golden Pagoda, **10**
Hemingway's, **15**
Island House, **6**
Island Taste, **22**
L'Escargot, **14**
TheLighthouse Club, **28**
Lobster Pot, **19**
Periwinkle, **11**
Ristorante Pappagallo, **5**
The Wharf, **16**

Lodging
Brac Reef Beach Resort, **33**
Caribbean Club, **7**
Cayman Kai Resort, **26**
Coconut Harbour, **23**
Grand Pavilion Hotel and Beach Club, **13**
Holiday Inn Grand Cayman, **8**
Hyatt Regency Grand Cayman, **9**
Pirates Point Resort, **31**
Radisson Hotel Grand Cayman, **18**
Ramada Treasure Island Resort, **14**
Sam McCoy's Guest House, **30**
Southern Cross Club, **32**
Sunset House, **24**
Tiara Beach Hotel, **34**
Tortuga Club, **29**
Villa Caribe, **27**

Canadian citizens are permitted items worth $300 duty-free once a year, or $100 quarterly, or $25 anytime. Forty ounces of liquor and two cartons of cigarettes may also be imported duty-free.

British subjects are entitled to £28 worth of merchandise duty-free, plus 200 cigarettes and one liter of alcoholic spirits.

Language English is spoken here with a slight Caribbean accent. The local daily newspaper, the *Caymanian Compass*, is also in English.

Precautions Remember that traffic is on the left in the Cayman Islands.

Locals make a constant effort to conserve fresh water, so don't waste a precious commodity.

Penalties for drug importation and possession of controlled substances include large fines and prison terms.

Though theft is uncommon in the Caymans, it is only prudent to watch your valuables when outdoors. Marauding blackbirds called "ching chings" have been known to carry off jewelry if it is left out in the open.

Staying in the Cayman Islands

Important Addresses **Tourist Information:** The main office of the **Department of Tourism** is located in the Tower Building (N. Church St., tel. 809/949–7999). There is also an information booth in the George Town Craft Market, on Cardinal Avenue, which is open when cruise ships are in port (tel. 809/949–8342).

Emergencies **Police:** The emergency number is 999.

Hospitals: For emergencies, call 555.

Pharmacies: The most central pharmacy is **Cayman Drug,** in downtown George Town on Panton Street (tel. 809/949–2597).

Airport Information: For flight information, call 809/949–7733.

Divers' Decompression Chamber: Call 809/949–4235.

Currency Although the American dollar is accepted everywhere, you'll save money if you go to the bank and exchange U.S. dollars for Cayman Island (C.I.) dollars, which are worth about $1.25 each. The Cayman dollar is divided into a hundred cents with coins of 1¢, 5¢, 10¢, and 25¢, and notes of $1, $5, $10, $25, $50, and $100. There is no $20 bill.

Prices are often quoted in Cayman dollars, so it's best to ask. All prices quoted here are in U.S. dollars unless otherwise noted.

Taxes and Service Charges Hotels collect a 6% government tax. The departure tax is $7.50.

Hotels add a 10% service charge to your bill. Many restaurants add a 10%–15% service charge.

Guided Tours The most impressive sights are underwater. Snorkeling, diving, glass-bottom-boat and submarine rides can be arranged at any of the major aquatic shops: **Bob Soto's Diving Ltd.** (tel. 809/947–4631), **Nick's Aqua Sports** and **Don Foster's Dive Grand Cayman** (tel. 809/949–5679 for both), **Aqua Delights** (tel. 809/947–4786), the **Watersports Center** (tel. 809/947–0762), and **Atlantis Submarine** (tel. 809/949–7700).

To see the island, rent a car or take a tour with a taxi driver or with a local tour service. **Evco Tours** (tel. 809/949–2118) offers six-hour, round-island tours from the Tortuga Club at the East End to the Turtle Farm and village of Hell in West Bay. **Majestic Tours** (tel. 809/949–7773) guide Buddy Wood takes vanloads of passengers to visit island high points on regular morning tours. All-day tours also can be arranged with **Tropicana Tours** (tel. 809/949–4599), **Rudy's** (tel. 809/949–3208), **Reids** (tel. 809/949–6531), and **GreyLine** (tel. 809/949–2791).

Getting Around If your accommodations are along Seven Mile Beach, you can walk to the shopping centers, restaurants, and entertainment spots along West Bay Road. Public buses run frequently into the downtown area—stops are marked with small white signs.

Taxis Taxis offer islandwide service. Fares are determined by an elaborate rate structure set by the government, and although it may seem pricey for a short ride (fare from Seven Mile Beach to the airport ranges from $7 to $11), cabbies rarely try to rip off tourists. Ask to see the chart if you want to double-check the quoted fare. **Cayman Cab Team** offers 24-hour service (tel. 809/947–0859), as does **Yellow Cab** (tel. 809/949–2026).

Rental Cars To rent a car, bring your current driver's license and the car-rental firm will issue you a temporary permit ($3). Most firms have a range of models available, from compacts to Jeeps to minibuses. The major agencies have offices in a building next to the airport terminal, where you can pick up and drop off vehicles.

Car-rental companies are **Ace Hertz** (tel. 809/949–2280), **Budget** (tel. 809/949–5605), **CICO-Avis** (tel. 809/949–2468), **Coconut** (tel. 809/949–4037), **Dollar** (tel. 809/949–2981), **Holiday Payless** (tel. 809/949–7074), and **National** (tel. 809/949–4790).

For mopeds, motorbikes, and bicycles: **Caribbean Motors** (tel. 809/949–4051 or 809/947–4466), **Cayman Cycle** (tel. 809/947–4020), **Honda** (tel. 809/947–4466), and **Soto Scooters** (tel. 809/947–4652).

Telephones and Mail For international dialing to Cayman, the area code is 809. To call outside, dial 0+1+ area code and number. You can call anywhere, anytime through the Cable and Wireless system and local operators. To make local calls, simply dial the last five digits of the number, excluding the country code and exchange.

Beautiful stamps and first-day covers are available at the main post office in downtown George Town weekdays from 8:30 to 4. Sending a postcard to the United States, Canada, the Caribbean, or Central America costs C.I. 10¢. An airmail letter is C.I. 25¢ per half ounce. To Europe and South America, the rates are C.I. 15¢ for a postcard and C.I. 50¢ per half ounce for airmail letters.

Opening and Closing Times Banking hours are generally Monday–Thursday 9–2:30 and Friday 9–1 and 2:30–4:30. Shops are open Monday–Saturday 9–5 and are usually closed on Sunday.

Beaches

Grand Cayman You may read or hear about the "dozens of beaches" of these islands, but that's more exaggeration than reality. Grand Cayman's west coast, the most developed area of the entire colony, is where you'll find its famous **Seven Mile Beach** (actually

5½ miles long) and its expanses of powdery white sand. The beach is litter-free and sans peddlers, so you can relax in an unspoiled, hassle-free atmosphere. This is also Grand Cayman's busiest vacation center, and most of the island's accommodations, restaurants, and shopping centers are located on this strip.

The seaside bar and pool at the Holiday Inn are "party central" to repeat visitors on the island; the bar features on-tap frozen piña coladas. Aqua Delights, the water-sport company operating out of the Holiday Inn, has one-of-a-kind rentals such as Aqua Trikes, Paddle Cats, and Banana Rides. You'll find headquarters for the island's aquatic activities scattered along the strip (*see* Participant Sports, below).

Grand Cayman has several smaller beaches that might better be called coves, including **Smith Cove,** off South Church Street, south of the Grand Old House—a popular bathing spot with residents on weekends .

The best snorkeling locations are off **the ironshore** (coral ledge area) south of **George Town** on Grand Cayman's west coast and in the reef-protected shallows of the island's north and south coasts, where coral and fish life are much more varied and abundant.

Other good beaches include **East End,** at Colliers, by the Tortuga Club, which can be lovely if it's kept clean of seaweed tossed ashore by trade winds. Seldom discovered by visitors unless they're staying out there are the beautiful beach areas of **Cayman Kai, Rum Point,** and, even more isolated and unspoiled, **Water Cay.** These are favored hideaways for residents and popular Sunday picnic spots.

Cayman Brac Both **Tiara Beach** and **Brac Reef Beach** resorts have fine small beaches, better for sunning than snorkeling. Excellent snorkeling can be found immediately offshore of the now-defunct **Buccaneer's Inn** on the north coast.

Little Cayman **Sandy Point,** on the eastern tip, and **Owen Island,** off the south coast, beaches are exquisite isolated patches of powder great for sunbathing and worth every effort to reach by boat.

Exploring the Cayman Islands

Numbers in the margin correspond with points of interest on the Grand Cayman and Cayman Brac and Little Cayman maps.

George Town Start to explore **George Town** at the **Cayman Maritime and**
❶ **Treasure Museum,** located on the waterfront on Harbor Drive, about 150 yards from the downtown area. This little museum is a real find. Dioramas show how Caymanians became seafarers, boat builders, and turtle breeders. An animated figure of Blackbeard the Pirate spins salty tales about the pirates and buccaneers who "worked" the Caribbean. Since the museum is owned by a professional treasure-salvaging firm, it's not surprising that there are a lot of artifacts from shipwrecks. There is even a gold bar that visitors can lift to appreciate its weight. *Harbour Dr., tel. 809/949–7470. Admission: C.I.$5. Open Mon.–Sat. 9–4:30.*

In the Freeport Building is **McKee's Treasure Museum,** which features the booty recovered from the deep by diver and salvager Art McKee. His collection of relics comes from the remains of sunken Spanish galleons, shipwrecked in the early 17th century. Artifacts are arranged by type—warfare, navigation, religious, everyday life, coins, and jewelry. *Goring Ave. tel. 809/949-7616. Guided tours are available. Admission: C.I.$5. Open Mon.-Sat. 9-4:30.*

Along the waterfront, heading along North Church Street toward town, notice part of the original wall of the old Fort George, which is being restored. Across the street is the Wholesome Bakery, which adds the homey smell of baking bread to the sea breezes off George Town Harbour. Try one of their delicious meat patties.

Turn left onto **Fort Street,** a main shopping street where you'll find the People's Boutique and a whole row of jewelry shops featuring black coral products—Bernard Passman, Island Treasures, Finiterre, Smith's, and the Jewellery Factory.

At the end of the block is the heart of downtown George Town. At the corner of Fort Street and **Edward Street,** notice the small clock tower dedicated to Britain's King George V and the huge fig tree, manicured into an umbrella shape. The Cayman Islands **Legislative Assembly Building** is next door to the 1919 **Peace Memorial Building,** which is the old town hall. You can have a look inside the Legislative Building during office hours (weekdays 8:30-5) or arrange a guided tour.

Turning right on Edward Street, the charming **Library,** built in 1939, has English novels, current newspapers from the United States, and a small reference section. It's worth a visit just for the Old World atmosphere. Across the street is the new **Court House.** Down the next block, a stroller enters the "financial district," where banks from all over the world have offices.

Straight ahead is the **General Post Office,** also built in 1939, with its strands of decorative colored lights and some 2,000 private mailboxes on the outside. (Mail is not delivered on the island.) Behind the post office is **Elizabethan Square,** a new shopping and office complex on **Shedden Road** that houses various food, clothing, and souvenir establishments. The courtyard has a pleasant garden and fountain as well as outdoor tables at La Fontaine, a French restaurant. In the evenings, a live band converts this spot into an outdoor nightclub.

If you walk out the side entrance of Elizabethan Square, you'll be in a parking lot from which you can see the main government office building, called the **Glass House.** At four stories, it was until recently the tallest structure and featured the only elevator on the island. Both claims to fame were stolen when the Hyatt opened its five-story luxury resort hotel in 1987.

Exiting Elizabethan Square onto Shedden Road and walking past Anderson Square and Caymania Freeport, turn right back onto Edward Street, then left at the Royal Bank of Canada onto **Cardinal Avenue.**

This street is the main shopping area. On the right is the chic Kirk Freeport Plaza, which is known for its emeralds and fancy watches. On the left is the George Town Craft Market, a tourist information office, and the Native Taste café with outdoor tables.

Turn left on **Harbour Drive** and make your way back to Shedden Road, passing the English Shoppe, a souvenir outlet that looks more as if it belongs on Shaftesbury Avenue in London than in the West Indies, and the Cayside Galleries, with its maritime antiques and cameras.

Walking back into town on Harbour Drive, you can enjoy a leisurely stroll along a waterfront sidewalk. A new public park with a circular wood structure is where visitors from the cruise ships disembark, but the park offers no shade from the sun.

Across the street is a pleasant church, the **Elmslie Memorial United.** Its vaulted ceiling with wood arches and a sedate nave should remind visitors of the quietly religious nature of island residents.

The Outer Districts   Venturing away from the Seven Mile Beach strip, travelers will encounter the more down-home character of the islands. Heading out on South Church Street, you can see some of the old houses, which feature elaborate Victorian gingerbread on modest frame homes. Heading east in a district called **Pantonville,** after the Pantons who live there, there are three pretty cottages with lacy woodwork. Then at **South Sound** you see larger residences, some with fine detail and gracious verandas.

In the Savannah district, **Pedro's Castle,** built in 1780, lays claim to being the oldest structure on the island. Pedro's is now a restaurant with a great view from the bar. At **Bodden Town,** you'll find an old cemetery on the shore side of the road. Graves with A-frame structures are said to contain the remains of pirates, but, in fact, they may be those of early settlers. A curio shop serves as entrance to what's called the **Pirate's Caves,** where you'll pass by a minizoo en route to these partially underground caves. The natural formations are interesting, but the place is more hokey than spooky.

Time Out   The large and airy **Lighthouse Club** (Breakers, tel. 809/947–2047) has booth seating around spectacular waterfront windows. Island dishes and German fare are served daily. The Key lime pie is memorable.

❷   The village of **East End** is the first recorded settlement on the island. Its major claim to fame these days is that it's where a renowned local musician called the "Violin Man," aka Radley and His Happy Boys, lives and occasionally performs his distinctive form of music (more akin to Louisiana's backwater zydeco than reggae). It's also the site of a number of shipwrecks and the **Tortuga Club,** now under reconstruction, whose guests are mostly avid divers.

❸   At the other end of the island is the **West Bay** community, whose main attraction is the **Turtle Farm.** The farm, which was started about 20 years ago, is the most popular attraction on the island today, with some 70,000 visitors a year. There are turtles of all ages, from day-old hatchlings to huge 600-pounders that can live to be 100 years old. The Turtle Farm was set up both as a conservation and a commercial enterprise; it releases about 5% of its stock back out to sea every year, harvests turtles for local restaurants, and exports the by-products. (Note: U.S. citizens cannot take home any turtle products due to a U.S. regulation banning their import.) In the adjoining café, you can sample turtle soup or turtle sandwiches while looking over an exhibit about turtles. *West Bay Rd., tel. 809/949–3893. Admission: $5 adults, $2.50 children 6–12. Open daily 9–5.*

❹ The other area of West Bay that is of brief interest is the tiny village of **Hell,** which is little more than a patch of incredibly jagged rock formations called ironshore. The big attraction here is a small post office and card shop, which does a land-office business selling stamps and postmarking cards from Hell. Souvenir shops called Devil's Den and Hades Hideaway also exploit the concept. Almost unbelievably, a nearby night-club, called the Club Inferno, is run by the McDoom family.

Cayman Brac

Brac, the Gaelic word for bluff, aptly identifies this island's most distinctive feature, a rugged limestone cliff that runs down the center of the island's 12-mile length. At the eastern end, the bluff soars to 140 feet—rather dramatic for the Caribbean. Cayman Brac lies 89 miles east of Grand Cayman and can be a pleasant day trip via a Cayman Airways package, which includes a morning flight, sightseeing tour, and lunch at a hotel with the afternoon free to swim, snorkel, and sun. Only 1,700 people live on this island, in rural communities with such names as Watering Place, Cotton Tree, Halfway Ground, and Spot Bay. The variety of flora includes unusual orchids and tropical fruits such as mangoes and papaya, and the Caymanian parrot lives among the Brac's bird population. Parts of the island are unpopulated, so visitors can explore truly isolated areas both inland and along the shore.

Two hotels catering to divers, the Tiara Beach and the Brac Reef Beach Resort, are located on sandy beaches in a lagoon on the south side.

Little Cayman

Only 2 miles away from Cayman Brac is Little Cayman Island, which boasts a population of only two dozen on its 12 square miles. This tiny place really is paradise for those intent on get-ting away from crowds—it has no shops, no restaurants, no movies, no gas stations or central electricity supply, and only three private phones and one pay phone on the entire island. It does have ample accommodations for visitors, however, in three small lodges—the Southern Cross Club, Sam McCoy's Diving and Fishing Lodge, and Pirate's Point. In addition to privacy, the real attractions of Little Cayman are diving, which is most spectacular off the north coast, and fishing, which includes angling for tarpon and bonefish.

And if Little Cayman ever gets too busy, there is one final retreat—**Owen Island,** which is just 200 yards offshore. Acces-sible by rowboat, it has a blue lagoon and a sandy beach. Take your own picnic if you plan to spend the day.

What to See and Do with Children

Don't miss the one-hour **Atlantis Submarine** (tel. 809/949–7700) ride, which takes 28 passengers, a driver, and a guide down along the Cayman Wall to depths of 150 feet. This $2.8 million submarine, which recorded its 100,000th guest in 1988, has all sorts of safety features, including a constantly circling surface monitor boat, and is air-conditioned. Through its large windows, you can see huge barrel sponges, corals of extraterrestrial-like configurations, strange eels, and schools of beautiful and beastly fish. Night dives are quite dramatic because the artificial lights of the ship make the colors more vivid than in daytime excursions.

Turtle Farm (*see* Exploring the Cayman Islands, above).

Older children can also enjoy many of the water sports and beach games available. Hotels politely say that they do not organize activities for children, so be prepared to do so on your own.

Off the Beaten Track

Two architectural curiosities are worth a look if you are driving around. One is the little pink-and-white house on West Bay Road just past the cemetery. This 100-year-old cottage is made of mahogany and ironwood. Another odd residence is the conch house, near the power plant. This house was covered with conch shells years ago, but a recent renovation has added modern skylights and a garish satellite dish in the front yard.

Carey Cayman Coral (no phone) is a workshop out in South Sound run by Carey Hurlstone. Carey, a gentle bear of a man with tattoos covering his skin, professes he was a biker with the Hell's Angels before coming home to Cayman to work as a craftsman. He also carves glass. Carey's workmanship is superb and his prices are quite reasonable for the quality.

Participant Sports

Deep-Sea Fishing   If you enjoy action fishing, Cayman waters have plenty to offer—blue and white marlin, yellowfin tuna, sailfish, dolphin, and wahoo. Bonefish and tarpon are also plentiful off Little Cayman. Some 25 boats are available for charter. Since 1984 a Million Dollar Month fishing tournament has been held in June, and registered anglers can win cash prizes by landing record-breaking catches. Each of the five tournaments has its own rules, records, and entrance fees. For information and applications, write Million Dollar Month Committee (Box 878, Grand Cayman, Cayman Islands, B.W.I.).

Diving   To say that the Cayman Islands are a scuba diver's paradise is not overstating the case. Everything a diver could want is here: pristine water (often exceeding 100-foot visibility), breathtaking coral formations, plentiful and exotic marine life, and a host of top-notch dive operations offering a variety of services, instruction, and equipment. Predictably, however, most of Grand Cayman's dive boats (at least during high season) tend to be packed. The sister islands are less crowded.

Divers are required to be certified and possess a "C" card or take a short resort or full certification course. A certification course, including classroom, pool, and boat sessions as well as checkout dives, takes about six days and costs up to $300. A resort course usually lasts a day and costs about $75. It introduces the novice to the sport and teaches the rudimentary skills needed to make a shallow, instructor-monitored dive.

All dive operations on Cayman are more than competent; among them are **Bob Soto's** (tel. 809/949–2022), **Don Foster's** (tel. 809/949–7025), **Aqua Delights** (tel. 809/947–4786), and **Nick's Aqua Sports** (tel. 809/949–8745). Literature on all operators can be obtained through the Department of Tourism.

On Cayman Brac, **Peter Hughes' Dive Tiara** (tel. 809/948–7553) offers scuba and snorkeling.

Most operations can rent all diving gear, including equipment for underwater photography; they also have facilities for film processing. Courses of instruction can be arranged at most shops.

Fitness A **Nautilus Fitness Center** (tel. 809/949–5132), with machines, weights, sauna, and whirlpool, is in operation on Crewe Road, in the Crighton Building just across from the airport. Daily membership is $10; weekly, $25. **Fitness Connection** (tel. 809/949–8485) offers aerobics classes, private instruction, and fitness counseling at three locations in George Town.

Golf The **Grand Cayman–Britannia** golf course, which is located next to the Hyatt Regency, was designed by Jack Nicklaus. The course is really three in one—a nine-hole championship course, an 18-hole executive course, and a Cayman course, which is played with a Cayman ball that goes about half the distance of a regulation ball. Greens fees range from $25 to $50.

Tennis Most hotels and condo complexes have tennis courts for guests.

Water Sports Waterskiing, windsurfing, Hobie Cats, and jet skis are available at many of the aquatic shops along Seven Mile Beach (*see* Diving, above).

Shopping

If your motto is "Born to Shop," then Grand Cayman has two money-saving attributes—duty-free merchandise and the absence of a sales tax. Prices on imported merchandise—English china, Swiss watches, French perfumes, and Japanese cameras and electronic goods—are relatively cheaper than elsewhere. Expensive jewelry is another good buy, and the selection is vast. If you've been postponing buying such luxury goods, you might consider this opportunity.

Good Buys Black coral products are popular and exquisite choices. There
Black Coral are a number of local craftsmen who create original designs and finish their own work. Among those who have retail outlets in downtown George Town are **Coral Art Collections by Mitzi** (tel. 809/949–7805), in the Old Fort building on North Church Street; **Bernard Passman** (tel. 809/949–0123), whose creations won the approval of the English royal family, on Fort Street; and **Black Coral Jewelry and Other Fine Gems** (tel. 809/949–7156), whose creators, Richard and Rafaela Barile, have attracted lots of celebrities to their shop on Harbour Drive (*see also* Off the Beaten Track, above).

Arts and Crafts Debbie van der Bol runs an arts and crafts shop called **Pure Art** (tel. 809/949–4433) in a home on South Church Street. She features the work of such local artists as Janet Walker, who does watercolors; woodworker Ralph Terry; and lacemaker Karin

Baur. Ms. van der Bol is also an artist, and her sketches and card series are among the best buys in the place.

The **Grand Cayman Craft Market** (tel. 809/949–2195), downtown on Cardinal Avenue, has an assortment of local crafts, as does the **Heritage Crafts Shop** (tel. 809/949–7093), upstairs on Shedden Road.

T-shirt shops abound all over town, especially along Harbour Drive, supporting the notion that they are the most popular souvenir.

Dining

Grand Cayman's restaurants should satisfy every palate and pocketbook. Gourmet Continental cuisine is available to the high rollers. Ethnic food can be had at moderate prices. West Indian fare in dining spots serving locals offers the best in meals and value. Fast-food franchises are there for those who must.

Seafood, not surprisingly, appears on most restaurant menus. Fish—including grouper, snapper, dolphin, tuna, wahoo, and marlin—is served either simply or Cayman style, with peppers, onions, and tomatoes. Conch, the meat of a large pink mollusk, is ubiquitous in stews and chowders—as fritters or pan-fried ("cracked"). Caribbean lobster is available but is often quite expensive, and other shellfish are in short supply in local waters. The only traditional culinary treat of the islands is turtle soup, stew, or steak, but only a few restaurants carry it these days.

Dining out on Grand Cayman can be expensive, so replenish your billfold because some places do not accept plastic. Prices are usually quoted in Cayman dollars.

All of the restaurants reviewed below are located on Grand Cayman. The most highly recommended restaurants are indicated by a star ★.

Category	Cost*
Expensive	over $20
Moderate	$15–$20
Inexpensive	under $15

per person, excluding drinks and service

★ **Caribbean Club.** The Continental menu of this quiet and well-appointed restaurant is one of the best in the Caymans. Among its seafood dishes, the lobster sausage is highly recommended, served as an appetizer or entrée. The service is meticulous and unhurried. The upstairs bar is worth a stop for the vista. *West Bay Rd., tel. 809/947–4099. Reservations are a must. Jacket and tie required. AE, MC, V. Expensive.*

★ **Chef Tell's Grand Old House.** TV celebrity chef Tell Erhardt has been running this popular establishment since 1986. His menu features Continental entrées and a few local specialties. Among the spicier appetizer choices is grouper Beignete, marinated and deep-fried grouper served with curry sauce and minted yogurt. On the bland side is Lobster Chef Fred's Way, dipped in egg batter and sautéed with shallots, mushrooms, and white wine. The back-porch dining room with its Victorian trim and ceiling fans is the liveliest and best spot for dining. The excellent service adds to this gracious dining experience. *S. Church St., tel. 809/949–2266. Reservations necessary for dinner, suggested for lunch. AE, MC, V. Closed for lunch weekends. Expensive.*

L'Escargot. Fine china, crystal, and silverware; waiters in tuxedos; and live piano music make this one of the island's most romantic dining spots. The view of the garden and pool competes with the elegant decor of the salon. The French and Continental menu features escargot in many forms. Sunday luncheon buffet is served from noon to 2:30. *Ramada Treasure Island Resort, tel. 809/949–7255. Reservations mandatory for dinner. Jacket and tie required for dinner. AE, MC, V. Expensive.*

Garden Loggia Cafe. The Hyatt's indoor-outdoor café opens onto the most beautifully landscaped garden courtyard on the island. The Caribbean decor includes pastel colors, ceiling fans, and marble-top tables. The menu combines European and Caribbean tastes. The Friday night seafood buffet and sumptuous Sunday champagne brunch feature everything from roast suckling pig, king crab, and lobster to waffles and custom-made omelets. Live music is featured at breakfast and dinner every day except Sunday. *Hyatt Regency Grand Cayman, West Bay Rd., tel. 809/949–1234. Reservations a must. AE, MC, V. Expensive.*

Lobster Pot. The second-floor terrace of this cozy restaurant overlooks the bay downtown, so the sunsets are an extra attraction. Its menu features both Continental dishes and such Caribbean specialties as conch chowder, turtle soup, steak, seafood curry, and, of course, lobster. This place is popular, so the constant turnover makes the atmosphere feel rushed. If you can't make dinner, drop by the pub and have a frozen banana daiquiri. *N. Church St., tel. 809/949–2736. Reservations recommended. MC, V. Expensive.*

Periwinkle. This Italian restaurant, decorated in soothing pink and gray, is quiet and romantic. The menu features such Italian fare as seafood lasagne and chicken cacciatore, grouper Caymanian style. During summer months, a grill is set up on the patio to charcoal dishes like fresh swordfish. *West Bay Rd., tel. 809/949–2927. Reservations accepted. AE, MC, V. Expensive.*

Ristorante Pappagallo. On a remote point near Spanish Cove, this thatch-roof restaurant's highlight is an exotic decor that includes macaws in cages. Curiously, its menu is northern Italian cuisine, with predictable antipasto, pasta, and veal dishes. The biggest drawbacks: its inconvenient location and inconsistency. *West Bay at Villas Pappagallo, tel. 809/949–3479. Reservations required. AE, MC, V. Expensive.*

The Cracked Conch. This popular seafood restaurant has the ambience of a crowded fish house. Specialties include conch fritters, conch chowder, spicy Cayman-style snapper, and three types of turtle steak. The Key lime pie is divine. Take-out service is available. The bar has live entertainment and is a local hangout. *Selkirk's Plaza, West Bay Rd., tel. 809/949–5717. Reservations suggested in winter. AE, MC, V. Moderate.*

Crow's Nest. With the ocean right in its backyard, this secluded small restaurant is a great spot for snorkeling as well as lunching. One drawback: Insect repellent is required for patio dining in the evening. The gourmet shrimp and conch dishes are highly recommended. The dessert of raisins and rum cake is scrumptious. *South Sound, tel. 809/949–6216. Reservations necessary during high season. MC, V. Closed Sun. Moderate.*

Golden Pagoda. The oldest Chinese restaurant in the Caymans features Hakka-style cooking. Among their specialties are Mahlah chicken, butterfly shrimp, and chicken in black bean sauce. Takeout is available. *West Bay Rd., tel. 809/949–5475. Reservations accepted. Dress: no shorts at dinner. AE, MC, V. Moderate.*

Hemingway's. Located right on Seven Mile Beach, this classy restaurant features open-air dining with a sea view and breezes. Zesty seafood dishes include Pirate's Stew Pot, conch and turtle steak prepared in coconut milk and green bananas, or beer-batter coconut shrimp. For a tropical drink, try the Seven Mile Meltdown, with dark rum, peach schnapps, pineapple juice, and fresh coconut. There is superb service and Caribbean decor. Buffet dinner is served on the *Spirit of Ppalu,* a glass-bottom catamaran. *Hyatt/Britannia Beach Club, tel. 809/949–1234. Reservations accepted. AE, MC, V. Moderate.*

The Lighthouse Club. This airy converted lighthouse offers oceanfront dining on the island's southeast coast. Seating is in comfy booths or at tables next to big screened windows overlooking the ocean. The menu includes such island specialties as mango shrimp, sea whelks, and conch, and such German fare as sauerbraten, schnitzel, and venison. The drive from town takes at least 15 minutes, but it's worth it. *Breakers, tel. 809/947–2047. Reservations accepted. AE, MC, V. Moderate.*

The Wharf. This restaurant, which opened in 1989, is stylishly decorated in blue and white and looks onto a veranda and the nearby sea. On the menu are such Caribbean specialties as turtle steak, conch chowder, and sea scallops Provençale. Daily specials include seafood paella and soft-shell and stone crabs. Live music entertains diners. The Ports of Call bar is a perfect spot from which to watch the sun set. *N. Church St., tel: 809/949–2231. MC, V. Moderate.*

★ **The Cook Rum.** This restaurant with a tin roof and a front-porch view of the bay features West Indian fare, including turtle stew, salt beef and beans, and pepper pot stew. Dessert specials are yam cake and coconut cream pie. *N. Church St., tel. 809/949–8670. No credit cards. Inexpensive.*

★ **Corita's Copper Kettle.** Here is a tidy downtown diner featuring Jamaican breakfasts and such native specialties as conch and lobster burgers. The fare is tasty and plain. *Edward St., tel. 809/949–2696. A second location (on Eastern Ave. in Georgetown) opened in 1990. No reservations. No credit cards. Inexpensive.*

Island House. The café atmosphere of this renovated 100-year-old Caymanian house is the main attraction. Standards have slipped in recent years, service is slow, and the food is unpredictable. Its best dishes are turtle steak and fillet of grouper. *Church St., West Bay, tel. 809/949–3017. No credit cards. Inexpensive.*

Island Taste. Caribbean decor (a hodgepodge of stone, bamboo, and rope) and island music set the laid-back pace here. A Caribbean luncheon buffet is served daily on a table made from the timbers of an old ship. Skip the bland seafood soup. *S. Church St., tel. 809/949–4945. AE, MC, V. Inexpensive.*

Lodging

The success of the Cayman Islands as a resort destination has an attendant problem—a scarcity of accommodations during the winter season. Visitors have to book ahead for holidays, especially at Christmastime. During the summer season, it is possible to find suitable lodging even on short notice. If you choose to stay in a condominium, you can book on a daily basis and stay any length of time. While about a third of the visitors come for the diving, a growing number are young honeymooners. There are few accommodations in the economy range, so guests must be prepared for resort prices. Cayman Islands Hotel Reservations: 800/327–8777.

Category	Cost*
Very Expensive	over $160
Expensive	$100–$160
Moderate	$85–$100
Inexpensive	under $85

All prices are for a standard double room for two, excluding 6% tax and a 10% service charge.

Hotels
Grand Cayman
★

Caribbean Club. Eighteen one- and two-bedroom villas (six located on the beach) comprise a quiet island getaway. All units are individually decorated and contain full kitchens, living and dining rooms, patios, and a bathroom for every bedroom. Secluded and luxurious. *Box 504, Grand Cayman, tel. 809/947–4099 or 800/327–8777. 18 villas. Facilities: tennis courts, water-sports center, restaurant, bar. AE, MC, V. Very Expensive.*

Grand Pavilion Hotel and Beach Club. This five-star hotel is where the English royal family stays when they are in the Cayman Islands. Rooms are exquisitely furnished with Louis XV–style furniture and canopy beds. The Pavilion is a favorite with international business travelers who return for the hotel's impeccable style and service. Guests have access to beach-club facilities across the road. *Box 1815, Grand Cayman, tel. 809/947–4666 or for reservations in U.S., 800/421–9999. 79 rooms and 3 suites. Facilities: 2 restaurants, 2 bars, meeting rooms, beach club, pool and pool bar. AE, MC, V. Very Expensive.*

★ **Hyatt Regency Grand Cayman.** One of the things that make this hotel special is that it's adjacent to the only golf course on Grand Cayman. The rooms are exquisite, each with a marble entrance, oversize bathtub, bar, French doors, and a veranda. The Hyatt's beach club offers every water sport imaginable. Regency Club accommodations include complimentary Continental breakfast, early evening hors d'oeuvres and 24-hour concierge service. *Box 1698, Grand Cayman, tel. 809/949–1234 or 800/553–1300. 236 rooms, 43 rooms in Regency Club, 1-, 2-, and 3-bedroom Britannia villas. Facilities: pool, golf course, tennis courts, private marina, full-service water-sports center, 3 restaurants, conference rooms. AE, MC, V. Very Expensive.*

Ramada Treasure Island Resort. Owned by a consortium of country music stars (Randy Travis and Larry Gatlin among other notables), the five-story resort aptly promotes itself as a place where the "fun never sets." All rooms are decorated in tropical colors and most have views of either the beach or the pool. *Box 1817, Grand Cayman, tel. 809/949–7777 or for reservations in U.S., 800/874–0027 or 800/228–9898. 290 rooms. Facilities: 2 restaurants, 3 bars, nightclub, 2 pools, Jacuzzi, water-sports center. AE, CB, DC, MC, V. Very Expensive.*

★ **Coconut Harbour.** There's only one drawback to this serious diver's retreat: It's located near a field of oil storage tanks. This delightful resort has a dive shop, waterfront thatch-roof bar, and an informal restaurant. There's excellent diving offshore at Waldo's Reef, which is known for its population of tame marine life. *Box 2086, Grand Cayman, tel. 809/949–7468, or for U.S. reservations, 800/552–6281. 35 rooms, all with kitchens. Facilities: bar/grill, dive shop. AE, MC, V. Expensive.*

Holiday Inn Grand Cayman. This hotel was the pioneer resort establishment on the beach, and it's still loose and fun. Don't miss the "Barefoot Man," who performs nightly outside on the patio. *Box 904, Grand Cayman, tel. 809/947–4444 or for reservations, 800/421–9999. 137 double and 78 king-size rooms. Facilities: restaurant, 3 bars, tennis, water-sports center. AE, MC, V. Expensive.*

Cayman Kai Resort. Nestled next to a coconut grove, each sea lodge features a full kitchen, dining and living areas, and two screened-in porches overlooking the ocean. *Box 1112, North Side, tel. 809/947–9056 or for reservations, 800/223–5427. 26 sea lodges, 11 villas. Facilities: restaurant, 2 bars, tennis court, diving, fishing and water-sports shop. AE, MC, V. Moderate.*

Radisson Hotel Grand Cayman. Due to open in the spring of 1990, this is a new luxury property on Seven Mile Beach. *Information and reservations: 800/333–3333. 306 rooms. Facilities: restaurant, bar, pool, nightclub, tennis court, water-sports center. All major credit cards. Very Expensive.*

★ **Sunset House.** Low-key and laid-back describes this motel on the ironshore south of George Town. A well-run dive operation, congenial staff, and popular bar make this resort a favorite with divers. The relaxed atmosphere on the deck in the evening makes it a great place to meet people. *Box 479, S. Church St., tel. 809/949–7111 and 800/854–4767. 42 rooms, 2 suites. Facilities: restaurant, bar, dive shop, fishing and sailing charters. AE, MC, V. Moderate.*

Villa Caribe. On the north coast, the Caribe offers Cayman-style and fine traditional cuisine. *Box 1410, North Side, tel. 809/947–9636 or for reservations, 800/367–0041. 14 rooms. Facilities: restaurant. Inexpensive.*

Cayman Brac **Brac Reef Beach Resort.** Designed, built, and owned by Bracker Linton Tibbets, the resort lures divers and vacationers who come to savor the special ambience of this tiny island. Quality accommodations, a pool, a beach, snorkeling, and the restaurant are additional reasons to stay here. *Box 235, Cayman Brac, tel. 809/948–7323. 42 rooms. Facilities: restaurant, 2 bars, pool, Jacuzzi, beach, dive shop. AE, MC, V. Moderate.*

Tiara Beach Hotel. This resort is dedicated to divers, with an excellent diving facility complemented by the DIVI chain's standards: tile floors, rattan furniture, louvered windows, balconies, and ocean views. *Box 238, Cayman Brac, tel. 809/948–7553 or for reservations, 800/FOR–DIVI. 70 rooms. Facilities: restaurant, bar, pool, Jacuzzi, tennis, dive operation, water-sports center, fishing. AE, MC, V. Moderate.*

Pirates Point Resort Opened in late 1989 by Texan Gladys Howard, this comfortably informal beach resort has six rooms in octagonal units just a few minutes from the airstrip. The voluble Ms. Howard is also a cordon bleu chef. "Relaxing" rates include meals only; all-inclusive rates include meals, wine, dives, fishing, and picnics on Owen Island. *Little Cayman, tel. 809/948-4210 or 800/654-7537. 6 rooms. Facilities: diving, fishing, restaurant. No credit cards. Very Expensive.*

Little Cayman **Sam McCoy's Diving and Fishing Lodge.** This small, cozy diving and fishing resort opened in 1985 on Little Cayman's north coast. Very reasonable rates and the owner's infectious good nature are the hallmarks of this locally run resort. Superb diving and snorkeling right offshore. Meals are included in rates. *Little Cayman, tel. 809/948-2249 or 809/948-3251; in the U.S.: 203/438-5663. 8 rooms. Moderate.*

Southern Cross Club. Three family-style meals a day are included with your room. A bus for tours, excellent bird-watching, and diving make a stay at the club all-inclusive and relaxing. *Little Cayman, tel. 809/948-3255 or 317/636-9501 in U.S. 10 rooms. Facilities: diving, fishing, bird-watching in sanctuary. Moderate.*

Condominiums The **Cayman Islands Department of Tourism** provides a complete list of condominiums and small rental apartments in the Moderate to Inexpensive range. Rates are higher during the winter season, so check before you book. **Cayman Rent a Villa** (Box 681, Grand Cayman, tel. 809/947-4144) can help you locate a rental house or cottage. **Reef House Ltd. Property Management** (Box 1540, Grand Cayman, tel. 809/949-7093) also rents villas, houses, and apartments on all three islands.

Nightlife

Each of the island hot spots attracts a different clientele. The rowdy crowd gathers at the **Wreck of the Ten Sails** at the Holiday Inn (tel. 809/947-4444), where the "Barefoot Man" entertains. The dance floor is always crowded, and it's also a great spot to people-watch. Admission is $5; hotel guests pay no admission charge.

Silver's Nightclub (tel. 809/949-7777) at the Treasure Island Resort is a spacious, tiered club that is usually filled to capacity. A lively house band plays Monday–Saturday nights.

Monkey Business (upstairs at the Falls Shopping Center, tel. 809/947-4024) is a disco with an ersatz jungle decor, complete with dummy monkeys. The flashing lights and pulsating beat keep the dance floor hopping.

For current entertainment, look at the freebie newspaper, *Cayman After Dark*, which gives listings of music, movies, theater, and other entertainment possibilities.

9 Curaçao

by Pamela Bloom

Forty miles north of Venezuela and 42 miles east of Aruba is Curaçao, the largest of the islands in the Netherlands Antilles. The sun smiles down on Curaçao, but it never gets stiflingly hot: the gentle trade winds refresh. Water sports attract enthusiasts from all over the world, and some of the best reef diving is here, though Curaçao's 38 beaches and coves hardly compare in size with those of its nearby sister islands of Aruba and Bonaire.

As seen from the Otrabanda of Willemstad by the first-time visitor, Curaçao's "face" will be a surprise—spiffy rows of pastel-colored town houses that look transplanted from Holland. Although the gabled roofs and red tiles show a Dutch influence, the absurdly gay colors of the facades, as novelist Christopher Isherwood once described them, are peculiar to Curaçao. It is said that the first governor of Curaçao developed a terrible allergy to the color white (it gave him migraines), so all the houses were painted in colors. The dollhouse look of the architecture makes a cheerful contrast to the stark cacti and the dramatic shrubbery dotting the countryside.

The history books still cannot agree on who discovered Curaçao—one school of thought believes it was Alonzo de Ojeda, another says it was Amerigo Vespucci, but they seem to agree that it was around 1499. The first Spanish settlers arrived in 1527. In 1634, the Dutch came via the Netherlands West India Company. They promptly shipped off the Spaniards and the few remaining Indians—survivors of the battles for ownership of the island, famine, and disease—to Venezuela. Eight years later, Peter Stuyvesant ruled as governor until he left for New York around 1645. Twelve Jewish families arrived from Amsterdam in 1651 and built a synagogue; today, it is the oldest synagogue still in use in the Western Hemisphere. Over the years, the city built massive fortresses to defend itself against French and British invasions—many of those ramparts now house unusual restaurants and hotels. The Dutch claim to Curaçao was finally recognized in 1815 by the Treaty of Paris. In 1954, Curaçao became an autonomous part of the Kingdom of the Netherlands, with an elected Parliament and island council, and is ruled by a governor appointed by the queen.

Today Curaçao's population is derived from more than 50 nationalities blending together in an exuberant mix of Latin and African roots. The island is known for its religious tolerance, and tourists are warmly welcomed. In the past few years, millions of dollars have been poured into restoring the old colonial landmarks and upgrading and modernizing hotels. The International Trade Center, a major convention hall that opened in 1989, is expected to attract enormous business to the island. Within the complex, construction on two new hotels—a Ramada and a Sonesta—should be finished sometime in 1990.

Before You Go

Tourist Information Contact the **Curaçao Tourist Office** (400 Madison Ave., New York, NY 10017, tel. 212/751–8266 or 800/332–8266) for information.

Arriving and Departing
By Plane If you're flying from New York, **American** (tel. 800/433–7300) and **ALM** (tel. 800/327–7230) will take you direct to Curaçao; only ALM flies nonstop to Curaçao from Miami and San Juan.

Curaçao

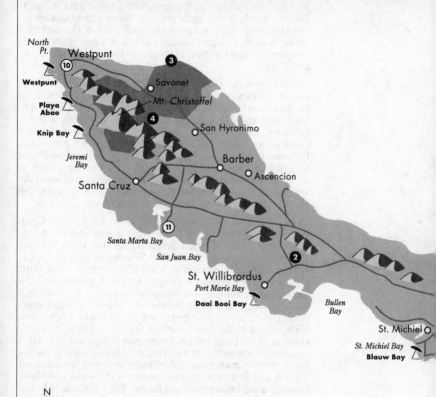

North Pt.

Westpunt
10

Westpunt

Playa Abao

Knip Bay

Jeremi Bay

3

Savonet

Mt. Christoffel

4

San Hyronimo

Barber
Ascencion

Santa Cruz

11

Santa Marta Bay

San Juan Bay

St. Willibrordus
Port Marie Bay
2

Daai Booi Bay

Bullen Bay

St. Michiel ○

St. Michiel Bay
Blauw Bay

N

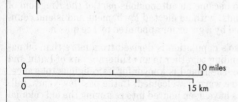

0   10 miles

0   15 km

Exploring

Arawak Clay
Products, **8**

Boca Tabla, **3**

Caracas Bay, **9**

Christoffel Park, **4**

Curaçao
Seaquarium, **5**

Curaçao Underwater
Park, **6**

Landhuis Brievengat, **7**

Landhuis Jan Kock, **2**

Willemstad, **1**

Dining

Bellevue
Restaurant, **18**

Belle Terrace, **17**

Bistro Le Clochard, **13**

Cozzoli's Pizza, **21**

De Taveerne, **14**

Fort Nassau
Restaurant, **16**

Gipsy, **22**

Golden Star
Restaurant, **19**

Janchi Christiaan's
Restaurant, **10**

La Bistroelle, **15**

Rijstaffel Indonesia
Restaurant, **20**

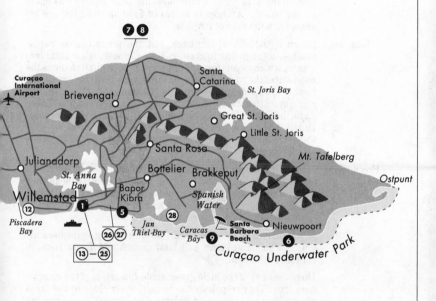

Caribbean Sea

Curaçao International Airport

Brievengat

Santa Catarina

St. Joris Bay

Great St. Joris

Little St. Joris

Mt. Tafelberg

Santa Rosa

Julianadorp

St. Anna Bay

Bottelier

Brakkeput

Ostpunt

Bapor Kibra

Spanish Water

Willemstad

Piscadera Bay

Jan Thiel-Bay

Caracas Bay

Santa Barbara Beach

Nieuwpoort

Curaçao Underwater Park

1 Exploring Sites

10 Hotels and Restaurants

Lodging

Avila Beach Hotel, **17**

Coral Cliff Resort and Beach Club, **11**

Curaçao Caribbean Hotel and Casino, **23**

Curaçao Plaza Hotel and Casino, **24**

Golden Tulip Las Palmas and Vacation Village, **12**

Holiday Beach Hotel and Casino, **25**

Lions Dive Hotel and Marina, **27**

Princess Beach Hotel and Casino, **26**

From Curaçao, ALM flies to the other Antilles islands, including Aruba, Bonaire, and St. Martin. **BWIA** (tel. 800/327–7401) flies to Antigua with a **LIAT** (tel. 809/462–0700) connection to Curaçao.

Passports and Visas U.S. and Canadian citizens traveling in Curaçao need only proof of citizenship. A voter's registration card or a notarized birth certificate (not a photocopy) will suffice—a driver's license will *not*. All British citizens must produce a passport. Visitors must show an ongoing or return ticket.

Customs and Duties U.S. residents returning to the United States may bring in $400 worth of duty-free articles. Included may be 200 cigarettes, one quart of liquor, locally made souvenirs and handicrafts, film, art, books, antiques, caviar, truffles, and jewelry made in the Netherlands Antilles (be sure to get a certificate from the place of purchase that your jewelry was made on the island). Articles in excess of $400 up to $1,000 are assessed at a flat rate of 10%.

Language Dutch is the official language, but the vernacular is Papiamento—a tough one to master. Like Chinese, it's a tonal language, which means that the slightest shift in pitch changes the meaning of the word. Developed during the 18th century by Africans, Papiamento evolved in Curaçao as the mode of communication between landowners and their slaves. These days, however, English, as well as Spanish, and, of course, Dutch, are studied by schoolchildren. Anyone involved with tourism—shopkeepers, restaurateurs, and museum guides—speaks English.

Precautions Mosquitoes in Curaçao do not seem as vicious and bloodthirsty as they do on Aruba and Bonaire, but that doesn't mean they don't exist. To be safe, you should douse yourself with insect repellent before dining alfresco and spray your hotel room at night—especially if you've opened a window.

If you plan to go into the water, beware of long-spined sea urchins, which can cause pain and discomfort if you come in contact with them.

Do not eat any of the little green apple-like fruits of the manchineel tree: They're poisonous. In fact, steer clear of the trees altogether; raindrops or dewdrops dripping off the leaves can blister your skin. If contact does occur, rinse the affected area with water and, in extreme cases, get medical attention. Usually, the burning sensation won't last longer than two hours.

Further Reading Before venturing into the Caribbean waters, pick up a copy of the *Guide to Corals and Fishes of Florida, the Bahamas and the Caribbean*, a waterproof paperback available through the publisher (Seahawk Press, 6840 S.W. 92nd St., Miami, FL 33156) and in bookstores and dive shops around Curaçao. Both children and adults will enjoy the easily understood text and the colorful drawings of more than 260 aquatic species. Tom van t' Hof's *Guide to the Curaçao Underwater Park* is an invaluable introduction to diving on the isle. *Curaçao: Scenes and Behind the Scenes* by Jos de Roo discusses the island's history and architecture.

Staying in Curaçao

Important   **Tourist Information:** The **Curaçao Tourism Development Foun-**
Addresses   **dation** has three offices on the island, where multilingual
guides are ready to answer questions. You can also pick up
maps, brochures, and a copy of *Curaçao Holiday*. The main office is located at Pietermaai #19 (tel. 599/961–6000); other
offices are in the Waterfort Arches (no phone) next to the Curaçao Plaza Hotel, and at the airport.

Emergencies   **Police** may be reached at tel. 599/94–4444.

Hospitals: For medical emergencies, call **St. Elisabeth's Hospital** (tel. 599/962–4900) or an ambulance (tel. 599/962–5822).

Pharmacies: Botica Popular (Madurostraat 15, tel. 599/61–
1269).

Currency   U.S. dollars—in cash or traveler's checks—are accepted nearly everywhere, so there's no need to worry about exchanging
money. However, you may need small change for pay phones,
cigarettes, or soda machines. The currency in the Netherlands
Antilles is the guilder, or florin, as it is also called, indicated by
an fl. or NAf. on price tags. The U.S. dollar is considered very
stable; the official rate of exchange at press time was NAf 1.77
to U.S. $1. Note: Prices quoted here are in U.S. dollars unless
indicated otherwise.

Taxes and   Hotels collect a 5% government tax.
Service Charges
The departure tax is $10.

Hotels add a 12% service charge to the bill; restaurants add
10%–15%.

Guided Tours You don't really need a guide to show you downtown Willemstad—it's an easy taxi or bus ride from most major hotels and
small enough for a self-conducted walking tour. To see the rest
of the island, however, a guided tour can save you time and energy. Most hotels have tour desks where arrangements can be
made with reputable tour operators. For very personal, amiable service, try **Casper Tours** (tel. 599/95–3010). For $25 per
person, you'll be escorted around the island in an air-conditioned van, with stops at the Juliana Bridge, the salt lakes,
Knip Bay for a swim, the grotto at Boca Tabla, and lunch at
Janchi Christiaan's, which is famous for its native cuisine. A
sunset cruise includes beer, wine, and cheese and runs $22.50
per head. **Taber Tours** (tel. 599/97–7637) offers a 3½-hour city
and country tour ($10), which includes visits to the Curaçao Li-
queur Factory, the Botanical Garden, the Breivennat Church,
and the old fort.

Taber Tours (tel. 599/97–7637) offers a two-hour sunset cruise,
costing $25 for adults and $15 for children, that includes a feast
of French bread, cheese, and wine. For a daytime excursion,
try the Coral sailing tour around Santa Marta Bay. The package includes transportation to and from your hotel, lunch at the
Coral Cliff Hotel, and beer and soft drinks during the trip. The
cost is $35 for adults, $25 for children.

Getting Around Taxi drivers have an official tariff chart, with fares from
Taxis   the airport vicinity running about $11 to Willemstad to $9 to
Picadera Bay. Taxis at other times are moderately priced, but
confirm the fare with the driver before departure. There is an

additional 25% surcharge after 11 PM. Taxis are readily available at hotels; in other cases, call Central Dispatch at 599/968–4574.

Rental Cars You can rent a car from **Budget** (tel. 599/98–3198), **Avis** (tel. 599/98–1163), and **National Car Rental** (tel. 599/98–3489) at the airport or have it delivered free to your hotel. A typical rate is about $28 a day for a Volkswagen Beetle to about $50 for a four-door sedan. If you're planning to do country driving or rough it through Christoffel Park, a Jeep is best. All you'll need is a valid U.S. or Canadian driver's license.

Telephones and Mail Phone service in Curaçao eventually does connect, but you can spend up to a half hour waiting to reach your party—and some of the connections will require yelling. Hotel operators will put the call through for you, but if you make a collect call, do check immediately afterward that the hotel does not charge you as well. To call Curaçao direct, dial 011–599–9 plus the number in Curaçao. To airmail a letter to the United States costs NAf 1; a postcard costs NAf .60.

To place a call from Curaçao to the United States, dial 1, area code, and local number. To place a local call on the island, dial the six- or seven-digit local number.

Opening and Closing Times Most shops are open Monday–Saturday 8–noon and 2–6. Banks are open on weekdays 8:30–noon and 1:30–4:30.

Beaches

Curaçao has some 38 beaches, and the best way to find "your" beach is to rent a Jeep, cycle, or heavy-treaded car. Ask your hotel to pack a picnic basket for you and go exploring. Getting lost and ending up in some undiscovered cove is half the fun. Curaçao doesn't have Aruba's long, powdery stretches of sand; instead, you'll discover the joy of inlets: tiny bay openings to the sea marked by craggy cliffs, exotic trees, and scads of interesting pebbles. Imagine a beach that's just big enough for your party of four—or a party of just two. Keep an eye out for flying fish. They propel their tails through the water until they reach a speed of 44 mph, then spread their fins and soar.

Hotels with the best beach properties include **The Avila Beach Hotel** (impressively long), the **Princess Beach** (impressively sensuous) and the **Coral Cliff Resort** (impressively deserted). No matter which hotel you're staying at, beach hopping to other hotels can be fun.

One of the largest, more spectacular beaches on Curaçao is **Blauwbaai** (Blue Bay). There's plenty of white sand and lots of shady places, showers, and changing facilities, but since it's a private beach, you'll pay an entrance fee of about NAf.4 per car. Take the road that leads past the Holiday Beach Hotel and the Curaçao Caribbean north toward Julianadorp. At the end of the stretch of straight road, a sign will instruct you to bear left for Blauwbaai and the fishing village of San Michiel. The latter is a good place to dive.

Starting from the church of St. Willibrordus, signs will direct you to **Daai Booi Bay,** a sandy shore dotted with thatched shelters. The road to this public beach is a small paved highway flanked on either side by thick lush trees and huge organpipe cacti. The beach is curved, with shrubbery rooted into the side of the rocky cliffs: a great place to swim.

Knip Bay has two parts: Big (Grote) Knip and Little (Kleine) Knip. Both are shaded with huge trees—these are manchineels, so steer clear of them. Both have alluring white sand, but neither has a place where you can change. Take the road to the Knip Landhouse, then turn right. Signs will direct you. In between the big and the little bay is a superb scenic route. The protected cove, backed by sheer cliffs, is usually a blast on weekends when there is live music.

Playa Abao boasts crystal-clear turquoise water; amenities include a snack center and public toilets. It is located at the northern tip of the island, near West Pointe Bay.

Santa Barbara on the eastern tip has changing facilities and a snack bar but charges a small fee, usually around $3.35 per car.

Westpunt, on the northwest tip of the island, is rocky but shady in the morning. It doesn't have much sand, but you can sit on a shaded ledge. On Sunday, watch the divers jump from the high cliff. The bay view is worth the trip. For lunch, stop at Janchie Christiaan's nearby (*see* Dining, below).

Exploring Curaçao

Numbers in the margin correspond with points of interest on the Curaçao map.

Willemstad ❶ The capital city, **Willemstad,** is a favorite cruise stop for two reasons: The shopping is considered the best in the Caribbean, and a quick tour of most of the downtown sights can be managed within a six-block radius. Santa Anna Bay slices the city down the middle: On one side is the Punda, and on the other is the Otrabanda (literally, the "other side"). Think of the Punda as the side for tourists, crammed with shops, restaurants, monuments, and markets. Otrabanda is for the natives—narrow winding streets full of private homes notable for their picturesque gables and Dutch-influenced designs.

There are three ways to make the crossing from one side to the other: (1) Drive or take a taxi over the Juliana Bridge, (2) traverse the Queen Emma Pontoon Bridge on foot, or (3) ride the free ferry when it's running. If you're staying in a hotel on the Otrabanda side, a free shuttle bus that stops by the lobby will leave you near the Rif Fort; you'll only need to take a short walk north to reach the foot of the Pontoon Bridge.

Our walking tour of Willemstad starts at the **Queen Emma Bridge,** affectionately called "the Lady" by the natives. During the hurricane season in 1988, the 700-foot floating bridge practically floated right out to sea; it was later taken down for major reconstruction. If you're standing on the Otrabanda side, take a few moments to scan Curaçao's multicolored "face" on the other side of Santa Anna Bay. If you wait long enough, the bridge will swing open (at least 30 times a day) to let the seagoing ships pass through. The original bridge, built in 1888, was the brainchild of the American consul Leonard Burlington Smith, who made a mint off the tolls he charged for the bridge. Initially, the charge was 2¢ per person for those wearing shoes, free to those crossing barefoot. Today it's free to everyone.

Take a breather at the peak of the bridge and look north to the 1,625-foot-long **Queen Juliana Bridge,** completed in 1974 and standing 200 feet above water. That's the bridge you drive over to cross to the other side of the city, and although the route is time-consuming (and more expensive if you're going by taxi), the view from this bridge is worth it. At every hour of the day, the sun casts a different tint over the city, creating an ever-changing panorama; the nighttime view, rivaling Rio's, is breathtaking.

When you cross the bridge and arrive on the Punda side, turn left and walk down the waterfront, along **Handelskade.** You'll soon pass the ferry landing. Now take a close look at the buildings you've seen only from afar; the original red tiles of the roofs came from Europe and arrived on trade ships as ballast.

Walk down to the corner and turn right at the customs building onto Sha Caprileskade. This is the bustling **floating market,** where each morning dozens of Venezuelan schooners arrive laden with tropical fruits and vegetables. Fresh mangoes, papayas, and exotic vegetables vie for space with freshly caught fish and unusual fabrics. It's probably too much to ask a tourist to arrive by 6:30 AM when the buying is best, but there's plenty of action to see throughout the afternoon. Any produce bought here, however, should be thoroughly washed before eating.

When the sun is beating down, the **Reading Corner** in the Maduro and Curiel's Bank building (right in front of the floating market) will feel like an oasis. It's an open-air reading room, where you can sit and catch up on the latest newspapers from the United States, Venezuela, and Holland. You might even be able to find a recent *Time* magazine or a *Business Week*.

Keep walking down Sha Caprileskade. Head toward the Wilhelmina Drawbridge, which connects Punda with the once-flourishing district of **Scharloo,** where the early Jewish merchants first built stately homes. Scharloo is now a red-light district.

At the bridge, turn left and walk up Columbusstraat to the **Mikveh Israel-Emanuel Synagogue,** founded in 1651 and the oldest temple still in use in the Western Hemisphere. One of the most important sights in Curaçao, it draws 20,000 visitors a year. Enter through the gates around the corner on Hanchi Snoa and ask the front office to direct you to the guide on duty. A unique feature is the brilliant white sand covering the synagogue floor, a remembrance of Moses leading his people through the desert; the Hebrew letters on the four pillars signify the names of the Four Daughters of Israel: Eve, Sarah, Rachel, and Esther. A quaint museum in the back displays Jewish antiques (including a set of circumcision instruments) and artifacts from Jewish families collected from all over the world. The gift shop near the gate has excellent postcards and commemorative medallions. *29 Kerkstraat, tel. 599/961–1067). Open weekdays 9–11:45 and 2:30–5. Services conducted by an American rabbi are held Fri. at 6:30 PM and on Sat. at 10 AM. Jacket and tie required.*

Continue down Columbusstraat till you reach the courthouse, with its stately balustrade, and the impressive Georgian facade of the Bank of Boston. The statue keeping watch over the park is of Queen Wilhelmina, a popular monarch of the Netherlands, who gave up her throne to her daughter Juliana after her Golden Jubilee in 1948. At Breedestraat, turn left and browse at two of the best jewelry shops in the Caribbean: **Spritzer & Fuhrmann** and **Gandleman's Jewelers.** Take Breedestraat down to the Pontoon Bridge, then turn left at the waterfront. At the foot of the bridge are the mustard-colored walls of **Fort Amsterdam.** Take a few steps through the archway and enter another century. The entire structure dates back to the 1700s, when it was actually the center of the city and the most important fort on the island. Now it houses the governor's residence, the Fort Church, the ministry, and several other government offices. Next door is the **Plaza Piar,** dedicated to Manuel Piar, a native Curaçaoan who fought for the independence of Venezuela under the liberator Simon Bolívar. On the other side of the plaza is the **Waterfort,** a bastion dating back to 1634. The original cannons are still positioned in the battlements. The foundation, however, now forms the walls of the Curaçao Plaza Hotel. Following the sidewalk around the plaza, you'll discover the most delightful shopping area on the island, newly built under the **Waterfort arches** (*see* Shopping, below, for details).

Western Side The road through the village of Soto that leads to the northwest tip of the island winds through landscape that Georgia O'Keefe might have painted—towering cacti, flamboyant dried shrubbery, and thatch-roof houses. Throughout this *cunucu,* or countryside, you'll see native fishermen hauling in their nets, women pounding cornmeal, and donkeys blocking traffic. Landhouses, large estate houses from centuries past, dot the countryside, though most are closed to the public. Their facades, though, can often be glimpsed from the highway. For a ❷ splendid view, food, drinks, and music, try to stop at **Landhuis Jan Kock** (tel. 599/964–8087), built in the mid-17th century, which is reputed to be haunted. Hours are irregular, so do call in advance.

Next, head toward Christoffel Park on the highway. Make a ❸ stop at **Boca Tabla,** where the sea has carved a magnificent grotto. Safely tucked in the back, you can watch and listen to the waves crashing ferociously against the rocks. About ❹ an hour from Willemstad, off the Westpunt highway, is **Christoffel Park,** a fantastic 4,450-acre garden and wildlife preserve with the towering Mt. Christoffel at its center. Open to the public since 1978, the park consists of three former plantations with individual trails that take about one to 1½ hours each to traverse. You may drive your own car (heavy-treaded wheels) or rent a Jeep with or without an accompanying guide. Start out early (by 10 AM the park starts to feel like a sauna), and if you're going solo, first study the *Excursion Guide to Christoffel Park* (sold at the front desk), which outlines the various routes and identifies the flora and fauna found here. No matter what route you take, you'll be treated to interesting views of hilly fields full of prickly pear cacti, divi-divi trees, bushy-haired palms, and exotic flowers that bloom unpredictably after April showers. There are also caves with ancient Indian inscriptions. For the strong of heart: Walk through the bat caves on the Savonet route (marked in blue); you'll hear bat wings rustling in the corners and see a few scary, but nonpoisonous, scorpion spiders scuttling over the walls. Make sure you're wearing the proper shoes; the ground is covered with *guano* (bird and bat droppings) that almost seems alive because of the millions of harmless mites. It's not all a shop of horrors, though—if you make it to the last chamber, you'll discover a magnificent white-faced barn owl.

As you drive through the park, keep a lookout for tiny deer, goats, and other small wildlife that might suddenly dart in front of your car. The snakes you could encounter—the whipsnake and the minute silver snake—are not poisonous. Whitetail hawks may be seen on the green route, white orchids and crownlike passion flowers on the yellow route.

Climbing up the 1,230-foot Mt. Christoffel on foot is an exhilarating experience and a definite challenge to anyone who hasn't grown up scaling the Alps. The guidebook claims the roundtrip will take you one hour, and Curaçaoan adolescent boys do make a sport of racing up and down, but it took this writer 2½ sweaty hours to make it back to camp. And the last few feet are deadly. The view from the peak, however, *is* thrilling—a panorama of the island, including Santa Marta Bay and the tabletop mountain of St. Hironimus. On a clear day, you can even see the mountain ranges of Venezuela, Bonaire, and Aruba. *Tel. 599/ 964–0363. Admission: $1.25 adults, 75¢ children 6–15, free after 2 PM. Open daily 8–3.*

Eastern Side   To explore the eastern side of the island, take the coastal road out from Willemstad past the zoo and botanical gardens (neither is exceptional) about 2 miles to Bapor Kibra. There you'll find the Seaquarium and the Underwater Park.

5 The **Curaçao Seaquarium** is *the* place to see the island's underwater treasures without getting your feet wet. In fact, it's the world's only public aquarium where sea creatures are raised and cultivated totally by natural methods. You can spend several hours here, mesmerized by the 75 freshwater tanks full of over 400 varieties of exotic fish and vegetation, including sharks, lobsters, turtles, corals, and sponges. Look out for their eight-foot mascot, Herbie the cewfish, a lugubrious fish who, with luck, has been moved to a bigger tank by the time you get there. Water slides designed for both adults and children are big pleasers. There's also an excellent Indonesian restaurant, steakhouse, and snack bar. A 495-yard, man-made beach of white sand is well suited to novice swimmers and children, and bathroom and shower facilities are available. A souvenir shop sells some of the best postcards and coral jewelry on the island. *Tel. 599/961–6666. Admission: $5 adults, $2.50 children. Open daily 9 AM–10 PM.*

6 **Curaçao Underwater Park** consists of about 12½ miles of untouched coral reef that have been granted the status of national park. Mooring buoys have been placed at the most interesting dive sites on the reef to provide safe anchoring and to prevent damage to the reef. The park stretches along the south shore from the Princess Beach Hotel in Willemstad to the eastern tip of the island. Admission is free.

7 **Landhuis Brievengat** (tel. 599/97–8344) is a 10-minute drive northeast of Willemstad, near the Centro Deportivo sports stadium. On the last Sunday of the month, it holds an open house with crafts demonstrations and folkloric shows. You can see the original kitchen still intact, the 18-inch-thick walls, fine antiques, and the watchtowers, once used for lovers' trysts. The restaurant serves a fine rijstaffel.

8 Nearby is the **Arawak Clay Products** (tel. 599/97–7658) with a factory showroom of native-made crafts. You can purchase a variety of tiles, plates, pots, and tiny replicas of landhouses. Tour operators can arrange trips.

Wind southward past Spanish Bay, where you'll pass several private yacht clubs that attract sports anglers from all over the world for international tournaments. And make a stop at **Santa Barbara Beach,** especially on Sundays, when the atmosphere approaches party time (*see* Beaches, above). **Caracas Bay,** off **9** Bapor Kibra, is a popular diving site, with a sunken ship so close to the surface that even snorkelers can balance their flippers on the helm.

Curaçao for Free

Located on the side of Willemstad in Cholobo, the **Senior Liqueur Factory** distills and distributes the original Curaçao liqueur. Don't expect to find a massive factory—it's just a small showroom in the open-air foyer of a beautiful 17th-century landhouse. There are no guides, but you can read the story of the distillation process on posters, and you'll be graciously offered samples in various flavors. If you're interested in buying—the chocolate liqueur is fantastic over ice cream—you can choose from a complete selection, which is bottled in a variety of fascinating shapes, including Dutch ceramic houses.

What to See and Do with Children

The **Curaçao Caribbean** and **Las Palmas** hotels work hard to provide a variety of activities for children—crafts, volleyball, water sports, and other group games. If you are staying elsewhere, talk to the activities director or hostess of your hotel for suggestions; they're usually very creative and might even plan a party for your child's birthday if other children are available.

Sports programs for youngsters can be found at **Chirino** (12 Orionweg, tel. 599/961–3346), a sport and recreation center. It also offers classes called *arte infantil*, where children sing, dance, act, and play. Also available is a fully equipped gym for adults, complete with aerobics classes, fitness training, jazz dancing, massage, and sauna.

Off the Beaten Track

Beth Haim, the oldest Jewish burial ground still in use in the Western Hemisphere, is a wonderful off-beat stop. Consecrated before 1659, it has more than 2,500 graves on 3 acres, and grand history can be read from the inscriptions on the magnificently carved tombstones.

Participant Sports

Horseback Riding No one in Curaçao offers romps down the beach, but you can ride the trail inside **Rancho Alegre** (tel. 599/97–9160) by the hour or longer by reservation. Or call **Joe Pineda** (tel. 599/98–1616) for a $10-an-hour ride at his ranch.

Jogging The **Rif Recreation Area** stretches from the water plant at Mundo Nobo to the Curaçao Caribbean Hotel along the sea. It comprises more than 1.2 miles of palm-lined beachfront, a wading pond, and a jogging track with an artificial surface, as well as a big playground. There is good security and street lighting along the entire length of the beachfront.

Tennis Most hotels (including Curaçao Caribbean, Las Palmas, Princess Beach, Holiday Beach, and the Lions Dive Hotel & Marina) offer well-paved courts, illuminated for day and night games.

Water Sports Curaçao has facilities for all kinds of water sports, thanks to the government-sponsored **Curaçao Underwater Park,** which includes almost a third of the island's southern diving waters. Scuba divers and snorkelers can enjoy over 12½ miles of protected reefs and shores, with normal visibility from 60 to 80 feet (up to 150 feet on good days). With water temperatures ranging from 70° to 80° F, wet suits are generally unnecessary. No coral collecting, spearfishing, or littering is allowed. An underwater nature trail, which is especially handy for snorkelers, has been chartered along the shallows between the Seaquarium and Jan Thiel Beach, but it's accessible only by boat. An exciting wreck to explore is the SS *Oranje Nassau,* which ran aground about 80 years ago and now hosts hundreds of exotic fish and unusually shaped coral.

Most hotels either offer their own program of water sports or will be happy to make arrangements for you. An introductory scuba lesson (or one-time dive) usually runs around $25–$30.

Underwater Curaçao (tel. 599/961–6666) is a world-renowned diving operation connected with the Divi Hotels and offers complete vacation/dive packages in conjunction with the Holiday Beach Hotel, Las Palmas, Princess Beach Hotel, and Lions Dive Hotel & Marina. Its fully stocked dive shop, located next to the Curaçao Seaquarium, offers equipment for both sale and rental. Personal instruction and group lessons are conducted on state-of-the art dive boats personally designed by "Dutch" Schrier. One dive will run you $25; packages are available. Glass-bottom-boat tours are also a fun way to go down under without getting your ears wet.

Seascape (tel. 599/962–5000, ext. 177), at the Curaçao Caribbean Hotel, specializes in snorkeling and scuba-diving trips to reefs and underwater wrecks in every type of water vehicle—from pedal boats and water scooters to waterskis and windsurf boards. A five-dive package costs $110. Snorkeling gear costs about $2 an hour to rent. Die-hard fishermen with companions who prefer to suntan will enjoy the day trip to Little Curaçao, the "clothes optional" island between Curaçao and Bonaire, where the fish are reputed to be lively: Plan on $40 per person. Deep-sea fishing for a maximum of six people can also be arranged; it costs $225 for a half day, $450 for a full day.

Seaquarium Dive Shop, at the Seaquarium, includes a spacious patio overlooking the marina and is equipped with personal storage bins and wash tanks. Take a dive/snorkeling trip on the *Coral Sea,* a 40-foot twin diesel yacht-style dive boat, or the *Coral View,* a monohull flat-top glass-bottom boat that makes regular 30-minute excursions. A full range of equipment can be rented.

Dive Curaçao & Watersports (tel. 599/961–4944, ext. 20) at the Princess Beach Hotel both rents equipment and conducts diving and snorkeling trips. Scuba lessons run $30, including equipment. Take a 1½-hour snorkeling tour around the under-water park for $10. Also available is a cabin cruiser for half-day or full-day deep-sea fishing excursions, for $150.

For windsurfing, check out the **Curaçao High Wind School** (Princess Beach Hotel, tel. 599/961–4944).

Spectator Sports

The graceful Windsurfers, bobbing sailboats, and commercial ships passing through the harbor make an ongoing sport spectacle in Curaçao. Soccer matches, and baseball games, from March through October, are held in the modern and comfortable **Centro Deportivo** stadium, located about 10 minutes from town. For more information, contact the Curaçao Tourist Board Office (400 Madison Ave., New York, NY 10017, tel. 212/751–8266 or 800/332–8266).

Shopping

Curaçao has long enjoyed the reputation of having some of the best shops in the Caribbean, but don't expect posh Madison Avenue boutiques. With a few exceptions (such as Benetton, which recently moved into the Caribbean with a vengeance), the quality of women's fashions here lies along the lines of sales racks.

If you're looking for bargains on Swiss watches, cameras, crystal, or electronic equipment, do some comparison shopping back home and come armed with a list of prices.

Shopping Areas Most of the shops are concentrated in one place—**Punda**—in downtown Willemstad, within about a six-block area. The main shopping streets are **Heerenstraat, Breedestraat,** and **Madurostraat. Heerenstraat** and **Gomezplein** are both pedestrian malls, closed to traffic, and their roadbeds have been raised to sidewalk level and covered with pink inlaid tiles.

The hippest shopping area lies under the **Waterfort arches,** along with a variety of restaurants and bars. Our three favorite shops under the arches are **Bamali** (tel. 599/961–2258), which sells Indonesian batik clothing, leather bags and briefcases, and charming handicrafts; **The African Queen** (no phone), an exotic bazaar of fine African jewelry, antiques, and artifacts; and **Gino's European Boutique** (tel. 599/961–5583), full of snazzy hats with plumes and trendy accessories that look wonderfully out of place on a Caribbean isle.

Good Buys The leading jewelers in the Netherlands Antilles, **Spritzer & Fuhrmann** (Heerenstraat 2, tel. 599/961–1511), carries Danish silver, delftware, Limoges, diamonds, emeralds, china, and Lladro figurines. The service is elegant.

Julius L. Penha & Sons (Heerenstraat 1, tel. 599/961–2266), in front of the Pontoon Bridge, sells French perfumes, Hummel figurines, linen from Madeira, delftware, and handbags from Argentina, Italy, and Spain. The store also has an extensive cosmetics counter.

Boolchand's (Heerenstraat 4B, tel. 599/961–2798) handles an interesting variety of merchandise behind a facade of red-and-white checked tiles. Stock up here on French perfumes, British cashmere sweaters, Italian silk ties, Dutch dolls, Swiss watches, and Japanese cameras.

Benetton (Madurostraat 4, tel. 599/961–4919) has winter stock in July and summer stock in December; both stocks are 20% off the retail price.

Crazy Look (Madurostraat 6, no phone) has French, Italian, and Dutch fashions with a hip Eurotrash look, as well as trendy sweat shirts and baggy pants.

Toko Zuikertuintje (tel. 599/97–0188), a supermarket built on the original 17th-century Zuikertuintje Landhuis, is where most of the local elite shop. Enjoy the free tea and coffee while you stock up on all sorts of European and Dutch delicacies.

Local Crafts Native crafts and curios are on hand at **Fundason Obra di Man** (Bargestraat 57, tel. 599/961–2413). Particularly impressive are the posters of Curaçao's architecture.

Black Coral (Princess Beach Hotel, tel. 599/961–4944) is owned by Dutch-born artisan Bert Knubben, one of Curaçao's true characters. For the past 30 years, he's been designing and sculpting the most exciting black-coral jewelery in the Caribbean—and even dives for it himself, with special permission from the government. Dolphin pendants and twiglike earrings finished in 14-karat gold are excellent buys. Call before you drop by.

Dining

Restaurateurs in Curaçao believe in whetting appetites with a variety of cuisines and intriguing ambience: Dine under the boughs of magnificent old trees, in the romantic gloom of wine cellars in renovated landhouses, or on the ramparts of 18th-century forts. Curaçaoans partake of some of the best Indonesian food in the Caribbean, and they also find it hard to resist the French, Swiss, Dutch, and Swedish delights. Dress in restaurants is almost always casual, but if you feel like putting on your finery, there will always be a place for you. Do take a wrap or a light sweater with you—for some reason, most restaurants have their air-conditioners going full blast.

The most highly recommended restaurants are indicated by a star ★.

Category	Cost*
Expensive	$15–$25
Moderate	$5–$15
Inexpensive	under $5

per person, excluding drinks and service

★ **Bistro Le Clochard.** The charming Dutch couple who own this harborside restaurant still laugh about the 1988 hurricane that blew out the big picture windows and sent ocean trout swimming through the dining area. A romantic gem, the bistro is built into the 18th-century Rif Fort and is suffused with the cool, dark atmosphere of ages past. The use of fresh ingredients in the consistently well-prepared French and Swiss dishes makes dining here a dream. Try the fresh-fish platters or the tender veal in mushroom sauce. Savor the fondue and let yourself get carried away by the unusual setting; just save room for the chocolate mousse. *On the Otrabanda Rif Fort, tel. 599/962–5666. Reservations required. Closed Sat. for lunch and Sun. off-season. AE, DC, MC, V. Expensive.*

★ **De Taveerne.** From the intricate detail of its centuries-old antiques to its impressive Continental menu, this restaurant rates as one of the most elegant, romantic spots on the island. Dining is in the whitewashed wine cellar of this magnificent renovated country estate, built in the 1800s by an exiled Venezuelan revolutionary. The best appetizer is the slices of tangy, smoked dolphin. The young Dutch chef, Hennie, also excels in grilled lobster and works wonders with veal. For dessert, there's better-than-average cheesecake and the absolutely unforgettable broiled pears, topped with vanilla ice cream and drenched with Curaçao chocolate liqueur. *LandhuisGroot Davelaar, on Fridsanusweg, near the Promenade Shopping Center, tel. 599/97–0669. Reservations required. AE, DC, MC, V. Closed Sun. Expensive.*

La Bistroelle. The rustic Victorian splendor of the chandeliers, dark wood beams, and plush velvet chairs here will make you think that you've wandered into a French country inn. A favorite of residents who can afford it, the marvelous French cuisine includes octopus, steak in champagne, mussels in whiskey sauce, and hearty bouillabaisse. The crepes Suzettes and *poires flambée* are not to be missed. The owners cater private parties in one of their plantation houses upon request. *Astroidenweg/Schottegatweg in the Promenade Shopping Center, tel. 599/97–6929. Reservations required. AE, DC, MC, V. Expensive.*

Fort Nassau Restaurant. This is *the* place to witness the twinkling magic of Curaçao at night. High on a hilltop overlooking Willemstad, the restaurant is built into an 18th-century fort and gives a 360-degree panoramic view of the city's rooftops. Go for a drink in the breezy, trendy Battery Terrace bar or dine in air-conditioned civility in front of the huge bay windows. The view might surpass the food, but best bets include the onion soup, the *keshi yena* (stuffed Edam cheese), and the red snapper. Afterward, check out the action in the Infinity Club downstairs, one of the sexiest, plushest discos we've ever seen. *Near Point Juliana, tel. 599/961–3086. Reservations required. AE, DC, MC, V. Expensive.*

Belle Terrace. Tucked into the quaint Avila Beach Hotel, this seaside restaurant sits right underneath the boughs of an ancient tree. Each night it features a different specialty, from Curaçao dishes like *keshi yena* to *sopito* (fish and coconut soup) to salted boiled breast of duck and filet mignon. In between stops at the creative salad bar, watch the fish jumping out of the sea—they fly up to 20 feet. *Penstraat 13–134, tel. 599/961–4377. Reservations required. AE, DC, MC, V. Moderate.*

Bellevue Restaurant. A mom, pop, and son operation that has acquired the reputation of serving some of Curaçao's best native cuisine—the queen of Holland and the president of Venezuela have even stopped by. Forty-three years ago, it started out as an American naval base—Charles Lindbergh landed his seaplane here. Choose from a lineup of soups, including oyster, iguana, turtle, okra, and papaya, as well as sauerkraut and goat-meat stews. The seafood-combination platter is so big you won't know where to start. And the caramel pudding is wicked. *Baai Macolaweg, Parera, tel. 599/95–4291. AE, DC, MC, V. Moderate.*

★ **Janchi Christiaan's Restaurant.** Tour buses stop regularly at this open-air restaurant for lunch and for weird-sounding, but mouth-watering, native dishes. For starters, try the okra soup, the cactus soup, or the goat-meat stew; the main-course specialty is a hefty platter of fresh-caught fish, potatoes, and vegetables. Curaçaoans joke that Janchi's "iguana soup is so strong it could resurrect the dead"—truth is, it tastes just like chicken soup, only better. But Janchi, Jr., says if you want iguana, you order iguana in advance "because we have to go out and catch them." He's not kidding. *Westpunt 14, tel. 599/964–0354. No reservations required. No credit cards. Moderate.*

Golden Star Restaurant. This place looks and feels more like a friendly roadside diner than a full-fledged restaurant, but the native food here is among the best in town. Owner Marie Burke turns out Antillean specialties like *bestia chiki* (goat stew), shrimp Creole, and delicately seasoned grilled conch, all served with generous heaps of rice, fried plantains, and avocado. Steaks and chops can be had for the asking. *Socratestraat 2, tel. 599/965–4795. No reservation required. AE, DC, MC, V. Moderate.*

★ **Rijstaffel Indonesia Restaurant.** No steaks or chops here, just one dish after another of exotic delicacies that make up the traditional Indonesian banquet called *rijstaffel.* Try some sweet-and-sour barbecue ribs at the mahogany bar first, then choose from 16–36 traditional dishes that are set buffet style around you. Wash it all down with Bintang, a tangy Indonesian beer. Lesser appetites will enjoy the lighter meals, such as the fried noodles, fresh jumbo shrimps in garlic, or combination meat-and-fish platters. Desserts are nearly mystical; a "ladies only" ice cream comes with a red rose. The coconut ice cream comes packed in a coconut shell you can take home. The walls are stocked with beautiful Indonesian puppets ($25–$40) that will make stunning gifts. Curaçaoans love this restaurant. *Mercurriusstraat 13–15, Salinja, tel. 599/961–2999. Reservations required. Happy hour daily 5–7. AE, DC, MC, V. Moderate.*

Cozzoli's Pizza. Fast, cheap, hearty New York–style pizzas oven-baked, just like they make them in Brooklyn, are offered here. Pig out on calzones, sausage rolls, and lasagna. It is right in the middle of downtown Willemstad. *Breedestraat 2, tel. 599/961–7184. No credit cards. Inexpensive.*

Gipsy. This is a spic-and-span fast-food counter in the middle of the shopping district—drop by if all you want is a diet Coke or a roast-beef sub. Amstel beer, cappuccinos, and espresso are quick pick-me-ups. *On Madurostraat, near the floating market. No phone. No credit cards. Inexpensive.*

Lodging

Hotels in Curaçao all have their pluses and minuses. If you're a business traveler, you'll appreciate the Curaçao Plaza, with easy access to the city center, but you'll have a long trek to the beach. Guests at the Curaçao Caribbean, Las Palmas, and Holiday Beach hotels enjoy their own beaches, but they're some distance from town. The Avila Beach Hotel has a beautiful beach, but the rooms are small and ascetic. Most hotels offer free shuttle bus services to downtown.

The most highly recommended lodgings are indicated by a star
★.

Category	Cost*
Expensive	over $75
Moderate	$55–$75
Inexpensive	under $55

*All prices are for a standard double room for two, excluding
5% tax and a 12% service charge.*

Hotels **Curaçao Caribbean Hotel and Casino.** Formerly a Hilton, this
★ hotel has a beach the size of a sandbox, but the lounging yard
behind it is sprawling and perfect for sunbathing. It's five minutes by car from the center of town. The high-rise complex is
self-contained, with one of the best organized activities program on the island, including crab races, Papiamento lessons,
crafts, walking tours, ping-pong and jousting tournaments,
and special theme nights for dinner and dancing. Adults can
safely leave their kids in the hands of friendly and energetic
hostesses who will entertain them. Water sports include everything imaginable. And the row of boutiques means you never
have to leave the premises to shop. Across the street is the new
International Trade Center. *Box 2133, Piscadera Bay, Willemstad, tel. 599/962–5000 or 800/444–1010. 200 rooms.
Facilities: 2 restaurants, 2 bars, pool, casino, beauty salon,
barbershop, lighted tennis courts, health spa, boutiques, drugstore, secretarial services, telex, meeting and convention
rooms. AE, DC, MC, V. Expensive.*

Golden Tulip Las Palmas and Vacation Village. The drive from
the main highway to the main building takes you through a luxurious tropical garden. Las Palmas has the feel of a laid-back
hacienda, with the three-story main building and compact
casitas spread out on the hilly gardens. However, you must be
an energetic walker to navigate the grounds; the private beach
is 800 yards from the main lobby, with a steep incline to negotiate, and the pool and casino are also a hike. A courtyard full of
vines, a lily pond, and bamboo arches makes for a relaxing dining experience. The air-conditioned rooms are comfortable,
but the acoustics—let's just say your room had better not be
next to a honeymoon couple's. The casino is tiny, but nightly
entertainment is usually big and noisy, with steel bands, fire-
eating limbo dancers, folklore shows, and exotic buffets. *Box
2179, Piscadera Bay, Willemstad, tel. 599/962–5200. 98 rooms;
94 2-bedroom villas. Facilities: restaurant, coffee shop, pool,
casino, private beach with snack bar, minimarket, lighted tennis courts, drugstore. AE, DC, MC, V. Expensive.*

Lions Dive Hotel & Marina. This recent addition to the Curaçao
vacation scene is located a hop, skip, and plunge away from the
Seaquarium. The pink-and-green caravansary is set on a
quarter mile of private beach with airy, light-filled rooms
overlooking the sea from spacious balconies or terraces. The atmosphere is lively; the young, attractive staff eager to please.
Dive packages are offered with Underwater Curaçao. *Bapor
Kibra, Curaçao, tel. 599/96–18100. 72 air-conditioned rooms
with color TV. Facilities: specialty restaurant, terrace bar,
pool. All major credit cards. Expensive.*

★ **Avila Beach Hotel.** The royal family of Holland and its ministers stay at this 200-year-old mansion for three good reasons: the privacy, the personalized service, and the austere elegance. Americans used to luxurious resorts might find the rooms stark, but the hotel's true elegance lies in the spectacular beach, the largest in Curaçao, as well as in the fabulous tree-shaded, outdoor dining area. The Danish chefs, who specialize in a Viking pot, local dishes, and weekly smorgasbord, also smoke their own fish and bake their own bread. Classical concerts, often performed by the owner, a budding tenor, take place on Sunday mornings. Recent renovations include a new coffee shop with an open-air sea view and a conference room. *Box 791, Penstraat 130134, Willemstad, tel. 599/961–4377. 87 rooms; 20 apartments with ocean view, some with kitchenettes. Facilities: restaurant, coffee shop, bar, elevator, conference room, shuttle bus to city center. AE, DC, MC, V. Moderate.*

Coral Cliff Resort and Beach Club. Seclusion and rustic simplicity are everything here. A half hour from the center of Willemstad, the grounds boast a beach so enticing that it even attracts native islanders who are desperate for a weekend retreat. The caged iguanas near the restaurant are the only ones you will see in captivity on the island, and you're apt to find low-flying trupials, parrots, and parakeets alighting on your dinner table. All rooms are air-conditioned and overlook the sea. Cottages are equipped with kitchenettes. *Box 3782, Santa Marta Bay, tel. 599/964–1820 or 800/223–9815. 35 rooms. Facilities: casino, pool, 2 restaurants, bar, car-rental agent, marina, water-sports center, and PADI 4-star dive shop. AE, DC, MC, V. Moderate.*

Curaçao Plaza Hotel and Casino. "Please don't touch the passing ships" is the slogan of the Curaçao Plaza, the only hotel in the world with marine-collision insurance. The ships do come close to the island's first high-rise hotel, which is built right into the massive walls of a 17th-century fort at the entrance of Willemstad's harbor. At the Plaza, you give up beachfront (you have beach privileges at major hotels, however) for walking access to the city's center—consequently, it's a business traveler's oasis, complete with executive floors and secretaries who will fax, telex, type, translate, and read out stock prices for you. The Queens and Kings Room is where the executives gather to network, read international papers, enjoy breakfast on the house, and indulge in the honor bar. The ramparts rising from the sea offer a fantastic evening view of the twinkling lights of the city. Most rooms are lacking in the decor department, but many have windows that provide a view of the Venezuelan coast. The new boutiques built under the adjacent arches are the best in Curaçao. *Box 229, Plaza Piar, Willemstad, tel. 599/961–2500. 254 rooms, 135 of which are in the tower, many with a sea view and some with balconies. All with bath, shower, color cable TV, air-conditioning, and 24-hr room service. Beach privileges with other hotels a taxi drive away. Facilities: 2 restaurants, nightclub, bar, casino, outdoor salt-water pool, discotheque, poolside barbecue and elaborate Sun. buffet, newsstand, drugstore, gift shop, and flower shop. Baby-sitter and house physician on call. AE, DC, MC, V. Moderate.*

Holiday Beach Hotel and Casino. This low-rise building was put up in 1966 and has undergone major reconstruction with an eye toward making beach life even more accessible. The lobby has been totally redesigned, and a beach bar and restaurant have been built close to the water. Despite the major renovations, however, the individual rooms remain uninspiring, not the kind you'd want to do more than sleep in. Clientele include business travelers and honeymooners, with a large cultural mix in the low season, including South Americans. *Box 2178, Otrabanda, Pater Euwensweg, Willemstad, tel. 599/962–5400. 197 rooms; 2 suites. Facilities: playground, beauty shop, boutique, drugstore, gift shop, car-rental agent, casino. AE, MC, V. Moderate.*

★ **Princess Beach Hotel and Casino.** The beach, lined with lime trees, is one of the most beautiful in Curaçao, and is located right in front of the underwater park and a short walk from the Seaquarium. The rooms are huge, most with breathtaking ocean or garden views. (The garden-view rooms are the more spacious of the two.) The pathway to guest rooms is through lush, tropical grounds full of chirping birds. The new freshwater pool has the added bonus of a staff to offer drinks to guests as they paddle about on floats. Dinner in the Ballroom is black tie. The casino is the most exciting in Curaçao. Time-sharing apartments with terraces are now available. The **Curaçao High Wind School** is on the premises. *M. L. King Blvd. 8, tel. 599/ 961–4944 or 800/223–9815. 203 rooms. Facilities: restaurant, special theme nights, pool with bar, boutiques, drugstore, dive shop, spa, refrigerators on request. AE, DC, MC, V. Moderate.*

Home and Apartment Rentals There are many rentals available on the island. Your best bet is to contact the **Curaçao Tourist Board** or write to **Caribbean Home Rentals** (Box 710, Palm Beach, FL 33480).

The Arts and Nightlife

The Arts **The Curaçao Museum,** housed in a century-old former plantation house, is filled with artifacts, paintings, and antique furnishings that trace the island's history. *Across from the Holiday Beach Hotel, off Pater Euwensweg, tel. 599/962–3777. Admission: $1.50. Open Tues.–Sun. 8–noon and 2–5. Closed last Sun. of the month.*

Gallery 86 (no phone), in the Bloksteeg (Punda) opposite the Bank of the Netherlands Antilles, features the works of local artists and occasionally those of South Americans and Africans.

Nightlife The once-a-month open house at Landhuis Brievengat (*see* Exploring, Curaçao, Eastern Side, above) is a great way to meet interesting locals—it usually offers a folkloric show, snacks, and local handicrafts. The Curaçao Plaza, Holiday Beach, Las Palmas, and the Princess Beach hotels all have casinos that are open 2 PM–4 AM, with the exception of San Marco and the Curaçao Caribbean, which are open 9 AM–4 AM.

Blue Note Jazz Cafe (Schout bij N. Doormanweg, tel. 599/937–0685) is a singles bar-cum-Dutch pub that fills up fast. There's likely to be more TV-watching than dancing. There is live jazz on Wednesday 9:30 PM–2 AM and Sunday noon–5 PM.

La Fontaine (78 Cas Coraweg, tel. 599/97–8596), about a 10-minute drive from town, is a psychedelic-lit disco that's popular with locals. Occasional live shows feature hard-rock acts that attract a teenage crowd.

Infinity (tel. 599/61–34–50), a tiny club underneath the Fort Nassau Restaurant, sets such a frisky mood you'll probably find yourself agitating your Adidas until the wee small hours.

Everything—from the plushy couches to the waterfall wall—makes the notion of "early to bed" downright unthinkable.

Considered the most colorful disco in town, **Naick's Place** (Lindbergweg 32, Salina, tel. 599/96–14640) is about as hip as Curaçao gets. It's dark and cool, with huge bamboo chairs for lounging. The men cruise and the women are dressed to kill. There are two disco floors with flashing lights and an intense aural assault. It's packed on Thursday, Friday, and Saturday nights.

The new nightclub and disco, **Sabine's** (Plaza Hotel, tel. 599/961–2500), is open daily 10 PM–3 AM. There's no cover charge for the live entertainment that's featured on Friday and Saturday nights.

10 Dominica

by Honey Naylor

The national motto emblazoned on the coat of arms of the Commonwealth of Dominica reads *"Après Bondi, c'est la ter."* It is a French-Creole phrase meaning "After God, it is the land." On this unspoiled isle, the land is indeed the main attraction . . . it turns and twists, towers to mountain crests, then tumbles to falls and valleys. It is a land that the Smithsonian Institute has called a giant plant laboratory, unchanged for 10,000 years.

The grandeur of Dominica (pronounced dom-in-*ee*-ka) is not man-made. This untamed, ruggedly beautiful land, located in the eastern Caribbean between Guadeloupe to the north and Martinique to the south, is a 290-square-mile nature retreat; 29 miles long and 15 miles wide, the island is dominated by some of the highest elevations in the Caribbean and has 365 rivers running through it. Much of the interior is covered by a luxuriant rain forest, a wild place where you almost expect Tarzan to swing howling by on a vine. This exotic spot is home to such unusual critters as the Sisserou (or Imperial) parrot and the red-necked (or Jacquot) parrot, neither of which can be found anywhere else in the world.

Dominica is home, too, to the last remnants of the Carib Indians, whose ancestors came paddling up from South America more than a thousand years ago. The fierce, cannibalistic Caribs kept Christopher Columbus at bay when he came to call during his second voyage to the New World. Columbus turned up at the island on Sunday, November 3, 1493. In between Carib arrows he hastily christened it Dominica (Sunday Island), and then sailed on.

For almost two centuries the British and French tried unsuccessfully to subdue the Caribs, and in 1748 they agreed to let the Caribs keep the island. However, French and English planters, unable to resist the lure of the fertile land, began to fight one another for squatter's rights. The Caribs had named their island *waitukubuli* ("tall is her body"), but it was *Dominica* that remained in history. In 1805, the English paid a "ransom" of 12,000 pounds to the French, and Dominica became a British possession. In 1967, the British colony became self-governing, and on November 3, 1978 Dominica became a fully independent republic, officially called the Commonwealth of Dominica. Despite (or perhaps because of) its ferocious past, Dominica today is a quiet, peaceful place. There are about 82,000 people living on the island, and they are some of the friendliest people in all of the Caribbean.

Before You Go

Tourist Information   The **Caribbean Tourism Association** (20 E. 46th St., New York, NY 10017, tel. 212/682–0435) has little information on hand, so you will do better to contact the **Dominica Tourist Board** (Box 73, Roseau, Dominica, WI tel. 809/448–2186, 809/448–2351. Telex 8649 TOURIST DO; fax 809/448–5840). However, if you write to the island allow at least two to three weeks for your letter to arrive as the mail is notoriously slow.

Arriving and Departing
By Plane   No major airlines fly into Dominica, but **LIAT** (tel. 809/462–0700) connects with flights from the United States on Antigua, Barbados, Guadeloupe, Martinique, St. Lucia, San Juan, and Puerto Rico. **Air Caribe** (tel. 809/449–1117) flies direct from San Juan, **Air Martinique** (tel. 809/449–1060) from Fort de France, and **Air Guadeloupe** (tel. 809/449–1060) from Pointe-à-

Pitre. **Air Anguilla** (tel. 809/497–2643) connects from Puerto Rico via Anguilla and **Air BVI** (tel. 809/774–6500) connects from Tortola, BVI, three days a week.

From the Airport **Canefield Airport** (about 3 miles north of the capital city of Roseau) at present can take only small aircraft, with lights available for night takeoffs only. Dominica's older and larger **Melville Hall Airport,** on the northeast (Atlantic) coast, can manage larger commercial aircraft and night landings; however, it is a rather harrowing 90-minute drive from there to Roseau, and the fare is about U.S.$50 for a private taxi. The usual system is a co-op cab, where all seats must be taken for about $15 a person, as opposed to the $6-per-car fare from Canefield to Roseau. The moral of the story: Opt for Canefield, if at all possible.

By Boat **The Caribbean Express** (Fort-de-France, Martinique, tel. 596/60–12–38) has scheduled weekly departures from St. Martin in the north to Grenada in the south, with stops at Antigua, St. Barts, St. Lucia, Guadeloupe, St. Vincent, and Martinique.

Passports and Visas The only entry requirements for U.S. or Canadian citizens are proof of citizenship, such as a birth certificate or voter registration card bearing a photograph, and an ongoing or return airline ticket. British citizens are required to have passports but visas are not necessary.

Customs and Duties In addition to items for personal use, you may bring in 200 cigarettes or 50 cigars and 8 ounces of tobacco, a quart of alcohol, and 6 ounces of perfume.

Language The official language is English, but most Dominicans also speak a French-Creole patois.

Precautions Be sure to bring insect repellent. If you are prone to car sickness, you will also want to bring along some pills. The roads twist and turn dramatically, and the (expert) local drivers barrel across them at a dizzying pace.

Staying in Dominica

Important Addresses **Tourist Information:** The main office of the **Division of Tourism** (Bath Estate, Roseau, tel. 809/448–2186 or 809/448–2351) and the tourist desks at the **Old Market Plaza** (Roseau, tel. 809/448–2186; hours: Mon. 8–5, Tues.–Fri. 8–4, Sat. 9–1), **Canefield Airport** (tel. 809/449–1242), and **Melville Hall Airport** (tel. 809/445–7051) are open weekdays 6:15–11 AM and 2–5:30 PM.

Emergencies **Police, Fire, and Ambulance:** Call 999.

Hospitals: Princess Margaret Hospital (Federation Dr., Goodwill, tel. 809/448–2231 or 809/448–2233).

Pharmacies: Jolly's Pharmacy (33 King George St., Roseau, tel. 809/448–3388).

Currency The official currency is the Eastern Caribbean dollar (E.C.), but U.S. dollars are accepted everywhere. At banks the rate is officially tied to the U.S. dollar, at a rate of E.C.$2.67 to U.S.$1. Hotels and restaurants often calculate exchanges at $E.C.$2.50–$2.60. Local prices, especially in shops frequented by tourists, are often quoted in both currencies, so be sure to ask. Prices quoted here are in U.S. dollars unless noted otherwise.

214

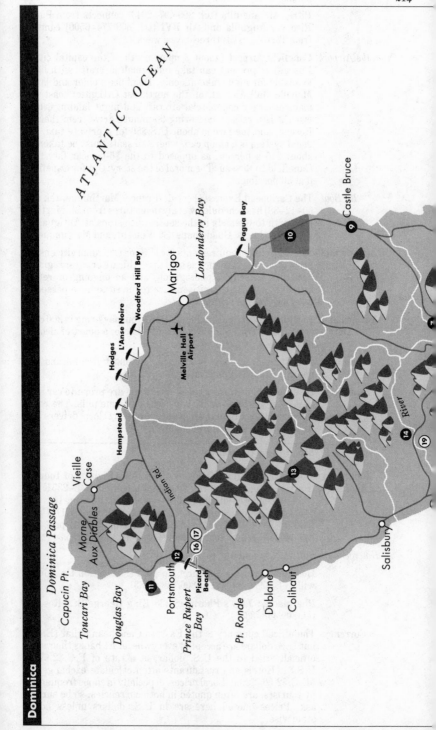

Dominica

ATLANTIC OCEAN

Dominica Passage

Capucin Pt.

Toucari Bay

Douglas Bay

Morne
Aux Diables

Vieille
Case

Indian Rd.

Portsmouth

Prince Rupert
Bay

Picard
Beach

Pt. Ronde

Dublane

Colihaut

Salisbury

Hampstead

Hodges

L'Anse Noire

Woodford Hill Bay

Marigot

Melville Hall
Airport

Londonderry Bay

Pagua Bay

Castle Bruce

River

11

12

16 17

13

14

19

9

10

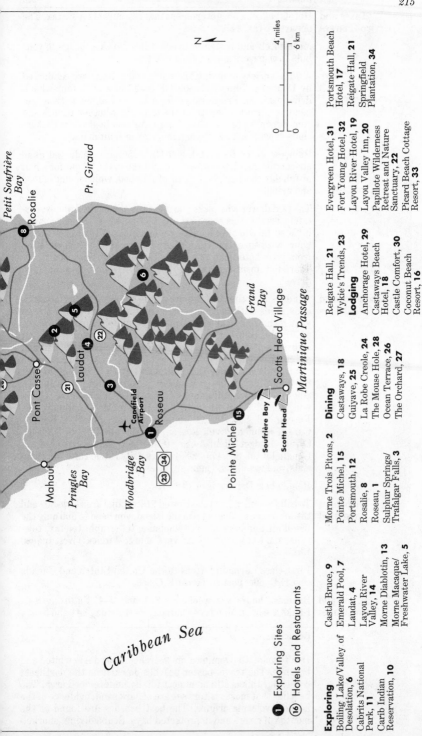

Caribbean Sea

Petit Soufrière Bay

Rosalie

Pt. Giraud

Pont Casse

Mahaut

Pringles Bay

Laudat

Canefield Airport

Roseau

Woodbridge Bay

Pointe Michel

Grand Bay

Scotts Head Village

Soufrière Bay

Scotts Head

Martinique Passage

N

0   4 miles
0   6 km

● Exploring Sites

⑯ Hotels and Restaurants

Exploring
Boiling Lake/Valley of Desolation, **6**
Cabrits National Park, **11**
Carib Indian Reservation, **10**

Castle Bruce, **9**
Emerald Pool, **7**

Laudat, **4**
Layou River Valley, **14**
Morne Diablotin, **13**
Morne Macaque/Freshwater Lake, **5**

Morne Trois Pitons, **2**
Pointe Michel, **15**
Portsmouth, **12**
Rosalie, **8**
Roseau, **1**
Sulphur Springs/Trafalgar Falls, **3**

Dining
Castaways, **18**
Guiyave, **25**
La Robe Creole, **24**
The Mouse Hole, **28**
Ocean Terrace, **26**
The Orchard, **27**

Reigate Hall, **21**
Wykie's Trends, **23**

Lodging
Anchorage Hotel, **29**
Castaways Beach Hotel, **18**
Castle Comfort, **30**
Coconut Beach Resort, **16**

Evergreen Hotel, **31**
Fort Young Hotel, **32**
Layou River Hotel, **19**
Layou Valley Inn, **20**
Papillote Wilderness Retreat and Nature Sanctuary, **22**
Picard Beach Cottage Resort, **33**

Portsmouth Beach Hotel, **17**
Reigate Hall, **21**
Springfield Plantation, **34**

Taxes and Service Charges   Hotels collect a 5% government tax; restaurants a 3% tax. The departure tax is $6.

Most hotels and restaurants add a 10% service charge to your bill. Taxi drivers appreciate a 10% tip.

Guided Tours   A wide variety of hiking and photo safari tours are conducted by **Dominica Tours** (tel. 809/448–2638) in sturdy four-wheel-drive vehicles. Prices range from $15 to $50 per person, depending upon the length of the trip and whether picnics and rum punches are included. There are also boat tours that include snorkeling, swimming, and rum or fruit drinks.

Rainbow Rover Tours (tel. 809/448–8650) are conducted in an air-conditioned Land Rover. Tours take in the island for a half or full day at a per-person cost of $30–$50, which includes food and drink.

The taxi driver who picks you up at the airport will almost certainly ask, "Is this your first visit to Dominica?" If your answer is "Yes," he will offer his services as a guide at the cost of $15 an hour, with tip extra. It's a good idea to get a recommendation from your hotel manager or the Dominica Tourist Board (*see* Tourist Information, above) before selecting a guide and driver.

Getting Around
Rental Cars   If it doesn't bother you to drive on the left on potholed mountainous roads with hairpin curves, rent a car and strike out on your own. Daily car-rental rates begin at $35 (weekly about $170), plus collision damage at $6 a day, and personal accident insurance at $2 a day, and you'll have to put down a deposit and purchase a visitor's driving permit for E.C. $20. You can rent a car from **Wide Range Car Rentals** (81 Bath Rd., Roseau, tel. 809/448–2198), **Valley Rent-A-Car** (Goodwill Rd., Roseau, tel. 809/448–3233), **Shillingford Car Rental** (10 Winston La., Goodwill, tel. 809/448–3151), **S.T.L. Rent-A-Car** (Goodwill Rd., Roseau, tel. 809/448–2340 or 809/448–4525), or **CNC Rent-A-Car** (37 Kennedy Ave., Roseau, tel. 809/448–2207 or 809/448–6375); **Budget Rent-A-Car** (Canefield Industrial Estate, Canefield, tel. 809/449–2080) offers daily rates, three-day specials, and weekly and monthly rates.

Remember: Driving is on the left.

Telephones and Mail   To call Dominica from the United States, dial area code 809 and the local access code, 44. On the island, you need to dial only the five-digit number. Direct telephone, telegraph, telefax, teletype, and telex services are via **Cable & Wireless (West Indies) Ltd.**

First-class (airmail) letters to the United States and Canada cost E.C. 60¢; postcards cost E.C. 35¢.

Opening and Closing Times   Business hours are weekdays 8–1 and 2–4, Saturday 8–1. Banks are open Monday–Thursday 8–1, Friday 8–1 and 3–5.

Beaches

Don't come to Dominica in search of powdery white-sand beaches. The travel-poster beaches do exist on the northeast coast, but this is still an almost totally undeveloped area. The beaches that most visitors see are of dark sand, evidence of the island's volcanic origins. The best beaches are found at the mouths of rivers and in protected bays. Scuba diving, snorkeling, and windsurfing are all excellent here. Check with Derek Perryman (**Dive Dominica,** tel. 809/448–2188) about scuba-diving expeditions and Fitzroy Armour, the owner of the **Waitukubuli Dive Centres** (tel. 809/448–2638).

Picard Beach, on the northwest coast, is the island's best beach. Great for windsurfing and snorkeling, it's a 2-mile stretch of brown sand fringed with coconut trees. The Castaways Picard Beach Cottage Resort, Portsmouth Beach, and Coconut Beach hotels are along this beach.

The scuba diving is excellent at **Soufrière Bay,** a sandy beach south of Roseau, and in the Scotts Head area.

Pagua Bay, a quiet, secluded beach of dark sand, is on the Atlantic coast.

Layou River has the best river swimming on the island, and its banks are great for sunbathing.

The beaches south of Roseau to **Scotts Head** at the southernmost tip of the island are good for scuba diving and snorkeling.

Woodford Hill Bay, Hampstead, L'Anse Noir, and **Hodges,** all on the northeast coast, are excellent beaches for snorkeling and scuba diving.

Exploring Dominica

Numbers in the margin correspond with points of interest on the Dominica map.

Given the small size of this almond-shape island, virtually any destination is within reach on any easy day trip. The amount of time you spend hiking, mountain climbing, bird-watching, or just enjoying the scenery will determine how much you can see during one round-the-island trip. The highways ringing the island's perimeter have been upgraded in recent years, making many sights and towns easier to reach driving on your own. However, when heading toward some of the more remote destinations, it is advisable to hire a car and driver or to take an escorted tour (*see* Guided Tours, above).

Roseau

①

All the hotels and virtually all the island's population are on the leeward, or Caribbean, side of the island. Twenty thousand or so inhabitants reside in **Roseau,** a town on the flat delta of the Roseau River. Stop first in the Tourist Office in the **Old Market Plaza.** Then stroll through the center of town, where craft shops and tiny cafés are tucked into old buildings made of wood, stone, and concrete. On Victoria Street is the **Fort Young Hotel,** which was originally built as a fort in the 18th century. Directly across the street is the **State House;** the **Public Library** and the **old Court House** are both nearby.

The National Park Office fittingly located in the 40-acre Botanical Gardens in Roseau, can provide tour guides, and a wealth of printed information. *Open Mon. 8–1 and 2–5, Tues.–Fri. 8–1 and 2–4.*

Heading north to Woodbridge Bay Harbour, stroll along the harbor, where you can watch bananas, citrus, and spices being loaded onto ships.

Time Out Sit in the garden of the late Jean Rhys, the Dominican-born novelist who won Britain's Royal Literary Award. It's now been turned into a garden bistro, the **World of Food** (Queen Mary St. and Field's La., tel. 809/448–3286). If you've never read Rhys, stop off at **Paperbacks** (6 Cork St.) and purchase her *Wide Sargasso Sea* or any of her many books.

Elsewhere on the Island
❷ Morne Trois Pitons is a blue-green hill of three peaks, the highest of which is 4,403 feet. The mountain is usually covered with swirling mists and clouds, and the 16,000-acre national park over which it looms is awash with cool mountain lakes, waterfalls, and rushing rivers. Ferns grow 30 feet tall and wild orchids sprout from trees. Sunlight leaks through green canopies, and a gentle mist rises over the jungle floor.

❸ The road from the capital to the Morne Trois Pitons National Park runs through the **Roseau River Valley.** About 5 miles out of Roseau, a side road branches, one direction leading to Wotten Waven, the other to **Sulphur Springs** (visible evidence of the island's volcanic origins) and the spectacular triple **Trafalgar Falls,** with a drop of 200 feet into a pool strewn with rocks.

❹ The village of **Laudat** (about 7 miles from Roseau) is a good starting point for a venture into the park. Two miles northeast ❺ of Laudat, at the base of **Morne Macaque** (3,500 feet), you'll find **Freshwater Lake,** with a fringe of greenery and purple hyacinths floating on the water.

❻ From Freshwater Lake there are several sights to be seen, but the hiking trails are not for the faint of heart. **Boiling Lake** and the **Valley of Desolation** are reached by a rugged 6-mile ramble, and you should go only with an experienced guide. There are *very* hot springs here that shift direction from time to time under an outer crust. Even experienced guides keep small groups of hikers (six to eight maximum) under their eye at all times (*see* Participant Sports, below).

Boiling Lake, the world's second-largest boiling lake, is like a caldron of gurgling gray-blue water. It is 70 yards wide, and the temperature of the water ranges from 180 to 197 degrees Fahrenheit. Its depth is unknown. It is believed that the lake is not a volcanic crater but a flooded fumarole—a crack through which gases escape from the molten lava below. This is a serious expedition for serious hikers (bring your own drinking water).

The Valley of Desolation lies below Boiling Lake, and it lives up to its name. Harsh sulfuric fumes have destroyed virtually all the vegetation in what was once a lush forested area. Hikers in the Valley of Desolation are advised to stay on the trail in order to avoid breaking through the crust that covers the hot lava below.

❼ **Emerald Pool** is 3½ miles northeast of Pont Casse, a 10-minute walk along the road that leads to Castle Bruce. Lookout points along the trail provide sweeping views of the windward coast and the forested interior. Emerald Pool is a swirling, fernbedecked basin into which a 50-foot waterfall splashes.

A good map and steady nerves are necessary for driving along the rugged, ragged windward (Atlantic) coast. A few miles east of Pont Casse there is a fork in the road where a right turn will take you to the southeast coast and a left to the northeast coast.

⑧ The south coast road goes to **Rosalie,** where there is a river for swimming, a black-sand beach, an old aqueduct, and a waterwheel. There is also a waterfall that dashes down a cliff into the ocean. A hike leads to **Petite Soufrière.**

⑨ The northerly road leads to the little fishing village of **Castle Bruce.** On the beach here you can watch dugout canoes being made from the trunks of gommier trees using traditional Carib methods (after the tree is cut it gets stretched). About 6 miles **⑩** north of Castle Bruce lies the **Carib Indian Reservation,** which was established in 1903 and covers 3,700 acres. Don't expect a lot in the way of ancient culture and costume. The folks who gave the Caribbean its name live pretty much like other West Indians, as fishermen and farmers. However, they have maintained their traditional skills at woodcarving, basket weaving, and canoe building. Their wares are displayed and sold in little thatch-top huts. The reservation's Roman Catholic church at Salibia has an altar that was once a canoe. Another point of interest on the reservation is **L'Escalier Tête Chien** ("trail of the snake staircase" in Creole patois)—a hardened lava flow that juts down to the ocean.

Time Out Stop for an hour or an overnight at the **Carib Territory Guesthouse** (tel. 809/445–7256), a very basic and fascinating wayside Carib house owned by Charles and Margaret Williams, who live on the premises with their children. There are some 10 bedrooms here for the adventurous traveler, lunch and a cold drink, or a good choice of Carib crafts. You can call Williams in advance and schedule a half-day or full-day walk with him through the territory.

Continuing north from the reservation you'll go past lovely **Pagua Bay,** with its beach of dark sand. A bit farther along, near Melville Hall Airport, is **Marigot,** the largest (population: 5,000) settlement on the east coast. On the northeast coast, steep cliffs rise out of the Atlantic, which flings its frothy waters over dramatic reefs, and rivers crash through forests of mangroves and fields of coconut. The beaches at **Woodford Hill, Hampstead, Anse Noir,** and **Hodges** are excellent for snorkeling and scuba diving, though all this wind-tossed beauty can be dangerous to swimmers since there are strong underwater currents as well as whipped-cream waves. From this vantage point you can see the French island of Marie Galante in the distance.

The road continues through banana plantations to Portsmouth, but a side road leads up to the village of **Vieille Case** and **Capuchin Point,** at the northernmost tip of the island. **Morne Au Diable** soars 2,826 feet over this area, and slopes down to **Toucari Bay** and **Douglas Bay** on the west coast, where there are spectacular dark-sand beaches.

⑪ Just 2 miles south of Douglas Bay, the 250-acre **Cabrits National Park** is surrounded on three sides by the Caribbean Sea. Local historian Lennox Honychurch has restored **Fort Shirley,** a military complex built between 1770 and 1815. Some of the buildings have been restored, and there is a small museum in the park. The park is connected to the mainland by a freshwater swamp, verdant with ferns, grasses, and trees, where you can see a variety of migrant birds.

A new cruise-ship pier development with both berthing and passenger facilities opens in the winter of 1991 at the port of Cabrits, below Fort Shirley. Present plans are to host only one ship at a time, which will make this a desirable stop on cruise itineraries.

Time Out The bar in the **Purple Turtle Guest House** (Portsmouth, tel. 809/445–5296) is a fine place for a rum punch before or after a tour through the town of Portsmouth.

⑫ **Portsmouth,** 2 miles south of Cabrits, is a peaceful little town with a population of about 5,000. **Prince Rupert Bay,** site of a naval battle in 1782 between the French and the English, is far and away the island's most beautiful harbor. There are more than 2 miles of sandy beaches fringed with coconut trees and the island's only beachfront hotels. The **Indian River** flows to the sea from here, and a canoe ride takes you through an exotic rain forest thick with mangrove swamps. Board a row boat (not power) for total tranquillity, to be able to hear fish jumping and exotic birds calling.

⑬ Just south of Indian River is **Pointe Ronde,** the starting point for an expedition to **Morne Diablotin,** the island's highest summit at 4,747 feet. This is not an expedition you should attempt alone; the uninhabited interior is an almost impenetrable primeval forest. You'll need a good guide (*see* Participant Sports, below), sturdy shoes, a warm sweater, and firm resolve.

⑭ The west coast road dips down through the little villages of **Dublanc,** (with a side road off to the Syndicate Estate), **Colihaut,** and **Salisbury** before reaching the mouth of the **Layou River.** The Layou River Valley is rich with bananas and cacao, citrus fruits, and coconuts. The remains of Hillsborough Estate, once a going rum-producing plantation, are here. The river is the island's longest and largest, with deep gorges, quiet pools and beaches, waterfalls and rapids—a great place for a full day's outing of swimming and shooting the rapids, or just sunning and picnicking.

The branch in the bend at Dublanc that leads to the Syndicate Estate also leads to the 200-acre site of the new **Project Sisserou.** This protected site has been set aside with the help of some 6,000 schoolchildren, each of whom donated 25¢ for the land where the endangered Sisserou parrot (found only in Dominica) flies free. At last estimate, there were only about 60 of these shy and beautiful birds, covered in rich green feathers with a mauve front.

⑮ Just south of Roseau the road forks, with a treacherous prong leading east to **Grand Bay,** where bay leaves are grown and distilled. If you continue due south from Roseau you'll go through **Pointe Michel,** settled decades ago by Martinicans who fled the catastrophic eruption of Mont Pelée. The stretch all the way from Roseau to Scotts Head at the southernmost tip of the island has excellent beaches for scuba diving and snorkeling.

Participant Sports

Boating Motorboat and sailing trips can be arranged through **Dominica Tours** (tel. 809/448–2638).

Hiking Trails range from the easygoing to the arduous. For the former, all you'll need are sturdy, rubber-soled shoes and an adventurous spirit.

For the hike to Boiling Lake or the climb up Morne Diablotin you will need hiking boots, a guide, and water. Guides will charge about $25–$35 per day, for individuals or small groups, and can be contacted through the Tourist Office or the Forestry Division (tel. 809/448–2401 or 809/448–2638).

Scuba Diving *Skin Diver* magazine recently ranked Dominica among the top five Caribbean dive destinations. **Dive Dominica** (Castle Comfort, tel. 809/448–2188) is one of the oldest dive shops in Dominica, run by NAUI-approved instructors. They offer snorkeling and resort dives for beginners, and for the advanced set, dives on drop-offs, walls, and wrecks—by day or night. The owners of the **Waitukubuli Dive Centres** (there are two: one at the Anchorage Hotel, the other at the Portsmouth Beach Hotel, tel. 809/448–2638) are PADI- and NAUI-certified, and specialize in dives of 6 to 1,000 feet. **The Castaways Hotel,** only 11 miles from Roseau, has added diving to its new water-sports center (tel. 809/449–6244 or 809/449–6245). The going rate at all of the above is about $65 for a two-tank dive or $90 for a resort course with two open-water dives.

Snorkeling Major island operators rent equipment: **Anchorage Limited** (tel. 809/448–2188), **Castaways Hotel** (tel. 809/449–6244 or 809/ 449–6245), **Coconut Beach Hotel** (tel. 809/445–5393), **Portsmouth Beach Hotel** (tel. 809/551–4255), **Sunshine Village** (tel. 809/445–5066), and **Picard Beach Cottage Resort** (tel. 809/445– 5142), or 809/445–5130).

Swimming River swimming is extremely popular on Dominica, and the best river to jump into is the Layou River (*see* Exploring Dominica, above). Also *see* Beaches, above, for our pick of the best beaches to swim, snorkel, or surf in.

Windsurfing Contact either **Anchorage Limited** or **Castaways Hotel** (*see* Snorkeling, above).

Shopping

Gift Ideas The handicrafts of the Carib Indians include traditional baskets made of dyed reeds and waterproofed with tightly woven banana leaves. One of our favorites is the "wife leader," a five- to six-inch lead made of woven straw that, in these days of liberation, can be used for anyone you can get to put their finger in the end, which tightens instantly. Their crafts are sold on the reservation, as well as in Roseau's shops. Dominica is also noted for its spices, hot peppers, and coconut-oil soap; its vetiver-grass mats are sold all over the world.

One of the nicest buys here (or anywhere) is a "then" and "now" book of photography and prose, *Views in the Island of Dominica, 1849*, that shows 1849 Dominica in sepia prints and again some 100 years later in color.

Good gifts are stylized candles from **Starbrite Industries** (Canefield Industrial Site, tel. 809/449–1006) that come in the shape of the Dominican parrot, cupids, and trees, as well as more traditional shapes. Open weekdays 8–1 and 2–4. **The Old Mill Cultural Centre and Historic Site** on Canefield Road presents wood carvings by a master carver, Louis Desire, and those of his students—all lovingly carved from Dominican woods. Open weekdays 8–4.

Shops Stop in **Caribana Handcrafts** (31 Cork St., Roseau, tel. 809/448–2761), where you'll find soaps, spices, stacks of handmade hats and baskets.

Siblings **Arnold** and **Roberta Toulon** hand-paint T-shirts at their studio-home (54 Queen Mary St., tel. 809/448–3740) that sell so well, stock is always limited. They will, however, make up a special order within two days. Arnold's canvases of fine art are also on display.

Dining

The fertile Dominican soil produces a cornucopia of fresh vegetables, and chefs here utilize them to great advantage, most often with a Creole flair. There are sweet green bananas, kushkush yams, breadfruit, and dasheen (a tuber similar to the potato known as taro elsewhere). You'll find fresh fish on virtually every menu, as well as "mountain chicken"—a euphemism for a large frog called *crapaud*.

The most highly recommended restaurants are indicated by a star ★.

Category	Cost*
Expensive	$25–$35
Moderate	$15–$25
Inexpensive	under $15

per person, excluding drinks, service, and sales taxes (3%)

★ **La Robe Creole.** A cozy place with wood rafters, ladderback chairs, and colorful Madras cloths, this restaurant has an eclectic à la carte listing. A specialty is callaloo and crab soup, made with dasheen and coconut. You can also have steak au poivre, crepes of lobster and conch, charcoal-grilled fish and meats, pizza, barbecued chicken, and salads. *3 Victoria St., Roseau, tel. 809/448–2896. Reservations advised. AE. Closed Sun. Expensive.*

★ **Reigate Hall.** In this stylish restaurant an old-fashioned waterwheel turns while you dine. While some new health-oriented dishes have been added, favored specialties remain breast of duck in port-wine sauce, mountain chicken in champagne sauce, and coq au vin. Dessert selections include crème caramel and poire Belle Hélène. *Reigate Hall Hotel, Roseau, tel. 809/445–4031. Reservations advised. AE, DC, MC, V. Expensive.*

Guiyave. Have a drink at the second-floor bar and then repair to the table-filled balcony for dining. Spareribs, lobster, rabbit, and mountain chicken are offered, along with homemade beef or chicken patties, spicy rotis, and a variety of light snacks and sandwiches. This restaurant is noted for its fresh tropical fruit juices (a local cherry, guava, passionfruit, and barbadine) and its homemade pies, tarts, and cakes. *15 Cork St., Roseau, tel. 809/448–2930. No credit cards. Moderate.*

Ocean Terrace. As the name suggests, this eatery in the Anchorage Hotel is on a terrace overlooking the ocean. Grilled lamb chops with mint jelly, Creole-style fish court bouillon, and chilled lobster in a chives-vinaigrette marinade are among the à la carte specialties. There is live Caribbean entertainment three nights a week. *Anchorage Hotel, Roseau, tel. 809/448-2638. Reservations advised. AE, DC, MC, V. Moderate.*

★ **The Orchard.** You can dine indoors in a spacious, unadorned dining room or in a pleasant covered courtyard surrounded by latticework. Chef Joan Cools-Lartique offers Creole-style coconut shrimp, lobster, black pudding, mountain chicken, and callaloo soup with crabmeat, among other delicacies. Sandwiches are also on the menu. *31 King George V St., Roseau, tel. 809/448-3051. MC, V. Moderate.*

The Mouse Hole. This is the place to pack for your picnic in the park. There are sandwiches, salads, and snacks, all for takeout only. It's downstairs from, and affiliated with, La Robe Creole (*see* above). *3 Victoria St., tel. 809/448-2396. No credit cards. Inexpensive.*

★ **Wykie's Trends.** Owner Thomas Wykie created this gathering spot for the island's movers and shakers (who also happen to be his pals). A cluster of six tables crowd the West Indian porch, with a Creole menu of *couchon braf* (smoked pork soup with dumplings), stewed chicken, lobster in a coconut sauce, *court bouillon* (boiled fish), or the fried fish of the day. Smooth jazz tapes provide background to the spicy food and equally spicy conversation. On Friday, there's usually a Jing-Ping, with accordion, quag (a sort of washboard instrument), and boom-boom players. *51 Old Street, Roseau, tel. 809/448-8015. No credit cards. Inexpensive.*

★ **Castaways.** The hotel's guests often lunch or dine here, but it's the Sunday brunch (which starts at 11 AM and goes to 6 PM) that's the real draw. The grill is fired up, and fresh fish, steak, chicken, and lobster are tossed on the fire. Side dishes of fresh fruits and vegetables, along with hot breads, round out the beach party. *Castaways Hotel, Roseau, tel. 809/449-6244 or 809/449-6245. AE, MC, V. Inexpensive.*

Lodging

Hotels on Dominica range from Spartan to chic, but even in the swankiest places informality is the rule. There are only 430 rooms on the entire island, but an additional 80 or so are planned for the near future. The only beachfront hotels are in the Portsmouth area, with the one exception outside Roseau being the Castaways on Mero Beach. Roseau's seaside facilities have a splendid view of the Caribbean but are beachless. There are also a few exceptional nature retreats perched in the rain forest. A variety of meal plans is available. It's a good idea to check current credit-card policy.

The most highly recommended lodgings are indicated by a star ★.

Category	Cost*
Expensive	$80–$120
Moderate	$50–$80

Inexpensive	under $50

All prices are for a standard double room for two, excluding 5% tax and a 10%–15% service charge.

Hotels ★ **Picard Beach Cottage Resort.** New for the 1990s is this resort of wood cottages built in 18th-century West Indian style, where the exterior colors (yellow and white) are carried through in a complementing interior. There's both beach and pool here, below the peaks of Morne Diablotin, on the northwest coast. *Box 34, Roseau, tel. 809/445–5131; fax 809/448–5640; in the U.S. 800/424–5500. 18 individual cottages with bedroom, bath, sitting/dining area, kitchen, and veranda. Facilities: beach, pool, dive center with scuba, snorkeling, and windsurfing, aerobics area, conference room for 120, bar, and restaurant. AE, MC, V. Very Expensive.*

Castaways Beach Hotel. This hotel is popular with young people, mostly because of its young and energetic manager, Linda Harris. The island's first resort hotel, it's located in Mero, 11 miles north of Roseau on a mile-long, dappled gray beach. Rooms have double beds, balconies overlooking tropical gardens, and come with or without air-conditioning. The restaurant serves French-Creole cuisine, island music plays nightly in the beach bar, and an all-day Sunday brunch/beach barbecue has a loyal following. *Box 5, Roseau, tel. 809/449–6245 or 800/223–9815 in U.S. 27 rooms with shower or bath. Facilities: beach, restaurant, 2 bars, tennis court, water-sports center. AE, MC, V. Expensive.*

★ **Fort Young Hotel.** This hotel reopened in the summer of 1989 following a total renovation. Now Dominican paintings and prints from the late 1700s meld with the massive stone walls of the 18th century, when this was Dominica's main fort. Set on a cliff in Roseau, it's a good location for business travelers who also appreciate the chance to dip into the swimming pool adjacent to the bar and restaurant. *Box 462, Roseau, tel. 809/448–5000; fax 809/448–5050. 33 air-conditioned rooms with telephone and TV. Facilities: pool, nightly entertainment, conference room, health club, bar, and restaurant. AE, MC, V. Expensive.*

★ **Papillote Wilderness Retreat and Nature Sanctuary.** You have to be in pretty good shape to navigate up the steep hill that leads to this inn, which is smack in the rain forest. The setting is spectacular, and Florida-born owner Anne Jean-Baptiste, who has lived on Dominica for more than 25 years, can provide all sorts of helpful tips about nature walks, tours, and such. Her inn is small and Spartan and has a loyal following of nature lovers. A hot tub bubbles right next to the open-air restaurant. *Box 67, Roseau, tel. 809/448–2287. 7 rooms, all share 4 baths. Facilities: restaurant, bar, boutique, nature tours. AE, MC, V. Expensive.*

★ **Reigate Hall.** Perched high on a steep cliff, this is a stunning stone-and-wood facility. The suite has a magnificent carved-wood four-poster bed, bar, and Jacuzzi (and the dubious distinction of being the most expensive accommodation on the island). All rooms have air-conditioning, private balconies, embroidered bedspreads on double or twin beds, bidets, and handsome hardwood floors. *Box 200, Roseau, tel. 809/448–4031, 800/223–9815 in U.S., 800/468–0023 in Canada. 17 rooms with bath. Facilities: restaurant, 2 bars, pool, lighted tennis* *court, sauna, exercise room, clock radios. AE, DC, MC, V. Expensive.*

★ **Springfield Plantation.** This former plantation home, complete with sweeping veranda, has been enlarged and is furnished in colonial style, including four-poster beds in some rooms. The setting (6 miles from Roseau) is some 1,200 feet in jungle-covered hills, with river bathing nearby. The compound includes hotel rooms as well as apartments with kitchens. The Anthurium River is right there for freshwater swimming. *Box 41, Roseau, tel. 809/449–1401. 7 rooms with bath. Facilities: restaurant, 2 bars. AE, Expensive.*

★ **Anchorage Hotel.** A three-story, galleried section of this hotel has spacious rooms, each with a double and a twin bed, and a private balcony overlooking the sea. Smaller, somewhat dark rooms are located by the swimming pool. The hotel is headquarters for Dominica Tours (*see* Guided Tours, above). *Box 34, Roseau, tel. 809/448–2638. 36 rooms with bath. Facilities: restaurant, bar, pool, squash court, yacht mooring. AE, DC, MC, V. Moderate.*

Coconut Beach Resort. The sprawling acerage of this informal beach hotel curves around its beachside location, on the north coast. It's casual and comfortable, if basic. Apartments and beachfront bungalows have double rooms that are cooled by air-conditioning or fans. *Box 50, Roseau, tel. 809/445–5393 or 809/445–5415. 11 rooms with bath. Facilities: beach, restaurant, bar, snorkeling. AE, MC, V. Moderate.*

★ **Evergreen Hotel.** A small gem perched on the Caribbean Sea, Mena Winston's hotel has air-conditioned rooms, simple traditional furnishings, and small vases of fresh flowers in each room; some rooms have private terraces. Winston and her family turn out exceptionally fine fare, and the spacious dining room is a popular spot where locals gather to watch cable TV. *Box 309, Roseau, tel. 809/448–3288. 10 rooms with bath. Facilities: restaurant, lounge. AE, DC, MC, V. Moderate.*

★ **Layou River Hotel.** A rambling estate property focused around the turbulent beauty of the Layou River, which rushes through a mountain funnel. Forty-eight rooms decorated in muted pastels (all with telephones) are scattered throughout a chalet-style main house and two-story bungalows. An Olympic-size swimming pool with adjacent bar dominates the back lawn, and thick jungle foliage contrasts with the modern architecture. *Box 8, Roseau, tel. 809/449–6281. 48 rooms with bath and shower, air-conditioned. Facilities: restaurant, bar, pool, island tours on request, good conference rooms. MC, V. Moderate.*

Portsmouth Beach Hotel. Many of the hotel's rooms are used by students from the nearby medical school, so things get a bit noisy here, but it *is* right on the beach. (The architecture has been accurately called "prison-like.") This hotel is a companion to the Anchorage Hotel in Roseau, and it's possible to arrange north-south stays. *Box 34, Roseau, tel. 809/445–5142. 76 rooms with bath. Facilities: beach, restaurant, 2 bars. AE, V. Inexpensive.*

Guest Houses **Layou Valley Inn.** Tasteful and splendid is this house that
★ Tamara Holmes and her late husband built in the foothills of the National Preserve, under the peaks of Morne Trois Pitons. She's a Russian who once translated for NASA but now devotes her talents to the kitchen. Mme. Holmes sums up this hideaway best: "My sheets are percale and my food is French." *Box 196,*

Roseau, tel. 809/449–6203. 10 rooms with bath. Facilities: restaurant, bar, swimming in mountain rivers, guided climbs to the Boiling Lake at extra cost. AE, MC, V. Expensive.

★ **Castle Comfort.** If this guest house is especially homey, it's because it is the home of the genial Mrs. Dorothy Perryman, whose sister owns the Evergreen Hotel next door. Completely redecorated, the blue and white colors throughout have a nautical feel; all rooms are air-conditioned and have twin beds and baths with showers. This is home to *Dive Dominica,* and the dive packages offered include room, meal plan, and diving excursions. *Box 63, Roseau, tel. 809/448–2188. 6 rooms with bath. Facilities: restaurant, dive shop. AE, MC, V. Moderate.*

Nightlife

Discos   If you're not too exhausted from mountain climbing, swimming, and such, you can join the locals on weekends at **The Warehouse** (tel. 809/449–1303) in Roseau and the **Shipwreck** in the Canefield Industrial area (tel. 809/449–1059), for weekend live reggae and taped music, with a Sunday bash that starts at noon and goes 'till 11 PM. both in Roseau.

Nightclubs   When the moon comes up, most visitors go down to the dining room in their resident hotel for the music or chat offered there, which is always liveliest on weekends. Newly reopened Ft. Young has upscale entertainment, as do many of the better hotels—the Castaways, Anchorage, and Reigate Hall in particular.

The best insider's spot is definitely **Trends** (51 Old St., Roseau, tel. 809/448–8015), where residents and visitors mingle during Friday's "Happy Hours" from 5 to 7, then stay on for a local calypso band or the Jing-Ping—groups that play local music on the accordion, drums, and quag (a washboardlike instrument). Another resident favorite is **Lenville,** in the village of Coulivistrie, a very basic rum shop with barbecued chicken and dancing (tel. 809/446–6598.)

11 Dominican Republic

by Honey Naylor

Sprawling over two-thirds of the island of Hispaniola, the Dominican Republic is the spot where European settlement of the Western Hemisphere really began. Santo Domingo, its capital, is the oldest continuously inhabited city in this half of the globe, and history buffs who visit have difficulty tearing themselves away from the many sites that boast of antiquity in the city's 16th-century Colonial Zone. Sun-seekers head for the beach resorts of Puerto Plata, Samaná, and La Romana; at Punta Cana, beachcombers tan on the Caribbean's longest stretch of white-sand beach. The highest peak in the West Indies is here: Pico Duarte (10,128 feet) lures hikers to the central mountain range, and ancient sunken galleons and coral reefs divert divers and snorkelers.

Columbus happened upon this island on December 5, 1492, and on Christmas Eve his ship, the *Santa María*, was wrecked on the Atlantic shore. He named it *La Isla Española* ("the Spanish island"), established a small colony, and sailed back to Spain on the *Pinta*. A year later, he returned, only to find that the Spanish colony had been destroyed by the Taino Indians, the island's original inhabitants. But Columbus established another colony nearby, leaving his brother Bartholomew in charge. Santo Domingo, which is located on the south coast where the Río Ozama spills into the Caribbean Sea, was founded in 1496 by Bartholomew Columbus and Nicolás de Ovando, and during the first half of the 16th century became the bustling hub of Spanish commerce and culture in the New World.

Hispaniola (a derivation of "La Isla Española") has had an unusually chaotic history, replete with bloody revolutions, military coups, yellow-fever epidemics, invasions, and bankruptcy. In the 17th century, the western third of the island was ceded to France; a slave revolt in 1804 resulted in the establishment there of the first black republic, Haiti. Dominicans and Haitians battled for control of the island on and off throughout the 19th century. The Dominicans finally declared themselves an independent republic in 1865, but the country was bankrupt by the turn of the century. The United States helped to administer the island's finances, and eventually U.S. Marines occupied the country from 1916 to 1924, until a new Dominican constitution was signed. Rafael Trujillo ruled the Dominican Republic with an iron fist from 1930 until his assassination in 1961. A short-lived democracy was overthrown soon thereafter, followed by another occupation by the U.S. Marines in 1965. The country has been relatively stable since the early 1970s, and administrations have been staunch supporters of the United States.

American influence looms large in Dominican life. If Dominicans do not actually have relatives living in the United States, they know someone who does; and many speak at least rudimentary English. Still, it is a Latin country, and the Hispanic flavor contrasts sharply with the culture of the British, French, and Dutch islands in the Caribbean. Racially mixed, the Dominican Republic also reflects a strong African and Haitian influence.

Dominican towns and cities are generally not quaint, neat, or particularly pretty. Poverty is everywhere; but the country is also alive and chaotic, sometimes frenzied, sometimes laid-back. Its tourist zones are as varied as they come—from extravagant Casa de Campo and the manicured hotels of Playa Dorada to the neglected streets of Jarabacoa in its gorgeous mountain setting and the world-weary beauty of the Samaná peninsula.

Dominicans love music—there is dancing in the streets every summer at Santo Domingo's Merengue Festival—and they have a well-deserved reputation for being one of the friendliest people in the region. This is a tropical country; there is less urgency to get things done and tempers don't flare up quickly. Blackouts, for instance, are a daily occurrence in much of the country, but this does not cause much discomfort for visitors, as hotels in the most affected area—Puerto Plata—have emergency generators.

The Dominican Republic has another asset: It is among the least expensive destinations in the Caribbean.

In recent years, tourism has played a more important role in the government's scheme of things. Like Puerto Rico, its cousin to the east across the Mona Channel, the Dominican Republic is gearing up for a grand and glorious 500th anniversary celebration of its "discovery" by Christopher Columbus.

Before You Go

Tourist Information Contact the **Dominican Tourist Information Center** at any of the following addresses: 485 Madison Ave., New York, NY 10022, tel. 212/826–0750; 2355 Sanzedo Ave., Suite 305, Coral Gables, FL 33134, tel. 305/444–4592; 29 Bellaire St., Toronto, Ontario, Canada M5R 2C7, tel. 416/928–9188; 1464 Crescent St., Montreal, Quebec, Canada H3G 2B6, tel. 514/289–9398.

Arriving and Departing
By Plane The Dominican Republic has two major international airports: Las Américas International Airport, about 20 miles outside Santo Domingo, and La Unión International Airport, about 25 miles east of Puerto Plata on the north coast. **American Airlines** (tel. 800/433–7300), **Pan Am** (tel. 800/221–1111), and **Dominicana** (tel. 718/632–0610) fly nonstop from New York to Santo Domingo; American, **Continental** (tel. 800/231–0856), and Dominicana fly nonstop from New York to Puerto Plata; American, Pan Am, and Dominicana fly nonstop from Miami to Santo Domingo; and American and Dominicana fly nonstop from Miami to Puerto Plata. Pan Am has connecting service from Santo Domingo to Puerto Plata and also flies nonstop from Santo Domingo to Port-au-Prince, Haiti; Continental has connecting service from Puerto Plata to Santo Domingo; and American offers connections to both Santo Domingo and Puerto Plata from San Juan, Puerto Rico.

Several regional carriers serve neighboring islands. There is also limited domestic service available from La Herrera Airport in Santo Domingo to smaller airfields in La Romana, Samaná, and Santiago. A new airport will open in Barahona in 1991.

Long-needed expansions and rehauls are under way at both Las Américas and Puerto Plata. In the meantime, be prepared for long lines and confusion. Overworked customs and immigration officials are often less than courteous, and luggage

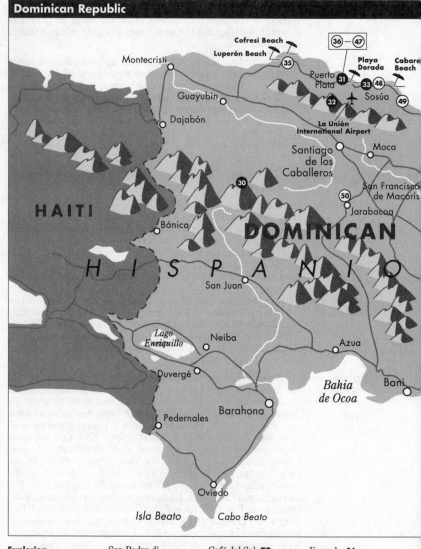

Cofresi Beach
Luperón Beach
Montecristi
(35)
Puerto Plata (31)
Playa Dorada (33) (48)
Cabarete Beach
(36) — (47)
Sosúa (49)
Guayubin
(32)
La Unión International Airport
Dajabón
Santiago de los Caballeros
Moca
San Francisco de Macorís
HAITI
Bánica
(30)
(50)
Jarabacoa
DOMINICAN
H I S P A N I O
San Juan
Lago Enriquillo
Neiba
Azua
Duvergé
Bani
Pedernales
Barahona
Bahia de Ocoa
Oviedo
Isla Beato
Cabo Beato

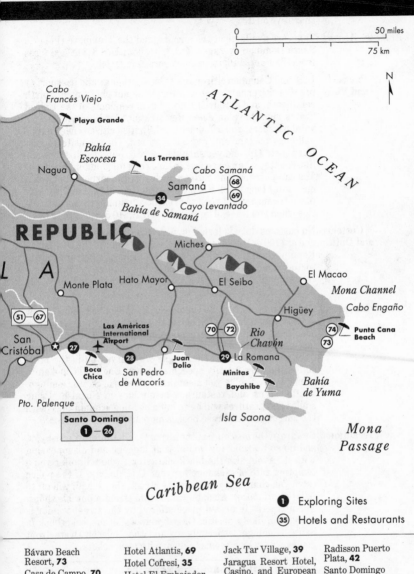

0 50 miles
0 75 km

Cabo
Francés Viejo

▲ **Playa Grande**

*Bahía
Escocesa*

Las Terrenas

Nagua

Cabo Samaná

Samaná **68**
69

34 *Cayo Levantado*

Bahía de Samaná

REPUBLIC

Miches

L A

Monte Plata Hato Mayor El Seibo El Macao

Mona Channel

Cabo Engaño

Higüey

51—**67**

San
Cristóba

★ **27**

Las Américas
International
Airport

70—**72** *Río
Chavón*

74 ▶ **Punta Cana
Beach**
73

28

**Boca
Chica**

San Pedro
de Macorís

**Juan
Dolio**

29 La Romana

Minitas

Bayahibe

*Bahía
de Yuma*

Pto. Palenque

Santo Domingo
1—**26**

Isla Saona

*Mona
Passage*

Caribbean Sea

1 Exploring Sites

35 Hotels and Restaurants

Bávaro Beach
Resort, **73**
Casa de Campo, **70**
Club Mediterranée, **74**
Dorado Naco, **36**
Eurotel Playa
Dorado, **37**
Gran Hotel Lina
and Casino, **65**
Hostal Nicolás
de Ovando, **67**
Hostal Jimessón, **38**

Hotel Atlantis, **69**
Hotel Cofresi, **35**
Hotel El Embajador
and Casino, **66**
Hotel Hogar, **50**
Hotel Montemar, **43**
Hotel Santo
Domingo, **62**

Jack Tar Village, **39**
Jaragua Resort Hotel,
Casino, and European
Spa, **63**
Playa Chiquita, **48**
Playa Dorada Beach
Resort, **40**
Puerto Plata Beach
Resort & Casino, **41**
Punto Goleta Beach
Resort, **49**

Radisson Puerto
Plata, **42**
Santo Domingo
Sheraton Hotel and
Casino, **64**

theft is rife. Try to travel with carry-on luggage, and keep a sharp eye on it.

From the Airport Taxis are available at the airport, and the 25-minute ride into Santo Domingo averages R.D.$80 (about U.S.$13). Taxi fares from the Puerto Plata airport average R.D.$40.

Passports and Visas U.S. and Canadian citizens must have either a valid passport or proof of citizenship, such as an original (not photocopied) birth certificate, and a Tourist Card. Legal residents of the United States must have an Alien Registration Card (green card), a valid passport, and a Tourist Card. British citizens need only a valid passport; no entry visa is required. The requisite Tourist Card costs $10, and you should be sure to purchase it at the airline counter when you check in, and then fill it out on the plane. You can purchase the card on arrival at the airport, but you'll encounter long lines. Keep the bottom half of the card in a safe place because you'll need to present it to immigration authorities when you leave. There is also a U.S.$10 departure tax.

Customs and Duties No customs duty is levied on personal belongings or gifts valued at $100 or less. Tortoiseshell is a big seller in the Dominican Republic, but the hawksbill turtle, which has a better grade of tortoiseshell, is on the U.S. list of endangered species: Anything manufactured from it that you bring home will probably be impounded by U.S. Customs.

Language Before you travel to the Dominican Republic, you should know at least a smattering of Spanish. Guides at major tourist attractions and front-desk personnel in the major hotels speak a fascinating form of English, though they often have trouble understanding tourists. The people who serve you in the hotel coffee shop are usually speechless when English is spoken to them, as are people you meet in the streets of Santo Domingo. Traffic signs and restaurant menus are in Spanish. Using smiles and gestures will help, but a nodding acquaintance with the language or a phrase book is more useful.

Precautions Beware of the *buscones* at the airports. They offer to assist you, and do so by relieving you of your luggage and disappearing with it. Avoid also the black marketers, who will offer you a tempting rate of exchange for your U.S. dollars. If the police catch you changing money on the street, they'll haul you off to jail (the *calabozo*). Also, buy amber only from reputable shops. The attractively priced piece offered by the street vendor is more than likely plastic. Guard your wallet or pocketbook in Santo Domingo, especially around the Malecón (waterfront boulevard), which seems to teem with pickpockets.

Staying in the Dominican Republic

Important Addresses **Tourist Information:** There is a **Tourist Information Center** in Santo Domingo (Av. George Washington, tel. 809/682–8181) and in Puerto Plata (Playa Long Beach, tel. 809/586–3676). Hours are weekdays 9–2:30.

Emergencies **Police:** In Santo Domingo, call 809/682–3000; in Puerto Plata, call 809/586–2804; in Sosúa, call 809/571–2233. However, do not expect too much from the police, aside from a bit of a hassle and some paperwork that they will consider the end of the matter.

Hospitals: Santo Domingo emergency rooms that are open 24 hours are **Centro Médico Universidad Central del Este** (UCE)

(Av. Máximo Gómez 66, tel. 809/682–0171), **Clínica Abreu** (Calle Beller 42, tel. 809/688–4411), and **Clínica Gómez Patino** (Av. Independencia 701, tel. 809/685–9131 or 685–9141). In Puerto Plata, you can go to **Clínica Dr. Brugal** (Calle José del Carmen Ariza 15, tel. 809/586–2519). In Sosúa, try the **Sosúa Medical Center** (1 Ocean Pl., tel. 809/571–2305).

Pharmacies: The following pharmacies are open 24 hours a day: in Santo Domingo, **San Judas Tadeo** (Av. Independencia 57, tel. 809/689–2851 or 809/685–8165); in Puerto Plata, **Farmacia Deleyte** (Av. John F. Kennedy 89, tel. 809/571–2515); in Sosúa, **San Rafael** (Pedro Clisante at Camino Libre).

Currency The coin of the realm is the Dominican peso, which is divided into 100 centavos. It is written R.D.\$, and fluctuates relative to the U.S. dollar. At press time, U.S.\$1 was equivalent to R.D.\$6.28. *Note:* prices quoted in this book are in U.S. dollars unless otherwise indicated. Always make certain you know in which currency any transaction is taking place (any confusion will likely not be to your advantage). There is a growing black market for hard currency, so be wary of offers to exchange U.S.\$ at a rate more favorable than the official one.

Taxes and Service Charges Hotels add a 21% government tax (which includes a 10% service charge) to your bill; restaurants add a 6% tax. The departure tax is \$10.

Although hotels add a 10% service charge, it is customary to leave a dollar per day for the hotel maid. Restaurants and nightclubs add a 10% service charge to your bill. However, you may want to leave an additional 5%–10% tip for a job well done. Taxi drivers expect a 10% tip. Skycaps and hotel porters expect at least three pesos per bag.

Guided Tours **Prieto Tours** (tel. 809/682–8426) operates Gray Line of the Dominican Republic. It offers half-day bus tours of Santo Domingo, nightclub tours, beach tours, tours to Cibao Valley and the Amber Coast, and a variety of other tours.

Turinter (Bahía Beach Hotel, Samaná, tel. 809/685–4020) tours include dinner and a show or casino, a full-day tour of Samaná, as well as specialty tours (museum, shopping, fishing).

Apolo Tours (tel. 809/586–2751) offers a full-day tour of Playa Grande and tours to Santiago (including a casino tour) and Sosúa.

Getting Around
Taxis Taxis, which are government-regulated, line up outside hotels and restaurants. The taxis are unmetered, and the minimum fare within Santo Domingo is R.D.\$30 (about U.S.\$5). You can also negotiate a fare with the driver, assuming there is no language barrier. Just be certain it is clearly understood in advance which currency is to be used in the agreed-upon fare. Taxis can also drive you to destinations outside the city. Rates are posted in hotels and at the airport. **Taxi la Paloma** (tel. 809/562–3460) or **Taxi Raffi** (tel. 809/689–5468) will transport you.

In a separate category are radio taxis, which are convenient if you'd like to schedule a pickup, and academic if you don't speak Spanish. The fare is negotiated over the phone when you make the appointment.

Avoid unmarked street taxis—there have been numerous incidents of assaults and robberies, particularly in Santo Domingo.

Buses   *Públicos* are small blue-and-white or blue-and-red cars that run regular routes, stopping to let passengers on and off. The fare is less than a peso. Competing with the públicos are the *conchos* or *colectivos* (privately owned buses), whose drivers tool around the major thoroughfares, leaning out of the window or jumping out to try to persuade passengers to climb aboard. It's a colorful, if cramped, way to get around town. The fare is about 50 centavos. Privately owned air-conditioned buses make regular runs to Santiago, Puerto Plata, and other destinations. Avoid night travel, as the country's roads are full of potholes. You should reserve by calling **Metro Buses** (Av. Winston Churchill, tel. 809/586–3736), **La Experiencia Bus Line** (Calle M. Aybar Av., tel. 809/594–0356), **Caribe Tours** (Av. 27 de Febrero at Leopoldo Navarro, tel. 809/687–3171), or **Dominican Express** (11 Av. Independencia, tel. 809/682–6610). One-way bus fare from Santo Domingo to Puerto Plata is R.D.$30.

Motorbike Taxis. Known as *motoconchos*, these bikes are a popular and inexpensive way to get around such tourist areas as Puerto Plata, Sosúa, and Jarabacoa. Bikes can be flagged down both on the road and in town; rates vary from R.D.$10 to R.D.$20, depending upon distance.

Rental Cars   You'll need a valid driver's license from your own country and a major credit card and/or cash deposit. Cars can be rented at the airports and at many hotels. Among the known names are **Avis** (tel. 809/533–3530), **Budget** (tel. 809/562–6812), **Hertz** (tel. 809/688–2277), and **National** (tel. 809/566–2747). Rates average U.S.$60 and up per day, depending upon the make and size of the car. Driving is on the right, but many Dominicans drive recklessly, often taking their half of the road out of the middle, and tend to screech suddenly to a halt for a cup of *café con leche*.

If for some unavoidable reason you must drive on the narrow, unlighted mountain roads at night, exercise extreme caution. The 80-kph (50-mph) speed limit is strictly enforced. Finally, keep in mind that gas stations are few and far between in some of the remote regions.

Plane   If you lack the time to travel overland, you can charter a small plane for trips around the island and to neighboring countries, and for surprisingly inexpensive rates. Contact Jimmy or Irene Butler at **Air Taxi** (Núñez de Cáceres 2, Santo Domingo, tel. 809/541–5333 or 809/541–7366).

Telephones and Mail   To call the Dominican Republic from the United States, dial area code 809 and the local number. Connections are clear and easy to make. Trying to place calls from the Dominican Republic, however, is another matter. The system is, to put it kindly, archaic. However, there is direct-dial service to the United States; dial 1, followed by area code and number.

Airmail postage to North America for a letter or postcard is R.D.$.50; to Europe, R.D.$1.

Opening and Closing Times   Regular office hours are weekdays 8 AM–noon and 2–5 and Saturday 8–noon. Government offices are open weekdays 7:30–2:30. Banking hours are weekdays 8:30–4:30.

Beaches

The Dominican Republic has more than 1,000 miles of beaches, including the Caribbean's longest strip of white-sand beach—Punta Cana.

Boca Chica is the beach closest to Santo Domingo (2 miles east of Las Américas Airport, 21 miles from the capital), and it's crowded with city folks on weekends. Five years ago, this beach was virtually a four-lane highway of fine white sand. "Progress" has since cluttered it with plastic beach tables, chaise longues, pizza stands, and beach cottages for rent. But the sand is still fine, and you can walk far out into clear blue water, which is protected by natural coral reefs that help keep the big fish at bay.

About 20 minutes east of Boca Chica is another beach of fine white sand, **Juan Dolio.** The Villas del Mar Hotel and Punta Garza Beach Club are on this beach.

Moving counterclockwise around the island, you'll come to the **La Romana** area, with its miniature **Minitas** beach and lagoon, and the long white-sand, palm-lined crescent of **Bayahibe** beach, which is accessible only by boat. La Romana is the home of the 7,000-acre Casa de Campo resort (*see* Lodging, below), so you're not likely to find any private place in the sun here.

The gem of the Caribbean, **Punta Cana** is a 20-mile strand of pearl-white sand shaded by trees and coconut palms. Located on the easternmost coast, it is the home of Club Med and the Bavaro Beach Resort (*see* Lodging, below).

Las Terrenas, on the north coast of the Samaná peninsula, looks like something from *Robinson Crusoe:* tall palms list toward the sea, away from the mountains; the beach is narrow but sandy; and best of all, there is nothing man-made in sight—just vivid blues, greens, and yellows. Two adjacent hotels are right on the beach at nearby Punta Bonita (see *Lodging,* below).

Playa Grande, on the north coast, is a long stretch of powdery sand that is slated for development. At present, it's undisturbed, but you'd better hurry if you want to enjoy it in solitude.

The beach at **Sosúa,** on the north coast, is lovely. Calm waters gently lap at long stretches of soft white sand. An unfortunate backdrop is a string of tents, and hawkers pushing cheap souvenirs. However, you can also get snacks and rent water-sports equipment from the vendors.

On the north Amber Coast, **Puerto Plata** is situated in a developed and still-developing area that is about to outdo San Juan's famed Condado strip. The beaches are of soft écru or white sand, with lots of reefs for snorkeling. The Atlantic waters are great for windsurfing, waterskiing, and fishing expeditions.

About an hour west of Puerto Plata lies **Luperón Beach,** a wide white-sand beach fit for snorkeling, windsurfing, and scuba diving. The Luperón Beach Resort is handy for rentals and refreshments.

Exploring the Dominican Republic

*Numbers in the margin correspond with points of interest on
the Santo Domingo map.*

Santo Domingo

❶ We'll begin our tour where Spanish civilization in the New
World began, in the 12-block area of **Santo Domingo** called the
Colonial Zone. This historical area is now a bustling, noisy district with narrow cobbled streets, shops, restaurants, residents, and traffic jams. Ironically, all the noise and congestion
make it somehow easier to imagine this old city as it was when it
was yet a colony—when the likes of Columbus, Cortés, Ponce
de León, and pirates sailed in and out, and colonists were settling themselves in the New World. Tourist brochures boast
that "history comes alive here"—a surprisingly truthful statement.

A quick taxi tour of the old section takes about an hour, but if
you're interested in history, you'll want to spend a day or two
exploring the many old "firsts," and you'll want to do it in the
most comfortable shoes you own. (Note: Hours and admission
charges are erratic; check with the Tourist Office for up-to-
date information.)

❷ One of the first things you'll see as you approach the Colonial
Zone is a statue, only slightly smaller than the Colossus of
Rhodes, staring out over the Caribbean Sea. It is **Montesina,**
the Spanish priest who came to the Dominican Republic in the
16th century to appeal for human rights for Indians.

❸ **Parque Independencia,** on the far western border of the Colonial Zone, is a big city park dominated by the marble and concrete **Altar de la Patria.** The impressive mausoleum was built in
1976 to honor the fathers of the country (Duarte, Sánchez, and
Mella).

❹ To your left as you leave the square, the **Concepción Fortress,**
within the old city walls, was the northwest defense post of the
colony. *Calle Palo Hincado at Calle Isidro Duarte, no phone.
Admission free. Open Tues.–Sun. 9–6.*

❺ From Independence Square, walk eight blocks east on Calle El
Conde and you'll come to **Parque Colón.** The huge statue of Columbus dates from 1897 and is the work of French sculptor
Gilbert. On the west side of the square is the **old Town Hall** and
on the east, the **Palacio de Borgella,** residence of the governor
during the Haitian occupation of 1822–44.

❻ Towering over the south side of the square is the coral limestone facade of the **Catedral Primada de América,** the first
cathedral in America. Spanish workmen began building the **Cathedral Santa María la Menor** in 1514 but left off construction to
search for gold in Mexico. The church was finally finished in
1540. Inside, the high altar is of beaten silver, and in the Treasury is a magnificent collection of gold and silver. In the nave are
four baroque columns, carved to resemble royal palms, which
for more than four centuries guarded the magnificent bronze
and marble sarcophagus containing (say Dominican historians)
the remains of Christopher Columbus. (Cuba and Spain also lay
claims to the famed remains.) The sarcophagus has recently
been moved to the Columbus Memorial Lighthouse (*see* Off the
Beaten Track, below)—only the latest in the Great Navigator's
posthumous journeys. When Columbus died in Spain in 1506,

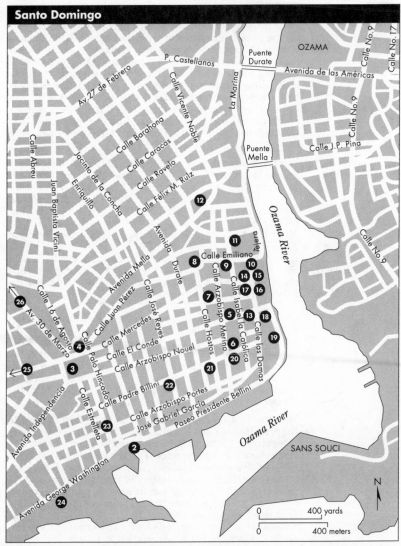

Santo Domingo

Alcázar de Colón, **10**

Calle Las Damas, **13**

Capilla de los
Remedios, **15**

Casa de Bastidas, **18**

Casa de Tostado, **20**

Casa del Cordón, **9**

Catedral Santa María
la Menor, **6**

Concepción Fortress, **4**

Hospital de San Nicolás
de Bari, **7**

Hostal Palacio Nicolás
de Ovando, **16**

Iglesia y Convento
Domínico, **21**

Jardín Botánico
Nacional Dr. Rafael M.
Moscoso, **26**

La Atarazana, **11**

La Iglesia de Regina
Angelorum, **22**

Malecón, **24**

Montesina, **2**

Museo de las Casas
Reales, **14**

National Pantheon, **17**

Parque Colón, **5**

Parque Indepen-
dencia, **3**

Plaza de la Cultura, **25**

Puerta de la
Misericordia, **23**

San Francisco
Monastery, **8**

Santa Bárbara
Church, **12**

Torre del
Homenaje, **19**

his last wish was to be buried in Santo Domingo, and, when the cathedral was finished, his remains were deposited there. After the French occupation of 1795, the Spaniards, determined to keep Columbus on Spanish soil, supposedly moved the remains to Cuba. Later, both Spain and Cuba got hold of exhumed corpses that they claimed were the remains of somebody named Columbus. Cuban and Spanish historians say it was Christopher; Dominican authorities say that it was Christopher's grandson Luís, and that Christopher's remains rest in Santo Domingo. *Calle Arzobispo Merino, tel. 809/689–1920. Admission free. Open Mon.–Sat. 9–6; Sun. masses begin at 6 AM.*

When you leave the cathedral, turn right, walk to Columbus Square and turn left on Calle El Conde. Walk one more block and turn right on Calle Hostos and continue for two more **7** blocks. You'll see the ruins of the **Hospital de San Nicolás de Bari,** the first hospital in the New World, which was built in 1503 by Nicolás de Ovando. *Calle Hostos, between Calle Las Mercedes and Calle Luperón, no phone. Admission free. Open Tues.–Sun. 9–6.*

Time Out   Stop at **Raffles** (Av. Hostos), a popular pub right across from the hospital. The lively back rooms of this cozy old house are much frequented by the young crowd.

Continue along Calle Hostos, crossing Calle Emiliano Tejera, and about mid-block on your left are the majestic ruins of the **8** **San Francisco Monastery.** Constructed between 1512 and 1544, the building contained the church, chapel, and convent of the Franciscan order. Sir Francis Drake's demolition squad significantly damaged the monastery in 1586, and in 1673 an earthquake nearly finished the job, but when it's floodlit at night the old monastery is indeed a dramatic sight.

Walk east for two blocks along Calle Emiliano Tejera. Opposite **9** the post office on Calle Isabel la Católica, the **Casa del Cordón** is recognizable by the sash of the Franciscan order carved in stone over the arched entrance. This house, built in 1503, is the Western Hemisphere's oldest surviving stone house. Columbus's son Diego Colón, viceroy of the colony, and his wife lived here until the Alcázar was finished. It was in this house, too, that Sir Francis Drake was paid a ransom to prevent him from totally destroying the city. The house is now home to the Banco Popular. *Corner of Calle Emiliano Tejera and Calle Isabel la Católica, no phone. Admission free. Open Tues.–Sun. 9–6.*

10   To reach the **Alcázar de Colón,** walk one block east along Calle Emiliano Tejera. You'll come across the imposing castle, with its balustrade and double row of arches. The castle of Don Diego Colón, built in 1514, was painstakingly reconstructed and restored in 1957. Forty-inch-thick coral limestone walls were patched and shored with blocks from the original quarry. There are 22 rooms, furnished in a style to which the viceroy of the island would have been accustomed—right down to the dishes and the viceregal shaving mug. Many of the period paintings, statues, tapestries, and furnishings were donated by the University of Madrid. *Just off Calle Emiliano Tejera at the foot of Calle Las Damas, tel. 809/689–5946. Admission: 50¢. Open daily 9–6.*

⓫ Across from the Alcázar, **La Atarazana** was once the colonial commercial district, where naval supplies were once stored. There are eight restored buildings, the oldest of which dates from 1507. It now houses crafts shops, restaurants, and art galleries.

Time Out Stop in for a pizza and a drink at **Drake's Pub** (Calle La Atarazana). There's a fine view from here of the Alcázar, and in the late afternoon the place fills up with congenial locals and foreigners.

⓬ To reach the **Santa Bárbara Church,** go back to Calle Isabel la Católica, turn right, and walk several blocks. This combination church and fortress, the only one of its kind in Santo Domingo, was completed in 1562. *Calle Mella, between Calle Isabel la Católica and Calle Arzobispo Merino, no phone. Admission free. Open Mon.–Sat. 9–6. Sun. masses begin at 6 AM.*

⓭ Retrace your steps to Calle Isabel la Católica, turn left on Calle Emiliano Tejera, and walk one block right to **Calle Las Damas,** where you'll make a right turn to the New World's oldest street. The "Street of the Ladies" was named after the elegant ladies of the court who, in the Spanish tradition, promenaded in the evening.

⓮ On your left you'll see a sundial dating from 1753, and across the street from it is the **Museo de las Casas Reales** (Museum of the Royal Houses). The collections in the museum are displayed in two early 16th-century palaces that have been altered many times over the years. Exhibits cover everything from antique coins to replicas of the *Niña*, the *Pinta*, and the *Santa María*. There are statue and cartography galleries, coats of armor and coats of arms, coaches and a royal court room, gilded furnishings, and Indian artifacts. The first room of the former Governor's Residence has a wall-size map marking the routes sailed by Columbus's ships on expeditions beginning in 1492. If you like museums, you may have a hard time taking leave of this one. *Calle Las Damas, corner Calle Mercedes, tel. 809/682–4202. Admission: 50¢ adults, 25¢ children. Open Tues.–Sun. 9–6.*

⓯ Across the street is the **Capilla de los Remedios** (Chapel of Our Lady of Remedies), which was originally built as a private chapel for the family of Francisco de Dávila. Early colonists worshiped here as well before the completion of the cathedral. Its architectural details, particularly the lateral arches, are evocative of the Castilian-Romanesque style. *Calle Las Damas, at the foot of Calle Mercedes, no phone. Admission free. Open Mon.–Sat. 9–6; Sun. masses begin at 6 AM.*

⓰ Just south of the chapel on Calle Las Damas, the **Hostal Palacio Nicolás de Ovando** (*see* Lodging, below), now a highly praised hotel, was once the residence of Nicolás de Ovando, one of the principal organizers of the colonial city.

⓱ Across the street from the hotel looms the massive **National Pantheon.** The building, which dates from 1714, was once a Jesuit monastery and later a theater. Trujillo had it restored in 1955 with an eye toward being buried there. Instead, it contains the remains of the martyrs who assassinated him. A commemorative mural of the assassination is painted on the ceiling above the altar, where an eternal flame burns. The impressive chandelier was a gift from Spain's Generalissimo Franco. *Calle Las Damas, near the corner of Calle Mercedes, no phone. Admission: 50¢. Open Mon.–Sat. 9–6.*

Continue south on Calle Las Damas and cross Calle El Conde. Look on your left for the **Casa de Bastidas,** where there is a lovely inner courtyard with tropical plants and temporary exhibit galleries. *Calle Las Damas, just off Calle El Conde, no phone. Admission free. Open Tues.–Sun. 9–6.*

You won't have any trouble spotting the **Torre del Homenaje** (Tower of Homage) in the Fort Ozama. The fort sprawls two blocks south of the Casa de Bastidas, with a brooding crenellated tower that still guards the Ozama River. The fort and its tower were built in 1503 to protect the eastern border of the city. The sinister tower was the last home of many a condemned prisoner. *On Paseo Presidente Bellini, overlooking Río Ozama, no phone. Admission free. Open Tues.–Sun. 9–6.*

When you leave the fortress, turn left off Calle Las Damas onto Calle Padre Billini. A two-block walk will bring you to **Casa de Tostado.** The house was built in the first decade of the 16th century and was the residence of writer Don Francisco Tostado. Its twin Gothic windows are the only ones that are still in existence in the New World. It now houses the **Museo de la Familia Dominicana** (Museum of the Dominican Family), which features exhibits on the well-heeled Dominican family in the 19th century. *Calle Padre Bellini, near Calle Arzobispo Merino, tel. 809/689–5057. Admission: 50¢ adults, 25¢ children. Open daily 9–6.*

Walk two blocks west on Calle Padre Bellini to the corner of Calle Duarte. The graceful building with the rose window is the **Iglesia y Convento Domínico** (Dominican Church and Convent), founded in 1510. In 1538, Pope Paul III visited here and was so impressed with the lectures on theology that he granted it the title of university, making it the oldest institution of higher learning in the New World. *Calle Padre Bellini and Av. Duarte, tel. 809/682–3780). Admission free. Open Tues.–Sun. 9–6.*

Continue west on Calle Padre Billini for two blocks, and at the corner of Calle José Reyes you'll see another lovely church, **La Iglesia de Regina Angelorum** (Church of Regina Angelorum), which dates from 1537. The church was damaged during the Haitian regime, from 1822 to 1844, but you can still appreciate its Baroque dome, Gothic arches, and traceries. *Corner of Calle Padre Bellini and Calle José Reyes, tel. 809/682–2783. Admission free. Open Mon.–Sat. 9–6.*

Walk four blocks west on Calle Padre Billini, turn left on Calle Palo Hincado, and keep going straight till you reach the **Puerta de la Misericordia** (Gate of Mercy), part of the old wall of Santo Domingo. It was here on the plaza, on February 27, 1844, that Ramón Mata Mella, one of the country's founding fathers, fired the shot that began the struggle for independence from Haiti.

Parque Independencia separates the old city from the new. Avenidas 30 de Marzo, Bolívar, and Independencia traverse the park and mingle with avenues named for George Washington, John F. Kennedy, and Abraham Lincoln. Modern Santo

Domingo is a sprawling, noisy city with a population of close to 2 million.

Avenida George Washington, which features tall palms and Las Vegas–style tourist hotels, breezes along the Caribbean Sea. The Parque Litoral de Sur, better known as the **Malecón**, borders the avenue from the colonial city to the Hotel Santo Domingo, a distance of about 3 miles. The seaside park, with its cafés and places to relax, is a popular spot, but beware of pickpockets.

Time Out Before leaving the seafront, check out the **Blues Bar** (Av. George Washington). Locals come here to watch TV *béisbol*, the ocean, and one another. There's a happy hour from 5 to 8, when jazz is played.

Avenida Máximo Gómez comes down from the north. Take a right turn on it, cross Avenida Bolívar, and you'll come to the landscaped lawns, modern sculptures, and sleek buildings of the **Plaza de la Cultura.** Among the buildings are the **National Theater** (tel. 809/687–3191), which stages performances in Spanish; the **National Library,** in which the written word is Spanish; and museums and art galleries, whose notations are also in Spanish. The following museums on the plaza are open Tuesday–Saturday from 10 to 5, and admission to each is 50¢: The **Museum of Dominican Man** (tel. 809/687–3622) traces the migrations of Indians from South America through the Caribbean islands. The **Museum of Natural History** (tel. 809/689–0106) examines the flora and fauna of the island. In the **Gallery of Modern Art** (tel. 809/682–8260), the works of 20th-century Dominican and foreign artists are displayed.

North of town in the Arroyo Hondo district is the **Jardín Botánico Nacional Dr. Rafael M. Moscoso** (Dr. Rafael M. Moscoso National Botanical Gardens), the largest garden in the Caribbean. Its 445 acres include a Japanese Garden, a Great Ravine, a gorgeous display of orchids, and an enormous floral clock. You can tour the gardens by train, boat, or horse-drawn carriage. *Arroyo Hondo, no phone. Admission: 50¢ adults, 25¢ children. Open daily 10–6.*

In the 320-acre **Parque Zoológico Nacional** (National Zoological Park), not far from the Botanical Gardens, animals roam free in natural habitats. There is an African plain, a children's zoo, and what the zoo claims is the world's largest bird cage. *Av. Máximo Gómez at Av. de los Proceres, tel. 809/562–2080. Admission: $1. Open daily 10–6.*

La Romana *Numbers in the margin correspond with points of interest on the Dominican Republic map.*

Head east on Las Américas Highway toward La Romana, about a two-hour drive along the southeast coast. About 1½ miles outside the capital, you'll come to the **Parque de los Tres Ojos** (Park of the Three Eyes). The "eyes" are cool blue pools peering out of deep limestone caves, and it's actually a four-eyed park. If you've a mind to, you can look into the eyes more closely by climbing down into the caves.

About 20 minutes east of the city is **Boca Chica Beach,** popular because of its proximity to the capital. Another 45 minutes or so farther east is the city of **San Pedro de Macorís,** where the national sport and the national drink are both well represented.

Some of the country's best *béisbol* games are played in **Tetelo Vargas Stadium,** which you can see off the highway to your left. The **Macorís Rum distillery** is on the eastern edge of the city.

The two big businesses around La Romana used to be cattle and sugarcane. That was before Gulf + Western created (and subsequently sold) the **Casa de Campo** resort, which is a very big business indeed, and **Altos de Chavón,** a re-creation of a 16th-century village and art colony.

Casa de Campo means "house in the country," and, yes, you could call it that. This particular "house" is a resort that sprawls over 7,000 acres and offers two golf courses (one of them, a teeth-clencher called Teeth of the Dog, has seven holes that skirt the sea), 16 tennis courts, horseback riding, polo, archery, trap shooting, and every imaginable water sport. Oscar de la Renta designed much of the resort and has a boutique in Altos de Chavón. He also owns a villa at Casa de Campo.

㉙ Altos de Chavón sits on a bluff overlooking the Rio Chavón, about 3 miles east of Casa de Campo. You can drive there easily enough, or you can take one of the free shuttle buses from the resort. In this re-creation of a medieval Spanish village there are cobblestone streets lined with lanterns, wrought-iron balconies, and courtyards swathed with bougainvillea. More than a museum piece, this village is a place where artists live, work, and play. There is an art school, affiliated with New York's Parsons School of Design, a disco, an archaeological museum, five restaurants, and a 5,000-seat outdoor amphitheater where Frank Sinatra and Julio Iglesias have entertained. The focal point of the village is **Iglesia St. Stanislaus,** which is named after the patron saint of Poland in tribute to the Polish Pope John Paul II, who visited the Dominican Republic in 1979 and left some of the ashes of St. Stanislaus behind.

The Amber Coast The Autopista cuts northwest across the country from Santo Domingo to the north, or Amber Coast, so-called because of the large deposits of amber in the region. The drive to the city of Puerto Plata on the north coast, a distance of about 240 kilome-
㉚ ters (150 miles), will take about four hours. **Pico Duarte** (10,128 feet), the highest peak in the West Indies, is to the west, and the mountainous road you'll be traveling on is lined with lush banana plantations, rice fields, fields of tobacco, and Royal Poinciana trees. Coconut palms are stuck in the hills like candles on a birthday cake. All along the road there are stands where, for just a few centavos, you can buy ripe pineapples, mangoes, avocados, *chicharrones* (fried pork rinds), and fresh fruit drinks.

About 144 kilometers (90 miles) north of the capital you'll come to the industrial city of **Santiago de los Caballeros,** where huge monuments guard the entrance to the city. Santiago, the capital of the province of Cibao, is the Dominican Republic's second-largest city but holds little of interest to tourists. Squeeze through the city's narrow teeming streets and contin-
㉛ ue northward to **Puerto Plata.**

The coastal area around Puerto Plata is a region of splashy resorts. The north coast boasts more than 70 miles of beaches, with condominiums and villas going up fast.

In the city of Puerto Plata, the **Museum of Dominican Amber,** housed in a lovely galleried mansion, is one of several tenants in the Tourist Bazaar. The museum displays and sells the Dominican Republic's national stone. Semiprecious, translucent amber is actually fossilized pine resin that dates back about 50 million years, give or take a few millennia. The north coast of the Dominican Republic has the largest deposits of amber in the world (the only other deposits are found in Germany and the U.S.S.R.), and jewelry crafted from the stone is the best-selling item on the island. *Calle Duarte 61, tel. 809/586–2848. Admission: $3. Open Mon.–Sat. 9–5.*

Southwest of Puerto Plata, you can take a cable car to the top of **32** **Mt. Isabel de Torres,** which soars 2,600 feet above sea level. On the mountain there is a botanical garden, a huge statue of Christ, and a spectacular view. *The cable car operates Tues., Thurs., Fri., Sat., and Sun. 8–6. Round-trip is 75¢.*

Take the Autopista east from Puerto Plata about 15 miles to **33** **Sosúa,** a small community settled during World War II by Austrian and German Jews. After the war, many of them returned to Europe or went to the United States, and most of those who remained married Dominicans. Only a few Jewish families reside in the community today, and there is only one small, one-room synagogue. The flavor of the town is decidedly Spanish. There are numerous hotels, condominiums, and apartments in Sosúa. (The roads off the Autopista, incidentally, are horribly punctured with potholes.)

Sosúa has become one of the most frequently visited tourist destinations in the country, favored by French Canadians and Europeans. Hotels and condos are going up at breakneck speed. It actually consists of two communities, **El Batey** and **Los Charamicos,** which are separated by a cove and one of the island's prettiest beaches. The sand is soft and white and the water gin-clear and calm. The walkway above the beach is packed with tents filled with souvenirs, pizzas, and even clothing for sale—a jarring note in this otherwise idyllic setting.

Time Out **P.J. International Bar** (Calle Pedro Clisante, El Batey, Sosúa, tel. 809/571–2325), in the center of Sosúa, is a hot spot for tacos, hamburgers, and a rum punch or two.

Continue east on the Autopista past **Playa Grande.** At press time, this powdery white beach was undisturbed and unspoiled. But the area is slated for development, and by the time you read these pages, business may be booming.

The Autopista rolls along eastward and rides out onto a **34** "thumb" of the island, where you'll find **Samaná.** Back in 1824, a sailing vessel called the *Turtle Dove,* carrying several hundred escaped American slaves from the Freeman Sisters' underground railway, was blown ashore in Samaná. The escapees settled and prospered, and today their descendants number several thousand. The churches here are Protestant, the worshipers live in villages called Bethesda, Northeast, and Philadelphia, and the language spoken is an odd 19th-century form of English.

About 3,000 humpback whales winter off the coast of Samaná from December to March. Plans are under way for organizing major whale-watching expeditions, such as those out of Massachusetts, that will boost the region's economy without scaring away the world's largest mammals.

In the meantime, sport fishing at Samaná is considered to be among the best in the world. A beautiful bay and beach round out Samaná's attractions.

Dominican Republic for Free

Concerts. The quadrangle of Santo Domingo's Plaza de la Cultura is the site of occasional classical music concerts that you can hear for a song. There are also open-air concerts along the Malecón. Check with local newspapers, your hotel, or the Tourist Office for dates and programs.

Colonial Zone. Many of the ancient buildings have no admission charge, notably the Catedral Santa María la Menor, the Tower of Homage, the San Francisco Monastery, and the Casa del Cordón (*see* Exploring the Dominican Republic, above).

Parque de los Tres Ojos. The Park of the Three Eyes, 10 minutes east of Santo Domingo, is free (*see* Exploring the Dominican Republic, above).

What to See and Do with Children

Jardín Botánica Nacional Dr. Rafael M. Moscoso (*see* Exploring the Dominican Republic, above).

Parque Zoológico Nacional (*see* Exploring the Dominican Republic, above).

Parque de los Tres Ojos (*see* Exploring the Dominican Republic, above).

Parque Quisqueya. Santo Domingo's amusement park has a merry-go-round, swings, seesaws, and other playground attractions. *Av. Bolívar and Av. Tiradentes, tel. 809/682–9191. Admission: $1. Open Thurs.–Sun. 10–10.*

Off the Beaten Track

Laguna Gri-Gri is a swampland smack out of the Louisiana, bayou country with the added attraction of a cool blue grotto that almost outdoes the Blue Grotto of Capri. Since Laguna Gri-Gri is only about 90 minutes west of Puerto Plata, in Río San Juan, you can board a boat for a peaceful trip through the swamps and into the grotto. Contact the Tourist Office for arrangements.

Nature lovers should consider a trip to **Jarabacoa,** in the mountainous region known rather wistfully as the Dominican Alps. There is little to do in the town itself but eat and rest up for excursions on foot, horseback, or by motorbike taxi to the surrounding waterfalls and forests—quite incongruous in such a tropical country. Accommodations in the area are rustic but comfortable.

Less accessible and vastly different is **Lago Enriquillo,** near the Haitian border. The lake encircles a wild, arid, and thorny island that serves as a sanctuary for such exotic birds and reptiles as the flamingo, iguana, and crocodile.

Just off the east coast of Hispaniola lies **Isla Saona,** now a national park inhabited by sea turtles, pigeons, and other wildlife. Caves on the island were once used by Indians. The beaches are beautiful, and legend has it that Columbus once strayed ashore here.

Just east of colonial Santo Domingo, across the Ozama River, in the San Souci district, is the **Columbus Memorial Lighthouse** (Av. España, no phone). This lighthouse monument and museum complex dedicated to the Great Navigator is scheduled for completion in 1992, its inauguration set to coincide with the 500th anniversary of Christopher Columbus's landing on the island. Along with its showpiece laser-powered lighthouse, the complex will hold the tomb of Columbus (recently moved there after 400 years in the Cathedral Santa María la Menor) and six museums featuring exhibits relating to Columbus and early exploration of the New World (one museum will focus on the long, rocky, and often controversial, history of the Lighthouse Memorial itself). The museums will be open to the public as each is completed between now and late 1992. At press time no admission fee or regular hours had been set. For more information, contact the Tourist Information Center (Av. George Washington, tel. 809/682–8181).

Las Terrenas, on the north coast of the Samaná peninsula, is only barely known to North American tourists. Meanwhile, French Canadians and Europeans, especially Germans, have begun making the long trek to this remote stretch of nearly deserted but beautiful beaches. The place is a sort of latter-day hippie haven that also attracts surfboarders and windsurfers. There are several modest restaurants and a dusty main street in the town of Las Terrenas, a small airfield at Portillo, and several congenial hotels right on the beach at Punta Bonita. If you're seeking tranquillity and are happy just hanging out drinking beer and soaking up sun, this is the place for you. You can also hire a motorbike taxi or bicycle to explore the rest of the peninsula. Las Terrenas is 4 ½ hours from Santo Domingo by bus.

Participant Sports

Although there is hardly a shortage of outdoor activities here, the resorts have virtually cornered the market on sports, including every conceivable water sport. In some cases, facilities may be available only to guests. You can check with the Tourist Office for more details. Listed below is a mere smattering of the island's athletic options:

Archery   Robin Hood never had it so good. Bows and arrows can be rented at **Club Med** (Punta Cana, tel. 809/567–5228) and **Bávaro Beach Resort** (Punta Cana, tel. 809/682–2162).

Bicycling   Pedaling is easy on pancake-flat beaches, but there are also steep hills in the Dominican Republic. Bikes are available at **Villas Doradas** (Playa Dorada, Puerto Plata, tel. 809/586–3000), **Dorado Naco** (Dorado Beach, tel. 809/586–2019), **Jack Tar Village** (Puerto Plata, tel. 809/586–3800), and **Cofresi Beach Hotel** (Puerto Plata, tel. 809/586–2898).

Boating   Hobie Cats and pedal boats are available at **Heavens** (Puerto Plata, tel. 809/586–5250). Check also at **Casa de Campo** (La Romana, tel. 809/682–2111) and **Club Med** (Punta Cana, tel. 809/567–5228).

Deep-Sea Fishing	Marlin and wahoo are among the fish that folks angle for here. Arrangements can be made through **El Mirador** (Puerto Plata) and **Casa de Campo** (La Romana). Fishing is best between January and June.
Golf	**Casa de Campo** resort (La Romana) has two 18-hole Pete Dye courses and a third one under way. In 1990, 18-hole courses are expected to open at both the **Punta Cana Beach Resort** and the **Bávaro Beach.** The Playa Dorada hotels have their own 18-hole Robert Trent Jones–designed course; there is also a 9-hole course nearby at the **Costambar.** Guests in Santo Domingo hotels are usually allowed to use the 18-hole course at the **Santo Domingo Country Club** on weekdays—*after* members have teed off. There is a 9-hole course outside of town, at Lomas Lindas.
Horseback Riding	**Casa de Campo** (La Romana) has a dude ranch on its premises, saddled with 2,000 horses.
Polo	You can arrange for lessons at **Casa de Campo** (La Romana).
Sailing	Sailboats are available at **Club Med** (Punta Cana) and **Casa de Campo** (La Romana).
Scuba Diving and Snorkeling	Ancient sunken galleons, undersea gardens, and offshore reefs are the lures here. For equipment and trips contact **Mundo Submarino** (Santo Domingo, tel. 809/566–0344). A new DIWA scuba-certification school has been opened at the **Demar Beach Club** in Boca Chica, outside the capital, offering three-day and one-week programs.
Tennis	There must be a million nets laced around the island, and most of them can be found at the large resorts (*see* Lodging, below).

Spectator Sports

Cockfights	For those who enjoy this grisly spectacle, there are fights at the Cockfighting Coliseum in Santo Domingo on Saturday afternoons and Wednesday evenings. *Tel. 809/565–3844; in Puerto Plata, Thurs. and Sat. at 1 PM, and Sun. at 2:30 PM in the coliseum on the first street south of the Malecón, on Calle Ramón Hernández.*
Greyhound Races	The dogs make tracks every Monday, Wednesday, Friday, and Sunday at **Canódromo El Coco.** *Av. Monumental, La Yuca— about 15 min north of the capital, tel. 809/560–6968 or 560– 8342. Admission: R.D.$1–R.D.$4. Races Mon.–Fri. 7:30 PM, Sun. and holidays 4 PM.*
Horse Racing	There are races year-round at the **Hipódromo Perla Antillana.** *Av. San Cristobal, Santo Domingo, tel. 809/565–2353. Admission free. Post time: Tues., Thurs., Sat. 3 PM.*
Polo	The ponies pound down the field at **Sierra Prieta** (Santo Domingo) and at **Casa de Campo** (La Romana). The season runs from October through May. For information about polo games, call 809/565–6880.

Shopping

The hot ticket in the Dominican Republic is amber jewelry. This island has the world's largest deposits of amber, and the prices here for the translucent, semiprecious stone are unmatched anywhere. The stones, which range in color from pale lemon to dark brown, are actually petrified resin from coniferous trees that disappeared from Earth about 50 million years ago. The most valuable stones are those in which tiny insects or small leaves are embedded. (Don't knock it till you've seen it.)

The Dominican Republic is the homeland of designer Oscar de la Renta, and you might want to stop at some of the chic shops that carry his creations. In the crafts department, hand-carved wood rocking chairs are big sellers, and they are sold unassembled and boxed for easy transport. Look also for the delicate ceramic lime figurines that symbolize the Dominican culture.

Bargaining is both a game and a social activity in the Dominican Republic, especially with street vendors and at the stalls in El Mercado Modelo. Vendors are disappointed and perplexed if you don't haggle. They also tend to be tenacious, so unless you really have an eye on buying don't even stop to look—you may get stuck buying a souvenir just to get rid of an annoying vendor.

Shopping Districts **El Mercado Modelo** in Santo Domingo is a covered market in the Colonial Zone bordering Calle Mella. The restored buildings of **La Atarazana** (across from the Alcázar in the Colonial Zone) are filled with shops, art galleries, restaurants, and bars. The main shopping streets in the Colonial Zone are **Calle El Conde** and **Calle Duarte.** (Some of the best shops on Calle Duarte are north of the Colonial Zone, between Calle Mella and Av. Las Américas). **Plaza Criolla** (corner of Av. 27 de Febrero and Av. Anacaona) is filled with shops that sell everything from scents to nonsense. Duty-free shops selling liquors, cameras, and the like are at the **Centro de los Héroes** (Av. George Washington), the **Embajador Hotel, Santo Domingo Sheraton,** and at **Las Américas Airport.**

In Puerto Plata, the seven showrooms of the **Tourist Bazaar** (Calle Duarte 61) are in a wonderful old galleried mansion with a patio bar. Another cluster of shops is at the **Plaza Shopping Center** (Calle Duarte at Av. 30 de Marzo).

In **Altos de Chavón,** art galleries and shops are grouped around the main square.

Good Buys **Ambar Tres** (La Atarazana 3, Colonial Zone, Santo Domingo,
Amber/Jewelry tel. 809/688-0474) carries a wide selection of the Dominican product.

Dominican Art Galleries in Santo Domingo are **Arawak Gallery** (Av. Pasteur 104, tel. 809/685-1661, and Conde 107, tel. 809/689-3651) and **Galería de Arte Nader** (La Atarazana 9, Colonial Zone, tel. 809/688-0969).

Macaluso's (Calle Duarte 32, and in Plaza Turisol, tel. 809/586-3433) and **The Collector's Corner Gallery and Gift Shop** (Plaza Shopping Center, Calle Duarte at Av. 30 de Marzo, no phone) are the better-known galleries in Puerto Plata.

Wood Crafts Visit the stalls of **El Mercado Modelo** in the Colonial Zone and **El Conde Gift Shop** (Calle El Conde 153, tel. 809/682-5909), both in Santo Domingo.

In Puerto Plata, browse and shop at **Macaluso's** (Calle Duarte 32, tel. 809/586-3433) and at the **Collector's Corner Gallery and Gift Shop** (Plaza Shopping Center, no phone). In Santiago, try **Artesanía Lime** (Autopista Duarte, Km 21-2, Santiago, tel. 809/582-3754).

Dining

Dining out is a favorite form of entertainment for Dominicans, and they tend to dress up for the occasion. Most restaurants begin serving dinner around 6 PM, but the locals don't generally turn up until 9 or 10. There are French, Italian, and Chinese restaurants, as well as those serving traditional Dominican fare. Some favorite local dishes you should sample are paella, *sancocho* (a thick stew), *arroz con pollo* (rice with chicken), *plátanos* (plantains) in all their tasty varieties, and *tortilla de jamón* (spicy ham omelet). Country snacks include *chicharrones* (fried pork rinds) and *calletas* (flat biscuit crackers). Many a meal is topped off with *majarete*, a tasty cornmeal custard. Presidente, Bohemia, and Quisqueya are the local beers; Bermúdez and Brugal the local rums. Wine is on the expensive side because it has to be imported.

The most highly recommended restaurants are indicated by a star ★.

Category	Cost*
Expensive	$30–$45
Moderate	$20–$30
Inexpensive	under $20

per person, excluding drinks, service, and sales tax (6%)

Santo Domingo
Continental
★

Alcázar. Oscar de la Renta designed this elegant Moorish setting. Start with lobster bisque, followed by sea bass with crabmeat au gratin or filet mignon with béarnaise sauce. A lunch buffet is served each day, with Mexican food on Tuesday, Chinese on Wednesday, Italian on Thursday, and so forth. *Hotel Santo Domingo, tel. 809/532–1511. Jackets and reservations required. AE, DC, MC, V. Expensive.*

Antoine's. In this *très intime* eatery, hotel guests rub shoulders with well-heeled Dominicans, with whom the restaurant is popular. Starters include black-bean soup, and among the main dishes on the extensive menu are lobster thermidor and imperial stew, made with lobster, shrimp, and scallops. There are no fewer than 20 dessert offerings. *Hotel Sheraton, Av. George Washington, tel. 809/686–6666. Jacket and reservations required. AE, DC, MC, V. Expensive.*

★ **Lina.** Lina was the personal chef of Trujillo, and she taught her secret recipes to the chefs of this stylish contemporary restaurant. Paella is the best-known specialty, but other offerings include steak au poivre and a casserole of mixed seafood flavored with Pernod. *Hotel Lina, Av. Máximo Gómez, tel. 809/ 686–5000. Jackets and reservations required. AE, DC, MC, V. Expensive.*

Mesón de la Cava. The capital's most unusual restaurant is more than 50 feet below ground in a natural cave complete with stalagmites and stalactites. Specialties include prime filet with Dijon flambé, tournedos Roquefort, and excellent seafood dishes. Live music and dancing nightly until 1 AM. *Av. Mirador del Sur, tel. 809/533–2818. Jacket and reservations required. AE, DC, MC, V. Expensive.*

Fonda de la Atarazana. This patio restaurant in the Colonial Zone is especially romantic at night when music and dancing are added. Try the kingfish, shrimp, or *chicharrones de pollo* (bits of fried Dominican chicken). *La Atarazana 5, tel. 809/689–2900. AE, MC, V. Moderate.*

Lucky Seven. Baseball is the big deal here. Owner Evelio Oliva has two satellite dishes, and telecasts of six major-league games go on at once. Incidentally, there's also steak, chicken, and seafood to satisfy pre- or postgame appetites. *Casimiro de Moya and Av. Pasteur, tel. 809/682–7588. No reservations. No credit cards. Moderate.*

Dominican **La Bahía.** An unpretentious spot where the catch of the day is
★ tops. Conch appears in a variety of dishes. For starters, try the *sopa palúdica*, a thick soup made with fish, shrimp, and lobster, served with tangy garlic bread. Then move on to kingfish in coconut sauce, or *espaguettis a la canona* (spaghetti heaped with seafood). *Av. George Washington 1, tel. 809/682–4022. No reservations. MC, V. Inexpensive.*

El Castillo del Mar. Another seafood restaurant on the Malecón, this one has an open-air setting by the sea. Start with fish soup, then feast on lobster thermidor or sea bass smothered in onions, tomatoes, peas, and basil. *Av. George Washington 2, tel. 809/688–4047. No reservations. MC, V. Inexpensive.*

French **Café St. Michel.** The cream of pumpkin soup and steak tartare
★ should clue you into why this popular restaurant has won many gastronomical awards. Desserts include a prize-winning chocolate torte and spectacular soufflés. *Av. Lope de Vega 24, tel. 809/562–4141. Jacket and reservations suggested. AE, MC, V. Moderate.*

Italian **Vesuvio.** Capital-city denizens flock to this superb Italian res-
★ taurant, where everything on the lengthy menu is either freshly caught, homemade, or homegrown. Start with antipasti, then try the seafood platter, *calamares al vino blanco* (squid in white wine sauce) or *scaloppina al tarragon* (veal with tarragon). (**Vesuvio II** is at Av. Tiradentes 17, tel. 809/562–6090.) *Av. George Washington 521, tel. 809/689–2141. Jacket required. No reservations. DC, MC, V. Expensive.*

Spanish **El Caserio.** An extensive menu lists specialties such as paella Valenciana, seafood zarzuela, bluefish with anchovies, and leg of lamb Segovia. For dessert, swallow your diet and order chocolate cake Caserio. *Av. George Washington 459, tel. 809/685–3392. Jackets and reservations required. AE, DC, MC, V. Expensive.*

La Romana **La Casa del Río.** In a dining room perched high on a cliff above
★ the Rio Chavón, you can feast on Continental specialties such as duck soup, ragout of lobster, and veal medallions. *Altos de Chavón, tel. 809/682–9656, ext. 2345. Jacket and reservations required. AE, DC, MC, V. Expensive.*

Tropicana. An elegant pavilion swept with cooling breezes, this eatery specializes in beef and fresh-caught seafoods. Shrimp and lobster are always offered, and sea bass is prepared in a variety of ways. *Casa de Campo, tel. 809/596–8885. Jackets and reservations required. AE, DC, MC, V. Expensive.*

Café del Sol. This is an outdoor café in a 16th-century village setting. You can sample pizza and assorted light dishes while enjoying the view of the distant mountain range. *Altos de*

Chavón, tel. 809/682–9656, ext. 2346. No reservations. AE, DC, MC, V. Moderate.

Puerto Plata **De Armando.** Here on the north coast, a restaurant in a pretty blue-and-white house dishes up steak, seafood, and Continental dishes, all served to the tune of a guitar trio. *Calle Separación, corner Calle Antera Mota, tel. 809/586–3418. Reservations required. MC, V. Expensive.*

Flamingo's. You can dine either indoors in a stately room or outside on the balcony overlooking the pool. In any case, you can feast on fettuccine al pesto, lobster fricassee in sherry sauce, and medallions of beef with béarnaise sauce. *Dorado Naco Hotel, tel. 809/586–2019. Reservations suggested. AE, DC, MC, V. Expensive.*

★ **Jimmy's.** Within this old Victorian house you'll be served chateaubriand, filet mignon, and a variety of creatures from the sea. Be sure to top it all off with something flambéed. *Calle Beller 72, tel. 809/586–4325. Jackets and reservations recommended. AE, MC, V. Moderate.*

Roma II. This is just an open-sided stand with a metal roof, but the pizzas, which are cooked in a wood-burning oven, are some of the best you'll ever eat. The pizza dough and pasta are made fresh daily. Other specialties include *spaghetti con pulpo* (octopus), *filete chito* (steak with garlic), and a host of other pastas and special sauces. *Corner Calle E. Prudhomme and Calle Beller, tel. 809/586–3904. No reservations. No credit cards. Inexpensive.*

Lodging

Your options here vary from the New World's first hotel to some of the world's newest and poshest resorts. An ambitious development plan continues, especially on the north coast; in Puerto Plata, there are already so many adjoining resorts that when you go out for a stroll you have to flag landmarks to find your way back to the one where your luggage is. Be sure to inquire about special packages when you call to reserve. Our prices, in U.S. dollars, are based on a double room during the high season.

The most highly recommended lodgings are indicated by a star ★.

Category	Cost*
Very Expensive	over $150
Expensive	$100–$150
Moderate	$75–$100
Inexpensive	under $75

All prices are for a standard double room for two, excluding 21% tax and a 10%–15% service charge.

Santo Domingo **Jaragua Resort Hotel, Casino and European Spa.** This palatial pink complex is set on 14 acres of gardens, waterfalls, and fountains. Top-name entertainers are booked into the 800-seat nightclub, master chefs from four countries tend to the cuisine, and a staff doctor supervises the diet program in the spa. Air-conditioned accommodations are in Garden or Tower rooms, and all have 3 phones, 21-channel satellite TVs, minibars, and hair dryers. Twelve cabañas surround the Olympic-size free-form pool, and the casino covers 20,000 square feet. *Av. George Washington 367, Santo Domingo, tel. 809/686–2222; 800/223–9815; or in Canada, 800/468–0023. 355 rooms, including 18 suites. Facilities: casino, pool, 6 restaurants, 5 bars, 4 tennis courts (1 lighted), golf (at the Santo Domingo Country Club), and European spa with exercise/diet programs, saunas, Jacuzzis, whirlpool. AE, MC, V. Very Expensive.*

★ **Hotel Santo Domingo.** Oscar de la Renta designed the interiors of this very *haut* hotel. There are acres of marble and tile, bold colors, ceiling fans, and hand-crafted Dominican furniture throughout. The air-conditioned hotel, on 14 beautifully land-scaped acres, overlooks the Caribbean. The rooms have balconies, cable TVs, and most have two double beds. The Alcázar is the elegant Continental restaurant; Las Palmas is the place for dancing. VIPs (and there are many who stay here) check into the Premier Club for extra perks. *Box 2112, Santo Domingo, tel. 809/535–1511 or 800/223–6620. 220 rooms. Facilities: 3 restaurants, 2 bars, pool, sun deck, sauna, 3 lighted tennis courts. AE, DC, MC, V. Expensive.*

★ **Santo Domingo Sheraton Hotel and Casino.** This 11-story, modern, air-conditioned hotel is on Avenida George Washington, next to the Jaragua, and many of the rooms have balconies overlooking the sea. Most of the rooms have a minibar, and all have a color TV with English-language movies. *Box 1493, Santo Domingo, tel. 809/686–6666 or 800/325–3535. 260 rooms. Facilities: casino, pool, Antoine's restaurant, bar, disco, 2 lighted tennis courts, beauty salon, saunas, health club, facilities for the handicapped. AE, DC, MC, V. Expensive.*

Hotel El Embajador and Casino. The rooms in this air-conditioned hotel are spacious, with carpeting, twin or king-size beds, radios, cable TVs, and balconies with either a mountain or ocean view (choose the latter). The pool is a popular weekend gathering place for resident foreigners. *Av. Sarasota 65, Santo Domingo, tel. 809/533–2131 or 800/457–0067. 316 rooms, including 12 suites. Facilities: casino, pool, free transport to beach, 4 tennis courts, 2 restaurants, 2 bars, shopping arcade, facilities for the handicapped. AE, DC, MC, V. Moderate.*

Gran Hotel Lina and Casino. This balconied hotel, on Avenida Máximo Gómez near the Plaza de la Cultura, has a staid but secure ambience. Rooms are air-conditioned, spacious, and carpeted, with double beds, minifridges, huge marble baths, and cable TVs. The staff is friendly and helpful. *Box 1915, Santo Domingo, tel. 809/686–5000. 220 rooms and suites. Facilities: casino, restaurant, piano bar, nightclub, coffee shop, health club, 2 tennis courts, pool facilities for the handicapped. AE, DC, MC, V. Inexpensive.*

★ **Hostal Palacio Nicolás de Ovando.** The oldest hotel in the New World, and one of the few in the Colonial Zone, was home to the first governor in the early 1500s. The decor is Spanish, with carved mahogany doors, beamed ceilings, tapestries, arched colonnades, and a courtyard with splashing fountain. Dominican specialties are served in the restaurant. *Calle Las Damas 44, Apdo. 89-2, Santo Domingo, tel. 809/687–3101. 55 air-conditioned rooms. Facilities: restaurant, bar, TV, pool. No credit cards. Inexpensive.*

The Amber Coast **Dorado Naco.** This is a sprawling complex of air-conditioned villas with spacious carpeted one- and two-bedroom apartments. The living/dining area has a sofa bed, cable TV, two phones, dining table that seats four, and a counter bar. Each apartment has a large patio or terrace surrounded by tropical flowers and plants. The Dorado's aggressive activities program arranges beach barbecues, bonfires, and the like. *Box 162, Playa Dorada, tel. 809/586–2019 or 800/322–2388. 150 rooms. Facilities: pool, restaurant, 3 bars, coffee shop, game room, minimarket, bicycle rental, horseback riding, tennis, golf, and water-sports center. AE, DC, MC, V. Expensive.*

★ **Eurotel Playa Dorada.** A cascading pool washes down to the two-mile beach and its clusters of small low-rise buildings. This large resort, completed in 1986, is done in bold, imaginative designs. Standard rooms have one double or two twin beds; one-bedroom apartments have a pull-out couch in the living room, and some have kitchens. There's always a lot going on at the beach club. *Box 337, Playa Dorada, tel. 809/586–3663 or 800/826–3447. 402 rooms, including 186 suites. Facilities: 3 restaurants, 3 bars, casino, 5 lighted tennis courts, golf, horseback riding, water-sports clinic, bicycles, scooters. AE, DC, MC, V. Expensive.*

Jack Tar Village. At this link in the all-inclusive chain of JTVs, everything, including drinks and golf greens fees, is included in the cost of your accommodations. The activities program is varied, enhanced by nightly entertainment and all manner of enjoyable pursuits. Accommodations are in Spanish-style villas near the beach. There is free transportation to town, but the all-inclusive deal will probably keep you on the premises. *Box 368, Playa Dorada, tel. 809/586–3800 or 800/527–9299. 240 rooms. Facilities: 2 pools, 3 restaurants, 5 bars, casino, golf, horseback riding, day and night tennis, water-sports center. AE, MC, V. Expensive.*

Playa Dorada Beach Resort. This beach resort is known for its lively nightlife. It's set on a mile-long white-sand beach, and there are a variety of social and sports programs. The grounds are beautifully landscaped, and the pool, with swim-up bar, is just a few steps from the beach. Air-conditioned rooms come with cable TVs and either two double or one king-size bed. *Box 272, Playa Dorada, tel. 809/586–3988 or 800/423–6902. 253 rooms, including 1 suite. Facilities: pool, 4 restaurants, 2 bars, disco, casino, ice-cream parlor, golf, tennis courts, horseback riding, bikes, jogging trail, water-sports center. AE, DC, MC, V. Expensive.*

★ **Puerto Plata Beach Resort and Casino.** This is a 7-acre village with cobblestone pathways, colorful gardens, and suites in 23 two- and three-story buildings. An activities center sets up water-sports clinics, rents bicycles, and so forth. The resort also caters to the little ones, with children's games and enclosures for them at the shallow end of the pool. La Lechuza is the resort's glitzy disco. It's just outside of town and a ways from Playa Dorada, which will be an added attraction to some. *Box 600, Av. Malecón, Puerto Plata, tel. 809/586–4243 or 800/223–9815. 216 suites. Facilities: pool, 4 restaurants, bar, outdoor Jacuzzi, horseback riding, 3 lighted tennis courts, water-sports center. AE, MC, V. Expensive.*

★ **Radisson Puerto Plato.** New in 1988, this is a luxurious resort with accommodations in 44 two-story pastel-colored villas. Rooms are air-conditioned, with remote-control cable TVs and minibars. The free-form pool has a swim-up terrace, and there's free shuttle service to the beach. Nightly entertainment and dancing in the patio lounge and lobby bar. *Playa*

Dorada, tel. 809/586–5350 or 800/777–7800. 336 rooms and junior suites. Facilities: 2 restaurants, 3 bars/lounges, pool, 7 lighted tennis courts, health club, gym, spa, Jacuzzi, golf. AE, MC, V. Expensive.

Hotel Cofresi. The rooms here are simply furnished (twin beds, bath with tub and shower), but the setting is breathtaking. The all-inclusive resort is built on the reefs along the Atlantic, which spritzes its waters into the peaceful man-made lagoon and pools along the beach. There are jogging and exercise trails, paddleboats for the lagoon, scuba-diving clinics, and evening entertainment, including a disco. Everything, including unlimited drinks, is included. *Box 327, Costambar, tel. 809/ 586–2898 or 800/828–8895; in NY, 212/840–6636; in Canada, 800/468–0023. 150 rooms. Facilities: 2 restaurants, 3 bars, disco, nightclub, 2 pools, (1 saltwater), bicycling, horseback riding, paddleboats, tennis, water-sports center. AE, MC, V. Moderate.*

★ **Playa Chiquita.** In this new Sosúa resort you register in a broad breezeway that leads past the free-form pool right to the small private beach. The all-suite, air-conditioned complex has contemporary tropical decor, with terra-cotta floors, cable TVs, double or king-size beds, wet bar, kitchenettes, and patios or balconies. A sun deck overlooks the ocean. The pool has a swim-up bar for adult guests and a shallow section for children. *Sosúa, tel. 809/689–6191. 90 rooms. Facilities: restaurant, coffee shop, pool, gift shop, horseback riding, water sports. MC, V. Moderate.*

Punta Goleta Beach Resort. The resort is set on 100 tropical acres across the road from the Cabarete beach, where windsurfing is the big deal. All the hotel's rooms are air-conditioned and most have terraces or patios with gingerbread trim. There is a lot of activity here, such as volleyball in the pool or on the beach, frog and crab racing, board games, merengue lessons, disco, and boating on the lagoon. *Box 318, Cabarete, tel. 809/ 571–0700 or 800/874–4637. 126 rooms plus 2- and 3-bedroom villas. Facilities: 2 restaurants, 4 bars, disco, jogging track, pool, lagoon, horseback riding, golf, tennis, water-sports center. AE, DC, MC, V. Moderate.*

★ **Hostal Jimessón.** One of the few hotels in downtown Puerto Plata, the Jimessón is a gingerbread, century-old clapboard house right out of New Orleans. There are rocking chairs on the front porch, and the parlor houses a veritable museum of antique grandfather clocks, victrolas, and mahogany and wicker furniture. Other superb, homey touches include a live parrot, hanging plants, and the owners' genuine hospitality. *Calle John F. Kennedy 41, Puerto Plata, tel. 809/586–5131. 22 air-conditioned rooms. Facilities: bar, cable TV. AE, MC, V. Inexpensive.*

Hotel Montemar. Located on the Malecón, between Puerto Plata and Playa Dorada, this is a good choice for a cost-conscious holiday. All rooms have an ocean view. Superior rooms are air-conditioned, but small standard rooms are not. There is a daily schedule of activities, and transportation to the beaches at Playa Dorada. It's a fine, inexpensive alternative to Playa Dorada. *Box 382, Puerto Plata, tel. 809/586–2800 or 800/332– 4872. 95 rooms. Facilities: restaurant, coffee shop, bar, 2 tennis courts, beach club, golf, horseback riding. AE, MC, V. Inexpensive.*

La Romana
★

Casa de Campo. This luxury resort is—in a word—awesome. It occupies 7,000 landscaped acres along the edge of the Caribbean. Much of the resort was designed by Oscar de la Renta, who owns a villa here and also has a boutique in Altos de Chavón, the re-created village and art colony on the property (*see* Exploring the Dominican Republic, above). There are 350 casitas, casita suites, and one-, two-, and three-bedroom golf and tennis villas, plus 150 condominium apartments. There is a ranch with 2,000 horses, three polo fields, and two 18-hole Pete Dye golf courses. Minibuses provide free transportation around the resort, but you can also rent electric carts, scooters, and bicycles. *Box 140, La Romana, tel. 809/523–3333 or 800/223–6620. 740 rooms. Facilities: 9 restaurants, 8 bars, 13 pools, 13 tennis courts (6 lighted), fitness center, Jacuzzi, sauna, polo fields, ranch, 2 18-hole golf courses, boutiques, marina, airstrip. AE, DC, MC, V. Very Expensive.*

Punta Cana
★

Bávaro Beach Resort. More than 20 miles of the Caribbean's best beach are to be found in front of this four-star luxury resort. Rooms are in five low-rise buildings by the beach or overlooking the gardens. Each room is air-conditioned and has a private balcony or terrace and refrigerator. A social director coordinates a wide variety of daily activities. *Higüey, tel. 809/ 682–2162. 1,001 rooms. Facilities: 3 restaurants, 3 bars, 2 pools, cable TV, archery, bicycles, horseback riding, tennis, disco, water sports. AE, MC, V. Expensive.*

Club Méditerranée. Everything but hard liquor is included in the price you pay for a stay in this 70-acre facility on the Punta Cana beach. Its air-conditioned, double-occupancy rooms are in three-story beach and coconut-grove lodgings, with twin beds and showers. There's a disco on the beach, plus the whole spectrum of Club Med activities, from archery to yoga. *Punta Cana, tel. 809/687–2767 or 800–CLUBMED; in NY 212/750–1670. 332 rooms. Facilities: 2 restaurants, bar, disco, pool, 14 tennis courts (6 lighted), golf driving range and putting green, archery, bocce ball, volleyball, boat rides, soccer, ping-pong, aerobics classes, water-sports center. AE, MC, V. Moderate.*

Samaná

Bahía Beach. On a cliff above the beach in one of the best game-fishing areas of the Caribbean, the Bahía offers air-conditioned rooms with ocean view on the mainland, plus fan-cooled cottages on Cayo Levantado, an offshore island. A favorite of young Dominicans, this is another all-inclusive resort. *Samaná Bay, tel. 809/685–6060. 85 rooms in the main hotel, 29 on the island. Facilities: restaurant, bar, pool, 2 tennis courts, disco, water sports. AE, MC, V. Inexpensive.*

★

Hotel Atlantis. There are only 10 rooms in this German-owned hotel in Las Terrenas, but each one is different—and the entire property has a refreshingly eccentric, informal air about it. Most of the spacious rooms overlook the sea; the proprietors stay up nights playing backgammon with their guests. Price includes breakfast. *Punta Bonita, Las Terrenas, tel. 809/586–3806. 10 rooms. Facilities: restaurant/bar. AE. Inexpensive.*

Jarabacoa
★

Hotel Hogar. Tasty home-cooked meals and very friendly staff add to the charm of this simple establishment right in the middle of town (only a block from the bus station). Look for the huge Montecarlo cigarette sign hanging out front. The rooms are spartan but serviceable, and come with their own mosquito netting. *Calle Mella 34, Jarabacoa, tel. 809/574–2739. 9 rooms. Facilities: restaurant. No credit cards. Inexpensive.*

The Arts and Nightlife

Check with your hotel and get a copy of the magazine *Vacation Guide* and the newspaper *Touring,* both of which are available free at the Tourist Office and at hotels, to find out what's happening around the island. Also look in the *Santo Domingo News* for listings of events.

Casinos Most of the casinos are concentrated in the larger hotels of Santo Domingo, but there are others here and there, and all offer blackjack, craps, and roulette. Casinos are open daily 3 PM–4 AM. You must be 18 to enter, and jackets are required. In Santo Domingo, the most popular casinos are in the **Dominican Concorde** (Calle Anacaona, tel. 809/562–8222), the **Jaragua** (Av. Independencia, tel. 809/686–2222), the **Embajador** (Av. Sarasota, tel. 809/533–2131), the **Gran Hotel Lina** (Av. Máximo Gómez, tel. 809/689–5185), the **Naco Hotel** (Av. Tiradentes 22, tel. 809/562–3100), and the **San Géronimo** (Av. Independencia 1067, tel. 809/533–8181).

12 Grenada

Grenada, a tiny island only 21 miles long and 12 miles wide, is bordered by dozens of beaches and secluded coves; crisscrossed by nature trails; and filled with spice plantations, tropical forests and select hotels clinging to hillsides overlooking the sea.

Known as the Isle of Spice, Grenada is a major producer of nutmeg, cinnamon, mace, cocoa, and many other common household spices. The pungent aroma of spices fills the air at the outdoor markets, where they're sold from large burlap bags; in the restaurants, where chefs believe in using them liberally; and in the pubs, where cinnamon and nutmeg are sprinkled on the rum punches. If the Irish hadn't beaten them to it, Grenada might have been called the Emerald Isle, for the lush pine forests and the thick brush on the hillsides give it a great, green beauty that few Caribbean islands duplicate.

Located in the Eastern Caribbean 90 miles north of Trinidad, Grenada is the most southerly of the Windward Islands. It is a nation composed of three inhabited islands and a few uninhabited islets: Grenada island is the largest, with 120 square miles and just under 100,000 people; Carriacou, 16 miles north of Grenada, is 13 square miles and has a population of 7,000; and Petit Martinique, 5 miles northeast of Carriacou, has 486 acres and a population of 600. Although Carriacou and Petit Martinique are popular for day trips and fishing and snorkeling excursions, most of the tourist action is on Grenada. Here, too, you will find the nation's capital, St. George's, and its largest harbor, St. George's Harbour.

Until 1983 when the United States/Eastern Caribbean invasion of Grenada catapulted this tiny nation into the forefront of international news, it was a relatively obscure island providing a quiet hideaway for those who love fishing, snorkeling, or simply lazing in the sun.

Today Grenada is back to normal, a safe and secure vacation spot with enough good shopping, restaurants, and pubs to make it a regular port of call for major cruise lines, and plenty of beaches and coves for those who want to scuba dive, snorkel, or just sit and stare at the waves.

Although Grenada's tourism industry is undergoing an expansion, it is a controlled expansion, counterbalanced by the island's West Indian flavor. No building can stand taller than a coconut palm, and new construction on the beaches must be at least 165 feet from the high-water mark. The hotels, resorts, and restaurants remain small and are mostly family-owned by people who get to know their guests and pride themselves on giving personalized service. They're typical of the islanders as a whole—friendly and hospitable.

Grenada was sighted by Columbus in 1498. Although he never stepped foot on the island, he nevertheless named it Concepción. Throughout the 17th century it was the scene of bloody battles between the indigenous Carib Indians and the French. The French finally captured the island in 1650, and lost it in 1762 to the British. This was the beginning of the seesaw of power between the two nations that became a familiar tale on many of the Windward Islands.

In 1967 Grenada became part of the British Commonwealth; seven years later it was granted total independence. The New Jewel Movement (NJM) seized power in 1979, formed the Peo-

Exploring

Dining

Lodging

Grenada

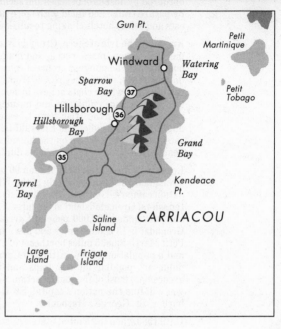

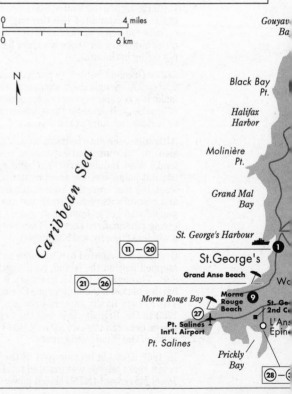

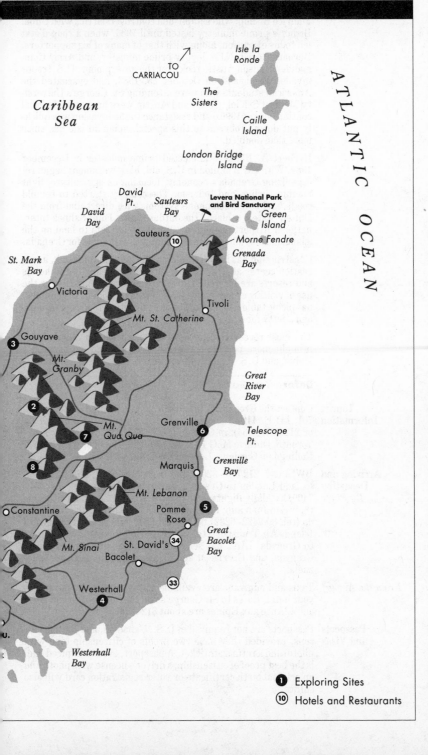

Isle la Ronde

The Sisters

Caille Island

ATLANTIC OCEAN

Caribbean Sea

TO CARRIACOU

London Bridge Island

David Pt.

David Bay

David Bay

St. Mark Bay

Sauteurs Bay

Levera National Park and Bird Sanctuary

Green Island

Sauteurs ⑩

Morne Fendre

Grenada Bay

Victoria

Tivoli

Mt. St. Catherine

❸ Gouyave

Mt. Granby

Great River Bay

❷

Mt. Qua Qua

Grenville ❻

Telescope Pt.

❼

Marquis

Grenville Bay

❽

Mt. Lebanon

Constantine

Pomme Rose ❺

Great Bacolet Bay

Mt. Sinai

St. David's ㉞

Bacolet

㉝

Westerhall ❹

Westerhall Bay

❶ Exploring Sites

⑩ Hotels and Restaurants

ple's Revolutionary Government, and named as prime minister Maurice Bishop, who established controversial ties with Cuba. Bishop's prime ministry lasted until 1983, when a coup d'état led to his execution, along with that of many of his supporters. Bernard Coard, NJM deputy prime minister, and Army Commander Hudson Austin took over the government. U.S. troops invaded the island on October 25, 1983, and evacuated the American students who were attending St. George's University Medical School. Coard and Austin were arrested (the trial continues as of 1990), and resistance to the invasion was quickly put down. Tourism to this special, splendid isle has since more than doubled.

Herbert A. Blaize was elected prime minister in December 1984. With $57.2 million in U.S. aid, his government began reorganizing Grenada's economy, focusing on agriculture, light manufacturing, and tourism. The country started to rebuild roads, and a new telephone system, with direct-dial from the United States, replaced the outdated one. Point Salines International Airport opened in 1984, enabling jets to land on the island and also allowing night landings, both firsts for Grenada.

Construction has been completed on Camerhogne Park, a recreation center at Grand Anse Bay, where many of the hotels and resorts are located. The park, designed primarily for the use of visiting cruise-ship passengers and resident Grenadians, has picnic tables, locker and shower facilities, food concessions, and a jetty for water taxis.

The most recent elections, which took place in March 1990, brought more peaceful progress to this island-nation with a stable, and U.S.-friendly government.

Before You Go

Tourist Information Contact the **Grenada Tourist Office:** in the United States (Suite 701, 141 E. 44th St., New York, NY 10017, tel. 800/638–9852, or 212/687–9554); in Canada (Suite 820, 439 University Ave., Toronto, Ontario M5G 1Y8, tel. 416/595–1339); or in Britain (1 Collingham Gardens, London SW5, tel. 1/370–516).

Arriving and Departing **BWIA** (tel. 212/581–3200) flies from New York, Miami, Toronto, and London to Grenada. **American Airlines** (tel. 800/334–7400) has daily flights from major U.S. and Canadian cities via their San Juan hub; **Pan Am** (tel. 800/421–5330), and **Air Canada** (tel. 800/422–6232) fly to Barbados, where **LIAT** (Leeward Islands Air Transport; tel. 809/462–0700) connects with flights to Grenada. LIAT has scheduled service between Barbados, Grenada, and Carriacou and also serves Trinidad and Venezuela.
By Plane

From the Airport Taxis and minivans are available at the airport to take you to your hotel. Rates to St. George's and the hotels of Grand Anse and L'Anse aux Epines are about $12–$14.

Passports and Visas Passports are not required of U.S., Canadian, and British citizens, provided they have two proofs of citizenship (one with photo) and a return air ticket. A passport, even an expired one, is the best proof of citizenship; a driver's license with photo *and* an original birth certificate or voter registration card will also suffice.

Customs and Duties You are allowed to bring into Grenada 200 cigarettes, 20 cigars, and 40 ounces of spirits.

If you're bringing in foreign-made articles, such as cameras, binoculars, and expensive timepieces, it's wise to keep the receipts with your travel documents. Otherwise, you may be charged duty when returning home.

Language English is the official language of Grenada.

Precautions Reasonable security with your personal property is a good idea. The only problem with walking late at night in the Grand Anse/L'Anse aux Epines (pronounced lance-au-peen) hotel districts is the lack of street lights (although 50 have recently been added). It's still dark enough to bump into things, maybe even into one of the cows that graze silently by the roadside. St. George's is equally safe.

Staying in Grenada

Important Addresses **Tourist Information:** The **Grenada Tourist Office** is located in St. George's (the Carenage, tel. 809/440–2001). It has maps, brochures, and information on accommodations, tours, and other services.

Emergencies **Police, Fire,** and **Ambulance:** In St. George's, Grand Anse, and L'Anse aux Epines, call 911. For other areas, check with your hotel.

Hospitals: St. George's Hospital (tel. 809/440–2051; 809/440–2052; 809/440–2053).

Pharmacies: Gittens (Halifax St., St. George's, tel. 809/440–2165); also Gittens Drug Mart (Grand Anse, tel. 809/444–4954).

Currency Grenada uses the Eastern Caribbean (E.C.) dollar. At press time, the exchange rate was E.C.$2.67 in banks to U.S.$1. Be sure to ask which currency is referred to when you make purchases and business transactions; prices are often quoted in E.C. Money can be exchanged at any bank or hotel. U.S. currency and traveler's checks are widely accepted. Most hotels and major restaurants accept credit cards. *Note:* Prices quoted here are in U.S. dollars unless indicated otherwise.

Taxes and Service Charges Hotels add an 8% government tax; restaurants add a 10% tax. The departure tax is E.C. $25.

Hotels and most restaurants add a 10% service charge to your bill. A 10%–15% gratuity should be added for a job well done.

Guided Tours **New Trend Tours** (Siesta Apartment Hotel, Grand Anse, tel. 809/444–1236) offers a wide selection of tours, as does **Arnold's Tours** (Siesta Apartment Hotel, Grand Anse, Tel. 809/444–1167). "Around the Island" is a 6½-hour trip up the west coast to a spice plantation at Gouyave, then to the Mascoll plantation house, Morne Fendue, for lunch. The return route is through the east-coast town of Grenville and across scenic St. David's Parish. The tour costs about $28 per person. The "Day Sail" tour includes a stop for swimming, snorkeling, and beachcombing in a deserted cove, plus lunch and rum punches, for $25. Deep-sea game-fishing expeditions cost about $20 per person, per hour, for a minimum of three hours. A day tour of the neighboring island of Carriacou includes air transportation, a barbecue lunch, and snorkeling for about $118 per person.

A number of car-rental agencies and tour operators in St. George's offer standard tours such as the "Royal Drive," which includes the town of St. George's; scenic Westerhall Point, across the island on the Atlantic; a small fishing village; a sugar-processing factory; and Grand Anse Beach. Agencies that offer such tours include **Otways Tours** (the Carenage, tel. 809/ 440–2558) and **Astral Tours and Travel** (the Carenage, tel. 809/440–5127). In Grand Anse, try **Carib Tours**, just south of the shopping center (tel. 809/444–4363 or 809/444–4364). **Henry's Tours** offers hiking trips for about $20 per person. Included are a trek to Fedon's Camp and an excursion to the Seven Sisters Falls (tel. 809/443–5313).

Getting Around Minivans ply the winding road between St. George's and Grand
Taxis Anse Beach, where many of the hotels are located. Hail one anywhere along the way, pay E.C.$1.25, and settle in for one of the most hair-raising rides of your life. Taxis are plentiful and rates are posted at the hotels and at the pier on the Carenage in St. George's. The trip from downtown to Grand Anse is about $6; from the airport to Grand Anse, about $12. Cabs are plentiful at all hotels, at the pier, and near the Tourist Office on the Carenage.

Rental Cars To rent a car, you will need a valid driver's license. Driving is on the left. Rental cars cost about $40 a day or $220 a week with unlimited mileage. Gas costs about $2.50 per gallon. Your hotel can arrange a rental for you. Car-rental agencies in St. George's include **David's** (Church St., tel. 809/440–2351), **Avis** at Spice Island Rentals (Paddock and Lagoon Rd., tel. 809/ 440–3936 or 809/444–4563), **MCR Car Rental** (Paddocks, 809/ 444–2832; after hours, 809/444–4486; 809/4405448 or 809/440– 5513), and **MacIntyre Brothers** (Young St., tel. 809/440–3316; 809/440–2514; after hours, 809/440–3428). In Grand Anse, try **Royston's** (tel. 809/444–4316 or 809/444–4592).

Telephones Telephone service on the island has much improved in the last
and Mail few years. Grenada can be dialed directly from the United States and Canada. Long-distance calls from Grenada must still be placed through hotel operators, but this is expected to change very soon.

Airmail rates for letters to the United States and Canada are E.C. $.90 for a half-ounce letter and E.C. $.60 for a postcard.

Opening and Store hours are generally from 8–noon and 1–4 weekdays; 8–
Closing Times noon, Saturday; they are closed Sunday. Banks are open weekdays 8–noon.

Beaches

Grenada has some 80 miles of coastline, 65 bays, and 45 white-sand beaches, many with secluded little coves. All the beaches are public and within an easy cab ride of St. George's. Most are located on the Caribbean, south of St. George's in the Grand Anse and L'Anse aux Epines areas, where most of the hotels are clustered. Virtually every hotel, apartment complex, and residential area has its own beach or tiny cove.

The loveliest and most popular beach is **Grand Anse,** about a 10-minute taxi ride from St. George's. It's a gleaming, 2-mile curve of sand and clear, gentle surf. At its southern end is a palm-covered point; to the north you can see the narrow mouth of St. George's Harbour and the pastel houses on the hillsides above it. The sunset is particularly beautiful at Grand Anse—enjoy it over cocktails at Spice Island Inn, where tables line the beach.

Levera National Park and Bird Sanctuary is at the northern tip of the island where the Caribbean meets the Atlantic. The first of the Grenadines is visible in the distance. The surf is rougher here than on the Caribbean beaches, but it is great for body surfing or watching the waves roll in. In 1990, this area, with its thick mangroves for food and protection, became an official sanctuary for nesting seabirds and seldom-seen tropical parrots.

Morne Rouge Beach is on the Caribbean side, about 1 mile south of Grand Anse Bay and 3 miles south of St. George's Harbour. The beach forms a ½-mile-long crescent and has a gentle surf excellent for swimming. A small café serves light meals during the day. In the evening, there's the disco, Fantazia 2001 (*see* Nightlife, below).

Exploring Grenada

Numbers in the margin correspond with points of interest on the Grenada map.

St. George's
❶

Grenada's capital city and major port is one of the most picturesque and truly West Indian towns in the Caribbean. Pastel warehouses cling to the curving shore along the horseshoe-shape Carenage, the harborside thoroughfare; rainbow-colored houses rise above it and disappear into the green hills. A walking tour of St. George's can be made in about two hours, particularly with the help of the Department of Tourism's free brochure, *Historical Walking Tour of St. George's*, which directs you to 21 points of historical interest. Pick it up.

Start on the **Carenage**, a walkway along St. George's Harbour and the town's main thoroughfare. Ocean liners dock at the pier at the eastern end, and the **Delicious Landing** restaurant (tel. 809/440–3948), with outdoor tables, is at the western end. In between are the **post office**, the **public library**, a number of small **shops**, the **Grenada Tourist Office**, and two more good restaurants, **Rudolf's** and the **Nutmeg** (*see* Dining, below), boasting a huge open window that provides a great view of the harbor.

You can reach the **Grenada National Museum** by walking along the west end of the Carenage and taking Young Street west to Monckton Street. The museum has a small, interesting collection of ancient and colonial artifacts and recent political memorabilia. *Young and Monckton Sts., no phone. Admission: 50¢ adults, 10¢ children. Open weekdays 9–3.*

Nearby are **York House** on Church Street (now the Supreme Court building) and the **Registry**, both built around 1800. Since both are used as public buildings, visits are unstructured. *Church and Young Sts., no phone. Admission free. Open weekdays 9–3:45.*

Walk west along Young Street, turn left on Cross Street, and you'll reach the **Esplanade**, the thoroughfare that runs along the ocean side of town. In the middle of the Esplanade you'll find **Grencraft**, the National Handicrafts Center (tel. 809/440–

2655), where local goods are sold. Also on the Esplanade, where Cross Street intersects, is a branch of the **Yellow Pouri Art Gallery** (tel. 809/440–3878), which keeps irregular hours. The main gallery, on Halifax Street (tel. 809/440–3001) is the larger of these two sister studios, which display art from Grenada, Jamaica, Trinidad, Guyana, and canvases by British, German, and French artists now living here. On the nearby Esplanade is a row of tiny shops that sell such treats as guava jelly (a soft candy) and coconut fudge. *Shopping hours: weekdays 8– noon and 1–4, Sat. 8–noon; closed Sun.*

Take the Esplanade north to Granby Street and turn right. Granby Street will take you to **Market Square,** which comes alive every Saturday morning from 8 to noon with vendors selling baskets and fresh produce, including tropical fruit you can eat on the spot.

Walk back on Granby Street to Halifax Street and turn left. At the intersection of Halifax and Church streets is **St. Andrew's Presbyterian Church,** built in 1830. Follow Church Street east to Gore Street, to **St. George's Anglican Church,** built in 1828. It's lined with plaques representing Grenada in the 18th and 19th centuries. **St. George's Methodist Church,** built in 1820, is on a hill a few blocks north, on Green Street near Tyrrel Street.

Take Tyrrel Street west to the corner of Park Lane to see the **Marryshow House.** Built in 1917, it combines Victorian and West Indian architecture. The Marryshow also houses the **Marryshow Folk Theatre,** Grenada's first cultural center. Plays, West Indian dance and music, and poetry readings are presented here on occasion. *Tyrrel St., near Bain Alley, tel. 809/440– 2451. Admission free. Open weekdays 10–4.*

Head west on Tyrrel Street and turn left onto Church Street. **Fort George** is at the southern tip of Church Street. The fort, rising above the point that separates the harbor from the ocean, was built by the French in 1708. The inner courtyard now houses the police headquarters. *Church St., no phone. Outer courtyard open to the public. Admission free. Open daily during daylight hours.*

The fastest way from the Carenage to the Esplanade is through the **Sendall Tunnel,** slightly north of Fort George. Take it if you're too tired to walk up the steep hill.

The West Coast The coast road north from St. George's winds past soaring mountains and valleys covered with banana and breadfruit trees, palms, bamboo, and tropical flowers. You can drive to
② **Concord Falls,** about 8 miles north of St. George's, and then hike 2 miles to the main falls, and another hour to a second, spectacular waterfall. About 15 minutes farther north is the town of **Gouyave,** center of the nutmeg industry.

③ **Dougaldston Estate,** near the entrance to the town, has a spice factory where you can see cocoa, nutmeg, mace, cloves, cinnamon, and other spices in their natural state, laid out on giant trays to dry in the sun. Old women walk barefoot through the spices, shuffling them so they dry evenly. *Gouyave, no phone. Admission free. Open weekdays 9–4.*

Time Out For lunch take the short drive to Betty Mascoll's old plantation house, **Morne Fendue** (St. Patrick's Parish, tel. 809/440–9330). The large, two-story house was built by Mrs. Mascoll's father in 1912 of hand-chiseled, colored stones mortared with lime and molasses. Outside, poinsettias grow in profusion; inside, amid Victorian antiques and dainty lace curtains, Mrs. Mascoll serves superb West Indian cuisine and one of the best rum punches on the island.

The East Coast Start your tour at **Westerhall**, a residential area about 5 miles
❹ southeast of St. George's, known for its beautiful villas, gardens, and panoramic views. From here, take a dirt road north
❺ to **Grand Bacolet Bay,** a jagged peninsula on the Atlantic where the surf pounds against deserted beaches. Some miles north
❻ is **Grenville,** the island's second-largest city. From here you can watch schooners set sail for the outer islands. As in St. George's, Saturday is market day, and the town fills with local people doing their shopping for the week. Cooking enthusiasts may want to see the town's spice-processing factory, which is open to the public.

If you take the interior route back to St. George's, you'll fully appreciate the lush, mountainous nature of the island. There is only one paved road that cuts across the island. Leaving Grenville and heading for St. George's, you'll wind upward through the rain forest until you're surrounded by mist, then you'll descend onto the sunny hillsides. In the middle of the island is
❼ **Grand Etang National Park.** The lake, in the crater of an extinct volcano, is a 13-acre glasslike expanse of cobalt-blue water. The area is a bird sanctuary and forest reserve, where you can go fishing and hiking. *Main interior rd., halfway between Grenville and St. George's, tel. 809/440–7425. Open Mon.–Sat. 8–4.*

❽ Another place to stop is **Annandale Falls and Visitors' Centre,** where a mountain stream cascades 50 feet into a pool surrounded by such exotic tropical flora as liana vines and elephant ears. This, too, is a good swimming and picnic spot. *Main interior rd., 15 min east of St. George's, tel. 809/440–2542. Open Mon.–Sat. 8–4.*

Grand Anse and Most of the island's hotels and its nightlife are in Grand Anse or
the South End the adjacent community of L'Anse aux Epines, which means Cove of Pines. Here you will find one of the two campuses of **St.**
❾ **George's University Medical School.**

The second campus is in **True Blue,** a residential area near L'Anse aux Epines. To reach it, take Grand Anse Road south toward the airport and turn left just before you reach the airport. Although the road is unnamed, it is the only road off Grand Anse Road.

The **Grand Anse Shopping Centre** has a supermarket/liquor store, a clothing store, shoe store, and several small gift shops with quality souvenirs and such luxury items as English china and Swedish crystal *(see* Shopping, below). Prices are competitive with duty-free shops elsewhere in the Caribbean.

Grenada's **Carriacou, Petit Martinique,** and a handful of uninhabited
Grenadines specks that comprise the nation of Grenada are north of Grenada island and part of the Grenadines, a chain of 32 tiny islands and cays.

Carriacou's colonial history parallels Grenada's; its tiny size has restricted its political role to a minor part in the area's history. It, too, is verdant and mountainous. A chain of hills cuts a wide swath through its center, from Gun Point in the north to Tyrrel Bay in the south. LIAT has daily flights to and from Grenada island, and schooners leave from St. George's Harbour twice a week. Hillsborough is the main town. In August, the Carriacou Regatta attracts yachts and sailing vessels from throughout the Caribbean.

Five miles northeast of Carriacou is Petit Martinique, the smallest of Grenada's inhabited islands. Like Carriacou and Grenada, Petit Martinique was settled by the French.

Grenada for Free

A good way to spend an afternoon without spending money is to watch fishing boats of all sizes and descriptions pull in and out of St. George's Harbour. On Tuesday afternoons you can watch the boats being loaded with crates and bags of fruit and vegetables bound for Trinidad. It's also fun to roam through the Saturday markets in St. George's and Grenville, which are ablaze with color and humming with activity. Farm women sitting under umbrellas sell bananas, papayas, oranges, yams, plantains, exotic roots and vegetables, and fresh spices; ask the women for their permission before grabbing a photo opportunity. At the nearby fish market, just a short stroll down the Esplanade, you can see the day's catch on display.

Participant Sports

Fishing
Deep-sea fishing around Grenada is excellent, with marlin, tuna, yellowfin, and dolphin topping the list of good catches. The annual **Game Fishing Tournament** is held in mid-January. Half-day and full-day excursions are available, plus tours to Sandy Island, Carriacou, and the Grenadines. Contact **Capt. Terry Lampert** (tel. 809/444–4657 or 809/440–2508) to set sail on one of his two fishing boats, the 30-foot *Royal Chappy* and the 41-foot *Free Spirit*.

Golf
The Grenada Golf and Country Club in Grand Anse (tel. 809/ 444–4244) has a nine-hole golf course that charges very low rates; your hotel will make arrangements for you.

Sailing, Diving, and Snorkeling
The Moorings (tel. 800/535–7289 in the United States; 800/633– 7348 in Canada) has recently taken over Secret Harbour on the southeast shore, added some of its finest charter yachts, and combined Shore 'n' Sail programs developed by America's cup racer Steve Colgate for beginning and experienced sailors.

You can rent 30- to 40-foot yachts, with or without crew, from **Go Vacations** at the Spice Island Marine Services (tel. 809/440– 3670; from the United States, 800/387–3998). Diving in this area is excellent, with visibility as much as 200 feet. Hundreds of varieties of fish and more than 40 species of coral await underwater explorers. Snorkeling can cost as little as $5 per person, per day, including equipment. A superb spot for scuba diving is at the site of the largest shipwreck in the Caribbean, the *Bianca C*, a cruise ship that caught fire and sank in 1961. It settled in waters more than 100 feet deep and is now home to giant turtles, spotted eagle rays with 15-foot wing spans, and a 350-pound grouper that lives in the ship's smokestack.

The **HMC Diving Centre** at Grand Anse Beach (at Spice Island Inn, tel. 809/444–4258; Ramada Renaissance, tel. 809/444–4372; and Coyaba, tel. 809/444–4129) and **World Wide Water Sports** (at Grand Anse, tel. 809/444–4371) both offer a variety of scuba courses, as well as certification for novices. HMC Diving Centre also takes expert divers to the reefs and shipwrecks.

Swimming Take your pick from Grenada's 45 beaches and secluded coves, but don't miss Grand Anse Beach. **Commodore Peter,** on Grand Anse Beach in front of Spice Island Inn (tel. 809/444–4258), will take you in his boat to a deserted island where he and his wife will prepare a delicious barbecue lunch while you swim, snorkel, or sunbathe.

Other Water Sports The major hotels on Grand Anse Beach have water-sports centers where you can rent small sailboats, Windsurfers, and Sunfish equipment. The centers are located in front of the hotels. Your hotel can make arrangements for you, or you can call one of the major hotels for information.

Tennis Several hotels have tennis courts that are free to their guests, including **Calabash** (tel. 809/444–4234), **Secret Harbour** (tel. 809/444–4548), **Coyaba** (tel. 809/444–4129), **Spice Island Inn** (tel. 809/444–4258), **Ramada Renaissance** (tel. 809/444–4371), and **Twelve Degrees North** (tel. 809/444–4580). If there are no courts where you're staying, you can play at some private clubs on the island. Two that accept guests are **Richmond Hill Tennis Club** (tel. 809/440–2537) in Richmond Hill, a suburb of St. George's, and **Tanteen Tennis Club** (tel. 809/440–3010) in St. George's. Your hotel desk clerk can contact them for you.

Shopping

The best souvenirs in Grenada are little spice baskets filled with cinnamon, nutmeg, mace, bay leaf, vanilla, and ginger. You can find them in practically every shop. Vendors who stroll the beach in Grand Anse also sell spice baskets as well as fabric dolls, T-shirts, hats, fans, and visors woven from green palm, and black-coral jewelry. Shops are open weekdays 8–4. Many are closed noon–1. Saturday hours are 8–noon. Shops are closed Sunday.

Good Buys The sister galleries of **Yellow Pouri** I on Halifax St.; II on Cross
St. George's St.) offer the most serious art finds, with canvases from Grenada, Jamaica, Guyana, Trinidad, and offerings by overseas artists who have settled here. Prices range from $2 to $2,000 in this excellent creation by James and Corry Rudin. In a less serious mood, **Noah's Arcade** (Gore St., tel. 809/440–2482) has prints of island scenes, books, and handmade necklaces for a pittance. **Grencraft,** the **National Handicrafts Centre** (Melville St. at the Esplanade, tel. 809/440–2655), sells locally made furniture, black- and white-coral jewelry, and jewelry made from tortoise shells; crafts of wood, wicker, straw, and fabrics; and T-shirts, postcards, local juices, preserves, candy, and sauces. **Spice Island Perfumes** on the Carenage (tel. 809/440–2006) is a treasure trove of local perfumes, body oils, natural extracts of spices and herbs, shampoos, suntan oils and lotions, teas, spices, and some nice batiks, and hand-screened T-shirts. **Sea Change,** also on the Carenage (tel. 809/440–2056), carries

books, magazines, postcards, stamps, film, paintings, and prints.

Grand Anse In Grand Anse, the **Grand Anse Shopping Centre** houses **The Gift Shop,** an outlet for such luxury items as watches, leather goods, fine jewelry, imported crystal and china, and framed prints, all at competitive prices. The center also has a clothing boutique for children and adults, with sportswear, novelty T-shirts, bathing suits, and some English wool sweaters; a record shop; and a shoe store.

Heading toward the village of St. Paul's, the **Comahogne Gallery** on the main road is the studio-home of sculptor John Pivott.

Dining

Unlike most Caribbean islands that have a scarcity of fresh produce, Grenada has everything from cabbages and tomatoes to bananas, mangoes, papaya (called pawpaw), plantains, melons, callaloo (similar to spinach), breadfruits, oranges, tangerines, limes, christophines (similar to squash), and avocados—the list is endless. In addition, fresh seafood of all kinds, including lobster and oyster, is also plentiful. Conch, known here as lambi, is very popular and appears on most menus in some form. Be sure to try one of the exotic ice creams made from avocado or nutmeg. Almost all the Grenadian restaurants serve local dishes, which are varied enough to be continually interesting.

Rum punches are served everywhere, but no two places make them exactly alike. The local beer, Carib, is also very popular.

The most highly recommended restaurants are indicated by a star ★ .

Category	Cost*
Expensive	$40–$60
Moderate	$20–$40
Inexpensive	under $20

per person, excluding drinks, service, and sales tax (10%)

★ **The Calabash.** The open-air restaurant here is small and pretty, surrounded by palms and tropical flowers. Try the callaloo soup. There is a fixed-price dinner and menu each evening. *L'Anse aux Epines, tel. 809/444–4234. Reservations suggested. AE, MC, V. Expensive.*
  Secret Harbour Hotel. This open-air restaurant is at the most elegant hotel on the island. Decorated in Spanish tile and red brick, it is cooled by the breezes of Mt. Hartman Bay. Allow time for cocktails or a nightcap in the cozy lounge. There is usually a fixed menu for dinner. *L'Anse aux Epines, tel. 809/444–4439 or 809/444–4548. Reservations suggested. AE, MC, V. Expensive.*
★ **Red Crab.** This establishment is a favorite meeting and eating spot (especially on Saturday nights) where guests dine in a relaxed pub or outside under trees and stars. The accent is on fresh seafood, local lobster in particular, but their spicy chicken and grilled meats are worth a try. Hot garlic bread comes with all orders. *L'Anse aux Epines (near the Calabash Hotel),*

tel. 809/444–4424. Lunch and dinner daily. AE, MC, V. Expensive.

★ **Spice Island Inn.** The dining room, open on three sides, is just a few steps from the beach. The Wednesday-night Grenadian buffet is exceptional and a great way to sample the various types of local seafood and salads. *Grand Anse, tel. 809/444– 4258 or 444–4423. Reservations required late Dec.–mid-Apr. AE, MC, V. Expensive.*

★ **La Belle Creole.** This restaurant is truly elegant and exceptional, both for its creative nouvelle West Indian cuisine and for the wraparound hilltop view of St. George's. Dishes change (both for lunch and dinner), but a few of the specialities are an appetizer made from Grenadian caviar (roe of the white sea urchin) and the lobster-egg flan. Entrées might be stuffed baked rainbow runner, Creole saffron pork chops, or lobster à la Creole. The Sunday barbecue features many of the delicate dishes and live entertainment. *Blue Horizons Cottage Hotel, Morne Rouge, St. George's, tel. 809/444–4316. Reservations required for nonhotel guests. AE, MC, V. Expensive.*

Balisier. You can dine poolside here on a large terrace that offers a sweeping view of St. George's. Dinner focuses on local specialties, such as shrimp Creole; curried or stewed lobster; lambi (conch); and fresh fish, which may be ordered broiled, poached, steamed, or fried, and with curry, white wine, or calypso sauces. *Richmond Hill, St. George's, tel. 809/440–2346. Reservations suggested. MC, V. Moderate.*

★ **Betty Mascoll's Great House.** Although it's a one-hour drive from St. George's, this restaurant is definitely worth the trip. The owner, Mrs. Mascoll, serves only lunch—and what a lunch! The buffet usually includes her legendary pepperpot, a stew of pork, oxtail, and other meats. The rum punches are among the best on the island. *St. Patrick's Parish, near Sauteurs, tel. 809/ 440–9330. Reservations required. No credit cards. Moderate.*

The Bird's Nest. This is a Chinese restaurant serving excellent food in a very relaxed setting. *Next to the Grand Anse Shopping Centre, tel. 809/444–4264. AE, MC, V. Moderate.*

The Boatyard. Smack in the middle of a marina, this restaurant is a lively place, filled with embassy personnel and expatriates. Lunches include burgers, fish and chips, and deep-fried shrimp. Dinner features club steaks, lobster, and different types of meat and seafood brochettes. In season (late Dec.–mid-Apr.) there's a steel band on Saturday night, jazz on Sunday, and disco music on Friday night. *L'Anse aux Epines, tel. 809/444– 4662. MC, V. Moderate.*

Coconut's Beach. Better known as "The French Restaurant," this cozy spot is set in a pretty Creole-style house on the beach, with tables of varying shapes and sizes set on the sand. Local cuisine is served with flair and with a French touch. In season, you can enjoy barbecues and listen to steel bands. It's also open for breakfast. *Grand Anse, tel. 809/444–4644. Reservations suggested. No credit cards. Moderate.*

Delicious Landing. This very informal place sits at the end of the Carenage overlooking the water. The menu includes seafood fritters, salads, lobster served a half-dozen different ways, barbecued chicken, sukiyaki, and some vegetarian specialties. *The Carenage, St. George's, tel. 809/440–3948. MC, V. Moderate.*

★ **Mama's.** This restaurant is more like a diner, West Indian style and very charming. There are no menus, and one of Mama's daughters will set before you whatever specialties Mama has cooked—probably some roast turtle, fried chicken, lobster salad, christophine salad, cabbage salad, or fried plantain. You will not leave hungry. *Lagoon Rd., St. George's, tel. 809/440–1459. Reservations required. No credit cards. Moderate.*

The Nutmeg. Fresh seafood is the specialty of this second-floor restaurant that has a great view of the harbor. Try the grilled turtle steaks. *The Carenage, St. George's, tel. 809/440–2539. Informal. AE, MC, V.*

Ristorante Italia. True to its name, this restaurant features delicious pizza, pasta, and other Italian dishes. Located above Spice Island Perfumes shop, the restaurant has broad windows overlooking scenic St. George's Harbour. *The Carenage, St. George's, tel. 809/440–3986. No credit cards. Moderate.*

Rudolf's. This informal, publike place offers both West Indian cuisine (crab back and lobster salad are specialties) and some Asian dishes such as Tung Po (breaded pork chops with honey, peaches, and rice). Try the cold tomato-and-orange soup. *The Carenage, St. George's. Closed Sun. No credit cards. Moderate.*

The St. James Hotel. This genteel old hotel was a private home 100 years ago. Its restaurant serves satisfying Grenadian cuisine on white linen tablecloths set with antique Sheffield silver. The chutney alone makes this restaurant worth a visit. *Lagoon Rd., St. George's, tel. 809/440–2041 or 809/440–2042. Reservations recommended. No credit cards. Moderate.*

Tropicana. You can dine on the terrace or in a small dining room here and enjoy an extensive list of both Chinese and West Indian specialties. Open for both lunch and dinner, it serves massive portions. The Tropicana also provides take-out service. *Lagoon Rd., St. George's, tel. 809/440–1586. AE, MC, V. Moderate.*

Lodging

Grenada's accommodations range from simply furnished kitchenette suites to suites representing Caribbean-style elegance. There are no pretentious hotels—Grenada is a simple place and its hotels have been furnished in "casual tropical" decor. Most of the hotels are owned and operated by Grenadians; those that aren't are usually run by British or American expatriates who thrive on the simplicity of Grenadian life. The hotels tend to be small (10 to 20 rooms in most cases), but they exude a sense of intimacy, with friendly managers or owners.

For confirmation on reservations at any of the 24 members of the **Grenada Hotel Association,** call, in the United States or Canada, 800/223–9815; in New York State, 212/545–8469.

During the winter season, some hotels offer MAP (Modified American Plan, two meals daily). Prices for the summer are discounted by 20% to 40%.

The most highly recommended lodgings are indicated by a star ★.

Category	Cost*
Very Expensive	over $200
Expensive	$150–$200

Moderate	$100–$150
Inexpensive	under $100

*All prices are for a standard double room for two, excluding
8% tax and a 10% service charge.*

Hotels   **The Calabash.** This all-suite hotel is set on a wide green lawn
Grenada overlooking a curved beach, a yacht harbor, and charter-boat
★   anchorage in Prickly Bay, L'Anse aux Epines. The deluxe
suites have their own private swimming pool. *Box 382, St.
George's, tel. 809/444–4234. 32 suites. Facilities: restaurant,
beach bar, pool, water-sports center, tennis. In season, MAP
only. AE, MC, V. Very Expensive.*

★   **Secret Harbour.** The Moorings (which specializes in sailing vacations) has taken over this deluxe resort, and it seems to be a
good match. The hotel has oversize rooms tucked into
Mediterranean-style villas on a bluff overlooking Mt. Hartman
Bay. Inside this proper property, it's four o'clock tea on the
veranda. Outside, yachts dock at the door (all with professional
crew), ready for a day at sea, or, if you opt for the hotel's
Club Mariner plans, four nights ashore and three cruising
the offshore islands. *Suite 402, 1305 U.S. 19 South, Clear-
water, Fl, 34624, tel. 800/535–7289 in U.S.; 813/535–1446 in
Florida; 800/633–7348 in Canada. 20 rooms. Facilities: restaurant, lounge, tennis, beach with bar, pool, sailboats (day
sailers, bareboat to crewed). Major credit cards. Very Expensive.*

★   **Spice Island Inn.** The suites here are sumptuous, each with a
supersized interior whirlpool and/or, a spa-Jacuzzi, or a 16- by
20-foot private swimming pool inside a walled garden. There's
over 1,600 feet of sprawling beach with sea-grape trees for
shade and small tables for afternoon tea. The rooms are well
decorated in soft pastels, with telephones, minibars, and
miniregfrigerators. *Bos 6, Grand Anse, St. George's, tel. 809/
444–4258 or 809/444–4423. 56 suites. Facilities: tennis courts,
water-sports center, restaurant, lounge, 2 boutiques, entertainment most nights, 9-hole golf course nearby. AE, MC, V.
Very Expensive.*

Horse Shoe Beach Hotel. Really a cluster of six Spanish-style
villas, this hotel clings to a hillside overlooking a small beach
and a pool. Each suite is furnished with antiques and giant, mahogany four-poster beds, fit for royalty. All the villas have
private patios and a kitchen in an outdoor courtyard where a
maid prepares breakfast each morning. *Box 174, St. George's,
tel. 809/444–4410 or 809/444–4244. 18 suites. Facilities: pool,
restaurant, lounge. AE, MC, V. Expensive.*

Ramada Renaissance Hotel. Since Ramada took over this resort, formerly the Grenada Beach Hotel, it has spent $15
million on renovation. It is the island's largest hotel and is
noted for its efficient, friendly service. All rooms have king-
size or extra-large beds and satellite TVs. *Box 441, Grand
Anse, St. George's, tel. 809/444–4371. 186 rooms, including 2
luxury suites. Facilities: 2 restaurants, lounge, pool, tennis,
hair dryers in rooms. AE, DC, MC, V. Expensive.*

Twelve Degrees North. Six apartments, with one and two bedrooms, sit atop a hill that slopes to a swimming pool and,
beyond that, a small beach that's good for snorkeling. Each
apartment is stocked with food staples, which are billed to you
at cost; a staff member is on hand to drive you to the supermar-

ket if you want to buy more food. There's no restaurant on the premises, but a maid prepares breakfast and lunch for you in your apartment. The complex is within walking distance or a short cab ride to the restaurants of Grand Anse and L'Anse aux Epines. Children under 12 are not allowed. A minimum stay of one week is required during high season. *Box 241, L'Anse aux Epines, St. George's, tel. 809/444–4580. 6 apartments. Facilities: pool, tennis, sailing dinghy for rent. No credit cards. Expensive.*

Blue Horizons Cottage Hotel. This comfortable hotel is set among the palms around a large, sunny lawn and swimming pool on 6½ acres. Grand Anse Beach is a six-minute walk down the hill, where their sister hotel, the Spice Island Inn, sprawls along 1,600 feet of beach. Water sports are free for guests at either hotel, with exchanging dining invitations and alternate-evening entertainment. *Box 41, Grand Anse, St. George's, tel. 809/444–4316 or 809/444–4592. 32 suites with terraces. Facilities: restaurant, 2 bars, lounge, pool. AE, MC, V. Moderate.*

Coral Cove. Secluded and serene, this hotel has cottages with one and two bedrooms, all with views of the sea, offshore islands, and the mountains. The nearby beach is excellent for snorkeling. *Box 187, St. George's, tel. 809/444–4217. 18 cottages. Facilities: pool, tennis courts. MC, V. Moderate.*

★ **Coyaba.** *Coyaba* means "heaven" in the Arawak Indian language. Guests will agree that the name is an apt one for this beachfront hotel. All the rooms have patios, satellite TVs, radios, telephones, and hair dryers. *Box 336, Grand Anse, St. George's, tel. 809/444–4129. 40 rooms. Facilities: pool with swim-up bar, tennis courts, water-sports center, restaurant, bar, lounge. AE, DC, MC, V. Moderate.*

Gem Apartments. Furnishings here are basic, but the one- and two-bedroom apartments on Morne Rouge Beach are spacious and comfortable, and all are air-conditioned. On the premises is the popular Fantazia 2001 disco, Sur La Mer restaurant, and Aquarius beach bar. *Gems BBC Ltd., Morne Rouge, St. George's, tel. 809/444–4224; 809/443–5536. 4 2-bedroom, 12 1-bedroom apartments. Facilities: disco, restaurant, beach bar. AE, DC, MC, V. Inexpensive.*

La Sagesse Nature Centre. Set on a bay 10 miles from Point Salines Airport, the center has a guest house with basic but spacious rooms. There's an old sugar mill and rum distillery at the entrance. Mangroves, a salt-pond bird sanctuary, and hiking trails provide a peaceful, unspoiled setting. *Box 44, St. David's, tel. 809/444–6458. 5 rooms. Facilities: restaurant, bar, art gallery. MC, V. Inexpensive.*

No Problem Apartment Hotel. "No problem" might refer to the convenient location of this small apartment complex just 1 mile from the airport, 2 miles from Grand Anse, and within walking distance of several deserted Point Salines beaches. Each apartment has twin beds, a sofa bed, well-equipped kitchen, TV, and telephone. Laundry service is provided. *Box 280, St. George's, tel. 809/444–4336. 20 suites. Facilities: pool, terrace restaurant, honor bar, barbecue, open kitchen, 14 bicycles. AE, DC, MC, V. Inexpensive.*

★ **The St. James Hotel.** This 100-year-old former private home has been a hotel since 1950. It's on the west end of St. George's, on a hill between the Carenage and the Esplanade, and is a gracious retreat amidst the bustle of town. There's shuttle-bus service to Grand Anse Beach. *Grand Etang Rd., St. George's, tel. 809/440–2041. 16 rooms, most with private bath; some share bath* *with adjoining room. Facilities: restaurant. MC, V. Inexpensive.*

Carriacou   **Cassada Bay Resort.** Set in a peaceful atmosphere, this resort has a panaromic view of the ocean. Privacy is the byword here. *Carriacou, tel. 809/443–7494. 18 suites with veranda. Facilities: restaurant, bar, water-sports center. AE, DC, MC, V. Inexpensive.*

Prospect Lodge. Located on the leeward coast of Carriacou, the lodge overlooks the Caribbean and provides a quiet setting for those who want to enjoy the beach and the sun. *Prospect, Carriacou, tel. 809/443–7380. 10 apartments. Facilities: restaurant, water sports. AE, DC, MC, V. Inexpensive.*

Silver Beach Resort. This 18-room hotel is tucked away on stretches of pristine beach on Carriacou, Grenada's sister isle. Totally refurbished, all rooms have private patios and ocean views. *Silver Beach, Carriacou, tel. 809/443–7337. 18 rooms, some self-contained apartments with kitchenettes. Facilities: snorkeling, windsurfing, spearfishing, tennis, day trip to offshore islets. AE, MC, V. Inexpensive.*

Villa and Private-Home Rentals   Two local agencies handle rentals of villas and private homes: **Bain and Bertrand Realtors** (Lagoon Rd., St. George's, tel. 809/440–2848) and **Grenada Property Management** (Melville St., St. George's, 809/440–1896). In-season rates range from about $600 a week for a two-bedroom home with a pool to about $3,500 for a six-bedroom home on the beach.

Nightlife

Grenada's nightlife centers on the hotel lounges and bars. During winter, many of the hotel lounges have steel, reggae, and pop bands in the evenings. **Spice Island Inn, The Calabash, Coyaba,** the **Ramada Renaissance,** and (on Wednesday for "jazz night") the **Village Hotel** are among the most lively (*see* Lodging, above). Check with your hotel or the Tourist Information Office to find out where various bands are performing on a given night.

Fantazia 2001 is a popular disco on Morne Rouge Beach where soca, reggae, and cadance are local steps, in addition to international tapes. Small cover charge on Friday and Saturday nights. *Gem Apartments premises, Morne Beach, tel. 809/444–4224. No cover or minimum.*

Club Paradise offers nightly entertainment that varies from sporting events on big-screen TV via satellite to a Wednesday Ladies' Night. *Lance aux Epines.*

Le Sucrier has reopened in the Sugar Mill on Wednesday, Thursday, Friday, and Saturday nights from 9 PM to 3 AM, with live jazz on Thursday and "oldies" night on Wednesday. *Grand Anse round-about.*

Friday night only is "the" night at the **Boatyard Restaurant and Bar,** from 11 PM till sunup, with international discs spun by a smooth-talkin' local DJ. *Lance aux Epines beach in the Marina.*

13 Guadeloupe

by Honey Naylor   It's a steamy hot Saturday in mid-August. There may be a tropical depression brewing somewhere to the west. It's that time
of year. But the mood in Pointe-à-Pitre, Guadeloupe's commercial center, is anything but depressing. Although Hurricane
Hugo swept full force onto the island of Guadeloupe in October
1989, a massive effort put the island back together so that by
December 1989 most hotels were fully operational. Now, amid
music and laughter, women adorned with gold jewelry and the
traditional madras and foulard parade through the streets.
Balanced on their heads are huge baskets decorated with miniature kitchen utensils and filled with mangoes, papayas,
breadfruits, christophines, and other island edibles. The procession wends its way to the Cathédrale de St-Pierre et St-Paul
where a high mass is celebrated. A five-hour feast with music,
song, and dance will follow.

The *Fête des Cuisinières* (Cooks' Festival) takes place annually
in honor of St. Laurent, patron saint of cooks. The parading
cuisinières are the island's women chefs, an honored group.
This festival gives you a tempting glimpse of one of Guadeloupe's stellar attractions—its cuisine. The island's more than
100 restaurants serve some of the best food in all of the Caribbean.

But there is more here than meets the palate. Night owls and
nature enthusiasts, hikers and bikers, scuba divers, sailors,
mountain climbers, beachcombers, and hammock potatoes all
can indulge themselves in Guadeloupe. Driving around the
island is the best way to fully appreciate the diversity of Guadeloupe.

Sugar, not tourism, is Guadeloupe's primary source of income.
As a result, the island's attractions are less commercialized
than those of neighboring isles. However, Guadeloupe is anxious to pull in a larger share of the tourist trade, and each year
more field workers opt for jobs in resorts and restaurants. Still,
at harvesttime in late January, the fields teem with workers
cutting the sugarcane, and the roads are clogged with trucks
taking the cane to distilleries. French is the official language
here. But even if your tongue twirls easily around a few French
phrases, you will sometimes receive a bewildered response.
The Guadeloupeans' Creole patois greatly affects their French
pronunciation. However their friendliness allows for repeated
attempts at communication, so that eventually you'll be understood. If not, don't despair—most hotels and many of the
restaurants have some English-speaking staff.

Guadeloupe looks like a giant butterfly resting on the sea between Antigua and Dominica. Its two wings—Basse-Terre and
Grande-Terre—are the two largest islands in the 659-square-
mile Guadeloupe archipelago, which includes the little offshore
islands of Marie-Galante, La Désirade, and Les Saintes, as well
as French St. Martin and St. Barthélemy to the north. Mountainous 312-square-mile Basse-Terre (lowland) lies on the
leeward side, where the winds are "lower." Smaller, flatter
Grande-Terre (218 square miles) gets the "bigger" winds on its
windward side. The Rivière Salée, a four-mile seawater channel flowing between the Caribbean and the Atlantic, forms the
"spine" of the butterfly. A drawbridge over the channel connects the two islands.

Guadeloupe

1 Exploring Sites

35 Hotels and Restaurants

La Mouette, **73**
Le Balata, **55**
Le Barbaroc, **50**
Le Flibustier, **64**
Le Foyal, **42**
Le Galion, **56**
Le Karacoli, **35**
Le Rocher de Malendure, **38**
Les Gommiers, **37**
Les Oiseaux, **40**
Relais des Iles, **43**
Relais du Moulin, **68**

Lodging
Auberge de la Distillerie, **48**
Auberge de la Vieille Tour PLM-Azur, **54**
Auberge des Anacardies, **45**
Auberge du Grand Large, **63**
Bois Joli, **46**
Callinago-PLM Azur, **61**
Cap Sud Caraibes, **62**
Club Med Caravelle, **66**
Fleur d'Epée Novotel, **60**
Grand Anse Hotel, **41**
Hamak, **72**
La Creole Beach, **59**
La Toubana, **67**
Los Santo-PLM Azur, **47**
Meridien, **71**
Relais du Moulin, **68**
Village Creole, **44**

If you're seeking resort hotels, casinos, and white sandy beaches, your target is Grande-Terre. By contrast, Basse-Terre's Natural Park, laced with mountain trails and washed by waterfalls and rivers, is a 74,100-acre haven for hikers, nature lovers, and anyone yearning to peer into the steaming crater of an active volcano. If you want to get away from it all, head for the offshore islands of Les Saintes, La Désirade, and Marie-Galante.

Christopher Columbus "discovered" Guadeloupe on November 4, 1493, when he landed at Ste-Marie on the southern shore of Basse-Terre and named the island Santa Marie de Guadeloupe de Estremadura. The Carib inhabitants, who had already polished off the peaceful Arawaks, had no intention of relinquishing the land they called *Karukera* (Island of Beautiful Waters). The Spaniards gave up on the island in 1604. In 1635, the French laid claim to it. They ran the Caribs off, brought in African slaves to work their sugar plantations, and in 1674 Guadeloupe was annexed by France. The British also had designs on the island, and they gained control of it from 1759 until 1763, when they relinquished it in exchange for all French rights to Canada. During the French Revolution battles broke out between royalists and revolutionaries on the island. In 1794, Britain responded to the call from Guadeloupe royalists to come to their aid, and that same year France dispatched Victor Hugues to sort things out. (In virtually every town and village you'll run across a "Victor Hugues" street, boulevard, or park.) After his troops banished the British, Hugues issued a decree abolishing slavery and guillotined recalcitrant planters. The ones who managed to keep their heads fled to Louisiana or hid in the hills of Grande-Terre, where their descendants now live. Hugues was soon relieved of his command, slavery was reestablished by Napoleon, and the French and English continued to battle over the island. The 1815 Treaty of Paris restored Guadeloupe to France, and in 1848, due largely to the efforts of Alsatian Victor Schoelcher, slavery was permanently abolished. The island has been a full-fledged *departement* of France since 1946, and in 1974 it was elevated to a *region*, administered by a prefect appointed from Paris by the Minister of the Interior.

Before You Go

Tourist Information Call or write to the **French West Indies Tourist Office** (610 5th Ave., New York, NY 10020, tel. 212/757–1125). You may also obtain information from the **French Government Office** at any of the following addresses: 628 5th Ave., New York, NY 10020, tel. 212/757–1125; 9454 Wilshire Blvd., Beverly Hills, CA 90212, tel. 213/272–2661; 645 N. Michigan Ave., Chicago, IL 60611, tel. 312/337–6301; 103 World Trade Center, Dallas, TX 75258, tel. 214/742–7011; 1 Hallidie Plaza, Suite 250, San Francisco, CA 94102, tel. 415/986–4161; 1981 Ave. McGill College (490), Montreal, Que., Canada H3A 2W9, tel. 514/288–4264; 1 Dundas St. W, Suite 2405, Toronto, Ont., Canada M5G 1Z3, tel. 416/593–4717; 178 Piccadilly, London, United Kingdom W1V 0AL, tel. 01/499–6911.

Arriving and Departing
By Plane **American Airlines** (tel. 800/433–7300) flies from more than 100 U.S. cities direct to San Juan with connections to Guadeloupe. **Minerve Airlines** (tel. 800/765–6065), a French charter carrier,

has twice-weekly direct service from New York during the December–March peak season. **Air Canada** (tel. 800/422–6232) flies direct from Montreal and Toronto. **Air France** (tel. 800/237–2747) flies nonstop from Paris and Fort-de-France, and has direct service from Miami, San Juan, and Port-au-Prince. **Air Guadeloupe** (tel. 599/5–44212) flies daily from St. Martin and St. Maarten, St. Barts, Marie-Galante, La Désirade, and Les Saintes. **LIAT** (tel. 212/269–6925) flies from St. Croix in the north and Trinidad in the south.

From the Airport You'll land at La Raizet International Airport, 2½ miles from Pointe-à-Pitre. Cabs are lined up outside the airport. The metered fare is about 35F to Pointe-à-Pitre, 60F to Gosier, and 170F to St-François. Or, for 5F, you can also take a bus from the airport to downtown Pointe-à-Pitre.

By Boat Major cruise lines call regularly, docking at berths in downtown Pointe-à-Pitre about a block from the shopping district. **Trans Antilles Express** (tel. 590/83–12–45) provides ferry service to and from Marie-Galante, Les Saintes, and La Désirade. The *Jetcat* and *Madras* ferries depart daily from the pier at Pointe-à-Pitre for Marie Galante at 6 AM and at 8 AM for Les Saintes, with return trips leaving the islands around 4 PM. Passage to either island from Pointe-à-Pitre takes about an hour. The *Princess Caroline* leaves Trois Rivières for the 30-minute trip to Les Saintes Mon.–Sat. at 8:30 AM, Sun. at 7:30 AM. The return ferry leaves at 3 PM. Allow 1½ hours to get from Pointe-à-Pitre to Trois Rivières. The *Socimade* runs between La Désirade and St-Francois, departing Mon., Wed., Fri.–Sun. at 8:30 AM, Tues. 3 PM, Thurs. at 4:30 PM. Return ferries depart Mon., Wed., Fri., Sat. at 6:15 AM and 4 PM, Tues. and Thurs. at 6:15 AM, Sun. at 4 PM. These schedules are subject to change and should be verified through your hotel or at the Tourist Office.

Passports and Visas U.S. and Canadian citizens need only proof of citizenship. A passport is best (even one that expired up to five years ago). Other acceptable documents are a notarized birth certificate with a raised seal (not a photocopy) or a voter registration card accompanied by a government-authorized photo ID. A free temporary visa, good only for your stay in Guadeloupe, will be issued to you upon your arrival at the airport. British citizens need a valid passport, but no visa. In addition, all visitors must hold an ongoing or return ticket.

Customs and Duties Items for personal use, such as tobacco, cameras, and film are admitted without tax or formalities, provided they are not in "excessive quantity."

Language The official language is French. Everyone also speaks a Creole patois, which you won't be able to understand even if you're fluent in French. In the major tourist hotels, most of the staff know some English. However, communicating may be more difficult in the smaller hotels and restaurants in the countryside. Some taxi drivers speak a little English. Arm yourself with a phrase book, a dictionary, patience, and a sense of humor.

Precautions Put your valuables in the hotel safe. Don't leave them unattended in your room or on the beach. Keep an eye out for motorcyclists riding double. They sometimes play the notorious game of veering close to the sidewalk and snatching shoulder bags. It isn't a good idea to walk around Pointe-à-Pitre at night because it's almost deserted after dark. If you rent a car, always lock it with luggage and valuables stashed out of sight.

The rough Atlantic waters off the northeast coast of Grande-Terre are dangerous for swimming.

Ask permission before taking a picture of an islander, and don't be surprised if the answer is a firm "No." Guadeloupeans are also deeply religious and traditional. Don't offend them by wearing short shorts or swimwear off the beach.

Staying in Guadeloupe

Important Addresses

Tourist Information: The **Office Departmental du Tourism** has offices in Pointe-à-Pitre (23 rue Delgrès, corner rue Schoelcher, tel. 590/82–09–30), in Basse-Terre (Maison du Port, tel. 590/81–24–83), and in St-François (Ave. de l'Europe, tel. 590/88–48–74). All offices are open weekdays 8–5, Saturday 8–noon.

Emergencies

Police: In Pointe-à-Pitre (tel. 590/17 or 590/82–00–17), in Basse-Terre (tel. 590/81–11–55).

Fire: In Pointe-à-Pitre (tel. 590/18 or 590/82–00–28), in Basse-Terre (tel. 590/81–19–22).

SOS Ambulance: Tel. 590/82–89–33.

Hospitals: There is a 24-hour emergency room at **Pointe-à-Pitre Central Hospital** (Abymes, tel. 590/82–98–80 or 590/82–88–88). There are 23 clinics and five hospitals located around the island. The Tourist Office or your hotel can assist you in locating an English-speaking doctor.

Pharmacies: Pharmacies alternate in staying open around the clock. The Tourist Office or your hotel can help you locate the one that's on duty.

Currency

Legal tender is the French franc, which is comprised of 100 centimes. At press time, U.S.$1 bought 5.96F, but the franc fluctuates relative to the dollar. Check the current rate of exchange. Some places accept U.S. dollars, but it's best to change your money into the local currency. Credit cards are accepted in most major hotels, restaurants, and shops, less so in smaller places and in the countryside. Prices are quoted here in U.S. dollars unless otherwise noted.

Taxes and Service Charges

A *taxe de séjour* varies from hotel to hotel but never exceeds $1 per person, per day.

Most hotel prices include a 10%–15% service charge; if not—it will be added to your bill.

Restaurants are legally required to include 15% in the menu price. No additional gratuity is necessary. Tip skycaps and porters about 5F. Many cab drivers own their own cabs and don't expect a tip. You won't have any trouble ascertaining if a 10% tip is expected.

Guided Tours

There are set fares for taxi tours to various points on the island. The Tourist Office or your hotel can arrange for an English-speaking taxi driver and even organize a small group for you to share the cost of the tour.

George-Marie Gabrielle (Pointe-à-Pitre, tel. 590/82–05–38) and **Petrelluzzi Travel** (Pointe-à-Pitre, tel. 590/82–82–30) both offer half- and full-day excursions around the island. A modern bus with an English-speaking guide will pick you up at your hotel.

At Raizet Airport, helicopter tours can be arranged through **Caraibe Air Tourisme** (tel. 590/91–61–24) and **Safari Tours** (tel. 590/84–06–74).

Organization des Guides de Montagne de la Caraibe, O.G.M.C., (Maison Forestière, Matouba, tel. 590/80–05–79) provides guides for hiking tours in the mountains.

Getting Around
Taxis Fares are regulated by the government and posted at the airport, at taxi stands, and at major hotels. During the day you'll pay about 35F from the airport to Pointe-à-Pitre, about 60F to Gosier, and about 170F to St-François. Between 9 PM and 7 AM, fares increase 40%. If your French is in working order, you can contact radio cabs at 590/82–15–09, 590/83–64–27, and 590/84–37–65.

Buses Modern public buses run from 5:30 AM to 7:30 PM. They stop along the road at bus stops and shelters marked *arrêtbus*, but you can also flag one down along the route.

Vespas or Bikes If you opt to tour the island by bike, you won't be alone. Biking is a major sport here (*see* Participant Sports, below, for rental information).

Vespas can be rented at **Vespa Sun** (Pointe-à-Pitre, tel. 590/82–17–80), **Location de Motos** (Meridien Hotel, St-François, tel. 590/88–51–00), and **Dingo Location Scooter** (Gosier, tel. 590/90–97–01).

Rental Cars Your valid driver's license will suffice for up to 20 days, after which you'll need an international driver's permit. Guadeloupe has 1,225 miles of excellent roads (marked as in Europe), and driving around Grande-Terre is relatively easy. However, you may be more comfortable with a Guadeloupean behind the wheel in the mountains of Basse-Terre. Guadeloupeans are skillful drivers, but they do like to drive fast. Cars can be rented at **Avis** (tel. 590/82–33–47 or 800/331–1212), **Budget** (tel. 590/82–95–58 or 800/527–0700), **Hertz** (tel. 590/82–00–14 or 800/654–3131), and **National-Europcar** (tel. 590/82–50–51 or 800/468–0008). There are rental offices at the airport as well as at the major resort areas. Car rentals cost a bit more on Guadeloupe than on the other islands.

Telephones and Mail To call from the United States, dial 011 + 590 + the local six-digit number. (To call person-to-person, dial 01–590.) It is not possible to place collect or credit card calls to the United States from Guadeloupe. Coin-operated phones are rare but can be found in restaurants and cafés. If you need to make many calls outside of your hotel, purchase a *Telecarte* at the post office or other outlets marked *Telecarte en Vente Ici*. Telecartes look like credit cards and are used in special booths marked "Telecom." Local and long-distance calls made with the cards are cheaper than operator-assisted calls.

To call the United States from Guadeloupe, dial 19 + 1 + the area code and phone number. To dial locally in Guadeloupe, simply dial the six-digit phone number.

Postcards to the United States need 2.80F; letters up to 20 grams, 4.40F. For Canada, postcards are 2F; letters, 2.70F. Stamps can be purchased at the post office, *café-tabacs*, hotel newsstands, or souvenir shops.

Banks are open weekdays 8–noon and 2–4. Credit Agricole, Banque Populaire, and Société Générale de Banque aux Antilles have branches that are open Saturday. During the summer most banks are open 8–3. Banks close at noon the day before a legal holiday that falls during the week. As a rule, shops are open weekdays 8 or 8:30–noon and 2:30–6, but hours are flexible when cruise ships are in town.

Beaches

Generally Guadeloupe's beaches, all free and open to the public, have no facilities. For a small fee, hotels allow nonguests to use changing facilities, towels, and beach chairs. You'll find long stretches of white sand on Grande-Terre. On the south coast of Basse-Terre the beaches are gray volcanic sand, and on the northwest coast the color is golden-tan. There are several nudist beaches (noted below), and topless bathing is prevalent at the resort hotels. Note that the Atlantic waters on the north-east coast of Grande-Terre are too rough for swimming.

Ilet du Gosier is a little speck off the shore of Gosier where you can bathe in the buff. Make arrangements for water-sport rentals and boat trips to the island through the Creole Beach Hotel in Gosier (tel. 590/84–26–26). Take along a picnic for an all-day outing. *Beach closed weekends.*

Some of the island's best beaches of soft white sand lie on the south coast of Grande-Terre from Ste-Anne to Pointe des Châteaux.

One of the longest and prettiest stretches is just outside the town of Ste-Anne at **Caravelle Beach.** Although it was severely hammered by Hurricane Hugo, it should be back to normal for the 1990/1991 season. Protected by reefs, the beach makes a fine place for snorkeling. At the hotel La Toubana (tel. 590/88–25–78) in the hills above you can rent fins and masks, as well as canoes and Windsurfers. Club Med, with its staggering array of activities, occupies one end of this beach.

Just outside of St-François is **Raisin-Clairs,** home of the Meridien Hotel (tel. 590/88–51–00), which rents Windsurfers, water skis, and sailboats.

Between St-François and Pointe des Châteaux, **Anse de la Gourde** is a beautiful stretch of sand that becomes very popular on weekends. A restaurant and snack bar are at the entrance to the beach.

Tarare is a secluded nudist strip just before the tip of Pointe des Châteaux. There is a small bar/café located where you park the car and a four-minute walk from the beach.

Located just outside of Deshaies on the northwest coast of Basse-Terre, **La Grande Anse** is a secluded beach of soft beige sand sheltered by palms. There's a large parking area but no facilities other than the Karacoli restaurant, which sits with its "feet in the water," ready to serve you rum punch and Creole dishes.

From **Malendure** beach, on the west coast of Basse-Terre, Pigeon Island lies just offshore. Jacques Cousteau called it one of the 10 best diving places in the world. The Nautilus Club (tel. 590/98–85–89) and Chez Guy (tel. 590/98–81–72) at Malendure are two of the island's top scuba operations. There are also glass-bottom boat trips for those who prefer keeping their heads above water.

Souffleur, on the west coast of Grande-Terre, on the north side of Port Louis, has brilliant flamboyant trees that bloom in the summer. There are no facilities on the beach, but you can buy the makings of a picnic from nearby shops. Be sure to stick around long enough for a super sunset.

Place Crawen, Les Saintes' quiet, secluded beach for skinny dipping, is a half mile of white sand on Terre-de-Haut. Facilities are within a five-minute walk at Bois Joli hotel (tel. 590/99–50–38).

Petit-Anse, on Marie-Galante, is a long gold-sand beach crowded with locals on weekends. During the week it's quiet, and there are no facilities other than the little seafood restaurant, La Touloulou.

Exploring Guadeloupe

Numbers in the margin correspond with points of interest on the Guadeloupe map.

Pointe-à-Pitre
❶

Pointe-à-Pitre is a city of some 100,000 people in the extreme southwest of Grande-Terre. It lies almost on the "backbone" of the butterfly, near the bridge that crosses the Salee River. In this bustling, noisy city, with its narrow streets, honking horns, and traffic jams, there is little of the relaxed, joyful mood one finds on many other Caribbean islands.

Life has not been easy for Pointe-à-Pitre. The city has suffered severe damage over the years as a result of earthquakes, fires, and hurricanes. The most recent damage was done in 1979 by Hurricane Frederick, 1980 by Hurricane David, and in 1989 by Hurricane Hugo. Standing on boulevarde Frébault you can see on one side the remaining French colonial structures and on the other the modern city.

Stop at the Office of Tourism, in Place de la Victoire across from the quays where the cruise ships dock, to pick up maps and brochures. *Bonjour, Guadeloupe,* the free visitors' guide, is very useful.

When you leave the office, turn left, walk one block along rue Schoelcher, and turn right on rue Achille René-Boisneuf. Two more blocks will bring you to the **Musée St-John Perse.** The restored colonial house is dedicated to the Guadeloupean poet who won the 1960 Nobel Prize in Literature. (Nearby, at No. 54, rue René-Boisneuf, a plaque marks his birthplace.) The museum contains a complete collection of his poetry, as well as some of his personal effects. There are also works written about him, and various mementos, documents, and photographs. *Corner rues Noizières and Achille René-Boisneuf, no phone. Admission: 10F. Open Mon.–Sat. 9–12:30 and 2–6.*

Rues Noizières, Frébault, and Schoelcher are Pointe-à-Pitre's main shopping streets. In sharp contrast to the duty-free shops is the bustling **Marketplace,** which you'll find by backtracking one block from the museum and turning right on rue Frébault. Located between rues St-John Perse, Frébault, Schoelcher, and Peynier, the market is a cacophonous and colorful place where housewives bargain for papayas, breadfruits, christophines, tomatoes, and a vivid assortment of other produce.

Take a left at the corner of rues Schoelcher and Peynier. The **Musée Schoelcher** honors the memory of Victor Schoelcher, the 19th-century Alsatian abolitionist who fought slavery in the French West Indies. The museum contains many of his personal effects and the exhibits trace his life and work. *24 rue Peynier, tel. 590/82–08–04. Admission: 5F. Open weekdays 9–noon and 2:30–5:30.*

Walk back along rue Peynier past the market for three blocks. You'll come to **Place de la Victoire,** surrounded by wood buildings with balconies and shutters. The square was named in honor of Victor Hugues's 1794 victory over the British. The sandbox trees in the park are said to have been planted by Hugues the day after the victory. During the French Revolution, Hugues's guillotine in this square lopped off the heads of many a white aristocrat. Today the large palm-shaded park is a popular gathering place. The Tourist Office is at the harbor end of the square.

Rue Duplessis runs between the southern edge of the park and La Darse, the head of the harbor, where fishing boats dock and fast motorboats depart for the choppy ride to Marie-Galante and Les Saintes.

Rue Bebian is the western border of the square. Walk north along it (away from the harbor) and turn left on rue Alexandre Isaac. You'll see the imposing **Cathedral of St. Peter and St. Paul,** which dates from 1847. Mother Nature's rampages have wreaked havoc on the church, and it is now reinforced with iron ribs. Hurricane Hugo took out many of the upper windows and shutters, but the lovely stained-glass windows survived intact.

Grande-Terre This round-trip tour of **Grande-Terre** will cover about 85 miles. Drive south out of Pointe-à-Pitre on Route N4 (named the "Riviera Road" in honor of the man-made beaches and resort hotels of Bas-du-Fort). The road goes past the marina, which is always crowded with yachts and cabin cruisers. The numerous boutiques and restaurants surrounding the marina make it a popular evening destination.

② The road turns east and heads along the coast. In 2 miles you'll sight **Fort Fleur d'Epée,** an 18th-century fortress that hunkers on a hillside behind a deep moat. This was the scene of hard-fought battles between the French and the English. You can explore the well-preserved dungeons and battlements, and on a clear day take in a sweeping view of Iles des Saintes and Marie-Galante.

③ The **Guadeloupe Aquarium** is just past the fort off the main highway. This aquarium, the Caribbean's largest and most modern, also ranks third in all of France. *Rte. N4, tel. 590/90–92–38. Admission: 15F adults, 10F children. Open weekdays 8:30–12:30 and 2:30–5:30, Sat. 8:30–5:30.*

④ **Gosier,** a major tourist center 2 miles farther east, is a busy place indeed, with big hotels and tiny inns, cafés, discos, shops, and a long stretch of sand. The Creole Beach, the Auberge de la Vieille Tour–PLM Azur, and its cousin the Callinago–PLM Azur are among the hotels here.

⑤ Breeze along the coast through the little hamlet of St-Felix and on to **Ste-Anne,** about 8 miles east of Gosier. Only ruined sugar mills remain from the days in the early 18th century when this village was a major sugar-exporting center. Sand has replaced sugar as the town's most valuable asset. The soft white-sand beaches here are among the best in Guadeloupe. The Club Med Caravelle occupies a secluded spot on the Caravelle Beach to the west of town, and there are several small Relais Creoles with their "feet in the sand." The hotel La Toubana sits on a bluff with its bungalows tumbling down to the beach, and the Relais du Moulin occupies one of the old sugar mills. On a more sober note, you'll pass Ste-Anne's lovely cemetery with stark-white above-ground tombs.

Don't fret about leaving the beaches of Ste-Anne behind you as you head eastward. The entire south coast of Grande-Terre is scalloped with white-sand beaches. Eight miles along, just before coming to the blue-roof houses of **St-François,** you'll come to the Raisins Clairs beach, another beauty.

St-François was once a simple little village primarily involved with fishing and tomatoes. The fish and tomatoes are still here, but so are some of the island's ritziest hotels. This is the home of the Hamak and the Meridien, two very plush properties. Avenue de l'Europe runs between the well-groomed 18-hole Robert Trent Jones municipal golf course and the man-made marina. On the marina side, a string of shops and restaurants cater to tourists.

To reach **Pointe des Châteaux,** take the narrow road east from St-François and drive 8 miles out onto the rugged promontory that is the easternmost point on the island. The Atlantic and the Caribbean waters join here and crash against huge rocks, carving them into castlelike shapes. The jagged, majestic cliffs are reminiscent of the headlands of Brittany. The only human contribution to this dramatic scene is a white cross high on a hill above the tumultuous waters. From this point there are spectacular views of the south and east coasts of Guadeloupe and the distant cliffs of La Désirade.

Time Out **Paillote** (no phone) is a tiny roadside stand right on the *pointe* where you can get libations and light bites.

About 2 miles from the farthest point, a rugged dirt road crunches off to the north and leads to the nudist beach, Pointe Tarare.

A mile closer to St-François is another beach, Anse de la Gourde, where at least half of a bikini is kept on. The half-mile stretch of coarse white sand and reef-protected waters makes it a choice beach and, off the car park, is **La Langouste** (tel. 590/88–52–19), a popular lunch spot on the weekends.

Take Route N5 north from St-François for a drive through fragrant silvery-green seas of sugarcane. About 4 miles beyond St-François you'll see **Zévalos,** a handsome colonial mansion that was once the manor house of the island's largest sugar plantation.

Four miles northwest you'll come to **Le Moule,** a port city of about 17,000 people. This busy city was once the capital of Guadeloupe. It was bombarded by the British in 1794 and 1809, and by a hurricane in 1928. Canopies of flamboyants hang over narrow streets where colorful vegetable and fish markets do a brisk business. Small buildings are of weathered wood with shutters, balconies, and bright awnings. The town hall, with graceful balustrades, and a small 19th-century neoclassical church are on the main square. Le Moule also has a beautiful crescent-shape beach.

10 North of Le Moule archaeologists have uncovered the remains of Arawak and Carib settlements. The **Edgar-Clerc Archaeological Museum,** 3 miles out of Le Moule in the direction of Campêche, contains Amerindian artifacts from the personal collection of this well-known archaeologist and historian. There are several rooms with displays pertaining to the Carib and Arawak civilizations. *La Rosette, tel. 590/23–57–43. Admission free. Open Mon., Wed.–Fri., and Sun. 9:30–12:30 and 2:30–5:30; Sat. 9:30–5:30.*

From Le Moule you can turn west on Route D101 to return to Pointe-à-Pitre or continue northwest to see the rugged north coast.

To reach the coast, drive 8 miles northwest along Route D120 to Campêche, going through Gros Cap.

Time Out **Château de Feuilles** (tel. 590/22–19–10), between Le Moule and Campêche (nearer Gros Cap), is an absolutely superb place for a long, lingering lunch. A miniestate, the château has style and excellent cuisine. Bring your swimming togs and use the pool while lunch is being prepared. (*See* Dining, below).

11 At 1½ miles beyond Campeche, turn north on Route D122. **Porte d'Enfer** (Gate of Hell) marks a dramatic point on the coast where two jagged cliffs are stormed by the wild Atlantic waters. One legend has it that a Madame Coco strolled out across the waves carrying a parasol and vanished without a trace.

12 Four miles from Porte d'Enfer, **La Pointe de la Grande Vigie** is the northernmost tip of the island. Park your car and walk along the paths that lead right out to the edge. There is a splendid view of the Porte d'Enfer from here, and on a clear day you can see Antigua 35 miles away.

13 **Anse-Bertrand,** the northernmost village in Guadeloupe, lies 4 miles south of La Pointe de la Grande Vigie along a gravel road. Drive carefully. En route to Anse-Bertrand you'll pass another good beach, Anse Laborde. The area around Anse-Bertrand was the last refuge of the Caribs. Most of the excitement these days takes place in the St-Jacques Hippodrome, where horse races and cockfights are held.

14 Route N6 will take you 5 miles south to **Port-Louis,** a fishing village of about 7,000. As you come in from the north, look for the turnoff to the Souffleur beach, once one of the island's prettiest, which, though, has become a little shabby. The sand is fringed by flamboyant trees whose brilliant orange-red flowers bloom during the summer and early fall. The beach is crowded on weekends, but during the week it's blissfully quiet. The sunsets here are something to write home about.

Time Out **Poisson d'Or** is a rustic seaside restaurant that features spicy Creole dishes. *Rue Sadi Carnot, Port-Louis, tel. 590/84–90–22. No credit cards.*

From Port-Louis the road leads 5 miles south through mangrove swamps to Petit Canal, where it turns inland. Three miles east of Petit Canal, turn right on the main road. Head 6 **15** miles south to **Morne-à-l'Eau,** an agricultural city of about

16,000 people. Morne-à-l'Eau's unusual amphitheater-shape cemetery is the scene of a moving (and photogenic) candlelight service on All Saint's Day. Take Route N5 out of town along gently undulating hills past fields of sugarcane and dairy farms.

Just south of Morne-à-l'Eau are the villages of **Jabrun du Sud** and **Jabrun du Nord,** which are inhabited by the descendants of the "Blancs Matignon," the whites who hid in the hills and valleys of the Grands Fonds after the abolition of slavery in 1848.

Continue on Route N5 to Pointe-à-Pitre.

Basse-Terre: The Southern Half

There is high adventure on the butterfly's west wing, which swirls with mountain trails and lakes, waterfalls, and hot springs. Basse-Terre is the home of the Old Lady, as the Soufrière volcano is called locally, as well as of the capital, also called Basse-Terre.

Guadeloupe's de rigueur tour takes you through the 74,100-acre Natural Park, a sizable chunk of Basse-Terre. Before going, pick up a *Guide to the Natural Park* from the Tourist Office, which rates the hiking trails according to difficulty.

The Route de la Traversée (La Traversée) is a good paved road that runs east–west, cutting a 16-mile-long swath through the park to the west coast village of Mahaut. La Traversée divides Basse-Terre into two almost equal sections. The majority of mountain trails falls into the southern half. Allow a full day for this excursion. Wear rubber-soled shoes, and take along both swimsuit and sweater, and perhaps food for a picnic.

Begin your tour by heading west from Pointe-à-Pitre on Route N1, crossing the Rivière Salée on the Pont de la Gabare drawbridge. At the Destrelan traffic circle turn left and drive 6 miles south through sweet-scented fields of sugarcane to the Route de la Traversée (aka D23), where you'll turn west.

As soon as you cross the bridge you'll begin to see the riches produced by Basse-Terre's fertile volcanic soil and heavier rainfall. La Traversée is lined with masses of thick tree-ferns, shrubs, flowers, tall trees, and green plantains that stand like soldiers in a row.

Five miles from where you turned off Route N1 you'll come to a junction. Turn left and go a little over a mile south to **Vernou.** Traipsing along a path that leads beyond the village through the lush forest you'll come to the pretty waterfall at **Saut de la Lézard,** the first of many you'll see.

Back on La Traversée, 3 miles farther, you'll come to the next one, **Cascade aux Ecrevisse.** Park your car and walk along the marked trail that leads to a splendid waterfall dashing down into the Corossol River (a fit place for a dip). Walk carefully—the rocks along the trail can be slippery.

Two miles farther along La Traversée you'll come to the **Parc Tropical de Bras-David,** where you can park and explore various nature trails. The **Maison de la Forêt** (admission free, open daily 9–5) has a variety of displays that describe (for those who can read French) the flora, fauna, and topography of the Natural Park. There are picnic tables where you can enjoy your lunch in tropical splendor.

19 Two and a half miles more will bring you to the two mountains known as **Les Mamelles**—Mamelle de Petit-Bourg at 2,350 feet and the Mamelle de Pigeon at 2,500 feet. (*Mamelle* means breast, and when you see the mountains you'll understand why they are so named.) There is a spectacular view from the pass that runs between the Mamelles to the south and a lesser mountain to the north. From this point, trails ranging from easy to arduous lace up into the surrounding mountains. There's a glorious view from the lookout point 1,969 feet up the Mamelle de Pigeon. If you're a climber, you'll want to spend several hours exploring this area.

20 You don't have to be much of a hiker to climb the stone steps leading from the road to the **Zoological Park and Botanical Gardens.** Titi the Raccoon is the mascot of the Natural Park. There are also cockatoos, iguanas, and turtles. *La Traversée, no phone. Admission: 20F adults, 10F children. Open daily 9–5.*

On the winding 4-mile descent from the mountains to **Mahaut** you'll see patches of the blue Caribbean through the green trees. In the village of Mahaut turn left on Route N2 for the drive south along the coast. In less than a mile you'll come to **Malendure.** The big attraction here is offshore on **Pigeon Island.** Club Nautilus and Chez Guy, both on the Malendure Beach, conduct diving trips, and the glass-bottom *Aquarium* and *Nautilus* make daily snorkeling trips to this spectacular site.

Time Out While there are a couple of café/bars on Malendure Beach, the restaurant for lunch is **Le Rocher de Malendure** (tel. 590/98–70–84). Perched on a bluff overlooking Pigeon Island, the open-air restaurant is a gem, with dining on a series of terraces affording marvelous views. The owner can also arrange deep-sea fishing expeditions.

21 22 From Malendure continue through neighboring **Bouillante,** where hot springs burst up through the earth, and **Vieux-Habitants,** one of the oldest settlements on the island. Pause to see the restored church, which dates from 1650, before driving 8 miles south to the capital city.

Basse-Terre **23** **Basse-Terre,** the capital and administrative center, is an active city of about 15,000 people. Founded in 1640, it has had even more difficulties than Pointe-à-Pitre. The capital has endured not only foreign attacks and hurricanes but sputtering threats from La Soufrière as well. More than once it has been evacuated when the volcano began to hiss and fume. The last major eruption was in the 16th century. But the volcano seemed active enough to warrant the evacuation of more than 70,000 people in 1975.

The centers of activity are the port and the market, both of which you'll pass along Boulevard Général de Gaulle. The 17th-century **Fort St. Charles** at the extreme south end of town, and the **Cathedral of Our Lady of Guadeloupe** to the north, across the Rivière aux Herbes, are worth a short visit. Drive along Boulevard Felix Eboue to see the colonial buildings that house government offices. Follow the boulevard to the **Jardin Pichon** to see its beautiful gardens. Stop off at **Champ d'Arbaud,** an Old World square surrounded by colonial buildings. Continue along the boulevard to the **Botanical Gardens,** another pleasant place to stop and smell the flowers. A steep, narrow road leads 4

㉔ miles up to the suburb of **St-Claude,** on the slopes of La Sou-frière. In St-Claude there are picnic tables and good views of the volcano. You can also get a closer look at the volcano by driving up to the Savane à Mulets. From there leave your car and hike the strenuous two-hour climb (with an experienced guide) to the summit at 4,813 feet, the highest point in the Lesser Antilles. Water boils out of the eastern slope of the vol-cano and spills into the Carbet Falls.

㉕ Drive 2 miles farther north from St-Claude to visit **Matouba,** a village settled by East Indians whose descendants still practice ancient rites including animal sacrifice. If you've an idle 10 hours or so, take off from Matouba for a 19-mile hike on a marked trail through the Monts Caraibes to the east coast.

Descend and continue east on Route N1 for 4 miles to
㉖ **Gourbeyre.** Visit **Etang As de Pique.** Reaching this lake, located 2,454 feet above the town, is another challenge for hikers, but you can also reach it in an hour by car via paved Palmetto Road. The 5-acre lake, formed by a lava flow, is shaped like an *as de pique* (ace of spades).

From Gourbeyre you have the option of continuing east along Route N1 or taking the roller-coaster Route D6 along the coast. Either route will take you through lush greenery to **Trois-Rivières** on the southeast coast.

㉗ Not far from the ferry landing for Les Saintes, the **Parc Archéologique des Roches Gravées** contains a collection of pre-Columbian rock engravings. Pick up an information sheet at the park's entrance. Displays interpret the figures of folk and fauna depicted on the petroglyphs. The park is set in a lovely botanical garden that was still recuperating from Hurricane Hugo at press time. *Trois-Rivières, no phone. Admission: 4F. Open daily 9–5.*

Continue through banana fields and the village of Bananier for 5 miles to reach the village of **St-Sauveur,** gateway to the mag-
㉘ nificent **Chutes du Cabaret** (Cabaret Falls). Three of the chutes, which drop from 65 feet, 360 feet, and 410 feet, can be reached by following the narrow, steep, and spiraling Habituée Road for 5 miles up past the **Grand Etang** (Great Pond). At the end of the road you'll have to proceed on foot. Well-marked but slip-pery trails lead to viewing points of the *chutes.*

Time Out You can have a hearty lunch of Creole chicken, curried goat, or crayfish at **Chez Dollin-Le Crepuscule** (Habituée Village, tel. 590/86–34–56) before or after viewing the falls. There's also a four-course menu.

㉙ Continue along Route N1 for 3 miles to **Capesterre-Belle-Eau.** You'll cross the Carbet River and come to **Dumanoir Alley,** lined with century-old royal palms.

㉚ Three miles farther along, through fields of pineapples, banan-as, and sugarcane, you'll arrive at **Ste-Marie,** where Columbus landed in 1493. In the town there is a monument to the Great Discoverer.

Seventeen miles farther north you'll return to Pointe-à-Pitre.

Iles des Saintes This eight-island archipelago, usually referred to as **Les**
㉛ **Saintes,** dots the waters off the south coast of Guadeloupe. The islands are Terre-de-Haut, Terre-de-Bas, Ilet à Cabrit, Grand

Ilet, La Redonde, La Coche, Le Pâté, and Les Augustins. Columbus discovered the islands on November 4, 1493, and christened them Los Santos in honor of All Saints' Day.

Of the islands, only Terre-de-Haut and Terre-de-Bas are inhabited, with a combined population of 3,260. Les Saintois, as the islanders are called, are fair-haired, blue-eyed descendants of Breton and Norman sailors. Fishing is the main source of income for Les Saintois, and the shores are lined with their fishing boats and *filets bleus* (blue nets dotted with burnt-orange buoys). The fishermen wear hats called *salakos*, which look like inverted saucers or coolie hats. They are patterned after a hat said to have been brought here by a seafarer from China or Indonesia. Almost no English is spoken on the islands.

With 5 square miles and a population of about 1,500, Terre-de-Haut is the largest island and the most developed for tourism. Its big city is Bourg, which boasts one street and a few bistros, cafés, and shops. Clutching the hillside are trim white houses with bright red or blue doors, balconies, and gingerbread frills.

Arrival on Terre-de-Haut is an exhilarating affair, whether by land or by sea. Air Guadeloupe has regularly scheduled flights, and your whole life may flash before your eyes as you soar down to the tiny airstrip. However, the flight is mercifully brief and you may prefer it to the choppy 35-minute ferry crossing from Trois-Rivières or the 60-minute ride from Pointe-à-Pitre. Ferries leave Trois-Rivières at about 9:30 AM and return about 3 PM. From Pointe-à-Pitre the usual departure time is 8 AM with return at 4 PM. Check with the Tourist Office for up-to-date ferry schedules.

Terre-de-Haut's ragged coastline is scalloped with lovely coves and beaches, including the nudist beach at Anse Crawen. The beautiful bay, complete with sugarloaf, has been called a "mini Rio." This is a quiet, peaceful getaway, but it may not remain unspoiled. At present, tourism accounts for 20%–30% of the economy. Although government plans call for a total of only 250 hotel rooms, the tourist-related industries are making a major pitch for tourists.

There are three paved roads on the island, but don't even think about driving here. The roads are ghastly, and backing up is a minor art form choreographed on those frequent occasions when two vehicles meet on one of the steep, narrow roads. There are four minibuses that transport passengers from the airstrip and the wharf and double as tour buses. However, the island is so small you can get around by walking. It's a mere five-minute stroll from the airstrip and ferry dock to downtown Bourg.

32 **Fort Napoléon** is a relic from the period when the French fortified these islands against the Caribs and the English, but nobody has ever fired a shot at or from it. The nearby museum contains a collection of 250 modern paintings. You can also visit the well-preserved barracks, prison cells, and museum, and admire the surrounding botanical gardens. From the fort you can see Fort Josephine across the channel on the Ilet à Cabrit. *Bourg, no tel. Admission: 10F. Open daily 9–noon.*

For so tiny a place, Terre-de-Haut offers a variety of hotels and restaurants. For details, *see* Dining and Lodging, below.

Marie-Galante The ferry to this flat island departs from Pointe-à-Pitre at 6 AM
33 with a return at 4 PM. You'll put in to Grand Bourg, its major
city with a population of about 8,000. A plane will land you 2
miles from Grand Bourg. If your French or phrase book are
good enough, you can negotiate a price with the taxi drivers for
touring the island.

With about 60 square miles, this is the largest of Guadeloupe's
offshore islands. It is dotted with ruined 19th-century sugar
mills, and sugar is still one of its major products (the others are
cotton and rum). One of the last refuges of the Caribs when
they were driven from the mainland by the French, the island is
a favorite retreat of Guadeloupeans who come on weekends to
enjoy the beach at Petit-Anse.

Columbus sighted the island on November 3, 1493, the day before he landed at Ste-Marie on Basse-Terre. He named it for his
flagship, the *Maria Galanda*, and sailed on.

There are several places near the ferry landing where you can
get an inexpensive meal of seafood and Creole sauce. If you
want to stay over, you can choose from La Salut, in St-Louis (15
rooms, tel. 590/97–02–67), Auberge de l'Arbre à Pain (7 rooms,
tel. 590/97–73–69), or Soledad (20 rooms, tel. 590/97–75–45) in
Grand Bourg. An entertainment complex in Grand Bourg El
Rancho has a 400-seat movie theater, restaurant, terrace grill,
snack bar, disco, and a few double rooms.

La Désirade According to legend, this island is the "desired land" of
34 Columbus's second voyage. He spotted it on November 3, 1493.
The 8-square-mile island, 5 miles east of St-François, was for
many years a leper colony. The main settlement is Grande
Anse, where there is a pretty church and a hotel called La
Guitoune. Nothing fancy, but the restaurant serves excellent
seafood. Most of the 1,600 inhabitants are fishermen.

There are good beaches here, notably Souffleur and Baie
Mahault, and there's little to do but loll around on them. The
island is virtually unspoiled by tourism and is likely to remain
so, at least for the foreseeable future.

Three or four minibuses meet the flights and ferries, and you
can negotiate with one of them to give you a tour. Ferries depart from St-François Mon., Wed., Fri.–Sun. 8:30; Tues. and
Thurs. 4:30. The return ferry departs (at varying hours) afternoons daily except Tuesday and Thursday. However, be sure to
check schedules.

Participant Sports

Bicycling The relatively flat terrain of Grande-Terre makes for easy
wheeling. See Christian Rolle at **Veló-Vert** (Pointe-à-Pitre, tel.
590/83–15–74) to rent bikes and maps that cover a 270-mile
tour. **Le Relais du Moulin** (near Ste-Anne, tel. 590/88–23–96)
offers bike tours. You can also rent bikes at **Cyclo-Tours**
(Gosier, tel. 590/84–11–34), **Le Flamboyant** (St-François, tel.
590/84–45–51), and **Rent-a-Bike** (Meridien Hotel, St-François,
tel. 590/84–51–00). For information about cycling tours from
the United States to Guadeloupe, contact **Country Cycling
Tours** (140 W. 83rd St., New York, NY 10024, tel. 212/874–
5151).

Boating If you plan to sail these waters, you should be aware that the winds and currents of Guadeloupe tend to be strong. There are excellent, well-equipped marinas in Pointe-à-Pitre, Bas-du-Fort, Deshaies, St-François, and Gourbeyre. Bare-boat or crewed yachts can be rented in Bas-du-Fort at **Locaraibes** (tel. 590/90–82–80), **Vacances Yachting Antilles** (tel. 590/90–82–95), and **Soleil et Voile** (tel. 590/90–81–81). All beachfront hotels rent Hobie Cats, Sunfish, pedal boats, motorboats, and water skis.

Deep-Sea Fishing Half- and full-day trips in search of bonito, dolphin, captain-fish, barracuda, kingfish, and tuna can be arranged through **Fishing Club Antilles** (Bouillante, tel. 590/84–15–00), **Le Rocher de Malendure** (Pigeon, Bouillante, tel. 590/98–73–25), and **Papyrus** (Marina Bas-du-Fort, tel. 590/90–92–98).

Fitness The **PLM-Azur Marissol** (Bas-du-Fort, tel. 590/90–84–44) offers gym facilities for calisthenics, stretching, water exercises in pool or sea, yoga, and beauty care.

Golf **Golf Municipal Saint-François** (St-François, tel. 590/88–41–87) has an 18-hole Robert Trent Jones course, an English-speaking pro, a clubhouse, a pro shop, and electric carts for rental.

Hiking Basse-Terre's Natural Park is laced with fascinating trails, many of which should be attempted only with an experienced guide. Trips for up to 12 people are arranged by **Organisation des Guides de Montagne de la Caraibe (O.G.M.C.)** (Maison Forestière, Matouba, tel. 590/80–05–79).

Horseback Riding Beach rides, picnics, and lessons are available through **Le Criolo** (St-Felix, tel. 590/84–38–90) and **Le Relais du Moulin** (Châteaubrun, between Ste-Anne and St-François, tel. 590/88–23–96).

Scuba Diving The main diving area is the Cousteau Underwater Park off Pigeon Island (west coast of Basse-Terre). Guides and instructors here are certified under the French CMAS rather than PADI or NAUI. To explore the wrecks and reefs, contact **Nautilus Club** (Bouillante, tel. 590/98–85–69) or **Chez Guy** (Bouillante, tel. 590/98–81–72). Both of these outfits arrange dives elsewhere around Guadeloupe. Chez Guy also arranges weekly packages that include accommodations in bungalows.

Sea Excursions and Snorkeling Most hotels rent snorkeling gear and post information about excursions. The *Papyrus* (Marina Bas-du-Fort, tel. 590/90–92–98) is a glass-bottom catamaran that offers full-day outings replete with rum, dances, and games, as well as moonlight sails. Glass-bottom boats also make snorkeling excursions to Pigeon Island (*see* Scuba Diving, above). The sailing school **Evasion Marine** (locations in St-François and Bas-du-Fort, tel. 590/84–46–67) offers excursions on board the *Ginn Fizz*, the *Ketch*, or the *Sloop*.

Tennis Courts are located at the following hotels: **Arawak** (2 courts), **Auberge de la Vielle Tour** (1 court), **Caravelle/Club Med** (6 courts), **La Creole Beach** (2 courts), **Golf Marine Club** (2 courts), **Hamak** (1 court), **Les Marines de St-François** (2 courts), **Meridien** (5 courts), **Novotel Fleur d'Epée** (2 courts), **PLM-Azur Marissol** (2 courts), **Relais du Moulin** (1 court), **Residence Karukera** (1 court), **Salako** (2 courts), and **Toubana** (1 court). Games can also be arranged through the **St-François Tennis Club** (tel. 590/88–41–87).

Windsurfing Immensely popular here, windsurfing rentals and lessons are available at all beachfront hotels.

Shopping

If shopping is your goal and you're headed for a French island, head for Martinique—the selection is larger and the language less of a barrier. But if you insist on shopping in Guadeloupe, visit Pointe-à-Pitre. Get an early start because it gets very hot and sticky around midday.

Many stores offer a 20% discount on luxury items purchased with traveler's checks or, in some cases, major credit cards. You can find good buys on anything French—perfumes, crystal, china, cosmetics, fashions, scarves. As for local handcrafted items, you'll see a lot of junk, but you can also find island dolls dressed in madras, finely woven straw baskets and hats, salako hats made of split bamboo, madras table linens, and wood carvings. And, of course, the favorite Guadeloupean souvenir—rum.

Shopping Areas In Pointe-à-Pitre the main shopping streets are **rue Schoelcher, rue de Nozières,** and **rue Frébault.** Bas-du-Fort's two shopping districts are the **Mammouth Shopping Center** and the **Marina,** where there are 20 or so boutiques and several restaurants. In **St-François** there are also several shops surrounding the marina. Many of the resorts have fashion boutiques. There are also a number of duty-free shops at Raizet Airport.

Good Buys For Baccarat, Lalique, Porcelaine de Paris, Limoges, and other
China, Crystal, upscale tableware, check **Selection** (rue Schoelcher, Pointe-à-
and Silver Pitre, no phone), **A la Pensée** (44 rue Frébault, Pointe-à-Pitre, tel. 590/82–10–47), and **Rosebleu** (5 rue Frébault, Pointe-à-Pitre, tel. 590/82–93–44).

Cosmetics Guadeloupe's exclusive purveyor of Orlane, Stendhal, and Germaine Monteil is **Vendome** (8–10 rue Frébault, Pointe-à-Pitre, tel. 590/83–42–84).

Native Crafts **Tim Tim** (16 rue Henri IV, tel. 590/83–48–71) is an upscale nostalgia shop with elegant (and expensive) antiques ranging from Creole furniture to maps. For doudou dolls, straw hats, baskets, and madras table linens, try **Au Caraibe** (4 rue Frébault, Pointe-à-Pitre). Anthuriums and other plants that pass muster at U.S. customs are packaged at **Casafleurs** (42 rue René-Boisneuf, tel. 590/82–31–23, and Raizet Airport, tel. 590/82–33–34) and **Floral Antilles** (80 rue Schoelcher, tel. 590/82–18–63, and Raizet Airport, tel. 590/82–97–65).

Perfumes Sweet buys can be found at **Phoenicia** (3 locations in Pointe-à-Pitre: 93 rue de Nozières, tel. 590/82–17–66; 8 rue Frébault, tel. 590/83–50–36; and 121 rue Frébault, tel. 590/82–22–22), **Au Bonheur des Dames** (49 rue Frébault, Pointe-à-Pitre, tel. 590/82–00–30), and **L'Artisan Parfumeur** (rue Schoelcher, Pointe-à-Pitre, no phone).

Rum and Tobacco **Delice Shop** (45 rue Achille René-Boisneuf, Pointe-à-Pitre, tel. 590/82–98–24), **Ets Azincourt** (13 rue Henry IV, Pointe-à-Pitre, tel. 590/82–21–02), and **Comptoir sous Douane** (Raizet Airport, tel. 590/82–22–76) have good choices of island rum as well as tobacco.

Dining

The food here is superb. Many of Guadeloupe's restaurants feature seafood (shellfish is a great favorite), often flavored with rich herbs and spices à la Creole. Favorite appetizers are *accras* (codfish fritters), *boudin* (highly seasoned pork sausage), and *crabes farcis* (stuffed land crabs). Christophine is a vegetable pear (as plantain is considered a vegetable banana—served as a side dish) that appears in a variety of costumes. *Blaff* is a spicy fish stew. Lobster, turtle steak, and *lambi* (conch) are often among the main dishes, and homemade coconut ice cream is a typical dessert. The island boasts 100 restaurants, including those serving classic French, Italian, African, Indian, Vietnamese, and South American fare. The local libation of choice is the *'ti punch* (little "poonch," as it is pronounced)—a heady concoction of rum, lime juice, and sugarcane syrup. The innocent-sounding little punch packs a powerful wallop.

The most highly recommended restaurants are indicated by a star ★.

Category	Cost*
Expensive	over $35
Moderate	$25–$35
Inexpensive	under $25

per person, excluding drinks

Grande-Terre

★ **Auberge de St-François.** Claude Simon's country home is set in an orchard and his tables are set with Royal Doulton china and fine crystal. Dining is indoors or on one of the flower-filled patios, with a superb view of Marie-Galante and Pointe des Châteaux. The house specialty is crayfish served several different ways. Also try brochette of smoked shark with a pepper sauce or conch. M. Simon has also developed a superior wine cellar to complement his cuisine. *St-François, tel. 590/88–51–71. Reservations advised. Closed Sun. MC, V. Expensive.*

★ **Auberge de la Vieille Tour.** Hurricane Hugo hit la Vieille Tour hard and the restaurant was holding off its grand reopening until after press time (Spring 1990). However, there is no reason to believe that the restaurant's repertoire or quality will change. Gilles Ballereau's superb cuisine is artistically presented in a stylish, air-conditioned room with intimate lighting. The large windows afford a splendid view of Ilet du Gosier. The highlights of the menu include fresh duck foie gras, sliced pork fillet in saffron sauce, and salmon and dorado with banana butter. There is an extensive (and expensive) wine list. *Gosier, tel. 590/84–23–23. Reservations advised. Jackets required. No lunch. AE, DC, MC, V. Expensive.*

Le Balata. Hugo also damaged this restaurant that sits high on a bluff above the main Gosier Bas-du-Fort highway. At press time, the new roof was in place and the restaurant's reopening had been scheduled for mid-summer 1990. Pierre and Marie Cecillon present classic Lyonnaise cuisine with Creole touches. Begin with chicken liver in aspic, then contemplate the catch of the day with parslied butter. A special businessman's lunch is available at 90F, including wine. Reserve early for one of the eight tables on the terrace with a view of Fort Fleur d'Epée. *Route de Labrousse, Gosier, tel. 590/90–88–25. Closed Sun. for dinner. AE, DC, V. Expensive.*

La Canne à Sucre. A favorite over the years for its innovative Creole cuisine, La Canne à Sucre is the best restaurant in Pointe-à-Pitre. Occupying an old town house in the center of the city, this small dining room serves the recipes of Gerard Virginius, which include chicken breast stuffed with conch and sea urchins sautéed with lime and spices. Partner Bruno Deligne created grilled lobster "Bruno-style." For more standard fare there are such items as red snapper in a pepper sauce. Among the lavish desserts is *coupe Canne à Sucre*, with rum, coconut sherbet, banana, caramel, whipped cream, and a dash of cinnamon. *17 rue Henri IV, Pointe-à-Pitre, tel. 590/82–10–19 or 590/83–58–48. Reservations advised. Jackets required. No lunch Sat.; closed Sun. AE, V. Expensive.*

★ **Château de Feuilles.** This restaurant is worth a special trip for lunch. You will savor no finer luncheon than is served in this relaxed, stylish, country setting hosted by Martine and Jean-Pierre Dubost. Take a dip in the pool or stroll around the 2-acre farm of this country home while waiting for your lunch. For aperitif, there are about 20 different punch concoctions made with different juices and flavors—sample all if you dare. The changing menu may include goose *rillettes*, breaded conch, tuna *carpaccio* (with olive and lemon), swordfish with sorrel, or *carpaccio* the deep-sea fish *capitan* grilled with lime and green pepper. For dessert, try the pineapple flan. The estate is located 15 km from Le Moule on the Campêche road, between Gros Cap and Campêche. *Campêche, tel. 590/22–19–10. Reservations advised. V. No dinner. Expensive.*

Le Flibustier. At press time, repairs were still under way as a result of Hurricane Hugo. This rustic hilltop farmhouse is a favorite with staffers from neighboring Club Med. A complete dinner of mixed salad, grilled lobster, coconut ice cream, petit punch, and half a pitcher of wine is $26. A lively, fun place. *La Colline, Fonds Thézan (between Ste-Anne and St-Felix), tel. 590/88–23–36. Closed Mon., no lunch Sun. No credit cards. Moderate–Expensive.*

★ **Le Galion.** The Ecotel Hotel's dining room is a training ground for student cooks, waiters, and waitresses. The menu changes with the visiting French master chefs and apprentices, but usually includes red snapper and lobster prepared in various ways. Gourmet galas are prepared twice a month by visiting chefs for about $36 per person. *Ecotel, Montauban, Gosier, tel. 590/84–15–66. Reservations suggested. Jackets required. No lunch. AE, DC, MC, V. Moderate–Expensive.*

La Louisiane. The owner, chef Hogon Damiel, hails from the Carlton in Cannes and offers such traditional favorites as duck-liver confit with raspberry vinaigrette or smoked fish as starters, then crayfish with cassis or roast rack of lamb. The dozen tables of this small restaurant are on a terrace decorated with paintings and hanging flower-filled pots. Since the restaurant is on the road to St-Marthe, about 2 miles from St-François, M. Damiel will send a car for you on request. *St-François, tel. 590/88–44–34. Reservations suggested. Closed Mon. MC, V. Expensive.*

Les Oiseaux. Claudette and Arthur Rolle's menu includes *filet en crôute* with red wine sauce, as well as some unusual dishes such as *Marmite de Robinson*, a fish fondue with dorado, kingfish, tuna, shrimp, and local vegetables. Shellfish aficionados should try *cigale de mer*, which is sea cricket, a member of the shrimp family. *Anse des Rochers, tel. 590/88–56–92. Reservations essential. Closed Thurs., Sun. dinner. V. Moderate–Expensive.*

★ **Relais du Moulin.** The restaurant of this inn overlooks a restored windmill. Inside, nouvelle cuisine includes the house specialty: grouper and lobster served with Creole sauce or stuffed with fresh homemade pâté. Crème caramel in coconut sauce is among the sumptuous desserts. By day sunlight floods through large windows; by night, candles flicker on crisp white cloths. *Châteaubrun (between Ste-Anne and St-Fraņois), tel. 590/88–13–78. Reservations advised. AE, DC, MC, V. Moderate–Expensive.*

La Grande Pizzeria. Open late and very popular, this seaside spot serves pizza, pasta, salads, and some Milanese, Bolognese, and other Italian seafood specialties. *Bas-du-Fort, tel. 590/92–82–64. No reservations. Moderate.*

La Mandingo. In a gardenside dining room, chef Gilles Dontevieux turns out smoked kingfish salad, spicy *palourdes Gouverneur* (squash), giant Guyanese grilled shrimp, and chicken with crayfish. At lunch, grilled meat and fish are served on an outdoor terrace. It's a popular disco by night. Severely damaged by Hurricane Hugo, this restaurant at the edge of the beach was still being repaired at press time. *Gosier Beach, tel. 590/84–35–59. MC, V. Moderate.*

La Mouette. Tables in a gazebo and in the front yard for barefoot and bathing-suit lunching. Grilled lobster, curried goat, ragouts, accras, and stuffed or roasted trunkfish are on the menu. *Pointe des Châteaux, tel. 590/88–62–52. Closed Tues. and Sun. dinner. No credit cards. Moderate.*

★ **Chez Violetta-La Creole.** Head of Guadeloupe's association of cuisinières (lady chefs), award-winning Violette Chaville presents an à la carte menu of traditional Creole dishes. You'll be served by waitresses in madras and foulard garb. The restaurant is popular with American visitors. *Eastern outskirts of Gosier Village, tel. 590/84–10–34. No credit cards. Moderate–Inexpensive.*

L'Amour en Fleurs. Close to Club Med (and very popular with its guests), this is an unpretentious little roadhouse where the award-winning Madame Tresor Amanthe prepares spicy blaffs, boudin, a tasty blend of conch, octopus, rice and beans, and court bouillon. Don't miss the homemade coconut ice cream. At press time the restaurant was still undergoing repairs from the damage done by Hurricane Hugo. *Ste-Anne, tel. 590/88–23–72. No credit cards. Inexpensive.*

Le Barbaroc. We have been assured that this restaurant will reopen in spring 1990 after the damage from Hurricane Hugo has been repaired. People come from all over the island to this rustic 12-table restaurant to feast on Félicité Doloir's imaginative Creole creations. Among the three dozen dishes listed are pureed breadfruit, *poulet du pays cuit fume* (smoked chicken), breadfruit and other vegetable soufflés, and sweet potato noodles. She also brews beer and concocts *moabie*, a nonalcoholic drink made from tree bark, and "punch de maison," a secret mixture of local fruits and rum. The energetic Madame Doloir also conducts culinary/historic tours of the area. *Petit Canal, tel. 590/22–62–71. Reservations advised. No credit cards. Dinner only, closed Wed. Inexpensive.*

Folie Plage. North of Anse-Bertrand, this lively spot is especially popular with families on weekends. In addition to the reliable Creole food of Prudence Marcelin, there is a children's wading pool, a boutique, and a disco on weekends. Superb court bouillon and imaginative curried dishes. *Anse Laborde, tel. 590/22–11–17. Reservations suggested. No credit cards. Inexpensive.*

Basse-Terre **Le Rocher de Malendure.** The setting on a bluff above
★ Malendure Bay and overlooking Pigeon Island makes this restaurant worth a special trip for lunch. The tiered terrace is decked with flowers and the best choices of the menu are the fresh fish, but there are also meat selections such as veal in raspberry vinaigrette and tournedos in three sauces. The owners, M. and Mme. Lesueur, also have five bungalows for rent at very reasonable prices and can arrange deep-sea fishing trips. *Malendure Beach, Bouillante, tel. 590/98–70–84. Reservations suggested on weekends. Lunch only. DC, MC, V. Moderate.*

★ **Chez Clara.** This restaurant is popular and crowded even in the off-season. Clara Laseur and her mother turn out Creole dishes with daily specials listed on the blackboard. Clara (whose English is excellent) gave up a jazz-dancing career in Paris to run her family's seaside restaurant. Clara takes the orders, and the place is often so crowded with her friends and fans that you may have to wait for her to get around to you. The food is worth the wait. *Ste-Rose, tel. 590/28–72–99. Reservations advised. Closed Wed., Sun. dinner, Oct. CB, MC, V. Moderate–Inexpensive.*

Le Karacoli. Lucienne Salcede's rustic seaside restaurant is well established and well regarded. The restaurant has its feet firmly planted in the sands of Grande Anse, a great place for a swim. Creole boudin is a hot item here, as are accras. Other offerings include coquilles Karacoli, court boullion, fried chicken, and turtle ragout. For dessert, try the banana flambé. *Grande Anse, north of Deshaies, tel. 590/28–41–17. No dinner Sat.–Thurs., closed Fri. CB, MC, V. Moderate–Inexpensive.*

Chez Jacky. Jacqueline Cabrion serves Creole and African dishes in her cheerful seaside restaurant. Creole boudin is featured, as are lobster (grilled, vinaigrette, or fricassee), fried crayfish, and ragout of lamb. There's also a wide selection of omelets, sandwiches, and salads. For dessert, try peach melba or banana flambé. *Anse Guyonneau, Pte. Noire, tel. 590/98–06 –98. Closed Sun. dinner. AE, MC, V. Inexpensive.*

Les Gommiers. Lovely peacock chairs grace the bar of this stylish restaurant. The changing menu may list beef tongue in mango sauce, lobster in sauce piquante, fillet beef Roquefort, escallopes of veal, and grilled entrecote. Banana split and profiteroles are on the dessert list. Light lunches include salade Niçoise. *Rue Baudot, Pte. Noire, tel. 590/98–01–79. Closed Mon., Wed. dinner. CB, MC, V. Inexpensive.*

Iles des Saintes, **Le Foyal.** This delightful seaside terrace restaurant serves a so-
Terre-de-Haut phisticated mélange of Creole and Continental dishes. Begin
★ with a warm crepe filled with lobster, conch, octopus, and fish; crabe farci; or a rillette of smoked fish. A house specialty is an assiette of smoked fish served cold; another is stuffed fish fillet served in a white-wine sauce. A special plate for children under 10 is also offered. *Anse Mirre, tel. 590/99–50–92. No credit cards. Moderate–Inexpensive.*

★ **Relais des Iles.** Select your lobster from the *vivier* and enjoy the splendid view from this hilltop eatery while your meal is expertly prepared by Bernard Mathieu. Imaginative things are done with local vegetables. For dessert try the melt-in-your-mouth chocolate mousse. Choose your spirits from an excellent wine list. *Rte. de Pompierre, tel. 590/99–53–04. Reservations suggested in high season. No credit cards. Moderate–Inexpensive.*

Lodging

Gosier and Bas-du-Fort are the main venues for resort hotels, but the areas around St-François and St-Anne also have their fair share of resorts. Guadeloupe doesn't have the selection of elegant, tasteful hotels found on other islands. You can choose between a splashy hotel with a full complement of resort activities or head for a small inn called a Relais Creole. All the inns have met certain guidelines for their beauty or location by the Guadeloupe tourist office and all have a decidedly Gallic accent. But if French is not your forte, you'll fare better in the large hotels. Most hotels include Continental breakfast in their rates (a few include full American breakfast).

The most highly recommended lodgings are indicated by a star ★.

Category	Cost*
Very Expensive	over $280
Expensive	$150–$280
Moderate	$110–$150
Inexpensive	under $110

All prices are for a standard double room for two, excluding a taxe de séjour *that varies from hotel to hotel, and a 10%–15% service charge.*

★ **Hamak.** Five landscaped acres, a private white-sand beach, and even a small fleet of twin-engine planes for transporting guests make this the glitziest place on Guadeloupe. One-bedroom suites are in bungalows. Each unit has a living room, small bedroom, kitchenette, a private rear patio with outdoor freshwater shower and a front terrace with hammock. All are air-conditioned, with large baths, twin beds, hair dryers, and international direct-dial phones. TVs and videos are available. *St-François 97118, tel. 590/88–59–99 or 800/366–1510). 56 units. Facilities: restaurant, 2 bars, lighted tennis court, water-sports center. AE, DC, MC, V. Very Expensive.*

★ **Auberge de la Vieille Tour PLM-Azur.** Taking advantage of the post-Hurricane Hugo shut-down, La Vieille Tour spent the winter season remodeling with the aim of making this countrylike inn one of Guadeloupe's top hotels. Located 3 blocks from the Gosier center, the main building occupies a hilltop on a 7-acre estate, with green hills rolling down to the rooms and small private beach. Some of the rooms are rather small and simply furnished, though outfitted with minibars, TVs, air-conditioners, and spacious baths. Eight rooms have upscale amenities, such as terry-cloth robes. In high season, breakfast, lunch, and barbecues are served at the terrace restaurant at the pool level. Robert Zarkis's orchestra plays nightly in the formal dining room. Water-sports equipment is available for guests Callinago PLM-Azur. *Montauban Gosier 97190, tel.*

590/84–23–23 or 800/223–9862. 80 rooms. Facilities: 2 restaurants, bar, boutiques, 2 lighted tennis courts, pool. AE, DC, MC, V. Expensive.

La Creole Beach. Set in 10 acres of tropical greenery, this Leader Hotel boasts two beaches and spacious rooms. All rooms have individually controlled air-conditioners, TVs, VCRs, radios, international direct-dial phones, and sliding glass doors that open onto a balcony. Water activities include boat excursions to Ilet du Gosier. Damaged by Hurricane Hugo, La Creole Beach is undergoing extensive repair and renewal. *Box 19, Gosier 97190, tel. 590/84–26–26 or 800/366–1510. 156 rooms. Facilities: restaurant, bar, pool, 2 lighted tennis courts, car-rental desk, boat excursions, water-sports center. Expensive.*

Fleur d'Epée Novotel. This beachfront property offers rooms with a queen-size and a single bed, blue onyx baths, satellite TV, radio, phones, and balconies (some with a sea view). An activities director organizes steel band shows and other entertainment. *Bas-du-Fort, Gosier 97190, tel. 590/90–81–49 or 800/221–4542. 186 rooms. Facilities: 2 restaurants, 1 snack bar, pool, 2 tennis courts, water-sports center. AE, DC, MC, V. Expensive.*

Club Med Caravelle. Occupying 50 secluded acres at the western end of a magnificent white-sand beach, this version of the well-known villages has air-conditioned twin-bed rooms, some with balconies. Activities include a French-English language lab, yoga, volleyball, calisthenics, and water sports. The grounds took a severe beating by Hurricane Hugo and though repair work is under way, they may not be at their best even by the 1990/1991 season. *Ste-Anne 97180, tel. 590/88–21–00 or 800/258–2633. 275 rooms. Facilities: restaurant, pub, boutiques, 6 lighted tennis courts (with pro), pool, water-sports center. AE. Moderate–Expensive.*

★ **Meridien.** This hotel is recommended for those who want to pack as much activity as possible into a vacation. The 150-acre resort puts out its own *A to Z Leisure Guide* and broadcasts from Radio Meridien to let you know about resort activities. The activities director organizes everything from bocci to book lending. The hotel's beach hut is a busy place even off-season. The spacious, breezy lobby is filled with Haitian artwork and fresh flowers. Standard rooms are rather modest, but all are air-conditioned with king-size or twin beds, radios, direct-dial phones, and balconies, about half of which face the sea. *St-François 97118, tel. 590/88–51–00 or 800/543–4300. 265 rooms, 10 suites. Facilities: 4 restaurants, 2 bars, disco, boutiques, pool, 5 tennis courts (3 lighted), bike rental, car-rental desk, water-sports center. AE, DC, MC, V. Moderate–Expensive.*

★ **La Toubana.** Red-roof bungalows are sprinkled on a hilltop overlooking the Caravelle Peninsula, arguably the best beach on the island. The bungalows are air-conditioned, and all rooms have private bath, phone, and an ocean view. Seven suites have kitchenettes and private terraced gardens. The pool is rather small. There's evening entertainment at the French-Creole restaurant, including a piano bar. Pets are welcome. Renovations necessitated by Hurricane Hugo spruced up this hotel. *Box 63, Ste-Anne 97180, tel. 590/88–25–78 or 800/223–9815. 57 rooms and suites. Facilities: restaurant, bar, pool, tennis court, water-sports center. AE, DC, V. Moderate–Expensive.*

Cap Sud Caraibes. This is a tiny Relais Creole on a country road between Gosier and Ste-Anne, just a five-minute walk from a quiet beach. Guests are presented with a welcome cocktail, and although English is not the first language here, every attempt is made to make you feel at home. Individually decorated rooms are air-conditioned, and each has a balcony and an enormous bath. There's a big kitchen that guests are welcome to share. *Gosier 97190, tel. 590/88–96–02, or 800/223–9815, 800/468–0023. 12 rooms. Facilities: transfer from airport to hotel, bar, drycleaning and laundry facilities, snorkeling equipment. Moderate.*

Relais du Moulin. A restored windmill serves as the reception room for this Relais Creole tucked in Châteaubrun, near Ste-Anne. A spiral staircase leads up to a TV/reading room from which there is a splendid view. Accommodations are in air-conditioned bungalows; rooms are immaculate and tiny, with twin beds, small terraces, and kitchenettes. The beach is a 10-minute hike away. Guests are advised to have their own rental car. Horseback riding can be arranged, and bikes are available. The fine restaurant serves West Indian nouvelle cuisine. *Châteaubrun, Ste-Anne 97180, tel. 590/88–23–96, 800/223–9815, or 800/468–0023. 40 rooms. Facilities: restaurant, bar, pool, tennis court, archery. AE, MC, V. Moderate.*

★ **Callinago-PLM Azur.** Within the Gosier resort compound on a peninsula 2 miles from town, this hilltop complex above the beach offers a choice between the Callinago Hotel and the Callinago Village. The former offers air-conditioned rooms with full baths, phones, and private balconies with views of the sea or the gardens. The village offers studios and duplex apartments with kitchenettes. You'll be offered a welcome drink. There's dancing in the bar, and frequent entertainment by folkloric groups and steel bands. Damage from Hurricane Hugo required extensive repair and remodeling that has smartened the property considerably. *Box 1, Gosier 97110, tel. 590/84–25–25 or 800/223–9862. 154 units. Facilities: 2 restaurants, 1 bar, car-rental desk, dive shop, pool, water-sports center. AE, DC, MC, V. Inexpensive–Moderate.*

★ **Auberge de la Distillerie.** This is an excellent choice for those who want to be close to the Natural Park and its hiking trails. The small country inn has air-conditioned studios with phones (you'll have to share a bath) and a TV lounge. There's also a rustic wood chalet that sleeps two-four people. Boat trips are arranged on the Lezarde River, in which you can also swim. Pets are welcome. *Vernou 97170, Petit-Bourg, tel. 590/94–01–56, 800/223–9815, or 800/468–0023. 7 studios, 1 chalet. Facilities: restaurant, bar, piano bar. AE, V. Inexpensive.*

Auberge du Grand Large. This casual family-style inn on the grand Ste-Anne beach has bungalows on the beach or tucked in a garden. All are air-conditioned with private baths. The restaurant serves Creole specialties. Pets are welcome. *Ste-Anne 97180, tel. 590/88–20–06, 800/223–9815, or 800/468–0023. 10 rooms. Facilities: restaurant, bar. AE, MC. Inexpensive.*

Grand Anse Hotel. Located near the ferry landing from which you leave for Les Saintes, this Relais Creole offers air-conditioned bungalows with shower baths, phones, and little balconies. The view of the mountains is spectacular. It's less than a mile from a black-sand beach, and water sports can be arranged. A good choice for nature lovers. *Trois Rivières 97114, tel. 590/92–92–21 or 800/468–0023. 16 bungalows. Facilities: restaurant, bar. V. Inexpensive.*

Les Saintes
★ **Village Creole.** Baths by Courreges, dishwashers, freezers, satellite TV/videos, and international direct-dial phones are among the amenities in this apartment hotel. Ghyslain Laps, the English-speaking owner, will help you whip up meals in the kitchen. If you'd prefer not to cook, he can provide you with a cook and housekeeper for an extra charge. A sailboat is available for excursions to Marie-Galante and Dominica. *Pte. Coquelet 97137, Terre-de-Haut, tel. 590/99-53-83 (telex 919671). 22 duplexes. Facilities: airport shuttle service, daily maid service, safe deposit, business center, scooter and boat rentals, water-sports center. MC, V. Moderate–Inexpensive.*

★ **Auberge des Anacardies.** Trimmed with trellises, topped by dormers, and owned by the mayor, this inn offers air-conditioned, twin-bed rooms with phones and baths. Casement windows open to a splendid view of the gardens, the hills, and the bay. This hostelry possesses the island's only swimming pool. Steak au poivre, grilled lobster, and steaks are among the restaurant's offerings. *La Savane 97137, Terre-de-Haut, Les Saintes, tel. 590/99-50-99. 10 rooms. Facilities: restaurant, bar, pool. AE, MC, V. Inexpensive.*

Bois Joli. In high season, you'll need to reserve a room here three months in advance. Facing the "Sugarloaf" on the island's beautiful bay, the hotel consists of modern rooms in bungalows, 14 of which are air-conditioned. You have to be pretty flexible about baths here. There are no private baths. Water sports can be arranged, and the Anse Crawen nudist beach is a five-minute walk away. Pets are allowed. *Terre-de-Haut 97137, tel. 590/99-52-53 or 800/223-9815. 21 rooms. Facilities: restaurant, 2 bars, airport transfers. MC, V. Inexpensive.*

★ **Los Santos-PLM Azur.** These red-top balconied bungalows are all air-conditioned, with phones and private baths; 10 have kitchenettes. Diving, boating, and cycling trips can be arranged. At press time the hotel was closed while it changed management. It is scheduled to be back in business by mid-1990 and is likely to remain the best inexpensive place to stay on Les Saintes. *Terre-de-Haut 97137, tel. 590/99-50-40 or 800/223-9862. 54 rooms. Facilities: restaurant, bar, boutique, TV lounge, video club, nursery, water-sports center. AE, DC, MC, V. Inexpensive.*

Home and Apartment Rental
For information about villas, apartments, and private rooms in modest houses contact **Gîtes de France** (tel. 590/82-09-30). For additional information about apartment-style accommodations, contact the **ANTRE Association** (tel. 590/88-53-09).

The Arts and Nightlife

Cole Porter notwithstanding, Guadeloupeans maintain the beguine began here (the Martinicans make the same claim for their island). Discos come, discos go, and the current music craze is "zouk," but the beat of the beguine remains steady. Many of the resort hotels feature dinner dancing, as well as entertainment by steel bands and folkloric groups.

Casinos
There are two casinos on the island. Neither has one-armed bandits, but both have American-style roulette, blackjack, and chemin de fer. The legal age is 21. Admission is $10, and you'll need a photo ID. Tie and jacket are not required, but "proper attire" means no shorts. The **Casino de Gosier les Bains** (Gosier,

tel. 590/84–18–33) has a bar, restaurant, and nightclub, and is open Monday–Saturday 9 PM–dawn. The **Casino de St-François** (Marina, St-François, tel. 590/84–41–40) has a snack bar and nightclub and is open Tuesday–Sunday 9 PM–3 AM.

Discos A mixed crowd of locals and tourists frequent the discos. Night owls should note that carousing is not cheap. Most discos charge an admission of at least $8, which includes one drink. Drinks cost about $5 each. Some of the enduring hot spots are **Le Foufou** (Hotel Frankel, Bas-du-Fort, tel. 590/84–35–59), **Ti Raccoon** (Creole Beach Hotel, Pointe de la Verdure, tel. 590/ 84–26–26), **Le Mandingo** (Gosier Beach, tel. 590/84–35–39), **Le Caraibe** (Salako, Gosier, tel. 590/84–22–22), the **Bet-a-Feu** (Meridien Hotel, St-François, tel. 590/88–51–00), and the very Parisian **Elysée Matignon** (Rte. des Hôtels, Bas-du-Fort, tel. 590/90–89–05).

Bars and If discos are not your dish, tune in to the **Auberge de la Vieille**
Nightclubs **Tour** (Gosier, tel. 590/84–23–23), where Robert Zarkis's orchestra plays for touch-dancing, which is never passé here. There's also a popular piano bar. **La Toubana** (Ste-Anne, tel. 590/88–25–78) offers a piano bar; there's nightly entertainment at the **Lele Bar** (Meridien, St-François, tel. 590/88–51–00); and an orchestra plays dance music at the **Marissol PLM-Azur** (Bas-du-Fort, tel. 590/90–84–44).

14 Jamaica

*by John DeMers
and Sandra Hart*

The third-largest island in the Caribbean (after Cuba and Puerto Rico), the English-speaking nation of Jamaica enjoys a considerable self-sufficiency based on tourism, agriculture, and mining. Its physical attractions include jungled mountaintops, clear waterfalls, and unforgettable beaches, yet the country's greatest resource may be the Jamaicans themselves. Although 95% of the population trace their bloodlines to Africa, their national origins lie in Great Britain, the Middle East, India, China, Germany, Portugal, South America, and many of the other islands in the Caribbean. Their cultural life is a wealthy one; the music, art, and cuisine of Jamaica are vibrant with a spirit easy to sense but as hard to describe as the rhythms of reggae or a flourish of the streetwise patois.

Jamaica is unusual in that, in addition to such pleasure capitals of the north coast as Montego Bay and Ocho Rios, it has a real capital in Kingston. For all its congestion, and for all the disparity between city life and the bikinis and parasails to the north, Kingston is the true heart and head of the island. This is the place where politics, literature, music, and art wrestle for acceptance in the largest English-speaking city south of Miami, its actual population of nearly 1 million bolstered by the emotional membership of virtually all Jamaicans.

The first people known to have reached Jamaica were the Arawaks, Indians who paddled their canoes from the Orinoco region of South America about a thousand years after the death of Christ. (It is possible that a more primitive group, the Ciboneys, had already spent time here on their trek from Florida to other Caribbean islands.) The Arawaks, who left their imprint on Jamaica, were basically a gentle folk who liked to hunt, fish, farm when the weather was good, and enjoy a rich collection of games and festivals. Then, in 1494, Christopher Columbus stepped ashore at what is now called Discovery Bay. Having spent four centuries on the island, the Arawaks had little notion that his feet on their sand would mean their extinction within 50 years.

What is now St. Ann's Bay was established as New Seville in 1509 and served as the Spanish capital until local government crossed the island to Santiago de la Vega (now Spanish Town). The Spaniards were never impressed with Jamaica; their searches found no precious metals, and they let the island fester in poverty for 161 years. When 5,000 British soldiers and sailors appeared in Kingston harbor in 1655, the Spaniards did not put up a fight.

The arrival of the English, and the three centuries of rule that followed, provided Jamaica with the surprisingly genteel underpinnings of its present life—and the rousing pirate tradition fueled by rum that enlivened a long period of Caribbean history. The British buccaneer Henry Morgan counted Jamaica's governor as one of his closest friends and enjoyed the protection of His Majesty's government no matter what he chose to plunder. Port Royal, once said to be the "wickedest city of Christendom," grew up on a spit of land across from present-day Kingston precisely because it served so many interests. Morgan and his brigands were delighted to have such a haven, and the people of Jamaica profited in being able to buy pirate booty at Port Royal at terrific bargains. In a sense, Port Royal may have been the world's first outlet store.

Morgan enjoyed a prosperous life; he was knighted and made lieutenant governor of Jamaica before the age of 30, and like every good bureaucrat, he died in bed and was given a state funeral. Port Royal fared less well. On June 7, 1692, an earthquake tilted two-thirds of the city into the sea, the tidal wave that followed the last tremors washed away millions in pirate treasure, and Port Royal simply disappeared. In recent years divers have turned up some of the treasure, but most of it still lies in the depths, adding an exotic quality to the water sports pursued along Kingston's reefs.

The very British 18th century was a time of prosperity in Jamaica. This was the age of the sugar baron, who ruled his plantation great house and made the island the largest sugar-producing colony in the world. Because sugar fortunes were built on slave labor, however, production became less profitable when the Jamaican slave trade was abolished in 1807 and slavery in 1838.

As was often the case in colonies, a national identity came to supplant the British allegiance in the hearts and minds of Jamaicans. This new identity was given official recognition on August 6, 1962, when Jamaica became an independent nation with loose ties to the Commonwealth. The island today has a democratic form of government led by a prime minister and by a cabinet of fellow ministers. The 60 members of the House of Representatives are chosen in general elections every five years; the 21 members of the Senate are nominated by the government and the opposition party, then appointed by the governor general.

The elections of February 1989 gave the People's National Party more than two-thirds of the seats in the House and made Michael N. Manley prime minister. Manley replaced Edward P.G. Seaga, leader of the Jamaica Labor Party, who was credited with the recovery of the national economy by instituting unpopular austerity measures. Under Seaga, tourism became Jamaica's major industry, with thousands of talented young Jamaicans choosing it as their career. The mining of bauxite is expected to expand in the near future, and agriculture has been given a fresh look with a new crop of winter vegetables intended to compete with those of Florida and Mexico.

Before You Go

Tourist Information
Contact the **Jamaica Tourist Board** (866 2nd Ave., New York, NY 10017, tel. 212/688–7650).

Arriving and Departing
By Plane
Donald Sangster International Airport in Montego Bay (tel. 809/952–5530) is the most efficient point of entry for visitors destined for Montego Bay, Round Hill-Tryall, Ocho Rios, Runaway Bay, and Negril. **Norman Manley Airport** in Kingston (tel. 809/924–8452) is better for visitors to the capital or Port Antonio. **Trans Jamaica Airlines** (tel. 809/929–5624) provides shuttle services on the island.

Air Jamaica (tel. 718/830–0303 or 800/523–5585) and **American Airlines** (tel. 212/619–6991 or 800/433–7300) fly nonstop from New York, and Air Jamaica also comes in from Miami, **BWIA** (tel. 800/327–7401) from San Juan, **Continental** (tel. 800/231–0856) flies in daily from Newark, and weekly from Houston and **Aeroflot** (tel. 809/929–2251) flies in from Havana. Air Jamaica

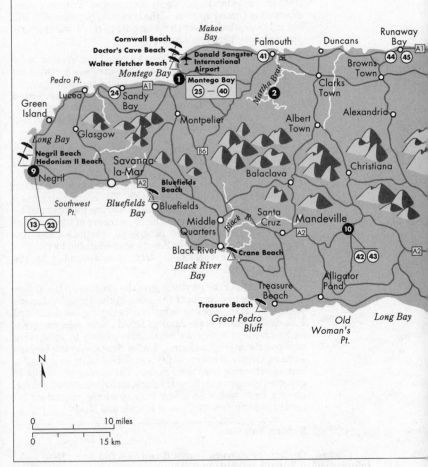

Mahoe Bay · Falmouth · Duncans · Runaway Bay

Cornwall Beach · Doctor's Cave Beach · Donald Sangster International Airport · **41** · Browns Town · **44** **45**

Walter Fletcher Beach · *Montego Bay* · **1** · Montego Bay · **25** — **40** · Martha Brae R. · **2** · Clarks Town

Pedro Pt. · Lucea · **24** · Sandy Bay · Montpelier · Albert Town · Alexandria

Green Island · Glasgow · · B6 · · Christiana

Long Bay · Negril Beach · Hedonism II Beach · Savanna-la-Mar · Balaclava

9 · Negril · A2 · Bluefields Beach · Santa Cruz · Mandeville

Southwest Pt. · **13** — **23** · *Bluefields Bay* · Bluefields · Middle Quarters · Black R. · **10** · A2

Black River · Crane Beach · **42** **43** · A2

Black River Bay · Treasure Beach · Alligator Pond

Treasure Beach · *Great Pedro Bluff* · *Old Woman's Pt.* · *Long Bay*

N

0 — 10 miles
0 — 15 km

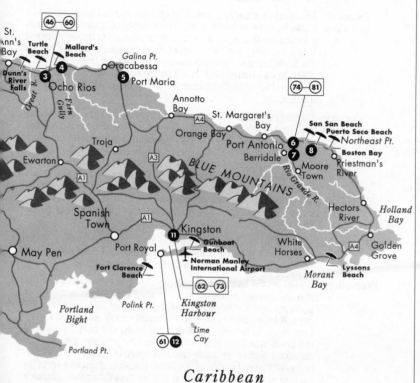

St. Ann's Bay
Turtle Beach
Dunn's River Falls
Mallard's Beach
46 — 60
Galina Pt.
Oracabessa
Ocho Rios
Port Maria
Annotto Bay
St. Margaret's Bay
Orange Bay
Port Antonio
Berridale
74 — 81
San San Beach
Puerto Seco Beach
Northeast Pt.
Boston Bay
Priestman's River
Troja
Ewarton
BLUE MOUNTAINS
Moore Town
Rio Grande R.
Hectors River
Holland Bay
Spanish Town
Kingston
White Horses
Golden Grove
May Pen
Port Royal
Gunboat Beach
Norman Manley International Airport
Lyssons Beach
Morant Bay
Fort Clarence Beach
62 — 73
Portland Bight
Polink Pt.
Kingston Harbour
Lime Cay
61 12
Portland Pt.

Caribbean Sea

1 Exploring Sites

13 Hotels and Restaurants

Fern Hill Club, **80**
Goblin Hill, **76**
Grand Lido, **15**
H.E.A.R.T. Country Club, **45**
Hedonism II, **16**
Hotel Oceana, **69**
Jamaica Inn, **54**
Jamaica, Jamaica, **44**
Jamaica Palace, **79**
Jamaica Pegasus, **67**
Mallards Beach Resort, **57**

Mandeville Hotel, **43**
Montevan Lodge, **81**
Morgan's Harbour Hotel, Beach Club, and Yacht Marina, **61**
Negril Gardens, **19**
Negril Inn, **17**
Plantation Inn, **55**
Sandals Ocho Rios, **52**
Sandals Negril, **18**
Sans Souci Hotel, Club, and Spa, **56**

Shaw Park Beach Hotel, **58**
Swept Away, **23**
Trelawny Beach Hotel, **41**
Trident Villas and Hotel, **74**
Tryall Golf, Tennis, and Beach Club, **24**
Wyndham Kingston, **68**

provides the most frequent service from U.S. cities, flying to the island from Philadelphia, Atlanta, Tampa, Los Angeles, New York, and Miami. The national carrier also flies from Toronto. **Air Canada** (tel. 800/422–6232) offers service from Toronto and Montreal, and both **British Airways** (tel. 800/247–9297) and Air Jamaica connect the island with London.

Passports and Visas
Passports are not required of visitors from the United States or Canada, but every visitor must have proof of citizenship such as a birth certificate or a voter registration card (a driver's license is *not* enough). British visitors need passports but not visas. Each visitor must possess a return or ongoing ticket and sufficient funds to maintain himself on the island. Declaration forms are distributed in flight in order to keep customs formalities to a minimum.

Customs and Duties
Luggage is searched upon arrival in Jamaica. The importation of illegal drugs, fresh fruits, flowers, meat, and rum (since it's produced here) is restricted. Jamaican law prohibits bringing arms or ammunition onto the island; firearms must be surrendered to authorities at the point of entry, to be returned at the time of departure. The laws forbidding the use of "ganja" (marijuana) in Jamaica are strict. Financial penalties, jail terms, and deportation await anyone who scoffs at the laws. Enforcement includes Coast Guard patrols and ganja-sniffing police dogs.

Language
The official language of Jamaica is English. Islanders sometimes speak a patois among themselves, and they may use it when they don't want you to understand something.

Precautions
Do not let the beauty of Jamaica cause you to relax the caution and good sense you would use in your own hometown. Never leave money or other valuables in your hotel room; use the safe deposit boxes that most establishments make available. Carry your funds in traveler's checks, not cash, and keep a record of the check numbers in a secure place. Never leave a rental car unlocked, and never leave valuables even in a locked car. Finally, resist the call of the wild when it presents itself as a scruffy-looking native offering to show you the "real" Jamaica. Jamaica *on* the beaten path is wonderful enough; don't take chances by wandering far from it. And ignore his efforts, however persistent, to sell you a ganja joint.

Staying in Jamaica

Important Addresses
Tourist Information: The main office of the **Jamaica Tourist Board** is in Kingston (Tourism Centre Bldg., New Kingston Box 360, Kingston 5, tel. 809/929–9200). There are also JTB desks at both Montego Bay and Kingston airports and JTB offices in all resort areas.

Emergencies
Police, Fire, Ambulance: Police and Air-Rescue is 119. Fire department and ambulance is 110.

Hospitals: University Hospital at Mona in Kingston (tel. 809/927–6621), **Cornwall Regional Hospital** (Mt. Salem, in Montego Bay, tel. 809/952–5100), and **Port Antonio General Hospital** (Naylor's Hill in Port Antonio, tel. 809/993–2646).

Pharmacies: Pegasus Hotel in Kingston (tel. 809/926–8174), **McKenzie's Drug Store** (16 Strand St. in Montego Bay, tel. 809/

952–2467), and **Great House Pharmacy** (Brown's Plaza in Ocho Rios, tel. 809/974–2352).

Currency By law, anything purchased in Jamaica must be paid for with Jamaican dollars. The Jamaican dollar is worth J$6.50 to U.S.$1 (although a further devaluation to J$7 is expected). Currency can be exchanged at airport bank counters, exchange bureaus, or a commercial bank. Be sure to keep all your exchange transaction receipts; you'll need them when you're ready to change your leftover Jamaican currency on leaving the country. Jamaican currency may not be taken out of the country. Prices quoted below are in U.S. dollars unless otherwise noted.

Taxes and Hotels collect a 5% government tax on room occupancy. The de-
Service Charges parture tax is $16.

Most hotels and restaurants add a 10% service charge to your bill. Otherwise, tips may average 15%–20%.

Guided Tours Half-day tours are offered by a variety of operators in the important areas of Jamaica. The best Great Houses tours include Rose Hall, Greenwood, and Devon House. Plantations to tour are Prospect and Brimmer's Hall. The Governor's Coach Tour uses a diesel rail car to visit villages, plantations, and a rum distillery. The increasingly popular waterside folklore feasts are offered on the Dunn's, Great, and White rivers. The significant city tours are those in Kingston, Montego Bay, and Ocho Rios. Quality tour operators include **Martin's Tours** (tel. 809/327–5767), **Tropical Tours** (tel. 809/952–1110), **Greenlight Tours** (tel. 809/926–2014), **Estate Tours Services** (tel. 809/974–2058), and **Jamaica Tours** (tel. 809/953–2476). A ride in a hot-air balloon is the highlight of the **Hilton High Day Tour** (tel. 809/952–3343), which has been dubbed "Up, Up, and Buffet." **Helitours Jamaica Ltd.** offers another way to see Jamaica from the air, with helicopter tours ranging from 10 minutes to an hour aloft at prices that vary accordingly ($45–$175). Contact their Ocho Rios office (tel. 809/974–2495), or the Kingston office (tel. 809/929–8150). **South Coast Safaris Ltd.** has guided boat excursions up the Black River for some 10 miles (round-trip), into the mangroves and marshlands, aboard the 25-passenger *Safari Queen* (tel. 809/962–0220 or 809/965–2513).

Getting Around Some but not all of Jamaica's taxis are metered. If you accept a
Taxis driver's offer of his services as tour guide, be sure to agree on a price *before* the vehicle is put into gear. All licensed taxis display red Public Passenger Vehicle (PPV) as well as regular license plates. Cabs can be summoned by telephone or flagged down on the street. Taxi rates are per car, not per passenger, and 25% is added to the metered rate between midnight and 5 AM. Licensed minivans are also available and bear the red PPV plates.

Rental Cars Jamaica has dozens of car-rental companies throughout the island. Because rentals can be difficult to arrange once you've arrived, you *must* make a reservation and send a deposit before your trip. (Cars are scarce, and without either a confirmation number or a receipt you may have to walk.) Best bets are the same names you would think of at home: **Avis** (tel. 800/331–2112), **Dollar** (tel. 800/421–6868), **Hertz** (tel. 800/654–3001), **National** (tel. CAR-EUROPE). In Jamaica, try the branch offices in your resort area or **United Car Rentals** (tel. 809/952–2636), or **Jamaica Car Rental** (tel. 809/924–8217). You must be at least 21 years old to rent a car, and you must have a valid driver's license (from any country). You may be required to post a security of several hundred dollars before taking possession of your car; ask about this when you make the reservation.

Traffic keeps to the left in Jamaica, and those who are unfamiliar with driving on the left will find that it takes some getting used to. Be cautious until you are comfortable with it.

Trains The diesel train between Kingston and Montego Bay reveals virtually every type of scenery Jamaica has to offer in a trip of nearly five hours.

Buses Buses are the mode of transportation Jamaicans use most, and consequently some buses are very crowded and slow. Yet the service is quite good between Kingston and Montego Bay and between other significant destinations. Schedule or route information is available at bus stops, or from the bus driver.

Cycles The front desks of most major hotels can arrange the rental of bicycles, mopeds, and motorcycles. Daily rates run from about $16 for a moped to $125 for a Honda 125. Deposits of $80 or more are required.

Telephones and Mail The area code for all Jamaica is 809. Direct telephone, telegraph, telefax, and telex services are available.

Airmail postage from Jamaica to the United States or Canada at press time was J$.55 for letters, J$.45 for postcards. Local mail is J$.25

Opening and Closing Times Normal business hours for stores are weekdays 8–4, Saturdays 8–1. Banking hours are generally Monday–Thursday 9–2, Friday 9–noon and 2:30–5.

Beaches

Jamaica has some 200 miles of beaches, some of them still uncrowded. The beaches listed below are public places, and they are among the best Jamaica has to offer. In addition, nearly every resort has its own private beach complete with towels and water sports. Some of the larger resorts sell day passes to nonguests.

Doctor's Cave Beach at Montego Bay shows a tendency toward population explosion, attracting Jamaicans and tourists alike; at times it may resemble Fort Lauderdale at spring break. The 5-mile stretch of sugary sand has been spotlighted in so many travel articles and brochures over the years that it's no secret to anyone. On the bright side, Doctor's Cave is well fitted out for all its admirers with changing rooms, colorful if overly insistent vendors, and a large selection of snacks.

Two other popular beaches in the Montego Bay area are **Cornwall Beach,** farther up the coast, which is smaller, also lively, with lots of food and drink available, and **Walter Fletcher Beach,** on the bay near the center of town. Fletcher offers protection from the surf on a windy day and therefore unusually fine swimming; the calm waters make it a good bet for children, too.

Ocho Rios appears to be just about as busy as MoBay these days, and the busiest beach is usually **Mallard's.** The Mallard's Beach and the Club Americana hotels are both here, spilling out their large convention groups at all hours of the day. To the south, it is **Turtle Beach** that the islanders consider the place to go swimming in Ocho Rios.

Not too long ago, the 7 miles of white sand at **Negril Beach** offered a beachcomber's vision of Eden. Today much of it is fenced off and littered with the debris of construction. The nude beach areas are sectioned off, and some new resorts are building accommodations overlooking their nude beaches, thereby adding a new dimension to the traditional notion of "ocean view."

Elsewhere in Negril, the action-oriented **Hedonism II** is a favorite of the young singles crowd, with facilities for a range of activities from jet-skiing to weight lifting and an array of social hoopla. Its reputation for the risqué may make it unappealing or unsuitable for some people. Hedonism's beach is a private hotel beach; nonguests must pay a fee to use the facilities.

In Port Antonio, head for **San San** or **Boston Bay.** Any of the shacks spewing scented smoke along the beach at Boston Bay will sell you the famous peppery delicacy jerk pork. **Puerto Seco Beach** at Discovery Bay is a sunny, sandy beach.

Kingston may seem an unlikely place for beach lovers, yet Kingstonians enjoy the water, too. **Gunboat Beach** is the most popular choice, and there are other options. **Fort Clarence,** a black-sand beach in the Hellshire Hills area southwest of the city, has changing facilities and entertainment. Sometimes Kingstonians are willing to drive 32 miles east to the lovely **Lyssons Beach** in Morant Bay or, for a small negotiable fee, to hire a boat at the Morgan's Harbor Marina at Port Royal to ferry them to **Lime Cay.** This island, just beyond Kingston Harbor, is perfect for picnicking, sunning, and swimming.

Those who seek beaches off the main tourist routes will want to explore Jamaica's unexploited south coast. Nearest to "civilization" is **Bluefields Beach** near Savanna-la-Mar, south of Negril along the coast. **Crane Beach** at Black River is another great discovery. And the best of the south shore has to be **Treasure Beach,** 20 miles farther along the coast beyond Crane.

Exploring Jamaica

Numbers in the margin correspond with points of interest on the Jamaica map.

Montego Bay ❶ The number and variety of its attractions make Montego Bay on the island's northwest corner the logical place to begin an exploration of Jamaica. Confronting the string of high-rise developments that crowd the water's edge, you may find it hard to believe that little of what is now Montego Bay (the locals call it MoBay) existed before the turn of the century. Today many explorations of Montego Bay are conducted from a reclining chair on Doctor's Cave Beach, a table nearby to hold frothy drinks.

Rose Hall Great House, perhaps the greatest in the West Indies in the 1700s, enjoys its popularity less for its architecture than for the legend surrounding its second mistress. Annie Palmer was credited with murdering three husbands and a plantation overseer who was her lover; the story is told in two novels sold everywhere in Jamaica: *The White Witch of Rose Hall* and *Ja-*

maica White. The great house is east of Montego Bay, just across the highway from the Rose Hall resorts. *Tel. 809/953–2323. Open daily 9:30–6.*

Greenwood Great House, 15 miles east of Montego Bay, has no spooky legend to titillate visitors, but it's much better than Rose Hall at evoking the atmosphere of life on a sugar plantation. The Barrett family, from which the English poet Elizabeth Barrett Browning was descended, once owned all the land from Rose Hall to Falmouth, and the family built several great houses on it. The poet's father, Edward Moulton Barrett ("the Tyrant of Wimpole Street"), was born at Cinnamon Hill, currently the private estate of country singer Johnny Cash. Highlights of Greenwood include oil paintings of the Barretts, china made especially for the family by Wedgwood, a library filled with rare books printed as early as 1697, fine antique furniture, and a collection of exotic musical instruments. *Open daily 9–6; admission is about $6.*

One of the most popular excursions in Jamaica is rafting on the **②** **Martha Brae River.** The gentle waterway takes its name from that of an Arawak Indian who killed herself because she refused to reveal the whereabouts of a local gold mine to the Spanish. According to legend, she finally agreed to take them there and, on reaching the river, used magic to change its course and drowned herself along with the greedy Spaniards. Her *duppy* (ghost) is said to guard the mine's entrance to this day. Bookings are made through hotel tour desks. The trip is $30 per raft (two per raft) for the 1½-hour river run, about 28 miles from most hotels in Montego Bay.

The **Governor's Coach Tour** takes you through the lush hills and countryside around Montego Bay in a diesel rail car. You'll get a look at Jamaican villages, plantations growing banana and coconut, coffee groves, and the facility that turns out Appleton Rum. The full-day excursion includes a riverside lunch and a rum punch. There are several ways to book a tour that picks guests up at MoBay hotels: The newest is from **Appleton Estate Express** (tel. 809/592–3692 or 809/592–6606), which leaves at 8:50 from MoBay and returns at 4:30 PM, for a cost of $50, on air-conditioned trains with musicians on board. **Jamaica Tours** (tel. 809/952–1398) also does a Tuesday through Friday departure from MoBay at 9:30 with a 5 PM return, for about $42. Both companies provide rum drinks and buffet lunch.

An Evening on the Great River is a must for tour groups, yet fun nonetheless. The adventure includes a boat ride up the torchlit river, a full Jamaican dinner, a native folklore show, and dancing to a reggae band. *Tel. 809/952–5047 or 809/952–5097. $41 per person with hotel pickup and return; $37 if you arrive via your own transport. Sun., Tues., and Thurs.*

Ocho Rios Perhaps more than anywhere else in Jamaica, **Ocho Rios**—67 **③** miles east of Montego Bay—presents a striking contrast of natural beauty and recreational development. The Jamaicans can fill the place by themselves, especially on a busy market day, when cars and buses from the countryside clog the heavily traveled coastal road that links Port Antonio with Montego Bay. Add a tour bus or three and the entire passenger list from a cruise ship, and you may find yourself mired in a considerable traffic jam.

Yet a visit to Ocho Rios is worthwhile, if only to enjoy its two chief attractions—Dunn's River Falls and Prospect Plantation. A few steps away from the main road in Ocho Rios await some of the most charming inns and oceanfront restaurants in the Caribbean. Lying on the sand of what will seem to be your private cove, or swinging gently in a rope chair with a tropical drink in your hand, you'll soon forget the traffic that's only a brief stroll away.

The dispute continues as to the origin of the name *Ocho Rios.* Some claim it's Spanish for "eight rivers"; others maintain that the name is a corruption of *chorreras,* which describes a seemingly endless series of cascades that sparkle from the limestone rocks along this stretch of coast. For as long as anyone can remember, Jamaicans have favored Ocho Rios as their own escape from the heat and the crowds of Kingston.

Dunn's River Falls is an eye-catching sight: 600 feet of cold, clear mountain water splashing over a series of stone steps to the warm Caribbean. The best way to enjoy the falls is to climb the slippery steps. Don a swimsuit, take the hand of the person ahead of you, and trust that the chain of hands and bodies leads to an experienced guide. Those who lead the climbs are personable fellows who reel off bits of local lore while telling you where to stop.

Prospect Plantation Tour (tel. 809/974-2058) is the best of several offerings that delve into the island's former agricultural lifestyle. It's not just for specialists; virtually everyone enjoys the beautiful views over the White River Gorge and the tour by jitney (a canopied open-air cart pulled by a tractor) through a plantation with exotic fruits and tropical trees planted over the years by such celebrities as Winston Churchill and Charlie Chaplin. Horseback riding over 1,000 acres is available.

The third "must" in Ocho Rios—and the newest—is **Carinosa,** a pet project of former prime minister Edward Seaga. This amazing 20-acre garden perched on a hillside above the town offers some of the loveliest orchids anywhere, a dramatic weave of streams and waterfalls, and a tropical aviary. *Eden Bower Rd., tel. 809/974-5346. Tours daily from 9 AM to 5 PM; cost $10.*

Time Out Try to plan your Carinosa visit around lunch or dinner, for the **Garden Restaurant** (tel. 809/974-5346) offers a delightful terrace and New Jamaican cuisine. Best bets are the smoked marlin and the Seville chicken julienne.

The only major historic site in Ocho Rios is **The Old Fort,** built in 1777 as a defense against invaders from the sea. The original "defenders" spent much of their time sacking and plundering as far afield as St. Augustine, Florida, and sharing their bounty with the local plantation owners who financed their missions.

4 **Golden Eye,** just east of Ocho Rios on the main coast road, was used in wintertime by Ian Fleming, the creator of James Bond, from 1946 until his death in 1964. Since then Golden Eye has served as home to reggae legend Bob Marley and to the founder of Island Records, Chris Blackwell. Today it can be seen only by those who can afford to rent it from the record company. It's an airy complex of deep-blue buildings, walls and bookcases bursting with Bond memorabilia, and a private cove reached by stone steps that would have delighted 007 (provided the Dom Perignon would not be badly shaken during the descent).

⑤ Two area residences are of more than passing interest. **Firefly,** about 20 miles east of Ocho Rios in Port Maria, was once Sir Noël Coward's vacation residence and is now preserved in all its hilltop wonder by the National Trust of Jamaica. Coward used to entertain jet-setters and royalty in the surprisingly spartan digs in an Eden-like setting. The Jamaicans who give impromptu tours of Firefly, for a cost of $1.75, used to work for Sir Noël, and they show a moving reverence for his simple grave on the grounds.

Port Antonio Every visitor's presence in Port Antonio pays homage to the **⑥** beginnings of Jamaican tourism. Early in the century the first tourists arrived here on the island's northeast tip, 133 miles east of Montego Bay, drawn by the exoticism of the island's banana trade and seeking a respite from the New York winters. The original posters of the shipping lines make Port Antonio appear as foreign as the moon, yet in time it became the tropical darling of a fast-moving crowd and counted Clara Bow, Bette Davis, Ginger Rogers, Rudyard Kipling, J. P. Morgan, and William Randolph Hearst among its admirers. Its most passionate devotee was the actor Errol Flynn, whose spirit still seems to haunt the docks, devouring raw dolphin and swigging gin at 10 AM. Flynn's widow, Patrice Wymore Flynn, owns a boutique in the Palace Hotel and also operates a working cattle farm.

Although the action has moved elsewhere, the area can still weave a spell. Robin Moore wrote *The French Connection* here, and Broadway's tall and talented Tommy Tune found inspiration for the musical *Nine* while being pampered at Trident.

With the help of recent renovations, a stroll through the town suggests a step into the past. A couple of miles north of Port Antonio's main street, **Queen Street** in the residential Titchfield area offers fine Georgian architecture. **DeMontevin Lodge** (21 Fort George, tel. 809/993–2604), owned by the Mullings family (the late Gladys Mullings was Errol Flynn's cook), and the nearby **Musgrave** are in the traditional sea-captain style that one finds along coasts as far away as New England.

The town's best-known landmark is **Folly,** on the way to Trident, a Roman-style villa in ruins on the eastern edge of East Harbor. The creation of a Connecticut millionaire in 1905, the manse was made almost entirely of concrete. Unfortunately, the cement was mixed with seawater, and it began to crumble as it dried. According to local lore, the millionaire's bride took one look at her shattered dream, burst into tears, and fled forever. Little more than the marble floor remains today.

Time Out **Navy Island** is the 64-acre island made infamous by Errol Flynn when he bought it. The present owners, Alice and Harry Eiler, welcome visitors who catch the private launch to their **Admiralty Club** for lunch (or dinner, by prior reservation: tel. 809/993–2667). Lunch can be as simple as a thick pepperpot soup and grilled fish with lime; dinner can be a five-course spectacular.

⑦ Rafting on the **Rio Grande River** (yes, Jamaica has a Rio Grande, too) is a must. This is the granddaddy of the river-rafting attractions, an 8-mile-long, swift green waterway from Berrydale to Rafter's Rest. Here the river flows into the Caribbean at St. Margaret's Bay. The trip of about three hours is made on bamboo rafts pushed along by a raftsman who is likely to be a character. You can pack a picnic lunch and eat it on the raft or along the riverbank; wherever you lunch, a vendor of Red Stripe beer will appear at your elbow. A restaurant, bar, and souvenir shop are at Rafter's Rest (tel. 809/993–2778). About $35 per two-person raft.

8 Another interesting excursion takes you to **Summerset Falls,** where you can climb the 400 feet with some assistance from a concrete staircase. A brief raft ride takes you part of the way. Tickets are sold just west of Rafter's Rest (tel. 809/993–2778). **Athenry Gardens,** a 16-acre tropical wonderland, and **Nonsuch Cave** are some 6 miles northeast of Port Antonio in the village of Nonsuch. The cave's underground beauty has been made accessible by concrete walkways, railed stairways, and careful lighting.

A short drive east from Port Antonio deposits you at **Boston Beach,** which is popular with swimmers and has been enshrined by lovers of jerk pork. The spicy barbecue was originated by the Arawaks and perfected by runaway slaves called the Maroons. Eating almost nothing but wild hog preserved over smoking coals enabled the Maroons to survive years of fierce guerrilla warfare with the English.

For as long as anyone can remember, Port Antonio has been a center for some of the finest deep-sea fishing in the Caribbean. Dolphins (the delectable fish, not the lovable mammal) are the likely catch here, along with tuna, kingfish, and wahoo. In October the week-long *Blue Marlin Tournament* attracts anglers from around the world. By the time enough beer has been consumed, it's a bit like the running of the bulls at Pamplona, except that fish stories carry the day.

Crystal Springs, about 10 miles west of Port Antonio, has over 15,000 orchids, and hummingbirds dart among the blossoms, landing on visitors' outstretched hands. It's a quiet, special corner of the world.

Negril Negril, situated 52 miles southwest of Montego Bay on the
9 winding coast road, is no longer Jamaica's best-kept secret. In fact, it has begun to shed some of its bohemian, ramshackle atmosphere for the attractions and activities traditionally associated with Montego Bay. Applauding the sunset from Rick's Cafe may still be the highlight of a day in Negril, yet increasingly the hours before and after have come to be filled with conventional recreation.

One thing that has not changed around this west coast center (whose only true claim to fame is a 7-mile beach) is the casual approach to life. As you wander from lunch in the sun to shopping in the sun to sports in the sun, you'll find that swimsuits are common attire. Want to dress for a special meal? Slip a caftan over your bathing suit.

Even though you may be staying at one of the charming smaller inns in Negril, you might enjoy spending a day at **Hedonism II,** a kind of love poem to health, Mother Nature, and good (mostly clean) fun. The owners love to publicize the occasional nude volleyball game in the pool at 3 AM, but most of the pampered campers are in clothes and in bed well before that hour. And what if Hedonism II is not the den of iniquity it likes to appear to be? What it is, and what your day pass ($40) gets you, is a taste of the spirit as well as the food—and participation in snorkeling, parasailing, and jet skiing.

Next to Hedonism II is a sister resort, the **Grand Lido,** that offers a "night pass" for nonguests that includes dinner at the Cafe Lido, live entertainment, dusk-to-dawn dancing, and midnight buffet. The price is a hefty $80, and reservations are a must.

After sunset, activity centers on **West End Road,** Negril's main (and only) thoroughfare, which comes to life in the evening with bustling bistros and ear-splitting discos. West End Road may still be unpaved, yet it leads to the town's only building of historical significance, the **Lighthouse.** All anyone can tell you about it, however, is that it's been there for a while. Even historians find it hard to keep track of the days in Negril.

Negril today stretches along the coast north from the horse-shoe-shaped **Bloody Bay** (named during the period when it was a whale-processing center), along the calm waters of **Long Bay** to the Lighthouse section and the landmark **Rick's Cafe** (tel. 809/957–4335). Sunset at Rick's is a tradition, one not unlike the event observed at Mallory Square in Key West. Here there are jugglers and fire-eaters, 50-foot cliffs, and divers who go spiraling downward into the deep green depths.

In the 18th century Negril was where the English ships assembled in convoys for the dangerous ocean crossing. Not only were there pirates in the neighborhood, but the infamous Calico Jack and his crew were captured right here, while they guzzled the local rum. All but two of them were hanged on the spot; Mary Read and Anne Bonney were pregnant at the time, and their execution was delayed.

Mandeville
⑩ More than a quarter of a century after Jamaica achieved its independence from Great Britain, Mandeville seems like a hilly tribute to all that is genteel and admirable in the British character. At 2,000 feet above sea level, 70 miles southeast of Montego Bay, Mandeville is considerably cooler than the coastal area 25 miles to the south. Its vegetation is more lush, thanks to the mists that drift through the mountains. The people of Mandeville live their lives around a village green, a Georgian courthouse, tidy cottages and gardens, even a parish church. The entire scene could be set down in Devonshire, were it not for the occasional poinciana blossom or citrus grove.

Mandeville is omitted from most tourist itineraries even though its residents are increasingly interested in showing visitors around. It is still much less expensive than any of the coastal resorts, and its diversions include horseback riding, cycling, croquet, hiking, tennis, golf, and people-meeting.

The town itself is characterized by its orderliness. You might stay here several days, or a glimpse of the lifestyle may satisfy you and you'll scurry back to the steamy coast. **Manchester Club** features tennis, nine holes of golf, and well-manicured greens; **Mrs. Stephenson's Gardens** are lovely, with orchids and fruit trees; the natural **Bird Sanctuary** shows off 25 species indigenous to Jamaica; and **Marshall's Pen Great House** offers an array of walking tours. The cool, crisp air will make you feel up to any stroll in Mandeville. Further information on Mandeville is available from the Mandeville office of the JTB (tel. 809/962–1072), or through the visitors information center at the Hotel Astra (tel. 809/962–3265 or 809/962–3377).

Time Out The **1907 Gallery** (tel. 809/962–0109) is nestled at 1907 Caledonia Meadows atop a gentle Mandeville Hill. It will take repeated inquiries to find, but the home-bar-boutique of John Deer and his daughter Rahjah is worth any hunt. Pull up an authentic barber chair to his bar, and listen to the story of this Rasta family as they moved from Jamaica to London to Jamaica and came to reside in a home filled with collectibles (that are also for sale).

Kingston The reaction of most visitors to the capital city, situated on the **⑪** southeast coast of Jamaica, is anything but love at first sight. In fact, only a small percentage of visitors to Jamaica see it at all. Kingston, for the tourist, may seem as remote from the resorts of Montego Bay as the loneliest peak in the Blue Mountains. Yet the islanders themselves can't seem to let it go. Everybody talks about Kingston, about their homes or relatives there, about their childhood memories. More than the sunny havens of the north coast, Kingston is a distillation of the true Jamaica. Parts of it may be dirty, crowded, often raucous, yet it is the ethnic cauldron that produces the cultural mix that is the nation's greatest natural resource. Kingston is a cultural and commercial crossroads of international and local movers and shakers, art-show openings, theater (from Shakespeare to pantomime), and superb shopping. Here, too, the University of the West Indies explores Caribbean art and literature, as well as science. As one Jamaican has put it, "You don't really know Jamaica until you know Kingston."

The best way to approach this city is from within, staying in one of the quiet residential sections and dining with the local inhabitants in restaurants that seem to have no names (people refer to them by their addresses, such as 73 or 64, and everyone knows where to meet). The first-time business or pleasure traveler may prefer to begin with New Kingston, a former racetrack property that now glistens with hotels, office towers, apartments, and boutiques. Newcomers may feel more comfortable settling in here and venturing forth from comfort they know will await their return.

Kingston's colonial past is very much alive away from the high rises of the new city. **Devon House** (tel. 809/929–6602), our first stop, is reached through the iron gates at 26 Hope Road. Built in 1881 and bought and restored by the government in the 1960s, the mansion has period furnishings. Shoppers will appreciate Devon House, for the firm Things Jamaican has converted portions of the space into some of the best crafts shops on the island. On the grounds you'll find one of the few mahogany trees to survive Kingston's ambitious but not always careful development.

Time Out Bob Marley's former cook has opened her own restaurant, **Minnie's Ethiopian Herbal-Health Food** (176 Old Hope Rd., tel. 809/927–9207), selling food and fresh juices (at last count, there were over 15 fresh fruit juices), prepared Rasta style. From early in the AM, this is the place for a true Jamaican breakfast of ackee with festival, or callaloo with "food," then on to a lunch of vegetable run-down or gungo-pea stew. On Friday nights musicians drop by to jam and juice.

Among nearby residences, **Kings House,** farther along Hope Road, is the home of Jamaica's governor-general, and **Vale Royal** on Montrose Road is home to the prime minister. The latter structure, originally built as a plantation house in the 1700s, is one of the few still standing in the capital that has a lookout tower for keeping an eye on ships in the harbor. *Tel. 809/927-6424. King's House is only open weekdays, 10–5.*

Once you have accepted the fact that Kingston doesn't look like a travel poster—too much life goes on here for that—you might see your trip here for precisely what it is, the single best introduction to the people of Jamaica. Near the waterfront, the **Institute of Jamaica** (tel. 809/922-0620) is a museum and library that traces the island's history from the Arawaks to current events. The charts and almanacs here make fascinating browsing; one example, famed as the Shark Papers, is made up of damaging evidence tossed overboard by a guilty sea captain and later recovered from the belly of a shark.

From the Institute, push onward to the **University of the West Indies** (tel. 809/927-1660) in the city's Mona section. A cooperative venture begun after World War II by several West Indian governments, the campus is set in an eye-catching cradle of often misty mountains. In addition to a bar and a disco where you can meet the students (they pay dues, while tourists enter free), the place seems a monument to the conviction that education and commitment lead to a better life for the entire Caribbean.

Jamaica's rich cultural life is evoked at the **National Gallery** (12 Ocean Blvd., tel. 809/922-1561), which was once part of Devon House and can now be found at Kingston Mall near the reborn waterfront section. The artists represented here may not be household words in other nations, yet the paintings of such intuitive masters as John Dunkley, David Miller, Sr., and David Miller, Jr., reveal a sensitivity to the life around them that transcends academic training. Among other highlights from the 1920s through the 1980s are works by Edna Manley and Mallica Reynolds, better known as Kapo.

Reggae fans touring the National Gallery will want to look for Christopher Gonzalez's controversial statue of Bob Marley, and they will feel transfixed by **Tuff Gong International** (56 Hope Rd.). Painted in Rastafarian red, yellow, and green, this recording studio was built by Marley at the height of his career. The house has since become the **Bob Marley Museum** (tel. 809/927-9152), with impromptu tours given by just about anyone who may be around. Certainly there is much here to help the outsider understand Marley, reggae, and Jamaica itself. The Ethiopian flag is a reminder that Rastas consider the late Ethiopian emperor Haile Selassie to be the Messiah, a descendant of King Solomon and the Queen of Sheba. A striking mural by Everald Brown, *The Journey of Superstar Bob Marley,* depicts the hero's life from its beginnings in a womb shaped like a coconut to enshrinement in the heart of the Jamaican people.

A distinct change of pace is offered by the **Royal Botanical Gardens at Hope** (tel. 809/927-1085), a cooling sanctuary donated to Jamaica by the Hope family following the abolition of slavery. Some 200 acres explode with tropical trees, plants, and flowers, each clearly labeled and lovingly discussed by qualified guides. Free concerts are given here on the first Sunday of each month.

⑫ Unless your visit must be very brief, you shouldn't leave Kingston without a glimpse of "the wickedest city in the world." **Port Royal** has hardly been that since an earthquake tumbled it into the sea in 1692, yet the spirits of Henry Morgan and other buccaneers add a great deal of energy to what remains. The proudest possession of **St. Peter's Church,** rebuilt in 1725 to replace Christ's Church, is a silver communion plate donated by Morgan himself.

You can no longer down rum in Port Royal's legendary 40 taverns, but you can take in a draft of the past at the **Archaeological and Historical Museum** (tel. 809/924–8706), located within the Police Training School building. In the same building are a small **Maritime Museum** and a tipsy, angled structure known as **Giddy House.** Nearby is a graveyard in which rests a man who died twice. According to the tombstone, Lewis Goldy was swallowed up in the great earthquake of 1692, spewed into the sea, rescued, and lived another four decades in "Great Reputation." Port Royal attractions are open daily 9–5.

Jamaica for Free

Fifteen years ago Jamaica introduced the *Meet the People* concept that has become so popular in the Caribbean. One of the best free attractions anywhere, it allows visitors to get together with islanders who have compatible interests and expertise. The nearly 600 Jamaican families who participate in Meet the People on a voluntary basis offer their guests a spectrum of activities from time at a business or home to musical or theatrical performances. The program's theme is Forget Me Not, the name of a tiny blue flower that grows on Jamaican hillsides. Once you've met these people, you're not likely to forget them. It's important to arrange your occasion in advance of your trip through the Jamaica Tourist Board.

Off the Beaten Track

The Cockpit Country, 15 miles inland from Montego Bay and one of the most primitive areas in the West Indies, is a terrain of pitfalls and potholes carved by nature in limestone. For nearly a century after 1655 it was known as the Land of Look Behind because British soldiers rode their horses back to back in pairs, looking out for the savage freedom fighters known as Maroons. Fugitive slaves who refused to surrender to the invading English, the Maroons eventually won a treaty of independence and continue to live apart from the rest of Jamaica in the Cockpit Country. The government leaves them alone, untaxed and ungoverned by outside authorities. The Jamaica Tourist Board has information on minibus tours from Montego Bay to Maroon headquarters at Accompong.

Admirers of Jamaica's wonderful coffee may wish to tour the **Blue Mountains.** The best way to do this is in your own rental car, driving into the mountains from Kingston along Highway A3. Before departing, you should obtain directions either to

Pine Grove or to the Jablum coffee plant at **Mavis Bank,** then follow the handlettered signs after you leave A3. It's an exciting excursion and a virtual pilgrimage for many coffee lovers. Pine Grove, a working coffee farm that doubles as an inn, has a restaurant that serves the owner Marcia Thwaites's Jamaican cuisine. Mavis Bank is delightfully primitive—considering the retail price of the beans it processes. There is no official tour; ask someone to show you around.

Spanish Town, 12 miles west of Kingston on the A1, was the island's capital under Spanish rule. British until 1872, the town boasts the noblest Georgian square (Government Square) and the oldest cathedral (St. James) in the Western Hemisphere. Spanish Town's original name was Santiago de la Vega, which the English corrupted to St. Jago de la Vega, both meaning St. James of the Plains.

Participant Sports

The Tourist Board licenses all operators of recreational activities, which should ensure you of fair business practices as long as you deal with companies that display the decals.

Fishing Deep-sea fishing can be great around the island. Port Antonio gets the headlines with its annual blue marlin tournament, and Montego Bay and Ocho Rios have devotees who talk of the sailfish, yellowfin tuna, wahoo, dolphin, and bonita. Licenses are not required. Boat charters can be arranged at your hotel.

Golf The best courses may be found at **Caymanas** and **Constant Spring** in Kingston; **Half Moon, Rose Hall, Tryall,** and **Ironshore** in Montego Bay; and **Runaway Bay** and **Upton** in Ocho Rios. A nine-hole course in the hills of Mandeville is called **Manchester Club** (tel. 809/962–2403).

Horseback Riding This is not only terrific recreation, it's also an ideal way to tour certain areas. The island is fortunate to have the best equestrian facility in the Caribbean, **Chukka Cove** (write Box 160, Ocho Rios, St. Ann, tel. 809/972–2506), near Ocho Rios. The resort, complete with stylishly outfitted villas, offers packages with full instruction in riding, polo, and jumping, as well as hourlong trail rides, three-hour beach rides, and overnight rides to a Great House. Weekends, in-season, this is the place for hot polo action and equally hot social action!

Tennis Many hotels have tennis facilities that are free to their guests, but some will allow you to play for a fee. The sport is a highlight at **Tyrall** in Sandy Bay, **Sans Souci Hotel, Club & Spa** in Ocho Rios, and **Half Moon Club** in Montego (*see* Lodging, below).

Water Sports The major areas for swimming, windsurfing, snorkeling, and scuba diving are Negril in the west and Port Antonio in the east. All the large resorts rent equipment for a deposit and/or a fee. Diving is perhaps the only option that requires training, for you need to show a C-card to participate. However, some dive operators on the island are qualified to certify you. **Blue Whale Divers** (Negril Tree House, tel. 809/957–4438), **Fantasea Divers** at the Beach Bar of the Sans Souci Hotel, Club & Spa (Ocho Rios, tel. 809/974–5344); also at Morgans Harbour (Port Royal Marina, Kingston, same tel.), and **Caribbean Amusement** (Trelawny Beach Hotel, Falmouth, tel. 809/954–2123) offer certification courses and dive trips. Some tour operators offer day trips that include an offshore trip, snorkel equipment, lunch, and cocktails. For the best swimming spots, *see* Beaches, above.

Shopping

by Sandra Hart

Shopping in Jamaica goes two ways: things Jamaican and things imported. The former are made with style and skill; the latter are duty-free luxury finds. Jamaican crafts take the form of resortwear, hand-loomed fabrics, silk screening, wood carvings, paintings, and other fine arts.

Jamaican rum is a great take-home gift. So is Tia Maria, Jamaica's world-famous coffee liqueur. The same goes for the island's prized Blue Mountain and High Mountain coffees, and its jams, jellies, and marmalades.

Some bargains, if you shop around, include Swiss watches, Irish crystal, jewelry, cameras, and china. The top-selling French perfumes are also available alongside Jamaica's own fragrances—Royal Lyme, Royall Spyce, and Royall Bay aftershave for men, and Khus Khus toilet water for women.

Shopping Areas
Kingston

A shopping tour of the Kingston area should begin at **Constant Spring Road** or **King Street.** No matter where you begin, keep in mind that the trend these days is shopping malls, and Jamaica has caught on with a fever and an ever-growing roster: **Twin Gates Plaza, New Lane Plaza,** the **New Kingston Shopping Centre, Tropical Plaza, Manor Park Plaza, The Village,** and the newest (and some say nicest), **The Springs.**

A day at **Devon House** (26 Hope Rd., Kingston, tel. 809/929–6602) should be high on your shopping list. This is the place to find old and new Jamaica. The Great House is now a museum with antiques and furniture reproductions, and the new Lady Nugent's Coffee Terrace outside. There are 10 boutiques in what were once the house's stables: a branch of Things Jamaican; Tanning and Turning for leather finds; first-rate furnishings and antique reproductions at Jacaranda; silver and pewter recreations (many from centuries-old patterns) at The Olde Port Royal; and some of the best tropical-fruit ice cream (mango, guava, pineapple, and passionfruit) at I-Scream.

Montego Bay and
Ocho Rios

A must to avoid are the "craft" stalls in MoBay and Ocho Rios that are literally filled with peddlers desperate to sell touristy straw hats, T-shirts, and cheap jewelry. You may find yourself purchasing an unwanted straw something in order to get out alive. If you're looking to spend money, head for Overton Plaza or Westgate Plaza in Montego Bay; in Ocho Rios, the shopping plazas are **Pineapple Place, Ocean Village,** the **Taj Mahal, Coconut Grove,** and **Island Plaza.** It's also a good idea to chat with salespeople, who can enlighten you about the newer boutiques and their whereabouts.

Special Buys
Arts and Crafts

The **Gallery of West Indian Art** (1 Orange La., MoBay, tel. 809/952–4547) is the place to find Jamaican and Haitian paintings. A corner of the gallery is devoted to hand-turned pottery (some painted) and beautifully carved birds and jungle animals. New for the '90s, owner Liz DeLisser has added a branch at Round Hill, a 10-minute drive outside MoBay (tel. 809/952–5150).

Cheap sandals are good buys in shopping centers throughout Jamaica. While workmanship and leathers don't rival the craftsmanship of those found in Italy or Spain, neither do the prices (about $20 a pair). In Kingston there are two booteries that share the same address, the **Shoe Scene** and **Taurus** (27 Half-Way Tree Rd., tel. 809/926–6476; 809/926–4168, respectively). There's also **Lee's** (New Kingston Shopping Center) and the **Landmark Shoe Store** (The Mall Plaza, no phone). In Ocho Rios, the **Pretty Feet Shoe Shop** (Ocean Village Shopping Centre, tel. 809/974–5040) is a good bet. In Montego Bay, try **Overton Plaza** or **Westgate Plaza.**

Things Jamaican (Devon House, Hope Rd., Kingston, tel. 809/ 929–6602; 68 Spanish Town Rd., Kingston, tel. 809/923–8928; Fort St., MoBay, tel. 809/952–5650) has three outlets and two airport stalls, which display and sell some of the best native crafts made in Jamaica. The Devon House branch offers items that range from carved wood bowls and trays to reproductions of silver and brass period pieces.

Books and Records   Books about Jamaica and the Caribbean, many not available in the United States, can be found at the three branches of **Sangster's Bookstores** (97 Harbour St., Kingston, tel. 809/922– 3640; Constant Spring Rd. Mall, Kingston, tel. 809/926–2271; Westgate Shopping Centre, MoBay, tel. 809/952–0319). Kingston also has a well-stocked new bookstore at The Springs Mall on Half-Way Tree Road, simply called **The Book Shop** (no phone). Jonathan Routh's *Jamaica Holiday: The Secret Life of Queen Victoria* makes a great gift and/or souvenir. For terrific beach reading dive into *The Book of Jamaica*, by Russell Banks, or anything by novelist Jean Rhys or V. S. Naipaul.

Reggae tapes by world-famous Jamaican artists, such as Bob Marley, Ziggy Marley, Ziggy Marley; Peter Tosh, and Third World, can be found easily in U.S. or European record stores, but a pilgrimage to **Randy's Record Mart** (17 N. Parade, Kingston, tel. 809/922–4859) should be high on the reggae lover's list. Also worth checking is the **Record Plaza** (Tropical Plaza, Kingston, tel. 809/926–7645) and **Record City** (Westgate Plaza, MoBay, tel. 809/993–2836). While Kingston is the undisputed place to make purchases, the determined somehow (usually with the help of a local) will find **Jimmy Cliff's Records** (Oneness Sq., MoBay, no phone), owned by reggae star Cliff.

Gift Ideas   Fine "macanudo" cigars, with monogrammed cigar bands, in beautiful wood humidors (also monogrammed), make sensational gifts. An order will take about one week to fill, so place an order with **Gore Brothers** (27 Upper Waterloo Rd., Kingston, tel. 809/925–0030) upon your arrival. (Cost is around $50 for the humidors alone.) In Ocho Rios, these fine cigars (as well as Petit Coronas, the Churchill cigars, and other notables) can be purchased without the humidor at **Jack-in-the-Box** at Island Plaza, or at their sister Jack-in-the-Box in MoBay on Main Street. The hard-to-find Blue Mountain coffee can sometimes be found at **John R. Wong's Supermarket** (1 Tobago Ave., Kingston, tel. 809/926–4811). If they're out of stock you'll have to settle for High Mountain coffee, the natives' second preferred brand. If you're set on Blue Mountain you might try **Magic Kitchen Ltd.** (Village Plaza, Kingston, tel. 809/929–6602).

Jamaican-brewed rums and Tia Maria can be bought at either the Kingston or MoBay airports before your departure. While the airport prices are no cheaper, there's no toting of heavy, breakable bottles from the hotel to the airport.

Specialty Shops Belts, bangles, and beads are the name of the game at the factory of **Ital-Craft** (Twin Gates Plaza Shopping Centre, Kingston, tel. 809/926-8291). Belts are the focus of this savvy operation, but they also produce some intriguing jewelry and purses (many made from reptile skins). While Ital-Craft's handmade treasures are sold in boutiques throughout Jamaica, we recommend a visit to the factory for the largest selection of these belts, made of spectacular shells, combined with leather, feathers, or fur. (The most ornate belts sell for about $70.)

Silk batiks, by the yard or made into chic designs, are at **Caribatik** (tel. 809/954-2314), the studio of Muriel Chandler, 2 miles east of Falmouth. Drawing on patterns in nature, Chandler has translated the birds, seascapes, flora, and fauna into works of art.

Teeny-weeny bikinis, which more than rival Rio's, are designed by **Sonia Vaz** and sold at her manufacturing outlet (77 East St., Kingston, tel. 809/952-5650) and at the Sandal's and Super Clubs resorts (*see* Lodging, below).

Sprigs and Things (St. James Pl., Gloucester Ave., MoBay, tel. 809/952-4735) is where artist Janie Soren sells T-shirts featuring her hand-painted designs of birds and animals. She also paints canvas bags and tennis dresses.

Annabella Proudlock sells her unique wood Annabella Boxes, the covers depicting reproductions of Jamaican paintings at a restored Great House, Harmony Hall (an eight-minute drive from Ocho Rios, east on A1; tel. 809/974-4222). Reproductions of paintings, lithographs, and signed prints of Jamaican scenes are also for sale along with shell work and hand-carved wood combs. Stay for high tea and enjoy the locally grown teas, jams, and jellies on the Great House's veranda.

Dining

Sampling the island's cuisine introduces you to virtually everything the Caribbean represents. Every ethnic group that has made significant contributions on another island has made them on Jamaica, too, adding to a Jamaican stockpot that is as rich as its melting pot. So many Americans have discovered the Caribbean through restaurants owned by Jamaicans that the very names of the island's dishes have come to represent the region as a whole.

Jamaican food represents a true cuisine, organized, interesting, and ultimately rewarding. It would be a terrible shame for anyone to travel to the heart of this complex culture without tasting several typically Jamaican dishes. Here are a few:

Rice and Peas. A traditional dish, known also as Coat of Arms and similar to the *moros y christianos* of Spanish-speaking islands: white rice cooked with red beans, coconut milk, scallions, and seasoning.

Pepperpot. The island's most famous soup—a peppery combination of salt pork, salt beef, okra, and the island green known as callaloo—is green, but at its best it tastes as though it ought to be red.

Curry Goat. Young goat is cooked with spices and is more tender and has a gentler flavor than the lamb for which it was a substitute for immigrants from India.

Ackee and Saltfish. Salted fish was once the best islanders could do between catches, so they invented this incredibly popular dish that joins saltfish (in Portuguese, *bacalao*) with ackee, a vegetable (introduced to the island by Captain Bligh of *Bounty* fame) that reminds most people of scrambled eggs.

Jerk Pork. Created by the Arawaks and perfected by the Maroons, jerk pork is the ultimate island barbecue. The pork (the purist cooks the whole pig) is covered with a paste of hot peppers, berries, and other herbs and cooked slowly over a coal fire. Many feel that the "best of the best" jerk comes from Boston Beach in Port Antonio.

Patties are spicy meat pies that elevate street food to new heights. While, in fact, they originated in Haiti, Jamaicans can give patty lessons to anybody.

Where restaurants are concerned, Kingston has the widest selection; its ethnic restaurants offer Italian, French, Rasta natural foods, Cantonese, German, Thai, Indian, Korean, and Continental fare. There are fine restaurants as well in all the resort areas, and the list includes many that are located in large hotels.

The most highly recommended restaurants are indicated by a star ★ .

Category	Cost*
Expensive	over $30
Moderate	$20–$30
Inexpensive	under $20

per person, excluding drinks and service charge (or tip)

Kingston

★ **Norma.** When Norma Shirley opened this lunch spot in the mid-'80s, it was an instant success with the ladies-who-lunch and the wives of the influential (both Mrs. Michael Manley and Mrs. Glen Holden, wife of the American ambassador, lunch here regularly). The reasons are obvious. This may be the finest restaurant in Jamaica, with some 12 tables scattered amid an outdoor garden under an open tent festooned with urns of ferns and fresh flowers. Mrs. Shirley once designed food pages for *Vogue*, and now "designs" each plate that leaves the kitchen—spicy chicken in parsley rice, a chicken breast stuffed with cream cheese, a perfect fillet of fish grilled in a caper sauce—and each dish is accompanied by a fresh flower. *8 Belmont Rd., tel. 809/929-4966, Reservations required. Open weekdays noon–4 PM. Open for dinner Thurs. and Fri. nights only. Very Expensive.*

★ **Blue Mountain Inn.** The elegant Blue Mountain Inn is a 30-minute taxi ride from downtown and worth every penny of the fare. (The inn operates a special limo, costing less than $5, from the Pegasus, Oceana, Courtleigh, and Terra Nova hotels.) A former coffee plantation Great House built in 1754, the inn complements its atmosphere with Continental cuisines. All the classics of the beef and seafood repertoires are here, including steak Diane and lobster Thermidor. *Gordon Town, tel. 809/927-7400. Reservations required. Dress: dressy. AE, CB, DC, MC, V. Expensive.*

The Palm Court. Nestled on the ground floor of the Wyndham

Kingston, the elegant Palm Court is the place to lunch or dine (lunch is noon to 3 PM; dinner from 7 PM onward). The menu is Continental, with a heavy Italian accent: ravioli stuffed with crabmeat, vegetarian linguine, fettuccine Alfredo, and pastas prepared in an ever-changing "pasta of the day." *Wyndham Kingston, tel. 809/926–5430. Reservations recommended. AE, DC, MC, V. Expensive.*

Talk of the Town. The view is terrific, with the lights of Kingston sparkling for miles below this restaurant on the 17th floor. The fare is international with a Jamaican flair. The wine list is excellent and costly, but you might try the locally blended Montpeliers (red) or Montereys (white). The Continental dishes are supplemented by intriguing Caribbean renditions, such as snapper wrapped in callaloo and served with a velouté sauce. *Jamaica Pegasus Hotel, tel. 809/926–3690. Reservations required. Dress: dressy. AE, CB, DC, MC, V. Expensive.*

Hotel Four Seasons. The Four Seasons has been pleasing local residents for more than 25 years with its cuisine from the German and Swiss schools and local seafood. The setting tries to emulate Old World Europe without losing its casual island character. *18 Ruthven Rd., tel. 809/926–8805. Reservations recommended. AE, CB, DC, MC, V. Moderate.*

Restaurant Korea. You'll meet more of Jamaica than you might expect in this popular Korean dining room, for the islanders love ethnic food. Bugoki is the specialty, a kind of marinated barbecue that can be made with beef, pork, or chicken. Chinese and Japanese dishes are also available. *73 Kuntsford Blvd., tel. 809/926–1428. Reservations optional. AE, CB, DC, MC, V. Moderate.*

St. Andrew Guest House. You won't see many tourists in this tucked-away old house. What you will see are Jamaicans who love good, home-style local specialties: gungo-pea soup, ackee and saltfish, mackerel run-down, tripe and beans, smoked pork chops, and pickled ox tongue. The small bar is a late-night place for drinks and the latest local gossip. *13 West Kings House Rd., tel. 809/926–6049. Reservations suggested. No credit cards. Inexpensive–Moderate.*

The Hot Pot. Jamaicans love the Hot Pot for breakfast, lunch, and dinner. Fricassee chicken is the specialty, along with other local dishes, such as mackerel run-down (salted mackerel cooked-down with coconut milk and spices) and ackee and salted cod. Their fresh juices "in season" are the best—tamarind, sorrel, coconut water, and cucumber. *Altamont Terr., tel. 809/926–3906. Reservations unnecessary. No credit cards. Inexpensive.*

Minnie's Ethiopian Herbal-Health Food. The late Bob Marley loved Minnie's cooking (she was his personal cook), and so does much of Kingston. Only fresh foods and Rasta-style cooking (no salt, no meat, etc.) are offered here. There are about 30 tables scattered over two floors of a simple wooden rondel, with local folk sipping fresh juices (soursop, carrot, beetroot, papaya, june plum, orange sorrel, neaseberry, Otaheite apple, mango, straight cane juice), or sampling red-pea stew, gungo-pea stew, steam fish, ackee, callaloo, and vegetable run-down. On Friday nights (from about 8 to 11 PM), there are reggae musicians or poetry readings. *176 Old Hope Rd., tel. 809/927–9207. No credit cards. Inexpensive.*

Montego Bay **Georgian House.** A landmark restaurant in the heart of town, the Georgian House occupies two restored 18th-century buildings set in a shady garden courtyard. An extensive wine cellar complements the Continental and Jamaican cuisine, the best of which are the steaks and the dishes made with the local spiny lobster. Free pickup from Montego Bay hotels. *Union and Orange Sts., tel. 809/952–0632. Reservations required. Dress: dressy. AE, CB, DC, MC, V. Expensive.*

Julia's. Even if Julia's didn't run a free minibus to hotels all over Montego Bay, visitors would have discovered it. The kitchen turns out fixed price dinner for $30 per person, lining up carefully prepared pastas (Alfredo, primavera, etc.) and quality veal. *Bogue Hill, tel. 809/952–1772. Reservations recommended. Dress: chic. AE, CB, DC, MC, V. Expensive.*

Pier 1. Despite its sharing a name with the American "import" store, Pier 1 writes the book daily on waterfront dining. After tropical drinks at the deck bar, you'll be ready to dig into the international variations on fresh seafood, the best of which are the grilled lobster and any preparation of island snapper. *Just off Howard Cooke Blvd., tel. 809/952–2452. Reservations recommended. AE, CB, DC, MC, V. Expensive.*

★ **Sugar Mill.** The Sugar Mill (formerly the Club House) is where seafood is served with flair—on a terrace. Steak and lobster are usually offered in a pungent sauce that blends Dijon mustard with Jamaica's own Pickapeppa. Other wise choices are the daily specials and anything flamed tableside—and the taste will rival the theater. *At Half Moon Golf Course, tel. 809/953–2560. Reservations required for dinner, recommended for lunch. AE, CB, DC, MC, V. Expensive.*

Calabash. The specialty of the Calabash, a casual eating place with seating for 80, is a kind of Caribbean casserole featuring lobster, shrimp, crabmeat, and whatever else strikes the chef as freshest, all baked in a cheese-and-brandy sauce. *Queen's Dr., tel. 809/952–3891. Reservations recommended. AE, CB, DC, MC, V. Dinner only. Moderate.*

Town House. Most of the rich and famous who have visited Jamaica over the decades have eaten at the Town House. You won't find innovative cuisine here, just good versions of standard ideas (red snapper papillot is the specialty, with lobster, cheese, and wine sauce) in a colonial setting of shuttered windows, high ceilings, and hard-to-get old brick. *16 Church St., tel. 809/952–2660. Reservations recommended. Dress: smart. AE, CB, DC, MC, V. Moderate.*

★ **Pork Pit.** This open-air hangout three minutes from the airport must introduce more travelers to Jamaica's fiery jerk pork than any other place on the island. The Pork Pit is a local phenomenon down to the Red Stripe beer, yet it's accessible in both location and style. Plan to arrive around noon, when the jerk begins to be lifted from its bed of coals and pimento wood. *Adjacent to Casa Montego Hotel, no phone. No reservations. No credit cards. Inexpensive.*

Ocho Rios **Casanova.** The Sans Souci Hotel is imaginative enough to serve
★ homemade pastas in a comfortable open-air setting. All the Italian items are fine, and so are the smoked marlin, the spiny lobster, and the "catch of the day." At lunch you must try chicken à la Deta, a spicy island version of barbecue; if it's not on the menu, ask for it. *Sans Souci Hotel, tel. 809/974–2353. Reservations recommended. Dress: dressy at dinner. AE, CB, DC, MC, V. Expensive.*

★ **Le Gourmand.** This French Provençale restaurant has ceiling fans whirling softly above tables dressed in the country man-

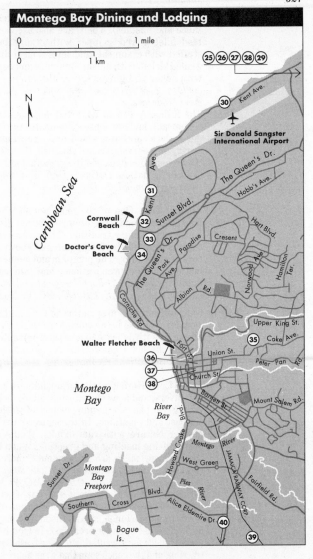

Montego Bay Dining and Lodging

ner—small-print fabrics, fresh flowers, glistening silver and crystal. Lunch or dinner, the menu changes, but it is always imaginative: *fillet de rouget* (red mullet); *queue de homard Provençale* (lobster tail); beef stroganoff flambé; chicken cordon bleu. Desserts are richly sinful: sabayon or crepes suzette. Soft taped music from France plays discreetly. *Coconut Grove Shopping Center, tel. 809/974–2717. Reservations required. AE, MC, V. Expensive.*

★ **Evita's.** The setting is a sensational, nearly 100-year-old gingerbread house high on a hill overlooking Ocho Rios's bay (but also convenient from MoBay). Owner Evita (from Venice) likes to have a good time, and she likes her friends to have a good time, too. They do, over 18-some pastas ranging from lasagna

Rastafari (vegetarian) to *rotelle alla Eva* (crabmeat with white sauce and noodles). There are also excellent fish dishes: sautéed fillet of red snapper with orange butter, red snapper stuffed with crabmeat, and several meat dishes—among them grilled sirloin with mushroom sauce and barbecued ribs glazed with honey-and-ginger sauce. *Mantalent Inn, Ocho Rios, tel. 809/974–2333. Reservations required. AE, V, MC. Inexpensive–Moderate.*

The Ruins. A 40-foot waterfall dominates the open-air Ruins restaurant, and in a sense it dominates the food as well. Surrender to local preference and order the Lotus Lily Lobster, a stirfry of the freshest local shellfish, then settle back and enjoy the tree-shaded deck and the graceful footbridges that connect the dining patios. *DaCosta Dr., tel. 809/974–2442. Reservations recommended. Dress: smart. AE, CB, DC, MC, V. Expensive.*

★ **Almond Tree.** One of the most popular restaurants in Ocho Rios, the Almond Tree offers Jamaican dishes enlivened by a European culinary tradition. The swinging rope chairs of the terrace bar and the tables perched above a lovely Caribbean cove are great fun. The pumpkin and pepperpot soups, the dramatic tableside preparations, and, among the entrées, the family mementos. *21 Fort George St., tel. 809/993–2604. Reservations required. AE, CB, DC, MC, V. Moderate.*

Negril **Cafe au Lait.** The proprietors of Cafe au Lait are French and Jamaican, and so is the cuisine. Local seafood and produce are prepared with delicate touches and presented in a setting overlooking the sea. *Charela Inn on Lighthouse Rd., tel. 809/957–4277. Reservations recommended. AE, CB, DC, MC, V. Moderate.*

Rick's Cafe. Here it is, the local landmark complete with cliffs, cliff divers, and powerful sunsets, all perfectly choreographed. It's a great place for a sunny brunch of omelets, eggs Benedict, or toast and plantains. In the sunset ritual, the crowd toasts Mother Nature with rum drinks, shouts and laughter, and ever-shifting meeting and greeting. When the sun slips below the horizon, there are more shouts, more cheers, and more rounds of rum. *Lighthouse Rd., tel. 809/957–4335. Reservations recommended. AE, CB, DC, MC, V. Moderate.*

Cosmos' Seafood Restaurant and Bar. Owner Cosmos Brown has made this seaside open-air bistro one of the best places in town to spend a lunch, an afternoon, and maybe stay on for dinner. (He's also open for breakfast. In fact, he only closes from 5 PM to 6:30 PM for a scrub-down.) The fresh fish is the featured attraction, and the conch soup that's the house specialty is a meal in itself. There's also lobster (grilled or curried), fish and chips, and a catch-of-the-morning. Customers often drop cover-ups to take a beach dip before coffee and dessert and return later to lounge in chairs scattered under almond and sea-grape trees. (There's an entrance fee for the beach alone, but it's less than $1.) *Norman Manley Blvd., tel. 809/957–4330. No credit cards. Inexpensive–Moderate.*

★ **Desi's Dread** (aka Desi's Dread One Stop Natural Vegetarian). After Rasta Desmond Clarke died, brother George took over and now, with the same gentle warmth, serves fresh fruit juices (beetroot, banana, carrot, orange, sorrel, papaya, mango, etc.) and an always-going stew pot over an open fire. (They only stew or steam, in the Rasta tradition, using fresh spices but never salt.) The broom-clean minikitchen serves dishes in carved calabash bowls with wooden spoons. *Negril Craft Park, then ask directions from any stall owner. No credit cards; no phone. Inexpensive.*

Lodging

The island has a variety of destinations to choose from, each of which offers its own unique expression of the Jamaican experience. **Montego Bay** has miles of hotels, villas, apartments, and duty-free shops set around Doctor's Cave Beach. Although it's lacking much cultural stimuli, MoBay presents a comfortable island backdrop for the many conventions and conferences it hosts.

Ocho Rios, on the northwest coast halfway between Port Antonio and Montego Bay, long enjoyed the reputation of being Jamaica's most favored out-of-the-way resort, but the late-blooming Negril has since stolen much of that distinction. Ocho Rios's hotels and villas are all situated within short driving distance of shops and one of Jamaica's most scenic attractions, Dunn's River Falls.

Port Antonio, described by poet Ella Wheeler Wilcox as "the most exquisite port on earth," is a seaside town nestled at the foot of verdant hills toward the east end of the north coast. The two best experiences to be had here are rafting the Rio Grande and a stop at the Trident, arguably the island's classiest resort.

Negril, some 50 miles west of Montego Bay, has become a byword for the newest crop of all-inclusive resorts (the first, Hedonism II, the Grand Lido, and Sandals Negril). Negril itself is only a small village, so there isn't much of historical significance to seek out. Then again, that's not what brings he sybaritic singles and couples here.

Mandeville, 2,000 feet above the sea, is noted for its cool climate and proximity to secluded south coast beaches.

The smallest of the resort areas, **Runaway Bay** has a handful of modern hotels and an 18-hole golf course.

Kingston is the most culturally active place on Jamaica. Some of the island's finest hotels are located here and those high towers are filled with rooftop restaurants, English pubs, serious theater and pantomime, dance presentations, art museums and galleries, jazz clubs, upscale supper clubs, and disco dives.

Jamaica was the birthplace of the Caribbean all-inclusive, the vacation concept that took the Club Med idea and gave it a lusty, excess-in-the-tropics spin. From Negril to Ocho Rios, resorts make their strongest statement by including everything, even drinks and cigarettes, in a single price of $150–$200 per night. At times they may feel a bit like Pleasure Island, where Pinocchio picks up long ears and a tail for doing everything bad he ever wanted to do. Yet their financial structure and their wealth of "free" recreation have a definite appeal. The all-inclusives are now branching out, some of them courting families, others going after an upper crust that would not even have picked up a brochure two or three years ago.

In the survey of accommodations that follows, the all-inclusives are listed first in each area, followed by other lodgings from the Very Expensive to the Inexpensive.

The most highly recommended lodgings are indicated by a star ★.

Category	Cost*
Very Expensive	over $340
Expensive	$250–$340
Moderate	$150–$250
Inexpensive	under $150

All prices are for a standard double room for two, MAP (breakfast and dinner), excluding 6% tax and any service charge.

Falmouth **Trelawny Beach Hotel.** The dependable Trelawny Beach resort offers seven stories of rooms overlooking 4 miles of beach. In recent years it has become an all-inclusive with an emphasis on families. Children under 14 get free room and board during the off-season when they share accommodations with their parents. *Box 54, Falmouth, tel. 809/954–2450. 350 rooms. Facilities: 2 dining rooms, tennis courts, pool, complimentary use of water-sports equipment. AE, CB, DC, MC, V. Moderate.*

Kingston **Jamaica Pegasus.** The Jamaica Pegasus is one of two fine business hotels in the New Kingston area. The 17-story complex near downtown is virtually a convention center, with some good restaurants and at least a little pampering. *Box 333, Kingston, tel. 809/926–3690. 350 rooms. Facilities: meeting rooms for 1,000, audiovisual services, restaurants, cocktail lounges, shops, pool, jogging track, health club, tennis courts. Meals not included. AE, CB, DC, MC, V. Expensive.*

★ **Wyndham Kingston.** The main competition to Jamaica Pegasus on the Kingston business beat, the high-rise Wyndham New Kingston also has 17 stories but adds seven cabana buildings. *Box 83, Kingston, tel. 809/926–5430. 400 rooms. Facilities: Olympic-size pool, gardens, conference space for 800, meeting rooms, tennis courts, health club, 3 restaurants, 2 bars, disco. Meals not included. AE, CB, DC, MC, V. Expensive.*

Hotel Oceana. The high-rise Hotel Oceana property affords convenient access to the National Gallery, government offices, and the ferry to Port Royal. *Box 986, Kingston, tel. 809/922–0920. 150 rooms. Facilities: meeting space for 1,200, cocktail lounge, shopping arcade, pool. Meals not included. AE, CB, DC, MC, V. Moderate.*

Mandeville **The Astra Hotel.** A hotel with guest-house charm, the Astra is
★ situated 2,000 feet up in the hills, providing an ideal getaway for nature lovers and outdoors enthusiasts. *Ward Ave., Box 60, Mandeville, tel. 809/962–3265. 20 rooms. Facilities: restaurant and bar, swimming pool, golf course and tennis courts nearby, horseback riding, bird-watching, fitness center. AE, CB, V. Inexpensive.*

Mandeville Hotel. The Victorian Mandeville Hotel, set in tropical gardens, has redecorated for the 1990s. There's now a flower-filled garden terrace for breakfast and lunch, and posh private rooms. *Box 78 Mandeville, tel. 809/962–2460 or 809/962–2138. 60 rooms. Facilities: restaurant, cocktail lounge, golf privileges at nearby Manchester Club. Meals not included. AE, MC, V. Inexpensive.*

Mahoe Bay **Sandals Royal Caribbean.** An all-inclusive for couples only, the Royal Caribbean is enlivened by Jamaican-style architecture arranged in a semicircle around attractive gardens. It's a sister in both theme and quality to other Sandals resorts. *Box 167, Montego Bay, tel. 809/953–2231. 165 rooms. Facilities: pool, private beach, tennis, putting green, dining room. AE, CB, DC, MC, V.*

Montego Bay **Carlyle on the Bay.** Now a part of the Sandals group, the Carlyle operates as an all-inclusive for singles, couples, and families; its rooms have balconies facing the sea. It is convenient to shopping in Montego Bay. *Box 412, Montego Bay, tel. 809/952–4140. 52 rooms. Facilities: beach privileges, pool, restaurants, pub. AE, CB, DC, MC, V. All-inclusive.*

★ **Sandals.** The largest private beach in Montego Bay is the spark that lights Sandals, one of the most popular couples resorts in the Caribbean. The all-inclusive, seven-day format includes airport transfers, government taxes, sports equipment, aerobics classes, meals, theme parties, and other entertainment. It's a bit like a cruise ship that remains in port, with air-conditioned rooms overlooking the bay. *Box 100, Montego Bay, tel. 809/952–5510. 243 rooms. Facilities: pool, water-sports center, dining room, nightclub. AE, CB, DC, MC, V. All-inclusive.*

★ **Half Moon Club.** For more than three decades the 400-acre Half Moon Club resort has been a destination unto itself with a reputation for doing the little things right. The villas on the beach, and the adjacent 13 tennis courts (7 are night-lighted), 4 lighted squash courts, Nautilus gym, and 14 boutiques, can give you the feeling of being in a private, pampered world, with individual swimming pools and expert room service. *East of Montego Bay (7 mi), tel. 809/953–2211. 197 rooms. Facilities: golf course, squash courts, health spa, water-sports center, pool, restaurants. AE, CB, DC, MC, V. Very Expensive.*

★ **Round Hill.** Eight miles west of town on a hilly peninsula, this resort is only open from mid-December through Easter, but when it's open, it's "the" place to be in Jamaica. The 27 villas are scattered over 98 acres. Each villa has a maid who cooks breakfast (and dinners, on request). There are also 36 hotel rooms in a two-story building overlooking the sea. *Box 64, Montego Bay, tel. 809/952–5150. 101 units. Facilities: tennis, horseback riding, water-sports center, restaurant. AE, CB, DC, MC, V. Very Expensive.*

Fantasy Resort. After a brief stint as an all-inclusive resort, this property has gone back to normal hotel status. The resort sports high-rise design and a Mediterranean flair. All nine stories have terraces. *Opposite Cornwall Beach, Box 16, Montego Bay, tel. 809/952–4150. 129 rooms. Facilities: open-air bar, dining room, saltwater pool, disco, shopping arcade. AE, CB, DC, MC, V. Expensive.*

★ **Wyndham Rose Hall Beach and Country Club.** The veteran Wyndham Rose Hall, a self-contained resort, has spent $10 million renovating in the hope of drawing more of the convention and meeting crowd, mixing recreation with a top-flight conference setup. *Box 999, Montego Bay, tel. 809/953–2650. 500 rooms. Facilities: pool, water sports, 6 tennis courts, golf course, 3 restaurants, coffee shop, nightclub, disco, 8 meeting rooms, audiovisual and teleconferencing equipment. AE, CB, DC, MC, V. Expensive.*

Holiday Inn Rose Hall. Here the great equalizer of hotel chains has done much to raise a run-down campground to the level of a full-service property with activities day and night and many tour facilities. *Box 480, Montego Bay, tel. 809/953–2485. 520 rooms. Facilities: pool, water-sports center, restaurant, shops. AE, CB, DC, MC, V. Moderate.*

★ **Richmond Hill Inn.** The hilltop Richmond Hill Inn attracts repeat visitors by providing spectacular views of the Caribbean and a great deal of peace, compared with MoBay's hustle. *Union St., Box 362, Montego Bay, tel. 809/952–3859. 22 rooms. Facilities: pool, terrace dining room. AE, CB, DC, MC, V. Inexpensive.*

Negril ★ **Grand Lido.** The opening of the Super Club's all-inclusive Grand Lido in 1989 broke new ground by extending this popular concept to upper income and taste levels. The dramatic entrance of marble floors and columns set a tone of striking elegance. The well-appointed oceanfront rooms, sports facilities, and 24-hour room service follow up in high style. For some, the pièce de résistance is a sunset sail on the resort's 147-foot yacht, *Zien,* which was a wedding gift from Aristotle Onassis to Prince Ranier and Princess Grace of Monaco, and now captained by Wynn Jones. *Box 88, Negril, tel. 809/957–4317. 200 suites. Facilities: 3 restaurants, satellite TV, 24-hour room service, valet, concierge, water-sports center, pools, clothed and nude beaches, use of squash courts at Hedonism II. AE, CB, DC, MC, V. All-inclusive.*

★ **Hedonism II.** Here is the resort that introduced the Club Med-style all-inclusive to Jamaica a little over a decade ago. Still wildly successful, Hedonism appeals most to vacationers who like a robust mix of physical activities, all listed daily on a chalkboard. *Box 25, Negril, tel. 809/957–4200. 280 rooms. Facilities: water-sports center, fitness center, open-air buffet dining room, disco and bar, horseback riding, lighted tennis courts, shuffleboard, volleyball, squash. AE, MC, V. All-inclusive.*

Negril Inn. One of the prettiest palm-speckled sandy beaches in Jamaica is the center of almost everything the all-inclusive Negril Inn does for its guests. *Negril, tel. 809/957–4209 or 800/634–7456. 46 rooms. Facilities: restaurant, dancing, entertainment, satellite TV, water-sports center. AE, CB, DC, MC, V. All-inclusive.*

Sandals Negril. The opening in 1989 of Sandals, built from the best parts of the old Sundowner and Coconut Cove resorts, made this 7-mile beach available to a new category of popular traveler. *Negril, tel. 809/957–4216; Unique Vacations, 7610 SW 61st St., Miami, FL 33143, tel. 800/327–1991. 186 rooms. Facilities: 2 freshwater pools, swim-up bar, private island, water-sports center, Jacuzzis, saunas, fitness center, movies, satellite TV, disco, piano bar. AE, CB, DC, MC, V. All-inclusive.*

★ **Swept Away.** The newest all-inclusive in Jamaica, and one of the best, this resort opened in early 1990. There are 130 suites in 26 cottages (all with sea view or private inner-garden atrium), plus villas with one to four bedrooms spread out along a half-mile of "drop-dead" beach, and a "total" sports complex just across the road. The compound's chefs concentrate on healthful dishes with lots of fish, white meat, fresh fruits, and veggies. *Long Bay, Negril, tel. 809/957–4040 or 800/526–2422. Facilities: 9 lighted tennis courts, 2 squash courts, 2 racquetball* courts, aerobics gym with cushioned floor, steam rooms and saunas, Jacuzzis, pool with lap lines. Full water-sports center, including scuba diving. AE, MC, V. All-inclusive for couples. Expensive.

Negril Gardens. A study in colonial pink and white, the new Negril Gardens bills itself as the "friendly alternative" to Negril's all-inclusive scene. It is attractive and refined, and it offers a nice beach with water sports. *Negril, Westmoreland, tel. 809/957–4408. 54 rooms. Facilities: terrace restaurant, disco. AE, CB, DC, MC, V. Very Expensive.*

Charela Inn. Intimacy is special at the Charela Inn, each of the quiet rooms offering a balcony or a covered patio. The owners' French-Jamaican roots find daily expression in the kitchen, and there's an excellent selection of wines. *Box 33, Negril, Westmoreland, tel. 809/957–4277. 26 air-conditioned rooms. Facilities: beach. AE, CB, DC, MC, V. Moderate.*

Ocho Rios
★

Boscobel Beach. Boscobel Beach is a parent's dream for a Jamaican vacation, an all-inclusive that makes families feel welcome. Everybody is kept busy all week for a single package price, and everyone leaves happy. *Box 63, Ocho Rios, tel. 809/ 974–3291 or 800/858–8009. 208 rooms, half of them suites. Facilities: Nautilus gym, Jacuzzi, windsurfing, sailing, snorkeling, tennis, volleyball, golf. AE, CB, DC, MC, V. All-inclusive.*

Couples. No singles, no children, no TVs: The emphasis at Couples is on romantic adventure for just the two of you, and the all-inclusive concept eliminates the decision making that can intrude on social pleasure. Couples has the highest occupancy rate of any resort on the island—and perhaps the most suggestive logo as well. There may be a correlation. *Tower Isle, St. Mary, tel. 809/974–4271. 152 rooms, 6 suites. Facilities: pool, island for nude swimming, tennis courts, Nautilus gym, 2 air-conditioned squash courts, a water-sports center that includes scuba diving, horseback riding, nightly entertainment, golf at Runaway Bay. AE, CB, DC, MC, V. All-inclusive.*

Sandals Ocho Rios. The Sandals concept follows its successful formula at one of their newer, couples-only all-inclusives at this nine-acre Sandals Ocho Rios resort. The mix of white and sand colors contrasts nicely with the vegetation and the sea. Accommodations are available in four grades, from deluxe ocean view to standard. *Ocho Rios, tel. 800/327–1991. 237 units. Facilities: restaurant, fitness center, water-sports center. AE, CB, DC, MC, V. All-inclusive.*

Chukka Cove. The battle cry at Chukka Cove is "Saddle Up." Chukka Cove earns its horse feed by maintaining some of the best equestrian facilities in the Western Hemisphere. In addition to polo, experienced riders will want to investigate Chukka Cove's Jamaican Riding Holiday, an exploration of the north coast by horseback. Less dedicated riders have a choice of trail rides, mountain trail rides, beach rides, or an overnight escorted ride to the Lillyfield Great House. *Box 160, Ocho Rios, tel. 809/972–2506. 6 villas with 12 sets of private suites, with cook and maid. Facilities: stables, equestrian instruction (all levels), cooks to prepare meals in villas, swimming from rocks. AE, CB, DC, MC, V. Very Expensive.*

Jamaica Inn. This vintage property is a special favorite of the privileged from both the United States and Europe, a clientele fascinated by the combination of class and quiet. There are weeks in season when every single guest is on at least his or her second visit. Each room has its own veranda on the beach. *Box 1, Ocho Rios, tel. 800/243–9420 or 203/438–3793. 50 rooms. Facilities: Continental and Jamaican dining, golf; tennis and horseback riding nearby. AE, CB, DC, MC, V. Very Expensive.*

★ **Plantation Inn.** This plantation actually looks like one—the Deep South variety à la *Gone with the Wind*. The whole place serves up a veranda-soft existence. All the rooms come with private balconies, and each has a dramatic view down to the sea. *Box 2, Ocho Rios, tel. 809/974–2501. 77 rooms. Facilities: dining and dancing by candlelight, shops, tennis courts, health club, afternoon tea, entertainment twice weekly. No children under 12. AE, CB, DC, MC, V. Very Expensive.*

★ **Sans Souci Hotel, Club, & Spa.** This pastel-pink cliffside fantasyland looks and feels like a lovely dream, if indeed the dreamer had absolute taste and no need to fret over the bill. Cuisine at the five-star Casanova Restaurant not only delights resort guests but attracts diners from other properties for breakfast, lunch, and dinner. It's all here—comfort, exoticism, celebrities getting away from the crush. *Ocho Rios, tel. 809/974–2353 or 800/237–3237. 80 rooms and suites. Facilities: health and fitness center, 2 freshwater pools, tennis courts, scuba diving, water-sports center. AE, CB, DC, MC, V. Very Expensive.*

Mallards Beach Resort. The largest hotel in Ocho Rios and formerly the Sheraton, this property draws most of its clientele from conferences and incentive travel. *Box 245, Ocho Rios, tel. 809/974–2201. 370 rooms. Facilities: Vivaldi's restaurant, water-sports center. AE, CB, DC, MC, V. Moderate.*

Shaw Park Beach Hotel. Another popular property with groups from Great Britain, Shaw Park offers a pleasant alternative to downtown high rises. The grounds are especially colorful and well-tended, while the Silks disco is a favorite for late-night carousing. *Cutlass Bay, Box 17, Ocho Rios, tel. 809/974–2552 or 800/243–9420. 118 rooms. Facilities: restaurant, water-sports center. AE, DC, MC, V. Moderate.*

Port Antonio **Trident Villas and Hotel.** If a single hotel had to be voted the
★ most likely for coverage by "Lifestyles of the Rich and Famous," this would have to be it. The pool, buried in a rocky bit of land jutting out into crashing surf, is a memory unto itself. The restaurant, on a scallop of beach reached through a stone arch, is also a classic. *Box 119, Port Antonio, tel. 809/993–2602 or 800/237–3237; fax 809/993–2590. 12 villas, 16 suites. Facilities: water-sports center, tennis courts, swimming pool. AE, MC, V. Very Expensive.*

Goblin Hill. For a while this was known as the Jamaica Hill resort, but it is once again going by its original, evocative name. It's a lush 13-acre estate atop a hill overlooking San San cove. Each villa comes with its own dramatic view, plus a maid and butler to handle the housekeeping, cooking, and general caretaking. *Box 26, Port Antonio, tel. 809/993–3286. 28 villas. Facilities: pool, beach, 2 tennis courts. AE, CB, DC, MC, V. Expensive.*

The Jamaica Palace. This 80-room, imposing property rises in an expanse of white pillared marble, with the all-white theme continued on the interior, broken only by the black lacquer and gilded oversize furniture. Each room has a semicircular bed and reproductions of Middle Eastern objets d'art and Oriental rugs. Although the hotel is not on the beach, there is a 114-foot swimming pool (shaped like the map of Jamaica) and the snazzy Designer's Gallery Boutique, owned by Patrice Wymore Flynn (widow of Errol). *Box 227, Port Antonio, tel. 809/993–2020 or 312/883–1020. 80 rooms, with 1 imperial suite, 5 full-size suites, 20 junior suites. Facilities: restaurant, 2 bars, swimming pool, baby-sitters on request. AE, CB, DC, MC, V. Expensive.*

The Fern Hill Club. This is an all-inclusive hilltop property that's well run and usually full. The newest rooms are split-level suites shaped into steep cliffs, with TVs, videos, small refrigerators, and a whirlpool-spa surrounded by a minigarden. *Box 28, Port Antonio, tel. 809/993–3222 or 416/620–4666. Facilities: 48 rooms; 4 swimming pools, 1 lighted tennis court, nightly entertainment, billiards, table tennis, shuffleboard, horseback riding, transport to and from nearby San San Beach, where scuba diving can be arranged. AE, MC, V. Moderate All-inclusive.*

Montevan Lodge. This place offers the ambience of a more genteel time, from the portrait of Queen Victoria that dominates the sitting room and knickknacks scattered about to the bubbling fish tank and friendly staff. The rooms are basic and spotless, with circular fans overhead. Outsiders are welcome for very tasty home cooking at lunch or dinner, with prior reservations. *Muscrave St. on Titchfield Hill, Port Antonio, tel. 809/993–2604. 15 rooms. Facilities: bar, restaurant. No credit cards. Inexpensive.*

Admiralty Club at Navy Island. This 64-acre private island was once the home of Errol Flynn, Port Antonio's most beloved "character." Casual elegance is the theme here, with a general sense of knowing the world's pleasures. Service is quite attentive. *Box 188, Port Antonio, tel. 809/993–2667 or 800/225–3614. 7 studio cottages, 6 villas. Facilities: beach, cove for nude swimming, dining. AE, CB, DC, MC, V. Moderate.*

Bonnie View Hotel. Though the main appeal of this property is to the budget, it does have a few nice rooms with private verandas overlooking spectacular scenery. Its restaurant atop a 600-foot hill offers the finest view of all. *Box 82, Port Antonio, tel. 809/993–2752. 30 rooms. Facilities: pool, sun deck. AE, CB, DC, MC, V. Inexpensive.*

Port Royal **Morgan's Harbour Hotel, Beach Club, and Yacht Marina.** A favorite of the sail-into-Jamaica set, the small Morgan's Harbour Hotel boasts 22 acres of beachfront at the very entrance to the old pirate town. Each room has been redecorated in a nautical style that the pirate Captain Morgan would have appreciated. *Port Royal, tel. 809/924–8464. 60 rooms. Facilities: full-service marina, pier bar, restaurant, access to Lime Cay. AE, CB, DC, MC, V. Moderate.*

Runaway Bay **Jamaica, Jamaica.** One of the best Super Clubs, this all-
★ inclusive was a pioneer in emphasizing the sheer Jamaican-ness of the island, rather than generic sensuality. The cooking is particularly first-rate. It used to be the Runaway Bay Hotel and Golf Club. *Box 58, Runaway Bay, tel. 809/973–2436. 152 rooms. Facilities: water-sports center, tennis, horseback riding, sightseeing tours, disco, nightly entertainment, 18-hole golf course nearby. Guests must be over 16. AE, CB, DC, MC, V. All-inclusive.*

H.E.A.R.T. Country Club. It's a shame more visitors don't know about this place, perched above Runaway Bay and brimming with Jamaica's true character. While providing training for young islanders interested in the tourism industry, it also provides a remarkably quiet and pleasant stay for guests. The employees make an effort to please. *Box 98, St. Ann, tel. 809/ 973–2671. 20 rooms. Facilities: satellite TV, golf, beach shuttle, restaurant. AE, CB, DC, MC, V. Inexpensive.*

Sandy Bay **Tryall Golf, Tennis, and Beach Club.** Part of a posh residential development 12 miles west of Montego Bay, Tryall clings to a hilltop overlooking the golf course and the Caribbean. Here you choose between accommodations in the former guest house of a 3,000-acre island plantation and one of the private villas dotted about the landscape. *Sandy Bay, Hanover, tel. 809/952–5110. 52 rooms, 40 villas. Facilities: golf course, tennis courts, pool with swim-up bar (bouillon served), terrace restaurant. AE, CB, DC, MC, V. Very Expensive.*

The Arts and Nightlife

Jamaica—especially in Kingston—supports a lively community of musicians. For starters there is reggae, popularized by the late Bob Marley and the Wailers and performed today by son Ziggy Marley, Jimmy Tosh (the late Peter Tosh's son), Greg Isaccs, the Third World, Jimmy Cliff, and many others. If your experience of Caribbean music has been limited to steel drums and Harry Belafonte, then the political, racial, and religious messages of reggae may set you on your ear; listen closely and you just might hear the heartbeat of the people. Those who already love reggae may want to plan a visit in mid-July to August for the Reggae Sunsplash. The four-night concert at the Bob Marley Performing Center in Montego Bay showcases local talent and attracts such performers as Rick James, Gladys Knight and the Pips, Steel Pulse, Third World, and Ziggy Marley and Company.

Nightlife and Bars For the most part, the liveliest late-night happenings throughout Jamaica are in the major resort hotels. Some of the best music will be found at **De Buss** (tel. 809/957–4405) and of course at the hot, hot spot, **Kaiser's Cafe** (tel. 809/967–4450), as well as at the **Disco** at Hedonism II (tel. 809/957–4200), the **Negril Tree House,** and **Club Kokua** in Negril (no phone). The most popular spots in Kingston today are **Mingles** at the Courtleigh (tel. 809/ 974–5524), **Illusions** in the New Lane Plaza (tel. 809/929–2125), and **Jonkanoo** in the Wyndham New Kingston (no phone).

In Port Antonio, if you have but one night to disco, do it at **The Roof Club,** 11 West Street. On weekends, from eleven-ish on, this is where it's all happening. If you want to "do the town," check out **Blue Jays,** Centre Point (no phones). The principal clubs in Ocho Rios are **Acropolis** on Main Street (no phone), also **Silks** in the Shaw Park Beach Hotel (tel. 809/974–2552), and the **Little Pub on Main Street** (tel. 809/974–5825). The hottest places in Montego Bay are the **Cave** disco at the Seawinds Beach Resort (tel. 809/952–4070), **Sir Winston's Reggae Club** on Gloucester Street (tel. 809/952–2084), and the **Rose Hall Beach Holiday Inn** (tel. 809/953–2485). Some of the all-inclusives (i.e., all the SuperClub properties) offer a dinner and disco pass from about $40. Like the daytime activity passes, these tickets allow you to sample one style of living without having to commit an entire vacation to it.

15 Martinique

by Honey Naylor

Not for naught did the Arawaks name Martinique *Mandinina*, which means "Island of Flowers." This is one of the most beautiful islands in the Caribbean, lush with exotic wild orchids, frangipani, anthurium, jade vines, flamingo flowers, and hundreds of vivid varieties of hibiscus. Trees bend under the weight of such tropical treats as mangoes, papayas, bright red West Indian cherries, lemons, limes, and bananas. Acres of banana plantations, pineapple fields, and waving green seas of sugarcane show the bounty of the island's fertile soil.

The towering mountains and verdant rain forest in the north lure hikers, while underwater sights and sunken treasures attract snorkelers and scuba divers. Martinique appeals as well to those whose idea of exercise is turning over every 10 or 15 minutes to get an even tan or whose adventuresome spirit is satisfied by finding booty in a duty-free shop. Francophiles in particular will find the island enchanting.

This 425-square-mile island, the largest of the Windward Islands, is 4,261 miles from Paris, but its spirit (and language) is French with more than a mere soupçon of West Indian spice. Tangible, edible evidence of that fact is the island's cuisine, which is a tempting blend of classic French and Creole dishes.

Columbus sailed near Martinique in 1493, but it was not until his fourth voyage in 1502 that he came ashore at Le Carbet. He paused long enough to remark, "My eyes would never tire of contemplating such vegetation," and to put ashore a number of goats to provide fresh meat for future visits. His eyes very quickly tired of the snakes he saw slithering about in his newfound Eden, so he weighed anchor and put water between him and them, never to return.

By the time Columbus made his way to Martinique, the cannibalistic Caribs had long since arrived on the island and eaten the Island of Flowers's Arawaks. Carib arrows kept outsiders at bay until 1635, when Pierre Belain d'Esnambuc, a Norman nobleman and adventurer, landed with a group of 100 settlers at the mouth of the Roxelane River. The French promised the Caribs the western half of the island, but instead polished them off and imported African slaves to work their sugarcane plantations.

By the mid-17th century, Martinique was an important sugar-producing island. Britain wanted to pluck the pearl away from the French, and the two nations fought over the island until the mid-19th century. In 1815, the island was ceded by treaty to France, and French it has remained ever since.

Martinique became an overseas department of France in 1946 and a *région* in 1974, a status not unlike that of an American state vis-à-vis the federal government. The Martinicans vote in French national elections and have all the benefits of France's social and economic systems. The island is governed by a prefect who is appointed by the French minister of the interior. Martinique has one of the highest standards of living in the Caribbean.

Before You Go

Tourist Information Contact the **French West Indies Tourist Office** (610 5th Ave., New York, NY 10020, tel. 212/757–1125). You may also obtain information from the **French Government Offices** (628 5th Ave., New York, NY 10020, tel. 212/757–1125; 9454 Wilshire Blvd., Beverly Hills, CA 90212, tel. 213/272–2661; 645 N. Michigan Ave., Chicago, IL 60611, tel. 312/337–6301; 103 World Trade Center, Dallas, TX 75258, tel. 214/720–4010; 1 Hallidie Plaza, Suite 250, San Francisco, CA 94102, tel. 415/986–4161; 1981 Ave. McGill College (490), Montreal, Quebec, Canada H3A 2W9, tel. 514/288–4264; 1 Dundas St. W, Suite 2405, Toronto, Ont., Canada M5G 1Z3, tel. 416/593–4717; and 178 Piccadilly, London, United Kingdom W1V 0AL, tel. 01/499–6911).

Arriving and Departing
By Plane

Minerve Airlines (800/765–6065), a French charter company, flies twice weekly nonstop from New York's JFK, winter season only (December through early April). Year round, **American** (tel. 800/433–7300) has daily service from more than 100 U.S. cities to San Juan, from which the airline's American Eagle wing flies on to Martinique. **Air France** (tel. 800/237–2747) flies direct from Miami and San Juan; **Air Canada** (tel. 800/422–6232) has service from Montreal and Toronto; **LIAT** (tel. 809/462–0700) flies in from neighboring islands; and **Air Martinique** (tel. 596/51–09–90) has service to and from St. Martin, Dominica, Barbados, St. Lucia, St. Vincent, Mustique, Union Island, and Trinidad.

From the Airport

You'll arrive at Lamentin International Airport, which is about a 15-minute taxi ride from Fort-de-France and about 40 minutes from the Trois-Ilets peninsula where most of the hotels are located.

Passports and Visas

U.S. and Canadian citizens must have a passport (an expired passport may be used as long as the expiration date is no more than five years ago) or proof of citizenship, such as an original (not photocopied) birth certificate or a voter registration card accompanied by a government-authorized photo identification. British citizens are required to have a passport and a visa. In addition, all visitors must have a return or ongoing ticket.

Customs and Duties

Items for personal use, including tobacco, cameras, and film, are admitted free.

Language

The official language is French, and you will have difficulty unless you have either a nodding acquaintance with the language or a good phrase book. While it is true that front-desk personnel in the tourist hotels speak some English, they often have difficulty understanding it. Most menus are in French, and even in the major tourist areas, waiters and waitresses often do not speak English. And rare is the Martinican in the countryside who speaks English. Outside the major tourist areas, you'll certainly have to resort to charades if you lack a smattering of French.

Precautions

Exercise the same safety precautions as you would in any other big city: Leave valuables in the hotel safe-deposit vault and lock your car, with luggage and valuables stashed out of sight. Also, don't leave jewelry or money unattended on the beach.

Beware of the *mancenillie* (manchineel) trees! These pretty trees with little green fruits that look like apples are poisonous. Sap and even raindrops falling from the trees onto your skin can cause painful, scarring blisters. The trees have red warning signs posted by the Forestry Commission.

340

Martinique

Legend (map)

- **1** Exploring Sites
- **24** Hotels and Restaurants

ATLANTIC OCEAN

Ste-Marie **13**
Caravelle Peninsula
Havre de la Trinité
Tartane **15**
Pointe Caracoli
La Trinité **14**
30
31
Baie du Galion
Gros-Morne
Le Robert
Havre du Robert
Pte. de la Rose
33 34
23
35
Lamentin
Le François
Lamentin International Airport
Mt. Vauclin
Ducos
Rivière Salée
N6
Le Vauclin
22
Rivière Salée
D7
D17
19
Rivière-Pilote
N6
D18
Ste-Luce
67
Le Mai
69
Le Diamant
D7
D18A
70
71
Pte. Figuier
68
Pte. Marin
72
73
Cul-de-Sac du Marin
20
Ste-Anne
Cap Chevalier
Grand Anse des Salines
21
Anse-Trabaud
Pte. d'Enfer
Pte. des Salines
St. Lucia Channel

If you plan to ramble through the rain forest, be careful where you step. Poisonous snakes, cousins of the rattlesnake, slither through this lush tropical Eden.

Except for the area around Cap Chevalier, the Atlantic waters are rough and should be avoided by all but expert swimmers.

Staying in Martinique

Important Addresses

Tourist Information: The **Martinique Tourist Office** (Blvd. Alfassa, tel. 596/63–79–60) is open Monday–Thursday 7:30–12:30 PM and 2:30–5:30, Friday 7:30–12:30 and 2:30–5, Saturday 8–noon.

Emergencies

Police: Call 596/17.

Fire: Call 596/18.

Ambulance: Call 596/70–36–48 or 596/71–59–48.

Hospitals: There is a 24-hour emergency room at **Hôpital La Meynard** (Châteauboeuf, just outside Fort-de-France, tel. 596/50–15–15)

Pharmacies: Pharmacies in Fort-de-France include **Pharmacie de la Paix** (corner rue Victor Schoelcher and rue Perrinon, tel. 596/71–94–83) and **Pharmacie Cypria** (Blvd. de Gaulle, tel. 596/63–22–25).

Consulate: The **United States Consulate** (14 rue Blenac, Fort-de-France, tel. 596/63–13–03).

Currency

The coin of the realm is the French franc, which consists of 100 *centimes* (for example, the cost of an airmail stamp is 4.40F: 4 francs, 40 centimes). At press time (Nov. 30, 1989), the rate was 6.08F to U.S. \$1, but check the current exchange rate before you leave home. U.S. dollars are accepted in some of the tourist hotels, but for convenience, it's better to convert your money into francs. Banks give a more favorable rate than do hotels. A currency-exchange service, **Change Caraibes,** is open daily at the Arrivals Building at Lamentin Airport, at the Galerie des Flibustiers in Fort-de-France, and at the entrance to Club Med in Ste-Anne (tel. 596/51–51–51, ext. 11–41, or 596/60–28–40). *Note:* Prices quoted here are in U.S. dollars unless indicated otherwise.

Major credit cards are accepted in hotels and restaurants in Fort-de-France and the Pointe du Bout areas; few establishments in the countryside accept them. There is a 20% discount on luxury items paid for with traveler's checks or with certain credit cards.

Taxes and Service Charges

A resort tax varies from hotel to hotel; the maximum is \$1 per person per day.

Rates quoted by hotels usually include a 10% service charge; some hotels add 10% to your bill. All restaurants include a 15% service charge in their menu prices.

Guided Tours

For a personalized tour of the island, ask the Tourist Office to arrange for a tour with an English-speaking taxi driver. There are set rates for tours to various points on the island, and if you share the ride with two or three other sightseers, the price will be whittled down.

Madinina Tours (tel. 596/73–35–35) offers half- and full-day jaunts, with lunch included in the all-day outings. Boat tours are also available, as well as air excursions to the Grenadines and to St. Lucia. Madinina has tour desks in most of the major hotels.

Hélicaraibes (tel. 596/73–30–03) provides charter tours by helicopter for a mere $700 or so per hour.

Parc Naturel Regional de la Martinique (Regional Nature Reserve, tel. 596/73–19–30) organizes inexpensive guided hiking tours year-round. Descriptive folders are available at the Tourist Office.

Getting Around

Taxis Taxi stands are located at Lamentin Airport, in downtown Fort-de-France, and at major hotels. Rates are regulated by the government, but local taxi drivers are an independent lot, and prices often turn out to be higher than the minimum "official" day charge of 9.50F. The cost from the airport to Fort-de-France is about 70F; from the airport to Pointe du Bout, about 150F. A 40% surcharge is in effect between 8 PM and 6 AM.

Buses Public buses and eight-passenger minivans (license plates bear the letters TC) are an inexpensive means of getting from point to point around the island. Buses are always crowded and are not recommended for the timid traveler. In Fort-de-France, the main terminal for the minivans is at Pointe Simon on the waterfront. There are frequent departures from early morning until 8 PM; fares range from $1 to $5.

Ferries Weather permitting, *vedettes* (ferries) operate daily between Fort-de-France and the Marina Meridien in Pointe du Bout and between Fort-de-France and Anse-Mitan and Anse-à-l'Ane. The Quai d'Esnambuc is the arrival and departure point in Fort-de-France. At press time, the one-way fare was 12F; round-trip 17F. Ferry schedules are listed in the visitors' guide, *Choubouloute*, available at the Office of Tourism.

The **Caribbean Express** (tel. 590/60–12–38) offers daily, scheduled interisland service aboard a 128-foot, 227-passenger motorized catamaran, linking Martinique with Grenada, Guadeloupe, Antigua, Dominica, St. Martin, St. Barts, St. Lucia, and St. Vincent. Fares run approximately 25% below economy airfares.

Bicycles or Motorbikes Bikes and motorbikes can be rented from **Vespa** (tel. 596/71–60–03), **Funny** (tel. 596/63–33–05), or **T. S. Autos** (tel. 596/63–42–82), all of which are located in Fort-de-France.

Rental Cars Martinique has about 175 miles of well-paved and well-marked roads (albeit the markings are *en Français*). Streets in Fort-de-France are narrow and clogged with traffic, country roads are mountainous with hairpin curves, and the Martinicans drive with abandon. If you drive in the country, be sure to take along a good phrase book and a copy of the detailed map, *Carte Routière et Touristique*, available in bookstores.

If you book a rental car from the United States at least 48 hours in advance, you can qualify for a hefty discount—sometimes with unlimited mileage.

A valid driver's license is needed to rent a car for up to 20 days. After that, you'll need an International Driver's Permit. Major credit cards are accepted by most car-rental agents. Rates are about $44–$50 per day (unlimited mileage). Lower daily rates with per-mile charges, which usually turn out to be higher overall rates, are sometimes available. Question agents closely. Among the many agencies are **Avis** (tel. 596/70–11–60 or 800/331–1212), **Budget** (tel. 596/63–69–00 or 800/527–0700), **Hertz** (tel. 596/60–64–64 or 800/654–3131), and **Europcar/ National Car Rental** (tel. 596/73–33–13 or 800/328–4567).

Telephones and Mail
To call Martinique station-to-station from the United States, dial 011 plus 596 plus the local six-digit number. For person-to-person calls, dial 01 plus 596 plus the local number. It is not possible to make collect or credit calls from Martinique to the United States. There are no coin telephone booths on the island. If you need to make calls outside your hotel, go to the post office and purchase a *Telecarte*, which looks like a credit card and is used in special booths marked *Telecom*. Long-distance calls made with *Telecartes* are less costly than are operator-assisted calls.

To place an intraisland call, dial the local six-digit number. To call the United States from Martinique, dial 19–596–1, area code, and the number you are trying to reach.

Airmail letters to the United States are 4.40F for up to 20 grams; postcards, 2.80F.

Opening and Closing Times
Stores that cater to tourists are generally open weekdays 8:30–6; Saturday 8:30–1. Banking hours are weekdays 7:30–noon and 2:30–4.

Beaches

All Martinique's beaches are open to the public, but hotels charge a fee for nonguests to use changing rooms and facilities. There are no official nudist beaches, but topless bathing is prevalent at the large resort hotels. Unless you're an expert swimmer, steer clear of the Atlantic waters, except in the area of Cap Chevalier and the Caravelle Peninsula. The soft, white-sand beaches begin south of Fort-de-France and continue; to the north the beaches are of hard-packed gray volcanic sand.

On the beach at **Anse-à-l'Ane,** you can spread your lunch on a picnic table, browse through the nearby shell museum, and cool off in the bar of the Calalou Hotel.

Anse-Mitan was created by Mother Nature, who placed it just to the south of Pointe du Bout and sprinkled it with white sand. The waters around this beach offer superb snorkeling opportunities. Small, family-owned bistros are half hidden in palm trees nearby.

Anse-Trabaud is on the Atlantic side, across the southern tip of the island from Ste-Anne. There is nothing here but white sand and the sea.

Diamant, the island's longest beach (2½ miles), has a splendid view of Diamond Rock, but the waters are rough and the currents are strong. This area is home to the Diamant-Novotel and Diamant les Bains hotels.

Les Salines is a 1½-mile cove of soft white sand lined with coconut palms. A short drive south of Ste-Anne, it's awash with families and children during holidays and on weekends, but quiet and uncrowded during the week even at the height of the winter season. Take along some picnic food and towels because there are no facilities.

The soft white beaches of **Pointe du Bout** are man-made, superb, and lined with luxury resorts, among them the Meridien and the Bakoua.

Near Les Salines, **Pointe Marin** stretches north from Ste-Anne. A good windsurfing and waterskiing spot, it also has campsites, sanitary facilities, and a 5F admission charge. Club Med occupies the northern edge, and the Manoir de Beauregard is in the nearby town of Ste-Anne.

Exploring Martinique

Numbers in the margin correspond with points of interest on the Martinique map.

The starting point of the tour is the capital city of Fort-de-France, where almost a third of the island's 320,000 people live. From here, we'll tour St-Pierre, Mont Pelée, and other points north, go along the Atlantic coast, and finish with a look at the sights in the south.

Fort-de-France ❶ **Fort-de-France** lies on the beautiful Baie des Flamands on the island's Caribbean (west) coast. With its narrow streets and pastel buildings with ornate wrought-iron balconies, the capital city is reminiscent of the French Quarter in New Orleans. However, where New Orleans is flat, Fort-de-France is hilly. Public and commercial buildings and residences cling to its hillsides.

Stop first at the **Office of Tourism,** which shares a building with Air France on the boulevard Alfassa, right on the bay near the ferry landing. English-speaking staffers provide excellent, free material, including detailed maps; a visitors' guide called *Chouboulute*, which lists events; *Bienvenue en Martinique (Welcome to Martinique);* and *Une Histoire d'Amour Entre Ciel et Mer*, an 18-page booklet in English, with a series of seven self-drive tours that are well worth your while.

Thus armed, walk across the street to **La Savane.** The 12½-acre landscaped park is filled with gardens, tropical trees, fountains, and benches. It's a popular gathering place and the scene of promenades, parades, and impromptu soccer matches. A statue of Pierre Belain d'Esnambuc, leader of the island's first settlers, is upstaged by Vital Dubray's flattering white Carrara marble statue of the Empress Josephine, Napoleon's first wife. Sculpted in a high-waisted Empire gown, Josephine gazes toward Trois-Ilets across the bay, where in 1763 she was born Marie-Joseph Tascher de la Pagerie. Near the harbor is a **marketplace** where high-quality local crafts are sold. On the edge of the Savane, you can catch the **ferry** for the beaches at Anse-Mitan and Anse-à-l'Ane and for the 20-minute run across the bay to the resort hotels of Pointe du Bout.

Rue de la Liberté runs along the west side of La Savane. Look for the main Post Office (rue de la Liberté, between rue Blenac and rue Antoine Siger). Just across rue Blenac from the Post Office is the **Musée Departementale de Martinique,** which contains exhibits pertaining to the pre-Columbian Arawak and Carib periods. On display are pottery, beads, and part of a skeleton that turned up during excavations in 1972. One exhibit examines the history of slavery; costumes, documents, furniture, and handicrafts from the island's colonial period are on display. *9 rue de la Liberté, tel. 596/71–57–05. Admission: 5F. Open weekdays 9–1 and 2–5, Sat. 9–noon.*

Leave the museum and walk west (away from La Savane) on rue Blenac to rue Victor Schoelcher. There you'll see the Romanesque **St-Louis Cathedral,** whose steeple rises high above the surrounding buildings. The cathedral has lovely stained-glass windows. A number of Martinique's former governors are interred beneath the choir loft.

Rue Schoelcher runs through the center of the capital's primary shopping district, which consists of a six-block area bounded by rue de la République, rue de la Liberté, rue de Victor Severe, and rue Victor Hugo. Stores feature Paris fashions (at Paris prices), and French perfume, china, crystal, and liqueurs, as well as local handicrafts.

Time Out **Drugstore de la Galerie** (46 rue Ernest Duproge, tel. 596/73–90–85) is a combination restaurant, cafeteria, and tearoom, where you can rest your feet and get a light repast every day from 7 AM to midnight.

Three blocks north of the cathedral, make a right turn on rue Perrinon and go one block. At the corner of rue de la Liberté is the **Bibliothèque Schoelcher,** the wildly elaborate Byzantine-Egyptian-Romanesque–style public library. It's named after Victor Schoelcher, who led the fight to free the slaves in the French West Indies in the 19th century. The eye-popping structure was built for the 1889 Paris Exposition, after which it was dismantled, shipped to Martinique, and reassembled piece by ornate piece on its present location.

Follow rue Victor Severe five blocks west, just beyond the Hotel de Ville, and you'll come to Place Jose-Marti. The **Parc Floral et Culturel** will acquaint you with the variety of exotic flora on this island. There's also an aquarium showing fish that can be found in these waters. *Place Jose-Marti, Sermac, tel. 596/71–66–25. Admission free. Open Mon.–Sat. 9–noon and 3–6.*

The Levassor River meanders through the park and joins the bay at **Pointe Simon,** where yachts can be chartered. The river divides the downtown area from the ritzy residential district of Didier in the hills.

The North The tour of the north is divided into two sections: a day trip and an overnight excursion. Martinique's "must do" is the drive north along the coast from Fort-de-France to St-Pierre. The 40-mile round-trip to St-Pierre can be made in an afternoon, although there is enough to see to fill an entire day. The drive to the north coast will appeal primarily to nature lovers, hikers, and mountain climbers. If you are interested in climbing Mont Pelée or hiking, plan to spend at least a night on the road *(see* Participant Sports, below, for guided hikes). Bear in mind that a 20-mile mountain drive takes longer than driving 20 miles on the prairie.

Tour 1 Head west out of Fort-de-France on Route N2. You'll pass
2 through the suburb of **Schoelcher,** home of the University of the French West Indies and Guyana. La Batelière Hotel, noted for its sports facilities, is also located here.

Just north of Schoelcher is Fond-Lahaye, where the road begins to climb sharply. About 4½ miles farther along, you'll come to the fishing village of **Case-Pilote,** named after a Carib chief to whom the French took kindly and called Pilote.

Time Out **La Guinguette** (coast road at Le Mouillage, St. Pierre, tel. 596/ 77–15–02) is a 20-table oceanside bistro where fishing boats bring fresh seafood to the kitchen doors and spicy Creole dishes are served on the wave-washed patio.

Continuing along the coastal road, you'll see red-roof houses
❸ clinging to the green mountainside on the way to **Bellefontaine,** 4 miles north. This is another fishing village, with pastel houses on the hillsides and colorful boats bobbing in the water. One of the houses here is built in the shape of a boat.

❹ Continue north along the coast until you get to **Le Carbet.** Columbus is believed to have landed here on June 15, 1502. In 1635, Pierre Belain d'Esnambuc arrived here with the first French settlers.

Le Carbet is home to the **Amazona Zoological Gardens,** which has crocodiles from the Amazon, armadillos, lions, and ocelots. *Le Coin, Le Carbet, tel. 596/78–00–64. Admission: adults 15F, children 10F. Open daily 9–6.*

Just north of Carbet is **Anse-Turin,** where Paul Gauguin lived for a short time in 1887 with his friend and fellow artist,
❺ Charles Laval. The **Musée Gauguin** traces the history of the artist's Martinique connection through documents, letters, and reproductions of some of the paintings he did while on the island. There is also a display of Martinican costumes and head-dresses. *Anse-Turin, tel. 596/77–22–66. Admission: 10F. Open daily 10–5.*

❻ Two miles farther brings you to **St-Pierre,** the island's oldest city, which now has a population of about 6,000. At the turn of this century, St-Pierre was a flourishing city of 30,000 and was called the Paris of the West Indies. In spring 1902, Mont Pelée began to rumble and spit out ash and steam. By the first week in May, all wildlife had wisely vacated the area. City officials, however, ignored the warnings, needing voters in town for an upcoming election. At 8 AM on May 8, 1902, the volcano erupted, belching forth a cloud of burning ash with temperatures over 3,600°F. In the space of three minutes, Mt. Pelée transformed the Paris of the West Indies into Martinique's Pompeii. The entire town was destroyed and its inhabitants were instantly calcified. There was only one survivor, a prisoner named Siparis, who was saved by the thick walls of his underground cell. (He was later pardoned and for some years afterward was a sideshow attraction at the Barnum & Bailey Circus.) You can wander through the site to see the ruins of the island's first church, built in 1640; the theater; the toppled statues; and Siparis's cell. *For a guided tour of the area, contact Syndicat d'initiative, La Guinguette Restaurant, tel. 596/77–15–02. Tours: 15F adults, 10F children. Open weekdays 9–noon.*

The **Musée Vulcanologique** was established in 1932 by American volcanologist Franck Perret. His collection includes photographs of the old town, documents, and a number of relics excavated from the ruins, including molten glass, melted iron, and contorted clocks stopped at 8 AM, the time of the disaster. *St-*

*Pierre, tel. 596/77–15–16. Admission: 5F adults, 1F children.
Open daily 9–noon and 3–5.*

In St-Pierre, Route N2 turns inland toward Morne Rouge, but
before going there, you may want to follow the coastal road 8
⑦ miles north to **Le Prêcheur.** En route, yóu'll pass what is called
the Tomb of the Carib Indians. The site is actually a formation
of limestone hills from which the last of the Caribs are said to
have flung themselves to avoid capture by the French. The village of Le Prêcheur was the childhood home of Françoise
d'Aubigné, later to become the Marquise de Maintenon and the
second wife of Louis XIV.

Return to St-Pierre and drive 4 miles east on Route 2 to reach
⑧ **Le Morne Rouge.** Lying on the southern slopes of Mont Pelée,
the town of Morne Rouge, too, was destroyed by the volcano. It
is now a popular resort spot with spectacular mountain scenery. This is the starting point for a climb up the 4,600-foot
mountain, but you must have a guide *(see* Participant Sports,
below).

At this point, you have the option of returning to Fort-de-
France or continuing on for a tour of the north and Atlantic
coasts.

If you choose to return to the capital, take the Route de la Trace
(Rte. N3) south from Le Morne Rouge. The winding, two-lane
paved road is one of the island's great drives, snaking through
dense tropical rain forests.

⑨ La Trace leads to **Balata,** where you can see the **Balata Church,**
an exact replica of Sacré-Coeur Basilica in Paris, and the **Jardin
de Balata** (Balata Gardens). Jean-Philippe Thoze, a professional landscaper and devoted horticulturalist, spent 20 years
creating this collection of thousands of varieties of tropical
flowers and plants. There are shaded benches where you can relax and take in the panoramic views of the mountains. *Rte. de
Balata, tel. 596/64–48–73. Admission: 30F adults, 10F children. Open daily 9–5.*

From Balata, Route N3 continues 8 miles south to the capital
city.

If you've opted to continue exploring the north and Atlantic
coasts, take Route N3 north from Morne Rouge. You'll pass
through Petite Savane and wind northeast to the flower-filled
⑩ village of **Ajoupa-Bouillon,** a 17th-century settlement in the
midst of pineapple fields.

A mile and a half east of Ajoupa-Bouillon, Route N3 deadends
at Route 1, which runs north–south. Turn left and drive 3 miles
through sugarcane, pineapple, and banana fields to **Basse-
Pointe,** which lies at sea level on the Atlantic coast. Just before
reaching Basse-Pointe you'll pass a Hindu temple, one of the
relics of the East Indians who settled in this area in the 19th
century. The view of the eastern slope of Mont Pelée is lovely
from here. Route D21 leads inland to the estimable **Leyritz
Plantation,** a fine place to stay, to play, and to eat.

⑪ The **Musée de Poupées Végétales** contains a collection of exotic
and unusual "doll sculptures," in which a local plant is shaped
into a figurine. The creative results, which depict famous wom-
en of French history, are made entirely of plants and leaves.

They are the work of local artisan Will Fenton. *Leyritz Plantation, tel. 596/78–53–92. Admission: 15F. Open daily 7–5.*

⑫ Three miles along, you'll come to **Macouba** on the coast. From here, the island's most spectacular drive leads 6 miles to **Grand-Rivière,** on the northernmost point. Perched on high cliffs, this village affords magnificent views of the sea, the mountains, and, on clear days, the neighboring island of Dominica. From Grand-Rivière, you can trek 11 miles on a well-marked path that leads through lush tropical vegetation to the beach at Anse-Ceron on the northwest coast. The beach is lovely and the diving is excellent, but the currents are very strong and swimming is not advised.

From Grand-Rivière, you can backtrack 13 miles to the junction of Routes N1 and N3 and continue down the Atlantic coast.

Time Out Stop in at **Chez Vava** (Rte. 1 on the eastern edge of Grand-Rivière, tel. 596/75–52–81) for a rum punch and a lunch of seafood and Creole dishes.

From the junction of Routes N1 and N3, continue 10 miles on Route 1 along the Atlantic coast, driving through the villages **⑬** of Le Lorrain and Marigot to **Ste-Marie,** a town of about 20,000 Martinicans and the commercial capital of the island's north. There is a lovely mid-19th-century church in the town and, on a more earthy note, a rum distillery.

The **Musée du Rhum,** operated by the St. James Rum Distillery, is housed in a graceful galleried Creole house. Guided tours of the museum take in displays of the tools of the trade and include a visit to the distillery. And, yes, you may sample the product. *Ste-Marie, tel. 596/75–30–02. Admission free. Open weekdays 9–5, weekends 9–1.*

⑭ **La Trinité,** a subprefecture in the north, is 6 miles to the south in a sheltered bay. From La Trinité, the **Caravelle Peninsula** thrusts 8 miles into the Atlantic Ocean. Much of the peninsula is under the auspices of the Regional Nature Reserve and offers places for trekking, swimming, and sailing. This is the home of the **Morne Pavilion,** an open-air sports and leisure center operated by the nature reserve *(see* Participant Sports, below). To reach it, turn right at Tartane on the Spoutourne Morne Pavilion road.

At the eastern tip of the peninsula, you can root through the **⑮** ruins of the **Dubuc Castle.** This was the home of the Dubuc de Rivery family, which owned the peninsula in the 18th century. According to legend, young Aimée Dubuc de Rivery was captured by Barbary pirates, sold to the Ottoman Empire, became a favorite of the sultan, and gave birth to Mahmoud II.

Tour 2 Return to La Trinité and take Route N4, which winds 20 miles through lush tropical scenery back to Fort-de-France.

The loop through the south is a round-trip of about 100 miles. This excursion will include the birthplace of the Empress Josephine, Pointe du Bout and its resort hotels, a few small museums, and many large beaches. You can spend an afternoon, a day, or a couple of weeks exploring this region, depending on the time at your disposal and your frame of mind.

From Fort-de-France, take Route N5, which leads south through Lamentin, where the airport is located. A 20-mile

drive will bring you to Rivière-Salée, where you'll make a right
16 turn on Route D7 and drive 4½ miles to the village of **Les Trois-Ilets.**

Trois-Ilets, named after the three rocky islands nearby, is a
lovely little village with a population of about 3,000. It's known
for its pottery, straw, and wood works and as the birthplace of
Napoleon's Empress Josephine. On the village square, you can
visit the simple church were she was baptized Marie-Joseph
Tascher de la Pagerie. To reach the museum and the old sugar
plantation on which she was born, drive a mile west on Route
D7 and turn left on Route D38.

A stone building that held the kitchen of the estate is now home
to the **Musée de la Pagerie.** (The main house blew down in the
hurricane of 1766, when Josephine was three.) It contains an
assortment of memorabilia pertaining to Josephine's life and
loves (she was married at 16 in an arranged marriage to Alexandre de Beauharnais). There are family portraits; documents,
including a marriage certificate; a love letter written to her in
1796 by Napoleon; and various antique furnishings, including
the bed she slept in as a child. *Trois-Ilets, tel. 596/68–34–55.
Admission: 15F adults, 3F children. Open Tues.–Sun. 9–5.*

The **Maison de la Canne** will teach you everything you ever
wanted to know about sugarcane. Exhibits take you through
three centuries of sugarcane production, with displays of tools,
scale models, engravings, and photographs. *Trois-Ilets, tel.
596/68–32–04. Admission: 15F. Open Tues.–Sun. 9–5:30.*

17 You can reach **Pointe du Bout** and the beach at **Anse-Mitan** by
turning right on Route D38 west of Trois-Ilets. This area is
filled with resort hotels, among them the Bakoua and the Meridien. The Pointe du Bout marina is a colorful spot where a
whole slew of boats are tied up. The ferry to Fort-de-France
leaves from this marina.

Time Out **Euromarche** (Lamentin) is one of the most complete supermarkets in the Western Hemisphere. For less than $2 (each), you
can stagger out with hot French bread, pâtés, cheeses, and
salmon flown in from Europe. Add some Creole boudin from
the deli counter and a chilled bottle of wine or the local dark
Rhum St. James, and have a gourmet picnic.

When you return to Route D7, turn right and head west. You'll
pass by the **Empress Josephine Golf Course** on the way to **Anse-
à-l'Ane,** where there is a pretty white-sand beach complete
with picnic tables.

South from Anse-à-l'Ane, Route D7 turns into a 10-mile roller
coaster en route to **Anse-d-'Arlets,** another popular beach.
You'll see fishermen's nets strung up on the beach to dry and
pleasure boats on the water.

From the center of town, take Route D37 along the coast down
to Morne Larcher and on to **Le Diamant.** Several hotels sit on
the 2½-mile beach (the island's longest, though not the best
18 beach), and from here, there is a splendid view of **Diamond
Rock** a couple of miles offshore.

In 1804, during the squabbles over possession of the island between the French and the English, the latter commandeered
the rock, armed it with cannons, christened it HMS *Diamond*

Rock, and proceeded to use it as a warship. For almost a year and a half, the British held the rock, bombarding any French ships that came along. The French got wind of the fact that the British were getting cabin fever on their isolated ship-island and arranged a supply of barrels of rum for those on the rock. The French easily overpowered the inebriated sailors, ending one of the most curious engagements in naval history.

The hotels Diamant Les Bains and Diamant-Novotel are both in this area. At Le Diamant, Route D37 joins up with Route D7, which strikes out in a northeasterly direction at Taupinière. A mile's drive will bring you to a fork in the road; one branch heads north to Fort-de-France and the other continues south along the coast. Take the southerly route.

⓳ Three miles down the coastline lies **Ste-Luce,** another fishing village with a pretty white beach. From Ste-Luce, you can take Route D17 north 1 mile to the **Forêt de Montravail,** where arrows point the way to Carib rock drawings.

Time Out   **La Vague du Sud** (Rue Schoelcher, Ste-Luce, tel. 596/62–44–96) is an unpretentious little eatery serving seafood.

You'll say good-bye to Route D7 in Ste-Luce and hook up with Route D18, which will take you northeast 4 miles to **Rivière Pilote,** a town of about 12,000 people. From there, Route D18A trickles down south to **Pointe Figuier,** where the scuba diving is excellent. Stay with Route D18A and curve around the beautiful Cul de Sac inlet through **Le Marin.** Just east of Le Marin, turn right on Route D9 and drive all the way down to the sea. En route you'll pass the turnoff to Buccaneer's Creek/Club Med ⓴ and the pretty village of **Ste-Anne,** where a Roman Catholic church sits on the square facing a lovely white beach. Not far away, at the southernmost tip, is the island's best beach, the **Grande Anse des Salines.** It's 1½ miles of soft white sand, calm waters, and relative seclusion (except on weekends).

In sharp contrast to the north, this section of the island is arid and dry. If you walk from Les Salines to Anse-Trabaud, you'll ㉑ go through the **petrified forest,** which would look eerie and otherworldly any place, but especially on the Island of Flowers.

㉒ Backtrack 9 miles to Le Marin. From there, Route N6 goes north 7 miles to **Le Vauclin,** skirting the highest point in the south, **Mt. Vauclin** (1,654 feet). Le Vauclin is an important fishing port on the Atlantic coast, and the return of the fishermen shortly before noon each day is a big event.

㉓ Continue north 9 miles on Route N6 to **Le François,** a sizable city of some 16,000 Martinicans. This is a great place for snorkeling. Offshore are a number of shallow basins with white-sand bottoms between the reefs.

There is a lovely bay 6 miles farther along at **Le Robert.** You'll also come to the junction of Route N1, which will take you west to Fort-de-France, 12½ miles away.

Participant Sports

Bicycling   The *Parc Naturel Regional de la Martinique* (tel. 596/64–42–59) has designed biking itineraries off the beaten track. Bikes can be rented from **Funny** (tel. 596/63–33–05), **Discount** (tel. 596/66–33–05), and **T S Location Sarl** (tel. 596/63–42–82), all located in Fort-de-France. In Sainte-Luce, try **Marquis Moto** (no phone).

Boating For boat rentals and yacht charters, check with **Ship Shop** (6 rue Joseph-Compère, Fort-de-France, tel. 596/71–43–40), **Carib Charter** (Habitation Croix du Sud, Pointe de Jaham, Schoelcher, tel. 596/71–58–96 or 73–08–80), **Soleil et Voile** (Marina Pointe du Bout, tel. 596/66–07–74 or 66–07–87), **Alizes Plus** (Marina Pointe du Bout, tel. 596/66–04–81), Shipchandling Division (6 rue Joseph Compère, tel. 596/70–11–39), **Voile et Vent aux Antilles** (Star Voyages, Marina Pointe du Bout, Trois-Ilets, tel. 596/66–00–72), **Dufour Antilles** (Marina Pointe du Bout, Trois-Ilets, tel. 596/66–05–35), **Caraibes Nautique** (Hotel Bakoua, Trois Ilets, tel. 596/66–06–06), **Captains Shop** (Marina Pointe du Bout, tel. 596/76–35–64), **Chimere Yachting** (Marina Pointe du Bout, Trois-Ilets, tel. 596/66–03–85), **Somatour** (14 rue Blenac, tel. 596/71–31–68), **Yachting Caraibe** (Cite Mansarde at Robert, tel. 596/65–18–18 or 8 Lotissement Bardinet, Fort-de-France, tel. 596/71–85–96), and **Agence Le Marin** (rue Osman Duquesnay, Marin, tel. 596/74–99–34).

Deep-Sea Fishing Fish cruising these waters include tuna, barracuda, dolphin, kingfish, and bonito. For a day's outing on the 37-foot *Egg Harbor*, with gear and breakfast included, contact **Bathy's Club** (Méridien Hotel, tel. 596/66–00–00). Charters of up to five days can be arranged on Captain Réné Alaric's 37-foot *Rayon Vert* (Auberge du Vare, Case-Pilote, north of Fort-de-France, tel. 596/78–80–56).

Golf At **Golf de l'Imperatrice Joséphine** (tel. 596/68–32–81), there is an 18-hole Robert Trent Jones course with an English-speaking pro, fully equipped pro shop, a bar, and restaurant. Located at Trois-Ilets, a mile from the Pointe du Bout resort area and 18 miles from Fort-de-France, the club offers special greens fees for hotel guests and cruise-ship passengers.

Hiking Inexpensive guided excursions in which tourists can participate are organized year-round by the *Parc Naturel Regional de la Martinique* (Regional Nature Reserve, Caserne Bouille, Fort-de-France, tel. 596/73–19–30).

Horseback Riding Excursions and lessons are available at **Ranch Jack** (near Anse-d'Arlets, tel. 596/68–63–97), the **Black Horse Ranch** (near La Pagerie in Trois-Ilets, tel. 596/66–00–04), and **La Cavale** (near Diamant on the road to the Novotel hotel, tel. 596/76–20–23), and **Ranch Val d'Or** (Quartier Val d'Or, Ste-Anne, tel. 596/76–70–58).

Sailing Hobie Cats, Sunfish, and Sailfish can be rented by the hour from hotel beach shacks. If you're a member of a yacht club, show your club membership card and enjoy the facilities of **Club de la Voile de Fort-de-France** (Pointe Simon, tel. 596/70–26–63) and **Yacht Club de la Martinique** (Carenage, Fort-de-France, tel. 596/70–23–60). Also check **Club Nautique du Marin** (tel. 596/74–92–48), **Cercle Nautique de Schoelcher** (Anse Madame, tel. 596/61–15–21), **Association Madiawind** (Madiana Plage, Schoelcher, tel. 595/73–55–07), **Windsurfing** (rue Martin Luther King, tel. 596/73–55–07), **Hotel Frantel** (tel. 596/66–04–04), and **ATM Yachts** (Club Nautique du Marin, tel. 596/74–98–17).

Scuba Diving To explore the old shipwrecks, coral gardens, and other under-sea sites, you must have a medical certificate and insurance papers. Among the island's dive operators are **Tropicasub** (La Guinguette, St-Pierre, tel. 596/77–15–02), **CSCP** (Le Port, Case Pilote, tel. 596/78–73–75), **Cressma** (Fort-de-France, tel. 596/61–34–36 or 596/58–04–48), **Bathis Club** (Hotel Meridien, tel. 596/66–00–00), **Planete Bleue** (La Marina, Trois-Ilets, tel. 596-66–08–79), **Sub diamant Rock** (Hotel Novotel, tel. 596/76–42–42), and **Oxygene Bleu** (Longpre, Lamentin, tel. 596/50–25–78).

Sea Excursions and Snorkeling The *Aquarium* (Fort-de-France, tel. 596/61–49–49) is a glass-bottom boat that does excursions. For information on other sailing, swimming, snorkeling, and beach picnic trips, contact **Affaires Maritimes** (tel. 596/71–90–05).

Sports Center The **Morne Pavilion** (tel. 596/73–19–30), on the Caravelle Peninsula, is an open-air sports and leisure center offering sailing, tennis, and other activities.

Tennis In addition to its links, the **Golf de l'Imperatrice Joséphine** (Trois-Ilets, tel. 596/68–32–82) has three lighted tennis courts. There are also two courts at the **Bakoua Beach Hotel** (tel. 596/66–02–02); six courts at **La Batelière Hotel** (tel. 596/61–49–49); seven courts at **Buccaneer's Creek/Club Med** (tel. 596/76–74–52); two courts at **Diamant-Novotel** (tel. 596/76–42–42); one court at the **Leyritz Plantation** (tel. 596/78–53–92); and two courts at the **Meridien Hotel** (tel. 596/66–00–00). Other hotels with tennis courts are **Novotel** (tel. 596/76–42–42), **Hotel PLM Azur Carayou** (tel. 596/66–04–04), **Le Calalou** (tel. 596/68–31–67), **Relais Caraibes** (tel. 596/74–44–65), **Anchorage Tobago** (tel. 596/76–73–74), **La Caravelle** (tel. 596/58–37–32), **Diamant Bleu** (tel. 596/76–42–15), **Rivage Hotel** (tel. 596/66–00–53), **La Margelle** (tel. 596/76–40–19), **Bungalow de la Prairie** (tel. 596/54–34–16), **Bungalow du Soleil Levant** (tel. 596/68–05–21), and **Brise Marine** (tel. 596/62–46–94). For additional information about tennis on the island, contact **La Ligue Regionale de Tennis** (Petit Manoir, Lamentin, tel. 596/51–08–00).

Shopping

French fragrances and designer scarves, fine china and crystal, leather goods, and liquors and liqueurs are all good buys in Fort-de-France. Purchases are further sweetened by the 20% discount on luxury items when paid for by traveler's checks and major credit cards. Among local items, look for Creole gold jewelry, such as loop earrings, heavy bead necklaces, and slave bracelets; white and dark rum; and handcrafted straw goods, pottery, and tapestries. In addition, U.S. Customs allows you to bring some of the local flora into the country.

Shopping Areas The area around the cathedral in Fort-de-France has a number of small shops carrying luxury items. Of particular note are the shops on **rue Victor Hugo, rue Moreau de Jones, rue Antoine Siger,** and **rue Lamartine.** There is also a duty-free shop at the airport. On the outskirts of Fort-de-France, shopping malls include **Centre Commercial de Cluny, Centre Commercial de Dillon, Centre Commercial de Bellevue,** and over 60 boutiques at **La Galleria** in Lamentin.

Good Buys
China and Crystal Look for Lalique, Limoges, and Baccarat at **Cadet Daniel** (72 rue Antoine Siger, Fort-de-France, tel. 596/71–41–48) and

Roger Albert (7 rue Victor Hugo, Fort-de-France, tel. 596/71–71–71).

Flowers Anthuriums, torch lilies, and lobster claws are packaged for shipment at **MacIntosh** (31 rue Victor Hugo, Fort-de-France, tel. 596/70–09–50, and at the airport, tel. 596/51–51–51) and **Les Petites Floralies** (75 rue Blenac, Fort-de-France, tel. 596/71–66–16).

Local Handicrafts A wide variety of dolls, straw goods, tapestries, pottery, and other items are available at the **Caribbean Art Center** (Centre de Metiers Arts, opposite the Tourist Office, Blvd. Alfassa, Fort-de-France (tel. 596/70–32–16). The **Galerie d'Art** (89 rue Victor Hugo, tel. 596/63–10–62) has some unusual and excellent Haitian art—paintings, sculptures, ceramics, and intricate jewelry cases—at reasonable prices.

Perfumes Dior, Chanel, and Guerlain are among the popular scents at **Roger Albert** (7 rue Victor Hugo, Fort-de-France, tel. 596/71–71–71). Airport minishops sell the most popular scents at in-town prices, so there's no need to carry purchases around.

Rum Rum can be purchased at the various distilleries, including **Duquesnes** (Fort-de-France, tel. 596/71–91–68), **St. James** (Ste-Marie, tel. 596/69–30–02), and **Trois Rivières** (Ste-Luce, tel. 596/62–51–78).

Dining

Martinique has, arguably, the best food in all the Caribbean, with restaurants serving classic French cuisine and Creole dishes and wine cellars filled with fine French wines. Some of the best restaurants are tucked away in the countryside, and therein lies a problem. The farther you venture from tourist hotels, the less likely you are to find English-speaking folk. If you don't speak French and want to savor the countryside cuisine, take along a sophisticated phrase book. The local Creole specialties are *colombo* (curry), *accras* (cod or vegetable fritters), *crabes farcies* (stuffed land crab), *écrevisses* (freshwater crawfish), *boudin* (Creole blood sausage), *lambi* (conch), *langouste* (clawless Caribbean lobster), *soudons* (sweet clams), and *oursin* (sea urchin). The local favorite libation is *le 'ti punch*, a "little punch," concocted of white rum, sugar, syrup, lime, ice, and a guaranteed hangover.

The most highly recommended restaurants are indicated by a star ★.

Category	Cost*
Expensive	over $50
Moderate	$30–$50
Inexpensive	under $30

*per person, excluding drinks and service

Fort-de-France **La Biguine.** Downstairs is a cozy, casual café with red-and-white check cloths and upstairs, a more formal candlelit dining room. Local fish poached in Creole sauce, shark cooked in tomato sauce, and duck fillet with pineapple or orange sauce are among the à la carte offerings, with homemade tarts for dessert. *11 Rte. de la Folie, tel. 596/71–40–07. Jackets required for* *dinner. Reservations required for dinner. AE. Closed Sun. Expensive.*

★ **La Belle Epoque.** The nine tables on the terrace of this turn-of-the-century house are much in demand. You can feast on duck fillet in mango sauce, hot spinach mousse, lobster medaillons with slices of leek, and a Creole swordfish fillet. Yves Coyac is the talented Martinican chef. *Km 2.5, Rte. de Didier, tel. 596/64–01–09. Jackets and reservations required for dinner. DC, MC, V. Closed Sun. and Mon. Expensive.*

Le Bristol. Selecting from a long list of rum drinks is the first order of business in this handsome terrace restaurant. The menu changes monthly, but you may find gazpacho or escargots in garlic butter for starters and main dishes, such as lobster fricassee and *magret de canard* as well as a variety of beef and fish dishes. Hot apple tarts and feathery coconut soufflés are usually on the dessert list. *0.2 km., rue Martin Luther King, tel. 596/63–66–76. Jackets and reservations required for dinner. AE. Expensive.*

★ **La Fontane.** In a pastoral setting, this lovely gingerbread house with a wraparound veranda is shaded by mango trees. Inside you'll find Oriental rugs, fresh flowers, and a display of antiques that includes a handsome gramophone and a grandmother's clock. *Le Bambou de la Fontane* is a mixed salad with fish, tomato, corn, melon, and crawfish. Other dishes served here are cream soup with crabs, crayfish bisque, red snapper with lemon/lime sauce, *magret de canard*, and steak au poivre. *Km 4 Rte. de Balata, tel. 596/64–28–70 or 596/71–38–28. Jackets and tie required. Reservations essential. AE, CB. Closed Sun. Expensive.*

La Grand 'Voile. Crisp white cloths, fine china and crystal, and lots of windows overlooking the harbor contribute to a lovely dining room. Starters include chilled chicken liver mousse and fresh steamed mussels. Main dishes include lobster in Creole sauce and fillet of beef Rossini (with artichoke hearts, foie gras, truffles, and Madeira sauce). The *Menu Degustation* (a variety of sample-size portions) is a practical way to savor the restaurant's specialties. Service here is sometimes on the slow side. *Pte. Simon, tel. 596/70–29–29. Jacket and reservations suggested. AE, MC, V. Open daily for lunch and dinner. Expensive.*

★ **Le Lafayette.** This is a true "salon" on the second story of a renovated hotel of the same name. Clusters of indoor greenery combine with white latticework and rich Haitian paintings as the setting for what may be the finest dining room in Fort-de-France. Begin the day with a chocolate brioche for breakfast, continue to a light fondu and salad for lunch, and end with a perfectly grilled lobster in a spicy sauce, or perhaps with imported sirloin in a black-pepper sauce. Dessert is something simple, like banana flambé in 20-year-old rum. *5 rue de la Liberté, tel. 596/60–97–75. Reservations required. AE, MC, V. Closed Sun. Expensive.*

Le Tiffany. Claude Pradine presides over the kitchen and the sleight-of-hand presentations every Friday night by the Martinique Academy of Magic. Dining is on candlelit terraces or in a cozy room filled with Pradine's collection of antiques. The menu consists of French cuisine as well as Creole dishes, which include terrine of red snapper, fish soup, crabe farci, breast of duck with mango, beef with Roquefort butter, Creole court bouillon, and curried lamb. Linger late over coffee, which is served with homemade chocolate truffles and Cognac. *An-*

cienne Rte. de Schoelcher, near Croix de Bellevue, tel. 596/71–33–82. Reservations required for dinner. MC, V. No lunch Sat.; closed Sun. Expensive.

★ **Le Coq Hardi.** Crowds flock here for the best steaks and grilled meats in town. You can pick out your own steak and feel confident that it will be cooked to perfection. Steak tartare is the house specialty, but there are tournedos Rossini (with artichoke hearts, foie gras, truffles, and Madeira sauce), entrecote Bordelaise, prime ribs, and T-bone steaks, among the wide selection of beef offerings. For dessert, there's a selection of sorbets, profiteroles, and pear Belle Hélène. *0.6 km., rue Martin Luther King, tel. 596/71–59–64. Reservations suggested. AE, DC, MC, V. Closed all day Wed. and Sat. at noon. Moderate.*

Diamant Creole. Claudine Victoire's popular seven-table restaurant is on the second floor of a little red-and-white house. The old-fashioned Creole dishes served include tiny local clams in white wine or with chives and shallots; fish or conch brochette; Creole paella; and soups and local vegetables not offered on most island menus. *7 Blvd. de Verdun, tel. 596/73–18–25. Reservations suggested. AE, MC, V. Closed Sun. Moderate.*

La Capresse. The colors are subdued (yellow and off-gray walls, slate-blue tablecloths with small clusters of daisies on each of the 10 tables); the food is French, Creole, and outstanding. At lunch, the menu might be a *coquilles de poisson* (shellfish), a grilled fish, or veal in a cream sauce. Over dinner, the soft sounds of the piano in the adjacent bar can be heard. *26 rue Perrinon, tel. 596/63–83–33. Reservations suggested for lunch and required for dinner. AE, MC, V. Breakfast, lunch, and dinner. Closed Sun. Moderate.*

Chez Gaston. Its cozy upstairs dining room, very popular with local residents, features a Creole menu. The brochettes are especially recommended. The kitchen stays open late, and there's a small dance floor. The downstairs section serves snacks all day. A French phrase book will be very helpful. *10 rue Felix Eboue, tel. 596/71–45–48. Reservations accepted. No credit cards. Inexpensive.*

Le Crew. Meals are served family style in rustic dining rooms, where the bill of fare features a few Creole dishes and lots of typical French bistro dishes: fish soup and stuffed mussels, snails, country pâté, frogs' legs, tripe, grilled chicken, and steak. The portions are ample, and there's a daily 60F three-course tourist menu that simplifies ordering. *42 rue Ernst Deproge, tel. 596/73–04–14. Reservations accepted. No credit cards. Closed Sat. evening and Sun. Inexpensive.*

Les Trois-Ilets **L'Amphore.** Dining is either on the front terrace, where there's a nice view of the bay, or in a gas-lit garden. Lobster is the menu's highlight, but there are Creole specialties and classic French dishes as well. During dinner, a guitarist strums and sings in several languages. *Anse-Mitan, tel. 596/66–03–09. Reservations accepted. No credit cards. Closed Mon.; no dinner Sat. Moderate.*

La Matador. Fresh flowers adorn each table in this simply furnished terrace restaurant. Creole boudin, quiche, or sea urchins are good for openers. Main dishes include turtle steak, Creole bouillaibaise, lobster Thermidor, and fillet of beef with port wine and mushrooms. *Anse-Mitan, tel. 596/68–05–36.*

Reservations suggested in high season. AE, DC, MC, V. Closed Wed. Moderate.

★ **La Villa Creole.** The steak béarnaise, curried dishes, conch, court bouillon, and other dishes are all superb. However, the real draw here is owner Guy Dawson, a popular singer and guitarist who entertains during dinner, either solo or en duo with Roland Manere or Guy Vadeleux. The setting is romantic, with oil lamps flickering in the lush back garden of this very popular place. *Anse-Mitan, tel. 596/66-05-53. Reservations essential. AE, DC, V. Closed Sun. Moderate.*

Bambou Restaurant. This casual place, right on the beach, serves omelets and salads, as well as lamb cutlets, curried chicken, steak au poivre, codfish pie, and sole meunière. For dessert, there's coconut flan or banana or pineapple flambé. *Anse-Mitan, tel. 596/66-01-39. Reservations accepted. AE, DC, MC, V. Inexpensive.*

Anse-d'Arlets **Tamarin Plage Restaurant.** The lobster *vivier* in the middle of the room gives you a clue to the specialty here, but there are other recommendable offerings as well. Fish soup or Creole boudin are good starters, then consider court bouillon, chicken fricassee, and curried mutton. The beachfront bar is a popular local hangout. *Anse-d'Arlets, tel. 596/68-67-88. Reservations accepted. No credit cards. Moderate.*

★ **Ti Sable.** This restaurant has a dramatic setting right on a beautiful beach and is shaded by a huge sea-grape tree. Seating is either on a broad seaside veranda or in an open pavilion with a billowing parachute ceiling. Specialties include grilled crawfish, poached sea urchins, and curried mutton. *Anse-d'Arlets, tel. 596/68-62-44. Reservations suggested. AE, V. Closed Sun. dinner (open for lunch) and all day Mon. Moderate.*

Ste-Anne ★ **Aux Filets Bleus.** This breezy open-air eatery is right on the beach, and you can go for a swim before or after dining. Turtle or fish soup, stuffed crab, and avocado vinaigrette are all good opening bids. In addition to an assortment of lobster entrées, there is grilled or steamed fish and octopus with red beans and rice. *Pointe Marin, tel. 596/76-73-42. Reservations essential. No credit cards. Closed Mon. Expensive.*

★ **L'Arbre a Pain.** Owner Rachel DesCloux offers unexpected dishes in her ground-floor dining room that opens onto a garden. The menu changes, but favorites are the inventive *fondu* dishes, *tartare de poisson*, and *écrevisses aux épices*. It's a leisurely place to lunch (or dine) in on a day of wandering the southern villages and beaches. *Rue du Bord de Mer, Ste-Anne, tel. 596/76-72-93. No credit cards. Inexpensive-Moderate.*

Le Petit Auberge. This country inn is hidden behind a profusion of tropical flowers, just across the main road from the beach. Fresh seafood is turned into such dishes as *filet de poisson aux champignons* (fish cooked with mushrooms), *crabe farci*, and fresh *langouste* in a Creole sauce. Or sample *canard à l'ananas*, *poulet Creole* or *entrecôte Creole*. They're all winners. *Plage du Gros Raisins, Ste-Luce, tel. 596/62-59-70. No credit cards. Moderate.*

La Dunette. Bright blue awnings shade the terrace, which is filled with wrought-iron chairs and tables, and there is an abundance of hanging plants. Your choices for lunch or dinner include fish soup, grilled fish or lobster, poached sea urchins, pork en brochette with pineapple, and several curried dishes. *Ste-Anne, tel. 596/76-73-90. Reservations suggested in high season. V. Closed Wed. Inexpensive.*

François **Club Nautique.** While this little place is not going to turn up in
★ *Architectural Digest*, the food that comes fresh daily out of the
sea is exquisitely prepared. Have a couple of rum punches, then
dig into turtle steak or charcoal-broiled lobster. The restaurant is right on the beach, and boat trips leave here for
snorkeling in the nearby coral reefs. *Le François, tel. 596/54–
31–00. Reservations accepted. AE, DC, MC, V. Open for lunch
only. Inexpensive.*

Diamant **Diamant Plage.** This split-level terrace faces the post office in
the village of Diamant. Octavia Gabrielle turns out, among
other things, Creole turtle, shark stew, stuffed shrimp or
conch, and superb grilled fish. *Le Diamant, tel. 596/76–40–48.
Reservations accepted. V. Inexpensive.*

Relais Caraibes. Parisians M. and Mme. Senez have opened this
individual bungalow colony *avec* restaurant but still manage to
spend enough time in Paris to gather original objets d'art for
decor and for sale. Dishes include chicken Antilloise, a half lobster in two sauces, fresh-caught fish in a basil sauce, and
fricassee of country shrimp. The crisply decorated dining
room, always awash in fresh flowers, commands an always-
clear view of Diamond Rock. *La Cherry, Diamant, tel. 596/76–
44–65. Open for lunch and dinner. No credit cards. Moderate.*

Lamentin **Le Verger.** An orchard is the setting for this green-and-white
★ country house, not far from the airport. Pheasant and duck, as
well as game, are on the extensive menu, which also includes
classic French and Creole dishes. Follow the signs for La
Trinité; the entrance to the restaurant is on the right immediately after the Esso and Shell stations. *Place d'Armes, tel. 596/
51–43–02. Reservations suggested. AE, DC, MC, V. Closed
Sat. afternoon and Sun. night. Moderate–Expensive.*

Morne-des-Esses **Le Colibri.** In the northwestern reaches of the island, this is the
★ domain of Clotilde Palladino, who presides over the kitch-
en while her children serve. Choice seating is at one of the
seven tables on the back terrace. For starters, try *buisson
d'écrevisses*, six giant freshwater crayfish accompanied by a
tangy tomato sauce flavored with thyme, scallions, and tiny
bits of crayfish. Stuffed pigeon, lobster omelets, suckling pig,
and coconut chicken are among the main dishes. *Morne-des-
Esses, tel. 596/69–91–95. Reservations essential. AE, DC,
MC, V. Closed Mon. Moderate–Expensive.*

Basse-Pointe **Leyritz Plantation.** The pride of Martinique is *the* place all the
★ cruise passengers head as soon as they disembark. The re-
stored 18th-century plantation has the ambience of a country
inn and a dramatic view of Mont Pelée. The menu is mostly Creole, featuring boudin, chicken with coconut, and several
curried dishes. *Basse-Pointe, tel. 596/75–53–92. Reservations
essential. DC, MC. Moderate–Expensive.*

Restaurant Mally. Unpretentious and popular, Mally Edjam's
home has a few tables inside and only four on the side porch under an awning. The lady is a legend on the island, and although
it's a long drive up, you'll be rewarded with the likes of papaya
soufflé, spicy Creole concoctions such as curried pork and
stuffed land crabs, and fresh local vegetables. Her exotic *confi-
tures* of guava, pineapple, and cornichon top off the feast, along
with a yogurt or light coconut cake. *Rte. de la Côte Atlantique,
tel. 596/75–51–18. Reservations required. No credit cards. Inexpensive.*

Le Morne Rouge   **Auberge de la Montagne Pelée.** The restaurant is open for dinner by reservation only, but the real treat is lunch on a clear day, when you can see Mont Pelée's summit from the terrace. Creole and French dishes are featured, including a Caribbean style pot-au-feu, with whitefish, scallops, salmon, crayfish, and tiny vegetables. *Rte. de l'Aileron, tel. 596/52–32–09. Reservations essential. MC, V. Moderate.*

La Trinité   **L'Ami Fritz.** Local gourmets flock to Fritz's for his Muenster
★ cheese, game, sauerkraut, and fine wines. The lovely country mansion nestles in rolling hills, surrounded by flowers and greenery. *Brin d'Amour, tel. 596/58–20–18. Jacket and tie required. Reservations suggested. V. Closed Mon. Expensive.*

St. Pierre   **La Factorerie.** Alongside the ruins of the Eglise du Fort, is this open-air restaurant connected to the agricultural training school, where students raise the crops. The food is pleasant and the view outstanding. Dishes include grilled langouste, grilled chicken in a piquant sauce, *fricassee de lambi* (conch), and the fresh catch of the day. *Quartier Fort, St-Pierre, tel. 596/79–72–50. Closed Sat. and Sun. evenings. No credit cards. Inexpensive.*

La Guinguette. Twenty-odd tables are tucked onto a patio that ends just feet above the beach at Le Mouillage, with a spectacular view of the Mont Pelée. The view makes it difficult to concentrate on the Creole dishes (but most diners manage), such as shark with a touffle sauce, jellyfish fricassee, grilled langouste, conch fricassee, and green bananas and salted fish. *Le Mouillage, St-Pierre, tel. 596/77–15–02. No credit cards. Inexpensive.*

Lodging

Martinique's range of accommodations runs from tiny French inns called *Relais Creoles* to splashy tourist resorts, with an 18th-century plantation to round things out. The majority of the hotels are clustered in Pointe du Bout and Anse-Mitan on the Trois-Ilets peninsula across the bay from Fort-de-France, but there are other notable lodgings scattered around the island. Attractive packages are offered by many of the hotels during the year, and it's a good idea to ask what's available when you call to reserve. Remember that in the small country inns, you'll need a French phrase book.

The most highly recommended lodgings are indicated by a star ★.

Category	Cost*
Very Expensive	over $220
Expensive	$150–$220
Moderate	$85–$150
Inexpensive	under $85

All prices are for a standard double room for two with Continental breakfast, excluding $1 per person per night tax and a 10% service charge.

Hotels   **Le Bakoua.** Named after the pointed straw hats worn by the
★ local fishermen, the Bakoua is locally owned and operated. Lo-

cated in Pointe du Bout, the hotel has accommodations in three hillside buildings and a fourth on its man-made white-sand beach. The decor is cushy-cum-rustic, with wooden furnishings and tile floors. All rooms have a balcony or patio, TV, radio, king-size bed, direct-dial phone, and air-conditioning. Most accommodations are spacious but some are small and less desirable; in hotel parlance these are known as mother-in-law rooms. Entertainment consists of live music and shows nightly, including dinner dancing, limbo, and Friday-night performances of Les Grands Ballets de la Martinique. Most of the staff speak commendable English. Be sure to inquire about special package deals. *Box 589, Fort-de-France, tel. 596/66–02–02; in NY, 212/696–1323; in U.K., 01/730–7144. 140 rooms, including 2 1-bedroom suites. Facilities: 2 restaurants, bar, pool, 2 lighted tennis courts, boutique, beauty salon, water-sports center. AE, DC, MC, V. Very Expensive.*

★ **Le Méridien Trois-Ilets.** There is a great deal of activity here, even in the low season, much of it revolving around the pool and the long strip of white-sand beach. All rooms are air-conditioned, with wall-to-wall carpeting, built-in hair dryers, and boat-size tubs; some have balconies with a splendid view of the bay and of Fort-de-France. English is spoken well here, and there's live entertainment nightly. *Trois-Ilets 97229, tel. 596/66–00–00 or 800/543–4300; in NY, 212/245–2920. 303 rooms including 10 suites. Facilities: 2 restaurants, bar, casino, disco, pool, 2 lighted tennis courts, duty-free shops, marina, car-rental desk, tour desk, water-sports center. AE, DC, MC, V. Very Expensive.*

La Batelière Hotel. This beachfront property boasts the island's largest rooms, and arguably the best tennis courts. The hotel overlooks the sea, and all rooms are air-conditioned, with direct-access phone, cable TV, radio, and private balcony or patio. Ask about the scuba and honeymoon packages. *Schoelcher 97233, tel. 596/61–49–49. 207 rooms and suites. Facilities: 2 restaurants, 3 bars, casino, pool, 6 lighted tennis courts, sauna, shops, water-sports center. AE, DC, MC, V. Expensive–Very Expensive.*

Diamant-Novotel. This self-contained resort occupies half an island in an ideal windsurfing location. Just beyond the registration area, a footbridge spans a large pool on the way to the guest rooms. Rooms are air-conditioned with wall-to-wall carpeting, twin beds, and large terraces. There are four beaches on the 5-acre property, and scuba packages offered by dive masters Claude and Dominique Colliat attract both French and U.S. visitors. A shuttle bus offers complimentary rides daily into Fort-de-France, and little pink monoplanes are available for soaring over the beach. The staff speaks English. *Le Diamant 97223, tel. 596/76–42–42 or 800/221–4242; in NY, 212/354–3722. 180 rooms. Facilities: 3 restaurants, 4 bars, 2 tennis courts, pool, dive shop, car-rental desk, water-sports center. AE, DC, MC, V. Expensive–Very Expensive.*

Club Med/Buccaneer's Creek. Occupying 48 landscaped acres, Martinique's Club Med is an all-inclusive village with plazas, cafés, restaurants, boutique, and a small marina. Air-conditioned pastel cottages contain twin beds and private shower/bath. The only money you need spend here is for bar drinks, personal expenses, and excursions into Fort-de-France or the countryside. There's a white-sand beach, a plethora of water sports, and plenty of nightlife. *Point Marin 97180, tel. 596/76–72–72 or 800/CLUBMED; in NY, 212/750–1670. 300 rooms. Fa-*

cilities: 2 restaurants and bars, 6 tennis courts (4 lighted), fitness and water-sports center, nightclub, disco. AE, V. Moderate–Expensive.

★ **Leyritz Plantation.** The pride of Martinique is an 18th-century restored plantation that occupies 16 acres on a lush tropical mountain. You can stay either in one of the antique-filled rooms in the manor house or opt for a rustic cabin, the carriage house, or one of the other restored buildings. But don't let the look of opulence fool you: The ambience here is of a cozy country inn. The management has done a superb job of retaining the old while keeping a foot firmly planted in the health-conscious late 20th century. The plantation maintains a well-equipped spa center with Jacuzzi, solarium, personalized nutrition and beauty programs, figure-improvement classes, facials, and massages. There's free transportation to the beach, which is about 30 minutes away. *Basse-Pointe 97218, tel. 596/78–53–08. 53 rooms. Facilities: restaurant, bar, spa, health-and-fitness center, horseback riding, tennis courts, pool. DC, MC. Moderate–Expensive.*

PLM Azur-Carayou. The style here is definitely tropical. The reception area has rattan furniture and, overhead, quaint wood rafters. The rooms, built around the large swimming pool in the garden, are air-conditioned, equipped with TVs, direct-dial phones, and well-stocked minibars. There are lots of sporting options for daytime activity, and a popular disco for evening. The hotel is well run, and the staff is helpful and friendly. *Pointe du Bout 97229, tel. 596/66–04–04. 200 double rooms. Facilities: 3 restaurants, 2 bars, 2 tennis courts, pool, archery, golf practice, scuba diving, fishing, waterskiing, sailing. AE, DC, MC, V. Moderate–Expensive.*

Bambou. The young and the hardy will enjoy this complex of rustic A-frame "chalets" with shingled roofs. The rooms are paneled in pink; they are tiny and Spartan, albeit with modern conveniences, such as air-conditioning, phones, and shower baths. The hotel is open year-round, and during high season, entertainment is featured five nights a week. *Anse-Mitan 97229, tel. 596/66–01–39; in NY, 212/757–1175. 118 rooms. Facilities: restaurant and bar, pool, water-sports center. AE, DC, MC, V. Moderate.*

★ **Diamant Les Bains.** Although manager Hubert Andrieu and his family go all out to make their guests comfortable, you won't feel quite at home unless you speak at least a little French. A few of the rooms are in the main house, where the restaurant is located, but most are in bungalows. All rooms are air-conditioned, with private baths, TVs, and phones; eight have kitchenettes. Fishing excursions and other sports activities can be arranged. *Le Diamant 97223, tel. 596/76–40–14; in the United States, 800/112–9815; in Canada, 800/468–0023; in NY, 212/840–6636. 24 rooms. Facilities: restaurant, bar, car rental, pool, water-sports center. DC, MC. Moderate.*

Diamant Marine. Here you'll find self-contained miniapartments (sleeping room with kitchenette and balcony) in a pristine stucco building, where the rooms are painted in strong Creole colors. Good for families who want to be self-sufficient. *Point de la Chery, near Diamant, tel. 596/76–46–00 or in the U.S. 800/221–4542. 149 rooms. Facilities: restaurant, 2 bars, 2 pools (1 for children), water sports, deep-sea fishing, 2 tennis courts. AE, V. Moderate.*

Imperatrice. Overlooking La Savane park in the center of the city, the Imperatrice's air-conditioned rooms are in a 1950s five-story building (with an elevator). The rooms in the front are either the best or the worst, depending upon your sensibilities: They are noisy, but they overlook the city's center of activity. All rooms have a TV and a private bath; 20 have balconies. Children under 8 stay free in the room with their parents, children 8–15 stay at 50% of the room rate. The hotel also has a popular sidewalk café. *Fort-de-France 97200, tel. 596/63–06–82; in the United States, 800/223–9815; in Canada, 800/468–0023; in NY, 212/840–6636. 24 rooms. Facilities: restaurant, café, bar. AE, DC, MC, V. Moderate.*

★ **Le Palais Creole.** There are only 11 rooms and 3 suites in this restored historic house in the heart of Fort-de-France, next to the Palais de Justice—but, oh, what rooms. Yves St. Laurent model Rosemane Mounia, who owns the hotel, the attached restaurant, and the hotel's upscale boutique, has decorated each room with an individual high-fashion flare. *26 rue Perrinon, Fort-de-France, tel. 596/71–65–29 or 596/63–83–33. 11 rooms, 3 suites. Facilities: restaurant, piano bar. AE, DC, V. Moderate.*

★ **Manoir de Beauregard.** Madame St. Cyr's hotel is an 18th-century manor house whose original walls and black-and-white tile floors date back to 1720. There are carved mahogany four-poster beds, some of which are a century old, and handsome old armoires. "Old" is the operative word, since the inn definitely shows its years, and the overall feeling is of a much-used castle. Touring groups cotton to the ambience, however, and come daily for a prix-fixe lunch. Modern conveniences include air-conditioning, phones, and private baths. *Ste-Anne 97227, tel. 596/76–73–40; in the United States, 800/223–6510. 27 rooms. Facilities: restaurant, bar, pool. AE, DC, MC, V. Moderate.*

★ **PLM Azur La Pagerie.** With its galleries, colonettes, and lush courtyard, La Pagerie looks as if it was plucked out of south Louisiana and planted near the marina in Pointe du Bout. Fully air-conditioned, the hotel has small rooms and studios, some with kitchenettes, all with private baths. It's within a short stroll of the resort hotels, restaurants, and activity. Continental breakfast is available. *Pointe du Bout 97229, tel. 596/66–05–30; in the United States, 800/223–9862; in NY, 212/757–6500. 98 rooms. Facilities: pool, water-sports center. AE, MC, V. Moderate.*

★ **Relais Caraibes.** This is a colony of bungalows on manicured grounds, with Diamond Rock dominating the seascape. Each of the 15 bungalows houses 2 separate suites and is decorated with objects the owner has brought from trips to her native Paris. *Point de la Chery, near Diamant, tel. 596/76–44–65. 30 rooms. Facilities: restaurant, bar, pool, private beach, boat, scuba instruction. AE, V. Moderate.*

★ **Saint Aubin.** This restored colonial house is in the countryside above the Atlantic coast. The rooms are modern, with air-conditioning, TVs, phones, and private baths. This is a peaceful retreat, and only 3 miles from La Trinité, 2 miles from the Spoutourne sports center and the beaches on the Caravelle Peninsula. The inn's restaurant is reserved for hotel guests and is closed during June and October. *Box 52, La Trinité, 97220, tel. 596/69–34–77; in the United States, 800/223–9815; in Canada, 800/468–0023; in NY, 212/840–6636. 15 double rooms. Facilities: restaurant, bar, pool. AE, DC, MC, V. Moderate.*

Auberge de l'Anse-Mitan. This beachfront hotel, established in 1930, is the island's oldest family-run inn. The rooms are Spartan, but all are air-conditioned and have a shower/bath. Views are either of the bay or the tropical garden, and some rooms have balconies. Informal meals are served on the terrace for guests. Things are peaceful and quiet here—even more so if you don't speak French. *Anse-Mitan 97229, tel. 596/66–01–12; in the United States, 800/223–9815; in Canada, 800/468–0023; in NY, 212/840–6636. 20 rooms. Facilities: restaurant, bar. AE, DC. Inexpensive.*

Auberge de la Montagne Pelée. There are three rooms and six studios with kitchenettes in this hillside inn that faces the famed volcano. Accommodations are simple; the view from the restaurant terrace is spectacular. *Le Morne Rouge 97260, tel. 596/53–32–09. 9 rooms. Facilities: restaurant. No credit cards. Inexpensive.*

The Last Resort. John and Véronique Deschamps's bed-and-breakfast on rue Osman Duquesnay is in the former gendarmerie annex. Language will be no problem here, since the Deschampses once lived in Sausalito, but you'll have to be flexible enough to share a bathroom with the other guests on your floor. A small communal kitchen is available, and an excellent family-style dinner is served nightly. *Le Marin 97290, tel. 596/74–83–88. 7 rooms. Facilities: restaurant. No credit cards. Inexpensive.*

Le Lafayette. This hotel's main claim to fame is its superb second-story dining room overlooking the Savane. For business travelers, or those who want to be right in the heart of town, this place is a real find. The choicest rooms are those with French windows, fronting the Savane. *5 rue de la Liberté, Fort-de-France, tel. 596/73–80–50. 24 rooms with TV, telephone, telex, and fax services. Facilities: restaurant, bar, complimentary use of Bakoua Hotel beach facilities. AE, DC, V. Inexpensive.*

Martinique Cottages. These garden bungalows in the countryside have kitchenettes, cable TVs, and phones. Operating the cottages is a family affair: The Arnauds built the bungalows, and son Jean-Marc and his sister Peggy speak English and Spanish as well as French. The restaurant here, La Plantation, is a gathering spot for gourmets. The beaches are about a 15-minute drive away. The cottages are difficult to find, and you should take advantage of the property's airport transfers. *Lamentin 97232, tel. 596/50–16–08. 16 rooms. Facilities: restaurant, bar, pool, Jacuzzi. AE, MC, V. Inexpensive.*

Rivage Hotel. Maryelle and Jean Claude Riveti's garden studios have kitchenettes, air-conditioning, TVs, phones, and private baths. It's located right across the road from the beach. Breakfast and light meals are served in the friendly, informal snack bar. You get good value for your money, and you should have no difficulty communicating: English, Spanish, and French are spoken. *Anse-Mitan 97229, tel. 596/66–00–53. 17 rooms. Facilities: snack bar, pool, poolside barbecue pit. No credit cards. Inexpensive.*

Home and Villa Rentals   The **Villa Rental Service** of the Martinique Tourist Office (tel. 596/63–79–60) can assist with rentals of homes, villas, and apartments. Most are in the south of the island near good beaches and can be rented on a weekly or monthly basis.

The Arts and Nightlife

The island is dotted with lively discos and nightclubs, but entertainment on Martinique is not confined to partying.

Be sure to catch a performance of **Les Grands Ballets de Martinique** (tel. 596/63–43–88). The troupe of young, exuberant dancers, singers, and musicians is one of the best folkloric groups in the Caribbean. They perform on alternate nights at the Bakoua, Méridien, La Batelièré, and Carayou-PLM Azur.

Discos As in most places, this season's hot spot may be history next season. Your hotel or the Tourist Office can put you in touch with the current "in" places. It's also wise to check on opening and closing times and admission charges. For the most part, the discos draw a mixed crowd of locals and tourists, the young and the not so young. Some of the currently popular places are **Le New Hippo** (24 blvd. Allegre, Fort-de-France, tel. 596/71–74–60), **Le Sweety** (rue Capitaine Pierre Rose, Fort-de-France, no phone), **Le Must** (20 blvd. Allegre, Fort-de-France, tel. 596/60–36–06), **Le Vesou** (Carayou-PLM Azur, tel. 596/66–04–04), **VonVon** (Hotel Méridien, tel. 596/66–00–00), **La Cabane de Pêcheur** (Diamant-Novotel, tel. 596/76–42–42), **L'Oeil** (Petit Cocotte, Ducos, tel. 596/56–11–11), and **Zipp's Dupe Club** (Dumaine, Le François, tel. 596/54–47–06).

Casinos The island's two casinos are open from 9 PM to 3 AM. You have to be at least 21 (with a picture ID); jacket and tie are not required. The **Casino Trois-Ilets** (Méridien Hotel, tel. 596/66–00–00) has American and French roulette, blackjack, and an admission charge of 58F.

16 Montserrat

by Sandra Hart

When Hurricane Hugo, the worst hurricane to hit the Caribbean in a century, roared into the pear-shaped, mountainous island of Montserrat on September 16, 1989, no corner of this 39-square Emerald Isle was left untouched.

Earlier visitors had been kinder: Christopher Columbus, who sailed by the Leeward coast in 1493, gave the island a glance and a name—Santa Maria de Monserrate—after a monastery in Barcelona. Hugo, however, was not so considerate. He roared in on Saturday night, at winds well over 150 mph (No one is certain of the exact wind speed, as the instruments atop Garibaldi Hill—guaranteed to withstand gusts of 250 mph—went out, as did everything else on the island.) The vicious wind and pounding rain continued well into Sunday night, ripping up foliage, washing out roads, and leaving 12 people dead. Some 95% of the buildings lost their roofs, and much of their contents. Others were leveled completely or tossed into neighboring fields.

When the worst was over, the island's 12,500 residents emerged from hiding, surveyed the damage, and began picking up the pieces. Amateur radio operators salvaged their equipment and reestablished contact with the outside world, reporting the island's needs. Teams of doctors, policemen, engineers, and electricians arrived from neighboring islands. The United States sent in building materials, and Great Britain announced her aid policy for her devastated colony.

George Martin, onetime Beatles producer and owner of Air Studios, the world-class recording studio he built on Montserrat in 1979, gathered together some of the stars who have recorded and vacationed here—Paul McCartney, Stevie Wonder, Elton John, Duran Duran, Boy George, the Mighty Arrow —and issued a collection of songs, *After the Hurricane: Songs for Montserrat*, with the proceeds going to an island relief fund.

Most of the lush greenery has already returned to Montserrat, aptly dubbed the Emerald Isle by its Irish settlers. The central mountains are again covered with rich vegetation, and the three mountain ranges—Silver Hills to the north, the Centre Hills, and the southern range—are again growing the limes for which the island is famous. Montserrat is known throughout the Caribbean as a food basket. Even in the days immediately following Hugo, when water was undrinkable and food scarce, restaurant owner John Fagon, who was stranded at his country farmhouse, got by on a diet of coconut water and fallen avocados.

A few residents attribute Hugo to the work of the devil ("church roofs go missing, liquor shops do fine"), but they do not fret. The Seventh Day Adventists in Plymouth, whose roof was among those that were missing, gather nightly in a tent next to the Flora Fountain Hotel and raise their choir song to the sky while their church is repaired. Elsewhere on the island, rebuilding continued throughout 1990, though even by the spring, many of the private villas—a big draw for visitors— had already been repaired and reopened, as had a handful of hotels. The reconstruction and repair of smaller, less sturdy structures, and some of the roads will take more time.

The visitor to Montserrat in 1991 will come across evidence of Hugo—both wreckage and renewal. Some residential areas are still a long way from normalcy, but the hurricane's churning up of offshore waters has resulted in some truly uncharted snorkeling and diving sites. For the most part, what you'll encounter is a newly refurbished island and its genuinely warm and welcoming people.

Before You Go

Tourist Information You can get information about Montserrat through **Tromson Monroe Public Relations** (110 E. 59th St., New York, NY 10022, tel. 212/750–9581).

Arriving and Departing *By Plane* Antigua is not only the gateway, it's the best way to reach Montserrat. **American Airlines** (tel. 800/334–7200), **BWIA** (tel. 212/581–3200), and **Pan Am** (tel. 800/421–5330) fly here from New York; **BWIA** and Pan Am fly from Miami; **Air Canada** (tel. 800/422–6232) and BWIA, from Toronto, **British Airways** (tel. 01/897–4000 in Britain, 800/247–9297 in the United States) from London; and **Lufthansa** transports visitors via Puerto Rico and Antigua (800/645–3880 in the United States).

From Antigua's **V.C. Bird International Airport,** you can make your connections with **LIAT** (tel. 809/491–2200) and **Montserrat Air** (tel. 809/491–2362) for the 15-minute flight to Montserrat, which departs at least three times a day.

Your knuckles and hair may turn white in the process, but you will land on the 3,400-foot runway at **Blackburne Airport,** on the Atlantic coast, about 11 miles from Plymouth.

From the Airport Taxis meet every flight, and the government-regulated fare from the airport to Plymouth is E.C.$21 (U.S.$10).

Passports and Visas U.S. and Canadian citizens only need proof of citizenship, such as a passport, a notarized birth certificate, or a voter registration card. A driver's license is *not* sufficient. British citizens must have a passport; visas are not required. All visitors must hold an ongoing or return ticket.

Customs and Duties You may bring into the country duty-free 200 cigarettes or 50 cigars or eight ounces of tobacco, and one quart of liquor, plus any personal items.

Language It's English with a brogue, a result of the Irish legacy. You'll also hear a patois that's spoken on most of the islands.

Precautions Ask for permission before taking pictures. Some residents may be reluctant photographic subjects, and they will appreciate your courtesy.

Most Montserrattians frown at the sight of skimpily dressed tourists; do not risk offending them by strolling around in shorts and swimsuits.

Staying in Montserrat

Important Addresses **Tourist Information:** The **Montserrat Department of Tourism** (Church Rd., Plymouth, tel. 809/491–2230) is open weekdays 8–noon and 1–4 PM.

Emergencies **Police** (tel. 809/491–2552).

Hospitals: There is a 24-hour emergency room at **Glendon Hospital** (Plymouth, tel. 809/491–2552).

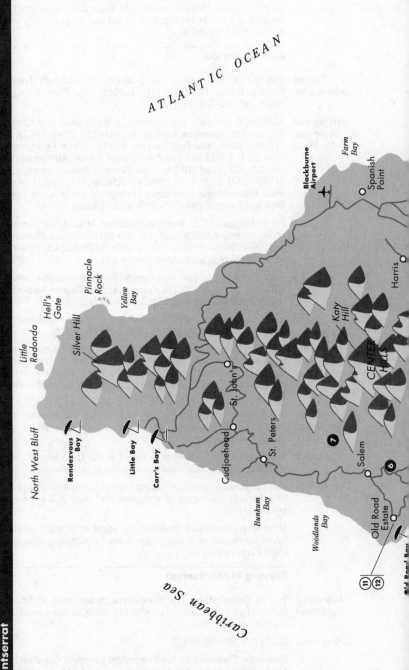

Montserrat

ATLANTIC OCEAN

Caribbean Sea

North West Bluff

Little Redonda

Hell's Gate

Pinnacle Rock

Yellow Bay

Silver Hill

Rendezvous Bay

Little Bay

Carr's Bay

Cudjoehead

St. John's

St. Peters

Bunkam Bay

Woodlands Bay

Old Road Estate

Salem

Center Hills

Katy Hill

Harris

Spanish Point

Farm Bay

Blackburne Airport

Old Road Bay

⑦

⑥

⑪

⑫

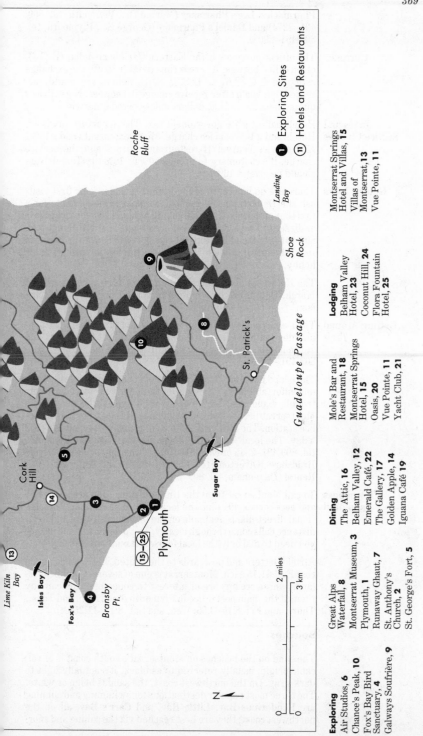

Roche Bluff

Landing Bay

Guadeloupe Passage

Shoe Rock

9

8

St. Patrick's

10

5

Cork Hill

14

3

Lime Kiln Bay

13

1
2
15–**25**

Plymouth

4

Isles Bay

Fox's Bay

Bransby Pt.

Sugar Bay

1 Exploring Sites

11 Hotels and Restaurants

N

0 | | | 2 miles

0 | | | 3 km

Exploring
Air Studios, **6**
Chance's Peak, **10**
Fox's Bay Bird Sanctuary, **4**
Galways Soufrière, **9**
Great Alps Waterfall, **8**
Montserrat Museum, **3**
Plymouth, **1**
Runaway Ghaut, **7**
St. Anthony's Church, **2**
St. George's Fort, **5**

Dining
The Attic, **16**
Belham Valley, **12**
Emerald Café, **22**
The Gallery, **17**
Golden Apple, **14**
Iguana Café **19**
Mole's Bar and Restaurant, **18**
Montserrat Springs Hotel, **15**
Oasis, **20**
Vue Pointe, **11**
Yacht Club, **21**

Lodging
Belham Valley Hotel, **23**
Coconut Hill, **24**
Flora Fountain Hotel, **25**
Montserrat Springs Hotel and Villas, **15**
Villas of Montserrat, **13**
Vue Pointe, **11**

Pharmacies: Lee's Pharmacy (Marine Dr., Plymouth, tel. 809/491–3274) and **Daniel's Pharmacy** (George St., Plymouth, tel. 809/491–2908).

Currency The official currency is the Eastern Caribbean dollar (E.C.$), often called beewee. At press time (winter 1989), the exchange rate was E.C.$2.67 to U.S.$1. U.S. dollars are readily accepted, but you'll often receive change in beewees. Note: Prices quoted here are in U.S. dollars unless noted otherwise.

Taxes and Service Charges Hotels collect a 7% government tax. The departure tax is $8. Hotels add a 10% service charge. Most restaurants add a 10%–15% service charge. If restaurants do not add the service charge, it's customary to leave a 10% or 15% tip. Taxi drivers should be given a 10% tip.

Guided Tours There are no bus tours of the island. If this is your first visit, ask the Department of Tourism to make arrangements for a taxi tour of the island. It will cost $8 per hour. Or contact a driver directly: Two in the highly recommended list are **Mango** (tel. 809/491–2134) and **B-Beep** (tel. 809/491–3787), who promises to find the elusive oriole birds for those interested in sharing his hobby.

The Rotary Club conducts garden tours during February and March. Details can be obtained from the Department of Tourism.

Getting Around *Taxis* The Department of Tourism issues a list of taxi fares to the popular destinations. Taxis are always available at the airport and at the hotels. You can also call the **Taxi Stand** in Plymouth (tel. 809/491–2261).

Car Rentals The island has more than 150 miles of good roads. Unless you're uncomfortable about driving on the left, you won't have any trouble exploring. You'll need a valid driver's license, plus a Montserrat license, which is available at the airport or the police station. The fee is E.C.$30. Rental cars cost about $28–$32 a day. The local Avis outlet is **Pauline Car Rentals** (Plymouth, tel. 809/491–2345 or 800/331–1084). Other agencies are **Neville Bradshaw** (Olverton, tel. 809/491–5270) and **Jefferson's Car Rental** (Dagenham, tel. 809/491–2126).

Telephones and Mail To call Montserrat from the United States, dial area code 809 and access code 491 plus the local four-digit number. International direct-dial is available on the island; both local and long-distance calls come through clearly. To call locally on the island, you need to dial only the local four-digit number.

Airmail letters and postcards to the United States and Canada cost E.C.$1.15 each. Montserrat is one of several Caribbean islands whose stamps are of interest to collectors. You can buy them at the main post office in Plymouth (open Mon. and Tues., Thurs. and Fri. 8:15–3:55; Wed. and Sat. 8:15–11:25AM).

Beaches

The sand on the beaches on Montserrat's south coast is of volcanic origin; usually referred to as black, it's actually light to dark gray. On the northwest coast, the sand is beige or white. The three most popular destinations for swimming and sunning are **Rendezvous Bay, Little Bay,** and **Carr's Bay,** all on the northwest coast; they are best reached via the sailing and snorkeling excursions arranged by the **Vue Pointe Hotel** (tel. 809/491–5210).

Fox's Bay has a lovely strip of gray sand on the bay just north of the Bird Sanctuary.

Old Road Bay and **Isles Bay** are on the coast north of Fox's Bay (4 miles north of Plymouth) and have stretches of gray-sand beaches.

Sugar Bay, to the south of Plymouth, is a beach of fine gray volcanic sand. The Yacht Club overlooks this beach.

Exploring Montserrat

Numbers in the margin correspond with points of interest on the Montserrat map.

Plymouth
❶

About a third of the island's population of 12,500 live in **Plymouth,** the capital city that faces the Caribbean on the southwest coast. The town is neat and clean, its narrow streets lined with trim Georgian structures built mostly of stones that came from Dorset as ballast on old sailing vessels. Most of the town's sights are set right along the water. On the south side, a bridge over the Fort Ghaut ("gut," or ravine) leads to Wapping, where most of the restaurants are located.

We'll begin at **Government House** on the south side of town just above Sugar Bay. The frilly Victorian house, decorated with a shamrock, dates from the 18th century. Beautifully landscaped gardens surround the building, but unfortunately the house and grounds are no longer open to the public.

Follow Peebles Street north and cross the bridge. Just over the bridge at the junction of Harney, Strand, and Parliament streets you'll see the **Market,** where islanders bring their produce every Saturday—a very colorful scene.

From the market, walk along Strand Street for one block to the tall white **War Memorial** with a bell turret. The memorial is a tribute to the soldiers of both world wars. Next to the monument is the **Post Office and Treasury,** a galleried West Indian-style building by the water, where you can buy stamps that make handsome souvenirs.

Walk away from the water on George Street, which runs alongside the War Memorial. The town's main thoroughfare, Parliament Street, cuts diagonally north-south through the town. A left turn onto Parliament Street, at the corner of George Street, will take you to the Methodist Church and the Court House. If you continue straight on George Street, you'll come to the Roman Catholic Church. North of the church is the **American University of the Caribbean,** formerly a medical school with many American students but now closed due to damages sustained in Hurricane Hugo.

Elsewhere on the Island

From here on, you'll need wheels. Take Highway 2, the main road north out of Plymouth. On the outskirts of town there's a stone marker that commemorates the first colony in 1632.

Tour 1
❷

St. Anthony's Church, which is just north of town, was consecrated some time between 1623 and 1666. It was rebuilt in 1730 following one of the many clashes between the French and the English in the area. Two silver chalices displayed in the church were donated by freed slaves after emancipation in 1834. An ancient tamarind tree stands near the church.

Richmond Hill rises northeast of town. Here you will find the **❸ Montserrat Museum** in a restored sugar mill. The museum contains maps, historical records, artifacts, and all sorts of memorabilia pertaining to the island's growth and development. *Richmond Hill, tel. 809/491–5443. Admission free. Open Sun. and Wed. 2:30–5 (but telephone to be sure; hours have been erratic since the hurricane).*

Take the first left turn past the museum to Grove Road; it will **❹** take you to the **Fox's Bay Bird Sanctuary,** a 15-acre bog area. Marked trails lead into the interior, which is aflutter with egrets, herons, coots, and cuckoo birds.

The **Bransby Point Fortification** is also in this area and contains a collection of restored cannons.

Backtrack on Grove Road to Highway 2, drive north and turn **❺** right on Highway 4 to **St. George's Fort.** It's overgrown and of little historical interest, but the view from the hilltop is well worth the trip, especially if the brush has been cleared by the time you visit.

Highway 2 continues north past the **Belham Valley Golf Course** to **Vue Pointe Hotel,** on the coast at Lime Kiln Bay. Head west to the green slopes of Centre Hills, almost in the center of the **❻** island, for **Air Studios,** a recording studio founded in 1979 by former Beatles producer George Martin. Sting, Boy George, and Paul McCartney have all cut records here, but sadly, following Hugo, Martin closed up shop and put the studio up for sale.

About 1½ miles farther north, a scenic drive takes you along **❼ Runaway Ghaut.** Two centuries ago, this peaceful green valley was the scene of bloody battles between the French and the English. **Little Bay, Carr's Bay,** and **Rendezvous Bay,** the island's three most popular beaches, are along the northwest coast. (Since driving in these parts can be treacherous, it's a good idea to sign up for one of the day sails through the Vue Pointe Hotel. In fact, it's a good idea to ask local management about any touring plans *après* Hugo.)

Tour 2 The next tour of the island will be considerably more arduous, taking in the mountains, rain forests, and *soufrières* (volcanic craters with sulfuric springs) to the south and east of Plymouth. Following the hurricane, all these paths were either washed out or strewn with unpassable debris, so it's all the more necessary to hire a knowledgeable guide. The Department of Tourism or your hotel can arrange one for you. The guide's fee will be about $6. Wear rubber-soled shoes.

A 15-minute drive south of Plymouth on Old Fort Road will bring you to the village of **St. Patrick's.** From there, a scenic drive takes you to the starting point of the tour's strenuous **❽** hike through thick rain forests to **Great Alps Waterfall.** The falls cascade 70 feet down the side of a rock and splash into a shallow pool, where you can see a rainbow in the mist.

❾ A rugged road leads eastward to **Galways Soufrière,** where another hike is involved, this one lasting about a half hour. Once there, you'll see volcanic rock, boiling water, and small vents of gurgling, molten sulfur. City people are fond of complaining in the summertime of streets so hot you could fry an egg on them. Here your guide will almost certainly fry an egg to demonstrate the intense heat of the rocks.

⑩ The island's highest point, **Chance's Peak,** pokes up 3,000 feet through the rain forests. The climb to the top is arduous—and you shouldn't attempt it without a guide—but if you do make it to the top, what little breath you may have left will be taken away by the view.

Also in this area is the old **Galways Estate,** a plantation built in the late 17th century by prosperous Irishmen John and Henry Blake, who came to Montserrat from Galway. All that now remains of the fine estate is the ruins of the house and factory and some rusted machinery. This is also the site of archaeological digs.

Off the Beaten Track

The place is **The Village Place,** and it is run by Andy Lawrence, a former DJ for Radio Montserrat and a knowledgeable music man, who now describes himself as owner, waiter, bartender, and cook. This was once the haunt of superstar musicians recording at Air Studios. Sting was a regular; Elton John proposed to his wife here, and Eric Clapton came and went. Now regular customers are locals, and almost all island visitors stop by. The Rolling Stones, who were the last heavies to record in Montserrat (*Steel Wheels*), knew finger lickin' chicken when they tasted it. (Andy's secret recipe—chicken spiced with paprika and thyme—is best munched with fries and beer.) There are a few crude wood picnic tables outside and a bar and a billiards table inside. Plain and simple it may be, but the Village Place is *the* place to be on Friday night. *Salem, tel. 809/491–5202. Open 6PM–11-ish. Closed Tues. No credit cards.*

Participant Sports

Boating | Boats are available through **Captain Martin,** who has a refurbished catamaran and takes guests for a full-day sail to neighboring islands from 10AM to 5PM for about $40 (tel. 809/491–5738); or through **Vue Pointe Hotel** (tel. 809/491–5210).

Golf | There is an 11-hole course at the **Montserrat Golf Course** (tel. 809/491–5220). The fairways run from the beach up the mountainside and are so well kept and challenging that most golfers go around twice, since it's possible to play 18 different tees.

Horseback Riding | Trail rides, lessons, and vacation packages are offered by **Sanford Farms** (contact Barbara Tipson, tel. 809/491–3301). Your hotel can arrange for riding on the beach or in the mountains for $14 an hour.

Sailing, Snorkeling and Scuba Diving | Snorkeling equipment is provided on the day cruises to the white-sand coves on the west coast; boats usually have an open bar. Arrangements can be made through **Vue Pointe Hotel** (tel. 809/491–5210) or **Captain Martin** (tel. 809/491–5738).

Dive Montserrat (tel. 809/491–5534) operates from the Vue Pointe Hotel, offering one or two tank dives, night dives, and instruction from a PADI-certified teacher. For the dives themselves, the cost begins at $40 and goes up to $250 for an instruction course. Contact Chris Mason.

Tennis There are lighted tennis courts at the **Vue Pointe Hotel** (tel. 809/491–5210) and the **Montserrat Springs Hotel** (tel. 809/491–2481).

Windsurfing Contact the **Vue Pointe Hotel** (tel. 809/491–5210) to rent boards.

Spectator Sports

Cricket is the national passion. Cricket and soccer matches are held from February through June in **Sturge Park. Shamrock Car Park** is the venue for volleyball and basketball games. Contact the Department of Tourism (tel. 809/491–2230) for schedules.

Shopping

Montserrat's sea-island cotton is famous for its high-quality excellence. Unfortunately, only a limited amount could be grown and that was *before* Hurricane Hugo. Since then, the supply has been even more limited. Several new boutiques have opened, however, and there are always good buys in hand-turned pottery, straw goods, and jewelry bits made from shells and coral. Possibly the best find are local books by local authors, who really know their subjects. Also, the album *After the Hurricane*—produced by Air Studios and recording artists the Mighty Arrow, Boy George, Duran Duran, The Police, Elton John, Paul McCartney and Stevie Wonder, and the Rolling Stones—is more than worth the $10 to $20 you'll pay for records, tapes or CDs. All monies from the sale of the album go to the Montserrat relief fund.

Good Buys **Just Looking** (George St., Plymouth, tel. 809/491–4076) is a
Clothes boutique that opened in 1989, featuring "sculpted," hand-painted pillows from Antigua; painted and lacquered boxes from Haiti; packaged spices from the British West Indies (including an Arawak love potion and a hangover cure); special teas; and Caribelle Batik's line of richly colored fabrics, shirts, skirts, pants, dresses and gowns for him and her. (These batiks originated in St. Kitts.)

The Lime Tree (Parliament St., tel. 809/491–3656) carries cotton clothing for men and boys, with some snappy styling. There are also "I Am Part of Reconstruction" T-shirts for $13, designed for owner Neville Bradshaw. **The Montserrat Sea Island Cotton Co.** (corner of George and Strand Sts., Plymouth, tel. 809/491–2557) has long been famous for its cotton creations, but this government-owned enterprise is being turned over to a private developer. They hope to remain open in the meantime. Telephone before making the trip to town.

Crafts **The Tapestries of Montserrat** (Parliament St., tel. 809/491–2520) provides a two-hour adventure wandering through this second-floor gallery of hand-tufted creations—from wall hangings and pillow covers to tote bags and rugs—all with fanciful yarn creations of flowers, carnival figures, animals, and birds. Owners Gerald and Charlie Handley will even help you create your own design for a small additional fee. **Carol's Corner** (Vue Pointe Hotel, tel. 809/491–5210) has finds by Carol Osborne that are first-rate: giant stuffed green frogs named Island Hoppers; copper bookmarks; and books (many signed by their authors) ranging from the *Montserrat Cookbook* to Frane

Lessac's books of prose and paintings. Drop by **Dutchers Studio** (Olde Towne, tel. 809/491–5253) to see their hand-cut, hand-painted objects made from old bottles. Should you really need a T-shirt, stop in at **Montserrat "T" Shirts** in Wappings (downstairs at the Plantation, no phone). **Island House,** on John Street, reopened last spring (following Hugo), with restocked finds of Haitian art, Caribbean prints, and clay pottery.

Dining

The national dish is goatwater, a thick stew made with goat meat and vegetables, similar to Irish stew. Goat meat is reminiscent of mutton. Mountain chicken (actually enormous frogs) is also a great favorite. Yam, breadfruit, christophine (a green vegetable), lime, mango, papaya, and a variety of seafood are served in most restaurants.

The most highly recommended restaurants are indicated by a star ★.

Category	Cost*
Expensive	over $30
Moderate	$20–$30
Inexpensive	under $20

per person, excluding drinks and service. If the service charge is not added to the bill, leave a 10% to 15% tip.

Montserrat Springs Hotel. Damaged by Hurricane Hugo, this hotel was at press time, still in the process of reopening. The split-level dining room at the Montserrat Springs Hotel, enclosed on three sides, faces a large pool and a sun deck. Openers include chilled melon; among the main courses is a variety of chicken and seafood dishes. *Richmond Hill, Plymouth, tel. 809/491–2481. Reservations suggested in season. AE, MC, V. Expensive.*

★ **Vue Pointe.** Candlelit dining in the hotel's restaurant overlooking the sea makes this a very romantic place, and with the 60% roster of return guests, the atmosphere is that of a house party. The menu may include West Indian curried chicken; beef Wellington; red snapper with Creole sauce; and, for dessert, a luscious lime pie or cheesecake. The Wednesday-night barbecue, accompanied by music from a steel band, is a popular island event. *Olde Towne, tel. 809/491–5210. Reservations suggested for dinner. AE, MC, V. Expensive.*

★ **Belham Valley.** The owning Daly family reopened a mere six months after Hugo, with a newly revitalized restaurant that seats up to 60 for lunch and dinner. The property itself is flower-filled with red, white, yellow, and pink hibiscus tumbling over the stone walls and sprouting from table vases. Once a private home, the restaurant has wood floors, a tiny terrace, and a large menu. Appetizers include conch fritters and liver pâté. Main dishes include Seafood Delight (sautéed lobster, red snapper, and sea scallops in a vermouth sauce) and broiled baby lobster tails. Scrumptious desserts are mango or lime mousse, lemon cake, and coconut-cream cheesecake. At lunchtime, the offerings are lighter: There are omelets, salads, and sandwiches. New this year is live jazz on Friday nights, with some of the backup musicians from Air Studios. *Olde Towne, tel. 809/*

491–5553. Reservations required for dinner. No lunch weekends; closed Mon. AE, V. Moderate–Expensive.

The Attic. The story of the Attic (since Hugo) is the story of Montserrat itself. The (formerly) third-story Attic had a sister restaurant on the second story called The Pantry. Compliments of Hugo, the Attic ended up in the Pantry, where owners John and Jeanne Fagon have decided it would stay! For breakfast, lunch, and dinner, twelve busy tables supply town folk with specialties of chicken, vegetable or shrimp quesadilla, ocean perch, pork chops with "pantry" sauce, breaded shrimp, and lobster tail. *Marine Dr., Plymouth, tel. 809/491–2008. No credit cards. Inexpensive.*

★ **Emerald Café.** Dining is relaxed at 10 tables inside and on the terrace, where there are white tables shaded by blue umbrellas. Burgers, sandwiches, goatwater stew, and plate lunches are served at lunchtime. Dinner dishes feature tournedos sautéed in spicy butter; broiled or sautéed Caribbean lobster; T-bone steak; mountain chicken Provençale; and kingfish, broiled or sautéed. The homemade pastries, such as Island Coconut Pie, are superb. There's also an ample list of liqueurs and wines. *Wapping, tel. 809/491–3821. Dinner reservations suggested in season. Closed Sun. No credit cards. Moderate.*

The Gallery. Pizza is the specialty here, but you can also get escargot, fish and chips, lasagna, and burgers. On Friday nights, the Masquerade band plays calypso, rhythm and blues, rock, and blues. *Wapping, tel. 809/491–2579. Reservations suggested in season. No credit cards. Closed Mon. and Tues. Moderate.*

★ **Iguana Cafe.** This is a real find for gourmets. Owners Michael and Sophie Bishop cook and serve creative dishes in a 200-year-old stone building with gardens (and a few tables) in back. He's American-born; she's French, with a family-owned vineyard. Dishes include blackened redfish, broiled sea scallops au gratin, mixed seafood mornay, swordfish steak, and filet mignon au poivre noir. There's also pizza, with 12 different toppings, and homemade ice cream. Hard hats left by repair volunteers after Hugo decorate the bar. *Wapping, tel. 809/491–3637. Closed Mon. and Tues. No credit cards. Moderate.*

Oasis. A 200-year-old stone building houses this restaurant, where you can dine indoors or on the patio. Entrées include mountain chicken, jumbo shrimp Provençale and red snapper with lime butter. *Wapping, tel. 809/491–2328. Reservations suggested in season. No credit cards. Moderate.*

Mole's Bar and Restaurant. You can get steak and eggs for breakfast in this upstairs country kitchen, but the emphasis is on basics: fried chicken and chips, fried fish and chips, and burgers with spicy toppings. *Lower Dagenham, tel. 809/491–2752. Closed Wed. No credit cards. Inexpensive.*

Golden Apple. In this large, galleried stone building, you'll be served huge plates of good, local cooking: their special goatwater stew, cooked over an outside, open fire; souse; *pelau* (chicken-and-rice curry); conch, stewed or curried; and mountain chicken. There's a small grocery store attached, and the decor includes beaded curtains and plastic covers to protect the white lace tablecloths. Fun and funky. *Cork Hill, tel. 809/491–2187. No credit cards. Inexpensive.*

Yacht Club. This simple, popular eatery and local hangout overlooks the water. Lunchtime offerings include curried chicken, sandwiches, and burgers. Mountain chicken, lasagna, and shrimp Creole are featured on the dinner menu. Friday-night entertainment consists of calypso, rhythm and blues, blues, and soul music played by a band. *Wapping, tel. 809/491–2237. Reservations required for dinner in season. No credit cards. Inexpensive.*

Lodging

Most of Montserrat's hotels operate on the modified American plan (MAP: Breakfast and dinner are included in the rate).

The most highly recommended lodgings are indicated by a star ★.

Category	Cost*
Very Expensive	over $170
Expensive	$135–$170
Moderate	$100–$135
Inexpensive	Under $100

*All prices are for a standard double room for two, excluding 7% tax and a 10% service charge.

Hotels

★ **Villas of Montserrat.** If you've ever wanted to do an island in style, this is the way to do it. You'll be flown in on a private plane, chauffeured to your villa, and treated to a lobster dinner at Belham Valley on the night of your arrival. Each three-bedroom villa is decorated island-style, and each has a color TV, microwave oven, dishwasher, three bathrooms, and a Jacuzzi. The cluster of villas overlooks Isle Bay and the Caribbean. *Plymouth, tel. 809/491–5165 or in the U.S. 212/752–8660. 3 villas. Facilities: pool. No credit cards. Very Expensive.*

Vue Pointe. This 7-acre property is on a spectacular point of land. If you feel as though you've arrived at an ongoing house party, you have. Accommodations are in 12 rooms or 28 octagonal cottages that spill down to the gray-sand beach on Old Road Bay. Each cottage has a large bedroom, great view, and privacy. There's a lounge in the main building where you can watch cable TV or chat with the other guests and the Osbornes, who own the hotel and who host Monday-night cocktail parties. The Vue Pointe is the center for water-sports activities on the island, and the Montserrat Golf Course adjoins the property. The Wednesday-night barbecue, with steel bands and other entertainment, is an island event for locals as well as tourists. There is a 150-seat conference center that also serves as a theater and a disco. *Box 65, Plymouth, tel. 809/491–5210. 12 rooms, 28 cottages. Facilities: restaurant, bar, gift shop, pool, 2 lighted tennis courts, water-sports center. AE, MC, V. Very Expensive.*

★ **Montserrat Springs Hotel and Villas.** This property suffered extensive damage under Hurricane Hugo and was still in the process of repair and renovation as this book went to press in the spring of 1990. The rooms, which are located in a wing of the main building and in the cottages along the steep hillside that slopes to the beach, are spacious (tubs are the size of rowboats). All have private balconies, phones, and TVs. The split-level restaurant overlooks the 70-foot pool. *Box 259, Plymouth, tel. 809/491–2482 or 800/223–9815; in Canada, 800/468–0023; in NY 212/840–6636. 29 rooms, including 6 suites. Facilities:*

restaurant, 2 bars, pool, hot/cold mineral-water Jacuzzi, 2 lighted tennis courts, 24-hr switchboard. AE, MC, V. Moderate–Expensive.

★ **Coconut Hill.** Built in the 1800s as a plantation house, this building has been a hotel since 1908 and, like everything in Montserrat, suffered damage during Hugo. The owning Osborne family are pros, however (they also own the Vue Pointe), and they are putting that professionalism to work to reopen in mint condition for the season. There are hardwood floors, galleries, beamed ceilings, and a marvelous Victorian parlor. Some rooms (No. 5 is one) have carved mahogany four-poster beds and open onto the upstairs gallery. All rooms have phones; you have a choice of twin or double beds. The restaurant serves West Indian-style cuisine. The hotel is a half mile outside Plymouth, 6 miles from the airport. *Box 337, Plymouth, tel. 809/491-2144. 9 rooms with bath. Facilities: restaurant, bar. AE, MC, V. Moderate.*

Belham Valley Hotel. On a hillside overlooking Belham Valley and the Belham Valley River, this hotel has three self-catering units. There is a cottage, often let on a long-term basis, and three apartments (a studio, a one-bedroom, and a two-bedroom). It's the restaurant here that's the big draw, particularly on Friday, which is Indian buffet night, with two meats and fish; two kinds of rice; *rathia* (yogurt and vegetables with pork and spices); and *sambosa* (meat patties). *Box 409, Plymouth, tel. 809/491-5553. 3 units. Facilities: restaurant, maid service. AE, MC. Inexpensive.*

Flora Fountain Hotel. This is a hotel for people coming on business, or for those who appreciate an old, rambling hotel in the heart of town. The two-story hotel has been created around an enormous fountain that's sometimes lighted at night, with small tables scattered in the inner courtyard. There are 18 serviceable rooms, all with tile bath and air-conditioning. The restaurant has a chef from Bombay who serves simple sandwiches and fine Indian dishes, particularly on Friday night, when it's Indian buffet night; several meat and fish dishes; at least two forms of rice; yogurt and vegetable dishes; and spicy meat patties. The staff couldn't be more helpful. *Box 373, Church Rd., Plymouth, tel. 809/491-8444. 18 rooms with air-conditioning. Facilities: restaurant and bar. MC, V. Moderate.*

Condominiums   **Shamrock Villas.** On a hillside overlooking the sea, the villas offer 45 one- and two-bedroom apartments and town-house condominiums. One-bedrooms in season are $350 per week; $1,350 by the month. *Contact Doug Kennedy, Montserrat Co., Ltd., Box 221, Plymouth, Montserrat, WI, tel. 809/491-2431 or 809/491-2432.*

Home and Apartment Rentals   Villas here tend to be luxurious, with sweeping views of the sea, private pools, and terraces. The services of a domestic helper and gardener are usually included in the rate. For information, contact **Neville Bradshaw Agencies Ltd.** (Box 270, Plymouth, tel. 809/491-2070), **D.R.V. Edwards** (Box 58, Plymouth, tel. 809/491-2431), **Lime Court Apartments** (Box 250, Plymouth, tel. 809/491-3656), or the **Montserrat Department of Tourism** (Box 7, Plymouth, tel. 809/491-2230).

Nightlife

The hotels offer regularly scheduled barbecues and steel bands, and the small restaurants feature live entertainment in the form of calypso, reggae, rock, rhythm and blues, and soul.

The **Yacht Club** (Wapping, tel. 809/491–2237) has live island music on Friday.

The Plantation Club (Wapping, upstairs over the Oasis, tel. 809/491–2892) is a lively late-night place with taped rhythm and blues, soul, and soca (Caribbean music).

La Cave (Evergreen Dr., Plymouth, no phone), featuring West Indian-style disco with Caribbean and international music, is popular among the young locals.

It's always worth checking the **Village Place** (Salem, tel. 809/491–5202) particularly on Friday nights, when the live entertainment is heavy and hot. This was where the famed Air Studios' all-star music crowd hung out.

17 Nevis

by Honey Naylor

In 1493, when the gentleman from Genoa spied a cloud-crowned volcanic isle during his second voyage to the New World, he named it *Nieves,* the Spanish word for "snows." It reminded him of the snowcapped peaks of the Pyrenees. Nevis (pronounced Neevis) rises out of the water in an almost perfect cone, the tip of its 3,232-foot central mountain smothered in clouds. It's lusher and less developed than its sister island of St. Kitts.

Tour groups are not attracted to an island that has no nonstop flights from the United States; that has virtually no glittering nightlife or shopping, and no high-rise hotels. Visitors tend to be self-sufficient types who know how to amuse themselves and who appreciate the warmth and character of country inns.

In 1607, Captain John Smith and his crew, on their way to establish the colony in Jamestown, Virginia, stopped off in Nevis to hang some mutineers; he noted: "Here we found a great poole, wherein bathing ourselves we found much ease." The mineral springs of the "great poole" didn't do much for the mutineers, but by 1778 the waters had become so famous that the luxurious Bath Hotel was built adjacent to them. This tiny, 36-square-mile island became known as the Spa of the Caribbean, attracting fashionable Europeans.

John Smith is not the only famous name associated with Nevis and with American history. Alexander Hamilton, who was to become treasury secretary under President George Washington, was born in Charlestown, Nevis, in 1755. His home in Charlestown has been restored and is now a museum.

Admiral Lord Nelson, who was headquartered in Antigua for a time, found Nevis a convenient stop for fresh water; it was where he met the comely Frances Nisbet. They were married at Montpelier Estate (as attested to in the records of St. John's Church in Fig Tree Parish). The Duke of Clarence, who later became King William IV of England, stood up for the admiral.

This island is known both for its natural beauty—long beaches with white and black sand, lush greenery—for a half-dozen mineral spa baths, and for the restored sugar plantations that now house some of the Caribbean's most elegant hostelries. In 1628, settlers from St. Kitts sailed across the 2-mile channel that separates the two islands. At first they grew tobacco, cotton, ginger, and indigo, but with the introduction of sugarcane in 1640, Nevis became the island equivalent of a boom town. As the mineral baths were drawing crowds, the island was producing an abundance of sugar. Slaves were brought from Africa to work on the magnificent estates, many of them nestled high in the mountains amid lavish tropical gardens.

The restored plantation homes that now operate as inns are the island's most sybaritic lures for the leisurely life. There is plenty of activity for the energetic—mountain climbing, swimming, tennis, horseback riding, snorkeling. But the going is easy here, with hammocks for snoozing, lobster bakes on palm-lined beaches, and candlelit dinners in stately dining rooms and on romantic verandas.

Nevis is linked politically with St. Kitts. The two islands, together with Anguilla, achieved self-government as an Associated State of Great Britain in 1967. In 1983, St. Kitts-Nevis became fully independent nations. Nevis papers sometimes

382

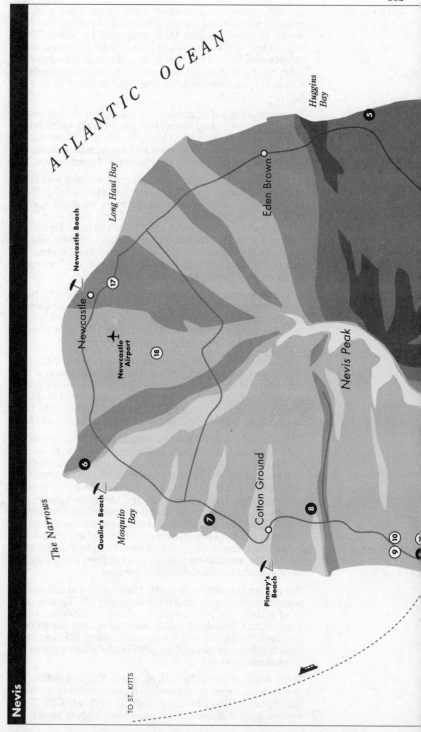

Nevis

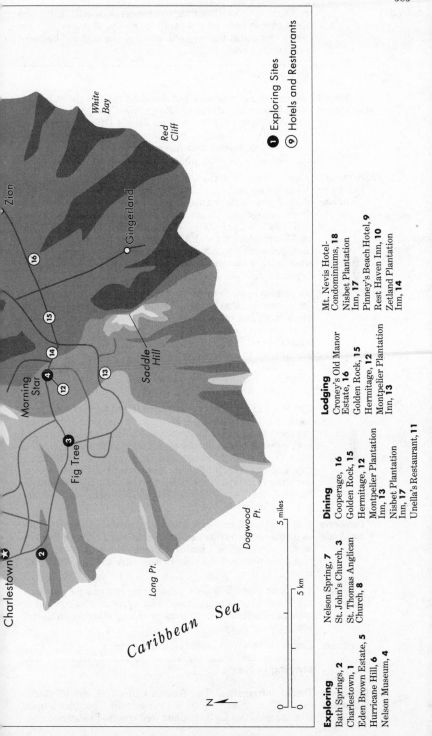

Exploring

Bath Springs, **2**
Charlestown, **1**
Eden Brown Estate, **5**
Hurricane Hill, **6**
Nelson Museum, **4**

Nelson Spring, **7**
St. John's Church, **3**
St. Thomas Anglican
Church, **8**

Dining

Cooperage, **16**
Golden Rock, **15**
Hermitage, **12**
Montpelier Plantation
Inn, **13**
Nisbet Plantation
Inn, **17**
Unella's Restaurant, **11**

Lodging

Croney's Old Manor
Estate, **16**
Golden Rock, **15**
Hermitage, **12**
Montpelier Plantation
Inn, **13**

Mt. Nevis Hotel–
Condominiums, **18**
Nisbet Plantation
Inn, **17**
Pinney's Beach Hotel, **9**
Rest Haven Inn, **10**
Zetland Plantation
Inn, **14**

● Exploring Sites

⑨ Hotels and Restaurants

run fiery articles advocating independence from St. Kitts, and the sister islands may separate someday. However, it's not likely that a shot will be fired, let alone one that will be heard around the world.

Before You Go

Tourist Information
You can get information about the island through the **St. Kitts & Nevis Tourist Board** (414 E. 75th St., New York, NY 10021, tel. 212/535–1234), **St. Kitts & Nevis Tourist Office** (11 Yorkville Ave., Suite 508, Toronto, Ont., Canada M4W 1L3, tel. 416/921–7717), and **Rosamund Bern Assoc.** (15 Wardour Mews, d'Arblay St., London W1V 3FF, United Kingdom, tel. 437/9475–7445).

Arriving and Departing
By Plane
Most visitors from the United States and Canada fly into St. Kitts and connect with **LIAT** (tel. 809/462–0700), which has two daily flights to **Newcastle Airport** on Nevis. LIAT also flies in from neighboring islands, as does **Windward Islands Airways** (tel. 599/5–44230 or 559/5–44237). Many hotels on the island make arrangements with **Air Caraibe** to bring guests over from Antigua, which avoids a lot of hassle. You can book through your hotel or contact **Caraibe Aviation** (Box 318, St. Johns, Antigua, tel. 809/462–3147).

From the Airport
Taxis meet every flight and ferry. The cabs are unmetered, but fares are regulated by the government and rates are posted at the airport and the ferry slip. Some sample posted fares are: from the ferry slip to Nisbet Plantation, U.S.$10; to Zetland Plantation, U.S.$6; and to Golden Rock, U.S.$7. The fare from the airport to Zetland Plantation is U.S.$12; to Montpelier Plantation, U.S.$13. Be sure that you and your driver understand whether the rate he quotes you is in Eastern Caribbean (E.C.) or U.S. dollars.

By Boat
The MV *Caribe Queen* is the Staten Island ferry of the Caribbean. Nevisians board the government-operated 150-passenger ferry to get to and from work on St. Kitts, and tourists take it to sightsee. It makes the 45-minute trip across the channel from St. Kitts daily except Thursday, which is maintenance day, and Sunday. Its schedule is as varied as a Chinese menu, so rather than trying to pick a departure hour from column B, just call the Tourist Office (tel. 809/469–5521) and ask for schedule information.

Passports and Visas
U.S. and Canadian citizens need only proof of citizenship, such as a voter registration card or a birth certificate. (A driver's license *won't* suffice.) British citizens need a passport, but a visa is not required. All visitors must have a return or ongoing ticket.

Customs and Duties
The government will allow you to bring in items for your personal use, plus 200 cigarettes or 50 cigars or a half pound of tobacco. There are no customs or immigration formalities if you arrive by ferry.

Language
English with a West Indian lilt is spoken here.

Staying in Nevis

Important Addresses
Tourist Information: The **Tourism Office** (tel. 809/469–5521, ext. 2049) is on Main Street in Charlestown. The office is open Monday and Tuesday 8–4:30 and Wednesday–Friday 8–4.

Emergencies **Police:** Call 809/469–5391.

Hospitals: There is a 24-hour emergency room at **Alexandra Hospital** (Charlestown, tel. 809/469–5473).

Pharmacies: Evelyn's Drugstore (Charlestown, tel. 809/469–5278) is open Monday–Saturday 8–5:30, Sunday 7 AM–8 PM; on Thursday it closes at 12:30 PM.

Currency Legal tender is the Eastern Caribbean dollar. The rate of exchange fluctuates but hovers around E.C.$2.65 or E.C.$2.70 to U.S.$1. The U.S. dollar is accepted everywhere, but you'll almost always get change in E.C.s. Prices quoted here are in U.S. dollars unless noted otherwise. Credit cards are not widely accepted on the island, though some of the inns will, inexplicably, take personal checks.

Taxes and Service Charges Hotels collect a 7% government tax. The departure tax is $5. Most hotels add a 10% service charge to your bill. For a job well done, a 10%–15% gratuity should be left in addition. Taxi drivers should be given a 10% tip.

Guided Tours The **taxi driver** who picks you up will offer to act as your guide to the island. Each driver is knowledgeable and does a 3½-hour tour for $40. He'll probably ask if you'd like him to make lunch reservations for you at one of the plantations, and you should say "Yes."

Another tour option is **Jan's Travel Agency** (Arcade, Charlestown, tel. 809/469–5578), which arranges half- and full-day tours of the island.

Getting Around *Rental Cars* Arrive in Nevis with a valid driver's license and your car-rental agency will help you obtain a local license at the police station. The cost is E.C. $30 (U.S. $12.).

Beware: The island's roads are pocked with crater-size potholes; driving is on the left; goats and cattle crop up out of nowhere to amble along the road; and if you deviate from Main Street you're likely to have trouble finding your way around. For all of the above reasons, we recommend that you take a taxi from point to point. Having said that, we won't withhold from you the information that **Skeete's Car Rental** (Newcastle Village, at the airport, tel. 809/469–9458) has Honda Civics, Toyota Corollas, Suzuki Jeeps, and minimokes; doesn't charge for mileage or gas; and accepts major credit cards.

Taxis Taxi service is readily available at the airport. Some of the island's fleet include **Kurtley Maynard** (tel. 809/469–1973), **Ralph Hutton** (tel. 809/469–1767), and **Luther Morton** (tel. 809/469–1858).

Telephones and Mail To call Nevis from the United States, dial area code 809, followed by 469 and the local number. Communications are excellent, both on the island and with the United States, and direct-dial long distance is in effect.

Airmail letters to the United States and Canada require E.C.60¢ per half ounce; postcards E.C.35¢. It'll take at least a week to 10 days for mail to reach home. Nevis and St. Kitts have separate stamp-issuing policies, but each honors the other's stamps.

Opening and Closing Times Shops are open Monday–Saturday 8–noon and 1–4. Most shops close earlier on Thursday. Banking hours are Monday–Thursday 8–1; Friday 8–1 and 3–5. **St. Kitts & Nevis National Bank** is open Saturday 8:30–11 AM.

Beaches

All of the beaches on the island are free to the public. There are no changing facilities, so you'll have to wear a swimsuit under your clothes. If you're doing a cab tour, you may arrange with your driver to drop you off at the beach and pick you up later.

Newcastle Bay is the beach location of Nisbet Plantation. Popular among snorkelers, it's a broad beach of soft, white sand shaded by coconut palms on the northernmost tip of the island, on the channel between St. Kitts and Nevis.

Pinney's Beach is the island's showpiece beach. It's almost 4 miles of soft, white sand backed by a cyclorama of palm trees, and it's on the calm Caribbean Sea. The palm-shaded lagoon is a scene right out of *South Pacific*. Several of the mountain inns have private cabanas and pavilions on the beach, but it is, nevertheless, a public beach.

Oualie's Beach, at Mosquito Bay, just north of Pinney's, is a black-sand beach where Oualie's Beach Pub (tel. 809/469–5329) can mix you a drink and fix you up with water-sports equipment.

Exploring Nevis

Numbers in the margin correspond with points of interest on the Nevis map.

Charlestown ❶ About 1,200 of the island's 9,300 inhabitants live in Charlestown, the capital of Nevis. It faces the Caribbean, about 12½ miles south of Basseterre in St. Kitts. If you arrive by ferry, as most people do, you'll walk smack onto Main Street from the pier.

You can tour the capital city in a half hour or so, but you'll need three to four hours to explore the entire island.

Turn right on Main Street and look for the **Nevis Tourist Office** (on your right as you enter the main square). Pick up a copy of the Nevis Historical Society's self-guided tour of the island and stroll back onto Main Street.

While it is true that Charlestown has seen better days—it was founded in 1660—it's easy to imagine how it must have looked in its heyday. The buildings may be weathered and a bit worse for wear now, but there are still evidences of past glory in their fanciful galleries, elaborate gingerbread, wood shutters, and colorful hanging plants.

The **Philatelic Bureau** is next door to the Tourist Board, just across a narrow alley. The stamps of St. Kitts and Nevis are lovely and make inexpensive souvenirs and gifts.

The stonework building with the clock tower at the corner of Main and Prince William streets houses the **courthouse and library.** A fire in 1873 severely damaged the building and destroyed valuable records. The current building dates from the turn of the century. You're welcome to poke around the second-floor library (open Mon.–Sat. 9–6), which is one of the coolest places on the island.

If you intend to rent a car, the **police station** across from the courthouse is the place to get your local driver's license.

The little park opposite the courthouse is **Memorial Square,** dedicated to the fallen of World Wars I and II.

Time Out   Drop into **Caribbean Confections** (across the street from the Tourist Office, tel. 809/469–5685) for coffee and homemade pastries. There are also sandwiches, peanut-butter cookies, and popcorn.

When you return to Main Street from Prince William Street, turn right and go past the pier. Main Street curves and becomes Craddock Road, but keep going straight and you'll be on Low Street. The **Alexander Hamilton Birthplace,** which contains the **Museum of Nevis History,** is on the waterfront, covered in bougainvillea and hibiscus. This Georgian-style house is a reconstruction of the statesman's original home, which was built in 1680 and is thought to have been destroyed during an earthquake in the mid-19th century. Hamilton was born here in 1755. He left for the American Colonies 17 years later to contrive his education; he became secretary to George Washington, and died in a duel with political rival Aaron Burr. The **Nevis House of Assembly** sits on the second floor of this building, and the museum downstairs contains Hamilton memorabilia and documents pertaining to the island's history. *Low St., no phone. Admission free. Open weekdays 8–4, Sat. 8–noon.*

Elsewhere on   You'll have to resort to wheels to see the other sights and sites.
the Island   The main road makes a 20-mile circuit, with various offshoots bumping and winding into the mountains. Take the road south out of Charlestown, passing **Grove Park** along the way, where soccer and cricket matches are played.

②   About ¼ mile along you'll come to the ruins of the **Bath Hotel** (built by John Huggins in 1778) and **Bath Springs.** The springs, some icy cold, others with temperatures of 108°F, emanate from the hillside and spill into the "great poole" that John Smith mentioned in 1607. Huggins's hotel was adjacent to the waters, with the Spring House built over the springs. The swanky hotel, which charged an outrageous price of sixpence, accommodated 50 guests. Eighteenth-century accounts reported that a stay of a few days, bathing in and imbibing the waters, resulted in miraculous cures. It would take a minor miracle to restore the decayed hotel to anything like grandeur —it closed down in the late 19th century—but the Spring House has been partially restored and some of the springs are still as hot as ever. *Bathing costs 50¢. Open daily 9–4.*

③   About 2 miles from Charlestown, in the village of Fig Tree, is **St. John's Church,** which dates from 1680. Among its records is a tattered, prominently displayed marriage certificate that reads: "Horatio Nelson, Esquire, to Frances Nisbet, Widow, on March 11, 1787."

④   At nearby Morning Star Plantation, the **Nelson Museum** contains memorabilia pertaining to the life and times of Admiral Lord Nelson, including letters, documents, paintings, and even furniture from his flagship. Nelson was based in Antigua, but returned often to court—and eventually marry—Frances Nisbet, who lived on a 64-acre plantation here. The museum's owner, Robert Abrahams, restored the plantation and collected the Nelson memorabilia. He lives on the estate, and when he is not home, the museum is closed. It's a good idea to check with the Tourist Office to see if it's open before making the trip to see it. *Morning Star, no phone. Admission free. Open Mon.–Sat. 9–1.*

⑤ At the island's east coast, you'll come to the government-owned **Eden Brown Estate,** built around 1740 and known as Nevis's haunted house, or, rather, haunted ruins. In 1822, apparently, a Miss Julia Huggins was to marry a fellow named Maynard. However, on the day of the wedding the groom and his best man had a duel and killed each other. The bride-to-be became a recluse, and the mansion was closed down. Local residents claim they can feel the presence of . . . someone . . . whenever they go near the old house. You're welcome to drop by. It's free.

⑥ Rounding the top of the island, west of Newcastle Airport, you'll arrive at **Hurricane Hill,** from which there is a splendid view of St. Kitts.

Time Out At **Oualie's Beach Club** (Mosquito Bay, tel. 809/469–5329), you can have a rum punch, a swim in the sea, and sign up for a snorkeling or scuba-diving trip.

About 1½ miles along the Main Road, **Fort Ashby,** overgrown with tropical vegetation, overlooks the place where the settlement of Jamestown fell into the sea after a tidal wave hit the coast in 1680. Needless to say, this is a favored target of scuba divers.

⑦ At nearby **Nelson Spring,** the waters have considerably decreased since the 1780s, when young Captain Horatio Nelson periodically filled his ships with fresh water here.

⑧ Before driving back into Charlestown, a little over a mile down the road, stop to see the island's oldest church, **St. Thomas Anglican Church.** The church was built in 1643 and has been altered many times over the years. The gravestones in the old churchyard have stories to tell, and the church itself contains memorials to the early settlers of Nevis.

Participant Sports

Boating Hobie Cats and Sunfish can be rented from **Oualie's Beach Club** (tel. 809/469–5329).

Deep-Sea Fishing The game here is kingfish, wahoo, grouper, and yellowtail snapper. **Jans Travel Agency** (tel. 809/469–5578) arranges deep-sea fishing trips.

Hiking The center of the island is Nevis peak, which soars up to 3,232 feet, flanked by Hurricane Hill on the north and Saddle Hill on the south. If you plan to scale Mt. Nevis, a daylong affair, it is highly recommended that you go with a guide. Your hotel can arrange it for you; you can also ask the hotel to pack a picnic lunch.

Horseback Riding You can arrange for mountain-trail and beach rides through **Cane Gardens** (tel. 809/469–5464) and **Nisbet Plantation** (tel. 809/469–5325).

Tennis There are two tennis courts at **Pinney's Beach Hotel** and one court each at **Nisbet, Montpelier, Golden Rock,** and **Zetland** (*see* Lodging, below).

Water Sports The village of **Jamestown** was washed into the sea around Fort Ashby; the area is a popular spot for snorkeling and diving. Reef-protected **Pinney's Beach** offers especially good snorkeling. **Montpelier Plantation** (tel. 809/469–5462) has a 17-foot Boston whaler for scuba and snorkeling trips. Snorkeling and waterskiing trips can also be arranged through **Oualie's Beach Club** (tel. 809/469–5329). Windsurfers can also be rented here.

Spectator Sports

Cricket and Soccer **Grove Park** is the venue for cricket (Jan.–July) and soccer (July–Dec.). Your hotel or the Tourist Board can fill you in on dates, times, and grudge matches of particular interest between Kittitians and Nevisians.

Shopping

Rare is the traveler who heads for Nevis on a shopping spree. However, there are some surprises here, notably the island's stamps, batik and hand-embroidered clothing, and the artwork of Dame Eva Wilkins, who died in 1989.

For more than 50 years Wilkins painted island people, flowers, and landscapes. An Eva Wilkins mural hangs over the bar at the Golden Rock *(see* Dining, below). Her originals sell for $100 and up, and prints are available in some of the local shops.

Stamp collectors should head for the **Philatelic Bureau,** just off Main Street opposite the Tourist Office. St. Kitts and Nevis are famous for their decorative, and sometimes lucrative, stamps. An early Kittitian stamp recently brought in $7,000.

Other local items of note are the batik caftans, scarves, and fabrics found in the Nevis branch of **Caribelle Batik** (in the Arcade of downtown Charlestown, no phone). **Caribee Clothes** (off Main St., tel. 809/469–5217) has resort clothing with hand-embroidered designs that have been praised by *Vogue*.

Dining

All of the plantation guest houses serve meals. Most of them have informal lobster bakes on the beach as well as romantic candlelit dinners in elegant dining rooms. (For more detailed descriptions of the plantations, *see* Lodging, below.) Meals in the plantations are prix fixe and run from about $25 to $35, including wine. In each case the menu changes daily.

The most highly recommended restaurants are indicated by a star ★ .

Category	Cost*
Expensive	$25–$35
Moderate	$15–$25
Inexpensive	under $15

per person, excluding drinks and service

★ **Cooperage.** An old stone dining room with high raftered ceilings provides an elegantly rustic setting. Among the specialties here are green-pepper soup, curried chicken breasts, seafood, and sorbets. *Croney's Old Manor, tel. 809/ 469–5445. Reservations required. AE, MC, V. Expensive.*

Golden Rock. Dinner is in an opulent dining room with handsome tablecloths and soft candlelight. West Indian and Continental dishes are served. *Golden Rock, tel. 809/469–5346. Reservations required. No credit cards, but personal checks are accepted. Closed Sun. Expensive.*

Hermitage. The atmosphere here is subdued, with white cloths, candlelight, and a backdrop of white latticework on the porch. Begin your meal with carrot-and-tarragon soup, then follow it with West Indian red snapper in ginger sauce, and fin-[ish off with a rum soufflé. *Hermitage Plantation, tel. 809/469–5477. Reservations required. AE, MC, V, personal checks. Expensive.*

Montpelier Plantation Inn. Dinner is served by candlelight on the veranda; your feast might include lobster, red snapper, or even roast beef and Yorkshire pudding. *Montpelier Plantation, tel. 809/469–5462. Reservations required. No credit cards. Expensive.*

Nisbet Plantation. The antiques-filled dining room at Nisbet has long been a popular place for lunch and dinner. At press time the inn had just changed ownership and was scheduled to reopen in early 1990. Be sure to ask about the current menu and credit card policies. *Nisbet Plantation, tel. 809/469–9325.*

★ **Mt. Nevis Hotel.** The attractive 60-seat dining room, where tables are set with fine china and silver, opens onto the terrace and pool, beyond which there is a splendid view of St. Kitts in the distance. Starters include fish chowder or lobster bisque. Entrées might include red snapper, lobster, or sirloin steak duded up with mushrooms and onions. The coffee and desserts are superb. *Mt. Nevis Hotel/Condominiums, Newcastle, tel. 809/469–9373. Reservations suggested. AE, MC, V. Expensive.*

Unella's Restaurant. Sit on the plain terrace overlooking the Charlestown harbor and take your pick of lobster bisque, fish chowder, filet mignon with mushroom sauce, barbecued ribs, and Caribbean lobster grilled and served with lemon butter. *Charlestown Harbour, tel. 809/469–5574. No reservations. No credit cards. Inexpensive.*

Lodging

The island is filled with restored sugar plantations that are now guest houses and inns. Most of them operate on the MAP (Modified American Plan: breakfast and dinner included in the room rate).

The most highly recommended lodgings are indicated by a star ★.

Category	Cost*
Very Expensive	over $200
Expensive	$150–$200

Moderate	$90–$150
Inexpensive	under $90

All prices are for a standard double room for two, MAP, excluding 7% tax and a 10% service charge.

Montpelier Plantation Inn. This old West Indian–style manor house is set in 650 beautifully landscaped acres. Neat brick paths lead through tropical gardens, and accommodations are in individual cottages, each with a patio and private bath. Transportation is provided to Pinney's Beach, where the estate has a cabana. There is a huge pool with a poolside bar, and the estate has a 17-foot Boston whaler for waterskiing, snorkeling, and fishing. *Box 474, Charlestown, tel. 809/469–5462 or 800/243–9420. 16 rooms. Facilities: restaurant, bar, pool, horseback riding, water-sports center. No credit cards. Very Expensive.*

Mt. Nevis Hotel/Condominiums. Author James Michener stayed in the elegant Hummingbird Suite of this sleek hotel, which opened in 1988. Standard rooms and suites are done up with handsome white wicker furnishings, glass-topped tables, and colorful island prints. Suites have full, modern kitchens and dining areas; all units have a balcony, safe-deposit box, direct-dial phone, cable TV, and VCR. At press time work was near completion on a beach club at Newcastle Beach, replete with shops, cocktail lounge, and full water-sports facilities. The hotel also has its own ferry, which will be used for moonlight cruises when not ferrying passengers to and from St. Kitts. There are literally flies in this ointment, however. The swarms of flies are a nuisance, making it difficult to enjoy morning breakfast or evening drinks. A good bug-zapper on the terrace would be of great benefit. *Box 494, Newcastle, tel. 809/469–9373 (collect). 16 rooms. Facilities: pool, restaurant, bar, water sports, beach club. AE, MC, V. Very Expensive.*

★ **Nisbet Plantation Inn.** From the manor house of this 18th-century plantation you can see the beach at the end of a long avenue of coconut palms, and from the bar, you look out over an old sugar mill covered with hibiscus, cassia, frangipani, and flamboyants. Rooms are in elegantly furnished cottages on Nisbet's long white-sand beach. At press time Nisbet had changed ownership and was scheduled to reopen in early 1990 with 12 additional rooms and two pools. When you call to reserve, ask about current credit-card policies. *Newcastle Beach, tel. 809/469–9325 or 800/344–2049 in USA. 45 rooms. Facilities: beach, 2 restaurants, 2 bars, free laundry, boutique, free snorkeling gear. Very Expensive.*

Croney's Old Manor Estate. Vast tropical gardens surround this restored sugar plantation, which is set 800 feet above the sea on the slopes of Mt. Nevis. Many guest rooms have high ceilings and hardwood floors, king-size canopy beds, and colonial reproductions. The outbuildings, such as the smokehouse and jail, have been imaginatively restored, and the old cistern is now the pool. This is the home of The Cooperage, one of the island's best restaurants (*see* Dining, above). There's transportation to and from the beach. The hotel is not recommended for children under 12. *Box 70, Charlestown, tel. 809/469–5445, 800/223–9815 in USA, 800/468–0023 in Canada. 10 rooms. Facilities: pool, 2 restaurants, 2 bars. AE, MC, V. Expensive.*

★ **Golden Rock.** The present owner, Pam Barry, is a direct descendant of the original owner of this 200-year-old estate. She has decorated the five cottages in a style befitting a once-flourishing plantation. There are handsome four-poster beds of mahogany or bamboo, hooked rugs, rocking chairs, and island-made fabrics of floral prints. All rooms have private baths and a patio. The restored sugar mill is a large suite for honeymooners or families, and the old cistern is now a spring-fed swimming pool. The estate covers 150 mountainous acres and is surrounded by 25 acres of lavish tropical gardens, including a sunken garden. The hotel has facilities on two beaches, and a shuttle bus that makes two trips daily to them. *Box 493, Gingerland, tel. 809/469–5346, 800/223–9815 in USA, 800/468–0023 in Canada. 16 rooms. Facilities: 2 beaches, 2 restaurants, bar, pool, bike rentals, tennis court, windsurfing. No credit cards, but personal checks are accepted. Expensive.*

★ **Hermitage.** This is a wonderful 250-year-old great house with modern facilities in the restored carriage house and cottages. Each cottage sleeps two, in twin beds or magnificent king-size canopy beds, and most have a small kitchenette. There are verandas and hammocks for loafing and enjoying the tropical gardens, and an antique-filled dining room for elegant dinners. *St. Johns, Fig Tree Parish, tel. 809/469–5477, 800/223–9815 in USA, 800/468–0023 in Canada. 11 suites. Facilities: pool, restaurant. AE, MC, V, personal checks. Expensive.*

Pinney's Beach Hotel. These bungalows are smack on Pinney's Beach, which is so spectacular you probably won't mind that the rooms are somewhat modest (though they have colorful bedspreads, carpeting, and private terraces). Some are air-conditioned, all have private baths, and some of the cottages are set around a garden. You'll be more comfortable in one that opens directly onto the beach. *Pinney's Beach, tel. 809/469–5207. 48 rooms. Facilities: beach, 2 restaurants, 3 bars, 1 tennis court, pool. AE, MC, V. Moderate.*

Zetland Plantation Inn. The big peach-colored great house and pastel cottages are set on 750 acres, 1,500 feet up the slope of Mt. Nevis. The restored sugar mill, with handsome brass beds and oriental rugs, can sleep up to six. Rooms and suites, all in contemporary tropical decor, are in seven double cottages. The suites have a bedroom, combination living room/dining room, and fully equipped kitchenette. The four deluxe suites have plunge pools as an extra added attraction. A shuttle bus takes guests to Charlestown and to Pinney's Beach. *Box 448, Gingerland, tel. 809/469–5454 or 800/243–2654 in USA. 22 suites. Facilities: pool, 2 restaurants, 2 bars, boutique, snorkeling and windsurfing equipment, tennis court. AE, MC, V. Moderate.*

Rest Haven Inn. This is a motelish facility on the outskirts of Charlestown. All rooms have two double beds, a terrace, bath with tub and shower, and a kitchenette. It's on the water, but not on the beach; however, there's a small free-form pool. The hotel is air-conditioned and well maintained. *Box 209, Charlestown, tel. 809/469–5208. 40 rooms. Facilities: restaurant, snack bar, lounge, pool, tennis court. AE. Inexpensive.*

Nightlife

The hotels usually bring in local calypso singers and steel or string bands one night a week. On Friday night the Shell All-Stars steel band entertains in the gardens at **Croney's Old Manor** (tel. 809/469–5445). The **Golden Rock** (tel. 809/469–5346) brings in the Honeybees String Band to jazz things up for the

Saturday-night buffet, and **Zetlands** (tel. 809/469–5454) has a beach barbecue every Tuesday, complete with string band. You can have dinner and a dance on Wednesday nights at **Pinney's Beach Hotel** (tel. 809/469–5207).

Apart from the hotel scene, there are a few places where young locals go on weekends for hi-fi calypso, reggae, and other island music; **Mariner's Pub & Bar** (tel. 809/469–1993) near Fort Ashby and **Dick's Bar** (no phone) in Brickiln are two such places.

18 Puerto Rico

by Honey Naylor

No city in the Caribbean is as steeped in Spanish tradition as Puerto Rico's Old San Juan. Old San Juan's attractions are myriad: restored 16th-century buildings, museums, art galleries, bookstores, 200-year-old houses with balustraded balconies of filigreed wrought iron overlooking quaint, narrow, cobblestone streets. This Spanish tradition also spills over into the island's countryside, from its festivals celebrated in honor of various patron saints in the little towns, to the paradors, those homey, inexpensive inns whose concept originated in Spain.

Puerto Rico has, in San Juan's sophisticated Condado and Isla Verde areas, glittering hotels, flashy, Las Vegas–style shows, casinos, and frenetic discos. It has the ambience of the Old World in the seven-square-block area of the old city and in its quiet colonial towns. Out in the countryside lie its natural attractions—the extraordinary, 28,000-acre Caribbean National Forest, more familiarly known as the El Yunque rain forest, with its 100-foot-high trees, more than 200 species of them, and its dramatic mountain ranges; there are forest reserves with trails to satisfy the most dedicated hiker, vast caves to tempt spelunkers, coffee plantations, old sugar mills, and hundreds of beaches.

Puerto Rico, 110 miles long and 35 miles wide, was populated by several tribes of Indians when Columbus landed on the island on his second voyage in 1493. In 1508, Juan Ponce de Léon, the frustrated searcher of the Fountain of Youth, established a settlement on the island and became its first governor, and in 1521, founded Old San Juan. For three centuries, the Dutch and the English tried unsuccessfully to wrest the island from Spain. In 1897, Spain granted the island dominion status. Two years later, Spain ceded the island to the United States, and in 1917 Puerto Ricans became U.S. citizens, part of the Commonwealth.

And so, if you're a U.S. citizen, you need neither passport nor visa when you land at the bustling Luis Muñoz Marín Airport, outside San Juan. You don't have to clear customs, and you don't have to explain yourself to an immigration official. English is widely spoken, though the official language is Spanish.

Puerto Rico also boasts hundreds of beaches with every imaginable water sport available, acres of golf courses and miles of tennis courts, and small colonial towns where you can quietly savor the Spanish flavor. If it's festivals you seek, every town honors its individual patron saint with an annual festival, which is usually held in the central plaza, and can last from one to 10 days. In San Juan, *LeLoLai* is a year-round festival celebrating Puerto Rican dance and folklore, with changing programs presented in major San Juan hotels. Having seen every sight on the island, you can then do further exploring on the offshore islands of Culebra, Vieques, Icacos, and Mona, where more aquatic activities, such as snorkeling and scuba diving, prevail.

Before You Go

Tourist Information
Contact the **Puerto Rico Tourism Company** at the following addresses: 575 5th Ave., 23rd Floor, New York, NY 10017, tel. 212/599–6262 or 800/223–6530; 3228–I Quails Lake Village La., Norcross, GA 30093, tel. 404/564–9362; 233 N. Michigan Ave.,

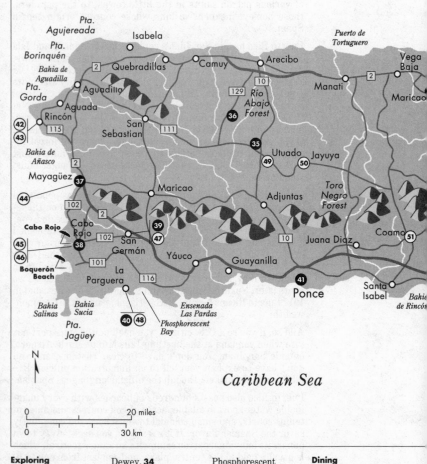

Pta. Agujereada

Pta. Borinquén

Bahia de Aguadilla

Pta. Gorda

Isabela

Puerto de Tortuguero

Vega Baja

Quebradillas

Camuy

Arecibo

2

Aguadilla

2

Manati

Maricao

Aguada

10

129

Río Abajo Forest

Rincón

42
43

115

San Sebastian

111

36

35

Bahia de Añasco

2

Mayagüez

37

44

102

Maricao

49

Utuado

Jayuya

50

Adjuntas

Toro Negro Forest

Cabo Rojo

39

Cabo Rojo

45
46

38

102

San Germán

47

10

Juana Diaz

Coamo

51

Boquerón Beach

101

Yáuco

Guayanilla

La Parguera

116

Ensenada Las Pardas

41

Ponce

Santa Isabel

Bahie de Rincón

40 48

Phosphorescent Bay

Bahia Salinas

Bahia Sucia

Pta. Jagüey

N

Caribbean Sea

0 _____ 20 miles
0 _____ 30 km

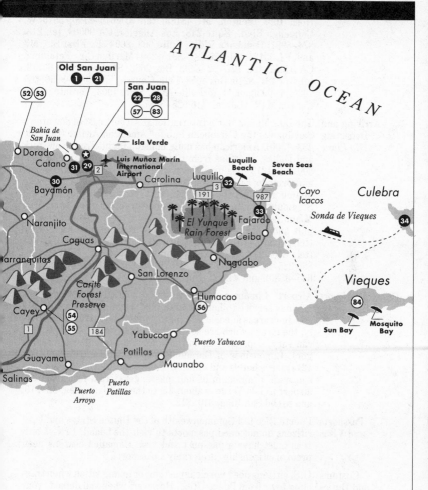

ATLANTIC OCEAN

Old San Juan
①—㉑

San Juan
㉒—㉘
㉗—㊸

㊿㊽

Bahia de San Juan

○ Dorado
Catano
Isla Verde
Luis Muñoz Marín International Airport

㉛ ㉙ ②

㉚ Bayamón

○ Naranjito

Caguas

Barranquitas

Carite Forest Preserve

○ Cayey

㊴ ㊵

1 184

Guayama

Salinas

Puerto Arroyo *Puerto Patillas*

Yabucoa ○
Patillas
Maunabo

Puerto Yabucoa

Carolina
Luquillo **Luquillo Beach** **Seven Seas Beach**
3 ㉜
191
987
Fajardo ㉝
Ceiba

El Yunque Rain Forest

○ Naguabo

San Lorenzo

Humacao
㊶

Cayo Icacos
Sonda de Vieques

Culebra

㉞

Vieques

㊴

Sun Bay **Mosquito Bay**

① Exploring Sites
㊷ Hotels and Restaurants

Lodging

Hilton International Mayagüez, **44**
Hyatt Dorado Beach, **53**
Hyatt Regency Cerromar Beach, **52**
Palmas del Mar, **56**
Parador Baños de Coamo, **51**

Parador Boquemer, **46**
Parador Casa Grande, **49**
Parador Hacienda Gripinas, **50**
Parador Oasis, **47**
Parador Villa Parguera, **48**
Sea Gate (Vieques), **84**

Suite 2204, Chicago, IL 60601, tel. 312/861–0049; 3386 Van
Horn 106, Trenton, MI 48183, tel. 313/676–2190; 3575 W.
Cahuenga Blvd., Suite 248, Los Angeles, CA 90068, tel. 213/
874–5991; Peninsula Bldg., Suite 903, 200 S.E. First St., Miami, FL 33131, tel. 305/381–8915; 2504 Marilyn Cir., Petaluma,
CA 94952, tel. 707/762–3468; Box 2662, St. Louis, MO 63116,
tel. 314/481–8216; Box 8053, Falls Church, VA 22041–8053, tel.
703/671–0930; or 11 Yorkville Ave., Suite 1003, Toronto, Ont.,
Canada M4W IL3, tel. 416/925–5587.

Arriving and Departing By Plane The Luis Muñoz Marín International Airport east of downtown
San Juan is the Caribbean hub for **American Airline** (tel. 800/
433–7300). American has daily nonstop flights from New York
and Dallas, and flies from Chicago via New York. **Delta** (tel.
800/221–1212) has direct service from Atlanta, Los Angeles,
and Orlando; **Eastern** (tel. 800/327–8376) flies from Atlanta and
Miami; and **TWA** (tel. 800/892–4141) flies from New York and
St. Louis. In late 1989, **Pan Am** began serving San Juan from
Miami, and **USAir** began daily nonstop service from Philadelphia and Charlotte, NC. Foreign carriers include **Air France**
(tel. 800/237–2747), **British Airways** (tel. 800/247–9297), **BWIA**
(tel. 800/327–7401), **Iberia** (tel. 800/772–4642), **LACSA** (tel.
800/225–2272), **LIAT** (tel. 809/791–3838), **Lufthansa** (tel. 800/
645–3880), and **VIASA** (tel. 800/327–5454).

From the Airport **Airport Limousine Service** (tel. 809/791–4745) provides
minibus service to hotels in the Isla Verde, Condado, and Old
San Juan areas at basic fares of $1, $1.50, and $1.75, respective-
ly; the fares, which are set by the Public Service Commission,
can vary, depending upon time of day and number of passengers. Limousines of **Dorado Transport Service** (tel. 809/796–
1214) serve hotels and villas in the Dorado area for $12 per per-
son with a minimum of four passengers. Taxi fare from the
airport to Isla Verde is about $5; to the Condado area, $8–$10;
and to Old San Juan, $10–$12.

Passports and Visas Puerto Rico is a Commonwealth of the United States and U.S.
citizens do not need passports to visit the island. British citizens must have a passport and visa. Canadian citizens need
proof of citizenship (preferably a passport).

Customs and Duties U.S. citizens need not clear customs or immigration when traveling to or from Puerto Rico. However, when you depart, your
luggage will be inspected by the U.S. Agriculture Department
as there are prohibitions against taking certain fruits and
plants into the United States.

Language The official language is Spanish, but almost everyone in and
around San Juan speaks English. If you plan to rent a car and
travel around the island, take along a Spanish phrase book.

Precautions San Juan, like any other big city and major tourist destination,
has its share of crime, so guard your wallet or purse on the city
streets. Puerto Rico's beaches are open to the public, and mug-
gings occur at night even on the beaches of the posh Condado
and Isla Verde tourist hotels. Don't leave anything unattended
on the beach. Leave your valuables in the hotel safe, and stick
to the fenced-in beach areas of your hotel. Always lock your car
and stash valuables and luggage out of sight. Avoid deserted
beaches day or night.

Staying in Puerto Rico

Important Addresses

Tourist Information: The government-sponsored **Puerto Rico Tourism Company** (tel. 809/721–2400) is an excellent source for maps, brochures, and other printed guide materials. Pick up a free copy of *¿Qué Pasa?* the official visitors guide.

Information offices are located at **Luis Muñoz Marín International Airport,** Isla Verde (tel. 809/791–1014 or 809/791–2551); **El Centro Convention Center,** Condado (tel. 809/723–3135 or 809/722–1513); **301 Calle San Justo,** Old San Juan (tel. 809/721–2400), and **La Casita,** near Pier One in Old San Juan (tel. 809/722–1709). Out on the island, information offices are located in **Ponce** (Casa Armstrong-Poventud, Plaza, Las Delicias, tel. 809/840–5695); **Aguadilla** (Rafael Hernandez Airport, tel. 809/890–3315); and each town's city hall on the main plaza, open weekdays from 8 AM to noon and 1 to 4:30 PM.

Emergencies

Police: Call 809/343–2020.

Medical Emergency: Call 809/343–2550.

Hospitals: Hospitals in the Condado/Santurce area with 24-hour emergency rooms are **Ashford Memorial Community Hospital** (1451 Ashford Ave., tel. 809/721–2160) and **San Juan Health Center** (200 De Diego Ave., tel. 809/725–0202).

Pharmacies: In San Juan, **Walgreen's** (1130 Ashford Ave., tel. 809/725–1510) is a 24-hour pharmacy. In Mayagüez there is another Walgreen's (16 Calle McKinley, tel. 809/833–6742), but it is not open 24 hours.

Currency

The U.S. dollar is the official currency of Puerto Rico.

Taxes and Service Charges

Hotels collect a 6% government tax on room charges. There is no departure tax.

Some hotels impose a 10% service charge. In restaurants, a 10%–15% tip is expected.

Guided Tours

Old San Juan can be seen either on a self-guided walking tour or on the free trolley. To explore the rest of the city and the island, consider renting a car. (We do, however, recommend a guided tour of the vast El Yunque rain forest.) If you'd rather not do your own driving, there are several tour companies you can call. Most San Juan hotels have a tour desk that can make arrangements for you. The standard half-day tours (at $10–$15) are of Old and New San Juan, Old San Juan and the Bacardi Rum Plant, Luquillo Beach and El Yunque rain forest. All-day tours ($15–$30) include a trip to Ponce, a day at El Comandante Racetrack, or a combined tour of the city and El Yunque rain forest.

Some of the leading tour operators are **Borinquén Tours, Inc.** (tel. 809/725–4990), **Gray Line of Puerto Rico** (tel. 809/727–8080), **Normandie Tours, Inc.** (tel. 809/725–6990 or 809/722–6308), **Rico Suntours** (tel. 809/722–2080 or 809/722–6090), and **United Tour Guides** (tel. 809/725–7605 or 809/723–5578). **Cordero Caribbean Tours** (tel. 809/799–6002) does tours (at hourly rates) out on the island in air-conditioned limousines.

Getting Around
Taxis

Metered cabs authorized by the Public Service Commission (tel. 809/751–5050) charge an 80¢ drop and 10¢ for each addi-

tional ⅛ mile. There is a 50¢ charge per suitcase. Waiting time
is $8 per hour.

Buses The **Metropolitan Bus Authority** (tel. 809/767–7979) operates
the buses (or *guaguas*) that thread through San Juan. The fare
is 25¢, and the buses run in exclusive lanes, *against the traffic*
on major thoroughfares, stopping at upright yellow posts
marked *Parada* or *Parada de Guaguas*. The main terminals
downtown are at Plaza Colón and the Catano Ferry Terminal.

Públicos Public cars (*públicos*) with license plates ending with "P" or
"PD" scoot to towns throughout the island, stopping in each
town's main plaza. The five-passenger cars operate primarily
during the day, with routes and fares fixed by the Public Service Commission. In San Juan, the main terminals are at the
airport and on the waterfront in Old San Juan.

Trolleys If your feet fail you in Old San Juan, climb aboard the free open-
air trolleys that rumble and roller-coast through the narrow
streets. Departures are from La Puntilla and from the marina,
but you can board them anywhere along the route.

Motor Coaches The **Puerto Rico Motor Coach Co.** (tel. 809/725–2460) makes
daily runs between San Juan and Mayagüez, with stops at Arecibo and Aguadilla. A bus leaves San Juan every two hours,
from 6 to 6, for a one-way fare of $6. Be sure to reserve in ad-
vance.

Ferries A round-trip ride between Old San Juan and Catano costs a
mere 20¢. The ferry runs every half hour from 6:15 AM to 10 PM.
The 400-passenger ferries of the **Fajardo Port Authority** (tel.
809/863–0705 or 800/462–2005) make the 80-minute trip twice
daily between Fajardo and Vieques (one way $2 adults, $1 children), the one-hour run between Fajardo and Culebra daily
(one way $2.25 adults, $1 children), and the half-hour trip between Vieques and Culebra on Saturday, Sunday, Monday,
and holidays (one way $2 adults, $1 children).

Rental Cars U.S. driver's licenses are valid in Puerto Rico for three months.
All major U.S. car-rental agencies are represented on the island, including **Avis** (tel. 809/721–4499), **Hertz** (tel. 809/791–
0840), **Budget** (tel. 809/791–3685), and **Thrifty** (tel. 809/791–
4241). Prices start at $19.95 (plus insurance), with unlimited
mileage. Most car rentals have shuttle service to or from the
airport and the pickup point. If you plan to drive across the island, arm yourself with a good map and be aware that there are
many unmarked roads up in the mountains. Many service stations in the central mountains do not take credit cards. Speed
limits are posted in miles, distances in kilometers, and gas
prices in liters.

Planes **Vieques Air-Link** (tel. 809/722–3736) flies from the Isla Grande
Airport to Vieques and to Culebra, with each trip costing
about $25 one way.

Telephones The area code for Puerto Rico is 809. Since Puerto Rico uses
and Mail U.S. postage stamps and has the same mail rates (17¢ for a
postcard, 25¢ for a first-class letter), you can save time by
bringing stamps with you. Post offices in major Puerto Rico cities offer Express Mail next-day service to the U.S. mainland
and to Puerto Rico destinations.

Opening and Shops are open from 9 to 6 (from 9 to 9 during Christmas holi-
Closing Times days). Banks are open weekdays from 8:30 to 2:30 and Saturday
from 9:45 to noon.

Beaches

By law, all of Puerto Rico's beaches are open to the public (except for the Caribe Hilton's man-made beach in San Juan). The
government runs 13 public beaches *(balnearios)*, which have
lockers, showers, picnic tables, and in some cases playgrounds
and overnight facilities. Admission is 25¢, parking is $1.
Balnearios are open Tuesday–Sunday 9–5 in the winter, 8–5 in
the summer. (When Monday is a holiday the balnearios are
closed on Monday and open Tuesday.) Listed below are some of
the major balnearios.

Boquerón Beach is a broad beach of hard-packed sand, fringed
with coconut palms. It has picnic tables, cabin rentals, bike
rentals, basketball court, minimarket, scuba diving, and snorkeling. *On the southeast coast, south of Mayagüez, Rte. 101,
Boquerón.*

A white sandy beach bordered by resort hotels, **Isla Verde** offers picnic tables and good snorkeling, with equipment rentals
nearby. *Near metropolitan San Juan, Rte. 187, Km 3.9, Isla
Verde.*

Luquillo Beach, a crescent-shape beach, comes complete with
coconut palms, picnic tables, and tent sites. Coral reefs protect
its crystal-clear lagoon from the Atlantic waters, making it
ideal for swimming. *30 mi east of San Juan, Rte. 3, Km 35.4.*

A recently opened beach of hard-packed sand, **Seven Seas** is already popular with bathers. It has picnic tables and tent and
trailer sites; snorkeling, scuba diving, and boat rentals are
nearby. *Rte. 987, Fajardo.*

Sun Bay, a white-sand beach on the offshore island of Vieques,
has picnic tables, tent sites, and offers such water sports as
snorkeling and scuba diving. Boat rentals are nearby. *Rte. 997,
Vieques.*

Surfing Beaches. The best surfing beaches are along the Atlantic coastline from Borinquén Point to Rincón, where the surfing
is best from October through April. There are several surf
shops in Rincón. Aviones and La Concha beaches in San Juan,
and Casa de Pesca in Arecibo, are summer surfing spots; all
have nearby surf shops.

Caution for snorkelers and scuba divers: Puerto Rico's coral-
reef waters and mangrove areas can be dangerous to novices.
Unless you're an expert, or have an experienced guide, avoid
unsupervised areas, and stick to the water-sports centers of
major hotels (*see* Participant Sports, below).

Exploring Puerto Rico

*Numbers in the margin correspond with points of interest on
the Old San Juan map.*

Old San Juan Old San Juan, the original city founded in 1521, contains au-
❶ thentic and carefully preserved examples of 16th- and 17th-
century Spanish colonial architecture, some of the best in the
New World. More than 400 buildings have been beautifully re-

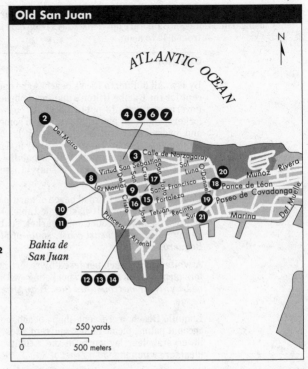

Old San Juan

stored. Graceful wrought-iron balconies, decorated with lush green hanging plants, extend over narrow streets paved with blue-gray stones (*adequines*, originally used as ballast for Spanish ships). The old city is partially enclosed by the old walls, dating from 1630, that once completely surrounded it. Designated a U.S. National Historic Zone in 1950, Old San Juan is chockablock with shops, open-air cafés, private homes, tree-shaded squares, monuments, plaques, pigeons, and people. The traffic is awful. Get an overview of the inner city on a morning's stroll (bearing in mind that "stroll" includes some steep climbs). However, if you plan to immerse yourself in history, or to shop, you'll need two or three days.

El Morro and Fort San Cristóbal are described in our walking tour: You may want to set aside extra time to see them, especially if you're an aficionado of military history. UNESCO has designated each fortress a World Heritage Site; each is also a National Historic Site. Both are looked after by the National Park Service; you can take one of their tours or wander around on your own.

Sitting on a rocky promontory on the northwestern tip of the old city is **San Felipe del Morro** ("El Morro"), a fortress built by the Spaniards between 1540 and 1783. Rising 140 feet above the sea, the massive six-level fortress covers enough territory to accommodate a nine-hole golf course. It is a labyrinth of dungeons, ramps and barracks, turrets, towers, and tunnels. Built to protect the port, El Morro has a commanding view of the harbor. Its small, air-conditioned museum traces the history of the fortress. *Calle Norzagaray, tel. 809/724–1974. Admission: $1 adults, children free. Open daily 8–6:15.*

❸ San José Plaza is two short blocks from the entrance to El Morro, but for the moment we'll bypass it and head for the **San Juan Museum of Arts and History,** which is a block east of the tour's path but a must. A bustling marketplace in 1850, this handsome building is now a modern cultural center that houses exhibits of Puerto Rican art. Multi-image audiovisual shows present the history of the island; concerts and other cultural events take place in the huge courtyard. *Calle Norzagaray, at the corner of Calle MacArthur, tel. 809/724–1875. Donation requested: $1 adults, 50¢ children. Open Tues.–Sat. 8–noon and 1–4. Audiovisual shows weekdays 11 AM and 1:15 PM.*

❹ Turn back west toward San José Plaza to **La Casa de los Contrafuertes,** on Calle San Sebastián. This building is also known as the Buttress House because wide exterior buttresses support the wall next to the plaza. The house is one of the oldest remaining private residences in Old San Juan. Inside is the Pharmacy Museum, a re-creation of an 18th-century apothecary shop. The building was closed for renovation at press time. *101 Calle San Sebastián, Plaza de San José, tel. 809/724–5949. Admission free. Open Wed.–Sun. 9–noon and 1–4.*

❺ The **Pablo Casals Museum,** a bit farther down the block, contains memorabilia of the famed cellist, who made his home in Puerto Rico for the last 20 years of his life. The museum holds manuscripts, photographs, and his favorite cellos, in addition to recordings and videotapes of Casals Festival concerts (the latter shown on request). *101 Calle San Sebastián, Plaza de San José, tel. 809/723–9185. Admission free. Open Tues.–Sat. 9:30–5:30; Sun. 1–5; closed Mon.*

❻ In the center of the plaza, next to the museum, is the **San José Church.** With its series of vaulted ceilings, it is a splendid example of 16th-century Spanish Gothic architecture. The church, which is one of the oldest Christian houses of worship in the Western Hemisphere, was built in 1532 under the supervision of the Dominican friars. The body of Ponce de León, the Spanish explorer who came to the New World seeking the Fountain of Youth, was buried here for almost three centuries before being removed in 1913 and placed in the cathedral. *Calle San Sebastián, tel. 809/725–7501. Admission free. Open Mon.–Sat. 8:30–4; Sun. noon mass.*

❼ Next door is the **Dominican Convent (Institute of Puerto Rican Culture).** Built by Dominican friars in 1523, the convent often served as a shelter during Carib Indian attacks in the past and, more recently, as headquarters for the Antilles command of the U.S. Army. Now home to the Institute of Puerto Rican Culture, the beautifully restored building contains an ornate 18th-century altar, religious manuscripts, artifacts, and art. Classical concerts are occasionally held here. *98 Calle Norzagaray, tel. 809/724–0700. Admission free. Chapel museum open Wed.–Sun. 9–noon and 1–4. Popular Arts Museum open Mon.–Sat. 9:15–4:15.*

❽ From San José Plaza walk west on Calle Beneficencia to **Casa Blanca.** The original structure on this site, not far from the ramparts of El Morro, was a frame house built in 1521 as a home for Ponce de León. But Ponce de León died in Cuba, never having lived in the house, and it was virtually destroyed by a hurricane in 1523, after which Ponce de León's son-in-law had the present masonry house built. His descendants occupied it for 250 years. From the end of the Spanish-American War in 1898 to 1966, it was the home of the U.S. Army commander in Puerto Rico. It is now a museum showcasing aspects of 16th- and 17th-century Puerto Rican family life. Guided tours are conducted Tuesday–Saturday. *1 Calle San Sebastián, tel. 809/724–4102. Admission free. Open Tues.–Sat. 9–noon and 1–4:30.*

⑨ San Juan Cathedral. This great Catholic shrine of Puerto Rico had humble beginnings in the early 1520s as a thatch-topped wood structure. Hurricane winds tore off the thatch and destroyed the church. It was reconstructed in 1540, when the graceful circular staircase and vaulted ceilings were added, but most of the work on the church was done in the 19th century. The remains of Ponce de León are in a marble tomb near the transept. *153 Calle Cristo. Open daily 6:30–5.*

Time Out Stop in at **María's** (204 Calle Cristo, no phone) for a papaya freeze, a chocolate frost, or a pitcher of Mexican sangría. Enchiladas and tacos are also served.

Across the street from the cathedral you'll see the Ramada Gran Hotel El Convento, which was a Carmelite convent more than 300 years ago. Go west alongside the hotel on Caleta de las **⑩** Monjas toward the city wall to the **Plazuela de la Rogativa.** In the little plaza, statues of a bishop and three women commemorate a legend, according to which the British, while laying siege to the city in 1797, mistook the flaming torches of a religious procession *(rogativa)* for Spanish reinforcements and beat a hasty retreat. The monument was donated to the city in 1971 on its 450th anniversary.

⑪ One block south on Calle Recinto Oeste you'll come to **La Fortaleza,** which sits on a hill overlooking the harbor. La Fortaleza, the Western Hemisphere's oldest executive mansion in continuous use, home of 170 governors and official residence of the present governor of Puerto Rico, was built as a fortress. The original primitive structure, built in 1540, has seen numerous changes over a period of three centuries, resulting in the present collection of marble and mahogany, medieval towers, and stained-glass galleries. Guided tours are conducted every hour on the hour in English, on the half hour in Spanish. *Tel. 809/721–7000. Admission free. Open weekdays 9–4.*

⑫ At the southern end of Cristo Street is **Cristo Chapel.** According to legend, in 1753 a young horseman, carried away during festivities in honor of the patron saint, raced down the street and plunged over the steep precipice. A witness to the tragedy promised to build a chapel if the young man's life could be saved. The man lived. Inside is a small silver altar, dedicated to the Christ of Miracles. *Open Tues. 10–4 and on most Catholic holidays.*

⑬ Across the street from the chapel, the 18th-century **Casa del Libro** has exhibits devoted to books and bookbinding. The museum's 5,000 books include rare volumes dating back 2,000 years; more than 200 of these books—40 of which were produced in Spain—were printed before the 16th century. *255 Calle Cristo, tel. 809/723–0354. Admission free. Open weekdays (except holidays) 11–4:30.*

⑭ Next door, the **Fine Arts Museum,** in a lovely colonial building, occasionally presents special exhibits. The museum usually holds the Institute of Puerto Rican Culture's collection of paintings and sculptures, but those pieces have been temporarily removed. *253 Calle Cristo, tel. 809/724–5949. Admission free. Open 9–noon and 1–4:30.*

⑮ Follow the wall east one block and head north on Calle San José two short blocks to **Plaza de Armas,** the original main square of Old San Juan. The plaza, bordered by Calles San Francisco, Fortaleza, San José, and Cruz, has a lovely fountain with statues representing the four seasons.

⑯ West of the square stands **La Intendencia,** a handsome three-story neoclassical building. From 1851 to 1898, it was home to the Spanish Treasury. Recently restored, it is now the headquarters of Puerto Rico's State Department. *Calle San José, at the corner of Calle San Francisco, tel. 809/722–2121. Admission free. Open weekdays 8–noon and 1–4:30.*

⑰ On the north side of the plaza is **City Hall,** called the *Alcaldía*. Built between 1604 and 1789, the alcaldía was fashioned after Madrid's city hall, with arcades, towers, balconies, and a lovely inner courtyard. A tourist information center and an art gallery are on the first floor. *Tel. 809/724–7171. Open weekdays 8–4.*

Time Out   **La Bombonera** (259 Calle San Francisco, no phone), established in 1903, is known for its strong Puerto Rican coffee and *Mallorca*—a Spanish pastry made of light dough, toasted, buttered, and sprinkled with powdered sugar.

⑱ Four blocks east on the pedestrian mall of Calle Fortaleza you'll find **Plaza de Colón,** a bustling square with a statue of Christopher Columbus atop a high pedestal. Originally called St. James Square, it was renamed in honor of Columbus on the 400th anniversary of the discovery of Puerto Rico. Bronze plaques in the base of the statue relate various episodes in the life of the great explorer. On the north side of the plaza is a terminal for buses to and from San Juan.

⑲ South of Plaza de Colón is the magnificent **Tapia Theater** (Calle Fortaleza at Plaza de Colón, tel. 809/722–0407), named after the famed Puerto Rican playwright Alejandro Tapia y Riviera. Built in 1832, remodeled in 1949 and again in 1987, the municipal theater is the site of ballets, plays, and operettas. Stop by the box office to see what's showing and if you can get tickets.

⑳ Walk two blocks north from Plaza de Colón to Calle Sol and turn right. Another block will take you to **San Cristóbal,** the 18th-century fortress that guarded the city from land attacks. Even larger than El Morro, San Cristóbal was known as the Gibraltar of the West Indies. *Tel. 809/724–1974. Admission free. Open daily 8–6:15.*

㉑ Stroll from Plaza de Colón down to the **Port,** where the esplanade is spruced up with flowers, trees, and street lamps. Across from Pier 3, where the cruise ships dock, local artisans display their wares at the Plazoleta del Puerto. At the marina, pay 20¢ and board a ferry for a round-trip ride to Catano.

New San Juan You'll need to resort to taxis, buses, públicos, or a rental car to
㉒ reach the points of interest in "new" San Juan.

*Numbers in the margin correspond with points of interest on
the San Juan map.*

Avenida Muñoz Rivera, Avenida Ponce de León, and Avenida
Fernández Juncos are the main thoroughfares that cross
Puerta de Tierra, just east of Old San Juan, to the business and
tourist districts of Santurce, Condado, and Isla Verde.

㉓ In Puerta de Tierra is Puerto Rico's **Capitol,** a white marble
building that dates from the 1920s. The grand rotunda, with
mosaics and friezes, was completed a few years ago. The seat of
the island's bicameral legislature, the Capitol contains Puerto
Rico's Constitution and is flanked by the modern buildings of
the Senate and the House of Representatives. There are spectacular views from the observation plaza on the sea side of the
Capitol. Pick up an informative booklet about the building from
the House Secretariat on the second floor. Guided tours are by
appointment only. *Avenida Ponce de León, tel. 809/721–7305 or
721–7310. Admission free. Open weekdays 8:30–5.*

At the eastern tip of Puerta de Tierra, behind the splashy Cari-
㉔ be Hilton, the tiny **Fort San Jeronimo** is perched over the
Atlantic like an afterthought. Added to San Juan's fortifica-
tions in the late 18th century, the structure barely survived the
British attack of 1797. Restored in 1983 by the Institute of
Puerto Rican Culture, it is now a military museum with dis-
plays of weapons, uniforms, and maps. *Tel. 809/724–5949.
Admission free. Open Wed.–Sun. 9:30–noon and 1:30–4:30.*

Dos Hermanos Bridge connects Puerta de Tierra with Miramar, Condado, and Isla Grande. Isla Grande Airport, from
which you can take short hops, is on the bay side of the bridge.

On the other side of the bridge, the Condado Lagoon is bordered by Avenida Ashford, which threads past the high-rise
Condado hotels and El Centro Convention Center, and
Avenida Baldorioty de Castro, which barrels all the way east to
the airport and beyond. Due south of the lagoon is Miramar,
a primarily residential area with fashionable, turn-of-the-century homes and a cluster of hotels and restaurants.

㉕ **Santurce,** which lies between Miramar on the west and the San
José Lagoon on the east, is a busy mixture of shops, markets,
and offices. Internationally acclaimed performers appear at the
㉖ **Fine Arts Center.** This completely modern facility, the largest
of its kind in the Caribbean, has a full schedule of concerts,
plays, and operas. *Centro de Bellas Artes, corner of De Diego
Ave. and Ponce de León St., tel. 809/724–4751.*

South of Santurce is the "Golden Mile"—Hato Rey, the city's
bustling new financial hub. Isla Verde, with its glittering
beachfront hotels, casinos, discos, and public beach, is to the
east, near the airport.

Time Out **Pescadería Atlántica** (81 Loiza St., tel. 809/726–6654) is a combination seafood restaurant and retail store. Stop in for a cool
drink at the bar and a side dish of calamares, lightly breaded
squid in a hot, spicy sauce.

Northeast of Isla Verde, Boca de Cangrejos sits between the
Atlantic and Torrecilla Lagoon—a great spot for fishing and

San Juan Exploring, Dining & Lodging

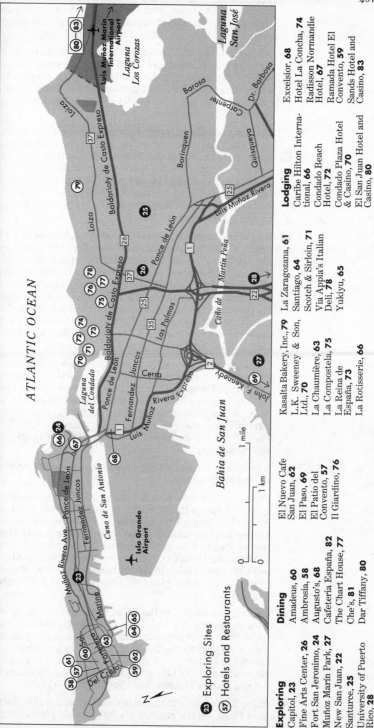

ATLANTIC OCEAN

Luis Muñoz Marín International Airport

Laguna Los Corozas

Laguna San José

Laguna del Condado

Bahía de San Juan

Caño de San Antonio

Isla Grande Airport

● 23 Exploring Sites

○ 57 Hotels and Restaurants

Exploring
Capitol, 23
Fine Arts Center, 26
Fort San Jeronimo, 24
Muñoz Marín Park, 27
New San Juan, 22
Santurce, 25
University of Puerto Rico, 28

Dining
Amadeus, 60
Ambrosia, 58
Augusto's, 68
Cafeteria España, 82
The Chart House, 77
Che's, 81
Dar Tiffany, 80
El Nuevo Cafe San Juan, 62
El Paso, 69
El Patio del Convento, 57
Il Giardino, 76
Kasalta Bakery, Inc, 79
L.K. Sweeney & Son, Ltd, 70
La Chaumière, 63
La Compostela, 75
La Reina de España, 73
La Rotisserie, 66
La Zaragozana, 61
Santiago, 64
Scotch & Sirloin, 71
Via Appia's Italian Deli, 78
Yukiyu, 65

Lodging
Caribe Hilton International, 66
Condado Beach Hotel, 72
Condado Plaza Hotel & Casino, 70
El San Juan Hotel and Casino, 80
Excelsior, 68
Hotel La Concha, 74
Radisson Normandie Hotel, 67
Ramada Hotel El Convento, 59
Sands Hotel and Casino, 83

snorkeling. This is the point of embarkation for the 30-passenger launch, *La Paseadora*, which tours the coast, the mangrove swamp, and the bird sanctuary at Torrecilla Lagoon.

Southeast of Miramar, Avenida Muñoz Rivera skirts along the northern side of **San Juan Central Park,** a convenient place for jogging, tennis, and calisthenics. The mangrove-bordered park was built for the 1979 Pan-American Games. *Cerra St. exit on Rte. 2, tel. 809/722–1646. Admission free. Open Tues.–Sat. 8–10, Mon. 2–10, Sun. 10–6.*

Las Américas Expressway, heading south, goes by Plaza Las Américas, the largest shopping mall in the Caribbean, and
㉗ takes you to the new **Muñoz Marín Park,** an idyllic tree-shaded spot dotted with gardens, lakes, playgrounds, and picnic areas. Cable cars connect the park with the parking area. *Next to Las Américas Expwy., west on Piñero Ave., tel. 809/763–0568. Admission free; parking $1 per vehicle. Open Tues.–Fri., 9–6, weekends 8:30–6; closed Mon.*

㉘ Río Piedras, a southern suburb of San Juan, is home to the **University of Puerto Rico,** located between Ponce de León Avenue and Barbosa Avenue. The university's campus is one of two sites for performances of the Puerto Rico Symphony Orchestra. Theatrical productions and other concerts are also scheduled here throughout the year. The University Museum has permanent archaeological and historical exhibits, and occasionally mounts special art displays. *Next to the university main entrance on Ponce de León Ave., tel. 809/764–0000, ext. 2452 or 2456. Open weekdays 9–9, weekends 9–3.*

The university's main attraction is the **Botanical Garden,** a lush garden with more than 200 species of tropical and subtropical vegetation. Footpaths through the thick forests lead to a graceful lotus lagoon, a bamboo promenade, an orchid garden, and a palm garden. *Intersection of Rtes. 1 and 847 at the entrance to Barrio Venezuela, tel. 809/766–0740. Admission free. Open Tues.–Sun. 9–4:30; when Mon. is a holiday, it is open Mon. and closed Tues.*

San Juan Environs *Numbers in the margin correspond with points of interest on the Puerto Rico map.*

From San Juan, follow Route 2 west toward Bayamón and you'll
㉙ spot the **Caparra Ruins,** where, in 1508, Ponce de León established the island's first settlement. The ruins are that of an ancient fort. Its small **Museum of the Conquest and Colonization of Puerto Rico** contains historical documents, exhibits, and excavated artifacts. (You can see the museum's contents in less time than it takes to say the name.) *Km 6.6 on Rte. 2, tel. 809/781–4795. Admission free. Open weekdays 9–5, weekends and holidays 10–6.*

㉚ Continue on Route 2 to **Bayamón.** In the Central Park, across from Bayamón's city hall, there are some historical buildings and a 1934 sugarcane train that runs through the park (open daily 8 AM–10 PM). On the plaza, in the city's historic district, stands the 18th-century Catholic church of Santa Cruz, and the old neoclassical city hall, which now houses the **Francisco Oller Art and History Museum** (open Tues.–Sat. 9–4).

㉛ Along Route 5 from Bayamón to Catano, you'll see the **Barrilito Rum Plant.** On the grounds is a 200-year-old plantation home and a 150-year-old windmill, which is listed in the National Register of Historic Places.

The **Bacardi Rum Plant,** along the bay, conducts 45-minute tours of the bottling plant, museum, and distillery, which has the capacity to produce 100,000 gallons of rum a day. (Yes, you'll be offered a sample.) *Km 2.6 on Rte. 888, tel. 809/788–1500. Admission free. Tours Mon.–Sat. 9:30–3:30; closed Sun.*

Out on the Island Puerto Rico's 3,500 square miles is a lot of land to explore. While it is possible to get from town to town via *público*, we don't recommend traveling that way unless your Spanish is good and you know exactly where you're going. The public cars stop in each town's main square, leaving you on your own to reach the beaches, restaurants, paradors, and sightseeing attractions. You'll do much better if you rent a car. Most of the island's roads are excellent. However, there is a tangled web of roads through the mountains, and they are not always well marked. Get a good road map.

East and South Our first excursion out on the island will take us east, down the coast to the south, and back up to San Juan. The first leg of the trip—to **Luquillo Beach** and the nearby **El Yunque rain forest**— can easily be done in a day. (There'll be heavy traffic and a crowded beach on weekends, when it seems as if the whole world heads for Luquillo.) The full itinerary will take two to three days, depending upon how long you loll on the beach and linger over the mountain scenery.

To take full advantage of the 28,000-acre El Yunque rain forest, go with a tour. Dozens of trails lead through the thick jungle (it sheltered the Carib Indians for 200 years), and the tour guides take you to the best observation points. Some of the trails are slippery, and there are occasional washouts.

However, if you'd like to drive there yourself, take Route 3 east from San Juan and turn right (south) on Route 191, about 25 miles from the city. The **Sierra Palm Visitor Center** is on Route 191, Km 11.6 (open daily 9:30–5). Nature talks and programs at the center are by appointment only—another good reason to go with a tour group.

El Yunque, named after the good Indian spirit Yuquiyu, is in the Luquillo Mountain Range. The rain forest is verdant with feathery ferns, thick ropelike vines, white tuberoses and ginger, miniature orchids, and some 240 different species of trees. More than 100 billion gallons of rainwater falls on it annually. Rain-battered, wind-ravaged dwarf vegetation clings to the top peaks. (El Toro, the highest peak in the forest, is 3,532 feet.) El Yunque is also a bird sanctuary and is the base of the rare Puerto Rican parrot. Millions of tiny, inch-long tree frogs *(coquis)* can be heard singing (or squawking, depending on your sensibilities). *For further information call the Catalina Field Office, tel. 809/887–2875 or 809/766–5335; or write Caribbean National Forest, Box B, Palmer, PR 00721.*

To reach Luquillo Beach, take Route 191 back to Route 3 and continue east 5 miles to Km 35.4. One of the island's best and most popular beaches, Luquillo was once a flourishing coconut plantation. Coral reefs protect its calm, pristine lagoon, making it an ideal place for a swim. The entrance fee is 25¢, parking is $1, and there are lockers, showers, and changing rooms *(see* Beaches, above).

If you want to continue exploring, get back on Route 3 and
③③ drive 5 miles to **Fajardo,** a major fishing and sailing center with
thousands of boats tied up to its three large marinas. Boats can
be rented or chartered here, and the *Spread Eagle* catamaran
can take you out for a full day of snorkeling, swimming, and
sunning *(see* Participant Sports, below). Fajardo is also the embarkation point for ferries to the offshore islands of Culebra (a
$2.25 fare) and Vieques ($2). Culebra has lovely white-sand
beaches, coral reefs, and a wildlife refuge. In the sleepy town of
③④ **Dewey,** on Culebra's southwestern side, check at the Visitor Information Center at city hall (tel. 809/742–3291) about boat
rentals. On Vieques, Sun Bay public beach has picnic facilities;
Blue Beach is superb for snorkeling; and Mosquito Bay is lumi-
nous even on moonless nights. You can stay overnight at the
government-sponsored Parador Villa Esperanza (tel. 809/741–
8675) on Vieques, which has, among other amenities, its own
marina and fleet of sailing ships.

Resume your ramble on Route 3, heading south past the U.S.
Naval Base and ride through the sugarcane fields to Humacao.
South of Humacao (take Route 906) is the 2,700-acre Palmas del
Mar, the island's largest residential resort complex.

Stay on Route 3 through Yabucoa, tucked up in the hills, and
Maunabo and Patillas, where you can pick up the routes to take
you through the Cayey Mountains. Route 184 north skirts Lake
Patillas and cuts smack through the Carite Forest Reserve.
Stay on Route 184 until it merges with Route 763. Turn left on
Route 763, then right on Route 765 to Route 1, where you'll
shoot northward back to San Juan.

Western Island If you're short of time, drive the 64 miles from San Juan to
Ponce in 90 minutes. Take the Las Américas Expressway,
which cuts through the splendid mountains of Cordillera Central.

If time is not a major problem, take a three- or four-day tour
exploring the western regions of the island. This route covers
Aguadilla, Mayagüez, San Germán, and Ponce. There's much
to see along the way—caves and coves, karst fields and coffee
plantations, mountains and beaches, and even a zoo.

③⑤ Outside Utuado, south of Route 10, is **Caguana Indian Ceremonial Park,** used 800 years ago by the Taino tribes for recreation
and worship. Mountains surround a 13-acre site planted with
royal palms and guava. According to Spanish historians, the
Tainos played a game similar to soccer, and in this park there
are 10 courts bordered by cobbled walkways. There are also
stone monoliths, some with colorful petroglyphs; a small museum; and a souvenir shop. *Rte. 111, Km 12.3. Admission free.
Open daily 8:30–4:30.*

From Utuado, drive west on Route 111 and then north on Route
③⑥ 129 to Km 18.9, where you'll find the **Río Camuy Cave Park,** one
of the world's largest cave networks. Guided tours take you on a
tram down through dense tropical vegetation to the entrance of
the cave, where you continue on foot over underground trails,
ramps, and bridges. The caves, sinkholes, and underground
rivers are all spectacular (the world's second-largest underground river runs through here), but this trip is not for those
with claustrophobia. Be sure to call ahead; the tours allow only
a limited number of people. *Rte. 129, Km 18.9, tel. 809/898–*

3100 or 809/756–5555. Admission: $4 adults, $2.50 children. Open Wed.–Sun. 8–4. Last tour starts at 4.

Route 111 twists from Utuado to **Aguadilla** on the northwest coast. In this area, somewhere between Aguadilla and Añasco, south of Rincón, Columbus dropped anchor on his second voyage in 1493. Both Aguadilla and **Aguada,** a few miles to the south, claim to have been the spot where his foot first hit ground, and both towns have plaques to commemorate the occasion.

Route 115 from Aguadilla to **Rincón** is one of the island's most scenic drives, through rolling hills dotted with pastel-colored houses. Rincón, perched on a hill, overlooks its beach, which was the site of the World Surfing Championship in 1968. Skilled surfers flock to Rincón during the winter, when the water is rough and challenging.

③⑦ Pick up Route 2 for the 6-mile drive to **Mayagüez,** Puerto Rico's third-largest city, with a population approaching 100,000. Mayagüez, known for its needlework, has plenty of shops to browse around in. (The Mayagüez Shopping Mall is one of the island's largest. The lounge of the hilltop Mayagüez Hilton is a popular gathering place for locals and tourists.)

North of town visit the **Mayagüez Zoo,** a 45-acre tropical compound that's home to about 500 animals. In addition to Bengal tigers, reptiles, and birds, including an Andean condor, there's a lake and a children's playground. *Rte. 108 at Barrio Miradero, tel. 809/834–8110. Admission: $1 adults, 50¢ children. Open Tues.–Sun. 9–4:30.*

③⑧ Due south of Mayagüez, via the coastal Route 102, is **Cabo Rojo,** once a pirates' hangout and now a favorite resort area of Puerto Ricans. The area has long stretches of white-sand beaches on the clear, calm Caribbean Sea, as well as many seafood restaurants. There are also several paradores in the region. **Boquerón,** at the end of Route 101, has one of the best beaches on the island, as well as two-room cabins for rent.

⑥① From Cabo Rojo continue east on Route 102 to **San Germán,** a quiet Old World town that's home to the oldest intact church under the U.S. flag. Built in 1606, Porta Coeli (Gates of Heaven) overlooks one of the town's two plazas (where the townspeople continue the Spanish tradition of promenading at night). The church is now a museum of religious art, housing 18th- and 19th-century paintings and statues. *Tel. 809/892–5845. Admission free. Open Wed.–Sun. 8:30–noon and 1–4:30.*

The fishing village of **La Parguera,** an area of simple seafood restaurants, mangrove cays, and small islands, lies south of San Germán at the end of Route 304. This is an excellent scuba-diving area, but the main attraction is **Phosphorescent Bay.**
④⓪ Boats tour the bay, where microscopic dinoflagellates (marine plankton) light up like Christmas trees when disturbed by any kind of movement. The phenomenon can be seen only on moonless nights. Boats leave the pier nightly at 7:30, and the trip costs $4 per person.

From San Germán, Route 2 traverses splendid peaks and valleys; pastel houses cling to the sides of steep green hills. East of Yauco, the road dips and sweeps right along the Caribbean and
④① into **Ponce.**

Puerto Rico's second city, with a population of about 150,000, has much to explore. You have not seen a firehouse until you've seen the red-and-black-striped **Parque de Bombas,** built in 1883 on the city's central plaza, with its bright yellow firetrucks. Stroll around the plaza, with its perfectly pruned trees, graceful fountains, gardens, and park benches. **Our Lady of Guadalupe Cathedral** would surely dominate the square, were it not for the firehouse. The white-columned **Casa Alcaldía** is the city hall, where you can stop in and pick up information.

Recent efforts to restore the city can be appreciated on the streets surrounding the plaza, where freshly painted houses with wrought-iron balconies, gas lamps, Corinthian columns, and Spanish arches may remind you of New Orleans's French Quarter.

Off the Beaten Track

The Blue Dolphin is a hangout where you can rub elbows with some offbeat locals. Located behind the Empress Oceanfront Hotel at the northern tip of Isla Verde, the Blue Dolphin offers one of the best views on the island. While strolling along the Isla Verde beach, just look for the neon blue dolphin on the roof— you can't miss it. *2 Amapola St., Isla Verde, tel. 809/791–3083. Open weekends noon–4 AM, weeknights noon–2 AM.*

What to See and Do with Children

Beaches.
Botanical Garden, University of Puerto Rico, Rio Piedras.
Catano ferry.
El Morro and **San Cristóbal** forts.
El Yunque rain forest.
The **Hyatt Regency Cerromar Beach** and **Hyatt Dorado Beach** offer chaperoned camps for children during the summer, as well as during Christmas and Easter holidays.
Mayagüez Zoo, Mayagüez.
Muñoz Marín Park. San Juan.
Río Camuy Caves, near Utuado.
Trolleys, Old San Juan.
Villa Coqui Wet N'Slide, A recreational park with pools, water slides, paddle boats, and canoes. *Rte. 763, Km 6, Caqua, tel. 809/747–4747. Open weekends and holidays 9 AM–5 PM.*

Participant Sports

Bicycling   The broad beach at Boquerón makes for easy wheeling. You can rent bikes at **Boquerón Balnearios** (Rte. 101, Boquerón, Dept. of Recreation and Sports, tel. 809/722–1551). In the Dorado area on the north coast, bikes can be rented at the **Hyatt Regency Cerromar Beach Hotel** (tel. 809/796–1234) or the **Hyatt Dorado Beach Hotel** (tel. 809/796–1234).

Boating   Virtually all the resort hotels on San Juan's Condado and Isla Verda strips rent paddleboats, Sunfish, Windsurfers, and the like. Contact **Condado Plaza Hotel Watersports Center** (tel. 809/721–1000, ext. 1361), **Caribbean School of Aquatics** (La Concha Hotel, Ashford Ave., Condado, tel. 809/723–4740), or **Castillo Watersports** (ESJ Towers, Isla Verde, tel. 809/791–6195). Sailing and boat rentals are also available at **Playita Boat Rental** (1010 Ashford Ave., Condado, tel. 809/722–1607). The 600-passenger **Reina de la Bahia** (tel. 809/721–6700) departs from the waterfront in Old San Juan for sightseeing, lunch, dinner, and disco excursions.

Fishing Half-day, full-day, split charters, and big- and small-game fishing can be arranged through **Benitez Deep-Sea Fishing** (Club Náutico de San Juan, Stop 9½, Fernández Juncos Ave., Miramar, tel. 809/723–2292), **Castillo Watersports** (ESJ Towers, Isla Verde, tel. 809/791–6195), and **San Juan Fishing Charters** (Stop 10, Fernández Juncos Ave., Miramar, tel. 809/723–0415).

Golf There are two 18-hole courses at **Hyatt Dorado Beach Hotel** (Dorado, tel. 809/796–1234, ext. 3238) and two 18-hole courses at the **Hyatt Regency Cerromar Beach Hotel** (Dorado, tel. 809/796–1234, ext. 3013). You'll also find 18-hole courses at **Palmas del Mar Resort** (Humacao, tel. 809/852–6000, ext. 54), **Club Ríomar** (Río Grande, tel. 809/887–3964), and **Punta Borinquén** (Aguadilla, tel. 809/890–2987).

Hiking Dozens of trails lace through **El Yunque** (information is available at the Sierra Palm Visitor Center, Rte. 191, Km 11.6). You can also hit the trails in **Río Abajo Forest** (south of Arecibo) and **Toro Negro Forest** (east of Adjuntas). Each reserve has a ranger station.

Horseback Riding Beach-trail rides can be arranged at **Palmas del Mar Equestrian Center** (Palmas del Mar Resort, Humacao, tel. 809/852–4785). Take to the rain-forest foothills trails, as well as the beaches, through **Hacienda Carabali** (tel. 809/793–8585).

Sailing Sailing instruction and trips are offered by **Palmas Sailing Center** (Palmas del Mar Resort, Humacao, tel. 809/852–6000, ext. 10310), **Calypso Watersports** (Sands Hotel, San Juan, tel. 809/791–6100), **Caribbean School of Aquatics** (La Concha Hotel, Ashford Ave., Condado, tel. 809/723–4740), **Caribe Aquatic Adventure** (Caribe Hilton Hotel, Puerta de Tierra, tel. 809/765–7444, ext. 3447), and **Castillo Watersports** (ESJ Towers, Isla Verde, tel. 809/791–6195).

Snorkeling and Scuba Diving Snorkeling and scuba-diving instruction and equipment rentals are available at **Caribbean School of Aquatics** and **Calypso Watersports** *(see* Sailing, above), **Coral Head Divers** (Marina de Palmas, Palmas del Mar Resort, Humacao, tel. 809/850–7208), **Cueva Submarina Training Center** (Plaza Cooperativa, Isabela, tel. 809/872–3903), **Caribe Aquatic Adventure** *(see* Sailing, above), **Castillo Watersports** *(see* Sailing, above), **Jack Becker's Spread Eagle** (Villa Marina Yacht Harbor, Fajardo, tel. 809/863–1905), and **Parguera Divers Training Center** (Lajas, tel. 809/899–4171).

Tennis There are 17 lighted courts at **San Juan Central Park** (Cerra St. exit on Rte. 2, tel. 809/722–1646), 6 lighted courts at the **Caribe Hilton Hotel** (Puerta de Tierra, tel. 809/721–0303, ext. 1730), 8 courts, 4 lighted, at **Carib Inn** (Isla Verde, tel. 809/791–3535, ext. 6), and 2 lighted courts at the **Condado Plaza Hotel** (Condado, tel. 809/721–1000, ext. 1775). Out on the island, there are 14 courts, 2 lighted, at **Hyatt Regency Cerromar Beach Hotel** (Dorado, tel. 809/796–1234, ext. 3040), 7 courts at the **Hyatt Dorado Beach Hotel** (Dorado, tel. 809/796–1234, ext. 3220), 20 courts, 2 lighted, at **Palmas del Mar Resort** (Humacao, tel. 809/852–6000, ext. 51), 3 lighted courts at the **Mayagüez Hilton Hotel** (Mayagüez, tel. 809/831–7575, ext. 2150), and 4 lighted courts at **Punta Borinquén** (Aguadilla, tel. 809/891–8778).

Windsurfing   Windsurfing rentals are available at **Caribbean School of Aquatics, Castillo Watersports, Palmas Sailing Center, Playita Boat Rental** (*see* Sailing, and Boating, above, for all information) and at **Lisa Penfield Windsurfing Center** (El San Juan Hotel, tel. 809/726–7274).

Spectator Sports

Cockfighting   It's the national sport of Puerto Rico, but it's not for the faint of heart. If you're curious about cockfights, head for **Club Gallístico.** *Rte. 37, Km 1.5, Isla Verde, tel. 809/791–6005. Open Sat. 1–7.*

Horse Racing   Races are run year-round at **El Comandante Racetrack.** On race days the dining rooms open at 12:30 PM. *Rte. 3, Km 15.3, Canovanas, tel. 809/724–6060. Open Wed., Fri., Sun., and holidays.*

Baseball   If you have a post–World Series letdown, you can fly down to the island, where the season runs October–April. Many major-league ballplayers in the United States made their start in Puerto Rico's baseball league and some return home in the off-season to hone their skills. Stadiums are in San Juan, Santurce, Ponce, Caguas, Arecibo, and Mayagüez. Contact the Tourist Office for details or call **Professional Baseball of Pureto Rico** (tel. 809/765–6285).

Shopping

San Juan is not a free port, and you won't find bargains on electronics and perfumes. You can, however, find excellent bargains in china, crystal, fashions, and jewelry.

Shopping for native crafts can be great fun. You'll run across a lot of tacky things you can live your whole life without, but you can also find some treasures, and in many cases you'll be able to watch the artisans at work. (For guidance, contact the Tourism Artisan Center, tel. 809/721–2400, ext. 248.)

The work of some Puerto Rican artists has brought them international acclaim: The paintings of Francisco Oller hang in the Louvre, and the portraits of Francisco Rodon are in the permanent collections of New York's Museum of Modern Art and the Metropolitan Museum. Look for their works, and those of other native artists, in San Juan's stylish galleries.

Popular souvenirs and gifts include *santos* (small, hand-carved figures of saints or religious scenes), hand-rolled cigars, handmade lace, carnival masks, and fancy men's shirts called *guayaberas.* Also, some folks swear that Puerto Rican rum is the best in the world.

Shopping Districts   **Old San Juan** is full of shops, especially on Cristo, Fortaleza, and San Francisco streets. The **Las Américas Plaza** south of San Juan is the largest shopping mall in the Caribbean, with 200 shops, restaurants, and movie theaters. Other malls out on the island include **Plaza del Carmen** in Caguas and the **Mayagüez Mall.**

Good Buys   You can get 30%–50% discounts on Hathaway shirts and cloth-
Clothing   ing by Christian Dior at **Hathaway Factory Outlet** (203 Cristo

St., tel. 809/723–8946); 40% reductions on men's, women's, and children's raincoats at the **London Fog Factory Outlet** (156 Cristo St., tel. 809/722–4334).

Jewelry There is gold, gold, and more gold at **Reinhold** (201 Cristo St., tel. 809/725–6878) and brand-name watches at **The Watch and Gem Palace** (204 San José, Old San Juan, tel. 809/722–2136.

Native Crafts For one-of-a-kind buys, head for **Puerto Rican Arts & Crafts** (204 Fortaleza St., Old San Juan, tel. 809/725–5596), **Plazoleta del Puerto** (marina, Old San Juan, tel. 809/725–3053), and **Don Roberto** (205 Cristo St., tel. 809/724–0194).

Paintings and Sculptures Popular galleries are **Galería Palomas** (207 Cristo St., Old San Juan, tel. 809/724–8904) and **Galería Botello** (208 Cristo St., Old San Juan, tel. 809/723–9987, and Plaza Las Américas, tel. 809/767–1525).

Dining

by Susan Fairbanks

A graduate of Cordon Bleu and Cornell Hotel School, Susan Fairbanks runs a food and beverage consulting business. She also teaches wine courses in Puerto Rico.

Over the past 10 years, phone book listings of restaurants in Puerto Rico have grown from 4 to 14 pages. As a result, there are many new places to try, many off the heavily beaten tourist's path. Whether you're dining at a fine restaurant or picking up fast food in a mall (be sure to visit the one in Plaza Las Américas to see the action), you'll find that every place is extremely busy at lunchtime. Dinner is more relaxed and leisurely, with dress casual to casually elegant; few establishments require a jacket.

On weekends it's common to see Puerto Rican families in their cars sightseeing in the hilly interior of the island and stopping for a late lunch on a beach or back up in the mountains. Visitors should do as the locals do and go out on the island for at least one meal. The drive is a curvy green adventure that is well worth the trip.

One unique aspect of Puerto Rican cooking is its generous use of local vegetables. Local vegetables include plantains cooked a hundred different ways: fried green, *tostones;* baked ripe, *amarillos;* and fried, plantain chips. Rice and beans with tostones or amarillos on the side are basic accompaniments to every dish. Locals cook white rice with *achiote* (annatto seeds) or saffron, brown rice with *gandules* (pigeon peas), and black rice with *frijoles* (black beans). Chickpeas and white beans are served in many daily specials. A wide assortment of yams are served baked, fried, stuffed, boiled, smashed, and whole. *Sofrito*—a garlic, onion, sweet pepper, coriander, oregano, and tomato puree—is used as a base for practically everything.

Beef, chicken, pork, and seafood are all rubbed with *adobo,* a garlic-oregano marinade, before cooking. *Arroz con pollo* (chicken stew), *sancocho* (beef and tuber soup), *asopao* (a soupy rice with chicken or seafood), *empanada* (breaded cutlet), and *encebollado* (steak smothered in onions) are all typical plates.

Fritters, also popular, are served in snack places along the highways as well as at cocktail parties. Assorted fritters include *empanadillas* (stuffed fried turnovers), *surrullitos* (cheese-stuffed corn sticks), *alcapurrias* (stuffed green banana croquettes), and *bacalaitos* (codfish fritters).

Local *pan de agua* is an excellent French loaf bread, best hot out of the oven. It is also good toasted and should be tried in the *Cubano* sandwich (made with roast pork, ham, Swiss cheese, pickles, and mustard).

Local desserts include flans, puddings, and fruit pastes served with native white cheese. Home-grown mangoes and papayas are sweet, and *pan de azucar* (sugar bread) pineapples make the best juice on the market. Fresh *parcha* juice (passionfruit), fresh *guarapo* juice (sugarcane), and fresh *guanabana* juice (a sweet juice similar to papaya) are also sold cold from trucks along the highway.

The best frozen piña coladas are served at the Caribe Hilton Hotel and Dorado Beach Hotel. Rum can be mixed with cola, soda, tonic, juices, water, served on the rocks, or even up. Puerto Rican rums range from light white mixers to dark, aged sipping liqueurs. Look for Bacardi, Don Q, Ron Rico, Palo Viejo, and Barillito. Puerto Rican coffee is excellent served espresso-black or generously cut *con leche* (with hot milk).

The most highly recommended restaurants are indicated by a star ★.

Category	Cost*
Very Expensive	over $50
Expensive	$25–$50
Moderate	$15–$25
Inexpensive	under $15

per person, excluding drinks and service

Old San Juan

★ **La Chaumière.** Reminiscent of an inn in the French provinces, this intimate yet bright white restaurant serves a respected onion soup, oysters Rockefeller, rack of lamb, and veal Oscar in addition to daily specials. *367 Tetuan St., tel. 809/722–3330. Reservations advised. AE, DC, MC. Closed Sun. Very Expensive.*

La Rotisserie. A bright peach room at its best for Tuesday and Thursday power lunches. Unfortunately, both the food and the service here are uninspired. Flambée specialties include steak Diane and *el pescador* (rice and seafood). The menu also includes Caesar salad, roast duck, and a selection of fresh seafood. *Caribe Hilton, Puerto de Tierra, tel. 809/721–0303. Jacket required. Reservations required. AE, CB, DC, MC, V. Very Expensive.*

Santiago. A very rosy and romantic restaurant featuring nouvelle Caribbean cuisine such as grouper-salmon terrine, pumpkin-tanier-plantain soup, and fresh fish in passionfruit sauce. *313 Recinto Sur., tel. 809/723–5369. Reservations recommended on weekends. AE, MC, V. Closed Sun. Very Expensive.*

La Zaragozana. One of the oldest restaurants around, this adobe hacienda re-creates an old Spanish atmosphere especially for tourists. The ambience is pleasant, with strolling musicians, murals, and vaulted archways. The food and service are tired, though. The menu offers the usual black-bean soup, steaks, lobster, paella, and flan. *356 San Francisco St., tel.*

809/723–5103. Reservations advised. AE, CB, DC, MC, V. Expensive.

★ **Yukiyu.** This is a new restaurant serving sushi, sashimi, and Japanese-inspired specials. The soft-shell crab, shrimp and vegetable tempura, tuna teriyaki, and cod steamed with ginger-and-orange béarnaise are all recommended. *311 Recinto Sur., tel. 809/721–0653. Reservations advised for lunch. AE, MC, V. Closed Sun. and Mon. Expensive.*

★ **Amadeus.** Featuring nouvelle Caribbean food, the atmosphere is sleek Old San Juan with a menu of 20 changing appetizers including tostones with sour cream and caviar, marlin ceviche, and crabmeat tacos. Entrées range from grilled dolphin with coriander butter to chicken lasagna and tuna or egg salad sandwich. Sit in the front room to be seen with beautiful people. *106 San Sebastian St., tel. 809/722–8635, or 809/721–6720. Reservations required. Closed Mon. AE, MC, V. Moderate.*

El Patio del Convento. Since the inner patio was covered with a plastic bubble, El Convento has lost its charm by spoiling the original architecture. The buffet lunch is a cattle train of cruise-ship tourists. The piña coladas are watery. The place is depressing. *100 Cristo St., tel. 809/723–9020. AE, MC, V. Moderate.*

Ambrosia. At the bottom of Cristo Street, the bar serves fresh, frozen fruit drinks while the menu features pastas, veal, and chicken. The daily lunch specials usually include quiche and lasagna served with large mixed salads for good value. *205 Cristo St., tel. 809/722–5206. AE, MC, V. Inexpensive.*

El Nuevo Cafe de San Juan. This café, which features a deli atmosphere, is good for sandwiches and grilled sausages. *152 Cruz St., tel. 809/725–5886. AE, MC, V. Inexpensive.*

San Juan

★ **Dar Tiffany.** This restaurant, just off the lobby of the glittering El San Juan Hotel, is a posh place with palm fronds etched in glass, voluptuous greenery and, yes, Tiffany lamps. Knock back a two-fisted martini from the bar before tackling superb aged prime rib, Maine lobster, or fresh Norwegian salmon. *El San Juan Hotel, Isla Verde., tel. 809/791–7272. Dress: Jackets suggested. Reservations suggested. AE, CB, DC, MC, V. Very Expensive.*

★ **La Compostela.** Contemporary Spanish food and a serious 9,000-bottle wine cellar are the draws to La Compostela. Specialties include mushroom pâté and Port *pastelillo* (meat-filled pastries), grouper fillet with scallops in salsa verde, roast lamb, and paella. This is a favorite restaurant with the local dining elite, and it is honored yearly in local competitions. *106 Condado Ave., tel. 809/724–6088. Reservations suggested. AE, CB, DC, MC, V. Very Expensive.*

La Reina de España. Step into a soft sea-green dining room serving imaginative Castillian cuisine. Chef-owner Jesus Ramiro has just published a new cookbook on Castillian cooking and each of his dishes is artfully arranged and decorated. Specialties include flower-shape peppers filled with fish mousse, a seafood fantasy caught under a vegetable net, roast duckling with sugarcane honey, and a kiwi dessert arranged to resemble twin palms. *1106 Magdalena Ave., tel. 809/721–9049. Reservations suggested. AE, MC, V. Very Expensive.*

Augusto's. Chef-owner August Schriener and his wife Claudia run an elegantly comfortable restaurant featuring classic cooking. Menus change weekly. Specialties include salmon baked in filo, lamb tenderloin with pepper-vodka fettuccine, and veal medallions with smoked mozzarella. The walls are hung with changing watercolor shows. *Excelsior Hotel, Miramar, tel. 809/725–7700. Reservations suggested. AE, MC, V. Expensive.*

The Chart House. Set in a restored Ashford mansion laced with graceful tropical verandas perfect for cocktails, the bar offers good drinks to a lively mix of people. Open-air dining rooms are upstairs, set at different levels. The menu includes prime rib, shrimp teriyaki, Hawaiian chicken, and the signature dessert: mud pie. *1214 Ashford Ave., tel. 809/728–0110. Reservations required. AE, CB, DC, MC, V. Expensive.*

★ **Il Giardino.** Overlooking Condado from atop the Dutch Inn, this roof-garden restaurant's Italian food and attentive service get rave reviews from the locals. Fresh pasta, a selection of veal dishes, and good wines make a moderate meal a pleasure. All ladies leave with a long-stemmed rose from maitre d'/owner Silverio Díaz. *Dutch Inn, 55 Condado Ave., tel. 809/722–1822. AE, MC, V. Expensive.*

L. K. Sweeney & Son Ltd. Brothers Larry and Tim Sweeney have opened a comfortable, casual, and Continental restaurant that overlooks the lagoon lights at night. You have your choice of live Maine or Caribbean lobster, beluga caviar, Norwegian salmon, and Florida stone crab. Thursdays feature a clambake (reservations are a must!). *Condado Plaza Hotel and Casino, 999 Ashford Ave., tel. 809/722–7977. AE, DC, MC, V. Expensive.*

Che's. The most established and casual of three Argentinian restaurants within a few blocks of each other, Che's features juicy churrasco steaks, lemon chicken, and grilled sweetbreads. The hamburgers are huge and the french fries are fresh. The Chilean and Argentinian wine list is also decent. *35 Caoba St., Punta Las Marias, tel. 809/726–7202. AE, CB, DC, MC, V. Moderate.*

★ **Scotch & Sirloin.** Tucked back among the tropical overgrowth overlooking the lagoon, the Scotch & Sirloin has been San Juan's most consistently fine steakhouse. Aquariums light up the bar and the fresh salad bar serves moist banana bread. Steaks are aged in-house and cooked precisely to order. *La Rada Hotel, 1020 Ashford Ave., Condado, tel. 809/722–3640. Reservations required. AE, DC, MC, V. Moderate.*

Cafeteria España. This is a busy Spanish cafeteria serving strong coffee, assorted croquettes, toasted sandwiches, soups, and a large selection of pastries. Spanish candies, canned goods, and other gourmet items for sale are packed into floor-to-ceiling shelves for a cozy, full feeling. *Centro Commercial Villamar, Baldorioty de Castro Marginal, Isla Verde, tel. 809/727–4517. No credit cards. Inexpensive.*

El Paso. Another family-run restaurant serving genuine criollo food seasoned for a local following. Specialties include asopao, pork chops, and breaded empanadas. Daily specials include tripe on Saturday and arroz con pollo on Sunday. *405 De Diego Ave., Puerto Nuevo, tel. 809/781–3399. AE, CB, DC, MC, V. Inexpensive.*

★ **Kasalta Bakery, Inc.** Walk up to the counter and order an assortment of sandwiches, cold drinks, strong café con leche, and pastries. Try the Cubano sandwich. There are plenty of stools for sitting, reading, or just looking out the window. *1966 McLeary St., Ocean Park, tel. 809/727–7340. No credit cards. Inexpensive.*

Via Appia's Italian Deli. The only true sidewalk café in San Juan serves pizzas, sandwiches, cold beer, and pitchers of sangria. It is a good place to people-watch and get something easy to eat. *1350 Ashford Ave., Condado, tel. 809/725–8711. AE, MC, V. Inexpensive.*

Out on the Island

The Horned Dorset Primavera. Lunch, served in a comfortable wicker room, is casual and à la carte. A fixed-price gourmet dinner is served in the upstairs dining room. Enjoy luxurious tropical architecture at its best as you feast on both food and ocean view. No children under age 12 are allowed. *Rte. 429, Km 3, Rincón, tel. 809/823–4030. Reservations required. AE, MC, V. Expensive.*

La Rotisserie. An institution in Mayagüez, this fine dining room offers the best value for the money in town with its lavish breakfast and lunch buffets. The restaurant is known for grilled steaks and fresh seafood. A different food festival is featured Wednesday through Friday: Wednesday, Italian; Thursday, Latin American; and Friday, seafood. *Hwy. 2, Km 152.5, Mayagüez, tel. 809/721–0303. Reservations suggested. AE, CB, DC, MC, V. Moderate–Expensive.*

★ **El Batey de Tonita.** Set up in the mountains for dining in the cool country air, this restaurant serves local *criollo* cooking with unique specials such as guinea hen fricassee, rabbit in garlic sauce, and crispy "aranita" plantains. *Rte. 7737, Km 2.1, Cayey, tel. 809/745–6312. MC, V. Moderate.*

The Black Eagle. Literally on the water's edge, you dine outside on the restaurant's veranda listening to the lapping waves under the stars. Specialties of the house include breaded conch fritters, fresh fish of the day, lobster, and prime meats that are imported by the owner. *Hwy. 413, Km 1, Barrio Ensenada, Rincón, tel. 809/823–3510. AE, MC, V. Moderate.*

★ **Goñzalez Seafood.** Nobody in Puerto Rico makes better crunchy tostones than Rosa Goñzalez. House specialties include fresh shark fillet in wine sauce, *mofongo* plantain stuffed with seafood, shrimps as big as lobsters, and grilled porterhouse steaks. *Hwy. 102, Km 9.8, Joyuda, Cabo Rojos, tel. 809/851–9000. AE, CB, DC, MC, V. Moderate.*

Sand and the Sea. Looking down onto Guayama and out across the sea, this mountain cottage is a retreat into Caribbean living with Kentucky host Hal Hester cooking, playing piano, and singing up a storm. The menu leans toward steaks and barbecues with a good carrot vichyssoise and excellent baked beans. Bring a sweater—it cools down to 50°F at night. *Hwy. 715, Km 5.2, Cayey, tel. 809/745–6317. AE, CB, DC, MC, V. Moderate.*

Lodging

Accommodations on Puerto Rico come in all shapes and sizes. Self-contained luxury resorts cover hundreds of acres. San Juan's high-rise beachfront hotels likewise cater to the epicurean; several target the business traveler. Out on the island, the government-sponsored paradors are country inns modeled after Spain's paradors. They are required to meet certain standards, such as proximity to a sightseeing attraction or beach and a kitchen serving native cuisine. (Parador prices range from $35 to $76 for a double room. Reservations for all paradores can be made by calling 800/443–0266 or 809/721–2884 in Puerto Rico.)

The most highly recommended lodgings are indicated by a star ★.

Category	Cost*
Very Expensive	over $200
Expensive	$125–$200
Moderate	$50–$125
Inexpensive	under $50

All prices are for a standard double room for two, excluding 6% tax and a 10% service charge.

San Juan

★ **Caribe Hilton International.** Built in 1949, this superb property occupies 17 acres on Puerta de Tierra and has been further enhanced by a $25 million face-lift in 1988. The spacious lobby is decorated with rose-color marble, waterfalls, and lavish tropical plants. The hotel boasts San Juan's only private, palm-fringed swimming cove. The airy guest rooms have balconies with ocean or lagoon views. The eighth and ninth floors provide VIP treatment. *Box 1872, 00903, tel. 809/721–0303 or 800/445–8667. 636 rooms, including 31 suites. Facilities: private beach, 2 pools, 6 lighted tennis courts, health club, 4 restaurants, disco, outdoor Jacuzzi, executive business center. AE, CB, DC, MC, V. Very Expensive.*

★ **El San Juan Hotel and Casino.** An immense chandelier shines over the hand-carved wood paneling and rose-color marble of the lobby in this sprawling 22-acre resort on the Isla Verde beach. You'll be hard pressed to decide if you want a spa suite in the main tower with whirlpool and wet bar; a garden lanai room, with private patio and spa; or a custom-designed casita with sunken Roman bath. (Some of the tower rooms have no view; your best bet is an oceanside lanai, with or without spa.) In any case, all rooms are air-conditioned, with three phones, remote-control TVs with VCRs, hair dryers, minibars, and many other amenities. *Box 2872, Isla Verde, 00902, tel. 809/791–1000 or 800/468–2818. 392 rooms. Facilities: pool, children's pool, 4 restaurants, 5 cocktail lounges, supper club, disco, casino, 3 lighted tennis courts with pro shop, activity center, water-sports center, shopping arcade, health club, non-smoking floor, facilities for handicapped, complimentary shuttle bus to Condado Plaza Hotel, courtyard Jacuzzi, concierge, valet parking. AE, CB, DC, MC, V. Very Expensive.*

Hotel La Concha. Looking like a large pink seashell, the hotel has individually air-conditioned rooms, all facing the ocean, furnished in contemporary tropical decor. In the main building and the 12 poolside cabanas there are 18 junior suites and 17 one- or two-bedroom corner suites. The VIP suites are on the top three floors. The ritzy Club Mykonos disco is perched right over the water. *Box 4195, 00905, tel. 809/721–6090 or 800/468–2822. 234 oceanfront rooms. Facilities: activity center, water-sports center, volleyball court on the beach, pool, poolside bar, 2 restaurants and lounges, disco, facilities for the handicapped, shopping arcade. AE, CB, DC, MC, V. Expensive.*

★ **Condado Beach Hotel.** Built in 1919 by Cornelius Vanderbilt, the hotel has a pale-pink lobby adorned with bouquets of flowers, a sweeping double staircase, and Victorian furnishings. Guest rooms, each decorated in the Spanish colonial style of the 1920s, have either an ocean, lagoon, or city view. The Vanderbilt Club floors, accessed by private elevator, provide all manner of pampering. *Box 41266, Minillas Station, 00940, tel. 809/721–6090 or 800/468–2775. 245 rooms, including 18 junior* *suites and 2 1- and 2-bedroom suites. Facilities: cable TV, 3rd-level pool, 2 restaurants and lounges, facilities for the handi-capped, water-sports center. AE, MC, V. Expensive.*

Condado Plaza Hotel and Casino. Nestled between the Atlantic Ocean and the Condado Lagoon, this stunning resort is two ho-tels in one, with a Lagoon Wing and an Ocean Wing. Standard rooms have walk-in closets, separate dressing areas, and amen-ity packages. There are a variety of suites (including spa suites with whirlpools) and a fully equipped executive service center. If that isn't posh enough, you can check into the Plaza Club, which has 24-hour concierge service and a dazzling display of pleasantries. The hotel's Isadora's Disco is a very hot night-club. *999 Ashford Ave., 00907, tel. 809/721–1000 or 800/468–8588. 585 rooms and suites. Facilities: 4 pools (1 saltwater), ca-sino, disco, 2 lighted tennis courts, 5 restaurants, 7 bars and lounges; fitness, water-sports, and business centers. AE, CB, DC, MC, V. Expensive.*

★ **Sands Hotel and Casino.** Puerto Rico's largest casino glitters just off the lobby, and a huge free-form pool lies between the hotel and its beach. The air-conditioned hotel has rooms with private balconies (ask for one with an ocean view), minibars, and many frills. The exclusive Plaza Club section offers a mas-seuse, private spas, and other enticements. Like its Atlantic City sister, the Sands books top entertainers—the Club Calyp-so is the top-name night spot here. *Isla Verde Rd. 187, Box 6676 Loiza Sta., Santurce 00914, tel. 809/791–6100 or 800/443–2009. 420 rooms. Facilities: pool, 4 restaurants, lounge, casi-no, disco, concierge, 24-hr room service, facilities for handi-capped, nightclub, water-sports center, business center, valet parking. AE, CB, DC, MC, V. Expensive.*

Radisson Normandie. Built in 1939 in the shape of the fabled ocean liner of the same name, this oceanfront hotel reopened in late 1988 under the Radisson banner. It's a national historic landmark, done up in Art Deco style, and each room comes with sunroom, minibar, and cable TV. Additional frills and pamper-ing can be found on the ritzy Club Normandie floor. *Box 50059, 00902, tel. 809/729–2929 or 800/333–3333. 180 air-conditioned rooms. Facilities: outdoor pool, 2 restaurants, lounge, ice-cream parlor, business center, health club, water-sports cen-ter. AE, MC, V. Expensive.*

★ **Excelsior.** Recently spruced up with English carpets in the cor-ridors and new sculptures in the lobby, this hotel is home to the estimable, award-winning Ali-Oli restaurant, which also oper-ates the new poolside El Gazebo restaurant. Each room has a private bath with phone and hair dryer. Complimentary coffee, newspaper, and shoeshine each morning. *801 Ponce de León Ave., 00907, tel. 809/721–7400, 800/223–9815 in U.S. or 800/468–0023 in Canada. 140 rooms, 60 with kitchenettes. Facili-ties: pool, cocktail lounge, 2 restaurants, free parking and free transportation to the beach. AE, MC, V. Moderate.*

Old San Juan **Ramada Hotel El Convento.** Puerto Rico's most famous hotel, ★ on Calle Cristo right across from the San Juan Cathedral. The pink stucco building, with its dark wood paneling and arcades, was a Carmelite convent in the 17th century. All of the rooms are air-conditioned, with twin beds and wall-to-wall carpeting. Fourteen rooms have balconies (ask for one with a view of the bay). This is a very romantic hotel and an architectural master-piece. *100 Cristo St., 00902, tel. 809/723–9020 or 800/468–2779.*

94 rooms. Facilities: pool, 2 restaurants and bar, free transport to beach. AE, CB, DC, MC, V. Moderate–Expensive.

Out on the Island
Cabo Rojos

Parador Boquemer. Located on Route 101 near the beach in a small, unpretentious fishing village, this parador has air-conditioned rooms, all with minifridges and private baths. *Box 133, 00622, tel. 809/851–2158. 64 rooms. Facilities: pool, restaurant. AE, CB, DC, MC, V. Inexpensive.*

Coamo

Parador Baños de Coamo. On Route 546, Km 1, northeast of Ponce, this mountain inn is located at the hot sulfur springs that are said to be the Fountain of Youth of Ponce de León's dreams. The springs were known to the earliest Taino Indians, as well as to Franklin D. Roosevelt, Thomas Edison, Alexander Graham Bell, and Frank Lloyd Wright. *Box 540, 00640, tel. 809/825–2186. 48 rooms. Facilities: pool, restaurant, lounge. AE, CB, DC, MC, V. Moderate.*

Dorado

Hyatt Regency Cerromar Beach. Located 22 miles west of San Juan at Route 693, Km 11.8, smack on the Atlantic, the Cerromar not only has a lovely reef-protected beach, it also claims that its $3 million river pool—with 14 waterfalls, an underwater Jacuzzi, grottoes, and all manner of flumes—is the world's longest freshwater pool. The completely modern seven-story hotel, done up in tropical style, has tile floors, marble baths, air-conditioning, and rooms with a king-size or two double beds. (You'll find somewhat quieter rooms on the west side, away from the pool activity.) Guests at the Cerromar and its sister facility, the Hyatt Dorado Beach a mile down the road, have access to facilities of both resorts, and colorful red trolleys (free, of course) make frequent runs between the two. *Dorado 00646, tel. 809/796–1234 or 800/228–9000. 508 rooms. Facilities: airport limo, casino, disco, 4 restaurants, 3 bars, 2 18-hole Robert Trent Jones golf courses, 14 tennis courts (2 lighted), pool, sauna, horseback riding, bike rentals, jogging and hiking trails, airport for private planes. AE, CB, DC, MC, V. Very Expensive.*

★ **Hyatt Dorado Beach.** The ambience is a bit more subdued and family-oriented at the Cerromar's sophisticated sister, where a variety of elegant accommodations are in low-rise buildings scattered over 1,000 lavishly landscaped acres. Most rooms have private patios or balconies, and all have polished terra-cotta floors, marble baths, air-conditioning, and many frills. Upper-level rooms in the Oceanview Houses have handsome king-size bamboo four-poster beds, in addition to a view of the two half-moon beaches. *Dorado 00646, tel. 809/796–1234 or 800/228–9000. 300 rooms. Facilities: 2 18-hole Robert Trent Jones golf courses, 7 tennis courts, horse-drawn carriage rides, horseback riding, hiking and jogging trails, 2 pools, wading pool, casino, 3 restaurants, 2 lounges, water-sports center, airport for private planes. AE, CB, DC, MC, V. Very Expensive.*

★ **Palmas del Mar.** This is an already luxurious but still developing resort community, on 2,700 acres of a former coconut plantation on the sheltered southeast coast (about an hour's drive from San Juan). In addition to private homes, town houses, condominiums, and villas, there are two hotels (the Palmas Inn and the Candelero), and the Ritz-Carlton plans to open a 75-room hotel in March 1991. A number of other multimillion-dollar projects are in the planning stage. *Box 2020, Rte. 906, Humacao 00661, tel. 809/852–6000, 800/221–4874, or in NY, 212/983–0393. 102 rooms, 85 villas, 1-, 2-, and*

3-bedroom suites. Facilities: beach, 18-hole Gary Player golf course, 20 tennis courts (4 lighted), casino, equestrian center, 6 pools, 6 restaurants, bike rentals, fitness center, watersports center. AE, CB, DC, MC, V. Very Expensive.

Jayuya **Parador Hacienda Gripinas.** It's a bit difficult to look for on
★ winding mountain roads, but in due time you'll find this treasure: a white hacienda with polished wood, beam ceilings, a spacious lounge with rocking chairs, and splendid gardens. The large airy rooms are decorated with native crafts—a very romantic hideaway. *Rte. 527, Km 2.5, Box 387, 00664, tel. 809/ 828–1717. 19 rooms. Facilities: restaurant, lounge, pool, hiking and horseback-riding trails. MC, V. Inexpensive.*

La Parguera **Parador Villa Parguera.** This parador is a stylish modern place on Phosphorescent Bay, with large colorfully decorated air-conditioned rooms. A spacious dining room, overlooking the swimming pool and the bay beyond, serves excellent native and international dishes. *Rte. 304, Box 273, Lajas 00667, tel. 809/ 899–3975. 50 rooms. Facilities: saltwater pool, restaurant, lounge, facilities for handicapped. AE, CB, DC, MC. Moderate.*

Mayagüez **Hilton International Mayagüez.** Built on 20 acres overlooking the Mayagüez Harbor, this resort on the island's west coast is about a 2½-hour drive from San Juan. All the rooms have a view of the sea. A recent $6 million renovation resulted in completely redecorated rooms, a new casino, and two executive floors. The hotel is 2 miles from the town of Mayagüez. Also close by are the Boquerón swimming beach, Punta Higuero surfing beach, the Mayagüez Marina for deep-sea fishing, seven excellent skindiving spots, and two golf courses. *Rte. 2, Km 152.5, Box 3629, 00709, tel. 809/831–7575 or 800/445–8667. 141 air-conditioned rooms and suites. Facilities: Olympic-size pool, 3 lighted tennis courts, casino, disco, restaurant, lounge. AE, CB, DC, MC, V. Expensive.*

San Germán **Parador Oasis.** The Oasis, not far from the town's two plazas, was a family mansion 200 years ago. You'll get a better taste for its history in the older front rooms; rooms in the new section in the rear are small and somewhat motelish. *72 Luna St., Box 144, 00753, tel. 809/892–1175. 50 rooms. Facilities: restaurant, pool, Jacuzzi, lounge, gym, sauna. AE, CB, DC, MC, V. Inexpensive–Moderate.*

Utuado **Parador Casa Grande.** The restored hacienda is on 107 acres of a former coffee plantation, with wood walkways leading to cottages snuggled among the lush green hills. Each unit has four spacious balconied rooms (No. 9 is way in the back, quiet, with a lovely mountain view). There are trails for hikers, hammocks for loafers, and occasional music for romantics. *Box 616, 00761, tel. 809/894–3939. 20 rooms. Facilities: pool, restaurant, lounge. AE, MC, V. Inexpensive.*

Vieques **Sea Gate.** Occupying 2 acres of a hilltop, this whitewashed hotel is a family-run operation. Proprietors John and Ruthye Miller will meet you at the airport or ferry, drive you to the beaches, arrange scuba-diving and snorkeling trips, and give you a complete rundown on their adopted home. Accommodations include three-room efficiencies with full kitchens and terraces. *Box 747, 00765, tel. 809/741–4661. 16 rooms. No credit cards. Inexpensive.*

The Arts and Nightlife

¿Qué Pasa? the official visitors guide, has current listings of events in San Juan and out on the island. Also, pick up a copy of the *San Juan Star*, and check with the local tourist offices to find out what's doing.

Music, Dance, and Theater LeLoLai is a year-round festival that celebrates Puerto Rico's Indian, Spanish, and African heritage. Performances take place each week, moving from hotel to hotel, showcasing the island's music, folklore, and culture. Sponsored by the Puerto Rico Tourism Company and major San Juan hotels, the festivities are free to visitors staying in a participating hotel for at least five nights. *Tickets can be purchased at the Condado Convention Center, tel. 809/723–3135. Admission: $8 for performances, $15–$35 for performances including dinner.*

Casinos By law, all casinos are in hotels, primarily in San Juan. The government keeps a close eye on them. Alcoholic drinks are not permitted at the gaming tables, although free soft drinks, coffee, and sandwiches are available. Dress for casinos tends to be on the formal side, and the atmosphere is refined. The law permits casinos to operate noon–4 AM, but individual casinos set their own hours, which change with the season.

Casinos are located in the following San Juan hotels (*see* Lodging, above): **Condado Plaza Hotel, Condado Beach Hotel, Caribe Hilton, Carib-Inn, Clarion Hotel, Ramada, Dutch Inn, Sands,** and **El San Juan.** Elsewhere on the island, there are casinos at the **Hyatt Regency Cerromar** and **Hyatt Dorado Beach hotels,** at **Palmas del Mar,** and at the **Hilton International Mayagüez.**

Discos In Old San Juan, young people flock to **Neon's** (203 Tanca St., tel. 725–7581) and to **Lazers** (251 Cruz St., tel. 723–6448).

In Puerta de Tierra, Condado, and Isla Verde, the 30-something crowd heads for **Juliana's** (Caribe Hilton Hotel, tel. 809/721–0303), **Isadora's** (Condado Plaza Hotel, tel. 809/722–5430), **Mykonos** (La Concha Hotel, tel. 809/721–6090), and **Amadeus** (El San Juan Hotel, tel. 809/791–1000).

Nightclubs The Caribe Hilton's **Club Caribe** books such headliners as Tony-award-winner Chita Rivera. The Sands Hotel's **Players Lounge** brings in such big names as Joan Rivers, Jay Leno, and Rita Moreno. El San Juan's **Tropicoro** presents international revues and top-name entertainers. (Young locals gather in the El San Juan's **El Chico** to dance to Latin music in a western saloon setting.) The Condado Plaza Hotel's **Copa Room** does a laser revue, and its **La Fiesta** sizzles with steamy Latin shows. In Old San Juan, the Ramada Hotel El Convento's **Ponce de Leon Salon** occasionally puts on flamenco shows.

19 Saba

by Honey Naylor

This 5-square-mile fairy-tale isle is not for everybody. If you're looking for exciting nightlife or lots of shopping, forget Saba, or take the one-day trip from St. Maarten. There are only a handful of shops, even fewer inns and eateries, and only 1,100 friendly, but shy, inhabitants. Beach lovers should also take note that Saba is a virtually beachless volcanic island, ringed with steep cliffs that fall straight down to the sea.

So, why Saba? Saba is a perfect hideaway, a challenge for adventurous hikers (Mt. Scenery rises above it all to a height of 2,855 feet), a longtime haven for divers, and, for Sabans, heaven on water. It's no wonder that they call their island the "Unspoiled Caribbean Queen."

The capital of Saba (pronounced *say*ba) is The Bottom, which is at the top, not the bottom, of a hill. Meandering goats have the right of way on The Road (there's only one); chickens cross at their own risk. In tiny, toylike villages, narrow paths are bordered by flower-draped walls and neat picket fences. Tidy houses with red roofs and gingerbread trim are planted in the mountainside among the bromeliads, palms, hibiscus, orchids, and Norwegian pines.

Saba is part of the Netherlands Antilles Windward Islands, located 28 miles—a 15-minute flight—from St. Maarten. The island is a volcano, extinct for 5,000 years (no one even knows where the crater was). Carib Indians may have hung out here around AD 800; Columbus spotted the little speck in 1493, but somehow Saba remained uninhabited until the first Dutch settlers arrived from Statia in 1640. Having established a foothold—no mean feat—they nestled into a bowl-shape valley and were soon joined by a handful of Scotch, English, and Irish settlers. *Botte* is Dutch for "bowl," but almost at the outset the word was Anglicized to "bottom."

In the 17th, 18th, and early 19th centuries the French, Dutch, English, and Spanish vied for control of the island. Saba changed hands 12 times before permanently raising the Dutch flag.

Sabans are a hardy lot. To get from Fort Bay to The Bottom, the early Sabans carved 900 steps out of the mountainside. Everything that arrived on the island, from a pin to a piano, had to be hauled up. Those rugged steps remained the only way to get about the island until The Road was built by Josephus Lambert Hassell (a carpenter who took correspondence courses in engineering) in the 1940s. The handmade road took 20 years to build, and if you like roller coasters you'll love The Road. The 6½-mile, white-knuckle route begins at sea level in Fort Bay, zigs up to 1,968 feet, and zags down to 131 feet above sea level at the airport.

After the success of the road venture, the Sabans, in 1963, constructed an airport on a flat point of land called (what else?) Flat Point. In 1965, the first television set arrived, and on Christmas Eve, 1970, Sabans received the gift of electricity, 24 hours a day! In spite of these modern conveniences, the island's uncomplicated lifestyle has persevered: Saban ladies still hand embroider the very special and delicate Saba lace, a reminder of Saban gentility that has continued to flourish since the 1870s, and brew the potent rum-based liquor, Saba Spice, sweetened with secret herbs and spices.

Before You Go

Tourist
Information

For help planning your trip, contact the **Saba Tourist Information Office** (c/o **Medhurst & Assoc. Inc.,** 271 Main St., Northport, NY 11768, tel. 516/261–7474, 212/936–0050, or 800/ 344–4606) or, in Canada, **New Concepts in Travel** (410 Queens Quai W, Suite 303, Toronto, Ont. M5V 2Z3, Canada tel. 416/ 362–7707).

Book reservations through a travel agent or over the telephone because mail can take from a week to a couple of months to reach the island.

Arriving and
Departing
By Plane

Unless you parachute in, you'll arrive from St. Maarten via **Windward Islands Airways** (tel. 599/5–44230 or 599/5–44237). The approach to Saba's tiny airstrip is the stuff that nightmares are made of. The strip is only 1,312 feet long, but the STOL (Short Takeoff and Landing) aircrafts are built for it, and the pilot only needs half of it. Try not to panic; remember that the pilot knows what he is doing and wants to live just as much as you do. Once you've touched down on the Band-Aid–like airstrip, the pilot taxis an inch or two, turns, and deposits you just outside a little shoebox called the Juancho E. Yrausquin Airport.

By Boat

Style, an open-air vessel with an open bar, departs St. Maarten's Great Bay Marina, Phillipsburg, Tuesday–Saturday at 9 AM and returns at 5 PM. The trip takes an hour and round-trip fare costs $45 (tel. 599/5–22167). If you take the watery way, however, you'll have lost more than an hour of sightseeing time on Saba.

Passports
and Visas

U.S. citizens need proof of citizenship. A passport is preferred, but a birth certificate or voter registration card will do (a driver's license will *not* do). British citizens must have a "British Visitors" Passport. All visitors must have an ongoing or return ticket.

Customs
and Duties

This is a free port, with no customs to clear, so you don't have to worry about bringing in receipts for expensive possessions.

Language

Saba's official language is Dutch, but everyone on the island speaks English.

Precautions

Everyone knows everyone else on the island, and crime is virtually nonexistent. Take along insect repellent, sunscreen, and sturdy, no-nonsense shoes that get a good grip on the ground.

Further Reading

Tales From My Grandmother's Pipe, by Senator Will Johnson, Saba's unofficial historian, is a treasure trove of Saba lore. *Saba, the First Guidebook,* by Natalie and Paul Pfanstiehl, takes you on a delightful exploration of the island, and even includes recipes. Dr. J. Hartog's *History of Saba* is filled with facts, figures, and fascinating photographs. All books are available at the **Saba Tourist Office,** Windwardside (*see* Important Addresses, below).

Staying in Saba

Important
Addresses

Tourist Information: The amiable Glenn Holm is at the helm of the **Saba Tourist Office** (Windwardside, tel. 599/46–2231) weekdays 8–noon and 1–5.

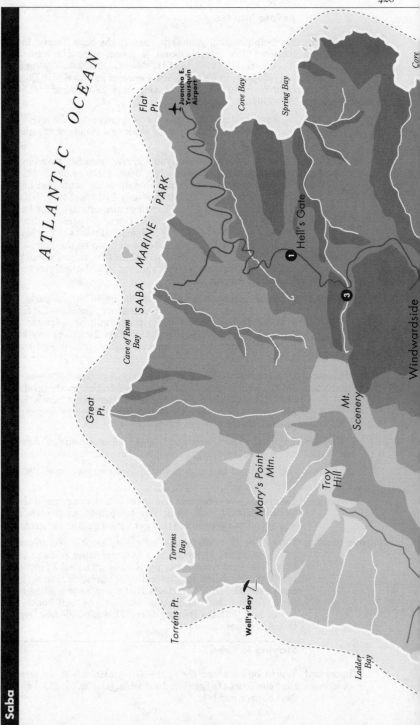

Saba

ATLANTIC OCEAN

SABA MARINE PARK

Flat Pt.

Juancho E. Yrausquin Airport

Cove Bay

Spring Bay

Core

Cave of Rum Bay

Great Pt.

Hell's Gate

1

3

Windwardside

Torrens Pt.

Torrens Bay

Mary's Point Mtn.

Mt. Scenery

Well's Bay

Troy Hill

Ladder Bay

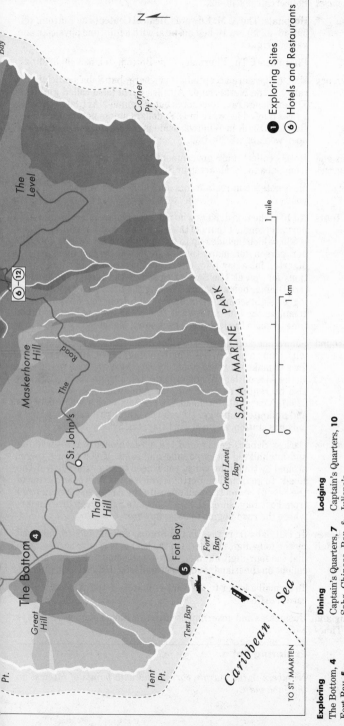

TO ST. MAARTEN

Caribbean Sea

N

Exploring
The Bottom, **4**
Fort Bay, **5**
Holy Rosary Church, **1**
Mt. Scenery, **3**
Windwardside, **2**

Dining
Captain's Quarters, **7**
Saba Chinese Bar &
Restaurant, **8**
Scout's Place, **9**
The Serving Spoon, **6**

Lodging
Captain's Quarters, **10**
Juliana's
Apartments, **11**
Scout's Place, **12**

1 Exploring Sites
6 Hotels and Restaurants

Emergencies	**Police:** call 599/46–3237.

Hospitals: The **A. M. Edwards Medical Center** (The Bottom, tel. 599/46–3288) is a 10-bed hospital with a full-time physician and various clinics.

Pharmacies: The **Pharmacy** (The Bottom, tel. 599/46–3289).

Currency U.S. dollars are accepted everywhere, but Saba's official currency is the Netherlands Antilles florin (also called guilder). The exchange rate fluctuates but is around NAf1.80 to U.S.$1. Prices quoted here are in U.S. dollars unless noted otherwise. **Barclays Bank** in Windwardside is the island's only bank; it's open weekdays 8:30–1:30.

Taxes and Service Charges Hotels collect a 5% government tax. The departure tax is $1 from Saba to St. Maarten or St. Eustatius.

Most hotels and restaurants add a 10%–15% service charge to your bill.

Guided Tours All 10 of the taxi drivers who meet the planes at Yrausquin Airport also conduct tours of the island. The cost for a full-day tour is $30, which includes up to four people; there is a charge of $7 per person for more than four. If you're just in from St. Maarten for a day trip, have your driver make lunch reservations for you at **The Serving Spoon** or the **Captain's Quarters** (*see* Dining, below) before starting the tour. After a full morning of sightseeing, your driver will drop you off for lunch, complete the tour afterward, and return you to Yrausquin in time to make the last flight back to St. Maarten.

Getting Around **Rental Cars** Saba's one and only road—The Road—is a serpentine affair with many a hairpin (read hair-raising) curve. However, if you dare to make your way about by car, there are nine rental cars at the **Avis** outlet (Windwardside, tel. 599/46–2289). Cars can also be rented at **Scout's Place** (Windwardside, tel. 599/46–2205). A car rents for about $30 per day, with a full tank of gas and unlimited mileage. (If you run out of gas, call the island's only gas station, down at Fort Bay, tel. 599/46–3272).

Hitchhiking Carless Sabans get around the old-fashioned ways—walking and hitchhiking (very popular and safe). If you choose to get around by thumbing rides, you'll need to know the rules of The Road. To go from The Bottom (which actually is near the top of the island), sit on the wall opposite the Anglican Church; to go from Fort Bay, sit on the wall opposite Saba Deep dive center, where the road begins to twist upward.

Telephones and Mail To call Saba from the United States, dial 011/599/46, followed by the four-digit number. On the island, it is only necessary to dial the four-digit number. Telephone communications are excellent on the island, and direct-dial long distance is in effect.

To airmail a letter to the United States costs NAf1.30; a postcard, NAf.60.

Opening and Closing Times Businesses and government offices on Saba are open weekdays 8–5.

Exploring Saba

Numbers in the margin correspond with points of interest on the Saba map.

Begin your driving tour with a trip from Flat Point, at the airport, up to Hell's Gate. Because there is only one road, we'll continue along its hairpin curves up to Windwardside, and then on to The Bottom and down to Fort Bay. This cross-island tour will give you a quick overview of tiny Saba, its limited cultural sights and varied natural settings.

There are 20 sharp curves on The Road between the airport and Hell's Gate. On one of these curves, poised on Hell's Gate's hill, ❶ is the stone **Holy Rosary Church,** which looks medieval but was built in 1962. In the **Community Center** behind the church, village ladies sell blouses, handkerchiefs, tablecloths, and tea towels embellished with the very special and unique Saba lace. These same ladies also turn out innocent-sounding Saba Spice, a rum-based liqueur that will knock your proverbial socks off.

The Road spirals past banana plantations, oleander bushes, ❷ and stunning views of the ocean below. In **Windwardside,** the island's second largest village, teetering at 1,968 feet, you'll see rambling lanes and narrow alleyways winding through the hills, and a cluster of tiny, neat houses and shops.

On your right as you enter the village is the **Church of St. Paul's Conversion,** a colonial building with a red-and-white steeple. Your next stop should be the **Saba Tourist Office** (next door to the post office), where you can pick up brochures and books about Saba. You may then want to spend some time browsing through the **Square Nickel,** the **Saba Shop,** and the **Island Craft Shop** *(see* Shopping, below).

The **Saba Museum,** surrounded by lemongrass and clover, lies just behind the Captain's Quarters. There are small signs marking the way to the 150-year-old house that has been set up to look much as it did when it was a sea captain's home. Its furnishings include a handsome mahogany four-poster bed with pineapple design, an antique organ, and, in the kitchen, a rock oven and a hearth. Among the old documents on display is a letter a Saban wrote after the hurricane of 1772, in which he sadly says, "We have lost our little all." *Windwardside, no phone. Admission: $1 donation requested. Open weekdays 10–3.*

Near the museum are the stone and concrete steps—1,064 of ❸ them—that rise to **Mt. Scenery.** The steps lead past giant elephant ears, ferns, begonias, mangos, palms, and orchids, up to a mahogany grove at the summit. On a cloudless day the view is spectacular. For a breathtaking journey, have your hotel pack a picnic lunch, wear nonslip shoes, take along a jacket and a canteen of water, and hike away. The round-trip excursion will take about a half day and is best begun in the early morning.

On the way from Windwardside to The Bottom, you'll pass through the small settlement of **St. John's.** As you round one of those many curves, look down on **Giles Quarter** by the ocean, where the Netherlands is funding a new airport to be built over a 10-year period.

❹ You'll be zigzagging downhill from Windwardside to **The Bottom,** which sits in its bowl-shape valley 820 feet above the sea. The Bottom is the seat of government and the home of the lieutenant-governor. The large house next to Wilhelmina Park has fancy fretwork, a high pitched roof, and wraparound double galleries.

Time Out   **Earl's Snack Bar** is the place to get grilled-cheese sandwiches, burgers, beer, ice-cream cones, and Eskimo pie. *The Bottom, no phone. Open daily 8:30–12:30, 3–4, and 7–9:30.*

On the other side of town is the **Wesleyan Holiness Church,** a small stone building with bright white fretwork, and dating from 1919. Stroll by the church, beyond a place called The Gap, and you'll come to a **lookout point** where you can see the rough-hewn steps leading down to Ladder Bay. Ladder Bay, with 524 steps, and Fort Bay, with its 200 steps, were the two landing sites from which Saba's first settlers had to haul themselves and their possessions. Sabans sometimes walk down to Ladder Bay to picnic. Think long and hard before you do, bearing in mind that it's 524 steps back *up* to The Road. (Hitchhiking from down there will get you nowhere!)

⑤   The last stop on The Road is **Fort Bay,** which is the jumping-off place for the island's two dive operations (*see* Scuba Diving and Snorkeling, below). There's also a gas station, a 277-foot deep-water pier that accommodates the tenders from ships that call here, and the information center for the **Saba Marine Park** (*see* Scuba Diving and Snorkeling, below).

Off the Beaten Track

It wasn't easy, but we found the only beach on Saba! Each April, a 20-foot strip of what's known as black (but is actually gray) sand appears at **Well's Bay,** down below Mary's Point. The beach is good for swimming and sticks around all summer and into early November. It used to take six hours to hike down there, but a new road, an extension of The Road, has shortened the travel time to 15 minutes from Windwardside.

Participant Sports

Boating   **Saba Deep** (tel. 599/46–3347 or 599/46–2201) conducts one-hour, round-island cruises that include cocktails, hors d'oeuvres, and a sunset you won't soon forget.

Deep-Sea Fishing   **Saba Deep** runs half- and full-day charters that include lunch, drinks, bait, and tackle.

Hiking   You can't avoid some hiking, even if you just go to mail a post-card. The big deal, of course, is Mt. Scenery, with 1,064 slippery steps leading up to the top (*see* Exploring Saba, above).

For information about Saba's 18 botanical hiking trails through the rain forest and up Mt. Scenery, check with Glenn Holm at the Tourist Office (*see* Important Addresses, above).

Scuba Diving   The island's first settlers probably found the **Saba Bank** (a fer-
and Snorkeling   tile fishing ground 3 miles southwest of Saba) a crucial point in their decision to set up house here. In more recent times, divers have enjoyed Saba's coral gardens and undersea mountains. **Saba Marine Park** was established in 1987 to preserve and manage Saba's marine resources. The park circles the entire island, dipping down to 200 feet, and is zoned for diving, swimming, fishing, boating, and anchorage. At press time, a snorkeling trail was in the planning stage and a guidebook on diving in Saba was also in the works. The park also offers talks and slide shows for divers and snorkelers, and provides brochures and

literature on marine life. *Harbor Office, Fort Bay, tel. 599/4–3295. Open weekdays 8–5. Call first to see if anyone's around.*

Saba Deep and **Sea Saba** (tel. 599/46–2246) will take you to explore Saba's 25 diving spots. Both offer rental equipment and certified instructors.

Wilson's Diving in Windwardside opened recently and specializes in shorter dive trips for visitors over from St. Maarten for the day.

Shopping

Gift Ideas   The island's most popular purchases are Saba lace and Saba Spice. The history of Saba lace (also called Spanish lace) goes back more than a century to Saban Gertrude Johnson, who attended a Caracas convent school where she learned the art of drawing and tying threads to adorn fine linens. When she returned home in the 1870s, she taught lacemaking to other Saban ladies, and the art has endured ever since. Collars, tea towels, napkins, and other small items are relatively inexpensive, but larger items, such as tablecloths, can be pricey. You should also know that the fabric requires some care—it is not drip-dry.

Saba Spice may *sound* as delicate as Saba lace, and the aroma is as sweet as can be. However, the base for the liqueur is 151-proof rum, and all the rest is window dressing.

Shops   Saba's famed souvenirs can be found in almost every shop. In Windwardside, stop in at **The Square Nickel, Island Craft Shop,** and **Saba Shop.** In The Bottom, the **Saba Artisan Foundation** (tel. 599/46–3260) turns out hand-screened fabrics that you can buy by the yard or already made into resort clothing for men, women, and children.

Dining

In most of Saba's restaurants you pretty much have to take potluck. If you don't like what's cooking in one place, you can check out the other restaurants. However, it won't take you long to run out of options.

The most highly recommended restaurants are indicated by a star ★.

Category	Cost*
Expensive	$25–$30
Moderate	$20–$25
Inexpensive	under $20

per person, excluding drinks and service

★ **Captain's Quarters.** Dining is comfortable on a cool porch surrounded by flowers and mango trees. There's usually a homemade soup and a choice of two entrées: the catch of the day, served with Creole sauce, and T-bone or sirloin steak. *Windwardside, tel. 599/46–2201. Lunch is served at 12:30, dinner at 7:30. Reservations required. MC, V. Closed Sept. Expensive.*

Saba Chinese Bar & Restaurant. A plain house with plastic tablecloths, where you can get, among other things, sweet-and-sour pork or chicken, cashew chicken, and some curried dishes. *Windwardside, tel. 599/46–2268. Reservations advised. No credit cards. Closed Mon. Inexpensive.*

Scout's Place. Chef Diana Medero turns out chicken cordon bleu, braised steak with mushrooms, and lobster (broiled or Newburg). You can get sandwiches all day long. *Windwardside, tel. 599/46–2295. Dinner is at 7:30. Reservations required. No credit cards. Inexpensive.*

★ **The Serving Spoon.** Queenie Simmons's chicken with peanut-butter sauce is famous throughout the islands. Her house adjoins her eight-table restaurant, where plates come heaped with huge portions. Stop by and ask her what she's preparing for the day. It might be meatballs with rice, seafood, french fries, steamed vegetables, or curried goat with butter. *The Bottom, tel. 599/46–3225. Reservations required. No credit cards. Inexpensive.*

Lodging

Like everything else on Saba, the guest houses are tiny and tucked into tropical gardens. The selection is limited and because most restaurants are located in the guest houses, you would do well to take advantage of meal plans.

The most highly recommended lodgings are indicated by a star ★.

Category	Cost*
Expensive	over $180
Moderate	$50–$65
Inexpensive	under $50

All prices are for a standard double room for two with breakfast and dinner, excluding 5% tax and a 10%–15% service charge.

Hotels **Captain's Quarters.** All the rooms here are spacious and airy, ★ with antique Victorian furnishings (including four-poster beds) and views of the tiny pool that's perched 1,500 feet above the sea. Four choice bedrooms are in a small house that was built by a Saban sea captain in 1832. Dining is in a shaded garden pavilion surrounded by hibiscus, poinsettia and papaya trees. *Windwardside, tel. 599/46–2201 or 800/468–0023. 10 rooms with bath. Facilities: pool, restaurant, gift shop, bar and lounge. MC, V. Expensive.*

Juliana's Apartments. Near the Captain's Quarters, Mrs. Juliana Johnson offers eight studio apartments and a 2½-room apartment with private bath, balcony, kitchenette, living/dining room, bedroom, and a large porch facing the sea. Guests have the use of facilities at the CQ, whose manager, Steve Hassell, is Mrs. Johnson's brother. *Windwardside, tel. 599/46–2269. AE, MC, V. Moderate–Expensive.*

★ **Scout's Place.** Billed as "Bed 'n Board, Cheap 'n Cheerful," Scout's Place, near the post office and within walking distance of Sea Saba Dive Center, was originally the Government Guest House. "Scout" is retired owner Scout Thirkield, who turned his place over to his longtime cook Diana Medero and who is still very much in evidence. Ten new rooms, all with four-poster beds, reproductions of antiques, private balconies, and private baths with hot water, have been added to the original four rooms, which have *no* hot water. There's a small breakfast room where you can have cheese omelets, bacon, and coffee. *Windwardside, tel. 599/46–2205. 14 rooms, 12 with private bath. Facilities: restaurant, pool, bar. No credit cards. Inexpensive.*

Apartments Twenty apartments and wood cottages, all with hot water and modern conveniences, are available for weekly and monthly rentals. For information, check with Glenn Holm, **Saba Tourist Office** *(see* Important Addresses, above).

The Arts and Nightlife

The arts can be summed up in two words: **Royal Cinema** (Windwardside, tel. 599/46–3263), which gets films about two weeks after they're released. If you're in a movie mood, ask around to find out what's showing.

As for nightlife, you can dance till 2 AM on Sunday at **Guido's** (Windwardside, tel. 599/46–2330), do the nightclub scene at **The Lime Tree Bar & Restaurant** (The Bottom, tel. 599/46–3256), or just hang out at **Scout's Place** or the **Captain's Quarters.**

20 St. Barthélemy

by Regina McGee

Regina McGee is a freelance writer living in New York City. She writes frequently on business and leisure travel.

Scale is a big part of St. Barthélemy's charm: a lilliputian harbor; red-roof bungalows dotting the hillsides; minimokes, not much bigger than golf carts, buzzing up narrow roads or through the neat-as-a-pin streets of Gustavia; exquisite coves and beaches, most undeveloped, all with pristine stretches of white sand. Just 8 square miles, St. Barts is for people who like things small and perfectly done. It's for Francophiles, too. The French cuisine here is tops in the Caribbean, and gourmet lunches and dinners are rallying points of island life. A French *savoir vivre* pervades, and the island is definitely for the style conscious—casual but always chic. This is no place for the beach-bum set.

Rothschild owns property and Rockefeller built an estate here, and for a long time the island, 15 miles from St. Martin in the French West Indies, was the haunt of the well-heeled and well-informed. In the past decade, the tourist base has expanded, and last year more than 100,000 visitors stopped by, including day-trippers from nearby islands and passengers from the occasional cruise ships that now anchor just outside the harbor.

Longtime visitors speak wistfully of the old, quiet St. Barts. While development *has* quickened the pace, the island has not been overrun with prefab condos or glitzy resorts. The largest hotel has only 64 rooms, and the remaining 566 rooms are scattered in cottages and villas around the island; no high rises are allowed. The tiny airport accommodates nothing bigger than 19-passenger planes, and there aren't any casinos or flashy late-night attractions. Moreover, St. Barts is generally not a destination for the budget-minded. Development has largely been in luxury lodgings and gourmet restaurants, and as the dollar continues to decline, island-wide prices have increased sharply in recent years.

When Christopher Columbus "discovered" the island in 1493, he named it after his brother, Bartholomeo. A small group of French colonists arrived from nearby St. Kitts in 1656 but were wiped out by the fierce Carib Indians who dominated the area. A new group from Normandy and Brittany arrived in 1694. This time the settlers prospered—with the help of French buccaneers, who took full advantage of the island's strategic location and well-protected harbor. In 1784 the French traded the island to King Gustav III of Sweden in exchange for port rights in Göteborg. He dubbed the capital Gustavia, laid out and paved streets, built three forts, and turned the capital into a prosperous free port. The island thrived as a major shipping and commercial center until the 19th century, when earthquakes, fire, and hurricanes brought financial ruin. Many residents fled for newer lands of opportunity, and in 1878 France agreed to repurchase its beleaguered former colony.

Today the island is still a free port, and, as a dependency of Guadeloupe, is part of an overseas department of France. Dry, sunny, and stony, St. Barts was never one of the Caribbean's "sugar islands," and thus never developed an industrial slave base. Most natives are descendants of those tough Norman and Breton settlers of three centuries ago. They are feisty, industrious, and friendly but insular.

You may hear some speak the old Norman patois of their ancestors or see the older women dressed in the traditional garb of provincial France. They have prospered with the tourist boom,

St. Barthélemy

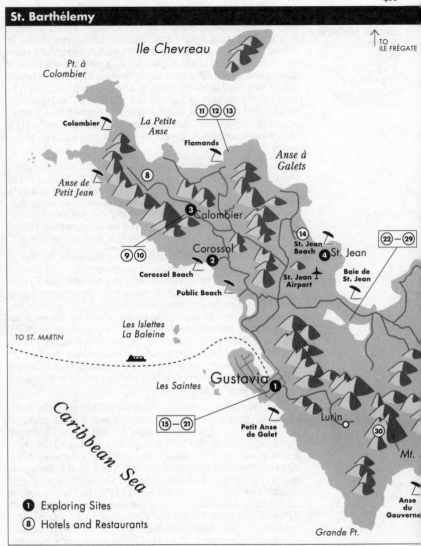

TO
ILE FRÉGATE

Ile Chevreau

Pt. à Colombier

Colombier

La Petite Anse

⑪ ⑫ ⑬

Flamands

Anse à Galets

⑧

Anse de Petit Jean

❸ Colombier

⑨⑩

Corossol

❷

Corossol Beach

Public Beach

⑭
St. Jean Beach

❹ St. Jean

St. Jean Airport

Baie de St. Jean

㉒ — ㉙

Les Islettes La Baleine

TO ST. MARTIN

Les Saintes

Gustavia

❶

⑮ — ㉑

Petit Anse de Galet

Lurin ○

㉚

Mt.

Caribbean Sea

Anse du Gouverne

Grande Pt.

❶ Exploring Sites

⑧ Hotels and Restaurants

Exploring
Colombier, **3**
Corossol, **2**
Grande Saline, **7**
Gustavia, **1**
Lorient, **5**
St. Jean, **4**
Toiny coast, **6**

Dining
Aux Trois Gourmands, **21**
Bamboo, **29**
Bartolomeo, **36**
Brasserie La Creole, **23**
Castelets, **30**
Chez Francine, **24**
Club Lafayette, **37**

Cote Jardin, **17**
Eddie's Ghetto, **20**
François Plantation, **9**
Gloriette, **38**
Hostellerie des Trois Forces, **44**
L'Escale, **15**
L'Hibiscus, **16**

La Langouste, **18**
La Marine, **19**
Le Flamboyant, **43**
Le Patio, **22**
Le Rivage, **39**
Marigot Bay Club, **34**
Taiwana, **11**
Topolino, **25**

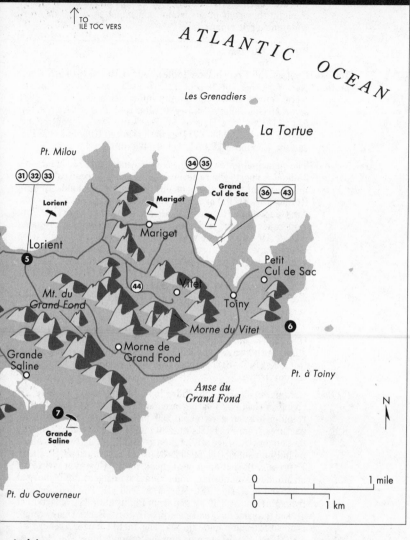

TO
ILE TOC VERS

A T L A N T I C   O C E A N

Les Grenadiers

La Tortue

Pt. Milou

③④ ③⑤

Grand
Cul de Sac

③⑥ — ④③

③① ③② ③③

Lorient

Marigot

Marigot

⑤

Lorient

Petit
Cul de Sac

Mt. du
Grand Fond

④④

Vitet

Toiny

Grande
Saline

Morne de
Grand Fond

Morne du Vitet

⑥

Pt. à Toiny

Anse du
Grand Fond

N

⑦

Grande
Saline

0 _____ 1 mile

0 _____ 1 km

Pt. du Gouverneur

Lodging

Auberge de la Petite
Anse, **8**
Baie des Flamands, **12**
Castelets, **30**
El Sereno Beach
Hotel, **41**
Filao Beach, **26**

François Plantation, **9**
Grand Cul de Sac
Beach Hotel and St.
Barts Beach Hotel, **42**
Guanahani, **40**
Hostellerie des Trois
Forces, **44**
Hotel la Banane, **31**
Hotel Manapany
Cottages, **14**

L'Hibiscus, **16**
La Normandie, **32**
Le P'tit Morne, **10**
Les Mouettes, **33**
Marigot Bay Club, **34**
Sea Horse Club, **35**
Tropical Hotel, **27**
Village St. Jean, **28**

White Sand Beach
Cottages, **13**

but some are worried that the upward swing of prices may threaten business, especially tour groups and families. So far, though, this gem of an island continues to draw an ever-widening circle of fans.

Before You Go

Tourist Information Contact the **French West Indies Tourist Board** (610 5th Ave., New York, NY 10020, tel. 212/757–1125). The **French Government Tourist Office** can supply information in Canada (1981 Ave., McGill College, Suite 490, Montreal, P.Q. H3A 2W9, tel. 514/288–4264, or 1 Dundas St. W., Suite 2405, Toronto, Ont. M56 1Z3, tel. 416/593–4717) or in the United Kingdom (178 Piccadilly, London W1V 0AL, tel. 01/499–6911).

Arriving and Departing

By Plane The principal gateway from North America is St. Maarten's Juliana Airport, where several times a day you can catch a 10-minute flight to St. Barts on either **Windward Islands Airways** (tel. 590/27–61–01) or **Air St. Barthélemy** (tel. 590/27–71–90). **Air Guadeloupe** (tel. 590/27–61–90) offers daily service from Espérance Airport in St. Martin, the French side of the same island. Air Guadeloupe also has direct flights to St. Barts from Guadeloupe and Antigua, while **Virgin Air** (tel. 590/27–71–76) operates daily flights between St. Barts and both St. Thomas and San Juan. Reconfirmation on all return interisland flights, even during off-peak seasons, is strongly recommended. Windward, Air St. Barthélemy, and Virgin Air also offer charter service.

From the Airport Airport taxi service costs $3 to $15 (to the farthest hotel). Since the cabs are unmetered, you may be charged more if you make stops on the way. Cabs meet all flights, and a taxi dispatcher (tel. 590/27–75–81) operates from 8:30 AM until the last flight of the day arrives.

By Boat Catamarans leave Philipsburg in St. Maarten at 9 AM daily, arriving in Gustavia's harbor around 11 AM. These are one-day, round-trip excursions (about $50, including open bar), with departures from St. Barts at 3:30 PM. If there's room, one-way passengers ($25) are often taken as well. Contact **Bobby's Marina** in Philipsburg (tel. 5995/2–3170) for reservations. **St. Barth Express,** a 12-seat open powerboat, leaves Gustavia at 8:15 AM on Monday, Wednesday, and Friday, arriving at Philipsburg at 9 AM and in Marigot (St. Martin) at 9:30 AM. The boat departs from Marigot at 3:30 PM and from Philipsburg (St. Maarten) at 4PM on the same days and goes directly to St. Barts. One-way fare is about $29 and round-trip $47. The **Yacht Charter Agency** (tel. 590/27–62–38) in Gustavia handles reservations. The *Princess* motorboat makes the same run every Wednesday and can be booked through **La Marine Service** (tel. 590/27–70–34) in Gustavia. La Marine also has boats for private charter, as does the Yacht Charter Agency.

Passports and Visas U.S. and Canadian citizens need either a passport (one that expired no more than five years ago will suffice) or other proof of citizenship, such as a notarized birth certificate with a raised seal or a voter registration card, both accompanied by photo identification. A visa is required for stays of more than three months.

Customs and Duties Items for personal use, including tobacco, film, and cameras, are admitted.

Language French is the official language, though a Norman dialect is spoken by some longtime islanders. Most hotel and restaurant employees speak English, but not all.

Precautions Roads are narrow and sometimes very steep, so check the brakes and gears of your rental car *before* you leave the lot. Some hillside restaurants and hotels require a bit of climbing, so if that's a problem, inquire ahead of time.

Staying in St. Barthélemy

Important Addresses **Tourist Information:** The **Office du Tourisme** (tel. 590/27–60–08) is in the Mairie de St. Barth (town hall), rue August Nyman, Gustavia. Hours are weekdays 7:30–noon and 2–6. The office is closed on weekends and Wednesday afternoons.

Emergencies **Hospitals: Gustavia Clinic** (tel. 590/27–60–35 or 590/27–60–00) is on the corner of rue Jean Bart and rue Sadi Carnot.

Pharmacies: There is a pharmacy in Gustavia on rue de la République (tel. 590/27–61–82), and one in St. Jean (tel. 590/27–66–61).

Currency The French franc is legal tender. Figure about 6.50F to the U.S. dollar. U.S. dollars are accepted everywhere; credit cards are accepted at most shops, hotels, and restaurants. Note: Prices quoted here are in U.S. dollars unless indicated otherwise.

Taxes and Service Charges Hotels add a 7% government tax. A 10F departure tax is charged if you are headed for St. Martin or Guadeloupe; 15F for other destinations.

Some hotels add a 10%–15% service charge to bills; others include it in their tariffs. All restaurants are required to include a 15% service charge in their published prices. It is especially important to remember this when your credit-card receipt is presented to be signed with the tip space blank, or you could end up paying a 30% service charge.

Most taxi drivers own their vehicles and do not expect a tip.

Guided Tours Tours are by minibus or taxi. An hour-long tour costs about $30 for one to two people and $40 for up to eight people. A five-hour island tour costs about $87 per vehicle. Itineraries are negotiable. Tours can be arranged at hotel desks, through the Tourist Office, or by calling any of the island's taxi operators, including **Hugo Cagan** (tel. 590/27–61–28) and **Florian La Place** (Taxi Drivers Group, tel. 590/27–63–58).

Getting Around *Taxis* You may arrange cab service by calling tel. 590/27–66–31, 590/27–60–59, or 590/27–63–12. Note: Fares are 50% higher from 8PM to 6 AM and on Sundays and holidays.

Rental Cars It's more fun to have your own car, though the steep, curvy roads require careful driving. **Avis** (tel. 590/27–71–43), **Budget** (tel. 590/27–67–43), and **Europcar** (tel. 590/27–73–33) are represented at the airport, among others. All accept credit cards. You must have a valid driver's license, and in high season there may be a three-day minimum. VW Beetles, open-sided Gurgels (VW Jeep), and minimokes—all with stick shift only—rent in season for $40–$45 a day, with unlimited mileage and limited collision insurance. Car-rental reservations are advised, especially during February and around Christmas. Some hotels have their own car fleets, and a car should be rented at the time you make your room reservation. The choice of vehicles may be limited, but many hotels offer 24-hour emergency road service, which most rental companies do not.

Motorbikes   Motorbike companies rent bikes for about $25 per day and require a $100 deposit. Call **Topolino's** (tel. 590/27–70–92) or **Rent Some Fun** (tel. 590/27–70–59).

Telephones and Mail   To phone St. Barts from the United States, dial 011–590 and the local number. To call the United States from St. Barts, dial 19–1, the area code, and the local number. For St. Martin, dial 3 and the number. For local information, dial 12. Automatic telephone booths around the island require "pay-in-advance" credit cards, which can be purchased at the post office. To dial a local number on the island, dial six digits; no area code is required.

Mail is slow. It can take up to three weeks for correspondence between the United States and the island. Post offices are in Gustavia and Lorient.

Opening and Closing Times   Businesses and offices close from noon to 2 during the week and all day Sunday. Shops in Gustavia are open weekdays 8:30–noon and 2–5, and until noon on Saturday. Shops across from the airport and in St. Jean also open Saturday afternoons and until 7 PM on weekdays. The two banks, both in Gustavia, are open weekdays 8–noon and 2–3:30.

Beaches

There are nearly 20 plages (beaches), each with a distinctive personality and all of them public. Topless sunbathing is common but nudism is forbidden. Here are the main attractions:

St. Jean is like a mini Côte d'Azur—beachside bistros, bungalow hotels, bronze beauties, and lots of day-trippers. The reef-protected strip is divided by Eden Rock promontory, and there's good snorkeling west of the rock. **Lorient** is popular with St. Bart's families and surfers, who like its rolling waves. **Marigot** is a quiet fishing beach with good snorkeling along the rocky far end. Shallow, reef-protected **Grand Cul de Sac** is especially nice for small children and windsurfers; it has excellent lunch spots and lots of pelicans. Around the point, next to the Guanahani Hotel, is tiny **Marechal Beach,** which offers some of the best snorkeling on the island. Secluded **Grande Saline,** with its sandy ocean bottom, is just about everyone's favorite beach and is great for swimmers. Despite the law, young and old alike go nude on this beach. It can get windy here, so go on a calm day. **Anse du Gouverneur** is even more secluded and equally beautiful, with good snorkeling and views of St. Kitts, Saba, and Statia.

A five-minute walk from Gustavia is **Petit Anse de Galet,** named after the tiny shells on its shore. Both **Public Beach** and **Corossol Beach** are best for boat- and sunset-watching. The beach at **Colombier** is the least accessible but the most private; you'll have to take either a rocky footpath from La Petite Anse or take the 30-minute climb down a cacti-bordered trail from the top. **Flamands** is the most beautiful of the hotel beaches—a roomy strip of silken sand. Back toward the airport, the surf at **Anse de Cays** is rough for swimming, but great for surfing.

Exploring St. Barthélemy

Numbers in the margin correspond to points of interest on the St. Barthélemy map.

Gustavia and the West **①** With just a few streets on three sides of its tiny harbor, Gustavia is easily explored in a two-hour stroll, including time to browse through shops or visit a café. This will leave you the rest of the afternoon for a trip to the west coast to enjoy a picnic and a swim.

Park your car harborside on the rue de la République, where flashy catamarans, yachts, and sailboats are moored, then head to the **Tourist Office** in the *Marie* (town hall) on rue August Nyman. Here you should pick up an island map and a free copy of *St. Barth Magazine*, a monthly publication on island happenings. Then settle in at either **Bar de L'Oubli** or **Gustavia's Le Select** (*see* Nightlife, below), two cafés at the corner of rue de la France and rue de la République, for coffee and croissants and a quick leaf through the listings of the week's events.

As you stroll through the little streets, you will notice that plaques sometimes spell out names in both French and Swedish, a reminder of the days when the island was a Swedish colony. Small shops along **rue du Roi Oscar II** and **rue du Général de Gaulle** sell French perfumes, resortwear, crystal, gold jewelry, and other luxury items. You might want to stop by **La Rotisserie** (rue du Lafayette and rue du Roi Oscar II) or **Taste Unlimited** (rue du Général de Gaulle) to pick up the makings for a picnic.

On the other side of the harbor, next door to the Trois Gourmands restaurant, a **market** has been set up where ladies from Guadeloupe and Dominica have arranged colorful displays of tropical fruits and vegetables. And if you feel like a swim, drive around the end of the harbor to **Anse de Galet.** This quiet little plage is also known as Shell Beach for the tiny shells heaped ankle-deep in some places.

Head back the way you came and turn off at the sign for Lurin. The views up the winding road overlooking the harbor are spectacular. After about five minutes, look for a sign to Plage du Gouverneur. A small rocky route off to the right will take you bumping and grinding down a steep incline to **Anse du Gouverneur,** one of St. Bart's most beautiful beaches, where pirate's treasure is said to be buried. If the weather is clear, you will be able to see the islands of Saba, St. Eustatius, and St. Kitts.

Time Out The hilltop **Sante Fe Restaurant** (Morne Lorne, at the turnoff to Gouverneur's Beach, tel. 590/27–61–04) is a favorite spot for sundowners, watching sunsets, and the island's best hamburgers.

Corossol, Colombier, Flamands **②** Starting at the intersection on the hilltop overlooking the airport (known as Tourmente), take the road to Public Beach and on to **Corossol,** a two-street fishing village with a little beach. Corossol is where the island's French provincial origins are most evident. Residents speak an old Norman dialect, and some of the barefoot older women still wear traditional garb— ankle-length dresses and starched white sunbonnets called *quichenottes* (kiss-me-not hats). The women don't like to be photographed. However, they are not shy about selling you some of their handmade straw work—handbags, baskets, broad-brim hats, and delicate strings of birds—made from lantania palms. The palms were introduced to the island 100 years ago by foresighted Father Morvan, who planted a grove in Corossol and Flamands, thus providing the country folk with a living that is still pursued today. Here, too, is the **Inter Oceans Museum** (tel. 590/27–62–97), which features a small but excellent collection of marine shells from around the world. *Tel. 590/27–62–97. Admission: 20F. Open daily 10–5.*

❸ Return to the main road and turn left for **Colombier.** Follow the signs illustrated with hummingbirds to reach island artist **Jean-Yves Froment's Studio** (tel. 590/27–61–72). Visitors are welcome, but call ahead to reserve a personalized demonstration in which the artist shows how his popular hand-blocked fabrics are created. Tropical fabrics and fashions are sold in his shop downstairs from the studio.

From Colombier, head down the main road about a mile to **Baie des Flamands,** a wide beach with a few small hotels. From here, take a brisk hike to the top of what is believed to be the now-extinct volcano that gave birth to St. Barts. From the peak you can take in the gorgeous view of the offshore islands.

Time Out Chef Solange Gréaux serves a delicious fish soup and home cooking at the **Baie des Flamands Hotel** (Anse des Flamands, tel. 590/27–64–85).

A drive to the end of Flamands Road brings you to a rocky footpath that leads to the island's most remote beach, **Anse de Colombier.** If you're not up to the 30-minute hike, take a 3 PM sail from Gustavia (*see* Participant Sports, below). You'll have time for a swim, and refreshments before the sunset sail back to the harbor.

St. Jean, Grand Cul de Sac, Saline Brimming with bungalows, bistros, sunbathers, and windsurfing sails, the half-mile crescent of sand at **St. Jean** is the **❹** island's most famous beach. Lunch at a beachside bistro such as **Le Pelican** or **Chez Francine** (*see* Dining, below), perhaps interrupted by a swim in the surf, is de rigueur, followed by a stroll through nearby boutiques.

❺ Leaving St. Jean, take the main road to **Lorient.** On your left are the royal palms and rolling waves of Lorient Beach. Lorient, site of the first French settlement, is one of the island's two parishes, and a newly restored church, historic headstones, a school, post office, and gas station mark the spot.

Bear left and continue along the coast. Turn left at the Mont Jean sign. Your route rolls around the island's pretty windward coves, past **Pointe Milou,** an elegant residential colony, and on to **Marigot,** where you can pick up a bottle of fine wine at **La Cave.** The bargain prices may surprise you (*see* Shopping, below).

The winding road passes through the mangroves, ponds, and beach of **Grand Cul de Sac,** where there are plenty of excellent beachside restaurants and water-sports concessions. Tucked beside the Club Lafayette is **Paulette Blardat's Magnolia Coiffure** (no phone), a beauty salon set right on the beach.

Time Out If you're in the mood to splurge, stop off at **L'Indigo Restaurant** at the Guanahani Hotel (tel. 590/27–66–60) for a truly special lunch. The poolside setting is stunning and the food, ranging from burgers to lobster, is superb.

6 Over the hills beyond Grand Cul de Sac is the much photographed **Toiny coast.** Drystone fences crisscross the steep slopes of Morne Vitet along a rocky shoreline that resembles the rugged coast of Normandy. The road turns inland and up the slopes of Morne de Grand-Fond. At the first fork (less than a mile), the road to the right leads back to Lorient. A left-hand turn at the next intersection will bring you within a few min-
7 utes to a dead end at **Grande Saline.** Ten years ago the big salt ponds of Grande Saline were shut down after a half-century of operation. The place looks desolate, but climb the short hillock behind the ponds for a surprise—the long arc of **Anse de Grande Saline.**

Time Out Stop for lunch, dinner, or drinks at **Le Tamarin** (Saline, tel. 590/ 27–72–12), a delightful spot by a huge tamarind tree. Paco the pet parrot greets guests. You may want to try your hand at archery between sipping drinks and ordering from the excellent specials listed on a blackboard.

Participant Sports

Boating St. Barts is a popular yachting and sailing center, thanks to its location midway between Antigua and St. Thomas. Gustavia's harbor, 13 to 16 feet deep, has mooring and docking facilities for 40 yachts, with good anchorages available at Public, Corossol, and Colombier. **Loulou's Marine** (tel. 590/27–62–74) is the place for yachting information and supplies. **Marine Service** (tel. 590/27–70–34), **La Maison de la Mer** (tel. 550/27–81–00), and the **Yacht Charter Agency** (tel. 590/27–62–38) offer sunset and half- and full-day sails. Marine and La Maison de la Mer also have unskippered motor rentals for about $220 a day.

Diving and Deep-sea fishing can be arranged through **Yacht Charter Agen-**
Deep-Sea Fishing cy (tel. 590/27–62–38), **Marine Service** (tel. 590/27–70–34), or with **Pierre Choisy** (tel. 590/27–61–22) on his *Bertram*. Marine also operates a PADI diving center, with scuba-diving trips for about $45 per person, gear included. **Club La Bulle** (tel. 590/27–68–93) and PADI-certified **Dive with Dan** (tel. 590/27–64–78) are other scuba options.

Tennis There are two tennis courts at the Guanahani (tel. 590/27–66–60), **Le Flamboyant Tennis Club** (tel. 590/27–69–82), and two at the **Sports Center of Colombier** (tel. 590/27–61–07). The Manapany (tel. 590/27–66–55), the **Taiwana** (tel. 590/27–65–01), and the **St. Barths Beach Hotel** (tel. 590/27–62–73) each have one court.

Windsurfing Windsurfing fever has definitely caught on here. Boards can be rented for about $11 an hour at water-sports centers along St. Jean and Grand Cul de Sac beaches. Lessons are offered for about $35 an hour at **St. Barth Wind School** (St. Jean, tel. 590/27–70–96), **Wind Wave Power** (St. Barths Beach Hotel, tel. 590/27–62–73), and at **Grand Bay Watersports** (Guanahani, tel. 590/27–66–60).

Shopping

St. Barts is a duty-free port and there are especially good bargains in jewelry, porcelain, imported liquors, and French perfumes, cosmetics, and designer resortwear.

Shopping Areas Shops are clustered in **Gustavia, St. Jean's Commercial Center,** and the **Villa Creole,** a cottage complex also in St. Jean. More shops and a gourmet supermarket are located across from the airport at **La Savane Commercial Center.**

Good Buys
Island Crafts Stop in Corossol to pick up some of the intricate straw work (wide-brim beach hats, mobiles, handbags) that the ladies of Corossol create by hand (*see* Exploring St. Barthélemy, above). For a very special kind of basket, visit **René Brin,** the last practitioner of a dying art form. His beautiful and sturdy fishermen's baskets each take three weeks to make and will last 30 years. For directions to his house/workshop in Lurin, contact Elise Magras at the Tourist Information Center (tel. 590/27–60–08). In Gustavia, look for hand-turned pottery at **St. Barth's Pottery** (tel. 590/27–62–74) and exotic coral and shell jewelry at the **Shell Shop** (no phone). In Colombier you'll find one of the best buys on the island, the hand-blocked prints of **Jean-Yves Froment** (*see* Exploring St. Barthélemy, above).

Wine and Gourmet
Shops Wine lovers will enjoy **La Cave** (Marigot, tel. 590/27–63–21), where an excellent collection of French vintages are stored in temperature-controlled cellars. Also check out **La Cave du Port Franc** (tel. 590/27–71–75) on the far side of the harbor for vintage wines, contemporary paintings, and objets d'art.

For exotic groceries or picnic fixings, stop by St. Barts's fabulous gourmet delis—**La Rotisserie** (tel. 590/27–63–13) on rue du Roi Oscar II (branches in Villa Creole and Pointe Milou) and **Taste Unlimited** (tel. 590/27–70–42) on rue du Général de Gaulle.

Dining

Dining out is a ritual on St. Barts. The quality of fare is generally high and so are the prices, which are reputed to be some of the steepest in the Caribbean. Many places offer prix fixe menus, which are usually a recommended choice. Italian, Creole, and French/Creole restaurants tend to be less expensive. *Accras* (salt cod fritters) with Creole sauce (minced hot peppers in oil), spiced *christophine* (a kind of squash), *boudin Créole* (a very spicy blood sausage), and a lusty *soupe de poissons* are some of the delicious and ubiquitous Creole dishes.

The most highly recommended restaurants are indicated by a star ★.

Category	Cost*
Expensive	over $45
Moderate	$25–$45
Inexpensive	under $25

per person, excluding drinks, service, and sales tax (4%)

Aux Trois Gourmands. This very pretty restaurant has an airy dining room overlooking Gustavia Harbor. The food is quite good nouvelle French cuisine. The chef trained with Paul Bocuse. *Next to produce market, Gustavia, tel. 590/27–71–83. Closed Sun. AE, CB, V. Expensive.*

Bartolomeo. There's a small bar as you enter, and at the rear is a pretty dining room that seats 35. The eclectic menu includes such pleasant surprises as lobster-stuffed ravioli and chicken breasts with ratatouille. For dessert, don't miss the luscious crème brûlée. *Hotel Guanahani, Grand Cul de Sac, tel. 590/ 27– 66–60. Reservations required. AE, MC, V. Expensive.*

★ **Castelets.** The romantic mountaintop setting, the first-class cooking of Marseilles-born Michel Viali, exceptional wines, and the soigné service make a meal at this classy *auberge* a St. Barts experience to savor. The cuisine is classic French and the tables are few and much in demand. *Morne Lurin, tel. 590/27– 61–73. Reservations required. AE, MC, V. Closed Tues., Wed. for lunch. Expensive.*

★ **François Plantation.** The approach to the dining room, through a flower-draped, lantern-hung arbor, is made for dramatic entrances. The menu is just as dramatic: quenelle of smoked salmon pâté, duck fillet with lemon and honey, a fan of prawns in a piquant Creole sauce. Tropical fruits with toasted sabayon sauce provides a perfect coda for a memorable evening *à table. Colombier, tel. 590/27–61–26. Reservations essential. AE, V. Expensive.*

L'Hibiscus. This popular in-town spot has a romantic terrace overlooking the harbor and a jazz trio playing nightly until 11:30. The food is disappointing for the price, but if you're looking for a cozy, lively atmosphere from which to catch a great sunset, this is the place. *Rue Thiers, Gustavia, tel. 590/27–64– 82. Dinner reservations required. AE, MC, V. Expensive.*

Club Lafayette. This "in" beach bistro offers simple but tasty lunch fare to a casually chic crowd. Grilled (barbecued in local parlance) lobster or crispy duck, followed by a fruit sherbet or *tarte tatin,* is the way to go. *Grand Cul de Sac, tel. 590/27–62– 51. Closed the end of May–mid-Nov. Reservations suggested. No credit cards. Expensive.*

Taiwana. A casual but exclusive beach club/hotel, this out-of-the-way lunch spot serves salads, lobsters, and grilled fish. Overnight patrons include a few celebrities and other folks invited by the owner. *Baie des Flamands, tel. 590/27–65–01. Reservations suggested. No credit cards. Expensive.*

Eddie's Ghetto. The combination of imaginatively prepared, modestly priced fare—crab salad, ragout of beef, crème caramel—served in a disarmingly fun-loving atmosphere turned Edward Stakelborough's restaurant into an instant success when it opened last year. The crowd is lively, the wine list impressive. *Gustavia, just off rue du Général de Gaulle. No phone. No credit cards. Reservations requested. Moderate.*

Gloriette. This beachside bistro serves delicious local dishes such as crunchy *accras* and grilled red snapper with Creole sauce. Light salads and Creole dishes are served at lunch and the house wine is always good. *Grand Cul de Sac, tel. 590/27– 75–66. No credit cards. Moderate.*

Hostellerie des Trois Forces. Fermented fruit juices, New Age chitchat, and a swim-up bar set the tone at this rustic mountaintop inn. A tasty Niçoise salad and omelet are excellent lunch choices, priced under $15. Dinner is served in a pretty country dining room. Especially good is the veal with cream butter and Calvados. Vegetarian dishes are also served. *Vitet, tel. 590/27–61–25. AE, MC, V. Moderate.*

★ **Le Flamboyant.** This restaurant features superb food on a charming, cozy terrace. Don't miss the tagliatelle St. Jacques for a starter. For dinner, the grilled lobster or fish accompanied by a bottle of chilled Sancerre is excellent. Be sure to get a table with a view. *Grand Cul de Sac, tel. 590/27–75–65. Closed Mon. Dinner only. AE, V. Moderate.*

La Langouste. Reserve a harborside table and order freely from the Creole and French menu, but save some room for the coconut flan dessert. The food is hearty and reasonably priced, and the airy pink dining rooms draw an eclectic crowd. *Rue Bord de la Mer, Gustavia 590/27–69–47. Reservations suggested. No credit cards. Closed for dinner Thurs. Moderate.*

★ **Le Patio.** Gourmet pizzas, salads, pastas, brochettes, and hamburgers are offered for lunch. In the evening there's all that plus fancier Italian fare—all reasonably priced. You'll like the breezy outdoor and indoor dining rooms, the views of the bay, and the friendly family service. *St. Jean, tel. 590/27–61–39. No credit cards. Closed Wed. Moderate.*

Marigot Bay Club. Generous portions and consistent quality help make this 16-table beachside place a favored lunch and dinner spot. Lightly spiced Creole dishes and simple fish and seafood entrées are featured. *Marigot, tel. 590/27–75–45. Reservations required. AE, V. Closed Sun. and for lunch on Mon. Moderate.*

★ **Bamboo.** Here relaxed picnic table–style dining on the beach at St. Jean sets the tone that is reasserted by the warm, friendly waiters. The menu ranges from burgers to lobsters. Sip an ice-cold beer as you watch the windsurfers and sunworshipers go by. *St. Jean, tel. 590/27–70–76. No credit cards. Lunch only. Inexpensive.*

Brasserie La Créole. Good breakfast omelets, croissants, and fresh fruit juices are served at open-air tables at this restaurant in the St. Jean shopping complex. For lunch and dinner there are salads, grilled dishes, and sandwiches. *St. Jean, tel. 590/27–68–09. AE. Inexpensive.*

Chez Francine. Swimsuit-clad patrons lunch on the terrace or at wood tables set in the sand. The lunch-only menu features grilled chicken, beef, and lobster, all served with crispy french fries for $15. *St. Jean Bay, tel. 590/27–60–49. MC, V. Inexpensive.*

Cote Jardin. Located on the hillside above Gustavia Harbor, this garden restaurant serves good Italian food at reasonable prices. Start with prosciutto and melon or tomatoes and mozzarella and move on to tortellini or a pizza. *Gustavia, tel. 590/27–70–47. Dinner only. MC, V. Inexpensive.*

★ **La Marine.** Mussels from France arrive on Thursday and in-the-know islanders are there to eat them at dockside picnic tables. The menu always includes fresh fish, hamburgers, and omelets. *Rue Jeanne d'Arc, Gustavia, tel. 590/27–70–13. No credit cards. Inexpensive.*

★ **L'Escale.** This pretty, cheery, and very popular restaurant is located harborside in Gustavia. Chef Eric Dugast cooks up the best pizza on the island, while Pierrie Lebrech prepares first-rate filet mignon, seafood, and pastas. With friendly service and low prices, it all adds up to a real winner! *Gustavia, tel. 590/27–70–33. Closed Tues. Dinner only. No credit cards. Inexpensive.*

★ **Le Rivage.** This new, popular, and very casual Creole establishment on the beach at Grand Cul de Sac serves delicious lobster salad, accras, and fresh grilled fish. The relaxed atmosphere and surprisingly low prices make for a very enjoyable time. *Grand Cul de Sac. tel. 590/27–60–70. Open for lunch and dinner. Closed Thurs. AE, MC, V. Inexpensive.*

Topolino. Popular with families. Topolino's offerings range from hearty Italian dishes to pizza. Trap your own lobster in the pond. *St. Jean, tel. 590/27–70–92. MC, V. Inexpensive.*

Lodging

The most highly recommended lodgings are indicated by a star ★.

Category	Cost*
Very Expensive	over $300
Expensive	$200–$300
Moderate	$125–$200
Inexpensive	under $125

*All prices are for a standard double room for two, excluding a 10%–15% service charge; there is no government room tax.

Hotels **Castelets.** Artists and dancers frequent this elegant hilltop inn with stunning views. Mme. Geneviève Jouany graciously presides over antiques-furnished rooms that are always in demand. You will need a car to go to the beach. *Box 60, Mt. Lurin, 97133, tel. 590/27–61–73. 10 rooms, some in 2 duplex villas. Facilities: small pool, restaurant. AE, MC, V. Very Expensive.*

Filao Beach. Comfortable duplex cottages surround a flower-filled garden on one of the island's most popular beaches. Service is very good and St. Jean's attractions are within easy walking distance. *Box 167, St. Jean, 97133, tel. 590/27–64–85. 30 rooms. Facilities: pool, luncheon, restaurant/bar. Very Expensive.*

★ **Guanahani.** This 7-acre resort adjoining the Rothschild estate is the island's largest. Grey-roof bungalows nestle in the hillside and some have lovely private pools. Beachside suites are much in demand. This is a full-service resort that knows how to pamper, pamper. *Box 109, Grand Cul de Sac, 97133, tel. 590/27–66–60. 17 double rooms, some with ocean views, 33 deluxe doubles, 3 spa suites with Jacuzzis, 10 1-bedroom suites with private pool and kitchens. Facilities: 2 restaurants, 2 lighted tennis courts, pool with Jacuzzi, beach, water-sports center. AE, MC, V. Very Expensive.*

Hotel Manapany Cottages. A ramshackle entry road ends at this luxury enclave, which is built around Anse des Cayes. Accommodations vary from St. Barts–style cottages and suites tucked into the hillside to much-in-demand beachfront suites with marble baths and four-poster beds. Bronze jet-setters line the pretty pool. The small beach sometimes has a strong undercurrent but the waves are great for surfing. *Box 114, tel. 590/27–66–59; 212/757–0225 in the U.S. 20 cottages and 12 club suites. Facilities: 2 restaurants, 2 bars, pool, Jacuzzi, beach,* *bocci-ball court, exercise room, boutique, lighted tennis court, water-sports center. AE, MC, V. Very Expensive.*

Hotel La Banane. Rustic luxury is the style of these romantic bungalows just off the beach. Rooms are tastefully decorated and especially popular with owner Jean Marie Rivière's celebrity friends. *Quartier Lorient, 97133, tel. 590/27–68–25. Facilities: restaurant, 2 pools, Jacuzzi. AE. Expensive.*

★ **François Plantation.** A colonial-era graciousness pervades this four-star complex of hilltop bungalows managed by longtime island habitués Françoise and François Beret. Everything is designed to take full advantage of the terrain, vegetation, and location high above Flamands. Rooms are air-conditioned and have refrigerators and satellite TV. You'll need a car for the beach and reservations for the elegant restaurant. *Colombier, 97133, tel. 590/27–78–82; 800/932–3222 in the U.S. 4 garden and 8 sea-view rooms. Facilities: pool, restaurant. AE, V. Expensive.*

L'Hibiscus. Air-conditioned bungalow rooms overlook Gustavia, though some of the patios look out on nearby buildings, too. A beach is within walking distance and the nightlife is always lively in the hotel's jazz lounge. *Rue Thiers, B. P. 86, Gustavia, 97133, tel. 590/27–64–82. 11 rooms with kitchenettes. Facilities: restaurant, pool, lounge. AE, DC, MC, V. Expensive.*

El Sereno Beach Hotel. A quiet, casually chic ambience pervades, and managers Christine and Marc Llepez are perfect hosts. Small but comfortable rooms with high-walled patios surround a central garden. The restaurant food is outstanding, and the clientele includes many repeats. *Box 19, Grand Cul de Sac, 97133, tel. 590/27–64–80. 20 rooms (3 sea-view). Facilities: restaurant, bar, pool, beach with water-sports center, boutique. DC, MC, V. Expensive.*

Grand Cul De Sac Beach Hotel and **St. Barths Beach Hotel.** These side-by-side properties owned by Guy Turbé stretch out on a narrow peninsula between lagoon and sea. Both are comfortable, unpretentious, and popular with families and tour groups who take advantage of the full range of sports available on the hotels' beach. Upper-level rooms are best at the two-story St. Barths Beach Hotel; the best rooms at Grand Cul de Sac Beach Hotel, a group of small air-conditioned bungalow units with kitchenettes, are right on the beach. The windows are screenless and if left open, mosquitoes can be a problem. There's limited parking for cars not rented through Turbé's agency. *Box 81, Grand Cul de Sac, 97133, tel. 590/27–62–73. 35 rooms; 16 bungalows. Facilities: 2 restaurants, bar, saltwater pool, tennis court, windsurfing school and water-sports center, TV/library room. AE, MC, V. Moderate–Expensive.*

Baie des Flamands. Upper-level rooms have balconies and lower-level ones have terrace kitchenette units in this newly refurbished motel-style hotel. One of the first hotels on the island, it is still run by a St. Barts family and is popular with families and tour groups. It has a good restaurant and an outstanding beach location. *Box 68, Anse des Flamands, 97133, tel. 590/27–64–85. 24 rooms with baths. Facilities: restaurant, bar, beach, saltwater pool, TV/library room, rental cars. AE, MC, V. Moderate.*

Marigot Bay Club. Jean Michel Ledee's pleasant apartments across from his popular seaside restaurant feature comfortable furniture, louvered doors and windows, air-conditioning, twin beds, kitchen/living areas, and large terraces with good views.

Marigot, 97133, tel. 590/27–75–45. 6 apartments. Facilities: restaurant, nearby beach. AE, V. Moderate.

Sea Horse Club. Next door to the Marigot Bay Club, this property has spacious suites and a beautifully landscaped garden. All rooms have living room, kitchen, terrace, shower/bath. *Marigot, 97133, tel. 590/27–75–36. 11 suites. Facilities: restaurant and beach within walking distance. AE, MC, V. Moderate.*

Le P'tit Morne. Families like these mountainside studios, each with a private balcony, air-conditioning, and good views. A snack bar serving breakfast and light lunches recently opened. *Box 14, Colombier, 97133, tel. 590/27–62–64. 14 rooms with kitchens. Facilities: pool, snack bar, reading room. AE, MC, V. Moderate.*

Tropical Hotel. Up the hill from St. Jean's Beach, this cozy gingerbread complex encircles a lush garden and small pool. The ambience is friendly; accommodations are air-conditioned. *Box 147, St. Jean, 97133, tel. 590/27–64–87. 20 rooms. Facilities: restaurant, reception bungalow with bar and wide-screen video lounge, pool. AE, MC, V. Moderate.*

★ **Village St. Jean.** This stone and redwood resort, up a short, steep hill from St. Jean's Beach, is now run by the second generation of the Charneau family. It has acquired a strong following over the years. The accent is on service, privacy, and wholesomeness. There are a variety of accommodations with air-conditioning and fine views of the town. Rounding out the picture will be a pool, which is scheduled for completion in 1990. This is a good value. *Box 23, St. Jean, 97133, tel. 590/27–61–39. 24 rooms. Facilities: restaurant, bar, small grocery, boutique, game and reading room. V. Moderate.*

★ **White Sand Beach Cottages.** The road in front of the place is a little ramshackle but these cottages are pleasant, air-conditioned, and well equipped. The cottage on the beach is the best. *Anse des Flamands, 97133, tel. 590/27–63–66. 4 cottages with kitchenettes. Facilities: beach, sun deck, MC, V. Inexpensive–Moderate.*

Auberge de la Petite Anse. Minimal decor but comfortable rooms with terraces and air-conditioning are offered in eight bungalows just above the beach. A grocery, bar, and restaurant are within walking distance. *Box 117, Anse des Flamands, tel. 590/27–64–60. 16 rooms with kitchenettes. AE, V. Inexpensive.*

La Normandie. This small inn offers reasonably priced rooms, a restaurant, and dancing in the evening on a glass floor set over the pool. Ask for one of the two air-conditioned rooms. *Lorient, 97133, tel. 590/27–61–66. 8 rooms. Facilities: pool, restaurant. V. Inexpensive.*

★ **Les Mouettes.** Good family accommodations are provided in bungalows overlooking the island's best surfing beach. *Lorient, 97133, tel. 590/27–60–74. 6 rooms. Each room has a shower, patio, and kitchenette. Facilities: car rental. Inexpensive.*

Villas, Condos, Apartments

For the price of an inexpensive hotel room, you can get your own little cottage, and for the price of a room at an expensive hotel, you'll get a villa with several bedrooms and your own swimming pool. On an island where the restaurants are so expensive, having a kitchen of your own makes sense. What you sacrifice in room service and the amenities of a hotel, you'll gain in privacy, more room, and money saved.

Villas, apartments, and condos can be rented through SIBARTH (tel. 590/27–62–38), which handles about 200 properties. WIMCO (800/932–3222) is the agency's representative in the United States. Rents average $700–$1,000 per week for one-bedroom villas, $3,500 for three-bedroom villas, and more for houses with pools.

Nightlife

St. Barts is a mostly in-bed-by-midnight island. However, some of the hotels and restaurants provide some late-night fun. Cocktail hour finds the barefoot boating set gathered in the garden of **Gustavia's Le Select;** the more sophisticated up at **L'Hibiscus's** jazz bar; the French at **Bar de l'Oubli.** Sunset-watchers head up to **Santa Fe** in Lurin or to **Chez Mayas's** terrace in Public. Then it's a long, leisurely meal, followed by an after-dinner drink on a breezy terrace—possibly **Castelets** in Lurin or your own. Roger Parat holds forth in **Manapany's** piano bar nightly, and there's a talented pianist at the **Guanahani** till midnight. The young and the hip gather after 10 at **Autour du Rocher** (tel. 590/27–60–73) in Lorient, a disco with billiards and backgammon. **La Licorne,** a newer disco also in Lorient, can be lively on weekends, as can **Pearl's Club** at the Jean Bart Hotel in St. Jean. At 10 PM on weekends the owner of Hotel La Banane emcees a Parisian-style revue made up of the waiters and waitresses at his **Club La Banane.** The audience participates, and—frequently—by the end of the show most of the performers, and some of the audience, wind up in the hotel swimming pool.

The owners of L'Escale have opened a very exclusive, very upscale club called **West** in Gustavia, featuring two floors of dancing to live music and a disco DJ.

21 St. Eustatius

by Honey Naylor

The flight approach to this tiny Dutch island of St. Eustatius, commonly known as Statia (pronounced Staysha) in the Netherlands Antilles, is almost worth the visit itself. The plane circles The Quill, a 1,968-foot-high extinct volcano that has an inviting rain forest within its crater. Here are giant elephant ears, ferns, flowers, wild orchids, fruit trees, wildlife, and birds hiding in the trees. The whole island is alive with untended greenery—bougainvillea, oleander, hibiscus, and alemanda.

During the American Revolutionary War, when the British blockaded the North American coast, food, arms, and other supplies for the American revolutionaries were diverted through the West Indies, notably through neutral Statia. (Benjamin Franklin had his mail routed through Statia to ensure its safe arrival in Europe.) On November 16, 1776, the brig-of-war *Andrew Doria*, commanded by Captain Isaiah Robinson of the Continental Navy, sailed into Statia's port flying the Stars and Stripes and fired a 13-gun salute to the Royal Netherlands standard. Governor Johannes de Graaff ordered the cannons of Fort Oranje to return the salute, and that first official acknowledgment of the new American flag by a foreign power earned Statia the nickname "America's Childhood Friend." Each year on November 16, Statian dignitaries in colonial-style garb participate in a colorful reenactment of the occasion at Fort Oranje; the festivities include parades, bands, picnics, and speeches.

Little 8-square-mile Statia, past which Columbus sailed in 1493, had prospered almost from the day the Dutch Zeelanders colonized it in 1636. In the 1700s, a double row of warehouses crammed with goods stretched for a mile along the bay, and there were sometimes as many as 200 ships tied up at the duty-free port. The island was called the "Emporium of the Western World" and "Golden Rock." There were almost 8,000 Statians on the island in the 1790s (today, there are about 1,700). Holland, England, and France fought one another for possession of the island, which changed hands 22 times. In 1816 it became a Dutch possession and has remained so to this day.

Four years after Statia's salute to the new American flag, Britain declared war on Holland, and on February 3, 1781, British Admiral George Rodney captured Dranjestad and proceeded to rob the island blind. Statia had aided, abetted, and acknowledged Britain's rebellious colony, and in revenge Rodney closed its shops, sealed its warehouses, auctioned off goods, and even confiscated the personal possessions of the islanders. For a month he kept the Dutch flag flying, thus luring and entrapping as many as 150 ships and confiscating their cargos. Less than a year later, having fattened his personal purse with about 4 million pounds sterling, Rodney departed. Statia bounced back, and flourished for another 10 years. Ironically, Statia's prosperity ended partly due to the success of the American Revolution. The island was no longer needed as a transshipment port, and its bustling economy gradually came to a stop.

Statia is in the Dutch Windward Triangle, 178 miles east of Puerto Rico and 35 miles south of St. Maarten. Oranjestad, the capital and only "city" (note quotes), is on the western side facing the Caribbean. The island is anchored at the north and the south by extinct volcanoes, like the Quill, that are separated by a central plain.

Statia is a wonderful playground for hikers and divers. There's as much to see underwater as on the island. Myriad ancient ships rest on the ocean floor alongside 18th-century warehouses that were slowly buried in the sea by storms. Much of the aboveground activity has to do with archaeology and restoration. Students from William and Mary's College of Archaeology converge on the island each summer; the University of Leyden in the Netherlands has a pre-Columbian program that includes the study of Statian Indian sites and artifacts; and the island's Historical Foundation is actively engaged in restoring Statian landmarks.

Most visitors will be content with a day visit from nearby St. Maarten, exploring some of the historical sights and enjoying a relaxed meal at the Old Gin House. Those who stay longer tend to be collectors of unspoiled islands with a need to relax and a taste for history.

Before You Go

Tourist Information
Contact the **Saba and St. Eustatius Tourist Information Office** (c/o Medhurst & Associates, Inc., 271 Main St., Northport, NY 11768, tel. 516/261–7474, 212/936–0050, or 800/344–4606). You may also contact the **Tourist Board** on the island (Oranjestad, St. Eustatius, Netherlands Antilles, tel. 599/38–2433.) While telephone communications are good, it can take anywhere from a week to two months for mail to get through.

Arriving and Departing
By Plane
Windward Islands Airways (tel. 599/5–44230 or 599/5–44237) makes the 20-minute flight from St. Maarten four times a day, the 10-minute flight from Saba daily, and the 15-minute flight from St. Kitts daily. **LIAT** (tel. 809/462–0700) has twice-weekly flights from St. Kitts.

From the Airport
Planes put down at the **Franklin Delano Roosevelt Airport,** where taxis meet all flights and charge about $3 for the drive into town.

Passports and Visas
All visitors must have proof of citizenship. A passport is preferred, but a birth certificate or voter registration card will do. (A driver's license will *not* do). British citizens need a "British Visitors" passport. All visitors need a return or ongoing ticket.

Customs and Duties
There is no customs, as Statia is a free port, so you don't have to worry about documentation for expensive possessions.

Language
Statia's official language is Dutch; it's used on government documents. However, everyone speaks English and Dutch is taught as a second language in the schools, and street signs are in both Dutch and English.

Further Reading
St. Maarten bookstores carry Dr. J. Hartog's book *St. Maarten, Saba and St. Eustatius.* At the Statia Historical Foundation you can get a copy of *St. Eustatius—A Short History,* by Ypie Attema.

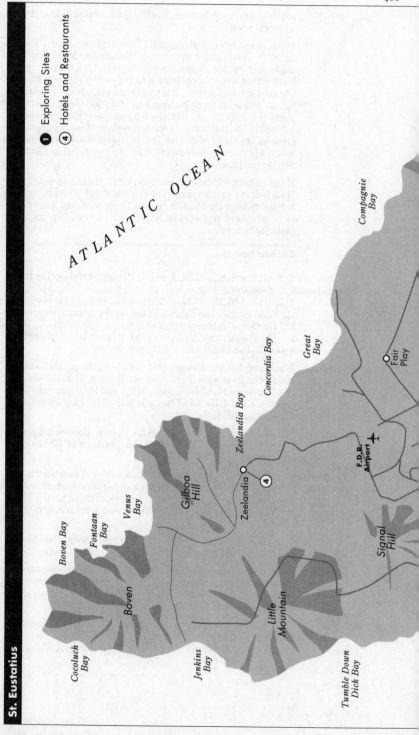

St. Eustatius

● Exploring Sites
④ Hotels and Restaurants

ATLANTIC OCEAN

Compagnie Bay

Fair Play

Great Bay

Concordia Bay

F.D.R. Airport

Zeelandia Bay

Zeelandia ④

Gilboa Hill

Venus Bay

Boven Bay

Fontaan Bay

Boven

Cocoluch Bay

Signal Hill

Little Mountain

Jenkins Bay

Tumble Down Dick Bay

457

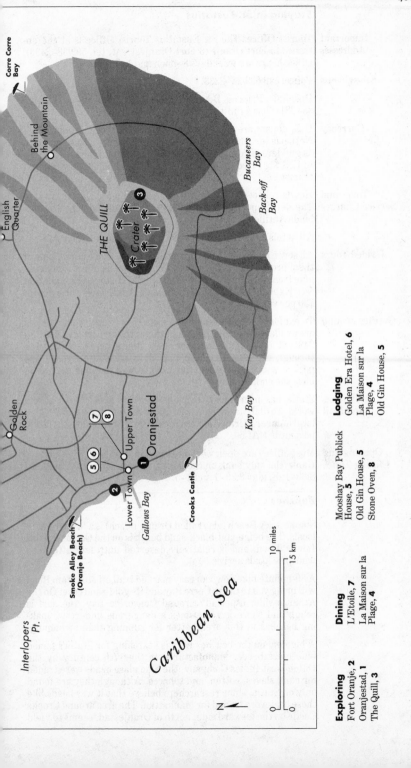

Exploring
Fort Oranje, **2**
Oranjestad, **1**
The Quill, **3**

Dining
L'Etoile, **7**
La Maison sur la
Plage, **4**

Mooshay Bay Publick
House, **5**
Old Gin House, **5**
Stone Oven, **8**

Lodging
Golden Era Hotel, **6**
La Maison sur la
Plage, **4**
Old Gin House, **5**

Staying in St. Eustatius

Important Addresses

Tourist Office: The **St. Eustatius Tourist Office** is at the entrance to Fort Oranje (3 Fort Oranjestraat, tel. 599/38–2433). Office hours are weekdays 8–noon and 1–5.

Emergencies **Police:** call 599/38–2333.

Hospitals: Princess Beatrix Hospital (25 Prinsesweg, tel. 599/38–2211) has a full-time licensed physician on duty.

Currency U.S. dollars are accepted everywhere, but legal tender is the Netherlands Antilles florin (NAf). Florins are also referred to as guilders. The exchange rate fluctuates but is about NAf1.80 to U.S.$1. Prices quoted here are in U.S. dollars unless noted otherwise.

Taxes and Service Charges Hotels collect a 5% government tax and a 5% electricity tax. The departure tax is $5 for destinations outside the Netherlands Antilles.

All hotels and restaurants add a 10%–15% service charge.

Guided Tours All seven of Statia's taxis are available for island tours. Some of them provide an audiocassette tape, which is otherwise available from the Tourist Office or from the Historical Foundation (*see* Exploring St. Eustatius, below). A full day's outing costs $30 per vehicle.

Getting Around To explore the island (and there isn't very much), car rentals are available through the **Avis** outlet at the airport (tel. 599/38–2421) at a cost of about $30 per day. Rentals are also available through the island's seven taxi drivers. Statia's roads are pocked with potholes and the going is slow and bumpy. Cattle have the right of way.

Telephones and Mail Statia has microwave telephone service to all parts of the world. To dial Statia from the United States, dial 011–599/38 + local number. Airmail letters to the United States are NAf1.30; postcards NAf.60.

Opening and Closing Times Most offices are open weekdays 8–noon and 1–4 or 5. **Barclays Bank** (the only bank on the island) is open Monday–Thursday 8:30–1; Friday 8:30–1 and 4–5.

Beaches

Smoke Alley Beach (also called Oranje Beach) is a favorite with locals. The beige-and-black-sand beach is on the Caribbean, off Lower Town, and is relatively deserted until late afternoon when the locals arrive.

A 30-minute hike down an easy marked trail off Mountain Road will bring you to **Corre Corre Bay** and its gold-sand cove. On the Atlantic side, especially around Concordia Bay, the surf is rough and there is sometimes a dangerous undertow, making beaches in this area better for sunning than swimming.

A big deal on the beaches here is searching for Statia's famed blue glass beads. Manufactured in the 17th century by the Dutch West Indies Company, the blue glass beads were traded for rum, slaves, cotton, and tobacco. Although they are found only on Statia, some researchers believe that it was beads like these that were traded for Manhattan. The area around **Crooks Castle** on the leeward side, north of Oranjestad, seems to yield the most treasure, although they are getting harder to find. (Glass beads in the sand should tell you something about running barefoot on the beach.)

Exploring St. Eustatius

Numbers in the margin correspond with points of interest on the St. Eustatius map.

Oranjestad, Statia's capital and only town, sits on the western coast facing the Caribbean. It's a split-level town: Upper Town and Lower Town. History buffs will enjoy poking around the ancient Dutch colonial buildings, which are being restored by the Historical Foundation, while hikers will want to head for the hills of The Quill. Both Oranjestad and Lower Town are easily explored on foot.

Oranjestad
① First stop is the **Tourist Office,** which is right at the entrance to Fort Oranje. You can pick up maps, brochures, and friendly advice, as well as a copy of the Historical Foundation's eight-page *Walking Tour* (50¢) and a listing of 12 marked hiking trails. You can also pick up the audiocassette tour, produced by the Historical Foundation in five languages, and available free on loan.

② When you leave the Tourist Office, you will be at the entrance to **Fort Oranje.** With its three bastions, the fort has clutched these cliffs since 1636. In 1976, Statia participated in the U.S. Bicentennial celebration by restoring the old fort, and now there are gleaming black cannons pointing out over the ramparts. In the parade grounds a plaque, presented in 1939 by Franklin D. Roosevelt, reads, "Here the sovereignty of the United States of America was first formally acknowledged to a national vessel by a foreign official." Various government buildings, including the post office, are within the fort, and restoration continues.

From the fort, cross over to Wilhelminaweg (Wilhelmina Way) in the center of Upper Town. The **St. Eustatius Historical Foundation Museum** is in the Doncker/de Graaff house, a lovely building with slim columns and a high gallery. British Admiral Rodney is believed to have lived here while he was stealing everything in sight. The house, acquired by the foundation in 1983 and completely restored, is Statia's most important intact 18th-century dwelling. Exhibits trace the island's history from the 6th century to the present and among the displays are Indian artifacts and a complete Amerindian skeleton. The eight-page *Walking Tour,* postcards, souvenirs, and books about Statia are sold here, and the foundation's audiocassette tour is available here also. *12 Van Tonningenweg, no phone. Admission: $1 adults, 50¢ children. Open weekdays 9–5.*

Return to Fort Oranjestraat (Fort Orange St.) and turn left. Continue to 4 **Fort Oranjestraat,** at the corner of Kerkweg (Church Way). The big yellow house, with a stone foundation, shingled walls, and gingerbread trim, is typical of the houses built in the West Indies around the turn of the century. Just behind it is **Three Widows Corner,** a tropical courtyard where you'll see two more examples of Statian architecture in a town house and another gingerbread house.

Now head west down Kerkweg to the edge of the cliff, where you'll find the **Dutch Reformed Church,** built in 1775. Once a ship's landmark, its square tower now houses a Historical Foundation information center. Ancient tales can be read on the gravestones in the 18th-century cemetery adjacent to the church.

Continue on Kerkweg and take the next two left turns onto Synagogepad (Synagogue Path) to **Honen Dalim** ("She Who Is Charitable to the Poor"), one of the Caribbean's oldest synagogues. Dating from 1738, it is now in ruins but is slated for restoration.

❸ The Quill, the volcanic cone rising in the northern sector, is 3 miles south of Oranjestad on the main road *(see Hiking, below).*

Time Out The **Kool Korner,** directly opposite the Tourist Office, is a cool spot to have a beer and shoot the breeze. It's also the place where locals pick up daily fresh-baked bread. *Fort Oranjestraat, no phone. Open daily 8:30 AM–10 PM.*

Follow Prinsesweg back to the main square and zigzag down the cobblestone Fort Road to Lower Town. Warehouses and shops that in the 18th century were piled high with European imports are now either abandoned or simply used to store local fishermen's equipment, but the restoration of the 18th-century cotton mill on the land side of Bay Road is impressive. The palms, flowering shrubs, and park benches along the water's edge are the work of the Historical Foundation members. As you walk along the water, imagine the time when this town was the center of commerce in the Caribbean.

Time Out Old Gin House (Lower Town, tel. 599/38–2319) is one of the nicest places on the island to rest, have a drink, or lunch.

Off the Beaten Track

For a dramatic view of the neighboring island of St. Kitts, drive south along "The Road to White Wall" as far as you can go. There you'll discover tiny Fort de Windt, whose solitary cannon points its muzzle across the narrow channel as if to challenge St. Kitts's massive Brimstone Hill fortifications, once called "The Gibraltar of the Caribbean."

Participant Sports

Hiking Trails range from the easy to the "Watch out!" The big thrill here is The Quill, the 1,968-foot extinct volcano with its craterful of rain forest. The Tourist Office has a list of 12 marked trails and can put you in touch with a guide (whose fee will be about $20).

Scuba Diving If you've never gone to an undersea supermarket, here's your chance. The "supermarket" is actually two parallel shipwrecks less than 50 yards apart. It's but one of the many wrecks and 18th-century submerged seaports you can see. **Surfside Statia,** (tel. 800/468–1708), a fully equipped dive shop offering certification courses, is operated by Americans Mike Guderian and Joe Donahue out of a warehouse next to the Old Gin House.

Snorkeling Crooks Point has several stands of pillar coral, giant yellow seafans, and seawhips. Jenkins Bay is another favorite with snorkelers. For equipment rental, contact **Surfside Statia** (*see* Scuba Diving, above).

Tennis There's a lone tennis court at the **Community Center** that's even lighted at night. There are changing rooms, but you'll have to bring your own racquets and balls. Cost is $2 (check with the Tourist Office for more information).

Shopping

Though shopping on Statia is duty-free, it is also somewhat limited. A handful of shops do offer unusual items, however. The boutique at **The Old Gin House** (tel. 599/38–2319) features handcrafts from around the Caribbean, as well as cottons silk-screened with traditional Statian motifs and sold both by the yard and made up into attractive resortwear. At **Hole in the Wall** on Van Tonningenweg in Upper Town (tel. 599/38–2265), owners Jana Morrison and Marianne Fitzsimmons hand-paint skirts, blouses, sundresses, and T-shirts in colorful and clever designs. Barbara Lane shows her own sophisticated ceramic pieces, together with paintings and woven sculptures by local artists at her **Park Place** (no phone) across from the Kool Korner in the center of town.

Dining

The variety of cuisines here is surprising, given the size of the island. Besides the traditional West Indian fare, you can find French and Italian cuisine.

The most highly recommended restaurants are indicated by a star ★.

Category	Cost*
Expensive	$25–$35
Moderate	$15–$25
Inexpensive	under $15

per person, excluding drinks and service

★ **La Maison sur la Plage.** The view is of the Atlantic, the cloths are crisp and white, and the fare is French. For dinner, openers include fish soup and quiche Lorraine. Among the entrées are duck breast with green-peppercorn sauce and *entrecôte forestière* (sirloin with mushrooms, cream, and red wine). Try the crepes à l'orange for dessert. *Zeelandia, tel. 599/38–2256. Reservations required. AE. Expensive.*

★ **Mooshay Bay Publick House.** The kitchen here has been praised by *Gourmet* magazine, and with justification. Your four-course, fixed-price feast likely will begin with warm grapefruit soup or a salad of smoked red snapper. The main course could be chateaubriand Dijonnaise, roast duck with sweet-and-sour sauce, or lobster mousse with caviar and horseradish. Two wines are included with the dinner. The setting is elegantly rustic, with old-brick walls, candlelight, pewter, and gleaming crystal. *Old Gin House, Lower Town, Oranjestad, tel. 599/38–2319. Reservations required. AE, DC, MC, V. Expensive.*

★ **Old Gin House.** Dining is delightful on the oceanside terrace of this hotel. The menu includes lobster Antillean (lobster chunks stewed with onions, red wine, Pernod, and a dash of hot pepper), plain burgers and dillyburgers (with sour cream and dill sauce), lobster salad, and sandwiches. *Old Gin House, Lower Town, tel. 599/38–2345. Reservations advised. AE, DC, MC, V. Moderate.*

Chinese Bar and Restaurant. Owner Kim Cheng serves up tasty Oriental and Caribbean dishes—*Bamigoreng* (Indonesian chow mein), pork chops Creole—in hearty portions at his unpretentious establishment. Dinging indoors can be slightly claustrophobic, but just ask your waitress if you may tote your Formica-top table out onto the terrace. She'll probably be happy to lend a hand and then serve you under the stars. *Prinsesweg, Upper Town, Oranjestad, tel. 599/38–2389. No credit cards. Inexpensive.*

★ **L'Etoile.** West Indian dishes such as spicy stuffed land crab and deep-fried meat turnovers are prepared by Caren Henriquez in a simple snack bar/restaurant. You can also get hot dogs, hamburgers, and spareribs. *Prinsesweg, Upper Town, Oranjestad, tel. 599/38–2299. No credit cards. Inexpensive.*

Stone Oven. West Indian specialties such as "goat water" (stew) are featured indoors. You can eat either indoors in the little house or outside on the palm-fringed patio. *16A Feaschweb, Upper Town, Oranjestad, tel. 599/38–2247. Reservations required. No credit cards. Inexpensive.*

Lodging

There are only three full-service hotels and a few apartment rentals on the island.

The most highly recommended lodgings are indicated by a star ★.

Category	Cost*
Very Expensive	over $100
Expensive	$80–$100
Moderate	$60–$80
Inexpensive	under $60

*All prices are for a standard double room for two, excluding 10% tax and a 15% service charge.

Hotels **Old Gin House.** American expatriate John May has fashioned a
★ comfortable inn out of the ruins of an 18th-century cotton-gin factory and warehouse. The cluster of buildings includes one that is two stories high, its bougainvillea-swathed double balconies overlooking a secluded tropical courtyard and pool; the highly acclaimed Mooshay Bay Publick House; a terrace restaurant and bar by the sea; and an additional six rooms in a two-story building with high ceilings, custom-made furnishings, and balconies that jut out over the ocean. The rooms are spacious and individually decorated with antique furnishings. There's a gallery with a library and lounge for cards and backgammon, and a cozy pub with beam ceilings and an 18th-century Bristol clock. *Box 172, Oranjestad, tel. 599/38–2319 or 800/223–5581 in USA. 20 rooms with bath. Facilities: pool, 2*

restaurants, bar, lounge, library, boutique. AE, DC, MC, V. Very Expensive.

Golden Era Hotel. This is a harborfront hotel whose rooms are neat, small, air-conditioned, and motel-modern. All have little terraces, but only half have a full or partial view of the sea. The other rooms look out over concrete or down on the roof of the restaurant. In the coffee-shop-style restaurant, fluorescent lights shine on curried dishes, fried chicken, spareribs, and conch and dumplings—all reasonably priced. Things pick up on Sundays, when a live band holds forth. *Box 109, Oranjestad, tel. 599/38–2345 or 800/223–6510. 19 rooms, 1 suite; all with private bath. Facilities: pool, restaurant, and bar. MC, V. Moderate–Expensive.*

La Maison sur la Plage. The plage is a 2-mile crescent of gray sand slapped by the wild waters of the Atlantic. The undertow here can be dangerous, so you should do your swimming in the pool. A cozy lobby has rattan furnishings, a checkerboard on the coffee table, and shelves filled with books. There's a stone-and-wood bar, and a *très* French dining room bordered by a trellis and greenery. French-born Michelle Greca's *maison* (house) is actually eight Spartan cottages where you have a choice of twin, double, or king-size beds. Each cottage has a bath and a private veranda, where a Continental breakfast is served. The most active thing in this isolated area is the Atlantic. *Box 157, Zeelandia, tel. 599/38–2256 or 800/845–9504. 10 rooms with bath. Facilities: pool, restaurant, bar, and lounge. AE. Moderate.*

Apartment Rentals Statia has only a handful of apartments, and the only luxury accommodation is **Cherry Tree Villa** (tel. 800/325–2222 or 813/787–2579), which sprawls over 17 lush acres. The moderately priced two-bedroom villa sleeps four, and its luxe touches include a Cuisinart, dishwasher, microwave oven, outdoor Jacuzzi facing the sea, and use of a car. A Hobie Cat and a 32-foot skippered yacht are available for an extra charge.

The **Henriquez Apartments** (tel. 599/38–2299), near the airport, are inexpensive studios with carpeted floors, small refrigerators, TVs, fans, coffeemakers, private baths, and either two double or twin beds. There's an outdoor patio with a barbecue pit and a meeting room that can accommodate 12. Check with the Tourist Office for information about these and other apartment rentals in Oranjestad.

Nightlife

Statia's three local bands divide their time among gigs at the occasional Saturday-night dances at the **Community Center** *(see* Participant Sports, above); alfresco soirees at the **Chinese Bar and Restaurant** *(see* Dining, above); and Sunday nights at the **Golden Era** *(see* Lodging, above). An alternative to all that activity is to just hang out at the **Kool Korner** till it closes *(see* Exploring St. Eustatius, above).

22 St. Kitts

by Honey Naylor

Tiny though it is, St. Kitts, the first English settlement in the Leeward Islands, crams some stunning scenery into its 65 square miles. St. Kitts is fertile and lush with tropical flora and has some fascinating natural and historical attractions: a rain forest, replete with waterfalls, thick vines, and secret trails; a central mountain range dominated by the 3,792-foot Mt. Liamuiga whose crater has been long dormant; and Brimstone Hill, the Caribbean's most impressive fortress, which was known in the 17th century as the Gibraltar of the West Indies. The island is home to 35,000 people and hosts some 60,000 visitors annually.

Until 1988, the island's official name was St. Christopher (Columbus named it after his patron saint), and its nickname was St. Kitts. Since everybody called it by its nickname anyway, the island officially changed its name to St. Kitts. The island is known as the Mother Colony of the West Indies, because it was from here that the English settlers sailed to Antigua, Barbuda, Tortola, and Montserrat, and the French dispatched colonizing parties to Martinique, Guadeloupe, St. Martin, St. Barts, Desirade, and Les Saintes. The French, who, inexplicably, brought a bunch of monkeys with them, arrived on St. Kitts a few years after the British.

As was the case on many Caribbean islands during the 17th and 18th centuries, the British and the French fell to squabbling. They joined forces long enough to massacre the cannibalistic Carib Indians and to reach an agreement by which the French held the north and south of the island and the British controlled the midsection, after which everybody (except the Caribs) set about growing tobacco, ginger, indigo, cotton, and later, sugar. Slaves were brought in from Africa, magnificent plantation homes were built, and sugar became the island's main export.

Things never were that friendly between the English and the French, and in the late 18th century, the French lay siege to Brimstone Hill and took it. Ultimately, the terms of the Treaty of Versailles in 1783 gave the British full control of the island. In 1967, St. Kitts and Nevis—together with Anguilla—became a self-governing state, from which Anguilla seceded later in the same year. St. Kitts-Nevis gained full independence from Britain in 1983.

The shape of St. Kitts has been variously compared to a whale, a cricket bat, and a guitar. It's roughly oval shape, 19 miles long and 6 miles wide, with a narrow peninsula trailing off toward Nevis, 2 miles across the strait. It's one of the Leeward Islands of the Lesser Antilles, in the eastern Caribbean.

As rich in history as it is fertile and lush with tropical flora, St. Kitts is just beginning to develop its tourism industry, and this quiet member of the Leeward group has that rare combination of natural and historic attractions and fine sailing, island hopping, and water-sports options offshore.

Before You Go

Tourist Information

Contact the **St. Kitts & Nevis Tourist Board** (414 E. 75th St., New York, NY 10021, tel. 212/535–1234), **St. Kitts & Nevis Tourist Office** (11 Yorkville Ave., Suite 508, Toronto, Ont., Canada M4W 1L3, tel. 416/921–7717), and **Rosamunde Bern**

St. Kitts

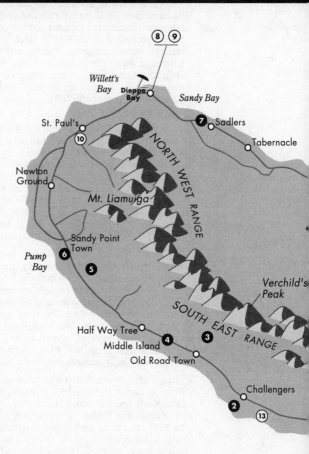

● Exploring Sites

⑧ Hotels and Restaurants

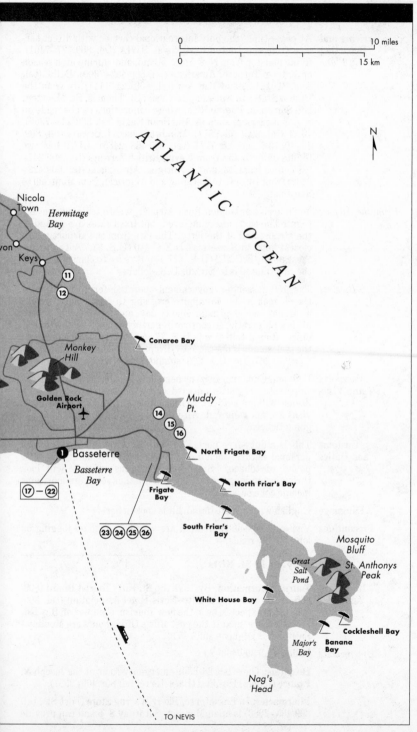

Association (15 Wardour Mews, d'Arblay St., London W1V, 3FF, United Kingdom, tel. 01/437–9475).

Arriving and Departing
By Plane

At press time, the only international carrier with direct service from the United States was **BWIA** (tel. 800/327–7401), flying nonstop from New York, Miami, and, during high season only, from Toronto. **American** (tel. 800/433–7300), **Delta**, (tel. 800/221–1212), and **Pan Am** (tel. 800/221–1111) fly from the United States to Antigua, St. Croix, St. Thomas, St. Maarten, and San Juan, Puerto Rico, where connections can be made on regional carriers such as **American Eagle** (tel. 800/433–7300), **LIAT** (tel. 809/465–2511), **Windward Island Airways** (tel. 809/465–0810), and **Air BVI** (tel. 800/468–2485). LIAT has two flights daily to and from Nevis, **British Airways** (tel. 800/247–9297) flies from London to Antigua, **Air Canada** (tel. 800/422–6232) from Toronto to Antigua, and American from Montreal to San Juan.

From the Airport

You'll arrive at Golden Rock Airport, where taxis meet every flight. The taxis are unmetered, but fixed rates are posted at the airport and at the jetty. The fare from the airport to the closest hotel in Basseterre is E.C.\$10 (U.S. \$3.70); to the farthest point, E.C.\$52 (U.S. \$17.40). Be sure to clarify whether the rate quoted is in E.C. or U.S. dollars.

By Boat

The 150-passenger government-operated ferry MV *Caribe Queen* makes the 45-minute crossing to Nevis daily except Thursday, which is maintenance day, and Sunday. The schedule is a bit erratic, so confirm departure times with the tourist office. Round-trip fare is U.S. \$7. A sea-taxi service between the two islands is operated by divemaster Kenneth Samuel (tel. 809/465–2670) for U.S. \$20 (summer), \$25 (winter).

Passports and Visas

U.S. and Canadian citizens need only produce proof of citizenship (voter registration card or birth certificate; a driver's license will not suffice). British citizens must have a passport; visas are not required. All visitors must have a return or ongoing ticket.

Customs and Duties

This is a duty-free port, and you can bring in any items of a personal nature, including 200 cigarettes or 50 cigars or ½ pound of tobacco. Stern-faced customs officials will look through your luggage to ascertain whether your personal items include coke or crack.

Language

English with a West Indian lilt is spoken here.

Precautions

Visitors, especially women, are warned not to go jogging on long, lonely roads.

Staying in St. Kitts

Important Addresses

Tourist Information: By 1991 the **St. Kitts Tourist Board** (809/465–2620) and the **St. Kitts-Nevis Hotel Association** (tel. 809/465–2754) expect to be in the new Tourism Complex on Bay Rd. in Basseterre, next to the post office. Office hours are Monday–Saturday 8 AM–noon and 1–5 PM.

Emergencies

Police: Call 809/465–99.

Hospitals: There is a 24-hour emergency room at the **Joseph N. France General Hospital** (Basseterre, tel. 809/465–2551).

Pharmacies: In Basseterre, **Skerritt's rug Store** (Fort St., tel. 809/465–2083) is open Monday–Saturday 8–5 and can provide

24-hour prescription service. **City Drug** (locations on Fort St., Basseterre, and at Sun 'n' Sand, Frigate Bay, tel. 809/465–2156) is open Monday–Wednesday and Friday 8–7; Thursday 8–5, Saturday 8–8, Sunday and holidays 8 AM–10 AM.

Currency Legal tender is the Eastern Caribbean (E.C.) dollar (often called "beewees.") At press time, the rate of exchange was E.C.$2.65 or E.C.$2.70 to U.S.$1. U.S. dollars are accepted practically everywhere, but you'll almost always get change in E.C.s. Prices quoted here are in U.S. dollars unless noted otherwise. Most large hotels, restaurants, and shops accept major credit cards, but small inns and shops usually do not. It's always a good idea to check current credit-card policies before turning up with only plastic in your pocket.

Taxes and Service Charges Hotels collect a 7% government tax. The departure tax is $5. (There is no departure tax from St. Kitts to Nevis.)

All hotels add a 10% service charge to your bill. In restaurants, a tip of 10%–15% is appropriate.

Guided Tours **Tropical Tours** (tel. 809/465–4167) can run you around the island and take you to the rain forest. **Delise Walwyn** (tel. 809/465–2631) also offers a variety of island tours. **Kriss Tours** (809/465–4042) and **Greg Pereira** (809/465–4121) both specialize in rain-forest and volcano tours.

Getting Around **Taxis** Taxi tours of the island take about three hours and cost about U.S.$35. **Jimmy Herbert** (tel. 809/465–4694) is a reliable, helpful driver.

Buses A privately owned minibus circles the island. Check with the tourist office about schedules.

Rental Cars and Scooters You'll need a local driver's license, which you can get by presenting yourself, your valid driver's license, and E.C.$30 (U.S.$12) at the police station, Cayon Street, Basseterre. Rentals are available at **Holiday** (809/465–6507) and **Caines** (tel. 809/465–2366). Delise Walwyn (tel. 809/465–2631) operates **Economy Car,** which also rents scooter bikes. **TDC Rentals** (tel. 809/465–2991) can put you in minimokes, as well as cars. Car rentals run about U.S.$35 per day. At press time, the price of gas was U.S.$1.72 per gallon. Remember to drive on the left!

Telephones and Mail To call St. Kitts from the United States, dial area code 809, then access code 465 and the local number. Telephone communications, both on the island and with the United States, are as clear as a bell, and you can dial long distance direct. To make an intraisland call, simply dial the seven-digit number.

Airmail letters to the United States and Canada cost E.C.$.60 per half ounce; postcards require E.C.$.35. Mail takes at least 7–10 days to reach the United States. St. Kitts and Nevis each issues its own stamps, but each also honors the other's. The beautiful stamps are collector's items, and you may have a hard time pasting them on postcards.

Opening and Closing Times Shops are open Monday–Saturday 8 AM–noon and 1–4 PM. Some shops close earlier on Thursday. Banking hours are Monday–Thursday 8 AM–1 PM; Friday 8 AM–1 PM and 3–5 PM. St. Kitts & Nevis National Bank is also open Saturday 8:30–11 AM.

Beaches

All beaches on the island are free and open to the public, even those occupied by hotels. The powdery white-sand beaches are all at the southern end of the island and on the peninsula.

The South East Peninsula Road leads from the foot of Timothy Hill to Majors Bay on the southern tip of the island, providing access to some of the island's best beaches. Among them are the twin beaches of **Banana Bay** and **Cockleshell Bay,** which together cover more than 2 miles. Sandals Banana Bay and Casablanca are two new luxury hotels slated for this area.

Other good peninsula beaches are **Friars Bay** (on both the Atlantic and the Caribbean sides) and **White House Bay.**

North of Banana Bay, the beaches of **Frigate Bay** are talcum-powder-fine. **North Frigate Bay,** on the Atlantic, is 4 miles wide and a favorite with horseback riders (*see* Participant Sports, below).

Beaches elsewhere on the island are of gray-black volcanic sand. **Conaree Bay** on the Atlantic side is a narrow strip of gray-black sand where the water is good for body surfing (no facilities). Snorkeling and windsurfing are good at **Dieppe Bay,** a black-sand beach on the north coast, where the Golden Lemon Hotel is located (*see* Participant Sports, below, for equipment rental).

Exploring St. Kitts

Numbers in the margin correspond with points of interest on the St. Kitts map.

The capital city of Basseterre, set in the southern part of the island, was once held by the French, hence its French name. It's an easily walkable town, graced with tall palms and small, beautifully maintained houses and buildings of stone and pastel-colored wood.

You can see the main sights of the capital city in a half hour or so; allow three to four hours for an island tour.

Basseterre
❶

Your first stop is at the **St. Kitts Tourist Board** (Tourism Complex, Bay St.) to pick up maps. Turn left when you leave there and walk past the handsome Treasury Building. It faces the octagonal **Circus,** which contains a fanciful memorial to Thomas Berkeley, a former president of the Legislative Assembly. Duty-free shops fill the streets and courtyards leading off from around the Circus. The **St. Kitts Philatelic Bureau** (open weekdays 8–4) is nearby on the second floor of the Social Security Building (Bay St.).

The colorful **Bay Street produce** market is open on weekends only. On the waterfront, next to the Treasury Building, is the air-conditioned **Shoreline Plaza,** with its tax-free shops, and nearby is the landing for the ferries to Nevis.

Time Out
Q.T.'s Delight (Shoreline Plaza, tel. 809/465–3423) is a charming spot for a drink and a light snack right on the waterfront.

From the Circus, Bank Street leads to **Independence Square,** with lovely gardens on the site of a former slave market. The square is surrounded on three sides by Georgian buildings, including the popular **Georgian House** restaurant (*see* Dining, below).

Walk up West Square Street, away from the bay, to Cayon Street, turn left, and walk one block to **St. George's Anglican Church.** This handsome stone building with crenelated tower was built by the French in 1670 and called Nôtre Dame. The British burned it down in 1706 and rebuilt it four years later, naming it after the patron saint of England. Since then, it has suffered fire, earthquake, and hurricanes and was once again rebuilt in 1859.

Elsewhere on the Island Main Road traces the perimeter of the island, circling the central mountain ranges. Head west on it out of Basseterre to explore the rest of St. Kitts. For the first few miles, you'll be driving through gently rolling hills, past old sugar plantations and ancient stone fences covered with vines, and through tiny villages with tiny houses of stone and weathered wood.

You won't have any trouble identifying the villages as you come across them; small white welcome signs are posted outside each village, placed by members of the 4-H Club. Just outside Challengers is **Bloody Point,** where in 1629, French and British soldiers joined forces to repel a mass attack by the Caribs. The scenery on the drive into **Old Road Town** is spectacular.

❸ From Old Road Town, take the road through the rain forest to visit **Romney Manor,** where batik fabrics are printed at **Caribelle Batik.** (*see* Shopping, below). The house is set in 6 acres of gardens, with exotic flowers, an old bell tower, and a 350-year-old saman tree (sometimes called a rain tree). Inside, you can watch artisans hand-printing fabrics by the 2,500-year-old Indonesian process known as *batik*.

❹ The village after Old Road Town is **Middle Island,** where Thomas Warner, the "gentleman of London" who brought the first settlers here, died in 1648 and is buried beneath a green gazebo in the churchyard of **St. Thomas Church.**

❺ The road continues through the village of Half-Way Tree to **Brimstone Hill,** the most important historic site on St. Kitts. From the parking area, it's a long walk to the 38-acre fortress, but the exercise is well worth it if military history and spectacular views interest you. After routing the French in 1689, the English erected a battery on top of Brimstone Hill, and by 1736, there were 49 guns in the fortress. In 1782, the French lay siege to the fortress, which was defended by 350 militia and 600 regular troops of the Royal Scots and East Yorkshires. A plaque in the old stone wall marks the place where the fort was breached. When the English finally surrendered, the French allowed them to march from the fort in full formation out of respect for their bravery. (The English afforded the French the same honor when they surrendered the fort a mere year later.) A hurricane did extensive damage to the fortress in 1843, and in 1852 it was evacuated and dismantled.

The citadel has been partially reconstructed and its guns remounted. You can see what remains of the officers' quarters, the redoubts, barracks, the ordnance store, and the cemetery. Its museums display, among other things, weaponry, uniforms, photographs, and old newspapers. In 1985, Queen Elizabeth visited Brimstone Hill and officially opened it as part of a national park. There's a splendid view from here that includes Montserrat and Nevis to the southeast, Saba and Statia to the northwest, and St. Barts and St. Maarten to the north. *Main Rd., Brimstone Hill. Admission: $2. Open Mon.–Sat. 9–6, Sun. 9–4.*

Time Out   **J's Place** (tel. 809/465–6264) across from the entrance to the fort is ideal for a drink, a sandwich, or a full meal.

Continuing on through seas of sugarcane, past breadfruit trees and old stone walls, you'll come to the town of **Sandy Point Town.** The houses here are West Indian–style raised cottages. The **Roman Catholic Church** has lovely stained-glass windows.

➏

Farther along, just outside the village of **Newton Ground,** are the remains of an old sugar mill and some ancient coconut palms. Outside the village of **St. Paul's** is a road that leads to **Rawlins Plantation,** a restored sugar plantation that's popular for dining and lodging. The fishing town of **Dieppe Bay** is at the northernmost point of the island. Its tiny black-sand beach is backed by the **Golden Lemon,** one of the Caribbean's most famous inns (*see* Lodging, below). The **Black Rocks** on the Atlantic coast just outside the town of Sadlers, in Sandy Bay, are lava deposits, spat into the sea ages ago when the island's volcano erupted. They have since been molded into fanciful shapes by centuries of pounding surf. The drive back to Basseterre around the other side of the island is a pleasant one, through small, neat villages with centuries-old stone churches and pastel-colored cottages.

➐

Participant Sports

Boating   Hobie Cats can be rented at **Pelican Cove Marina** (tel. 809/465–2754 or **R. G. Watersports** (tel. 809/465–2670).

Deep-Sea Fishing   Angle for yellowtail snapper, wahoo, mackerel, dolphin, and barracuda, with **Tropical Tours** (tel. 809/465–4167) or **Pelican Cove Marina.**

Golf   There is an 18-hole championship course in the Frigate Bay area (Tourist Board, tel. 809/465–4040).

Hiking   Trails in the central mountains vary from easy to don't-try-it-by-yourself. Monkey Hill and Verchild's Mountain are not difficult, although the Verchild's climb will take the better part of a day. Don't attempt Mt. Liamuiga without a guide. You'll start at Belmont Estates on horseback, then proceed on foot to the lip of the crater at 2,600 feet. You can go down into the crater, clinging to vines and roots. **Kriss Tours** (tel. 809/465–4042) takes small groups into the crater and to Dos d'Anse Pond on Verchild's Mountain.

Horseback Riding   Frigate Bay and Conaree Beach are great for riding. Guides from **Trinity Stable** (tel. 809/465–3226) will lead you into the hills at a more leisurely gait.

Scuba Diving and Snorkeling   Kenneth Samuel of **Kenneth's Dive Centre** (tel. 809/465–2670) is an independent dive operator who takes small groups of divers with C cards to nearby reefs. Equipment, rentals, and trips are also available through **Caribbean Watersports** (tel. 809/465–8050) and **Fisherman's Wharf** (tel. 809/465–2754).

Sea Excursions **Tropical Tours** (tel. 809/465–4167) offers moonlight cruises on the 52-foot catamaran *Cileca III* and glass-bottom-boat tours. The **OTI** (tel. 809/465–2754) has a fleet of boats, based at Fisherman's Wharf, that run daily shuttles to Banana Bay on the peninsula. **Kantours** (tel. 809/465–2098) takes you on a Banana Bay Beach Safari for a day of snorkeling and swimming and an evening barbecue.

Tennis There are three lighted courts at **Jack Tar Village/Royal St. Kitts** (tel. 809/465–2651) and a grass court at **Rawlins Plantation** (tel. 809/465–6221).

Waterskiing and Windsurfing Rentals are available at **Fisherman's Wharf** (tel. 809/465–2754).

Spectator Sports

Cricket matches are played in Warner Park from January to July; **soccer** from July to December, **softball** from January to August. Contact the Tourist Board (tel. 809/465–4040) for schedules.

Shopping

St. Kitts has limited shopping, but there are a few duty-free shops where you can find some good buys in jewelry, watches, perfume, china, and crystal. Among the island crafts, the best known are the batik fabrics, scarves, caftans, and wall hangings of Caribelle Batik. There are also locally produced jams, jellies, herb teas, and handicrafts of local shell, straw, and coconut. And, available only on St. Kitts, CSR (Cane Spirit Rothschild) is a "new cane spirit drink" that's distilled from fresh sugarcane.

Shopping Districts Most shopping plazas are near The Circus in downtown Basseterre. Some shops have outlets in other areas, particularly in Dieppe Bay. **T.D.C. Mall** is just off The Circus in downtown Basseterre. **Shoreline Plaza** is next to the Treasury Building, right on the waterfront in Basseterre. **Palms Arcade** is on Fort Street, also near The Circus.

Good Buys **T.D.C.** (T.D.C. Plaza, on Bank St., tel. 809/465–2511) carries fine china and crystal, along with cameras and other imports.

Slice of the Lemon (Palms Arcade and Dieppe Bay, tel. 809/465–2889) carries fine perfumes but is better known for its elegant jewelry.

Caribelle Batik (Romney Manor, tel. 809/465–6253), **The Kittitian Kitchen** (Palms Arcade, Basseterre, and at the Golden Lemon, Dieppe Bay, no phone), and **Palm Crafts** (also in Palms Arcade, tel. 809/465–2599) all sell that special something (island crafts, jams and jellies, batik) to take home as gifts and souvenirs.

Dining

St. Kitts restaurants range from funky little beachfront bistros to elegant plantation dining rooms.

The most highly recommended restaurants are indicated by a star ★.

Category	Cost*
Expensive	over $25
Moderate	$15–$25
Inexpensive	under $15

Per person, excluding drinks and service. There is no sales tax on St. Kitts.

The Georgian House. Dining is by candlelight in a restored, antiques-filled British manor house. There is a changing à la carte menu that might include cucumber soup, roast leg of lamb, and lobster Thermidor. *S. Independence Sq., Basseterre, tel. 809/465–4049. Dress: casually elegant. Reservations advised. No credit cards. Closed Sun. Expensive.*

★ **Frigate Bay Beach Hotel.** The piña coladas are sensational in this split-level restaurant overlooking the hotel pool. Candlelight dinners are romantic and dishes are beautifully presented. The à la carte menu includes curried chicken with rice, lobster with lemon butter, and shrimp Creole. *Frigate Bay Beach Hotel, tel. 809/465–8935. Reservations suggested. AE, MC, V. Expensive.*

The Patio. Owner Peter Mallalieu prepares six-course meals, by reservation only, in his flower-filled home. The fixed-price feast includes wine and liqueurs. Fresh seafood and vegetables are prepared to order, and the menu changes nightly. *Frigate Bay Beach, tel. 809/465–8666. Reservations required. AE, MC, V. Expensive.*

★ **Rawlins Plantation.** Elegant dinners are served in a lovely white room with high, vaulted ceilings. The fixed-price (U.S.$35 per person) meal might include curried egg mousse, fresh tomato soup, fish and shrimp kebabs, and chocolate profiteroles. This is also a popular lunch spot, where you might find breadfruit salad, flying fish fritters, or *bobote* (ground beef, eggplant, spices, curry, and homemade chutney). *Mt. Pleasant, tel. 809/465–6221. Reservations required. No credit cards, but personal checks are accepted. Expensive.*

★ The **Golden Lemon.** Owner Arthur Leaman creates the recipes himself for the West Indian, Continental, and American cuisine served in his hotel, and he never repeats them more than once in a two-week period. The patio, lush with bougainvilles and ferns, is a popular spot for Sunday brunch, which can include banana pancakes, rum beef stew, and spaghetti with white clam sauce. *Dieppe Bay, tel. 809/465–7260. Dress: casually elegant. Reservations required. AE. Moderate–Expensive.*

The Anchorage. This is an informal beachside eatery where lobster is king, but burgers, steaks, salads, and sandwiches are also offered. *Frigate Bay Beach, tel. 809/465–8235. Reservations not required. No credit cards. Moderate.*

★ **Ballahoo.** Curried conch, beef Stroganoff, salads, and sandwiches are served in a delightful upstairs gallery overlooking Pelican Gardens and The Circus. *Bay Rd., Basseterre, tel. 809/465–4197. Reservations not required. AE, MC, V. Closed Sun. Moderate.*

★ **Fisherman's Wharf.** At the Ocean Terrace Inn, this waterfront eatery serves the island's best Friday-night buffet. Steak barbecue alternates with West Indian specialties, grilled lobster, and fish. Dinner is followed by dancing and entertainment.

Fortlands, Basseterre, tel. 809/465–2754. Reservations not required. No credit cards. Moderate.

Ocean Terrace Inn. This is a popular place with locals and visitors, where you can dine by candlelight inside or on a balcony overlooking the bay. Lobster is the specialty here—grilled, broiled, and Thermidor. Curried chicken, conch chowder, and other West Indian dishes are served, as well as Continental offerings. *Fortlands, Basseterre, tel. 809/465–2754. Reservations required. AE, MC, V. Moderate.*

★ **Sou Tai.** Cantonese cuisine is served in the great house of an erstwhile estate on a hill overlooking the Atlantic. *Canada Estate, tel. 809/465–8456. Reservations advised. No credit cards. Moderate.*

Jong's Oriental Restaurant. It's pronounced *yong's*, it's on the sands at Conaree Beach, and it's got a spectacular view of the Atlantic. *Conaree Beach, tel. 809/465–2062. Reservations advised. No credit cards. Closed Sun. and Mon. Inexpensive.*

PJ's Pizza. You'll find excellent pizza right next to the Island Paradise Condominiums. Other Italian dishes are also served, as well as sandwiches. *Frigate Bay, tel. 809/465–8373. No credit cards. Closed Sun. and Mon. Inexpensive.*

Victor's Hideaway. Hidden behind the Church of the Immaculate Conception, this friendly dinner spot specializes in stews—mutton, curried goat, or lobster—but deep-fried fish and beef and chicken dishes are also on the menu. The restaurant changed ownership in 1989, and there are those who feel that the quality of the food has declined. *9 Stainforth St., tel. 809/465–2518. No credit cards. Closed Sun. Inexpensive.*

Lodging

Choices run from guest houses to full-service hotels to elegant inns in restored plantation homes. Some of the inns include breakfast and dinner in their rates, which will be indicated in the descriptions that follow.

The most highly recommended lodgins are indicated by a star ★.

Category	Cost*
Very Expensive	over $250
Expensive	$175–$250
Moderate	$125–$175
Inexpensive	under $125

*All prices are for a standard double room for two, excluding 7% tax and a 10% service charge.

Hotels
★ **The Golden Lemon.** Arthur Leaman, a former editor of *House and Garden*, has created a hotel that is internationally famous, and with good reason. The four original rooms have high ceilings, hardwood floors, and galleries overlooking the black-sand beach, palm trees, and the ocean. Each room in the hotel is different; there are wonderful white-iron four-posters, carved armoires, chaise lounges, ceiling fans, mosquito nets, rocking chairs, and a fine collection of Meissen china in a display case. Solar-heated water guarantees that showers (there are no tubs) are always hot. Rates include breakfast (served in your

room or on the veranda), afternoon tea, and an elegant dinner. There's a staff of 38, and the maximum stay is two weeks. **The Lemon Court** and **Lemon Grove Condominiums** are sleek, secluded studios and one- and two-bedroom, two-story units that surround manicured gardens. Some have private Grecian pools, and all are decorated with a collection of antiques and Caribbean art. *Box 17, Dieppe Bay, tel. 809/465–7260 or 800/845–9504. 27 rooms and suites. Facilities: beach, pool, restaurant, duty-free shop, free laundry service, one tennis court. AE. Very Expensive.*

Jack Tar Village/Royal St. Kitts. Once you've registered and had your picture taken for the ID card you'll have to wear at all times, you're all set for the island's most action-packed hotel. The schedule of daily activities includes horseshoe pitching, volleyball, shuffleboard, horseback riding, biking, and hiking. This is also the home of the island's only casino. Entertainment often includes folkloric shows and steel bands. This is an all-inclusive resort, which means that everything is included in the room rate—meals, taxes, snacks, greens fees, drinks—everything. *Box 406, Frigate Bay, tel. 809/465–8651; 214/670–9888 or 800/527–9299 in USA. 250 rooms. Facilities: casino, 2 pools, 2 restaurants, bars and lounges, horseback riding, 3 lighted tennis courts, facilities for handicapped, water-sports center. AE, DC, MC, V. Very Expensive.*

★ **Rawlins Plantation.** This lovely inn is set 350 feet above sea level in 12 acres of a once-flourishing sugar plantation. The view from the veranda is splendid, and there is a cozy parlor, done in stylish tropical decor, with bookshelves lining the walls. Guests take dinner in a formal dining room (breakfast, afternoon tea, and dinner are included in the rate). Accommodations (with double, queen-size, or king-size beds), are in cottages tucked into the hillside. All are individually decorated with delicate prints and come equipped with mosquito nets on four-poster beds. A 17th-century stone windmill contains the split-level honeymoon suite with sunken bathroom. Paul and Claire Rawson became the new owners of Rawlins in 1989. *Box 340, Mt. Pleasant, tel. 809/465–6221 (617/367–8959 in USA). 9 rooms. Facilities: pool, restaurant, tennis court, croquet. No credit cards, but personal checks are accepted. Very Expensive.*

Frigate Bay Beach Hotel. The third fairway of the island's golf course adjoins the property, but the beach, about a mile away, is reached by complimentary shuttle buses. The cluster of whitewashed, air-conditioned buildings contain standard rooms as well as condominium units with fully equipped kitchens. There are hillside and poolside units, the latter preferable. Standard rooms are large but simply furnished, with tile floors and sliding glass doors leading to a terrace or balcony. There's a pool with swim-up bar and a friendly staff. *Box 137, Basseterre, tel. 809/465–8936, 809/465–8935, or 800/622–7836. 64 rooms. Facilities: pool, restaurant, bar. Moderate–Expensive.*

★ **Ocean Terrace Inn.** Affectionately called OTI, this is one of the island's most luxurious hotels, offering an assortment of rooms, all of which are air-conditioned, with cable TVs and radios. There are rooms with kitchenettes and condominium units with private terraces overlooking one of the inn's two pools. In a section called Fisherman's Village are luxury one- and two-bedroom split-level suites overlooking Basseterre's harbor. Fisherman's Wharf restaurant is famed island-wide for its buffets, and the hotel's Pelican Cove Marina has its own fleet of boats. Modified American Plan available. *Box 65, Basseterre, tel. 809/465–2754 or 800/223–5695. 52 rooms. Facilities: beach, 2 pools, outdoor Jacuzzi, 2 restaurants, 2 bars, cable TV, fleet of boats, water-sports center. AE, MC, V. Moderate.*

Fairview Inn. This hotel celebrated its 20th anniversary in 1988. The main building is an 18th-century great house, with graceful white verandas and Oriental rugs on hardwood floors. Rooms are in cottages sprinkled around the backyard, which happens to be a mountain of considerable size. The rooms have functional furnishings, with either twin or double beds, private patios, and radios. All have private baths with showers or bath tubs. Some have air-conditioning, some fans, some neither. The Fairview is well known for its superb West Indian cuisine. *Box 212, Basseterre, tel. 809/465–2472 or 800/223–9815; 212/840–6636 in NY; 800/468–0023 in Canada. 30 rooms. Facilities: 2 restaurants, bar, pool. AE, DC, MC, V. Inexpensive.*

Fort Thomas Hotel. This hotel is on the site of an old fort. Popular with tour groups, it's set in 8 acres on a hillside at the outskirts of Basseterre. Rooms are spacious, and all have private baths, air-conditioning, radios, and phones; TVs can be rented. There's a free shuttle bus to the beach. *Box 407, Basseterre, tel. 809/465–2695; 800/223–9815 in USA; 800/468–0023 in Canada. 64 rooms. Facilities: pool, game room, restaurant, bar. AE, CB, DC, MC, V. Inexpensive.*

★ **Sun 'n Sand Beach Village.** These studio and two-bedroom, self-catering cottages are immaculately clean and right on the beach on the Atlantic side of the island. Furnishings are simple and tropical, with tile floors, terraces, twin or queen-size beds, and private baths (shower only). Studios are air-conditioned; apartments have window air-conditioners in bedrooms and ceiling fans in living rooms. Bedroom apartments have convertible sofas in living rooms and fully equipped kitchens with microwave ovens and full-size refrigerators. *Box 341, Frigate Bay, tel. 809/465–8037 or 800/621–1270. 32 studios, 18 2-bedroom cottages. Facilities: beach, restaurant, pool, children's pool, 2 lighted tennis courts, grocery store, drugstore, gift shop. AE, MC, V. Moderate–Expensive.*

Condos and Guest Houses This little island has a number of condominiums and guest houses available to visitors. For information, contact the St. Kitts Tourist Board (Box 132, Basseterre, St. Kitts, tel. 809/465–4040).

Nightlife

Most of the Kittitian nightlife revolves around the hotels, which host such live entertainment as folkloric shows, calypso music, and steel bands.

Casinos The only game in town is at the **Royal St. Kitts Casino** in Jack Tar Village (*see* Lodging, above), where you'll find blackjack tables, roulette wheels, craps tables, and one-armed bandits. Dress is casual, and play continues till the last player leaves.

Discos Kittitian and Italian dishes are served in **The Lighthouse** (Deepwater Port Rd., tel. 809/465–8914), but come after 11 PM Thursday–Saturday when the place spins into a disco, attracting a mostly local crowd. At **J's Place** (across from Brimstone Hill, tel. 809/465–6264), you and the locals can dance the night away Friday and Saturday.

23 St. Lucia

by Honey Naylor

Oval, lush St. Lucia, 27 miles long and 14 miles wide, sits at the southern end of the Windward Islands. It has two topographical features, apart from its beaches, that earn it a special place in the Caribbean tableaux of islands: the twin peaks of the Pitons (Petit and Gros), which rise to more than 2,400 feet, and the bubbling sulfur springs in the town of Soufrière, part of a low-lying volcano that erupted thousands of years ago, and now attracts visitors for the springs' curative waters.

This is a ruggedly beautiful island, with towering mountains, lush green valleys, and acres of banana plantations. Yachtsmen put in at Marigot Bay, one of the Caribbean's most beautiful secluded bays. The diving is good, and so is the liming—the St. Lucian term for "hanging out."

Believing that Columbus came upon their island on December 13, 1502, St. Lucians celebrate that date as Discovery Day. But in recent years doubts have been cast on the theory. Some historians think St. Lucia (pronounced *loo*-sha) was found in 1499 by Juan de la Cosa, Columbus's navigator.

The first inhabitants were the Arawaks, who paddled up from South America sometime before AD 200. The ferocious Caribs followed them, killed them off, and were still living on the island when the first Europeans began to arrive.

In 1605, 67 English settlers bound for Guiana were blown off course and landed near Vieux Fort. Within a few weeks the cannibalistic Caribs had devoured all but 19, who escaped in a canoe. Another group of English settlers arrived 30 years later, but their attempt at colonization was also unsuccessful. It was the French who, in 1660, managed to sign a treaty with the Caribs and gain control of the island.

Thus began a 150-year period of battles between the French and the English for control of the 238-square-mile island. In the late 18th century, English Admiral George Rodney had his headquarters on St. Lucia. The island changed hands 14 times before the British took permanent possession in 1814.

During those battle-filled years, Europeans colonized the island. They developed sugar plantations, using slaves from West Africa to work the fields. Most of today's 140,000 St. Lucians are descendants of those West Africans. The coal industry was begun on the island in 1883, and by the turn of the century Castries, the capital, had become the leading coal port in the West Indies. In 1960, banana plantations began to flourish, and bananas are now the island's leading export.

On February 22, 1979, St. Lucia became an independent state within the British Commonwealth of Nations, with a resident governor-general appointed by the queen. Still, there are many relics of French occupation, notably in the island patois, the Creole cuisine, and the names of the places and the people.

Before You Go

Tourist Information Contact the **St. Lucia Tourist Board** (820 2nd Ave., 9th Floor, New York, NY 10017, tel. 212/867–2950. In Canada: 151 Bloor St. W, Suite 425, Toronto, Ont., Canada M5S 1S4, tel. 416/961–5606. In the United Kingdom: 10 Kensington Court, London W8 5DL, tel. 01/370–0926).

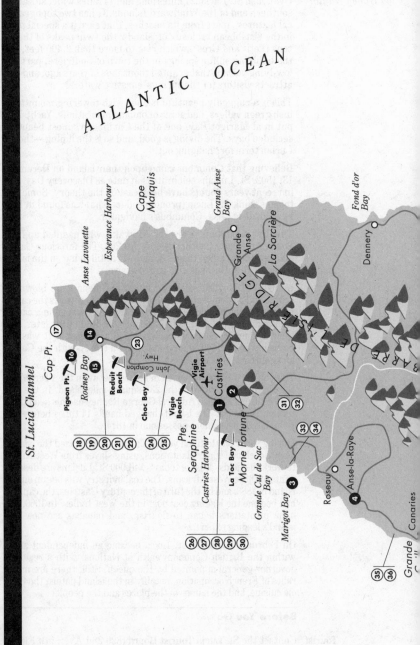

St. Lucia

480

ATLANTIC OCEAN

St. Lucia Channel

Cap Pt.

⑰ Pigeon Pt. ⑯

⑭

Rodney Bay ⑮

Reduit Beach

Choc Bay

John Compton Hwy

Vigie Beach

Vigie Airport

Pte. Seraphine

Castries Harbour

① Castries

②

Morne Fortune

La Toc Bay

Grande Cul de Sac Bay

Marigot Bay ③

Roseau

Anse-la-Raye ④

Canaries

Grande

Anse Lavouette

Esperance Harbour

Cape Marquis

Grand Anse Bay

Grande Anse ○

La Sorcière

BARRE DE L'ISLE RIDGE

Fond d'or Bay

Dennery ○

⑱ ⑲ ⑳ ㉑ ㉒

㉔ ㉕

㉓

㉖ ㉗ ㉘ ㉙ ㉚

㉛ ㉜

㉝ ㉞

㉟ ㊱

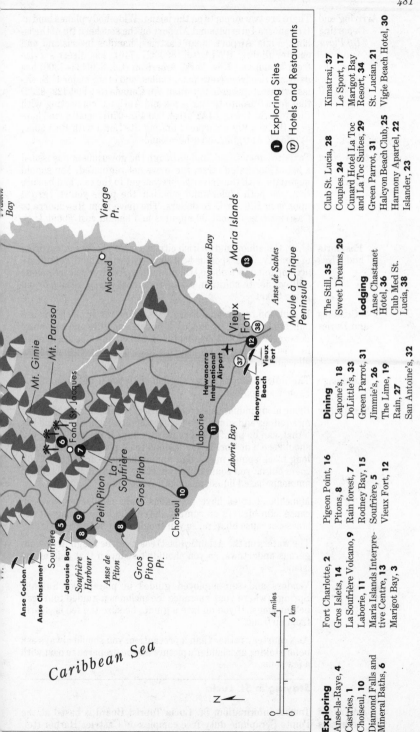

Exploring Sites

17 Hotels and Restaurants

Exploring
Anse-la-Raye, 4
Castries, 14
Choiseul, 10
Diamond Falls and
Mineral Baths, 6

Fort Charlotte, 2
Gros Islets, 14
La Soufrière Volcano, 9
Laborie, 11
Maria Islands Interpre-
tive Centre, 13
Marigot Bay, 3

Pigeon Point, 16
Pitons, 8
Rain forest, 7
Rodney Bay, 15
Soufrière, 5
Vieux Fort, 12

Dining
Capone's, 18
DoLittle's, 33
Green Parrot, 31
Jimmie's, 26
The Lime, 19
Rain, 27
San Antoine's, 32

The Still, 35
Sweet Dreams, 20

Lodging
Anse Chastanet
Hotel, 36
Club Med St.
Lucia, 38

Club St. Lucia, 28
Couples, 24
Cunard Hotel La Toc
and La Toc Suites, 29
Green Parrot, 31
Halcyon Beach Club, 25
Harmony Apartel, 22
Islander, 23

Kimatrai, 37
Le Sport, 17
Marigot Bay
Resort, 34
St. Lucian, 21
Vigie Beach Hotel, 30

Arriving and There are two airports on the island. Wide-body planes land at
Departing Hewanorra International Airport on the southern tip of the is-
By Plane land. Vigie Airport, near Castries, handles interisland and
charter flights. **BWIA** (tel. 800/327–7401) has direct service
from Miami and New York. **American** (tel. 800/433–7300) has
daily service from New York, Dallas, and other major U.S. cities, with a stopover in San Juan. **Air Canada** (tel. 800/422–6232)
flies from Toronto to Barbados and Antigua, connecting with
flights to St. Lucia. **LIAT's** (tel. 809/462–0701) small island hoppers fly into Vigie Airport, linking St. Lucia with Barbados,
Trinidad, Antigua, and other islands.

From the Airport **Taxis** are unmetered, and although the government has issued
a list of suggested fares, these are not regulated. You should
negotiate with the driver *before* you get in the car, and be sure
that you both understand whether the price you've agreed
upon is in E.C. or U.S. dollars. The drive from Hewanorra to
Castries takes about 90 minutes and should cost about U.S.
$35.

Passports U.S., Canadian, and British citizens must produce some proof
and Visas of identity. A passport is best, but a notarized birth certificate
accompanied by a photo ID will suffice. A driver's license alone
will *not* do. In addition, all visitors must have a return or ongoing ticket.

Customs In addition to personal items, 200 cigarettes or 50 cigars or 8
and Duties ounces of tobacco, 40 ounces of liquor, and gifts and souvenirs
not exceeding E.C.$50 (about U.S. $18.50) in value are allowed
in. Visitors under 18 are not entitled to the tobacco and alcohol
allowances.

Language The official language is English, but you'll also hear some
French and patois.

Precautions Bring along industrial-strength insect repellent to ward off the
mosquitoes and sand flies. Centipede bites, while rare and not
lethal, can be painful and cause swelling. If you're bitten, you
should see a doctor. If you happen to step on a sea urchin, its
long black spines may lodge under the skin; don't try to pull
them out as you could cause infection. Apply ammonia, or an
ammonia-based liquid, as quickly as possible.

Manchineel trees have poisonous fruit and leaves that can
cause skin blisters on contact. Even raindrops falling off the
trees can cause blisters, so you shouldn't sit beneath the trees.

The waters on the Atlantic (east) coast can be rough, with dangerous undertows, so you shouldn't swim on that side of the
island.

Vendors and self-employed guides in places like Sulphur
Springs (where your entrance fee includes a guided tour) can
be tenacious. If you do hire a guide, be sure the fee is clearly
fixed up front.

As a courtesy rather than a precaution, you should always ask
before taking an islander's picture and be prepared to part with
a few coins.

Staying in St. Lucia

Important **Tourist Information: St. Lucia Tourist Board** is based at the
Addresses Pointe Seraphine duty-free complex on Castries Harbor (tel.

809/452–4094 or 809/452–5968). The office is open weekdays from 8–4:30. There is also a tourist information desk at each of the two airports (**Vigie**, tel. 809/452–2596, and **Hewanorra**, tel. 809/454–6644).

Emergencies **Police:** Call 999.

Hospitals: Hospitals with 24-hour emergency rooms are **Victoria Hospital** (Hospital Rd., Castries, tel. 809/452–2421) and **St. Jude's Hospital** (Vieux Fort, tel. 809/454–6041).

Pharmacies: The largest pharmacy is **Williams Pharmacy** (Williams Bldg., Bridge St., Castries, tel. 809/452–2797).

Currency The official currency is the Eastern Caribbean dollar (E.C.$). Figure about E.C.$2.70 = U.S. $1.00. U.S. dollars are readily accepted, but you'll usually get change in E.C. dollars. Major credit cards are widely accepted, as are traveler's checks. Prices quoted here are in U.S. dollars unless indicated otherwise.

Taxes and Hotels collect an 8% government tax.
Service Charges
The departure tax is $8; $4 if you're headed to another Caribbean destination.

Hotels add a 10% service charge to your bill; most restaurants add 10%. Taxi drivers expect a 10% tip.

Guided Tours **Taxi drivers** take special guide courses and offer the most personalized way to see the island. A tour around the island costs about $14 an hour, not including tip.

The **Carib Touring Company** (tel. 809/452–2689) offers a variety of half- and full-day tours.

Barnard's Travel (Bridge St., Castries, tel. 809/452–2214) also offers a full range of half- and full-day island tours, as well as excursions to Dominica, Martinique, St. Vincent, and the Grenadines.

St. Lucia Representative Services Ltd. (tel. 809/452–3762) offers a full range of half- and full-day island tours, as well as excursions to a number of neighboring islands.

Getting Around This is a cheap means of transportation. There's no organized
Buses service, but minivans cruise the island and, like a taxi, will stop when hailed. You can also catch a minivan in Castries by hanging around outside Clarke Cinema (corner Micoud and Bridge Sts.).

Taxis Taxis are always available at the airport, the harbor, and in front of the major hotels. Most hotels post the names and phone numbers of drivers.

Rental Cars To rent a car you have to be 25 years old and hold a valid driver's license. You must buy a temporary St. Lucian license at the airports or police headquarters (Bridge St., Castries) for $11. Rental agencies include **Avis** (tel. 809/452–2700 or 800/331–2112), **Budget** (tel. 809/452–0233 or 800/527–0700, **Hertz** (tel. 809/452–4777 or 800/654–3131), **National** (tel. 809/452–8028 or 800/328–4567), and **Carib Touring Ltd.** (tel. 809/452–3184).

Telephones To call St. Lucia from the United States, dial area code 809, ac-
and Mail cess code 45, and the local five-digit number. You can make direct-dial long-distance calls from the island, and the connec-

tions are excellent. To place intraisland calls, dial the local five-digit number.

Postage for airmail letters to foreign countries is E.C.$.65 for up to one ounce; postcard postage is E.C.$.15.

Opening and Shops are open weekdays 8–12:30 and 1:30–4, Saturday 8–
Closing Times noon. Banks are open Monday–Thursday 8–1, Friday 8–noon and 3–5.

Beaches

All of St. Lucia's beaches are public, and many are flanked by hotels where you can rent water-sports equipment and have a rum punch. There are also secluded beaches, accessible only by water, to which hotels can arrange boat trips. It is not advisable to swim along the windward (east) coast because the Atlantic waters are rough and sometimes dangerous.

Anse Chastanet is a black-sand beach just north of Soufrière with a backdrop of green hills and the island's best reefs for snorkeling and diving. The wooden gazebos of the Anse Chastanet Hotel are nestled among the palms, with a dive shop and bar on the beach (*see* Lodging, below).

Anse Cochon, on the Caribbean coast, is a black-sand beach accessible only by boat. The waters are superb for swimming and snorkeling.

Jalousie Bay, south of Soufrière, is a bay several miles deep between the Pitons. Accessible only by boat, it offers great snorkeling and diving.

La Toc Bay is near Castries Harbour. The sand here is gray.

Pigeon Point off the northern shore has secluded white-sand beaches, fine for picnicking and swimming.

Reduit Beach is a long stretch of beige sand between Choc Bay and Pigeon Point and is home to the St. Lucian Hotel, which offers numerous water sports.

Vieux Fort, at the southernmost tip, has a long secluded stretch of gray volcanic sand and waters protected by reefs. **Honeymoon Beach** is another sandy escape just west of Vieux Fort.

Vigie Beach and **Choc Bay,** north of Castries Harbour, have fine beige sand and calm waters (*see* Lodging, below).

Exploring St. Lucia

Numbers in the margin correspond with points of interest on the St. Lucia map.

Castries **Castries,** on the northwest coast, is a busy city with a popula-
❶ tion of about 60,000. It lies in a sheltered bay surrounded by green hills. Ships carrying bananas, coconut, cocoa, mace, nutmeg, and citrus fruits for export leave from **Castries Harbour,** one of the busiest ports in the Caribbean. Cruise ships dock here, too.

Take a cab or drive to **Pointe Seraphine,** the Spanish-style complex of 23 duty-free shops by Castries Harbour. Pick up maps, arrange tours, and find out anything you want to know about St. Lucia at the information desk of the **Tourist Board** just inside the main terminal. This is the starting point for many of the island tours.

The John Compton Highway connects the duty-free complex to downtown Castries. To reach the downtown center from Pointe Seraphine's transportation terminal, you can stroll for 20 minutes, or you can drive or take a cab.

Castries, with Morne Fortune (the Hill of Good Luck) rising behind it, has had more than its share of bad luck over the years, including two hurricanes and four fires. As a result, Castries lacks the colorful colonial buildings found in other island capitals. Most of Castries's buildings are modern, and the town has only a few sights of historical note.

Head first to **Columbus Square,** a green oasis ringed by Brazil, Laborie, Micoud, and Bourbon streets. At the corner of Laborie and Micoud streets there is a 400-year-old saman tree. A favorite local story is of the English botanist who came to St. Lucia many years ago to catalogue the flora. Awestruck by this huge old tree, she asked a passer-by what it was. "Massav," he replied, and she gratefully jotted that down in her notebook, unaware that "massav" is patois for "I don't know."

Directly across the street is the Roman Catholic **Cathedral of the Immaculate Conception,** which was built in 1897.

Some of the 19th-century buildings that managed to survive fire, winds, and rains can be seen on Brazil Street, the southern border of the square.

Time Out   In the courtyard of the Victorian building that houses Rain Restaurant, the **Pizza Park** (Columbus Sq., tel. 809/452–3022) sells takeout or eat-in pizza all day.

Head north on Laborie Street and walk past the government buildings on your right. On the left, William Peter Boulevard is one of Castries's shopping areas. "The Boulevard" connects Laborie Street with Bridge Street, which is another shopping street.

Continue north for one more block on Laborie Street and you'll come to Jeremie Street. Turn right, and you'll see the **market** on the corner of Jeremie and Peynier streets. The market is a busy place, especially on Saturday mornings when farmers bring their produce to town.

Elsewhere on   To reach **Morne Fortune,** head due east on Bridge Street. The
the Island   drive will take you past the **Government House,** the official resi-
Morne Fortune   dence of the governor-general of St. Lucia. If you want to take a picture of the house, ask the guard on duty before focusing your camera. You cannot take pictures when the governor-general is in residence.

Driving up the Hill of Good Fortune, you'll see some of the Caribbean's most beautiful tropical plants—frangipani, lilies, bougainvillea, hibiscus, and oleander—along the road.

Two hundred years ago the Vigie Peninsula had the island's heaviest concentration of fortifications. That former battleground and the area to the north of it now have the island's greatest concentration of resort playgrounds. The island rising on the horizon is Martinique. To the south you'll see the twin peaks of the Pitons.

2 **Fort Charlotte** on the Morne was begun in 1764 by the French as the *Citadelle du Morne Fortune*. It was completed 20 years later, but during those years many battles were fought here, and the fortress changed hands a number of times. The Inniskilling Monument is a tribute to one of the most famous battles, fought in 1796, when the 27th Foot Royal Inniskilling Fusiliers wrested the Hill of Good Fortune from the French. Admission to Fort Charlotte is free, and you can wander at will to see the Four Apostles Battery; the Combermere Barracks, which are now part of an educational complex; and the redoubts, guard room, stables, and cells. Stop in the Military Cemetery. It was first used in 1782, and the faint inscriptions on the tombstones tell the tales of the French and English soldiers who died here. Six former governors of the island are buried in this cemetery.

South of Castries The road from Castries to Soufrière travels through beautiful country. Keep in mind, though, that the many hairpin curves make this road a difficult drive. You'll also be handling a right-hand drive vehicle on the left side of a curving road.

3 In the village of Roseau, make a detour and drive to **Marigot Bay.** In 1778, British Admiral Samuel Barrington took his ships into this secluded bay within a bay and covered them with palm fronds to hide them from the French. The resort community today is a great favorite of yachtspeople. You can arrange to charter a yacht, swim, snorkel, or lime with the yachting crowd at one of the bars on the bay. A 24-hour water taxi connects the various points on the bay.

Time Out Stop for rum punch, lunch, and atmosphere at the **Rusty Anchor** (Hurricane Hotel, tel. 809/453–4230), a happy haunt of boaters.

If you continue south, you'll be in the vicinity of one of the island's two rum distilleries. Major production of sugar ceased here in about 1960, and distilleries now make rum with imported molasses. You're still in banana country, with acres of banana trees covering the hills and valleys. More than 127 different varieties of bananas are grown on the island.

In the mountainous region ahead you'll see **Mt. Parasol,** and if you look hard enough through the mists, you may be able to make out **Mt. Gimie,** St. Lucia's highest peak, rising to 3,117 feet.

4 The next village you'll come to is **Anse-la-Raye.** The beach here is a colorful sight, with fishing nets hanging on poles to dry and brightly painted fishing boats bobbing in the water. The fishermen of Anse-la-Raye still make canoes the old-fashioned way, by burning out the center of a log.

Soufrière
5 As you approach the town of **Soufrière,** you'll be in the island's breadbasket, where most of the mangoes, breadfruit, tomatoes, limes, and oranges are grown.

The town of Soufrière, which dates from the mid-18th century, was named after the nearby volcano and has a population of about 9,000 people. The Soufrière Harbour is the deepest harbor on the island, accommodating cruise ships that nose right up to the wharf. The government and the Soufrière Development Committee are working to give the town a face-lift and boost tourism in the area. The **Soufrière Tourist Information**

Centre (Bay St., tel. 809/454–7419) can provide information about the attractions in the area, which, in addition to the Pitons, include La Soufrière, billed as the world's only drive-in volcano, and sulfur springs; the Diamond Mineral Baths; and the rain forest. You can also ask at the Tourism Centre about Soufrière Estate, on the east side of town, where construction of botanical gardens and a zoo is under way.

6 Adjoining Soufrière Estate are the **Diamond Falls and Mineral Baths,** which are fed by an underground flow of water from the sulfur springs. Louis XVI provided funds for the construction of these baths for his troops to "fortify them against the St. Lucian climate." During the Brigand's War, just after the French Revolution, the baths were destroyed. They were restored in 1966, and you can see the waterfalls and the gardens before slipping into your swimsuit for a dip in the steaming curative waters. *Soufrière. Admission: E.C.$5. Open daily 10–5.*

7 The island's dense tropical **rain forest** is to the east of Soufrière on the road to Fond St. Jacques. The trek through the lush landscape takes three hours, and you'll need a guide. Mt. Gimie (St. Lucia's highest peak), Piton Canaries, Mt. Houlom, and Piton Tromasse are all part of this immense forest reserve. The views of the mountains and valleys are spectacular.

8 For the best land view of the **Pitons,** take the road south out of Soufrière. The road is awful and leads up a steep hill, but if you persevere, you'll be rewarded by the sight of the twin peaks. The perfectly shaped pyramidal cones, covered with tropical greenery, were formed of lava from a volcanic eruption 30 million to 40 million years ago. The tallest is Petit Piton (2,619 feet) and its twin, Gros Piton (2,461 feet). Gros Piton is so named because although it is shorter, it is fatter than its twin.

9 To the south of Soufrière, your nose will note the left turn that takes you to **La Soufrière,** the drive-in volcano, and its **sulfur springs.** There are more than 20 pools of black, belching, smelly sulfurous waters, and yellow-green sulfur baking and steaming. Take the guided tour offered by the Tourist Board. *La Soufrière. Admission: E.C.$5 (including guided tour). Open daily 9–5.*

10 Follow the road farther south and you'll come next to the coastal town of **Choiseul,** home to wood-carving and pottery shops. At the turn of the road past the Anglican Church, built in 1846, a bridge crosses the River Doree, so named because the riverbed is blanketed with fool's gold.

11 The next stop is **Laborie** a little fishing village where you can buy cheese, bread, and fish. There is also an underground passage that leads from an old fort at Saphire, up the coast, to an opening at the sea.

12 Now drive along the southern coast of the island to **Vieux Fort,** St. Lucia's second-largest city and home of the Hewanorra International Airport. Drive out on the **Moule-à-Chique Peninsula,** the southernmost tip of the island. If you look to the north, you can see all of St. Lucia and, if the day is especially clear, you can spot the island of St. Vincent 21 miles to the south. Looking straight down, you can see where the waters of the Caribbean blend with the bluer Atlantic waters.

Time Out **Chak Chak** (Beanfield Rd., Vieux Fort, tel. 809/454–6260) is a casual, airy restaurant that serves Creole dishes.

⑬ At the **Maria Islands Interpretive Centre** you can find out all there is to know about the Maria Islands Nature Reserve. The reserve consists of two tiny islands in the Atlantic off the southeast coast of St. Lucia. The 25-acre Maria Major and its little sister, 4-acre Maria Minor, are inhabited by rare species of lizards and snakes that share their home with frigate birds, terns, doves, and other wildlife. *Moule-à-Chique, no phone. Admission: Wed.–Sat. E.C.$3, Sun. E.C.$.50. Open Wed.– Sun. 9:30–5.*

A good road leads from Vieux Fort through the towns on the Atlantic coast. The road will take you past **Honeymoon Beach,** a wide, grassy, flat Anse l'Islet peninsula jutting into the ocean. Drive through Micoud and, a few miles farther north, Dennery, both of which are residential towns overlooking the Atlantic. At Dennery the road turns west and climbs across the Barre de l'Isle Ridge through a tiny rain forest with dense vegetation. There are trails along the way that lead to lookout points where you can get a view of the National Forest Preserve. This bumpy road will take you all the way back to Castries.

The North End For another tour up the coast north of Castries, take the John
and Gros Islet Compton Highway north out of town for about five minutes to the Vigie Airport. This whole northwest stretch of the Caribbean coast is of far more interest to the hedonist than to the historian. This area features some of the island's best beaches and it's loaded with resort hotels.

⑭ **Gros Islets** to the north is a quiet little fishing village not unlike Anse-la-Raye to the south. But on Friday nights, Gros Islets hosts a street festival to which everyone is invited.

⑮ **Rodney Bay,** named after Admiral Rodney, is an 80-acre manmade lagoon that boasts a host of hotels and restaurants. The St. Lucian Hotel and Club St. Lucia are in this area, as are Capone's, Lime, and other popular restaurants.

Pigeon Point **Pigeon Point,** jutting out on the northwest coast, was Pigeon
⑯ Island until a causeway was built to connect it to the mainland. Tales are told of the pirate Jambe de Bois (wooden leg), who used to hide out here. This 40-acre area, a strategic point during the struggles for control of the island, is now a national park, with long sandy beaches, calm waters for swimming, and areas for picnicking.

The **Pigeon Point Museum** includes the ruins of barracks, batteries, and garrisons dating from the French and English battles. *Pigeon Point, no phone. Admission: E.C.$3. Open Mon.–Sat. 9–4.*

Off the Beaten Track

If you want a closeup look at a working banana plantation, and are willing to get a little wet and muddy in the process, you can tour the island's largest—the **Marquis Plantation.** St. Lucia Plantation Tours (tel. 809/542–8658) or **St. Lucia Representative Services Ltd.** (*see* Guided Tours, above) will pick you up at your hotel in an air-conditioned bus. Wear your most casual clothes, and be prepared to rough it.

Participant Sports

Most hotels have Sunfish, water skis, fins, masks, and other water-sports equipment offered free to guests and for a fee to nonguests.

Boating **Captain Mike's** (tel. 809/452–0216) has a fleet of Bertram's charter boats for snorkeling and swimming cruises and private charter parties. Bare-boat or skippered yacht charters are available through **Stevens Yachts** (tel. 800/638–7044), which has a fleet of 39- to 56-foot sailing yachts; **Trade Wind Yacht Charters** (Rodney Bay, tel. 809/452–8424 or 800/222–6656); and the **Moorings Yacht Charter** (Marigot Bay, tel. 809/453–4357 or 800/535–7289).

Deep-Sea Fishing Among the sea creatures in these waters are dolphin, Spanish mackerel, barracuda, and white marlin. Contact **Captain Mike's** (tel. 809/452–0217) to steer you in the right direction.

Golf There is a nine-hole course at **Cunard La Toc Hotel** (tel. 809/452–3081) and a nine-plus-nine course at **Cap Estate Golf Club** (tel. 809/452–8523). Greens fees at both are about E.C.$15, and clubs are available for rental.

Hiking The island is laced with trails, but you should not attempt the challenging peaks on your own. Your hotel or the Tourist Board can provide you with a guide.

Horseback Riding For trail rides on the beach, contact **Trim's Riding Stables** (Cas-En-Bas and Cap Estate, tel. 809/452–8273) and **Sunset Riding School** (Cap Estate, tel. 809/452–8628).

Jogging You can jog on the beach by yourself or team up with the **Roadbusters** (tel. Jimmie at 809/452–5142 or evenings at 809/452–4790).

Parasailing Contact **Jacob's Watersports** (tel. 809/452–8281).

Scuba Diving **Scuba St. Lucia** (tel. 809/454–7355) is a PADI five-star training facility that offers daily beach and boat dives, resort courses, underwater photography, and day trips. **Marigot Bay Resort** (tel. 809/453–4357) offers a full scuba program. Dive trips are also arranged through **Buddies Scuba** (tel. 809/452–5288) and through most of the hotels.

Sea and Snorkeling Excursions The 140-foot square-rigger *Brig Unicorn* (tel. 809/452–6811) sails to Soufrière, with steel bands, a swim stop, rum punch, and soda. Its sister schooner, the *Buccaneer,* also does outings. **Captain Mike's** (tel. 809/452–0216) does swimming and snorkeling cruises; the *Sailing Bus* (tel. 809/452–8725) offers a full-day sail from Rodney Bay to Marigot; and **Jacob's Watersports** (tel. 809/452–8281) features speedboat and snorkeling cruises. Sea and snorkeling excursions can also be arranged through **Maho** (tel. 809/452–3762) and **The Surf Queen** (tel. 809/452–3762 or through your hotel).

Squash There is one squash court at **Cap Estate Golf Course** (tel. 809/452–8523; open 8–4).

Tennis The largest tennis center is at **Cunard La Toc Hotel** (tel. 809/452–3081), where there are five lighted courts and bookings are essential. Additional courts are available at most major hotels for a fee.

Waterskiing Contact **Jacob's Watersports** (tel. 809/452–8281). Rentals are also available at most of the hotels.

Windsurfing The **St. Lucian Hotel** is the local agent for Mistral Windsurfers (tel. 809/452–8351). Also contact **Marigot Bay Resort** (tel. 809/453–4357) and **Jacob's Watersports** (tel. 809/452–8281). Most hotels rent Windsurfers to nonguests.

Spectator Sports

Contact the Tourist Board (tel. 809/452–4094) for specific information regarding schedules.

Cricket and **soccer,** the two national pastimes, are played at **Mindoo Philip Park** in Marchand, 2 miles east of Castries.

Shopping

Shopping on St. Lucia is low-key, but the island's best-known products are the unique hand-silk-screened and hand-printed designs of Bagshaw Studios. Bagshaw products are designed, printed, and sold only on St. Lucia. The island is also home to Windjammer Clothing, which is sold on virtually every Caribbean island. Apart from those indigenous products, there are native-made wood carvings, pottery, and straw hats and baskets.

Shopping Areas St. Lucia entered the duty-free market with the opening of **Pointe Seraphine,** a Spanish-style complex by the harbor, where 23 shops sell designer perfumes, china and crystal, jewelry, watches, leather goods, liquor, and cigarettes. Native crafts are also sold in the shopping center. Castries has a number of shops, mostly on **Bridge Street** and **William Peter Boulevard,** selling locally made souvenirs. There are also shopping arcades at the **La Toc** and **St. Lucian hotels.**

Good Buys In Pointe Seraphine, look for designer perfumes at **Images** (tel.
Duty-Free 809/452–6883). **J. Q. Charles** (tel. 809/452–2721) carries fine china and crystal, as does **Touch of Class** (tel. 809/452–7443). Leather handbags, jewelry, crystal, and perfumes can be found at **Meli** (tel. 809/452–7587).

Fabrics and Bagshaw's silk-screen fabrics and clothing can be found at
Clothing Pointe Seraphine and at the **La Toc** shop (tel. 809/452–2139). **Windjammer Clothing Company** (tel. 809/452–1040) has its main store at Vigie Cove and an outlet at Pointe Seraphine. **Caribelle Batik** (Old Victoria Rd., The Morne, Castries, tel. 809/452–3785) creates batik clothing and wall hangings. Visitors are welcome to watch the craftspeople at work.

Native Crafts Trays, masks, and figures are carved from mahogany, red cedar, and eucalyptus trees in the studio adjacent to **Eudovic's** (Morne Fortune, 15 min south of Castries, tel. 809/452–2747). Hammocks, straw mats, baskets and hats, carvings, as well as books and maps of St. Lucia are at **Noah's Arkade** (Bridge St., Castries, and Pte. Seraphine, tel. 809/452–2523).

Dining

If you stop by the Castries market (*see* Exploring St. Lucia, above) on a Saturday, you'll see the riches produced in this fertile volcanic soil. Mangoes, plantains, breadfruits, limes, pumpkins, cucumbers, pawpaws (pronounced poh-poh here, known as papaya elsewhere), green figs, yams, christophines (a green vegetable), and coconuts are among the fruits and vegetables that appear on menus throughout the island. Every menu lists the catch of the day (especially flying fish), along with the ever-popular lobster. Chicken, pork, and barbecues are also big-time here. Most of the meats are imported—beef from Argentina and Iowa, lamb from New Zealand. The French influence is strong in St. Lucian restaurants, and most chefs cook with a Creole flair.

The most highly recommended restaurants are indicated by a star ★.

Category	Cost*
Expensive	$15–$20
Moderate	$10–$15
Inexpensive	under $10

*per person, excluding drinks, service

Green Parrot. The Green Parrot Inn comes complete with sommelier and crisp white napery. The Continental menu includes poached fish fillet with mushroom cream and white-wine sauce glaze; tournedos cordon rouge (steak fillet topped with foie gras and Madeira sauce); and entrecote sautéed in butter and embellished with pineapple and cherries in red-wine sauce. There is lively entertainment on Wednesday and Saturday nights, with limbo and belly dancers. *Red Tape La., Morne Fortune, tel. 809/452-3399. Jacket required. Reservations essential. AE, MC, V. Expensive.*

Capone's. The gang here does a skillful job of blending the tropics, the Jazz Age, and Art Deco touches. There are black-and-white tile floors, a polished wood bar, and a player piano. Waiters and waitresses dressed like gangsters serve rum drinks called Valentine's Day Massacre and Mafia Mai Tai and bring your check in a violin case. The pasta is fresh, and the meat dishes include *osso buco alla Milanese* (veal knuckle) and chicken rotisserie. The **Pizza Parlour** turns out burgers and sandwiches, as well as pizza. *Rodney Bay, across from the St. Lucian Hotel, tel. 809/452-0284. Reservations suggested. AE, MC, V. No lunch; closed Mon. Moderate–Expensive.*

★ **San Antoine's.** High on the Morne, with splendid views of Castries below and Martinique in the distance, this restored historic building was originally the great house of the San Antoine Hotel, built in the mid-1800s and destroyed by fire in 1970. Now there is fine china and crystal on the tables and a superb wine list. Guests must choose from a 60-page menu, which contains such specialties as escargots in pastry, smoked-salmon mousse, and hazelnut meringue cake. After coffee and liqueurs, stroll down the nature trail through the bamboo forest. *Morne Fortune, tel. 809/452-4660. Jacket required.*

Reservations suggested. AE, V. No lunch; closed Sun. Moderate–Expensive.

Dolittle's. Take the ferry across from the Hurricane Hotel to this waterside eatery, named after the Rex Harrison movie shot here. Callaloo soup is among the openers. Main dishes include marinated red snapper; ask about the daily specials. *Marigot de Roseau on Marigot Bay, tel. 809/453–4246. Reservations suggested. AE, MC, V. Moderate.*

Jimmie's. The bar here is a popular meeting place and the restaurant is a romantic spot for dinner. Specialties include Madras fish and seafood risotto, but there's also a wide choice of seafood, meat, chicken, and vegetable dishes. *Vigie Cove, Castries, tel. 809/452–5142. No reservations. No credit cards. Moderate.*

The Lime. Across the street from Capone's, the Lime is a favorite place to lime. A casual place with lime-colored gingham curtains, straw hats decorating the ceiling, and hanging plants, it offers a fixed-price three-course dinner. Starters might include homemade pâté or stuffed crab back. Entrée choices might be medallions of pork fillet with the chef's special orange-and-ginger sauce or fish fillet poached in white wine and mushroom sauce. There's an extensive wine list. *Rodney Bay, tel. 809/452–0761. Reservations suggested for dinner. MC, V. Closed Tues. Moderate.*

★ **Rain.** This is one of the island's stellar attractions. The restaurant is in a Victorian building, and the balcony overlooking Columbus Square is a favored spot. It's usually crowded and the tables are a tad too close together, but you can still soak up the atmosphere. Lunchtime offerings include Creole soup, crab farci, rainburgers, quiches, and salads; Creole chicken is a specialty. At night, the "Champagne Buffet of 1885" is a lavish but moderately priced seven-course feast. For dessert there's old-fashioned, hand-cranked ice cream. *Columbus Sq., Castries, tel. 809/452–3022. Reservations advised. AE, MC, V. Moderate.*

The Still. Converted from an old rum distillery, this restaurant is on the grounds of a working plantation, which supplies most of the meats and produce served. The emphasis is on local foods— christophines, breadfruits, yams, and callaloo, as well as seafood, pork chops, and beef dishes. A popular Creole buffet is served at lunch. *Soufrière, tel. 809/454–7224. Reservations suggested. MC, V. Moderate.*

Sweet Dreams. Sweet, indeed. More than 150 kinds of sweets are offered here, including soft ice cream, 30 varieties of milk shakes, muffins, cookies, candies, and doughnuts. There's a children's playground where children can play while parents enjoy an uninterrupted sundae. *Rodney Bay, no phone. No reservations. No credit cards. Closed Mon. Inexpensive–Moderate.*

Lodging

St. Lucia's Caribbean coast is splashed with hotels, most of them along the strip from Castries to Cap Estate. There are hotels with social directors who will have you doing calisthenics on the beach at dawn, and West Indian guest houses where hanging out is the day's only scheduled activity. You should reserve four months in advance for a room during the winter season.

The most highly recommended lodgings are indicated by a star ★.

Category	Cost*
Very Expensive	over $150
Expensive	$100–$150
Moderate	$50–$100
Inexpensive	under $50

All prices are for a standard double room for two, excluding 8% tax and a 10% service charge.

Hotels **Club St. Lucia.** Everything is included in the price here, which means meals and unlimited drinks, golf greens fees and clubs, horseback riding, a full-day boat cruise, and a supervised children's miniclub. The resort sits on 12 acres, with rooms and suites in bungalows scattered over the hillside, and has two beaches. The accommodations are spacious, with king-size beds (twins on request), tile floors, patios, baths with tubs and showers, and air-conditioning in all but the standard rooms, which have ceiling fans only. There are clock radios in all of the rooms, but no phones. Live entertainment is scheduled nightly. *Box 915, Smugglers Village, Castries, tel. 809/452–0551 or 800/223–9868 in Britain. 154 rooms and suites. Facilities: restaurant, 2 bars, pool, 2 tennis courts, disco, minimart, water-sports center, transport to stables, golf club, squash court. AE, DC, MC, V. Very Expensive.*

Couples. Exactly as the name suggests, this all-inclusive resort is for couples only. Things tend to be quite active, with volleyball in the pool and on the beach, aerobics, and water exercises. The activities desk can arrange anything, including a wedding. Rooms and suites are on the chic side, with king-size four-poster beds and marble baths. There is an oceanfront wing with 24 air-conditioned rooms and 12 fan-cooled rooms. Other accommodations are in the three-story air-conditioned main building. There is nightly live music for dancing, and a piano bar that closes when the last couple leaves. Once you've paid the up-front fee, your hands need not touch money again during your stay. *Box 190, Malabar Beach, tel. 809/452–4211 or 800/221–1831. 100 rooms. Facilities: restaurant, 2 bars, pool, 2 lighted tennis courts, sauna, Jacuzzi, exercise room, bicycles, horseback riding, water-sports center. MC, V. Very Expensive.*

★ **Cunard Hotel La Toc and La Toc Suites.** In a secluded 110-acre valley, this posh air-conditioned resort's reception area is done in rose colors with fresh flowers, statuary, Oriental rugs, and artwork. Spacious standard rooms in the hotel section, furnished with artwork and upscale rattan and pine, have king-size or twin beds, clock radios, and baths with amenity packages, tubs, and showers. The La Toc Suites, adjacent to the hotel, originally intended to be sold as condominiums but used as the hotel's suites, are now being operated as a separate hotel. A resident host and hostess are on hand, as are 24-hour attendants who help you unpack, turn your bed down and serve you breakfast in it, and pamper you throughout your stay. The two-bedroom suites have private plunge pools, wet bars, refrigerators, TVs and VCRs, plus all of the facilities of the sister hotel. When you call to reserve ask about Cunard's land-and-sea packages. *Box 399, Castries, tel. 809/452–3081 or Cunard 800/222–0939. 192 rooms in the hotel; 54 La Toc Suites. Facilities: 3 restaurants, 3 bars, 2 pools, 6 lighted tennis courts, fitness center, beauty salon, boutiques, 9-hole golf course, water-sports center. AE, DC, MC, V. Very Expensive.*

Halcyon Beach Club. You register in a wood-paneled breezeway, and a path leads from there to the small sandy beach. Located on Choc Bay, 3 miles north of Castries, this hotel has accommodations in chalet-style buildings with simple tropical furnishings, two double beds, air-conditioning, clock radios, and patios or balconies. Standard rooms are in the gardens and superior rooms line the beach. The Chanticleer Wharf Restaurant sits out on a jetty, where there is also a disco. There's a children's playground (children under 12 stay for free with their parents), and a pool just off the beach. There's plenty of entertainment. By noon the music is revved up and going strong. *Box 388, Castries, tel. 809/452–5331 or 800/223–9815. 140 rooms. Facilities: 2 restaurants, 2 bars, disco, 2 lighted tennis courts, pool, horseback riding and golf nearby, children's playground, water-sports center. AE, DC, MC, V. Very Expensive.*

Le Sport. A $15 million investment transformed the Cariblue Hotel into this resort, which bills itself as the Body Holiday. If you've been dying to dip into thalassotherapy (seawater massages, thermal jet baths, and such), this is the place to do it. In addition to the beauty treatments, eucalyptus inhalations, and seaweed nutrient wraps, the all-inclusive resort offers a daily program involving everything from aerobics to yoga. Cushy air-conditioned rooms are done in luscious pastels, all with twin beds, marble baths, hair dryers, and fridges. A band plays nightly, and there's a piano bar. *Box 437, Cariblue Beach, tel. 809/452–8551 or 800/544–2883. 128 rooms and suites. Facilities: restaurant, 2 bars, 2 pools, bicycles, 2 lighted tennis courts, water-sports center, thalassotherapy, beauty and rejuvenation treatments, Jacuzzi, Turkish baths, exercise rooms, health shop, boutique, bank, medical facilities. AE, DC, MC, V. Very Expensive.*

★ **Marigot Bay Resort.** Villas, an inn, and a hotel comprise this village, which is located on a lovely bay, surrounded by green hills with lush tropical trees and flowers. A little trolley edges up the hill from Dolittle's Restaurant and the market to the one-, two-, and three-bedroom villas with wide plank verandas and fully equipped kitchens. The West Indian–style Marigot Inn next to the restaurant has lanai studios, each with kitchenette and balcony overlooking the marina. Fan-cooled stone cottages with wicker, bamboo, and rattan furnishings, king-size beds, and kitchenettes comprise the harborside Hurricane Hole Hotel, which has the ambience of a hunting lodge. A 24-hour water taxi connects the resort's facilities. *Box 101, Castries, tel. 809/453–4357 or 800/535–7289. 47 rooms. Facilities: 2 restaurants, 2 bars, market, dive shop, yacht charters, sailing, water-sports center. AE, DC, MC, V. Very Expensive.*

★ **St. Lucian.** The lobby is broad and white, with Oriental rugs and upholstered sofas. This was once two hotels and the rooms are spread out over considerable acreage, some on Reduit Beach, some in gardens. All have individually controlled air conditioners, two double beds, clock radios, direct-dial phones, and patios or terraces. This is the home of Splash, one of the island's hottest discos, and the local agent for Mistral Windsurfers. Water sports, including windsurfing lessons, are free to hotel guests. *Box 512, Castries, tel. 809/452–8351 or 800/221–1831. 192 rooms. Facilities: 2 restaurants, 4 bars, disco, pool, laundry/dry cleaning, 2 lighted tennis courts, dive shop, boutiques, ice-cream parlor, beauty salon, minimarket, water-sports center. AE, DC, MC, V. Expensive–Very Expensive.*

Vigie Beach Hotel. A glassed-in bar sits on the mile-long Vigie Beach, and a path leads through gardens up to the hotel. Rooms are spacious with modern decor, double beds, balconies with garden or beach view, and individually controlled air conditioners. Meals are served buffet style, and there is nightly entertainment. TVs are available for rent, and guests can use the tennis courts at the Halcyon Beach Hotel. You'll be sunning to the sound of small planes, as the hotel is located adjacent to Vigie Airport. *Box 395, Castries, tel. 809/452–5211 or 800/468–0023. 49 rooms. Facilities: restaurant, 2 bars, pool, Jacuzzi. AE, DC, MC, V. Expensive–Very Expensive.*

★ **Anse Chastanet Hotel.** Rooms are in a cluster of octagonal gazebos planted in a tropical hillside forest. In addition to the gazebos, there are 12 suites, some with plunge pools. All have ceiling fans and verandas. The hotel is on a 400-acre estate near Soufrière and the Pitons. From the main restaurant, 125 steps lead to a lovely white-sand crescent where there is another restaurant, a thatch-roof bar, and a dive shop. Sunfish and Windsurfers are gratis to guests. The restaurants serve fine West Indian fare. The hotel is quiet, peaceful, and secluded. *Box 216, Soufrière, tel. 809/454–7355. 37 rooms and suites. Facilities: 2 restaurants, 2 bars, tennis court, dive shop, water-sports center. AE, DC, MC, V. Expensive.*

Club Med St. Lucia. The four-story air-conditioned hotel is on a 95-acre beachfront property on the southeast coast, where the rough Atlantic waters are not recommended for swimming. All of the usual Club Med activities are here, including nightly entertainment. Hewanorra International Airport is five minutes away. *Vieux Fort, tel. 809/455–6001 or 800/CLUBMED. 256 rooms. Facilities: restaurant, bar, boutique, fitness center, 8 tennis courts, pool, horseback riding, water-sports center. AE, DC, MC, V. Expensive.*

Harmony Apartel. On Rodney Bay Marina, this two-story apartment hotel has accommodations ranging from small studios to two-bedroom apartments with fully equipped electric kitchens. All have wall-to-wall carpeting, twin beds, showers, TVs with VCRs, balconies or patios, and token-operated air conditioners. The two-bedroom apartments sleep up to six, and you've a choice of one or two baths. Poolside rooms, away from the marina, are quieter. Windsurfing is free; other water sports are available. There's a manager's rum-punch party every Tuesday. The Mortar and Pestle restaurant serves fine Caribbean food. *Box 155, Castries, tel. 809/452–8756 or 800/223–6510. 21 units. Facilities: restaurant, minimarket, maid service, pool, water-sports center, VCR library and books library. AE, MC, V. Moderate–Expensive.*

★ **Green Parrot.** There are green velvet chairs in the small reception room, a popular sunken bar, and a formal wood-paneled dining room. The stone and stucco inn sits high up in the Morne above Castries, and the view is spectacular. A free bus scoots you to town and the beach. Large rooms have patio, phone, air-conditioning, and bath with tub/shower and vanity. The hotel arranges boat trips to Jambette Beach for barbecue and snorkeling for about $30. *Box 648, Castries, tel. 809/452–3399. 30* rooms. *Facilities: 2 restaurants, bar, game room, nightclub. AE, MC, V. Moderate.*

★ **Islander.** An upscale motel just 300 yards from Reduit Beach, the Islander offers standard air-conditioned rooms with clock radios, wall-to-wall carpeting, king-size beds, refrigerators, balconies, and phones. There are also suites with kitchenettes. The Islander is in the Rodney Bay area. Supermarkets, restaurants, and nightlife are a few steps away. *Box 907, Castries, tel. 809/452–8757 or 800/223–9815. 60 units. Facilities: restaurant, bar, pool, movie room. AE, MC, V. Moderate.*

Kimatrai. This is a clean, family-owned and -operated hotel on the southeast coast, just above Vieux Fort. The Hewanorra International Airport is five minutes away. Accommodations include double rooms, self-contained apartments and bungalows. All are air-conditioned with private showers. The hotel operates only on the European Plan (no meals included). *Box 238, Vieux Fort, tel. 809/454–6328. 25 units. Facilities: restaurant, bar. No credit cards. Inexpensive–Moderate.*

Home and Apartment Rentals For private-home rentals, contact **Carribbean Home Rentals** (Box 710, Palm Beach, FL 33480) or **Happy Homes** (Box 12, Castries, St. Lucia).

Nightlife

Most of the action is in the hotels, which offer entertainment of the island variety—limbo dancers, fire-eaters, calypso singers, and steel band jump-ups.

Splash (St. Lucian Hotel, tel. 809/452–8351) is a sophisticated place with a good dance floor and splashy lighting effects. Open Monday–Saturday from 9 PM. At the **Halcyon Wharf Disco** (Halcyon Beach Club, tel. 809/452–5331), you can dance on the jetty under the stars every night. If you're looking for local flavor, **Monroe's** (Grande Rivière, Gros Islets, tel. 809/452–8131) is a strictly local place that welcomes visitors.

On weekends, locals usually hang out at **The Lime** (Rodney Bay, tel. 809/452–0761) before heading to the discos. If you're a nostalgia buff, you'll have a hard time leaving **Rain** (Columbus Sq., Castries, tel. 809/452–3022), where locals and tourists hang out nightly. **Capone's** (Rodney Bay, tel. 809/452–0284) is an Art Deco place right out of the Roaring Twenties, with a player piano and rum drinks. **The Charthouse** (Rodney Bay, tel. 452–8115) has a popular bar, jazz on stereo, and live music on Saturday. **San Antoine's** (Morne Fortune, tel. 809/452–4660), overlooking Castries Harbor, is a slightly formal place for after-dinner liqueurs and small talk. The **Rusty Anchor** (Marigot Bay, tel. 809/453–4357) is an informal hangout for the yachting crowd. Young boaters tie up at the **A-Frame** (Rodney Bay, tel. 809/452–8725) for drinks, chess, darts, and backgammon. (You can take the ferry for E.C.$2, which leaves every hour across the road from The Islander Hotel.) The **Green Parrot** (The Morne, tel. 809/452–3399) is in a class all by itself. Chef Harry Edwards hosts the floor show, which features limbo dancers. Harry has been known to shimmy under the pole himself. There are also belly dancers. Great fun; formal attire.

24 St. Martin St. Maarten

by Honey Naylor   What are the pros and cons of a visit to St. Maarten/St. Martin?

On the positive side, there are frequent nonstop flights from the United States, so you don't have to spend half your vacation getting here—a critical advantage if you have only a few days to enjoy the sun. The 37-square-mile island is home to two sovereign nations, St. Maarten (Dutch) and St. Martin (French), so you can experience two cultures for the price of one.

The island, particularly the Dutch side, is ideal for people who like lots of things to do. Whatever can be done in or on the water—snorkeling, windsurfing, waterskiing—is available here; and there is golf and tennis as well. Especially on the French side, there are enough quality restaurants for serious diners to try a different one each night, even on a two-week stay. The duty-free shopping is as good as anywhere in the Caribbean, except perhaps in the U.S. Virgin Islands. There's an active nightlife, with discos and casinos. Water-sports enthusiasts will love Simpson Bay Lagoon, the largest inland body of water in the Caribbean. Day trips can be taken by ship or plane to the nearby islands of Anguilla, Saba, St. Eustatius, and St. Barthélemy. There are hotels for every taste and budget—from motel-type units for the package tour trade to some of the most exclusive resorts in the Caribbean. The standard of living is one of the highest in the Caribbean, so the islanders can afford to be honest and to treat visitors as welcome guests.

On the negative side, the island is not one of the most beautiful the Caribbean has to offer, and there is little indigenous art, architecture, or culture. St. Maarten/St. Martin has been thoroughly discovered; unless you stay in an exclusive resort, you are likely to be sharing beachfronts with tour groups or conventioneers. Yes, there is gambling, but the table limits are so low that hard-core gamblers will have a better time gamboling on the beach. It can be fun to shop, and there's an occasional bargain, but many goods, particularly electronics, are cheaper in the United States.

Perhaps what makes this island unique is the opportunity it affords the visitor to lead an active life one moment and to come to a complete halt the next. For all its bustle, St. Martin/St. Maarten is still a Caribbean island brushed by gentle trade winds. You can do nothing at all and enjoy yourself immensely.

Before You Go

Tourist Information   For information about the Dutch side, contact the **St. Maarten Tourist Office** (275 7th Ave., New York, NY 10001, tel. 212/989–0000) or the **St. Maarten Information Office** (243 Ellerslie Ave., Willowdale, Toronto, Ont., Canada M2N 1Y5, tel. 416/223–3501). Information about French St. Martin can be obtained through the **French West Indies Tourist Board** (610 5th Ave., New York, NY 10020, tel. 212/757–1125). **In Canada:** 1981 Ave. McGill College, Montreal, Quebec H3A 2W9, tel. 514/288–4264. **In the United Kingdom:** 178 Piccadilly, London W1Z 0AL, tel. 01/493–6594.

Arriving and Departing
By Plane   There are two airports on the island. L'Esperance on the French side is small and handles only island-hoppers. Bigger planes fly into Juliana International Airport on the Dutch side. **American Airlines** (tel. 800/433–7300) has daily nonstop flights from New York and connections from more than 100 U.S. cities

via its San Juan hub. **Pan Am** (tel. 800/221–1111) has daily non-stop service from New York. **BWIA** (tel. 800/327–7401) flies in via Antigua from New York, Toronto, Jamaica, San Juan, Trinidad, and Miami. **LIAT** (tel. 809/462–0701) flies from Antigua; **ALM** (tel. 800/327–7230) from Aruba, Bonaire, Curaçao, the Dominican Republic, and four times a week from New York, **Air Martinique** (tel. 596/51–08–09) connects the island with Martinique twice a week. **Windward Islands Airways (Winair,** tel. 599/54–42–30), which is based on St. Maarten, has daily scheduled service to Saba, St. Eustatius, St. Barts, Anguilla, St. Thomas, and St. Kitts/Nevis. **Air Guadeloupe** (tel. 590/90–37–37) has several flights daily to St. Barts and Guadeloupe from both sides of the island. **Air St. Barthélemy** (tel. 590/27–71–90) has frequent service from Juliana. Tour and Charter services are available from Winair and **St. Martin Helicopters** (Dutch side, tel. 599/4–4287).

By Boat Motorboats zip several times a day from Anguilla to the French side at Marigot; three times a week from St. Barts. Catamaran service is available daily from the Dutch side to St. Barts. The 50-passenger *Style* (tel. 599/5–22167) slaps across from Saba four times a week.

Passports and Visas U.S. citizens need proof of citizenship. A passport (valid or not expired more than five years) is preferred. An original birth certificate with raised seal (or a photocopy with notary seal), or a voter registration card are also acceptable. All visitors must have a confirmed room reservation and an ongoing or return ticket. British and Canadian citizens need valid passports.

Customs and Duties There are no customs as St. Martin/St. Maarten is a free port.

Language Dutch is the official language of St. Maarten and French is the official language of St. Martin, but almost everyone speaks English. If you hear a language you can't quite place, it's Papiamento, a Spanish-based Creole of the Netherlands Antilles.

Further Reading Dr. J. Hartog's *St. Maarten, Saba, and St. Eustatius,* usually available in paperback in the island's bookstores, gives you a rundown on the islands' history and includes interesting photographs.

Staying in St. Martin/St. Maarten

Important Addresses **Tourist Information:** On the Dutch side the **Tourist Information Bureau** is on Cyrus Wathey (pronounced watty) Square in the heart of Philipsburg, at the pier where the cruise ships send their tenders. *Tel. 599/5–22337. Open weekdays 8–noon and 1–5, except holidays.*

On the French side, there is a small **Tourist Information Office** on the Marigot pier. *Tel. 590/87–53–26. Open weekdays 9–noon and 2–3:30; closed holidays and the afternoon preceding a holiday.*

Emergencies **Police:** Dutch side (tel. 599/5–22222), French side (tel. 590/85–50–10).

Ambulance: Dutch side (tel. 599/5–22111), French side (tel. 590/87–54–14).

Hospitals: St. Rose Hospital (Front St., Philipsburg, tel. 599/5–22300) is a fully equipped 55-bed hospital.

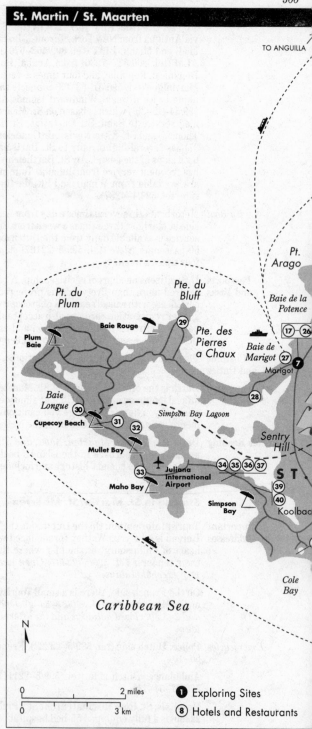

St. Martin / St. Maarten

TO ANGUILLA

Pt. Arago

Baie de la Potence

Pt. du Plum

Pte. du Bluff

Pte. des Pierres a Chaux

Baie Rouge

Baie de Marigot

Marigot

Plum Baie

Baie Longue

Cupecoy Beach

Simpson Bay Lagoon

Sentry Hill

Mullet Bay

S T

Juliana International Airport

Maho Bay

Simpson Bay

Koolbac

Cole Bay

Caribbean Sea

N

0   2 miles
0   3 km

① Exploring Sites

⑧ Hotels and Restaurants

Pharmacies: Pharmacies are open Monday–Saturday 7–5. **Central Drug Store** (Philipsburg, tel. 599/5–22321), **Mullet Bay Drug Store** (tel. 599/5–42801, ext. 342), and **Pharmacie** (Marigot, tel. 590/87–50–79).

Currency Legal tender on the Dutch side is the Netherlands Antilles florin (guilder), written NAf; on the French side, the French franc (F). The exchange rate fluctuates, but in general is about 1.80 NAf to U.S. $1 and 5.5F to U.S. $1. On the Dutch side, prices are usually given in both NAf and U.S. dollars, which are accepted all over the island, as are credit cards. Note: Prices quoted here are in U.S. dollars unless otherwise noted.

Taxes and Service Charges On the Dutch side, there is a 5% government tax added to hotel bills. On the French side, a *taxe de sejour* (visitor's tax) is tacked onto hotel bills (the amount differs from hotel to hotel, but the maximum is $1 per day, per person). All visitors pay a $5 departure tax from Juliana Airport. It will cost you 10 French francs to depart by plane from l'Esperance Airport or by ferry to Anguilla from Marigot's pier.

In lieu of tipping, service charges are added to hotel bills all over the island, and, by law, are included in all menu prices on the French side. On the Dutch side, most restaurants add 10%–15% to the bill.

Hotels on the Dutch side add a 15% service/energy charge to the bill. Hotels on the French side add 10%–15% for service.

Taxi drivers expect a 10% tip.

Guided Tours A 2½-hour taxi tour of the island costs $30 for one or two people, $7 for each additional person. Your hotel or the Tourist Office can arrange it for you. Best bet is the 20-passenger vans of **St. Maarten Sightseeing Tours** (Philipsburg, tel. 599/5–22753), which offer, among other options, a 2½-hour island tour for $6 per person. You can tour in deluxe comfort with **St. Maarten Limousine Service** (tel. 599/5–24698 or 599/5–22698) for $40–$50 per hour with a three-hour minimum. Fully equipped Lincoln Continentals accommodate up to six people and are furnished with stereo, fully stocked bar, and air-conditioning. The limo service also offers transportation to and from Juliana Airport at rates ranging from $30 to $65 one way. (They include one hour of waiting time free of charge for late arrivals.)

Getting Around **Taxis** Taxi rates are government-regulated and authorized taxis display stickers of the St. Maarten Taxi Association. There is a taxi service, headed by Raymond Helligar, at the Marigot port near the Tourist Information Bureau. Fixed fares apply from Juliana Airport and the Marigot ferry to the various hotels and around the island. Fares are 25% higher between 10 PM and midnight; 50% higher between midnight and 6 AM.

Buses One of the island's best bargains at 85¢, buses operate frequently between 7 AM and 7 PM and run from Philipsburg through Cole Bay to Marigot.

Rental Cars You can book a car at Juliana Airport, where all major rental companies have booths. There are also rentals at every hotel area. Rental cars are inexpensive–approximately $30 a day for a subcompact car plus Collision Damage Waiver. All foreign driver's licenses are honored, and major credit cards are accepted. The cost is about $30 a day, plus collision insurance, with unlimited mileage. **Avis** (tel. 800/331–1212), **Budget** (tel. 800/527–0700), **Dollar** (tel. 800/421–6868), **Hertz** (tel. 800/223–6472), and **National** (tel. 800/328–4567) all have offices on the island. Most hotels will reserve a car for guests in advance, an offer that you should take advantage of, especially during the height of the winter season.

Telephones and Mail To call the Dutch side from the United States, dial 011–599 + local number; for the French side, 011–590 + local number. To phone from the Dutch side to the French, dial 06 + local number; from the French side to the Dutch, 3 + local number. Keep in mind that a call from one side to another is an overseas call, not a local call. Telephone communications, especially on the Dutch side, leave something to be desired. On the French side, it is not possible to make collect or credit-card calls to the United States, and there are no coin phones. If you think you'll need to use public phones on the French side, go to the special desk at Marigot's post office and buy a Telecarte (it looks like a credit card), which gives you 40 units for around 31F or 120 units for 93F.

Letters from the Dutch side to the United States and Canada cost NAf 1.30; postcards, NAf .60. From the French side, letters up to 20 grams, 4.10F; postcards, 2.80F.

Shops on the Dutch side are open Monday–Saturday, 8–noon and 2–6; on the French side, Monday–Saturday 9–noon or 12:30, and 2–6. Some of the larger shops on both sides of the island open Sunday and holidays when the cruise ships are in port. Some of the small Dutch and French shops set their own capricious hours.

Banks on the Dutch side are open Monday–Thursday 8–1 and Friday 4–5. French banks open weekdays 9–noon and 2–3 and close afternoons preceding holidays.

Beaches

The island's 10 miles of beaches are all open to the public. Beaches occupied by resort properties charge a small fee (about $3) for changing facilities, and water-sports equipment can be rented in most of the hotels. The island has as many beaches as it has square miles. Some of the 37 beaches are secluded, some are located in the thick of things. Topless bathing is virtually de rigueur on the French side. If you take a cab to a remote beach, be sure to arrange a specific, clearly understood time for your driver to return to pick you up, and don't leave valuables unattended on the beach.

Hands down, **Baie Longue** is the best beach on the island. It's a beautiful, mile-long curve of white sand on the westernmost tip of the island. This is a good place for snorkeling and swimming, but beware of a strong undertow when the waters are rough. You can sunbathe in the buff, though only a few do. Pack a lunch. There are no facilities.

Baie Rouge is one of the most secluded beaches on the island. This little patch of sand is located at the base of high cliffs and is backed by private homes rather than by hotels. Some rate it the prettiest beach of the island. A small snack/soda stand is located at the entrance.

Cupecoy Beach is a narrower strip of white sand with a backdrop of cliffs and caves. It's just south of Baie Longue on the western side of the island, near the Dutch-French border. There are no facilities.

You have to approach the **Dawn Beach-Oyster Pond** area through the Dawn Beach Hotel. This long white-sand beach is partly protected by reefs (good for snorkeling), but the waters are not always calm. When the waves come rolling in, this is the best spot on the island for bodysurfing. There are water-sports rentals at **Red Ensign Watersports** (*see* Participant Sports, below), a snack bar, and facilities.

Ilet Pinel is a little speck off the northeast coast, with about 500 yards of beach, where you can have picnics and privacy. There are no facilities.

Ecru-color sand, palm and sea-grape trees, calm waters, and the roar of jets lowering to nearby Juliana Airport distinguish the beach at **Maho Bay.** Concession stand, beach chairs, and facilities are available.

At **Mullet Bay,** the powdery white-sand beach is crowded with guests of the Mullet Bay Resort, where you can get refreshments. Rentals are available at the hotel through **Maho Watersports** (*see* Participant Sports, below).

Orient Beach is the island's best-known "clothes optional" beach—it's on the agenda for voyeurs from visiting cruise ships. You can enter from the parking area or through the **Club Orient** (tel. 590/87–33–85), which has chalet self-catering bungalows for rent, shops, and rental water-sports equipment.

Beyond Baie Longue is **Plum Beach,** where the beach arcs between two headlands and the occasional sunbather discloses all.

Simpson Bay is a long half-moon of white sand near Simpson Bay Village, one of the last undiscovered hamlets on the island. In this small fishing village you'll find refreshments, the **Ocean Explorers** (*see* Participant Sports, below) for water-sports rentals, and the opportunity to take a small tour of the neat little ultra-Caribbean town homes.

Exploring St. Martin/St. Maarten

Numbers in the margin correspond with points of interest on the St. Martin/St. Maarten map.

Philipsburg The Dutch capital of Philipsburg, which stretches about a mile along an isthmus between Great Bay and the Salt Pond, has three more or less parallel streets: Front Street, Back Street, and Pond Fill. Your first stop should be the **Tourist Office** on **Wathey Square.** After arming yourself with maps, brochures, and friendly advise, stroll out on the pier. **Great Bay** is rolled out before you, and the beach stretches alongside it for about a mile. The square bustles with vendors, souvenir shops, and tourists. There's a taxi stand where you can arrange for a driver to take you around if you'd rather not rent a car. Philipsburg should be explored on foot, but you'll need wheels to get around the island.

Directly across the street from Wathey Square you'll see a striking white building with a cupola. It was built in 1793 and has since served as the commander's home, a fire station, and a jail. It now serves as Town Hall and the post office.

The square is in the middle of the isthmus on which Philipsburg sits. To your right and left the streets are lined with hotels, duty-free shops, fine restaurants, and cafés, most of them in pastel-colored West Indian cottages gussied up with gingerbread trim. Narrow alleyways lead to arcades and flower-filled courtyards where there are yet more boutiques and eateries.

Little lanes called *steegjes* connect Front Street with Back Street, which is considerably less congested because it has fewer shops.

Time Out Behind a filigree facade you can get a Haagen Dazs "fix" at **Donchee's Ice Cream Parlor.** (Back St., tel. 599/5–22452). There are oven-warm pastries, too.

Our drive begins at the western end of Front Street. The road (it will become Sucker Garden Rd.) leads north along Salt Pond and begins to climb and curve just outside of town. Take the first right to **Guana Bay Point,** from which there is a splendid view of the island's east coast, tiny deserted islands, and small St. Barts, which is anything but deserted.

Sucker Garden Road continues north through spectacular scenery. Continue along a paved roller-coaster road down to **Dawn Beach,** one of the island's best snorkeling beaches.

Oyster Pond is the legendary point where two early settlers, a Frenchman and a Dutchman, allegedly began to pace in opposite directions around the island to divide it between their respective countries. (The official boundary marker is on the other side of the island.)

Elsewhere on the From Oyster Pond, follow the road along the bay and around
Island Etang aux Poissons (Fish Lake), all the way to **Orléans.** This settlement, which is also known as the French Quarter, is the oldest on the island. Noted local artist and activist Roland Richardson makes his home here. He holds open studio on Thursdays from 10 to 6 to sell his art. He's a proud islander ready to share his wealth of knowledge about the island's cultural history.

A rough dirt road leads northeast to **Orient Beach,** the island's best-known nudist beach. Offshore, little Ilet Pinel is an uninhabited island that's fine for picnicking, sunning, and swimming.

Farther north you'll come to **French Cul de Sac,** where you'll see the French colonial mansion of St. Martin's mayor nestled in the hills. Little red-roof houses look like open umbrellas tumbling down the green hillside. The scenery here is glorious, and the area is great for hiking. There is a lot of construction, however, as the surroundings are slowly being developed. The descent to L'Habitation, the elegant resort at Anse Marcel on the north coast, may turn your knuckles white.

The road swirls south through green hills and pastures, past flower-entwined stone fences. Past Esperance Airport is the town of **Grand Case.** Though it has only one mile-long main street, it's known as the "Restaurant Capital of the Caribbean": More than 20 restaurants serve French, Italian, Indonesian, and Vietnamese fare, as well as fresh seafood.

Grand Case Beach Hotel is at the end of this road and has two beaches to choose from for a short dip.

Follow the signs south from Grand Case to Rue de la République, which brings you to the French capital of **Marigot.** If you're a shopper, a gourmand, or just a Francophile, you'll want to tarry here awhile. Marina Port La Royale is the shopping complex at the port, but Rue de la République and Rue de la Liberté, which border the bay, are also filled with duty-free shops, boutiques, and bistros.

The road due south of Marigot to Philipsburg passes the official boundary, where a simple border marker, erected by the Dutch and French citizenry to commemorate 300 years of peaceful co-existence, bears the dates "1648 to 1948." The only formality at the border is an occasional pause to allow a herd of cows to meander across the road.

At the airport, the road from Marigot to the north and Simpson Bay to the west join together and lead to Philipsburg, passing the cut-off to Divi Little Bay Beach Resort.

The other road from Marigot leads west and hugs the coastline to cross a small bridge to Sandy Ground and then along Marigot Bay. Soon thereafter, on the right, will be the Mediterranean-style village resort of **La Belle Creole** commanding Pointe du Bluff. Then come some of the island's best beaches—**Baie Rouge, Plum Bay,** and **Baie Longue**—clinging to the westernmost point of the island. They are all accessible down bumpy but short dirt roads and perfect for swimming and picnicking.

At the end of Baie Longue and running eastward along the south coast is **La Samanna,** the once-fashionable jet-set resort. Just after this hotel you enter back into Dutch territory at **Cupecoy Beach.** You'll have to endure the huge, garish vacation condo-hotel complexes of Mullet Bay and Maho Bay before you reach Juliana Airport and Philipsburg.

What to See and Do with Children

Live Eagle Spectacular (*see* Off the Beaten Track, below).

Fun City. An entertainment center with local limbo and fire dancers, Caribbean folkloric dancers, and steel drum players. Shows daily at 11 AM and 2 PM. For further information call **The Caribbean Entertainment Center** (Philipsburg, tel. 599/5–22261 or 599/5–23194).

Off the Beaten Track

No doubt about it, Jean-Pierre Bordes has a way with birds. For more than 20 years he's been talking to them, listening to them, and teaching them to straighten up and fly right. What kinds of birds? Oh, vultures, falcons, eagles—your basic birds of prey. And why? You can see for yourself high on a hilltop overlooking St. Maarten, where Bordes presents his **Live Eagle Spectacular.** This is one of only six places in the world where falconry is performed publicly. Bordes's hooded peregrine falcon rises high in the sky and dives toward Earth at a speed of 200 miles an hour. Each of his four griffin vultures has a wing span of nine feet. There's no show unless the weather's right, so ask at your hotel or at the Tourist Office before you drive up the narrow dirt road that leads to it. *In Maho Bay on the road to*

Pointe Pirouette, just past Casino Royale (follow the yellow signs). Admission: $8 adults, $4 children. Shows daily, weather permitting, at 10:30, 2:30, and 4.

Participant Sports

All the resort hotels have activities desks that can arrange virtually any type of water sport.

Boating Motorboats, speedboats, Dolphins, pedal boats, sailboats, and canoes can be rented at **Lagoon Cruises & Watersports** (tel. 599/5–42801, ext. 337) and **Caribbean Watersports** (tel. 599/5–44387).

Sun Charters (tel. 800/772–3500) has a fleet of 30 Centurion sailboats for hire. A new yacht charter company is **Dynasty** (Marigot's Port La Royale Marina, tel. 590/87–85–21).

Deep-Sea Fishing Angle for yellowtail, snapper, grouper, marlin, tuna, and wahoo on half-day deep-sea excursions, including bait and tackle, instruction for novices, and open bar. Contact **Wampum** (Bobby's Marina, Philipsburg, tel. 599/5–22366).

Golf **Mullet Bay Resort** (tel. 599/5–42081) has an 18-hole championship course.

Horseback Riding Contact **Crazy Acres Riding Center** (Wathey Estate, Cole Bay, tel. 599/5–22061) or **Caid & Isa** (Anse Marcel, tel. 590/87–32–92).

Jet- and Waterskiing Rent equipment through **Caribbean Watersports** (tel. 599/5–42801 or 599/5–44363) and **Maho Watersports** (tel. 599/5–44387).

Parasailing A great high can be arranged through **Lagoon Cruises & Watersports** (tel. 599/5–42801).

Running The **Road Runners Club** (Pelican Resort Activities Desk, tel. 599/5–42503) meets weekly for its 5K or 10K run.

Scuba Diving On the Dutch side is Proselyte Reef, named for the British frigate H. M. S. *Proselyte*, which sank south of Great Bay in 1802. In addition to wreck dives, reef, night, cave, and drift dives are popular. Off the northeast coast of the French side, dive sites include Ilet Pinel, for good shallow diving; Green Key, a prolific barrier reef; and Flat Island (also known as Ile Tintamarre) for sheltered coves and subsea geologic faults. NAUI and PADI certified dive centers offer instruction, rentals, and trips at **Tradewinds Dive Center** (tel. 599/5–22167), **Maho Watersports** (tel. 599/5–44387), **St. Maarten Divers** (tel. 599/5–23008, ext. 536), **Under the Waves Watersports** (tel. 590/87–51–87), **Watersports Unlimited** (tel. 599/5–23434), and **Little Bay Watersports** (tel. 599/5–22333).

Sea Excursions You can take a day-long picnic sail (wine, beer, soft drinks, lunch, and snorkeling equipment are included) to offshore islands or secluded coves aboard the 45-foot ketch *Gabrielle* (tel. 599/5–23170); the 41-foot ketch *Pretty Penny* (tel. 599/5–2167); or the 60-foot schooner *Gandalf.* The catamaran *Bluebeard II* (tel. 599/5–42801 or 599/5–42898), moored in Marigot, sails around Anguilla's south and northwest coasts to Prickley Pear, where there are excellent coral reefs for snorkeling and powdery white sands for sunning. Included in the deal are mixed drinks, snacks, beer, the use of underwater cameras, and a chicken and seafood barbecue.

The luxurious 75-foot motor catamaran *White Octopus* (tel. 599/5–23170) does full-moon and cocktail cruises, complete with calypso music. In St. Martin, sailing, snorkeling, and picnic excursions to offshore islands can be arranged through **Pat Turner Watersports** (Le Galion, tel. 590/87–51–77), **Papagayo** (Club Orient, tel. 590/87–33–85), **L'Habitation** (tel. 590/87–33–33), **La Belle Creole** (tel. 590/87–58–66), and **La Samanna** (tel. 590/87–51–22).

Snorkeling Coral reefs teem with marine life, and clear water allows visibility of up to 200 feet. Some of the best snorkeling on the Dutch side can be had around the rocks below Fort Amsterdam off Little Bay Beach, the west end of Maho Bay, Pelican Key and the rocks near the Caravanserai Hotel, and the reefs off Dawn Beach and Oyster Pond. On the French side, the area around Orient Bay, Green Key, Ilet Pinel, and Flat Island (or Tintamarre) is especially lovely for snorkeling, and has been officially classified a regional underwater nature reserve. Arrange rentals and trips through **Watersports Unlimited** (tel. 599/5–23434), **Red Ensign Watersports** (tel. 599/5–22929), **Ocean Explorers** (tel. 599/5–45252), and **Little Bay Watersports** (tel. 599/5–22333).

Tennis There are two lighted courts at **Dawn Beach Hotel** (tel. 599/5–22944), two lighted courts at **Pelican Resort** (tel. 599/5–42503), three asphalt courts at **Little Bay and Belair Beach Resorts** (tel. 599/5–22333 or 599/5–23362), four courts at **Maho Reef & Beach** (tel. 599/5–42115), four lighted courts at **Le Privilege** (Anse Marcel, 590/87–59–28), and 16 all-weather courts at **Mullet Bay Resort** (tel. 599/5–42081).

Windsurfing Rental and instruction are available at **Little Bay Beach Hotel** (tel. 599/5–22333, ext. 186), **Maho Watersports** (tel. 599/5–44387), and **Red Ensign Watersports** (tel. 599/5–22929).

Shopping

About 180 cruise ships call at St. Maarten each year, and they do so for about 500 reasons. That's roughly the number of duty-free shops on the island.

Prices can be 25%–50% below those in the United States and Canada on French perfumes, liquor, Cognac and fine liqueurs, cigarettes and cigars, Swedish crystal and Finnish stoneware, Irish linen, Italian leather, German cameras, European designer fashions, plus thousands of other things you never knew you wanted. But check prices before you leave home, especially if you live in the New York City area—Manhattan's prices for cameras and electronic equipment are hard to beat anywhere.

St. Maarten's best-known "craft" is its guavaberry liqueur, made from rum and the wild local berries (not to be confused with guavas) that grow only on this island's central mountains.

Prices are quoted in florins, francs, and dollars; shops take credit cards and traveler's checks. Most shopkeepers, especially on the Dutch side, speak English. (If more than one cruise ship is in port, avoid Front Street. It's so crowded you won't be able to move.)

Shopping Areas In St. Maarten: **Front Street,** Philipsburg, is one long strip lined with sleek boutiques and cozy shops gift wrapped in gingerbread. **Old Town,** near the end of Front Street, has 22 stores, boutiques, and open-air cafés. The newest addition, just outside of Philipsburg, is **Amsterdam Shopping Center,** with 22 pastel West Indian-style shops and restaurants on cobblestone streets. And there are almost 100 boutiques in **Mullet, Mayo,** and **Treasure Island Cupecoy Piazza.**

In St. Martin: Wrought-iron balconies, colorful awnings, and gingerbread trim decorate Marigot's smart shops, tiny boutiques, and bistros in the **Marina Port La Royale, Galerie Perigourdine,** and on the main streets, **Rue de la Liberté** and **Rue de la République.**

Good Buys **Little Switzerland** (Marigot and Philipsburg, tel. 800/524–2010) and **Spritzer and Fuhrmann** (Marigot, tel. 590/87–59–62; Philipsburg, tel. 599/5–44381) handle the finest in crystal and china.

Jewelry and watches can be found at **Oro del Sol** (Marigot, tel. 590/87–57–02; Treasure Island Cupecoy Piazza, tel. 599/5–22602), **Carat** (Marigot, tel. 590/87–73–40; Philipsburg, tel. 599/5–22180), **Little Switzerland** (Marigot and Philipsburg, tel. 800/524–2010), and **Little Europe** (Philipsburg, tel. 599/5–23062).

Pick up a bottle of wine for your picnic at **La Cave du Savour Club** (Marigot, tel. 590/87–58–51).

Lipstick (Marigot, tel. 590/87–73–24) and **Oro del Sol** (Marigot, tel. 590/87–57–02) carry perfumes and cosmetics.

For designer fashions head to **La Romana** (2 locations on Front St., tel. 599/5–22181) and **Havane** (Marigot, tel. 590/87–70–39).

New Amsterdam Store (Philipsburg, tel. 599/5–22787) and **The Yellow House** (Philipsburg, tel. 599/5–23438) handle fine linens and porcelain.

The Lil' Shoppe (Philipsburg, tel. 599/5–2177) carries eel-skin wallets, handbags, perfumes, and a large selection of swimwear. Shoes, belts, and handbags are also sold at **Maximoflorence** (Philipsburg, tel. 599/5–23735).

Island Specialties Caribelle batik, hammocks, handmade jewelry, herbs and spices are stashed at **The Shipwreck Shop** (Philipsburg, tel. 599/5–22962); sculpture, oils, and watercolors, plus "a few of a kind of attire and sundries" are on display at American mystery writer De Forbes's **Pierre Lapin** (Grand Case, tel. 590/87–52–10); and T-shirts, beach towels, native dolls, Indian glass bangles, and hand-painted Delft souvenirs can all be found at **Sasha's** (Philipsburg, tel. 599/5–24331).

K-Dis (Marigot, tel. 590/87–52–23) is a supermarket with French wines and liqueurs, cheeses, pâtés, heat-and-serve dishes, salads, and cold cuts.

Dining

It may seem that this island has no monuments. Au contraire, there are many of them, all dedicated to gastronomy. You'll scarcely find a touch of Dutch; the major influences are French and Italian. This season's "in" eatery may be next season's remembrance of things past, as things do have a way of changing rapidly. In high season, unless otherwise noted in our text, be sure to make reservations, and call to cancel if you can't make it. Many restaurants close during August and/or September.

The most highly recommended restaurants are indicated by a star ★.

Category	Cost*
Very Expensive	over $50
Expensive	$40–$50
Moderate	$25–$40
Inexpensive	under $25

per person, excluding drinks and service

Dutch Side

Antoine's. This is an elegant, airy terrace overlooking Great Bay. You might start your meal, which is served by candlelight, with French onion soup, then move on to steak au poivre, veal sweetbreads in vermouth sauce, or lobster Thermidor. For dessert, try cheesecake with raspberry melba sauce. *Front St., Philipsburg, tel. 599/5–22964. AE, MC, V. Very Expensive.*

La Rosa. An intimate dining room with piano music, where Italian specialties begin with a mixed antipasto or prosciutto and melon. Pasta offerings include *rigatoni la Rosa* (young fennels done up with fresh sardines, onions, tomato sauce, raisins and Parmesan cheese). Among the best meat dishes are broiled veal rolls. Save room for the tartufo. *Sea Palace Hotel, Front St., Philipsburg, tel. 599/5–23832. AE, MC, V. Very Expensive.*

Le Bec Fin. To reach the well-known upstairs restaurant, you stroll through a flowery courtyard where La Coupole's croissants and cakes are baked daily (a nice thing to bear in mind come breakfast time). A new chef has taken over the kitchens of Le Bec Fin, but the fare remains much the same. Starters include warm chicken mousse with tarragon and tomato sauce and snails baked in mushroom caps with hazelnut sauce. Try the fresh red snapper fillet with mussel sauce, or the duck breast in cranberry sauce, although fish is your best bet. The meringue swan with mint ice cream is as delightful to the eye as to the palate. *Front St., Philipsburg, tel. 599/5–22976. AE. Expensive.*

★ **Oyster Pond Yacht Club.** Reopened in September 1988 after renovation, the hotel and its dining room are even more elegant than before. You'll find fine linens and china, fresh flowers, and a delightful terrace with wonderful sea views. Chef Paul Souchette, originally from Martinique, cooks with an island flair. His specialties include salad with a mint and yogurt dressing, coquilles St. Jacques, fillet of red snapper in sauce piquante, and sweet, billowy soufflés for dessert. The hotel's guests have priority in this romantic dining room, so you should reserve well in advance. *Oyster Pond, tel. 599/5–22206 or 599/5–23206. Reservations advised. AE, MC, V. Very Expensive.*

Red Snapper. A breezy terrace restaurant on Great Bay with white rattan chairs, salmon-color cloths, fine china, and a splendid view. Try goat cheese in pastry shells for openers. Chef Lionel's specials include baked red snapper fillet served with thinly sliced potatoes, and sea scallops on a bed of braised endive. For dessert, chocolate amaretto cake is a must. *93 Front St., Philipsburg, tel. 599/5–23834. AE, MC, V. Very Expensive.*

Spartaco. Northern Italian cuisine is served in a 200-year-old stone plantation house. Everything here is either homemade or imported from Italy. Some of the specialties are black angelhair pasta with shrimp and garlic, tagliata of swordfish baked with pink pepper and rosemary, and veal Vesuviana, with mozzarella, oregano, and tomato sauce. *Almond Grove, Cole Bay, tel. 599/5–45379. No lunch. MC, V. Very Expensive.*

Felix. This classy little beachside eatery serves dinner by candlelight. At lunchtime, take a dip before feasting on salad Felix (an imaginative concoction of bananas, sweet potatoes, and avocado), rack of lamb Provençale, or steak au poivre. The restaurant is on the road to Pelican Resort. *Pelican Key, tel. 599/5–45237. AE. Closed Tues. Expensive.*

L'Escargot. A lovely 19th-century house wrapped in verandas is home to one of St. Maarten's oldest French restaurants. Starters include homemade pâté with pink peppercorns. There are also, of course, a variety of snail dishes. For an entrée, try the duck in pineapple-banana sauce or the poached yellowtail in cream sauce with fresh mint. *76 Front St., Philipsburg, tel. 599/5–22483. AE, MC, V. Expensive.*

Le Perroquet. In a cool green-and-white West Indian-style house on the peaceful lagoon, chef Pierre Castagna turns out such exotic specialties as breast of ostrich. *Airport Rd., Simpson Bay, tel. 599/5–44339. Closed Mon. AE, V. Expensive.*

★ **West Indian Tavern.** A local favorite, famous for its guavaberry drinks, this is a casual tavern with gingerbread frill, verandas, and hanging plants. For starters, try crisp fried local cristophine (a vegetable fruit) or coconut fried prawns. Entrées include grouper sautéed with bacon, chopped hazelnuts and light cream, and curried chicken with homemade mango-and-bamboo chutney and fresh coconut. Don't miss the Key-lime pie. If you're on the island on St. Patrick's Day, this is the place to be (the owner's Irish). *Front St., Philipsburg, tel. 599/5–22965. No lunch, but open until midnight for dinner. AE, MC, V. Expensive.*

Cafe Royal. Owner Rene Florijn once coordinated a little lunch for Princess Margaret and a few (400) friends. The café's few tables sprinkle the sidewalk, and inside brass ceiling fans whir over a pink-and-green garden set in the atrium. The menu includes smoked Norwegian salmon, snails in garlic butter, fresh lobster salad, and hamburgers. Breakfasts range from simple to sumptuous, and afternoon tea is refreshing. For picnics, have the deli in the back pack a basket for you. *Palm Plaza, Front St., Philipsburg, tel. 599/5–23443. AE, MC, V. Moderate.*

Chesterfield's. Burgers and salads are served at lunch, but menus are more elaborate for dinner on this indoor/outdoor terrace overlooking the marina. Menu offerings include French onion soup, roast duckling with fresh pineapple and banana sauce, and chicken cordon bleu. The Mermaid Bar is a popular spot with yachtsmen. *Great Bay Marina, Philipsburg, tel. 599/5–23484. AE, MC, V. Moderate.*

Le Pavillon. Creole and French specialties, such as *Assiette Tricolore* (lobster, snapper, and shrimp with three sauces) and duckling in pineapple sauce, are served in this little beachside bistro. *Simpson Bay Village, tel. 599/5–44254. No lunch. AE, MC, V. Moderate.*

Callaloo. You can find a little bit of everything except callaloo. There's a pizza piazza, the lively Gazebo Bar, and a little air-conditioned café where you can get quiche, burgers, oversize sandwiches, barbecued chicken, and charbroiled steaks. *Promenade, Front St., Philipsburg, no phone. Reservations not required. Closed Sunday. No credit cards. Inexpensive.*

★ **Sam's Restaurant and Pub.** Sam's is enormously popular with a motley crowd of locals, tourists, the boating crowd, and especially American expatriates. Featured are thick-cut onion rings, charbroiled shrimp and steak kebabs, pork chops and apple sauce, and big burgers. Come here for a huge American breakfast. Also, the downstairs bar is one of *the* places to be at night for live music. *Front St., Philipsburg, tel. 599/5–22989. AE, MC, V. Inexpensive.*

Wajang Doll. Indonesian dishes are served in the garden of this West Indian–style house. The specialty is rijstaffel—the Indonesian rice table that offers 14 or 19 dishes in a complete dinner. *Front St., Philipsburg, tel. 599/5–22687. AE, MC, V. Inexpensive.*

French Side **Alizéa.** With justification, those who have tried this terrace
★ restaurant have come away claiming that the cuisine is the best on the island. Trained in France, chef Guy de Corre describes his cooking as "refined contemporary cuisine that respects tradition." The menu changes constantly, but some outstanding dishes have been goat-cheese ravioli with truffle butter, mousse of pheasant with medallions of lobster, hot duck liver on a chutney of figs, and a galette of quail breast with cinnamon and quail legs stuffed with pistachios. *In Alizéa Hotel, Mont Vernon 25, tel. 590/87–33–42. Reservations suggested. AE, MC, V. Very Expensive.*

La Belle France. This gourmet restaurant within the stunning L'Habitation resort offers a spicy lobster pâté served with an assortment of island fish, homemade foie gras, sliced monkfish in a light sauce of green leeks, and, for dessert, mano delight in sweet pineapple sauce. *Anse Marcel, tel. 590/87–32–32. No lunch. AE, MC, V. Very Expensive.*

Le Poisson d'Or. Posh and popular, this restaurant is in a restored stone house with a 20-table terrace. You can feast on terrine of foie gras, snails wrapped in a crepe, a cassoulet of lobster with oysters and a champagne sauce, followed by sautéed yellowtail served with a zucchini mousse. The young chef, Francoise Julien, cooks with enthusiasm, but his cuisine has stiff competition from the setting—the waters of the bay lapping the terrace. Closed for lunch during off-season. *Off rue d'Anguille on the sea, Marigot, tel. 590/87–72–45. Closed Tues. for lunch in high season. AE, MC, V. Very Expensive.*

La Provence. Dining is on an upscale terra-cotta terrace that steps down from the stone plaza of La Belle Creole with a sweeping view over the pool and beyond the gardens into the bay. The new chef, Georges LaVigne, hails from the south of France, though his cuisine is more Continental than innovative French. Two nights a week are buffet dinners, (Monday's beef isn't as good as Friday's seafood). The rest of the week is à la carte dining with such entrées as fresh fish, or veal with fresh forest mushrooms. *Pointe des Pierres a Chaux, tel. 590/87–58–66. AE, CB, DC, MC, V. Very Expensive.*

La Rhumerie. The chef turns out Creole and traditional French fare, with specialties including crab farci, curried goat, herbed conch, boudin, frogs' legs, snails, and duck à l'orange. *Colombier, no phone. No credit cards. Very Expensive.*

La Samanna. This restaurant has an exquisite setting in the celebrated hotel. A brilliantly colored Indian wedding tent billows over the octagonal bar, and you can dine by candlelight on a tented terrace surrounded by bougainvillea. Chef Jean-Pierre Jury's à la carte menu might include Beluga caviar, broccoli terrine with carrots and chives, sautéed filet mignon with walnuts, or grilled red snapper with Creole sauce (the latter a low-calorie offering). The clientele is chic, international, and often famous. A meal here is perhaps the most expensive you can have in St. Martin—easily $200 for dinner for two including wine. *Baie Longue, tel. 590/87-51-22. Jackets suggested. AE, DC, MC, V. Very Expensive.*

La Vie En Rose. This is a popular and reputable second-floor restaurant. Try to reserve a table on the balcony overlooking Marigot harbor. The menu rewards adventurous eaters with mint-flavored vichyssoise with mussels, lobster salad with celery and truffles, breaded sautéed foie gras with pears, and sliced breast of duck in lemon-ginger sauce. Save room for chocolate mousse cake topped with vanilla sauce. The ground-floor tearoom and pastry shop serve an excellent luncheon with wine for $7. *Blvd. de France, Marigot, tel. 590/87-54-42. AE, MC, V. Very Expensive.*

Auberge Gourmande. A cozy setting on the main street of Grand Case. Chef Daniel Passeri, a native of Burgundy, is also in charge of Le Tastevin across the street. For openers, try the escargots de bourgogne or frogs' legs in puff pastry, then move on to beef tenderloin in Roquefort sauce or duck breast with three-berry sauce. Reservations can be made by phoning Le Tastevin (tel. 590/87-55-45). *Grand Case, no phone. Closed Aug., Sept., and Wed. MC, V. Expensive.*

La Residence. An intimate setting with soft lighting, a tinkling fountain, and such specialties as fresh snapper baked in foil with olive oil and spices, bouillabaisse, and fresh lobster in a Cognac sauce. The soufflés are sensational. *Marigot, tel. 590/87-70-37. AE, MC, V. Expensive.*

Le Privilege. High on a hill, with a commanding view, Le Privilege is a sports and entertainment complex that is open 24 hours a day. Its various restaurants serve everything from burgers and fries to lobster cannelloni in truffle sauce. The pool is available for day or night dips; the disco is one of the island's hot boîtes on weekends. *Anse Marcel, tel. 590/87-37-37. AE, V. Expensive.*

Le Tastevin. The setting here is elegant: a chic pavilion, with tropical plants and ceiling fans, overlooks the water. Dine on lobster soup with basil, snails in white-wine sauce, medallions of pork in black-currant sauce, or duck breast with apples and cider. *Grand Case, tel. 590/87-55-45. MC, V. Expensive.*

★ **Bistrot Nu.** A friendly and enormously popular late-night spot that serves traditional brasserie-style food from coq au vin to fish soup, snails, pizza, and seafood until 2 AM. For simple, unadorned fare at a reasonable price, this may be the best spot on the island. *Rue de Hollande, Marigot, no phone. No credit cards. Moderate.*

Cas' Anny. Creole cooking is the specialty of Anne-Marie Boissard's seaside terrace restaurant. She turns out Creole boudin, crabe farci, and lambi (conch) Provençale. *Rue d'Anguille, tel. 599/87-53-38. AE, MC, V. Moderate.*

★ **Don Camillo da Enzo.** Country-style decor and excellent service distinguish this small eatery. Both northern and southern Italian specialties are featured. Some favorites are the carpaccio, green gnocchi in Gorgonzola cream sauce, and veal medallions in marsala sauce. *Port La Royale, Marigot, tel. 590/87-52–88. AE, MC, V. Moderate.*

L'Aventure. This is a handsome restaurant with a veranda smothered in bougainvillea and a gull's-eye view of the harbor. This is the fourth restaurant brothers Roger Petit and Ray Peterson have presented to the island. Come for the view, not the cuisine which is American steak-house fare. Lunch is served Sundays only in high season. *On the port, Marigot, tel. 590/87–72–89. AE, MC, V. Moderate.*

Maison sur le Port. Watching the sunset from the palm-fringed terrace is not the least of the pleasures in this old West Indian house. The meat of the matter has to do with duck (a house specialty), *trois filets* (lamb, veal, or steak in a light sauce), and poached lobster in pink-pepper sauce. Try the fresh-fish mousse served with a carrot sauce. There is also a tempting three-course prix fixe menu. Chef Christian Verdeau's imaginative salads are lunchtime treats. *On the port, Marigot, tel. 590/87–56–38. AE. Moderate.*

Mini Club. The popular upstairs terrace is virtually a treehouse nestled in the coconut palms. A pleasant eatery anytime, but especially Wednesday and Saturday, when there is a sumptuous buffet of almost 30 dishes—salads, roast pork, suckling pig, beef, fish, lobster—all for $30 per person, with wine. *Rue d'Anguille, Marigot, tel. 590/87–50–69. AE. Moderate.*

Le Palmier. Tosélita takes care of diners while her mother, Ketty, cooks up Creole dishes with your choice of fish, lobster, chicken, or goat as their base. Located on the Nettle Bay side of the small bridge leading out of Marigot, the restaurant is a small, one-story cabin with tables on the veranda. Everything is basic, simple, and authentic. *Sandy Ground, Marigot, tel. 590/87–59–04. Closed Mondays. No credit cards. Inexpensive.*

Lodging

Until very recently, the Dutch side commanded all of the big, splashy resorts. The casinos are still to be found exclusively on the Dutch side—gambling is illegal on the French side. However, St. Martin is having something of a building boom, especially in the area around Nettle Bay. There are also small inns and Mediterranean-style facilities on both sides of the island. Many of the hotels offer enticing packages that are worth investigating. You'll also save substantially if you travel off-season; the downside of this is that many hotels and restaurants are closed for refurbishing or just plain recovering from the winter onslaught.

As a rule, rooms on the beach command the highest prices.

The most highly recommended lodgings are indicated by a star ★.

Category	Cost*
Very Expensive	over $300
Expensive	$140–$300

Moderate	$80–$140

Inexpensive	under $80

*All prices are for a standard double room for two, excluding
5% tax (Dutch side), a taxe de sejour (set by individual hotels
on the French side), and a 10%–15% service charge.*

Hotels
Dutch Side

Belair Beach Hotel. On Little Bay beach, this air-conditioned,
all-suites oceanfront hotel is done in tropical decor with soft island prints. All suites are identical, with a living and dining
room, master bedroom with king-size bed, small guest room,
two baths, color TV, two direct-dial phones, full kitchen, serve-
through bar, and sliding glass doors opening onto a terrace that
overlooks the sea. *Box 140, Philipsburg, tel. 599/5–23362 or
800/622–7836. 72 suites. Facilities: beach, 2 restaurants, 2
bars, boutique, gift shop, food and liquor store, laundry service, car-rental desk, water-sports center. AE, CB, DC, MC, V.
Very Expensive.*

Caravanserai. The lobby, which is decorated with artwork, Oriental rugs, potted palms, and peacock chairs, opens onto a
breezeway with a view of the reefs of Maho Bay. Choose from a
variety of accommodations: spacious rooms, villas, suites, or
studios. Rooms are individually furnished and some have private lagoons. Water sports are available at sister facility
Mullet Bay Resort, and a shuttle bus runs nightly to the casino
there. High tea is served each afternoon in the Palm Court. *Box
113, Philipsburg, tel. 599/5–42510 or 800/223–9815; 800/468–
0023 in Canada. 84 rooms. Facilities: 2 restaurants, 2 pools (1
saltwater). AE, DC, MC, V. Very Expensive.*

La Vista. All of the accommodations are air-conditioned suites
with cable TVs, direct-dial phones, balconies, and lovely white
iron queen-size beds. A junior suite in low season is less than
$100, but the seven-day minimum stay catapults this facility
into the most expensive category. *Box 40, Pelican Key, tel. 599/
5–43005, 800/223–9815, 212/840–6636 in NY, or 800/468–0023
in Canada. 24 suites. Facilities: horseback riding, pool, restaurant, tennis. AE, MC, V. Very Expensive.*

Maho Beach Hotel & Casino. A variety of accommodations are
available at this facility. All have two double beds or a king-size
bed and a private balcony. The Casino Royale is the island's
largest casino, and Studio 7, atop the casino, is currently the
rage. The trick here is to get a room far enough away from the
airport's landing strip (those in the tennis complex are the quietest). *Maho Bay, tel. 599/5–42115 or 800/223–9815. 247
rooms. Facilities: beach, casino, 4 restaurants, 3 bars, disco,
pool, boutiques, 4 lighted tennis courts, shopping arcade, all
water sports. AE, DC, MC, V. Very Expensive.*

★ **Oyster Pond Yacht Club.** The hotel, which had a face-lift in 1988,
and a new enthusiastic manager in 1989, still retains its refined,
low-key gentility, quite out of character with the rest of St.
Maarten. Built around a courtyard, each of the two towers has
two split-level suites and individually decorated rooms with
terra-cotta floors, white wicker furnishings, ceiling fans, and
pastel French cottons. All rooms have a secluded balcony or
terrace and a view of the ocean, the courtyard, or the yacht basin. Rooms have screened louvers for those who prefer sea
breezes to air-conditioning. The hotel is on a mile-long beach
that's excellent for snorkeling. The dining room opens onto the
Atlantic Ocean; the pool perches right on the ocean's edge.
You'll find hammocks instead of TVs, and the hotel's only phone

is manned by a staff member at the front desk. *Box 239 Philipsburg, tel. 599/5–22206, 599/5–23206, or 800/372–1323. 20 rooms. Facilities: restaurant, bar, saltwater pool, 2 tennis courts, water-sports center. AE, MC, V. Very Expensive.*

Treasure Island Hotel & Casino at Cupecoy. Accommodations in this 17-acre Mediterranean-style village are in villas in a hilltop complex and suites in the Beach Club, which offers garden or ocean views. Lovely Cupecoy Beach lies at the foot of the sandstone cliffs. *Box 14, Philipsburg, tel. 599/5–43219 or 800/535–2929. 260 rooms and suites, some with TV and radio. Facilities: bank, beauty salon, boutiques, casino, convention center, 2 tennis courts, 3 pools, water-sports center. AE, CB, DC, MC, V. Very Expensive.*

Dawn Beach Hotel. Rooms are air-conditioned and are located on the hillside or on the beach. All are spacious, with handsome rattan furnishings, combination living room/bedroom with king-size bed, kitchenettes, closed-circuit color TV, radio, and private patio. (If you prefer tubs to showers, opt for the hillside villa.) The pool has a waterfall and the white-sand beach is one of the island's best for snorkeling, but the breeze is often strong and can whip up the waves. Since the hotel is off by itself, there's bus service to town twice daily. *Box 389, Philipsburg, tel. 599/5–22929, 800/351–5656 in U.S., or 800/468–0023 in Canada. 155 rooms. Facilities: restaurant, 2 beach bars, pool, 2 lighted tennis courts, car-rental desk, water-sports center. AE, CB, DC, MC, V. Expensive.*

Divi Little Bay Beach Resort & Casino. Air-conditioned one-, two-, and three-bedroom casitas and villas stretch along the 1,000-foot beach, surround the pool, and nestle in tropical gardens. The rooms are large, with king-size beds, minifridges, satellite color TVs, radios, terraces, modern rattan furniture, and carpeted or tile floors. There's live entertainment nightly and a pricey New York-style deli. The Little Bay Beach & Racquet Club, a time-share resort, completes the picture. *Box 61, Philipsburg, tel. 599/5–22333 or 800/367–3484. 120 rooms (plus 40 time-shares). Facilities: beauty salon, casino, 2 restaurants, 2 bars, shopping arcade, car-rental desk, pool, 3 lighted tennis courts, water-sports center. AE, DC, MC, V. Expensive.*

Pelican Resort & Casino. Walk into the reception area and one-armed bandits and gaming tables greet you. On the lower level is a sales office enticing guests to buy into this hotel-condo complex. An assortment of white stucco buildings house the resort's air-conditioned apartments, suites, and deluxe studios, all of which have a sweeping view of the Caribbean. Each has a fully equipped kitchen (including hibatchi and microwave), satellite TV, king-size beds, rattan furniture, and many frills (some have hot tubs). The resort has 1,400 feet of ocean frontage, though not good for bathing, and its own 60-foot catamaran, *El Tigre*, which is available for charters. *Simpson Bay, tel. 599/5–44309, 800/451–5510, or 212/354–5510 in NY. 342 suites and studios. Facilities: casino, 2 restaurants, 2 bars, 5 pools, health spa, Jacuzzi, 4 lighted tennis courts, children's playground, grocery store and shopping area, water-sports center. AE, DC, MC, V. Expensive.*

Pointe Pirouette Villa Hotels. This complex of four Mediterranean-style villas is located on a privately owned peninsula. Point Pirouette, Point Petite, Venezia, and the newest, Punta Venezia, contain ultramodern accommodations, ranging from studios to suites. The hotel's location at the back of Mullet

Bay facing Simpton Bay Lagoon, not the sea, might explain why management has reduced room rates considerably this year. A rental car is included with your stay during peak season. Continental breakfast is offered in the reception area, but there is no restaurant. *Box 484, Philipsburg, tel. 599/5–44207. 50 units. Facilities: private boat dock, tennis court, commissary, 24-hr security, rental cars. AE, MC, V. Expensive.*

Holland House. This is an ideally situated hotel, with the shops of Front Street at its doorstep and a mile-long backyard called Great Bay Beach. (Rooms 104 through 107 open directly onto the beach.) Each room has contemporary tropical furnishings, balcony, kitchenette, satellite cable TV, and air-conditioning. Its delightful open-air restaurant overlooking the water serves reasonably priced dinners. *Box 393, Philipsburg, tel. 599/5–22572, 800/223–9815, or 212/840–6636 in NY. 52 rooms, 2 suites. Facilities: beach, restaurant, lounge, gift shop. AE, DC, MC, V. Moderate.*

Mary's Boon. This informal inn has enormous rooms with kitchenettes, seaside patios, and ceiling fans. Meals are served family style, and there is an honor bar. Pets are welcome. The inn is on Simpson Bay's big beach. The many repeat guests don't seem fazed by the roar of the jets landing at the nearby airport. *Box 2078, Philipsburg, tel. 599/5–44235 or 212/986–4373 in U.S. 12 studios. Facilities: beach, restaurant, bar. No credit cards. Moderate.*

★ **Passangrahan Royal Guest House.** It's entirely appropriate that the bar here is named Sidney Greenstreet. This is the island's oldest inn, and it looks like a set for an old Bogie-Greenstreet film. The building was once Queen Wilhelmina's residence (there's a picture of her in the lobby) and the government guest house. Wicker peacock chairs, slowly revolving ceiling fans, balconies shaded by tropical greenery, king-size mahogany four-poster beds, and a broad tile veranda are some of the hallmarks of this guest house. Afternoon tea is served. There are no TVs or phones in the guest house. *Box 151, Philipsburg, tel. 599/5–23588 or 800/622–7836. 30 rooms and suites. Facilities: Great Bay Beach, rental bikes, bar, restaurant. AE, MC, V. Moderate.*

Seaview Hotel & Casino. Another good buy on Front Street and Great Bay Beach. The air-conditioned, twin-bed rooms are modest, cheerful, and clean. All rooms have baths (some with showers only), satellite TV, and phones. The four rooms above the sea have the best views. *Box 65, Philipsburg, tel. 599/5–22323, 800/223–9815, 212/840–6636 in NY, or 800/468–0023 in Canada. 45 rooms. Facilities: beach, breakfast room, casino. AE, MC, V. Moderate.*

Caribbean Hotel. You expect Sadie Thompson to vamp through those beaded glass curtains any minute. Frankly, this hotel is recommended more for its atmosphere, which is funky, almost campy, than for its facilities, which are passable and clean. It's on a second floor above Front Street, across the street from the beach. Rooms have tile floors, air-conditioning, TVs, kitchenettes, private baths. *Box 236, Philipsburg, tel. 599/5–22028. 34 rooms. Facilities: restaurant, bar. AE, MC, V. Inexpensive.*

French Side **La Samanna.** This luxurious, secluded hotel looks as if it was
★ transported to St. Martin from Morocco. Briefly a favorite of the "in crowd," the hotel's exorbitant prices keep it very exclusive. The hotel is set in a tropical garden on a slope overlooking Baie Longue. Red hibiscus is everywhere. There is a rich (the

word is used advisedly) variety of accommodations from which to choose. There are nine rooms and two suites in the air-conditioned main building, all with private terraces. You can choose an apartment, a two-story beachfront villa, or a secluded three-bedroom villa with private patio, private beach, or split-level terrace. *Box 159, Marigot 97150, tel. 590/87–51–22 or 212/696–1323. 85 rooms. Facilities: restaurant, lounge, pool, 3 lighted tennis courts. AE. Very Expensive.*

★ **La Belle Creole.** This 25-acre re-creation of an old Mediterranean village is replete with a stone central plaza. Although this hotel was completed in 1988, work continues on such features as transporting a coral reef to within swimming distance of the beach, importing peacocks and macaws, and planting fruit trees. The enormous rooms and 17 suites have every modern convenience, including air-conditioning, direct-dial phones, and minibars. Accommodations (king-size or two double beds) are in 27 one- to three-story villas linked by stone-paved streets and graceful courtyards. Most villas have private balconies with a view of the ocean, the island, or Marigot Bay. Grand as it is, La Belle Creole has a casual, relaxed atmosphere even when it's crowded. *Box 118, Marigot 97150, tel. 590/87–58–66 or 800–HILTONS. 156 rooms and suites. Facilities: 3 beaches, activities desk, shopping arcade, free-form pool, 4 lighted tennis courts, restaurant, 2 bars, 5 rooms with facilities for the disabled. AE, CB, DC, MC, V. Expensive–Very Expensive.*

Grand Case Beach Club. This informal condo complex is situated on Grand Case's crescent-shape beach. Air-conditioned studios and one- and two-bedroom apartments all have balconies or patios and kitchenettes. The 62 oceanfront units are much in demand. There's satellite TV in the lounge and complimentary Continental breakfast is included in the rate. There are lots of repeat guests, so reserve well in advance. Attractive packages are offered. *Box 339, Grand Case 97150, tel. 590/87–51–87 or 800/223–1588. 75 studios and apartments. Facilities: 2 beaches, restaurant, lounge, 1 lighted tennis court, billiards, car rental, catamaran. AE, MC, V. Expensive–Very Expensive.*

★ **Alizéa.** One of the island's most attractive hotels opened in time for the 1989–1990 season. The Alizéa, located on Mont Vernon hill, offers splendid views over Orient Bay. An open-air feeling pervades the hotel from its terrace restaurant, where the food is superb, to the 26 guest apartments done up with contemporary wood furnishings and pastel fabrics. Rooms vary in style and design. *Mont Vernon 25, 97150, tel. 590/87–33–42, fax 590/87–70–30. 26 rooms. Facilities: pool, restaurant. AE, MC, V. Expensive.*

L'Habitation. A white-knuckle road leads down to this resort, which is set in a 150-acre nature reserve with 1,600 feet of white-sand beach. The two-story main building is a white-column structure with red-tile roof and graceful galleries. All of the air-conditioned rooms, suites, and apartments have spacious baths, balconies, wall safes, TVs, and fridges. One-bedroom apartments have fully equipped kitchens and private patios. Guests have complimentary access to the facilities of Le Privilège, a sports and entertainment complex on the hill (a minibus makes frequent trips to it). *Box 581, Marcel Cove 97150, tel. 590/87–33–33, 87–78–80, 800/847–4249 in U.S. and Canada, 212/747–0225 in NY. 200 rooms, 50 apartments. Facilities (including Le Privilège): beach, boutiques, aerobics,* *car rental, disco, 3 restaurants, 3 bars, 6 lighted tennis courts, 2 pools, 2 squash courts, 1 racquetball court, 100-slip marina, water-sports center. AE, CB, DC, MC, V. Expensive.*

Captain Oliver. At Oyster Pond facing a beautiful horseshoe-shape bay, this small hotel, with bungalows featuring a view of the bay or garden, is for those who want to be away from the hustle of St. Maarten. The exceptionally clean, fresh rooms—those facing the bay are the choicest—have their own patio decks and kitchenettes. The restaurant on the yacht basin has good, fresh dishes at dinner and is also open for breakfast and lunch. *Oyster Pond, 97150, tel. 590/87–40–26 or 800/223–9862. 25 rooms. Facilities: restaurant, snack bar. AE, DC, MC, V. Moderate–Expensive.*

★ **Hevea.** This is a small, white guest house with smart awnings in the heart of Grand Case. Rooms are dollhouse small but will appeal to romantics.   There are beam ceilings, washstands, carved wood beds with lovely white coverlets and mosquito nets. The air-conditioned rooms, studios, and apartment are on the terrace level; fan-cooled studios and apartments are on the garden level. *Grand Case 97150, tel. 590/87–56–85 or 800/423–4433. 8 units. Facilities: restaurant. MC, V. Moderate.*

La Residence. Located in Marigot and popular with business travelers, this soundproof hotel is an excellent choice. All of the accommodations have baths (with showers only), phones, and air-conditioning. You've a choice among double rooms, studios, mezzanine loft beds, and apartments with or without kitchenettes. You'll have to take a cab to get to the beach. *Rue du Général de Gaulle, Marigot 97150, tel. 590/87–70–37. 20 rooms. Facilities: restaurant, lounge. AE, MC, V. Moderate.*

★ **La Royale Louisiana.** Located in downtown Marigot in the boutique shopping area, this upstairs hotel is as fresh as a spring breeze. White and pale green galleries overlook the flower-filled courtyard. There's a selection of twin, double, and triple air-conditioned duplexes, all with private baths (tubs and showers), TVs, VCRs, and phones. *Rue du Général de Gaulle, Marigot 97150, tel. 590/87–86–51. 68 rooms. Facilities: restaurant, snack bar, beauty salon. AE, DC, MC, V. Moderate.*

Bertine's. This is a simple, isolated guest house on a hilltop near La Savane. Christine and Bernard Piticha have many repeat guests who gather in the excellent restaurant for cocktails, conversation, and dinner. *La Savane, Grand Case 97150, tel. 590/87–58–39. 4 rooms, 1 bedroom apartment. Facilities: lounge, restaurant. No credit cards. Inexpensive.*

Palm Plaza Hotel. Right in the center of Marigot, this hotel is upstairs above a patio. All rooms have air-conditioning, white wicker furniture, and private baths (with either shower or tub). Rooms are rather small. *Rue de la République, Marigot 97150, tel. 590/87–51–96. 21 rooms. AE, MC, V. Inexpensive.*

Home and Apartment Rentals
Both sides of the island offer a wide variety of homes, villas, condominiums, and housekeeping apartments. Information in the United States can be obtained through **Caribbean Home Rentals** (Box 710, Palm Beach, FL 33480, tel. 407/833–4454), **Jane Condon Corp.** (211 E. 43rd St., New York, NY 10017, tel. 212/986–4373), or **St. Maarten Villas** (707 Broad Hollow Rd., Farmingdale, NY 11735, tel. 516/249–4940). On the island, contact **Carimo** (tel. 590/87–57–58), **Ausar** (tel. 590/87–51–07), or **St. Maarten Rentals** (tel. 599/5–44330).

Nightlife

To find out what's doing on the island, pick up any of the following publications: *St. Maarten Nights, What to Do in St. Maarten, St. Maarten Events,* or *St. Maarten Holiday,* all distributed free in the tourist office and hotels. *Discover St. Martin/St. Maarten,* also free, is a glossy magazine, put together by artist Roland Richardson and friends, that includes articles about the island's history and the latest on shops, discos, restaurants, and even archaeological digs.

Each of the resort hotels has a Caribbean spectacular one night a week, replete with limbo and fire dancers and steel bands. Often the same group of entertainers moves from hotel to hotel, so if you happen to miss it in your resort, you can catch the act elsewhere.

Casinos are the main focus on the Dutch side, but there are discos that usually start late and keep on till the fat lady sings. Discos here have a high turnover rate; one season's hottest spot can burn out and almost literally disappear by dawn's early light. There are a lot of bars, some with live music.

Casinos   All eight of the casinos have craps, blackjack, roulette, and slot machines. You must be 18 years old to gamble. The casinos are located at the **Great Bay Beach Hotel, Divi Little Bay Beach Hotel, Pelican Resort, Mullet Bay Hotel, Seaview Hotel, St. Maarten Beach Club, Treasure Island at Cupecoy,** and (the largest) **Casino Royal at Maho Beach.**

Discos   **The Tropics** is a hot disco that draws a mixed crowd of locals (by Madame Estate in Royal Inn Motel). **Studio 7** (tel. 599/5–42115) attracts a young crowd in its ultramodern digs atop Casino Royale across from Maho Beach Resort. **Le Club** (Mullet Bay, tel. 599/5–42801) draws a mixed crowd of locals and tourists, and features a floor show, "Les Folies de Sint Maarten." French nationals and locals flock to **L'Atmosphere** (no phone) on the second floor of L'Auberge de Mer in Marigot. **Le Privilege** (Anse Marcel, tel. 590/87–38–38) caters to the young and hip French. **Night Fever** (Colombier, outside Marigot, no phone) attracts a young crowd of locals.

Bars and   The boating crowd seems to favor **Sam's Restaurant & Pub**
Nightclubs   (Front St., Philipsburg, tel. 599/5–22989) for live jazz, R&R, and island music nightly (*see* Dining, above). **The Blue Note** (Front St., Philipsburg, tel. 599/5–22166), in Pinocchio's Arcade, pulls young people in nightly for live jazz, R&R, and pop. A mixed crowd of locals and tourists, all ages, hangs out at the **Heartbreak Bar** (St. Maarten Beach Club Hotel, tel. 599/5–23434).

25 St. Vincent and the Grenadines

by Joan Iaconetti

St. Vincent and the Grenadines form a necklace of volcanic islands that beckon the traveler, sailor, and day-tripper who are more intrigued by blooming flowers than by Bloomingdale's. The fertile volcanic soil has helped to create the oldest botanical gardens in the Western Hemisphere, and rich aromatic valleys of bananas, coconuts, and arrowroot cover this relatively undeveloped island.

St. Vincent, with a population of about 112,000, is only 18 miles long and 11 miles wide, but it delights those who have discovered its stunning natural beauty, both below and above its crystal seas. Equipped with little more than a snorkel and a sense of adventure, visitors can discover unrivaled underwater landscapes; a pair of comfortable shoes and a little stamina are enough to hike mountains that are so verdant they rival Hawaii's. In contrast to St. Vincent's beaches of black volcanic sand, the Grenadines offer numerous powdery white bays and coves on both calm leeward and surfy windward shores.

The Grenadines' peaceful, laid-back atmosphere is due to its residents' hospitality rather than to five-star amenities or designer shopping. Hotels are small, food is simple; and the islands appeal to adventurous singles and couples who prefer active sports to glitz and gambling.

While the islands have their share of the poor and unemployed, the superfertile volcanic soil allows everyone to grow enough food to eat and trade for necessities. Since the locals haven't come to regard tourists as meal tickets, beggars and hawkers are few.

Historians believe that in 4300 BC, long before King Tut ruled Egypt, the Ciboney Indians first inhabited St. Vincent. Unhampered by passports and political unrest, the Ciboney made their way to Cuba and Haiti, leaving St. Vincent to the Arawaks. Columbus sailed by in 1492, while the Arawaks were involved in intermittent skirmishes with the bellicose Caribs; his arrival, named Discovery Day (or St. Vincent and the Grenadine's Day), is still commemorated on January 22.

Declared a neutral island by French and British agreement in 1748, St. Vincent became something of a political football in the years that followed. Ceded to the British in 1763, it was captured by the French in 1779 and restored to the British by the Treaty of Versailles in 1783. By the 19th century, St. Vincent was quite sure it was more British than French.

On October 27, 1979, St. Vincent gained independence from Great Britain. The current prime minister of St. Vincent is James "Son" Mitchell, whose New Democratic Party replaced the Labor Party. Mitchell won another landslide victory in May 1989.

In contrast to its colorful history, the 32 islands and cays that make up the Grenadines seem timeless, as free from politics as the beaches are free from debris. Nine miles south of St. Vincent is Bequia, the second-largest Grenadine. Admiralty Bay is one of the finest anchorages in the Caribbean. With superb views, snorkeling, hiking, and swimming, the island has much to offer the international mix of backpackers and luxury yacht owners who frequent its shores.

A 90-minute sail south is Mustique, equipped with a small airstrip. More arid than Bequia, Mustique does not seek tourists, least of all those hoping for a glimpse of the rich and famous (Princess Margaret, Mick Jagger) who own houses here. The appeal of Mustique is seclusion and privacy: Here you can rent an elegant villa all to yourself.

Just over 3 square miles, Canouan is an unspoiled island that offers travelers an opportunity to relax, snorkel, and hike.

Numerous yachts and catamarans can be chartered for day sails from any of the Grenadines to the tiny uninhabited islets known as The Tobago Cays (pronounced toe-bay-go keys). Avid snorkelers claim that the Cays have some of the best hard and soft coral formations found outside the Pacific Ocean. The beaches here are perfect for secluded picnics.

The tiny island of Mayreau (pronounced my-ro) has 170 residents, no phones, and one of the area's most beautiful beaches. The Caribbean is often mirror-calm, yet just yards away on the southern end of this narrow island is the rolling Atlantic surf. The Tobago Cays are just 30 minutes away by sailboat.

John Caldwell has spent 20 years turning Palm Island from a mosquito-infested mangrove swamp into a small island paradise for couples and families. The Caldwell family also hosts day-tripping cruise passengers who come to lounge on the wide white beaches, which are dotted and fringed with over a thousand palm trees that Caldwell has planted over the years.

Petit St. Vincent is another private luxury resort island, reclaimed from the jungle by manager Haze Richardson. It's actually possible to spend your entire vacation in one of the resort's widely spaced stone houses without ever seeing another human being. Those who enjoy socializing and activities might be happier at Palm, Mayreau, or Young Island.

Union Island isn't really a place for landlubbers: The island caters almost completely to French sailors, who keep very much to themselves. Surface transport is limited, and to see the island you need a boat. You won't find the laid-back friendliness of the other Grenadines here.

Before You Go

Tourist Information The **St. Vincent and the Grenadines Tourist Office** (801 2nd Ave., 21st Floor, New York, NY 10017, tel. 212/687–4981 or 800/696–9611; in Canada: 100 University Ave., Suite 504, Toronto, Ont. M5J 1V6, tel. 416/971–9666 or 416/971–9667; in the United Kingdom: 10 Kensington Court, London W8 5DL, tel. 01/937–6570). Write for a visitors guide, full of useful, up-to-date information.

Arriving and Departing *By Plane* Most U.S. visitors fly via **American** (tel. 800/433–7300) or **Pan Am** (tel. 800/221–1111) into Barbados or St. Lucia, then take a small plane to St. Vincent's E.T. Joshua Airport (formerly Arnos Vale Airport) or to Mustique, Canouan, Union, or Palm, the only islands with airstrips. (Other destinations require a boat ride on either a scheduled ferry, a chartered boat, or your hotel's launch.) Other airlines that connect with interisland flights are **BWIA** (tel. 800/327–7401), **British Airways** (tel. 800/247–9297), **Air Canada** (tel. 800/422–6232), and **Air France** (tel. 800/237–2747).

LIAT (Leeward Islands Air Transport, tel. 809/457–1821), **Air Martinique** (tel. 809/458–4528), fly interisland. Delays are common but usually not outrageous. A surer way to go is with **Air St. Vincent** (aka **Air Mustique;** tel. 809/458–4380 or 809/458–4818. In the U.S., 800/526–4789). Its six- or eight-seat charter flights meet and wait for your major carrier's arrival even if it's delayed (bring earplugs if you're supersensitive to noise).

From the Airport Taxis and/or buses are readily available at the airport on every island. A taxi from the airport to Kingstown will cost $5–$7 (E.C. $15–$20); bus fare is less than 40¢. If you have a lot of luggage, it might be best to take a taxi—buses are very short on space.

Passports and Visas U.S. and Canadian citizens must have a passport; a voter registration card, birth certificate, or driver's license will *not* do. All visitors must hold return or ongoing tickets. Visas are not required.

Language English is spoken everywhere in the Grenadines, often with a Vincentian patois or dialect.

Precautions Insects are a minor problem on the beach during the day, but when hiking and sitting outdoors in the evening, you'll be glad you brought industrial-strength mosquito repellent.

Plants to watch out for include the manchineel tree, whose little green apples look tempting but are toxic. Even touching the sap of the leaves will cause an uncomfortable rash. Most trees on hotel grounds are marked with signs; on more remote islands, the bark may be painted red. Hikers should watch for Brazil wood trees/bushes, which look and act similar to poison ivy.

When taking photos of market vendors, private citizens, or homes, be sure to ask permission first and expect to give a gratuity for the favor.

There's little crime on these islands, but don't tempt fate by leaving your valuables lying around.

Further Reading *Exploring the Windward Islands,* by Chris Doyle, is available on the islands at most large hotels and shops. Doyle covers off-the-beaten-track sites, recipes, and island lore.

Staying in St. Vincent and the Grenadines

Important Addresses **Tourist Information:** The **St. Vincent Board of Tourism** (tel. 809/457–1502) is located in a marked building on Egmont Street, on the second floor.

Emergencies **Police:** (tel. 809/457–1211).

Hospitals: (tel. 809/456–1185).

Pharmacies: Deane's (tel. 809/457–1522), **Reliance** (tel. 809/456–1734), both in Kingstown.

Currency Although U.S. and Canadian dollars are taken at all but the smallest shops, Eastern Caribbean currency (E.C.$) is accepted and preferred everywhere. At press time, the exchange rate was U.S.$1 = E.C.$2.67; banks give a slightly better rate of exchange.

Price quotes are normally given in E.C. dollars; however, when you negotiate taxi fares and such, be sure you know which type of dollar you're agreeing on. All prices here are in U.S. dollars unless noted otherwise.

Taxes and Service Charges The departure tax from St. Vincent and the Grenadines is $6 (E.C.$15). Restaurants charge a 5% government tax, and if a 10% service charge is included in your bill, no additional tips are necessary.

Guided Tours Tours can be informally arranged through taxi drivers who double as informal but knowledgeable guides. Your hotel or the Tourism Board will recommend a driver. When choosing a driver/guide, look for the Taxi Driver's Association decal on the windshield and talk with the driver long enough to be sure you'll be able to understand his patois over the noise of the engine. Settle the fare first ($30–$40 is normal for a two- or three-hour tour). To prearrange a taxi tour, contact the Taxi Driver's Association (tel. 809/457–1807).

Grenadine Tours (St. Vincent, tel. 809/456–4176) arranges air, sea, and land excursions throughout the islands.

Getting Around
Taxis Many of the roads in the Grenadines are not in the best condition, so you may prefer taxis to a rented car.

Minivans Public buses come in the form of brightly painted minivans with names like "Struggling Man" and "Who to Blame." Bus fares run E.C.$1–$5 in St. Vincent, with the route direction indicated on a sign in the windshield. Just wave from the road, and the driver will stop for you.

Smaller islands also have taxi-vans and pickup trucks with benches in the back and canvas covers for when it rains.

Rental Cars Rental cars cost an average of $35 per day; driving is on the left. Although major improvements are being made, St. Vincent's roads are not well marked or maintained. To orient yourself, consider taking a half-day taxi tour (*see* Guided Tours, above).

To rent a car you'll need a temporary Vincentian license (unless you already have an International Driver's License), which costs E.C.$20. Among the rental firms are **Johnson's U-Drive** (tel. 809/458–4864) at the airport and **Kim's Auto Rentals** (tel. 809/456–1884), which has a larger selection of slightly more expensive rental cars that must be rented by the week.

Telephones and Mail The area code for St. Vincent and the Grenadines is 809. If you use Sprint or MCI in the United States, you may need to access an AT&T line to dial direct to St. Vincent and the Grenadines. From St. Vincent, you can direct-dial to other countries; ask the hotel operator for the proper country code and for the probable charge, surcharge, and government tax on the call. Local information is 118; international is 115.

When you dial a local number from your hotel in the Grenadines, you can drop the 45-prefix. Only Mayreau has no telephones; on other islands, few hotels have phones in the rooms.

Mail between St. Vincent and the United States takes two–three weeks. Airmail postcards cost 45¢; airmail letters cost 65¢ an ounce.

Bic-Pac, an overnight courier service that's part of Federal Express, is located on Bay Street in Kingstown.

Opening and Closing Times Stores and shops in Kingstown are open weekdays 8–4. Many close for lunch from noon to 1 or so. Saturday hours are 8–noon. Banks are open weekdays 8–noon, Fridays from 2 or 3–5. The post office is open weekdays 8:30–3, Saturdays 8:30–11:30.

St. Vincent

Beaches

Most of the hotels and white-sand beaches are near Kingstown; black-sand beaches ring the rest of the island. The placid west coast, site of **Villa Beach** (white sand), **Questelle's Bay** (black sand), and **Buccament Bay** (black sand), are good for swimming; the beaches at Villa and the CSY Yacht Club are small but safe, with dive shops nearby. The exposed Atlantic coast is dramatic, but the water is rough and unpredictable. No beach has lifeguards, so even experienced swimmers are taking a risk. There are no beach facilities on the windward side of the island.

Exploring St. Vincent

Numbers in the margin correspond with points of interest on the St. Vincent map.

Kingstown's shopping/business district, cathedrals, and sights can easily be seen in a half-day tour. Outlying areas, botanical gardens, and the Falls of Baleine will each require a full day of touring.

Kingstown Kingstown, the capital and port of St. Vincent's, is located at
Tour 1 the southeastern end of the island.

❶ Begin your tour on **Bay Street,** near Egmont Street, a shopping mecca. Kingstown's boutiques feature such local crafts as cotton batik hangings and clothing, floor mats, baskets, and black coral jewelry.

Saturday's **fish/vegetable market** on Bay Street is a hectic, lively place. Arrive before 11 AM to catch all the action. Note: Keep a tight grip on your valuables in the market.

Unusual gifts for stamp collectors are at the **post office** on Granby Street east of Egmont. St. Vincent is known worldwide for its particularly beautiful and colorful issues, which commemorate flowers, undersea creatures, and architecture.

Follow Back Street (also called Granby Street) west past the Methodist Church to **St. George's Cathedral,** a yellow Anglican church built in the early 19th century. The dignified Georgian architecture includes simple wood pews, an ornate hanging candelabra, and stained glass windows. The gravestones tell the history of the island.

Across the street is **St. Mary's Roman Catholic Cathedral,** built in 1823 and renovated in the 1930s. The renovations resulted in a strangely appealing blend of Moorish, Georgian, and Romanesque styles. When the adjacent school lets out between 2 and 3, local children are eager to pose for photos.

A few minutes away by taxi or bus is St. Vincent's famous **Botanical Gardens.** Founded in 1765, it is the oldest botanical garden in the Western Hemisphere. Captain Bligh brought the first breadfruit tree to this island, a direct descendant of which is in the gardens. St. Vincent parrots and green monkeys are housed in cages, and unusual trees and bushes cover the well-kept grounds. Local guides offer their services for a few dollars an hour. *Information: c/o Minister of Agriculture, Kingstown, tel. 809/457–1003. Tours: 75¢ for 1 person, $1.10 for 2. Open weekdays 7–4, Sat. 7–11 AM, Sun. 7–6.*

The tiny **National Museum** houses ancient Indian clay pottery found by Dr. Earle Kirby, St. Vincent's resident archaeologist. Dr. Kirby's historical knowledge is as entertaining as it is extensive. Contact him for a guided tour, as the labels in the museum offer little information. *Tel. 809/456–1787. Open Wed. 9–noon, Sat. 3–6.*

② Flag another taxi for the 10-minute ride to **Fort Charlotte,** built in 1806 to keep Napoleon at bay. The fort sits 636 feet above sea level, with cannons and battlements perched on a dramatic promontory overlooking the city and the Grenadines to the south, Lowman's Beach and the calm east coast to the north. The fort saw little military action; it was used mainly to house paupers and lepers.

Outside Kingstown The coastal roads of St. Vincent offer panoramic views and insights into the island way of life. Life in the tiny villages has changed little in centuries. This full-day driving tour includes Layou, Montreal Gardens, Mesopotamia Valley, and the Windward coast. Be sure to keep your eyes on the narrow road and to honk your horn before you enter the blind curves.

Beginning in Kingstown, take the Leeward Highway about 45 minutes north through hills and valleys to **Layou,** a small fish-**③** ing village. Just north of the village are **petroglyphs** (rock carvings) left by the Caribs 13 centuries ago. If you're seriously interested in archaeological mysteries, you'll want to stop here. Phone the Tourism Board to arrange a visit with Victor Hendrickson, who owns the land. For E.C.$5, Hendrickson or his wife will meet you and escort you to the site.

④ Half an hour farther north is **Barrouallie** (pronounced Bar-relly), a whaling village where whaling boats are built and repaired year-round.

Time Out Ten minutes away from Barrouallie is **Wallilabou** (wally-la-boo), a particularly beautiful bay where you can stop for a bring-your-own picnic, sunbathe, and swim (there are no showers, though).

Tour 2 Backtrack to Kingstown and continue toward Mesopotamia to **⑤** the **Montreal Gardens,** another extensive collection of exotic flowers, trees, and spice plants. It's not as well-maintained as the Botanical Gardens, but the aroma of cocoa and nutmeg wafting on the cool breeze is enticing. Spend an hour with well-informed guides or wander on your own along the narrow paths. Vincentian newlyweds often spend their honeymoon in the Garden's tiny cottage appropriately named "Romance." *Tel. 809/458–5452. Open daily.*

Now drive southeast (roads and signs aren't the best, so ask di-**⑥** rections at Montreal Gardens) to the **Mesopotamia region.** The rugged, ocean-lashed scenery along St. Vincent's windward coast is the perfect counterpoint to the lush, calm west coast. Mesopotamia is full of dense forests, streams, and bananas, which are St. Vincent's major exports. The blue plastic bags on the trees protect the fruit from damage in high winds. Coconut, breadfruit, sweet corn, peanuts, and arrowroot grow here

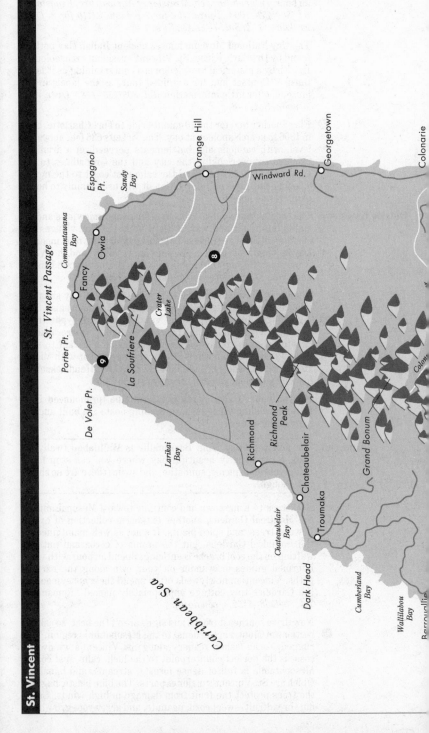

St. Vincent

St. Vincent Passage

Caribbean Sea

Orange Hill

Georgetown

Colonarie

Espagnol Pt.

Sandy Bay

Windward Rd.

Commantawana Bay

Owia

Porter Pt.

Fancy

De Volet Pt.

Crater Lake

La Soufriere

8

9

Larikai Bay

Richmond

Richmond Peak

Grand Bonum

Colon

Chateaubelair

Troumaka

Chateaubelair Bay

Dark Head

Cumberland Bay

Wallilabou Bay

Barrouallie

529

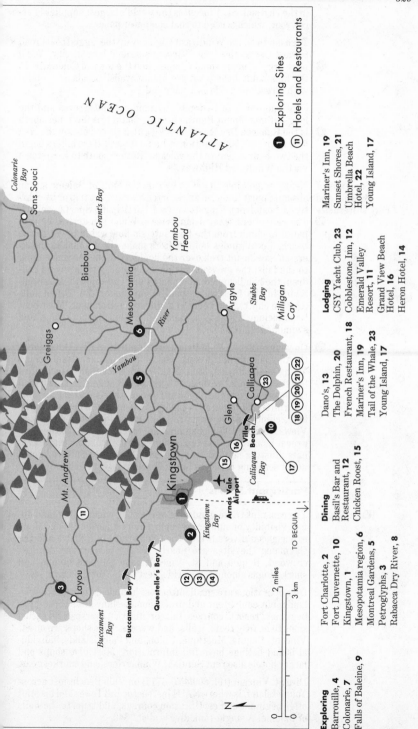

ATLANTIC OCEAN

Exploring Sites

Hotels and Restaurants

Exploring
Barrouille, **4**
Colonarie, **7**
Falls of Baleine, **9**
Fort Charlotte, **2**
Fort Duvernette, **10**
Kingstown, **1**
Mesopotamia region, **6**
Montreal Gardens, **5**
Petroglyphs, **3**
Rabacca Dry River, **8**

Dining
Basil's Bar and
Restaurant, **1**
Chicken Roost, **15**
Dano's, **13**
The Dolphin, **20**
French Restaurant, **18**
Mariner's Inn, **19**
Tail of the Whale, **23**
Young Island, **17**

Lodging
CSY Yacht Club, **23**
Cobblestone Inn, **12**
Emerald Valley
Resort, **11**
Grand View Beach
Hotel, **16**
Heron Hotel, **14**
Mariner's Inn, **19**
Sunset Shores, **21**
Umbrella Beach
Hotel, **22**
Young Island, **17**

in the rich soil. St. Vincent is the world's largest supplier of arrowroot, which is used to coat computer paper.

7 Turn north on the Windward Highway up the jagged coast road toward Georgetown, St. Vincent's second-largest city. You'll pass Argyle, many small villages, and the town of **Colonarie.** In the hills behind the town are hiking trails. Locals are helpful with directions as signs are limited.

8 Continue north to **Georgetown,** amid coconut groves and the long-defunct Mount Bentinck Sugar factory. A few miles north is the **Rabacca Dry River,** a rocky gulch carved out by the lava flow from the 1902 eruption of La Soufrière. Here hikers begin the two-hour ascent to the volcano. Return south to Kingstown via the Windward Highway.

The Falls of Baleine and Fort Duvernette 9 Nearly impossible to get to by car, the **Falls of Baleine** are an absolute must to see on an escorted all-day boat trip or by chartered boat from Kingstown (*see* Participant Sports, below). The ride offers scenic island views. When you arrive, be prepared to climb from the boat into shallow water to get to the beach. Local guides help visitors make the 15-minute sneakers-and-swimsuit trek over the boulders in the stream leading to the falls; the government recently built a walkway so children, the handicapped, and photo buffs can enjoy them as well. Swim in the freshwater pool, climb under the 63-foot falls (they're chilly), and relax in a hidden environment. Most boat trips include a stop at a calm bay for lunch, snorkeling, and swimming.

10 On your return to Villa Beach, catch sunset at **Fort Duvernette,** the tiny island that juts up like a loaf of pumpernickel behind Young Island Resort. Take the *African Queen*–style ferry for a few dollars from the dock at Villa Beach near Kingstown (call the boatman from the phone on the dock) and set a time for your return (60–90 minutes is plenty). When you arrive at the island, climb the 100 or more steps carved into the mountain. Views from the 195-foot summit are terrific, but avoid the overgrown house near the top, where you'll encounter (harmless) bats. Rusting cannons from the early 1800s are still here, aimed not at seagoing invaders but at the marauding Caribs.

Participant Sports

Water Sports The constant trade winds are perfect for windsurfing, and 80-foot visibility on numerous reefs means superior diving. Many experienced divers prefer the Grenadines to Bonaire and the Caymans; the sites are nearly as spectacular and far less crowded. Bequia and St. Vincent have the best diving, and snorkeling is among the world's best in the Tobago Cays.

Dive operations are small, often less luxurious than on other islands, but competent and professional. Many offer three-hour beginner "resort" courses, full certification courses, and excursions to nearby reefs, walls, and wrecks. Dive shops are on St. Vincent, Bequia, Mustique, Union, and Palm Islands; individual island listings have full information. Most dive shops and larger hotels also rent Sunfish, Windsurfers, and snorkel gear.

Dive St. Vincent (tel. 809/457–4714) on Villa Beach, just across Young Island, is where NAUI instructor Bill Tewes and his staff offer beginner and certification courses, and trips to the Falls of Baleine. A single-tank dive is about $40.

Mariner's Watersports (tel. 809/458–4228), on Villa Beach, offers complete scuba trips and gear as well as beginner's resort courses and full certification. They also rent water skis and Windsurfers and offer full instruction on the use of this gear.

Young Island has some of the most colorful snorkeling in the Caribbean. If you're not a guest on this private island, phone the resort for permission to take the ferry and rent equipment from their water-sports center (*see* Lodging, below).

Hiking Dorsetshire Hill, about 3 miles from Kingstown, rewards you with a sweeping view of city and harbor; picturesque Queen's Drive is nearby. Mt. St. Andrew, on the outskirts of the city, is a pleasant climb through a rain forest on a well-marked trail.

But the queen of climbs is La Soufrière, St. Vincent's active volcano (which last erupted, appropriately enough, on Friday the 13th in 1979). Approachable from both windward and leeward coasts, this is *not* a casual excursion for inexperienced walkers; you'll need stamina and sturdy shoes for this climb of just over 4,000 feet. Be sure to check the weather before you leave; hikers have been sorely disappointed to reach the top only to find the view completely obscured by enveloping clouds.

Climbs are all-day affairs; a LandRover and guide can be arranged through your hotel or a knowledgeable taxi driver. The four-wheel-drive vehicle takes you past Rabacca Dry River through the Bamboo Forest. From there it's a two-hour hike to the summit, and you can arrange in advance to come down the other side of the mountain to the Chateaubelair area.

Sailing and Charter Yachting Unless you're plagued with motion sickness, the Grenadines are the perfect place to charter a sailboat or catamaran (bareboat or complete with captain, crew, and cook) to weave you around the islands for a day or a week. Boats of all sizes and degrees of luxury are available; we recommend CSY Yacht Club (Caribbean Sailing Yachts, tel. 809/458–4308) in the Blue Lagoon area of St. Vincent.

Shopping

Noah's Arkade (tel. 809/457–1513), on Bay Street, features such local crafts as batiks and baskets. The best batiks are at **Batik Carib** (tel. 809/456–1666) and **Sprotties** (tel. 809/458–4749), also on Bay Street. The **St. Vincent Craftsmen Center** (tel. 809/457–1288), in the northwest end of Kingstown on James Street above Granby Street, sells grass floor mats and other woven items. Swiss watches and clocks, perfumes, crystal, bone china, and gold and silver jewelry can be found at **Stecher's** (tel. 809/457–1142) on Bay Street in the Cobblestone Arcade (a branch is at the airport). Across the way is **Giggles** (tel. 809/457–1174), a boutique with a wide selection of contemporary clothing and accessories for men and women.

Dining

The most highly recommended restaurants are indicated by a star ★.

Category	Cost*
Expensive	over $20
Moderate	$10–$20
Inexpensive	under $10

per person, excluding drinks and sales tax (5% on credit-card purchases only)

★ **Basil's Bar and Restaurant.** This air-conditioned restaurant, downstairs in the Cobblestone Inn, opens at 8 AM for Kingstown's version of the power breakfast. Basil's also serves a buffet lunch with hearty callaloo soup, lobster, and barbecued conch, plus seafood pasta and chicken in fresh ginger and coconut milk. *Bay St., Kingstown, tel. 809/457–2713. Reservations recommended. AE, MC, V. Expensive.*

★ **French Restaurant.** Referred to as "The French," this open-air place has what is unanimously acclaimed to be the best food in the Grenadines. A nearby lobster pool assures freshness, and the chef does wonders with locally available ingredients (garlic soup instead of onion soup, for example). Choose from crepes, lobster bisque, and grilled lamb chops; the lunch menu includes quiche and sandwiches. There's also a varied wine list and a bar inside. *Villa Beach, tel. 809/458–4972. Dinner reservations recommended. AE, V. Expensive.*

Tail of the Whale. The Tail serves excellent soups and delectably spicy West Indian lobster, probably the island's best. The bar is lively and sociable. *CSY Yacht Club, Blue Lagoon, tel. 809/ 458–4308. V. Expensive.*

Young Island. Five-course chef's-choice dinners include seafood, whole roast pig, beef, and chicken. A barbecue with a steel band is featured on Saturday night. *Young Island, tel. 809/458–4826. Reservations required. AE, MC, V. Expensive.*

Mariner's Inn. Hearty, homemade West Indian food is served on a veranda with a view of Young Island. The Friday night barbecue and jump-up is among the best for quality, quantity, and desserts. *Villa Beach, tel. 809/458–4287. AE, MC, V. Moderate.*

Chicken Roost. This eatery is handy if you're waiting at the airport across the street, and worth a visit even if you're not. The *rotis* (Caribbean burritos), sandwiches (including shark), pizzas, and ice cream can't be beat. Open daily till midnight. *Opposite airport, tel. 809/457–1032. No credit cards. Inexpensive.*

Dano's. Stop in while you're strolling Kingstown for good, cheap Caribbean burritos and lots of local color. *Middle St., Kingstown, tel. 809/457–2020. No credit cards. Inexpensive.*

Lodging

Luxury resorts require booking about six months in advance, but most St. Vincent hotels can squeeze you in with far less notice. There's a bit of a lull in January, between the Christmas week and February rush, when rooms are sometimes available on a day's notice. Many hotels offer MAP (Modified American Plan, with breakfast and dinner included).

The most highly recommended lodgings are indicated by a star ★.

Category	Cost*
Very Expensive	over $200
Expensive	$115–$200
Moderate	$60–$115
Inexpensive	under $60

*All prices are for a standard double room for two, excluding 5% tax and a 10% service charge.

Young Island
★

Young Island. A 36-acre privately owned island just 200 yards off the Villa Beach dock in St. Vincent, Young Island is an upscale resort that attracts mostly over-35 couples who prefer casual elegance to the glitzy atmosphere of traditional luxury resorts. Airy rooms are set in the hills amid flowering almond and hibiscus trees. Each room has lovely views, though cottages No. 30 and 17 near the summit have the most dramatic vistas (also the longest walk uphill). Sail-hotel packages and day sails are available on Young Island's two yachts, and snorkeling around Young Island is superior. Dive St. Vincent is just across the channel. All meals are included. *Box 211, Young Island, tel. 809/458–4826; U.S. agent: Ralph Locke Associates, Box 800, Waccabuc, NY 10597, tel. 914/763–5526 or 800/223–1108. 29 rooms. Facilities: scuba diving, saltwater pool, watersports center, lighted tennis court. AE, MC, V. Very Expensive.*

Emerald Valley

Emerald Valley Resort. About 30 minutes from Kingstown, up in the hills, Emerald Valley is the one place in the Grenadines where you can gamble—but don't expect Las Vegas glitz. New management is downplaying gaming in favor of family activities that take advantage of the natural beauty of the site. Hikers will enjoy the nature trail in the surrounding hills. Simple accommodations are in chalets with kitchens. *Penniston Valley, St. Vincent, tel. 809/458–7421. 12 chalets. Facilities: casino, restaurant, 2 tennis courts, grass volleyball court, croquet, pool. AE, MC, V. Expensive.*

Villa Beach
★

Grand View Beach Hotel. The original plantation house of the Sardine family is still run by managers Tony and Heather Sardine. A charmingly homey hotel with fantastic views, it sits on eight secluded acres about five minutes from the airport. There's a trail down to the beach, good snorkeling, and the picture-perfect pool sits atop Villa Point. *Box 173, St. Vincent, tel. 809/458–4811. 12 rooms. Facilities: tennis and squash courts, pool, reading room, restaurant, water-sports center nearby. AE, MC, V. Expensive.*

Sunset Shores. Everything in this very simple but livable hotel is arranged around the pool. Business travelers appreciate the clipboard in the central sitting area that carries daily Caribbean, financial, sports, and international news from the wire services. The better rooms have patios. *Box 849, across from Young Island on Villa Beach, St. Vincent, tel. 809/458–4411. 27 air-conditioned rooms. Facilities: restaurant, pool, watersports center nearby. AE, MC, V. Expensive.*

Mariner's Inn. A bit scruffy around the edges, the Mariner's is a sprawling, multibuilding hotel at the end of Villa Beach. Popular with old salts and adventurous younger couples, it's getting a much-needed renovation by new management. Lots of socializing goes on around the outdoor bar that is fashioned from a lifeboat of the *Antilles*, which sank off Mustique 20 years ago. The dining room's cuisine is on the upswing. The beach is a 10-minute stroll away. *Box 868, St. Vincent, tel. 809/458–4287. 25 rooms. Facilities: bar, restaurant. AE, MC, V. Moderate.*

Umbrella Beach Hotel. The hotel's small, simple, and charming rooms with kitchenettes are set in a garden on Villa Beach. The three best rooms face the water. Excellent breakfast is served outdoors in a garden overlooking the beach. Here you'll find superior value and location for the price. Next door is The French, St. Vincent's best restaurant. *Box 530, St. Vincent, tel. 809/458–4651. 9 rooms. Facilities: bar, restaurant. MC, V. Inexpensive.*

Blue Lagoon **CSY Yacht Club.** Located in Blue Lagoon, about 15 minutes
★ from the airport, this is the place for chartering a sailboat or trading stories with the yacht owners and former charter-yacht-owner-turned-manager Mike O'Brien. The spacious, modern rooms have cathedral ceilings and private patios. The long shallow-water beach that curves around Blue Lagoon offers a view of anchored sailboats. A beach bar has music and dancing on weekends. The secluded swimming pool is up a circuitous stone walk, set among flowering bushes. *Box 133, St. Vincent, tel. 809/458–4308 or 800/631–1593; U.S. agent: Anchor Reservations, 795 Franklin Ave., Franklin Lakes, NJ 07417, tel. 800/526–4789. 19 air-conditioned rooms. Facilities: pool, bar, restaurant, conference room. MC, V. Moderate.*

Kingstown **Heron Hotel.** Right out of a Somerset Maugham novel, this Kingstown inn is on the second floor of a converted Georgian plantation's warehouse. Pleasantly eccentric travelers, young and old, stay here to be near the dock for the early boat. Rooms are faded but atmospheric, and No. 15 is large and has a sitting area. *Box 226, St. Vincent, tel. 809/457–1631. 15 air-conditioned rooms. Facilities: courtyard, dining room. AE, MC, V. Moderate.*

Cobblestone Inn. This pre-1814 stone building used to be a sugar warehouse; wicker furniture now fills its large, airy rooms. Room No. 5 overlooks the street and is sunny but a bit noisy. The nearest beach is 3 miles away. The plant-filled courtyard leads to a rooftop bar that's popular for breakfast and lunch. Rates include breakfast. *Box 862, St. Vincent, tel. 809/456–1937. 19 rooms. Facilities: bar, restaurant. AE, V. Inexpensive.*

Nightlife

Don't look for fire-eaters and limbo demonstrations on St. Vincent. Nightlife here consists mostly of hotel barbecue buffets and jump-ups, so called because the lively steel-band music makes listeners jump up and dance.

The Attic (on Grenville St., tel. 809/457–2558), a new jazz club with modern decor, offers international artists and steel bands. There is a small cover charge; call ahead for hours and performers.

Vidal Browne, manager of **Young Island** (tel. 809/458–4826), hosts sunset cocktails and hor d'oeuvres each Thursday on Fort Duvernette, the tiny island behind the resort. On that night 100 steps up the hill are lit by flaming torches and a string band plays. Reservations are necessary for nonguests.

The Friday night barbecue and jump-up at **Mariner's Inn** (tel. 809/458–4287) draws both tourists and locals.

Basil's Too (tel. 809/458–4025) opened in late 1989, and this newest addition offers lunch, dinner and dancing amid painted murals, all set on Villa Beach overlooking Young Island.

The Grenadines

The Grenadines are wonderful islands to visit for fine diving and snorkeling opportunities, good beaches, and unlimited chances to laze on the beach with a picnic waiting for the sun to set so you can go to dinner. For travelers seeking privacy, peace and quiet, or an undisturbed holiday, these are the islands of choice.

For price information on restaurants and hotels, see the price charts in the Dining and Lodging sections of St. Vincent, above.

Bequia

Arriving and Departing   Your flight may arrive in St. Vincent too late in the day to make the *Admiral* ferry's last departure from Kingstown to Bequia at 4:15 PM. This means either an overnight stay in St. Vincent or chartering a sail or speedboat. Take a taxi to the Villa Beach Dock or the CSY Yacht Club. Charters cost about $80 and up.

All scheduled transportation departs from the main dock in Kingstown. The SS *Admiral* motor ferry leaves Monday–Friday at 9, 10:30, 4:30 and 7PM; Saturday's departure is at 12:30 PM. The trip takes 70–90 minutes and costs less than $3. The SS *Snapper* mail boat travels south on Mondays and Thursdays at about 10 AM, stopping at Bequia, Canouan, Mayreau, and Union, and returns north on Tuesdays and Fridays. The cost is under $10, and you can stay in a cabin aboard the *Snapper* for E.C.$20 if you're worried about missing its 6 AM departure from Union. Weekday service between St. Vincent and Bequia is also available on the island schooner *Friendship Rose*, which leaves about 12:30 PM. The "St. Vincent and the Grenadines Visitor's Guide" available in hotels and at the airport, has complete interisland schedules.

Important Addresses   **Tourist Information:** The **Bequia Tourism Board** (tel. 809/458–3286) is located on the main dock.

Emergencies   **Police:** (tel. 809/456–1955).
Medical Emergencies: (tel. 999).

Guided Tours   To see the views, villages, and boat-building around the island, hire a taxi and negotiate the fare in advance. Water taxis, available from any dock, will also take you by Moonhole, a private community of stone homes with glassless windows, some decorated with bleached whale bones. The fare is about $11.

For those who prefer sailboats to motorboats, Arne Hansen and his catamaran *Toien* can be booked through the **Sunsports Dive Shop** (tel. 809/458–3577). Day sails to Mustique run $35–$40 per person, including drinks. An overnight snorkel/sail trip to the Tobago Cays costs about $150 for two people, including breakfast and drinks. Longer custom charters can also be arranged.

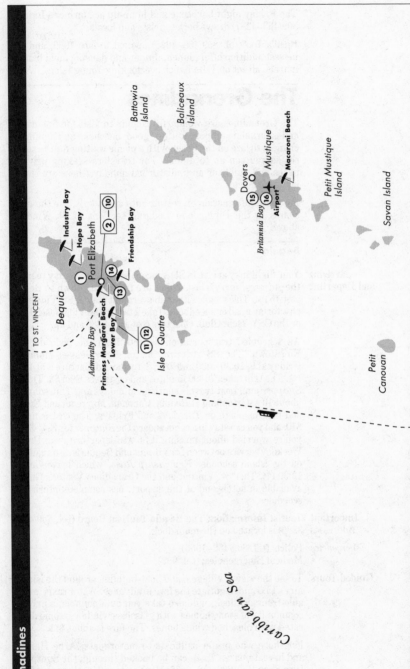

The Grenadines

TO ST. VINCENT

Bequia

Industry Bay
Hope Bay
Port Elizabeth
Admiralty Bay
(1)
Friendship Bay
(2)—(10)
(14)
(13)
Princess Margaret Beach
Lower Bay
(11)(12)
Isle a Quatre

Battowia
Island

Baliceaux
Island

Mustique
Macaroni Beach
Dovers
(15)
Britannia Bay
(16)
Airport
Petit Mustique
Island

Savan Island

Petit Canouan

Caribbean Sea

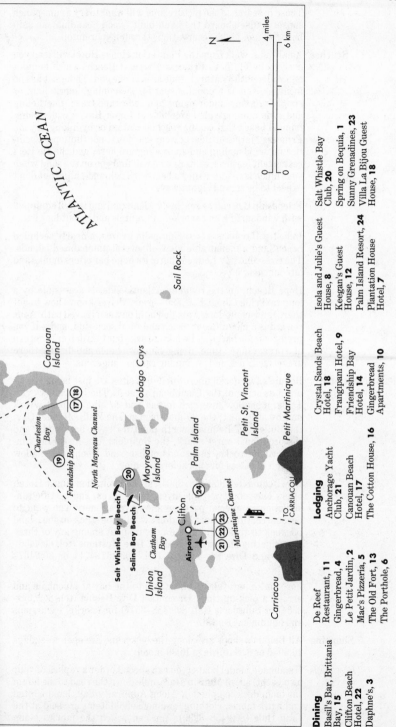

Those in search of the picturesque will want to try a rum-punch sunset cruise aboard the hand-built, wood Scandinavian sailboat *Fredag*. Make reservations through your hotel.

Beaches A half-hour walk from the Plantation House Hotel will lead you over rocky bluffs to **Princess Margaret Beach,** which is quiet and wide, with a natural stone arch at one end. Though it has no facilities, this is a popular spot for swimming, snorkeling, or simply relaxing under palms and sea-grape trees. Snorkeling and swimming are also excellent at **Lower Bay,** a wide, palm-fringed beach that can be reached by taxi or by hiking beyond Princess Margaret Beach; wear sneakers, not flipflops. Facilities for windsurfing and snorkeling are here, and the De Reef restaurant features waiters who will find you on the sand when your lunch is ready. Enjoy a beer with fish-and-chips, but don't expect to be served right away.

Friendship Bay can be reached by land taxi and is well equipped with windsurfing and snorkeling, rentals and an outdoor bar.

Industry Bay boasts towering palm groves, a nearly secluded beach, and a memorable view of several uninhabited islands. The Crescent Bay Lodge is here; its huge bar offers drinks and late lunches.

Hope Beach, on the rougher Atlantic side, is accessible by a long taxi ride (about E.C.$20—every driver knows how to get there) and a mile-long walk downhill on a semipaved path. Your reward is a magnificent beach and total seclusion, and—if you prefer—nude bathing. Be sure to ask your taxi driver to return at a prearranged time. Bring your own lunch and drinks; there are no facilities, and swimming can be dangerous.

Participant Sports Bequia's two dozen uncrowded dive sites are just being recog-
Water Sports nized as some of the Caribbean's finest. The best are Devil's Table, a shallow dive rich in fish and coral; a sailboat wreck nearby at 90 feet; the 90-foot drop at The Wall, off West Cay; the Bullet, off Bequia's north point for rays, barracuda, and the occasional nurse shark; the Boulders for soft corals, tunnel-forming rocks, thousands of fish; and Moonhole, shallow enough in places for snorkelers to enjoy.

Dive Bequia (tel. 809/458–3504), at the Plantation House Hotel, offers one- and two-tank dives, night dives, and certified instruction. A special package allows vacationers who want to become certified divers but don't want to be stuck on one island all week to spread the five-day course out among any of three participating shops: **Dive Bequia, Dive Mustique** (tel. 809/456–4777), and **Dive St. Vincent** (tel. 809/457–4714 or 809/457–4948).

For snorkeling, take a water taxi to the bay at Moonhole and arrage a pick-up time. Or contact **Dive Bequia** (tel. 809/458–3504) or **Sunsports** (tel. 809/458–3577) for snorkel excursions and equipment rental.

Shopping All Bequia's shops are along the beach and are open weekdays 10:30–5 or 6, Saturdays 10:30–noon.

Best Buys Handmade model boats (you can special order a replica of your own yacht) are at **Mauvin's** (a ¼-mile down the road to the left of the main dock, no phone). Along Admiralty Bay, handprinted and batik fabric, clothing, and household items are sold at the **Crab Hole** (809/458–3290). You can watch the fabrics being made in the workshop out back. **Solana's** (tel. 809/458–3554) offers attractive beachwear, saronglike pareos, and handy plastic beach shoes. **Local Color** (tel. 809/458–3202), above the Porthole restaurant in town, has an excellent and unusual selection of handmade jewelry, wood carvings, resort clothing, and scrimshaw (ink drawings on ivory). **Wearable Art** (above the Frangipani Hotel, tel. 809/458–3368) offers hand-painted Egyptian cotton beachwear and jewelry. The **Bequia Bookstore** (tel. 809/458–3258) has novels, books on island lore, postcards, and decorative maps. **Melinda's** (tel. 809/458–3895) is a new shop, with hand-painted T-shirts and silk items.

Dining Dining on Bequia ranges from West Indian to gourmet cuisine, and it's consistently good. Barbecues at Bequia's hotels mean spicy West Indian seafood, chicken, or beef, plus a buffet of spicy side dishes and sweet desserts. Restaurants are occasionally closed on Sundays; phone to check.

★ **Le Petit Jardin.** This new chalet-style French restaurant offers gourmet lobster and fish prepared with West Indian touches and ingredients. The elegant style and service here are welcome in this part of the world. *Port Elizabeth, tel. 809/458–3318. Reservations necessary. No credit cards. Expensive.*

The Old Fort. Overlooking the Atlantic from Mt. Pleasant, the building dates from the mid-1700s. Otmar and Sonja Schaedle restored it and created a gourmet restaurant and small hotel. *Mt. Pleasant, tel. 809/458–3440. Expensive.*

★ **The Gingerbread.** Lunches and dinners are served upstairs, but your best bet is to stick with the gourmet shop's cappuccino and baked goods for breakfast. *Port Elizabeth, tel. 809/458–3577. Dinner reservations suggested. MC, V. Moderate.*

De Reef Restaurant. On Lower Bay Beach, De Reef serves casual lunches and exceptional dinners, including gingered lamb and seafood. *Lower Bay, tel. 809/458–3800. No credit cards. Inexpensive–Moderate.*

★ **Mac's Pizzeria.** The island's best lunches and casual dinners are enjoyed amid fuschia bougainvillea on the covered outdoor terrace overlooking the harbor. Choose from mouthwatering lobster pizza, quiche, pita sandwiches, lasagna, home-baked cookies, and muffins. Friendly cats and amiable service add to the pleasurable experience. *On the beach, Port Elizabeth, tel. 809/458–3475. Dinner reservations necessary. No credit cards. Inexpensive–Moderate.*

★ **Theresas Restaurant.** On Monday nights, Theresa and John Bennett offer a rotating selection of enormous and tasty Greek, Indian, Mexican, or Italian buffets . . . plus West Indian dishes at lunch and dinner the rest of the week. *At the far end of Lower Bay beach, no phone. Dinner reservations by VHF radio necessary. No credit cards. Inexpensive–Moderate.*

The Porthole. Located in town, this is where sailors gather for drinks, chicken and rice, or rotis (Caribbean burritos). *Port Elizabeth, tel. 809/458–3458. No credit cards. Inexpensive.*

Lodging **Plantation House Hotel.** A 1988 fire destroyed the main house
★ but left the pink cottages intact; manager Jaques Ducau has sped rebuilding, adding a new beach cottage and a bigger Dive Bequia scuba shop. The new building, which resembles the original but has modern conveniences, should be completed before the 1990 winter season and five more rooms should be added. The cottages are being completely refurbished. The

Plantation House attracts mostly older couples who enjoy its relatively secluded, spacious, palm-filled grounds. The restaurant serves good French-accented food, and a room-size cage of parakeets near the bar keeps imbibers entertained. *Box 16, Admiralty Bay, Bequia, St. Vincent, W.I., tel. 809/458–3425. 17 cottages. Facilities: diving, pool, bar, restaurant. AE, MC, V. Very Expensive.*

Spring on Bequia. The only Bequia hotel not on the water, Spring is nestled in green hills overlooking groves of tall palms and grazing goats. The hotel is about a mile above town (a pretty walk, though you may want to take a taxi back uphill), and the nearest beach, lovely but too shallow and occasionally seaweedy for serious swimming, is a 10-minute stroll away. The large wood and stone rooms attract upscale travelers who want serenity and seclusion. The airy veranda bar is the site of manager Candy Leslie's deservedly famous Sunday curry lunch (reservations necessary). *Bequia, St. Vincent, W.I., tel. 809/458–3414; U.S. agent: Spring on Bequia, Box 19251, Minneapolis, MN 55419, tel. 612/823–1202 or 612/823–9925. 11 rooms. Facilities: pool, bar, restaurant, tennis. AE, MC, V. Expensive.*

Friendship Bay Hotel. This 27-unit white hotel on the hill features rooms with large terraces and sweeping views and rooms built of coral stone closer to the beach. While the service has been wildly uneven on recent visits, Friendship offers a long white-sand beach and improved food by a new Argentine chef. On Saturday nights owners Joanne and Eduardo Guadagnino still hold the liveliest beachside barbecue/jump-up in the Grenadines. Enjoy a rum punch at the MauMau Beach Bar, a cozy establishment equipped with swings instead of seats (the swings have backs and armrests, a safety plus after several potent rum punches). *Box 9, Bequia, St. Vincent, W.I., tel. 809/458–3222; U.S. agent: Ralph Locke, Box 800, Waccabuc, NY 10597, tel. 800/223–1108. 27 rooms. Facilities: water-sports center, restaurant, 2 bars; boutique. AE, MC, V. Moderate–Expensive.*

★ **The Frangipani Hotel.** The Frangi has long since gained the status of venerable institution, that rare combination of comfortable hotel and local gossip center where absolutely everyone ends up to share drinks and stories. Managed by Marie Kingston and Lou Keane, the main building used to be Prime Minister Son Mitchell's family home. Surrounded by tropical trees and flowering bushes, the garden units are built of stone, and the rooms, with private verandas and baths, are some of the nicest obtainable. Four simple, less expensive rooms are in the main house, although only one has a private bath. A two-bedroom, two-bath house with a patio overlooks the tennis court and another apartment with a large bedroom and kitchen is nearby. Several more garden units and two-bedroom dwellings are planned. At the beachside terrace bar and dining area, string bands appear on Mondays with folk songs on Friday nights during tourist season. The Thursday night steel-band jump-up, which draws throngs of visitors and locals, is a must. *Box 1, Bequia, St. Vincent, W.I., tel. 809/458–3255. 11 rooms. Facilities: tennis, bar, restaurant, water-sports center; yacht services. AE, MC, V. Inexpensive–Moderate.*

Keegan's Guest House. This is the place for budget-minded beach lovers who want quiet, friendly surroundings. Located on Lower Bay, John Keegan's house offers family-style West Indian breakfasts and dinners for its guests. Rooms 3, 4, and 5 have a shared bath and are cheaper, although there is no hot water to be found (you really do get used to it). *Bequia, St. Vincent, W.I., tel. 809/458–3254. 7 rooms. Facilities: dining room. No credit cards. Inexpensive.*

Isola and Julie's Guest House. Right on the water in Port Elizabeth, these two separate buildings share a small restaurant and bar. Furnishings (which are few) run to early Salvation Army, but the rooms are airy and light with private baths; some have hot water. *Box 12, Isola's Guest House, Bequia, St. Vincent, W.I., tel. 809/458–3304, 809/458–3323, or 809/458–3220. 25 rooms. Facilities: bar, restaurant. No credit cards. Inexpensive.*

Nightlife   Most nights there's a jump-up at: **Mac's** on Tuesday, the **Frangipani** on Thursday, **Plantation House** on Friday, **Friendship Bay** on Saturday.

Canouan

This is an island where goatherding is still a career option and organized activities are nil. Walk, loaf, swim, or snorkel; Canouan still lives in the 18th century.

Dining and Lodging   **Canouan Beach Hotel.** In Charlestown Bay on a golden-sand beach, the CBH recently completed a marina. Airy little cottages with brightly colored decor are available, and windsurfing and snorkeling are best at Friendship Point. Day sails on the hotel's catamaran leave Monday–Saturday for a different destination to nearby islands and the Cays. Steel bands perform on Mondays and Thursdays. From April to October, scuba-diving instruction and rentals are available. *Canouan, St. Vincent, W.I., tel. 809/458–8888. 35 rooms. Facilities: air-conditioning, bar, restaurant, marina, windsurfing, snorkeling. AE, V. Very Expensive.*

Crystal Sands Beach Hotel. Locally run and extremely simple, Crystal Sands is located on Charleston Bay and has a veranda bar and dining area. Cottages share a connecting door for larger groups and are equipped with private baths and patios. Fishing, sailing, and great snorkeling can be found off the fine beach. Phone the managers to arrange for air pickup in St. Vincent. If you take the mail boat from Kingstown (*see* Arriving and Departing in Bequia, above), pack light and be prepared to climb from the large ferry into a small rowboat to get to shore. *Canouan, St. Vincent, W.I., tel. 809/458–8015. 20 beds in rooms and cottages. Facilities: bar, dining area, snorkeling, fishing. No credit cards. Moderate.*

Villa La Bijou Guest House. Up the hill and only a 10-minute walk from Friendship Bay (15 minutes from the airstrip; pack light—taxis are rarely available), La Bijou is the mosaic-stone "dream house" of the de Roche family, who treat their guests more like friends than paying customers. A great view of the Cays and good French food make for a pleasant stay. *M. de Roche, Villa La Bijou, Canouan, St. Vincent, W.I., tel. 809/458–8025. 6 rooms. No hot water in the shared baths. Facilities: snorkeling, Sunfish, windsurfing, dining room. No credit cards. Inexpensive–Moderate.*

Nightlife   Surprise: There's a bar/disco at **La Bijou.**

Mayreau

Farm animals outnumber citizens on tiny Mayreau (pronounced *my-ro*). Except for water sports and hiking, there's nothing to do, and visitors like it that way. This is the perfect place for a meditative or vegetative vacation.

Guided Tours You can swim and snorkel in the Cays or nearby islands on day trips with Chuck Burghard on his spacious, rainbow-striped catamaran *Carnival*. Contact Chuck through **Undine Potter** at the Salt Whistle Bay Resort (from the U.S., tel. 800/387–1752; in the Grenadines, marine radio VHF channel 68 or 16). Note that the Salt Whistle Bay's snorkel equipment has seen better days. Buy or rent your own before you arrive.

Beaches Top honors go to **Salt Whistle Bay Beach**—the Caribbean's prettiest. The beach is an exquisite half-moon of powdery white sand, shaded by perfectly spaced palms and flowering bushes, with the rolling Atlantic a stroll away. Hike 25 minutes over Mayreau's mountain (wear shoes; bare feet or flip-flops are a big mistake) to a good photo opportunity at the stone church atop the hill. Once you've put your camera away, you can investigate Mayreau's one tiny town (have a drink at Dennis Hideaway) and enjoy a swim at beautiful **Saline Bay Beach.** No facilities; the mail boat's tender stops at the dock here.

Participant Sports NAUI instructor Bill Tewes of Dive St. Vincent opened a new scuba shop on Salt Whistle Bay in late 1989.

Dining and Lodging Set far back from the water, the roomy stone cottages at the **Salt Whistle Bay Club,** Mayreau's only hotel, are so cleverly hidden that sailors need binoculars to be sure a hotel is there at all. With names like "Oleander" and "Ivora," the cottages sport round-stone showers (no hot water) that look like large, medieval telephone booths. You can dry your hair on the breezy, shared second-story veranda atop each two-room building. The outdoor dining area has stone tables covered by thatched palms. On top of these tables, duck, fish-and-chips, and coconut cake are served while music from the bar drifts in. There used to be a jump-up, but guests preferred peace and quiet. *Salt Whistle Bay Club, 610 Reynolds St., Toronto, Ont., Canada L1N 6H8, tel. 416/430–1275, fax 416/430–8988; in the Caribbean, marine radio channel 16 or 68. 14 units, 5 double cottages, 8 smaller rooms, 1 suite. Facilities: windsurfing, snorkeling, catamaran charter, bar, restaurant. No credit cards. Very Expensive.*

Mustique

This island has no town and no activities, though horseback riding is available and motorbikes can be rented from **TechServe** (tel. 809/458–4621; ask for TechServe). If you're not a hotel or villa guest, it's easiest to arrange for these via marine radio from Basil's Bar when you arrive.

Beaches **Macaroni Beach** is Mustique's most famous stretch of sand, offering surfy swimming (no lifeguards, so be careful) with trees and mountains rising behind you. There's not much shade, and no facilities, which also describes Mustique's smaller, nameless beaches. Daytrippers can also swim near **Basil's Bar.**

Dining **Basil's Bar, Britannia Bay.** Day sailors are welcome for lunch at the famous if exorbitantly priced Basil's, another Grenadines institution. Homemade ice cream, lobster, and occasional glimpses of the rich and famous provide gastronomic and visual distractions. Wednesday features a jump-up and barbecue; Monday night, live music. The restaurant also has a boutique with designer batiks and Basil's T-shirts. *Tel. 809/458–4621. Reservations suggested. AE, MC, V. Moderate.*

Lodging **The Cotton House.** This restored 18th-century stone and coral Georgian house accommodates half the guest rooms, while three guest cottages near the "Roman ruin" pool and a two-story wing houses eight other rooms. Custom-designed furnishings accent the light, breezy rooms, all of which have patios or balconies. Manager Cristophe Lajus continues the Cotton House's tradition of excellent food. Full water sports, tennis, and horseback riding are available here, and shopping can be found at the Treasure Boutique, which features chic international designer resort wear and accessories. *Mustique, St. Vincent, W.I., tel. 809/456–4777. U.S. agent: Ralph Locke Associates, Box 800, Waccabuc, NY 10597, tel. 914/763–5526 or 212/696–1323. 30 rooms. Facilities: pool, bar, restaurant, boutique, diving, windsurfing, tennis, horseback riding. AE, V. Very Expensive.*

Villa Rentals. Leasing an elegant villa of your own (complete with maid and cook) can be expensive, but sharing the cost with another couple makes the price more reasonable. Where else can you vacation in the house Princess Margaret owns? Contact the Manager of the Mustique Company (Mustique, St. Vincent, W.I., tel. 809/457–1531) for listings and information.

Palm Island

One of the area's most beautiful islands, this private resort offers many activities. **Palm Island Resort's** new fitness walk circles past private homes, hills, and deserted Atlantic beach. The 12 stone cottages with outdoor showers all have a beach view, verandas, and newly refurbished pastel/rattan interiors. Recently added solar power now provides hot water, and a full health spa with indoor/outdoor exercise area is planned. Tea is served on your terrace every day at 4 PM, and West Indian meals in the refurbished outdoor dining/bar area are good. *Palm Island, St. Vincent, W.I., tel. 809/458–8824. U.S. Agent: Scott Calder, 152 Madison Ave., NY 10016, tel. 212/535–9530. 12 cottages, 24 rooms. Facilities: minifridge, bar, ceiling fans, mosquito netting; diving, snorkeling, windsurfing, Zodiac and Sunfish rentals, fitness course; fishing, catered day sails or extended trips, yacht provisioning. AE, MC, V. Very Expensive.*

Petit St. Vincent

Many upscale travelers consider Petit St. Vincent the finest private island in the Grenadines, and the privacy is as perfect as the food: The imported duck and game hen are worthy of any four-star Manhattan restaurant. Here the clientele communicates with flags. A yellow flag hoisted outside your stone and wood house means that you want room service. If you have food delivered, make sure you don't confuse your Jeep-driving waiter by raising the red "leave me alone" flag.

Meals are served the old-fashioned way in the Pavilion (without the aid of flags). You can play table tennis and listen to occasional live piano music in the outdoor bar, while manager Haze Richardson's six Labradors stroll the grounds.

Beaches Small, secluded beaches surround the island, now hidden from the jogging/fitness trail by skillful new landscaping. The hotel will drop you for the day at Mopion, a tiny sandbar with one thatch-roof shelter for shade. There is good swimming all over.

Participant Sports Activities include tennis, croquet, windsurfing, waterskiing (small extra charge), snorkeling, sailing trips, and jogging on a new 20-stop, 32-exercise fitness trail that runs along the beaches and around a wooded area. Shaded hammocks are strung up every 100 feet along the trail. *PSV, Box 12506, Cincinnati, OH 45212, tel. 513/242-1333, 800/654-9376, or 809/458-8801. 22 houses. No credit cards. Closed Sept. and Oct. Very Expensive.*

Union

Union's airstrip is right behind the Anchorage Yacht Club.

Beaches The beach around Clifton Harbour is narrow, unattractive, rocky, and shadeless. Other beaches have no facilities and are virtually inaccessible without a boat; the desolate but lovely Chatham Bay offers good swimming.

Participant Sports **Dive Anchorage,** run by NAUI instructor Glenroy Adams and his brother Rick on the grounds of the Anchorage Yacht Club, offers reef dives at Mayreau and in the Tobago Cays and wreck dives at the *Purina,* a sunken WWI English gunship. Resort courses, certification courses, glass-bottom boat trip, and snorkel trips are offered. *Tel. 809/458-8221. Cost: about U.S.$40 per dive. No credit cards.*

Dining **Clifton Beach Hotel.** Excellent West Indian food is served here, thanks to new chefs who formerly worked on Mustique. The outdoor bar-restaurant area is pleasant and faces the harbor. *Tel. 809/458-8235. AE, V. Inexpensive–Moderate.*

Lodging **Anchorage Yacht Club.** Sprawling between the airstrip and what little beach there is are rooms and bungalows with concealed outdoor showers and terraces facing the water, all comfortably refurbished and full of French yachtsmen. Scuba, fishing, windsurfing, and Hobie Cats are available, plus yacht charters to nearby islands and provisioning for visiting boats. The expensive boutique offers French fashions and accessories not found on other islands, and new manager Charlotte Honnart has improved the restaurant's French and Creole cuisine. The enormous bar area is fronted by a pool inhabited by dozens of nurse sharks so docile that a sign warns, PLEASE DO NOT TOUCH THE SHARKS. *Union, St. Vincent, W.I., tel. 809/458-8221. 15 rooms, 6 bungalows. Facilities: water-sports center, restaurant, bar, boutique, air-conditioning, yacht provisioning and charters. AE, MC, V. Expensive.*
Sunny Grenadines. Simply furnished, airy, and appealing, the dozen rooms are in several two-story stone buildings arranged around a plant-filled garden. A few rooms have kitchens, some big enough for four or five people, and all have small porches and twin beds. The harbor view is pleasant if not spectacular. Hospitable manager Augustus Mitchell arranges boat trips to

the Cays. *Union, St. Vincent, W.I., tel. 809/458–8327. 10 rooms, some with kitchens. Facilities: bar and restaurant. MC, V. Inexpensive–Moderate.*

Nightlife A steel band plays Monday and Friday nights at the **Anchorage Yacht Club.**

26 Trinidad and Tobago

by Mark Rowland

Mark Rowland is Pacific Editor of Musician *magazine. His feature articles have appeared in* Esquire, American Film, Americas, *and other publications.*

Trinidad and Tobago, the southernmost islands in the West Indies chain, could not be more dissimilar. Trinidad's cosmopolitan capital, Port-of-Spain, bustles with shopping centers, modern hotels, sophisticated restaurants, and an active nightlife. It is also home of Carnival, the birthplace of steelband music, and a busy port. The 1.2 million Trinidadians know prosperity from oil (it is one of the biggest producers in the Western Hemisphere), a steel plant, natural gas, and a multiplicity of small businesses. More than half of them—Indians, Africans, Europeans, Asians, and Americans, each with their own language and customs—live in Port-of-Spain. The Trinidadians are heavy on cricket and horse racing. But you have to leave the capital to find a good beach. And because it is one of the most active commercial cities in the West Indies, most visitors are business travelers.

Tobago, 22 miles away, offers the lazier life most tourists seek. The Robinson Crusoe island is more laid-back, the pace slower, with beautiful, near-deserted beaches, secluded bays, small hotels, and little fishing villages. Goats outnumber cars. Tobago is popular with snorkelers and divers; its Buccoo Reef is an underwater wonderland.

Columbus reached these islands on his third voyage in 1498. Three prominent peaks around the southern bay where he anchored prompted him to name the land La Trinidad, after the Holy Trinity. Trinidad was formally ceded to England in 1802, ending 300 years of Spanish rule.

Tobago's history was more complicated. It was "discovered" by the British in 1508. The Spanish, Dutch, French, and British all fought for it until it was ceded to England under the Treaty of Paris in 1814. In 1962, both islands—T & T, as they're commonly called—gained their independence within the British Commonwealth, finally becoming a republic in 1976.

In 1986, the National Alliance for Reconstruction (NAR) won a landslide victory, toppling the People's National Movement (PNM), which had been in power for 30 years but had brought the country to the brink of economic ruin. The NAR is now in the process of reconstruction and development.

Trinidad's capital may be noisy and its way of life somewhat frenetic, but its countryside is rich in flora and fauna, home to more than 400 species of birds and 700 varieties of orchids.

Before You Go

Tourist Information

Contact the **Trinidad and Tobago Tourism Development Authority** (Cruise Ship Complex, #1D Wrightson Rd., Port of Spain). In the United States: Forest Hills Tower, 118–35 Queens Blvd., Queens, NY 11375, tel. 718/575–3909; 330 Biscayne Blvd., Suite 310, Miami, FL 33122, tel. 305/374–2056 or 800/325–1337, ext. 700. In the United Kingdom: 48 Leichester Sq., London WC2H 7QD, tel. 01/930–6566. In Canada: 40 Holly St., Suite 102, Toronto, Ont. M4S 3C3, tel. 416/486–4470 or 800/268–8986.

Arriving and Departing
By Plane

There are daily direct flights to Piarco Airport, about 30 miles east of Port-of-Spain, from New York, Miami, and Toronto on **BWIA** (tel. 800/327–7401), Trinidad and Tobago's national airline. You can also fly from one or more of these cities on **Pan Am** (tel. 800/221–1111), **American** (tel. 800/433–7300), and **Air Can-**

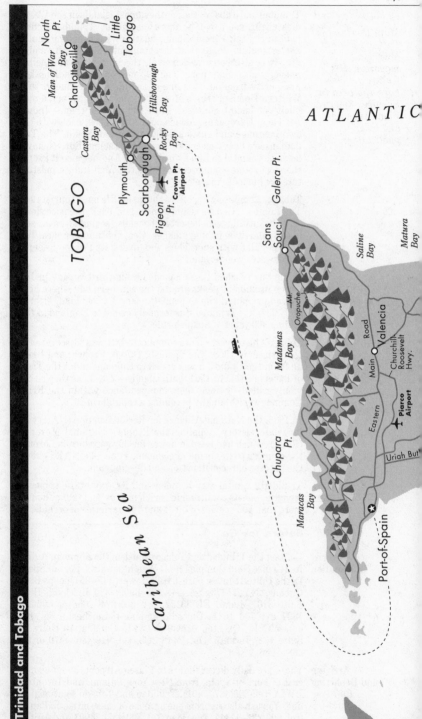

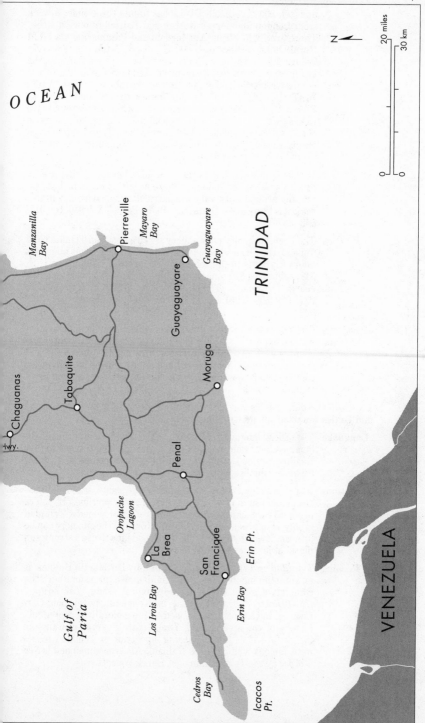

ada (tel. 800/422–6232). BWIA has flights three times a week from London and serves Boston and Baltimore once a week. There are flights from Amsterdam and Paramaribo via **KLM Royal Dutch Airlines** (tel. 800/777–5553). **ALM** (tel. 800/327–7230) and Pan Am have flights from New York via Curaçao, the latter at a lower cost than most standard fares. There are numerous interisland flights in the Caribbean by BWIA and **LIAT** (tel. 809/462–0701). All flights to Trinidad alight at Piarco Airport. Most round-trip fares include a free round-trip ticket to Tobago from Piarco, about a $30 value, so be sure to check with your agent. BWIA flights from Trinidad to Crown Point Airport in Tobago take about 15 minutes and depart about six to 10 times a day.

Package tours aren't generally touted as heavily as they are for other Caribbean islands, but there are bargains to be had, especially around Carnival. One particularly good agency in this regard is **Pan Caribe Tours** (Box 46, El Paso, TX 79940, tel. 915/542–3370).

By Boat The Port Authority runs a ferry service between Trinidad and Tobago; the ferries leave twice a day. The trip takes about six hours (flying is preferable); return fare is TT$50, about U.S. $12; cabin fare $19 (one-way double occupancy), with an extra charge for vehicles. Tickets are sold at offices in Port-of-Spain (tel. 809/625–4906) and at Scarborough, in Tobago (tel. 809/639–2181).

Passports and Visas Citizens of the United States, the United Kingdom, and Canada who expect to stay for less than two months may enter the country with an original birth certificate (not a photocopy) and some other identification with a photograph. Citizens of other countries need passports. A visa is required for a stay of more than two months.

Customs and Duties Adult visitors may carry out 50 cigars or 200 cigarettes and one quart of spirits without paying a duty.

Language The official language is English, although there is no end of idiomatic expressions used by the loquacious Trinis *(see* Further Reading, below). You will also hear smatterings of French, Spanish, Chinese, and Hindi.

Precautions Insect repellent is a must during the rainy season (June–December) and is worth having around anytime. If you're prone to car sickness, bring your preferred remedy. Trinidad is only 11 degrees north of the equator, and the sun here can be intense. Even if you tan well, it's a good idea to use a strong sun block, at least for the first few days.

Further Reading *Trinidad and Tobago Dialect (Plus)*, by Dr. Martin Haynes, is an entertaining dictionary of Trinidadian expressions with the cumulative effect of an anthropological study. *The Dragon Can't Dance*, by Earl Lovelace, is an engaging novel about Carnival set in Laventille and based on the generally accepted folk history of the steel bands. *The Middle Passage* contains an insightful—if rather unsparing—portrait of Trinidad by its most famous writer, V. S. Naipaul. Also recommended is *Sea Grapes* by the Trinidadian poet Derek Walcott.

Staying in Trinidad and Tobago

Important Addresses

Tourist Information: Information is available from the **Trinidad & Tobago Tourism Development Authority,** (Cruise Ship Complex, #1D Wrightson Rd., Port-of-Spain, tel. 809/623–1932, fax 809/623–3848; Piarco Airport, tel. 809/664–5196). For Tobago, write to the **Tobago Division of Tourism** (Tobago House of Assembly, Scarborough Hall, Scarborough, tel. 809/639–2125).

Emergencies

Police: Call 999.

Fire and Ambulance: Call 990.

Hospitals: Port-of-Spain General Hospital is on Charlotte Street (tel. 809/625–7869). **Tobago County Hospital** is on Fort Street in Scarborough (tel. 809/639–2551).

Pharmacies: Oxford Pharmacy (tel. 809/627–4657) is at Charlotte and Oxford streets near the Port-of-Spain General Hospital. **Ross Drugs** (tel. 809/639–2658) is in Scarborough. For a complete list of other pharmacies, check the T&T Yellow Pages.

Currency

The Trinidadian dollar (TT$) has been devalued twice in recent years. The current exchange rate is about U.S.$1 to TT$4.20. The major hotels in Port-of-Spain have exchange facilities whose rates are comparable to official bank rates. Most businesses on the island will accept U.S. currency if you're in a pinch. Note: All prices quoted here are in U.S. dollars unless indicated otherwise.

Taxes and Service Charges

Restaurants and hotels add a 15% Value Added Tax (VAT). The airport departure tax is TT$50, or about U.S. $12.

Many hotels and restaurants add a 10% service charge to your bill. If the service charge is not added, you should tip 10%–15% of the bill for a job well done.

Guided Tours

Trinidad and Tobago Sightseeing Tours (Galleria Shopping Centre, Western Main Rd., St. James, Port-of-Spain, tel. 809/628–1051) has a variety of sightseeing packages, from a tour of the city to an all-day drive to the other side of the island. Another reputable agency is **Hub Travel Limited** (Hilton Hotel lobby, tel. 809/625–3155; Piarco Airport, tel. 809/664–4359). Almost any **taxi driver** in Port-of-Spain will be willing to take you around the town and to the beaches on the north coast, and you can haggle for a cheaper rate. For a complete list of tour operators and sea cruises, contact the Tourism office. For nature guides *see* Participant Sports, below.

Getting Around

Taxis

Taxis in Trinidad are easily identified by their license plates, which begin with the letter *H*. Passenger cars and vans called Maxi Taxis pick up and drop off passengers as they travel. They are easily hailed day or night along most of the main roads near Port-of-Spain. For longer trips you will need to hire a private taxi. There are set rates, though they are not always observed, particularly at Carnival. To be sure, pick up a rate sheet from the Tourism office. On the whole, the drivers are honest, friendly, and informative, and the experience of riding in a Maxi Taxi with a souped-up sound system during Carnival is worth whatever fare you pay.

Buses

Buses cover the island and are inexpensive, but they are very old and very crowded.

Rental Cars/ Scooters If you are a first-time visitor to Port-of-Spain, where the streets are often jammed with traffic and drivers who routinely play "chicken" with one another, taxis are your best bet. But if you're set on wheels and not prone to headaches, you can call on several car-rental services around town. Try **Premier Auto Rental Limited** (10 Nook Ave., St. Ann's, Port-of-Spain, tel. 809/624–7265) or **Bacchus Taxi Service** (37 Tragerete Rd., Port-of-Spain, tel. 809/622–5588). All agencies require a large deposit and you must make reservations well in advance of your arrival. Figure on paying about $30–$45 per day.

In Tobago you will be better off renting a car or Jeep than relying on taxi service, which is less frequent and ultimately much more expensive. Try **Sweet Jeeps** (Sandy Point, tel. 809/639–8533) or **Tobago Travel** (Box 163, Tobago, tel. 809/639–8778). You can also rent **motor scooters** from **Banana Rentals** (c/o Kariwak Village, Crown Point, tel. 809/639–8441). Rentals average $25–$35 a day.

As befits one of the world's largest exporters of asphalt, Trinidad's roads are fairly well paved. In the outback, however, they are often narrow, twisting, and prone to washouts in the rainy season. Inquire about conditions before you take off, particularly if you're heading toward the north coast. Never drive into downtown Port-of-Spain during afternoon rush hour. Don't forget to drive on the left.

Telephones and Mail The area code throughout the two islands is 809. For telegraph, telefax, teletype, and telex, contact **Textel** (1 Edward St., Port-of-Spain, tel. 809/625–4431). Cables can be sent from the Tourism office and major hotels. **Postage** for first-class letters to the United States is TT$2.25; postcards, TT$2.00.

To place an intraisland call, dial the local seven-digit number. To reach the United States by phone, dial 1, the appropriate area code, and the local number.

Opening and Closing Times Most shops open weekdays 8–6:30 and Saturday 8–noon. Banking hours are Monday–Thursday 9–2 and Friday 9–1 and 3–5.

Carnival

Trinidad always seems to be either anticipating, celebrating, or recovering from a festival, the biggest of which is **Carnival.** It occurs each year between February and early March. Trinidad's version of the pre-Lenten bacchanal is reputedly the oldest in the Western Hemisphere; there are festivities all over the country but the most lavish is in Port-of-Spain.

Carnival officially lasts only two days (from *J'ouvert* at sunrise on Monday through the *las lap* to midnight the following day). If you're planning to go, it's a good idea to arrive in Trinidad a week or two early to enjoy the events leading up to Carnival. Not as overwhelming as its rival in Rio, or as debauched as Mardi Gras in New Orleans, Trinidad's fest has the warmth and character of a massive family reunion.

Carnival is about extravagant costumes: Individuals prance around in imaginative outfits. Colorfully attired troupes—called *mas*—that sometimes number in the thousands march to the beat set by the steel bands. You can visit the various mas "camps" around the city where these elaborate costumes are put together—the addresses are listed in the newspapers—

and perhaps join one that strikes your fancy. Fees run anywhere from $35 to $100; you get to keep the costume. Children can also parade in a Kiddie Carnival that takes place on Saturday morning a few days before the real thing.

Throwing a party is not the only purpose for Carnival; it's also a showcase for calypso performers. Calypso is music that mixes dance rhythms with social commentary, sung by characters with such evocative names as Shadow, the Mighty Sparrow, and Black Stalin. As Carnival approaches, many of these singers perform nightly in calypso tents, which are scattered around the city. You can also visit the pan yards of Port-of-Spain, where steel orchestras, such as the Renegades, Desperadoes, Catelli All-Stars, Invaders, and Phase II, rehearse their arrangements of calypso.

For several nights before Carnival, costume makers display their talents, and the steel bands and calypso singers perform in spirited competitions in the grandstands of the racetrack in Queen's Park, where the Calypso Monarch is crowned. At sunrise, or J'ouvert, the city starts filling up with metal-frame carts carrying steel bands, flatbed trucks hauling sound systems, and thousands of revelers who squeeze into the narrow streets. Finally, at the stroke of midnight on "Mas Tuesday," Port-of-Spain's exhausted merrymakers go to bed. The next day everybody settles back to business.

Beaches

Trinidad Contrary to popular notion, Trinidad has far more beaches than Tobago; the catch is that Tobago's beaches are close to hotels, and Trinidad's are not. There are, however, four worthy sites within an hour's drive of Port-of-Spain, spread out along the north coast road.

Tyrico Bay is a small beach lively with surfers who flock here to enjoy the excellent surfing. The strong undertow may cow some swimmers. **Maracas Bay** is a long stretch of sand with a cove and a fishing village at one end. It's a local favorite, so it can get crowded on weekends. Parking sites are ample, and there's a snack bar and rest facilities.

A few miles up the north coast road is **Las Cuevas Bay,** a narrow, picturesque strip of sand fanned by palms. A stand offers tasty snacks, and vendors hawk fresh fruit across the road. It's less crowded here, and seemingly serene, although, like Maracas, the current can be treacherous. About 8 miles east, along the north coast road, is another narrow beach. **Blanchisseuse Bay** is palm-fringed and the most deserted of the lot. Facilities are nonexistent, but the beach is ideal for a romantic picnic.

The drive along the northeast coast toward Toco takes several hours but does reward the persistent traveler with gorgeous vistas and secluded beaches. **Balandra Bay,** sheltered by a rocky outcropping, is popular among bodysurfers. **Salibea Bay,** just past Galera Point, which juts toward Tobago, is a gentle beach with shallows and plenty of shade—perfect for swimming. Snack vendors abound in the vicinity. The road to **Manzanilla Beach** and **Cocos Bay** to the south is lined by stately coconut palms and the longest continuous stretch of beach in the country. Manzanilla has picnic facilities, and a postcard-pretty view of the Atlantic, though its water is occasionally muddied by the Orinoco River, which flows in from South America.

Tobago Traveling to Tobago without sampling the beaches is like touring the south of France without drinking the wine. So, starting from the town of Plymouth and gravitating—slowly—counterclockwise, we'll explore a dozen of the island's more memorable sand spots.

Great Courland Bay, near Fort Bennett, is a long stretch of clear, tranquil water, bordered on one end by **Turtle Beach,** so named for the turtles that lay their eggs here at night between April and May. (You can watch; the turtles don't seem to mind.) A short distance west, there's a side road that runs along **Stone Haven Bay,** a gorgeous beach that's across the street from Grafton Beach Resorts, a new luxury hotel complex.

Mt. Irvine Beach, across the street from the Mt. Irvine Beach Hotel, is an unremarkable setting that has the best surfing in July and August. It's also ideal for windsurfing in January and April. There are picnic tables surrounded by painted concrete pagodas and a snack bar.

Pigeon Point is the locale inevitably displayed on Tobago travel brochures. It's the only privately owned beach on the island, part of what was once a large coconut estate, and you must pay a token admission (about $1) to enter the grounds. The beach is lined with royal palms, and there's a food stand, gift shop, and paddleboats for rent. The waters are calm.

Store Bay, where boats depart for Buccoo Reef, is probably the most socially convivial setting in the area. Next to the bustling Crown Reef Hotel, the beach is little more than a small sandy cove between two rocky breakwaters. Farther west along Crown Point, **Sandy Beach** is abutted by several hotels, including the Tropikist, Crown Point, and Sandy Point Beach Club. You won't lack for amenities around here.

Just west of Scarborough, take Milford Road off the main highway to the shores of **Little Rocky Bay.** The beach is craggy and not much good for swimming, but it is quiet and offers a pleasing view of Tobago's capital across the water.

After driving through Scarborough, continue south on Bacolet Street 4 miles to **Bacolet Beach,** a dark-sand beach that was the setting for the film *Swiss Family Robinson*.

The road from Scarborough to Speyside has plenty of swimming sites of which **King's Bay Beach,** surrounded by steep green hills, is the most visually satisfying—the bay hooks around so severely that you feel as if you're swimming in a lake. It's easy to find because it's marked by a sign about halfway between Roxborough and Speyside.

Man of War Bay in Charlotteville is flanked by one of the prettiest fishing villages in the Caribbean. You can lounge on the sand and purchase the day's catch for your dinner. Farther west across the bay is **Lover's Beach,** so called because of its pink sand and because it can be reached only by boat. You can hire one of the locals to take you across.

Parlatuvier, on the north side of the island, is best approached via the road from Roxborough. The beach here is a classic Caribbean crescent, a scene peopled by villagers and local fishermen.

Exploring Trinidad

Numbers in the margin correspond with points of interest on the Trinidad map.

Port-of-Spain
❶
It is not really surprising that a sightseeing tour of Port-of-Spain begins at the port. (If you're planning to explore by foot, which will take two to four hours, start early in the day; by mid-afternoon Port-of-Spain can be hot.) Though it is no longer as frenetic as it was during the oil boom of the 1970s, **King's Wharf** entertains a steady parade of cruise and cargo ships, a reminder that the city started from this strategic harbor. Across Wrightson Road is **Independence Square,** which is not a square at all: It's a wide, dusty thoroughfare crammed with pedestrians, car traffic, taxi stands, and peddlers of everything from shoes to coconuts. Flanked by government buildings and the familiar towers of the Financial Complex (familiar because its facade also adorns one side of all TT dollar bills), the square is representative of this city's chaotic charm.

Near the east end of Wrightson Road stands the Roman Catholic **Cathedral of the Immaculate Conception,** built in 1832 under the aegis of an Anglican governor, Sir Ralph Woodford. Its treasures consist of a Florentine-marble altar, iron framework from England, and stained glass from Ireland.

Up Picton Road are **Fort Chacon** and **Fort Picton,** erected to ward off invaders by the Spanish and British regimes, respectively. The latter is a martello tower with a fine view of the gulf.

At the corner of Prince and Frederick streets, look across **Woodford Square** toward the magnificent **Red House,** a Renaissance designed building that takes up an entire city block. Trinidad's House of Parliament takes its name from a paint job done in anticipation of Queen Victoria's Diamond Jubilee in 1897. Woodford Square has served as the site of political meetings, speeches, public protests, and occasional violence. The original Red House, in fact, was burned to the ground in a 1903 riot. The present structure was built four years later. The chambers are open to the public.

The view of the south side of the square is framed by the Gothic spires of **Trinity,** the city's other cathedral, and by the impressive **public library** building. *Tel. 809/623–6142. Open weekdays 7–3.*

Continue north along Pembroke Street and note the odd mix of modern and colonial architecture, gingerbread and graceful estate houses, and stucco storefronts. Pembroke crosses Keate Street at **Memorial Park.** A short walk north leads to the greater green expanse of **Queen's Park,** more popularly called the **Savannah.**

Time Out
Buy a cool coconut drink—called "cold nut"—from any of the vendors operating out of flatbed trucks along the Savannah. For about 50¢, he'll lop off a green coconut with a deft swing of the machete and provide you with a straw. Sit under one of the park's shady trees and reflect on all the roads that brought you here.

Trinidad

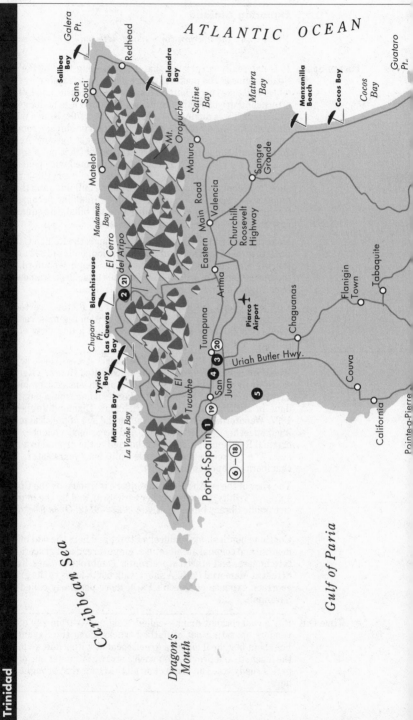

Caribbean Sea

ATLANTIC OCEAN

Galera Pt.

Salibea Bay *Galera Pt.*

Redhead

Sans Souci

Matelot

Balandra Bay

Saline Bay

Matura Bay

Madamas Bay

Mt. Oropuche

Matura

Manzanilla Beach **Cocos Bay**

Cocos Bay

Guataro Pt.

Sangre Grande

El Cerro del Aripo

Blanchisseuse

Eastern Main Road

② **㉑**

Valencia

Churchill Roosevelt Highway

Chupara Pt. **Las Cuevas Bay**

Arima

Flanigin Town

Tabaquite

Tyrico Bay

Tunapuna

Piarco Airport

Chaguanas

㉚

Uriah Butler Hwy.

③
④

San Juan

⑤

Couva

Maracas Bay

El Tucuche

⑲

①

Port-of-Spain

California

⑥ — ⑱

Pointe-à-Pierre

La Vache Bay

Dragon's Mouth

Gulf of Paria

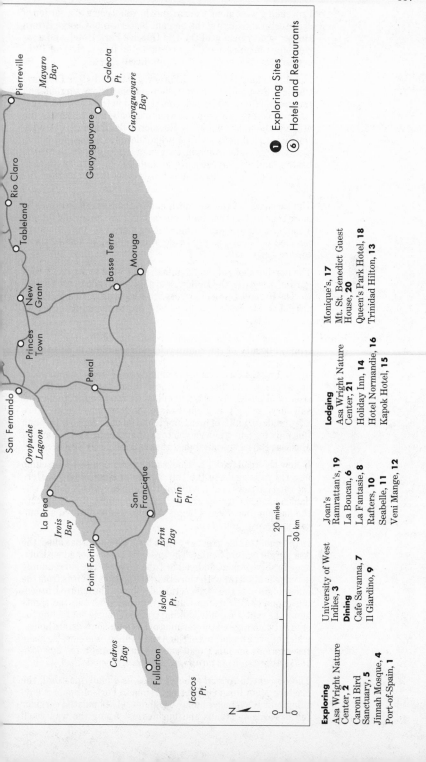

557

Proceeding west along the Savannah, you'll come to a garden of architectural delights: the elegant lantern-roof **George Brown House;** what remains of the **Old Queen's Park Hotel;** and a series of astonishing buildings constructed in a variety of 19th-century styles, known as the **Magnificent Seven.**

Notable among these are **Killarney,** patterned after Balmoral Castle in Scotland, with an Italian-marble gallery surrounding the ground floor; **Whitehall,** constructed in the style of a Venetian palace by a cacao-plantation magnate and currently the office of the prime minister; **Roomor,** a flamboyantly Baroque colonial-period house with a preponderance of towers, pinnacles, and wrought-iron trim that suggests an elaborate French pastry; and the **Queen's Royal College,** in German Renaissance style, with a prominent tower clock that chimes on the hour.

The **racetrack** at the southern end of the Savannah serves as more than just a venue for horse racing. It is the setting for music and costume competitions during Carnival, and, when not jammed with calypso performers, costumes, or horses, tends toward quietude.

The northern end of the Savannah is devoted to plants. A rock garden, known as the **Hollow,** and a fish pond add to the rusticity. The **Botanic Gardens,** across the street, date from 1820. The official residences of the president and prime minister are on these grounds.

Out on the Island The intensely urban atmosphere of Port-of-Spain belies the tropical beauty of the countryside surrounding it. It's there, but you will need a car, and six to eight hours, to find it. Begin by circling the Savannah—seemingly obligatory to get almost anywhere around here—to Saddle Road, the residential district of **Maraval.** After a few miles the road begins to narrow and curve sharply as it climbs into the Northern Range. Here are undulating hills of lush, junglelike foliage. An hour through this hilly terrain will lead you to the beaches at **Tyrico Bay** and **Maracas Bay;** a few miles past that is **Las Cuevas Beach.**

Follow the road past Las Cuevas for several miles, then climb into the hills again to the tiny village of **Blanchisseuse.** Here the road narrows again, winding through canyons of moist, verdant foliage and mossy grottoes. As you painstakingly execute the hairpin turns, you'll begin to think you've entered a tropical rain forest. You have.

In the midst of this greenery lies a bird-watcher's paradise, the ❷ **Asa Wright Nature Center.** The grounds are festooned with delicate orange orchids and yellow tube flowers. The surrounding acreage is atwitter with more than 100 species of birds from the hummingbird to the rare nocturnal oilbird. The oilbirds' breeding grounds in Dunston Cave are included among the sights along the center's guided hiking trails. If you're not feeling too energetic, lounge on the veranda of the handsome estate house, which offers a panorama of the Arima Valley. You can also make reservations for lunch (call one day in advance). *tel. 809/667–4655. Admission: $5 adults, $3 children. Open daily 9–5.*

The descent to **Arima,** about 7 miles, is equally pastoral; the Eastern Main Road connecting Arima to Port-of-Spain is anything but: It's a busy, bumpy, and densely populated corridor full of roadside stands and businesses. Along the way you'll

❸ pass the **University of West Indies** campus in Curepe and
❹ the majestic turrets and arches of the **Jinnah Mosque** in St. Joseph.

Proceed west from Arima along the Churchill-Roosevelt Highway, a limited-access freeway that runs parallel to the Eastern Main Road a few miles to the south. Both avenues cross the Uriah Butler Highway just outside Port-of-Spain in San Juan; a few miles south on Butler Highway, take the turnoff for the
❺ **Caroni Bird Sanctuary.** Across from the sanctuary's parking lot is a sleepy canal with several boats and guides for hire; the smaller boats are best.

The Caroni is a large swamp with mazelike waterways bordered by mangrove trees, some plumed with huge nests of termites. In the middle of the sanctuary are several islets that are home to Trinidad's national bird, the scarlet ibis. Just before sunset they arrive by the thousands, their richly colored feathers brilliant in the gathering dusk, and, as more flocks alight, they turn their little tufts of land into bright Christmas trees. It's not something you see every day. Bring a sweater and insect repellent for your return trip. The boat fee is usually about $6–$10. Advance reservations can be made with boat operators Winston Nanan (tel. 809/645–1305) or David Ramsahai (tel. 809/663–2207).

Exploring Tobago

Numbers in the margin correspond with points of interest on the Tobago map.

A driving tour of Tobago, from Scarborough to Charlotteville and back, can be done in about four hours.

❶ **Scarborough** is as pretty as a picture, and just about as alive. It is nestled around the aptly named **Rocky Bay,** and it gives the feeling that not much here has changed since the area was settled two centuries ago. This is its charm.

The road east from Scarborough soon narrows as it twists
❷ through **Mt. St. George,** a village that clings to a cliff high above the ocean. There's an overlook where you can eye the black-sand beach of **Fort Granby.** The sea dips in and out of view as you pass through a series of small settlements and the town of
❸ **Roxborough.** About an hour's drive will bring you to **King's Bay,** an attractive crescent-shape beach. Just before you reach the bay is a bridge with an unmarked turnoff that leads to a gravel parking lot; beyond that, a landscaped path leads to a waterfall with a rocky pool where you can refresh yourself. You may meet enterprising locals who'll offer to guide you to the top of the falls, a climb that you may find not worth the effort.

After King's Bay the road rises dramatically; just before it dips
❹ again there's a marked lookout with a vista of **Speyside,** a small fishing village.

Time Out **Jemma's Sea View Kitchen** (tel. 809/660–4066), a stand along the main road in Speyside, offers tasty West Indian lunches served on a picnic table by the ocean.

Past Speyside the road cuts across a ridge of mountains that separates the Atlantic side of Tobago from the Caribbean. On the far side is **Charlotteville,** a remote fishing community, albe-

Tobago

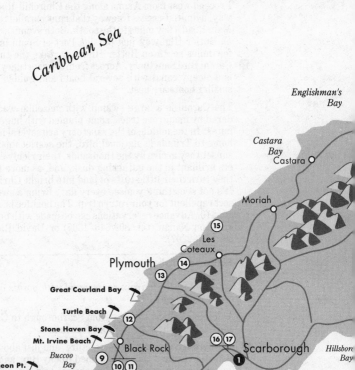

Caribbean Sea

Englishman's Bay

Castara Bay

Castara

Moriah

15

Les Coteaux

14

Plymouth

13

Great Courland Bay

Turtle Beach

12

Stone Haven Bay

Mt. Irvine Beach

Black Rock

9

16 **17**

Scarborough

Hillsboro Bay

Buccoo Bay

10 **11**

1

Pigeon Pt.

Little Rocky Bay

Rocky Bay

18

Bacolet Bay

Store Bay

7

Bacolet Beach

Sandy Beach

Crown Pt. Airport

8

Canaan

Columbus Pt.

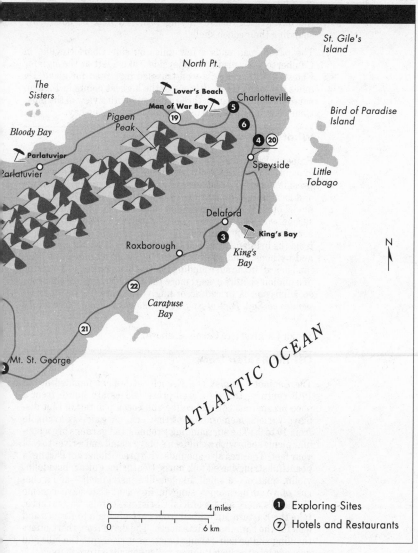

0 | 4 miles
0 | 6 km

1 Exploring Sites

7 Hotels and Restaurants

it the largest village on the island. Fishermen here announce the day's catch (usually flying fish, red fish, or bonito) by sounding their conch shells.

The paved road ends a few miles outside Charlotteville, in Camberton; Returning to Speyside, take a left at the sign for **Flagstaff Hill.** Follow a well-traveled dirt road for about 1½ miles to a radio tower. It's one of the highest points in Tobago, surrounded by ocean on three sides and with a view of the hills, Charlotteville, and Bird of Paradise Island in the bay.

What to Do and See with Children

Emperor Valley Zoo and the **Botanical Gardens** are a cultivated expanse of parkland just north of the Savannah, the site of the president's official residence. A meticulous lattice of walkways and local flora, the parkland was first laid out in 1820 and is a model of what a tropical garden should be. In the midst of this serene wonderland is the zoo, leisurely apportioned on eight acres and largely featuring birds and animals of the region— from the brilliantly plumed scarlet ibis to slithering anacondas and pythons; wild parrots breed in the area and can be seen (and heard) in the surrounding foliage. The zoo draws a quarter of a million visitors a year; more than half of them are children, so admission is priced accordingly—a mere TT$1. *80 Independance Sq., Port-of-Spain, tel. 809/625-2264. Open daily 9:30-6.*

Junior Carnival (*see* Carnival, above)

Off the Beaten Track

The Lopinot Complex is a French settlement founded in the 19th century; there's a well-preserved estate house from a once-prosperous colonial coffee and cocoa plantation that displays various memorabilia of that era. (A guide is available from 10 to 6.) The surrounding grounds and gardens are a popular picnic spot, with a children's playground and a river to cool your feet. The area also abounds with practitioners of Parang, a beautiful string-based folk music (featuring guitar, mandolin, violin, quatro— a small, ukelele-like instrument—and a chorus of vocal harmonies sung in Spanish) that have become Trinidad's more or less official Christmas carols. To get there, take the Eastern Main Road from Port-of-Spain to Arouca and look for the sign that points north. The drive from there offers thrilling and/or hair-raising twists as it rises into the hills and decends into the lush Lopinot valley–an adventure in itself.

Participant Sports

Bird-watching   Bird-watchers can fill up their books with notes on the variety of species to be found in Trinidad at the **Asa Wright Nature Center,** the **Caroni Bird Sanctuary** (*see* Exploring Trinidad, above), and at the **Pointe-à-Pierre Wild Foul Trust,** which is located within the confines of a petrochemical complex (42 Sandown Rd., Pt. Cumana, tel. 809/637-5145). In Tobago, naturalist **David Rooks** offers walks inland and trips to offshore bird colonies (tel. 809/639-9408).

Deep-Sea Fishing   The islands off the northwest coast of Trinidad offer excellent waters for deep-sea fishing; the ocean here was a favorite angling spot of Franklin D. Roosevelt. Members of the **Trinidad and Tobago Yacht Club** (Bayshore, tel. 809/637–4260) may be willing to arrange a tour. Contact Riad Shakeer. The Tourism office also recommends **Mr. Pouchet** (tel. 809/622–8974).

In Tobago, contact **Dillon Tours and Charters** (tel. 809/639–8765). Dillon's the most expensive, about $350 per day.

Golf There are nine golf courses in the country, the best of which are the **Mt. Irvine Golf Club** (tel. 809/639–8871) in Tobago and **Moka Golf Course** in Maraval (tel. 809/629–2314), just outside Port-of-Spain.

Scuba Diving Tobago draws scuba-diving aficionados from around the world. You can get information, supplies, and instruction at **Dive Tobago** (tel. 809/639–2266 or 809/639–3695), **Tobago Marine Sports Ltd.** (tel. 809/639–0291), **Tobago Scuba** (tel. 809/660–4327), and **Tobago Dive Experience** (Crown Point, tel. 809/639–0343; in Trinidad, tel. 809/639–1263). Also in Trinidad is **Scuba Shop Ltd.** (Mirabella, tel. 809/658–2183).

Snorkeling The best spots for snorkeling are on Tobago, of which **Buccoo Reef** is easily the most popular—perhaps a bit too popular. Over the years the reef has been damaged by the ceaseless boat traffic and by the thoughtless visitors who take pieces of coral for souvenirs. Even so, it's still a trip worth experiencing, particularly if you have children. For $8 (tickets are available in almost any hotel), you board a Plexiglas-bottom boat at either Store Bay or Buccoo Beach; the 15-minute trip to the reef, 2 miles offshore, is made only at low tide. Operators provide rubber shoes, masks, and snorkels but not fins, which are helpful in the moderate current.

There is also good snorkeling by the beach near the **Arnos Vale Hotel** and at **Blue Waters.**

Tennis The following hotels have tennis courts: **The Trinidad Hilton, Turtle Beach, Arnos Vale, Crown Point, Mt. Irvine,** and **Blue Waters Inn** (*see* Lodging, below); so does the **Trinidad Country Club** (tel. 809/622–3470).

Shopping

Thanks in large part to Carnival costumery, there's no shortage of fabric shops on the islands. The best bargains for Oriental and East Indian silks and cottons can be found downtown on **Frederick Street** and around **Independence Square.** Other good buys are such duty-free items as Angostura Bitters and Old Oak or Vat 19 rum, all widely available throughout the country.

Good Buys Upscale boutiques at the **Hilton** and in the **Long Circular Mall**
Boutiques make for more relaxed browsing. Luxury items are available at **Y. de Lima,** with branches on High Street and at the West Mall, and at **Stecher's** at the Hilton Hotel—on Lady Young Street, in the Long Circular Mall, and in the Cruise Ship Complex (#ID Wrightson Rd.), all in Port-of-Spain; and at the Crown Reef Hotel in Tobago. No real bargains, though.

Local Crafts The Tourism office can provide an extensive list of local artisans who specialize in everything from straw and cane work to miniature steel pans. **The Village** (Nook Ave. by the Hotel Normandie) has several shops that specialize in indigenous fashions, crafts, and a gallery of contemporary Trinidadian art.

Records For the best selection of calypso and soca music, check out
Rhyner's Record Shop (54 Prince St., 809/623–5673, and at the
Cruise Ship Complex) or **Metronome** (2 Madras St., 809/622–
4157), both in Port-of-Spain.

Dining

Trinidad Port-of-Spain doesn't lack for variety when it comes to
eateries. Two devaluations of the Trinidad dollar in recent
years have persuaded some of the more expensive dining establishments to trim their prices, resulting in more reasonable
rates as well as imaginative hybrids of European and Caribbean cuisines. In addition to the establishments listed below,
there is also no shortage of East Indian and Chinese restaurants and pizzerias (but don't expect New York–style pizza).

Trinidadians are particularly fond of *callaloo*, a soup or stew
of dasheen leaves (similar to spinach) and okra, flavored with
anything from pork to coconut, pureed and served at every
restaurant in the country. It's hard to believe anything this
green and swampy looking can taste so delicious. Other items
in a Trinidadian menu worth sampling are *coocoo*, a dumpling
of cornbread and okra; *roti*, a sandwich of East Indian origin,
on flat bread or in a pocket pita, usually filled with curried
chicken and potatoes; *pelau*, a rice-and-peas dish inspired by
Chinese cuisine; *tamarind ball*, a dessert made from the sweet-
sour tamarind; and *peanut shake*, a peanut butter–flavor milk
shake that really does taste better than it sounds.

No Trinidadian dining experience can be complete, of course,
without a rum punch with fresh fruit, and the legendary Angostura Bitters, made by the same company that produces the
excellent Old Oak rum. Carib beer and Stag are recommended
for washing down the spicier concoctions.

Tobago With few exceptions, the restaurants in Tobago are located in
hotels and guest houses; several of the large resort complexes
also feature some form of nightly entertainment. The food isn't
as eclectic as on Trinidad, generally favoring local styles, but in
terms of quality and service Tobagonian "home cooking" more
than holds its own.

The most highly recommended restaurants are indicated by a
star ★.

Category	Cost*
Expensive	over $25
Moderate	$15–$25
Inexpensive	under $15

*per person, excluding drinks, service, and sales tax (3%)

Trinidad **La Boucan.** This place has long been considered the best restaurant in town, in part because of its sophisticated decor. A
large mural of a social idyll in the Savannah dominates one wall
of a room. The restaurant strives for elegance: silver service,
uniformed waiters, candlelight, pink tablecloths, and the soft
tinkling of a grand piano. The chef has an imaginative touch
that extends to presenting some of his culinary creations in fantastic shapes. Specialties run from smoked duck breast to

Creole dishes and French crepes. The meals here tend toward good-but-not-really-gourmet, suggesting an Anglicized French restaurant. In a setting this civilized, you probably won't mind. *Trinidad Hilton, Lady Young Rd., Port-of-Spain, tel. 809/624–3211. Jackets recommended. Reservations recommended. AE, DC, MC, V. Expensive.*

★ **Cafe Savanna.** Caribbean style, with bare wood walls and Sade on the sound system, this cozy den consistently serves the best fare on the island. The menu specializes in Trinidadian dishes with a distinctive flair: coconut curried shrimp and fillet of grouper marinated in fresh herbs. The callaloo soup here sets the standard for other island delicacies. The three-course lunch special for about $9 is a bargain. *Kapok Hotel, 16–18 Cotton Hill, Port-of-Spain, tel. 809/622–6441. AE, DC, MC, V. Expensive.*

La Fantasie. A pastel dining room with high ceilings seeks to mix postmodern design with a sense of fun. The menu calls itself Cuisine Créole Nouvelle and tends toward Trinidadian dishes of fresh fish and poultry, seasoned and presented in the French manner. Customers are invited to name dishes. The selections change often; if you happen to dine here on a night when fresh homemade ice cream is offered, you're in luck. *Normandie Hotel, 10 Nook Ave., St. Ann's, Port-of-Spain, tel. 809/624–1181. AE, DC, MC, V. Expensive.*

Il Giardino. This restaurant is run by an Italian chef in a setting that resembles a greenhouse; potted plants of all varieties fill display shelves and trellises support orchids. Chef Luciano holds forth in the kitchen, creating pasta specialties to the sounds of opera. *6 Nook Ave., St. Ann's, Port-of-Spain, tel. 809/624–1459. AE, DC, MC, V. Moderate.*

Rafters. Behind a stone facade with green rafters is a pub that has become an urban institution. Once it was a rum shop; currently under the proprietorship of Paul Mowser, it's a bar and a restaurant. The pub is the center of activity. In late afternoons the place begins to swell with Port-of-Spainers ordering from the tasty selection of burgers and barbecue and generally loosening up. On Fridays the place is packed; a more convivial introduction to the city would be difficult to replicate. *6A Warner St., Port-of-Spain, tel. 809/628–9258. AE, DC, MC, V. Moderate.*

Seabelle. This restaurant is hard to find—there's no sign or street number. The entrance looks like the door to a private home—which is part of its charm. The ambience is beatnik with 1950s jazz on the stereo, a pool in the back, and a darkened bar where time almost stands still. The accent is on seafood. It has only seven tables so you must call for reservations—and directions. *27 Mucurapo Rd., St. James, Port-of-Spain, tel. 809/622–3594. No credit cards. Moderate.*

★ **Veni Mange.** The best lunches in town are served inside this small stucco house. Credit Allyson Hennessy, a Cordon Bleu-trained cook who has become a celebrity of sorts because of a TV talk show she hosts, and her sister/partner Rosemary Hezekiah. The cuisine here is Creole. It is open for lunch only, unfortunately, and it is often crowded, especially on Fridays when no one wants to leave. *13 Lucknow St., St. James, Port-of-Spain, no phone. No credit cards. No dinner. Moderate.*

Joan Ramrattan's. Although it looks like a roadside bar there's delicious home cooking inside, courtesy of the proprietress. A good place to waft the flavors of city living, it is well off the tourist beat. *164 Eastern Main Rd., corner of Hammersmith*

St., Port-of-Spain, tel. 809/623–0168. No credit cards. No Dinner. Inexpensive.

Tobago

★ **Blue Crab.** Perched on a wide porch above a busy corner of downtown Scarborough, this is the spot for lunch. Best bets here are the fresh kingfish or flying fish with callaloo and vegetables, prepared with élan by cook Ken Sardinha. While nominally closed for dinner, the proprietors will open the restaurant and serve a supper upon the request of even one couple. *Corner of Main and Fort Sts., Scarborough, tel. 809/639–2737. No credit cards. Moderate.*

Cocrico Inn. A café with a bar against one wall, the Cocrico offers Southern-style home cooking. The chefs frequently use fresh fruits and vegetables grown in the neighborhood. There is nothing fancy here, just warm and delicious food. *Corner of North and Commissioner Sts., Plymouth, tel. 809/639–2691. AE, V. Moderate.*

★ **Papillon.** Named after one of the proprietor's favorite books, this restaurant is a homey room with an adjoining patio. The menu is the most varied on the island, with such unusual items as banana-vichyssoise soup. There's also an astute selection of wines. *Bucco Bay Rd., Mt. Irvine, tel. 809/639–0275. AE, DC, MC, V. Moderate.*

The Old Donkey Cart House. The name is something of a curiosity, since this attractive restaurant is set in and around a green and white colonial house, about a 2-mile drive south of Scarborough. There's an outdoor dining in a garden with twinkling lights. The cuisine is a mélange of German and Caribbean delights, including a cheese board, an extensive selection of imported wines, and rich desserts. *Bacolet St., Scarborough, tel. 809/639–3551. No credit cards. Moderate.*

Sugar Mill Restaurant. This restaurant is housed in a converted 18th-century mill with walls constructed from sea coral; a conical, shingle roof descends like an enormous hat over an expansive outdoor patio. The prix fixe dinner is usually a choice of grilled meats or the catch of the day, expertly prepared, with extras including a tasty pâté. Dining is by candlelight, sometimes to the accompaniment of a steel band, while the refreshing Caribbean breeze wafts in. *Mt. Irvine Bay Hotel, tel. 809/639–8871. AE, DC, MC, V. Moderate.*

Lodging

On Trinidad most lodging establishments are located within the vicinity of Port-of-Spain, far from any beach. On Tobago, it's the opposite; every establishment listed here, with one exception, is either on or within walking distance of the ocean. Carnival week is one of two times in the year (the other is Christmas) you should book reservations far in advance; expect to pay twice the price charged during the rest of the year.

Most places do offer breakfast and dinner for an additional flat rate (MAP), but on the whole these offer less variety than you'll get if you strike out for meals on your own. If you're lodging on the east side of Tobago, however, MAP is almost essential because of the dearth of restaurants.

The most highly recommended lodgings are indicated by a star ★.

Category	Cost*
Very Expensive	over $150
Expensive	$90–$150
Moderate	$55–$90
Inexpensive	under $55

All prices are for a standard double room for 2, excluding 3% tax and a 10% service charge.

Trinidad
Hotels
★

Trinidad Hilton. Perched over Port-of-Spain, the Hilton radiates an air of luxury. Each room either has a balcony, which opens to a fine view and the distant murmur of the city below, or overlooks the equally inviting Olympic-size pool, shaded by trees harboring brightly crested cornbirds. This is easily Port-of-Spain's most elegant hotel, with prices to match. It frequently bustles with conventioneers, which may be its only drawback. The good news is that it's usually available for last-minute Carnival bookings. The Aviary bar serves the creamiest drinks in town. *Lady Young Rd., Box 442, Port-of-Spain, tel. 809/624–3211. 442 rooms. Facilities: 2 restaurants, bar, conference rooms, satellite TV, pool, health club, tennis courts, drugstore, gift shops, car rental, taxi service. AE, DC, MC, V. Expensive.*

Holiday Inn. This hotel is located at the port and close to Independence Square, which affords lodgers a pastel view of the old town and of ships idling in the Gulf of Paria. There's not a whole lot to do within walking distance, and traffic during rush hour is not a pretty sight. (An exception is during Carnival; then you're in the middle of all the festivities.) The hotel's rooftop restaurant, **La Ronde,** has recently reopened; it's a revolving bistro that offers a striking panorama of the city at night and provides the only charm on the premises. *Wrightson Rd., Box 1017, Port-of-Spain, tel. 809/625–3361. 235 rooms. Facilities: satellite TV, pool, health spa, conference rooms, beauty salon, taxi service. AE, DC, MC, V. Expensive.*

Asa Wright Nature Center. Set in a lush rain forest about 90 minutes east of Port-of-Spain, this handsome lodge, constructed in 1908 by a tycoon for his young bride, attracts international legions of bird-watchers and nature photographers. There are impressive views of the verdant Arima Valley and the Northern Range from the veranda, where tea is served each afternoon. The rooms are uncomplicated and comfortably furnished; some of the beds have hand-carved frames cut from trees from the surrounding forest, which is now protected by a private trust. Three meals a day and an evening rum punch are included in the rates. Reservations at least six months in advance are recommended. (For more information about the center, *see* Exploring, above.) *Bag 10, Port-of-Spain; write: Caligo Ventures, Box 21, Armonk, NY 10504, tel. 914/273–6333. No credit cards. Moderate.*

★ **Hotel Normandie.** Built in the 1930s by French Creoles on the ruins of an old coconut plantation, the Normandie has touches of Spanish, English-colonial, and even postmodern architecture, giving the place an agreeably artsy patina. Fittingly, it has become the linchpin of a complex in St. Ann's that includes a gallery, a café, and an array of shops. *10 Nook Ave., St. Ann's Village, Port-of-Spain, tel. 809/624–1181. 61 rooms. Facilities:*

restaurant and bar, pool, meeting rooms, gallery, café, shops, car rental, taxi service. AE, DC, MC, V. Moderate.

★ **Kapok Hotel.** This hotel has been run by the Chan family for years and all but gleams with cheerful efficiency. It's a great location, just off the north end of the park, near the zoo and Presidential Palace, and away from the worst traffic. Its two distinctive restaurants, the *Savanna* and *Tiki Village*, are among the best in town. Rooms are comfortably furnished in a wicker motif and command a pleasing view on the park side. The Kapok is a good bargain for your buck. *16–18 Cotton Hill, Port-of-Spain, tel. 809/622–6441. 71 rooms. Facilities: TV, pool, 2 restaurants, taxi service. AE, DC, MC, V. Moderate.*

★ **Monique's.** This homey lodging is a nest of congeniality only minutes from downtown. Mike and Monique Charbonne have been running their home as a guest house for 10 years. They have recently expanded the place to 12 rooms, one specifically designed for the disabled. All rooms have private baths. Their philosophy is to make their house your own, and it's not unusual for hosts and lodgers to be found fraternizing in the living room. Meals are available on request, and Mike will occasionally organize a picnic to the couple's 100-acre plantation near Blanchisseuse. *114 Saddle Rd., Maraval, tel. 809/628–3334. 12 rooms. Facilities: common-room area with TV. AE. Inexpensive.*

Mt. St. Benedict Guest House. A country-style guest house that feels like a retreat, this nonsectarian lodging is situated on a hill overlooking the valley about 10 miles east of Port-of-Spain. The flat fee of $45 a day per person includes three meals, mostly local cuisine. Rooms are tidy, with shared baths. There is a steady breeze along the hillside that negates the need for air-conditioning. A good getaway while visiting the city, but a car is necessary. *Tunapuna, tel. 809/662–4084. 20 rooms. Facilities: TV room. AE, DC, MC, V. Inexpensive.*

Queen's Park Hotel. Constructed in 1895 and once the belle of Port-of-Spain, what beauty remains here is awaiting renovation; the section of the hotel that is open was built in the 1950s, and suggests a cross between art deco and a housing project. The rooms are cozy and include refrigerators, though the halls feel more like a dormitory; a few rooms have balconies that overlook the southern end of the Savanna. The service here is gracious and attentive, and the location is ideal. *5 Queen's Park W, Port-of-Spain, tel. 809/625–1061. 74 rooms. Facilities: pool, open-air dining, lounge. AE, DC, MC, V. Inexpensive.*

Bed-and-Breakfasts The number of private homes in Trinidad offering bed-and-breakfast accommodations is growing each year. For a complete listing of homes in Trinidad approved for guest accommodation, contact the **Trinidad and Tobago Bed and Breakfast Association** (Box 3231, Diego Martin, or Park Lane Court, Amethyst Dr., El Dorado, Tunapuna, *tel. 809/663–5265*).

Tobago **Arnos Vale Hotel.** The hotel is an attractive hideaway that
Hotels crosses Tobago horticulture with Mediterranean design. White stucco cottages are set on a hill that descends through a series of winding paths to a secluded beach, a newly constructed pool, and a handy bar. The hilltop restaurant, with iron lattice tables, a chandelier, and a hand-painted piano, leads to a crescent-shape patio that offers a sweeping view of the sea. The grounds are getting a face-lift, which will include a disco and several new rooms. *Arnos Vale, tel. 809/639–2881; for*

reservations contact: M.G. Benati, Vacanze SRL, Via Rastrelli-2, 20122 Milan, tel. 02–85391. 32 rooms. Facilities: pool, bar, restaurant, tennis, beach, snorkeling. AE, DC, MC, V. Expensive.

Grafton Beach Resorts. This new luxury complex overlooks one of the finest—formerly secluded—beaches on the island. Most rooms have king-size or double beds and a minibar. It also boasts a shopping arcade on the premises and a bird sanctuary nearby—pure getaway stuff. *Black Rock, Tobago. tel. 809/639 –0191 or 9944–6, fax 809/639–0030. 120 rooms. Facilities: on the beach, pool and beach bar, night lounge, satellite TV, gym with sauna. AE, V. Expensive.*

★ **Mt. Irvine Bay Hotel.** Once the site of a 17th-century sugar plantation, the mill has been deftly recast as a restaurant. There's open-air dining on the surrounding patio, which overlooks a magnificent pool, a cabana bar, and the quiet water of the Caribbean. The balcony rooms of this rambling, two-story complex afford the same view as the restaurant with broader horizons, or else survey the adjacent Mt. Irvine golf course, considered among the finest in the world. The Mt. Irvine gently pampers guests with a panache that puts its own brochures to shame. Rates are steep by Tobago standards. Candlelight suppers to the sounds of a steel band, however, soon put the cost in context. *Mt. Irvine Bay, Box 222, Tobago, tel. 809/639– 8871. 64 rooms, 42 cottages. Facilities: pool, 2 bars, 2 restaurants (1 formal), tennis courts, convention facilities, beach across the street, beauty parlor, shops, taxi service. AE, DC, MC, V. Expensive.*

Turtle Beach Hotel. The ranch-style lobby of this hotel leads to a seemingly endless bar, which in turn empties onto a wide beach peppered with thatch cabanas. The rooms have easy access to the beach. The restaurant is expanding its menu, which boasts a reputable Creole buffet on Sundays. There are two bars (one on the beach) and a tiny pool that is a good place from which to watch the sun set. *Great Courland Bay, tel. 809/639– 2851; write: Box 201, Scarborough, Tobago. 125 rooms. Facilities: restaurant, 2 bars, beach, pool, tennis court, water-sports center, bike rentals, gift shop. AE, DC, MC, V. Expensive.*

★ **Blue Waters Inn.** It's easy to miss the sign for this gem of a hotel nestled on the shore of Batteaux Bay; the entrance road appears to drop over a cliff. It's all part of the charm of this rustic retreat, where birds fly through a dining room ornamented with driftwood. A variety of beamed rooms and cabins include new apartments with kitchenettes. The beach here is free of currents; nature walks are popular along the 48 acres of grounds. Anyone craving peace and quiet will welcome the news that the place doesn't have a pool, air-conditioning, TV, or phone. The home cooking is dependably delicious. *Batteaux Bay, Speyside, Tobago, tel. 809/660–4341. 20 rooms. Facilities: tennis, beach, dive instruction. No credit cards or personal checks. Moderate.*

Cocrico Inn. Named after the national bird of Tobago, this comfortable inn is set on a quiet side street in the village of Plymouth, a short walk from a local bird sanctuary as well as a beach. The accent here is on native culture; the café-style restaurant prepares Tobagonian dishes using homegrown fruits and vegetables (including a delicious guava punch). *North and Commissioner Sts., Box 287, Plymouth, Tobago, tel. 809/639–2961. 16 rooms. Facilities: restaurant, bar, pool. AE, V. Moderate.*

★ **Kariwak Village.** The resort's motif attempts to recapture the spirit of the Carib and Arawak Indians who originally lived here, without diminishing creature comforts. There's a suitably tropical bar, highly touted Caribbean cooking, and open-air dining. The gift shop features a thoughtful selection of local crafts and books; there are often shows on the premises by Tobago artists. Nine cabanas, which resemble equatorial igloos, have been divided into 18 cozy apartments, all of which look onto the pool. *Crown Point, tel. 809/639–8545; write: Box 27, Scarborough, Tobago. 18 rooms. Facilities: shuttle service to beach, pool, restaurant, bar, scooter rentals. AE, V. Moderate.*

Man O' War Bay Cottages. Seven separate apartments are set along the sleepy shoreline of an overgrown cacao plantation. The clientele runs to scientists and travelers who want to escape the rigors of urban living. The local amenities include fishermen who will take you out fishing for a fee and nature guides. Watch for the flocks of wild parrots that fly by in the late afternoon. *Charlotteville, tel. 809/639–4327. 7 cottages with kitchens. Facilities: beach, snorkeling and fishing nearby, access to Marine Institue lab. No credit cards. Moderate.*

Richmond Great House. This is a restored 19th-century plantation house with high, beamed ceilings on a 1,500-acre citrus estate. Common rooms have a great view, but what holds your gaze are the African art sculptures and furniture collected by the professor who owns the place. You can also stop by for lunch; just call in the morning. *Belle Garden, Tobago. tel. 809/660–4467. 5 rooms. Facilities: 10-minute drive to beach, pool, TV, and music. No credit cards. Moderate.*

Della Mira Guest House. Proprietor Neville Miranda built this establishment in 1954, and he's still running the place. The restaurant off the main lobby has a marvelous view of Rocky Bay. A walk lined with mango and banana trees leads to *La Tropicale,* a dance club along the water that's very romantic; unfortunately, it's rarely open. The bedrooms are clean but far from fancy. The beach is a short drive from the hotel. The Della Mira is very economical, and Mr. Miranda is a warm and ingratiating host. *Box 203, Scarborough, Tobago, tel. 809/639–2531. 14 rooms. Facilities: restaurant, lounge, pool, nightclub, beauty salon. No private phones or TVs. No credit cards. Inexpensive.*

The Golden Thistle Hotel. The look here is that of a respectable 1950s motel. There's a surprisingly huge auditorium in the back that's a popular site with locals for weekend entertainment. Several of the rooms include kitchenettes, making this spot particularly attractive to travelers on a budget. Proprietor Clyde St. Louis is attentive to all requests, even driving elderly guests to the beach at nearby Pidgeon Point (it's a 10-minute walk). It's that kind of place. *Store Bay Rd., Crown Point, Tobago, tel. 809/639–8521. Facilities: pool, bar, TV room, restaurant, kitchenette. No credit cards. Inexpensive.*

The Arts and Nightlife

Trinidad Trinidadian culture doesn't end with music, but it definitely begins here. While both calypso and steel bands are best displayed during Carnival, the steel bands play at clubs, dances, and fetes throughout the year. There's no lack of nightlife in Port-of-Spain.

Mas Camp Pub (corner of Ariapata and French Sts., Woodbrook, tel. 809/627–8449) is Port-of-Spain's most comfortable and dependable night spot. There are tables, a bar, an ample stage in one room, and an open-air patio with more tables and a bar with a TV. There's a kitchen if you're hungry and **Hush,** which makes delicious fruit-flavor ice cream, is right next door.

Cricket Wicket (149 Tragarete Rd., tel. 809/622–1808), a popular watering hole with a cupola-shape bar in the center, is a fine place to hear top bands, dance, or just sit and enjoy the nocturnal scenery.

In the late afternoons the locals come to **Rafters** (6A Warner St., tel. 809/628–9258) to wind down and wind up.

Tobago Nightlife on Tobago is generally confined to hotel-sponsored entertainment, which runs the gamut from steel band performances to limbo dancers. In addition, **Kariwak Village** features a mélange of calypso and jazz. There are nightclubs at the **Della Mira Guest House** in Scarborough and at the **Golden Thistle Guest House** in Crown Point, both of which feature dancing on weekends and occasional live performances, usually during Carnival season.

27 Turks and Caicos Islands

by Honey Naylor

The Turks and Caicos Islands are relatively unknown except to collectors of beautiful beaches and scuba divers, who religiously return to these waters year after year.

First settled by the English more than 200 years ago, the British Crown Colony of Turks and Caicos (population 8,000) is renowned in two respects: Its booming banking and insurance institutions lure investors from the United States and elsewhere, and its offshore reef formation entices divers to a world of colorful marine life surrounding its 40 islands, only eight of which are inhabited.

The Turks and Caicos are two groups of islands in an archipelago lying 575 miles southeast of Miami and about 90 miles north of Haiti. Some 8,000 people live on the eight large islands and over 40 small cays (pronounced "keys"), which have a total land mass of 193 square miles. The Turks Islands include Grand Turk, which is the capital and seat of government, and Salt Cay, with a population of about 400. According to local legend these islands were named by early settlers who thought the scarlet blossoms on the local cactus resembled the Turkish fez.

Some 22 miles west of Grand Turk, across the 7,000-foot-deep Turks Island Passage, is the Caicos group, which includes South, East, West, Middle, and North Caicos, and Providenciales. South Caicos, Middle Caicos, North Caicos, and Providenciales (nicknamed Provo) are the only inhabited islands in this group; Pine Cay and Parrot Cay are the only inhabited cays. "Caicos" is derived from *cayos*, the Spanish word for cay.

In the years following Ponce de León's landing in 1515, a band of pirates also established communities in the archipelago. Around 1678, Bermudians, lured by the wealth of salt in these islands, began raking salt from the flats and returning to Bermuda to sell their crop. Despite French and Spanish attacks and pirate raids, the Bermudians persisted and established a trade that became the bedrock of the Bermudian economy. In 1766, Andrew Symmers settled here to hold the islands for England. Later, Loyalists from Georgia obtained land grants in the Caicos Islands, imported slaves, and continued the lifestyle of the pre–Civil War American South.

With an eye toward tourism dollars to create jobs and increase the standard of living, the government has devised a long-term development plan to improve the Turks and Caicos' visibility in the Caribbean tourism market. Providenciales, in particular, is slated not only for tourism development, but also for development of banking, registration of business companies, and offshore insurance.

Before You Go

Tourist Information Contact the **Turks and Caicos Islands** (c/o Medhurst & Assoc., Inc., 271 Main St., Northport, NY 11768, tel. 516/261–7474 or 212/936–0050). You can also reach the **Turks and Caicos Tourist Board** on Grand Turk toll-free at 800/441–4419. They can provide more complete and up-to-date information. **The Caribbean Tourist Organization** (20 E. 46th St., New York, NY 10017, tel. 212/682–0435) is another reliable source of information.

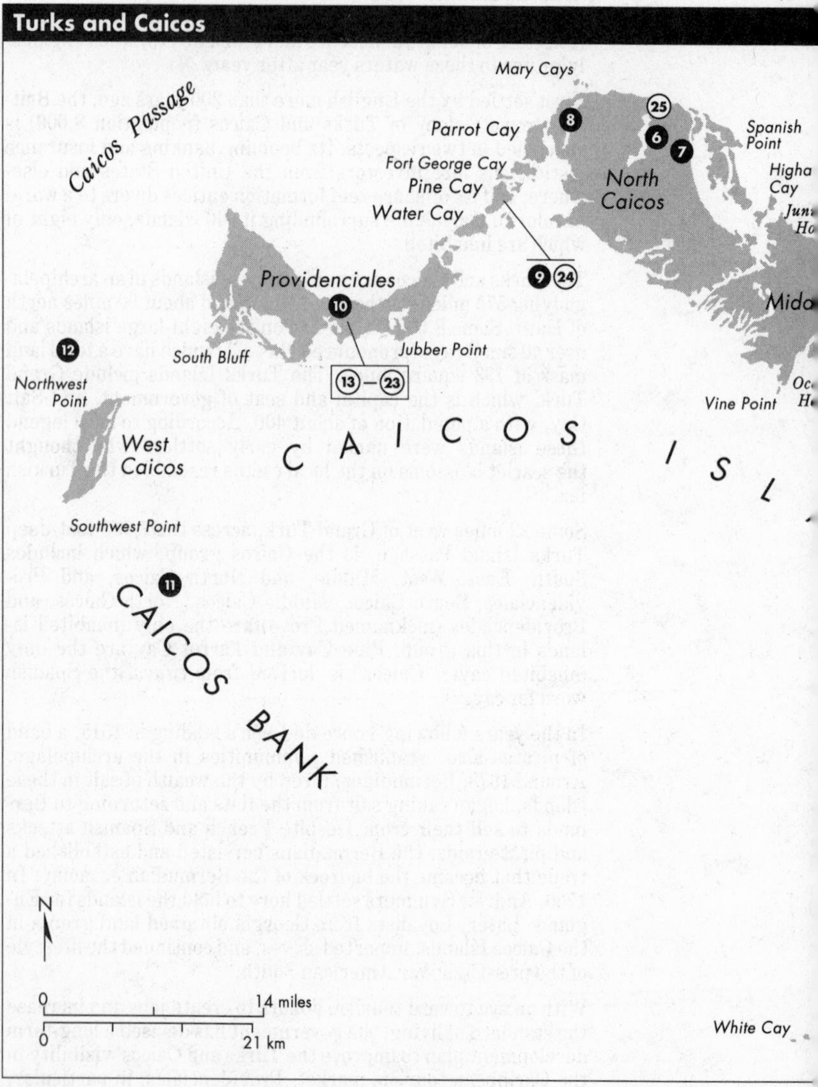

Turks and Caicos

Mary Cays

Caicos Passage

Parrot Cay

⑧

㉕

⑥ ⑦

Spanish
Point

Fort George Cay
Pine Cay

North
Caicos

Higha
Cay

Jun
Ho

Water Cay

⑨ ㉔

Providenciales

⑩

Mida

⑫

South Bluff

Jubber Point

⑬—㉓

Northwest
Point

Ocs
Ho

West
Caicos

Vine Point

C A I C O S   I S L

Southwest Point

⑪

C A I C O S   B A N K

N

0   14 miles

0   21 km

White Cay

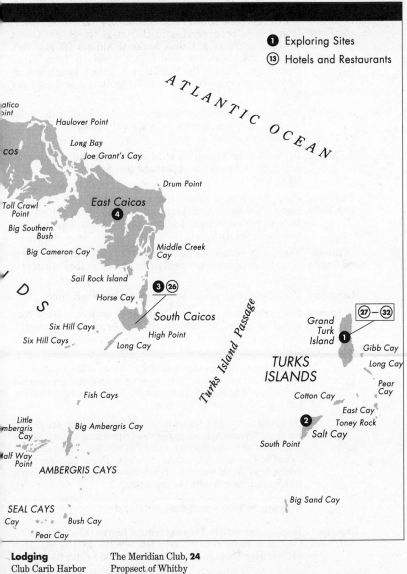

● Exploring Sites

⑬ Hotels and Restaurants

ATLANTIC OCEAN

atico point

Haulover Point

Long Bay

Joe Grant's Cay

cos

Drum Point

Toll Crawl Point

East Caicos ④

Big Southern Bush

Middle Creek Cay

Big Cameron Cay

Sail Rock Island

③ ㉖

Horse Cay

DS

South Caicos

Turks Island Passage

Grand Turk Island ❶

㉗—㉜

Six Hill Cays

High Point

Gibb Cay

Six Hill Cays

Long Cay

Long Cay

TURKS ISLANDS

Pear Cay

Fish Cays

Cotton Cay

East Cay

Little mbergris Cay

Big Ambergris Cay

Toney Rock

❷ Salt Cay

alf Way Point

South Point

AMBERGRIS CAYS

SEAL CAYS

Big Sand Cay

Cay

Bush Cay

Pear Cay

Lodging

Club Carib Harbor Hotel, **26**

Club Med Turkoise, **19**

Erebus Inn, **15**

Evan's Inn, **31**

Hotel Kittina, **30**

Island Princess, **18**

Island Reef, **27**

Mariner's Hotel, **20**

The Meridian Club, **24**

Propsect of Whitby Hotel, **25**

Salt Raker Inn, **29**

Third Turtle Inn, **21**

Treasure Beach Villas, **22**

Turtle Cove Yacht and Tennis Resort, **23**

Arriving and Departing **By Plane**	**Pan Am** (tel. 800/221–1111) has several weekly flights from Miami to Provo and Grand Turk. **Bahamasair** (tel. 809/327–8451) offers turbo-prop service from Nassau to South Caicos weekly. The **Turks & Caicos National Airlines** (TCNA) (tel. 809/946–2082) makes several flights weekly to Grand Turk from Puerto Plata in the Dominican Republic. Interisland air service is provided by TCNA on a regularly scheduled daily basis.
From the Airport	Taxis are available at the airports; expect to share a ride. Rates are fixed. A typical fare from the airport to the Island Reef hotel might be around $5.
By Boat	Because of the superb diving, two live-aboard dive boats call regularly. Contact the *Aquanaut* (c/o See & Sea, tel. 800/DIV–XPRT).
Passports and Visas	U.S. citizens need some proof of citizenship such as a voter registration card, birth certificate, or passport. British subjects require a current passport. All visitors must have an ongoing or return ticket.
Customs and Duties	There is no restriction on the import of cameras, film, sports equipment, or other personal items so long as they are not for resale.
Language	The official language of the Turks and Caicos is English.
Precautions	Petty crime does occur here, and you're advised to leave your valuables in the hotel safe-deposit box. Bring along a can of insect repellent. Deer and sand flies are ubiquitous and sadistic critters.

If you plan to explore the uninhabited island of West Caicos, be advised that the interior is overgrown with dense shrubs that include manchineel, which has a milky, poisonous sap that can cause painful, scarring blisters.

On Grand Turk, Salt Cay, and South Caicos, signs are posted reading, "Please help us conserve our precious water." Those islands have no freshwater supply other than rainwater collected in cisterns, and rainfall is scant. Drink only from the decanter of fresh water your hotel provides, and avoid even rinsing your mouth with the tap water.

Staying in Turks and Caicos Islands

Important Addresses	**Tourist Information:** The **Government Tourist Office** (Front St., Cockburn Town, Grand Turk, tel. 809/946–2321 or 800/441–4419) is open Monday–Thursday 8–4:30 and Friday 8–4.
Emergencies	**Police:** Grand Turk, tel. 809/946–2299. Providenciales, tel. 809/946–4259. South Caicos, tel. 809/946–3299.
	Hospitals: There is a 24-hour emergency room at **Grand Turk Hospital** (Hospital Rd., tel. 809/946–2333) and the **Providenciales Health-Medical Center** (Leeward Hwy. and Airport Rd., tel. 809/946–4201).
	Pharmacies: Prescriptions can be filled at the **Government Clinic** (Grand Turk Hospital, tel. 809/946–2040) and in Provo, at the **Providenciales Health-Medical Center** (Leeward Hwy. and Airport Rd., tel. 809/946–4201).
Currency	The unit of currency is U.S. dollars.

Taxes and Service Charges	Hotels collect a 7% government tax. The departure tax is $10. Hotels add a 10% service charge to your bill. In restaurants, a tip of 10%–15% is appropriate. Taxi drivers expect a 10% tip.
Guided Tours	A **taxi** tour of any one of the islands costs $20 an hour. The drivers are friendly and know everything and everybody. **Executive Tours** (tel. 809/946–4524) offers a variety of bus and small-plane tours. A bus tour takes in all of Provo, stopping off for drinks at Le Deck and at the Seven Dwarfs at Turtle Cove Marina. Another tour is of the conch farm. The Flying Pirates airlift you to Middle Caicos, the largest of the islands, for a visit to its mysterious caves. They'll put you in a boat and take you to Parrot Cay, and in a donkey cart to tour one of the smaller isles. If you want to island-hop on your own schedule, air charters are available through **Charles Air Service** (tel. 809/946–4352), **Blue Hills Aviation** (tel. 809/946–4226), **Flamingo Air Services** (tel. 809/946–2109), and **Turks & Caicos National Airlines** (tel. 809/946–2606).
Getting Around *Taxis*	Taxis are unmetered, and rates, posted in the taxis, are regulated by the government.
Planes	Daily hops to all of the inhabited islands are via **Turks & Caicos National Airlines'** (tel. 809/946–2606) five-seaters. Round-trip airfare from Grand Turk costs from $20 to $90.
Rental Cars	**Hertz** has outlets on Grand Turk at the **Island Reef Hotel** (tel. 809/946–2055) and on Provo in **BCP Plaza** (tel. 809/946–4475). Local rental agencies on Provo are **Pride** (tel. 809/946–4325) and **Provo** (tel. 809/946–4404). Rates average $25–$35 per day. To rent cars on South Caicos, check with your hotel manager for rates and information.
Scooters	You can scoot around Provo by contacting **Holiday Scooter Rentals** (tel. 809/946–4422) or **Scooter** (tel. 809/946–4684.)
Telephones and Mail	You can call the islands direct from the United States by dialing 809 and the number, but the volume of commercial activity in the business capital of Grand Turk often creates lengthy delays during weekday office hours. International credit card calls can be made from the **Cable and Wireless (WI) Ltd.** exchange on Front Street, Cockburn Town, Grand Turk.
	Postal rates for letters to the United States, Bahamas, and Caribbean are 25¢ per half ounce; postcards 15¢; letters to the United Kingdom and Europe, 40¢ per half ounce; postcards, 20¢; letters to Canada, Puerto Rico, and South America, 30¢; postcards, 15¢.
Opening and Closing Times	Most offices are open weekdays from 8 or 8:30 till 4 or 4:30. Banks are open Monday, Tuesday, Thursday, and Friday 8:30–noon and 2–4:30.

Beaches

There are more than 230 miles of beaches in the Turks and Caicos Islands, ranging from secluded coves to mile-long stretches. Most beaches are soft coralline sand. Tiny uninhabited cays offer complete isolation for nude sunbathing and skinny-dipping. Many are accessible only by boat.

Big Ambergris Cay, an uninhabited cay about 14 miles beyond the **Fish Cays,** has a magnificent beach at Long Bay.

East Caicos, an uninhabited island accessible only by boat, boasts a magnificent 17-mile beach.

Governor's Beach is a long white strip on the west coast of **Grand Turk.** Hotel Kittina/Omega Divers and the Salt Raker Inn/Blue Waters Divers are located on this beach.

The entire island of **North Caicos** is bordered by great beaches for swimming, scuba diving, snorkeling, and fishing.

Pine Cay, an upscale retreat, has a 2½-mile strip of beach—the most beautiful in the archipelago.

A fine white-sand beach stretches 12 miles along the northeast coast of **Providenciales.** Other splendid beaches are at **Sapodilla Bay,** and rounding the tip of the northwest point of the island.

There are superb beaches on the north coast of **Salt Cay,** as well as at **Big Sand Cay** 7 miles to the south.

The north end of **South Caicos** is only a few hundred yards wide and is fringed with fine white sand.

Exploring Turks and Caicos Islands

Numbers in the margin correspond to points of interest on the Turks and Caicos Islands map.

Grand Turk Chickens skitter across the road, horses and cattle wander around as if they owned the place, and the occasional donkey cart clatters by, carrying a load of water or freight. Front Street, the main drag, lazes along the western side of the island **❶** and eases through **Cockburn Town,** the colony's capital and seat of government. Buildings in the capital reflect the 19th-century Bermudian style of architecture, and the narrow streets are lined with low stone walls and old street lamps, now powered by electricity.

Time Out The **Pepper Pot** (no phone) is a little blue shack at the end of Front Street, where Peanuts Butterfield is famous for conch fritters.

About half of the colony's 8,000 residents live on this 7-square-mile island. Diving is definitely the big deal here. Grand Turk's Wall, with a sheer drop to 7,000 feet, is well known to divers.

Salt Cay This tiny 2½-square-mile dot in the water is home to about 400 **❷** people. The island boasts one telephone, a few stores in **Balfour Town,** and splendid beaches on the north coast. Old windmills, salt sheds, and salt ponds are silent reminders of the days when the island was a leading producer of salt.

South Caicos **Cockburn Harbour,** the best natural harbor in the Caicos chain, **❸** is home to the Commonwealth Regatta, held each year in May. This 8½-square-mile island was once an important salt producer; today it's the heart of the fishing industry. Spiny lobster and queen conch may be found in the shallow Caicos bank to the west and are harvested for export by local plants. Bonefishing here is some of the best in the West Indies.

At the northern end of the island there are fine, white-sand beaches; the south coast is great for scuba diving along the drop-off; and the windward (east) side is excellent for snorkeling, where large stands of elkhorn and staghorn coral shelter a variety of small tropical fish.

East Caicos Uninhabited and accessible only by boat, this island has on its
④ north coast a magnificent 17-mile beach. It was once a cattle range and the site of a major sisal-growing industry.

Middle Caicos The largest (48 square miles) and least-developed of the inhabited Turks and Caicos Islands, Middle Caicos is home to
⑤ limestone **Conch Bar Caves,** with their eerie underground salt lakes and milky-white stalactites and stalagmites. Archaeologists have discovered Arawak and Lucayan Indian artifacts in the caves and the surrounding area. The boats that dock here and the planes that land on the island's little airstrip provide the island's 500 residents with their only connection to the outside world. **Executive Tours** can fly you over and take you through the mysterious caves (*see* Guided Tours, above).

North Caicos The **Prospect of Whitby Hotel** is on the north end of this 41-
⑥ square-mile island. To the south of Whitby is **Flamingo Pond,** a nesting place for the beautiful pink birds. If you take a taxi tour of the island, you'll see the ruins of the old plantations and, in
⑦ ⑧ the little settlements of **Kew** and **Sandy Point,** a profusion of tropical trees bearing limes, papayas, and custard apples. The beaches here are superb for shelling, snorkeling, scuba diving, swimming and fishing, as well as for lolling.

Pine Cay One of a chain of small cays connecting North Caicos and Provo,
⑨ 800-acre **Pine Cay** is privately owned and under development as a planned community. It's home to the exclusive **Meridian Club** resort, playground of jet-setters, and its 2½-mile beach is the most beautiful in the archipelago. The island has a 3,800-foot airstrip, and electric carts for getting around.

Providenciales In the mid-18th century, so the story goes, a French ship was
⑩ wrecked near here and the survivors were washed ashore on an island they gratefully christened La Providentielle. Under the Spanish, the name was changed to Providenciales.

Provo's 37½-square miles are by far the most developed in the Turks and Caicos. With its rolling green hills and 12-mile beach, the island is a prime target for developers. More than 15 years ago a group of U.S. investors, including the DuPonts, Ludingtons, and Roosevelts, opened up this island for visitors and those seeking homesites in the Caribbean. A new Sheraton and a new Ramada are under construction, and work on Frenchman Pierre Gely's Leeward Development of villas and condominiums is proceeding. Provo is also the home of Club Mediteranée's showpiece, Club Med Turkoise, which was built in 1984.

Downtown Provo, located near Ludington International Airport, is a cluster of stone and stucco buildings that house car-rental agencies, law offices, boutiques, banks, and other businesses.

Time Out Stop in **Fast Eddie's** (Airport Rd., no phone) for a relaxing drink and a platter of seafood.

Provo is home to the **Caicos Conch Farm,** a major mariculture operation where the mollusks are farmed commercially. You can tour the farm's facilities and geodesic dome, watch a slide show, and browse in the gift shop.

About 1,700 people live on Provo, a considerable number of which are expatriate U.S. and Canadian business people and retirees.

West Caicos Over the past few centuries numerous wrecks occurred in the area between West Caicos and Provo, and author Peter Benchley is among the treasure-seekers who have been lured to this ⑪ island. **Molasses Reef** is now a restricted area currently being surveyed by an underwater marine-archaeology group who believe they may have located the *Pinta*, which is thought to have been wrecked here in the early 1500s.

Charter planes can put down on a 3,000-foot dirt airstrip, but this island is uninhabited, untamed, and there are no facilities whatsoever. A glorious white beach stretches for a mile along the northwest point, and offshore diving is the most exotic in the islands. A wall inhabited by every kind of large marine life ⑫ begins a quarter-mile offshore, and the **Northwest Reef** offers great stands of elkhorn coral and acres of staghorn brambles. But this area is only for experienced divers. The wall starts deep, the currents are strong—and there are sharks in the waters.

If you do tour West Caicos, take along several vats of insect repellent. It won't help much with the sharks, but it should fend off the mosquitoes, deer flies, and sand flies. Be advised, too, that the interior is overgrown with dense shrubs, including manchineel.

Participant Sports

Bicycling Provo has a few steep grades to conquer, but very little traffic. Bikes can be rented at **Sun Cycles** (Airport Rd., next to **Touch of Class** boutique, tel. 809/946–4612).

Boat Rentals You can rent a boat with private pilot for a half or full day of sportsfishing through **Executive Tours** (Provo, tel. 809/946–4524). Catamarans and power boats can be rented at the **Hotel Kittina** (Grand Turk, tel. 809/946–2232).

Fishing **Executive Tours** (Provo, tel. 809/946–4524) will take a maximum of four people out for half- or full-day fishing expeditions, bait and tackle included. The same outfit will arrange half- or full-day deep-sea fishing trips in search of shark, marlin, kingfish, sawfish, wahoo, and tuna, with all equipment furnished. Deep-sea, bonefishing, and bottom fishing are also available aboard the *Sandbox* (Third Turtle Inn, tel. 809/946–4683), **Seatopia** (tel. 305/442–1396), and the *Sakitumi* or the *Safari* (tel. 809/946–4684).

Horseback Riding Horses roam lazily around the main roads on Grand Turk. If you see one that appeals to you, find out who owns it, get permission to ride it, and hop on.

Scuba Diving Diving is the top attraction here. (All divers must carry and present a valid certification card before they'll be allowed to dive.) These islands are surrounded by a reef system of more than 200 square miles, and much of it is unexplored. Grand Turk's famed wall drops more than 7,000 feet. There are undersea cathedrals, coral gardens, and countless tunnels. Among the operations that provide instruction, equipment rentals, underwater video equipment, and trips are **Omega Divers** (Hotel Kittina, Grand Turk, tel. 809/946–2232 or 800/255–1966), **Blue Water Divers** (Salt Raker Inn, Grand Turk, tel. 809/946–2432), **Dolphin Cay Divers** (Prospect of Whitby Hotel, North Caicos, tel. 800/346–4295), **Provo Turtle Divers** (Provo, tel. 809/946–4232 or 800/328–5285), and **Seatopia** (tel. 305/442–1396).

Sea Excursions   **Seatopia** (tel. 305/442–1396) does glass-bottom boat excursions and sails to uninhabited islands. The 56-foot trimaran *Tao* (tel. 809/946–4393) runs sunset cruises, as well as sailing and snorkeling outings. The Provo Turtle Divers' 20-foot glass-bottom *Grouper Snooper* (Provo, tel. 809/946–4232) offers sightseeing and snorkeling excursions.

Snorkeling   **Wet Pleasures** (Provo, tel. 809/946–4455), **Blue Water Divers** (tel. 809/946–2432), **Omega Divers** (Grand Turk, tel. 809/946–2232), and **Provo Turtle Divers** (Provo, tel. 809/946–4232) all provide rentals and trips.

Tennis   There are two lighted courts at **Turtle Cove Yacht & Tennis Club** (Provo, tel. 809/946–4203), eight courts (four lighted) at **Club Med Turkoise** (Provo, tel. 809/946–4491), one court at the **Meridian Club** (Pine Cay, tel. 800/225–4255), and two courts at the **Erebus Inn** (Grand Turk, tel. 809/946–4240).

Waterskiing/   Equipment is available at the **Island Princess** (Provo, tel. 809/
Jet-skiing   946–4260), **Third Turtle Inn** (Provo, tel. 809/946–4230), and **Wet Pleasures** (Provo, tel. 809/946–4455).

Windsurfing   Rental and instruction are available through **Dolphin Cay Divers** (Prospect of Whitby Hotel, North Caicos, tel. 800/346–4295), **Seatopia** (tel. 305/442–1396), **Salt Raker Inn** (Grand Turk, tel. 809/946–2260), and **Wet Pleasures** (Provo, tel. 809/946–4455).

Spectator Sports

The only game in town is cricket. The season runs from June to November.

Dining

Like everything else on these islands, dining out is a very laid-back affair, which is not to say that it is cheap. Because of the high cost of importing all edibles, entrées in all of the restaurants are more expensive than on other islands, and all of the menus are à la carte. A 7% government tax and a 10% service charge are added to your check. Reservations are not required, and dress is casual.

The most highly recommended restaurants are indicated by a star ★.

Category	Cost*
Very Expensive	over $35
Expensive	$25–$35
Moderate	$20–$25
Inexpensive	under $20

*per person, excluding drinks, service, and sales tax (7%)

Grand Turk **Island Reef.** This stone-and-glass building with beam ceilings
★ sits right on the water's edge. The owner is a transplanted
Texan, and you know it the minute you bite into the country-
fried steak. Other offerings are lobster, panfried grouper, seafood platter, burgers, and sandwiches. *Island Reef Hotel, tel.
809/946–2055. AE, MC, V. Expensive.*

★ **Papillon's Rendezvous.** This is a rustic French restaurant overlooking the water. Begin with onion soup or escargots, then
try grilled quail, snapper fillet, or filet mignon. *Front St., tel.
809/946–2088. No credit cards. Closed Sun. and Mon. Expensive.*

Sandpiper. Candles flicker on the Sandpiper's terrace beside a
flower-filled courtyard. Its blackboard specialties might include pork chops with applesauce, lobster, filet mignon, or
seafood platter. *Hotel Kittina, tel. 809/946–2232. AE, MC, V.
Moderate.*

Salt Raker Inn. In this informal open dining pavilion, you might
start with tomato and mozzarella salad or melon and ginger.
Popular entrees include lobster in cream and sherry sauce, barbecue steak, and seafood curry. For dessert, try oranges in
caramel or banana splits. *Salt Raker Inn, tel. 809/946–2260.
AE, MC, V. Moderate.*

Providenciales **Erebus Inn.** The inn's starters include snails in garlic and pars-
★ ley butter. Among the main dishes are duck à l'orange, grilled
steak, broiled lobster tail, cracked conch, and veal cutlet with
mustard sauce. *Erebus Inn, tel. 809/946–4240. MC, V. Very
Expensive.*

★ **Island Princess.** This is a very special place, with crisp pink napery, a sweeping view of the beach and the sea, and a friendly
staff. The grouper cordon bleu is special—so are the lobster
and the turtle steak. *Island Princess Hotel, The Bight, tel. 809/
946–4260. MC, V. Expensive.*

Banana Boat. This casual spot has a varied menu including
chicken français, spaghetti and meatballs, chicken cutlet par-
migiana, meatball hoagies, cracked conch, lemon chicken,
hamburgers, and hot dogs. *Turtle Cove Marina, tel. 809/946–
4312. AE, MC, V. Moderate–Expensive.*

Hong Kong Restaurant. A no-frills place with plain wood tables
and chairs, the Hong Kong offers lobster with ginger and
green onions, chicken with black-bean sauce, sliced duck with
salted mustard greens, and sweet-and-sour chicken. *Leeward Rd., tel. 809/946–4695. AE, MC, V. Closed Sun. Moderate.*

★ **Hey, Jose.** This canopied outdoor restaurant is popular for Tex-
Mex treats like tacos, tostados, nachos, burritos, and margaritas. You can build your own pizza. *Leeward Rd., no phone. No
credit cards. Inexpensive–Expensive.*

Dora's. Small vases of hibiscus sit on blue plastic cloths in
Dora's cheerful white room. Appetizers include conch fritters
and fish chowder, and among the main dishes are pork chops,
fish and chips, lobster salad, and turtle steak. *Leeward Hwy.,
no phone. No credit cards. Closed weekends. Inexpensive–
Moderate.*

Lodging

Hotel accommodations are available on Grand Turk, South Caicos, Pine Cay, and Provo. There are also some small guest
houses on Salt Cay. Accommodations range from small island

inns to the splashy Club Med Turkoise. Because of the popularity of scuba diving here, virtually all the hotels have dive shops and offer very attractive dive packages.

The most highly recommended lodgings are indicated by a star ★.

Category	Cost*
Expensive	$85–$140
Moderate	$55–$85
Inexpensive	under $55

All prices are for a standard double room for two, excluding 7% tax and a 10% service charge.

Grand Turk

★ **Hotel Kittina.** Choose between the sleek, balconied, air-conditioned suites with kitchens, which sit on a gleaming white-sand beach, or the older main house across the street, which oozes island atmosphere. Rooms in the latter are simple; strong winds blow through the rooms and keep things so cool you don't need the ceiling fans. *Box 42, tel. 809/946–2232 or 800/548–8462. 54 rooms and suites. Facilities: restaurant, 2 bars, pool, boutique, Omega Dive Shop, T&C Travel Agency. AE, MC, V. Expensive.*

★ **Island Reef.** These modern air-conditioned efficiency and one-bedroom units sit on a ridge on the eastern coast, where you can stroll out of your room and onto the beach. Furnishings are contemporary, and each unit has a complete electric kitchen. *Box 10, tel. 809/946–2055 or 800/243–4954. 20 rooms. Facilities: restaurant, bar, tennis, pool, boutique, water sports arranged with dive operations. AE, MC, V. Moderate.*

Evan's Inn. These rooms and apartments are situated on a ridge overlooking the ocean inlet of North Creek. Some rooms are air-conditioned. There is a patio for outdoor barbecues, and free transportation to the beach and into town. *Box 65, tel. 809/946–2098. 16 rooms. Facilities: restaurant, bar, saltwater pool. AE, DC, MC, V. Moderate.*

Salt Raker Inn. Across the street from the beach, this renovated, galleried house was the home of a Bermudian shipwright 150 years ago. The rooms and suites are not elegant, but are individually decorated and have a home-like atmosphere. Accommodations include a garden house with screened porches and three one-bedroom suites, some with air-conditioning. *Box 1, tel. 809/946–2260. In U.K., 44 Birchington Rd., London NW6 4LJ, tel. 01/328–6474. 9 rooms and suites. Facilities: restaurant, bar, dive packages. AE, MC, V. Moderate.*

Pine Cay

★ **The Meridian Club.** High-rollers get away from it all in high style on this privately owned 800-acre island. Club guests enjoy, among other things, an unspoiled cay with 2½ miles of soft white sand and a 500-acre nature reserve, with tropical landscaping, freshwater ponds, and nature trails that lure birdwatchers and botanists. There are seaside cottages, each with twin beds and a patio fronting on the beach, and a round cottage with two ocean-view atrium units. *Pine Cay, tel. 800/225–4255. Drawer 114; Box 52–6002, Miami, FL 33152, tel. 212/696–4566 in U.S. 15 rooms and cottages. Facilities: restaurant, bar, pool, tennis court, dive packages, water-sports center. No credit cards. Expensive.*

Providenciales **Club Med Turkoise.** This lavish $23 million resort is one of the most sumptuous of all of Club Med's villages. One-, two-, and three-story bungalows line a mile-long beach, and all of the usual sybaritic pleasures are here. *Providenciales, tel. 809/946–4491 or 800–CLUBMED; 212/750–1687 in NY. 306 rooms. Facilities: restaurant, bar, disco, boutique, 8 tennis courts (4 lighted), bicycles, Jacuzzis, TV/video room, library, fishing, water-sports center. AE, MC, V. Expensive.*

★ **Erebus Inn.** All units in this stylish resort have two double beds and modern wicker furnishings. Some rooms are in the older chalet; units in the newer section are air-conditioned, with 13-channel cable TV and phones. The hotel sits on a cliff overlooking Turtle Cove, which affords a wonderful view of the marina and the Caribbean beyond. The excellent French restaurant and lively bar make this a popular gathering spot. *Turtle Cove, Box 238, Providenciales, tel. 809/946–4240. 30 rooms. Facilities: restaurant, bar, 2 pools (1 saltwater), 2 tennis courts, miniature golf, dive packages. MC, V. Expensive.*

★ **Third Turtle Inn.** Wood walkways lace around the limestone hillside upon which this small, serene resort sits. One of Provo's oldest resorts, it is a long-time haunt of the rich and famous. It's also a favorite hangout of a colorful cast of pilots, yachtsmen, and local characters, and many a tall tale is told in the famous Seven Dwarfs Bar. Rooms have minibars and many amenities, and there is a heavy emphasis on water sports. *Providenciales, tel. 809/946–4230 or 800/323–7600. Box 526002, Miami, FL 33151. 15 rooms. Facilities: restaurant, bar, tennis court, boutique, marina, dive shop/dive packages. AE, MC, V. Expensive.*

Treasure Beach Villas. These one- and two-bedroom self-catering apartments have fully equipped kitchens, fans, and Provo's 12 miles of white sandy beach for beachcombing and snorkeling. *The Bight, tel. 809/946–4211 or 800/227–2157. Box 8409, Hialeah, FL 33012. 8 single, 10 double rooms. Facilities: pool, tennis court. AE. Expensive.*

★ **Island Princess.** Wood walkways at the hotel lead up to and around the rooms, which are situated in two wings. All rooms have cable TV and private balconies. There is an excellent restaurant overlooking the beach and the sea. *The Bight, tel. 809/946–4260. 80 rooms. Facilities: restaurant, bar, 2 pools, game room, children's playground, dive packages, boat rentals, water-sports center. MC, V. Moderate.*

Mariner's Hotel. A gravel road leads to the hotel, which has contemporary tropical furnishings in fan-cooled rooms and baths with showers. The hotel is on the south end of the island, with easy access to a white-sand beach; there's a dive shop on the premises. *Sapodilla Point, tel. 809/946–4488. 25 rooms. Facilities: restaurant, bar, pool, bakery and pastry shop, dive shop. AE, MC, V. Moderate.*

★ **Turtle Cove Yacht and Tennis Resort.** Occupying 1½ acres, this air-conditioned recreation facility has rooms and condominium units facing the marina. All rooms have TVs and phones. *Providenciales, tel. 809/946–4203. 12 rooms and condominiums. Facilities: restaurant, 2 bars, 2 lighted tennis courts, pool, marina. AE, MC, V. Moderate.*

South Caicos **Club Carib Harbor Hotel.** Within walking distance of the township, this small resort overlooking Cockburn Harbour and the fishing district has simple, functional rooms. *Box 1, South Cai-*

cos, tel. 809/946–3251. 12 rooms. Facilities: restaurant, bar. AE, MC, V. Moderate.

North Caicos
★

Prospect of Whitby Hotel. This is a secluded retreat with a pool near a 7-mile-long beach. Some rooms are air-conditioned, some have kitchenettes, but the focus here is on diving. The hotel is home to Dolphin Cay Diving, whose 40-foot catamaran *Surfbreaker* and 28-foot *Formula* spirit guests out to the reefs. *Box 21, Grand Turk, tel. 809/946–4250 or 800/346–4295. 28 rooms. Facilities: restaurant, bar, pool, dive shop. MC, V. Expensive.*

Nightlife

On Grand Turk, check out **The Ladies** (Hospital Rd., no phone), where there are dart boards and dancing to live island music on weekends. Another island favorite is the **Uprising** (Lighthouse Rd., no phone), which also has live music and dancing on weekends.

On Provo, the **Banana Boat** (tel. 809/946–4312) has live Top 40s, reggae, and soca (rock-influenced calypso), on Thursday, Friday, and Saturday nights. On Tuesday nights you can hear live calypso at the **Erebus Inn** (tel. 809/946–4240), and on Thursday nights **The Third Turtle** (tel. 809/946–4230) has live island music. **Le Deck** (tel. 809/946–4547) offers varied evening entertainment, from open-air dancing every night and live bands to one-armed bandits.

28 The U.S. Virgin Islands

by David Grambs   Your destination here will be either St. Thomas (13 miles long); its neighbor St. John (9 miles long); or, 40 miles to the south, St. Croix (23 miles long). These are the big three of some 75 bits and pieces of volcanic land that make up the northern hook of the Lesser Antilles, just east of Puerto Rico. Whichever you visit, there are bracing breezes, courtesy of the trade winds.

A pro/con thumbnail sketch of the three main U.S. Virgin Islands might put it that St. Thomas is bustling (hustling) and the place for shopping and discos (commercial glitz and overdevelopment); St. Croix is more Danish, picturesque, and rural (more provincial and duller, particularly after dark); and St. John is matchless in the beauty of its National Park Service–protected land and beaches (a one-village island mostly for the rich or for campers).

St. Thomas may be building too much and too quickly and have oppressive cruise-ship crowds (Wednesdays, notably) and even some sewage problems, but it also has a lively nightlife scene, secluded beach resorts, and frequent 20-minute ferries to St. John. St. Croix, for all its slower and steadier pace, has elegant resort dining, horseback riding, and three golf courses, Buck Island and its reef, and a more small-town atmosphere. St. John, though small and relatively upscale, has a tasteful new harborside mall and reasonable restaurants in one village, which is cozy and lively; 20 hiking trails; and lustrous beaches.

The United States bought its half of the Virgin Islands in 1917. English, seasoned with Creole, is the language; the U.S. dollar is the currency. Even Cable TV with HBO and fast-food outlets will make you feel at home here.

Long before the Virgin Islands were Americanized, they had to be "discovered"—by Columbus, of course, in 1493, the beginning of a colorfully hybrid and unimaginably complicated history that turned out to be a round dance (after the Arawak, Taino, and Carib Indians left) among the European powers, along with the Knights of Malta. It is a history of slave trading, pirates and privateers, sugar plantations, and slave revolt and liberation. Through it all, the Danes had the staying power; from the 17th to the 19th centuries, they oversaw a plantation economy that produced molasses, rum, cotton, and tobacco.

Remnants and whiffs of this history are everywhere in the U.S. Virgin Islands today, from the ruins of the stone sugar-mill right next to the St. Croix airport runway to the graceful Danish architecture and arcades of Christiansted and Charlotte Amalie. Many of the stones that you see in buildings or tread on in the streets were once used as ballast on sailing ships. Pirate watchtowers grace the grounds of two popular hotels overlooking the St. Thomas harbor, and there are forts or ruins of forts on all three islands. St. John has a partially restored sugar-mill and petroglyphs left by slaves—or are they pre-Columbian? Old plantation names, such as Sally's Fancy, Bonne Esperance, Sweet Bottom, and Parasol, are alive and well in St. Croix.

Before You Go

Tourist Information   Information about the U.S. Virgin Islands is available through the **U.S. Virgin Islands Government Tourist Office** (1270 Ave. of the Americas, New York, NY 10020, tel. 212/582–4520) and at the **U.S. Virgin Islands Division of Tourism** offices in Atlanta

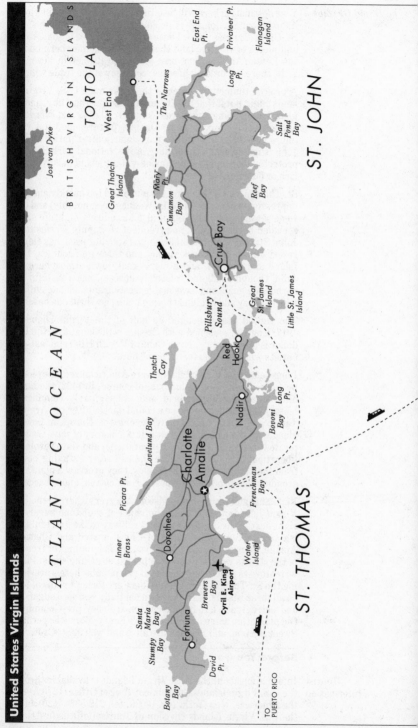

United States Virgin Islands

ATLANTIC OCEAN

Jost van Dyke

BRITISH VIRGIN ISLANDS

TORTOLA

West End

Great Thatch Island

The Narrows

Mary Pt.

East End Pt.

Privateer Pt.

Flanagan Island

Long Pt.

Salt Pond Bay

Cinnamon Bay

Cruz Bay

Reef Bay

ST. JOHN

Pillsbury Sound

Great St. James Island

Little St. James Island

Thatch Cay

Red Hook

Nadir

Long Pt.

Bovoni Bay

Picara Pt.

Lovelund Bay

Charlotte Amalie

Frenchman Bay

Inner Brass

Dorothea

Santa Maria Bay

Stumpy Bay

Fortuna

Brewers Bay

Cyril E. King Airport

Water Island

ST. THOMAS

Botany Bay

David Pt.

TO PUERTO RICO

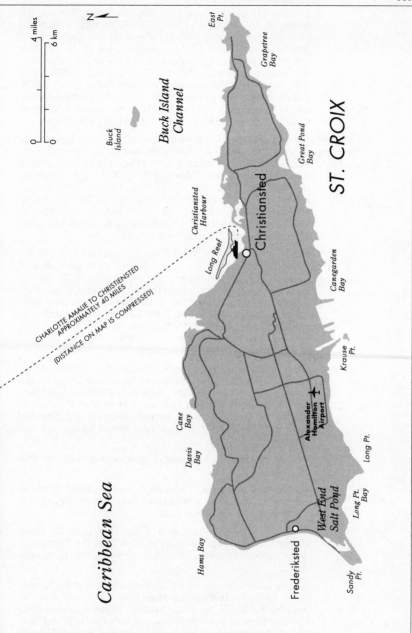

Caribbean Sea

N

4 miles
6 km

Buck Island

Buck Island Channel

East Pt.

Grapetree Bay

Great Pond Bay

ST. CROIX

Christiansted Harbour

Long Reef

Christiansted

Canegarden Bay

Krause Pt.

CHARLOTTE AMALIE TO CHRISTIENSTED APPROXIMATELY 40 MILES
(DISTANCE ON MAP IS COMPRESSED)

Cane Bay

Davis Bay

Alexander Hamilton Airport

Long Pt.

Long Pt. Bay

West End Salt Pond

Hams Bay

Frederiksted

Sandy Pt.

(235 Peachtree Ctr., Suite 1420, Gaslight Tower, Atlanta, GA 30303, tel. 404/688–0906), Chicago (122 S. Michigan Ave., Suite 1270, Chicago, IL 60603, tel. 312/461–0180), Los Angeles (3460 Wilshire Blvd., Suite 412, Los Angeles, CA 90010, tel. 213/739–0138), Miami (2655 Le Jeune Rd., Suite 907, Coral Gables, FL 33134, tel. 305/442–7200), and Washington, DC (1667 K St., NW, Suite 270, Washington, DC 20006, tel. 202/293–3707). British travelers can write or visit the **U.S. Virgin Islands Division of Tourism** office in London (2 Cinnamon Row, Plantation Wharf, York Pl., London SW 11 3TW, tel. 071/978–5262).

Arriving and Departing

By Plane **American Airlines** (tel. 800/433–7300) offers direct flights to St. Thomas/St. Croix from New York, Boston, and Raleigh/Durham. **Pan Am** (tel. 800/221–1111) also has nonstop service from New York and Miami. **Midway** (tel. 800/621–5700) flies from Chicago to St. Thomas/St. Croix. (Note that St. John, a popular destination and a short ferry ride from St. Thomas, has no airport.) **Eastern Airlines** (tel. 800/474–8330) flies into St. Thomas daily from Miami. **Continental Airlines** (800/525–0280) arrives daily in St. Thomas from Newark.

Most flights to the U.S. Virgin Islands from other U.S. cities—including Baltimore, Chicago, Hartford, Los Angeles, Minneapolis/St. Paul, Philadelphia, and Washington, DC—are via San Juan, Puerto Rico, where connections can be made with intraisland commuter service on **Air BVI** (tel. 800/468–2485), **American Eagle** (tel. 800/433–7300), **Leeward Islands Air Transport (LIAT)** (tel. 809/774–2313), **Virgin Air** (tel. 809/791–4898), and **Eastern Metro Express** (tel. 809/776–9322 or 800/474–8330).

Passengers leaving from Albany, Buffalo, New Orleans, Pittsburgh, Rochester, St. Louis, and Syracuse can make the connecting service at Maimi. **Delta** (tel. 800/221–1212) offers connecting service to San Juan via Atlanta from Charleston, Cincinnati, Dallas, Denver, Detroit, Houston, and New Orleans, and flies direct to San Juan from Chicago and Los Angeles.

British Airways flies London/San Juan twice a week (tel. 800/247–9297).

Eastern Metro Express, in addition to the intraisland flights already mentioned, flies several times daily from St. Croix to St. Thomas, St. John, and San Juan.

By Boat Some 20 cruise-ship lines stop at St. Thomas or St. Croix throughout the year; a number of ships from the West Coast make regular runs to St. Thomas/St. Croix via the Panama Canal.

Among the cruise-ship lines that offer stopovers at St. Thomas or St. Croix are **Holland American Line** (300 Elliott Ave. W, Seattle, WA 98119, tel. 206/281–3535), **Princess Cruises** (2029 Century Park E, Suite 3000, Los Angeles, CA 90067, tel. 800/421–0522 or 213/553–1770), **Royal Caribbean Cruises** (903 South America Way, Miami, FL 33132, tel. 800/327–6700, or, in Canada, 800/245–7225), **Royal Viking Line** (1 Embarcadero Ctr., San Francisco, CA 94111, tel. 800/422–8000), **Cunard Line** (555 Fifth Ave., New York, NY 10017, tel. 800/528–6273, 800/458–9000, or 212/661–7777), and **Home Lines** (1 World Trade Ctr., Suite 3939, New York, NY 10048, tel. 212/432–1414, or, in Canada, 514/842–1441).

There is a regular ferry service from Charlotte Amalie and Red Hook Harbor on St. Thomas to St. John.

Passports and Visas U.S. and Canadian citizens are required to present some proof of citizenship, if not a passport then a birth certificate or voter registration card. If you are arriving from the U.S. mainland or Puerto Rico, you need no inoculation or health certificate.

Customs and Duties Before you leave the U.S. Virgin Islands to return to the U.S. mainland, your baggage will be subject to inspection by U.S. Customs in St. Thomas or St. Croix; however, if you are making a connecting flight in San Juan, you will go through Customs in Puerto Rico. A U.S. resident may bring back up to $800 worth of duty-free imports (goods not made in the U.S. Virgin Islands or United States) every 30 days, twice the limit allowed those coming from other Caribbean islands. This includes an allowance of 200 cigarettes and 100 cigars (non-Cuban). Residents 21 years or older may bring back five bottles of liquor duty-free, or six bottles if one was produced in the U.S. Virgin Islands. If you exceed your $800 exemption in foreign-made goods brought home, you will pay a duty of 5% for the next $1,000; thereafter, the duty changes somewhat, up to your maximum "take-home" of $2,000 worth. Apart from the $800 exemption, you may mail home up to $50 worth of gifts to friends or relatives on any one day. Keep your sales slips conveniently handy, just in case any questions arise at Customs.

Language English, often with a Creole or West Indian lilt, is the medium of communication in these islands.

Precautions Crime exists here, but not to the same degree that it does in larger cities on the U.S. mainland. In Charlotte Amalie, pickpockets recognize a big spender when they see one, and it's best to stick to well-lit streets at night. If you plan on carrying things around, rent a car, not a jeep, and lock possessions up in the trunk. Keep your rental car locked wherever you park.

Aside from an ornery donkey or two, there are no dangerous animals or snakes in the U.S. Virgin Islands. Tap water is quite safe. The trade winds prevent insects from becoming a major problem in these climes, though mosquitoes and no-see-ums are not yet extinct.

Further Reading The word-of-mouth classic about life in the Virgin Islands is Herman Wouk's novel *Don't Stop the Carnival*.

Staying in the U.S. Virgin Islands

Important Addresses **Tourist Information:** The **U.S. Virgin Islands Division of Tourism** has an office in St. Thomas (Box 6400, Charlotte Amalie, U.S. Virgin Islands 00804, tel. 809/774–8784), St. Croix (Box 4538, Christiansted, U.S. Virgin Islands 00822, tel. 809/773–0495, and at the Customs House Bldg. Strand St., Frederiksted, U.S. Virgin Islands 00840, tel. 809/772–0357), and St. John (Box 200, Cruz Bay, U.S. Virgin Islands 00830, tel. 809/776–6450).

There is a **Visitors Center** in Charlotte Amalie, across from Emancipation Square and at Havensight Mall. In St. Croix, go to the Old Scalehouse at the waterfront, across from Fort Christiansvaern. The **National Park Service** also has visitor centers at the ferry areas on St. Thomas (Red Hook) and St. John (Cruz Bay).

Emergencies **Police:** Call 915. The number is the same for all three islands.

Hospitals: The emergency room of **St. Thomas Hospital and Community Center** in Charlotte Amalie (tel. 809/776–8311) is open 24 hours a day. On St. Croix there is the **St. Croix Hospital and Community Health Center** in Christiansted (tel. 809/778–6311 or 809/778–5895) and the **Ingeborg Nesbett Clinic** (tel. 809/772–0260) in Frederiksted. For medical emergencies on St. John, contact the **Murah Keating Smith Clinic** (tel. 809/776–6222) located in the De Castro Building in Cruz Bay or call an emergency medical technician direct (tel. 809/776–6400).

Pharmacies: St. Thomas has numerous pharmacies, among them **Cathedral Pharmacy** (tel. 809/776–4080), **Sunrise Pharmacy** (tel. 809/774–5333), and **St. Thomas Apothecary Hall** (tel. 809/774–5432).

Currency The U.S. dollar is the medium of exchange here.

Taxes and Service Charges A 7.5% tax is added to hotel rates. There is no departure tax for the U.S. Virgin Islands.

Some hotels and restaurants add a 10% to 15% service charge to your bill.

Guided Tours Hotels can provide information about group tours or about private taxi guides. (On St. Thomas and St. Croix, group tours in open safari vehicles are popular among cruise-ship passengers; on St. John, the passengers are mainly visitors from St. Thomas who come over by ferry.)

Bus tours on St. Thomas are offered by **Grayline** (tel. 809/776–1515) and **Tropic Tours** (tel. 809/774–1855). On St. Croix, contact **St. Croix Safari Tours** (tel. 809/773–5922 or 809/778–3727), **St. Croix Sun Tours** (tel. 809/773–9661), and **Travelers Tours** (tel. 809/778–1636). On St. John, you can book an extensive safari bus tour through the **National Park Service** (tel. 809/776–6201) or **Cool Breeze** (tel. 809/776–6588).

If you want to leave the driving to a knowledgeable local and are willing to pay a bit more not to be part of a camera-laden tourist herd on a safari bus, a personal taxi tour is the answer. Plenty of drivers offer this service, for a half day or a full day, for a prearranged price. Ask the management at your hotel for a recommendation (or, better yet, ask a fellow guest who has just taken such a tour).

One recommended private limousine van service on St. Thomas, for personalized island tours or airport pickups, is **Executive Transportation, Inc.** (or **Extra, Inc.**, tel. 809/775–6974 or 809/775–5204), run by Bob Kirkpatrick, a former New Yorker who knows this island as few others do. On St. John, the one-woman operation called **Miss Lucy's Taxi** (tel. 809/776–6804) is a delightful service. Lucy is something of a mellow philosopher who wears a flower in her hair. Her taxi is the van with the blossom-bedecked goat horns. Don't take too long to make up your mind—she may retire soon.

Getting Around Taxis of all shapes and sizes are available at various ferry,
Taxis shopping, resort, and airport areas on St. Thomas and St. Croix and respond quickly to a call. U.S. Virgin Islands taxis do not have meters, but you need not worry about fare gouging

if you (1) check a list of standard rates to popular destinations, often posted in hotel and airport lobbies and printed in free tourist brochures and periodicals, such as *St. Thomas This Week;* (2) ask a resident or someone at your hotel what it should cost (roughly) to where you want to go; and (3) settle the final fare with your driver before you start. Taxi drivers are required to carry a copy of the official rates and must show it to you when asked. Remember, too, that you can signal to a taxi that is already occupied. The drivers take multiple fares and sometimes even trade passengers at midpoints: This can can keep your fare low.

Buses   Public buses are not the best or quickest way to get around on the islands, and the service is minimal. (There is no service on St. John.) On St. Thomas, the **Manassah Country Bus** makes hourly trips (75¢) between Charlotte Amalie and Red Hook, site of the main ferry dock.

Mopeds   For two-wheel motoring on St. Thomas, call **A-1 Scooter and Jeep Rental** (tel. 809/776–4872) or **Paradise Scooter Rentals** (tel. 809/775–2724). On St. John, call **Cruz Bay Scooter Rental** (tel. 809/776–6493). You must be at least 15 years old to rent a scooter.

Rental Cars   Any U.S. driver's license is good for 90 days here; the minimum age for drivers is 18.

Driving is on the *left* side of the road (although your steering wheel will be on the left side of the car). Many of the roads are narrow and the islands are dotted with hills, so there is ample reason to drive carefully. Even at the sedate speed of 20 miles per hour, driving can be an adventure—for example, you may find yourself in a stick-shift Jeep slogging behind a slow tourist-packed safari bus at a steep hairpin turn on St. John. Give a little beep at blind turns. Note that the general speed limit on these islands is only 25 to 35 mph, which will seem fast enough for you on most roads.

On St. Thomas, you can rent a car from **ABC Rentals** (tel. 809/776–1222 or 800/524–2080), **Anchorage E-Z Car** (tel. 809/775–6255), **Aristocrat** (tel. 809/776–0021), **Avis** (tel. 809/774–4616), **Budget** (tel. 809/776–5774), **Caribbean Jeep & Car** (tel. 809/776–6811), **Cowpet Car Rental** (tel. 809/775–7376 or 800/524–2072), **Dependable** (tel. 809/774–2253 or 800/522–3076), **Discount** (tel. 809/776–4858), **Dollar** (tel. 809/776–0850), **Econo-car St. Thomas** (tel. 809/775–6763), **Hertz** (tel. 809/774–1879), **Paradise** (tel. 809/775–2724), **Sea Breeze** (tel. 809/774–7200), **Sun Island** (tel. 809/774–3333 or 800/233–7941), **Thrifty** (tel. 809/776–3500), and **V.I. Auto Rental** (tel. 809/776–3616 or 800/843–3571).

On St. Croix, call **Avis** (tel. 809/778–9365), **Budget** (tel. 809/778–4663), **Caribbean Jeep & Car** (tel. 809/773–4399 or 809/778–1000), **Charlie's** (tel. 809/778–8200 or 809/773–1678), **Hertz** (tel. 809/778–1402), **Olympic** (tel. 809/773–2208), and **St. Croix Jeep & Honda** (tel. 809/773–0161, 809/773–8370, or 809/773–1351).

On St. John, call **Cool Breeze** (tel. 809/776–6588), **Dalmidia by the Sea** (DBS) (tel. 809/776–6374), **Delbert Hill Jeep & Auto** (tel. 809/776–6637 or 809/776–7947), **O'Connor Jeep** (tel. 809/776–6343), **Roosevelt Jeep Rental** (tel. 809/776–6628), **St. John Car Rental** (tel. 809/776–6103), or **Spencer's Jeep** (tel. 809/776–6628).

Telephones and Mail The area code for the U.S. Virgin Islands is 809, and there is direct dialing to the mainland. Local calls from a public phone cost 25¢ for each five minutes. On St. John, the place to go to for *any* telephone or message needs is **Connections** (tel. 809/776–6922).

Postal rates are the same as they are elsewhere in the United States: 25¢ for a letter, 15¢ for a postcard. **Post offices** on St. Thomas are located near Emancipation Square and Frenchtown; on St. Croix, at the King's Wharf area of Christiansted and within walking distance of the pier in Frederiksted; and on St. John, near the ferry dock in Cruz Bay.

Opening and Closing Times On St. Thomas, Charlotte Amalie's Main Street area shops are open from 9 A.M. to 5 P.M. Monday through Saturday, and the same applies to shops at Havensight Mall. Cruise-ship arrivals, however, also dictate shop hours. Shops at hotels—notably the two-story arcade of 24 shops at Frenchman's Reef—are usually open evenings as well. St. Croix store hours are usually 9 or 9:30 to 5 or 5:30 Monday through Friday, but you will definitely find some shops in Christiansted open in the evening. On St. John, like everything else, store hours are "casual."

Beaches

All beaches in the U.S. Virgin Islands are open to the public, including those in front of hotels. (This means the *beaches only*, not the resort's beach chairs, sailboards, etc.) Each island also has some beaches with picnic facilities and rest rooms. You can always find truly remote and untrammeled beaches if you are willing to drive on some unpaved roads (four-wheel drive is recommended) and do a little walking. Exercise caution in swimming or snorkeling since there are few lifeguards. Among the three islands, there are more than 50 recognized and commonly visited beach areas you can consider for a visit.

St. Thomas **Magens Bay** is a public beach that's usually crowded and busy because of its spectacular loop of white sand, more than a half-mile long, and its calm waters—two peninsulas protect it. The bottom is flat and sandy, so this is a place for sunning and swimming rather than snorkeling. Food, changing facilities, and rest rooms are available.

The condo resort at **Secret Harbour** doesn't at all detract from the attractiveness of this covelike East End beach. Not only is it pretty, it is also superb for snorkeling—go out to the left, near the rocks.

At **Morningstar Beach,** close to Charlotte Amalie, many young residents show up for body surfing or volleyball or less. The sandy-bottom water is in the shadow of the huge, cliffside Frenchman's Reef Hotel. Snorkeling is good here when the current doesn't affect visibility.

From **Sapphire Beach** there is a fine view of St. John and other islands. Snorkeling is excellent at the reef to the right or east, near Pettyklip Point. All kinds of water-sports gear are for rent.

Hull Bay, on the north shore, has a rugged beach that faces Inner and Outer Brass cays and attracts fishermen and beachcombers. Surfing and snorkeling are good.

St. Croix **Buck Island** and its reef, which is under environmental protection, can be reached only by boat; nonetheless, it is a must outing on any visit to St. Croix. Its beach is beautiful, but its finest treasures are those you can see when you plop off the boat and adjust your face mask, snorkel, and flippers.

The waters are not always gentle at **Cane Bay,** a breezy north-shore beach, but the scuba diving and snorkeling are wondrous, and there are never many people around. Just swim straight out to see elkhorn and brain corals. Less than 200 yards out is the dropoff or so-called Cane Bay Wall.

Tamarind Reef Beach is a small but attractive hotel beach east of Christiansted. Both Green Cay and Buck Island seem smack in front of you and make the view arresting. Snorkeling is good.

Sandy Point, the largest beach in the U.S. Virgin Islands, is a must on your itinerary. The shallow, calm water makes for wonderful swimming, and you won't see that many people around. Also are the mangroves and birds of West End Salt Pond, prized by bird-watchers and environmentalists.

Isaac Bay, at St. Croix's east end, is tricky to get to but worth it if you want some seclusion and calm swimming plus a barrier reef for snorkeling. You can get here via footpaths from Jacks Bay.

St. John **Trunk Bay** is the main beach draw on the island because of its underwater snorkeling trail. Crowds or not, it's still beautiful. Though veteran snorkelers pooh-pooh the "picked clean" trail reef, the reef fish are definitely still there. Lifeguards are on duty here.

Hawksnest Bay has a narrow but lovely beach. The water seems especially clear, and both swimming and snorkeling are good. Scenes for the movie *The Four Seasons* were shot here.

Cinnamon Bay beach, at a campground site, has some wide parts and looks out on several green cays. There is a snack bar here.

Salt Pond Bay, on the southeastern coast of St. John, is a scenic area to explore, being next to Coral Bay and rugged Drunk Bay. There is shade if you want it, as well as picnic tables and charcoal grills and few people. Swimming and snorkeling are good.

Exploring St. Thomas

Numbers in the margins correspond with points of interest on the St. Thomas and Charlotte Amalie maps.

Our first suggested itinerary, of town and on foot, does entail a bit of uphill walking, but it mixes sights of historic buildings related to both church and state affairs with duty-free shopping and one spectacular view of the island's most important town. The second tour—north and east of Charlotte Amalie—is to be made in a car.

Charlotte Amalie Start by enjoying the good harbor breeze at **Frenchtown,** where the Frenchies, descendants of immigrants from St. Barthélemy (or St. Barts), pull up their boats and slap down yellowtail, squirrelfish, old wife, and other fish for sale. The island you see out there is **Hassel Island,** now a Virgin Island National Park, where you can view military ruins; you can

St. Thomas

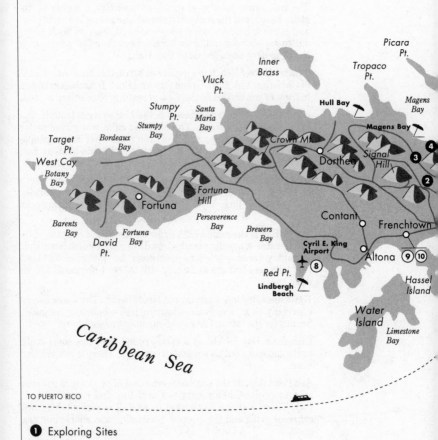

1 Exploring Sites

8 Hotels and Restaurants

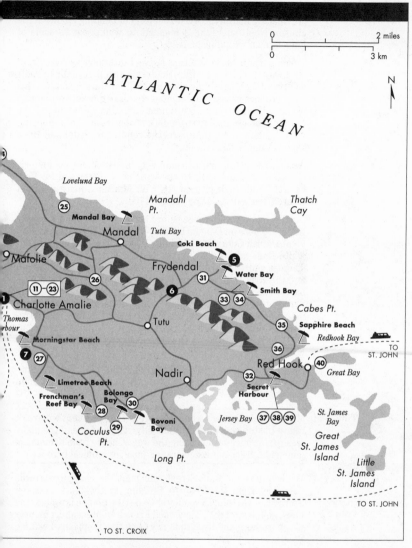

Galleon House, **23**
Heritage Manor, **22**
Hotel 1829, **13**
Island Beachcomber
Hotel, **8**
Limetree Beach
Resort, **28**
Maison Greaux, **10**
Pavilions & Pools, **36**

Pastel's, **24**
Point Pleasant
Resort, **34**
Sapphire Beach, **35**
Sea Horse Cottages, **38**
Secret Harbour, **39**
Stouffer Grand Beach
Resort, **33**
Villa Blanca Hotel, **26**
Watergate Villas, **29**

reach it by ferry ($3 round-trip). You may see a number of people cleaning fish on the wood-roof jetty or bending elbows at the Maison Noel bar. Take a moment to walk west to some of Frenchtown's winding streets.

Turning north, cross Veterans Drive, also known as Waterfront Highway (watch the traffic!), and walk east before turning left on Strand Gade to see the open-air stalls of **Market Square.** This busy produce bazaar was an infamous slave market two centuries ago. You'll begin to see vendors here, as you're now at the western end of Charlotte Amalie's feverish duty-free shopping district along both **Main Street** (Dronnigens Gade) and **Back Street** (Vimmelskaft Gade).

Among the retail and discount stores are numerous historic churches. A few blocks to the west is **St. Peter and St. Paul Church,** built in 1844, and right off Market Square is **Christ Church Methodist,** dating back to 1700.

Stroll east on Back Street before turning left and up Raadet's Gade. Up here on Denmark Hill, you will see the old Greek Revival **Danish Consulate** building (1830)—look for the red-and-white flag—and Villa Santana (1858). Two more notable St. Thomas churches are here: **All Saints Anglican Church** (1848) and the 1844 **Dutch Reform Church,** whose congregation goes back to at least 1660. Perhaps more singular, however, is the **Synagogue** nearby on Crystal Gade. The second-oldest temple in the Western Hemisphere (the oldest is in Curaçao), it was rebuilt several times—Jews have lived on St. Thomas since at least 1665. The sand on the floor commemorates the biblical Exodus.

Once you've caught your breath from this hilly, interdenominational adventure head back down Raadet's Gade to Main Street.

Time Out	Main Street shoppers who are in need of refreshment but aren't ready to stop shopping can take advantage of one of the many fresh-fruit juice stands along the way. Choose from homemade lemonade, fresh-squeezed orange juice, or tropical fruit ices.

While you're on Main Street, don't let the shopping crowds keep you from the **Pissarro Building** in the block between Storetvaer Gade and Trompeter Gade (the plaque is around the block on Back Street). The famed French Impressionist painter was born here and lived upstairs (now the Tropicana Perfume Shop).

After browsing at Bakery Square (off Back Street between Nye Gade and Garden Street), go back down to Main Street and turn left. Just past Garden Street turn left again and go up some steps to the beautiful Spanish-style **Hotel 1829,** whose restaurant is one of the best on St. Thomas. You may want to take a peek into its cool, dark bar and picturesque courtyard. Now walk to the right and you'll find yourself at the foot of the **99 Steps,** on Government Hill, a staircase "street" built by the Danes in the 1700s. If you're feeling energetic, go for it and start up—they're low steps and you can lean on the railing while you catch your breath. Now that you're at the top, we can tell you that there are a few more than 99 steps. Continue ahead on the street to the right and U-turn up the drive to **Blackbeard's Castle,** originally Fort Skytsborg and now a small hotel. The massive five-story stone watchtower here was built in 1679 and possibly was used by the notorious pirate Edward Teach. If you walk past it to the other end of the hotel's pool, you'll get your reward for taking on those 99-plus steps: an unsurpassed view of Charlotte Amalie and its impressive harbor.

With gravity now on your side, head back down the steps. To the right, down Kongen's Gade, you'll come to **Government House** (1867), the official residence of the governor of the U.S. Virgin Islands. (The first two floors are open to the public.) Inside you'll find murals and paintings with a historical motif by Camille Pissarro, whose birthplace you passed on Main Street. Continue down to Norre Gade, where you'll see the **Frederik Lutheran Church,** the second-oldest Lutheran church in the Western Hemisphere. Its walls date back to 1793.

You can mail letters and postcards across the way at the **Post Office,** which is worth entering to see the early murals of Stephen Dohanos, who once did covers for the *Saturday Evening Post*. Walk down Tolbod Gade toward the water, and you'll find yourself at historic **Emancipation Park** (or Garden or Square), so called because it honors the freeing of the slaves in 1848. Various official ceremonies are still held here. You'll also find a smaller version of the Liberty Bell here. Sit on a bench near the gazebo and relax a bit. On the north side of the park is the 19th-century **Grand Hotel** building, now housing offices, shops, and a visitors' hospitality lounge. In the large corner shop, you'll find souvenirs, ranging from exotic seashells and Haitian wood carvings to message (tropical) T-shirts.

Closer yet to the harborfront is **Fort Christian,** St. Thomas's oldest standing structure (1672–87) and a U.S. national landmark. The clock tower was added in the 19th century. This remarkable redoubt has, over time, seen use as a jail, governor's residence, town hall, courthouse, and church. Its dungeons now house a museum featuring artifacts of Virgin Islands history. The St. Thomas Arts Council sponsors the works of local artists at the fort monthly, with a reception open to the public on the first Tuesday of each month when the exhibits change.

From outside the fort you can see the waters of the harbor and if you now cross back over Veterans Drive, you'll be at **Kings Wharf.** Also situated near the pier is the lime-green **Legislature Building** (1874), since 1957 the seat of the 15-member USVI Senate. Built originally by the Danish as a police barracks, the building was later used to billet U.S. Marines and, much later, housed a public school. Look across the harbor and you'll see Frenchtown, where this tour began.

North and East of Charlotte Amalie Having explored Charlotte Amalie, you may want to rent a car and explore the north side of the island, far more beautiful, the northsiders will tell you, than anything on the Caribbean side. Head northwest out of Charlotte Amalie—it's all uphill!—on Mafolie Road (Route 34) to Route 35, turn left onto Route 33, ❷ and bear west to **Fairchild Park,** which was a gift to the people of this island from philanthropist Arthur Fairchild. Wind ❸ around to **Mountain Top,** where you will be afforded a splendid view of the northern side of St. Thomas: Magens Bay, Tortola, and, if the sky is clear, some 18 other islands. You're at 1,547 feet elevation here. There's a full-service restaurant at Mountain Top, as well as souvenirs and clothing to buy. If it isn't too early for you, you can drink one of the half-million banana daiquiris served here annually.

❹ From Mountain Top, drive east; Route 40 or Route 37 brings you to an overlook called **Drake's Seat** and another spectacular vista of the island's Atlantic coastline, Magen's Bay, and outlying islands. Sir Francis Drake, who was one of Queen Elizabeth's privateers, used this place as a vantage point over his anchored fleet, and you will even find an actual chair ensconced here to symbolize the idea (you may sit in it).

❺ Take Route 35 east to Route 42 and the lovely scenery of **Mahogany Run** and its championship golf course. Proceed east on Route 42 and left on Route 38 until you come to a fork and a sign for **Coki Beach** and **Coral World Marine Park.** The snorkeling is excellent at Coki, with reefs at its eastern and western ends, and you may want to dash in for a swim (you'll find shower facilities here) or just do some people watching while nibbling on a meat pâté snack from one of the vendors. Just down from the beach, you will find the entrance to Coral World, an experience not to be missed. The domed tower you see at the end of the pier is a three-level underwater observatory. If you arrive by 11 AM, you'll be lucky enough to see divers feeding barracudas, sharks, and other sea creatures. Yet some of the most colorful fish to be seen here are those in the smaller tanks surrounding you. (The lowest level is the real thing, the sea bottom, not a tank.) You can take a break upstairs at the restaurant and bar before you walk outside to the nature path, museum, and Marine Gardens Aquarium. There are rest rooms, lockers, showers, and changing rooms here.

❻ Going back the way you came, west on Route 38, stop at **Jim Tillett's Art Gallery and Boutique,** an old sugar-mill site on Estate Tutu, where you can watch crafts people working at silkscreening, ceramics, and painting. You can buy fabrics or articles of clothing with artful prints.

Time Out At the Tillett's Mexican restaurant, **El Papagayo** (at the entrance to Tillett's, tel. 809/775–1550), relax near the fountain on the patio and enjoy a taco, burrito, hamburger, or some chicken wings. A strawberry Margarita is a good liquid option.

Drive east again on Route 38 and take the right hand of the fork, the continuation of Route 38. This road loops around the eastern end of St. Thomas and takes you past many of the island's best hotels and beaches, including the Stouffer Grand Beach Resort (Water Bay), Point Pleasant (Smith Bay), and Sapphire Beach Resort. You'll also pass, on the right side of the road, Pavilions & Pools, where each room has its own private swimming pool. At **Red Hook Harbor,** you can get a quick ferry to St. John (20 minutes each way, departures on the hour).

From here, Route 32 brings you west toward Charlotte Amalie and past turnoffs for other fine hotels and beaches, among them Secret Harbour Beach Resort, Bolongo Bay Beach and Tennis Club (Bovoni Bay), and Limetree Beach Hotel (Frenchman's Cove). Proceeding west, you will also pass the road to the spectacular and huge Frenchman's Reef–Morningstar hotel complex, which looks like a cross between a promontory fortress and a mammoth cruise ship and has, among other things, a cliffside elevator tower.

7 Speaking of cruise ships, you may now see one or two ahead as you approach the **West Indian Dock** at the eastern edge of Charlotte Amalie. Pull in to **Havensight Mall** for some major duty-free shopping with an ambience that is a little spiffier than that in town around Main Street. Also here is the headquarters for the *Atlantis* submarine, on which you can book an unforgettable underwater ride (it's best to call ahead for reservations, tel. 809/776–5650).

Four doors down from the *Atlantis* is Dockside Book Shop, a friendly bookstore crammed to the ceiling with best sellers, mysteries, travel guides, children's, and Caribbean books. A tip: Unlike the majority of the other bookstores you'll find on St. Thomas, particularly at hotels, Dockside does not mark up its books from the stateside cover price.

Time Out   Drop into the cool **Cafe Havensight** (next to the *Atlantis* Submarine office, tel. 809/774–5818). Behind the high bar are six metal dispensers, each of which holds a first-rate frozen tropical drink. Which shall it be—the fuzzy navel, virgin peach, piña colada, white Russian, mad mongoose, or lime squeeze?

Exploring St. Croix

Numbers in the margin correspond with points of interest on the St. Croix map.

This tour will take you to many worthwhile St. Croix sights except for those of downtown Christiansted (which is easily explored on foot—pick up a copy of the *Walking Tour Guide)* and the more remote eastern end of the island. You'll visit historic plantation settings; a botanical garden; a rum distillery; the largest and one of the most beautiful beaches in the West Indies; Frederiksted; and, in addition, you'll enjoy some scenic coastal driving.

If you're trying to escape the tight-squeeze traffic of Christiansted, head from the main waterfront area up Company Street and right out to Route 75, Northside Road. A few miles up the road, you can make a detour by turning right onto Route 751, which leads you to **St. Croix by the Sea,** a beautifully landscaped hotel with one of the most spectacular sea views on St. Croix. Have breakfast at the room off the majestic pink-and-white lobby and feast on the view, to the east, of Christiansted and Buck Island. Before you leave, be sure to walk outside for a look at the 154-foot ocean-fed swimming pool, the largest saltwater pool in the Caribbean.

1 A bit farther down Route 75 is **Judith's Fancy,** where you can see the ruins of an old great house and the tower left from a 17th-century château. This was once home to the governor of the Knights of Malta. The "Judith" comes from the first name of a woman buried on the property. Here, too, you have a good view of **Salt River Bay,** where Christopher Columbus landed in 1493. The Salt River estuary draws many scuba divers and a few years ago had an operational Hydrolab 50 feet down.

After driving back to Route 75, continue west and then north on Route 80 toward the coast and pull over at windy **Cane Bay.** This is one of St. Croix's best beaches for scuba diving, and

St. Croix

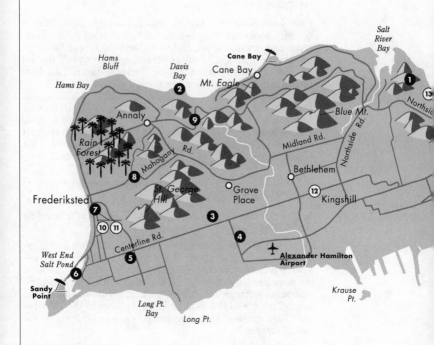

● Exploring Sites

⑩ Hotels and Restaurants

Exploring
Cruzan Distillery, **4**
Davis Bay, **2**
Frederiksted, **7**
Judith's Fancy, **1**
St. Croix Leap, **8**

St. George Village
Botanical Gardens, **3**
Scenic Road West, **9**
West End Salt Pond, **6**
Whim Greathouse, **5**

Dining
Captain's Table, **14**
Club Comanche, **15**
Cormorant Beach
Club, **13**
King's Alley, **16**
Serendipity, **17**
Top Hat, **18**

Lodging
Anchor Inn, **24**
The Buccaneer, **21**
Carambola Beach
Resort and Golf Club, **12**
Club Comanche, **15**
Cormorant Beach
Club, **13**

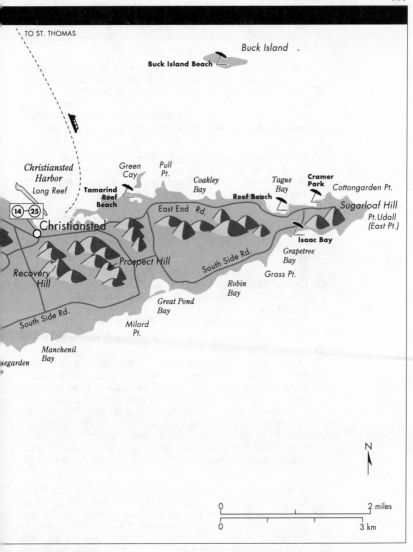

TO ST. THOMAS

Buck Island

Buck Island Beach

Christiansted Harbor

Long Reef

Tamarind Reef Beach

Green Cay

Pull Pt.

Coakley Bay

Tague Bay

Reef Beach

Cramer Park

Cottongarden Pt.

14 — 25

Christiansted

East End Rd.

Sugarloaf Hill

Pt. Udall (East Pt.)

Isaac Bay

Recovery Hill

Prospect Hill

South Side Rd.

Grapetree Bay

Grass Pt.

Robin Bay

Great Pond Bay

South Side Rd.

Milord Pt.

Manchenil Bay

aegarden

N

0 — 2 miles
0 — 3 km

near the small stone jetty you may see a few wet-suited, tank-backed figures making their way out to the "drop-off" (a bit farther out there is steeper drop-off to 12,000 feet). Other than divers, you won't see too many people here.

Rising behind you is **Mt. Eagle,** St. Croix's highest peak, at 1,165 feet. Leaving Cane Bay and passing North Star beach, follow the beautiful coastal road to **Davis Bay.** First, you will enjoy the panoramic views of the sea along this winding corniche. Second, it's worth getting a glimpse of the strikingly beautiful setting of Carambola, a luxurious new Rockresort hotel.

The road comes to an end here. Drive back about a mile and follow Route 69, River Road, to the right, inland, continuing on it all the way to Centerline Road (Route 70, or Queen Mary Highway). This is the island's central superhighway, the quickest route between Christiansted and Frederiksted. After driving about 1½ miles, you can turn off to the right for a visit to the **St. George Village Botanical Gardens,** 17 acres of lush and fragrant flora amid the ruins of a 19th-century sugarcane plantation village.

Just across the Centerline Road, off of Route 64, you'll find the **Cruzan Distillery,** which is, well, a rum business. The rum is made with pure rain water. Visitors are welcome for a tour and a free piña colada. If you hear a whoosh in your head, it's not the rum but the sky traffic at nearby Alexander Hamilton Airport.

Return to Centerline Road and drive west to Frederiksted. On the way, the **Whim Greathouse** is a must stop. The lovingly restored estate, with a windmill, cookhouse, and other buildings, will give you a true sense of what life was like on St. Croix's sugar plantations in the 1800s. The singular oval-shape and high-ceiling great house has antique furniture, decor, and utensils well worth seeing. Notice that it has a fresh and airy atmosphere. (The waterless moat around the great house was used not for defense but for gathering cooling air.) It is built of stone, coral, lime, and molasses. Its apothecary exhibit is the largest in all the West Indies. You will also find a museum gift shop.

Now let's head for the beach—the largest in all the U.S. Virgin Islands. **Sandy Point,** a National Natural Landmark site at St. Croix's southwestern tip, has a splendid beach and the **West End Salt Pond,** rife with mangroves and little blue herons. In the spring, large leatherback sea turtles clamber up the white sand to lay their eggs here. You will also find seashells and brown pelicans.

A short drive up the placid western coast of the island brings you to correspondingly placid **Frederiksted,** founded in 1751. A single long cruise-ship pier juts into the sparkling sea from this historic coastal town, noted less for its Danish than for its Victorian architecture (dating from after the uprising of former slaves and the great fire of 1878). A stroll around will take you no more than an hour.

Restored **Fort Frederik,** next to the pier, was completed late in the 18th century. Here, in 1848, the slaves of the Danish West Indies were freed by Governor General Peter van Scholten. Right at the end of the pier, you can stop at the **Customs House,** which has a Division of Tourism Visitors Bureau. Walk down

Market Street to the **Market Place,** where you can buy fresh fruits and vegetables early in the morning, and around the corner on Prince Street to the **Old Danish School,** designed in the 1830s by a Danish architect named Hingleberg and now part of Frederiksted's Ingeborg Nesbett Clinic. **St. Paul's Episcopal Church,** a mixture of classic and Gothic Revival architecture, is two blocks south on Prince Street; it survived several hurricanes after its construction in 1812 and became Episcopal when the United States purchased the island in 1917. A few steps away, on King Cross Street, you'll come to **Apothecary Hall,** which survived the fire of 1878. Walk south and turn right on Queen Cross Street to the **Old Public Library,** or **Bell House,** which now houses an arts and crafts center and, in a more recent addition, the **Dorsch Cultural Center** for performing arts.

You're back at the waterfront again and if you walk up Strand Street, you'll come to **Victoria House,** once a private residence and now a landmark that is Frederiksted's best-known example of Victorian gingerbread architecture.

The whole west end of the island, from Sandy Point on the south to Ham's Bluff on the north, is lined with one inviting empty beach after another. The area north and east of Frederiksted is **rain forest,** much of it private property but laced with roads open to the public. Just north of Frederiksted, turn right on Route 76, or **Mahogany Road** (the best of the roads in this area), and watch for the sign on the right to **St. Croix Leap,** a place where you can see or purchase handsome articles of mahogany, saman, or thibet wood crafted by local artisans. You'll find that the rain-forest air is surprisingly cool.

Return west to the coast road (Route 63) and head north to **Sprat Hall Plantation,** owned and run for generations by the Hurd family and famed for its home-cooked food (you can stay here as a guest). The beautiful great house is the oldest in the Virgin Islands. This is also the place to arrange a few hours of horseback riding.

Time Out Pull up a chair at the breezy **Sprat Hall Beach Restaurant** (across the road from Sprat Hall Plantation, tel. 809/772–0305) and have a cooling soda or rum drink and an order of its famous pumpkin fritters while you gaze through the beach sea grapes at the calm and glistening Caribbean. A friendly banana quit with a sweet tooth may hop onto your table.

From here, you can return to Christiansted the easy and swift way, south on Route 63 to Frederiksted and then left onto Centerline Road. But if time allows and you have four-wheel drive, zip north toward Hams Bluff and take the marvelous **Scenic Road West** to its end at Route 69, near North Star Beach and Cane Bay.

Exploring St. John

Numbers in the margin correspond with points of interest on the St. John map.

St. John is a conveniently small island. While many of its southern-coast beaches and other sites can be reached only on foot, most of the island's famed beaches are easily accessible by car or Jeep. This suggested itinerary takes you along much of

St. John

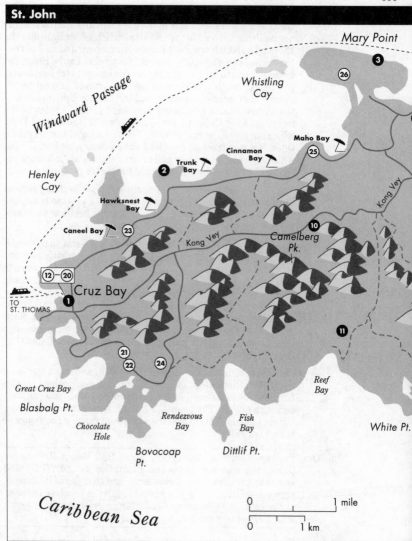

Mary Point

Windward Passage

Whistling Cay

Henley Cay

Maho Bay ㉕

Cinnamon Bay

Trunk Bay ②

Hawksnest Bay

Caneel Bay ㉓

Kong Vey

Camelberg Pk. ⑩

⑫—⑳

Cruz Bay ①

TO ST. THOMAS

⑪

Kong Vey

㉖ ③

Reef Bay

Great Cruz Bay

Blasbalg Pt.

㉑ ㉒ ㉔

Chocolate Hole

Rendezvous Bay

Fish Bay

Bovocoap Pt.

Dittlif Pt.

White Pt.

Caribbean Sea

0 _____ 1 mile
0 _____ 1 km

Exploring	Fortsberg, **7**	Pusser's, **12**
Annaberg Plantation, **4**	Kong Vey, **10**	Shipwreck Landing, **27**
Bordeaux Mountain, **9**	Minna Neger Ghut, **3**	The Upper Deck, **24**
Christ of the Caribbean Statue, **2**	Reef Bay Trail, **11**	
Coral Bay, **5**	Salt Pond, **8**	**Lodging**
Cruz Bay, **1**		Caneel Bay, **23**
East End, **6**	**Dining**	Cinnamon Bay Campground, **25**
	The Back Yard, **14**	
	Fred's, **15**	
	Fronds, **21**	
	Lime Inn, **13**	

Lodging
The Cruz Inn, **19**
Cruz Views, **17**
Gallows Point, **16**
The Inn at Tamarind Court, **20**
Maho Bay Camp, **26**
Raintree Inn, **18**
Virgin Grand Beach Hotel, **22**

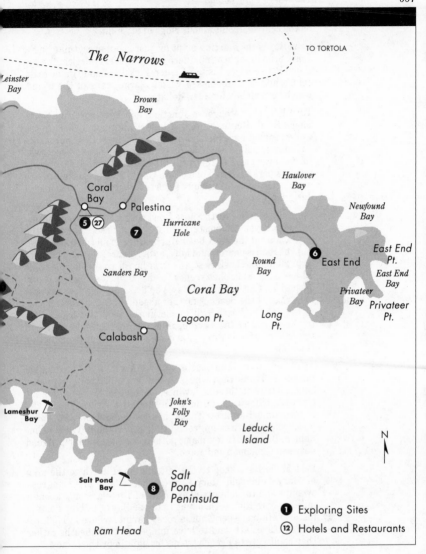

The Narrows

TO TORTOLA

Leinster
Bay

Brown
Bay

Coral
Bay

Palestina

5 **27**

7

*Hurricane
Hole*

*Haulover
Bay*

*Newfound
Bay*

*East End
Pt.*

6 East End

*East End
Bay*

Sanders Bay

*Round
Bay*

*Privateer
Bay* *Privateer
Pt.*

Coral Bay

Lagoon Pt.

*Long
Pt.*

Calabash

*John's
Folly
Bay*

*Leduck
Island*

**Lameshur
Bay**

N

**Salt Pond
Bay**

8

*Salt
Pond
Peninsula*

Ram Head

1 Exploring Sites

12 Hotels and Restaurants

the scenic northern coast before a return trip over a paved road on the central, mountainous ridge of St. John.

❶ **Cruz Bay** is the starting point for just about everything on St. John. Stop first at the northern side of the ferry dock at the **National Park Service Visitors Center.** Pick up a handy guide to St. John's hiking trails or see various large maps of the island, which you can buy for a few dollars.

Turn left, past Mongoose Junction, and head north on North Shore Road, Route 20. A half mile ahead, you'll come to the well-groomed gardens and beaches of **Caneel Bay,** purchased and developed in the 1950s by Laurance Rockefeller (who turned over much of the rest of the island to the U.S. government as parkland) and one of the Caribbean's best-known and most ecologically conscious resorts. Visitors are welcome at designated areas.

Continue east on North Shore Road with all the sense of anticipation that you can muster: you are about to see, one after the other, four of the most beautiful beaches in all the Caribbean. But the road is narrow and hilly, so drive carefully (and no more than 20 mph). **Hawksnest,** the first beach you will come to, is where Alan Alda shot scenes for his film *The Four Seasons*. Though it is closer to Cruz Bay, you'll usually find fewer people here than at the beaches farther ahead. Just past Hawksnest, swing left to Peace Hill (sometimes called Sugarloaf Hill)
❷ to the *Christ of the Caribbean* statue and an old sugar-mill tower. The area is grassy, and views do not get much better than this.

Your next stop—and that of quite a few tourist-filled safari buses—is **Trunk Bay,** whose famed beach has an underwater snorkeling trail (those red, white, and blue markers you see out there) and lifeguards on duty. This beach is worth a return visit. **Cinnamon Bay,** after Trunk, has a wider and more sweeping beach and is also a campground site, as is **Maho Bay,** after Cinnamon. Beware of a few major potholes on the level strip of road between Cinnamon and Maho.

Past Maho Bay, keep to the left and head north to the area of **Mary Point** and **Mary Creek,** where there are mangrove swamps and the mountainous island of Tortola is only about a mile away to the northeast of Leinster Bay. At Mary Point is
❸ historic **Minna Neger Ghut,** a rocky ravine, where in 1733, rebelling slaves are said to have jumped to their deaths rather than capitulate to French troops brought in by the Danes.

❹ The partially restored **Annaberg Plantation,** built in the 1780s and once an important sugar mill, is just ahead on North Shore Road. Pick up a guide pamphlet and stroll around. Slaves, Danes, and Dutchmen toiled here for years to produce crude sugar, molasses, and rum for export. If you want to get your feet literally wet, be here on Monday at 2 PM for a 1½-hour guided seashore walk along beaches and mangrove lagoons.

From Annaberg, keep to the left and swing south; then go east,
❺ on Route 10 to the lovely, sleepy area of **Coral Bay,** where St. John's first sugar plantations were established. This being the dry end of the island, you'll see quite a few cacti. If you wish, detour here past Hurricane Hole to the remote and pristine
❻ **East End,** only a 15- or 20-minute ride from Coral Bay, where two millennia ago there were Indian settlements. At Haulover

Bay, only a couple of hundred yards separate the Atlantic Ocean from the Caribbean.

7 South of the ball field at Coral Bay is **Fortsberg.** This is the site of Fort Frederik, which was taken by oppressed slaves during a bloody revolt in 1733.

8 From Coral Bay, Route 107 takes you south to the peninsula of **Salt Pond,** which is only about a foot above sea level. If you're weary of driving, you can hike a trail south to the spectacular cliffs of **Ram Head.** In any case, you—or your rented car—can't proceed much farther on 107 without venturing onto a truly rocky road west. But be sure to get at least a view of beautiful **Lameshur Bay,** one of the best snorkeling places on St. John and an area used for underwater training by the U.S. Navy.

Time Out Pull over to airy and tidy **Shipwreck Landing and Bar** (on Rte. 107, just south of Coral Bay, tel. 809/776–8540) for some conch fritters or a burger and some friendly chitchat with Mike, the affable young owner.

Go north on Route 107 to Centerline Road, Route 10. Go west or left, over the heights of the island toward Cruz Bay. On your left, past the turnoff for the North Shore Road, you'll pass the **9** bumpy road leading to **Bordeaux Mountain,** at 1,277 feet St. John's highest peak. This is also an area of rain forest. Stop for a moment hereabouts and you'll find bay trees (*Pimenta racemosa*). Crackle a leaf from one and you'll get a whiff of the bay rum for which St. John is famous. A mile ahead, stop on the **10** right at **Kong Vey** ("King's Road") for a good view of some of the British Virgin Islands to the northeast.

To appreciate the Bordeaux Mountain region fully, return **11** when you have time and hike down the **Reef Bay Trail** (off Centerline Road), which ultimately leads you to some sugar-estate ruins and St. John's mysterious petroglyphs, pool-surrounded rock carvings that have been attributed to both pre-Columbian Arawak Indians and later island slaves.

Off the Beaten Track

Third World Electronics (Four Winds Plaza, tel. 809/775–5510). This jam-packed music store at Four Winds Plaza is where to go if you're looking for the latest trends in Caribbean music. It's especially easy to find on Saturday nights, when speakers set up outside the store cause the plaza to vibrate with soca (rock-influenced calypso). The sales staff will gladly acquaint you with what's happening in calypso, reggae, soca, and zouk (the latter a fusion of all the former, with a dash of French melody thrown in).

Participant Sports

For water sports, especially, you've come to the right islands. Your hotel, if it doesn't have its own boats, dive shop, etc., will usually have arrangements with sailing, scuba, and other enterprises to meet your wishes.

Golf The U.S. Virgin Islands has three 18-hole golf courses and one 9-hole course, none of them on St. John.

St. Thomas   Scenic **Mahogany Run** (tel. 809/775–5000), with a par-70 18-hole course and a view of the British Virgin Islands, lies to the north of Charlotte Amalie and has one "Devil's Triangle" trio of holes.

St. Croix   **The Buccaneer's** (tel. 809/773–2100) 18-hole course is conveniently close to (east of) Christiansted. Yet more spectacular is **Carambola** (tel. 809/778–0747), in the valleyed northwestern part of the island, designed by Robert Trent Jones. **The Reef Club** (tel. 809/773–9250), at the northeastern part of the island, has nine holes.

Horseback Riding   St. Thomas has little to offer the equestrian, but St. Croix and St. John both have stables and beautiful countryside to trot through.

St. Croix   At Sprat Hall, near Frederiksted, Jill Hurd runs **Jill's Equestrian Stables** (tel. 809/772–2880 or 809/772–2627) and will take you clip-clopping through the rain forest, along the coast, or on moonlit rides. Sunday-morning brunch rides are one of the options offered by **Hidden Valley Equestrian Center** (tel. 809/778–8670), just east of The Buccaneer.

St. John   **Pony Express Riding Stables** (tel. 809/776–6922 or 809/776–6494), rides out on scenic trails around Bordeaux Mountain and along beaches.

Sailboarding   Most of the major water-sports centers on the three islands can accommodate the Windsurfer.

St. Thomas   The **St. Thomas Diving Club** (tel. 809/776–2381 or 809/775–1800, ext. 185), at Bolongo Bay, caters to sail-boarders as well as scuba divers.

St. Croix   Call either **Caribbean Sea Adventures,** at Kings Wharf in Christiansted (tel. 809/773–5922), or **Sea Shadows,** at Cane Bay (809/778–3850).

St. John   Contact **St. John Watersports,** in Cruz Bay (tel. 809/776–6256).

Sailing/Boating   The U.S. Virgin Islands constitutes the biggest charter-boat fleet base in the Western Hemisphere, and you can choose among ketches, yawls, schooners, sloops, cutters, catamarans, power boats, and trimarans. More than 175 professionally crewed charter yachts are associated with the **Virgin Islands Charteryacht League,** at Homeport, St. Thomas (tel. 809/774–3944 or 800/524–2061).

St. Thomas   Most boats operate out of Red Hook, at the eastern end of the island. **Watersports Center** (Sapphire Bay, tel. 809/775–6755) will book you a full-day or half-day sail; so will **Sea Adventures** (Frenchman's Reef Hotel, tel. 809/774–9652; 809/776–8500, ext. 625; or 800/524–2096). **Coconut Cruises** (at Stouffer Grand Beach Resort, tel. 809/775–5959) has half-day, full-day, and sunset cruises aboard a 51-foot trimaran, with an open bar. Snorkeling, fishing gear, and underwater cameras are provided.

St. Croix   **Mile-Mark Charters** (tel. 809/773–2285) has both a sloop and a trimaran for full- or half-day sails. **Caribbean Sea Adventures** (tel. 809/773–5922) arranges bareboat and crewed charters and rents small boats as well.

St. John   **St. John Watersports** (Mongoose Junction, Cruz Bay, tel. 809/776–6256) handles both day sails and charters.

Scuba Diving and Snorkeling	There are more than 20 dive operators on the three islands, and many of the hotels on St. Thomas and St. Croix offer dive packages. For drop-offs or walls, St. Croix, where 18 hotels have scuba packages, is the place.

St. Thomas **Joe Vogel Diving Co.** (tel. 809/775–7610), the oldest scuba-certification school in the U.S. Virgin Islands, is run by an ex-navy frogman who personally conducts all classes and dives and is something of a legend on St. Thomas; among Joe's offerings is a sunrise shore dive to an airplane wreck. Other reliable scuba and snorkel operators are **Aqua Action** (Secret Harbour, tel. 809/775–6285), **Underwater Safaris** (Ramada Yacht Haven Motel and Marina, tel. 809/774–1350 and 809/774–9700), and **St. Thomas Diving Club** (Bolongo Bay, tel. 809/775–1800 and 800/524–4746).

St. Croix **Caribbean Sea Adventures** has year-round dive packages for 6, 10, or 14 boat dives and is headquartered at The Buccaneer (tel. 809/773–6011 or 809/773–5922). You are also in good hands with Steve Fordyce and **Sea Shadows** (tel. 809/778–3850 or 809/773–1441) right at Cane Bay and its splendid wall. **The Belangers Virgin Dive** (tel. 809/778–9764) headquarters is at Salt River Marina, near where Columbus once landed. If you're a beginning snorkeler, try Dick Mooney's **Snorkeling Safari** (Tamarind Reef, tel. 809/773–0951).

St. John **Low Key Watersports** (Wharfside Village, (tel. 809/776–6042) dives three different wrecks, including that of the *Rhone*. Other scuba operators are **Cruz Bay Watersports** (tel. 809/776–6234) and **St. John Watersports** (tel. 809/776–6256).

If you'd like to get introduced to the feel of scuba diving but would rather stay in shallow water and have an air-hose tether to a "buoyant flotation unit," try **Snuba** (tel. 809/775–4063 or 809/776–6922).

Sportfishing In the past quarter-century, some 20 world records—many for blue marlin—have been set in these waters. Sailfish, skipjack, bonito, tuna (allison, blackfin, and yellowfin), and wahoo are abundant. On St. Thomas and St. John, there are also more than a hundred government-listed spots for shoreline fishing where you may hook up with tarpon, crevalle, snook, bonefish, snapper, or even barracuda.

St. Thomas Call **American Yacht Harbor** at Red Hook (tel. 809/775–6454) if you're interested in some serious angling. Or you may join **Captain Don Merton** (through Island Holiday Tours, (tel. 809/775–6500) for a day on St. Thomas's famous North Drop.

St. Croix **Caribbean Sea Adventures,** at Kings Wharf (tel. 809/773–5922), has deep-sea fishing charters. **Ruffian Enterprises,** also at Kings Wharf (tel. 809/773–6011 or 809/773–0917), will take you out on a 41-foot Hatteras. Or join Captain Bunny Jones aboard the *Catch 22* (tel. 809/773–0576, 809/773–4482, or 809/778–6987). At Kings Alley Dock, you will find the *Lady Mac K* (tel. 809/778–6118 or 809/778–0487), a custom-rigged Hatteras Fisherman.

St. John **Caneel Bay** (tel. 809/776–6111), at the edge of Cruz Bay, will arrange fishing outings.

Tennis Numerous hotels on St. Thomas and St. Croix have tennis courts for both day and night play, and there are a few public courts on all three islands.

St. Thomas Among the hotels that have tennis courts are **Bluebeard's Castle, Bolongo Bay Beach, Frenchman's Reef, Limetree Beach, Sapphire Beach, Secret Harbour, Stouffer Grand Beach,** and **Virgin Isle.** There are also two public courts at Long Bay and two at Sub Base.

St. Croix There are courts at **The Buccaneer, Carambola Beach,** Divi St. **Croix, Hotel on the Cay, St. Croix by the Sea, Cormorant Beach Club,** and **Queen's Quarter** hotels. Public courts can be found at Conegata Park (two) and Fort Frederik (two), on the western side of St. Croix.

St. John Resorts that have courts are **Caneel Bay, Cruz Inn, Edie's Eden,** and **Virgin Grand.** There are also four public courts in Cruz Bay.

Shopping

St. Thomas:
Charlotte Amalie

There are well over 400 shops in Charlotte Amalie alone, and in the Havensight area, where the cruise ships dock, there are at least 50 more clustered in converted warehouses. Even diehard shoppers won't want to cover all the boutiques, since a large percentage peddle the same T-shirts and togs. Many visitors devote their shopping time on St. Thomas to the stores that sell handicrafts and luxury items. Even if you don't intend to buy a fur coat, it's fun to say you tried one on in St. Thomas, and there are now several furriers where you can do just that.

Although those famous "give away" prices no longer abound, shoppers on St. Thomas can still save money. Today, a realistic appraisal puts prices on many items at about 20% off stateside prices. What's more, there is no sales tax in the U.S. Virgin Islands, and visitors can take advantage of the $800 duty-free allowance and the additional 5% discount on the next $800 worth of goods. Remember to save receipts.

You won't need to spend a lot of time comparison shopping since some luxury items—perfumes, cosmetics, liquor—are uniformly priced throughout the U.S. Virgin Islands. Prices on almost everything else, from leather goods to leisure wear, vary very little from shop to shop. The prices on jewelry do vary quite a bit, however, and it's here that you'll still run across some real "finds."

Shopping Districts. The major shopping area is in downtown Charlotte Amalie in centuries-old buildings that once served as merchants' warehouses and that for the most part have been converted to retail establishments. Both sides of **Main Street** are lined with shops, as are the side streets and walkways between Main Street and the Waterfront. These narrow lanes and arcades have names like Drake's Passage, Royal Dane Mall, Palm Passage, Trompeter Gade, Hibiscus Alley, and Raadet's Gade.

The **Bakery Square Shopping Mall** (one block north of Main St. off Nye Gade) has about 15 boutiques. The streets adjacent to Bakery Square, notably Back Street, Nye Gade, Garden Street, Kongens Gade, and Norre Gade, are also very good areas for browsing. At **Havensight Mall,** which is close to the deep-water port where the cruise ships dock, you'll find many branches of downtown stores as well as specialty shops and boutiques.

Charlotte Amalie Shopping

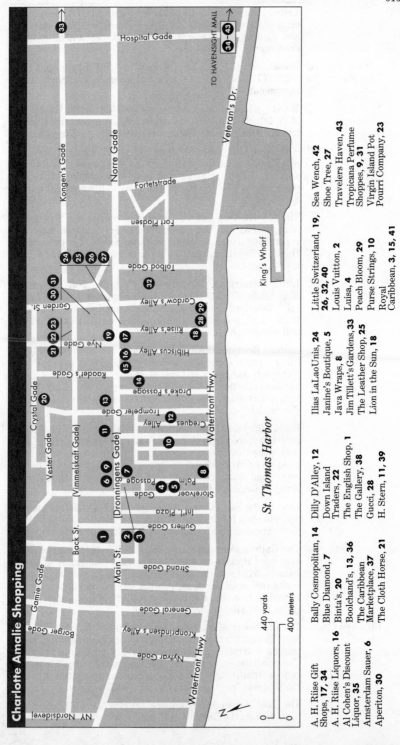

To Havensight Mall

Hospital Gade

St. Thomas Harbor

King's Wharf

Veteran's Dr.

Kongen's Gade

Norre Gade

Fortetstrade

Fort Pladsen

Tolbod Gade

Garden St.

Nye Gade

Cardow's Alley

Riise's Alley

Hibiscus Alley

Raadet's Gade

Crystal Gade

Vester Gade

Drake's Passage

Trompeter Gade

Creques Alley

Waterfront Hwy.

(Vimmelskaft Gade)

(Dronningens Gade)

Back St.

Main St.

Gutters Gade

Strand Gade

General Gade

Storetvaer Gade

Palm Passage

Int'l. Plaza

Gamle Gade

Borger Gade

Kronprindsen's Alley

Nyvar Gade

Waterfront Hwy.

NY Nordsidevel

440 yards

400 meters

N

A. H. Riise Gift
Shops, **17, 34**
A. H. Riise Liquors, **16**
Al Cohen's Discount
Liquor, **35**
Amsterdam Sauer, **6**
Aperiton, **30**

Bally Cosmopolitan, **14**
Blue Diamond, **7**
Binta's, **20**
Boolchand's, **13, 36**
The Caribbean
Marketplace, **37**
The Cloth Horse, **21**

Dilly D'Alley, **12**
Down Island
Traders, **22**
The English Shop, **1**
The Gallery, **38**
Gucci, **28**
H. Stern, **11, 39**

Ilias LaLaoUnis, **24**
Janine's Boutique, **5**
Java Wraps, **8**
Jim Tillett's Gardens, **33**
The Leather Shop, **25**
Lion in the Sun, **18**

Little Switzerland, **19,
26, 32, 40**
Louis Vuitton, **2**
Luisa, **4**
Peach Bloom, **29**
Purse Strings, **10**
Royal
Caribbean, **3, 15, 41**

Sea Wench, **42**
Shoe Tree, **27**
Travelers Haven, **43**
Tropicana Perfume
Shoppes, **9, 31**
Virgin Island Pot
Pourri Company, **23**

Listed here are many of the major shops and the types of merchandise they carry. Virtually all stores accept MasterCard and Visa, and most accept American Express and other major credit cards.

Cameras and Electronics **Boolchand's** (31 Main St., tel. 809/776–0794; Havensight Mall, tel. 809/776–0302) carries all kinds of cameras and audio-video equipment.

Royal Caribbean (33 Main St., tel. 809/776–4110; Havensight Mall, tel. 809/776–8890) has attractive prices on some cameras and accessories; Sony Walkmans are usually good buys here.

China and Crystal **A.H. Riise Gift Shops** (37 Main St. and Havensight Mall, tel. 809/776–2303) carries Waterford and Wedgwood, Royal Crown and Royal Doulton at good prices. For example, a five-piece place setting of Royal Crown Derby's Old Imari goes for under $350.

The English Shop (Main St. at Market Square and Havensight Mall, tel. 809/774–3495) offers china and crystal from major European and Japanese manufacturers. Spode, Limoges, Royal Doulton, Royal Crafton, Royal Worcester, and Villeroy & Boch are featured.

Little Switzerland (3 locations on Main St., 1 at Havensight Mall, tel. 809/776–2010) has crystal pieces from Lalique, Baccarat, Waterford, Swarovski, Riedel, and Orrefors and china from Villeroy & Boch, Aynsley, Wedgwood, Royal Doulton, and Wedgwood.

Clothing **Janine's Boutique** (8A-2 Palm Passage, tel. 809/774–8243) features women's and men's dressy and casual apparel from European designers and manufacturers, including the Louis Feraud collection. They also carry accessories. A men's-only corner has select finds from Valentino, Christian Dior, and Pierre Cardin.

Binta's (Crystal Gade) features batik fabrics or bright African prints that are perfect for a jumpsuit, halter/skirt or long pants with wrap top. Shoppers can place their orders in the morning and pick up in the afternoon. In addition to being a talented designer and seamstress, Binta delights in conversation. A wide array of earrings of unusual design is also available.

Lion in the Sun (Riise's Alley, tel. 809/776–4203) is another place to shop for designer fashions for men and women. Some items are available for about 25% less than stateside prices.

Galleries **The Gallery** (Veteran's Dr., tel. 809/776–4641) carries some very good Haitian art along with works by a number of Virgin Islands artists. Items on display include oil paintings, metal sculpture, wood carvings, painted screens and boxes, figures carved from stone, and oversize papier-mâché figures. Prices range from $100 to $5,000.

Gifts and Crafts **The Caribbean Marketplace** (Havensight Mall, Bldg. III, tel. 809/776–5400) is the place to look for Caribbean handicrafts, including Caribelle batiks from St. Lucia; bikinis from the Cayman Islands; and Sunny Caribee spices, soaps, teas, and coffees from Tortola. Visitors can make an appointment to tour the adjacent fragrance factory (tel. 809/774–2166).

The Cloth Horse (Bakery Square, tel. 809/774–4761) has signed pottery from the Dominican Republic; wicker and rattan furniture and household goods from the island of Hispaniola; and pottery, rugs, and bedspreads from all over the world.

Down Island Traders (Bakery Square and Frenchman's Reef, tel. 809/774–3419) offers hand-painted calabash bowls ($5); jams, jellies, spices, and herbs; herbal teas made of rum, passion fruit, and mango; high-mountain coffee from Jamaica; and a variety of handicrafts from throughout the Caribbean.

Jim Tillett's Gardens (Estate Tutu, tel. 809/775–1405) is more than worth the cab fare to reach the complex. Tillett's artwork is on display, and you can watch craftsmen and artisans produce silk-screened fabrics, pottery, candles, watercolors, and other handicrafts.

Java Wraps (24 Palm Passage, tel. 809/774–3700) has Indonesian batik creations. This store offers a complete line of beach cover-ups, swimwear, and leisure wear for women, men, and children. The most interesting items are the signed sarongs ($35–$120) and the ceremonial puppets from Java ($60).

The **Virgin Islands Pot Pourri Company** (Bakery Sq., tel. 809/776–1038) displays the owner's own snazzy batik and tie-dye creations as well as the work of other Virgin Islands fabric artists.

Jewelry **A.H. Riise Gift Shops** (37 Main St. and Havensight Mall, tel. 809/776–2303), St. Thomas's oldest and largest shop for luxury items, offers jewelry, pearls, ceramics, china, crystal, flatwear, perfumes, and watches, as well as an unusual collection of artwork, books, and historic prints.

Amsterdam Sauer (14 Main St., tel. 809/774–2222) displays many fine, one-of-a-kind designs.

Aperiton (3A Main St., tel. 809/776–0780) is a good spot for lovely jewelry made by Greek and Italian designers.

Blue Diamond (25A Main St., tel. 809/776–4340) is favored by many locals; this store shows many of its own 14K and 18K designs crafted by European goldsmiths.

H. Stern (12 Main St., Havensight Mall, Frenchman's Reef, Stouffer Grand Beach Resort, and Bluebeard's, tel. 809/776–1939) is one of the most respected names in gems. The boutique at the Havensight Mall has one of the best collections of tennis bracelets available anywhere.

Ilias LaLaoUnis (37 Main St., tel. 809/774–5294) includes collections of 18K- and 22K-gold pieces designed by its Greek owner.

Little Switzerland (2 locations on Main St., 1 on Emancipation Sq., tel. 809/776–2010) is the sole distributor for Rolex watches. The store also does a booming mail-order business; ask for a catalogue.

The **Peach Bloom** boutique (Post Office Alley, tel. 809/776–2788) shows select pieces of antique jewelry and one-of-a-kind pieces from the United States and Europe ranging in price from $50 into the thousands. The selection includes bracelets, rings, pendants, lockets, pins, watches, fobs, and Victorian silver baby spoons and teething rings.

Leather Goods **Gucci** (A.H. Riise Gift Alley, 37 Main St., tel. 809/774–7841) offers traditional Gucci insignia designs in wallets, bags, briefcases, totes, walking shoes, and loafers for men and women.

The Leather Shop (Main St. at Dronningens Gade, tel. 809/776–3995; Havensight Mall, Bldg. II, tel. 809/776–0040) has some big names at big prices: Fendi and Bottega Veneta are prevalent.

Louis Vuitton (24 Main St. in Palm Passage, tel. 809/774–3644) is an example of St. Thomas shopping at its most elegant. From scarves and umbrellas to briefcases and steamer trunks, all Vuitton workmanship is the finest.

Luisa (Palm Passage, tel. 809/776–1085) has shoes and bags exclusively from Italy.

At **Purse Strings** (2A-1 Royal Dane Mall, tel. 809/774–1219) handbags ranging from designs by Christian Dior, Carlo Fiori, and Lesandro Saraso to straw and canvas Caribbean creations hang from the walls, counters, and ceiling. There is also a large selection of eelskin and snakeskin bags and accessories; eelskin attachés are a good buy for $160.

The **Shoe Tree** (37 Main St., tel. 809/774–3900) carries women's shoe styles under a top price of $70—one of the Caribbean's best-kept shopping secrets. Designers include Bandolino, Pierre Cardin, Evan Picone, and Liz Claiborne.

Travelers Haven (Havensight Mall, tel. 809/775–1798) has leather bags, backpacks, vests, and money belts.

Liquor Liquor prices are standard throughout all the Virgin Islands, and U.S. citizens can carry back a gallon of liquor or five "fifths" duty-free.

A.H. Riise Liquors (34 Main St. and Havensight Mall, tel. 809/774–6900) has a large selection of liquors, cordials, wines, and tobacco, including rare vintage Cognacs, Armagnacs, ports, and Madeiras; they also stock imported cigars, fruits in brandy, and barware from England.

Al Cohen's Discount Liquor (across from Havensight Mall, Long Bay Rd., tel. 809/774–3690), a warehouse-style store with a large wine department, is open seven days a week.

Perfumes Fine fragrances from France waft around every bend in the cobblestoned roads; where you buy hardly matters, since prices are the same in all shops.

The **Tropicana Perfume Shoppes** (2 Dronningen Gade, tel. 809/774–0010; 14 Dronningen Gade, tel. 809/774–1834) offers the largest selection of fragrances for men and women in the Virgin Islands; both shops give small free samples to customers.

A.H. Riise Gift Shop (tel. 809/774–6900) is the best bet for perfumes in the Havensight Mall.

Sportswear **Bally Cosmopolitan** (Drake's Passage, tel. 809/776–2040) may have the largest collection of Gortex swimsuits outside Israel: the inventory includes about 300 different styles of bikinis, maillots, and "constructed" one-piece suits. For men, this store offers one of the best selections of knit sport shirts from Italy (Fila, Ellesse) and the finest sea-island cotton shirts from the London firm of Smedley.

At the **Dilly D'Alley** boutique (Trompeter Gade, tel. 809/776–5006) shoppers can select from over 20 lines of swimwear. Definitely a best buy are the unusually comfortable, tie-dyed cotton wrap-around dresses.

Sea Wench, at the Havensight Mall (Building III, tel. 809/776–1088), mixes known names in swimwear (Cacharel, Roxanne, Jantzen) with California-casual designs and Brazilian briefs. They also import some very lacy lingerie from France, Austria, and the United States.

St. Croix While St. Croix does not have nearly as many shops as St. Thomas does, the selection of duty-free goods is still fairly large. Many of St. Thomas's leading shops have branches in St. Croix, but there are also plenty of independent merchants that have items you may not be able to find in Charlotte Amalie. In Christiansted, most of the shops are clustered in the historic district near the harbor. **King Street, Strand Street,** and the arcades that lead off them comprise the major shopping district. The longest arcade is **Caravelle Arcade,** located in the hotel of the same name.

Gallows Bay, located halfway between Christiansted and Fredriksted, has developed an attractive boutique area that features unusual silver jewelry and gift items made on the island.

St. John The opportunities for duty-free shopping are more limited— and the prices a bit higher—on St. John compared with the other islands. One spot popular with visitors is **Wharfside Village,** an attractive, compact mall of some 30 shops overlooking Cruz Bay Harbor. **Mongoose Junction,** a shopping center just north of Cruz Bay across from the Park Service Visitor Center, has a number of shops that sell handicrafts designed and fashioned by resident artisans.

Dining

Just about every kind of cuisine you can imagine is available in the U.S. Virgin Islands, and the price range is broad enough to match any visitor's pocketbook. With so much air traffic between the mainland and the islands, supplies are as fresh as they are in most major cities of the United States. Beef, pork, and poultry are as good as you will find them at home; the unusual and delicious variety of local fruits, vegetables, and seafood is a culinary bonus here.

St. Thomas is the most cosmopolitan of the islands and has the most visitors, so it is not surprising that the island also has the largest number and greatest variety of restaurants. St. Croix restaurants are both more relaxed, and, in some ways, more elegant. Dining on St. John is, in general, more casual; the emphasis is on simple food prepared to order in an informal setting at reasonable prices.

The most highly recommended restaurants are indicated by a star ★.

Category	Cost*
Very Expensive	over $35
Expensive	$25–$35

Moderate	$15–$25
Inexpensive	under $15

average cost of a three-course dinner, per person, excluding drinks, service, and sales tax

St. Thomas   **Fiddle Leaf.** American and French nouvelle cuisine is featured at this elegant Art Deco restaurant. Selections range from New Orleans blackened fish and Wisconsin veal to more embellished, sauce-rich fare. The desserts are highly praised. *Government Hill, tel. 809/775–2810. Reservations required. AE, MC, V. Very Expensive.*

★ **Hotel 1829.** The seafood, prime ribs, and venison dishes at Hotel 1829 make dining here one of the best experiences to be had on St. Thomas. The chef's soufflés have won awards. *Government Hill, a few steps up from Main St., Charlotte Amalie, tel. 809/776–1829. Reservations required. AE, MC, V. Very Expensive.*

Eden Paradise Grill. At this lovely terrace restaurant in a sheltered cove, you will dine seated in majestic peacock chairs. The cuisine is French Caribbean. Lobster, veal, and fresh fish dishes are featured, as is duckling flambéed at your table. *Secret Harbour Resort, east end of the island, tel. 809/775–6198. Reservations required. AE, MC, V. Expensive.*

Entre Nous. The view here, high over Charlotte Amalie's harbor, is exhilarating, and the dining is elegant. The Caesar salad is outstanding, and the entrées include rack of lamb, Caribbean lobster, veal, and Chateaubriand. Try Grand Marnier–flamed baked Alaska for dessert. *Bluebeard's Castle, Charlotte Amalie, tel. 809/776–4050. Reservations required. AE, MC, V. Expensive.*

Moghul's Restaurant. This air-conditioned spot is distinctly Chinese in decor, but the new owner has added lots of spicy Indian specialties to the Hunan and Szechuan menu. *Wheatley II Shopping Plaza, at the foot of Raphune Hill, Charlotte Amalie, tel. 809/776–3939. AE, MC, V. Moderate–Expensive.*

The Chart House. On the premises of an old great house called Villa Olga, this restaurant features kabob and teriyaki dishes, lobster, Hawaiian chicken, and a large salad bar. Mud pie is a favorite dessert. *Villa Olga, Frenchtown, tel. 809/774–4262. No reservations except for 10 or more. AE, MC, V. Moderate.*

For the Birds. The beer is served in Mason jars and the Margaritas are available in 46-ounce servings at this beach restaurant with a disco dance floor. You can have sizzling fajitas, barbecued baby back ribs, seafood, or steaks. *Scott Beach, near Compass Point on the east end of the island, tel. 809/775–6431. Reservations only for a party of 6 or more. AE, MC, V. Moderate.*

Harbourfront. Here, right at the waterfront, you can sit next to saltwater aquariums and feast on Caribbean seafood or prime ribs. If you bypass the dolphin (the food fish) or mako shark and choose the prime ribs, you'll soon see that the Godzilla-size portion will feed three and then some. *72 Kronprindsens Gade, Charlotte Amalie, tel. 809/776–0200. Reservations advised. AE, MC, V. Moderate.*

★ **Piccola Marina Cafe.** Dockside dining at its friendliest is the trademark of this open-air restaurant close to the St. John ferry dock at Red Hook. The clientele is a mix of sailors and fishermen who live on the boats you see along the docks. Specialties are fresh fish—you can watch your dinner being unloaded from the boat and carried to the kitchen during happy hour—and homemade pasta dishes. *Red Hook, tel. 809/775-6350. Reservations suggested. AE, MC, V. Moderate.*

Sugar Reef Cafe. This café at the water's edge is the brainchild of three chefs who got their training at the elegant Hotel 1829 in Charlotte Amalie. The menu is "eclectic/American," with soufflés and homemade ice cream among the specialties. The blue-and-white striped ceiling and vibrant tropical fabrics make for a cheerful dining experience. *Crown Bay, tel. 809/776-4466. Reservations suggested. AE., MC, V. Moderate.*

Zorba's. A waterfall punctuates your conversation at this courtyard Greek restaurant. Souvlaki and moussaka are on the lunch menu, and fish dishes and roast leg of lamb are among the dinner selections. *Government Hill, Charlotte Amalie, tel. 809/776-0444. AE, DC, MC, V. Moderate.*

Eunice's Terrace. The West Indian menu at this lively bar and restaurant includes conch strips sautéed in butter-and-garlic sauce, snapper or grouper fillet, and a seafood combination plate. For dessert there is rum cake, Key lime pie, or sweet potato pie. *Rte. 38, near the Coral World turnoff, tel. 809/775-3975. AE. Moderate–Inexpensive.*

Little Bo Peep. The French West Indian fare at this restaurant includes curried beef, goat, or chicken; conch Creole, callaloo, and, of course, rice and peas, fungi, fried plantain, or potato stuffing as side dishes. *7B Back St., Charlotte Amalie, tel. 809/774-1959. AE, DC, V. Closed Mon. Inexpensive.*

Sparky's Waterfront Saloon. This is a lively and inexpensive place for chili, burgers, or fish 'n' chips at lunchtime or steak, fresh fish, or pasta at dinner. *Waterfront, Charlotte Amalie, tel. 809/774-8015. MC, V. Inexpensive.*

St. Croix **Captain's Table.** Seafood is the forte at this pleasant courtyard restaurant, from shellfish appetizers to island conch, wahoo with white wine, shrimp done Indonesian style, and bouillabaisse. You can also have steak or surf and turf. *Company St., Christiansted, tel. 809/773-4532. Reservations required. AE, MC, V. Expensive.*

★ **Cormorant Beach Club.** Candlelight and the sounds of the night surf create the atmosphere here, where a California chef brings her own touch to Continental and Cruzan dishes. The boneless breast of chicken is blackened with Creole spices and served with black beans and avocado *salsa.* Among the appetizers are conch fritters and carrot-orange soup. *La Grande Princesse, west of Christiansted, tel. 809/778-8920. Reservations suggested. AE, MC, V. Expensive.*

Club Comanche. The atmosphere is very friendly and casual at this upstairs terrace restaurant, where the decor includes an outrigger canoe hanging from the ceiling. The curry of beef fillet is a popular dish, as is the stuffed shrimp Savannah. There are some 15 appetizers on the varied menu. *Strand St., Christiansted, tel. 809/773-2665. Reservations advised. AE, MC, V. Moderate.*

King's Alley. Some nice shrubbery and trees surround this open-air place at the waterfront, where you can get chicken wings, stuffed potato skins, sandwiches, burgers, barbecued ribs or chicken, steak, and even a few Mexican and Japanese selections. *King's Alley, Christiansted, tel. 809/773-0468. AE, MC, V. Moderate.*

★ **Serendipity.** This cozy, iron-gated beach restaurant has brick walls and a front-and-center bar with high rattan arm-stools.

The house specialty is a shrimp-stocked pasta delight, but you can also have Barbadian flying fish, filet mignon, or a special, such as chicken breast sautéed with a cranberry–Grand Marnier sauce. Friday-night barbecues and Sunday brunches are very popular. *Mill Harbour, Christiansted, tel. 809/773–5762. Reservations advised. AE, MC, V. Moderate.*

Top Hat. Many locals consider this restaurant to be the best on the island. It's been in business for 20 years, serving international cuisine with an emphasis on Danish specialties—roast duck, crepes with shrimp, and smoked eel. The old West Indian structure complete with gingerbread trim is nicely accented in gray, white, and pink. The photographs on the walls are the work of owner and European-trained chef Hans Rasmussen. *52 Company St., tel. 809/773–2346. Reservations suggested. AE, MC, V. Closed May–Oct. Moderate–Expensive.*

St. John   **Fronds.** If you have to ask how much, don't come. At this gourmet restaurant at the Virgin Grand Beach Hotel, a five-course meal is served on Fitz and Lloyd china. The chefs' masterpieces include Swedish rainbow trout Laplandia sauté meunière with cream chives and dill sauce. Live classical guitar or piano music accompanies the dining "experience." *Virgin Grand Beach Hotel, tel. 809/776–7171. Reservations advised. Jacket required. AE, DC, MC, V. Very Expensive.*

Pusser's. On an upper level and overlooking the Cruz Bay harbor, this is a lovely place to dine in the cool of an evening. British lunch specialties are shepherd's pie and steak and ale pie. For dinner there is steak, chicken, lamb or pork chops, lobster tail, or a chef's special, such as skewers of fillet chicken with curry sauce, beef with peanut sauce, and monkfish with barbecue sauce. *Wharfside Village, Cruz Bay, tel. 809/774–5489. Reservations advised for 6 or more. AE, MC, V. Expensive.*

★ **Lime Inn.** This busy, roofed open-air restaurant has a nice ornamental garden and beach-furniture chairs. There are several shrimp and steak dishes and such specials as sautéed chicken with artichoke hearts in lemon sauce. On Wednesday nights, there is an all-you-can-eat shrimp feast. *Downtown, Cruz Bay, tel. 809/776–6425. Reservations advised. AE, MC, V. Moderate.*

The Upper Deck. It *is* like a deck, and the view from here at sunset is excellent. Herring and New England fish chowder are appetizers, and besides steak or chops you can have fried scallops, clams, or shrimp, as well as baked local fish or pan-fried liver with bacon and onions. *Up in the hills off South Shore Rd., tel. 809/776–6318. Closed Mon. and Tues. MC, V. Moderate.*

The Back Yard. This open-air, down-to-earth bar/restaurant has a limited menu: burgers, barbecued ribs, kingfish. Miss Maggie cooks on Monday, Wednesday, and Friday. Stop by for what many locals claim is the best conch on the island. *Downtown, Cruz Bay, tel. 809/776–8553. No credit cards. Inexpensive.*

Fred's. This simple place, offering West Indian dishes, is in the center of town. Chicken and fish dishes are complemented by johnnycake and fungi. *Downtown, Cruz Bay, tel. 809/776–6363. No credit cards. Inexpensive.*

★ **Shipwreck Landing.** If you're tooling around St. John east of Cruz Bay, this is a pleasant oasis to stop in for food or refreshment. Burgers, chicken teriyaki, sandwiches, taco salad, and conch fritters are choices for lunch. There is a regular dinner special, along with Cajun dishes and a chicken cordon bleu that comes with banana cream sauce. *Rte. 107, Coral Bay, tel. 809/ 776–8540. Dress: informal. No credit cards. Inexpensive.*

Lodging

The U.S. Virgin Islands win the numbers game. They have more hotels per square inch than any other area in the Caribbean. The concentration is at Charlotte Amalie, St. Thomas, and Christiansted, St. Croix, but almost every beach has its hotel as well. The government rate sheet, published twice yearly (for low summer and high winter rates) lists 52 choices on St. Thomas, 37 on St. Croix, and about a dozen on St. John. Places range from luxury hotels to small guest houses, apartments, and campsites.

St. Thomas leads in the field of smaller accommodations, with more inns than any other island in the Caribbean; St. Croix has beach resorts and places scattered around the countryside; St. John has Caneel Bay and the Virgin Grand for elegance and comfort and, at the opposite end of the spectrum, Cinnamon Bay and Maho Bay offer campsites and cabins in the national park if you want to "rough it."

High-season rates are generally in effect from December 15 to April 15. Rates are from 25% to 50% lower the rest of the year.

The most highly recommended lodgings are indicated by a star ★.

Category	Cost*
Very Expensive	over $200
Expensive	$125–$200
Moderate	$65–$125
Inexpensive	under $65

*All prices are for a standard double room, excluding 7.5% accommodations tax.

Hotels
St. Thomas
★ **Frenchman's Reef** (and **Morning Star Beach Club**). Sprawling, luxurious, and situated on a prime harbor promontory east of Charlotte Amalie, Frenchman's Reef is St. Thomas's American superhotel par excellence. There are cavernous restaurants and ballrooms, 23 duty-free shops, a helicopter pad, and an elevator to the beach. Most rooms have sea views, and Morning Star offers on-the-beach villas. There are guest activities and live entertainment galore. Baby-sitting can be arranged ($5 an hour). There are no organized activities for children, but G- and PG-rated movies are shown on Sunday and Monday nights. *Box 7100, Charlotte Amalie, 00801, tel. 809/776–8500 or 800/524– 2000. 518 rooms. Facilities: beach, 7 restaurants, 6 bars, 2 Olympic-size pools, 4 tennis courts, water sports, aerial tours by helicopter. AE, DC, MC, V. Very Expensive.*

★ **Sapphire Beach.** This resort is on one of St. Thomas's prettiest beaches. There is a marina for boating enthusiasts and, for divers, good snorkeling. An interesting bonus is the opportunity to watch sea turtles feed at an area set aside for the purpose. All villas and suites have beachfront balconies and come with fully equipped kitchens, air-conditioning, telephones, and cable TVs. Children under 12 are welcome. They eat free and can join the Little Gems Kids Klub. *Box 8088, Red Hook, 00801, tel. 809/775–6100 or 800/524–2090. 141 rooms. Facilities: beach, restaurant, bar, 4 tennis courts, water sports, nearby golf. AE, MC, V. Very Expensive.*

Stouffer Grand Beach Resort. The resort's zigzag architectural angles spell luxury, from the marble atrium lobby to the one-bedroom suites with private whirlpool baths. The beach is excellent, and there is a new health club with Nautilus machines. The Ultimate Lifestyle Package includes a private secluded-island picnic and a flight to San Juan for a dinner-and-casino evening. The 34-acre resort is diligently managed. Daily organized activities for children include iguana hunts, T-shirt painting, and sand-castle building. *Smith Bay Rd., Box 8267, 00801, tel. 809/775–1510 or 800/468–3571. 290 rooms. Facilities: beach, 6 lit tennis courts, 2 pools, water sports, nearby golf. AE, DC, MC, V. Very Expensive.*

★ **Point Pleasant Resort.** Perched high over Smith Bay, affording a great view of St. John and Drake Passage to the east and north, this resort offers a wide range of accommodations—from simple bedrooms to multiroom suites scattered in several hillside units. The air-conditioned rooms have balconies and most have kitchens. Every guest gets four hours' free use of a car daily. There are monthly full-moon jazz concerts at the main pool. You can sign up for daily guided walks over the hilly property, which offers spectacular views of the British Virgin Islands and St. John. *Estate Smith Bay, 00802, tel. 809/775–2000, 800/524– 2300, or 800/645–5306. 148 rooms. Facilities: 2 beaches, restaurant, bar, 3 pools, tennis court (lit), water sports. AE, MC, V. Expensive–Very Expensive.*

Bluebeard's Castle. Though not exactly a castle, this large, red-roof complex offers kingly modern comforts and is on a steep hill overlooking the town, which from here glistens at night like a Christmas tree. All rooms are air-conditioned and equipped with cable TV and a refrigerator; most have terraces. Havensight Mall, where the cruise ships come in, is not far. The hotel offers free transportation to Magens Bay Beach. *Box 7480, Charlotte Amalie, 00801, tel. 809/774–1600 or 800/524–6599. 167 rooms. Facilities: 2 restaurants, bar, pool, 2 tennis courts, nearby golf. AE, DC, MC, V. Expensive.*

Bolongo Bay Beach and Tennis Club. A mecca for water-sports enthusiasts and the headquarters of the St. Thomas Diving Club, Bolongo has oceanfront and garden-view rooms with efficiency kitchens, cable TVs, telephones, air-conditioning, and balconies. At the shaded poolside patio you can watch breakers dashing against the promontory to the left while you rest your feet and discuss life's vicissitudes with amiable bar manager Tony Hunt. Kid's Corner entertains the young ones for three hours in the morning and three hours in the evening. Activities are divided between the playroom and the beach. *Box 7337, 00801, tel. 809/775–1800 or 800/524–4746. 78 rooms. Facilities: beach, restaurant, 4 tennis courts (2 lit), pool, water sports. AE, DC, MC, V. Expensive.*

Fairway Village. The villas, banked on a lush, green hillside, are right at the Fazio-designed Mahogany Run 18-hole golf course. Studios and one-bedroom apartments have fully equipped kitchens. This is a golfer's heaven; for swimmers, there is a wooden-decked swimming pool and Magen Bay Beach is nearby. *Property Management Caribbean, Inc., Rte. 6,*

00802, tel. 809/775–1220 or 800/524–2038. 25 rooms. Facilities: golf, pool. AE. Expensive.

Hotel 1829. This historic Spanish-style hillside inn has a lovely courtyard and, outside, a handsome bar and a terrace shaded by a green awning. The less expensive rooms are near the terrace; the suites and deluxe rooms come with cable TVs, wet bars, and balconies. All rooms are air-conditioned. No children under 12 are admitted. *Box 1567, Charlotte Amalie, 00801, tel. 809/776–1829 or 800/524–2002. 15 rooms. Facilities: pool, restaurant. AE, MC, V. Expensive.*

Limetree Beach Resort. The surf is gentle at the quiet inlet of Limetree Beach, and the hotel is known for the stone-faced but friendly vegetarian iguanas on its tropically landscaped grounds. Now a part of Bolongo Beach Resorts, Limetree is an all-inclusive resort, offering three- and seven-night packages that include all meals, car rentals, and all types of water sports —including day sails. Standard (first-floor), superior, and deluxe rooms have air-conditioning, cable TVs, telephones, Servi-bars, and electronic safes; most have an ocean view. All guests receive a complimentary scuba lesson. *Box 7337, 00801, tel. 809/776–4770, or 800/524–4746. 84 rooms. Facilities: beach, restaurant, 2 tennis courts, volleyball, shuffleboard, water sports. AE, DC, MC, V. Expensive.*

Pastels. Situated on the crest of the hills overlooking the Mahagony Run Golf Course, these one- or two-bedroom condominiums offer not only golfing privileges but specialized service that allows you to do as little or as much as you please. There's a fully stocked bar, microwaves, answering machines, and VCRs. Balconies look down island through the British Virgin Islands. The kitchen is stocked with everything you need for your first breakfast, and transporation is available to town or nearby Magen Bay Beach. *Box 12260, St. Thomas, USVI 00801, tel. 809/775–5285. 10 units. AE, MC, V. 7-day minimum. Expensive.*

Pavilions & Pools. Simple, tropical-cool decor and immured privacy are ambient here, where each island-style room has its own 20-foot-by-14-foot or 18-foot-by-16-foot pool. The unpretentious accommodations include air-conditioning, telephones, full kitchens, and VCRs. Water sports are available at Sapphire Beach on the adjacent property. The management is particularly attentive to your wishes and does everything to preserve the general quiet. *Rte. 6, 00802, tel. 809/775–6110 or 800/524–2001. 25 rooms, each with a private pool. AE, DC, MC, V. Expensive.*

★ **Secret Harbour.** The white buildings, with air-conditioned studios and suites, are nestled around an inviting, perfectly framed cove on Nazareth Bay, where you can watch the marvelous sunsets. In the one-bedroom suites, equipped with kitchenettes, the decor consists of pastel-hued fabric art on the walls and a chandelier. You'll find hardcover fiction on the bookshelves. The restaurant has majestic peacock chairs. The beach is no secret to local residents who appreciate good snorkeling. Children under 12 can stay for free. *Box 7576, St. Thomas, USVI 00801, tel. 809/775–6550 or 800/524–2250 (10 AM–4 PM). 60 rooms. Facilities: beach, restaurant, bar, tennis court, water sports. No credit cards. Expensive.*

Watergate Villas. The air-conditioned villas, east of Charlotte Amalie at Bolongo Bay, have modern studios and suites with one, two, or three bedrooms, all with a large living–dining room and fully equipped kitchen. *Estate Bolongo Bay, Proper-*

ty Management Caribbean, Inc., Rte. 6, 00802, tel. 809/775–6220 or 800/524–2038. 140 rooms. Facilities: restaurant, bar, beach, 2 pools, tennis, water sports. AE. Expensive.

★ **Blackbeard's Castle.** This small inn on Government Hill has a tiptop view of Charlotte Amalie and the harbor and an intimate atmosphere. All the rooms, many with handsome wall hangings, have air-conditioning, new telephones, and cable TVs. The picturesque piratical lookout tower is the oldest structure on the island. Continental breakfast is complimentary and transportation to the beach is free as well. The restaurant is excellent. Order a tropical cocktail and sip it while listening to romantic piano music. *Box 6041, Charlotte Amalie, 00801, tel. 809/776–1234. 16 rooms. Facilities: pool, restaurant, bar. AE, MC, V. Moderate.*

★ **Heritage Manor.** This regally immaculate, air-conditioned European-style guest house has gleaming 1837 tile floors, brass beds, wall-mounted hair dryers, and city-theme prints. The Tokyo room is coziness incarnate. Suites have refrigerators. Continental breakfast is complimentary. The house has its own parking strip, and it is a short walk downhill to the shops. Children under 10 are not admitted. *Box 90, Charlotte Amalie, 00804–0090, tel. 809/774–3003. 7 rooms, 3 with private bath. Facilities: pool. AE, DC, MC, V. Moderate.*

Island Beachcomber Hotel. This hotel, whose air-conditioned rooms have refrigerators and patios or balconies, is close to the airport but right on Lindbergh Beach. (Unlike most hotels on St. Thomas, it is west of Charlotte Amalie.) It is especially casual: You can live here in your swimsuit—but do put on a cover-up at the garden restaurant. The restaurant cuisine is Caribbean. *Box 1618, Charlotte Amalie, 00801, tel. 809/774–5250 or 800/982–9898. 50 rooms. Facilities: beach, restaurant, water sports. MC, V. Moderate.*

Sea Horse Cottages. These simple cottages, located at the eastern end of the island, look across to St. John. There is a rocky, irregular beach and a pool that overlooks a marina. All rooms have kitchens and ceiling fans. *Box 2312, 00801, tel. 809/775–9231. 25 rooms. Facilities: beach, pool. No credit cards. Moderate.*

Villa Blanca Hotel. Located above Charlotte Amalie on Raphune Hill, the hotel is surrounded by an attractive garden and has modern, balconied rooms with rattan furniture, kitchenettes, cable TVs, and ceiling fans. The eastern rooms face the Charlotte Amalie harbor; the western ones look out on rolling hills and a partial view of Drake's Channel and the British Virgin Islands. *Box 7505, Charlotte Amalie, 00801, tel. 809/776–0749. 12 rooms. Facilities: pool. AE, DC, MC, V. Moderate.*

Maison Greaux. Up the hill and not far from Frenchtown, this guest house has reasonable rates and a harbor view. Six of the 10 rooms are air-conditioned. *Box 1856, Charlotte Amalie, 00801, tel. 809/774–0063. 10 rooms. No credit cards. Inexpensive–Moderate.*

Galleon House. This small hotel has a panoramic view of St. Thomas and offers a variety of accommodations, some with private verandas; similarly, some have air-conditioning and cable TV, and some do not. A Continental breakfast is served, and there is a player piano on the main veranda. *Box 6577, Charlotte Amalie, 00801, tel. 809/774–6952 or 800/524–2052. 14 rooms. Facilities: pool, restaurant. AE, MC, V (plus 5% service charge). Inexpensive.*

St. Croix **The Buccaneer.** If you like tropical golf or a 240-acre self-contained beach resort offering all water sports, tennis, basketball, a nature/jogging trail, shopping arcade, health spa, and several restaurants, this is the place for you. All rooms have refrigerators and safes. The hotel's newsletter informs guests of scheduled island tours, pig roasts, terrace jazz concerts, and bartender "drink demos." *Box 218, Christiansted, 00821–0218, tel. 809/773–2100 or 800/223–1108. 147 rooms. Facilities: beach, 4 restaurants, golf, health spa, pool, tennis, basketball, horseback riding, jogging trail, water sports, shopping arcade, special holiday activities for children. AE, DC, MC, V. Very Expensive.*

Carambola Beach Resort and Golf Club. This horticulturally lush Rockresorts property looks like a red-roof village in a green valley next to the sea. (It's between Christiansted and Frederiksted.) The air is redolent of exotic gardens and of the beautiful wood of which everything seems to be made. The villa rooms—three upstairs, three downstairs—are spacious and elegant in an island way, with bench showers and screened porches. *Box 3031, Kingshill, 00850, tel. 809/778–3800 or 800/223–7637. 156 rooms plus 1 suite. Facilities: beach, 2 lighted tennis courts, golf course, pool, water sports, 2 Jacuzzis, 2 restaurants. AE, DC, MC, V. Very Expensive.*

★ **Cormorant Beach Club.** Breeze-bent palm trees, hammocks, the thrum of the north-shore waves, and a blissful sense of respected privacy rule here. All beachfront villa rooms have a patio or balcony, air-conditioning, telephone, and double-sink bath. Coffee is set out daily in the building breezeways, and you have a "CBC" terry-cloth robe to wear when you walk to the beautifully ledged polygonal pool. The airy, high-ceiling restaurant is one of St. Croix's best. *108 LaGrande Princesse, Christiansted, 00820, tel. 809/778–8920 or 800/548–4460. 38 rooms. Facilities: beach, pool, restaurant, bar, water sports, 2 tennis courts. AE, MC, V. Very Expensive.*

St. Croix by the Sea. The hotel's coastal landscape and view east to Christiansted and Buck Island are spectacular, as is its huge, curved seawater pool. Standard, superior, and ocean-view rooms all have air-conditioning, cable TVs, telephones, and shower-massage heads. *Box 248, Christiansted, 00820, tel. 809/778–8600, 800/524–5006, or 800/223–5695. 65 rooms. Facilities: 3 restaurants, 2 lounges, 154-ft saltwater pool, 4 tennis courts. AE, DC, MC, V. Expensive–Very Expensive.*

Hotel on the Cay. This resort on Protestant Cay is the visual centerpiece of Christiansted's harbor and has two fine beach areas that guests at other hotels boat to. Canal-like garden "ponds" flow outside the rooms, which have air-conditioning, telephones, and cable TVs, and have just been redone. Ferry service is incredibly frequent. The sheltered beach is especially suitable for children. *Box 4020, Christiansted, 00820, tel. 809/773–2035 or 800/524–2035. 55 rooms. Facilities: 2 restaurants, pool, 4 tennis courts, water sports. AE, MC, V. Expensive.*

★ **The Pink Fancy.** This is a homey, restful place right in town. The oldest of the four buildings here is a 1780 Danish town house, and old stone walls and foundations enhance the setting. The inn's efficiency rooms are very clean and well-tended; four have air-conditioning. Articulate host Wendall Snyder may reveal to you why St. Croix scuba diving is the Caribbean's best-kept secret. *27 Prince St., Christiansted, 00820, tel. 809/773–*

8460 or 800/524–2045. 13 rooms. Facilities: pool, bar. MC, V. Expensive.

Anchor Inn. Here stairs and porchways lead to motel-like rooms with small balconies, air-conditioning, cable TVs, small refrigerators, and bedspreads in orange-brown shades. Your harbor window may overlook a corrugated roof, but bathrooms have tubs and showers and the inn is right at the heart of the Christiansted waterfront. *58 King St., Christiansted, 00820, tel. 809/773–4000 or 800/524–2030. 30 rooms. Facilities: restaurant, bar, pool, water sports nearby. AE, DC, MC, V. Moderate.*

★ **Sprat Hall.** This seaside Frederiksted establishment is a restored plantation estate, the oldest in the U.S. Virgin Islands. The Hurd family serves stylish meals in the homey, antique-furnished great house (no smoking, please). You can stay at a family cottage or modern duplex suite on the extensive grounds. This is the place for horseback riding; across the road is a beach restaurant dappled with sunlight. *Box 695, Frederiksted, 00840, tel. 809/772–0305 or 800/843–3584. 17 rooms. Facilities: beach, restaurant, horseback riding, water sports. No credit cards. Moderate.*

Club Comanche. The picturesque stone mill (looking like a topless lighthouse) at dockside houses only canoes, and guests' rooms are anything but uniform. A split-level suite can be had, as can a room with a four-poster or (in Room 52) a waterbed. Evenings bring the sounds of cocktail piano music from the balcony of the Comanche Restaurant. The pool is long enough for decent lap swimming. *1 Strand St., Christiansted, 00820, tel. 809/773–0210 or 800/524–2066. 42 rooms with private bath. Facilities: restaurant, bar, saltwater pool, water sports. AE, MC, V. Inexpensive–Moderate.*

King's Alley Hotel. This slatted, brown-painted hotel has angled, recessed balconies; some of its rooms look out on the Christiansted waterfront and marina; all have telephones, air-conditioning, and cable TVs. The adjacent courtyard is lovely on a breezy morning and is romantically lighted at night. *King's Alley, Christiansted, 00820, tel. 809/773–0103 or 800/843–3574. 23 rooms. Facilities: pool, restaurant, water sports, AE, DC, MC, V. Inexpensive–Moderate.*

★ **The Frederiksted.** Ask for the ocean view: Traffic on the street outside is usually light, and you can gaze across to the tranquil western sea through a floor-to-ceiling window. All the inn's rooms have air-conditioning, cable TVs, wet bars, and refrigerators. The Frederiksted's pool is a small splash, but the lanterned and awninged red-tile courtyard is very pretty and cozy. *20 Strand St., Frederiksted, 00840, tel. 809/772–0500 or 800/524– 2025. 40 rooms. Facilities: pool, bar. AE, DC, MC, V. Inexpensive.*

★ **Hotel Caravelle.** There is a tidy European elegance about the Caravelle. All rooms have air-conditioning, cable TVs, and refrigerators (under the bathroom counter), and the matching blues, grays, and purples of the bedspreads and wall hangings are tastefully cool and summery, as a northerner might put it. Superior rooms overlook the harbor. Manager Elsie Galloway is friendly and helpful. *44A Queen Cross St., Christiansted, 00820, tel. 809/773–0687 or 800/524–0410. 43 rooms. Facilities: waterfront restaurant and bar, pool, water sports. AE, DC, MC, V. Moderate.*

Moonraker Hotel. Squirreled away downtown, the Moonraker has simple rooms with air-conditioning, cable TVs (with free

HBO), telephones, and small refrigerators; all are the same price. You'll find white bedspreads, oval mirrors, and nifty small, bureau-ledge lamps. *43A Queen Cross St., Christiansted, 00820, tel. 809/773–1535. 15 rooms. AE, MC, V. Inexpensive.*

St. John **Caneel Bay.** The beauty of St. John virtually begins here at this ★ 170-acre peninsula, developed in the 1950s by Laurance Rockefeller. It is like an ecologist's park, but one with tropical gardens, seven beaches, three restaurants, and an 18th-century sugar mill. Rustic rooms have simple interiors of regional woods and handwoven fabrics. No telephone or TV in the rooms, since this is the prototypical Rockresort. Male guests are asked to wear jackets after 6 PM. *Caneel Bay (St. John's North Shore), 00830, tel. 809/776–6111 or 800/223–7637. 171 rooms. Facilities: beach, 3 restaurants, 11 tennis courts, water sports. AE, DC, MC, V. Very Expensive.*

Virgin Grand Beach Hotel. St. John's major new big resort, this 34-acre property has impressively landscaped suites and luxurious town houses with marble-platform whirlpool baths, a long beach and marina, and a quarter-acre pool. Some units have full kitchen facilities. The Fronds restaurant offers gourmet dining. It all has the aspect of a semi-neo-Aztec royal city. Morning, afternoon, and evening children's programs that include beach olympics, stargazing, island tours, and arts and crafts are planned daily. *Great Cruz Bay, 00830, tel. 809/776–7171 or 800/323–7249. 264 rooms. Facilities: beach, marina, 2 restaurants, pool, water sports, tennis. AE, DC, MC, V. Very Expensive.*

★ **Gallows Point.** These gray quadragonal-roof buildings with jalousied windows grace the peninsula south of the Cruz Bay ferry dock. Garden apartments have spacious garden showers, and upper-level apartments have loft bedrooms. The kitchen facilities are excellent. There's a fine little snorkeling beach below the pool. The entranceway is bridged by Ellington's restaurant. *Box 58, Cruz Bay, 00830, tel. 809/776–6434 or 800/323–7229. 60 rooms. Facilities: beach, pool, snorkeling. AE, DC, MC, V. Expensive.*

Cruz Views. The views are from a hill close to Cruz Bay Village. Five of the 10 one-bedroom condo units have lofts, and all have covered decks and garden showers. Sofas have pull-out beds. The rooms are island-simple and neat but, without air-conditioning, not always as cool as one would like. No telephone or TV in the rooms. *CDC Realty & Management Company, Box 458, Cruz Bay, 00830, tel. 809/776–6152, 800/524–2095, or 800/338–0987. 10 rooms. Facilities: pool. MC, V. Moderate.*

Raintree Inn. If you want to be right at the action in town and bunk at an affordable, island-style place, go no farther. The dark-wood rooms have a nicely simple, tropical-cabin feeling to them. Three efficiencies here have kitchens and—if you don't mind climbing an indoor ladder—a comfortable sleeping loft. A restaurant, The Fish Trap, is next door. *Box 566, Cruz Bay, 00830, tel. 809/776–7449. 11 rooms. MC, V. Inexpensive–Moderate.*

The Cruz Inn. The buildings here are only a few blocks away from the Cruz Bay ferry dock and have a view of Enighed Pond. One building has seven carpeted guest rooms that share two baths. There are also suites with or without cooking facilities, an air-conditioned apartment, and an efficiency with cold water only. Continental breakfast is complimentary.

*Box 566, Cruz Bay, 00830, tel. 809/776–7688. 14 rooms, 5
with private bath. Facilities: restaurant, bar. MC, V, D. Inexpensive.*

The Inn at Tamarind Court. If you can only barely afford a vacation on St. John, try this inexpensive hostelry located right in
town. It's especially suited to singles. There is an "inn" part,
with six rooms and two shared baths, and a "hotel" part, with
11 rooms with private bath and shared-bath family rooms. The
front-courtyard bar is a friendly hangout: Darts, Ping-Pong,
and a horseshoe pit are provided. *Box 350 Cruz Bay, 00830, tel.
809/776–6378. 20 rooms, 11 with private bath. AE, MC, V. Inexpensive.*

Campgrounds   **Cinnamon Bay Campground.** Tents, one-room cottages, and
bare sites are available at this National Park Service location
on an attractive beach. The tents are 10 feet by 14 feet, with
flooring, and come with living, eating, and sleeping furnishings
and necessities; the 15-foot-by-15-foot cottages have twin
beds. Bare sites, which come with a picnic table and a charcoal
grill, must be reserved in writing no earlier than eight months
prior to arrival. *Cruz Bay, 00830–0720, tel. 809/776–6330 or
800/223–7637. Facilities: beach, commissary, bathhouses
(showers and toilets), restaurant, water sports. MC, V.*

Maho Bay Camp. Eight miles from Cruz Bay, this National
Park Service campground is a lush hillside community of
three-room tent cottages linked by boardwalk stairs and
ramps, which also lead down to the beach. The 16-foot-by-16-
foot shelters have beds, dining table and chairs, electric
lamps (and outlets), propane stove, ice cooler, and kitchen-
ware and cutlery. *Box 310, Cruz Bay, 00830, tel. 809/776–
6240, 809/776–6226, or 800/393–9004. 99 tent-cottages. Facilities: beach, restaurant, commissary, barbecue areas, bathhouses (showers, sinks, and toilets), water sports. No credit
cards.*

Nightlife

Don't look for brassy casino shows in these isles. Nightlife
in the U.S. Virgin Islands consists of a choice between town
and resort, resort being one of the large or even small hotels
that have local bands or limbo shows one or more nights each
week.

Charlotte Amalie on St. Thomas has the biggest club scene,
with the music ranging from disco and live rock to West Indian
pop, steel bands, and cocktail piano. But you can also find varied entertainment, including occasional stage shows, from
night to night at the luxury hotels. Call ahead to be sure when
and which things are happening.

St. Thomas   Among the most popular clubs in downtown Charlotte Amalie
are **The Greenhouse, Barnacle Bill's,** and the **Old Mill.** For a
disco that's a little dressier, try **Club Z.** You can enjoy more local or island music at the **Hillside Club** or **Walter's Living Room.**
St. Thomas hotels offering quite a menu of entertainment,
from combos to calypso, include **Frenchman's Reef, Bluebeard's
Castle, Limetree Beach,** and **Stouffer Grand Beach.** For romantic piano—and great views—head uphill to **Bluebeard's Castle**
or **Blackbeard's Castle.**

In the realm of the arts, major concerts and shows on St. Thomas are held at the **Reichhold Center for the Arts,** on the campus of the College of the Virgin Islands (tel. 809/774–4482).

St. Croix   Christiansted has a lively and eminently casual club scene near the waterfront (Frederiksted has considerably less to offer). At **Hondo's Backyard** you'll hear live guitar and vocals in an open-air courtyard with a bar and Cinzano tables or move along to **Casa Loco** for blues and reggae. The upstairs **Moonraker Lounge** brings in lively performers for periods of several weeks, such as Gary Loyd from Nashville. Milder piano music can be enjoyed on the broad veranda of **Club Comanche.** For jazz there is the **Bombay Club,** with Jimmy Hamilton and his band. St. Croix hotels worth checking out for nightly music and weekly shows are **The Buccaneer** and **Divi St. Croix.**

St. John   For live or recorded music in the little village of Cruz Bay, try **Fred's,** which has live local sounds a couple of nights a week, or **World Headquarters,** at Mongoose Junction, which is lively pretty late on weekends. A solid late-hours hangout is **The Back Yard.** At new Wharfside Village, there is Pusser's **Crow's Nest** pub, where you might hear folk singer–entertainer Jeff Cahill, and the spacious pool-table bar **Larry's Landing.** For resort entertainment a little outside of town, try the luxurious **Virgin Grand.**

Index

Personal Itinerary

Departure *Date*

Time

Transportation

Arrival *Date* *Time*

Departure *Date* *Time*

Transportation

Accommodations

Arrival *Date* *Time*

Departure *Date* *Time*

Transportation

Accommodations

Arrival *Date* *Time*

Departure *Date* *Time*

Transportation

Accommodations

Personal Itinerary

Arrival	*Date*	*Time*
Departure	*Date*	*Time*
Transportation		
Accommodations		

Arrival	*Date*	*Time*
Departure	*Date*	*Time*
Transportation		
Accommodations		

Arrival	*Date*	*Time*
Departure	*Date*	*Time*
Transportation		
Accommodations		

Arrival	*Date*	*Time*
Departure	*Date*	*Time*
Transportation		
Accommodations		

Addresses

Name	*Name*
Address	*Address*
Telephone	*Telephone*
Name	*Name*
Address	*Address*
Telephone	*Telephone*
Name	*Name*
Address	*Address*
Telephone	*Telephone*
Name	*Name*
Address	*Address*
Telephone	*Telephone*
Name	*Name*
Address	*Address*
Telephone	*Telephone*
Name	*Name*
Address	*Address*
Telephone	*Telephone*
Name	*Name*
Address	*Address*
Telephone	*Telephone*
Name	*Name*
Address	*Address*
Telephone	*Telephone*

Fodor's Travel Guides

U.S. Guides

Alaska
Arizona
Boston
California
Cape Cod
The Carolinas & the
  Georgia Coast
The Chesapeake
  Region
Chicago
Colorado
Disney World & the
  Orlando Area

Florida
Hawaii
The Jersey Shore
Las Vegas
Los Angeles
Maui
Miami & the Keys
New England
New Mexico
New Orleans
New York City
New York City
  (Pocket Guide)

New York State
Pacific North Coast
Philadelphia
The Rockies
San Diego
San Francisco
San Francisco
  (Pocket Guide)
The South
Texas
USA
The Upper Great
  Lakes Region

Virgin Islands
Virginia & Maryland
Waikiki
Washington, D.C.

Foreign Guides

Acapulco
Amsterdam
Australia
Austria
The Bahamas
The Bahamas
  (Pocket Guide)
Baja & the Pacific
  Coast Resorts
Barbados
Belgium &
  Luxembourg
Bermuda
Brazil
Budget Europe
Canada
Canada's Atlantic
  Provinces
Cancun, Cozumel,
  Yucatan Peninsula
Caribbean
Central America
China

Eastern Europe
Egypt
Europe
Europe's Great
  Cities
France
Germany
Great Britain
Greece
The Himalayan
  Countries
Holland
Hong Kong
India
Ireland
Israel
Italy
Italy's Great Cities
Jamaica
Japan
Kenya, Tanzania,
  Seychelles
Korea

Lisbon
London
London Companion
London
  (Pocket Guide)
Madrid & Barcelona
Mexico
Mexico City
Montreal &
  Quebec City
Morocco
Munich
New Zealand
Paris
Paris (Pocket Guide)
Portugal
Puerto Rico
  (Pocket Guide)
Rio de Janeiro
Rome
Saint Martin/
  Sint Maarten
Scandinavia

Scandinavian Cities
Scotland
Singapore
South America
South Pacific
Southeast Asia
Soviet Union
Spain
Sweden
Switzerland
Sydney
Thailand
Tokyo
Toronto
Turkey
Vienna
Yugoslavia

Special-Interest Guides

Bed & Breakfast
  Guide to the Mid-
  Atlantic States

Bed & Breakfast
  Guide to New
  England
Cruises & Ports
  of Call

A Shopper's Guide
  to London
Health & Fitness
  Vacations
Shopping in Europe

Skiing in North
  America
Sunday in New York
Touring Europe

T A Today

A New Introduction to
Transactional Analysis

Ian Stewart
Vann Joines

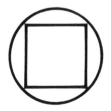

Lifespace Publishing
Nottingham and Chapel Hill

First published 1987
by Lifespace Publishing,
Nottingham, England,
and Chapel Hill, North Carolina, USA.
Reprinted 1998, 1990, 1991 (with revisions), 1992, 1993, 1994, 1995, 1996, 1997, 1999, 2000, 2002, 2003, 2005.

Made and printed in England
by Russell Press Ltd., Nottingham.

ISBN 1-870244-00-1

British Library Cataloguing in Publication Data

Stewart, Ian, *1940-*
    TA today : a new introduction to
    transactional analysis.
    1. Transactional analysis.
    I. Title II. Joines, Vann
    158'2 RC489.T7

Library of Congress Cataloging in Publication Data

Stewart, Ian, 1940-
    TA today.

    Bibliography: p.
    Includes index.
    1. Transactional analysis. I. Joines, Vann.
II. Title.
RC489.T7S74 1987 616.89'145 87-16977

CONTENTS

6. Structural Pathology / 50

Contamination *50*
Exclusion *53*

Part III COMMUNICATING: Transactions, Strokes and Time Structuring

7. Transactions / 59

Complementary transactions *60*
Crossed transactions *62*
Ulterior transactions *65*
Transactions and non-verbals *68*
Options *69*

8. Strokes / 72

Stimulus-hunger *72*
Kinds of strokes *73*
Stroking and reinforcement of behavior *74*
Giving and taking strokes *75*
The stroke economy *78*
The stroking profile *81*
Self-stroking *82*
Are there 'good' and 'bad' strokes? *84*

9. Time Structuring / 87

Withdrawal *88*
Rituals *88*
Pastimes *89*
Activities *90*
Games *91*
Intimacy *93*

Part IV WRITING OUR OWN LIFE-STORY: Life-Scripts

10. The Nature and Origins of Life-Script / 99

Nature and definition of life-script *99*
Origins of the script *101*

11. How the Script is Lived Out / 107

Winning, losing and non-winning scripts *107*
The script in adult life *110*
Why script understanding is important *113*
The script and the life course *115*

APPENDICES

PREFACE

In this book, we introduce you to the current theory and practice of transactional analysis (TA).

We have presented the material in a way that will be useful to you whether you are learning about TA on your own or taking part in a taught course. If you are an independent reader meeting TA for the first time, we hope you will appreciate the book's informal and conversational style. We have used examples liberally to illustrate points of theory.

If you are reading the book as background to an 'Official TA 101' course in TA, you will find coverage of the full '101' syllabus.

TA today is international. We hope that the readership of this book will also be international. With this in mind, we have chosen language and examples that will be familiar to people all over the world.

The exercises

When we are teaching TA courses, we run frequent exercises along with the taught material. Each block of teaching is followed immediately by a relevant exercise. We find that this is the most effective way of letting students practice and reinforce the theoretical ideas.

In this book we follow the same pattern. Exercises are incorporated in the text. Each exercise comes immediately after the related theory. *To get most benefit from the book, do each exercise as you come to it.*

We signal exercises by a printers' 'blob' and a change to a different typeface.

● When you see this style of print, you are reading an exercise. Do it as soon as you come to it. Then go on to the next block of teaching. The end of the exercise is shown by the same sign as you saw at the beginning. ●

We suggest you keep a loose-leaf notebook in which you can compile your responses to the written exercises, together with the other thoughts and ideas you bring to mind while reading the book. This will help you learn TA in the most effective way possible — by using it for yourself.

What this book is and is not

When you have read this book through and completed the exercises, you will certainly know a lot more about yourself than you did when you started. You may also find you can use this knowledge to make some changes in your life which you had been wanting to make. If so, congratulations.

But this book is not intended as a substitute for therapy. If you have substantial personal problems, you are advised to seek out a reputable therapist who can give you the expert personal attention you need.

TA therapists encourage their clients to learn the ideas of TA. If you decide to enter TA therapy, you can use this book as a source of that learning.

If your wish is to provide TA therapy or services to others, this book will likewise be useful to you as your first introduction to the basic ideas of TA. But this basic knowledge does not qualify you to offer professional help. To be accredited as a TA practitioner, you have to complete prescribed hours of advanced study, practical experience and supervision. You must pass the examinations set by TA accrediting organizations. We give more details of these in Appendix E.

Our theoretical approach

The material we present here represents the broadly accepted mainstream of present-day TA theory. In a basic text, it would not be appropriate to explore areas at the 'cutting edge' of TA theorizing, areas that are still controversial. Yet TA today is very different from the TA of ten years ago. There are some important concepts, now at the very heart of the TA mainstream, that Eric Berne had never heard of by the time he died in 1970. One of our main enthusiasms in writing this book is to present these new ideas to you. Berne was an innovator above all. We think he would have applauded the way in which TA practitioners have continued to innovate.

There has also been a less desirable current of change in TA thinking and writing, dating from the earliest years of the discipline. We mean the trivialization of some of TA's original and most fundamental ideas.

Berne wanted TA to be accessible to everyone. He chose to use simple words to describe his thinking. Though the words were simple, the ideas were complex and subtle.

As TA attained the dubious status of a 'pop psychology' in the 1960s, some writers took advantage of TA's surface simplicity to present it in an over-simplified version. TA has not yet fully recovered from the damage done during those years. Despite the fine work of TA writers and practitioners over two decades, the image of TA as a superficial cookbook psychology has proven hard to shake off.

In writing *TA Today*, our objective has been to correct that false image. We have aimed to describe TA theory in its original subtlety and depth without sacrificing any of the clarity or simplicity in language which Berne prized so much.

This is true above all of the foundation of TA theory, the ego-state model itself. In his original work, Berne emphasized again and again that ego-states had a *time* dimension. Parent and Child were both echoes of the past. Adult was a response to the here-and-now, using the person's full grown-up resources. All three of the ego-states entailed thinking, feeling and behaviors. There is a world of difference between this and the later, trivialized version of the model which proclaims: 'Adult is thinking, Child is feeling, Parent is oughts and shoulds.'

In this book, we return to Berne's original formulation of the ego-state model. We have used it as a consistent base for the explanation of other areas of theory.

Cases and names

Wherever we give case illustrations, the names used are fictitious. If they bear any relationship to the real name of any person, this is purely by chance.

Thanks and acknowledgements

Our 'expert reader' was Erika Stern, PhD, of the Department of Counseling Studies, University of Utrecht, The Netherlands. It's difficult to imagine anyone who could have been better qualified for the task. She made available to us her acute understanding not only of TA but also of other psychological approaches. She is herself an accomplished editor. And, being multi-lingual, she was able to alert us to uses of language that would have posed problems to readers who are not native speakers of English. In all these ways, Erika has made a major contribution to this book.

Our 'lay readers' were Andrew Middleton, PhD, and Christine Middleton. They commented on the manuscript from their viewpoint as new learners of TA. They drew our attention to passages where we had assumed that because *we* knew the map, other people would not need signposts. They pointed out where our explanation was overdetailed or repetitive, and did a fine job in suggesting clarifications. Andy and Christine have had a great influence on the final shape of the book.

Richard Erskine, PhD, and Marilyn Zalcman, MSW, ACSW, read the draft chapter on the Racket System and made valuable suggestions for re-wording.

Jenni Hine, MAOT, provided current data on TA organizations.

Emily Hunter Ruppert, ACSW, suggested the collaboration in authorship of which this book is the result.

We gratefully acknowledge the permission of the following authors to use copyright material originally published in the *Transactional Analysis Journal* or *Transactional Analysis Bulletin*, issues as shown:

John Dusay, MD, for the *Egogram*: TAJ, 2, 3, 1972.

Franklin Ernst Jr, MD, for the *OK Corral*: *TAJ, 1,* 4, 1971.
Richard Erskine, PhD, and Marilyn Zalcman, MSW, ACSW, for the *Racket System*: *TAJ, 9,* 1, 1979.
Taibi Kahler, PhD, for the *Miniscript*: *TAJ, 4,* 1, 1974.
Stephen Karpman, MD, for the *Drama Triangle*: *TAB, 7,* 26, 1968.
Jim McKenna, MSW, for the *Stroking Profile*: *TAJ, 4,* 4, 1974.
Ken Mellor, Dip. Soc. Studs., and Eric Sigmund, for the *Discount Matrix*: *TAJ, 5,* 3, 1975.

Your comments, please!

We intend this book to be the standard basic textbook of TA from now on. As it goes through successive editions, we plan to update it, so that each edition will merit its title of *TA Today*.

We ask you for your help in this project. Will you let us have your critique and feedback?

Are there any places where you think we could have been more clear? Anything you'd have liked to see in the book that we do not have in? Anything we do have in that you'd have liked to see out? Did you find any factual blunders, anachronisms, incongruities? All of them we'd like to hear about.

And if there are features of our book you particularly like, we'd value hearing about those too.

Please contact us in care of Lifespace Publishing, either at Nottingham, England, or Chapel Hill, USA. You can find full addresses on the page of 'ordering information' at the back of the book.

Ian Stewart and Vann Joines

June 1987

Part I
INTRODUCING TA

Chapter 1
WHAT TA IS

'Transactional analysis is a theory of personality and a systematic psychotherapy for personal growth and personal change'.

That's the definition of TA suggested by the International Transactional Analysis Association.[1] In fact, TA today is all this and much more. Among psychological approaches, transactional analysis is outstanding in the depth of its theory and the wide variety of its applications.

As a *theory of personality*, TA gives us a picture of how people are structured psychologically. To do so it uses a three-part model known as the *ego-state model*. The same model helps us understand how people function — how they express their personality in terms of behavior.

TA also provides a *theory of communication*. This can be extended to give a method of *analyzing systems and organizations*.

TA offers a *theory of child development*. The concept of *life-script* explains how our present life patterns originated in childhood. Within the framework of life-script, TA develops explanations of how we may continue to re-play childhood strategies in grown-up life, even when these produce results that are self-defeating or painful. Thus TA gives us a *theory of psychopathology*.

In the area of practical applications, TA does indeed offer us a system of psychotherapy. It is used in the treatment of all types of psychological disorders, from everyday living problems to severe psychosis. It provides a method of therapy for use with individuals, groups, couples and families.

Outside the therapeutic field, TA is used in educational settings. It helps teachers and learners to stay in clear communication and avoid setting up unproductive confrontations. It is particularly suitable for use in counseling.

TA is a powerful tool in management and communications training and in organizational analysis.

Among the many other applications of TA are its uses by social workers, police and probation authorities, and ministers of religion.

TA can be used in any field where there is a need for understanding of individuals, relationships and communication.

Key ideas of TA

There are a few key ideas which form the foundation of TA theory. They serve to distinguish TA from any other psychological system. In the coming chapters, we shall examine all these ideas in detail and illustrate them by examples. Here they are first in summary. We suggest you simply read this section through to become acquainted with the terms and general ideas.

The ego-state model (PAC model)

Most basic of all is the *ego-state model*. An *ego-state* is a set of related behaviors, thoughts and feelings. It is a way in which we manifest a part of our personality at a given time.

The model portrays three distinct ego-states.

If I am behaving, thinking and feeling in response to what is going on around me here and now, using all the resources available to me as a grown-up person, I am said to be in my *Adult ego-state*.

At times, I may behave, think and feel in ways which are a copy of one of my parents, or of others who were parent-figures for me. When I do so, I am said to be in my *Parent ego-state*.

Sometimes I may return to ways of behaving, thinking and feeling which I used when I was a child. Then I am said to be in my *Child ego-state*.

Note the initial capital letters. They are always used when we want to indicate that we are referring to the ego-states (Parent, Adult, Child). A small letter beginning the word shows we mean a real-life parent, adult or child.

The ego-state model is often known alternatively as the *P-A-C model*, after these three initial letters.

When we use the ego-state model to understand various aspects of personality, we are said to be employing *structural analysis*.

Transactions, strokes, time structuring

If I am communicating with you, I can choose to address you from any one of my three ego-states. You can reply in turn from any one of your ego-states. This exchange of communications is known as a *transaction*.

The use of the ego-state model to analyze sequences of transactions is referred to as *transactional analysis proper*. The word 'proper' is added to show that we are talking about this branch of TA in particular, rather than TA as a whole.

When you and I transact, I signal recognition of you and you return that recognition. In TA language, any act of recognition is called a *stroke*. People need strokes to maintain their physical and psychological well-being.

When people are transacting in groups or pairs, they use time in various specific ways which can be listed and analyzed. This is the analysis of *time structuring*.

Life-script

Each of us, in childhood, writes a life-story for himself or herself. This story has a beginning, a middle and an end. We write the basic plot in our infant years, before we are old enough to talk more than a few words. Later on in childhood, we add more detail to the story. Most of it has been written by the age of seven. We may revise it further during adolescence.

As grown-ups, we are usually no longer aware of the life-story we have written for ourselves. Yet we are likely to live it out faithfully. Without being aware of it, we are likely to set up our lives so that we move towards the final scene we decided upon as infants.

This unaware life-story is known in TA as the *life-script*.

The concept of life-script ranks with the ego-state model as a central building-block of TA. It is especially important in psychotherapeutic applications. In *script analysis*, we use the concept of life-script to understand how people may unawarely set up problems for themselves, and how they may set about solving those problems.

Discounting, redefining, symbiosis

The young child decides on a life-script because it represents the best strategy that the child can work out to survive and get by in what often seems a hostile world. In our Child ego-state, we may still be believing that any threat to our infant picture of the world is a threat to the satisfaction of our needs, or even to our survival. Thus we may sometimes distort our perception of reality so that it fits our script. When we do so, we are said to be *redefining*.

One way of ensuring that the world seems to fit our script is to selectively ignore information available to us about a situation. Without conscious intention, we blank out the aspects of the situation that would contradict our script. This is called *discounting*.

As a part of maintaining our script, we may sometimes get into relationships as grown-ups which re-play the relationships we had with our parents when we were children. We do this without being aware of it. In this situation, one of the partners in the relationship plays the part of Parent and Adult, while the other acts Child. Between them, they function as though they had only three instead of six ego-states available. A relationship like this is called a *symbiosis*.

Rackets, stamps and games

As young children, we may notice that in our family, certain feelings are encouraged while others are prohibited. To get our strokes, we may decide to feel only the permitted feelings. This decision is made without conscious awareness. When we play out our script in grown-up life, we continue to cover our authentic feelings with the feelings that were permitted to us as children. These substitute feelings are known as *racket feelings*.

If we experience a racket feeling and store it up instead of expressing it at the time, we are said to be saving a *stamp*.

A *game* is a repetitive sequence of transactions in which both parties end up experiencing racket feelings. It always includes a *switch*, a moment when the players experience that something unexpected and uncomfortable has happened. People play games without being aware they are doing so.

Autonomy

To realize our full potential as grown-ups, we need to update the strategies for dealing with life which we decided upon as infants. When we find that these strategies are no longer working for us, we need to replace them with new ones which do work. In TA language, we need to move out of script and gain *autonomy*.

The tools of TA are designed to help people achieve that autonomy. Its components are *awareness, spontaneity*, and the *capacity for intimacy*. It implies the ability to solve problems using the person's full resources as a grown-up.

The philosophy of TA

TA rests upon certain philosophical assumptions. These are statements about people, life and the objectives of change.[2]

The philosophical assumptions of TA are:

People are OK.
Everyone has the capacity to think.
People decide their own destiny, and these decisions can be changed.

From these assumptions there follow two basic principles of TA practice:

Contractual method.
Open communication.

People are OK

The most fundamental assumption of TA is that *people are OK*.

This means: you and I are both have worth, value and dignity as people. I accept myself as me and I accept you as you. This is a statement of essence rather than behavior.

At times, I may not like nor accept what you *do*. But always, I accept what you *are*. Your essence as a human being is OK with me, even though your behavior may not be.

I am not one-up to you, and you are not one-up to me. We are on a level as people. This is true even though our accomplishments may differ. It is true even though we may be of different race, age or religion.

Everyone has the capacity to think

Everyone except the severely brain-damaged has the capacity to think. Therefore it is the responsibility of each of us to decide what he or she wants from life. Each individual will ultimately live with the consequences of what he or she decides.

Decisional model

You and I are both OK. We may sometimes engage in not-OK behavior. When we do, we are following strategies we *decided* upon as young children.

These strategies were the best ways we could work out as infants to survive and get what we wanted from a world which may have seemed hostile. As grown-ups, we still pursue these same patterns at times. We may do this even though the results are unproductive or even painful for us.

Even when we were young children, our parents could not *make* us develop in one particular way rather than another. They could certainly exert strong pressures on us. But we made our own decisions whether to comply with these pressures, to rebel against them or to ignore them.

For us as grown-ups, the same is true. We cannot be *made* to feel or behave in particular ways by others, or by 'the environment'. Other people, or our life circumstances, may exert strong pressures on us. But it is always our own decision whether to conform to these pressures. We are responsible for our own feelings and behavior.

Any time we make a decision, we can change that decision later. This is true of the early decisions we make about ourselves and the world. If some of these infant decisions are producing uncomfortable results for us as grown-ups, we can trace the decisions and change them for new and more appropriate decisions.

Thus, people can change. We achieve change not merely by insight into our old patterns of behavior, but by actively deciding to change those patterns. The changes we make can be real and lasting.

Contractual method

If you are a TA practitioner and I am your client, then we take *joint responsibility* for achieving whatever change I want to make.

This follows from the assumption that you and I relate on equal terms. It is not up to you to do things *to* me. Nor do I come to you expecting you will do everything *for* me.

Since we both take part in the process of change, it is important that we both know clearly how the task will be shared. Therefore we enter into a *contract*.

This is a statement of the responsibility of each party. As client, I say what I want to change and what I am willing to do in order to bring about that change. You, as practitioner, confirm that you are willing to work with me in this task. You undertake to use the best of your professional skills in doing so, and say what recompense you want from me in return for your work.

Open communication

Eric Berne insisted that the client, as well as the practitioner, should have full information about what was going on in their work together. This follows from the basic assumptions that people are OK and that everyone can think.

In TA practice, case notes are open to the client's inspection. The practitioner encourages the client to learn the ideas of TA. Thus the client can take an equal role in the process of change.

To help in communication, the ideas of TA are expressed in simple language. Instead of the long Latin- or Greek-derived words customary in some other branches of psychology, TA speaks in familiar words: *Parent, Adult, Child, game, script, stroke.*

Some people have assumed that this straightforward language must reflect superficial thinking. Their view is mistaken. Though TA's language is simple, its theory is profound and closely reasoned.

Part II
PICTURING
PERSONALITY

The Ego-State Model

Chapter 2
THE EGO-STATE MODEL

Think back over the past twenty-four hours of your life.

Were there moments during that time when you acted, thought and felt just as you did when you were a child?

Were there other times when you found yourself behaving, thinking and feeling in ways you copied long ago from your parents, or from other people who were parent-figures for you?

And were there still other occasions when your behavior, thoughts and feelings were simply a direct here-and-now response to what was happening around you at that moment? On these occasions, you responded as the grown-up you now are, rather than dipping back into your childhood.

● Take time now to write down at least one example of each of these three ways of behaving plus thinking plus feeling which you recall from the past twenty-four hours. ●

You have just completed your first exercise in using the *ego-state model*.

Let's consider what you have just done. You examined three different ways of being in the world. Each of these consisted of a set of *behaviors, thoughts and feelings*.

When I am behaving, thinking and feeling as I did when I was a child, I am said to be in my *Child ego-state*.

When I am behaving, thinking and feeling in ways I copied from parents or parent-figures, I am said to be in my *Parent ego-state*.

And when I am behaving, thinking and feeling in ways which are a direct here-and-now response to events round about me, using all the abilities I have as a grown-up, I am said to be in my *Adult ego-state*.

Often in everyday TA practice, we say simply that I am 'in my Child', 'in my Parent', or 'in my Adult'.

Putting the three ego-states together, we get the three-part *ego-state model* of personality which is at the heart of TA theory. It is conventionally pictured as the set of three stacked circles shown in Figure 2.1. Because the three ego-states are often labeled with their initial letters, the model is alternatively known as the *PAC model*.

This simple version of the diagram, in which the three ego-state

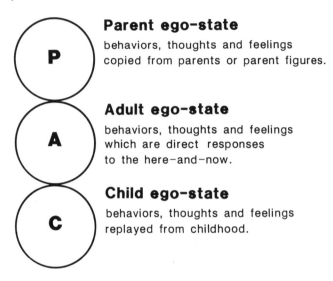

Parent ego-state

behaviors, thoughts and feelings
copied from parents or parent figures.

Adult ego-state

behaviors, thoughts and feelings
which are direct responses
to the here-and-now.

Child ego-state

behaviors, thoughts and feelings
replayed from childhood.

**Figure 2.1 First-order structural diagram:
The ego-state model**

circles are not subdivided, is called a *first-order structural diagram*. We shall meet the more detailed second-order diagram in a later chapter.

The process of analyzing personality in terms of ego-states is called *structural analysis*.[1]

Examples of ego-state shifts

Jane is driving her car along a road crowded with traffic. Second by second, she is observing the position and speed of other vehicles around her. She is looking out for road signs. She controls her own car in response to what is going on round about her, here and now. Jane is in her *Adult ego-state*.

Just then, another driver passes Jane and cuts in sharply in front of her. For a fraction of a second, Jane feels scared that the two cars will crash. She flashes a glance at her driving mirror, sees the road behind is clear and slows slightly so that the crash is avoided. All the time, she has stayed in her *Adult* ego-state. Her feeling of scare was an appropriate response to the here-and-now danger, helping her body react more quickly in order to avoid a collision.

Now, with the other driver vanishing up the road ahead, Jane shakes her head and purses her lips in disapproval. Turning to her passenger, she says: 'Drivers like that ought not to be allowed on the road!' At this moment Jane has moved into her *Parent ego-state.* When she was little, she had often sat beside her father as her drove his car and watched him as he showed his disapproval of other drivers' errors by shaking his head and pursing his lips in just this way.

A minute or two later, Jane pulls off the road at her office. Looking at her watch, she sees that because of the heavy traffic, she is late for an important meeting with her boss. Her heart sinks and for a moment she feels panic-stricken. Now Jane has shifted into her *Child ego-state.* She has contacted old memories of arriving at school late and feeling scared of the punishment she imagined she might get from her schoolteacher. Her feeling of panic is a response to these old memories, not to anything that is likely to happen in her grown-up situation.

At this instant, Jane is not consciously *aware* that she is re-playing her childhood. If you were to ask her 'Does this situation remind you of anything in your childhood?' she might then bring that old schoolroom scene back to conscious memory. Alternatively, she might have buried those painful recollections so thoroughly that she would not be able to remember them immediately. She might have to take longer, even perhaps go into therapy, if she wanted to bring those deeper memories back into consciousness.

As she now re-experiences her childhood feelings and thoughts, Jane also shows some behaviors which she first showed all these years ago as a schoolgirl. Her heart races. She lifts her hand to beside her mouth, and widens her eyes. From close up, you would be able to see that she has broken out into a light sweat.

Then after a moment or two, Jane thinks to herself: 'Wait a minute! What am I getting scared of? My boss is a reasonable woman. She'll understand why I'm late. Anyway, we can make up the lost time by taking a bit off the coffee break.' Jane is back in her Adult ego-state. Her passenger sees her relax and take her hand away from her mouth. Jane's face breaks into a smile, and she laughs. Her laugh is the laugh of the grown-up woman she is. It sounds quite different from the nervous giggle of a scared child.

● Before reading further, go back to the examples you have noted of when you were in Child, Parent and Adult ego-states during the past twenty-four hours.

Child ego-state
Think of each time you were in your Child ego-state. Note down what *feelings* you experienced. It may help if you role-play the occasion to yourself.

Record next what you were *thinking.* Often, you can get most easily to Child thoughts by asking yourself: 'What was I saying to myself inside my head?' Explore what you were saying inside your head about yourself, about other people and about the world in general.

Lastly, note down how you were *behaving* while you were in Child. A good way is to role-play yourself in Child while sitting in front of a mirror.

Check that these feelings, thoughts and behaviors were re-plays of how you felt, thought and behaved when you were a child. You may even be able to identify which past occasions you were re-playing. What age were you on each of these occasions?

Parent ego-state

In the same way, note down the set of related feelings, thoughts and behaviors for each time you were in your Parent ego-state. Again, role-play the occasion if you like.

You can often get to Parent thoughts most readily by asking yourself: 'What do I hear my mother or father saying inside my head?' Or perhaps the voice you hear inside your head may belong to another relative like an aunt, uncle or grandparent, or to a schoolteacher.

Check that on those occasions when you were in Parent, you were copying your behaviors, thoughts and feelings from your actual parents or parent-figures. You will probably find it quite easy to identify the specific person you were copying on each occasion.

Adult ego-state

Finally, record the sets of related behaviors, thoughts and feelings which you have identified with the times when you were in your Adult.

To distinguish Adult from Child or Parent, ask yourself: 'Was this behavior, or thought, or feeling, appropriate as a grown-up way of dealing with what was going on round me at that present moment?' If the answer is 'yes', then note that response as Adult. ●

You may find that for these occasions when you were in Adult, you are able to list behaviors and thoughts, but not feelings. For much of the time, we can deal effectively with here-and-now reality without experiencing feelings. However, we can and do feel emotions at times while in Adult.

How can you tell Adult from Child feelings? *Adult feelings are appropriate as a way of dealing with the immediate situation.* Recall Jane's moment of scare as the car cut too close in front of her. Her emotional reaction sharpened her responses, helping her to avoid an accident.

If you have not met the idea of ego-states before, you may be in doubt whether some thoughts, feelings or behaviors you listed were Adult as compared to Child or Parent. If so, don't worry. As you read on and complete more of the exercises, you will have plenty of opportunity to develop this important skill of distinguishing between ego-states.

For a healthy and balanced personality, we need all three of our ego-states. We need Adult for the here-and-now problem-solving that enables us to tackle life in a competent, effective way. To fit comfortably into society, we need the sets of rules we carry in our Parent. In our Child ego-state, we have access again to the spontaneity, creativity and intuitive power we enjoyed in our childhood.

Definition of ego-states

Eric Berne defined an ego-state as *a consistent pattern of feeling and experience directly related to a corresponding consistent pattern of behavior.*[2]

Berne was exact in his choice of words. It's worth while taking some time now to be clear what he was conveying in this definition.

First, Berne is saying that each ego-state is defined by a combination of feelings and experience which *consistently* occur together.

For instance, when Jane realized she was late for her meeting, she began to *experience* memories of feared punishment from her childhood. As she did so, she *felt* panicky. If you were to ask Jane about this, she would confirm that while re-experiencing her childhood in this way, she consistently also feels these childhood emotions. All the memories Jane has of her childhood experiences, plus the feelings that go with them, are classed as belonging in Jane's Child ego-state.

Next, Berne is suggesting that the *behaviors* typical of each ego-state are consistently shown together. If I observed Jane over some time, I would be able to confirm that she shows three separate sets of behavioral signals. One set defines her Adult, another her Parent, and another her Child. The signals making up each set are consistently shown together. There is a clear and consistent difference between one set and another.

For instance, when Jane widens her eyes and begins to sweat lightly, while her heartbeat speeds up, it's predictable that she will also lift her hand to somewhere near her mouth. These signals make up part of the set which defines Jane's Child ego-state. Were I to observe Jane for some time, I would be able to list a whole range of other behaviors which also belong in that set. For instance, Jane may also tilt her head to one side and start waggling her foot. When she speaks, her voice may be high and quavering.

I could go on to make up similar lists of the behaviors that consistently signal Jane's Adult and Parent ego-states.

Now let's return to Berne's definition, and focus on the phrase 'directly related to'.

Berne is saying that when I am in touch with the feelings and experience defining a particular ego-state, I will also be showing the behaviors which define that same ego-state. For instance, while Jane is *experiencing* her childhood memories of being late for school and *feeling*

15

the panic she felt then, she will also show the set of *behaviors* she showed as a child. The behaviors are directly related to the feelings and experience, and together they mark off Jane's Child ego-state.

The whole point of the ego-state model is that it allows us to make reliable connections of this kind between behavior, experience and feelings. If you see me showing the consistent set of behaviors that mark off my Child ego-state, you can reliably suppose that I am also re-playing experiences and feelings from my childhood. If you see me change my behavior and begin showing the signals which define my Adult ego-state, you can reasonably assume that my experience and feelings are those of a grown-up person responding to the here-and-now. When I outwardly show behaviors that I copied from my parents, you can predict that I will internally be re-playing feelings and experience I also copied from them.

● Go back now to the personal examples you noted of being in your own Child, Parent or Adult ego-states during the past twenty-four hours.

Check whether the feelings and thoughts you noted for your Child ego-state make up a set which hangs together consistently for you.

Check whether the behaviors you noted for your Child ego-state also make up a consistent set.

Check whether your Child behaviors are consistently associated with your Child feelings and thoughts.

Carry out the same three steps for your Parent and for your Adult behaviors, thoughts and feelings.

Compare the three sets of behaviors, thoughts and feelings you have noted as defining your three ego-states. Check whether the three sets are distinctively different one from another. ●

Are ego-state distinctions real?

By completing the exercises in this chapter so far, you have been able to check whether your own behaviors, feelings and experiences hang together in the way the ego-state model suggests. But what evidence is there that the model applies to people generally?

To collect this evidence, we need to use methods of observing people which keep the observer's pre-conceived ideas out of the picture as far as possible. We need to analyze the results in a way that allows us to judge whether they could have arisen by mere chance. When we have chosen appropriate methods of observation and analysis, we need to use them to investigate two questions.

(1) Do people show three consistent and clearly distinguishable sets of behaviors that correspond to our definitions of the three ego-states?

(2) Do the person's reported experience and feelings correlate with

the sets of behavioral clues in the way we would expect from the model?

There is now a substantial body of observational work that supports the answer 'yes' to both these questions. It's outside the scope of this book to describe these studies in detail. You can follow them up, if you wish, from the References list for this chapter.[3]

Ego-states and superego, ego, id

The three-way division of personality in the ego-state model reminds us of another famous three-part model. Sigmund Freud suggested the existence of three 'psychic agencies': superego, ego and id.

It's obvious that the two models are similar. At first sight, the Parent looks like the judgmental superego, which 'observes, orders, corrects and threatens'. The Adult has similarities to the reality-testing ego. And the Child seems to resemble the id, home of uncensored instincts and drives.

The resemblance between the two models is not surprising, given that Berne was trained initially as a Freudian analyst. But some commentators have gone further and suggested that Berne's Parent, Adult and Child are merely trivialized versions of Freud's three psychic agencies. In this they are mistaken. In his early writings, Berne was at pains to point out the differences between his model and that of Freud.

First and most important: the Parent, Adult and Child ego-states are each defined in terms of *observable* behavioral clues. By contrast, the superego, ego and id are purely theoretical concepts. You cannot look at me or listen to me and judge whether I am 'in my superego'. But you can judge by observation whether I am in my Parent ego-state.

Next, the ego-states relate to persons with specific identities, while Freud's three psychic agencies are generalized. When a person is in her Parent ego-state, she is not just acting in a way that is generally 'parental'. She is re-enacting the behaviors, feelings and thoughts of one of her *own* parents or parent-figures. When she is in Child, she will not simply be behaving in a 'childlike' manner. She will be reproducing behaviors she performed during her *own* childhood, along with their accompanying feelings and experience.

The Parent, Adult and Child ego-states will each *include* influences from superego, ego and id. Berne pointed out that someone in Parent will be reproducing the parent's 'total behavior, including her inhibitions, her reasoning, and ... her impulses'. Adult and Child ego-states likewise entail their own inhibitions, reasoning and impulses.

Berne built upon Freud's model by adopting Paul Federn's idea of ego-states, i.e. distinct states in which the ego is manifested at a given time. He further classified these into three behaviorally observable ego-states, which he labeled Parent, Adult and Child.

Freud's model and the ego-state model are not one and the same

17

thing. Neither do they contradict each other. They are simply different ways of portraying personality.[4]

Ego-states are names, not things

You cannot put an ego-state in a wheelbarrow. You cannot weigh it nor touch it. You cannot find it in any particular location in the body or brain.

This is because an ego-state is not a *thing*. Instead, it is a *name*, which we use to describe a set of phenomena, i.e. a set of related feelings, thoughts and behaviors. In the same way, Parent, Adult and Child are not things. They are names. We use these three words as labels to distinguish the three different sets of feeling-thinking-behaving which you have met in this chapter.

Quite often in everyday TA practice, people talk about ego-states as if they *were* 'things we have'. You may hear statements like:

'My Kid wants some fun,' or

'You have a strong Adult.'

The trouble with talking this way is that we may slip into believing that ego-states have some kind of existence of their own, separate from the person we are talking about. Of course, this isn't so. It's not that 'my Kid' wants some fun. *I* want some fun, and I may be in my Child ego-state while I want it. It's not that 'I have a strong Adult'. Rather, *I* have a good ability to do the things that are usually associated with the Adult ego-state, like reality-testing and assessing probabilities.

Throughout this book, we avoid the habit of talking as though ego-states were 'things'. We suggest that you do the same.

The over-simplified model

After *Games People Play* became a best-seller in the mid-1960s, TA became in part a 'pop psychology'. Certain writers and speakers jumped on the commercial bandwagon. To make TA an even more marketable commodity, they watered down some of Berne's original ideas. They emphasized features that were striking and immediately obvious. They left out the aspects that required deeper thought or closer observation.

It was in this period that an over-simplified version of the ego-state model became current. That trivialized model is still with us. It has been at the root of endless misunderstanding, both among TA people themselves and among professional observers from other fields.

In this section, we take a look at the over-simplified model. *We do NOT suggest that you use it. It will NOT be used at any point in this book.* We present it here solely because you are likely to meet it in some earlier TA literature. You will also discover it in the thinking of many people who learned their TA during that heady time of the 1960s.

What does the over-simplified model suggest?

It says merely: 'When I'm thinking, I'm in Adult. When I'm feeling, I'm in Child. When I'm making value-judgments, I'm in Parent.'

And that's it! Small wonder that professional observers from outside TA, hearing this model presented as TA's main building-block, have asked in bewilderment: 'Is *this* all there is?'

Having read this chapter's account of what the ego-state model actually says, you may be wondering whether the over-simplified model bears any resemblance at all to the actual version. The fact is that there are resemblances. The over-simplified model presents *some* of the typical characteristics of each ego-state. But it misses out other characteristics that are essential to the model.

Let's look first at the grains of truth in the over-simplified model. How is it similar to the actual model?

You know that when I am in my Adult ego-state, I am responding to the here-and-now with all the resources available to me as a grown-up. Usually, this entails some kind of problem-solving. I am likely to experience myself as 'thinking'. Someone observing my behavior would probably interpret it by saying I am 'thinking'.

If I go into Child, I begin re-playing behaviors, feelings and thoughts from my own childhood. Children, especially young ones, deal with the world mainly from a feeling position. Therefore, when I'm in Child, I will most often experience myself as 'feeling'. At these times, anyone observing me would likely confirm I seemed to be 'expressing feelings'.

When I am in Parent, I am copying my behaviors, thoughts and feelings from a parent or parent-figure, as that person appeared to me in my own childhood. To a child, parents appear to spend a lot of their time laying down rules about what ought and ought not to happen, or issuing judgments about how the world is. So for a lot of the time when I am in Parent, I will be doing what my parents did and making value-judgments about 'oughts and shoulds'.

It turns out, then, that the over-simplified model gives us some simple first clues to recognizing ego-states. When I am in Adult, I will *often* be thinking. In Child, I will *often* be into feelings. And when I'm in Parent, I will *often* be making value-judgments.

But these obvious clues to ego-states fall far short of giving us a full description of each ego-state. The over-simplified model completely omits to mention that I can think *and* feel *and* make value-judgments from *any* of my ego-states.

An even more serious fault of the over-simplified model is that it says nothing about the *time* dimension of ego-states. Again and again, Berne emphasized that Parent and Child are echoes of the *past*. In Child, I am replaying behaviors, thoughts and feelings *from my own past* — my childhood. When I am in my Parent ego-state, I am engaging in behaviors, thoughts and feelings which I copied *in the past* from my parents and parent-figures. Only when I am in my Adult am I responding to situations with all my *present* resources as a grown-up.

With that brief look, we turn away from the over-simplified model. It was fine as a topic for lightweight books and after-dinner speeches. But it did not give much clue to what TA is really about. From now on in this book, we stay with Berne's original version of the ego-state model.

Chapter 3
FUNCTIONAL ANALYSIS OF EGO-STATES

In this and the next chapter, we go on to build more detailed versions of the ego-state model. These view ego-states in terms of either *structure* or *function*.

A *structural* model shows *what* there is in each ego-state. A *functional* model divides the ego-states to show us *how* we use them.

Putting the same idea in more formal language: a structural ego-state model is concerned with the *content* of ego-states. A functional model is concerned with their *process*.

STRUCTURE = 'WHAT' = CONTENT.

FUNCTION = 'HOW' = PROCESS.

The functional model is probably easier to understand at first acquaintance, so we will look at that first.[1] It is pictured in Figure 3.1.

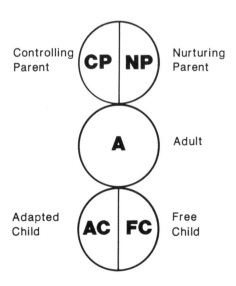

Figure 3.1 Functional analysis of ego-states

Adapted Child and Free Child

Imagine that I am in my Child ego-state. I am behaving, thinking and feeling just as I used to in my childhood.

For a lot of the time when I was a child, I was adapting to the demands of parents or parent-figures. I had learned that in order to get by, I had better be polite to the neighbors even though I might not have liked them very much. When I needed to wipe my nose, I used my handkerchief instead of my sleeve, even though the sleeve might be more convenient. Very early on in my life, I had worked out that Father liked me better when I was quiet, so when he was around I was mostly quiet. Mother liked me to laugh and didn't seem to like me crying or getting angry. So when I was with Mother I laughed most of the time, even when sometimes I was sad and wanted to cry, or angry and wanted to shout at her.

Now as a grown-up, I often re-play these ways of behaving that I decided on as a child so as to fit in with what my parents expected. When I do so, I am said to be in the *Adapted Child* part of my Child ego-state.

There were other times in my childhood when I rebelled against these rules and expectations that my parents seemed to be setting for me. When Father's back was turned, I made rude faces at the neighbor's little girl next door. And sometimes when I was on my own, I gave my nose a really good wipe on my sleeve, just because I was so tired of using that handkerchief. There were even days when I felt so bad about always having to laugh when Mother was around that I made a point of sulking all day, just to show her.

When I behaved in these ways, it was as if I was taking my parents' rules and turning them around backwards. Instead of adapting to their expectations, I was doing as much of the opposite as I could.

In grown-up life, I may still be rebelling in ways like these. Quite often, I may not be aware that my behavior is a rebellion. When the boss gives me a tough work assignment, I may discover that I 'don't have enough time' to get it finished by the deadline. In fact, I have as much time as anybody ever has, twenty-four hours in each day. Telling the boss I didn't get the job finished, I may feel an obscure satisfaction that says 'That'll show you!' When I was four years old, I may have felt the same rebellious satisfaction as I showed Mother she *couldn't* make me eat that last potato on my plate.

When I engage in this kind of rebellion, I am nevertheless still responding to childhood rules. Therefore I am said to be still in the *Adapted Child* ego-state.

Some earlier TA writers portrayed rebellion in a separate ego-state division, which they called the *Rebellious Child*. You may still find the name in some modern sources. In this book, we shall follow the more usual current practice and regard rebellion as part of the Adapted Child set of behaviors.

There were times in my childhood when I behaved in ways which were independent of parental pressures. At these times, I was neither adapting to my parents' expectations, nor rebelling against them. I was simply acting as I myself wanted to. When my pet mouse died, I cried because I was sad. When my little sister pushed me, I got angry and pushed her back. I enjoyed many hours of reading stories and learning how to do jigsaw puzzles, not to please my parents but just for myself.

When I am in my Child ego-state as a grown-up, I may sometimes behave in these uncensored childhood ways. At these times I am said to be in the *Free Child* part of my Child ego-state. Sometimes the alternative name of *Natural Child* is used to describe this ego-state part.

In the functional model, then, the Child ego-state is divided into *Adapted Child* and *Free Child*. In the picture of the ego-state model, we show this by dividing the Child circle in two (see Figure 3.1).

Positive and negative Adapted Child

As grown-ups, we are all in Adapted Child a fair amount of the time. There are thousands of rules we follow about how to live and be accepted in the world. In everyday living, we don't think consciously about these rules before deciding to follow them. Before I cross the road, I look right and left in the way my father and teachers insisted I do when I first went to school on my own. When I'm at table during a dinner party and want the vegetables, I say 'please'. As a child I learned to do this as if it were automatic, because I correctly learned that people would judge me 'rude' if I didn't. And if they judged me rude, I would take longer to get the vegetables.

Our Adapted Child behaviors may work for us in ways like these. By replaying these rule-following patterns, we often get what we want comfortably for ourselves and other people. And we save a great deal of mental energy. Just imagine what it would be like if you had to think out your table manners afresh every time you sat down at the table!

We can speak of *positive Adapted Child* to describe these productive ways of behaving from our Adapted Child ego-state. Some writers use the alternative phrase *OK Adapted Child*.

By contrast, we are said to be in *negative (or not-OK) Adapted Child* when we replay childhood patterns of behavior which are no longer appropriate to our grown-up situation. As a young child, I may have learned that a powerful way to get attention from Mother and Father was to sulk. Now as a grown-up, I may sometimes still sulk in the hope of getting what I want. When I do so, I ignore my grown-up option of simply asking for what I want directly.

Or I may have decided as a child that it wasn't safe to make any kind of show of myself in front of people. Maybe I got slapped down by Mother for 'showing off'. Perhaps my playmates teased me when I had to recite in class. Now as a grown-up, asked to speak in public, I may turn red, stammer and stutter, while I feel embarrassed and think to myself 'I'm no good as a speaker!' In here-and-now reality, I am perfectly capable of speaking and the situation carries no risk for me.

All of us, for some of the time, display negative Adapted Child patterns of behavior. Later in the book, you will learn why this is. An aim of personal change in TA is to replace these old outdated patterns with new ones which make full use of our grown-up options.

Positive and negative Free Child

Free Child behaviors too can be classed as positive (OK) or negative (not-OK). To say I am 'in Free Child' means I am engaging in behaviors from my childhood that pay no attention to Parental rules or limits. Sometimes these can be productive and life-enhancing for me as a grown-up, and so are classed as positive. For instance, suppose that as a child I decided to adapt to my parents by never showing I was angry. In grown-up life, without realizing it, I may have been following the same strategy. Bottling up my anger, I may have become depressed or physically tense. Then, perhaps in the course of therapy, I decide to let myself express how angry I feel. Beating furiously on a cushion, I at last mobilize the uncensored Free Child energy I have been hanging on to for all these years. I'm likely to find afterwards that I feel better and more relaxed physically.

In a similar way, many of us reach grown-up life still hanging on to unexpressed Child feelings of grief, scare or desire for physical contact. When we express these emotions in a safe situation, we engage in positive Free Child behavior.

There are other times when Free Child behavior is clearly negative. If I belch loudly at a formal dinner-party, I am satisfying my uncensored Child urges. But the social consequences will probably be more uncomfortable for me than if I had held down the belch. At a more serious extreme, I might engage in the negative Free Child behavior of driving a motor-cycle at full speed along a crowded road, endangering my own life and that of others.

● Think back through the past twenty-four hours. Make a note of occasions when you were in positive Adapted Child. What were your behaviors on each occasion? Do you recall what childhood situations you were replaying?

Do the same for occasions when you were: in negative Adapted Child; in positive Free Child; in negative Free Child.

Take one minute to write down all the words you can think of to describe someone in positive Adapted Child. (If you are working in a group, brainstorm for a minute with someone writing the words up).

Do the same for someone in: negative Adapted Child; positive Free Child; negative Free Child. ●

Controlling Parent and Nurturing Parent

For some of the time when I was a child, my parents were telling me what to do, controlling me or criticizing me. 'Go to bed! Don't run out into the road! Blow your nose! That's clever, silly, good, naughty, fair, not fair...' When I behave in ways which copy my parents in this role, I am said to be in *Controlling Parent* (sometimes called *Critical Parent*).

At other times, my parents were caring for me or looking after me. Mother might cuddle me. Father might read me bedtime stories. When I fell and cut my knee, one of my parents would comfort me and bring the bandages. When I replay the behaviors my parents showed when they were looking after me, I am said to be in *Nurturing Parent*.

We diagram this two-way division in the functional Parent by dividing the ego-state circle in two, in the same way as we did for Child (see Figure 3.1).

Positive and negative Controlling and Nurturing Parent

Some TA writers distinguish positive and negative subdivisions in each of these parts of the Parent. (Again, the terms 'OK' and 'not-OK' are sometimes used instead). They would say we are in *positive Controlling Parent* when our Parental directives to others are genuinely aimed at protecting them or promoting their well-being. A doctor might command his patient: 'Stop smoking! It's bad for you.' He is re-playing the kind of command he got from his parents when he was small: 'Don't walk out on the road in front of the cars!'

Negative Controlling Parent describes Parental behaviors which entail a put-down (discount) of the other person. The boss who snarls to his secretary: 'You've made a mistake *again!*' may be reproducing the tones and gestures of the irritable schoolteacher who said the same to him when he was in class at six years old.

Positive Nurturing Parent implies caring which is provided from a position of genuine regard for the person helped. *Negative Nurturing Parent* means that 'help' is given from a one-up position that discounts the other person. A positive Nurturing Parent behavior might be to say to a workmate: 'Do you want help with that job? If you do, let me know.' The negative counterpart might be to walk up to him and say: 'Here, I'll help you with that,' take the work out of his hands and complete it for him. The 'smother-mother' is the classic example of negative Nurturing Parent behavior.

● Thinking back through your day, note occasions when you showed Controlling Parent towards others. On which of these occasions were you coming from positive Controlling Parent? Negative Controlling Parent? Do you recall which parent or parent-figure you were copying each time?

Do the same for times in the day when you were showing positive or negative Nurturing Parent.

Take one minute to write down all the words you can think of to describe someone in positive Controlling Parent. (In a group, brainstorm for a minute).

Do the same in turn for: negative Controlling Parent; positive Nurturing Parent; negative Nurturing Parent. ●

Adult

The Adult in the functional model is usually not subdivided. We class any behavior as Adult which is a response to the here-and-now situation, using all the person's grown-up resources.

We have now assembled the whole of the functional model. You can review it in Figure 3.1.

If I want to say which functional ego-state part you are using, I have to judge from your behavior. For that reason, these functional subdivisions can alternatively be called *behavioral descriptions*.

Egograms

How important is each of these functional ego-state parts in your personality? Jack Dusay has devised an intuitive way of showing this. He calls it the *egogram*.[2]

To make an egogram, you begin by drawing a horizontal line. Label it along its length with the names of the five main functional ego-state parts. To save spelling them out in full, use their initial letters. Thus Controlling Parent becomes CP, Free Child becomes FC, and so on. Draw them in the order shown on Figure 3.2.

The idea is to draw a vertical bar above each ego-state label. The height of the bar shows how much of the time you use that functional part.

Start with the part you judge you use most, and draw its vertical bar. Next, take the part you think you use least and draw its bar. Make the *relative* heights of the two bars fit your intuitive judgment of the relative amounts of time you spend in each part.

Figure 3.2

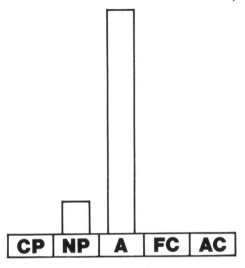

Figure 3.3

For instance, if I judge I am in Adult most and Nurturing Parent least, I might draw my first two bars as in Figure 3.3.

Now complete the egogram by drawing in the other three bars. Make the height of each one represent the relative time you spend in that functional ego-state part. My completed egogram might look like Figure 3.4.

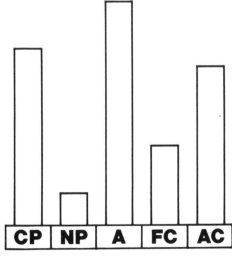

Figure 3.4

The exact height of each bar is not important. What matters is the relative height of each bar as compared to the others.

Jack Dusay did not suggest dividing up the bars into positive and negative parts, but it can be interesting to do so. You can shade in a part of the bars for CP, NP, FC and AC to show 'negative'. This leaves the rest of the bar showing 'positive'. For instance, I believe that most of my time in Adapted Child is spent in positive rule-following. When I behave in uncensored Free Child ways, most of these behaviors also lead to comfortable and productive outcomes. I am not often in Nurturing Parent, but when I am, I hardly ever 'smother' people in a negative way. I am often in Controlling Parent. Most of this Controlling Parent time is spent in positive ways of directing others. My final egogram looks like Figure 3.5.

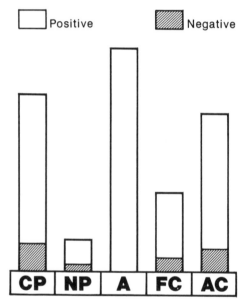

Figure 3.5

● Go ahead and draw your own egogram.

If you are working in a group, share your ideas with another group member as you draw. Work quickly and by intuition.

What do you learn about yourself?

Some people find that one egogram fits them in every situation. Others find they need to draw two or even more different egograms. Perhaps they will have a 'work' and a 'home' egogram. If this is true of you, go ahead and draw each one. What do you learn?

Explain egograms to someone who knows you well. Ask this person to draw *your* egogram. What do you learn by comparing their version with your own? ●

The constancy hypothesis

Jack Dusay suggested a *constancy hypothesis*:

'When one ego-state increases in intensity, another or others must decrease in order to compensate. The shift in psychic energy occurs so that the total amount of energy may remain constant.'

The best way to change my egogram, says Dusay, is to set about *raising* the part I want to have more of. When I do so, energy will automatically shift out of other parts I want to have relatively less of.

Suppose I look at my egogram and decide I would like to be more in Nurturing Parent and less in Controlling Parent. I begin practicing more Nurturing Parent behaviors. Perhaps I offer someone a back-rub once each day. Or at work I experiment with making open offers of guidance instead of ordering people to do things. I don't make any attempt to cut down on my Controlling Parent behavior. By the constancy hypothesis, I can expect this will go down anyway as I put more energy into Nurturing Parent.

● Is there anything you want to change about your egogram?

If there is, decide which bar you need to raise to achieve this change.

List at least five new behaviors which you can practice to increase this ego-state part. Make a point of doing these behaviors in the week following.

Then re-draw your egogram. If possible, get a re-drawn egogram from the person who knows you well. (Do not tell them which changes you aimed to make in the egogram.) Does your new egogram fit the constancy hypothesis? ●

Chapter 4
THE SECOND-ORDER STRUCTURAL MODEL

In the last chapter's functional model, we divided the ego-states up to indicate *how* they were shown in behavior — their *process*. Now in looking at the second-order *structural* model, we examine *what* the ego-states have in them — their *content*.

Right from the moment I am born, I am experiencing the world. I store those experiences away in memory.

Do we actually record every moment of our life experience somewhere in memory? Have we the potential to recall all of it? Nobody knows for sure. Nor is it clear yet how the storage is accomplished. We do know that everyone retains memories of their past. Some can be brought easily back into awareness. Others are more difficult to recover. Memories of early childhood especially may only come back to us in dreams and fantasies.

Each one of us has an uncountable number of experiences of thoughts, feelings and behaviors stored away in memory. The purpose of the second-order structural model is to *classify* these memories in a useful way, within our familiar framework of ego-states.

If you like, you can think of the second-order structural model as a kind of *filing system*. Imagine a businessman sitting at his desk. Each day he deals with many different pieces of paperwork — letters in, replies out, bills, staff records and so on. At the end of the day's work, he doesn't just throw all these bits of paper randomly into a sack on the floor. He stores them away systematically in his filing system.

It's obvious why he does so. By means of the filing system, he can *organize* his records in a way that is useful to his business. Suppose for instance that he needs to draw up his financial accounts. He simply needs to go to the file labeled 'bills', and there are the records of all his outgoings ready for the accountant.

In just the same way, the TA practitioner uses the second-order structural model to 'file away' a person's memory traces of thoughts, feelings and behaviors in a way that will be useful in his understanding of personality through structural analysis.[1]

The second-order structural model is pictured in Figure 4.1. How does it operate as a 'filing system'?

As children, all of us receive messages from our parents. For each message we receive, we have a certain way of thinking about it and certain

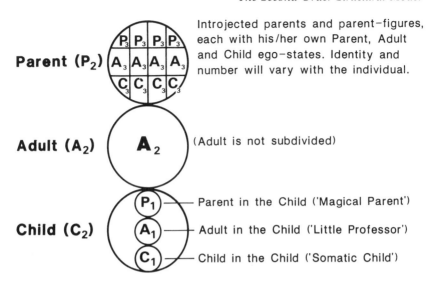

Parent (P$_2$) — Introjected parents and parent-figures, each with his/her own Parent, Adult and Child ego-states. Identity and number will vary with the individual.

Adult (A$_2$) — (Adult is not subdivided)

Child (C$_2$)
— Parent in the Child ('Magical Parent')
— Adult in the Child ('Little Professor')
— Child in the Child ('Somatic Child')

Figure 4.1 Second-order structural model

fantasies which we form in relation to that message. We have feelings which we experience about the message, and we make a decision about what we will do in response to it. In addition, our parents may give us reasons why the message is important. They may convey feelings which imply a covert message additional to the one they are conveying overtly.

In the second-order structural model, the messages we received from our parents or parent-figures are 'filed away' in P$_3$. The reasons they gave us for why they are important are stored in A$_3$. Any secret or covert implications are stored in C$_3$.

Our own thinking about the messages becomes part of our A$_2$ content.

The fantasy we formed about what would happen if we did or did not follow these messages becomes part of P$_1$. The feelings we have in response to our fantasy are stored in C$_1$, and our early decision about what we will do comes from A$_1$.

In the following sections, we look in more detail at each of these 'filing compartments' in the model.

Second-order structure: Parent

You already know that the Parent ego-state means the entire set of thoughts, feelings and behaviors which you have copied from parents and parent-figures. Thus in the structural model, the *content* of the Parent is defined as the set of memory traces of these parental thoughts, feelings and behaviors.

In formal language, we say that these are parental *introjects*. To introject something is like swallowing it whole instead of chewing and digesting it. Typically this is what children do with their parental modeling.

A child experiences her parents for a lot of the time as issuing commands and defining the world. So the content of the Parent will consist largely of these commands and definitions. 'Don't put your hand in the fire.' 'It's wrong to steal.' 'The world is a good, bad, beautiful, scary place.' Along with the words go memories of the gestures, tones and emotional expressions that went with them.

In the second-order structural model, we first divide the Parent according to whom each remembered message came from. For most people, this will be Mother or Father. Maybe grandparents were also important figures. Teachers often play a part. The number and identity of the people who gave you your Parent content are unique to you.

Next we register that each of your parent-figures had a Parent, Adult and Child ego-state. This gives us the second-order picture of the Parent shown in Figure 4.1.

Notice that the whole Parent ego-state is conventionally labeled P_2 in this diagram. Different TA writers have used different ways of labeling the P, A and C subdivisions in P_2. Here, we call them P_3, A_3 and C_3.

Parent in the Parent (P_3)

My father had a whole set of slogans and commands which he had introjected from his own parents. He passed some of these on to me, and I stored them away in my Parent, along with those I got from my mother. In this way the Parent in the Parent is a storehouse of messages which may be passed down through generations. For instance, Scottish parents may tell their children: 'Porridge will make you strong and you should eat all of it up every morning.' You can imagine their remote ancestors, dressed in skins, saying the same to *their* children as they stirred the pot in their cave each morning.

Adult in the Parent (A_3)

We picture the Adult in the Parent as being the collection of statements about reality which a person has heard from the figures in her Parent and has copied from them. Many of these statements will be true in objective fact. Others will reflect the parents' misapprehensions or fantasies about the world. Still others will be statements about things that were once factually true but are no longer so. For instance, the statement 'You can't walk on the moon' used to be a reality.

Child in the Parent (C₃)

Mother, Father and teacher each had a Child ego-state. When I introjected them into my own Parent, I included my perception of their Child as part of the introject. Accessing my stored memories of them, I may come in contact with their Child feelings, thoughts or behaviors. I may experience myself feeling or reacting as that parent did when I was little.

When my mother was a little girl, she decided she could get what she wanted from people by sulking and looking sour. Later on when I was a child and she wanted something from me, she would often sulk and look sour in the same way. Now in my own Parent ego-state, I carry a message that when I'm in charge of people I can get them to do what I want by sulking and looking sour.

Second-order structure: Adult

The content of my Adult is defined as the thinking, feeling and behaving which I engage in as a response to the here-and-now. This implies that the Adult is the 'filing compartment' in which is placed the whole set of strategies for reality-testing and problem-solving which I have available to me now as a grown-up person.

In the Adult we locate not only the reality-testing we apply to the world outside ourselves, but also our grown-up evaluation of the content of our own Parent and Child ego-states. For instance, I carry a Parent command in P_2 that says: 'Look right and left before you cross the road!' As a grown-up I have assessed this message and have concluded that it makes sense in reality. This conclusion is filed in A_2.

For much of the time I am in Adult, I and others will experience that I am 'thinking'. But you'll recall from Chapter 2 that Adult content is defined to include here-and-now *feeling* responses, as well as here-and-now thinking. You may wonder: how can feelings be a way of problem-solving? Imagine that at this moment a tiger, escaped from a circus, were to leap through the window of your room. If you are like most people, your here-and-now feeling would be scare. And that emotion would be a great help to the speed at which you ran away.

Or imagine you are on a crowded bus. The person next to you keeps on elbowing you until you are in danger of falling out of the door. Here-and-now anger is your stimulus for elbowing him in return, to regain your rightful place and your safety.

If I feel here-and-now sadness, that is my way of resolving a different kind of problem: namely, the loss of someone or something important to me.

In the second-order structural model, we usually make no divisions in the Adult. We show A_2 on the diagram as simply a plain circle.

Second-order structure: Child

We define any stored experience from the person's own childhood as being part of the content of the Child ego-state.

There are many different ways in which these millions of memories could be classified. One obvious way would be to group them according to the age they date from. Some TA writers, notably Fanita English, have done just this.[2]

More often, we divide the structural Child ego-state in a different way, pictured in Figure 4.1. The reasoning behind it is simple. When I was a child, I already had Parent, Adult and Child ego-states.

Every child has basic needs and wants (Child). She has fantasies about how best to get these met (Parent). And she possesses intuitive problem-solving skills (Adult).

To signal this, we draw circles for Parent, Adult and Child *within* the larger circle showing the Child ego-state.

These three internal divisions of the Child ego-state are conventionally labeled P_1, A_1 and C_1. The whole Child ego-state in the second-order model is given the label C_2.

Parent in the Child (P_1)

Every child learns early in life that there are rules which must be followed. These rules are laid down by Mother and Father.

Unlike a grown-up, the young child doesn't have the reasoning power to examine the rules and check whether it makes sense to follow them. Instead, she simply knows they must be followed. But often she doesn't feel at all keen on following them. So she finds ways of scaring or seducing herself into obedience.

'If I don't say my prayers at night, the Devil will come out of the fire and get me.'

'If I don't eat all of my dinner, Mother will go away and leave me and never come back.'

'If I act nice, everybody will love me.'

It is in this magical form that younger children store away their own version of messages from their parents. Since these impressions are the child's fantasies of the implications of his parents' messages, they are grouped together in the model as the content of the child's Parent ego-state. Later as a grown-up, I may go back into Child and access these magical messages, which make up the Parent in my Child, P_1.

This fantasized version of the parent may often be far more threatening than the actual parent. Even when parents love their child and are parenting him as well as they are able, the young child may perceive them as giving him destructive messages like:

'Drop down dead!'

'Never enjoy anything!'
'You aren't supposed to think!'
To reflect this quality of harshness, P_1 was given several different scary nicknames by earlier TA writers. It has been called the Witch Parent, the Ogre and the Pig Parent.

But the child's grandiose fantasy may be positive as well as negative. The Parent in the Child is also associated with the Fairy Godmother, the Good Fairy and Santa Claus. For this reason we prefer the term 'Magical Parent' for P_1.

Berne called P_1 the Electrode. This refers to the way the Child responds almost compulsively to these magical images of reward and punishment.

Adult in the Child or 'Little Professor' (A_1)

A_1, the Adult in the Child, is a label for the whole collection of strategies the child has available for solving problems. These strategies change and develop as the child grows. Researchers into child development have studied these changes in detail. Their work is necessary reading if you want thorough understanding of the Adult in the Child.[3]

As a young child, I was certainly interested in checking out the world around me. But my ways of doing so didn't entail the processes grown-ups call 'logical'. I relied more on intuition, instant impressions. At the same time, I learned new things far faster than any grown-up can learn. This stored capability earns A_1 its alternative name of 'Little Professor'.

In grown-up life, I can still go back into my Child ego-state and access the intuition and creativity which I hold in A_1.

Child in the Child (C_1)

Six-year-old Jean is lying on the floor, busy reading the book she has just been given at school. In comes the cat. Jean looks up from her book, reaches out to stroke him. But the cat has had a bad day that day. He swipes Jean on the arm, and blood wells up from a scratch.

In the next second, Jean's six-year-old thinking is forgotten. She rolls herself up in a ball, and her wordless scream brings Mother running from the next room. Until the scratch is bandaged and Mother has given comfort, Jean is a baby again. As a child of six, she is back in her one-year-old Child ego-state.

As a grown-up, Jean will have a stored memory of this scene. If she recalls it, she will contact first the Adult in her six-year-old Child ego-state (reading the book). Then she will shift into C_1, the earlier Child within the Child, as she re-lives her pain and panic on being scratched.

Very young children experience the world mainly in terms of body sensations. These will form the bulk of the memories stored in the Child in the Child. For this reason, C_1 is sometimes called the *Somatic Child*.

35

Have you ever seen one of those sets of Russian dolls? You unscrew the top of the outside doll and find another smaller one inside. Then you unscrew the top of the second doll and see an even smaller doll inside. You unscrew that one and...

The second-order model of the Child is like that. In the structure of my six-year-old Child I have an earlier Child of, say, three. Inside that in turn is an even earlier Child, and so it goes on. When we draw the diagram for the model, we don't usually bother showing this in full detail. But particularly if you are a therapist, keep this feature in mind. It is often important to track the various ages of the Child which a client may move through in therapy.

Putting C_2 together with the pictures we developed of the Adult and Parent, we get the complete second-order structural diagram shown in Figure 4.1.

Distinguishing structure from function

To use the ego-state model effectively, you need clear understanding of the differences between structure and function. Confusion between the two has been a longstanding problem in the development of TA theory.

Yet the differences themselves are easy to understand. They all arise from one simple fact, which you already know about.

The functional model classifies observed behaviors, while the structural model classifies stored memories and strategies.

So long as you keep this in mind, you will distinguish accurately between structure and function.

One of us (VJ) explained the distinction more fully in a 1976 *TA Journal* article.[4] He wrote:

'Berne was careful in his presentations to differentiate structural and functional diagrams. I believe he had a solid logical basis for being so. Many present-day writers are attempting to equate these two modifying categories. This is like attempting to equate a "wheel" with "revolving". The two categories refer to different aspects of reality. In analyzing ego-states, "structural" refers to the component parts of the personality while "functional" or "descriptive" refers to the way in which the personality is functioning at a given point in time. An analogy would be the different ways to look at a heat pump used to heat and cool a house. One could look at the heat pump "structurally" and point to its various components such as the compressor, the air ducts, the thermostat, etc. One could also look at the heat pump "functionally" or "descriptively" and talk about it heating the house, cooling the house transferring air from one place to another, using electricity, etc. These are descriptions of how the total system is functioning at a given point in time.'

Any time you want to clarify the difference between structure and function, think of that wheel and that heat-pump.

You also know another way of wording the distinction:

STRUCTURE = 'WHAT' = CONTENT

FUNCTION = 'HOW' = PROCESS.

What is so important about making the correct distinction?

Any time we are talking about interactions between people, we must use the *functional* model. The *structural* model fits when we are considering what goes on inside the individual.

Saying the same things in technical language: *interpersonal* aspects of TA work require the functional model. *Intrapsychic* matters need to be studied in terms of the structural model.

In this book, our discussion of 'Communicating' in Part III will be almost entirely about function. The account of 'Life-script' in Part IV will relate principally to structure.

When I look at you and listen to you and judge what ego-state you are in, I can make my judgment only in terms of the functional model. Perhaps I see you put your head to one side, crease your brow and put the end of one finger in your mouth. From these observations I judge that you are in your Adapted Child functional ego-state.

There is no similar way I can observe you and try to judge whether you are 'in your Little Professor' or 'coming from your Parent-in-the-Parent'. These names define collections of memories, not sets of behaviors. Only by listening to the *content* of what you are saying can I begin to get evidence about second-order structure.

If I do want to know about the content of your Little Professor or Parent-in-the-Parent — the *what* rather than the *how* — I need to do some detective work. Principally, I need to ask you a lot of questions. I may also use my general knowledge about different kinds of personality and about how children develop.

In the next chapter, we shall list Eric Berne's four ways of diagnosing ego-states and relate them to the structure-function distinction.

Relationship between structure and function

It is possible for two things to be *different*, yet to be *related* to each other. This is true of structure and function. Obviously, the way I behave at any moment will depend partly on the set of memories and strategies I am contacting internally.

Suppose I am showing a set of behaviors corresponding to the negative Adapted Child functional ego-state division. Let's say I am sitting scrunched up with arms and legs tightly folded. I'm clenching my teeth and my face is going red, while sweat breaks out on my brow. If you looked at me then, what could you tell about the structural ego-state part I might be contacting internally?

You might reasonably guess I am experiencing body sensations of the sort which fit with the definition of Somatic Child, C_1. And so I may be. But perhaps I am also accessing internal images of the scary ogre or witch parent figures I built for myself at the age of three and stored away to make up my P_1.

It's also possible that I am replaying the way my father used to scrunch up and go red when he felt under threat as a child. If so, I am accessing part of my own Parent ego-state, the Child in my Father Parent (C_3 of Father).

And for all you know, I may be a skilful actor and be setting up the whole charade for some grown-up purpose which you don't know about yet. If so, then I am likely to be switching internally between the content of my Adult, A_2, and Little Professor, A_1.

To repeat: when you look at me and listen to me, you can *observe* function. But you can only *infer* structure.

Chapter 5
RECOGNIZING EGO-STATES

Eric Berne listed four ways of recognizing ego-states. He called them:

Behavioral diagnosis
Social diagnosis
Historical diagnosis
Phenomenological diagnosis.

Berne stressed that it was best to use more than one of these ways at a time. For a complete diagnosis, all four should be used, in the order shown above. Behavioral diagnosis is the most important of the four. The other three act as checks upon it.[1]

Behavioral diagnosis

In behavioral diagnosis, you judge which ego-state a person is in by observing his behavior. As you do so, you can see or hear:

words
tones
gestures
postures
facial expressions.

You would diagnose the person's functional ego-state by observing several of these at one time. Are the various clues consistent with each other?

For instance, suppose you see me sitting upright in my chair. My body is balanced evenly round a vertical mid-line. Both feet are planted firmly on the floor. From these body clues, you would form a first judgment that my behavior is Adult.

You look at my face and see that my gaze is even, my facial muscles relaxed. As I begin speaking, you hear a level tone of voice. Now you have consistent clues from expression and voice tone which help confirm your behavioral diagnosis of Adult.

No one clue is sufficient in itself. Perhaps I am sitting there discussing the philosophy of the ego-state model. If you wrote my words down, they would seem Adult. But as you look at me, you note that I have now shifted my feet so that the toes of one are resting on the toes of the other. I have tilted my head to one side. With the fingers of my left hand I am rapping on the arm of my chair. The clues from gestures and postures let you know that I am most likely in my Adapted Child, despite my Adult-sounding words.

Are there 'standard clues' to ego-states?

It's traditional for books about TA to give tables of standard clues for behavioral diagnosis. For instance, a wagging finger is said to fit with Controlling Parent. A whining voice is supposed to show Adapted Child. Shouting 'Wow! Yippee!' is given as a clue to Free Child, and so on.

But this idea of 'standard clues' raises a cautionary point, concerning the fundamental nature of the ego-state model.

The tables of 'standard clues' rely on the suggestion that when I am, for instance, in Adapted Child, I will be behaving *like a child* complying with the demands of his parents. Likewise, in Nurturing Parent I will be behaving *like a parent* looking after a child.

But this is not what the ego-state model says. What do I mean when I use the model's language accurately?

When I say I am 'in my Child', I mean I am behaving, thinking and feeling as the child *I* once was — not just like *any* child. When I am 'in Nurturing Parent', I am behaving, thinking and feeling as one of *my* parents did, not just like 'parents generally'.

It follows that for a reliable behavioral diagnosis of my Adapted Child ego-state, you would need to know how *I* looked and sounded back in my childhood when I was obeying my parents. To recognize me in Nurturing Parent, you would need to have observed my mother or father as they looked after me all these years ago.

The set of behavioral clues that define my Adapted Child or Free Child will be different from yours, because we were different children. Because we had different parents, we will each have our own unique set of behaviors to mark Controlling or Nurturing Parent.

Does this mean that tables of 'standard clues' are useless?

Luckily, the answer is 'no'. There are some kinds of behavior that are typical of *children in general* when they are obeying their parents or acting spontaneously. There are behaviors which *parents in general* will often show when they are controlling or nurturing their children. So if we look for these typical behaviors, we can make a useful start in diagnosing functional ego-states. We simply need to be aware that it is only a start.

To firm up our diagnosis, we need to get to know the person. Over time we can draw up a list of their own unique sets of behaviors signaling ego-state changes.

In this book we prefer not to give a table of 'standard clues'. Instead we invite you to draw up your own.

● Take a big sheet of paper and draw six vertical columns on it. Head the left-hand column 'Clues from — '. Head the other five columns with the five functional ego-state labels you used in the egogram — CP, NP, A, FC, AC.

Go back to the column headed 'Clues from — '. Evenly spaced down it, write five headings:

Words
Tones
Gestures
Postures
Facial expressions.

Draw in horizontal lines so that you finish up with five empty boxes down each column. One box will be for 'Words', one for 'Tones', and so on.

The idea is that you fill in the behavioral clues *for yourself* in each column.

Let's take the Controlling Parent column. In it you enter behavioral clues that you show when you copy your parents' ways of controlling or commanding others. Think of situations when you typically get into CP. Maybe this will be when you are in charge of subordinates at work. If you are a parent, consider the behaviors you show when you are telling your children what to do.

Here are a few examples of what I might enter for myself under CP.

Words: 'Don't! Stop! Do! Here's how it is. That's good. That's bad. You should. You must.'

Tones: deep, resonant, harsh.

Gestures: chopping the air with right hand. Propping fingers together in a 'steeple' shape. Linking hands behind head.

Postures: leaning far back in chair. Tilting head back, 'looking down nose'.

Expressions: corners of mouth pulled down slightly. Eyebrows raised.

You may find that some of these clues fit for you too. The main thing is to draw up your own unique list. Go ahead with it now.

List only what people can see and hear. Do not interpret. For instance, under 'expressions', put down only what people see you doing with your face. Do not enter words like 'condescending, bossy, supercilious...'. These would be interpretations. As you look at me and listen to my voice, maybe you do feel I'm being bossy. But the bossiness is not something you are observing. It is an interpretation you are making inside your own head. Practice awareness always of what you observe. If you then go on to interpret your observation, stay aware that the interpretation is something separate from what you are observing.

When you have filled in the column for Controlling Parent, go on to fill the other columns in the same way. For Nurturing Parent, list the behaviors you show when you are copying your parents' ways of looking after people. Again, if you are a parent yourself, you are likely to do this some of the time when you are caring for your children.

For Adapted Child, put down behavioral clues you show when you are re-playing ways you had of following other people's rules when you were a child. You may do this when you are conforming in company, talking to the boss at work, and so on.

For Free Child, think of a recent time when you acted like the child you once were, neither conforming to others' rules nor rebelling against them. Maybe you were on the roller-coaster, hid your face and shrieked as it shot down the slope. Perhaps you were visiting the doctor for a routine inoculation and found yourself shaking with fright as the nurse produced the needle.

Recall that the functional divisions of Parent and Child can be shown in negative ways as well as positive ways. Are there behaviors you show when you're squashing people from negative Controlling Parent? If you're a parent, do you sometimes smother your kids? If so, how do they see and hear you in negative Nurturing Parent? Talking to the boss, do you sometimes crawl to him while wishing he were a hundred miles away? If you do, how would you see and hear yourself on a video film in negative Adapted Child?

In the Adult column, enter behaviors you show when you are acting as your here-and-now grown-up self. This might be a recent situation when you were at work exchanging information with a colleague. You might be in the supermarket buying what you had down on your shopping list. Perhaps you were reading this book and learning about ego-states. Remember that the Adult ego-state relates to here-and-now feeling as well as to thinking. Therefore, Adult behaviors may include expressions of emotion, where the feelings expressed are appropriate responses to the present situation.

Keep the Free Child column for behaviors you show when you are acting as though you were a spontaneous child again instead of a spontaneous grown-up. ●

Sometimes when you are observing my behavioral clues, you may need to ask more questions to help you judge which of my ego-states a particular behavior fits with. Suppose you see me sitting in a drooping pose. I'm leaning forward, head in hands. The corners of my mouth are turned down. I'm sighing deeply, and my eyes are filling with tears.

From all these clues, you gather that I'm expressing sadness. But what ego-state am I in? Have I perhaps just heard that a close relative has died? My sadness then would be an appropriate response to the here-and-now, hence Adult. Or have I got back in contact with some memory of a loss I experienced when I was a child, and which I've never let myself be sad about until now? In that case, my feeling expression is from Free Child. Still another possibility is that I am replaying a negative Adapted Child pattern, in which I droop and get sad as a way of manipulating the people around me.

To back up your assessment of my behavioral clues, you may want to ask questions about how other people relate to me. You may ask about my personal history and what my parents were like. And you may explore what I can re-experience from my own childhood.

● As we now look at Berne's other three ways of diagnosis, use them to check back on the behavioral list you have made up for yourself. Alter and add to your list according to what you learn. ●

Social diagnosis

The idea behind social diagnosis is that other people will often relate to me from an ego-state that complements the one I am using. Therefore, by noting the ego-state they respond from I can get a check on the ego-state I have come from.

For instance, if I address you from my Parent ego-state, chances are you will respond to me from your Child. If I open communication with you from my Adult, you will likely come back also in Adult. And if I approach you from my Adapted Child, you may well respond from your Parent.

Thus if I realize that people often seem to be giving me Child responses, I have reason to think that I may often be addressing them from Parent. Maybe I am a supervisor and find my supervisees either crawl to me or find ways of sabotaging my orders behind my back. Both of these look like Adapted Child responses. Possibly, then, I am being more of a Controlling Parent with them than I had realized. If I want to change the situation, I can list the Controlling Parent behaviors I have been using in the work situation. Then I can experiment with, say, Adult behaviors instead. My supervisees' ego-state responses to me will give me a social diagnosis of how far I have managed to change from my Parental approach.

● Think of a recent occasion when someone seemed to be responding to you from their Child. What behavioral clues did the other person show which you interpreted as indicating they were in Child?

Did you invite this response by coming from your Controlling Parent or Nurturing Parent? If so, look at your list of behavioral clues and pick out how the other person saw and heard you in Parent.

How might you have altered your own behavior to invite them to respond from a different ego-state?

Do the same exercise for recent occasions when someone seemed to be responding to you from their Adult; their Parent. ●

Historical diagnosis

In historical diagnosis, we ask questions about how the person was as a child. We ask about the person's parents and parent-figures. This lets us double-check on our impressions of the person's functional ego-states. It also lets us know about ego-state structure. *Historical diagnosis deals with both process and content.*

I might see you in a group, hunching forward with a frown on your face. Your hand is up covering your eyes. I hear you say: 'I'm confused. I can't think.' Behaviorally, I judge you to be in Adapted Child.

For historical diagnosis, I might ask you: 'How did you feel as a child when somebody asked you to think?' Or perhaps I might say: 'To me, you look like you're about six right now. Do you connect with anything in your childhood?' You might recall: 'Yes, Dad used to badger me to read books, then laugh because I couldn't get all the words right. So I used to play stupid just to spite him.'

At another moment you may be leaning back in your chair. Tilting your head back, you look down your nose at your neighbor. You tell her: 'What you've just said isn't right. Here's how things really are...' Perhaps she cowers down, hunches her shoulders and raises her eyebrows in Adapted Child style. Now I have both behavioral and social clues that you are in Controlling Parent. For a historical check, I might ask: 'Will you freeze your position a second? Did either of your parents sit like that when they were telling you how things were?' Maybe you burst out laughing and reply, 'Yeah, it's Dad again!'

Your reports thus give me a double-check on my behavioral diagnosis. Seeing you showing the sets of behaviors which I think fit with your Adapted Child ego-state, I have confirmed that your internal experience is a replay of the way you responded to parental pressures in your childhood. As you show Parent clues behaviorally, you report to me that you are copying the behaviors of one of your own parents.

● Look back at the list of behavioral clues you have drawn out for yourself. Use historical diagnosis to check the clues for each ego-state.

As you go through the Controlling Parent and Nurturing Parent clues, find if you recall what parent or parent-figure you are copying with each behavior. What are the copied thoughts and feelings which accompany the behavior?

For Adapted Child and Free Child clues, recall situations in your childhood when you behaved in that same way. How old were you? What were you thinking and feeling at these times?

For Adult, check that the behaviors you have listed are *not* a replay of your childhood nor a parental behavior you have swallowed whole.

You may find that you want now to shift some of your behavioral clues to a different column. For instance, some of the clues you first listed for Adult may turn out to fit better in Adapted Child. ●

Phenomenological diagnosis

Sometimes I may re-experience the past instead of just remembering it. Berne wrote that '...phenomenological validation only occurs...if the individual can re-experience the whole ego state in full intensity with little weathering.'

Suppose you had just recalled that time when Dad badgered you to read and then laughed at you for getting the words wrong. If you and I were working in therapy, I might invite you to get back into that childhood scene. Perhaps you put Dad in front of you in imagination and tell him what you couldn't tell him when you were six. You might find yourself first whining to Dad. Then you might re-contact furious anger and start yelling 'It's not fair!' while beating on a cushion in the way you would have liked to beat on Dad. You and I have a phenomenological diagnosis of part of the content of your Child ego-state.

Berne used the word 'phenomenological' here in a sense which is different from its usual dictionary definition. He never explained why he had chosen to do this. Simply register Berne's technical meaning as described above.

Ego-state diagnosis in practice

Ideally, we would use all four ways of diagnosis. But in practice, this is often impossible. When it is, we simply diagnose as best we can.

When we use TA in work with organizations, education or communications training, or simply to help our own everyday relations with others, we need to rely mainly on behavioral diagnosis. Social diagnosis gives us some back-up. Even in TA therapy, behavioral diagnosis is the first and most important way of recognizing ego-states.

● To develop your effectiveness in using TA, practice continually refining your behavioral diagnosis. Keep referring back to the table of ego-state clues you have made out for yourself, revising it as you become more and more aware of your own ego-state shifts.

If you have the equipment, make audio-tapes or video-tapes of yourself. Analyze your ego-state clues second by second. Relate your changes in words, voice tone, and body signals if you have video, to what you were experiencing internally.

Get into the habit of doing behavioral diagnosis when you are communicating with others. Do it when you are in meetings or classes. Do it when you are talking with your spouse, your boss, your employees. Keep track of the other person's ego-state shifts and your own. This may feel awkward at first. Persist until it becomes second nature.

Keep your analysis to yourself unless you are sure the other person wants to know about it!

Take every available chance to check your behavioral diagnosis against historical and phenomenological evidence. *But only do this with others if you have their explicit agreement in advance.* The more often you check in this way, the more accurate will your behavioral diagnosis become. ●

The executive and the real Self

For simplicity in our discussion of ego-states, we have assumed until now that a person can be in only one ego-state at a time. In reality, the position is less straightforward. It's possible for someone to *behave* in a way that fits one ego-state, while he *experiences himself* as being in a different ego-state.

For example, imagine that I am at work, discussing a planned assignment with a colleague. For the first few minutes of the discussion, I have my attention fully on the task in hand. If you were watching my behavioral signals, you would make a secure judgment that I am in Adult. My own internal experience also is that I am in Adult — responding to the here-and-now, exchanging and assessing information.

But as the talk goes on longer and longer, I begin to feel bored. I say to myself in my head: 'I wish I were out of here. It's such a nice day outside — I'd rather be taking a walk in the fresh air. But I don't suppose I can...' Now I am experiencing myself in Child. I am replaying times from my schooldays when I had sat indoors in class, feeling bored with the lesson and wishing I could go out and play.

Bored though I feel, I keep on with the job in hand. As you observe my behavior, you see me continuing to exchange information. Thus outwardly, I am still behaving in Adult. But my behavior no longer fits with the ego-state I am experiencing.

To describe this situation, Eric Berne suggested a distinction between the *executive* and the *real Self.*[2]

When an ego-state is dictating a person's behavior, that ego-state is said to *have executive power.*

When a person experiences himself to be in a particular ego-state, we say he is experiencing that ego-state as his *real Self.*

Most often, the ego-state with executive power will also be experienced as the real Self. In the example above, as I began my work discussion, I had executive power in Adult and simultaneously experienced Adult as my real Self.

But then, as I began to feel bored, I shifted my experience of real Self into my Child ego-state. Nevertheless, I continued to act in a way that was consistent with Adult. Thus I kept executive power in the latter ego-state.

Suppose my work colleague had kept up the discussion for even longer. I might then have yawned and lost track of what he was saying. As he waited for me to reply to one of his points, I might have blushed and said 'Oh, sorry, I'm afraid I wasn't with you.' Now I would have executive power in Child, while also experiencing Child as my real Self.

● Make up at least three more examples which illustrate someone having executive power in one ego-state while experiencing a different ego-state as her real Self.

Do you recall any examples of this from your own experience in the past week? ●

Incongruity

This division between the executive and the real Self obviously poses extra problems for ego-state diagnosis. Since the ego-state with executive power is the one which determines behavior, you would expect that the person's behavioral clues would indicate that ego-state. So long as that ego-state is being experienced also as real Self, your behavioral diagnosis will give you an accurate view of the person's internal experience.

But what if the person then switches into a different ego-state as real Self, while still keeping executive power in the original ego-state? How can you detect this using behavioral diagnosis?

The fact is that sometimes you can't detect it. This is most likely at moments when the person's overall behavior is relatively inactive. For instance, you may see me sitting listening to a lecture. I'm sitting upright, not moving much and not saying anything. At first guess you might judge me behaviorally to be in Adult. But internally, I might be in a Child daydream. Without further enquiry, you have no means of knowing this.

More often, however, the person does show behavioral clues to indicate what is going on. You'll realize that when someone has executive power in a different ego-state from that experienced as real Self, there is a split between his behavior and his internal experience. Externally, he usually shows this in the following way: his most obvious behavioral signals will indicate the ego-state that has executive power. But at the same time, he will exhibit other and more subtle signals which do not match those of the executive ego-state. Instead, they fit the ego-state he is experiencing as real Self.

In technical language, we say then that his behavior shows *incongruity*.

When I was having the discussion with my colleague at work, my most obvious behaviors matched the ego-state I had in executive throughout, i.e. Adult. But if you had watched and listened to me with close attention, you would have noted some changes at the moment I became bored and shifted into Child as my real Self. Up to that point, the pitch of my voice had varied noticeably through my sentences. Now, it became monotonous. My gaze, which until then had been switching regularly between the work document and my colleague's face, now lost focus and stared at one point on the table. These incongruities would help you judge that I had shifted my experience of real Self out of Adult and into Child.

Recognizing incongruity is one of the most important skills you can develop as a user of TA. We shall return to this topic when we look at transactions in Chapter 7.

Berne's energy theory

Eric Berne developed a theoretical explanation of what happens when we shift executive power and our sense of real Self between one ego-state and another. It is outside the scope of this book to discuss his theory in detail. We will sketch it out in this section, and you can follow it up if you wish from the References list.

Berne followed Freud in hypothesizing the concept of psychic energy, or *cathexis*. He suggested that this energy exists in three forms: bound, unbound and free. The additional term 'active cathexis' is applied to the sum of unbound plus free cathexis.

To illustrate the difference between these three forms of cathexis, Berne used the metaphor of a monkey in a tree. When the monkey is sitting on a high branch, it possesses *potential* energy — the energy that would be released if the monkey fell to the ground. This potential energy is analogous to bound cathexis.

If the monkey then does fall off the branch, the potential energy is released as *kinetic* energy. This illustrates the nature of unbound cathexis.

However, a monkey is a living organism. Rather than just falling off the branch, it can exercise the choice to jump to the ground. Berne suggests that this voluntary use of energy is analogous to free cathexis.

Each ego-state is envisaged as having a boundary. Free cathexis can move readily between one ego-state and another across these boundaries. In addition, each ego-state contains a certain measure of energy which is resident within its boundary. If that energy is not being used at any given moment, it corresponds to bound cathexis. When the resident energy is brought into use, the bound cathexis is converted to unbound cathexis.

For instance, when I began my conversation at work, I was actively using the energy that resides in my Adult ego-state. The cathexis in that ego-state was unbound. By directing my attention to the task at hand, I was also shifting free cathexis into Adult.

Throughout the scene in the example, I *could* have been employing some of the energy resident within the boundaries of my Parent ego-state. For example, I might have begun replaying Parental judgments in my head about whether I was working hard enough. However, I did not do so. The cathexis within the boundary of my Parent ego-state remained bound.

Berne hypothesized that an ego-state will take over executive power when it is the one in which the sum of unbound plus free cathexis (i.e. active cathexis) is greatest at a given moment. The ego-state experienced as real Self will be the one which at a particular moment has the greatest amount of free cathexis.

At the beginning of my discussion at work, I had executive power in Adult and also experienced Adult as my real Self. We can infer, therefore, that I had the highest active cathexis *and* highest free cathexis in Adult during this time.

When I started paying attention to feeling bored, I moved some free cathexis into Child. I continued doing so until that ego-state came to contain higher free cathexis than either my Adult or my Parent. At that point I began experiencing Child as my real Self. But I kept executive power in Adult, showing that I still had the highest total of active cathexis in my Adult ego-state.

If the discussion had gone on much longer, I might have unbound more and more of the bound cathexis resident in Child, until finally that ego-state had more active cathexis than Adult and so took over executive power.

You'll realize that it is possible at times for a person to have some active cathexis in *all three* ego-states at once. For instance, I might continue to keep executive power in Adult, exchanging technical information with my colleague. While doing so, I might also unbind some cathexis in Parent and start criticizing myself internally for not understanding the task well enough. At the same time I might unbind some Child cathexis and begin feeling ashamed that I was not complying with those Parental demands.

If you found this section's theoretical exposition tough going at first sight, don't worry. If you like theory, you'll want to pursue the more detailed treatment of the topic in the writings of Berne and other theorists. If theory is not so much to your taste, simply pass this section by. It's not essential to your understanding of anything else in this book.

Chapter 6
STRUCTURAL PATHOLOGY

So far we have assumed that you can always tell the content of one ego-state clearly from that of another. We have assumed also that people can move at will between ego-states.

But what happens if the content of two ego-states gets jumbled up? Or if a person cannot get into or out of a particular ego-state? Eric Berne named these two problems *contamination* and *exclusion*. Together they go under the heading of *structural pathology*.[1]

Contamination

At times, I may mistake part of the content of my Child or Parent ego-states for Adult content. When this happens, my Adult is said to be *contaminated*.

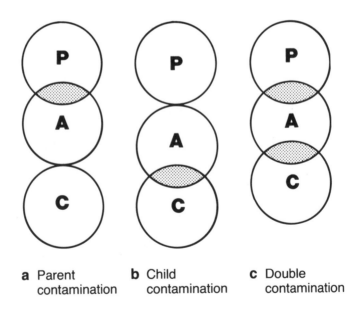

a Parent
 contamination

b Child
 contamination

c Double
 contamination

Figure 6.1 Contamination

It is as though one ego-state intrudes into the boundary of another. On the ego-state diagram, we picture this by drawing the circles overlapping and shading in the overlap. The shaded area stands for the contamination.

Figure 6.1a shows Parent content intruding into the Adult, a *Parent contamination*. Figure 6.1b shows *Child contamination*. And Figure 6.1c shows *double contamination*, with both Parent and Child overlapping the Adult.

Parent contamination

I am in Parent contamination when I mistake Parental slogans for Adult reality. These are taught beliefs that are taken as facts. Berne called this *prejudice*. For example:

'All Scotsmen are mean.'
'Blacks are idle.'
'Whites exploit you.'
'The world is a bad place.'
'People can't be trusted.'
'If at first you don't succeed, try, try, try again.'

If I believe that a statement like this is an expression of reality, I am in contamination.

When a person is speaking about herself and says 'you' instead of 'I', it's likely that the content of what follows will be Parent-contaminated. For instance, Madge is describing her life:

'Well, you've just got to keep on going come what may, haven't you? And you can't let people see your feelings.' Chances are that Madge learned these two slogans from her parents. Probably, her parents also believed they were statements about reality.

Child contamination

When I am in Child contamination, I cloud my grown-up thinking with beliefs from my childhood. These are fantasies, evoked by feelings, that are taken as fact. Maybe I am leaving a party and hear people laughing as I walk out of the door. I say to myself: 'They're laughing at me behind my back!'

At that moment I am re-playing a time from my early childhood when I decided without words: 'There's something wrong with me. Everybody knows what it is except me. But nobody will tell me.'

I am not aware that it is a re-play. In contamination, I mistake that childhood situation for grown-up reality.

If I chose, I could go back into the room and check whether the party-goers had actually been laughing at me. If they truthfully said 'No', I might move out of contamination. Doing so, I would separate my Adult appraisal of the present situation from my outdated Child pictures of the world. I might realize the people in the room had been laughing at a joke that had nothing to do with me. Perhaps I might also recall the childhood memories of being teased, but now would identify them as being from the past.

Suppose even that the people in the room had been having a good laugh at my expense. I might move out of contamination by realizing 'So what? If they choose to laugh at me, that's their affair. I'm still OK.'

But I might not be ready that day to move out of my Child contamination. In that case, when the revellers told me 'No, we weren't laughing at you', I might say to myself internally: 'Huh! Bet they're lying just to be nice to me.'

Berne sometimes used the word *delusion* to describe the kind of belief that typically arises from Child contamination. Some common delusions are:

'I'm no good at spelling/arithmetic/languages.'

'People just don't like me.'

'There's something wrong with me.'

'I was born fat.'

'I can't stop smoking.'

When the content of a Child contamination comes from earlier childhood, the delusion is likely to be more bizarre. This is especially likely if the person's childhood was full of traumatic events.

'I can kill people just by being around.'

'If I drop dead, then Mother will love me.'

'People are trying to kill me with cosmic rays.'

Double contamination

Double contamination occurs when the person re-plays a Parental slogan, agrees to it with a Child belief, and mistakes both of these for reality. For instance:

(P) 'People can't be trusted,' paired with:

(C) 'I can never trust anyone.' Or:

(P) 'Children should be seen and not heard,' paired with:

(C) 'To get by in the world, I have to keep quiet.'

Some modern TA writers see all contamination as being double. To them, the content of the double contamination consists of all the outdated, distorted beliefs a person holds about himself, other people and the world. In TA language, these are the *script beliefs*.[2]

● Take a piece of paper and head it: 'I am the sort of person who....' Then take two minutes to write down all the ways you think of to finish the sentence.

At the end of the two minutes, relax, breathe and look round the room for a while. Help yourself get into Adult by sitting vertically balanced in your chair. Plant both feet flat on the ground. Look at what you have written. For each of the ways you finished the sentence, check whether it is a statement about reality or a Child contamination.

If you decide any of the statements about yourself do come from Child contamination, think what the reality of the matter is. Strike out the Child-contaminated words and put in the Adult up-date. For instance, if you had put:

'I am the sort of person who can't get along with people,'
you could strike it through and write instead:

'I am intelligent and friendly and I'm very well able to get along with people.'

Update all Child-contaminated statements in this way.

Now take another piece of paper. Take two minutes to write down all the slogans and beliefs you remember hearing from your parents and parent-figures.

Get into Adult as before. Look through your list of Parental slogans and beliefs. Check whether each one is a statement about reality or a Parent contamination. If you decide there are any you want to up-date to fit with grown-up reality, strike them out and substitute your new version. For example, you might strike out:

'If at first you don't succeed, try, try, try again,'
and write instead:

'If at first you don't succeed, change what you're doing so that you do succeed.'

This exercise is fun and useful. You can do it in moments of leisure. ●

Exclusion

Sometimes, Berne suggested, a person will shut out one or more of her ego-states. He called this *exclusion*.

Figures 6.2a — 6.2c show the three possibilities for exclusion of one ego-state. In the diagrams, we show the excluded ego-state by crossing it through and drawing a line between it and the neighboring circle.

People who *exclude Parent* will operate with no ready-made rules about the world. Instead, they make their own rules afresh in every situation. They are good at using Little Professor intuition to sense what is going on around them. These people are often 'wheeler-dealers'. They may be top politicians, successful executives, or Mafia bosses.

If I *exclude Adult*, I switch off my grown-up power of reality-testing. Instead, I hear only an internal Parent-Child dialogue. My resulting actions, feelings and thoughts will reflect this constant struggle. Because I am not using my full Adult powers of reality-testing, my thoughts and actions may even become bizarre, with the possibility that I may be diagnosed psychotic.

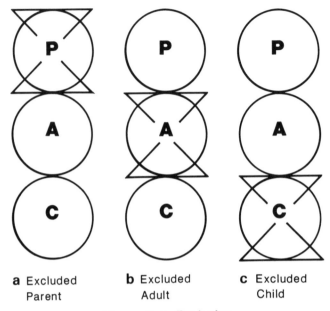

a Excluded   **b** Excluded   **c** Excluded
Parent   Adult   Child

Figure 6.2 Exclusion

Someone who *excludes Child* will shut out the stored memories of his own childhood. Asked 'How was life for you as a child?', he will reply 'I don't know. I don't remember anything about it.' When we express feelings as grown-ups, we are often in our Child ego-state. Therefore the person with excluded Child will often be regarded as a 'cold fish' or 'all head'.

If two out of the three ego-states are excluded, the one operational ego-state is labeled *constant* or *excluding*. It is shown on the diagram as a thicker circle. Figures 6.3a — 6.3c show the three possibilities.

A person with *constant Parent* will deal with the world solely by accessing a set of Parental rules. Asked 'How do you think we could develop this plan?', she might answer 'Well, I think it's a good plan. Keep at it, that's what I say.' In response to 'How do you feel?', her reply might be 'At times like this, you've got to keep calm, haven't you?'

According to Berne, someone with *constant Adult* is 'unable to join in the fun'. Instead he functions 'almost solely as a planner, information-collector, and data-processor'.[3]

Anyone in *constant Child* will at all times behave, think and feel as though they were still in childhood. Meeting a problem, this person's strategy will be to escalate feelings. They will shut out both grown-up reality-testing and sets of Parental rules. This person is likely to be seen by others as 'immature' or 'hysterical'.

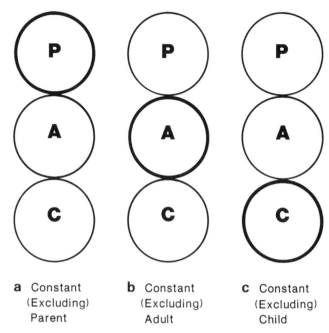

a Constant   **b** Constant   **c** Constant
   (Excluding)   (Excluding)   (Excluding)
    Parent   Adult   Child

Figure 6.3   Constant (excluding) ego-states

Exclusion is never total. Instead, it is specific to particular situations. For instance, if we talk of someone as 'having an excluded Child', what we really mean is that they seldom get into their Child ego-state, except in some select situations.

People cannot function without having some Child ego-state. They cannot function outside of institutions without some Adult. They don't get along in society very well without having some Parent.

Part III
COMMUNICATING

Transactions,
Strokes and Time
Structuring

Chapter 7
TRANSACTIONS

You are sitting reading this book. I come into the room and say 'Hi there!' You look up and reply 'Hi!' We have just completed a simple *transaction*.

A transaction takes place when I offer some kind of communication to you and you reply to me. In formal language, the opening communication is called the *stimulus*. The reply is called the *response*.

This gives us the formal definition of a transaction as *a transactional stimulus plus a transactional response*. Berne referred to the transaction as the 'basic unit of social discourse'.

You and I might continue our conversation. In response to your 'Hi!' I might ask 'Had a good day?' and you might reply in turn. Now we have a chain of transactions. The response of each one serves as stimulus to the next. Communication between people always takes the form of such chains of transactions.

In the *analysis of transactions*, we use the ego-state model to help explain what goes on during this process of communication.[1]

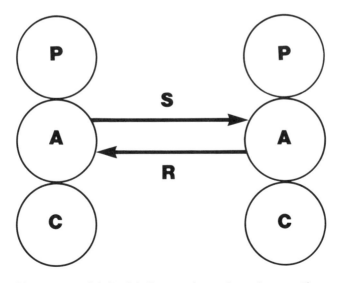

Figure 7.1 Adult–Adult complementary transaction

Complementary transactions

I ask you 'What's the time?' You reply 'One o'clock.' We have exchanged here-and-now information. Our words are Adult. Our voice tones and body signals confirm the Adult ego-state.

Figure 7.1 pictures this Adult-Adult transaction. The arrows show the direction of each communication. In formal language, these arrows are known as *vectors*. The label S stands for 'stimulus', R for 'response'.

Asking you for information, I was in my Adult ego-state. We show this by having the 'S' vector start from the Adult circle on my PAC diagram. I intended my communication to be heard by you in your Adult. Thus the vector ends up at the Adult on your diagram.

With your matter-of-fact reply, you also were coming from Adult and expected me to receive the information in my Adult. Hence the 'R' vector comes back from your Adult circle to my own.

This illustrates one kind of *complementary transaction*. We define such a transaction as follows:

A complementary transaction is one in which the transactional vectors are parallel and the ego-state addressed is the one which responds. Check how this definition applies to the Adult-Adult transaction in our example. Because a complementary transaction always has the vectors parallel in the diagram, it is often called by the alternative name *parallel transaction*.

Figure 7.2 shows another kind of complementary transaction. This time it features Parent and Child ego-states.

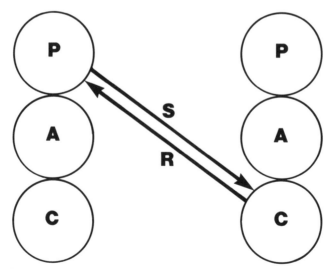

Figure 7.2 P→C, C→P complementary transaction

The store manager looks up as the clerk comes through the door, ten minutes late. Shifting into Parent, the manager growls: 'Late *again*! This just won't do!' Cowering and blushing in Child, the employee mutters: 'Sorry. I'll try not to do it again.'

With his Parental growl, the manager means his stimulus to be heard by the clerk in Child. So the 'S' vector starts from his Parent circle and goes to the clerk's Child circle. Sure enough, the clerk does go into Child. His muttered apology is for the benefit of the manager in Parent. This is shown by the placing of the 'R' vector.

You'll see that this example also fits the definition of a complementary transaction.

● Two other possibilities for complementary transactions are Parent-Parent and Child-Child. Go ahead and draw a transactional diagram for each. Think of words to fit the stimulus and the response in each case. ●

We can get a more detailed analysis of transactions by using the functional model. For instance:

Bob (slumps in chair): 'Phew, I'm tired! I'd love you to give me a back-rub. Will you?'

June (warm tone, smiles, opens arms): 'Yes, sure I will.'

Their transaction is complementary. The stimulus is FC to NP, and the response comes back from NP to FC (Figure 7.3).

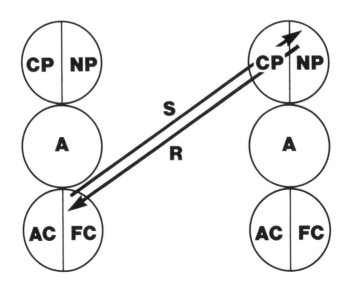

Figure 7.3 FC → NP, NP → FC
complementary transaction

First rule of communication

A complementary transaction has a quality of expectedness about it. Asking you for information about the time, I expected you to respond from your Adult, and you did. When the manager told off his clerk, he expected a Child apology and he got it.

A conversation may consist of a chain of complementary transactions. If so, the whole chain will have this feel of something predictable happening.

Manager: 'I should think you would be sorry, too! This is the third time this week.'

Clerk (whines): 'I said I was sorry, boss. Anyway, I was held up in the traffic.'

Manager: 'Huh! Don't come that stuff with me! You should have left earlier...'

An exchange like this can go on 'in a groove' until the transactors run out of steam or decide to do something else.

This is formalized in the *first rule of communication*:

So long as transactions remain complementary, communication can continue indefinitely.

Notice we don't say 'will continue', but 'can continue'. Obviously any conversation will draw to a close after a certain time. But as long as the transactions stay complementary, there is nothing in the process of communication to break the smooth flow of stimulus and response.

● Make up an imaginary conversation consisting of a chain of Adult-Adult complementary transactions. Do the same for Parent-Child, Parent-Parent and Child-Child exchanges. Check that each fits with the first rule of communication.

If you are working in a group, get into pairs and role-play each kind of exchange. See how long you can keep going in a chain of parallel transactions. ●

Crossed transactions

I ask you 'What's the time?' You stand up, go red in the face, and yell: 'Time! Time! Don't ask me about the time! You're late *again*! What on earth do you think you're doing?'

This is not the Adult response I had invited with my Adult question. Instead, you have moved into an angry Parent ego-state. With your scolding, you invite me to move out of my Adult and into my Child. The transactional diagram for our exchange is given in Figure 7.4.

This is an example of one kind of *crossed transaction*. It is so called because the vectors on the diagram for this type of transaction usually cross.

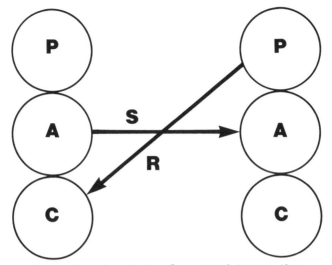

Figure 7.4 A→A, P→C crossed transaction

Also, 'crossed' is an apt description for the feel of this sort of exchange. When you cross our transaction by yelling at me, I feel as though you had cut across the flow of our communication.

Formally, *a crossed transaction is one in which the transactional vectors are not parallel, or in which the ego-state addressed is not the one which responds.*

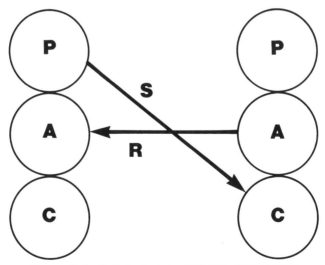

Figure 7.5 P→C, A→A crossed transaction

Let's re-run the scene between the manager and the late-arriving clerk. The clerk comes in and the manager growls at him Parentally. But instead of cowering and apologizing, the clerk looks evenly at the boss. He replies in a level voice: 'I can hear that you're angry. I understand why you may feel that way. Please tell me what you want me to do about this now.'

He has crossed the manager's P — C stimulus with an A — A response. We see it in Figure 7.5. Once again the response cuts across the flow of communication which had been expected by the person sending the stimulus.

Sometimes we need to use the detailed functional model to see whether a transaction is crossed. For example:

Bob (slumps in chair): 'Phew, I'm tired! I'd love you to give me a back-rub. Will you?'

June (harsh voice, frowns, looks down nose at him): 'You're crazy! You think I have time to give back-rubs?'

She replies to Bob's C — P stimulus with a P — C response. On a first-order model, the transaction would appear parallel. But it feels crossed. The nature of the cross is revealed in Figure 7.6. June has come back from CP and not NP. She addresses Bob in his AC instead of his FC.

Second rule of communication

When a transaction is crossed, chances are that the person receiving the cross will shift into the ego-state that the crosser has invited. He will likely

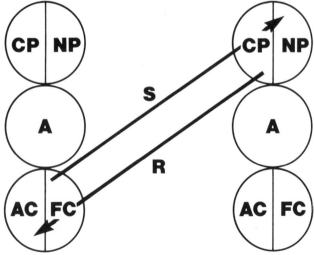

Figure 7.6 FC → NP, CP → AC crossed transaction

then move into a parallel transaction from that new ego-state. When I ask you the time and you yell at me for being late, I will probably get into Adapted Child and apologize. Or I may be rebellious from that same ego-state: 'Well, I couldn't help it. Don't know what you're making so much fuss about.' My original Adult request for information is forgotten for the time being.

The *second rule of communication* says:

When a transaction is crossed, a break in communication results and one or both individuals will need to shift ego-states in order for communication to be re-established.

The 'break in communication' may be felt as only a mild jolt. At the other extreme, it may entail the two people storming furiously out of the room, slamming the doors and never speaking to each other again.

Eric Berne calculated that in theory there are 72 possible varieties of crossed transaction. Luckily, two of those are by far the most common in practice. They occur when an A — A stimulus is crossed either by a C — P response or by a P — C response.

● Make up your own example of an A — A stimulus crossed by a C — P response. How might the conversation continue if the person receiving the response moved into Parent and opened a parallel transaction from that ego-state?

Do the same exercise for an A — A stimulus crossed by a P — C response.

Make up an example of an A — A stimulus crossed by a C — C response. Draw the transactional diagram. Notice from this example that parallel vectors do not *always* mean a parallel transaction.

If you are working in a group, get into pairs and role-play a conversation in which every transaction is crossed. Each time the other person speaks, decide which ego-state she was inviting in you. Get into a different ego-state and respond. She then crosses you in return. See how long you can keep up the sequence without slipping into parallel transactions. When you finish, discuss your experience during this exercise. How was it different from the earlier one in which you kept all the transactions parallel? ●

Ulterior transactions

In an *ulterior transaction*, two messages are conveyed at the same time. One of these is an overt or *social-level* message. The other is a covert or *psychological-level* message.

Most often, the social-level content is Adult-Adult. The psychological-level messages are usually either Parent-Child or Child-Parent.

Husband: 'What did you do with my shirt?'

Wife: 'I put it in your drawer.'

Simply looking at the written words, we'd say this was an Adult-Adult complementary transaction. And so it is, at social level. But now let's re-run it with sound and visuals.

Husband (harshly, voice tone dropping at end of sentence; tense facial muscles, drawing brows together): 'What did you do with my shirt?'

Wife (voice quavering, rising tone; hunches shoulders, drops head forward, looks out from under raised eyebrows): 'I put it in your drawer.'

The psychological level is a parallel P — C, C — P exchange. If we put words to the messages conveyed at this level, they might read:

Husband: 'You're always messing with my things!'

Wife: 'You're always unjustly criticizing me!'

This gives the transactional diagram shown in Figure 7.7. We show the social-level stimulus and response as solid arrows and label them S_s and R_s. The dotted arrows stand for the psychological-level stimulus and response, S_p and R_p.

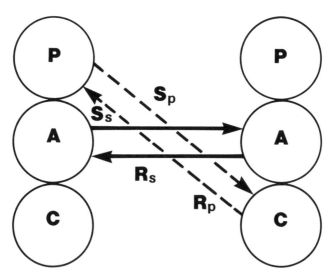

Figure 7.7 Duplex ulterior transaction: social level
A→A, A→A; psychological level P→C, C→P

Any ulterior transaction like this, in which an A — A social message overlies a psychological-level exchange between P and C (less often, C — C or P — P), is called a *duplex transaction.*

Eric Berne pictured another kind of ulterior, which he called the *angular transaction.* Here, I may address you with a social-level stimulus from Adult to Adult. But my secret message is from my Adult to your

Child. I hope you will take my invitation and come back with a Child response. The textbook example is that of a salesperson hoping to hook a customer into an impulse purchase.

Salesperson: 'Of course, Sir, that camera is the top of our range. But I guess it's probably beyond your budget.'

Customer (defiantly): 'I'll take it!'

The transactional diagram at Figure 7.8 shows the angle between the S_s and S_p vectors which gives this transaction its name.

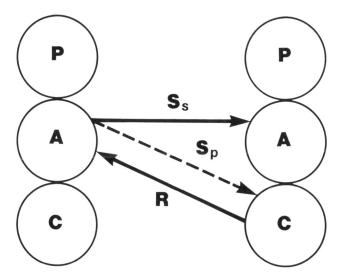

Figure 7.8 Angular ulterior transaction

It's always possible that the exchange might have gone differently:

Salesperson: '...it's probably beyond your budget.'

Customer (thoughtfully): 'Well, now you mention it, you're right. It is beyond my budget. Thanks anyway.'

Here, the salesperson's maneuver has not succeeded in 'hooking' the customer into Child.

The example illustrates an important general point about transactions. *When I offer you a transactional stimulus, I can never MAKE you go into a particular ego-state. The most I can do is INVITE you to respond from that ego-state.*

Third rule of communication

Berne's 'third rule' says: *The behavioral outcome of an ulterior transaction is determined at the psychological and not at the social level.*

67

Berne wrote 'is determined', not 'may be determined'. He is suggesting that when people communicate on two levels, what actually happens is *always* the outcome of the secret messages. If we want to understand behavior, we must pay attention to the psychological level of communication.

In TA language, we talk of this as *'thinking Martian'*. Berne pictured a little green man from Mars coming down and observing Earthlings. This Martian has no preconceptions of what our communications are supposed to mean. He simply observes how we do communicate, then notes the behavior which follows.

● Practice being that Martian. Be aware always of the psychological as well as the social level. Check on Berne's striking claim. Was he right in believing that the behavioral outcome is always determined at the psychological level? ●

Transactions and non-verbals

In an ulterior transaction, the social-level message is given by the words. To 'think Martian' at the psychological level, you need to observe non-verbal clues. These are found in voice tones, gestures, postures and facial expressions. There are also more subtle clues in breathing, muscle tension, pulse rate, pupil dilation, degree of sweating and so on.

We have referred to psychological-level messages as 'secret messages'. In fact they are not secret at all if you know what to look for. The non-verbal clues are there for you to read.

Young children read these clues intuitively. As we grow up, we are systematically trained to blank out this intuition. ('It's not polite to stare, dear.') To be effective in using TA, we need to re-train ourselves in noting body clues. You have made an important start by practicing behavioral diagnosis of ego-states.

The truth is that every transaction has a psychological as well as a social level. But in an ulterior transaction, the two do not match. The messages conveyed by the words are belied by the non-verbal messages.

You learned in Chapter 5 that *incongruity* is the technical name for this kind of mis-match. To 'think Martian', practice watching out for incongruity.

And this leads us to a more general point. *To analyze ANY transaction accurately, you need to consider non-verbal clues as well as words.*

Recall our example of the husband asking his wife where his shirt was. Simply reading the words, it looked Adult-Adult. With non-verbal clues, it turned out to be a Parent-Child exchange. We could have re-run the same words with different sets of non-verbals to give a different kind of transaction each time.

● Test this out. Keep the same words between husband and wife. Find out how many different kinds of transaction you can generate by putting in different non-verbals.

In a group, role-play the husband-wife transaction with different sets of non-verbal clues. ●

Options

No one kind of transaction is 'good' or 'bad' in itself. If you want to maintain a smoothly predictable flow of communication, keep your transactions parallel. If you find that your communication with someone is often jerky and uncomfortable, check whether you and she cross your transactions frequently. If so, decide whether to smooth out your interchanges by avoiding the crosses.

But suppose the office's prime bore is only too keen to set up a smooth flow of communication with you? Or that your next-door neighbor has just settled down to start her daily tale of woe while drinking your coffee? In these cases you might be glad to interrupt their flow by deliberately crossing transactions.

In his article *Options*, Stephen Karpman developed the idea that we can choose to transact in whatever way we like. In particular, we can choose new ways of transacting so as to break out of familiar, uncomfortable 'locked' interchanges with others.[2]

At work, Mary always seems to be apologizing or justifying herself. Her supervisor takes the other end of this set-up by continually criticizing Mary and telling her how things should be.

Supervisor: 'You see, this report should have been on smaller-size paper.'

Mary: 'Oh, sorry. My mistake.'

Supervisor: 'Well, I suppose you couldn't help it. But I did put round a memo about this.'

Mary: 'I do try to read these memos, but honestly, I've been so busy lately...'

The two seem locked into this Controlling Parent — Adapted Child groove. If Mary finally decides to break loose, how does she use Options?

Karpman writes: 'The object is "to change what is going on and get free in whatever way you can." To get this you have to get the other person out of their ego state, or change your ego state, or both.' He sets out four conditions that need to be met for this strategy to work:

One or both ego-states must actually change.
The transaction must be crossed.
The subject must change.
The previous topic will be forgotten.

We would suggest that the first and second of these conditions are the essential ones. We think the other two are 'optional extras', though they will usually apply.

Supervisor: 'You should really have written this report on smaller paper.'

Mary (feigns falling off her chair. Lies on her back on the floor, waving arms and legs in the air): 'Aaargh!! Mean to say I've done it *again*? What on earth are you going to do with me, boss?'

Supervisor: (Cracks up laughing).

Mary has switched into Free Child playing instead of Adapted Child apologies. The supervisor in turn accepts Mary's invitation into Free Child.

Crossing from Free Child is only one option. Maybe Mary would first test out a more conventional cross from Adult:

Mary (takes pencil and memo pad): 'Please tell me what size of paper you want these reports on in future?'

Any time you feel locked into an uncomfortable set of transactions, you have the option of crossing from any of your five functional ego-state parts. And you can address any of those five parts in the other person. Karpman even suggests that you can choose to use negative as well as positive ego-state divisions. Mary might have chosen to cross her supervisor's negative Controlling Parent scolding by coming back with a negative Controlling Parent squelch of her own:

Supervisor: 'You should have used a smaller size of paper.'

Mary (draws self up, frowns; speaks in harsh tone): 'Now just wait a minute. This is *your* fault. You should have made sure we all knew about this.'

We suggest that in beginning practice with Options, you keep to positive ego-state parts. In any case, use Adult to decide which way of crossing is most likely to get the results you want safely and appropriately.

You can never guarantee that your cross will succeed in inviting the other person into a new ego-state. If it doesn't, test shifting your own ego-state and issuing a different cross.

● Think of a situation where you have felt 'locked' into a familiar, uncomfortable groove of parallel transactions with someone. Maybe this will be a work situation. Perhaps it will be happening in a closer relationship. Using the functional model, locate the ego-states you and the other person have been coming from.

Now work out at least four ways you could use your ego-state Options to cross this flow of transactions. For the moment, list any possible cross even though it may seem 'way-out'.

From this list of possibles, pick one or several that seem likely to get results safely and appropriately. If you have excluded any Options as being 'inappropriate', look at them again. Remember that you have the ability to use any of your ego-states. Sometimes an unconventional cross is the one most likely to work. Use Adult to separate the unconventional from the genuinely unsafe.

If you want to, go ahead in the situation to test out your Options and discover the results.

In a group, anyone who wants to can describe a 'locked' situation he wants to get free from. The other group members brainstorm possible Options, role-playing the cross in each case. The person who brought the problem should take note of each brainstorm idea but not pass comment on any until all suggestions have been given. It's then up to him to choose to take one, several or none of the suggestions. If he acts on a suggestion, the outcome is his own responsibility. ●

Chapter 8
STROKES

You are walking along the street. You catch sight of a neighbor of yours coming in the other direction. As you and the neighbor pass, you smile and say: 'Nice day!' Your neighbor smiles back and replies: 'Yes, it is.'

You and your neighbor have just exchanged *strokes*. A *stroke* is defined as *a unit of recognition*.[1]

We are all so familiar with this kind of exchange that we usually don't give it a thought. But suppose this scene were re-run with only a slight difference. As your neighbor approaches, you smile and say: 'Nice day!' Your neighbor makes no response whatever. He or she walks past as if you weren't there. How would you feel?

If you are like most people, you would be surprised at your neighbor's lack of response. You might ask yourself: 'What's gone wrong?' We need strokes, and we feel deprived if we don't get them.

Stimulus-hunger

Eric Berne described certain *hungers* which are experienced by all of us. One of these is the need for physical and mental stimulation. Berne called this *stimulus-hunger*.

He pointed to the work of researchers in human and animal development. In a well-known investigation, Rene Spitz had observed babies reared in a children's home.[2] They were fed well, kept clean and warm. Yet they were more likely to experience physical and emotional difficulties than were children brought up by their mothers or other direct caretakers. Spitz concluded that what the children in the home lacked was stimulation. They had little to look at all day except the white walls of their rooms. Above all, they had little physical contact with those who looked after them. They lacked the touching, cuddling and stroking which babies would normally get from their caretakers.

Berne's choice of the word 'stroke' refers to this infant need for touching. As grown-ups, he said, we still crave physical contact. But we also learn to substitute other forms of recognition in place of physical touching. A smile, a compliment, or for that matter a frown or an insult — all show us that our existence has been recognized. Berne used the term *recognition-hunger* to describe our need for this kind of acknowledgement by others.

Kinds of strokes

We can classify different kinds of strokes. They can be:

Verbal or non-verbal
Positive or negative
Conditional or unconditional.

Verbal v. non-verbal strokes

In the example at the beginning of the chapter, you and your neighbor exchanged both verbal and non-verbal strokes. You spoke to each other, and you smiled.

You could have traded many other verbal strokes, ranging all the way from 'Hello!' to a full-scale conversation.

Different non-verbal strokes might have been to wave, nod, shake hands or hug each other.

Referring back to the last chapter, you'll realize that *any transaction is an exchange of strokes.* Most transactions involve both verbal and non-verbal exchanges. They may be wholly non-verbal. It's difficult to imagine a transaction which is purely verbal and has no non-verbal content, except perhaps a telephone conversation.

Positive v. negative strokes

A *positive stroke* is one which the receiver experiences as pleasant. A *negative stroke* is one experienced as painful. In our opening example, you and your neighbor exchanged positive strokes, both verbal and non-verbal.

If your neighbor had responded to your greeting by frowning at you instead of smiling, he would have given you a negative non-verbal stroke. He could have given you a more intense non-verbal by punching you in the eye. To deal you a negative verbal stroke, he might have responded to your cheerful 'Nice day!' with 'Huh!', or even 'It was until *you* came along.'

You might imagine that people would always seek positive strokes and avoid negatives. In reality, we work by a different principle: *any kind of stroke is better than no stroke at all.*

This idea is supported by various gruesome studies of animal development. In one, two sets of baby rats were kept in identical featureless boxes. One group were given electric shocks several times a day. The other group were not. Rather to the experimenters' surprise, the group receiving the shocks developed better than those left without this stimulation, painful as it was.[3]

We are like those rats. To satisfy our stimulus-hunger, we can use negative strokes just as readily as positives.

As infants, we know this instinctively. For almost all of us, in early childhood, there were times when we experienced not getting the positive strokes we needed or wanted. At such times, we figured out ways to get negative strokes. Painful as they were, we preferred them to the dreaded alternative of being left stroke-deprived.

In grown-up life, we may re-play this infant pattern, and continue to seek out negative strokes. This is the source of some behaviors that seem on the face of it to be self-punishing. We shall meet this idea again when we discuss games, rackets and script.

Conditional v. unconditional strokes

A *conditional stroke* relates to what you do. An *unconditional stroke* relates to what you are.

> *Positive conditional:* 'That was a good piece of work you did.'
> *Positive unconditional:* 'You're lovely to have around.'
> *Negative conditional:* 'I don't like your socks.'
> *Negative unconditional:* 'I hate you.'

● Make up five examples each of these four kinds of strokes — positive conditional and unconditional, negative conditional and unconditional. Think of non-verbal as well as verbal examples of each.

In a group, have a round in which each person gives a positive conditional stroke to the person on his or her left. Notice each time how the stroke is given and how it is received. When the round is finished, discuss what you observed. Then do a round in the other direction. Again discuss how the strokes were given and taken. ●

Stroking and reinforcement of behavior

As infants, we test out all sorts of behaviors in order to find out which ones yield us the strokes we need. When a particular behavior does turn out to earn strokes, we are likely to repeat that behavior. And each time we get a further stroke from it, we become even more ready to use that behavior in future.

In this way, stroking *reinforces* the behavior which is stroked. Grown-ups, needing strokes just as much as infants, are just as ready to mould their behavior in whatever ways seem most effective to keep the strokes coming.

Recall that we work by the principle 'any kind of stroke is better than no stroke at all'. If there do not seem to be enough positive strokes to fulfil our need for stroking, we will go ahead and seek out negative strokes. Suppose I decided as a child that I had better seek negatives rather than risk being stroke-deprived. Then when I receive a negative stroke as a grown-up, that negative will act as a reinforcement to my behavior *just as effectively as a positive stroke*. This helps us further in understanding why people may tenaciously repeat behavior-patterns which appear to be self-punishing.

The same knowledge gives us guidance on how we can break free from these negative patterns. We can do so by changing our ways of seeking strokes. Instead of setting up to get painful negative strokes, we can set up to get enjoyable positive strokes. And each time we do get a positive stroke for a new behavior, we become more ready to repeat that new behavior in future.

Here, the *quality* and *intensity* of strokes are important. Neither of these concepts can be measured numerically. But it's common sense to suppose that people will attach different subjective values to strokes according to who those strokes come from and how they are given.

For instance, suppose we two authors get a positive stroke for the value of this book from a respected practitioner in TA who has just read it from cover to cover. We will certainly experience that stroke as higher in quality than one we might get from someone not interested in TA who has merely scanned the Preface and the chapter titles.

Again, imagine a child getting a negative stroke from his father for behaving in some way the parent doesn't like. That stroke may be conveyed by a stern voice and wagging finger. Or it may be accompanied by furious yelling and a physical assault. Clearly, the child is likely to experience the latter negative as more intense than the former.

Giving and taking strokes

Some people have a habit of giving strokes that start off sounding positive, but have a negative 'sting' at the end.

'I can see you understand this, more or less.'

'That's a lovely coat — did you buy it in the second-hand shop?'

Strokes like these are called *counterfeit strokes*. It's as though they give something positive, then take it away again.

There are also people who are very liberal in doling out positives, but do so insincerely. This person will spot you across the room, rush up and smother you in a bear-hug. Grinning from ear to ear, he says: 'Wow! I'm touched that you're here! The room just lit up since you came in! And you know, I read that article you wrote and I just thought it was *so* inspired, *so* insightful...' And so on.

Eric Berne described this as *marshmallow-throwing*. Other writers use the term *plastic strokes* to describe these insincere positives.

There are other people who go to the opposite extreme, and have trouble in giving any positive strokes at all. Typically, this person comes from a family where positive stroking was scarce. Cultural background also plays a part. Someone from Britain or Scandinavia is likely to be sparing with positives, especially positive physical strokes. Persons from a Latin or Caribbean culture, more liberal in positive stroking, may experience these northern people as cold and reserved.

When it comes to taking strokes, we all have our own preferences. I may like to hear strokes for what I do rather than what I am. You may prefer strokes that are unconditional. Maybe I am quite ready to take a fair number of negatives, while you feel upset at even a slight negative stroke. You may revel in being stroked physically, whereas I squirm at anything more than a handshake.

Most of us have certain strokes which we are used to getting. Because of their familiarity, we may devalue these strokes. At the same time we may secretly want to receive other strokes which we seldom get. Perhaps I am used to getting positive verbal conditional strokes about my ability to think clearly. I do like these, but I feel they are 'small change'. What I may really want is for somebody to tell me: 'You look great!' and give me a hug.

I may even go a step further, and deny *to myself* that I want the strokes I most want. Suppose that as a small child I wanted Mother to give me big hugs and she seldom did. To ease the pain of this, I might decide to blank out my longing for hugs. As a grown-up, I may keep up this strategy without being aware I am doing so. I may steer clear of physical strokes, denying to myself the need for them that is still unsatisfied.

In TA terms, we say that everybody has their preferred *stroke quotient*. The proverb 'Different strokes for different folks' is another way of saying this. We see, too, why the quality of a stroke can't be measured objectively: a high-quality stroke to you may be a low-quality stroke to me.

Stroke filter

When someone gets a stroke that doesn't fit in with her preferred stroke quotient, she is likely to ignore it or belittle it. We say that she *discounts* or *filters out* the stroke. When she does this, you are likely to observe some incongruity in the way she receives the stroke.

For instance, I may sincerely say to you: 'I admire your clear thinking in the way you've written this report.' But suppose when you were a child, you decided: 'I'm good-looking and I'm fun, but I'm no good at thinking.' My stroke doesn't fit with your preferred stroke quotient. Hearing my stroke, you may say 'Thanks.' But as you say it, you curl up your nose and twist your mouth as if something tasted bad. Another frequent way of discounting a stroke is to laugh or giggle: 'Thanks, huh huh!'

It's as if each of us holds up a *stroke filter* between ourselves and incoming strokes. We filter out strokes selectively. We let in those strokes that fit with our preferred stroke quotient, and keep out those that don't. In turn, our stroke quotient serves to maintain our existing picture of ourselves.

Some people decide as children that positive strokes are scarce or untrustworthy, and decide to survive on negatives instead. In grown-up life, they may continue to filter out positives and take in negatives. These people prefer the stick to the carrot. Offered a compliment, they are likely to discount it.

'I do like your hair.'

'Huh! Yeah, well, must remember to wash it sometime.'

Persons who have had a specially painful childhood may decide it is unsafe to let in any strokes at all. These people keep up a stroke filter so tight that they turn aside virtually all the strokes they are offered. In doing so they maintain their Child security, but deprive themselves of the strokes they could get quite safely as grown-ups. Unless they find ways of opening up their stroke filter, they are likely to end up withdrawn and depressed.

● In a group: think back to the rounds of the group in which you gave and took strokes.

Of the strokes given, which were straight and which were counterfeit? Did anybody throw marshmallows?

When people were taking strokes, who received the stroke with open appreciation? Who discounted the offered stroke? How did you see and hear them doing so?

Did anyone openly refuse a stroke they did not want, rather than discounting it?

Now get into sub-groups of four. Decide whether, in the coming exercise, you will work with positive strokes only, or with both positives and negatives. If anyone in the four wants positives only, their want must be respected.

Take turns at being 'it'. For three minutes, the person who is 'it' listens while the other three deliver verbal strokes. The strokes can be conditional or unconditional.

When the three minutes is up, 'it' shares her or his experience with the others. Consider these questions:

Which of the strokes I got did I expect to get?

Which strokes didn't I expect?

Which strokes did I like?

Which strokes did I dislike?

Are there any strokes I'd have liked to get and didn't?

Then go on to the next 'it' and repeat. ●

The stroke economy

Claude Steiner suggests that as children, we are all indoctrinated by our parents with five restrictive rules about stroking.

Don't give strokes when you have them to give.
Don't ask for strokes when you need them.
Don't accept strokes if you want them.
Don't reject strokes when you don't want them.
Don't give yourself strokes.

These five rules together are the basis of what Steiner calls the *stroke economy.*[4] By training children to obey these rules, says Steiner, parents ensure that '...a situation in which strokes could be available in a limitless supply is transformed into a situation in which the supply is low and the price parents can extract for them is high.'

Steiner believes parents do this as a way of controlling their children. By teaching children that strokes are in short supply, the parent gains the position of stroke monopolist. Knowing that strokes are essential, the child soon learns to get them by performing in ways which Mother and Father demand.

As grown-ups, says Steiner, we still unawarely obey the five rules. As a result we spend our lives in a state of partial stroke-deprivation. We use much energy in seeking out the strokes we still believe to be in short supply.

Steiner suggests that we are readily manipulated and oppressed by agencies who manage to set themselves up in the role of stroke monopolists. These may be governments, corporations, advertisers or entertainers. Therapists, too, may be seen as stroke purveyors.

To re-claim our awareness, spontaneity and intimacy, Steiner urges, we need to reject the restrictive 'basic training' our parents imposed on us regarding stroke exchange. Instead, we can be aware that strokes are available in limitless supply. We can give a stroke whenever we want. No matter how many we give, they will never run out. When we want a stroke, we can freely ask for it and we can take it when it is offered. If we don't like a stroke we are offered, we can reject it openly. And we can enjoy giving ourselves strokes.

Not everyone in TA would go all the way with Steiner in his stark portrayal of the 'stroke economy' as a basis for commercial and political oppression. You can arrive at your own view.

What is certain is that most of us restrict our stroke exchange in accordance with our early childhood decisions. These decisions were made in response to our infant perceptions of pressure from parents. As grown-ups we can re-assess these decisions and change them if we want to.

● In a group: think back over the stroking exercises you have already done. In the whole group or in sub-groups, discuss how you experienced giving, accepting and rejecting strokes. Which were you comfortable with? Uncomfortable? When you were uncomfortable, do you trace that back to rules you remember your parents setting for you as a child? These rules are likely to have been modeled rather than expressed in words. ●

Asking for strokes

There is one myth about stroking that almost all of us are taught. The myth is: 'Strokes that you have to ask for are worthless.'

Here is the reality: *strokes that you get by asking are worth just as much as strokes you get without asking.*

If you want a cuddle, ask for it and get it, it is just as good a cuddle as one you get by waiting and hoping.

You may object: 'But if I ask, maybe the other person will give me the stroke just to be nice.'

Appraising from Adult, we can see this is a possibility. Alternatively, the stroke may be sincere. There's a good chance that others may have been wanting to stroke you but had been hearing their own Parent proclaiming 'Don't give strokes.'

You always have the option of checking with the other person whether or not their stroke was genuine. If it was not, you have further options. You can choose to take it anyway. Or you can reject their marshmallow and ask for a stroke that is genuine, from the same person or from someone else.

● In a group: get into sub-groups of four. If you like, they can be the same fours as for the exercise in which three people stroked and the fourth listened.

This will be an exercise in asking for strokes. Again, take turns to be 'it'. This time, 'it' takes three minutes to ask the others for strokes.

The three strokers respond by giving the stroke asked for *if they are genuinely willing to give it.* If you are a stroker and are not willing to give the stroke genuinely, say to the person asking: 'I'm not willing to give you that stroke right now.' Do not offer any explanation.

When time is up, 'it' shares his or her experience with the others. Then go on to the next 'it' and continue.

If you are working individually: write down at least five positive strokes you want but don't usually ask for. They can be verbal, non-verbal or a mixture of both. In the following week, ask at least one person for each of these strokes.

If you get the stroke, thank the stroker. If you do not, it's OK to ask for Adult information about why the other person did not want to give the stroke you asked for.

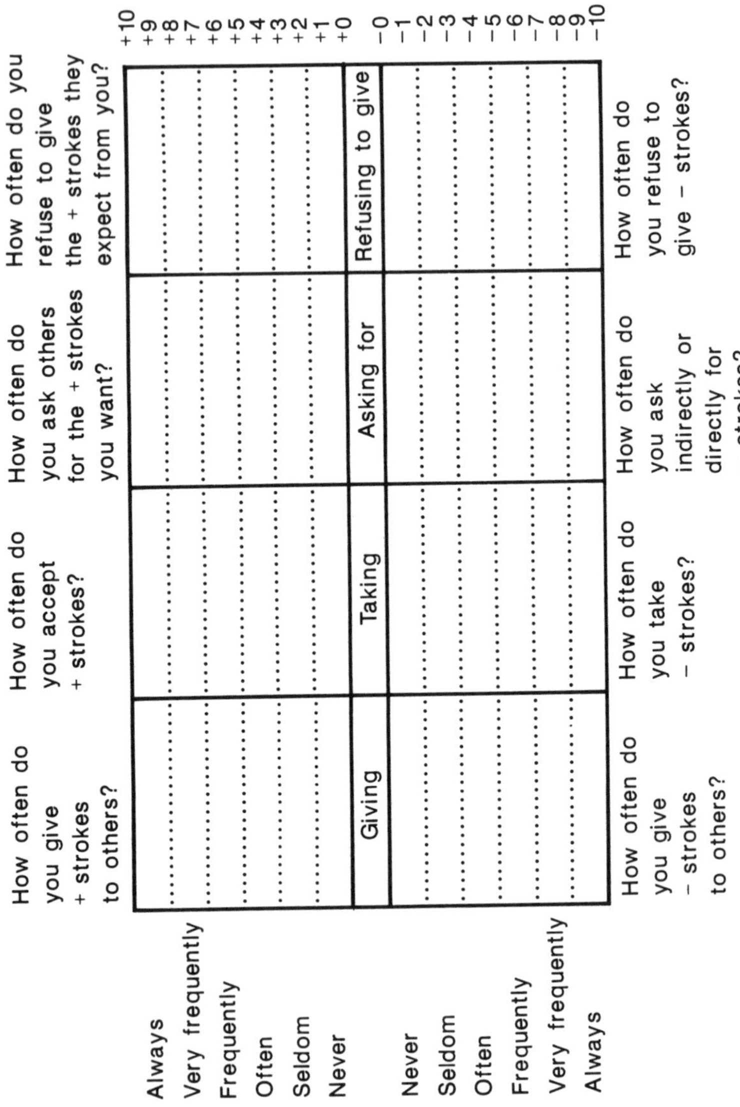

	How often do you give + strokes to others?	How often do you accept + strokes?	How often do you ask others for the + strokes you want?	How often do you refuse to give the + strokes they expect from you?
Always				
Very frequently				
Frequently				
Often				
Seldom				
Never				
	Giving	Taking	Asking for	Refusing to give
Never				
Seldom				
Often				
Frequently				
Very frequently				
Always				
	How often do you give – strokes to others?	How often do you take – strokes?	How often do you ask indirectly or directly for – strokes?	How often do you refuse to give – strokes?

+10 +9 +8 +7 +6 +5 +4 +3 +2 +1 +0
–0 –1 –2 –3 –4 –5 –6 –7 –8 –9 –10

Figure 8.1 The stroking profile

The exercise is complete when you have *asked for* the strokes, whether or not you got all of them. When you have asked for all the strokes on your list, give yourself a stroke for doing the exercise. ●

The stroking profile

Jim McKenna has devised a diagram which he calls the *stroking profile*.[5] It analyzes stroking patterns in rather the same way as Dusay's egogram analyzes the use of functional ego-states, by use of a bar-chart.

To make out a stroking profile, you begin with the blank diagram shown in Figure 8.1. You draw bars in each of the four columns to represent your intutitive estimate of how frequently you: give strokes; take them when they are offered; ask for strokes; and refuse to give strokes.

You make separate estimates under each heading for positive and for negative strokes. The frequency for positives is shown by drawing a bar upwards from the central axis of the diagram. For negatives, draw the bar downwards.

Figure 8.2 shows one possible example of a completed stroking profile. This person doesn't give many positive strokes, but is liberal with negatives. She is keen to take positives from others, and often asks for them. She perceives herself as seldom taking or asking for negatives. Frequently she refuses to give positive strokes that other people expect, but she is not so ready to refuse giving negatives. How would you feel about relating to the person who drew this stroking profile?

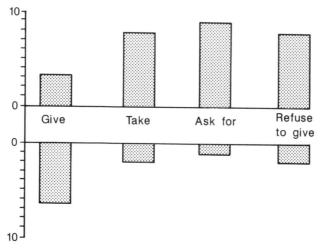

Figure 8.2 Example of a stroking profile

81

● Go ahead and draw your own stroking profile. Work rapidly and intuitively.

Under 'asking for strokes', in the negative column, include times when you set up in some indirect way to get attention from others that was painful or uncomfortable for you. At these times, you would be replaying a Child belief: 'any stroke is better than no stroke at all'. In the same way, when you are completing the negative column under 'refuse to give', include occasions when you refused to give others negatives which they were setting up indirectly to get from you.

Jim McKenna suggests that the negative and positive scales under each heading show an inverse relationship. For instance, if a person is low in taking positive strokes, he will likely be high in taking negatives. Does this pattern apply to your completed stroking profile?

Discover if there is anything about your stroking profile that you want to change.

If so, the way to proceed is to increase the bars you want more of. This, says McKenna, is more likely to work than aiming to reduce the bars you think you have too much of. In Child, you are likely to be unwilling to give up old stroking patterns until you have something better to replace them.

If you do want to change your stroking profile, note down at least five behaviors designed to increase any bar you want more of. Carry out these behaviors in the coming week. For instance, if you decide you want to give more positive strokes to others, you might note down one compliment you could genuinely give to each of five of your friends, but have never given. Then go ahead and give those compliments during the week.

Is McKenna right in suggesting that as you increase the bar you want more of, the bar you want less of in the same column decreases automatically? ●

Self-stroking

There's no doubt that many of us as children were taught Steiner's fifth rule: 'Don't give yourself strokes.' Parents told us: 'Don't show off! It's rude to boast!' School continued the indoctrination. When we came out at the top of the class or won prizes on sports day, it was OK for others to say how good we were. But we ourselves were supposed to shrug and say modestly: 'Oh, it was nothing.'

As grown-ups, we may continue this Adapted Child behavior. By the time we reach adulthood, most of us are so used to it that we belittle our own achievements even to ourselves. By doing so, we restrict an important source of strokes: *self-stroking*.

We can stroke ourselves at any time. Here are some ways of practicing this pleasant skill.

● In a group: do a round of the group in which each person tells the group one good thing about himself or herself. Anyone who isn't willing to do this should simply say 'pass' when their turn comes.

It's OK for you to brag openly and sincerely during this exercise.

When each person is giving their brag, the rest of the group listen closely and show their appreciation of whatever good thing the boaster is sharing.

When you have the feel of telling the group one good thing about yourself, go on to a more extended brag exercise. In this, each member of the group in turn goes into the centre of the circle and brags non-stop for an agreed length of time. The bragger should talk directly to various people around the circle, loudly enough so that everyone can hear. If you run out of ideas, simply repeat yourself.

The rest of the group encourage the bragger by good-natured comments like: 'Yeah! Great stuff! Tell us more!'

A variant of this is the 'self-stroking carousel.' The group splits into two. Sit down in two circles, one inside the other. The inside circle face out, so that people are facing each other in pairs.

The group leader or a volunteer needs to keep time. For three minutes, the inside person of each pair brags continuously to the outside person, who listens and appreciates. The time-keeper calls 'Change', and the outside partner takes over as bragger while the inside person listens.

After another three minutes, the time-keeper calls 'Move.' Everybody in the inside circle shifts round one place to the left so that they get a new partner, and begins bragging again for another three minutes. Then the new outside partner brags for three minutes. The inside circle moves round one place again, and so on.

Continue until each person has bragged to everyone in the other circle, or as long as time and energy last.

Working individually: get a large sheet of paper. On it write everything good about yourself. Take as much time to do this as you want. If appropriate in your living circumstances, pin the paper up where you can see it often. Otherwise, keep it somewhere ready to hand. Each time you think of another good thing about yourself, add it to the list on the paper.

Make a list of at least five ways you can stroke yourself positively. Maybe you will take time to relax in a warm bath with your favorite music playing. Perhaps you will treat yourself to a special meal or a trip away somewhere. Don't regard these strokes as 'rewards' for anything. Give them to yourself for your own sake.

Use Adult appraisal to check that these strokes are really positives.

Confirm that they are affordable, safe and healthy for you. Then go ahead and give yourself each one. ●

The 'stroke bank'

Though self-stroking is an important stroke source, it is never a complete replacement for the strokes we get from other people. It's as if each of us has a *stroke bank*.[6] When we get a stroke from someone, we not only take that stroke at the time it is given, but store the memory of it away in our stroke bank. Later we can go back to the bank and pull the stroke out to use again as a self-stroke. If the stroke was one we specially appreciated, we may re-use it many times over. But eventually these saved-up strokes lose their effectiveness. We need to top up our bank with new strokes from others.

Are there 'good' and 'bad' strokes?

It's tempting to assume that positive strokes are 'good', negative strokes 'bad'. In the literature of TA, this assumption has often been made. People have been urged to get and give unlimited numbers of positives, preferably unconditional. Parents have been advised that if they dole out a diet of positive strokes, their children will grow up OK. In reality, the matter is not so simple.

Recall that our need for strokes is based on recognition-hunger. Recognition in itself is a stroke. By censoring out whole areas of another person's behavior which we regard as 'negative', we give only partial recognition to that person. A selective diet of unconditional positive strokes may not fit the person's internal experience. And so, curiously, he may feel stroke-deprived while apparently surrounded by positive strokes.

Conditional strokes, both positive *and* negative, are important to us because we use them as a way of learning about the world. This is true in our childhood and in our grown-up lives. As a child, I threw my bowl of strained carrots all over the floor. Mother yelled at me, and I didn't like that. I learned that if I wanted Mother to smile instead of yelling, I could do it by keeping my carrots in their bowl.

For me as a grown-up, conditional strokes perform the same signaling function. A negative conditional tells me that someone doesn't like the way I am behaving. I can then take my own option of whether or not to change my behavior so that they do like it. A positive conditional signals that someone else does like what I am doing. Getting positive conditional strokes helps me feel competent.

If negative conditionals are absent, I have no grounds to change a behavior even though it may be counter-productive for me. This is what happens when people are 'too polite' to tell someone he has bad breath or needs to wash his shirts more often. This person may be avoided by others but not know what to do about it.

I do not need negative unconditional strokes, but even they carry messages that I can use for my own good. If someone tells me 'I can't stand you', I know that no change in my behavior is going to alter their view. To look after myself, I need to withdraw from their company.

There is some evidence that when parents actually manage to rear children on an unchanging regime of positive strokes, the child eventually becomes unable to distinguish positives from negatives.[7] He has consistently had part of his internal experience denied or not recognized by his parents. This may lead to a range of problems in later life. Luckily, most parents follow their urges and enforce rule-setting by a mixture of negatives and positives.

A healthy stroke quotient thus will include both positives and negatives, conditionals and unconditionals.

This said, there are some good reasons for the traditional TA emphasis on positive stroking. Especially in northern cultures, people tend to be miserly with positives. In the office, the boss may tell his employees off when they come in late. He's less likely to praise them when they arrive on time. The schoolteacher, marking Johnny's spelling test, may point out the one word he got wrong and say nothing about the other nine words he got right.

Both boss and teacher would improve the effectiveness of their feedback by giving positives for what is good as well as negatives for what is bad. Overall, we need more positives than negatives if we are to feel consistently good about ourselves.

Strokes v. discounts

A *straight negative stroke* must be clearly distinguished from a *discount*.[8] A discount always entails some distortion of reality. In the context of stroking, I discount you if I criticize you in a belittling or distorting way. Unlike a straight negative stroke, the discount takes away from the reality of what you are or what you do.

We shall take a detailed look at discounts in a later chapter. For now, here are some examples of straight negatives contrasted with discounts.

Negative conditional stroke: 'You spelled that word wrong.'
Discount: 'I see you can't spell.'

Negative conditional stroke: 'I feel uncomfortable when you do that.'
Discount: 'You make me feel uncomfortable when you do that.'

Negative unconditional stroke: 'I hate you.'
Discount: 'You're hateful.'

Unlike a straight negative, a discount gives me no signal on which I can base constructive action. It cannot, because the discount itself rests on a distortion of reality.

Chapter 9
TIME STRUCTURING

Whenever people get together in pairs or groups, there are six different ways in which they can spend their time. Eric Berne listed these six modes of *time structuring* as:

> *Withdrawal*
> *Rituals*
> *Pastimes*
> *Activities*
> *Games*
> *Intimacy.*[1]

These, Berne suggested, are all ways of satisfying *structure-hunger*. When people get into a situation where no time-structure is placed upon them, the first thing they are likely to do is to provide their own structure. Robinson Crusoe, arriving on his desert island, structured his time by exploring and setting up living quarters. Prisoners in solitary confinement make themselves out calendars and daily timetables.

If you have ever taken part in a group dynamics exercise where the group's time was initially completely unstructured, you'll know the discomfort of this situation. Typically, people will ask: 'But what are we here to *do*?' Eventually each group member will resolve this question by engaging in one of the six ways of time-structuring.

As we look at each of the six ways, we can relate it to what we already know about ego-states and strokes. The intensity of stroking increases as we move down the list from withdrawal to intimacy.

In TA literature, it has sometimes been suggested that the degree of psychological *risk* also increases as we go down the list. Certainly, the unpredictability of stroking does tend to increase. In particular, it becomes less predictable whether we will be accepted or rejected by the other person. From Child, we may indeed perceive this unpredictability as a 'risk' to ourselves. When we were children, we depended for our OKness on the stroking we got from our parents. We perceived rejection by them as a threat to our survival.

For us as grown-ups, there is no such risk in *any* of the ways of time-structuring. Nobody can 'make' us feel. If another person chooses to act in a rejecting way towards me, I can enquire why and ask them to change.

If they do not, I can leave the relationship with that person and find another relationship where I am accepted.

Withdrawal

Let's suppose I am taking part in that group dynamics exercise. A dozen people, including me, have turned up in a room. We have no agenda other than to be there. For a time, we sit in silence.

I may turn my attention inward. Perhaps I carry on a monologue in my head. 'Wonder what we're here for? Ah well, I suppose somebody else knows. Ouch, this chair is uncomfortable! Maybe if I asked that woman over there, she'd tell me what this exercise is for...'

Maybe I go right away from the room in my imagination. While I sit there in body, I'm off in spirit to next year's holiday or yesterday's row with the boss.

I am engaging in *withdrawal*. When a person withdraws, she may stay with the group physically, but does not transact with other group members.

While I withdraw, I may be accessing any ego-state. It may not be possible for others to make a behavioral diagnosis of my ego-state at this time, because of the lack of external clues.

During withdrawal, the only strokes I can get or give are self-strokes. Since I do not engage with others, I avoid the psychological 'risk' of rejection which I may perceive in my Child. Some people habitually withdraw in groups because they decided as children that it was risky to exchange strokes with others. They may develop a large and well-used *stroke bank*. Like a camel in the desert, these people may be happy to go for long periods without any external stroke input. Nevertheless, if I withdraw for a lot of the time, I run the eventual risk of drawing down my stroke bank and becoming stroke-deprived.

Rituals

As we sit there in the group room, a man across from me in the group breaks the silence. Turning to his neighbor, he says: 'Well, I suppose we might as well introduce ourselves. I'm Fred Smith. Nice to meet you.' He offers his hand for a handshake.

Fred has chosen to structure his time with a *ritual*. This is a familiar social interaction that proceeds as if it were pre-programmed.

All children learn the rituals appropriate in their family culture. If you are from a Western country and someone holds out their hand for a handshake, you know you are supposed to take the hand and shake it. An Indian child learns the *namaste* gesture in the same way. British girls and boys learn that when somebody says 'How do you do?', you respond by asking the same ritual question.

Rituals vary in complexity. Simplest of all is the American one-stroke exchange: 'Hi!' 'Hi!' At the other extreme are some religious rituals. Here, the sequence actually is written down, and the priest and worshippers follow detailed directions during a ritual that may last for hours.

Structurally, the program for rituals belongs in the Parent ego-state. In carrying out a ritual, we are in Child listening to these Parent directions. Functionally, rituals are usually performed in Adapted Child. Most often, a ritual brings comfortable results in terms of our adapting to expected norms, and so will be classified as positive Adapted Child behavior. Because of the stereotyped words, tones and body signals used in rituals, it may be difficult to confirm this with behavioral diagnosis.

Rituals are perceived from Child as involving more psychological 'risk' than withdrawal. However, they provide familiar positive strokes. The participants in a ritual will often keep a close count of the strokes exchanged. Though low in intensity, these strokes can be important as a way of topping up our stroke bank. If you doubt this, imagine how you might feel if you held out your hand for a handshake and the other person ignored you. The predictability of ritual strokes may be a plus for people who decided in childhood that it was risky to exchange strokes within a closer relationship.

Pastimes

Back in the group, the ice has been broken. Now several people are chatting about their experiences in groups.

'I did a group like this before, in high school. We never did get to know what it was about.'

'Yes, I know what you mean. What I don't like is the long silences.'

'Tell you what, I think it's easy money for the people who set these things up. Why, when I enrolled for this group I expected that...' And so on.

The speakers have moved into a *pastime*. Often, we use the verb and say they are *pastiming*.

A pastime, like a ritual, proceeds in a way that is familiar. But the content of a pastime is not programmed so strictly as that of a ritual. The pastimers have more leeway to make their own embellishments.

In any pastime, the participants talk *about* something but engage in no action concerning it. The pastimers in the group exercise are discussing the group and groups generally. They give no sign that they are going to do anything about what is happening in the group.

A frequent clue to pastiming is 'pastime = past time'. Most often, pastimers will be discussing what happened yesterday somewhere out there, rather than now and here. Pastiming is typified by the light superficial conversation heard at cocktail parties.

Berne gave witty names to some familiar pastimes. Men may pastime around 'General Motors', while women may prefer 'Kitchen' or 'Wardrobe' if they are comfortable in traditional sex roles. When parents get together, there's usually a session of 'P.T.A.' (Parent-Teacher Association):

'Johnny's just getting his second set of teeth through. We were up most of the night last night.'

'Oh, yes, I remember when our two were that age...'

For Britishers, the best-known pastime of all is one which Berne didn't name: 'The Weather'.

Pastimes are usually conducted from Parent or Child ego-states. In a Parental pastime, people voice sets of pre-judged opinions about the world.

'The young people today, don't know what they're coming to.'

'Yes, I know. Why, only yesterday...'

Child pastimers go back and re-play thoughts and feelings from when they were children.

'This silence is making me feel really uncomfortable.'

'Mm. I wonder what we're supposed to be doing here?'

Some pastimes sound on the social level as though they were Adult. But when you 'think Martian', they turn out to be Child.

'You know, as we sit here, I'm experiencing that we may all be in our Adapted Child. What do you think?'

'Well, I think I'm in my Adult now. But maybe I was in Child a few minutes ago.'

This is the pastime that Berne called 'TA Psychiatry'. The social-level exchange of information is covering the real agenda, which is a Child avoidance of what is really going on between the group members. Obviously, we would need to check this assessment by observing tones and non-verbal signals.

Pastiming yields mainly positive strokes, with some negatives. By comparison with strokes from rituals, pastime strokes are more intense but somewhat less predictable. Therefore we perceive them from Child as carrying a slightly greater 'risk'.

In social interchanges, pastiming serves an additional function. It is a way in which people 'sound each other out' as possible partners for the more intense stroke exchanges which take place in games or intimacy. We will say more about these below.

Activities

A woman across the group from me speaks up. 'So far, we've been spending our time talking about what we might be supposed to do here. But I'm wondering what we *are* going to do. Here's a suggestion. How's about we brainstorm for two minutes on things we could do, then take a vote and do one of those things?'

Her neighbor responds: 'I think that's a good idea. I'll stand by the board and be the recorder.' People all round the group agree, and start calling out their suggestions.

Now we are in *activity*. The communication between the group members is directed at achieving a goal, not just talking about it. This is the difference between activities and pastiming. In activity, people are directing their energy towards some material outcome.

We are likely to be in activity for much of the time at our workplace. Other examples would be repairing an appliance, changing the baby or writing a cheque. Someone who plays a sport 'seriously', or works hard to become a skilful player of a musical instrument, is engaging in an activity.

The Adult is the predominant ego-state in activity. This follows from the fact that activities are concerned with achieving here-and-now goals. Sometimes in activity we may follow appropriate rules. At such times we switch into positive Adapted Child or positive Parent.

Strokes from activity can be both conditional positive and conditional negative. They are usually delayed strokes, given at the end of the activity for a job well or poorly done. The degree of psychological 'risk' perceived in activity can be greater or less than in pastiming, depending on the nature of each.

Games

In the group room, the brainstorm is over. A dozen or so suggestions are scribbled on the board. 'OK, now let's vote,' says the recorder. 'I'll call out each suggestion. Hold your hand up if it's one you want to do.'

Voting completed, the recorder counts. 'Well, that's clear,' he says. 'We start by having a round of the group. Each of us is going to say who we are and what we want to get from being here.'

'Just a minute,' comes another voice. Everybody looks round at the speaker, a man who has told us his name is John. Right now he is leaning forward, elbows on knees. He scrunches his brows together in a frown. 'I'm utterly confused by all this. Who said the vote was to be binding on everybody?'

The recorder screws his mouth up into a tense smile, tilts his head back and looks down his nose at John. 'Ah, well, you see,' he says, 'that's just how things are with votes. The minority have to go with the majority. It's called democracy. Clear now?'

'No, sorry, I'm not,' John says. 'In fact, you've confused me even more. What's democracy got to do with it?' He screws up his brow even tighter and squints across the room.

The recorder sags and gives out a sigh. Shrugging his shoulders, he looks around the group. 'Well, so much for that idea,' he says sadly.

But now John, too, changes his position. Sitting up straight, he widens his eyes, while his mouth falls open. He slaps himself on the side of the head. 'Oh, *no*,' he says. 'This is the story of my life. Look, I'm afraid I've messed up this exercise for all you people. I'm *sorry*, I really am.'

John and the recorder have each just played a *game*.

The analysis of games is a major part of TA theory. We shall look at games in detail in later chapters. For now, simply notice the main features of that interchange between John and the recorder.

They exchanged a sequence of transactions. At the end of that sequence, they both felt bad.

Immediately *before* they got into those bad feelings, they seemed quite suddenly to switch roles. John had started by protesting his confusion and sounding irritable. He switched into self-blaming and sounding apologetic. At the same moment the recorder switched from patronising explanation into drooping helplessness.

For both parties, there was a split second just after the switch when each had a sense that something unexpected was happening. Had they had time to express this sense in words, each might have asked: 'What on earth is going *on* around here?'

Despite this sense of the unexpected, both John and the recorder will actually have run similar sequences many times before. The surroundings and the people may be different from one occasion to the next. But each time, the nature of the switch will be the same, and so will the bad feelings which each person experiences.

In fact, John and the recorder had signaled their willingness to play the game with each other right at the beginning of their interchange. They did this by exchanging ulterior transactions. Their social-level messages sounded like an exchange of information. But at psychological level, John invited the recorder to play the game, and the recorder accepted.

We all play games from time to time. When you are identifying your own time-structuring patterns in the exercises below, label as 'Games' the time you spend in the kind of interchange we have just described. It's repetitive for you. It ends up with you feeling bad. And at some point, it entails a moment when you ask yourself 'What just happened?' and get a sense of having switched roles in some way.

All games are re-plays of childhood strategies that are no longer appropriate to us as grown-ups. Therefore, by definition, games are played from any negative ego-state part: negative Adapted Child, negative Controlling Parent or negative Nurturing Parent. Also by definition, games cannot be played from Adult.

Games always entail an exchange of *discounts*. These discounts are on the psychological level. At social level, the players experience the game as an exchange of intense strokes. In the opening stages of a game, the strokes experienced may be either positive or negative. At the close of the game, both players experience intense negatives. The degree of psychological 'risk' perceived is greater than in activities or pastimes.

Intimacy

As I listen to John protesting his confusion then switching to apology, I start to feel angry. Instead of holding down my anger, I express it. Turning to John, I tell him: 'I'm really angry at you for what you've just said. You can think just as well as anybody else. I want you to get on and do it.' I speak these words in a harsh, loud voice. Leaning over toward John, I feel myself going red in the face. My tones and body signals are congruent with what I am expressing.

John's face goes as red as mine. Leaning towards me and almost rising from his chair, he waves his arms above his head. 'Well, I'm angry too!' he yells. 'I've been feeling that way since I came in here. Yes, I can think, and right now I want some space to myself to do that without you shouting at me.'

John and I have been in *intimacy*. We have expressed our authentic feelings and wants to each other without censoring.

In intimacy, there are no 'secret messages'. The social level and the psychological level are congruent. That is an important difference between intimacy and games.

Just as important is that in intimacy, the feelings expressed are appropriate to finish the situation. When John and I got angry with each other, each let the other know what he wanted through emotions as well as words. Neither of us could *make* the other behave in a particular way. But we had each made as clear as possible what we wanted, on a feeling as well as a thinking level.

By contrast, the feelings experienced at the end of a game do nothing to resolve the situation for the players. We know this because games are played over and over again.

When we come to look in more detail at games and rackets, we shall return to this distinction between productive and unproductive feelings.

Berne's choice of the word *intimacy* here should be understood as a specialized technical usage. Intimacy as a time structure may or may not have much to do with 'intimacy' in the usual dictionary sense. When people are being sexually or personally 'intimate', they may perhaps also be sharing their feelings and wants openly with each other. In that case, they are structuring their time in intimacy. But it's common also for intense emotional relationships to be founded mainly on game-playing.

Games are sometimes used as a substitute for intimacy. They involve a similar intensity of stroking (though game strokes are mainly negative) but without the same degree of perceived 'risk'. In a game, each person shifts the responsibility for the outcome to the other. In intimacy, each accepts his own responsibility.

Writing of the ego-states concerned in intimacy, Berne said:

'Intimacy is a candid Child-to-Child relationship with no games and no mutual exploitation. *It is set up by the Adult ego-states of the parties concerned*, so that they understand very well their contracts and commitments with each other...'

We have supplied the italics in this quotation to emphasize the importance of the Adult in intimacy. Some TA writers since Berne have simplifed his presentation and portrayed intimacy as being *purely* a Child-Child interchange. As usual, Berne's original idea turns out to be more subtle and significant. To relate in intimacy, we first need to establish the relationship with our full Adult powers of thinking, behaving and feeling. Within this protective framework, we can go back into Child if we want to, sharing and satisfying some of the unmet needs we carry from our early years.

Some TA writers have suggested that intimacy also entails mutual caring and protection from Parent.[2] The message from this ego-state is: 'I won't discount you, and I won't allow you to discount me.'

Stroking in intimacy is more intense than in any other form of time-structuring. Either positive or negative strokes may be exchanged. But there will be no discounting, since intimacy is by definition an exchange of authentic wants and feelings.

When we were describing intimacy earlier in this section, we deliberately chose an example in which the strokes exchanged were straight negatives. This was to counter the impression, given by some TA writers after Berne, that intimacy must *always* be a kind of seventh-heaven of positive stroking.

When intimacy does entail an exchange of positive strokes, they are experienced as especially pleasant and gratifying. For example, we can imagine one way in which that scene in the group might continue. Having let fly my anger against John, I relax, look him in the eye and smile. I say: 'Hey, I feel I know you better now. I'm glad you were open with me about how you felt.' John looks back at me just as directly. He smiles and says: 'I'm glad too. And I like that you listened to me.' We lean towards each other and clasp hands.

Because intimacy is not pre-programmed, it is also the most unpredictable of all the ways of time-structuring. Thus from Child, I may perceive intimacy as being the most 'risky' way to relate to another person. Paradoxically, it is actually the *least* risky. When I and the other person are in intimacy, we are communicating without discounting. Therefore, the outcome of intimacy must always be constructive for the people concerned. Whether or not they will always find it *comfortable* is another matter. It is likely to depend on whether the strokes exchanged are straight positives or straight negatives.

● Make a 'time-structuring pie chart'. To do this, draw a circle. Divide the circle into slices representing the amounts of your typical waking day that you spend in the six different forms of time structuring.

Find out whether you want to change the look of your time-structuring pie. If so, draw the version you want to achieve. Write down at least five ways in which you will increase the amount of the time-structure you most want to increase. In the coming week, carry out these behaviors. Then re-draw your time-structuring pie.

Be alert each day to how you and others structure time. Analyze time-structuring during meetings, at work, in conversations with neighbors, at parties, or wherever. Do not tell others what you are doing unless you are sure they want to know.

In a group: make up sub-groups of six. Choose any topic of conversation. Talk about it for three minutes, with each person role-playing one of the six ways of time-structuring. At the end of time, discuss your experience. Choose another topic, shift time-structuring roles and repeat.

In the large group, count off round the room from 'one' to 'six'. All the 'ones' are to role-play withdrawing, the 'twos' rituals, the 'threes' pastiming, and so on. Then mill around and have a 'time-structure cocktail party' for five minutes, with everyone in role. At the end of time, share your experience with the rest of the group. ●

Part IV
WRITING OUR
OWN LIFE-STORY

Life-Scripts

Chapter 10
THE NATURE AND ORIGINS OF LIFE-SCRIPT

You have written your own life-story.

You began writing it at birth. By the time you were four years old, you had decided on the essentials of the plot.

At seven, you had completed your story in all its main details. From then until you were about twelve years of age, you polished it up and added a few extras here and there. In adolescence you revised your story, updating it with more real-life characters.

Like all stories, your life-story has a beginning, a middle and an end. It has its heroes, heroines, villains, stooges and walk-on characters. It has its main theme and its sub-plots. It may be comic or tragic, enthralling or boring, inspiring or inglorious.

Now that you are an adult, the beginnings of your story are out of reach of your conscious memory. You may not have been aware, until now, that you wrote it at all. Yet without that awareness, you are likely to live out the story you composed all those years ago. That story is your *life-script*.

● Suppose for now that you have, indeed, written the story which is your own life.

Take pencil and paper and write down answers to the following questions. Work quickly and intuitively, accepting the first answers you bring to mind.

What is the title of your story?

What kind of story is it? Happy or sad? Triumphant or tragic? Interesting or boring? Use your own words, putting them down just as you bring them to mind.

In a few sentences, describe the closing scene: how does your story end?

Keep your answers. You can refer to them again as you read more about the nature of life-script. ●

In everyday TA language, we usually refer to life-script simply as *script*.

Nature and definition of life-script

The theory of script was first developed by Eric Berne and his co-workers, notably Claude Steiner, in the mid-1960s. Since then many writers have built on those original ideas. The concept of script has grown in importance as a part of TA theory, until now it ranks with the ego-state model as a central idea of TA.[1]

In *Principles of Group Treatment*, Berne defined life-script as 'an unconscious life plan'. Later, in *What Do You Say After You Say Hello*, he gave a more complete definition: 'a life plan made in childhood, reinforced by the parents, justified by subsequent events, and culminating in a chosen alternative'.

To develop understanding of script, it's worth taking time to explore the detail of these definitions.

Script is a life plan

The notion that people's grown-up life patterns are affected by childhood experience is central not only to TA but to many other psychological approaches. Where TA script theory is distinctive is in its suggestion that the child lays down a *specific plan* for her life, rather than simply a general view of the world. This life plan, the theory suggests, is laid out in the form of a drama, with a clear-cut beginning, middle and end.

Script is directed towards a payoff

Another distinctive assertion of script theory is that the life plan 'culminates in a chosen alternative'. When the young child writes his life drama, he writes the closing scene as an integral part of it. All the other parts of the plot, from the opening scene onwards, are then planned to lead up to this final scene.

In the technical language of script theory, this closing scene is called the *payoff* of the script. The theory suggests that when as adults we play out our script, we are unawarely choosing behaviors which will bring us closer to our script payoff.

Script is decisional

Berne defines the script as 'a life plan *made* in childhood'. This is to say that the child *decides* upon the life plan. It is not determined solely by external forces such as the parents or by the environment. In technical TA language, we express this by saying that the script is *decisional*.

It follows that even where different children are brought up in the same environment, they may decide upon quite different life plans. Berne relates a story of two brothers who were both told by their mother: 'You'll finish up in an asylum.' One of the brothers became an in-patient in a mental hospital; the other became a psychiatrist.

In script theory, the term 'decision' is used in a technical sense, different from the usual dictionary meaning of the word. The child's script decisions are not made in the deliberate thinking way which we associate with adult decision-making. The earliest decisions result from feelings, and are made before the child has words. They depend also on a different kind of reality-testing from that used by adults.

Script is reinforced by the parents

Though the parents cannot determine a child's script decisions, they can exert a major influence upon them. From a child's earliest days, her parents are giving her messages, on the basis of which she forms conclusions about herself, others and the world. These *script messages* are non-verbal as well as verbal. They form the framework in response to which the child's main script decisions are made. In Chapters 13 and 14 we shall look at the various kinds of script message and how they relate to script decisions.

Script is outside of awareness

In grown-up life, the nearest we come to a memory of our earliest years is in dreams and fantasies. Unless we take time to work with and discover our script, we are likely to remain unaware of the early decisions we made, even though we may be living them out in our behavior.

Reality is redefined to 'justify' the script

When Berne wrote that the script is 'justified by subsequent events', he might have done better to put quotation marks around 'justified'. What we often do is to interpret reality in our own frame of reference so that it *appears* to us to justify our script decisions. We do this because, in our Child ego-state, we may perceive any threat to our script-based view of the world as a threat to the satisfaction of our needs or even a threat to our survival. When we look at *discounting, redefining and frames of reference* in later chapters, we shall see how this distortion occurs and how it relates to life problems.

Origins of the script

Why do we make these sweeping infant decisions about ourselves, others and the world? What function do they serve? The answers lie in two crucial features of script formation.

(1) Script decisions represent the infant's best strategy for surviving in a

101

world which often seems hostile, even life-threatening.
(2) Script decisions are made on the basis of an infant's emotions and
reality-testing.

In our discussion of these in the following sections, we acknowledge our debt to the work of Stan Woollams.[2]

Response to a hostile world

The infant is small and physically vulnerable. To her, the world is populated by lumbering giants. An unexpected noise may signal that her life is in immediate danger. Without words or coherent thinking, she knows that if Mother and Father go away, she will die. If they get too angry with her, they may annihilate her. And the infant does not have grown-up understanding of time. If she is hungry or cold, and Mother does not come, then perhaps Mother will never come, and that means death. Or it could mean what is worse than death — being left alone for ever and ever.

When the child is two or three years old, perhaps a brother or sister is born. The toddler, now that she is bigger, knows she will probably not die because of this. But all Mother's attention seems to be taken up by the new arrival. Maybe there is not enough love to go round? Will the baby take it all? The threat now is the loss of Mother's love.

Right through the years of script formation, the child is in a one-down position. She perceives her parents as having total power. In her infancy, that power is of life or death. Later, it is to satisfy her needs or leave them unsatisfied.

Her response is to decide upon strategies for staying alive and getting her needs met as best she can.

Early reality-testing and emotion

A young child does not think like a grown-up. Nor does she experience emotion in the same way. Script decisions are made on the basis of a child's distinctive ways of thinking and feeling.

The baby's emotional experience is of rage, utter misery, terror or ecstasy. He makes his early decisions in response to these intense feelings. Thus it is not surprising that the decisions are often extreme. Say for instance he has to be in hospital for an operation. This is not a pleasant experience even for a grown-up. But for the infant it may be a terrifying disaster. As well as his scare, he feels abject sadness that Mother is not there and perhaps never will be again. And he is filled with rage because she has let this happen to him. He may decide: 'These people want to kill me. Mother let it happen, so she wants to kill me too. I'd better kill them all before they get me.'

In the logic of the infant, the rule is to reason from the particular to the general. For instance, suppose the child's mother is inconsistent in responding to his demands. Perhaps she comes sometimes when he cries but ignores him at other times. The child doesn't just conclude 'Mother is untrustworthy.' Instead he may decide 'People can't be trusted', or perhaps 'Women can't be trusted.' A girl of four or five may feel furious at Father for ceasing to give her the warm attention he lavished on her when she was a toddler. She is likely to decide not just 'I'm furious at Father', but 'I'm furious at men.'

The child may compensate for his feeling of powerlessness by imagining he is omnipotent or can work magic. Maybe he senses that Mother and Father get along badly with each other. Particularly if he is an only child, he may decide 'It's my fault.' If his parents get into physical fights, he may believe it is his job to protect one parent from the other.

If the child senses he is being rejected by a parent, he may attribute the fault to himself, deciding 'There's something wrong with me.'

Young children have difficulty in distinguishing between urges and deeds. A toddler may feel 'I want to kill this new baby who's getting all the attention!' To her, this amounts to saying 'I have killed the new baby.' She may then conclude: 'As a murderer, I am bad and horrible.' In grown-up life, this person may carry a vague feeling of guilt for the 'crime' she never committed.

A central skill of TA is to develop a sense for this kind of infant logic. Linguists talk of *Sprachgefuehl*, the 'feeling for a language'. Particularly if you want to use TA in therapy, it pays to acquire a feeling for the child's language of script.

To improve your understanding of this language, you can read the work of Erikson, Piaget and other investigators of child development.³ To get a feel of what it means for *you*, pay attention to your dreams. They are the nearest we come in grown-up life to a memory of what that hostile world was like to us as infants.

● EXERCISES: DISCOVERING YOUR OWN SCRIPT

Dreams, fantasies, fairy-tales and childhood stories can all give us clues to our script. Here are some exercises using these.

When you are doing the exercises, let your imagination run free. Don't bother thinking what they are for or what they mean. Don't censor or try to figure out what you are supposed to say. Just accept your first images and the feelings that may come with them. You can do your interpreting and deciphering afterwards.

You will get the most from the exercises if you find a group or partner to work with. Whether in a group or working individually, it's also a good idea to record your responses on tape. Just turn the recorder on and let it run during the exercise. Afterwards, play it back several times and let your intuition bring meanings to the surface. You will be amazed at the amount you learn about yourself and your script.

While doing any of these exercises, it is possible that you may begin to experience strong emotions. These will be childhood feelings which you are bringing to the surface along with your script memories. If you do have this experience, you can decide at any point to stop or continue the exercise. If you choose to stop, cease the exercise and fix your attention on some prominent object in the room. Tell yourself (or your partner) what the object is, what colour it is, and what it is used for. Think of some routine grown-up topic such as what you will be having for your next meal, or when you next need to be at your workplace. While doing this, stand or sit up straight with your head and body balanced around a vertical mid-line.

Hero or heroine

Who is your favorite character? It may be someone from a childhood story. Perhaps it is a hero or heroine from a play, book or film you remember. Maybe it is a real person.

Choose the first character you bring to mind.

Now turn on your recorder and/or get attention from your partner or group. Become your chosen character. Talk about yourself for as long as you like. Use the word 'I...'

For example: suppose my story hero is Superman. I may start off: 'I'm Superman. My job is to help people with problems. I fly in from nowhere, do all sorts of miraculous things, then disappear again. Most of the time, nobody knows I'm Superman, because I go around in disguise...'

Whoever your chosen character is, now go ahead, be him or her and talk about yourself.

Story or fable

A variation of the first exercise is to tell a story or fable. Again, choose any one you like — the first one you bring to mind is best. It may be a childhood fairy-tale, a classic myth, or anything else you want.

You might begin: 'Once upon a time, there was a beautiful girl who was sent to sleep for ages and ages by her evil stepmother. She lay in a room deep inside a castle. Round the castle was a prickly hedge. Kings and princes came looking for the girl, but none of them was strong enough to hack through the hedge...'

To get even more from the story, you can go on and become each one of the people and things in the story. Each time, talk about yourself. From the story above, you could choose to be the girl, the stepmother, the room, the castle, one of the princes, and the hedge.

As the hedge, you might say: 'I'm a hedge. I'm sturdy, rough and prickly. All my prickles point outwards, so that people can't hack me around. My job is to protect that young girl who's asleep inside me...'

Dream

Choose a dream of yours. You are likely to learn most from a recent dream or one which recurs, but any dream will do.

Tell the dream. Relate it in the *present* tense, not the past.

Then, just as you did with your story, become each of the people and things in the dream and talk about yourself.

Recall how you felt immediately after you awoke from the dream. Was it a pleasant or unpleasant feeling?

Did you like how the dream ended? If you did not, you can continue the exercise by re-writing your dream ending. Tell the re-written ending just as you told the dream, using the present tense.

Test whether you're now fully satisfied with the dream's ending. If not, re-write it again, as many times as you want to.

Object in the room

Look around the room. Choose any object you see. The best one is the first one you think of. Now be that object and talk about yourself.

For example: 'I'm the door. I'm hard, square and wooden. Sometimes I get in people's way. But when I do, they just push me to one side...'

To get even more from this exercise, ask a partner to conduct a conversation with you as the object you have chosen. The partner is *not* to make interpretations. He is just to talk with you as the door, the fireplace or whatever you have chosen to be. For instance:

'I'm the door. When I stand in people's way, they push me aside.'

'Well, door, how do you feel when people push you aside?'

'I feel angry. But I'm a door and I can't talk. I just let them do it.'

'Aha. So is there anything you want to change, door, to feel better?'

See your life as a play

For this exercise, you need someone to act as a 'guide' and talk you through it while you relax. Alternatively, record the cues on tape and listen to them while relaxed. One guide can lead a group of people through the exercise.

The guide need not follow the cues as written here word for word. In fact it is better if she simply jots down a few reminders of the sequence to follow, then improvises the wording. She should allow plenty of pauses between sentences. This gives the participants time to develop their visualizations.

Get relaxed in a chair or on the floor. It may help to close your eyes. The guide then goes ahead on these lines:

'Imagine you're in a theatre. You're waiting for a play to start. This play is your very own life story.

'What kind of play is this you're going to watch? Is it a comedy, a tragedy? Is it a high drama or a kitchen-sink opera? Is it interesting or boring, heroic or matter-of-fact — or what?

'Is the theatre full, half-empty, empty? Are the audience going to be enthralled or bored? Happy or sad? Are they going to applaud or walk out — or what?

'What's the title of this play of yours — your very own life-story?

'So now the lights are going down. The curtain is opening. Your very own play is just beginning.

'And you see the first scene. This is the very first scene of your life. You are very, very young in this scene. What do you see round you? Who is there? Do you see faces or parts of faces? If you see a face, see the expression on that face. What do you hear? Be aware of what you feel. Maybe you feel some feeling in your body. Maybe you feel some emotion. Do you smell or taste anything? Give yourself time now to be aware of this very first scene in your play.' (Pause)

'Now the scene changes. In this next scene of your play, you are a young child — maybe three to six years old. Where are you? What can you see round about you? Are there any other people there? Who is there?

'Are they saying anything to you? Are you saying anything to them? Do you hear any other sounds?

'What do you feel in this scene? Do you feel any sensations or feelings in your body? Do you feel any emotions?

'Maybe you smell something or taste something?

'Take time now to be aware of all you see, hear, feel, taste or smell in this second scene of your play — the scene when you are three to six years old.' (Pause)

Then the 'guide' runs through the same cues for the following scenes in the play, one after the other:

Teenage scene, about ten to sixteen years old;

Present scene, the age you are now;

Scene ten years in the future;

The last scene of your play — your death scene. In giving the cues for this scene, the 'guide' should also ask 'How old are you in this last scene of your play?'

Finally the 'guide' asks you to come back to the present, taking all the time you need.

Share as much of your experience as you want to with the group or a partner. ●

Chapter 11
HOW THE SCRIPT IS LIVED OUT

Having written our infant life-story, we are likely to go ahead and live it out for at least some of the time in our adult life.

In this chapter, we describe how you may live out your script as a *winner, loser* or *non-winner*. We show how people may move into and out of script-determined behavior, and explain why knowledge of script is important in understanding people's life patterns.

Your script has both *content* and *process*. You'll remember that content refers to *what*, while process refers to *how*.

The content of your script is different from anyone else's. It is as unique as a fingerprint. Script process, on the other hand, seems to fall into a relatively small number of distinctive patterns. We shall look at these in a later chapter.

Winning, losing and non-winning scripts

In terms of content, we can classify scripts under three headings:

winning
losing or hamartic
non-winning or banal.[1]

Winning script

Berne defined a 'winner' as 'someone who accomplishes his declared purpose'. (Robert Goulding added: 'and makes the world a better place as a result.') 'Winning' also implies that the 'declared purpose' be met comfortably, happily and smoothly. If I decide as a child that I am going to be a great leader, and eventually I become a successful, fulfilled general or politician basking in public praise, I am a winner. If I decide to be a millionaire, then I win if I grow up to be a happy, comfortable millionaire. If I decide to become a penniless hermit, and go on to become that hermit living happily in my cave, I am a winner. 'Winning' is always relative to the goals I set for myself.

Losing script

By contrast, a 'loser' means 'someone who does not accomplish a declared purpose'. Once again, it's not just the accomplishment or otherwise that matters, but the degree of comfort that goes with it. If I decide to become a great leader, join the army and finish up being drummed out in disgrace, I am a loser. If my political life is ended by a scandal over which I am thrown out of office, I am a loser. If I decide to be a millionaire and finish up as a penniless hermit, I am a loser.

But I am also a loser if I decide to be a millionaire, become one, and feel perpetually miserable because of my ulcer and the pressure of business. If I get my hermit's cave and live there complaining of my poverty, the dampness and the lack of company, I'm a loser.

Berne was careful to define 'winner' and 'loser' in relation to 'accomplishing declared purposes' because he wanted to emphasize that 'winners' were not simply to be equated with people who piled up material goods and money. Nor were 'losers' necessarily those people who were short of material things.

The fact is, though, that some of us in childhood may decide to achieve a purpose which *cannot* be attained without misery, self-limitation or even physical harm. For example, the infant may decide without words: 'I'm supposed to fail at whatever I do', and then go ahead to live out that script decision. To achieve his declared purpose, he fails at things. Another child may decide early in life: 'To be loved by Mother and Father, I have to drop dead', and go on to achieve that tragic purpose. Scripts with this kind of payoff would be called 'losing' by everyone, even though they do not fit the letter of Berne's definition.

Losing scripts can be broadly classified as first-, second- and third-degree, according to the severity of the payoff. A first-degree losing script is one where the failures and losses are mild enough to be discussed in the person's social circle. Examples might be repetitive quarrels at work, mild depression with out-patient treatment, or failure at college examinations.

Second-degree losers experience unpleasant script outcomes that are serious enough to be unacceptable topics for social conversation. This might mean being fired from a series of jobs, being hospitalized for severe depression, or being expelled from college for misconduct.

A third-degree losing script culminates in death, serious injury or illness, or a legal crisis. Third-degree payoffs might be imprisonment for stealing the firm's funds, lifelong hospitalization for a psychiatric disorder, or suicide after failing final examinations.

We often use the term *hamartic* to describe third-degree losing scripts and their payoffs. The word is derived from the ancient Greek *hamartia*, meaning 'a basic flaw'. It reflects the way in which a losing script, like an ancient Greek drama, seems to lead inexorably from the early negative decision to the tragic final scene.

Non-winning script

Someone with a non-winning script is a 'middle-of-the-roader'. He plods along from day to day, not making any big wins but not making any big losses either. He doesn't take risks. This kind of script pattern is often called *banal*.

At work, a non-winner will not become the boss. He will not be fired either. Instead, he will likely serve out his working years, be awarded a marble clock, and go into quiet retirement. He may sit in his rocking-chair reflecting: 'I *could* have been the boss if only I'd been in the right place at the right time. Ah well, I didn't do so bad, I suppose.'

Winners, losers and non-winners

Berne suggested that you could tell a winner from a loser by asking him what he would do if he lost. He said a winner knows but doesn't talk about it. A loser doesn't know, and all he can talk about is winning: 'When I make my first million...', 'When my horse comes in....' He stakes everything on one option, and that is how he loses.

A winner always has additional options, and that is how he wins. If one thing doesn't work out, he does something else until he is successful.

A non-winner sometimes wins and sometimes loses, but never very big in either direction, because he doesn't take risks. He plays it safe, and that is how he remains a non-winner.

Cautions on classification

This classification of scripts as winning, non-winning and losing is only approximate. What may count as a non-winning payoff to you may be a winning payoff to me. What is unacceptable in my social circle may be OK in yours.

In fact, most of us decide on scripts which are a mixture of winning, non-winning and losing. In my unique set of childhood decisions, I perhaps set myself up to be a winner at brainwork, a non-winner at physical activity, and a first-degree loser at personal relationships. Your personal combination of decisions may be entirely different.

Most important of all is to realize that *any script can be changed*. By becoming aware of my script, I can discover any areas in which I made losing decisions, and change them to winning decisions. The winning-nonwinning-losing classification is useful information about the past. It gives me a valuable road-map for present changes. In no way is it an unchangeable statement about the future.

● Review what you discovered about your own script when you did the exercises in the last chapter.

Would you say your script has been mainly winning, mainly losing, or mainly banal?

Do you identify specific areas in your life where you have set yourself up to be a winner, a loser, a nonwinner?

Are there areas in which you have so far been a loser or nonwinner and would like to be a winner?

If so, for each of these areas, write down how you would *know* you were winning instead of losing or nonwinning in that area. What would be your winning outcomes?

Then for each area, write down at least five actions you can take to bring about your winning outcomes. Do one of these actions each day. If you are working in a group, report back on your successes. ●

The script in adult life

As grown-ups, we sometimes re-play the strategies we decided upon as infants. At these times we respond to here-and-now reality as if it were the world we pictured in our early decisions. When we do so, we are said to *be in script*. Another way of saying this is that we are engaging in *scripty* behavior or feelings.

Why do we do this? Why don't we just leave our infant decisions behind as we grow up? The primary reason is that we are still hoping to resolve the basic issue that was left unresolved in our infancy: how to get unconditional love and attention. Thus as adults, we frequently react as if we were still infants. In common with many other therapies, TA sees this fact as the source of most life-problems.

When we get into script, we are usually not aware that we are re-enacting infant strategies. We can develop this awareness by understanding our script and discovering our own early decisions.

It is not possible to predict accurately whether someone will get into script at a particular moment. But there are two factors that make it more likely:

(1) When the here-and-now situation is perceived as stressful.

(2) When there is some resemblance between the here-and-now situation and a stressful situation in childhood.

These two factors reinforce each other.

Stress and the script

Stan Woollams has suggested the idea of a *stress scale*.[2] The greater the stress, the more likely the person is to get into script. If we grade stress, say from 1 to 10, I may get into script in a situation that is stressful at level 6 or higher. You may be able to go up to 8 before moving into script.

Say I have a disagreement with my immediate line manager. This represents only a level 3 stress. So I stay out of script. I discuss our differences in an Adult way. I reason that my manager and I will either work out a compromise, or have to agree to differ. If it's the latter, then no disaster.

But say now the line manager calls in the Director. An argument with the boss counts as level 6 on the stress scale. I flip into script. Faced with the Director, I activate the same physical reactions, feelings and thoughts I used to have as a child when my angry father loomed over me like a giant, shouting words of abuse I couldn't understand. Without realizing it consciously, I have made the Director 'become' my father. And I respond as if I were a terrified kid of three again.

The 'stress scale' is a good way of pointing up the relationship between stress and scripty responses. It does *not* mean that stress can 'make' anyone go into script. The movement into script is decisional, even though the decision is out of awareness.

It's probable that simply by learning about script, I will become able to take greater stress before I move into scripty behavior. If I undertake personal therapy, I can further improve my ability to problem-solve rather than reverting to scripty behavior.

Rubberbands

When I went into script in my argument with the Director, it wasn't just because the situation was stressful. It was also that the here-and-now scene *resembled* a painful scene from my childhood.

In TA language, we say that the present situation is a *rubberband* back to the early situation.

This expresses graphically how we respond at times as though we had been catapulted back to early childhood scenes. Imagine a gigantic rubber band stretching through time. It hooks on to some feature of the present that recalls childhood pain, and twang! — off we go into the past.

Usually we have no conscious memory of the childhood scene. Thus we also don't recognize the point of resemblance. For me, the rubberband stretched from the Director back to my angry father. But while I was quailing before the Director's wrath, I didn't consciously realize my father was there behind him.

Because Mother and Father are such important figures in our early life, they are often to be found at the far end of rubberbands. So are our siblings, and other parent-figures like grandparents, aunts and uncles. Whenever we join a group of people, we are likely to cast each of the group in the role of a parent or sibling. Talking to anyone with whom we relate significantly, we identify them some of the time with figures from the past. We do so without conscious awareness.

This is the phenomenon that Freudians call *transference*. In TA, we refer to it colloquially as 'putting a face on someone'. When I went into script in my argument with the boss, I was putting my father's face on him.

111

Rubberbands do not always stretch back to people. We can also hook back to sounds, smells, particular surroundings, or anything else that reminds us unawarely of stressful situations in childhood.

One of the goals of change in TA is to *disconnect rubberbands*. Through script understanding and personal therapy, I can resolve the original trauma and free myself of the pull back to old childhood scenes. By doing so, I allow myself to tackle here-and-now situations with all the grown-up resources at my command.

● Think of a recent situation in which you were under stress and which ended unpleasantly or unsuccessfully for you. In particular, think what bad feeling you experienced during that situation. You need not actually experience that feeling again while you do this exercise.

Now recall a situation during the past year which turned out badly for you in a similar way, and in which you felt the same bad feeling.

Go back about five years and recall a similar situation in which you felt that same bad feeling.

Now bring back the memory of a similar unpleasant situation, with the same bad feeling, from your teenage years.

Recall now a similar scene, with a similar bad feeling, from your childhood. What age were you?

If you can, think back to a similar scene or scenes from even earlier in your childhood. What age were you? Who was there? What was happening?

The aim of this exercise is to trace the far end of the rubberband. What was the similarity between the recent experience and your childhood experience? If another person was involved in the recent experience, what 'face' from the past were you putting on him or her?

Once you are aware what past situation you were replaying, you can begin disconnecting the rubberband. Use Adult awareness to remind yourself that people in the here-and-now are in fact different from Father, Mother or others whose faces you may have put on them. If you begin experiencing that same bad feeling, let yourself be aware that the present situation is different from that in the past. You now have the resources and options of a grown-up person, as well as those of the child you were in the early scene. ●

Script and the body

It seems that we make some of our earliest decisions with our body as well as our mind. Perhaps the infant wants to reach out for Mother. But he discovers that Mother often draws away from him. To quell the pain of this rejection, he suppresses his bodily urge. To stop himself reaching out, he tenses his arms and shoulders.

Many years later as a grown-up, he may still hold this tension. But he will be unaware he is doing so. He may experience aches and pains in his shoulders or his neck. Under deep massage or in therapy, he may feel the tension and then release it. With that release, he is likely to release also the flood of feeling he had repressed since infancy.

Eric Berne wrote of *script signals*. These are bodily clues that indicate a person has moved into script. Perhaps she will sigh deeply, change position, or tense up part of her body. Berne drew attention especially to tensions in the sphincters, the muscles that close the various body openings.

Some TA therapists have specialized in this area of *bodyscript*.[3]

Why script understanding is important

Why is the life-script such an important concept in TA theory?

The reason is that it gives us a way of understanding why people behave in the ways they do. We specially need this understanding when we are examining ways of behaving that seem on the face of it to be painful or self-defeating.

For instance, when we look at *games* later in the book, we shall find people getting into painful interchanges that they repeat over and over. Why do we keep doing this sort of thing when it is so uncomfortable?

Script theory suggests an answer: we do it to reinforce and further our script. When we are in script, we are clinging to infant decisions. For us as infants, these decisions seemed the best possible way of surviving and getting needs met. As grown-ups, we still hold this belief in our Child ego-state. Without conscious awareness, we seek to set up the world so that it appears to justify our early decisions.

When in script, we attempt to meet adult problems by re-playing infant strategies. Necessarily, these bring the same results as they brought when we were infants. When we get those uncomfortable results, we can say to ourselves in our Child ego-state: 'Yes. The world *is* like I decided it was.'

And each time we 'confirm' our script beliefs in this way, we can take a step closer to our script payoff. For example, I may have decided as a baby: 'There's something wrong with me. People reject me. The ending of my story will be to die sad and alone.' In grown-up life, I may further this life-plan by setting up to be rejected time and time again. With each rejection, I tick up another 'confirmation' that my closing scene is a lonely death. Outside of my awareness, I may be holding the magical belief that if I play out this ending, Mother and Father will change and love me at last.

The script as 'magical solution'

The script offers a magical solution for resolving the basic issue that was unresolved in childhood: how to get unconditional love and acceptance. As adults we have a hard time letting go of that magic, because as kids we often identified with a fairy-tale and our fantasy is that if we can make our life go like the fairy-tale we too can end up living 'happily ever after'.

The only problem is that fairy-tales perpetrate a hoax on kids. They teach that if you want to have something good happen to you, you first have to be a big enough victim to deserve it.

For example, if you want to marry a prince you have some interesting choices. You can work hard, suffer, sit in the ashes and weep, and wait for your fairy godmother to come along and send you off to the ball. Or you can eat a poisoned apple, or prick your finger on a poisoned spindle and wait for some guy to come along who has an investment in kissing dead women. Or you can get locked up in a tower, grow long hair and wait for somebody to come by who has an investment in finding women who are institutionalized. Or you can go around kissing toads or trying to turn beasts into princes.

If you want to marry a princess, the choices are equally appealing. You can go around kissing dead women, or looking for women who are locked up. Or you can try to find women who run away from you, or go around acting beastly or froggy. If you want to end up being successful and well liked, you first have to start out being ugly and made fun of.

The positive thing that fairy-tales do is to give kids a sense of power and control over their lives at a time when they feel powerless. The only problem is that the solution offered is magical and does not work in reality, but at least it enables the child to survive in a situation that might otherwise seem hopeless.

Later, in adult life, the Child in us continues to hold on to that magical belief and keeps trying to make it work. If it hasn't worked yet, then maybe we haven't suffered enough to deserve the rescue. A part of moving out of the script is to give up the belief in a perfect world. Instead, we can begin to use our Adult to problem-solve and figure out how to get our needs met in a world that won't ever be perfect, but can be beautiful and enjoyable.

The script as 'protection against disaster'

There is still another reason why people cling so tenaciously to script beliefs. Suppose I am faced with the possibility of behaving, thinking or feeling in some way that does not fit with my script. To me in Child, this would mean having to give up the 'magical solution', and that seems bad enough. But it would also mean I had to face up to what I feared might happen *instead* of the magical outcome I had been hoping for.

When I made my script decisions as an infant, it seemed to me that the only alternative to following these decisions would be some terrible, unspeakable disaster. I had no clear conception of what that disaster might be. I knew only that I was terrified of it. At all costs, it had to be avoided. And the only way I knew of avoiding it was to cling to the decisions I had made about myself, others and the world. Each time I could 'confirm' these decisions, I made it seem less likely that the catastrophe would overtake me.

When we play out our script in grown-up life, we are still following this infant motivation. That is why people will often report that they feel 'more comfortable' continuing to follow ways of behaving which, at the same time, they recognize as self-damaging. Without being aware of it, they are acting out the belief: 'The way I'm behaving now is painful. But it's not nearly as bad as the unknown disaster that would happen if I changed my behavior.'

All this helps us see why script understanding is so important to the process of personal change. To move out of script, I have to identify the needs I did not have met as a child. I have to find ways of getting those needs met now, using my grown-up resources instead of relying on the script's 'magical solution'. And I have to assure myself that I can break free of my script patterns without having to face the disaster I so much dreaded when I was an infant.

The script and the life course

Berne wrote: 'The script is what the person planned to do in early childhood, and the life course is what actually happens.'

Your life course is the result of four interacting factors:

heredity
external events
script
autonomous decisions.

My inheritance of genes largely determines my physical make-up. It may also help determine my mental characteristics, though there is still no agreement in the 'nature vs. nurture' argument. Perhaps I decide as a child that my destiny in life is to be a famous athlete. If heredity has given me a body that is only moderately fast and strong, then I may do better to find a different way of fulfilling myself.

Perhaps my early decision was to live to a healthy old age. I may be unfortunate enough to be caught in a fire, earthquake or plane crash, even though I have not set up in any way for such an outcome. A chance external event has cut across my decision to live.

Sometimes, external influences disrupt negative script patterns. For instance, when a country's population is 'pulling together' during wartime, fewer people suffer from neurotic complaints than in peacetime. (This is not an argument in favor of war. There are more comfortable ways of curing neurosis.)

Whether or not I undertake formal therapy, many of my life decisions can be taken with full use of my grown-up resources. We say that these decisions are *script-free* or *autonomous*. When I make an autonomous decision, I am dealing with here-and-now reality as the adult I now am.

How do you know whether you are acting in script or autonomously? As you continue to read this book and work through the exercises, you will develop ways of judging this. If in doubt, assume that you are in script. Especially if you get into a situation that repetitively seems to 'go wrong' for you, take it as your first assumption that you have been setting that situation up without being aware you were doing so. Then test out ways of setting up to make the situation go right instead of wrong.

Chapter 12
LIFE POSITIONS

Berne suggests that the young child, early in the process of script formation, '...already has certain convictions about himself and the people around him.... These convictions are likely to stay with him the rest of his life, and may be summarized as follows:
(1) I'm OK, or
(2) I'm not-OK;
(3) You're OK, or
(4) You're not-OK.'
By putting these together in all their possible combinations, we get four statements about self and others:

(1) I'm OK, you're OK;
(2) I'm not-OK, you're OK;
(3) I'm OK, you're not-OK;
(4) I'm not-OK, you're not-OK.

These four views are known as *life positions.*[1] Some writers call them *basic positions, existential positions*, or just *positions*. They represent fundamental stances a person takes up about the essential *value* he perceives in himself and others. This means more than simply having an opinion about his own and other people's *behavior*.

Once the child has adopted one of these positions, she is likely to construct all the rest of her script to fit in with it. Berne wrote: 'Every game, script and destiny is based on one of these four basic positions.'

The child who chooses 'I'm OK, you're OK' is likely to build a winning script. He views himself as lovable and good to have around. He decides that his parents are lovable and trustworthy, and later extends this view to people generally.

If the infant takes up the position 'I'm not-OK, you're OK', she is more likely to write a banal or losing life-story. To fit with her basic position, she will construct her script round themes of being victimized and losing out to others.

'I'm OK, you're not-OK' may form the basis for a script that seems on the face of it to be winning. But this child will have the conviction that he needs to be one-up and put others one-down. He may manage to do this for some of the time, achieving his wants but only with a continual

117

struggle. At other times, the people around him will get tired of being one-down and reject him. Then he will switch from apparent 'winner' to heavy loser.

The position 'I'm not-OK, you're not-OK' is the most likely foundation for a losing script. This child has become convinced that life is futile and full of despair. She views herself as being one-down and unlovable. She believes no-one will help her because they are not-OK as well. Thus she will write her script around scenes of rejecting and being rejected.

Origins of life position

There's some disagreement among TA authorities on how life positions originate, and at what age.

Berne believed that '...the position is taken in early childhood (third to seventh year) in order to justify a decision based on early experience.' In other words, for Berne, the early decisions come first, and the life position is adopted later in childhood to make the world appear to justify what has been decided.

For instance, the infant might decide without words: 'Never again will I risk loving anyone, because Mother showed me I was unlovable.' Later he justifies this by adopting the conviction 'I will never be loved', which translates to 'I'm not OK.' If a little girl is physically abused by her father, she may decide 'Never again will I trust a man, because of Father's ill-treatment.' She then generalizes to the conviction 'All men are untrustworthy', or 'You (they) are not-OK.'

In the view of Claude Steiner, life position is adopted much earlier. He sees its origins in the earliest months of nursing. For Steiner, the position 'I'm OK, you're OK' reflects the comfortable, mutual interdependence between the feeding infant and her mother. He equates this to the position of 'basic trust' described by child development authority Erik Erikson. This is '...a state of affairs in which the infant feels that she is at one with the world and that everything is at one with her.'

Steiner suggests that all children begin in the position 'I'm OK, you're OK'. The child shifts to another position only if something interrupts the mutual interdependence between child and mother. Maybe the child perceives Mother as withdrawing the protection and acceptance she had offered in earlier days. For some infants, birth itself may be felt as such a threat. The baby may respond to these discomforts by deciding that she is not-OK or that others are not-OK. She has moved from Erikson's state of 'basic trust' into 'basic mistrust'. The child then goes on to build her script upon this fundamental view of self and others.

Thus Steiner agrees with Berne in suggesting that the life position 'justifies' script decisions. But in Steiner's version, the life position is adopted first in time and the decisions come later.

Life position can be defined as *one's basic beliefs about self and others, which are used to justify decisions and behavior.*

Life position in adulthood: the OK Corral

Each of us arrives in adulthood having written a script based on one of the four life positions. But we don't stay in that position every hour of the day. Minute by minute, we shift between positions.

Franklin Ernst has developed a way of analyzing these shifts. He calls it the *OK Corral* (Figure 12.1).[2]

Ernst uses the phrase 'OK-with-me' instead of just 'OK'. This helps emphasize that OKness is a matter of *my* convictions about *me*, and *my* convictions about *you*.

The vertical axis of the Corral indicates 'You're OK' in the upwards direction, 'You're not-OK' going downwards. On the horizontal axis, we get 'I'm OK' on the right, 'I'm not-OK' on the left. Each of the four quadrants then corresponds to a life position.

Often, TA writers shorthand 'OK' by a '+' sign, and 'not-OK' by a '-'. Sometimes the word 'You' is shortened to 'U'. The four life positions are then written simply I+U+, I-U+, I+U- and I-U-.

On the version of the Corral shown in Figure 12.1, each of the four positions is given a name. These names were not on Ernst's original diagram, but are often used by other writers.

Franklin Ernst points out that each of the childhood positions is reflected in grown-up life by a particular kind of social interaction. He calls this an *operation*. The names for the four operations are shown on the Corral. If we get into one of these operations without awareness, from our Child ego-state, we are likely to create a scripty 'justification' for the corresponding life position. But we also have the choice of getting into Adult and using any of the operations with awareness. By doing so we can invite the social outcomes we desire.

I'm OK, You're OK: Get-On-With

I've just arrived at my workplace. In comes the boss with a stack of papers. 'Here's the report we've been waiting for,' she says. 'I've marked points for your action. Will you see to these and report back, please?' 'Right,' I say, 'I'll do that.'

In agreeing to the boss's request, I have checked with myself that I am competent to do what she asks and feel good about doing it. I see her as being fair and reasonable in asking me to do it. Thus I am in the position of 'I'm OK, you're OK'. In our social interaction, the boss and I are *getting-on-with* what we are both there to do.

Each time I have an interaction from this position, I reinforce my belief that I and others in the world are OK.

119

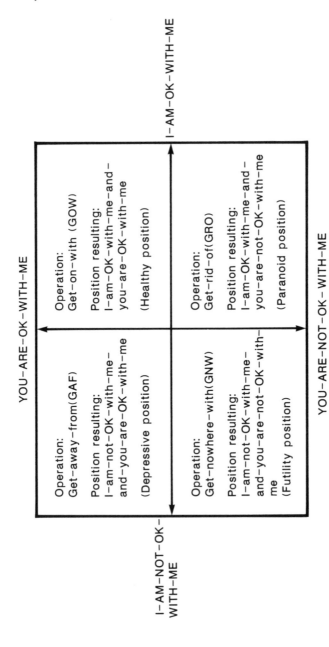

Figure 12.1 The OK Corral: Grid for What's Happening

I'm not-OK, You're OK: Get-Away-From

I've just settled down and opened the report at the first page. From the corner of my eye, I see somebody bearing down on me. It's one of my workmates. He's wearing a worried frown. Having seen that look before, I can make a good guess what he's coming for. He wants to spend a lot of time moaning about his work situation, asking my advice and then not taking it. As he arrives at my desk and opens his mouth, I have two choices. I can get into script or respond from Adult.

Scripty operation: Suppose I get into script and adopt the position 'I'm not-OK, you're OK'. I say to myself: 'I just can't cope with this fellow's complaints. I'm not up to it. But he's somebody who just seems to keep on talking no matter what I do. I have to get out of here!' I tense up my stomach and start sweating. Not really hearing what my workmate is saying, I mumble: 'Sorry, Jim, have to go out to the bathroom a minute!' and make for the door. Only when I'm outside do I relax and heave a sigh of relief. I have *got-away-from* Jim in a scripty way. In doing so, I have reinforced my Child conviction that I am not OK while others are OK.

Adult operation: If I choose to stay in Adult, I say to myself: 'Right now, I'm not willing to listen to Jim. He's got problems, but it's not my job to settle them. Once he gets started talking, it's difficult to stop him. I think the best thing I can do is move out of range.' As Jim opens his mouth and gets halfway through his first complaint, I say: 'Hey, Jim, that sounds bad. Can't stop now, though. I've got to get down to the library and check some sources on this report. Hope you manage to solve your problems.' I pick up the report and walk out. With Adult awareness, I have chosen the operation of *getting-away-from*.

I'm OK, You're Not-OK: Get-Rid-Of

Ten minutes later, I'm back in my office with a cup of coffee, well into the report. The door opens again. This time it's my assistant. He looks downcast. 'Afraid I've got some bad news,' he says. 'You know that printing job you gave me to set up? I was busy and forgot to get it off. We've missed the printer's deadline. What do I do?'

Scripty operation: I may respond from a position of 'I'm OK, you're not-OK'. I go red in the face and snarl at my assistant: 'What do you *do*? What you do is you sort this out right away! So get a move on — I don't want to hear a word more from you till you've got that job done, understand?' As I say this my heart-rate soars and I literally 'go hot under the collar'. When my assistant has disappeared back through the door, I say to myself: 'Can't trust anybody to do a job these days unless I do it myself!' I have *gotten-rid-of* my assistant, while creating a scripty 'justification' for believing that I am OK while others are not.

121

Adult operation: I reply to my assistant: 'Well, it's your job to get this sorted out. Right now I'm doing something urgent. So go and find some ways of getting this job finished as soon as possible. Come back at four o'clock and report to me.' I look back down at the report to signal that our interview is finished. Here, I've *gotten-rid-of* my assistant in a way that lets me look after myself and leaves us both OK.

I'm not-OK, You're not-OK: Get-Nowhere-With

The phone rings. It's my partner calling from home. 'Something awful has happened! A water-pipe burst and the whole carpet got soaked before I could turn the water off!'

Scripty operation: at this, I may go all the way into 'I'm not-OK, you're not-OK'. I say to myself: 'I've had enough. I can't take this any longer. And my partner's no help either. It's hopeless.' I sigh into the phone: 'Look, I just can't take this. It's just too much after the day I've had.' Without waiting for an answer, I hang up the phone. I feel drained and depressed. Internally, I have reinforced my view that I and others are not-OK.

Adult operation: Deciding to stay in Adult, I reply: 'Look, the harm's done now. Just go on hold till I get home. Then we'll see what we can do.' I have chosen the operation of *getting-nowhere-with*.

Personal change and the OK Corral

Though we switch between quadrants on the Corral, we each have one 'favorite' quadrant where we spend most of our time while in script. This will be the one we decided on in childhood as our basic position.

'I'm OK, you're OK' is the *healthy* position. Here, I get-on-with living and problem-solving. I act to achieve the winning outcomes I desire. This is the only position based on reality. If my childhood position was 'I'm not-OK, you're OK', I am likely to play out my script mainly from the *depressive* position of feeling one-down to others. Unawarely, I will choose my bad feelings and repetitive behaviors to 'confirm' that this is my rightful position in the world. If I experience psychiatric problems, I am likely to be diagnosed neurotic or depressed. Should I have written a hamartic script, my probable payoff is self-harm or suicide.

An early position of 'I'm OK, you're not-OK' will mean that I live my script mostly from the defensive position of trying to stay one-up on others. Those around me are likely to experience me as overbearing, insensitive, aggressive. Though the name *paranoid* is often applied to this position, it also corresponds to the psychiatric diagnosis of character-disorder. In a third-degree losing script, my closing scene may entail killing or harming others.

If I took up a basic position of 'I'm not-OK, you're not-OK' as an infant, my script will be played through principally from the *futility* position. Here, I am believing that the world and others are no good, and neither am I. If I wrote a banal script, my pattern will be to get-nowhere-with most of the things I set out to do in life. If my script is hamartic, the likely payoff is 'go crazy', with a psychotic diagnosis.

Like all aspects of the script, life position can be changed. This is likely to happen only as a result of script insight, therapy or some powerful external experience.

The process of change often entails a movement through the Corral in a specific sequence. If the person starts off by spending most time in I-U-, her next move is likely to be into I+U-. After some time with that as her most important quadrant, she will shift to I-U+. The final goal is to increase the time spent in I+U+ until it becomes the favorite position.

It may seem strange that people often need to shift through I-U+ in order to get from I+U- to I+U+. But the experience of therapy shows that I+U- is often a *defense* against I-U+. The infant who concluded 'I'm OK and all those others are not-OK' took up that position to defend against the painful realization of being one-down and powerless in the face of her parents. To change as a grown-up, she needs to face that infant pain and then let it go.

● EXERCISES WITH THE OK CORRAL

Draw the axes of the OK Corral and label the quadrants.

Now draw an enclosure on the axes to show how much time you spend in each quadrant during an average day. For instance, if you think you spend most time in I-U+, next most in I+U+, third most in I+U- and least of all in I-U-, your enclosure would look like Figure 12.2. Franklin Ernst called this picture the *Corralogram*.[3]

What are the circumstances in which you are likely to get into each quadrant? What do you typically do and say, and how do you feel, when you are in each one?

What ego-states do you come from in each quadrant? (Use the functional model). What ego-states are you inviting in others?

What kinds of stroke do you give and get in each quadrant?

Now that you have drawn your Corralogram, is there anything you want to change about it?

If you do want to make changes, think how you could choose any of the four Adult operations to use instead of getting into scripty responses. Decide on at least one occasion when you will test out an Adult operation in the coming week, and do it. If you are working in a group, report back on the results. ●

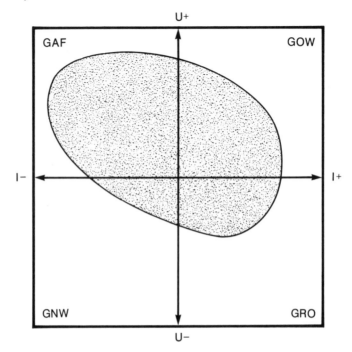

Figure 12.2 Corralogram example

Chapter 13
SCRIPT MESSAGES AND THE
SCRIPT MATRIX

You know that the life-script consists of a set of *decisions*. These are made by the child in response to *script messages* about self, others and the world. The script messages come mainly from the child's parents.

In this chapter we look at the nature of script messages and the ways in which they can be transmitted. We meet a model, the *script matrix*, which gives us a standard method for analyzing the messages underlying each individual's script.

Script messages and the infant's perception

It's important to recall that the infant makes her script decisions in response to her own *perception* of what is going on around her. This perception is founded on an infant's ways of feeling and reality-testing. Therefore the messages that the infant perceives as coming from the parents and the world around her may be quite different from any that a grown-up would perceive. The young baby, startled by a sudden loud noise, may conclude without words: 'Somebody out there is trying to kill me!' At that same moment her loving parents may be congratulating themselves on the safe environment they are providing for her.

Kinds of script message

Script messages may be conveyed *verbally*, *non-verbally*, or in these two ways combined.[1]

Both verbal and non-verbal messages may contain an element of *modeling*.

Verbal script messages can be transmitted in the form of *commands* or *attributions*.

Verbal v. non-verbal messages

Before the infant has words, he interprets other people's messages in terms of their non-verbal signals. The young baby has acute perception of expressions, body tensions, movement, tones and smells.

If Mother holds him close and warm, letting him mould to the shape of her body, he is likely to perceive her message to him as 'I accept and love you!' But if she tenses up and holds him stiffly a little away from her,

he may read her as conveying: 'I reject you and don't want you close!'
The mother herself may be quite unaware of her tension and distancing.

Sometimes the infant may construe script messages from events
around her that are not of the parents' making. Loud noises, sudden
movements, separations from the parents such as a stay in hospital, may
all appear to the baby as life-threatening. Because she assumes that her
parents are in charge of reality, she may conclude that the threats also
come from them.

Later in childhood, when the child understands language, non-
verbal communication is still important as a component of script
messages. Physical abuse, or the threat of it, may mean to the child that
his parents reject him or possibly want him dead. When parents speak to
the child, he will interpret the script meaning of what they say according
to the non-verbals that go with it. Recall Berne's Third Rule of
Communication: when transactions are ulterior, the significant message
is on the psychological level.

Picture the young schoolchild coming home with the new reading
book she's just been given by teacher. She starts reading it to her parents
and stumbles over a word she hasn't met before. Father says: 'You got
that word wrong.' With those words could go many different sets of non-
verbals. Each of these would carry its own meaning to the child in terms of
possible script decisions.

Father might speak in a harsh, loud voice, while curling his lip and
screwing his face up. At the same time he might knock the book out of her
hand or even deal her a blow. To the child, his message reads: 'I don't
want you around and would prefer you dead.'

He might say the words in a flat voice, without looking up from the
newspaper he himself is reading. Reading the non-verbals, his daughter
interprets his message as: 'You're not important to me.'

He might accompany his words with a wink and a giggle. Using Little
Professor strategy, the little girl tests out giggling back. Sure enough,
Father smiles even more. She reads his message: 'To please me, you have
to act stupid.'

Father might say the words in an even voice, while sitting beside her
pointing the words out in her book. He then gives her time to look at the
word again. His 'Martian' conveys to the child: 'It's OK for you to think.'

Modeling

Young children are perceptive observers of the way people behave.
Particularly, they note how Mother and Father relate to each other and to
other family members. Using Little Professor strategies of reality-testing,
the child continually tries out solutions to the question: 'How do I best get
what I want around here?'

Maybe a little girl notes that when Mother wants something from

Father, she usually gets it by starting a fight and then bursting into tears. The child ticks off the conclusion: 'To get what I want from people, especially men, what I need to do is start a fight and then burst out crying.'

Perhaps a little boy had a brother who died. He notes that his parents go to the cemetery each week with flowers. They seem to be sad most of the time and to be thinking more of the one who died than the other who is still alive. The child concludes: 'People who die get all the attention.' He doesn't have the grown-up capacity to understand the finality of death. So he may then decide: 'In order to get the attention I want from my parents, I need to die like my brother did.'

Commands v. attributions

Script messages can be in the form of direct commands. 'Don't bother me! Do what you're told! Get lost! Hurry up! Don't be naughty! If at first you don't succeed, try, try, try again!' Most parents bombard their children with hundreds of commands like these. Their potency as script messages will depend on how often they are repeated and on the non-verbals that go with them.

At other times, the child may be told not just what he should *do*, but what he *is*. This kind of message is called an *attribution*.

'You're stupid!'

'You're my little girl!'

'You'll end up in jail.'

'You'll never make it.'

'You're good at reading!'

These are examples of attributions spoken directly to the child. Their content may be positive or negative. As always, their power as script messages will be affected by the non-verbal signals that accompany them. 'You're stupid', spoken harshly along with a blow, conveys a different script message from the same words spoken in a light tone accompanied by a smile and a cuddle.

Sometimes attributions may be delivered indirectly. This means that the parent speaks *about* the child to someone else, either when the child is present or in a way that will be communicated back to the child.

'This one is the quiet one.'

'Jill is so cute!'

'He's not strong, you know.'

'She worries us because she's so naughty.'

'Father says you're just a nuisance!'

Indirect attributions like these are especially likely to be read by the child as potent script messages. She views her parents as determining reality. Hearing them talking to other people about how she is, she takes it for granted that what they say has to be fact.

In some families, attributions are passed on from one generation to the next by psychological-level messages. These may be based on such features as position in the family or the giving of names. For example, Ellen came into therapy because she feared she might be going mad. Through script analysis, she registered that two other women in her family had been christened Ellen: her aunt and her grandmother. Both had become psychotic at about Ellen's present age. The psychological-level message, never spoken in words, was: 'Anybody in our family christened Ellen goes mad at 35.'

Traumatic event v. repetition

The child may make a central script decision in response to a single event which she experiences as especially threatening. Perhaps a little girl is sexually abused by her father. She may read that single episode as an overpowering script message, and decide: 'Never again will I trust men.' Earlier in life, a period of separation from the mother may often form the basis for non-verbal decisions like 'I can't trust anyone' or 'People want me dead.' Some TA therapists believe that the single traumatic event of birth is itself a potent influence on script decisions.

Probably more often, decisions are arrived at over a period of time, in response to script messages which the child experiences repetitively. Perhaps the infant reaches out to Mother and she turns away from him. He reaches out again, and again gets no response. Not until he has done this many times may he begin to form the conclusion: 'Mother doesn't want me close.' The little boy who hears the attribution 'This is the shy one' may need to hear it repeated for months and years before deciding firmly that he is indeed shy.

Eric Berne compared the build-up of script messages to a pile of coins, stacked one on the other. A few of the coins in the stack are skewed. The more skewed ones there are, the more likely is the whole stack to go off line and fall over. One badly skewed coin can throw the stack off true. So can a number of slightly skewed coins, particularly if they are all arranged to lean the stack in one direction. This is a graphic picture of the way in which traumatic events and repeated messages combine to form the basis for life-script.[2]

The script matrix

Your mother and father both had their own Parent, Adult and Child ego-states. They transmitted script messages to you from all three of these ego-states. You received these messages and filed them away in your own three ego-states. From this realization, Claude Steiner developed what is now one of the central models of TA: the *script matrix*. It is shown in Figure 13.1.[3]

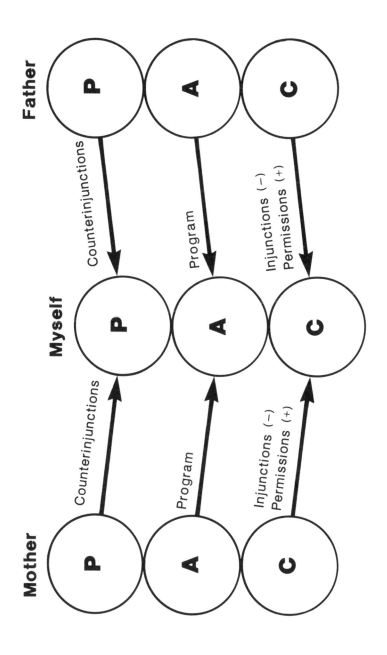

Figure 13.1 The script matrix

Messages which originate from mother's and father's Parent ego-states are called *counterinjunctions*. You file them away as part of the content of your own Parent.

Modeling or 'here's how' messages from the Adult of the parent to the Adult of the child make up what is called the *program*.

Messages sent from the Child ego-state of mother and father can be of two kinds: *injunctions* or *permissions*. We picture these as being filed away in the content of your own Child ego-state.

Different TA writers have drawn script matrix diagrams which differ from each other in minor details. The one we show here is a collated version.

Counterinjunctions

These Parent-to-Parent messages were originally called *counterinjunctions* because they were thought to 'run counter to the injunctions'. We know now that these messages *may* sometimes contradict injunctions, but may just as often reinforce injunctions or be irrelevant to them. Still, the name 'counterinjunctions' has stuck.

The *counterscript* is the set of decisions made by the child in compliance with the counterinjunctions. Counterinjunctions consist of commands about what to do or not do, plus definitions of people and the world. We all get thousands of these from our parents and parent-figures. Typical ones are:

'Be good!'
'Don't be naughty!'
'Be my princess!'
'Work hard!'
'Come top of the class!'
'It's bad to tell lies.'
'Keep things in the family.'

Most of the time, we use our counterscript in a positive way, to look after ourselves and fit in comfortably with society. As grown-ups, we don't need to think whether we should belch at the table or whether it's polite to throw unwanted food over our shoulder; the knowledge is already there in our positive counterscript. In the same way, we don't run out in the road in front of traffic or stick our hand into the fire.

Most of us, though, have a few counterscript messages which we have decided to use as part of a negative script set-up. Suppose I carry the Parental command 'Work hard!' around in my head. I may use it to win success at school and college. In my career I may go on working hard and get a good promotion. But I may also work so hard that I overstress myself. I may sacrifice leisure, relaxation and friendships to the demands of work. If my script is hamartic, I may use my 'Work hard' message to further a payoff of ulcer, high blood-pressure or heart attack.

There are five commands in particular which play a special role in the counterscript. They are:

Be Perfect
Be Strong
Try Hard
Please (people)
Hurry Up.

These are called *driver messages* or simply *drivers*. The name 'driver' is used because the child feels a compulsion to follow these commands. He believes he can stay OK so long as he obeys the driver. All of us carry these five messages around in our counterscript, though in varying proportions. When I replay a driver message internally, I exhibit a set of behaviors that typically accompany that driver. These *driver behaviors* are consistent from person to person. By studying someone's driver behavior, we can reliably predict some important features of their script. In a later chapter, we look at drivers in more detail.

Program

The *program* consists of messages about how to do things. In compiling the script matrix, we phrase these as sentences beginning: 'Here's how to...' Each of us learns many thousands of program messages from parents and parent-figures. For instance, 'Here's how to...

count to 10
write your name
make porridge
tie your shoes
be a man (a woman)
be cute
come top of class
hide your feelings.'

As with counterscript, we use most of our program messages in a constructive, positive way. But we may also carry around some negative program. For instance, a boy may learn from his father's modeling: 'Here's how to work hard, overstress yourself and die young.' A little girl may learn from Mother: 'Here's how to sit on your feelings and end up depressed.'

These negative program messages might be shown more accurately in the matrix diagram as coming from the *contaminated* Adult in the parent, and being filed away in the *contaminated* Adult of the child. Also, many of the 'here's how' messages in the program might better be seen as forming part of the content of the Little Professor (A_1) of the parent and being stored in A_1 of the child, rather than A_2. However, the diagram is not usually drawn with this detail.

Injunctions and permissions

Picture a mother with her new baby. As she looks after her child, the mother may be replaying messages from her own Parent ego-state, such as: 'Children need to be protected. Their needs come first.' For much of the time also she may be in her Adult ego-state, practicing techniques of child care she has read up in books. But what's going on in her Child ego-state?

As the mother goes back and replays her own infancy, she may be feeling: 'Great! Now there's another kid to play with around here!' She may be enjoying the physical interchange of strokes between the baby and herself, just as she enjoyed stroking and being stroked when she was the infant. Picking up her non-verbal messages, the baby is likely to conclude: 'Mother wants me and likes me being close to her.'

In script language, we say that the mother is giving her baby *permissions* — here, permission to exist and permission to be close.

But the Child in mother may feel instead: 'This is dangerous. Now this new baby is around, she has to get all the attention. When am *I* going to get attention? Maybe there isn't enough attention to go round?' Replaying the uncensored feelings and urges of her own infancy, the mother may be scared and furious at the new arrival. She may want, deep in her Child ego-state, to reject the baby or even kill him.

She is likely not to have the slightest awareness of these feelings. In her own consciousness and to any outside observer, she is a loving and caring mother.

But the baby knows. With his acute awareness of nonverbal cues, he picks up Mother's scare and anger. Little by little he may form the conclusion, without words: 'Mother doesn't want me close to her. In fact, she would rather I weren't around at all.'

These negative messages from the parent's Child are examples of *injunctions*. In this case, the injunctions are 'Don't exist' and 'Don't be close'.

As grown-ups, we each carry around a set of injunctions and permissions, filed away in the content of our Child ego-state. The decisions we made in response to these messages are the principal foundations of our life-script. This whole complex of injunctions and permissions, plus the decisions made upon them by the child, is sometimes called the *script proper*.

Distinguishing injunctions/permissions from counterinjunctions

How do you tell the difference in practice between a negative counterinjunction and an injunction? Or between a positive counterinjunction and a permission? There are two ways of distinguishing them.

132

(1) Counterinjunctions are verbal, injunctions/permissions are (originally) preverbal. If you listen inside your head, you will be able to hear your counterinjunctions being spoken in words. Often you will be able to hear the actual parent or parent-figure who originally spoke them to you.

If you go against a counterinjunction, and listen again in your head, you are likely to hear verbal scolding from the parent-figure who gave the command.

Injunctions and permissions, by contrast, are not necessarily heard in words. Instead, you feel them in emotions and body sensations, and reflect them in behavior.

If you defy an injunction, you are likely to experience bodily tension or discomfort. Your heart may race, you may start sweating or feel 'knots in the stomach'. You are likely to find all sorts of ways of avoiding the behavior which goes against the injunction. These ways may seem Adult to you, but are actually rationalizations.

For instance, suppose I received the injunction 'Don't be close' from my mother and made the early decision that, indeed, I had better not get close to anybody. Now as a grown-up, I am taking part in an encounter group. The leader invites us to close our eyes, find a partner by touch alone, and get to know that person by feeling their hands. I start sweating gently and my pulse-rate goes up. As I feel another person reach out for my hand, I open my eyes and say: 'Hm. Don't see the point in this exercise. What do you think it's for?'

Sometimes injunctions are heard in words also. For instance, a person who has been given the injunction 'Don't exist' may recall his parents saying things like 'I wish you had never been born!' or 'Drop dead!'

(2) Injunctions/permissions are given in early childhood, counterinjunctions later. Developmentally, injunctions and permissions are earlier than counterinjunctions. This of course is related to the 'verbal — preverbal' distinction. As a general rule, the child takes in injunctions and permissions in the years before she has command of language. There is no one age that marks a sharp end-point to this period. In our experience, injunctions may continue to be given until the child is between six and eight years old. Counterinjunctions may be given between the ages of three and twelve.

Chapter 14
INJUNCTIONS AND DECISIONS

In their work as therapists, Bob and Mary Goulding found that twelve themes emerged again and again as the basis for people's negative early decisions. They developed the list of these twelve injunctions which we give below.[1]

Each injunction has its corresponding permission. Traditionally in script analysis, injunctions are written beginning with the word 'Don't...' and permissions with the phrase 'It's OK to...'

Notice that 'Don't...' and 'It's OK to...' are not simple opposites. 'Don't...' conveys a blanket prohibition, a command not to do something. But 'It's OK to...' is not a command to do something. Instead, it invites the receiver of the message to *choose* whether to do something or not do it.

Realize too that these names for the injunctions and permissions are only verbal labels we apply for convenience in script analysis. The injunctions and permissions themselves are conveyed to the child in ways that are mainly non-verbal.

Twelve injunctions

Don't Be (Don't Exist)

If you have ever contemplated suicide, it's most likely that your script messages include a Don't Exist injunction. The same is probably true if you have ever felt worthless, useless or unlovable.

You may remember a parent saying things to you like: 'I'll kill you for that!', or 'I wish I'd never had you!' These verbal messages help confirm the presence of this injunction, though its main impact will have been through non-verbal signals earlier in your life.

Why should parents deliver Don't Exist to a child? It's likely to be because the parent, in his or her own Child ego-state, feels deprived or threatened by having the child around. Maybe a young man marries and becomes a father. Seeing his wife give most of her energy and attention to the new baby, the father may experience a rubberband back to his own childhood. Without awareness, he re-lives the time when he was two, and a new baby had just arrived in his family. As that two-year-old, he was profoundly scared in case there would never again be enough attention for him. How could he ever get Mother's love back? The only hope seemed to be if he could get the baby out of the way, and preferably dead. Now as a grown-up, he may signal these same homicidal urges non-verbally to his own baby.

Or perhaps a woman already has several children and doesn't want more. Because of family pressures, or 'by accident', she does have a new child. In her own Child ego-state, she is screaming: 'No! Not another one! I want attention to *my* needs for a change!' She will likely suppress her Child fury, denying it even to herself. But in subtle ways, she conveys rejection to the baby. Maybe she never smiles and seldom talks to him, even as she does all the right things to look after him materially.

Where a parent physically or mentally abuses a child, the Don't Exist message is being conveyed overtly.

The Don't Exist injunction turns up frequently during script analysis. This may seem surprising, considering its death-laden implications. But recall that it is quite easy for an infant to read a threat of death into all sorts of parental behavior or external events which to a grown-up might appear quite harmless. Remember also how the young child may confuse deeds with urges. Perhaps wanting a younger sibling dead, she may decide 'I'm a murderer and so I deserve to die.' She delivers Don't Exist *to herself.*

The same may happen where a mother subtly conveys to her child 'You hurt me badly when you were born.' (Berne called this the 'Torn Mother script'). The child may decide 'Just by being born, I harmed Mother or maybe even killed her. Therefore, I'm dangerous and can harm or kill people just by being around. So I deserve to be hurt or killed myself.'

Parents may also say things like: 'If it weren't for you, I could have gone to college, or taken that trip to foreign countries, or wouldn't have had to marry that so-and-so...'

If Don't Exist is a common injunction, why don't most people commit suicide? Luckily, people are extremely ingenious at staying alive. In his early years, the child carrying a Don't Exist is likely to make *compound decisions* to defend against its fatal outcome. These decisions will be of the form: 'It's OK for me to go on existing *so long as I...*' The blank can be completed in many ways, such as: '...keep on working hard' or '...don't get close to people.' In a later section we shall look at compound decisions in more detail.

Don't Be You

This injunction can be conveyed to a child by parents who have a boy when they wanted a girl, or *vice versa*. Their non-verbal message is 'Don't be the sex you are'. This may be reflected in their choice of a name for the child. Maybe a girl is called Jacky or a boy is christened Vivian. Parents may dress their daughter in 'butch' clothes or their son in frilly collars and bows. In grown-up life, the person carrying 'Don't be the sex you are' may continue to cultivate dress or manners that suggest the opposite sex. Don't Be You may be more general, and simply convey 'Don't be you, be some other child'. Parents may prefer a younger to an elder child, or a brother to a sister. A mother who feels rejecting towards her child may continually compare him with other children: 'Little Johnny down the road can ride a two-wheel bicycle — isn't he clever? And he's a year younger than you are, too.' Here, the parent may be holding an image of the 'ideal child' she wishes. She reacts positively only to the aspects of her actual child which resemble that image, and discounts the rest.

Parents may also make statements like: 'You're just like your no-good Uncle Harry.' Then, the more the child acts like Uncle Harry the more strokes he gets.

Don't Be a Child

This is another injunction handed out by parents who, in their Child ego-state, feel threatened by having their child around. But instead of wanting the baby right out of the way, the Child in the parent says: 'There's only room for one kid around here — and that's me. But I'll put up with you, so long as you behave like a grown-up instead of a child.' This may be reflected later on by verbal messages like 'You're too old to...', or 'Big boys don't cry'.

Don't Be a Child is also given out by parents who were never allowed to be child-like themselves and feel threatened by child-like behavior. They may have been reared in times of depression or in a stern home where worth and value were related to doing.

Sometimes eldest or only children give themselves this injunction. Seeing Mother and Father arguing, an only child may decide: 'The only other person around here is me. So I must be the cause of the fight. Therefore, it's up to me to do something about it. I'd better grow up quickly so I can take charge.' An eldest child may decide similarly that she is responsible for her younger brothers and sisters.

If you feel awkward relating to children, you probably carry Don't Be a Child. The same is probably true if you stiffen up when you are at parties or in similar 'fun' situations among other adults. 'Don't have fun' and 'Don't enjoy' are sometimes listed as variants of Don't Be a Child. For sure, we don't need to be in our Child ego-state in order to have fun or enjoy. But if you decided as a child that having fun and enjoying were things children did, and that *you* were supposed to be a solemn little grown-up, you may well rubberband to that decision when the chance arises of having fun at your present age.

In some families, if you are having too much fun you are labeled lazy or sinful. There may be a magical belief that if you feel *too* good, something bad will happen. So the way you magically ward off evil is to not feel too good.

Don't Grow Up

It is often the youngest child who gets a Don't Grow Up injunction. The parents, in their Child ego-state, may not want to let go of having a young kid around in the family. They may define their whole worth in terms of being a good father or good mother. If their child grew up, they would no longer feel valuable. Alternatively, this injunction may be given out by parents who never grew up themselves. Their message is 'stay my little playmate'.

Sometimes Don't Grow Up is read as 'Don't leave me'. The woman who stays at home into her middle age, caring for a demanding aged mother, may be carrying this message.

Another variant of Don't Grow Up is 'Don't be sexy'. This is often given by a father to his daughter, at the stage of her childhood when she is old enough to become noticeably feminine. In his Child, her father is scared of his own sexual response to her. He puts out non-verbal messages of physical distancing, which the little girl may read as an injunction against growing up and becoming a sexual woman.

Don't Make It

This injunction is given by a parent who, in his own Child, is jealous of the accomplishments of his son or daughter. Suppose a father comes from a poor family. He had to go out to work when he was fifteen years old, and he never got the chance to go to college. Now, as a result of his hard work, he and his children are financially comfortable. He is paying for his daughter to go to a good school, so that one day she will have the chance to go on to a university.

Seeing her excel at her lessons, the father may feel parental pleasure. But outside of his awareness, in his Child ego-state, he is bitterly jealous that his daughter is getting chances that he never got. What if she does succeed in her studies? Maybe that will prove she is better than he is? Non-verbally, he may convey the Don't Make It injunction to his daughter, even while on an overt level he is urging her to work hard and do well.

A student who has made a script decision to obey a Don't Make It injunction will typically work hard in class and do all her assignments competently. But come the examinations, she is likely to find some way of sabotaging herself. Maybe she will panic and walk out of the exam. Maybe she will 'forget' to hand in a crucial piece of work. She may even come down with a psychogenic illness, or find she has suddenly become unable to read.

Don't (Don't Do Anything)

The blanket message 'Don't!' implies: 'Don't do anything, because anything you do is so dangerous that you're safer doing nothing at all'. If someone in adult life continually dithers between courses of action, always feeling he's getting nowhere but never taking any action to change this, he may be carrying this script message.

The 'Don't' injunction is given by a parent who, in Child, is terrified that her child will come to harm if he is allowed to run free of the parental apron-strings. The grounds for the terror lie in the parent's own script rather than in reality. A parent with this fear may say things like: 'Johnny, go see what your little sister is doing and tell her not to.'

Don't Be Important

People carrying this message may become panicky when they are asked to take on any kind of leadership role. They may 'dry up' when called upon to speak in public. In her career, the person complying with Don't Be Important may work excellently in a subordinate post, but either not seek promotion or sabotage herself when there is a chance of getting it. A variant of this injunction is 'Don't ask for what you want'.

This is another script message arising from parents' impulse of rejection towards their child. Non-verbally, the parent conveys from his Child ego-state: 'I'll put up with having you around, kid, just as long as you realize that you and your wants are not important around here.'

Don't Belong

The Indian statesman Pandit Nehru used to say: 'When I am among Europeans, I feel like an Indian. When I am among Indians, I feel like a European.' The chances are that Nehru had received a Don't Belong injunction from his parents. The person complying with Don't Belong feels 'out of it' in groups, and so is likely to be seen by others as a 'loner' or 'unsociable'.

This message may be conveyed as an attribution by parents who continually tell their child he is 'different from other children', 'shy', or 'difficult'. Or the parents may model the injunction through their own social ineptitude. The message may be conveyed either by scapegoating the child or by continually telling him how special he is.

Don't Be Close

The injunction Don't Be Close may imply a ban on physical closeness. In this form it is often modeled by parents who seldom touch each other or the child. Alternatively, it may signify 'don't be emotionally close'. This form of the message may be passed down through the generations in families who never talk to each other about their feelings.

A child may give herself Don't Be Close as a response to continual physical distancing by the parent. The child may reach out time and again, only to get no response. Eventually she may decide that her seeking for closeness is not worth the pain of rejection.

A variant of Don't Be Close is 'Don't trust'. This message is sometimes read by the young child when a parent abruptly goes away or dies. Unable to understand the true reason for the parent's disappearance, the infant may conclude: 'Never again will I trust anyone to be here when I want them.' 'Don't trust' can also be picked up if the parent is abusive or tries to trick or take advantage of the child. The decision is: 'I'll stay away from you in order to protect myself.'

Carrying decisions like these in adult life, the person may be continually suspicious of others he relates to. Even when they warmly accept him, he may have his feelers out for signs of rejection. If the other person refuses to reject him, he may 'test the relationship to destruction' and then say: 'I told you so!'

Don't Be Well (Don't Be Sane)

Imagine that Mother and Father are two busy people, both out all day working. They love their daughter but don't have much energy to give her attention when they get home in the evenings and she comes back from the day-care center.

Then she gets ill. Mother takes time off work to look after her sick daughter. Father does what he's seldom done before and reads her stories while she falls asleep at night.

In her astute Little Professor, the little girl stores away the conclusion: 'To get the attention I want around here, I have to be ill.' Without realizing it or intending it, her parents have given her the injunction Don't Be Well. If she complies with this message in grown-up life, their daughter may use the scripty strategy of getting sick whenever things go wrong in her relationships or at work.

Sometimes Don't Be Well is given by attribution, as when parents continually tell a child's relatives and neighbors: 'This one isn't strong, you know.'

The variant Don't Be Sane is often modeled for the child by a psychotic parent or relative. The child may only get attention if he acts crazy enough. This injunction may be made more potent by unspoken rules about how insanity is to be passed on in a particular family.

Don't Think

The Don't Think injunction may be given by a parent who consistently belittles his child's thinking. Little James proudly shows Father his first efforts at writing his own name. Father snorts: 'Huh! Clever-pants, you are!' Sometimes Don't Think may be modeled, as by a hysterical mother who models for her daughter: 'When women want to get something from men, they can do it by switching off their thinking and escalating feelings.' Don't Think may also convey: 'Obsess about everything in creation except the immediate problem at hand.'

An adult complying with a Don't Think injunction is likely to respond to problems by getting confused, or by feeling bad about the problem instead of thinking how to solve it.

Two variations of Don't Think are 'Don't think about *x*' (where *x* may stand for sex, money, etc.) and 'Don't think what *you* think, think what *I* think.'

Don't Feel

Don't Feel may be modeled by parents who themselves bottle up their feelings. Sometimes there is an embargo on any show of feeling in the family. More often, particular feelings are prohibited while others are allowed. Thus the Don't Feel injunction may be interpreted as 'Don't feel anger', 'Don't feel fear', and so on.

Sometimes the message is read as 'experience the feeling but don't show it'. Other children receive a more extreme version which enjoins them not even to experience a particular emotion. Little boys, for instance, are often instructed time and time again by their fathers: 'Big boys don't cry', or 'Be a brave soldier!' These mottoes translate to 'Don't experience sadness' and 'Don't experience fear'.

In some families the Don't Feel message implies 'Don't experience physical sensations'. This injunction is often given early in infancy. If given powerfully, it can be the source of some severe problems in adulthood. For instance, a child enjoined against feeling hunger may later develop an eating disorder. In the opinion of some TA therapists, the 'Don't feel sensations' message lies at the root of certain kinds of psychosis.

Some parents convey a version that goes: 'Don't feel what *you* feel, feel what *I* feel'. Mother says to young son: 'I'm hungry. What do you want to eat?' or 'I'm cold, go put on your sweater.'

Episcript

Fanita English has described a specially virulent kind of script message which she calls *episcript*. Here, a parent conveys an injunction and adds to it the non-verbal message: 'I hope this happens to you, so that it won't have to happen to me.'[2]

For instance, a mother scripted with Don't Exist during her own childhood may pass a Don't Exist on to her son or daughter. In her Little Professor, the mother may believe that this buys a magical release from her own injunction. At psychological level she conveys to her child: 'If you drop dead, maybe I won't have to.' Thus the injunction here is like a 'hot potato', passed on from generation to generation.

Sometimes episcript may take the form of a family task or family curse, with every generation supposed to end up the same way. Fanita English gives the example of a young man who at one time had been taking psychedelic drugs. He became interested in psychology, came off the drugs and started working as a therapist. However, it soon became apparent that he was sabotaging some of his clients, giving them covert messages that said: 'Crack up and go into a madhouse!'

His supervisor detected this set-up, and the young man came into therapy for himself. Through script analysis, he realized he had received the command 'Go into a madhouse!' (Don't Be Sane) as a 'hot potato' passed on by his mother. He had sought to obey her injunction by taking drugs. In becoming a therapist, he had been trying to pass on the same 'hot potato' to his clients. When he and his therapist explored his family history, they found that the same 'go crazy' episcript had been handed down through at least two previous generations. Nobody had actually gone into a madhouse. Each generation believed it had avoided that outcome by the magical device of passing the 'hot potato' along to someone else.

How decisions relate to injunctions

We have emphasized that a parent's injunctions cannot *make* the child write her script in a particular way. It is the child who *decides* what to do with the injunctions she receives. One child may accept an injunction as it stands. Another may modify it ingeniously to ease its impact. Still another may simply refuse to accept the injunction at all.

For instance, suppose a little boy picks up Don't Exist from his mother. He may simply take on board the whole impact of the injunction, and commit suicide either as a child or in adulthood. The suicide may be overt or may take the form of an 'accident', as where someone drives his car fast while drunk.

Another possibility is that the child may make a magical early decision to shift the impact of Don't Exist by deciding to kill someone else instead of killing himself. This results in a hamartic script in which the payoff is homicide instead of suicide.

Alternatively, the magical belief may be of the form: 'If I can stop existing as a sane person, maybe I won't actually have to die.' This gives the script the hamartic payoff of 'go-crazy'.

At the other extreme from these tragic decisions, the infant may already be able to realize: 'This message is my mother's problem, not mine,' and thus reject the Don't Exist injunction altogether. Children who do this may, in the Gouldings' words, '...become little psychiatrists or priests, as they study the family and attempt to cure it, while saving their own lives by recognizing the pathology is not of their doing.' Many of these 'little psychiatrists or priests' go on to become big psychiatrists or priests, and good ones too.

The child always has the option of turning an injunction around in this way to create positive instead of negative outcomes. For instance, a little boy who gets 'Don't be the sex you are' may grow into a man rich in positive qualities that are conventionally pictured as 'feminine' — sensitivity, physical warmth, openness to feelings.

Another way of avoiding the impact of injunctions is to make *compound decisions*. This means that the child uses Little Professor ingenuity in combining different script messages, with the objective of staying alive and getting her needs met as well as she can. These compound decisions come up frequently in script analysis, and are important in understanding how the script works. In the sections below, we look at various kinds of compound decision and see how they are used to defend against harmful injunctions. Practical experience suggests that Don't Exist is the message most often defended against, and so we use it in most of the examples.

Counterinjunction covering an injunction

Consider the script matrix shown in Figure 14.1.

You'll notice Jack has been given the Don't Exist injunction by his mother. To Jack in his Little Professor, the main priority is to work out a way of staying alive. How might he do this?

One way is to take a counterinjunction and use it to cover up the Don't Exist. Jack might take his mother's 'Work Hard!' counterinjunction and make the compound decision: 'So long as I work hard, it's OK for me to stay alive.'

What is this likely to mean for Jack as a grown-up? He is likely to grow into a man who drives himself hard at whatever he does. At his job, he will be seen as a glutton for work. When he plays sports, he may work hard at being good at them. In personal relationships he may work hard to be good company, and when having sex he is likely to work hard to satisfy his partner.

Now suppose Jack starts getting high blood pressure, ulcers or other stress symptoms. He decides to work less hard. Maybe he takes extra holidays or starts delegating work to other people. Everything seems fine for a while. But strangely enough, Jack finds it very difficult to stick to his

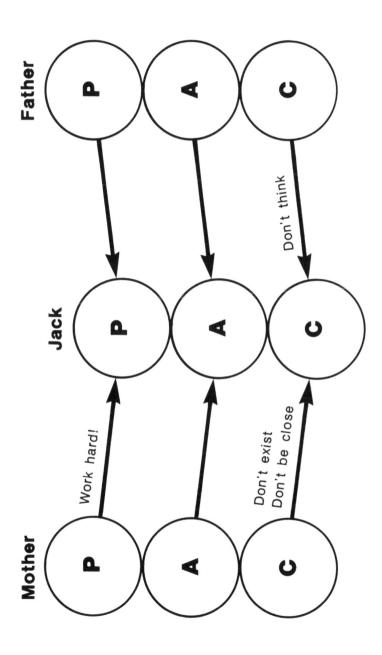

Figure 14.1 Partial script matrix for Jack

new pattern. Almost without knowing it, he fills his new-found leisure time with commitments. Maybe he takes up a voluntary position, and within a week or two is taking it so seriously that he's pressuring himself more than he was before. What's going on?

The clue is that Jack has disturbed the dynamic balance of his script. In his conscious awareness, he sees himself as having taken a positive step by dropping some of his workload. But in his unaware Little Professor, he perceives this same change as a threat to his life. His scripty belief is: 'Now I've stopped working so hard, I have to listen to Mother telling me to drop dead.' It's no wonder that he soon finds ways of starting to overwork again.

We say that Jack has been *covering* Mother's Don't Exist with the counterinjunction Work Hard. When he starts to work less hard, he *uncovers* the injunction.

This kind of script set-up sometimes has a paradoxical and particularly unpleasant outcome. In keeping on working hard, Jack is following a Little Professor strategy for staying alive. But after years of overwork, he may drop dead from a heart attack, or become disabled by ulcers or high blood pressure. The very set-up which is designed to *defend* against a hamartic payoff has resulted in that payoff being reached.

To see how Jack can make changes that truly release him from this negative set-up, we need to understand the dynamics of his compound decision. If he sets out to drop his overworking but does nothing about the underlying Don't Exist message, the chances are great that he will soon slip back into working too hard. This may appear like 'self-sabotage' to an outside observer. But to Jack in his Little Professor, it's the exact opposite of sabotage; it appears to be his only way of avoiding Mother's death threat.

To dismantle this part of his script, Jack needs to defuse the Don't Exist message *first*. Once he has taken permission to keep on living despite Mother's curse, he can go ahead and reduce his work commitments. Now he will find he can keep the pressure off comfortably and permanently.

One injunction covering another injunction

Don't Exist was not the only injunction Jack got from his mother. She also gave him Don't Be Close. Jack might use this lighter injunction to defend against the heavier one. As an infant he might make the compound decision: 'It's OK for me to go on living, so long as I don't get close to anyone.'

When in his script as an adult, Jack will unawarely play out this early decision. He will appear to others as physically distant and unwilling to share his feelings. He will likely find it difficult to give or take strokes, especially physical ones.

144

Jack may not be comfortable with this pattern. He may feel stroke-deprived or lonely, and set out to get closer to someone in a relationship. But it's probable that he will prevent himself from doing this for more than a short time. Then he is likely to find a way of drawing away from the other person, perhaps setting up to reject or be rejected.

Consciously, Jack feels sad and upset about being alone again. But in his unaware Little Professor, he is breathing a sigh of relief. Had he kept on being close, thus breaking Mother's Don't Be Close injunction, he would have had to face her homicidal command 'Don't Exist.'

Here again, if Jack wants to abandon this scripty set-up and enjoy closeness, he needs to begin by taking the sting out of the Don't Exist injunction. He can do this by deciding to live, no matter what.

Playing one parent against the other

Father did not hand Jack a Don't Exist message. Instead, he gave the lighter injunction Don't Think. This afforded Jack yet another infant strategy for staying alive. He might decide: 'So long as I play stupid for Father, I won't have to drop dead for Mother.'

In adult life, Jack may sometimes seem to 'switch off' his thinking. At these times he plays confused and says things like: 'I can't get my thoughts together. My mind must be going.' Unawarely, he is seeking to keep Father around to protect him from Mother's lethal injunction.

Antiscript

Some people may take one of their script messages and turn it round to its opposite. They then follow this opposite instead of the original message. Most often, this is done with counterscript. When we act in this way we are said to be in *antiscript*.[3]

A person may go into and out of antiscript at different times in her life in response to any one script message. Teenage is a common time for antiscript. An example is the girl who has gone through childhood obeying the counterscript 'Be quiet and do what parents say'. At fourteen she suddenly switches, becoming brash and loud, staying out late, going round with what her parents call 'bad company'.

It might seem that she has broken free of her counterscript. In reality, she is following it just as much as she did before. She has merely turned her script message round, as you might turn a color slide round to view it from the back.

Antiscript may be thought of as what the rebellious child decides to do when she has had enough of the script and counterscript. At this point, she stops caring what happens if she no longer follows these early decisions.

Later on, when she got married, this same girl might move back out of antiscript and revert to her script and counterscript. Once again she would become quiet and conventional, this time acting the 'little woman' for her husband.

● DRAWING YOUR OWN SCRIPT MATRIX

Take a big sheet of paper and draw a blank script matrix like that in Figure 13.1. On it you can enter script messages you received from your parents.

This self-analysis is not meant to be an exact exercise. Nor does it give answers that are graven in stone. You should regard your script matrix as an important source of *information about your past*. It gives you a road-map of the ways in which you can *change your own future*. Like any map, your matrix can be revised and made more complete as you get more information. And like a map also, it can be changed as new roads are built and broadened, old ones done away with.

Work quickly and rely on your intuition.

Injunctions

Look through the list of 'twelve injunctions'. Consider whether you have experienced the living problems or discomforts associated with each one. Note the injunctions you think have been important for you. Enter them on the matrix according to the parent they came from. Some may have come from both parents. Do you remember the parent modeling the injunction for you? Giving you injunction-laden commands or attributions? If in doubt, go on your hunches.

When entering up your injunctions, keep to the twelve standard names used in the Gouldings' list. If you think a variant name fits best, put it in brackets after the standard name. An example might be: 'Don't Be a Child (Don't Enjoy)'.

Counterscript

Recall the do's and don'ts, slogans and mottoes, your parents frequently gave you as a child. When was each parent pleased with you? Angry with you? What words did they use to let you know they were pleased or angry? What advice did they give you for how to be a success and bring credit to the family?

From this evidence, enter up your counterscript. You will likely find it quite easy to remember which parent gave you which command. Listen for the voice in your head. If in doubt, simply guess. Some counterscript may come from other relatives, older siblings, or schoolteachers.

Program

When compiling the script matrix, we conventionally only enter up the parts of the program that are negative. (There would not be space to enter all the thousands of positive 'How to's' all of us learn from our parents). Recall that the negative program comes from the contaminated Adult of the parent, though on the diagram it is shown as coming simply from the Adult circle.

Did either parent model for you how to achieve some scripty outcome? Frequently, one parent models how to obey an injunction or counterinjunction you have got from the other parent. For instance, Mother may have handed you a Don't Feel message, while Father models: 'Here's how to deny your feelings'.

Enter up your negative program as a set of statements beginning 'Here's how to...' Some people do not have any obvious negative program messages. If you cannot identify any, leave that part of your matrix blank.

Using fantasy, story and dream data

Now look back through the material you gathered while you were doing the exercises with fantasies, stories and dreams in Chapter 10. This will be in freehand form, just as you brought it to mind.

Look at it now in terms of the formal script matrix. Use your thinking and intuition to check how it relates to what you have already entered on the matrix diagram. Alter or fill out your matrix entries accordingly. ●

It has been traditional in TA to use formal *script questionnaires* to identify script data of the kind which you have been discovering in the exercise above. We do not include a script questionnaire here, since we think formal questionnaires are more suitable for interview use than for self-directed script exploration. If you want to look at examples of formal questionnaires, follow up the References list for this chapter.[4]

Chapter 15
SCRIPT PROCESS

So far in Part IV, we have been discussing the 'what' of the life-script — its *content*. Now in this and the remaining chapter, we turn to look at the *process* of the script — how we live it out over time.

Study of the life-script has revealed a fascinating fact. It is that there seem to be only six main patterns of script process. Whether I am Chinese, African or American, I will live out my script according to one or more of these six patterns. The same is true whatever my age, sex, education or culture.

The six types of process script were originally listed by Berne.[1] Some alterations to his classification have since been suggested by other TA theorists, notably Taibi Kahler.[2]

Six process scripts

Here are the six patterns of script process:

> *Until*
> *After*
> *Never*
> *Always*
> *Almost*
> *Open-ended.*

Each of these has its own theme, describing the way in which the person lives her script over time. Berne, always fond of the classics, listed a Greek myth illustrating each of these process themes.

Until script

If I live out my script according to the Until pattern, my motto in life is: 'I can't have fun *until* I've finished my work.' There are all sorts of possible variants of this, but they all share the notion that 'something good can't happen *until* something less good has been finished.'

'I have to understand myself fully before I can change.'
'Life begins at forty.'
'After I retire, I'll be able to travel.'

'My reward is in the next world.'

Like all the process themes, the Until pattern is lived out both short-term and long-term. Jonathan believes: 'Once the children grow up and leave, I'll have time to relax and do all the things I've been wanting to do.' Day by day as he waits for his lifetime Until, he lives out the same pattern over shorter time-spans. He says to his wife: 'OK, I'll come and have a drink with you, but just wait a minute until I've finished washing the dishes.'

Jonathan shows the Until pattern even in the structure of the sentences he uses. Frequently he will put in a *parenthesis*. He says things like: 'I told my wife — *and, mind you, I said the same to my daughter only yesterday* — that we'd have to do something about the house.' He interrupts himself in mid-sentence to put in the extra thought. With this sentence pattern, Jonathan is reflecting the Until belief: 'I have to cover everything before I can finish.'

The Greek hero Hercules had an Until script. Before he could be promoted to become a demi-god, he had to complete a set of arduous tasks — not least of which was cleaning a mountain of manure out of the King's stables.

After script

The After pattern is the obverse of Until. The person with an After script follows the motto: 'I can have fun today, but I'll have to pay for it tomorrow.'

'This is a great party! But oh, dear, what a headache I'm going to have in the morning.'

'After you're married, life is just one round of obligations.'

'I like to start the day bright and early, but I get tired by evening.'

Frequently, the After-script person will use the sentence pattern illustrated in the first and third of these examples. The sentence begins with a 'high'. Then comes a fulcrum, often represented by the word *but*. After that point, all the rest is a 'low'. A sentence like this is a miniature re-play of the After script.

The After pattern is illustrated by the myth of Damocles. This Greek potentate lived a round of eating, drinking and being merry. But all the time, above his head there hung a sword suspended on a single horse-hair. Once he looked up and saw it, he could never be happy again. He lived in constant dread of when it would fall. Like Damocles, the person with an After script believes he can have a good time today, but only at the cost of the sword falling tomorrow.

Never script

The theme of Never is: 'I can never get what I most want.' Andrew often says he would like to get into a steady relationship with a woman. But he has never done so. In fact, he never seems to get started going to places where he might meet new women. He's often thought he would like to go back to college and study for a degree. But he hasn't got round yet to submitting application papers.

In his Never script pattern, Andrew is like Tantalus, who was condemned to stand eternally in the middle of a pool of water. To one side of the pool was a store of food, to the other side a crock of water. But both were just out of Tantalus' reach, and he stayed hungry and thirsty.

In the myth, Tantalus didn't seem to realize that he could get hold of food and water by just taking a step to either side. A person in the Never script pattern is like this. He could get what he wanted by simply taking a step, but he doesn't take it.

No distinctive sentence pattern has been discovered for the Never script. However, people with a Never script often talk about negative script content in a repetitive, 'broken-record' manner. They tell you their troubles one day, then next day they tell them again as if the first time hadn't happened.

Always script

The person with an Always script asks: 'Why does this always happen to me?' The Greek myth for Always is that of Arachne, who was good at embroidery. She was unwise enough to challenge the goddess Minerva to an embroidering contest. The outraged deity changed Arachne into a spider, condemned to spin her web for all eternity.

Martha follows the Always pattern. She's been married three times and divorced twice. Her first marriage was to a man who was quiet, retiring and not very sociable. Martha broke with him, she told her friends, because she really wanted someone more dynamic. But to the surprise of those same friends, she was soon announcing her engagement to another man who seemed to them like a carbon-copy of the first one. That marriage didn't last long either. Martha's third husband is retiring, quiet and not very dynamic, and she's already complaining to her friends about him.

People with the Always pattern may play it out like Martha, by going from one unsatisfactory relationship, job or locality to another. A variant is to stay with the original unsatisfactory choice instead of moving on to a better one. The person with an Always script may say: 'I've not got much out of working with this therapist. But, well, I suppose I'll keep on and just hope we get somewhere.'

Martha often uses a sentence pattern which typically accompanies an Always script. She begins the sentence, then goes off on a tangent. She switches to another tangent and goes off on that one, and so on. 'Well, what I've come to see you for is...huh, when I was on the way here I saw my friend and she — oh, by the way, I've got some money with me and...'

Almost

Sisyphus was another character to fall foul of the touchy Greek gods. He was condemned to spend eternity pushing a huge rock up a hill. Every time he almost got to the top, he lost his grip on the rock and it rolled all the way down to the bottom again. Like Sisyphus, the modern-day person with an Almost script says: 'I almost made it this time.'

Fred borrows a book from his friend. Giving it back, he says: 'Thanks for the book. I've read it all except the last chapter.' When Fred cleans his car, he gets it almost clean, except for a few patches of mud which he's missed. Living his Almost pattern over the longer term, Fred has almost been promoted at work. But though he's got near the boss's chair, he's not quite made it in there. Each time he gets to the short-list, and each time he somehow fails to perform at the interview.

Berne called this script pattern 'Over and Over'. However, later writers have pointed out that *all* the patterns are lived over and over, and so the title 'Almost' has been adopted instead.

Taibi Kahler has suggested that there are two types of Almost pattern. He calls the one we have just described 'Almost Type 1'. In his 'Almost Type 2', the person actually *does* make it to the top of the hill. But instead of parking his rock and sitting down with a sigh of relief, this person hardly even notices he's got to the top. Without a pause, he looks around for an even higher hill to push the rock up, and off he goes. At the top of that one in turn, he looks around to spy a still higher mountain to tackle.

The person with Almost Type 2 will often be a material high achiever. Janet, for instance, sailed through her examinations at school. She went straight on to win a scholarship to college. By the time she graduated with a first-class degree, she had already decided to begin her PhD studies. Now holding her doctorate, she is working hard for a Fellowship to her learned society. Though the envy of her colleagues, Janet herself does not feel she has 'made it'. Once she's a Fellow, she tells her friends, she's got her eye on a Professorship. Of course it will mean still more hard work, and she never seems to have time to socialize.

There are two different sentence patterns that signal the Almost script. The speaker may start a sentence, then go off on one tangent which he finishes. 'What I'm lecturing to you about today is — oh, by the way, I have a page of notes which I'll give you.'

Alternatively, the person with an Almost script may come out with a string of positives followed by a single negative. 'Aren't the trees lovely in Autumn? It's really warm, too, and such bright sunshine. Mind you, the air's cold.'

Open-ended script

This pattern resembles the Until and After scripts in having a particular cut-off point after which things change. But for the person with an Open-ended script, the time after that point is just one big void. It's as if the closing pages of a theatrical script had gone missing.

Alfred has just retired after 40 years' service to his firm. Now he's at home with his tributes and marble clock. He had been looking forward to his extra leisure. But instead of enjoying it, he feels strangely uneasy. What's he going to do with himself? How will he fill his time?

Margery says goodbye to the youngest of her four children as he leaves home for the last time, now a young adult. She heaves a sigh of relief. After all these years, no more child-rearing chores! But a day or two later, Margery is feeling a bit down. Without the extra washing-up, the dirty clothes lying around for her to tidy away, she's at a loss what to do with her time.

The Open-ended script pattern may be lived out over the short as well as the long term. Some people typically set only short-term goals. Once they have completed these, they flounder, not knowing what to do until something else comes along. Then they set another short-term goal, and the process is repeated.

The motto of the Open-ended script is: 'Once I get to a certain point in time, I won't know what to do with myself afterwards.' It recalls the myth of Philemon and Baucis. This elderly couple welcomed the gods in the form of travel-worn strangers when others would not. As a reward for their kindness, the gods extended their lives by turning them into trees planted beside each other with their branches entwined.

Combinations of process themes

We all show all six of the process script patterns. But for most of us, one of the patterns is predominant. Jonathan shows mainly the Until script, Martha clearly lives out the Always pattern, and so on.

Some people combine two of the patterns. Usually one of these will be the main one, with a second one also important. For instance, people with Almost Type 2 may also show the Until pattern. This is true of Janet in our example. Her unspoken motto is: 'I can't rest until I've made it to the top. And I never really make it to the top, because there's always an even higher top somewhere. Therefore, I can never rest.'

A person who combines the Until and Never scripts will follow the belief: 'I can't have fun until I've finished my work. But I never finish my work. Therefore, I can never have fun.'

Other frequent combinations are After plus Almost Type 1, and Always plus Never. You may care to work out the scripty 'mottoes' that go with each.

Origins of process script

Why are there only six process themes? Why are they so uniform across cultures? Nobody knows. Finding the answers to these questions is a challenging task for TA research.

We do have some idea about how process script is transmitted from parents to children. It seems to be part of the counterscript, passed on mainly by parental modeling.

Breaking out of process script patterns

If you are uncomfortable with your process script, you can step out of it. Of all the personal changes TA makes feasible, this is one of the easiest to accomplish. You need to begin by establishing what your own main process patterns are. Once you have this insight, you simply take Adult control and behave in ways that break the pattern.

If your main pattern has been Until, you break it by going ahead and having fun even before you have finished all your work. (Daniel Casriel calls this 'riding the pony without waiting until you've cleaned out the stables').

For the person with an After script, the step out of process script is to go ahead and enjoy today, having first decided to enjoy tomorrow also. For instance, if you are at a party, drink enough to enjoy yourself but not so much that you finish up with a sore head the next day.

To break the Never pattern, decide what it is you want. Make a list of five specific things you can *do* to attain your want. Then do one of these things each day.

If you have been living out the Always theme, realize that you do not have to keep repeating the same mistakes or persist when things are awful. If you want to, you can leave an unsatisfying job, relationship or locality and look for something new.

You can step out of Almost Type 1 by making sure you complete what you do. If you clean a room, clean it all. When you are reading a book, read all the chapters. To dismantle Almost Type 2, take the pleasant step of recognizing each of your own successes as you achieve it. Keep a list of your aims. Each time you fulfil one, strike it off the list. Do not start on the next aim without having a celebration for the one you have just achieved.

If you think you may have been handed an Open-ended pattern, realize that your parents have given you a gift in disguise. Since the closing pages of your original script are missing, you are free to write your own ending in whatever way you like.

Each time you complete a behavior that contradicts your process pattern, you weaken that pattern for the future. You make it easier for yourself to step further out of your old process script theme.

● YOUR PROCESS SCRIPT PATTERN

Look through the descriptions given above for the different process script types. Pick out the pattern or patterns that have been typical of you.

Are you comfortable with this pattern or patterns as a way of behaving in the future?

If not, decide on at least five behaviors that go contrary to your process script. Begin now, and do at least one of these behaviors each day. Continue until you are satisfied with your change. ●

Chapter 16
DRIVERS AND THE MINISCRIPT

Working in the early 1970s, clinical psychologist Taibi Kahler made an intriguing discovery. He had followed up Berne's idea that the script may be played out over very short time periods. Second by second, Kahler noted his subjects' words, tones, gestures, postures and facial expressions. He found that there were certain distinctive sets of these behaviors which people consistently showed just before they moved into any kind of scripty behavior or feelings.

Kahler and his co-workers listed five of these second-by-second behavior sequences. They called them *drivers*.[1]

Further study showed that driver behavior was part of a wider pattern which Kahler called the *miniscript*. This is a sequence of script behaviors, feelings and beliefs. It is played out over a time-scale ranging from a few seconds to a few minutes. Invariably it begins with one of the driver behaviors. The miniscript reproduces, over a short time-period, the process of the entire life-script. Each time I run through my miniscript, I reinforce my script process. Whenever I step out of my miniscript pattern, I help defuse my script process.

The five drivers also turned out to be distinctively related to the six process script types. By observing someone's driver patterns, you can predict reliably what her process script will be.

Thus by learning how to detect the five driver behaviors, you can tell a lot about a person in a short space of time. In this chapter we describe how drivers can be observed. We discuss how drivers fit into the overall life-script, and study the workings of the miniscript sequence.

How to detect driver behavior

The five drivers are:

Be Perfect
Please (others)
Try Hard
Be Strong
Hurry Up.

Each of these is signaled by a distinctive set of *words, tones, gestures, postures and facial expressions.*

155

You have already learned to use these clues in making a behavioral diagnosis of ego-states. In looking for driver behaviors, you need to shrink your time-scale. Driver behaviors are typically shown within half-a-second to one second. Observing within this short time-span takes some initial practice if you are not used to it. But it soon becomes second nature.

The caution 'don't interpret' applies here, just as it did when we were discussing behavioral diagnosis in general. Stay with the behaviors you can actually see and hear. For instance, as you look at me you may be tempted to say I 'look stern'. But what am I doing with my face, body and voice which you interpret as 'sternness'? Where do you see muscle tension? Is my voice low, high, loud, harsh? Are my eyebrows up or down? In what direction am I looking? What hand gestures do you see me making? To become skilful at detecting drivers, stay with observable clues like these. Following is a list of the clues for each driver.

Be Perfect

Words: the person in Be Perfect will often use *parentheses*. For example:
'I'm here today, *as I said*, to teach you about drivers.'
'TA is, *we might say*, a theory of personality.'
The wording for Be Perfect frequently includes words and phrases like these, whether in parentheses or not. They act as qualifiers but add no new information to what's being said. Typically: *as it were, probably, possibly, certainly, completely, one might say, as we have seen.*

Another clue is that the speaker may count points off by numbers or letters. 'Our topics today are — *one* — to discuss drivers; and — *two* — to study their relationship to script.'

Tones: often sound Adult. Well-modulated, neither high nor low.

Gestures: counting on the fingers to accompany the points counted off by letters or numbers in the wording. Hand may stroke chin in the traditional 'thinker's' gesture. Fingertips may be placed together in a V shape, the gesture called 'steepling'.

Postures: often looks like Adult. Upright, evenly balanced round midline.

Facial expressions: eyes look upwards (less often, downwards) and to one side, usually while the person is making a pause in speech. It's as though the person were trying to read the 'perfect answer' written somewhere on the ceiling or floor. At the same time, the mouth is often slightly tensed, with the corners drawn a little outwards.

Please Others

Words: the person in Please Others often uses the 'high-*but*-low' sentence structure we have already met as a clue to the After script.

'I've really enjoyed your teaching, but I don't know if I'll remember what you said.'

'What a terrific party! But, by golly, I'm going to regret it in the morning.'

Frequently she will put in querying words and phrases like *OK? hmm? all right by you? kind of...? sort of...?*

Tones: high voice, squeaky tone, typically rising at the end of each sentence.

Gestures: reaching out with the hands, usually palms up. Head nodding.

Postures: shoulders hunched up and forward. Leaning towards the other person.

Facial expressions: the person in Please Others will very often look at you with her face turned slightly downwards. Thus she needs to look up at you with her eyebrows raised. This in turn means that she crinkles her brow up into horizontal lines. At the same time she shapes her mouth in an expression similiar to a smile. However, as compared to a non-driver genuine smile, the Please Others expression is more tense. The upper teeth are bared, and sometimes the lower teeth are shown as well.

Try Hard

Words: often the person in Try Hard will use the word *try*.

'What *I'm trying* to tell you is...'

'*I'll try* and do what we agreed.'

When used in this driver fashion, 'try' always conveys 'I'll try to do it instead of doing it.' Other typical words are: *difficult, can't, what? what's that again? don't get you, it's hard to...*, and interrogative grunts like *huh? uh?*.

Tones: the person will sometimes tense up the throat muscles so that the voice sounds muffled or strangled.

Gestures: often one hand is placed beside the eyes or beside one ear, as though the person were straining to hear or see something. Fists may be clenched.

Postures: with Try Hard as with Please Others, the person often strains forward. Hands may be placed on the knees. General impression is of a hunched-up pose.

Facial expressions: a frequent clue for Try Hard is that the person crunches his brow up so that two vertical lines appear above his nose. The eyes and sometimes the whole face may be screwed up into tight wrinkles.

Be Strong

Words: a person in Be Strong will often use words that convey: 'my feelings and actions are not my responsibility, but are caused by agencies outside me.'

'You're making me angry.'

'This book bores me.'

'The thought strikes me that...'

'His attitude forced me to fight back.'

'The inner-city environment brings about violence.'

Often, too, he uses distancing words like *one, you, people, it, that*, when he is talking about himself.

'That feels good' (meaning 'I feel good').

'You have to keep your feelings to yourself' (meaning 'I have to').

'Situations like this put pressure on one.'

Tones: flat, monotonous, usually low.

Gestures: Be Strong is marked by an absence of gesture.

Postures: frequently the posture is 'closed'. The arms may be folded or crossed in front of the body. Legs may be crossed, or placed in the 'figure-four' position, with the ankle of one leg resting on the knee of the other. The whole body conveys immobility.

Facial expressions: the face is expressionless and immobile.

Hurry Up

Words: hurry, quick, get going, let's go, no time to...

Tones: staccato, machine-gun-like. Sometimes the person in Hurry Up will rush the words out so quickly that she scrambles them up.

Gestures: finger-tapping, foot-tapping or wagging, wriggling round in the chair, repetitive checking of watch.

Postures: no specific posture, but the overall impression is of agitated movement.

Facial expressions: frequent, rapid changes in direction of gaze.

No one clue necessitates a driver

For reliable diagnosis of a driver, you need to look for *several clues for that driver occurring together*. Do not go on just one clue. For instance, hearing me say 'I'll try to...', you may conclude: 'Aha! He's in Try Hard driver.' But that does not necessarily follow. Were you to look at my other behavioral clues, you might see me tensing my mouth, looking upwards at the ceiling, and ticking off points on my fingers. These signals would make it more likely that I was actually in the Be Perfect driver. Alternatively, I could speak the words 'I'll try to...' while my other behavioral clues signaled that I was in Adult, not in any driver.

Primary driver

Each of us shows all five of the driver behaviors. But most people have one driver which they show most frequently. Often this will also be the driver they show *first* when they respond to a transactional stimulus. This is called their *primary driver*.

Some people have two main drivers which are about equal in frequency. Much less often, you meet someone who shows an even spread of three or more drivers.

● PRACTICING DRIVER DETECTION

If you have a television set, watch an interview program. Use it as practice in detecting the second-by-second clues of driver behavior.

If you have a video recorder, record the program while you are doing this. Later, play back the recording in slow motion or with stop-frames. Check your second-by-second observations against this.

Experiment to see whether different TV personalities typically show different primary drivers. Does your favorite comedian have a different primary driver from your least favorite politician?

What do you think is your own primary driver? Write your answer down.

Now get an objective check. Either have yourself observed by someone else who knows driver clues, or have yourself recorded on video and play back the recording. Were you right in your initial guess of your own primary driver?

If you are working in a group, get into sub-groups of three. Decide who will be 'client', who 'counselor' and who 'observer'. The client talks to the counselor for three minutes on any light topic. The counselor listens and responds in any way she wishes, and is also responsible for timekeeping. The observer, with pencil and paper, notes down which drivers he detects in the behavior of client and counselor. (To simplify the exercise first time through, the observer can concentrate on the client's driver behaviors only). When the three minutes is up, the observer feeds back what driver clues he observed. Then switch roles and repeat the exercise.

Look out for driver behavior in all sorts of everyday interaction. Practice detecting drivers as you work, shop, travel, have casual conversations with friends. *Do not tell people you are doing this* unless you know for sure they are interested. ●

Drivers and process script types

By noting my primary driver, you can tell my main process script type.[2] The correspondences between the two are shown in the following list.

Primary driver	*Process script*
Be Perfect	Until
Please Others	After
Be Strong	Never
Try Hard	Always
Please Others + Try Hard	Almost Type 1
Please Others + Be Perfect	Almost Type 2
Please Others + Be Perfect	Open-ended

The two types of Almost script are shown by people who have Please Others ranking first-equal with Try Hard and Be Perfect respectively. For the Open-ended script, the person will also show Please Others plus Be Perfect, but both drivers will be shown more intensely than for Almost Type 2.

Why is driver behavior related so closely to process script type? The answer is that the driver behaviors themselves are miniature versions of the process scripts. Each time I go into a driver behavior, I play out the corresponding process script pattern within the space of half-a-second.

As Taibi Kahler expresses it: 'The five drivers are the functional manifestations of not-OK (structural) counterscripts.'

For instance, suppose I am teaching a class about TA. I say: 'TA — which was first developed by Eric Berne, in approximately the years from the late 1950s onwards — is a system, or should we say model, for understanding personality; that, at least, is a beginning definition.' As I come out with this mouthful of parentheses, I am looking upwards at the ceiling, as though I expected to see the perfect definition written there. I am ticking off with my fingers the two concepts 'system' and 'model', to make sure I've said it in every way possible.

In the instant I carry out this set of Be Perfect behaviors, I am obeying an internal Parental voice that says: 'You're only OK around here if you get everything right.' Listening to this voice from my Adapted Child, I am believing that I can't finish my sentence *until* I've covered the entire waterfront.

Thus, in those few seconds, I have lived out my main script process of Until. In doing so, I have reinforced that process.

Now let's re-run that sequence. As I face the class, I look squarely at them and relax. I say: 'TA is a model for understanding personality. It was developed by Eric Berne. His first studies on it were in the late 1950s.'

Saying it this way, I stay in Driver-free Adult. I have tuned out the old Parent voice in my head that tells me I have to Be Perfect. Instead I have listened to a new tape which I have installed. It says: 'You're already good enough as you are!'

Through my understanding of driver behavior, I have deliberately avoided using parentheses. Instead, I have delivered my information in smaller chunks. I haven't managed to say quite as much as I said in the driver-ridden version. But if you were a student in my class, which version would you find more understandable?

In stepping out of my driver pattern, I have also stepped out of my Until script. And in doing so, I have weakened my Until pattern. I have made it even more easy for myself to step outside it the next time round.

This driver-script relationship holds also for the other four drivers. Each time I show the Please Others driver, I am living out the After pattern. The Parental voice in my head repeats the counterscript: 'You're only OK around here if you please people.' With raised eyebrows and toothy smile, I hope from Adapted Child I am being pleasing enough. *But* I'm scared that sooner or later I'll run out of energy to please, and then will come the 'downer' as the sword of Damocles falls on my head.

To step out of Please Others, I keep myself aware of the Please Others driver behaviors. In particular, I relax my eyebrows instead of raising them, and thus keep my forehead smooth instead of crinkling it in horizontal lines. As I do this, I play a new message to myself in my head. It says: 'You're OK to please yourself!' Since I'm no longer basing my OKness on pleasing people, I can also let go my scare of what may happen tomorrow if I don't please them enough.

In showing Be Strong, I am tuning in a counterscript message: 'You're only OK if you hide your feelings and wants from people. Don't let them see you're weak.' Listening to this in Adapted Child, I obey by shutting down external signals. I keep my face impassive, move little, speak in a flat voice.

As I show this set of Be Strong behaviors, I live out and reinforce the Never process pattern. I may be wanting contact and strokes from the others around me. But by keeping up my expressionless front, I give them no clue of this. Like Tantalus, I stop myself from making the move I would need to make to get what I want.

If I get tired of copying Tantalus, I let down my facade. I practice how to show my feelings in voice, expression and gesture. Especially, I explore the pleasure of moving freely in all kinds of ways. Breaking out of my Be Strong behavior patterns, I am also breaking free of my Never script. I have installed a new voice in my head that says: 'Go ahead and show how you feel. Be open about what you want.'

Suppose my primary driver is Try Hard. As you ask me a question, I hunch forward, crunching my brow into two vertical lines above my nose. I squint my eyes. My hand is up beside my head, as though I had difficulty in hearing you. I say: 'Huh? What? Didn't get you.' Actually my hearing is fine. I am in the Try Hard driver. During those few seconds, I am listening to a Parental voice from the past. It tells me: 'To be OK around here, you have to keep trying hard to do things.' In order to obey this command, I 'know' in Adapted Child that I can't let myself actually get

161

around to doing anything. If I did do it, I couldn't keep on trying hard to do it any more.

As I try to do things but don't, I continue to go round and round in the Always script pattern. Maybe I don't much like where I am at the moment. I try hard to get somewhere else, but don't actually do what I'd need to do to get there.

I can disable Try Hard and Always by setting up a new tape for myself that says: 'You're OK to go ahead and do it!' Each moment I feel myself beginning to make those two vertical lines in my brow, I relax and let them smooth out again. I listen so I hear what people say to me. If at times they do speak indistinctly, I say: 'I didn't hear you. Will you say that again?'

The connections between script and driver for the two Almost scripts and the Open-ended script are not so clear. By conjecture, it isn't difficult to see how the combined counterscript mottoes for the drivers might add up to the script patterns. (You may care to work out what the combined mottoes are, and do your own conjecturing). In any case, I can step out of these process patterns also by taking action to disable the driver behaviors.

There is no direct driver-script connection for the Hurry Up driver. In many ways, Hurry Up is an odd-man-out among the drivers. It seems to turn up most often along with another driver as primary, and to act as a reinforcer of that primary.

● YOUR PRIMARY DRIVER AND SCRIPT PROCESS

You have already noted which process script was most typical for you. You have noted also your primary driver. Do the two correspond in the way we have described in the section above?

What if they do not seem to correspond? The listed connections between driver and process script are generalizations, and it is conceivable they may simply not apply to you. But they have proved to apply reliably in thousands of observed cases. If they appear at first not to fit for you, it is worth while to review your initial judgment on your primary driver and your process script type. In our experience, the most common reason for an apparent mis-fit is that the person has not identified her primary driver accurately. ●

Drivers and life position

From the examples we gave in the section on 'Drivers and process script type', you'll see that the driver messages in the counterscript carry a special implication about life position. The Parental message is: 'You're OK *if* you...are perfect, please others, etc.'

Thus when I am in script and listening to this Parental message in my Adapted Child, my position is: 'I'm OK *as long as* I...am perfect, please others, etc.'

We say that drivers reflect a position of *conditional OKness*.

The five allowers

For each of the driver messages there is an antidote called an *allower*.[3] If you were lucky with your parents, you got some of these allowers from them. If not, you can install them yourself. We have met each of them above. Here they are in summary.

Driver	Allower
Be Perfect	You're good enough as you are
Please Others	Please yourself
Be Strong	Be open and express your wants
Try Hard	Do it
Hurry Up	Take your time

Each time you consciously step out of a driver behavior and substitute a driver-free behavior, you affirm the allower non-verbally.

You can also repeat the allower to yourself before you go to sleep at night and when you wake in the morning. Write it up on a big notice and put the notice where you see it frequently.

Caution: if you begin experiencing bad feelings or discomfort on affirming your allower, back off from doing so for a while. By feeling uncomfortable, you may be letting yourself know that your counterscript driver has been covering a heavier script decision. It is advisable for you to discover and defuse that heavier decision before you continue with movement out of the driver.

Origins of drivers

Why are there five and only five driver behaviors? Why are they the same for everybody, regardless of culture, age, or education? Why does each driver consistently accompany its own specific counterscript message? Nobody knows.

Taibi Kahler himself is now beginning to think that the drivers may be partly inborn, a result of 'nature' as well as 'nurture'.[4] Hedges Capers has suggested that drivers may be viewed as a survival strategy for the infant during script-making.[5] This would certainly help to account for their apparently 'automatic' quality. Other theorists have speculated that the five drivers are mottoes which the child first hears from his parents during toilet training.

163

But these ideas are still in the realm of conjecture. One of the most challenging tasks of current TA research is to produce a convincing account of the origins of driver behavior.

The miniscript

Drivers reflect a position of conditional OKness. They are manifestations of counterscript messages. As with any other counterinjunctions, drivers may perform the script function of defending against heavier decisions, formed around injunctions.

But this function cuts two ways. While I am in a driver, I am believing 'I'm OK as long as I...am perfect, please others, etc.' As long as I can keep on obeying the driver counterscript command, I believe I don't need to listen to the injunction. However, there will be some occasions when I don't have enough energy to keep myself in the driver. At these times, I fail to be perfect enough, please people enough, etc., to satisfy the Parent in my head. Then, in terms of my script beliefs, it *must* follow that I have to listen to the injunction. As I do so, I will experience bad feelings as I replay the early decision I made around that injunction.

Each time I carry this sequence through, I play out my script in miniature. I also reinforce my script.

This process is represented by Taibi Kahler in the model which he called the *miniscript*. It is shown diagramatically in Figure 16.1.[6]

Position 1: driver

The miniscript sequence always begins with a driver. As I listen to the counterscript message in my head, I show the corresponding driver behavior. It lasts from half-a-second to seven seconds at most.

While I am in the driver, *I experience no emotion*. My Adapted Child belief is that I remain OK as long as I am obeying the driver.

Two possible outcomes may follow. I may manage to try hard enough, hurry up enough, etc., to satisfy the demands of my internal Parent. If so, I end the driver behavior. I will then move either into non-scripty behavior or into another driver.

Alternatively, I may not summon up enough energy to fulfil the driver command. I have not satisfied my internal Parent's condition for OKness. With that conditional protection withdrawn, I now believe I must listen to the injunction I had been guarding against.

On the miniscript model, this is marked by a movement from the driver (position 1) to one of the other three positions. We say that I *go through the driver* to the next position.

Position 2: stopper

For instance, suppose that as an infant I made the combined decision 'I'm OK to belong, so long as I'm perfect.' Imagine I am at a party. As I talk to

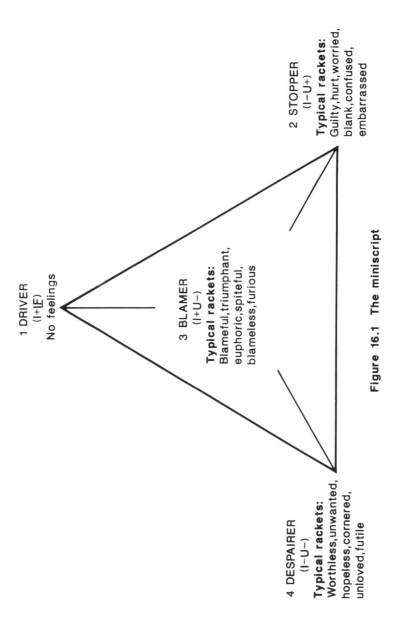

1 DRIVER
(I+IF)
No feelings

2 STOPPER
(I–U+)
Typical rackets:
Guilty,hurt,worried,
blank,confused,
embarrassed

3 BLAMER
(I+U–)
Typical rackets:
Blameful,triumphant,
euphoric,spiteful,
blameless,furious

4 DESPAIRER
(I–U–)
Typical rackets:
Worthless,unwanted,
hopeless,cornered,
unloved,futile

Figure 16.1 The miniscript

the group around me, I move in and out of my Be Perfect driver. Eventually I run low on the energy I have been using to keep on getting things right. Maybe I slip and stumble over some words, or say something that people laugh at.

I now go through the Be Perfect driver. Internally I judge myself: 'I've not managed to be perfect. So I'm not-OK. Anybody like me, who gets things wrong, can't possibly belong in this group.' As I re-run my early decision not to belong, I feel again the sense of inadequacy that I first felt at the time I made this decision in childhood.

In the language of the miniscript, the injunction I hear when I go through my driver to position 2 is called a *stopper*. It may be any of the twelve injunctions, depending on the unique content of my own script. The term *stopper* is also used to describe position 2 itself.

As I shift from driver to stopper, I change life position. Instead of the driver's 'I'm OK if...', I now move to 'I'm not-OK, You're OK'.

Re-playing the early decision I made around the injunction, I also re-experience a bad feeling from my childhood — a *racket feeling*. The specific racket I feel will depend on the content of my own script. All the racket feelings at Position 2 will reflect the I-U+ life position. Some examples are listed in Figure 16.1.

Position 3: blamer

Suppose that as a child I decided I was more comfortable blaming others for not-OK occurrences than blaming myself. In that case, I may rapidly shift to the third position on the miniscript, the *blamer*. Here my life position is 'I'm OK, You're not-OK'. I will experience a racket feeling that fits with this blaming life position. For example, as I stumble over my words during the party conversation, I may feel irritated with the others in the group because they don't seem to have understood me.

When Taibi Kahler first drew the miniscript, he called this third position 'vengeful Child'. However, the I+U- life position may be expressed functionally from negative Controlling Parent as well as from negative Adapted Child, so we think that Kahler's revised name 'blamer' is more appropriate.

Position 4: despairer

If my early childhood experiences led me to conclude 'I'm not-OK and neither are you', I may move to this I-U- life position during my miniscript sequence. If so, I arrive at miniscript position 4, the *despairer*. I may get there directly from position 2, or take a detour via position 3.

Here, my racket feelings will be in tune with my belief that life is futile. I may feel despairing, helpless, hopeless or cornered. If I shift to the despairer position while speaking to my group at the party, I may droop and say to myself: 'Oh, what's the use? I never seem to get through to people. And they don't understand me anyway.'

In Kahler's original version of the miniscript, position 4 was called 'final miniscript payoff'. We prefer his revised name 'despairer', since for many people position 4 is not the 'final' position. I may habitually play out my miniscript sequence to end up in stopper or blamer. If I was lucky with my parents or if I have resolved my script issues in therapy, I may seldom go below the driver level.

Movement through the miniscript

Miniscript theory does not predict any specific sequence of movement from one position to another. Each individual has her own typical patterns. For instance, a frequent pattern of mine may be to go through the Be Perfect driver and immediately feel irritated. I have shifted directly to blamer. Once I have spent long enough in my script, I typically shift straight back into the driver for half-a-second, then revert to non-scripty behavior.

My partner's most usual pattern may be to go through the Please Others driver to the stopper position. There she experiences racket feelings of inadequacy. Just occasionally she may move from position 2 over to position 4, where she feels hopeless and unloved. She will stay with those feelings for a while, then return to feeling inadequate and finally shift back out of the miniscript via a flash of the Please Others driver.

The four myths

Taibi Kahler suggests there are *four myths* which underlie drivers and rackets.[7] They consist of two pairs. One of each pair comes from Parent. The other is a Child response.

As I get into a driver, I replay a voice from my negative Nurturing Parent that says: *'I can make you feel good by doing your thinking for you.'* This is the first myth.

In my Adapted Child I respond: *'You can make me feel good by doing my thinking for me.'* So long as I am believing this second myth, I maintain my conditional OKness.

Perhaps I go through the driver and into a racket feeling. As I do so, I hear an internal voice from my negative Controlling Parent. It repeats the third myth: *'I can make you feel bad by what I say to you.'*

Shifting into negative Adapted Child, I echo this with the fourth myth. I begin believing: *'You can make me feel bad by what you say to me.'*

When we get into drivers and rackets while communicating with others, we are re-running these mythical beliefs. Suppose you and I are having an argument. I yell at you: 'Now you're making me feel annoyed!' At that instant I'm believing the fourth myth, 'Other people can make me feel bad by what they say to me.'

In reality, there is no means by which this can happen. I am responsible for my own feelings and actions. For sure, I am responding to your words by feeling annoyed. But you are not *making me feel* annoyed. If I chose, I could feel amused, blank, scared, excited, or any other of a thousand feelings.

In your turn, you may actually believe that you are 'irritating me'. Perhaps you want me to be irritated. But you cannot *make me* feel that way. You can issue me with a strong *invitation*. Whether I respond to your invitation is up to me.

● YOUR MINISCRIPT PATTERNS

Think of some recent situations in which you responded to stress by feeling bad.

In your imagination, re-play each situation up to the point when you just began experiencing the bad feeling. You don't have to re-play the bad feeling itself. For each situation, check answers to the following questions.

What driver did you go through?

What position on the miniscript did you go to first? What bad feeling did you experience there?

Did you shift to a second or third position on the miniscript? If so, again register what bad feelings you experienced.

After checking several situations, determine whether you have one or more typical patterns of movement round the miniscript.

Do you want to change any of these patterns? If so, you can make changes at any point. It may take some initial practice.

Get used to detecting your own driver clues as you show them. With this ability, 'catch' the driver behavior at the instant you begin doing it. By Adult decision, step out of the driver. Instead, behave in a way which fits the corresponding allower.

If you miss the driver clues, you may go through the driver and begin feeling bad. If so, simply choose to change the way you feel. In place of the bad feeling, substitute a good one of your own choice. You can do this at any time.

Each time you choose to follow an allower instead of a driver, you help extinguish your miniscript pattern in future. You do the same each time you choose to feel good instead of feeling a racket.

Do you find it difficult to believe that the third and fourth myths are really myths? Many people do on first acquaintance. If you are one of them, do a pencil-and-paper exercise. Simply write down any way in which you believe one person could *make* another person feel bad by what they say to that person.

If you think you have found such a way, ask yourself another question: could the person spoken to have chosen to feel any *other* feeling? If so, then the speaker could not have been *making* the other person feel in a particular way.

In this exercise, we are not talking of physical assault. If somebody hits me with a brick, it's obvious that they are making me feel bad. But words aren't bricks. ●

Part V
MAKING THE WORLD FIT OUR SCRIPT

Passivity

Chapter 17
DISCOUNTING

In the process of living, I am continually being presented with problems. How do I get across the road without being killed? How do I deal with the work assignment I've just been given? How do I respond to a friendly or an aggressive approach from someone?

Each time I meet a problem, I have two options. I can use the full power of my grown-up thinking, feeling and actions to solve the problem. Or I can go into script.

If I do move into script, I begin perceiving the world so that it seems to fit the decisions I made as an infant. I am likely to blank out my awareness of some aspects of the real situation. At the same time, I may blow up other aspects of the here-and-now problem into giant proportions. Instead of taking action to solve the problem, I rely on the 'magical solution' which my script offers. I hope in Child that by working this magic, I can manipulate the world into providing a solution for me. Instead of being active, I become passive.

In Part V, we look at this contrast between passivity and problem-solving. This area of TA theory is known as *Schiffian* or *Cathexis* theory, after the 'Schiff family' who first developed it, and the Cathexis Institute which they founded. The Schiffs define *passivity* as 'how people don't do things, or don't do them effectively'.[1]

Nature and definition of discounting

Discounting is defined as *unawarely ignoring information relevant to the solution of a problem.*[2]

Imagine I am sitting in a crowded restaurant. I begin to feel thirsty and think I'd like a glass of water. I try to catch the eye of the waiter. He pays no attention. I gesture again. Still no response.

At this instant I go into script. Without being aware of it, I begin replaying a time in my infancy when I had wanted to call my mother to me and she had not come. I put my mother's face on the unresponsive waiter. At the same time I begin acting, feeling and thinking as though I were still a young child. I droop and feel hopeless. I say to myself in my head: 'It's no good. No matter how much I try, he's not going to come.'

To get to this conclusion, I have had to ignore some information about here-and-now reality. I have *discounted* several options I have as a grown-up, options I did not have as a baby. I could have stood up, walked over to the waiter and shouted in his ear. I could have gone to the nearest table where there was a water-jug, asked for it and poured myself a drink. Had I acted in these ways, I would have been active in problem-solving instead of passive.

A friend is sitting with me in the restaurant. Seeing the waiter's lack of response to my gestures, my friend gets angry. He snorts: 'That fellow is obviously incompetent. If I had my way, I'd see him fired!'

My friend has also gone into script. But as a child he decided upon the life position I+U-, rather than my own I-U+. Now he sees the waiter through the spectacles of his own script. He discounts the waiter's competence to respond to my call. Like me, my friend is being passive. His sitting there snarling about the waiter will do nothing to get me my glass of water.

Grandiosity

Every discount is accompanied by *grandiosity*. This is an exaggeration of some feature of reality. The expression 'making a mountain out of a molehill' aptly describes grandiosity. As one feature of the situation is blotted out or diminished through discounting, so another feature is blown up out of proportion by grandiosity.

When I sat in the restaurant feeling hopeless because the waiter wasn't bringing my glass of water, I was not only discounting my own options. I was also crediting the waiter with power he didn't have, the power to determine whether or not I got any water.

As my friend discounted the waiter's competence, he was also being grandiose about himself. He was taking on himself the role of judge and jury, when he had neither adequate evidence nor responsibility to do so.

● Think back to a recent situation in which the outcome was unsatisfactory for you. That situation represents a problem which you didn't solve.

Looking back, do you now identify a feature or features of reality that you were discounting? Could you have acted in a different way that you 'didn't think of at the time'? Were you ignoring somebody else's ability to act in a particular way? Were there resources in the situation that were available but which you didn't think of using?

Do you identify where you were being grandiose? What features of yourself, others or the situation were you blowing up out of proportion?

If you are working in a group, or if you have a friend who is willing to help you, get a second opinion on your answers. It is often easier for us to spot other people's discounting and grandiosity than to spot our own.

Whether or not you have got immediate answers to these questions, keep your problem situation in mind. You can refer to it again as background to the further discussion in this chapter. ●

The four passive behaviors

When I discount, I do so by making a statement to myself in my own head. Thus *a discount itself is not observable.* Since you can't thought-read, you have no way of knowing I am discounting unless I speak or act in some way which indicates the presence of the discount.

There are four types of behavior which always indicate that the person concerned is discounting. These *four passive behaviors* are:

Doing nothing
Overadaptation
Agitation
Incapacitation or violence.

Doing nothing

The members of a TA group are sitting in a circle. The group leader says: 'Let's go round the group and each person say what he or she appreciates or resents about today's session. If you don't want to take part, it's OK to say "pass".'

The exercise begins. People round the group each give an appreciation or resentment. One or two say 'pass'.

Then comes Norman's turn. There's a silence. People wait for Norman to say something, but he doesn't. He sits unmoving and silent, staring into space. Since he doesn't seem to want to speak any appreciation or resentment, the person next to him waits for him to say 'pass'. But Norman doesn't do that either. He continues to sit as if dumb.

Norman is showing the passive behavior called *doing nothing*. Instead of using energy to take problem-solving action, he is using it to stop himself from acting. A person exhibiting this passive behavior feels uncomfortable and experiences himself as not thinking. He is discounting his own ability to do anything about the situation.

Overadaptation

Amy comes into the house after a hard day's work. Her husband Brian is sitting reading a newspaper. Looking beyond him into the kitchen, Amy sees a huge pile of unwashed dishes beside the sink.

'Hi,' says Brian. 'Hope you've had a good day. Just about time for tea, isn't it?' Taking her coat off, Amy goes straight through to the kitchen. She washes the pile of dishes and gets down to making tea.

Neither Brian nor Amy notice that he has not asked her to wash the dishes and make tea. Nor has she asked him if he wants her to. Still less has she paused to think whether she herself *wants* to wash the dishes, or whether it might be more appropriate if Brian washed them.

Amy's passive behavior is *overadaptation*. When someone overadapts, she is complying with what she *believes* in Child are the wishes of others. She does so without checking with them what their wishes are in reality, and without any reference to what her own wishes are. The person in overadaptation, unlike the person who is doing nothing, experiences herself as 'thinking' during the passive behavior. Her 'thinking', though, actually proceeds from a contamination.

Someone in overadaptation will often be experienced by others as helpful, adaptable or accommodating. Thus overadaptation is frequently stroked by those to whom the person relates. Because of this social acceptability and because the person appears to be thinking, overadaptation is the most difficult to detect of the four passive behaviors.

The person in overadaptation is discounting her ability to act on her own options. Instead, she follows options she believes others want.

Agitation

The class of students is listening to the lecturer. At the back of the room sits Adam. The lecturer is speaking rather quietly, and Adam has difficulty in hearing him. As the lecture period goes on, Adam has more and more trouble following what the lecturer is talking about. He puts down his pen and starts drumming his fingers on the desk. If we could see underneath that desk, we'd notice that Adam is waggling his foot rapidly up and down in time to his finger-drumming.

Adam is showing *agitation*. In this passive behavior, the person is discounting his ability to act to solve a problem. He feels acutely uncomfortable, and engages in purposeless, repetitive activity in an attempt to relieve the discomfort. Energy is directed into the agitated activity instead of into action to solve the problem. During agitation, the person does not experience himself as thinking.

If Adam were using his clear Adult, he could simply attract the lecturer's attention and ask him to speak up. As it is, his finger-drumming and foot-waggling do nothing towards solving his problem.

Many common habits entail agitation. Nail-biting, smoking, hair-twiddling and compulsive eating are all examples.

Incapacitation and violence

Betty is in her late thirties. The younger of two daughters, she still lives at home with her aged mother, whom she looks after. The old woman, despite her age, is really in pretty sound health.

Out of the blue, Betty meets a man and they fall in love. Happily she announces to her mother that she intends to move out to live with him and perhaps get married.

A couple of days later, the mother begins having dizzy spells and has to take to her bed. The doctor can find nothing physically wrong with her. But Betty begins to feel guilty about her intention to move out.

Mother's passive behavior is *incapacitation*. Here, the person disables herself in some way. Discounting her own ability to solve a problem, she hopes in Child that by incapacitating herself she can get someone else to solve it.

Incapacitation can sometimes be in the form of psychosomatic ailments, as here. Alternatively it can be achieved by mental breakdown or by abuse of drugs or alcohol.

Robert has just had a furious row with his girlfriend. He storms out of the house and walks the streets for a long while. He goes down town, has a few beers. Then he picks up a chair and smashes all the plate-glass windows in the bar.

Robert's passive behavior is *violence*. It may seem strange to refer to violence as a 'passive' behavior. But it is passive, because it is not directed at solving the problem in hand. When Robert smashes the windows, he does nothing to resolve his differences with his girlfriend.

Incapacitation can be viewed as violence directed inwards. In both incapacitation and violence, the person is discounting his ability to solve a problem. He releases a burst of energy, directed against self or others, in a desperate attempt to force the environment to solve the problem for him.

Incapacitation or violence will often follow a period of agitation. When the person is agitating, he is building up energy which he may then discharge destructively by either incapacitating or getting violent.

● Review the problem situation you considered in the last section. Do you identify which of the passive behaviors you engaged in?

Now re-run the situation in your mind's eye. When you come to the moment where you began the passive behavior, imagine yourself instead staying in Adult and using the full power of your grown-up thinking, feeling or behaving to solve the problem. How do you then act differently? ●

Discounting and ego-states

Discounting can be related to what you already know about ego-state pathology (Chapter 6).

Discounting may indicate the presence of *contamination*. That is to say: when I am discounting, I may be mis-perceiving reality to fit Parent or Child script beliefs, which I mistake for Adult thinking.

Exclusion may be another source of discounting. Here, I am ignoring aspects of reality because I am blanking out one or more of my ego-states. If I am excluding my Child, I will ignore the wants, feelings and intuitions I carry from my own childhood, which might in reality be relevant to the problem I have to solve in the present. With excluded Parent, I will blank out the rules and definitions of the world I learned from my parent-figures, though these also can often be useful in problem-solving. An excluded Adult means that I discount my own ability to assess, feel or act in direct response to any feature of the here-and-now situation. As you would expect, excluded Adult is the most disabling of the three exclusions in terms of the person's intensity of discounting.

Often discounting can occur without any ego-state pathology. In these cases, it is simply the result of the person's Adult being uninformed or misinformed. For instance, an over-weight lady decides to go on a slimming diet. She stops eating bread, potatoes and pasta. Instead, she takes nuts and cheese. In fact, the nuts and cheese have more calories per ounce than the foods she's given up. She discounts this fact simply because she doesn't know about it.

In terms of the functional model of ego-states, discounting can be straighforwardly expressed. Whenever I am coming from any negative ego-state part, I am discounting. And whenever I am discounting, I am coming from a negative ego-state part. The one idea defines the other.

To say 'I am coming from a negative part of my personality' means I am thinking, feeling or behaving in some way that gets me uncomfortable, unsuccessful or ineffective results. It means I have not solved a problem. And when I stop myself solving a problem, I necessarily have been discounting.

Detecting discounts

You know that discounting, not observable in itself, can be inferred by the person's showing any of the four passive behaviors. There are many other ways of detecting discounts.

Driver behavior always indicates a discount. Remember that when I show a driver, I am internally replaying the script belief: 'I'm only OK *if* I...Try Hard, Please Others, etc.' The reality is that I am OK whether or not I follow these driver messages.

The Schiffs specify certain *thinking disorders* as clues to discounting. One of these is *over-detailing*. Asked a simple question, the person showing this disorder will reply with a long tirade of minute details. *Over-generalization* is the opposite to this, in which the person expresses ideas only in sweeping, global terms. 'Well, my problem is something huge. People are after me. Things are getting me down.'

In Part VI we shall look at *rackets, games* and *behaviors from the Drama Triangle*. All these also confirm the presence of discounting.

Verbal clues

One of the skills of TA is to identify discounting by listening to the words people use. In the examples we have given in this chapter, we have chosen words that made it clear the speaker was discounting. In everyday conversation, the verbal clues to discounting are usually more subtle.

In theory, what we are listening for is straightforward. We know the speaker is discounting when she says something in which information about reality is ignored or distorted. The difficulty in practice is that everyday speech is full of discounts, so much so that we become desensitized to them. We need to re-learn the skill of listening to what is really being said and testing each statement against reality.

For instance, when someone says 'I can't...' he will most often be discounting. The test is to ask yourself: 'Well, can he, either now or some time?'

'I'll try to...' is usually a discount, since what it implies is usually 'I'll try to, but I won't do it.' The same is true of all other driver wording. Be Strong discounts are particularly common.

'What you say is boring me.'

'I'm baffled by this problem.'

'A thought just crossed my mind.'

Sometimes a discount is signaled by leaving out a part of the sentence. For instance, a member of a TA group may look around the other group members and announce: 'I want a hug.' She doesn't say whom she wants the hug from. She is omitting information relevant to the solution of her problem — how to get the hug she wants — and her request thus entails a discount.

Nonverbal clues

Equally important is the skill of identifying discounts from nonverbal clues. Here, the discount is signaled by a mis-match between the words being said and the nonverbal signals that go with them. You'll recall from Chapter 5 that this mis-matching is called *incongruity*.

For example, a teacher asks his pupil: 'Do you understand the assignment I've set you?' The pupil replies 'Sure.' But at the same time he puckers his brow and scratches his head. If the teacher is alert to 'thinking Martian', he will ask more questions to check whether his pupil is discounting.

Incongruity does not always indicate discounting. For instance, the chairman of a meeting stands up and pronounces: 'Today, we have a lot of work ahead of us.' But as he makes this serious statement, he beams round the table. His 'Martian' signals simply: 'And I'm glad to see you all here.'

Gallows

One frequent indication of a discount is *gallows laughing*. Here, the person laughs when making a statement about something unpleasant.

'Oh! That was silly of me, ha ha!'

'Hee, hee, hee — I sure got the better of *him*.'

'Had a bit of a bump in the car on the way over here, ho ho!'

In gallows there is incongruity between the laugh and the painful content of the words. Whenever someone gives a gallows laugh, smile or chuckle, he is making a non-verbal invitation to the listeners to reinforce one of his script beliefs. The invitation is accepted on psychological level if the listeners join in the gallows laughing. For instance, the person who says 'I'm silly, ha ha' is in script, inviting the listeners to join his laughter and thus 'confirm' his script belief: 'I can't think'.

The straight response to gallows is to refuse to join in the laughing or smiling. You may also say: 'That's not funny', if you are in a situation where it is socially appropriate to do so.

● You have already practiced the skill of 'thinking Martian'. Now you can refine this skill by distinguishing the nonverbals that signal discounts from those that do not. In fact, it is not always possible to tell clearly from someone's nonverbal signals whether he is discounting. If it is important for you to know, you may have to check your impressions by verbal questioning. ●

Chapter 18
THE DISCOUNT MATRIX

Discounting results in unsolved problems. Thus if we can devise a systematic way of identifying the nature and intensity of discounting, we will have a powerful tool for problem-solving. Such a tool exists. It is called the *discount matrix*, and was developed by Ken Mellor and Eric Sigmund.[1]

The discount matrix starts from the idea that we can classify discounts according to three different criteria:

area
type
level.

Areas of discounting

There are three *areas* in which people can discount: *self, others,* and the *situation.*

In the example given above, where I was sitting in the restaurant drooping bècause the waiter wasn't bringing my glass of water, I was discounting myself. I was ignoring my own ability to take action to get what I wanted.

My friend, who got angry and started criticizing the waiter, was discounting not himself but the other person. In judging the waiter 'incompetent', he was blanking out any aspects of the waiter's actions that might have contradicted his criticism.

Suppose that after drooping for a while, I'd turned to my friend and said: 'Well, there we are. It really isn't fair that these other people are getting served and I'm not. But then, this world is an unfair place, isn't it?' Here, I'd have been discounting the situation.

Types of discounting

The three *types* of discounting are of: *stimuli, problems* and *options.*

To discount a *stimulus* is to blank out perception that something is happening at all. As I sat in the restaurant, I might simply not have allowed myself to feel that I was thirsty. I would have been discounting the stimulus of my own thirst. Maybe my friend, in calling the waiter incompetent, had 'not seen' the way in which the waiter had actually succeeded in serving many other customers, even though the evidence was right there in front of him.

The person who discounts a *problem* realizes that something is happening, but ignores the fact that whatever is happening poses a problem. Feeling thirsty there in the restaurant, I might have said to my friend: 'I feel very thirsty right now, but, oh well, it doesn't matter.'

When discounting *options*, the person is aware that something is happening and that it constitutes a problem. But she blanks out the possibility that anything can be done about the problem. This is where I was discounting in the original version of the restaurant scene. As I sat drooping, I knew that I felt thirsty. I was aware that my thirst was a problem to me. But I was unawarely ignoring the many options I had, other than just sitting and hoping the waiter would respond.

Levels (modes) of discounting

The terms *level* and *mode* are interchangeable, but *level* gives a clearer idea of what is meant. The four levels of discounting are: *existence, significance, change possibilities* and *personal abilities*.

Let's apply those four levels to my discounting of my own options in our example. In the original version of the scene, I was discounting the *existence* of my own options to solve the problem. I didn't even consider the possibility of, for example, walking over and speaking to the waiter instead of gesturing to him.

If I had been discounting the *significance* of my options, I might have said to my friend: 'I suppose I could go over and ask him. But I bet asking him wouldn't make any difference.' Here, I'd have realized there was something different I could do, but blanked out the possibility that this action could have any effect.

Discounting my options at the level of *change possibilities*, I might have said: 'Of course, I *could* walk across and collar the fellow. But people just don't do that in restaurants.' In this case I would have let myself realize that the option existed and that it might have results, while ignoring the possibility that anyone could actually put the option into practice.

At the level of *personal abilities*, I might have discounted by saying: 'I know I could go across and ask him for some water. But I just don't have the nerve to do it.' Here, I am aware the option exists and could bring results. I realize that some people in the world might well use that option. But I dismiss my own ability to do so.

The discount-matrix diagram

The discount matrix is compiled by listing all the possible combinations of

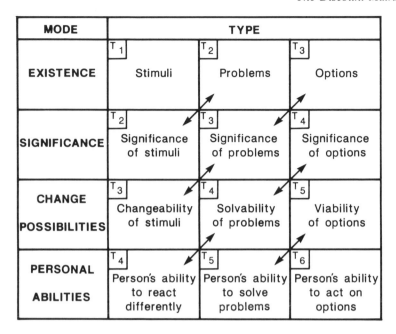

MODE	TYPE		
EXISTENCE	T 1 Stimuli	T 2 Problems	T 3 Options
SIGNIFICANCE	T 2 Significance of stimuli	T 3 Significance of problems	T 4 Significance of options
CHANGE POSSIBILITIES	T 3 Changeability of stimuli	T 4 Solvability of problems	T 5 Viability of options
PERSONAL ABILITIES	T 4 Person's ability to react differently	T 5 Person's ability to solve problems	T 6 Person's ability to act on options

Figure 18.1 The discount matrix

types and *levels* of discount. When we do so, we get the diagram shown in Figure 18.1.

You'll see that the matrix has three columns for the three types of discount, and four rows for the four modes or levels. The wording in each of the resulting twelve boxes indicates the combination of type and level.

Let's take another example to help explain the meaning of the matrix. Suppose two friends are talking. One of them is a heavy smoker. As he lights up yet another cigarette, he is convulsed by a bout of coughing. His friend says to him: 'That's a terrible cough. I'm concerned about you. Please, give up smoking.' What might the smoker reply if he were discounting in each of the twelve different boxes on the matrix?

If the smoker were discounting the *existence of stimuli*, he might reply: 'What cough? I wasn't coughing.'

Discounting the *existence of the problem*, he might say: 'Oh, no, I'm fine, thanks. I've always had a cough.' He is letting himself be aware of his cough, but blotting out the possibility that this may constitute a problem for him.

Notice next that in doing this, the smoker *is also discounting the significance of the stimulus*. In discounting the possibility that his cough may be a problem, he is also discounting the fact that the cough may have some meaning (significance) for him.

This is indicated on the matrix diagram by the diagonal arrow connecting the boxes for 'existence of problems' and 'significance of stimuli'. The arrow means that one of these discounts will always entail the other.

All the diagonal arrows on the diagram have this meaning. The 'T' numbers, entered at the top left of each box, are labels for the different diagonals. For instance, discounts of the existence of problems and of the significance of stimuli correspond to diagonal T_2.

Let's test this out on the next diagonal down, T_3. We can take the top-right box on this diagonal, where the smoker is discounting the existence of options. He might show this by replying: 'Well, yes, but we smokers do cough, you know? A short life and a happy one, that's what I say, ha ha.'

Now he is admitting that he has a cough and that the cough may well indicate a problem, namely that smoking can kill people. But he is blanking out the possibility that anyone can do anything to avoid smokers' cough.

In doing so, he also blanks out any perception that the possibility of being killed by smoking is something he might be concerned about. He discounts the significance of the problem.

And by his denial that anything can possibly be done by anyone to get rid of a smokers' cough, he discounts the changeability of the stimulus.

Check that the same equivalence of discounts also applies along the other diagonals. On T_4, the smoker might say: 'Well, yes, I suppose I should give up really. But I've been smoking so long, I don't think my giving up now is going to make any difference.'

On T_5 he might respond: 'Sure, you're right, I need to give up. But I can't figure out how to do it.'

And on T_6 the smoker might say: 'Yes! I've been telling myself for ages I should throw my cigarettes and lighter away. But I just can't seem to get round to it.'

Another feature of the matrix is that *a discount in any box also entails discounts in the boxes below it and to its right*.

For instance, suppose a person is discounting the existence of a problem. Since he is not allowing himself to be aware that the problem even exists, he's obviously also going to blank out any perception that the problem may be significant. Nor will he be thinking whether he or anyone else can solve the problem. He is thus discounting in the entire column of boxes related to 'problems'.

And since he is ignoring the existence of the problem, why should he consider whether there are options for solving it? Because he thus discounts the existence of options, he will also discount all the other boxes in the 'options' column.

Finally, recall that a discount of the existence of problems is equivalent to discounting the significance of stimuli, along diagonal T_2. Therefore the other two boxes below it in the 'stimuli' column will be discounted also.

To summarize: *a person discounting on any diagonal will also be discounting in all the boxes below and to the right of that diagonal.*

You may wish to go back to the 'smoker' examples and confirm this *hierarchy of discounts.*

● Make up the discount matrix for another imaginary case. Wife and husband have just settled down in bed for the night. Then, in the next room, their baby starts crying. The husband says to his wife: 'Do you think one of us should go and see why the baby's crying?'

Work out the responses his wife might give if she were discounting on each of the diagonals in the discount matrix.

Confirm that the 'hierarchy of discounts' applies. ●

Using the discount matrix

Whenever a problem is not being solved, some information relevant to the solution of that problem is being ignored. The discount matrix gives us a systematic way of pinpointing what information is being missed. This in turn provides guidance to the specific actions we need to take to solve the problem.

You'll recall that if a person is discounting on any given diagonal of the matrix, she will also be discounting in all the boxes below and to the right of that diagonal. This gives us an important clue to the process of problem-solving. When a problem remains unsolved despite efforts to solve it, this is often because the person *is addressing the problem on too low a diagonal of the discount matrix.*

It follows that in using the matrix as a problem-solving tool, we need to begin by looking for discounts *on the highest diagonal first.* We step into the matrix at the top left-hand corner. If we discover a discount there, we need to deal with that discount before going any further downwards or to the right.

Why? Because if we miss that initial discount and try to deal with a discount on any lower diagonal, *our intervention will itself be discounted.*

Let's illustrate this by referring back to the example about the smoker and his concerned friend. Suppose you are that friend. As you listen to the smoker's hacking cough, you say to yourself: 'He's going to kill himself if he doesn't stop smoking. Something needs to be done about this.'

So you say out loud: 'I'm concerned about you. Please give up smoking.'

With your intervention, you have addressed the problem on the lowest diagonal of the box. The issue is whether the smoker is going to act on a specific option.

But suppose the smoker is discounting much higher on the matrix? For example, he may be on diagonal T_2. This will mean he is aware that he has a hacking cough. But he does not regard this as being of any concern to him. He does not perceive it as a problem. In terms of the discount matrix, he is discounting the significance of the stimulus and the existence of the problem.

It's obvious, then, that he will also discount any relevance in what you have just said to him. Why should he have any investment in stopping smoking when, as far as he is aware, his smokers' cough is not a problem?

Since you can't read his mind, you have no way of knowing where he is discounting until he responds to you. And notice here an important point: he may respond from the highest diagonal on which he is discounting, but may also respond *from any diagonal below it.*

For instance, suppose he replies: 'Hm, yes, I know I should give up, but I think once you're hooked on this habit, you're hooked on it.' This is a discount of the solvability of problems, making it look as though he is discounting on diagonal T_4.

The temptation for you then is to start into an exposition of the evidence that people can, in fact, give up smoking. But you will get nowhere with this. The smoker is really discounting on T_2. Thus, outside of his awareness, he is saying to himself: 'So, people can give up smoking. What's that got to do with me? This cough of mine is no problem anyway.'

Suppose now you wanted to help your smoking friend by systematically using the discount matrix. You would begin by checking for a discount on diagonal T_1. 'Are you aware that you've got a really bad cough?'

If he confirms he is aware of the cough, you would go down to the next diagonal. You might ask: 'Is that cough of yours something you bother about?' Were he to reply 'No, not really, it's something I just take for granted,' you would have located his discount on T_2. This lets you know that if your smoker friend is to give up his habit, he first needs to become aware that his cough may indicate a problem. He needs to realize too that this problem may be a cause for his concern.

● Use this technique to review your personal example of a problem situation you did not solve at the time.

Beginning at the top left of the discount matrix, check each box, working downwards on successive diagonals, until you identify the box in which you were discounting. As before, if you are working in a group or with a willing friend, it may be helpful if you get a second opinion.

Test whether you were also discounting in all the other boxes on the same diagonal and those below it.

What was the area of the discount? Were you discounting yourself, others or the environment?

When you have identified the discount, consider its ego-state source. Did it come from a contamination? An exclusion? Or were you uninformed or misinformed?

Let yourself be aware of whatever part of reality you had previously been discounting. If you need accurate or new information, get it.

Now re-run the situation in your mind's eye. When you come to the point at which you began to discount, replace the discount with your full awareness of reality. How do you now act, think or feel differently? How does this alter the outcome of the situation? ●

The discount matrix was originally developed for use in psychotherapy. But it provides an equally effective tool for problem-solving in organizations and education. In these settings also, it is common for problems to remain unsolved because they are being addressed on too low a diagonal in the discount matrix. The remedy remains the same: to identify the information which is being missed, start at the top left corner of the matrix and check downwards through the diagonals. Bear in mind that people often discount because they are misinformed or uninformed, rather than because they are getting into script.

For instance, picture a university teacher with a class of his students. He asks them questions to check their understanding of his recent lectures. To his dismay, they can answer hardly any. When the class finishes, the lecturer tells himself: 'These students just haven't been working. What's the trouble? Why have they no motivation?'

By assuming that the students have not been working, he is addressing a discount in the area of 'others', on diagonal T_5 or T_6 of the discount matrix. He has assumed that his students know they may have problems if they don't work, but that they either don't feel they can handle the work or just aren't getting started to it.

If the lecturer were to check through the discount matrix, he would discover that the real problem is quite different. The fact is that when he is lecturing, he mumbles. The students can't hear what he is saying. The discount is on diagonal T_2 of the matrix. To address the problem, the lecturer simply needs to speak up.

Chapter 19
FRAME OF REFERENCE AND REDEFINING

I have my way of perceiving the world. You have your way, and it will be different from mine.

Suppose you and I stand outside a window, and look at the room within. We report to each other what we see.

I say: 'It's a fairly small room. It's square in shape. There are people in it. The carpet is green and the curtains brown.'

You report: 'It's a family scene. The whole atmosphere is warm. There's Mother, Father and two kids, and they're talking and laughing. It's a big room, so they have plenty of space.'

Judging by these reports, a listener might think you and I were looking at two completely different rooms. But the room is the same. It is our perception of it that is different. Were we each to report on what we were hearing, feeling, smelling or tasting as we looked into that room, the chances are that our reports of these perceptions would differ also.

What is more, it's probable that you and I would respond to that scene in different ways. I might feel nothing in particular, and walk away after viewing the room for a few minutes. You might feel happy, knock on the window and open a conversation with the people inside.

Thus, you and I differ in how we perceive the scene and how we respond to it. Your *frame of reference* is different from mine.

The frame of reference

The frame of reference is defined by the Schiffs as *the structure of associated responses which integrates the various ego-states in response to specific stimuli.* It provides the individual with '...an overall perceptual, conceptual, affective and action set, which is used to define the self, other people and the world...'[1]

To help explain this formal definition, the Schiffs say that the frame of reference can be thought of as a 'filter on reality'. As you and I looked at the room, each of us filtered out certain parts of the scene. For instance, I noted the color of the carpet, but filtered out the identities of the people in the room. From your frame of reference, you did the opposite.

We also *defined* the size of the room differently. To me, it was 'fairly small'. To you, it was 'big'. It so happens that I was brought up in an old house in the country, where all the rooms had been large. You spent your childhood in a city flat where the rooms were pocket-sized. Thus the definition of 'a big room' in our respective frames of reference is different.

You added another definition. You said: 'The whole atmosphere is warm'. I had not defined 'atmosphere', and had not even perceived it as part of the scene.

Now suppose you ask me if I agree with you that the atmosphere is warm. I might reply: 'No, I certainly don't.' You may wonder how I could possibly disagree with you so flatly. Aren't the family in the room talking and laughing openly with each other? How could there be a warmer atmosphere than that?

But then I add: 'Warm atmosphere? No, that carpet is completely the wrong color. They need an orange or red one. And look at those grey walls!' You and I have encountered another way in which people's frames of reference often differ. We have each used the same words. But the *meanings* we attach to the words are quite different. The definition of 'a warm atmosphere', in this case, differs between your frame of reference and mine.

Frame of reference and ego-states

As a further aid to understanding the frame of reference, the Schiffs suggest that it can be thought of as a 'skin that surrounds the ego-states, binding them together'. As I perceive the world according to my unique frame of reference, I make my own unique set of ego-state responses to that perceived world. It's in this way that the frame of reference 'integrates the various ego-states'.

As you and I looked into the room, I got into Adult and made a comment on shapes, sizes and colors I saw in the here-and-now. You were in Child, re-playing happy memories of family scenes like this which you had enjoyed in your own childhood. Having made these ego-state shifts internally, we transacted with each other externally from the ego-states we had chosen.

Our frame of reference gives us the patterns in which we integrate our ego-state responses so as to express our overall personality.

Role of the Parent

The Parent ego-state plays a particularly important part in the formation of the frame of reference. This is because our frame of reference consists of *definitions* of the world, self and others. It is from our parents and parent-figures that we originally learn these definitions. Depending on the age at which we receive them, they may be filed away as part of the content of our own Parent ego-state (P_2) or of the Parent in the Child (P_1).

Each of us has a personal set of Parental definitions of what is good, bad, wrong, right, scary, easy, difficult, dirty, clean, fair, unfair, and so on. It is on this set of definitions that we base our views of self, others and the world. We choose our responses to situations accordingly.

Frame of reference and the script

What is the relationship between the script and the frame of reference? The answer is that the script *forms part of* the frame of reference. The frame of reference in total is made up of a large number of definitions. Some of these definitions will entail discounts, while others will not. The script consists of *all the definitions in the frame of reference which entail discounts.*

When I get into script, I am ignoring features of the here-and-now situation which would be relevant to the solution of a problem. I am discounting. In doing so, I am replaying outdated definitions of myself, others and the world which include those discounts.

For instance, as a child I may have received messages from my parents telling me I was not able to think. Now suppose that as a grown-up, I am about to take an examination. If I get into script at this point, I begin internally replaying the old Parental definition of myself that says: 'You can't think!' Agreeing with this in my Child ego-state, I accept the discount of my own thinking ability. I begin to feel inadequate and confused.

Nature and function of redefining

In this example, the reality of the situation is that I am able to think. Thus in accepting the old definition of myself as unable to think, I have *distorted my perception of reality so that it fits my script.* This process is called *redefining.*[2]

You learned in Part IV that the child makes script decisions because they seem to be the best way of surviving and getting by in a hostile world. In my Child ego-state as a grown-up, I may cling to these early decisions, because I am still clinging to the belief that they are necessary for my survival. Thus if some feature of reality seems to challenge my script decisions, I am likely to defend against it. Putting this idea into Schiffian language, we say: when my scripty frame of reference is threatened, I defend against the threat by redefining.

As a child, I accepted my parents' definition of me as 'unable to think'. I made this script decision because I believed it was the only way I had of surviving and getting my needs met. Now as I get into script as a grown-up, I re-run this old survival strategy. I redefine reality by discounting my own ability to think.

This does not help me solve the problem, which is to pass the examination. But outside my awareness, in my Child ego-state, I am following a motive that seems more important than any examination could be. That is: to defend against the unspeakable disaster I fear may happen if I challenge my parents' definition.

Redefining transactions

When I redefine, I do so internally. How will you know from my outward behavior whether or not I am redefining?

The only external clue is that you will see or hear me discounting. Thus, the signals of discounting are the external manifestation that redefining is taking place internally. Every discount represents a distortion of reality.

In Chapter 17, you learned to recognize a whole range of behavioral clues which indicate that someone is discounting. These same clues, then, also tell you that the person is redefining. We also know someone is redefining if he shows grandiosity or a thinking disorder, which are typical accompaniments to discounting.

There are two distinctive transactions that give clear verbal evidence of redefining. They are the *tangential transaction* and the *blocking transaction.*

Tangential transactions

A tangential transaction is one in which *the stimulus and response address different issues, or address the same issue from different perspectives.*

For example, a therapist asks a group member: 'How do you feel?' She replies: 'Well, when we spoke about this in the group yesterday, I felt angry.' With her response, she addresses the issue of how she feels, but from the perspective of yesterday instead of today.

Or, at a wage negotiation, a union representative asks: 'What do you want from our side so we can conclude this agreement?' The personnel manager answers: 'We're not at all satisfied with the conditions you've proposed so far.' Here, the issue has been shifted from 'wanting' to 'feeling satisfied with'.

Everyday conversation is full of tangential transactions. When people are in situations they perceive as stressful, they are even more likely to redefine in this way. This is not surprising, because in stressful situations people are likely to begin perceiving threats to their frame of reference. The covert purpose of going off on a tangent is to divert the other person away from the issue which constitutes the threat. The person who initiates the tangential transaction will not be consciously aware she is doing so.

Often, the other person will follow the tangent, rather than sticking with the original topic. He may even go off on a further tangent of his own. For example:

Union representative: 'What do you want from our side so we can conclude this agreement?'

Personnel manager: 'We're not at all satisfied with the conditions you've proposed so far.'

U.R.: 'No, and we're not satisfied with what you've proposed either.'

P.M.: 'Oh? So what would you need from us that would satisfy you?'

U.R.: 'Ah, the trouble is, I'm not sure you can deliver what we need...'

When people get into an exchange of tangential transactions, they are likely to have an uncomfortable sense that their conversation is 'getting nowhere', or 'going around in circles'. On the psychological level, that is exactly what is intended. Conversations like these can go on for a long time. The participants may feel they have been working hard, and end up feeling drained. By the close of their discussion, they may have never gotten back to the original issue they had intended to address.

Blocking transactions

In a blocking transaction, *the purpose of raising an issue is avoided by disagreeing about the definition of the issue.*

Examples might be:

Therapist: 'How do you feel?'
Group member: 'Do you mean emotionally or physically?'

Union representative: 'What do you want from our side so we can conclude this agreement?'
Personnel manager: 'Are you talking about what we want, or what we think we can get?'

You will seldom hear long exchanges of blocking transactions. It is more likely that after the initial block, the parties will begin detailed arguments over the definition of the issue. Or, if one of the people concerned is a really determined blocker, the conversation may come to a halt in a dumbfounded silence. At the psychological level, the aim of the blocking transaction is the same as that of the tangential: to avoid addressing issues that would threaten the frame of reference of either or both participants.

● In a group: form small groups of three. In each small group, decide who is going to be 'client', who 'counselor' and who 'observer'.

The client chooses any topic he wishes. He and the counselor talk about that topic for three minutes. (The observer, or the group leader if there is one, keeps time.)

The client's task is to respond tangentially to *everything* the counselor says. Each time the client goes off on a tangent, the counselor is to follow him off on the new topic. The client then takes off on yet another tangent, and so on. The aim is for the client to keep up a continuous chain of tangential transactions for the whole three minutes.

When that time is up, take another two minutes for the client and counselor to discuss their experience, and for the observer to report what she heard and saw.

Change roles and repeat until everyone has had a turn in each role.

Now re-run the exercise, but with one difference: this time, the counselor is *not* to go with the client's tangents. Instead, each time the client offers a tangent, the counselor is to find ways of pulling the client back to the original topic. The client's task is still to entice the counselor away on as many tangents as he can manage. Repeat as before until everyone has played each role.

Now do a similar two-part exercise, but using blocking transactions instead of tangential transactions. Again, in the first part of the exercise the counselor is to allow the client to block her. In the second part, the counselor is to use her ingenuity to avoid being blocked, while the client keeps up his efforts to block every transaction.

Finally discuss how your experience of the exercise using blocking transactions differed from that of the exercise using tangential transactions. ●

Because you are doing this exercise with Adult awareness, your exchanges will be role-plays of tangential and blocking transactions, rather than actual instances of these transactions. But the exercise gives you practice in recognizing and confronting the tangents and blocks which people may use without awareness.

Chapter 20
SYMBIOSIS

In Schiffian theory, a *symbiosis* is said to occur *when two or more individuals behave as though between them they form a single person.*[1]

In a relationship like this, the people concerned will not be using their full complement of ego-states. Typically, one of them will be excluding Child and using only Parent and Adult. The other will take the opposite position, staying in Child while shutting out her other two ego-states. Thus they have access to a total of only three ego-states between them. This is pictured in Figure 20.1.

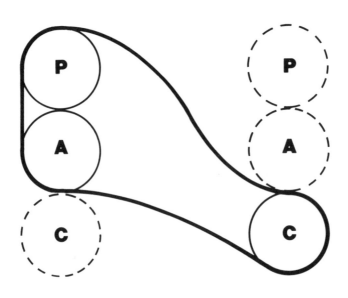

_ _ : Ego—states not utilized

━━ : Symbiosis

Figure 20.1 Symbiosis

For instance, imagine a lecturer taking a tutorial class with his students. They are working through some exercises on theory. The lecturer writes an exercise up on the board. Turning to one of the students, he asks: 'OK, Jim, will you tell us how you'd work through the next steps of this and get to the solution?'

Jim says nothing. Instead, he sits silent and unmoving for a while. Then he begins to waggle his foot rapidly up and down and rub the side of his head. Still he does not say a word.

The silence drags on. The other students in the class start to fidget as well. Finally the lecturer says: 'Seems like you don't know this one, Jim. Really, you *should* be working harder on your revision. Now, here's what we do to get the solution...' And he completes the exercise on the board.

Jim relaxes, stops waggling his foot, and dutifully makes notes of the solution the lecturer has provided.

At this point, student and lecturer have moved into a symbiosis. By denying his own ability to reason out a solution, and covertly manipulating for the lecturer to take charge of the situation, Jim has discounted his own Adult and Parent ego-states.

The lecturer, obligingly providing the solution while giving Jim a 'should' about his revision, has stepped into the complementary role of Adult and Parent. In doing so, the lecturer has discounted his own Child ego-state. Had he allowed himself to use his Child resources, he'd have become aware that he was feeling uncomfortable and unsatisfied with the exchange that was going on between Jim and himself. He would have tuned in to an intuition: 'Hey, I've just been conned into doing all the work around here, and I don't like it!' Using that Child perception, he might have been able to find a creative way of facilitating Jim and the other students to work out the problem for themselves.

As it was, the lecturer shut out his own Child feeling of discomfort. Instead, he sought comfort by taking up his familiar symbiotic role of Adult and Parent.

Jim, too, relaxed and felt more comfortable as soon as he had settled into his familiar Child role.

That's the trouble with symbiosis. Once a symbiosis has been established, the participants *feel* comfortable. There's a sense that everybody is in the role that is expected of them. But that comfort is acquired at a price: the people in the symbiosis are each shutting out whole areas of their own grown-up resources.

In everyday relating, people move into and out of symbiosis with each other from moment to moment. Sometimes also, a long-term relationship is founded upon symbiosis. This is true of Bill and Betty, who exemplify one picture of a 'traditional' married couple. Bill is the strong, silent type. With a pipe clamped in his jaw, he expresses himself in grunts. Come joy or disaster, Bill keeps his feelings firmly behind a granite facade. He looks after all the household finances, giving Betty a weekly allowance. When there's a decision to be made, Bill makes it, and tells Betty afterwards.

Betty, for her part, sees her mission in life as being to please her husband. She's happy to go along with his decisions, because, she tells her friends, 'she likes a strong man to lean on'. If a household emergency arises, Betty dissolves into tears, panic or giggles, and waits for Bill to come home and sort it out.

Some of their friends wonder occasionally how Bill manages to get along with Betty's helplessness. Others marvel that Betty can keep relating to Bill when he's so unfeeling. But in fact, their marriage has lasted a good many years, and looks set to last for many more. They gain their stability from being in symbiosis. Bill plays Parent and Adult to Betty's Child. Within that symbiosis, each 'needs' the other. And as always in symbiosis, the stability they experience is bought at the price of discounting a part of each person's capabilities. Over time, they will each build up resentment at having been discounted, which is likely to cause some distancing in their relationship.

● If you are working individually, find someone who is willing to do this pairwork exercise with you. In a group, get into pairs.

For the first part of the exercise, find a way of making contact in your pair so that each of you is propping the other one up physically. For instance, you might turn back-to-back and lean together. Or you might put the palms of your outstretched hands against those of your partner, then both move your feet back so that each person is bearing part of the other's weight.

Once you have found this mutual leaning position, stay in it a while. Be aware what you are feeling and thinking as you do so, but do not put this in words to your partner yet.

Next, one of you should make just the beginning of a movement out of the leaning position. Make the movement large enough to give the other person the feel of how it would be if you moved away completely. (Do not move away so far that the other person actually falls down). Then the one who has moved gets back into the mutual leaning position, and the other person takes a turn to make a move out. Register what you experience when you are the person who remains in the leaning position and the other person begins to move away from you.

For the second part of the exercise, find a way of making contact in your pair so that you are still touching, but each is bearing his or her own weight. For example, you might again place the palms of your hands against your partner's, but this time have each person stand upright instead of leaning on each other. Stay in this self-balanced position for a while. Register to yourself what you experience. How does this differ from what you experienced in the first part of the exercise?

Now have one partner break the contact. For example, if you have been standing with your hands touching, one of you might simply lower his hands. Register your experience when you are the person who is staying still and the other person breaks contact with you. How does this experience differ from that in the first part of the exercise, when the two of you were leaning together and the other person began to move away?

After a while, the partner who has broken contact makes that contact again. Repeat several times breaking and re-making contact, all the while with both partners bearing their own weight.

Run through this sequence again, with the other partner being the one who breaks and makes contact.

Take time to share your experiences with your partner. ●

The first part of this exercise is designed to literally 'give you the feel' of symbiosis. When the two of you are leaning on each other, most people report they feel 'comfortable' or 'supported'. But some also say they feel apprehensive in case the other person will move away and let them fall down. Almost everyone becomes aware of this apprehension when their partner does draw away slightly.

This illustrates another feature of actual symbiosis. When one of the partners perceives that the other is about to withdraw from the symbiotic pairing, she is likely to defend against this withdrawal. Her belief is: 'Without the other, I won't be able to stand on my own'. Paradoxically, it's this belief which gives symbiosis its apparent quality of stability.

Recall Bill and Betty, the strong silent husband and little-woman wife. Imagine that some of Betty's friends tell her about a women's group they have started, and that she joins it. She becomes uncomfortable with her Child role in the symbiosis. She starts questioning some of Bill's decisions. Instead of pleasing him all the time, she starts pleasing herself also. She learns assertiveness techniques, and starts practicing some of them on her husband. What do you guess Bill's reaction will be?

The chances are that he will start escalating in an attempt to keep Betty in the symbiosis. He is likely to ignore or ridicule Betty's new assertiveness. He may get coldly withdrawn or openly angry when she fails to have the dinner ready for him or doesn't bring his slippers.

Bill may succeed in his attempts to invite Betty back into the symbiosis. If he does not, their relationship may be in for a stormy period.

Another possibility is that Bill himself will change his attitudes and move out of the symbiosis. Perhaps he will do this on his own, perhaps by joining a group or going into therapy.

If so, the relationship between Betty and himself will change and become more like what you experienced in the second part of the exercise. Now, you were still making contact with the other person, but the two of you were standing up independently instead of leaning on each other. One of you could break contact, and the two of you were still standing. The contact could be made and broken at will, and yet neither person fell down.

There's no guarantee that you will feel more *comfortable* in this independent position than you did in the mutual leaning position. In fact, many people report feeling less comfortable in the second part of the exercise than in the first. They are aware that they have more options — of moving, breaking and making contact — than they had when they were propping each other up. That's how it often is when two people move out of symbiosis in a relationship. They have more options, more flexibility, less predictability, and no guarantee of feeling more comfortable initially.

'Healthy' v. 'unhealthy' symbiosis

There are some situations in which it's appropriate for people to be in symbiosis. For example, suppose I have just come out from under the anaesthetic after an operation. I'm lying on a trolley being wheeled down a hospital corridor. I'm not very sure yet where I am, but I am sure of one thing: I'm hurting. Apart from the pain, the main thing I'm aware of is that a nurse is walking along beside me, holding my hand and telling me: 'You'll be all right. Just hang on to my hand.'

At that point, my Adult and Parent are out of commission. I am in no condition to start assessing here-and-now problems. I don't have the energy to access the messages I got from my parents about how to look after myself. I am doing what is appropriate for me to do: regressing to being a child again, feeling my pain and letting myself be cared for.

The nurse is giving me the Adult and Parent input that I need. She is dealing with current problems while giving me protection and reassurance. This is her job, so she also is appropriately in her symbiotic position.

In Schiffian terms, we say that the nurse and I are in a *healthy symbiosis*. This is contrasted with *unhealthy symbiosis*, illustrated by the examples given earlier in this chapter. When the word 'symbiosis' is used alone, it normally implies unhealthy symbiosis.

How do we distinguish formally between healthy and unhealthy symbiosis? The answer is that a symbiosis will be unhealthy whenever it involves *discounting*. In the examples of symbiosis between the student and the lecturer, and between Bill and Betty, the parties were each discounting reality by acting as though they only had three ego-states between them. By contrast, when I was being wheeled along on that hospital trolley, the reality was that my Adult and Parent were out of action because of the trauma and the effects of the anaesthetic. The nurse was indeed using her Parent and Adult. But she wasn't necessarily discounting her own Child while she did so.

Symbiosis v. normal dependency

One obvious example of a healthy symbiosis is that which exists between a child and his parent. When the baby is born, he is all Child. He doesn't yet have the capacity to solve problems or protect himself. These functions need to be performed by the parent, who will appropriately use Adult and Parent ego-states in doing so. Stan Woollams and Kristy Huige have suggested the term *normal dependency* to denote this healthy parent-child symbiosis.[2]

Recall that in a healthy symbiosis, the parties are not discounting *any* of their ego-states. The infant does not yet have a functioning Parent or Adult, so they cannot be discounted. However, the parent does have a Child ego-state. To avoid slipping into unhealthy symbiosis, she needs to stay aware of her own Child needs and find some way of getting these met, even while she is closely involved in caring for her infant.

Symbiosis and the script

Thus in ideal parenting, the child's caretaker will be employing Parent and Adult resources appropriately, while still not discounting her own Child. As the child grows, the parent will provide him with what is needed to complete each stage of development. At each stage, the child acquires more and more of his own resources, and so has less and less need to lean on the parent. Ideally, the parent encourages the child in this appropriate separation, while continuing to provide support in the areas where the child still needs it.

In this ideal process, the initial intense symbiosis between child and parent is progressively broken.[3] The final result is that by the time the child reaches young adulthood, both parties are relating without symbiosis. Each is able to stand independently, making or breaking contact at will.

The trouble is that there are no ideal parents. No matter how good a job Mother and Father make of parenting, every child goes through the process of development with some needs unmet along the way.

This fact reveals the scripty *function* of symbiosis in adult life. *Every symbiosis is an attempt to get developmental needs met which were not met during the person's childhood.*

As always with scripty behavior, the person in symbiosis is using outdated strategies in his attempt to get needs met. These strategies were the best he could work out as a young child, but are no longer appropriate in grown-up life. In symbiosis, the person is *discounting* grown-up options. The discounting is outside his awareness.

Whenever we get into symbiosis, we are unwittingly re-playing old childhood situations where we felt an unmet need. We once again set up the relationship that existed in the past between ourselves and a parent or parent-figure, and re-run the situation in an attempt to manipulate the other into satisfying the need which was not met.

Choice of symbiotic position

You may be thinking: 'OK, so if symbiosis is a re-play of old childhood situations, I can see why people get into the Child role in symbiosis. But why should anybody choose to be in the Parent role?'

The answer is that some children make an early decision: 'The parenting around here is so ineffective that my best option is to take over as parent myself.' Perhaps Mother, in her own Child ego-state, was scared to set firm boundaries for her children. Instead, she blackmailed them by saying things like: 'If you do that, you'll hurt me', or 'Look — you're making Father angry!' The child was being asked to take responsibility for the parents' feelings and welfare. He might respond by deciding that his job in life was to look after his parents. Thus, in effect, he became a little parent himself. In grown-up life, he may re-enter this role in symbiosis.

Other children, who perceive their parents as abusive or oppressive, may take up the life position 'I'm OK, you're not-OK' and fantasize about putting their parents down from a Parental position. This, again, is replayed in their grown-up symbiotic relationships.

Symbiotic invitations

When people meet, they are adept at signaling to each other what symbiotic role they want to take up. These *symbiotic invitations* are often conveyed without words. Usually, one or more of the four passive behaviors will be shown.

In the example which opened this chapter, Jim made his symbiotic invitation first by doing nothing, then by agitation. When he sat silent and then began to fidget, he was conveying to the lecturer the covert message: 'I need you to think for me and tell me how things are.' His symbiotic invitation was for the lecturer to take up Parent and Adult roles, while he took up Child.

By going ahead and completing the exercise, the lecturer was agreeing on that same psychological level: 'Yes, you're right. You do need me to think for you and tell you how things are.' As he did so, he accepted Jim's symbiotic invitation.

Sometimes a symbiotic invitation may be conveyed in words. When this happens, the person will be heard manipulating for what she wants, rather than asking directly. This is often done subtly. For instance, a member of a therapy group may look forlornly down at the floor and say: 'I need a hug.' The temptation is for other group members to go ahead and give her the hug she seems to have asked for. But if they do so, they will have accepted her symbiotic invitation. Had she asked for the hug in a non-symbiotic manner, she would have looked at one particular member of the group and said: 'Will you give me a hug?'

Competitive symbiosis

But what happens when two people meet who both want to take up the same symbiotic role? If they both want to be Parent, or both seek to act Child?

When this is so, the parties will begin 'jockeying for position' in the hope of taking up their preferred symbiotic role. For example, you may have heard this kind of exchange in a restaurant as two people prepare to pay up after the meal:

'Now, put that money away. I'll pay for this.'

'No, no, come on, *I'll* pay.'

'I absolutely insist! Not another word!'

These transactions may go on for some time, with each party escalating insistence on paying. Each is seeking to be Parent to the other. They are in a *competitive symbiosis* — in this case, competing for the Parent position.

By its nature, competitive symbiosis is unstable. Exchanges like this usually last only for a relatively short time. They may conclude in two possible ways. The parties may storm away from each other, slamming doors as they go. Or one of them may back down and yield the desired symbiotic position to the other. The one who has backed down then takes the complementary position in the symbiosis.

For instance, the exchange in the restaurant might end with one of the parties saying: 'Ah, well, if you insist...' and putting away his wallet with a show of reluctance. He has backed down to the Child position, allowing himself to be 'looked after' by the other person.

● Make up another example of a competitive symbiosis for the Parent position, ending with one of the parties backing down to Child.

Diagram the transactions that take place during the exchange.

What positions on the OK Corral would you say each party visits during the competition, and after one of them backs down?

Make up an example of a Child-competitive symbiosis, ending with one of the parties backing down and reluctantly taking the Parent role. Again diagram the transactions and analyze the OK-Corral positions.

Draw a transactional diagram for the exchange between Jim and the lecturer, in which Jim issued his symbiotic invitation and the lecturer accepted it.

What do you think might be important counterinjunctions and injunctions in Jim's script matrix? In the lecturer's? In Bill's and in Betty's? ●

Second-order symbiosis

In some symbiotic relationships, there's a second symbiosis going on underneath the first. It takes the form shown in Figure 20.2. This kind of

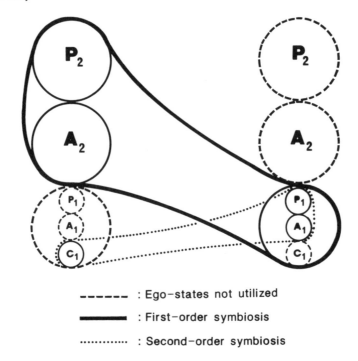

------ : Ego-states not utilized

▬▬▬ : First-order symbiosis

············ : Second-order symbiosis

Figure 20.2 Second-order symbiosis

symbiosis is called a *second-order symbiosis* because it occurs within the second-order structure of the Child ego-state.

Relationships between couples like Bill and Betty often entail second-order symbiosis. On first impression, it seems clear that Bill is in the Parent-Adult role in their symbiosis, while Betty plays Child. He gets to be in control and to deal with practical problems. She gets to be controlled and express feelings. And on the level of first-order symbiosis, that is indeed what is going on. Bill is re-playing an early decision: 'The only way I can get by is to be in charge and in tight control of everybody, including myself.' Betty's decision was: 'My mission in life is to please others, especially men, and not to think about things.' The first-order symbiosis represents their joint efforts to get their needs met through these script decisions.

However, Bill has yet another need. It is even further below his awareness than the need to be in charge and in control, and it comes from an earlier stage of his development. That is the need for physical strokes and comfort. We show this as part of the content of Bill's C_1, the early Child in the Child.

The trouble for Bill is that in making his later script decisions, he shut out those early Child needs. So how is he to get them met now? The answer is that in choosing Betty as his symbiotic partner, he adeptly picked someone who would take up the complementary role in the second-order symbiosis.

Betty's mother, like Betty herself, had married a strong, silent man who was not keen to give physical strokes. When Betty was an infant, her father had not been around much. He had preferred to spend his time at work or out drinking with his friends. Mother had had no other grown-up to satisfy her own early Child needs for stroking and being looked after.

With her acute infant perception, Betty had decided without words: 'To keep Mother around and in good shape, I'd better look after her myself.' Using her own rudimentary Parent and Adult, P_1 and A_1, she became caretaker to her mother's Somatic Child. Now in grown-up symbiosis, she replays this pattern with Bill.

A symbiosis like this may be particularly difficult to break. Recall that stroking is a survival issue for the early Child. Thus in this example, if Betty makes to break out of the symbiosis, Bill in his Somatic Child may experience mortal terror. His Child belief is that he is about to lose his only source of physical strokes, and that means death.

At the same early Child level, Betty may perceive breaking the symbiosis as meaning the loss of Mother. To the infant, this also implies a death sentence.

It's likely that neither Bill nor Betty will allow this early Child terror into their awareness. Instead, they are likely to find rationalizations of why they should continue in their symbiotic relationship. If they do want to break out of that relationship, they may need script insight and therapeutic help.

Part VI
JUSTIFYING OUR
SCRIPT BELIEFS

Rackets and Games

Chapter 21
RACKETS AND STAMPS

Here's an exercise to start this chapter. We suggest you do it before reading on. If you are working in a group, have the group leader or a volunteer lead the rest of the group through the scene, improvising on the instructions which follow.

● In this exercise, you will be asked to imagine a scene, and then to answer a few questions about it. There are no 'right' or 'wrong' answers.

Imagine that tomorrow is going to mark the beginning of a holiday period in your area, a time when all the shops will be shut for several days.

Imagine too that it's quite some time since you did any shopping. You are almost out of essential food and provisions. Looking at the time, you realize with relief that you've just got long enough to get down to the supermarket and get around it before it closes.

Mentally checking a list of the things you need to buy, you set off for the supermarket. Arriving there, you see a crowd of other shoppers on the same mission as yourself, stocking up before the holiday closing period begins.

Keeping an eye on the time, you go round the shelves collecting the items you want. As you finish, you note with satisfaction that there are still just a few minutes to go before the store closes. You'll have plenty of time to get through the checkout.

You get to the checkout desk. The clerk enters your purchases on the cash-till, and tells you the total cost.

You reach for your money. And you can't find it. You search again, and still it isn't there. You realize why: you have left it at home. In your haste, you have come to the supermarket without any money. You don't have a credit card or cheques either.

As a line of shoppers builds up behind you, you tell the clerk what's happened. You ask: 'Would it be OK for me to leave my name and address, take the goods away and come back to pay you after the holiday?' The clerk replies: 'No, I'm afraid that isn't possible.'

You don't have time now to go home and get your money before the store closes. So you won't get your goods. You'll have to go without them. And it will be several days before the shops open again.

As you realize this, *how do you feel?*

Register how you are feeling, and give a name to that emotion. Then come out of the imagined scene. ●

Keep note of the feeling you registered. Whenever people do this exercise, the emotions they report at the end have certain typical characteristics. We will list these below. Check whether each one applies to the emotion that you registered.

(1) Different people report different feelings. If you are working in a group, go around and ask each member to name the emotion he or she felt at the end of the scene. Have someone note these up as each person reports.

The scene itself was the same for everybody. But you'll discover that the people in the group report a whole range of different emotions. Typically, the list of different feelings may read: 'Angry at myself, panicky, embarrassed, angry at the clerk, sick, blank...' The bigger the group, the greater the range of different feelings that will be reported.

If you are working individually, you can test this by finding some willing friends who will go through the scene and report their feelings at the end.

(2) The feeling registered is one that you experience in a wide range of different stress situations. For example, if I report at the end of this scene that I feel 'angry at myself', it's likely that I would also report feeling angry at myself in many other situations where I felt under stress. If you reported feeling 'panicky', then you would probably report that same bad feeling in different situations.

It's as if each of us has a 'favorite bad feeling' which we bring up for all-purpose use when we perceive things getting tough. Some people have a choice of two or three bad feelings to use in this way. They may keep one for use at home, another for work, and so on.

(3) The feeling registered is one that was modeled or encouraged in your family, while other feelings were discouraged or prohibited. For instance, if you registered feeling 'angry at someone else', it's likely that this feeling was shown frequently by your parents and family members when you were a child. When you yourself showed it, you would get some kind of recognition for doing so.

There would be a whole range of other feelings that were seldom or never shown in your family. In this example, while it was acceptable to be angry in your family, it may not have been considered OK to be sad, scared or happy. If you showed any of these other feelings you'd find that you either got scolded for it, or — worse still for you as a child — just got ignored.

(4) The emotion you felt did nothing towards solving your problem. If I got angry and started shouting at the clerk, that would do nothing to get me the goods I'd wanted. Whether I felt panicky, sick, blank, angry at myself, or any of the other feelings people typically report, none of these

emotions would help me in the slightest to get my purchases out of that supermarket.

These characteristics are typical of the kind of emotion that TA calls a *racket feeling.*[1]

In the sections which follow we discuss the nature and function of racket feelings. They are important to understand, because they play a central role in the way people live out their scripts.

Definitions of 'racket' and 'racket feeling'

There has been a lot of confusion in the TA literature about the meaning of the terms 'racket' and 'racket feeling'. Some writers have used the two terms interchangeably.

In this book, we don't do this. We follow another school of thought that says there is a useful distinction to be made between rackets and racket feelings.

We define a *racket feeling* as *a familiar emotion, learned and encouraged in childhood, experienced in many different stress situations, and maladaptive as an adult means of problem-solving.*

We define a *racket* as *a set of scripty behaviors, employed outside awareness as a means of manipulating the environment, and entailing the person's experiencing a racket feeling.*

In other words, a racket is a process in which someone sets up to feel a racket feeling, and feels that feeling. The set-up is outside the person's conscious awareness.

For instance, in our imagined scene where I came away without my money, I had set up to feel the bad feeling I experienced at the end. I *could* have made sure I had the money with me, but I didn't. If you were to ask me why I didn't, I might answer: 'I just didn't think of it.'

The outcome of the events which the person has set up is seen as 'justifying' the racket feeling. Suppose that as I stood at the checkout desk, I felt furious at the clerk. You might ask me: 'How come you're angry at the clerk?' My answer might be: 'Well, I'm not going to get my goods, am I?'

Anger at others is my favored racket feeling in stress situations. Five other people might well feel five different bad feelings in that same situation. And they'd all be likely, as I did, to assume that *their* favored racket feeling was the 'natural' way to feel in those circumstances.

Do people always need to set up a racket in order to feel a racket feeling? No. We can also experience a racket feeling in response to independently occurring stress situations, ones which we have genuinely done nothing to set up. For example, imagine yourself making a journey on some form of public transport — plane, train or bus — with a time deadline to meet at your destination. Because of a mechanical fault, your journey is delayed. As you sit there watching the minutes tick away, how do you feel? Chances are that I would feel angry at the transport company. You might feel panicky, another person feel sick, and so on.

Rackets and script

Realize first one universal connection between scripts and rackets: *any time you experience a racket feeling, you are in script.*

Why do racket feelings play such an important part in the mechanism of the script? The answer lies in the way children learn to use racket feelings as a means of getting needs met in their families.

We've seen that racket feelings are learned and encouraged in childhood. Every family has its own restricted range of permitted feelings, and another wider range of feelings that are discouraged or prohibited.

Sometimes the permitted feelings will differ according to whether the child is a boy or girl. Often, little boys are taught that it's OK to be angry and aggressive, but not to be scared or tearful. Little girls may learn that they are supposed to react to stress by crying or being sweet and bubbly, even though they may feel like showing anger.

So what happens, then, if the child does go ahead and show one of the prohibited feelings? Suppose for instance that the little boy gets scared, and shows it. Maybe he's being chased by the local bully. He comes running to Mother, shaking with fright and looking for her protection. Mother looks down her nose at him and says: 'Now, now! Be a brave soldier! Out you go and stand on your own two feet.' Then she gets on with the chores.

The child registers: 'If I get scared and show it, I don't get the results I want around here. I wanted protection and I got ignored instead.'

In his acute Little Professor, the boy casts around for ways he *can* get results in the way he wants. He is likely to test out a whole range of feelings day by day as responses to stress situations. He tries out sadness, cheerfulness, aggressiveness, confusion, blankness, and as many other different feelings as you can name. Suppose he discovers that aggressiveness gets the best response from Mother. Now if the neighborhood bully chases him, he fights back (and loses, because the bully is bigger than he is). Though he's hurting from the bruises, at least he gets approval from Mother: 'That's right. Big boys don't cry!'

He has discovered a feeling that 'gets him the results' he most wants: recognition from his parents. To get the strokes he wants, he needs to show aggression. For sure, he buys these strokes at the cost of hurting. This sequence of events is likely to be repeated over and over again as the little boy continues to grow. With each repetition, he gradually comes to a further conclusion about feelings and their results. 'Except for aggressiveness, no other kinds of feeling seem to be any use around here.

In fact, if I do show any other feelings, my parents take away their support, and that's dangerous. Therefore, I'd best not even let myself *feel* any feelings except aggressiveness.'

Now, each time he begins to feel scared or sad, he hides the feeling even from himself. Instead, he switches straight into getting aggressive.

Rackets and rubberbands

Suppose I was that little boy, and suppose I'm now standing at the checkout desk in the supermarket as the clerk refuses my request for credit.

As I experience the stress of this situation, I hook on to the end of a *rubberband*. I begin reacting as though I were a small child again, back in a stress situation of the past. For me, it's as if the clerk and indeed the whole world were threatening me, just as that neighborhood bully used to threaten when I was little.

In an instant, I do what I learned to do as a child. I get aggressive. Facing up to the clerk, I yell: 'It's disgraceful! Are you trying to say you don't trust me?' The clerk shrugs.

Still fuming with anger, I march stiffly off out of the supermarket. For a few moments I feel a certain grim sense of satisfaction. I say to myself: 'Well, at least I told that clerk where to get off!' But at the same time, I know that all my shouting will not change the fact that I've had to leave my goods behind. I'm still burning up inside, and later that day I get acid indigestion.

My feeling reaction was not of the slightest use to me in solving my here-and-now problem. But outside of awareness, I had been pursuing a motive that was much more important to me than that. *I was attempting to manipulate the environment so as to gain the parental support I gained in childhood by experiencing and showing these racket feelings.*

This is always the function of racket feelings in adulthood. Each time I experience a racket feeling, I am re-playing an outdated childhood strategy. In other words, I am in script.

Setting up rackets

In our example, I had set up the racket, the sequence of events which 'justified' me in experiencing my racket feeling. I had 'accidentally' forgotten to bring my money with me.

Now that we know the script function of racket feelings, we can see why I did so. I set up the racket *so that I could experience the racket feeling*. In my Child, I had been experiencing a need for strokes. So I had arranged to manipulate for those strokes in the way I had learned as a child. I had set up to feel the same feeling that 'got results' for me in my family.

In this way, racket theory gives us an entirely new perspective on why people get bad feelings. Let's return to our supermarket example. The everyday explanation of this would be: 'I went without the goods I needed, therefore I felt angry.'

But with a knowledge of rackets, we'd say instead: 'I wanted to justify feeling angry, therefore I set myself up to go without the goods I needed.'

Racket feelings and authentic feelings

We have explained how children learn that certain feelings are encouraged in their family, while others are discouraged or prohibited. When the child experiences any of the prohibited feelings, he makes a rapid switch into an alternative feeling which is permitted. He may not even allow himself to be aware of the prohibited feeling. When we experience racket feelings in adulthood, we go through the same process. In this way, a racket feeling is always a *substitute* for another feeling, one which was prohibited in our childhood.

To convey this quality of substitution, we refer to racket feelings as *inauthentic* feelings. By contrast, *authentic* feelings are those feelings we experience as young children, *before* we learn to censor them as being discouraged in the family.

This distinction between racket and authentic feelings was first suggested by Fanita English.[2] In her original work, she used the phrase 'real feelings' as a contrast to racket feelings. However, it's more usual nowadays to talk of 'authentic' rather than 'real' feelings. The point here is that when I am experiencing a racket feeling, that feeling is certainly 'real' as far as I am aware. When I started bawling out the clerk, I wasn't feigning anger: I was really angry. But my anger was a racket feeling, not an authentic feeling.

We often speak of a racket feeling as being used to *cover* an authentic feeling. Say for instance that a little girl learns: 'In my family, it's permitted for a girl to be sad, but never angry.' When in script as a grown-up, suppose she is in a situation where she might be about to get angry with somebody. For instance, suppose she is elbowed rudely by somebody on a crowded bus. The instant she begins to feel angry, she moves into her learned childhood pattern almost like a conditioned reflex. Instead of getting angry, she starts feeling sad and perhaps bursts into tears. She has *covered* her authentic anger with inauthentic racket sadness.

Some people not only cover authentic feelings with racket feelings, but also cover one racket with another racket. For example, Robert spent a lot of his early childhood feeling scared in case Mother might abandon him. Without words, he learned that if he showed anger every time he felt scared, he at least got some strokes from Mother. So while he was still an infant, he began covering fear with anger.

When he got a bit older, he discovered that for everybody in his family except small babies, there was a prohibition on showing any feelings at all. In order to fit in with family norms, you were supposed to keep a stiff upper lip and stay blank. Robert then decided: 'I'd better stop even feeling angry, because if I get angry I *will* be in danger of ending up outside the family.' So he joined in with the rest of the family, suppressed his anger just as he had his scare, and covered it with blankness.

Now suppose Robert, in adult life, gets into a situation where his uncensored feeling would be scare. Maybe he perceives that a partner in a relationship is making signals of rejection, and thus is threatening to leave Robert in the position he didn't want to be as a child — alone. The instant Robert begins to feel scared of this, he covers the scare with anger. Just as rapidly, he covers the anger with blankness. As far as he is aware, the blankness is his 'real' feeling. Were you to ask him how he feels, he'd reply: 'I don't feel much, really.'

Naming racket and authentic feelings

What are the authentic feelings, those emotions that we feel when we are not censoring? In TA it's usual to list four of them:

mad
sad
scared
glad.

The word 'mad' is used here in the American sense of 'angry', not the English sense of 'crazy'.

To these we would add various physical sensations that a child can feel, e.g. relaxed, hungry, full, tired, turned-on, disgusted, sleepy, etc.

In contrast to this short list of names for the authentic feelings, you could fill pages and pages with names that people give to their racket feelings. Perhaps you'd like to test this for yourself.

You could start with the inauthentic feelings that would usually be categorized as 'emotions': embarrassment, jealousy, depression, guilt, etc. Then you can add the vaguer terms that express how people feel about themselves when they are in script: lost, stuck, cornered, helpless, desperate, and so on.

Some racket names relate more obviously to thinking than to feeling: confused, blank, puzzled, etc.

Not all racket feelings would be categorized as 'bad' by the people who are experiencing them. Recall our example of the little girl who learned that she was supposed to be sweet and bubbly, even when she really felt angry. As a grown-up, she'll have a reputation of being 'everybody's ray of sunshine'. She may get a lot of strokes for her racket happiness, just as she did when she was a child. Other racket feelings that may be experienced as 'good' are triumphancy, aggressiveness, blamelessness, or euphoria. Nevertheless, all these feelings are inauthentic. They have been learned during childhood and are used in grown-up life as an attempt to manipulate support from the environment.

Another complication in naming feelings is this: the names given to the authentic feelings are *also* given to racket feelings. For instance, you can get authentic anger or racket anger, authentic sadness or racket sadness, and so on. Perhaps I learned as a child to cover anger with confusion, while you learned to cover anger with sadness. Your racket feeling happens to have the same name as one of the authentic feelings. Mine does not. But your inauthentic sadness and my confusion are both racket feelings.

Racket feelings, authentic feelings, and problem-solving

So if racket feelings aren't always experienced as 'bad', why is it important to distinguish between racket and authentic feelings?

The answer is: *expression of authentic feelings is appropriate as a means of here-and-now problem-solving, while expression of racket feelings is not.*

In other words, when we express an authentic feeling, we do something that helps finish the situation for us. When we express a racket feeling, we leave the situation unfinished.

George Thomson has explained the problem-solving function of three of the authentic feelings: fear, anger and sadness.[3] He points out that these feelings deal respectively with the future, the present, and the past.

When I feel authentic *fear* and act in some way to express that emotion, I am helping solve a problem that I foresee arising in *future*. For sure, that future may be very close. Suppose I'm crossing a road, having checked to see the way is clear. Suddenly, a car shoots out of a side road, being driven much too fast, and skids towards me. Galvanized by fear, I leap to one side. I have avoided the *future* event of being struck by the car.

Authentic *anger* is for solving problems in the *present*. Maybe I am waiting in line to be served in a shop. A woman tries to push ahead of me, shoving me to one side with her shopping-basket. Expressing my anger, I react appropriately to look after myself in the *present*. I push her back with equal force, and growl: 'I got here before you. Get to the end of the line, please.'

When I feel authentically *sad*, I am helping myself get over a painful event that has happened in the *past*. This will be some kind of loss, something or someone that I will never regain. By allowing myself to be openly sad, to cry for a while and talk out my loss, I free myself from that past pain. I finish the situation and say goodbye. Then I am ready to go on to whatever the present and future have to offer me.

George Thomson does not discuss the function of happiness. We'd suggest that authentic happiness signals: 'No change needed.' In this sense, happiness has a timeless quality. It means: 'What was happening in the past is OK to be happening now, and to keep on happening in future.' The expression of authentic happiness is to relax, feel comfortable, enjoy the present, and when satiated fall asleep.

In sharp contrast to this problem-solving function of authentic feelings, racket feelings never help finish the situation. You can check this from the many examples already given in this chapter. When I shouted at the clerk, I didn't help myself get my purchases home in the future. I didn't get any productive result in the present. And I didn't help myself say goodbye to the past possibility of getting my goods before the supermarket closed. Any time you begin feeling fear, anger or sadness out of their appropriate time-frame, *you know the emotion is a racket feeling.* For instance, some people go through life feeling angry about things that have happened in the past. But the past cannot be changed. Therefore, this anger is non-productive as a means of solving problems, i.e. it is a racket feeling. Check that the same applies to any of the other possible mis-matches between feelings and time-frames.

● What would you say would be the authentic feeling that would have helped finish the situation for you in our opening example? Once you had realized you weren't going to get your purchases, would you authentically have felt angry, sad, scared or happy? Check whether each of these feelings would have helped you finish the situation. ●

Because rackets represent the re-playing of an outdated Child strategy, the expression of racket feelings in the here-and-now is bound to result in the same unsatisfactory outcome over and over again. While in script, the person may temporarily feel satisfied at having manipulated some strokes from the environment. But the underlying need, which would be addressed by expressing the authentic feeling, has still not been met. Thus the person is likely to *re-cycle* the entire pattern, playing it out anew in each stress situation. We shall meet this idea again when we look at the Racket System in a coming chapter.

Racketeering

Fanita English coined the word 'racketeering' to describe a way of transacting which people may use as a means of seeking strokes for their racket feelings.[4]

A racketeer invites others into exchanges in which he expresses a racket feeling and aims to extract strokes for that feeling from the other person. These transactions will go on as long as the other person is willing to keep dealing out strokes to the racketeer.

Fanita English suggests that racketeering can be of two types, both of which entail parallel transactions between Parent and Child. In Type I, the racketeer takes up the Child role initially. His life position is 'I'm not-OK, you're OK (ha ha)'. In Type II, he comes from Parent, with a life position of 'I'm OK (ha ha), you're not-OK'.

The Type I racketeer may sound sad and pathetic, a mode of racketeering that Fanita English labels Type Ia and calls 'Helpless'. For example, you might hear this sort of exchange:

Racketeer (C — P): 'I'm feeling down again today.'
Partner (P — C): 'Oh, dear, sorry to hear that.'
Racketeer: 'And the boss was getting at me again.'
Partner: 'Tut, tut, that's bad.'

Alternatively, the Child racketeer may come from a whiny, complaining position. This is Type Ib, 'Bratty'. Typically, the partner may respond with strokes from negative Controlling Parent instead of negative Nurturing Parent:

Racketeer: 'And you weren't much help, either.'
Partner: 'Huh! Can't you stand up for yourself?'
Racketeeer: 'What do you expect me to do? He's the boss, isn't he?'
Partner: 'Well, why didn't you complain to the union?'

The Type II racketeer also has two possible modes of operating. In Type IIa, 'Helpful', he takes up a negative Nurturing Parent stance, aiming to extract strokes of gratitude from the other person in Child:

Racketeer (P — C): 'Sure you've had enough to eat?'
Partner (C — P): 'Ooh, yes, thanks.'
Racketeer: 'Come on, now, how about finishing this slice of pie?'
Partner: 'Well, honestly, it was great, but I'm full, thanks.'

'Bossy' describes the Type IIb racketeer, who initiates the transactions from negative Controlling Parent. He seeks apologetic Child strokes from his partner.

Racketeer: 'You're late again!'
Partner: 'Sorry!'
Racketeer: 'What do you mean, sorry? This is the fourth time this week...'

Though Fanita English does not say so, we would suggest that people can also racketeer Parent-to-Parent, on themes such as 'Ain't It Awful', or Child-to-Child with an escalation of feeling exchanges.

You'll see that racketeering is one kind of pastime, where the exchanges carry a charge of racket feelings. The parallel transactions will only cease when one of the participants withdraws or crosses a transaction. Often, the person initiating the cross will be the racketeer and not the partner. That's because habitual racketeers become adept at sensing when the other person is about to withdraw from the exchange. Rather than have his source of strokes run out in this way, the racketeer prefers to keep the initiative.

The frequent result is to transform the racketeering exchange into a *game*. When we look at games in a later chapter, we'll consider how this happens.

● Did you racketeer during the past week?

If so, were you Helpless or Bratty, Helpful or Bossy? Or did you test out several of these positions?

Do you want to keep on racketeering like this? If not, how will you get non-rackety strokes that will be acceptable in place of the strokes you got from racketeering?

Did you accept anyone else's invitation to be a partner to their racketeering? If so, which of the four modes were they in?

Do you want to keep on stroking their racket feelings? If not, how will you cross the transactions next time? ●

Stamps

When I experience a racket feeling, there are two things I can do with it. I can express it there and then. Or I can store it away for use later. When I do the latter, I am said to be saving a *stamp*.[5]

● In the past week, was there an occasion when you felt a racket feeling and saved it up instead of expressing it there and then?

If so, you saved a stamp. What was the name of the racket feeling written on this stamp? Was it a jealous, triumphant, angry, irritated, gloomy, helpless stamp...or what?

How big a collection do you have of this kind of feeling?

How long do you intend building up your collection?

When you decide to cash in your collection, what are you going to cash it in for? ●

The word 'stamp' is short for 'psychological trading stamp'. It refers to a practice popular with supermarkets in the 1960s, whereby customers were given stamps of different colors along with the goods they were buying. These trading stamps could be pasted in stamp books. When you'd saved up a certain number, you could cash the collection in for a prize.

Some people preferred to cash the stamps frequently in small lots, for small prizes. Others saved books and books full and finally cashed them in for a really big prize.

When people save up psychological trading stamps, they have the same kind of choice about cashing them. For instance, suppose I save anger stamps. At work, the boss criticizes me. I feel angry at him, but don't show it. I hang on to the stamp until I get home that night. Then I yell at my dog for getting under my feet. Here, I've only saved a single stamp, which I've cashed within the day.

The example illustrates another common feature of stamp-cashing: the person who eventually gets the collection dumped on them is frequently not the person who was the object of the racket feeling in the first place.

My workmate may also save up angry stamps. But suppose he prefers to make a much bigger collection before cashing them in. He may save up his anger against the boss for months and years. Then, collecting his mountain of angry-stamp books, he may march into the boss's office, bawl the boss out, and get fired.

Stamps and the script

Why do people save up stamps? Eric Berne suggested the answer. They do so because *by cashing in the stamps, they can move towards their script payoff.*

If a person's script is hamartic, he is likely to favor making big collections of stamps which he can then cash in for his heavy payoff. For instance, he may collect depression stamps for years and years, then finally cash them in for a suicide. Someone whose hamartic payoff is 'harming others' may stack up a huge collection of rage stamps, then use them to 'justify' homicide. On a lighter level but still as part of a losing script, a business executive might save harrassed stamps and cash them for a heart attack, ulcer or high blood pressure.

People with banal scripts will keep smaller collections of stamps and trade them in for lighter payoffs. A woman who saves 'misunderstood' stamps may cash them in every few months for a huge quarrel with her husband. Someone like my workmate, who collects anger stamps against authority figures, may trade them in for getting into disputes at work and occasionally getting fired.

There are varying opinions in TA on whether stamp-collecting has any place in a winning script. Some writers have referred to 'gold stamps', meaning stamps which are saved up for a positive outcome. (They contrast these with 'brown stamps', the negative ones we have been talking about so far.) For instance, they suggest, a hard-working executive might save gold stamps for jobs well done, and cash them in for a well-deserved holiday.

We believe that stamp-saving is not needed at all in a genuinely winning script. That hard-working executive doesn't need to justify his holiday, for 'jobs well done' or on any other grounds. He can go ahead and have his holiday just because he wants it.

● With this knowledge of the script function of stamps, review your own stamp collection and the payoff you may have in view when you cash it in. Do you still want this payoff?

If not, you can simply let your collection go. But before deciding to let it go, be sure that you genuinely want to let go of the expected payoff. Be clear that, if you do choose to let go of your stamp collection, you must also say a permanent goodbye to the payoff you had been planning.

Having thought about this, do you still want to let the stamps go?

If your answer is 'yes', then choose a way in which you will dispose of the stamps permanently. Some people throw them on a fire. Others flush them down the toilet. Still others drop them in a fast-flowing river and watch them being carried away to sea. Choose your own way. Whatever you choose, it must be a way that will make it impossible for you ever to get the stamps back.

Once you have decided on your means of disposal, get comfortable and close your eyes. Visualize yourself holding your stamp collection. See how many books or bags of stamps there are. Note their colors. See written across them the name of the racket feeling you have been saving up. If you have been saving the stamps against a particular person or group of people, see their name also written on the stamps.

Are you ready to let the stamps go? Then go ahead and make your disposal in whatever way you have decided. Throw them on the fire and watch till they have disappeared in smoke. Or flush them down the toilet, maybe flushing several times to make sure they've all gone down. If you throw them in a river, watch them until the last stamp has been carried away out of your sight.

In imagination, now look at your hands and confirm that they are empty of the stamps you had been carrying.

Now visualize that you turn around and look up. You'll see someone or something very pleasant that you had not seen before. Say hello to that pleasant someone or something. That's where you'll get the good strokes which will mean that you don't feel the need to save stamps in future.

Welcome these strokes. Feel the relief of not carrying the stamp collection around any longer. Then come out of the exercise. ●

Chapter 22
THE RACKET SYSTEM

The Racket System is a model which explains the nature of life-scripts and shows how people may maintain their script throughout life. It was devised by Richard Erskine and Marilyn Zalcman.[1]

In this chapter, the diagrammatic presentation of the Racket System, and the factual explanations of the diagram's meaning, are drawn directly from Erskine and Zalcman's article 'The Racket System: a model for racket analysis', for which they won the Eric Berne Memorial Scientific Award. The case illustrations and supporting interpretations have been supplied by the present authors.

The Racket System is defined as *a self-reinforcing, distorted system of feelings, thoughts and actions maintained by script-bound individuals.* It has three inter-related and interdependent components: the *Script Beliefs and Feelings,* the *Rackety Displays* and the *Reinforcing Memories.* It is shown diagrammatically in Figure 22.1.

Script Beliefs and Feelings

When I am in script, I will be replaying outdated beliefs about *myself, other people* and the *quality of life.* Erskine and Zalcman suggest that script decisions are adopted in childhood as a means of 'explaining away' unfinished feelings. When under stress in grown-up life, I may re-run this infant strategy. To defend against experiencing the feeling, I 'explain it away' by reviving those childhood conclusions and experiencing them as being true in the present. These then constitute my Script Beliefs.

Erskine and Zalcman picture the Script Beliefs and Feelings, taken in total, as representing a *double contamination* of the Adult. If you wish to check your understanding of this, refer back to Chapter 6.

The Script Beliefs under each heading are divided into *Core Script Beliefs* and *Supporting Script Beliefs.*

Core Script Beliefs

The Core Script Beliefs correspond to the child's earliest and most fundamental script decisions. For every infant, there are times when the expression of uncensored feelings fails to get the infant's needs met. We saw in the previous chapter how the child then tests out a range of

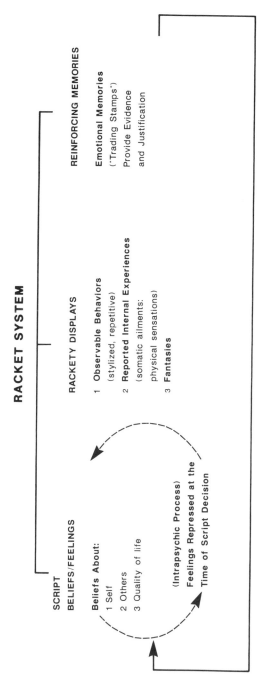

Figure 22.1 The Racket System

substitute feelings until she discovers those which do 'get results' in terms of parental attention. These substitute feelings are adopted as racket feelings, and the original uncensored feeling is suppressed.

Yet because the original feeling has not been responded to, the infant's emotional experience is left unfinished. In an attempt to make sense of this, she comes to conclusions about herself, others and the world. These form the Core Script Beliefs. They rest on the kind of concrete and magical thinking of which young children are capable.

Let's take the example of a client whom we will call David. In his late twenties, David had been though several living-in relationships with women. Each time, the woman had walked out on David after a year or so. He himself recognized he had invited this outcome, by picking fights with his girlfriends, getting jealous, and acting in a touchy, aggressive manner. Now David was in yet another relationship, with a woman he loved and valued. He was scared he was going to break up that relationship in the same old way. Though he was aware of his own aggressiveness and jealousy, he didn't feel he was able to control himself when he began feeling these emotions. Recently he had struck his girlfriend, and she was threatening to leave him. At this point, he came to therapy.

A Racket System analysis of this problem takes us right back to David's infancy. In the earliest months of his life, David enjoyed the intimate physical closeness that exists between a very small baby and his mother. But when David got a little older, just after his first birthday, Mother began feeling that he was not any longer just the cuddlesome bundle he had been when he was smaller. He was more mobile now, and often got grubby. He drooled, and when he made messes he got smelly. Though she was not aware of it, Mother reacted by pushing David away physically.

With his acute infant awareness, David picked up Mother's signals of rejection. He felt a sense of shock and disorientation: what had gone wrong with the world? Worst of all, was Mother going to leave him quite alone? Contemplating that possibility, David felt sheer terror and abject hurt. Yet still, each time he reached out for Mother to give him comfort, she seemed to reject him yet again. Expressing his scare and hurt, David did not get his needs met.

Unable to comprehend the factual reasons for Mother's withdrawal, David 'made sense of' his own unfinished feelings by concluding: 'I'm unlovable. There's something wrong with me.' Thus he formed a Core Script Belief about himself.

In line with this, he also adopted the Core Script Beliefs: 'Other people (especially important women) reject me. The world is a scary, lonesome, unpredictable place.'

Concluding that his expression of hurt and scare was not going to get his needs met, David gave up after a while and adopted a second-best strategy. He discovered that if he expressed anger, he at least got some attention from Mother. By flying into a tantrum, or by grizzling, he could at least get her to shout or scowl at him. Though this negative attention was painful, it was better than nothing at all. David decided: 'The best way for me to get my needs met is to act angry.' He had learned to cover his authentic feelings of scare and hurt with racket anger, and in so doing had laid the foundation for his Rackety Display.

Supporting Script Beliefs

Once the infant has arrived at his Core Beliefs, he begins to interpret his experience of reality in accord with these beliefs. They influence what experiences he attends to, the meaning he attaches to these experiences, and whether he regards them as significant. In this way, he begins to add Supporting Script Beliefs which re-affirm and elaborate upon the Core Script Beliefs.

David had a brother who was a couple of years older than himself. Because of the age difference, he was naturally bigger than David, as well as being more advanced in thinking ability. With the reasoning power of a toddler, David came to some further conclusions. 'Now I think I know what it is that is so wrong with me. It's that I'm not big enough or smart enough. I can tell this because my brother, who *is* big and smart, gets all the attention.'

Thus David had begun to build up some of his Supporting Script Beliefs. 'I am stupid. I'm physically weak and too small. My needs are not important. Others are bigger and smarter than I am. Because of this, they are more important than me and they get all the attention, especially from important women. Life is very, very unfair.'

Recycling Script Beliefs and Feelings

Now David is an adult. At moments of stress, he may go into script. As we've seen, this is especially likely if the here-and-now situation somehow *resembles* a stress situation in childhood — if there is a *rubberband*.

At such times, David re-experiences the feelings and beliefs of his early childhood. Suppose he perceives his girlfriend as 'pushing him off' in their relationship. Unknowingly, he responds as he did when Mother pushed him away as an infant. Below the level of awareness, he begins experiencing hurt and terror.

As he does so, he replays his Script Beliefs. He 'explains' the rejection he has perceived by saying to himself internally, outside of awareness: 'I'm unlovable, because there's something fundamentally wrong with me. This important woman wants to reject me utterly. If she does, I'll be left all alone.'

Each time David makes these statements to himself, he 'justifies' his feelings of scare and hurt. And each time he re-experiences these feelings, he re-states the Script Beliefs in order to 'explain' to himself how he feels. In this way, the Script Beliefs and Feelings are continually *recycled*. This is illustrated by the dotted arrows on Figure 22.1. Erskine and Zalcman stress that this process goes on *intrapsychically* — that is, inside the person's own head. Because David already has an internal scripty 'explanation' of what he has perceived as a rejection, he does not make his Script Beliefs available for updating against here-and-now reality. On the contrary: every time he repeats this recycling process, he reinforces his perception that reality has 'confirmed' the Script Beliefs.

Rackety Displays

The Rackety Displays consist of *all the overt and internal behaviors which are manifestations of the Script Beliefs and Feelings.* They include *observable behaviors, reported internal experiences* and *fantasies.*

Observable behaviors

The observable behaviors consist of the displays of emotion, words, tones, gestures and body movements which the person makes in response to the intrapsychic process. These displays are repetitive and stylized because they reproduce the scripty behaviors which the child learned to use in a wide range of situations as a way of 'getting results' in his or her family.

The Rackety Displays may entail behaviors which are in accord with the Script Beliefs or which defend against them. For example, David, who concluded in childhood 'I am stupid', acts confused and stupid when replaying this Script Belief as an adult. Someone else who reached the same childhood conclusion might defend against it by working long hours at studies, getting high grades at school and college then going compulsively through one professional qualification after another.

David's Rackety Displays of aggression towards his girlfriend arise from his early conclusion: 'The way for me to get my needs met is to get angry whenever I start feeling hurt or scared.' When his girlfriend behaves in any way which he perceives as a slight or rejection, he begins replaying his Core Script Beliefs and the feelings of terror and hurt that go with them. But, just as he learned to do as an infant, he instantly covers those emotions with anger. In the manner of a 'conditioned reflex', he becomes angry and aggressive. He may start a furious argument with his girlfriend, shout at her or push her about. Or he may choke back his anger, and storm out of the house to walk the streets fuming with rage.

This behavior gives David's girlfriend no way of knowing that his authentic emotions are hurt, scare and a longing for closeness. Indeed,

David himself has suppressed these feelings from awareness. He comes across instead as a touchy, physically aggressive individual. In the history of David's relationships, the end-result has been that his girlfriends have eventually walked out on him. Each time, David has used this response to 'justify' his Script Beliefs 'I'm unlovable, women reject me, and I get left on my own.'

Reported internal experiences

We have seen that the infant adopts the Script Beliefs in an attempt to make sense of an unfinished emotional experience, and thus finish that experience as best he can. As well as this *cognitive* process, the person may go through a similar sequence *somatically* — in terms of what he does in his body. In order to divert energy away from his unfinished need, he may use that energy to set up some kind of held physical tension or discomfort.

We gave an example of this in an earlier chapter. You'll recall the infant who repeatedly reaches out for Mother but gets no response. So after a while he tenses up his shoulders to stop himself from reaching out. Though this is uncomfortable, it's not so distressing as it would be to keep on reaching out and facing Mother's apparent rejection. He then suppresses both his awareness of his original need and his awareness of holding tension in his shoulders. As a grown-up he is likely to experience aches and pains in his shoulders, neck and upper back. This is true for David in our case example.

People have a whole range of tensions, discomforts and somatic ailments that are responses to the Script Beliefs in this way. They may not be apparent in observable behavior, but can be reported upon by the person. Sometimes, muscular tensions may have been so thoroughly suppressed that they do not come into the person's awareness except under massage.

Fantasies

Even when nobody is actually behaving in accordance with a person's Script Beliefs, the person may go ahead and fantasize such behavior. The imagined behavior may be his own or someone else's.

For instance, David sometimes fantasizes being punished or imprisoned for having committed a physical assault on a girlfriend. He frequently imagines that people are belittling him behind his back, dwelling on a whole range of things that they find wrong with him. Sometimes his fantasy is a grandiose picture of 'the best that could happen': he imagines having met the perfect girlfriend, who will accept him one hundred per cent and will never behave in a way that he could interpret as a rejection.

Reinforcing Memories

When in script, the individual consults a collection of memories which reinforce the Script Beliefs. Each of these remembered occurrences will be one in which the person re-cycled Script Beliefs and Feelings. As she did so, she would engage in the accompanying Rackety Display, either by experiencing a racket feeling or engaging in any of the other overt and internal behaviors which typify her own Racket System. As the event is remembered, the racket feeling or other rackety manifestation is recalled along with it. In other words, each Reinforcing Memory is accompanied by a *stamp*.

The events remembered may be other people's responses to the individual's Rackety Displays, as when successive girlfriends have abandoned David in response to his aggressive behavior. They may also include responses which the individual has interpreted internally as confirming the Script Beliefs, even though in reality they were neutral or even contrary to these beliefs. For example, a girl might invite David to a party. Internally he might tell himself: 'She didn't really mean it. She was only saying it to be nice to me.' Making this interpretation, he might feel angry at yet another 'rejection'. Thus he would notch up another 'confirmation' of his Script Beliefs, and collect another Reinforcing Memory with its associated trading stamp.

There are some events that not even the most ingenious Little Professor can construe as fitting the Script Beliefs. But in that case, the individual may adopt another strategy: to selectively forget such events. For instance, there have been occasions when a woman has openly told David she values him just for himself, and would love to stay close to him. But while in script, he blanks those memories out of his recollection.

We have seen also that the individual may construct fantasies of scenes which fit the Script Beliefs. Memories of these fantasies serve as Reinforcing Memories just as effectively as do memories of actual events. Each time David makes mental pictures of people talking about him behind his back because of whatever is 'wrong with him', he adds another Reinforcing Memory to his stock.

Here again, we see how the Racket System is self-reinforcing. The Reinforcing Memories serve as *feedback* to the Script Beliefs. This is shown by the solid arrow on Figure 22.1.

Each time a Reinforcing Memory is recalled, the person replays a Script Belief, which itself is strengthened by the Reinforcing Memory. As the Script Belief is replayed, the underlying suppressed feeling is stimulated, and the process of intrapsychic 'recycling' is set in motion once more. As this takes place, the person engages in Rackety Displays. These may include observable behaviors, internal experiences, fantasies, or a combination of the three. In turn, the outcome of the Rackety Display enables the person to collect more Reinforcing Memories, with their accompanying emotional stamps.

● COMPILING YOUR OWN RACKET SYSTEM

Take a big sheet of paper and draw out a replica of Figure 22.1. Leave plenty of space below each sub-heading in each of the three columns. On this blank diagram, you can begin to fill in the content of your own Racket System.[2]

If you want to proceed with the exercise, think of a recent situation that was unsatisfactory or painful for you and in which you finished up feeling bad. You need not re-experience the bad feeling now if you do not want to.

Imagining yourself back in that situation, fill in the details of the Racket System as they applied to you. Work quickly and intuitively.

To get to the Script Beliefs, a good way is to ask yourself: 'In that situation, *what was I saying in my head* about myself? About the other people concerned? About the quality of life and the world in general?'

How do you enter up the 'Feelings repressed at the time of script decision'? By the very fact that these feelings are being repressed while you are in the Racket System, you will *not* have been clearly aware of them during the scene which you are analyzing. However, there are various clues you can use. Sometimes, you may have experienced a brief flash of the authentic feeling before you went into the racket feeling. For instance, if your racket feeling in the scene was irritation, you may have felt scared for a split second beforehand. Another way is to ask yourself: 'If I were an infant and had no concept of censoring my feelings, how would I have felt in this situation? Would I have felt rage? Desolate sadness? Terror? Ecstasy?' If in doubt, guess. As a final check, look back at the previous chapter's section on 'Racket feelings, authentic feelings and problem-solving'. Which of the authentic feelings would have been appropriate to finish this situation for you?

Now move to the column on Rackety Displays. To list your observable behaviors, imagine you are seeing the scene on a video, with yourself in it. Note your words, tones, gestures, postures and facial expressions. What rackety emotion are you expressing? Check this against your memory of the racket feeling you were experiencing during the scene.

Under 'reported internal experiences', note any tensions or discomforts anywhere in your body. Did you have a headache? Churning stomach? Pain in the neck? Bear in mind that 'no sensation' is one kind of sensation. Thinking back, were there any parts of your body that you were blanking out of your awareness?

Enter any fantasies that you were experiencing. A good way here is to imagine yourself back in the scene, then ask yourself: 'What is the *worst* thing I feel could happen here?' Put down whatever you first bring to mind in response, no matter how fanciful it may seem. Next, ask yourself: 'What is the *best* thing I feel could happen here?' *This fantasy also is part of the Racket System*, so note it down in the same way.

Finally, go to the column for Reinforcing Memories. Letting your memory run free, note down your recollections of past situations similar to the scene you are analyzing. These may be from the recent past or from longer ago. In all of them, you will recall experiencing the same racket feeling, the same physical discomfort or tension, etc., which you have noted above under 'Rackety Displays'.

You may find it interesting to check your Racket System details against the script matrix you compiled for yourself in an earlier exercise. How much do they have in common? You can use each of them to refine and revise the other. ●

Breaking out of the Racket System

As well as being a tool for analysis, the Racket System is an instrument for change. Erskine and Zalcman say:

'Any therapeutic intervention which interrupts the flow in the Racket System will be an effective step in the person's changing their Racket System and therefore their script.'

In other words, you can step in at *any* point in the Racket System and make a change at that point that begins to move you out of script. When you effect that change, you break the old feedback loops. Thus further change becomes easier. The process is still self-reinforcing, but now you are reinforcing movement out of script instead of staying stuck in script.

You don't need to stop at just one point of intervention. If you want, you can break the flow of the Racket System at several different points. The more of these you change, the greater your movement out of script.

In their article, Erskine and Zalcman describe various specific interventions that therapists can use to interrupt the Racket System. You can use a similar approach in self-therapy. If you want to use the Racket System in this way, here is an exercise to give you a starting framework. You can add to it and modify it in whatever creative ways you like.[2]

● Take a big sheet of paper like the one on which you drew out your Racket System. On it, you are going to draw a diagram that looks like a Racket System, but is actually its *positive* counterpart. If you like, you can call this new diagram 'The Autonomy System'.

Once again, draw up three columns. Head the left-hand column 'Updated Beliefs and Feelings'. The middle column gets the title 'Autonomous Displays', and the third column has the same title as on the Racket System, 'Reinforcing Memories'.

Under 'Updated Beliefs and Feelings', enter sub-headings for beliefs about self, others and the quality of life, as on the Racket System.

Think back once more to the scene you recalled when compiling your Racket System. Start with 'beliefs about self'. What is the positive reality about yourself that you will now enter as your updated belief?

For example, suppose David were to do this exercise. He might enter under this heading: 'I am thoroughly lovable, and I'm every bit good enough just as I am.'

Here and throughout, it's important to use *positive wording* of this kind. Avoid negative words like *not, stop, lose, without*. If your first version of the entry has any such words in it, take time to re-phrase so that you say it in positive words only. In the example for David, his Script Belief was 'There's something wrong with me.' Instead of changing this to 'There's nothing wrong with me,' he would change it to a positive statement such as 'I'm every bit good enough.'

Go on and update your beliefs about others and the quality of life in the same way, using positive words. Watch out for grandiosity, which would still be part of your Racket System. But if in doubt, err on the side of optimism.

At the foot of the left-hand column, where you entered up 'Repressed feelings' in your Racket System, now write the heading 'Authentic feelings expressed'. Write in the same authentic feelings as you entered in your Racket System. Imagining yourself back in the scene, visualize how you could have expressed your authentic feeling in a safe way that would have finished the situation for you.

Go next to the middle column, 'Autonomous Displays'. Once again, see the scene with yourself in it as on a video. But this time re-run it so that you are behaving in a positive way, out of script and feeling an authentic emotion instead of a racket. Enter up under 'observable behaviors' the words, gestures, etc. which you see and hear yourself using in this updated version.

In the same way, complete 'reported internal experiences' for the revised scene. In place of discomforts, what comforts do you feel? Do you become aware of any tensions you had not been aware of before? If so, do you choose to relax these tensions? What happens when you do?

In the Autonomy System, you do not enter 'fantasies'. As we saw, grandiose fantasies of 'the best' *and* 'the worst' outcomes are both part of the Racket System. Instead, now enter here 'Plans and positive visualizations.' This is a heading to complete at leisure. It refers to the Adult life-planning you can do to ensure that future situations are run in the positive way you are now constructing, instead of the rackety way you analyzed in your Racket System. In place of fantasies, you can employ creative visualization techniques to empower and advance your life plans.

Finally, complete the column for Reinforcing Memories. It's almost certain that you will be able to recall *some* past instances in your life of positive situations that resemble the re-run situation you are now compiling. Maybe, when you think of it, you will be able to recall many.

229

And what if you really can't recall any? Just make some up. Recalling made-up positive situations is every bit as effective as recalling actual ones.

Now you have a starting version of your Autonomy System. As with the Racket System, you can revise and refine it as time goes on.

Imagine the completed diagram for your Racket System held a few inches above the diagram for your Autonomy System. In future, you can make a trap-door at any point in the Racket System, and step down through it to land at the corresponding point in the Autonomy System. From that point, you will go with the flow of the Autonomy System, instead of going round the rackety feedback loops that you went round in the past.

Maybe you will make yourself several trap-doors. The more you have, the easier you will find it to step out of your Racket System and into autonomy. And each time you do make this step, it will become even easier to make in future. ●

Chapter 23
GAMES AND GAME ANALYSIS

Have you ever had an interaction in which you and the other person both ended up feeling bad, and afterwards you said to yourself something like:
'Why does this keep on happening to me?'
'How on earth did *that* happen again?'
'I thought he/she was different from the others, but...'
Did you feel surprised at the painful way things had turned out — yet, at the same time, realize that the same sort of thing had happened to you before?

If you have had an interaction like this, it's most likely that in TA language you were playing a *game*.[1]

Just like a game of football or a game of chess, a psychological game is played according to predetermined rules. It was Eric Berne who first drew attention to this predictable structure of games, and suggested ways in which they could be analyzed.

In this chapter, we look at methods of game analysis devised by Berne and other TA writers.

Examples of games

Here are two examples of how people play games.

Example 1: Jack meets Jean. They fall in love and decide to live together. All goes well early on. But as the months go by, Jack begins giving his partner a hard time. He ignores her wants and feelings. He shouts at her, sometimes pushes her about. He gets drunk and comes home late. He spends Jean's money and 'forgets'to pay her back.

Jean stays with him despite his ill-treatment. The more aggressive he becomes, the more she makes allowances for his behavior.

This goes on for almost three years. Then, without warning, Jean leaves Jack for another man. Jack comes home to find a note on the kitchen table saying she has gone for good.

Jack is dumbfounded. He says to himself, 'How on earth did this happen to me?' He traces Jean, pleads unsuccessfully with her to come back. The more he begs her, the more harshly she rejects him, and the worse he feels. Jack spends a long time feeling depressed, abandoned and worthless. He tries to work out what is wrong with him: 'What has this other man got that I haven't got?'

The strange thing is that all this has happened to Jack before. He has been through two relationships, and two rejections, that followed the same pattern. Each time he has said to himself, 'Never again.' But it does happen again, and each time Jack feels surprised and rejected.

Jack is playing the game called *Kick Me*.

Jean also has been through this all before. She has had several other relationships with men before meeting Jack. Somehow, she seems to pick men who are good to her when they first know her, but who soon start ill-treating her as Jack did. Each time, she has put up with the man's behavior, acting the 'little woman' — for a while. Each time too, she has eventually had a sudden change of mind and has rejected the man abruptly. When she does so, she feels blameless and somehow triumphant. She says to herself: 'I thought so. Men are all the same.' Nevertheless, after a while she starts a relationship with somebody new, and the whole sequence is played through again.

Jean's game is *Now I've Got You, Son of a Bitch* — known for short as *NIGYSOB*.

Example 2: Molly is a social worker. She is in her office, talking to a client who has just come in. He looks dejected.

The client says: 'I'm afraid something awful has happened. My landlord has thrown me out, and I've nowhere else to go. I don't know what to do.'

'Oh, dear, that's bad,' says Molly, with a worried frown. 'What can I do to help?'

'I don't know,' says her client gloomily.

'I'll tell you what,' says Molly. 'Why don't you and I look through the evening paper and find a room for you to rent somewhere in town?'

'That's the trouble,' says Molly's client, looking even more downcast. 'I don't have enough money to pay the rent.'

'Well, I'm sure I could arrange for you to get some welfare help with that.'

'Nice of you,' says the client. 'But honestly, I don't want to take anybody's charity.'

'Ah. Well, how's about I fix you up a bed in the hostel until you get somewhere else to stay?'

'Thanks,' says the client, 'but really I don't think I could put up with being among all those other people when I'm feeling like this.'

A silence falls as Molly racks her brain for more ideas. She can't think of any.

Her client heaves a long sigh, gets up and makes to leave. 'Well, thanks anyway for trying to help,' he says glumly as he disappears through the door.

Molly asks herself 'What on earth happened?' She feels first astonished, then inadequate and depressed. She tells herself she is no good as a helper.

Meantime, her client is walking down the street feeling indignant and angry at Molly. He says to himself: 'Didn't think she was going to be able to help me, and she hasn't!'

Both for Molly and for her client, this scene is a replay of many others that have happened in the past. Molly quite often gets into this kind of interaction. She offers help and advice to clients then feels bad when they don't accept it. Her client is equally familiar with the receiving end. He somehow ends up again and again rejecting the offered help while feeling angry at being let down by the helper.

Molly and her client are playing a pair of games which very often go together. Molly's game is *Why Don't You...?*. Her client plays *Yes, But...*[2]

Typical features of games

From these examples, we can pick out some features that are typical of games.

(1) *Games are repetitive.* Each person plays her favorite game through time and time again. The other players and the circumstances may change, but the pattern of the game remains the same.

(2) *Games are played without Adult awareness.* Despite the fact that people repeat games over and over, they go through each replay of their game without being aware they are doing it. It's not until the closing stages of the game that the player may ask himself: 'How did *that* happen again?' Even at that point, people usually don't realize that they themselves have helped set up the game.

(3) *Games always end up with the players experiencing racket feelings.*

(4) *Games entail an exchange of ulterior transactions between the players.* In every game, there is something different happening at the psychological level from what seems to be happening at the social level. We know this from the way people repeat their games again and again, finding others whose games interlock with their own. When Molly's client comes for help and she offers it, they both believe that is their real purpose. But the outcome of their interaction shows that their unaware motivations were very different. At the psychological level, they were sending each other 'secret messages' which declared their true intentions. Molly was setting out to offer help which was not going to be accepted. Her client had come to ask for her help and then not take it.

(5) *Games always include a moment of surprise or confusion.* At this point, the player has the sensation that something unexpected has happened. Somehow, people seem to have changed roles. This was what Jack experienced when he discovered Jean had left him. Jean, for her part, left because she had quite suddenly changed her mind about Jack.

233

● Think of a painful interaction in your own recent experience which fits this description of a game.

Take a pencil and paper and note down what the situation was. Check that it had the five features we have given as being typical of games.

Note too how you felt at the end of it. Is this a familiar feeling of yours? ●

Sweatshirts

It's uncanny how people manage to seek out others who will play games which interlock with their own games. Jack consistently finds women who will leave him for someone else. Molly picks clients who will ask for her help and then not take it.

It's as if each person were wearing a *sweatshirt* with her game invitations printed on it. The sweatshirt has a motto on the front which is the one we consciously want the world to see. On the back is the psychological-level 'secret message'. The message on the back is the one that actually determines whom we pick for our relationships.

We can imagine that on the front of Jean's sweatshirt there's a motto something like: 'I'll be sweet and longsuffering.' On the back her motto reads: 'But just wait till I get you!'

● What do you think are the mottoes on the front and back of Jack's sweatshirt? Of Molly's?

Go back to your own personal game example. What do you imagine was the motto on the front of your sweatshirt? On the back?

What do you think were the front and back messages on the sweatshirts of any others you related to in that situation?

If you are working in a group, get into a subgroup with two or three other people. Each member of the small group uses intuition to jot down the front and back sweatshirt messages of the other members. Then share with each other what you wrote down.

Don't worry if the other people in the small group are not well known to you. It's usual for us anyway to read sweatshirt messages from first impressions.

If you want, you can repeat the exercise with others you know well. You may find out some interesting things about yourself by comparing the different mottoes which different people read on your sweatshirt. ●

Different Degrees of Games

Games can be played at different degrees of intensity.[3]

A *first-degree game* has an outcome which the player is willing to share with her social circle. In the game examples at the beginning of this chapter, all the players were playing at a first-degree level. You can guess that while Molly is unloading her feelings of self-doubt on her colleagues at coffee break, her one-time client will be down in the bar grumbling to *his* friends about how useless she is. The friends and colleagues will regard this as quite acceptable behavior. In fact, first-degree games usually make up a big proportion of the time-structuring at parties and social gatherings.

Games played at a *second-degree* level bring heavier outcomes, of a kind which the player would rather not make public in her social circle. For instance, suppose Molly's client had not just grumbled, but had gone off and entered a formal complaint of incompetence? Molly might then have experienced deep depression, perhaps even resigning her job. She'd also have been less likely to talk casually to her friends about what had occurred.

A *third-degree* game, in Berne's words, '...is one which is played for keeps, and which ends in the surgery, the courtroom or the morgue.' If Jack and Jean had been playing at this grim intensity, Jack might have physically maltreated Jean. Jean in turn might have saved up her anger until one day she picked up the kitchen knife and stabbed him with it.

Formula G

Berne discovered that every game goes through a sequence of six stages.[4] He named them as follows:

Con + Gimmick = Response → Switch → Crossup → Payoff

or just using their initials:

C + G = R → S → X → P

He called this sequence *Formula G* or the *Game Formula*.

Let's apply Formula G to the games played between Molly and her client. He opens by telling her his landlord has thrown him out. Under this social-level message lies his *Con*. It is delivered non-verbally, and conveys: 'But when you try to help me, I'm not going to be helped, ha ha!'

As Molly buys into the game set-up, she signals her willingness to play by revealing her *Gimmick*. Berne used this word to describe a scripty 'weak spot' that leads someone to buy into someone else's Con. For Molly, it's a Parent message in her head that says 'You *have* to help someone who is in such bad shape!'

Listening to this message internally, she responds to her client on the psychological level: 'OK, I'm going to try to help you, but we both know that in the end you aren't going to let yourself be helped.' At the social level, she covers this by saying 'What can I do to help?'

The *Response* stage of a game consists of a series of transactions. They may only last for a second or two or may go on for hours, days or years. In this case, Molly offers several pieces of advice to her client. He counters with justifications of why each one won't work. At social level, these transactions seem like straightforward exchanges of information. But at psychological level, they repeat the Con-Gimmick exchange that opened the game.

The *Switch* is pulled when Molly runs out of suggestions and her client says 'Thanks for trying to help.'

At the next instant, Molly feels as though she had been taken by surprise. This moment of confusion is the *Crossup*. Her client has a similar experience.

Straight away, both players collect their *Payoff* of racket feelings. Molly feels depressed and inadequate. Her client feels righteously indignant.

● What were the stages of Formula G in the interlocking games played by Jack and Jean?

Identify the stages of Formula G in your own personal example of a game. What were the psychological-level messages exchanged at each stage? ●

The Drama Triangle

Stephen Karpman devised a simple yet powerful diagram for analyzing games, the *Drama Triangle* (Figure 23.1).[5] He suggests that whenever people play games, they are stepping into one of three scripty roles: *Persecutor, Rescuer or Victim.*

A *Persecutor* is someone who puts other people down and belittles them. The Persecutor views others as being one-down and not-OK.

A *Rescuer*, too, sees others as being not-OK and one-down. But the Rescuer responds by offering help from a one-up position. She believes: 'I have to help all these others because they're not good enough to help themselves.'

To a *Victim*, it is himself who is one-down and not-OK. Sometimes the Victim will seek a Persecutor to put him down and push him around. Or the Victim may be in search of a Rescuer, who will offer help and confirm the Victim's belief 'I can't cope on my own.'

Every one of the Drama Triangle roles entails a *discount*. Both the Persecutor and Rescuer discount others. The Persecutor discounts others' value and dignity. Extreme Persecutors may discount other people's right to life and physical health. The Rescuer discounts others' abilities to think for themselves and act on their own initiative.

A Victim discounts herself. If she is seeking a Persecutor, then she agrees with the Persecutor's discounts and views herself as someone worthy to be rejected and belittled. The Victim seeking a Rescuer will believe that she needs the Rescuer's help in order to think straight, act or make decisions.

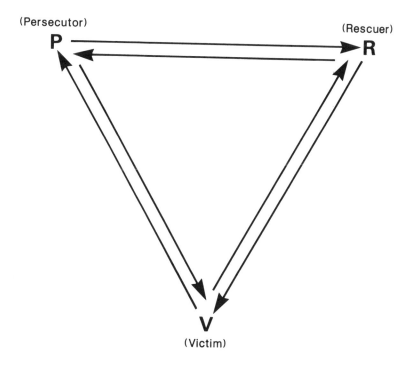

(Persecutor)

(Rescuer)

P

R

V

(Victim)

Figure 23.1 The Drama Triangle

● Take one minute to write down all the words you can think of that might be applied to a Persecutor.
Do the same for a Rescuer and for a Victim. ●

All three Drama Triangle roles are *inauthentic*. When people are in one of these roles, they are responding to the past rather than to the here-and-now. They are using old, scripty strategies they decided upon as children or took on board from their parents. To signal the inauthenticity of the Triangle roles, the words Persecutor, Rescuer and Victim are spelled with initial capitals. If we spell the words beginning with small letters, we mean real-life persecutors, rescuers or victims.

● Can you think of a real-life persecutor who would not also be a Persecutor?

What would be examples of the difference between an authentic rescuer and a person playing the role of Rescuer?

Would you say it is possible for anyone to be a victim without also being a Victim? ●

Usually, someone who is playing a game will start at one of the positions and then will switch to another. This switch in Drama Triangle positions takes place at the moment of the Switch in the Game Formula.

In the Kick Me game played by Jack, he began in the Persecutor position and stayed there through the Response stage of his game. When the Switch was pulled, Jack switched to Victim.

● What Drama Triangle switches were made by Jean in her NIGYSOB game? By Molly and her client in their game interaction?

What Drama Triangle switches did you make in your own personal game example? ●

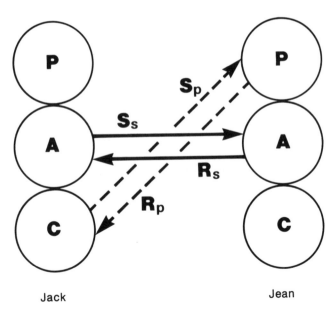

Jack   Jean

Figure 23.2 Example of Berne's transactional game diagram

Transactional analysis of games

Another way to analyze games is to use a transactional diagram. This is specially useful in bringing out the ulterior transactions between the players.

Berne's transactional game diagram

Figure 23.2 shows Eric Berne's version of the transactional game diagram.[6] It describes the opening exchanges between Jack and Jean.

Jack *(social level, S_s):* 'I'd like to get to know you better.'
Jean *(social level, R_s):* 'Yes, I'd like that too.'
Jack *(psychological level, S_p):* 'Kick Me, please!'
Jean *(psychological level, R_p):* 'I'll Get You, You S.O.B.!'

The ulterior 'secret messages' of S_p and R_p stay outside the awareness of each player until they are revealed at the moment of the Switch.

The Goulding-Kupfer diagram

Bob Goulding and David Kupfer developed a different version of the transactional game diagram (Figure 23.3).[7] For them, games have five required features.

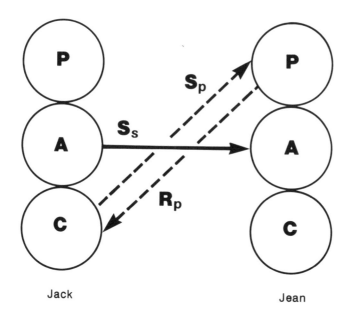

Jack   Jean

Figure 23.3 Example of Goulding-Kupfer game diagram

(1) First comes the social-level 'opener' of the game (S_s). Goulding and Kupfer call it the 'ostensible straight stimulus'. In this case, Jack says: 'I'd like to get to know you better.'

(2) The second element of the game is the simultaneous psychological-level message (S_p) which is the game's Con. It is called the 'secret message', and includes a scripty statement about the self. Jack's 'secret message' is 'I deserve to be rejected, and I'm going to test you out till I prove it. Kick Me, please!'

(3) As always, the outcome is determined at the psychological level. Jean reads Jack's 'Kick Me' message and responds accordingly, by stringing him along for a while and then rejecting him. In the Goulding-Kupfer sequence, this is the 'response to the secret message'.

(4) Both players end up experiencing racket feelings, the 'bad-feeling payoff'.

(5) The entire series of ulterior transactions stays outside the Adult awareness of the players.

The Gouldings point out that if anyone has enough investment in getting into his favorite game, he can twist the actual responses he is getting from the other person so as to read the game response into them. Thus he can take his racket payoff even if the other person's responses were not gamey.

For instance, suppose Jean had steadfastly refused to reject Jack despite all his pushing. He might redefine her response by saying to himself: 'She's only pretending to want me around. I *know* she really wants rid of me, and she's probably going round with someone else in secret.' In this way he might manufacture the discount he had been expecting and go ahead to take his bad-feeling payoff anyway.

● Use Berne's transactional game diagram and the Goulding-Kupfer diagram to analyze the games played by Molly and her client.
Use them to analyze your own personal game example. ●

The Game Plan

John James has developed a set of questions which give us another way of understanding the progress of a game. He calls it the *Game Plan*.[8]

The following exercise uses a variation of the Game Plan that includes two additional 'mystery questions'. It was devised by Laurence Collinson.

You can use the Game Plan questions to analyze the personal game example which you have already noted. Or, if you like, use it to examine a different gamey situation which you recognize in your life.

● Take a pencil and paper and note down the answers to the following questions, as they apply to your chosen example. It's a good idea if you find someone else to share your ideas with as you complete the Game Plan questions.

The 'mystery questions' are printed at the end of this chapter. *Do not look at them until you have answered all the other Game Plan questions.* Then add the answers to the two 'mystery questions'.

1. What keeps happening to me over and over again?
2. How does it start?
3. What happens next?
4. (Mystery question)
5. And then?
6. (Mystery question)
7. How does it end?
8a. How do I feel?
8b. How do I think the other person feels? ●

Interpretation

The sequence of answers to the Game Plan questions should show you the Drama Triangle switches and Formula G stages in the game.

The feelings you listed at Questions 8a *and* 8b are *both* likely to be racket feelings of yours. It may be that you recognize the feeling at 8a as being familiar, but are surprised to think that the one named at 8b is also your own racket. If this is true of you, check with someone who knows you well.

The answers to the two 'mystery questions' are the psychological-level messages of the transactional game diagram. However, Laurence Collinson suggests that *both these statements are also likely to be messages which your parents conveyed to you while you were a young child.* Check whether this is true for you.

A second possibility is that one or both of the 'mystery question' answers may be a message which *you* conveyed to your parents when you were very young.

Keep your Game Plan answers. You can use them again as you read the following two chapters.

Definitions of Games

There's disagreement among TA writers about the proper definition of a game.[9] Perhaps this is because Berne himself defined games differently at different stages of his thinking.

In his last book, *What Do You Say After You Say Hello*, Berne spells out Formula G and explains the six stages as we have done above. Then he adds:

'Whatever fits this formula is a game, and whatever does not fit it is not a game.'

As a definition, this couldn't be clearer. Yet in an earlier book, *Principles of Group Treatment*, Berne had defined a game in different words:

'A game is a series of ulterior transactions with a gimmick, leading to a usually well-concealed but well-defined payoff.'

You'll see the crucial difference between the two definitions. The later version, in *What Do You Say...*, refers to the *Switch* and *Crossup* as essential features of a game. The earlier definition does not.

In fact, it wasn't until quite late on in his development of game theory that Berne introduced the idea of the Switch. It appears first in *Sex in Human Loving*. In the earlier *Games People Play*, he used a definition similar to the one in *Principles of Group Treatment*, making no reference to the Switch or Crossup.

Since Berne, some writers have used definitions that follow his earlier version. In various different words, they have defined a 'game' as any sequence of ulterior transactions that ends up with the parties feeling bad (experiencing racket feelings).

We prefer to follow the alternative school of thought, and use Berne's later definition. We define as 'games' only those sequences that follow all the stages of Formula G, *including* the 'switch of roles' and 'moment of confusion' represented by the Switch and Crossup.

Why? Because Berne's earlier definition, without the Switch, is already described in modern TA by another concept: *racketeering*. And there's a clear distinction between the process of racketeering and the process of a game, in a way which Fanita English has described. Racketeers resemble game-players in that they exchange ulterior messages, taking racket-feeling payoffs at the same time. But in racketeering, no Switch is pulled. The parties may keep on racketeering as long as they both want or have energy to, and then simply stop or do something different.

It's only if one of the parties does pull a Switch that the racketeering exchange is transformed into a game. (In the coming chapter, we'll say more about why people may do this).

We think that this distinction between racketeering and game-playing is a useful one to make. It gives us practical help in understanding how people get into painful exchanges and how they can get out of them. Therefore, it's useful also to have two distinct definitions, so that we can always make it clear which of the two concepts we're talking about.

Suppose you want to define a 'game' to somebody who doesn't know the technical language of Berne's Formula G? You can use this way of saying it, suggested by Vann Joines:

'A game is the process of doing something with an ulterior motive that:

242

(1) is outside of Adult awareness;

(2) does not become explicit until the participants switch the way they are behaving; and

(3) results in everyone feeling confused, misunderstood, and wanting to blame the other person.'

The 'mystery questions'

Mystery question 4: What is my secret message to the other person?

Mystery question 6: What is the other person's secret message to me?

Chapter 24
WHY PEOPLE PLAY GAMES

Games are no fun. So why do we play them?

TA writers have suggested several answers to this question.[1] They all agree on one point. That is: in playing games, we are following outdated strategies. Game-playing was one of the devices we adopted as young children to get what we wanted from the world. But in adult life we have other, more effective options.

Games, stamps and script payoff

Above all, people play games to further their life script.

Eric Berne suggested the sequence by which we achieve this. At the payoff of every game, the player experiences a *racket feeling*. Each time he does this, he can store the feeling away as a *stamp*.

You learned the rest of the story in Chapter 21. When the game-player has built up a big enough collection of stamps, he feels 'justified' in cashing it in for whatever negative *script payoff* he decided upon as a child.

Thus each person chooses her games to yield the kind of stamps that will advance her towards the script ending she has decided upon. As usual with scripts, the script story may be played through in miniature many times during the player's life.

Consider Jean's NIGYSOB game. Each time she plays it, she collects anger stamps and then cashes them in for a rejection of the other person. Her long-run script payoff is to end up old and alone, having rejected all the men she has known.

People choose the degree of their games to suit the degree of their script payoff. Suppose Jean's script were hamartic instead of banal. She would likely play her NIGYSOB at third degree. The men she chose would batter her physically instead of with words. At the game switch, she in turn would cash her anger stamps by harming the man physically. Her script payoff would be homicide or seriously harming others.

● Look back at your own game example. What feeling stamp did you save?

How might you have been saving up these stamps for a negative script payoff? ●

Reinforcing script beliefs

You know that the child views her early decisions as being the only way to get by and survive. So it is not surprising that when we are in script as grown-ups, we want to confirm time and time again that our script beliefs about self, others and the world are 'true'. Each time we play a game, we use the payoff to reinforce those script beliefs. For example, when Molly was an infant she decided non-verbally that her job in life was to help others, but that she could never help them well enough. Each time she plays out her Why Don't You...? game, she ends up repeating this decision in her head. In the language of the Racket System, she stacks up another Reinforcing Memory to further her Script Beliefs about self, others and the quality of life.

Games and life position

We can also use games to 'confirm' our basic life position. (To review this concept, see Chapter 12). For instance, people like Jack who play Kick Me are reinforcing a life position of 'I'm not-OK, you're OK'. This position 'justifies' the player in getting-away-from others. A NIGYSOB player such as Jean believes she is confirming 'I'm OK, you're not-OK' each time she reaches her Persecutor payoff, and thereby 'justifies' her strategy of getting-rid-of other people.

If a person's position is down in the lower-left quadrant of the OK Corral, at 'I'm not-OK, you're not-OK', she will most likely use her games to 'justify' getting-nowhere-with people. For example, this is where Molly ends up each time she plays out her game of Why Don't You...?

● In your own game example, what script beliefs about self, others and the world might you have been reinforcing at the payoff?
Which of the life positions do these beliefs fit?
Does that check with the basic life position you saw yourself in when you were learning about the OK Corral? ●

Games, symbiosis and the frame of reference

The Schiffs suggest that games result from unresolved symbiotic relationships, in which each player discounts both himself and the other.[2] The players maintain grandiose beliefs in order to 'justify' the symbiosis, such as 'I can't do anything' (Child) or 'I only live for you, dear!' (Parent). Thus every game is either an attempt to maintain an unhealthy symbiosis, or an angry reaction against that symbiosis.

We can draw a symbiotic diagram to analyze the interlocking games

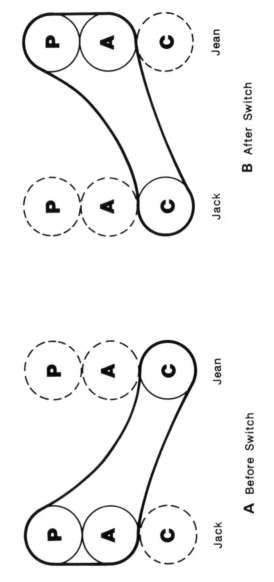

A Before Switch   **B** After Switch

Figure 24.1 Example of use of symbiotic diagram in game analysis

which Jack and Jean are playing (Figure 24.1). In Figure 24.1a, we see their initial symbiotic positions. Jack takes the Parental role, while Jean plays Child. In line with the standard way of drawing the symbiotic diagram, we show Jack also taking on ownership of the Adult ego-state. However, when the partners are playing through the early stages of their respective games, neither is aware of what is going on. You could therefore imagine re-drawing the diagram to show the Adult out of commission for both Jack and Jean.

At the Switch, the symbiotic positions are switched also. Now Jack takes on the role of hurt Child. Jean switches into rejecting Parent. This gives the closing symbiotic picture shown in Figure 24.1b.

Without knowing it, Jack has been replaying his childhood symbiosis with his mother. When he was an infant, he picked up non-verbally that his mother was rejecting him. Without words, Jack decided: 'It seems I only get attention from Mother when she does something to reject me. Otherwise, I might get no attention at all. So I'd better set up to keep the rejections coming.' He had soon worked out a range of strategies to get this result. Sometimes he would whine and grizzle, on and on. At other times he would fly into a tantrum. Either way, Mother eventually got angry with him. When she did, she would shout at Jack or even slap him. This kind of attention hurt. But it was better than no attention at all.

As a grown-up, Jack still follows the same infant strategy outside of awareness. He seeks out women who are likely to reject him from a Parental position. If the rejection is slow in coming, he helps it along by Persecuting the woman, in the same way as he Persecuted his mother when he was fifteen months old.

Jean, too, has been replaying a childhood symbiosis. As an infant and a toddler, she had enjoyed getting lots of playful strokes from her father. But there came a time when Jean became not just a baby, but a feminine little girl. In his Child, Father began feeling uncomfortable at his own sexual response to her. Without awareness, he withdrew from Jean physically.

Jean felt betrayed and hurt. To blank out the pain, she covered her hurt with anger, and decided she'd feel less uncomfortable if she became the one who did the rejecting. She got into her Parent to put down her father's Child. As a grown-up woman, she unknowingly acts out this same decision. She 'puts Father's face' on men she relates to, and rejects them while once again feeling her childhood anger.

● Draw the symbiotic diagrams for the games played by Molly and her client.

Find what symbiotic position you took up at the beginning of the game in your own personal example, and what position you moved into at the Switch. Do you identify what childhood symbiosis you were replaying or reacting against? ●

When people use games to replay a childhood symbiosis, they 'justify' and maintain the problem which is being discounted. In so doing, they defend their frame of reference.

Thus games are played in order to 'justify' what the players are already feeling and believing (their racket feelings and life position) and to shift the responsibility on to someone or something else. Each time a person does this, he reinforces and furthers his script.

Games and strokes

You know that the Child needs strokes for survival. Every child gets scared at times that the supply of strokes may run out. To guard against this, she develops a repertoire of manipulations to keep the strokes coming.

Games are a reliable way of getting a supply of intense strokes. The strokes exchanged in the opening stages of the game may be positive or negative, depending on the game. At the switch, each player gets or gives intense negative strokes. Whether positive or negative, every stroke exchanged during a game entails a discount.

Games, strokes and racketeering

Fanita English suggests that people begin seeking game strokes when their strokes from *racketeering* are in danger of running out.[3] Perhaps I may have been getting into a Helpless role with you, while you have been acting Helpful. I may tell you all the bad things people have been doing to me that day, while you offer Rescuing sympathy. For a while, we exchange these racketeering strokes.

Then you get tired of the exchange and signal that you want to move on. Feeling scare in my Child, I may respond by pulling a NIGYSOB game switch, saying something like 'Huh! I always thought you were somebody I could rely on, but now I see I was wrong.' Outside of my awareness, I'm hoping you will come back with a Kick Me and keep the supply of strokes coming.

Whenever people get into games to manipulate for strokes, they are discounting reality. They are ignoring the many grown-up options they have to get strokes in positive ways.

● What strokes were you getting and giving at each stage of your own game example?

Did you get into the game when racketeering strokes were in danger of running out? ●

Berne's 'six advantages'

In *Games People Play*, Eric Berne listed 'six advantages' of game-playing.[4] Nowadays, they are not often referred to in practical TA work.

Each can be understood more simply in terms of other TA ideas. Let's review them briefly. For illustration, say I am a Kick Me player.

(1) Internal psychological advantage. By playing games, I maintain the stability of my set of script beliefs. Each time I play Kick Me, I reinforce my belief that I need to be rejected in order to get attention.

(2) External psychological advantage. I avoid situations that would challenge my frame of reference. Thus I avoid the anxiety I would feel at the challenge. By playing Kick Me, I avoid facing up to the question: 'What would happen if I did ask others for straight positive strokes?'

(3) Internal social advantage. In Berne's words, games 'offer a framework for pseudo-intimate socializing indoors or in privacy.' Part of my Kick Me game may be long, agonizing 'heart-to-heart' exchanges with my gaming partner. We feel as though we are being open with each other. In reality, this is not intimacy. Beneath the social-level messages are the ulteriors which confirm that we are in a game.

(4) External social advantage. Gaming gives us a theme for gossiping in our wider social circle. When I am in the bar with a crowd of other male Kick Me players, we may pastime or racketeer on the theme 'Ain't Women Awful?'.

(5) Biological advantage. This refers to the game's yield of strokes. Kick Me yields mainly negatives. As a child, I decided that since positive strokes seemed hard to come by, I had better set up reliable ways of getting kicks in order to survive. Also, each time I replay the game, I am satisfying structure-hunger as well as stroke-hunger.

(6) Existential advantage. This is the function of the game in 'confirming' the life position. Kick Me is played from a position of 'I'm not-OK, you're OK'. Each time I take a gamey kick, I reinforce this position.

● What are the 'six advantages' of Jean's NIGYSOB game?
  What were the 'six advantages' in your own game example? ●

Positive payoffs of games

John James has developed the idea that games have real advantages as well as scripty ones. He points out that every game brings a *positive payoff* as well as its negative payoff.[5]

A game represents the child's best strategy for getting something from the world. When we play games in adulthood, we are attempting to meet a genuine Child need. It's just that the means of satisfying that need are outdated and manipulative.

James suggests that the positive payoff comes *after* the negative payoff in the Game Formula. For instance, what's the positive Child need which I am satisfying by playing my Kick Me game? It's that each time I play the game, after I have collected my bad-feeling payoff, I say to myself in Child: 'Phew! Thank goodness for a bit of time and space for myself!'

Other Kick Me players may gain different positive payoffs from mine. The positive payoff is unique to each game player. But, says John James, it is always there to be found.

● What positive payoffs might Molly and her client have been seeking when they got into their Why Don't You? — Yes, But exchange?

What positive payoff did you get at the close of your own game example? You may realize the answer immediately, or it may take you some time and thought. ●

Chapter 25
HOW TO DEAL WITH GAMES

You have already taken the most important steps in defusing game-playing. You have learned what games are and how they can be analyzed. You know the covert motives people have in playing games.

In this chapter, we outline a 'tool-kit' of practical ways to counter games.

Need we name the game?

In his bestselling *Games People Play*, Eric Berne fascinated his readers by giving catchy names to the games he listed.[1] Others followed Berne's lead, and game-naming became a fashion in TA that lasted for some years. Literally hundreds of games were 'discovered', each with its own name.

With over twenty years' hindsight, we can see now that only a few of these represented genuine additions to our understanding of games. Many of the suggested names turn out to describe interactions that are not games at all, according to the definitions we met in Chapter 23. In particular, many do not have a Switch, and so can be more consistently classified as pastimes or racketeering. This is the case with many of the 'games' listed in *Games People Play*.

When we eliminate these non-games, we discover that the remaining games can be classified into a relatively small number of basic patterns. Each of these patterns can be represented by one well-known game title. All the other names represent variations on these, and the variation is in *content* rather than *process* — in the details of *what* goes on during the game rather than *how* the game is being played.

Most TA practitioners nowadays prefer to economize on the number of game names they use. We favor this approach. We think you can best develop an understanding of games by concentrating on the general patterns that define *how* games are played. This also allows you to work out general principles for countering games, instead of having to develop a separate 'antithesis' specific to the content of each game, as Berne did.

Some familiar games

In this section we list some of the most commonly-used game names.

251

They are classified according to the shift in Drama Triangle positions which the player makes at the moment of the Switch.[2]

Persecutor-to-Victim switch

This is typified by *Kick Me*, which we have already illustrated by examples.

Cops and Robbers is a version of the same game played in a legal setting. Here, the player opens by seeking to Persecute the forces of law and order. But eventually he sets up to get caught, thus finishing up as Victim.

In *Blemish*, the player finds fault with others, criticizing their appearance, work, dress, etc. He may keep this up indefinitely as a theme for racketeering, without necessarily pulling a game Switch. However, the blemisher may eventually get himself rejected by those he has been criticizing, or set up to be 'accidentally' overheard as he dwells on someone's faults behind their back. Then he makes the move from Persecutor to Victim on the Drama Triangle, converting his racketeering into a game.

The player of *If It Weren't For You* is always moaning to others about how they prevent her from doing something she wants. For instance, a mother may tell her children: 'If it weren't for you, I could be away traveling in foreign countries.' Now suppose something happens to interrupt her racketeering on this theme. Maybe she inherits a sum of money large enough to pay for child care. Or her children simply get old enough not to need her around. Do you think she then goes on those foreign travels? No. She discovers she's too scared to leave her own country. In so doing, she makes a Switch to the Victim position.

Victim-to-Persecutor switch

This pattern is exemplified by *Now I've Got You, Son of a Bitch (NIGYSOB)*. You'll recall this as the game played by Jean in one of our opening examples. In this and all its variations, the player gives some sort of 'come-on' from a Victim position. When the gaming partner takes the bait, the player delivers a Persecuting kick.

In *Yes, But...*, the player starts by asking for advice while fending off all the suggestions that are given. The Switch comes when the advice-giver runs out of suggestions and the Yes, But... player deals out a rejection of the helper. You'll remember how Molly's client played this in our example. It's a common game in social work and other 'helping' settings.

Rapo is the sexual version of NIGYSOB. Here, the player signals a sexual come-on. When the gaming partner responds with a sexual advance, the Rapo player comes back with an indignant rejection. The Rapo player wears a sweatshirt that says on the front: 'I'm available!' On the back it reads: 'But not to *you*, ha ha!' First-degree Rapo is a common source of game strokes at parties, and has a mild sexual rebuff as its outcome. At third degree, the Rapo player may wait until there has been physical sexual contact, then pull the Switch by crying 'Rape!'.

There are several games of the NIGYSOB pattern in which the initial Victim position is taken up as a racketeering stance, and the Switch is usually not pulled unless that stance is confronted. Players of *Stupid* and *Poor Me* begin by racketeering from postures of 'I can't think' and 'I can't help myself' respectively. They may be content to stay in this Victim position for as long as the strokes keep coming. However, if someone confronts these players with demands to think or do things for themselves, they may pull the Switch by becoming angry or accusing: 'Huh! Should have known better than to think I'd get any help from *you*!'

Wooden Leg is a variation of Poor Me, with a sweatshirt motto that runs: 'What can you expect from someone who...had a mother like mine/ is an alcoholic like me/was brought up in the inner city/(supply any other excuse).'

The player of *Do Me Something* seeks covertly to manipulate other people into thinking or acting for him. For example, a student who is asked a question in class may sit dumbly, chewing his pencil and waiting for the lecturer to supply the answer. As long as the hoped-for assistance is produced, the player may stay in the position of helpless Victim. But later, he may pull the Switch and collect a further harvest of game strokes by accusing the helper of giving bad advice. For example, that same student might go to the principal after the examination and complain that he'd scored a low mark because the lecturer had been unclear in his teaching. This end-of-game stance has sometimes been given a different game name, *See What You Made Me Do*.

Rescuer-to-Victim switch

The prototype game here is *I'm Only Trying To Help You*. This title can be used for any game in which someone begins by offering 'help' from a Rescuing position, then switches to Victim when the person they are 'helping' either rejects the help, goes ahead and gets into a mess anyway, or signals that the help offered has not been good enough. The would-be 'helper' then collects a payoff of inadequacy stamps.

The game Molly was playing in our opening example, *Why Don't You...?*, is a variation on this theme that involves the giving of advice which is rejected by the gaming partner.

Rescuer-to-Persecutor switch

See How Hard I've Tried begins like I'm Only Trying To Help You, with the 'helper' in the Rescuer role. But at the Switch, the one-time Rescuer changes to an accusing Persecutor instead of a woeful Victim. For instance, imagine a woman who has acted the 'smother-mother' to her son right through his childhood. Now he's a rebellious teenager and has just announced he intends to leave home. Pulling her game Switch, the mother screams: 'After all I've done for you! I hope you get just what you deserve! I'm washing my hands of you, do you hear?'

Using Options

In Chapter 7, you learned about Options. If you have practiced them, you will be skilled in their use by now. This skill, combined with a knowledge of game analysis, gives you an effective armory for countering games.

Options can be used to break the flow of a game at *any* stage in the Game Formula. If you realize that you yourself are part-way through a game of your own, you can take your Option of shifting out of a negative and into a positive functional ego-state. If someone else has invited you into their game, use Options to come back with a response that cuts across their expectations of what you are 'supposed' to do at that stage of the game.

We suggest you use only positive ego-state Options. Rather than engage in a dance around the Drama Triangle with the other person, step off the Triangle altogether.

You cannot *make* anyone else stop playing games. Nor can you stop them trying to hook you into a game. But by using Options, you can stay out of game-playing yourself, or get back out of it if you find that you have already gotten in. And you maximize the chance that you will also invite the other person out of their game, if this aim matters to you.

Catching the 'opening Con'

Bob and Mary Goulding have stressed the importance of catching the game right at the beginning, at the 'opening Con'.[3] If you immediately come back with an Option to confront this, you're likely to forestall the rest of the game.

This calls for skill in 'thinking Martian'. You need to pick up the ulterior message that forms the Con, and cut across that instead of responding to the social level.

You can use a cross from straight Adult. For example, consider the start of the game between Molly and her client. When he came out with his request for assistance, Molly might have responded: 'You sound like you have a problem. What do you want me to do about it?' With this question, she would address the covert agenda directly. If her client were to redefine in a further attempt to hook her into his game, she could simply repeat the same cross until he either gave an Adult answer or gave up and left. In the latter case, he might take his own game payoff anyway. But Molly would have avoided taking a payoff for herself.

If it fits the setting, a specially effective way of cutting across the opening Con is to come back with an exaggerated, 'over-the-top' response from either Child or Parent. For instance, Molly might have greeted her client's opening complaint by slithering down in her chair until she vanished below her desk, groaning: 'Oh, *dear*! You are in bad shape again, aren't you?' When a client tells Bob Goulding that she has come into therapy to 'work on' a problem, Bob's frequent response is to assume an expression of pained boredom, and drone: 'Work on, and work on, and work on...' Responses like these cross the opening Con at psychological level, conveying: 'I've seen through your game, so let's have some fun instead.'

Watching for discounts and drivers

The opening Con always entails a discount. There are further discounts at each stage of the game. Therefore, the skill of detecting discounts helps you identify game invitations and defuse them with Options.

If you accept the discount offered in the Con, you will have exposed your Gimmick and the game will be under way. Thus the way to disable the game is to confront the other person's discount.

In the split second before moving into a game, the player will exhibit driver behavior. You learned in Chapter 16 how to identify drivers. This skill also will assist you in catching the opening Con and forestalling subsequent game moves. To stay out of the game, refuse to respond to the other person's driver behavior with a driver of your own. Instead, give yourself an allower.

Disowning the negative payoff

What if you miss the opening Con, get into the game, and become aware of it only at the Switch? All isn't lost. You can still refuse to take your bad-feeling payoff. Better still, you can give yourself a good-feeling payoff instead. For instance, suppose I'm attending a lecture given by a well-known speaker. When the time comes for discussion, I put up a spirited attack on his ideas. In fact, though I'm not aware of it yet, I've started Persecuting him. When I'm through, the lecturer smiles quietly and demolishes my critique with one well-chosen sentence. The audience laughs.

At this point, my script calls for me to hit the Switch of my Kick Me game. I'm 'supposed' to feel rejected and useless. Instead of that, I step out of script. I tell myself: 'Interesting! I've just identified that I've been setting up Kick Me for the past three minutes. How clever I am to have realized that!' I award myself a bundle of good feelings for my own cleverness in spotting the game.

255

Note that I don't congratulate myself for having gotten into the game. I congratulate myself for being clever enough to realize I've gotten into it.

The interesting thing is that if you use this technique consistently, you will find you play the game less often and less intensely as time goes on. And this is no surprise, given the role games play in relation to the script. Each time I disown the bad-feeling payoff of a game and give myself a good-feeling payoff instead, I throw away a negative stamp. I collect a positive Reinforcing Memory in place of the negative one called for in the game. Thus I help defuse my Script Beliefs and reduce the intensity of my Rackety Displays, of which the game itself is one.

Going straight to the positive payoff

A similar technique is suggested by John James.[4] You'll recall his idea that every game has a positive payoff as well as a negative one. When you identify a particular game as one you have often played, you can work out what authentic Child need you have been meeting in the past by doing so. Then you can find ways of satisfying that need in straight instead of scripty ways.

For instance, suppose the positive payoff of my Kick Me game is to get time and space for myself. Knowing this, I can use my grown-up options to get these benefits without getting kicked first. I may begin taking ten minutes' quiet time for myself each morning and afternoon, or block out time in my schedule to go for walks alone in the country. As I do so, I meet my Child needs in a straight way. As a result I'm likely to find myself playing Kick Me less and less often. Furthermore, when I do play the game, I will most likely play it at a lesser degree than I did previously.

Moving to intimacy at the Switch

Once you have become accustomed to tracking the successive stages of a game, you will find it particularly easy to recognize the Switch. You will realize that you and the other person seem to have switched roles in some way, and you will almost simultaneously recognize the moment of confusion which constitutes the Crossup.

At this point you have yet another strategy for stepping out of the game. When a person remains in script at the moment of the Switch and Crossup, he believes his *only* option is to move to the Payoff. But with Adult awareness you can take a different route. Instead of moving into racket feelings, you can be open with the other person about your authentic feelings and wants. Thus you invite intimacy in place of the game Payoff.

For instance, imagine I had played my Kick Me game through in a relationship, and that I had just arrived at the Switch in the game. I might say to the other person: 'I've just realized what I've been setting up — to push you away until you reject me. Now I'm scared you're going to leave me, and I really want you to stay close to me.'

By this open statement, I cannot *make* the other person stay with me. I cannot even *make* her move out of her own game if she is invested in staying in it. But I *invite* her to respond with her own authentic feelings and wants. If she does, we may move back into the relationship with feelings of happiness and relief. Alternatively, we may decide to part anyway, though for straight rather than gamey reasons. If we make the latter decision, both of us may have to face up to a period of sadness at our loss. As always, intimacy is less predictable than game-playing, and we may or may not experience it as more comfortable.

Replacing game strokes

Game-playing is seen by the Child as a reliable way of getting strokes. So what may happen when, for good Adult reasons, you reduce your game-playing?

Outside of awareness in Child, you may feel panic and ask yourself: 'What's happening to my stroke supply?' Recall that to the Child, loss of strokes means a threat to survival.

Thus without knowing it, you may begin using Little Professor strategies to regain the lost strokes. Perhaps you find other ways of playing the same old games. Or you start playing different games with the same Drama Triangle switch. Or you 'forget' to confront discounts. Superficially, these actions might be interpreted as 'self-sabotage'. As far as the early Child is concerned, their purpose is just the opposite. The motive is to maintain the supply of strokes, hence ensure survival.

For this reason, it's important that you not merely set out to 'stop playing games'. You also need to find a way of *replacing* the yield of strokes which you previously got from game-playing. Stan Woollams has drawn attention to an additional catch here.[5] Game strokes are plentiful and intense. By contrast, the strokes we can get from game-free living are relatively mild, and sometimes may not be in such reliable supply. For sure, these new strokes are straight ones instead of involving discounts. But as we know, the stroke-hungry Child is more concerned with quantity than quality.

There's no way around this, other than to take time to convince yourself in Child that the new stroke supply is acceptable and is going to last. During this transition period, it may be a good idea to set up extra sources of strokes that you can draw on to tide you over. This is one way in which the support of a group can help personal change.

In the longer term, you will become accustomed in Child to this new and less intense stroke input. Game-freedom may entail the loss of some familiar sources of excitement. But it allows us to use grown-up options which we denied ourselves through game-playing. And by moving out of games, we make it easier to move into the authentic closeness of intimacy.

● Look back at the game example that you analyzed by means of the Game Plan (Chapter 23).

Do you identify it with one of the named games given above? Check this against the switch in Drama Triangle positions you made at the Switch in the game.

Refer to the various techniques for countering games which you have learned in this chapter. Apply each of them to your game example. You will end up with a list of ways to disarm this game in the future.

If you want to apply these techniques, decide first how you are going to get strokes to replace those you will lose when you move out of the game. Set up this alternative stroke supply.

Then go ahead and begin countering the game. Choose one technique and use it consistently for a week. Then test out others in the same way. If you are working in a group, report back on your successes. ●

Part VII
CHANGING

TA in Practice

Chapter 26
CONTRACTS FOR CHANGE

It is outside the scope of this book to give detailed guidance on the professional uses of TA. Our aim in this final Part is to present you with a brief overview of the ways in which TA is used to promote change.

We begin in this chapter by looking at one of the central features of TA practice: the use of contracts.[1]

Berne defined a *contract* as *an explicit bilateral commitment to a well-defined course of action.* We also like James and Jongeward's definition: *'A contract is an Adult commitment to one's self and/or someone else to make a change.'*

Contracts specify:

— who both parties are;

— what it is they are going to do together;

— how long this will take;

— what the goal or outcome of that process will be;

— how they will know when they have gotten there; and

— how that will be beneficial and/or pleasing to the client.

TA practitioners distinguish two different kinds of contract: the *administrative* or *business contract* and the *clinical* or *treatment contract.*

The business contract is an agreement between the practitioner and client about the details of payment and administrative arrangements for their work together.

In the treatment contract, the client sets out clearly what changes he wants to make, and specifies what he is willing to do to help bring about these changes. The practitioner says whether she is willing to work with the client in the achievement of his desired changes, and states what her input to this process will be.

Steiner's 'four requirements'

Claude Steiner has set out four requirements for sound contract-making. They were derived from the practice of contract-making in legal settings.

(1) Mutual consent. This means that both parties must agree to the contract. The practitioner does not impose business arrangements nor treatment goals on the client. Nor can the client impose them on the practitioner. Instead, the contract is arrived at by negotiation between the two parties.

(2) Valid consideration. In legal language, a 'consideration' means some form of recompense given in return for someone's time or work. In TA settings, the consideration will usually be in the form of money paid by the client to the practitioner. Sometimes the parties may contract for the consideration to be made in kind. For example, the client might agree to do a certain number of hours' clerical work for the practitioner in return for each hour of treatment. Whatever the details, the nature of the consideration must be explicit and be agreed by both parties to the contract.

(3) Competency. Both the practitioner and the client must be competent to carry out what has been agreed upon in the contract. For the practitioner, this means having the specific professional skills needed to facilitate the client in his desired change. The client must be able to understand the contract and have the physical and mental resources to carry it through. This implies that, for example, a severely brain-damaged person might not be able to enter competently into a treatment contract. Nor can a competent contract be made by anyone who is under the influence of alcohol or mind-altering drugs.

(4) Lawful object. The goals and conditions of the contract must be in conformity with the law. For the practitioner, 'lawful object' also implies adherence to ethical principles laid down by the professional body to which she belongs.

Why use contracts?

First and foremost, the emphasis on contracts in TA practice arises from the philosophical assumption *'People are OK'*. The practitioner and client relate to each other as equals. Hence they share responsibility for the change the client wants to make.

This follows from the belief that everyone has the capacity to think and is ultimately responsible for her own life. She is the one who will live with the consequences of what she decides. Therefore it is up to the client, not the practitioner, to decide what she wants for her life. The practitioner's job is to point out everything that seems dysfunctional.

If this sharing of responsibility is to be meaningful, both parties need to be clear about the nature of the change that is desired and the contribution each will make to its achievement.

Contracts and the covert agenda

You know that in any relationship, the parties may exchange ulterior messages. This is especially likely to be true in situations where personal or organizational change is being sought, since such changes usually mean a challenge to someone's frame of reference. Both practitioner and client are likely to come into their working relationship with a *covert agenda* as

261

well as their social-level agenda. One important function of a contract is *to make the covert agenda explicit.* By exposing ulterior messages, clear contract-making cuts through psychological games and helps both the client and the practitioner to stay off the Drama Triangle.

The practitioner has her own frame of reference, and it will be different from that of the client. Therefore she will come into their relationship bringing her own internal definitions of what kinds of change are 'good' for people. Without a contract, it would be tempting for her to assume that her client's definitions were the same as her own. Further, because the definitions in her frame of reference might not be fully in her awareness, she might not be fully aware that she *was* making assumptions about the 'proper' goals for her client to pursue.

In this situation, it is likely that the practitioner would move into a Drama Triangle role. She might begin 'railroading' the client in a particular direction, thus playing Persecutor to the client's Victim. In Bob Goulding's words, working without a contract may mean that a therapist becomes *the rapist.*

Alternatively, the practitioner might say internally: 'This client obviously needs to make such-and-such a change. He hasn't made it yet. Therefore, he's in a sorry plight and can't get by without my help.' With this, she would step into the Rescuer role.

The client also is likely to have a covert as well as an overt agenda. By coming to the practitioner, he has declared on social level that there is some change he wants to make. (In some cases, he comes because there's a change that other people want him to make.) But he hasn't yet made the change. This may be because he genuinely doesn't know how to. Or it may be that he does know how to, but is defending on a covert level against making the change. In the latter case, he will be giving the practitioner ulterior messages like: 'I've come to change, but I'm helpless to do it,' or 'I've come to change, but you can't make me.'

If the covert agenda goes ahead on both sides, practitioner and client will take up complementary roles on the Drama Triangle, opening the way for racketeering and games.

One function of the contract is to forestall this. In *negotiating* clear objectives and methods of change, practitioner and client are forced to compare frames of reference. This process helps bring the covert agenda into Adult awareness, so that both parties can assess it against reality. Since neither the practitioner nor the client is perfect, it is unlikely that either will bring his full hidden agenda to light at the initial negotiation. Instead, the contract may have to be reviewed and if necessary re-negotiated many times during the process of change.

Contracts and goal-orientation

Most clients come to the practitioner bringing a *problem* which they want to tackle. One of the purposes of contract-making is to shift the focus of attention away from the problem, and center instead on the *goal of change*.

In the process of making a contract, both client and practitioner must necessarily construct a mental picture of the desired outcome of their work together. When they orient themselves to a clear goal in this way, they automatically mobilize the personal resources they need to achieve that outcome. This is the principle behind all systems of 'creative visualization'.

By contrast, if practitioner and client had given their attention mainly to 'the problem', they would have had to construct a mental picture of that problem. Without intending to, they would have been engaging in negative visualization, directing their resources to examining the problem rather than solving it.

There is still another advantage in setting a clearly-stated contract goal: it gives both parties a way of knowing when their work together has been completed. It also allows them to assess the progress they are making along the way. Thus the use of contracts prevents the situation where treatment might drag on interminably, with the client and practitioner spending months and years 'working on' the client's problems.

Making an effective contract

Here in summary are the main features which TA practitioners would look for in an effective contract. Rather than just stating these in the abstract, we invite you to put them into practice on a desired change of your own. As James and Jongeward point out, you can make a contract for change with yourself as well as with a therapist.

The exercise sequence which follows is based on a contract-making procedure for self-therapy devised originally by Muriel James.[2] It has been further developed by one of the present authors (IS). You need writing materials, plenty of paper, and time to work.

● Decide on a personal change you want to make. Write it down, using whatever words you bring to mind. ●

A contract goal must be *phrased in positive words*. Often, the initial wording of a goal will contain negatives. For example, the person may want to *stop* smoking or *control* drinking, to *lose* weight, or *not* to be scared of authority figures. Such 'stop contracts' and 'not contracts' never work in the long term. Partly, this is because of the way in which the contract goal acts as a visualization. You cannot visualize 'not something'. (If you doubt this, go ahead and visualize 'not a red elephant'.) When you try to do so, you automatically make a mental picture of whatever follows the 'not', or any other negative word. For instance, if a person takes on a contract to 'stop smoking', she cannot address that contract without continually visualizing the problem activity she is setting out to stop.

There's also a good reason in TA theory for the ineffectiveness of 'stop contracts'. Remember that all scripty behavior represents the Child's best strategy for surviving, getting strokes and getting needs met. So what happens if you simply contract to 'stop doing' that scripty behavior? At the very least, you have failed to give yourself in Child any clear directive on what you *are* going to do instead; you have simply added one more to the endless list of 'don'ts' and 'stops' you got from your parents when you were young. At worst, you may be contracting to give up a behavior which in Child you have been perceiving as essential to your survival.

To get to an effective contract, you must specify the *positive* which will provide you in Child with a clear directive to action. It must provide a new option for surviving and getting needs met that is at least as good as the old scripty option.

● If your stated want contains any negative words, re-phrase it to contain only positives. Your re-phrased statement will say what positive you are going to use to *replace* the negative. ●

The contract must be for a goal that is *achievable*, given your present situation and resources. Generally speaking, we deem 'achievable' anything that is physically possible. Note that this condition implies that you can only contract for a change you want to make in *yourself*. It is not physically possible to 'make' anyone else change.

● Check whether your desired change is possible for you. As a check question, ask: has at least one other person in the world achieved it? If so, list it as being possible. (Be sure to specify fully, however, what the 'it' entails). ●

The goal must be *specific and observable*. Both you and other people must be able to tell clearly whether you have achieved the goal. Beware of *over-generalized* goals and of *comparatives*. Often, people will start with global goals like: 'I want to be a warm, outgoing person' or 'I want to get closer to others.' To take a contract like this would be to buy into endless 'working on', since the stated goals are not specific enough to let anyone know whether they have been achieved.

● How will you and others know when your desired change has been achieved? State your answer with full detail of what you and others will be able to *see* and *hear* you doing differently. If your goal concerns the way you relate to other people, specify *which people, by name.* ●

The change you are aiming for must be *safe*. Use Adult appraisal, and consider both physical safety and social appropriateness.

● Is this desired change safe for you? ●

The contract goal must be made *from Adult, with Free Child co-operation*. In other words, it must be appropriate to your grown-up situation and abilities, and help satisfy your authentic Child needs rather than denying them. *A contract made from Adapted Child will almost always have the effect of furthering your script.* Adapted Child contracts are therefore to be avoided.

● Check: how much do you want this change for *you*, rather than to please others, get someone's approval, or rebel against someone? The 'others' and 'someone' may be people from your past or your present. Another way of asking this check question is: 'What's in this change for *me*?' ●

To achieve the goal, you need to mobilize your Child resources as well as those of your Adult and Parent. Therefore, contract goals in TA are phrased in 'eight-year-old language' — in words understandable to the Child part of you.

● Is your goal stated in words that an intelligent eight-year-old would understand? If not, re-phrase to make it so. ●

Achieving your goal *will always involve some cost*. This may be in terms of time, money, commitment, upheaval, saying goodbye, or facing the scare of change.

● Check: what will this change cost you to achieve? Now that you have worked out the cost, do you still want the change? ●

The remaining steps of the sequence concern a *commitment to specific action*.

● Write down at least five things you will *need to do* to achieve your contract goal. Again be specific in stating actions which you and others will be able to see and hear you taking. If these actions involve people, say *which* people by name.
Now, from the list of things you need to do, select and write down the ones you *will* do in the coming week.
Write down: 'The people who might support me in this change are...' and add their names. ●

Chapter 27
AIMS OF CHANGE IN TA

You saw in the previous chapter how specific contract goals are negotiated between the TA practitioner and the client. But what end-product are they to aim for in the change process? How will client and practitioner know when their work together is complete?

Autonomy

Eric Berne's suggested ideal was *autonomy*.[1] He never offered a definition of the word, but he described autonomy as being 'manifested by the release or recovery of three capacities: *awareness, spontaneity* and *intimacy.*'

Awareness

Awareness is the capacity to see, hear, feel, taste and smell things as pure sensual impressions, in the way a new-born infant does. The aware person does not interpret nor filter his experience of the world to fit Parental definitions. He is in contact with his own bodily sensations as well as with external stimuli.

As we grow up, most of us are systematically trained to deaden our awareness. We learn instead to devote energy to naming things and criticizing our own or other people's performance. For instance, suppose I am at a concert. As the musicians play, I may be engaged in an internal monologue: 'This was written in 1856, wasn't it? Hm, the tempo is a bit too fast. I wonder when this is going to finish? I must get an early night, lot of work to do tomorrow...'

If I let myself become aware, I switch off this voice in my head. I simply experience the sound of the music and my own bodily responses to it.

Spontaneity

Spontaneity means the capacity to choose from a full range of options in feeling, thinking and behaving. Just as the aware person experiences the world, so the spontaneous person responds to the world: directly, without blanking out portions of reality or re-interpreting it to fit Parental definitions.

266

Spontaneity implies that the person can respond freely from any of her three ego-states. She can think, feel or behave as her grown-up self, using her Adult ego-state. If she wants to, she can go into Child and get back in touch with the creativity, intuitive power and intensity of feeling she possessed in her own childhood. Or she may respond from Parent, re-playing the thoughts, feelings and behavior she learned from her parents and parent-figures. Whatever ego-state she uses, she will choose her response freely to suit the present situation, not to comply with outdated Parental commands.

Intimacy

You learned in Chapter 9 that intimacy means an open sharing of feelings and wants between you and another person. The feelings expressed are authentic, so intimacy excludes the possibility of racketeering or game-playing. When a person is in intimacy he is likely to move into Free Child, having first assured a safe setting for this through Adult contract-making and Parental protection.

Becoming free from the script

Though Berne didn't say so explicitly, he implied that autonomy was the same thing as *freedom from the script*. Most TA writers since Berne have also equated these two ideas. Thus we can suggest a definition of autonomy: *behavior, thinking or feeling which is a response to here-and-now reality, rather than a response to script beliefs.*

You may ask: 'But isn't the Adult ego-state defined as the set of behaviors, thoughts and feelings that are a direct response to the here-and-now? So does being autonomous mean being in Adult all the time?'

The answer is 'No.' We have already seen how the spontaneous person may sometimes *choose* to respond to the here-and-now by moving into Child or Parent ego-states. In autonomy, this *choice* is itself made freely in response to the present situation. By contrast, when a person is in script she will make her ego-state shifts in response to her own self-limiting childhood decisions about the world, her script beliefs.

Though autonomy doesn't mean being in constant Adult, it does imply processing all incoming data about the world through your Adult ego-state, then maintaining Adult awareness as you choose which ego-state to respond from. Like any other new skill, this may feel awkward at first. Autonomy always offers more options than does the script. Intimacy may well seem less comfortable initially than game-playing or racketeering, because intimacy is less predictable. However, autonomous ego-state choice becomes easier with practice. It can become so swift and natural that it's almost as though the person's Adult

267

ego-state had positive Child and positive Parent qualities incorporated into it. Berne suggested the phrase *integrated Adult* to convey this idea.²

Problem-solving

In Schiffian terms, we can say that the autonomous person engages in *problem-solving* instead of *passivity*. Here, 'problem-solving' doesn't only imply *thinking* to work out the solution to the problem; it means also taking effective *action* to bring that solution about. As we saw in Chapter 21, the expression of authentic *feelings* also serves a problem-solving function. When someone is problem-solving, he is accurately perceiving and responding to reality. Thus he is neither discounting nor redefining. And this in turn means he is script-free.

For TA work in organizational, educational or other settings outside therapy, it can be particularly appropriate to set 'effective problem-solving' as the goal for change, rather than 'autonomy' or 'being script-free'. In these settings, discounting and unsolved problems may often arise because people are *misinformed*, rather than because they are in script. Thus the practitioner needs to focus attention not on script-work, but on information exchange and the development of effective ways for people to act on that information.

Views of 'cure'

Another of Berne's enthusiasms was his emphasis on *cure*. He stressed time and again that the TA practitioner's job was to 'cure the patient', not merely to help him 'make progress'.³

In his book *Principles of Group Treatment*, Berne uses the metaphor of 'frogs and princes' to underline his own concept of cure. He suggests that 'cure' means casting off the frog skin and resuming the interrupted development as prince or princess, whereas 'making progress' means becoming a more comfortable frog. In *What Do You Say After You Say Hello?*, he describes cure as breaking out of the script entirely and 'putting a new show on the road'.

A few years ago, the *TA Journal* produced a symposium issue in which various TA writers gave their own interpretations of 'cure'.⁴ There were almost as many differing views as there were contributors. Here are just a few of the ideas that emerge from that discussion.

Some writers take the down-to-earth view that 'cure' can best be defined in terms of *contract completion*. Rather than have any global goal for change, the practitioner and client simply work together until the client has completed as many mutually-agreed contract goals as she wants.

More widely held is the view that, in therapy applications at least, 'cure' must entail some kind of movement out of script. Such *script cure* can be *behavioral, affective* or *cognitive*, or a combination of the three. In other words, someone who moves out of script can do so by acting, feeling or thinking in new ways.

Several writers suggest a fourth dimension to script change: *somatic cure*. This means that the person moving out of script will change the ways she uses and experiences her body. For instance, she may release chronic tensions or be relieved of psychosomatic ailments.

Cure: progressively learning new choices

No matter how you define 'script cure', it is seldom a once-for-all event. Much more often, cure is a matter of progressively learning to exercise new choices.

Whenever anyone makes a significant change in their script, they usually experience a natural 'high' for a few weeks or months. Then after a while they often go back to experiment with the old behavior. It's as though a part of them wants to see if there are any goodies left in that old behavior. The difference is that they recognize where they are and don't stay there as long. The old behavior is no longer as satisfying as it used to be and they have new options, so they move out sooner. Pretty soon it no longer has any appeal and they skip it altogether.

Perhaps this process is best summarized by the following poem:[5]

Autobiography in Five Short Chapters

by Portia Nelson

I

I walk down the street.
    There is a deep hole in the sidewalk.
I fall in
I am lost...I am helpless
It isn't my fault.
It takes forever to find a way out.

II

I walk down the same street.
    There is a deep hole in the sidewalk.
    I pretend I don't see it

I fall in again
I can't believe I am in the same place.
    But, it isn't my fault.
It still takes a long time to get out.

III

I walk down the same street.
    There is a deep hole in the sidewalk.
    I see it is there
    I still fall in...it's a habit
My eyes are open.
I know where I am.
    It is my fault.
I get out immediately.

IV

I walk down the same street.
    There is a deep hole in the sidewalk.
    I walk around it.

V

I walk down another street.

Chapter 28
TA THERAPY

Therapy is a process designed to help people in achieving personal change. In this chapter, we look at the nature and techniques of therapy in TA practice.

Self-therapy

If you have read this book and worked through the exercises, you have already done a great deal of *self-therapy*. You have examined the typical patterns of your own behavior, feelings and thinking. To help understand these, you have learned to use the many analytical devices that TA offers. You have recognized the outdated Child strategies that you now realize are not the most effective options for you as a grown-up, and you have tested active ways of replacing these with new and more successful options.

Some TA writers have given special attention to developing ways in which TA can be used in self-therapy. Notable among these is Muriel James. She won the Eric Berne Memorial Scientific Award for her work on *self-reparenting*.[1] This is a system by which the person can build a 'new Parent', providing positive new messages to overcome the negative, restrictive messages that may have been given by the actual parents. It employs a combination of techniques, including questionnaires, contract-making, fantasy and visualization, and behavioral change assignments.

In a sense, all therapy is self-therapy. TA recognizes that everyone is responsible for his own behavior, thoughts and feelings. Just as nobody can make you feel, so nobody can make you change. The only person who can change you is you.

Why therapy?

So, given that people are responsible for their own change, what is the point of working with a therapist?

One way to answer this question is in terms of *discounting* and the *frame of reference*. We all have some investment in blanking out aspects of reality that would threaten the picture of the world we put together in childhood. Any time I get into script in adulthood, I will be discounting to defend my frame of reference. If I am to solve problems and change effectively, I need to become aware of the aspects of reality I have been discounting.

But that's where the catch comes. By the very fact that I am discounting them, these features of reality are 'blind spots' for me. I *may* be able to detect and correct my discounting by my own Adult effort. TA's armory of analytical tools can help me greatly in this.

However, there are likely to be some parts of my frame of reference that I see in Child as being particularly important to my survival. These I will defend with especial energy. I will do this outside of awareness, by maintaining blind spots on any perceptions of reality that would confront these crucial discounts. In order to change in these areas, I need input from someone else who does not have the same blind spots.

Friends and family members are not likely to be the best source of this input. Families typically have blind spots that all the members of the family are brought up to share. I am also likely to select my friends, and my spouse or partner, because they have blind spots in common with my own. One purpose of working with a therapist, or of joining a therapy group, is that it gives me a source of feedback which is not subject to my own blind spots.

If I go on to use this feedback and begin altering my frame of reference, I am likely to begin feeling scared in Child. To see me through the change, I may need support and protection. I may also benefit from further confrontation as I employ all kinds of diverting tactics outside of my awareness as ways of defending against change. I will find it easier to make the change, and establish it as permanent, if I get strokes and encouragement from others. All of these benefits I can get from working with a therapist or group.

Who can benefit from therapy?

There's a TA saying: 'You don't need to be sick in order to get better.' You do not have to be disabled, disadvantaged or disturbed to get benefit from therapy. In fact, you do not even need to 'have problems'. You can be a well-functioning, fulfilled person, and enter therapy simply to get even more of what you want from life. Nobody is one hundred per cent script-free, no matter how lucky they were with their parents. For most of us, there are some areas of life where we have been setting up problems for ourselves by getting into script. If so, we may find it worth the time, money and commitment involved in going into therapy to resolve these script issues.

This said, TA therapy may also be sought by anyone who is experiencing personal problems, ranging from temporary relationship or work difficulties to severe mental disturbance. Treatment of the more serious disorders requires an appropriate setting, with psychiatric support.

272

Characteristics of TA therapy

If you decide to go into TA therapy, your first step is to find a qualified therapist and contract to attend for a certain number of sessions. These may be individual consultations, or you may become a member of a group. TA was originated by Berne as a method of group therapy, and most TA therapists still favor group treatment as the setting of choice.

In earlier chapters, you have already learned the main characteristics of TA therapy. Let's review these.

The practice of therapy in TA is founded upon a coherent *theoretical framework*, which you have learned in this book. You know that the main building-blocks of this theory are the *ego-state model* and the concept of *life-script*.

Personal change is seen in terms of a *decisional model*. In Part IV, you met TA's account of how each of us decides in childhood upon script patterns of behaving, thinking and feeling. A premise of all TA therapy is that that these early decisions can be changed.

You learned in Chapter 26 how TA treatment is based on a *contractual method*. The client and therapist take *joint responsibility* for achieving contract goals. These goals are chosen to promote movement out of script and into *autonomy*, in the way described in Chapter 27.

The therapeutic relationship in TA rests on the assumption that *people are OK*. The client and therapist are viewed as being on a level with each other, neither one-up nor one-down.

Open communication is fostered. Therapist and client speak a common language, using the simple words which you have met in this book. The client is encouraged to learn about TA. Therapists will usually ask their clients to attend introductory courses or read books on TA such as this one. If the therapist takes case notes, these are open to the client's inspection. In all these ways, the client is empowered to take an active and informed part in the the treatment process.

An additional feature of TA therapy is that it is oriented to *change*, rather than simply to the achievement of insight. Certainly, TA lays stress on understanding the nature and sources of problems. But this understanding is never viewed as an end in itself. Instead, it is a tool to use in the active process of change. The change itself consists in making a decision to act differently, then going ahead and doing so.

With this orientation, TA practitioners have never attached value to long-drawn-out therapy for its own sake. It's not expected that a client must necessarily take months and years of on-going work to achieve insight before he can change. Berne underlined this in a famous recommendation to clients: 'Get well first, and we'll analyze it later if you still want to.'

At the same time, TA is not solely a 'brief-therapy' approach. For the resolution of some problems, a long-term relationship needs to be set up between client and therapist, and this also can be done within a TA framework.

Three schools of TA

It's usual to distinguish three main 'schools' in present-day TA. Each of these has its own distinctive theoretical emphasis and its preferred range of therapeutic techniques.[2]

Few individual TA therapists nowadays belong exclusively to any one of these 'schools'. In fact, in order to gain professional accreditation, the therapist must demonstrate the ability to draw freely on the thinking and techniques of all three. The following 'thumbnail sketches' bring out the central features of each school, deliberately making them seem more sharply distinct than they really are.

The classical school

The classical school is so called because it follows most closely the approach to treatment developed in TA's early days by Berne and his associates. Classical practitioners use a whole range of analytical models to facilitate Adult understanding and at the same time 'hook' Child motivation. You learned many of these devices in the earlier chapters of this book: the Drama Triangle, the egogram, the stroking profile, Options, etc.

Thus in the classical approach, the first step is for the client to develop understanding of how he has been setting up problems. He then contracts to make behavioral changes which will mark movements out of his old scripty patterns and into autonomy. It is recognized that as the client changes his behavior, he is likely also to begin feeling differently, but encouragement to express feelings is not itself a central focus of classical TA.

Group treatment is strongly favored by the classical school. The *group process* is viewed as centrally important. This means that the client's interactions with other group members are assumed to be a re-play of the problem which the client has brought to therapy, which in turn is a re-play of problem situations left unresolved in childhood. The therapist's role is to allow the group process to develop, then feed in interventions which help the group members become aware of the games, racketeering and other scripty patterns they have been exhibiting in their relationships with other members and with the therapist.

In the view of the classical school, an important function of the therapist is to give the client new Parental messages. Pat Crossman has suggested 'three P's' that the therapist must provide in order to do this effectively: *permission, protection* and *potency*.[3]

In giving *permission*, the therapist gives the client messages that actively contradict injunctions or negative counterinjunctions in the script. These may be delivered verbally, as for example: 'It's OK for you to feel what you feel!' or 'Stop working so hard!' Permissions may also be modeled by the therapist.

If he is to accept the therapist's permission, the client in Child must perceive the therapist in Parent as being more powerful — having greater *potency* — than the actual parent from whom the original negative messages came. The client must also see the therapist as being able to provide *protection* against the disastrous consequences he fears may result from disobeying his parents' negative commands.

The redecision school

Bob and Mary Goulding are the orginators of a therapeutic approach that combines the theory of TA with the techniques of gestalt therapy, developed by Frederick (Fritz) Perls. The Gouldings point out that early decisions are made from a feeling rather than a thinking position. Therefore, in order to move out of script, the person must re-contact the Child feelings he experienced at the time of the early decision, finish the business by expressing those feelings, and change the early decision for a new and more appropriate *redecision*. This may be accomplished through fantasy or dreamwork, or by 'early scene work', in which the client tracks back in recollection to an early traumatic scene and re-experiences it.

Bob and Mary Goulding follow Perls in believing that when someone is 'stuck' with a problem, this indicates that two parts of their personality are pushing in opposite directions with equal force. The net result is that the person is using a great deal of energy, but getting nowhere. This situation is called an *impasse*. The Gouldings elaborated Perls' theory by picturing impasses as occurring between different ego-states. In therapy, impasse resolution is usually carried out using the gestalt technique known as 'two-chair work'. The client imagines the conflicting parts of himself in different chairs, 'becomes' each part in turn, and carries on a dialogue with the object of resolving the conflict. During this process, suppressed Child feelings may often be brought to the surface.

Even more than TA practitioners generally, redecision therapists emphasize personal responsibility. In redecision work, the therapeutic contract is not viewed as a two-sided agreement between client and therapist; it is a commitment made by the client to himself, with the therapist as witness. The therapist does not 'give the client permissions'. The client *takes* permission to behave and feel in new ways, with the therapist acting as a positive model. Likewise, *potency* is seen as a resource which the client already has, rather than being provided by the therapist.

Redecision therapists frequently work with groups, but they do not focus on group process. Instead, therapy is done one-to-one, with the rest of the group acting as witnesses and providing positive strokes to encourage and reinforce change.

While the expression of feeling is central to redecision work, therapists in this school stress that it is also important for the client to understand what is going on. Typically, the feeling work will be followed immediately by an 'Adult de-brief'. Equally important is for the client to make a contract for behavioral change to practice and consolidate his new decisions.

The Cathexis school

In Part V, we met the important contributions to TA theory made by the Cathexis school. The Schiffs originally founded the Cathexis Institute as a center for the treatment of psychotic clients. They used an approach which they called *reparenting*. It is based on the premise that 'craziness' is the result of destructive, inconsistent Parental messages. In treatment, the client is encouraged to regress to early infancy. In so doing, he *decathects* his 'crazy Parent' ego-state, i.e. withdraws all energy from it. He is then literally given the chance to re-do his growing up, this time with the therapist providing positive and consistent Parent input. Luckily, this second time of growing up proceeds much more quickly than the first time around. Even so, reparenting means that the fully-grown 'infant' will be heavily dependent for some time on his new 'mother' and 'father'. This style of treatment, then, requires a secure setting and a high degree of commitment on the part of the therapist, as well as psychiatric back-up. In the early days of Cathexis, the Schiffs legally adopted their 'children', so that there is now a widespread 'Schiff family'. Among them are counted some of the most respected theorists, therapists and teachers in present-day TA.

Schiffian method has also proven effective in therapy with non-psychotic clients. The emphasis here is on the consistent confronting of discounts and redefinitions. Instead of being passive, people are urged to think and act in order to solve problems. The intense therapeutic commitment of reparenting is not appropriate in work with non-psychotic clients. However, the Schiffian therapist may enter into a *parenting* contract with such clients. The therapist contracts to be consistently available to the client, within specified time boundaries, and serve as a 'replacement parent', giving the client new and positive Parental definitions in place of the restrictive messages that may have been received from the actual parents.

When Schiffian therapy is done in groups, the group is seen as providing a *reactive environment*. This means that all the members of the group, including the therapist, are expected to respond actively to the actions of other members. If you do something in the group that I don't like, I am expected to tell you: 'I don't like what you just did. I want you to do (x) instead.' If anyone in the group gets into passive behavior or discounting, the other group members are expected to confront this immediately, and call for active problem-solving. Here, 'confronting' does not mean Persecuting. It implies a straight demand on the other person, made from an I+U+ position. The person who makes the confrontation does so with the genuine motive of looking after herself *and* of helping the other person. Shea Schiff has used the phrase 'caring confrontation' to convey this idea.

Beyond the 'three schools'

Some of the major developments in today's TA lie outside the boundaries of any one of the 'three schools'. Two prime examples are Erskine and Zalcman's Racket System and Kahler's Miniscript. Each of these theoretical models has generated its own distinctive therapeutic approach.

One of TA's most positive features has been its ability to incorporate ideas and techniques from other therapies. These have proven readily compatible with the theoretical foundations of TA. The result is that the modern-day TA therapist possesses a large, adaptable 'tool-kit' of techniques which he can draw upon according to the client's needs. Most TA practitioners have also trained in other modalities, and bring these into their TA work. We have already spoken of the TA-gestalt combination used in redecision therapy. TA therapists may also use concepts and techniques drawn from psychoanalytic and brief-therapy approaches, bioenergetics, neuro-linguistic programming, systems theory, visualization and self-image modification techniques, Ericksonian therapy, behavioral psychology, developmental theory, and numerous other fields, according to the practitioner's background and interests. Always, the ego-state model and the theory of life-script act as organizing principles, guiding the use of these varied techniques within a TA framework.

Chapter 29
TA IN EDUCATION AND ORGANIZATIONS

From the earliest days of Eric Berne's development of TA, he regarded it as 'a theory of social action' and as a method of working with groups. TA can enhance effectiveness in almost any human endeavor where people are dealing with other people.

TA is employed in a great diversity of educational and organizational settings. Each of these has its own individual characteristics and needs. In this chapter, we give only a brief overview of the ways in which TA can be useful to educators, managers and organizational analysts. The list of References for this chapter will give you a guide to the literature on these applications.

Differences between educational-organizational and clinical applications

The basic theory of TA is the same for educational and organizational (EO) work as for clinical applications, but there are differences in emphasis and in techniques.[1] The training and accreditation of TA practitioners takes account of these differences (see Appendix E).

In clinical work, the *contract* is usually two-handed, being negotiated between the therapist and the individual client. By contrast, contracts in EO settings are most often three-handed. The business contract will be negotiated between the practitioner and the sponsoring agency, for the benefit of the members of the agency. For example, a business firm may hire a TA trainer to work with their employees. The treatment contract also is likely to be negotiated at least in part between the practitioner and the paying agency, rather than with the individuals or groups with whom the practitioner is actually working.

This implies that all parties must be particularly careful to maintain clear, above-board contract procedures to avoid three-handed game-playing. For example, a business firm may assign employees to a TA training course even though the employees themselves have no initial motivation to attend. Unless this starting-point is made overt in the contract negotiations between the firm, the trainer and the group members, there are immediate possibilities for all three parties to take up Drama Triangle roles, with subsequent game switches.

In EO work, the practitioner operates as a facilitator, trainer or coach rather than as a therapist. He will most often invite his group members to deal with what is going on at the *social level*, rather than the *psychological level*. Another way of saying this is that EO work addresses the *overt* rather than the *covert* agenda. Needless to say, the practitioner himself needs to be keenly aware of the 'Martian' messages that underlie what is happening at social level, but it is usually not appropriate for him to bring these messages directly to his clients' awareness.

One reason for this difference in emphasis is that in an EO setting the practitioner usually cannot provide the *protection* that is needed if the covert level is to be laid bare. In an in-house team-building course, for example, the participants may only be with the practitioner for two or three days. Were he to invite the group members back into unfinished script material, they might be left with the associated painful feelings but with no obvious means of resolving them. In any case, work at script level is by no means always necessary to achieve effective problem-solving. Recall from Chapter 17 that discounting can arise from *misinformation* just as easily as from contamination or exclusion.

In EO work, then, the practitioner will most often focus on how the individual or group can most effectively solve problems by thinking and acting in the present, rather than exploring what past business a person may need to finish. When ego-state diagnosis is used, it will be behavioral and social, rather than historical or phenomenological. The practitioner may teach his group members the concept of life-script, as a way of explaining why people may act in ways that appear self-defeating or painful. But individual script-work will seldom be used. In the sections which follow, we review some of the ways in which TA concepts can be applied in organizational and educational settings.

Organizational applications

Does organizational work in TA[2] have any overall goal which corresponds to the goal of autonomy in TA therapy? Roger Blakeney suggests the criterion of *effectiveness*. He points out that organizations, like individuals, may develop dysfunctional or ineffective patterns of behavior, analogous to a person's scripty behavior. Movement out of this 'organizational script' will be marked by an improvement in the organization's effectiveness in achieving its desired outcomes.

Ego-states

Organizations do not themselves have ego-states, but they do have elements that function in an analogous way. They have patterns of beliefs, etiquette and rules that correspond to the Parent ego-state. They have technologies and problem-solving strategies that are analogous to the Adult. And they have patterns of behavior and feelings that parallel the Child ego-state. The organizational analyst can examine the amount of energy that the organization devotes to each of these three elements, in the same way as the therapist examines the distribution of cathexis among a person's ego-states.

On a more obvious level, communication and interactions between individuals in an organization can be enhanced by knowledge of the ego-state model. Managers, for instance, may realize they are taking up a negative Parental stance, while their employees respond from a negative Adapted Child by being rebellious or overly compliant. To improve effectiveness, both managers and employees might take action to raise their use of Adult. They might make a clear contract on when it was appropriate for the managers to use positive Parent and the employees to be in positive Adapted Child (in situations where safety was involved, perhaps). Free Child, hence job satisfaction, might be encouraged by such means as making the workplace brighter and more comfortable. It's reported that some Japanese firms provide their employees with stuffed dummies of the management, together with large wooden clubs. When a worker is feeling sore at the boss, he can take time out in work hours to go and beat up his replica manager. This is Free Child release *par excellence*.

Transactions, strokes, time structuring

The analysis of *transactions* has been widely applied in training personnel who are in direct contact with the public, e.g. receptionists and booking clerks. They learn how to keep the flow of communication smooth and comfortable by maintaining parallel transactions, or how to thwart a potential Parent-Child argument by crossing a transaction.

The analysis of *stroking* patterns has obvious application in enhancing job motivation. Managers may need to learn to give positive strokes for jobs done well, rather than giving only negatives for jobs done badly. The principle of 'different strokes for different folks' applies: while you may get your greatest satisfaction from the praise of respected superiors, I may prefer to get my strokes in the form of a bigger wage-packet or longer holidays.

When *time structuring* at meetings is examined, it may sometimes turn out that these gatherings consist of much pastiming and little activity. As for games, they probably account for the greatest waste of time and human resources in organizations. Individuals often resort to games when they feel bored, not recognized or not sufficiently challenged within the organization. Changing stroking patterns and increasing the opportunities for positive challenge can do wonders to eliminate game-playing and increase productivity. TA procedures of *contract-making* can also help direct organizational energy into constructive action rather than the pursuit of hidden agendas.

Confronting passivity

Schiffian concepts have proven widely useful in organizational applications. The Discount Matrix provides a means of systematic problem-solving. It is particularly useful in situations where information and instructions are 'passed down the line', with the accompanying tendency for details to get lost or distorted on the way. An awareness of verbal discounts, tangential and blocking transactions can enhance communication and improve the effectiveness of meetings.

TA in education

Autonomy implies clear thinking and effective problem-solving. The educator aims to help her students develop these abilities. Therefore, autonomy as an overall goal is as relevant in educational settings[3] as it is in clinical work.

The educator will usually be able to relate to her students over a longer period and in a more personal way than is possible for the organizational practitioner. By the nature of educational settings, it is especially likely that the students may 'put a face on' the teacher, and that she in turn may buy into these replays of the past by taking on a Parental role. She can help avoid this by acquiring a knowledge of script theory and by learning the content of her own script.

TA theories of child development can guide the educator in dealing effectively with young people at various developmental stages.

Ego-states

The basic ego-state model is readily understood by children from early school age onwards. TA's simple language helps in this learning. By examining the content and motivations in all three of their ego-states, students become better able to learn with a clear knowledge of their own intentions and desires. Learning experiences themselves are most likely to be effective if they appeal to all three ego-states. It is especially important to recognize that the Free Child is the source of creativity and energy in the personality and needs to be included in the learning process.

The educator herself needs to have free access to all her ego-states. For much of the time, she will be demonstrating Adult problem-solving. Often she will need to set firm boundaries from positive Controlling Parent, or to show caring from positive Nurturing Parent. She can get into Child to model spontaneity, intuitive ability and the enjoyment of learning.

Transactions, strokes, time structuring

The analysis of transactions is useful in keeping communication between teachers and students clear, productive and free of hidden agendas. Using *Options* can help both teachers and students to break out of 'locked' Parent-Child interactions.

Detecting and avoiding *driver* behavior can also be a great help in clearing communication. There is a big difference between learning something and trying to learn it. Lecturers come over more clearly when they are taking their time instead of hurrying up. Students improve their study technique when they are satisfied with covering enough, rather than setting out to Be Perfect by covering everything.

Attention to patterns of *stroking* and *time structuring* is relevant to education in much the same way as to organizational work. The classroom and lecture-hall are especially rich breeding-grounds for *games* and *racketeering*. Students may play games such as Stupid, You Can't Make Me, or Do Me Something (with its potential Switch into See What You Made Me Do). Teachers can play See How Hard I've Tried, I'm Only Trying To Help You, Why Don't You..., or Blemish. A knowledge of game analysis enables students and teachers to avoid these unproductive exchanges and get on with the activities of teaching and learning.

The use of *contract-making* helps educators and learners to reach clear, overt agreement about what they are each there to do and how best they can do it.

Confronting passivity

In educational settings, it is especially likely that people may be expecting symbiosis. This expectation may even be overt in some cultures, where teachers are traditionally pictured as playing the Parent and Adult role while the student plays Child. Current approaches to education agree with TA in viewing this as a discount of the abilities of both parties.

A knowledge of Schiffian concepts helps teachers and students to stay out of symbiosis and make full use of all three ego-states. Educators can learn to recognize the four passive behaviors and confront them instead of buying into games. If the institutional setting makes it possible, tutorial groups and classes may be set up to provide a reactive environment where teachers and students take mutual responsibility to promote clear thinking and active problem-solving.

Chapter 30
HOW TA HAS DEVELOPED

At the date of this book's first publication, it is thirty years since Eric Berne delivered the first professional paper to bear the title 'Transactional Analysis'. Of that thirty-year span, more than half has gone by since Berne's early death in 1970. TA, like Berne himself, has had to face the premature loss of a father.

In this chapter, we trace Berne's life and the origins of his thinking in the 1950s and earlier. The thirty years following that 1957 paper saw first a phase of early development, in the fertile minds of a handful of TA professionals centered on America's West Coast. The publication of Berne's bestselling *Games People Play*, in the mid-1960s, catapulted TA into the public eye, and marked the beginning of a decade of mass popularity.

The years from the late 1970s until the present have been a period of consolidation. The numerical following of TA has declined from a 1976 peak to a current level which, though lower, is stable and still much higher than in the early years. Theory and practice have been refined and developed. Perhaps most striking of all has been the worldwide spread of interest in TA. No longer confined to the West Coast, to America, or to English-speaking countries, the TA community has become truly international.

Eric Berne and the origins of TA

Eric Berne[1] was born Eric Lennard Bernstein in Montreal in 1910. His father was a general practitioner and his mother a professional writer. His early years were happy, and he especially enjoyed accompanying his father on his medical rounds. Then, when Eric was only nine, his father died. His loss affected the little boy deeply, and this may have been a major influence in Berne's later development.

Encouraged by his ambitious mother, Berne went on to enter medical school, and qualified as a doctor in 1935. Shortly afterwards he moved to America and began psychiatric residency. He became an American citizen and changed his name to Eric Berne.

In 1941 he began training as a psychoanalyst, becoming an analysand of Paul Federn. This was interrupted by the outbreak of World War II, and Berne joined the Army Medical Corps in 1943 as a psychiatrist.

During this period of service, he began practicing group therapy. He had already started compiling critical notes on psychiatry and psychoanalysis which were to form the basis for later writings.

Following his release from the Army in 1946, Berne resumed his psychoanalytic training, this time under Erik Erikson. He began the regime of hard work which marked the rest of his life, combining a private practice with several official appointments and a crowded schedule of writing commitments. His first book, *The Mind in Action*, was published in 1947; it was to be revised in 1957 as *A Layman's Guide to Psychiatry and Psychoanalysis.*[2]

In 1949, Berne published the first of six professional journal articles concerning the nature of intuition. Appearing from that year until 1958, these were to present the emerging ideas on which Berne founded his development of TA.

All this time, Berne had continued training in psychoanalysis. In 1956 he applied for membership of his professional psychoanalytic institute, but was turned down.

Spurred on by this rejection, Berne resolved to go ahead by himself and construct a new approach to psychotherapy. By the end of that year, he had completed two more in his series of papers on intuition, in which he first presented his concept of Parent, Adult and Child ego-states and used the term 'structural analysis'. These articles were published in 1957. Berne went on to write a further paper, which he presented to the American Group Psychotherapy Association in November 1957. It was entitled 'Transactional Analysis: A New and Effective Method of Group Therapy'.

In this article, which appeared in print the following year, Berne re-stated his concepts of Parent, Adult and Child ego-states, and introduced the notions of games and script. Thus the basic framework of TA theory was already complete.

What kind of man was Berne? Different people who knew him have different memories of his complex personality. Some say he was genial, supportive, fun-loving. Others recall him as sharp-tongued, competitive and personally distant.[3] What is certain is that he was a clear thinker, and demanded clear thinking in others. This quality has come down to us in the coherent structure of TA theory.

Throughout his career, Berne kept up a keen interest in the function of intuition. As well as providing the impetus to Berne's original formulation of TA concepts, this was reflected in the stress he laid on 'thinking Martian': understanding covert as well as overt messages.

Berne was an individualist, even a rebel. We can only guess whether his rejection by the psychoanalytic establishment was genuinely the spur for his development of TA. But he did succeed in originating a method of psychotherapy that 'broke the rules' of the establishment, as Berne saw them at the time. His ideal was to cure people quickly, rather than having them 'make progress' during years of therapy. He determined that TA should speak the language of the layman, instead of cloaking itself in Latin and Greek, so that client and therapist could more readily co-operate in the process of cure.

Paradoxically, some of Berne's most deeply-felt ideals sprang directly from a medical background. Perhaps this reflected not only his own medical training, but also his memories of a happy childhood spent with his father. When Berne wrote *Transactional Analysis in Psychotherapy*, he gave it a Latin dedication: 'To the memory of my father David, Doctor of Medicine and Master of Surgery, and doctor to the poor'.

To Berne, the effective therapist had to be a 'real doctor'. Berne was not suggesting that only medically-qualified persons should become therapists. On the contrary, he meant that *any* therapist had to accept the responsibilities expected of a medical doctor. The 'real doctor', said Berne, is always oriented first and foremost towards curing his patients. He must plan his treatment so that at each phase he knows what he is doing and why he is doing it. These qualities are still demanded today in the accreditation of TA practitioners.

The early years

Since the early 1950s, Berne and his associates had been holding regular clinical seminars.[4] In 1958 they formed the San Francisco Social Psychiatry Seminars (SFSPS), meeting each Tuesday at Berne's home. With several changes of name and venue, their meetings have continued to this day.

In those early years, the San Francisco seminars provided a fertile breeding-ground for the emerging ideas of TA. Berne's *Transactional Analysis in Psychotherapy*, the first book entirely devoted to TA, appeared in 1961. It was followed in 1963 by *The Structure and Dynamics of Organizations and Groups*. The *Transactional Analysis Bulletin* began publication in January 1962, with Berne as Editor.

The membership of the SFSPS included many who are now well-known figures in the 'Classical school' of TA, such as Claude Steiner, Jack Dusay, Stephen Karpman and Franklin Ernst.

Also among the participants in the early seminar meetings was Jacqui Lee Schiff. In addition, Bob Goulding entered clinical supervision with Berne in the early 1960s. Thus were sown the seeds of development of the other two main 'schools' of current TA, which we described in Chapter 28.

In 1964, Berne and his colleagues decided to form the International Transactional Analysis Association (ITAA) in recognition of the fact that TA was now being practiced by a growing number of professionals outside the USA. At the same time, the name of the San Francisco seminar was changed to the San Francisco Transactional Analysis Seminar (SFTAS).

The year 1964 also saw what was to be a landmark in TA's history: the publication of *Games People Play*. Berne had intended the book to be a reader for a relatively small circle of professionals. Instead, it became a best-seller. As its sales boomed worldwide, so the language and ideas of TA caught the imagination of a mass audience.

The years of expansion

The commercial success of *Games People Play* did not produce an immediate explosion in the number of professionals using TA. The 1965 membership roll of ITAA contained a mere 279 names. However, these small numbers of practitioners continued a steady development of TA theory and practice. In 1965 the Schiffs, now based in the Eastern USA, began their work with psychotic clients. Berne's *Principles of Group Treatment* was published in 1966, and the same year saw the appearance of Steiner's seminal article on 'Script and Counterscript' in the *TA Bulletin*.

In 1968, the membership of ITAA had grown to more than 500, and Stephen Karpman's Drama Triangle made its first public appearance in a *TAB* article.

All the while, Berne continued with his unremitting routine of hard work. By June 1970, he had completed the manuscripts of two books, *Sex in Human Loving* and *What Do You Say After You Say Hello?*. But he was never to see them in print. Late in June he suffered a heart attack and was rushed to hospital. Thought at first to be recovering, he had a second attack and died on July 15, 1970.

The first issue of the *Transactional Analysis Journal*, in January 1971, was a memorial volume in honor of Berne. In that same issue, Aaron and Jacqui Schiff published their pathbreaking article on 'Passivity', and Stephen Karpman presented his concept of 'Options'.

As well as Berne's own works, two other best-selling books helped swell public interest in TA. Thomas Harris's *I'm OK, You're OK* had appeared in 1967. Unlike *Games People Play*, it was aimed specifically at a lay readership, and presented the basic theory of TA in a way that was immediately appealing if sometimes idiosyncratic. In 1971, Muriel James and Dorothy Jongeward's *Born To Win* brought TA ideas together with the gestalt approach of Fritz Perls.

Thus the snowball of public interest began rolling. ITAA's membership, which numbered around 1,000 in 1971, grew to over 5,000 by 1973. It continued to rise until it reached a peak of almost 11,000 in 1976.[5]

Meantime, all three 'schools' of TA were busy with further advances in theory and practice. Jack Dusay's original article on 'Egograms' appeared in the *TA Journal* in 1972. In the same year, Bob and Mary Goulding published the article which presented their ideas on redecision and injunctions, and the Schiffs founded the Cathexis Institute.

Taibi Kahler's work on drivers and the miniscript, first presented in a 1974 *TA Journal* article, represented a major new departure for TA. Kahler's ideas fell outside the framework of any of the main 'schools'. And though the miniscript is firmly rooted in basic TA theory, it introduces some crucial concepts that Berne had never heard of by the time of his death in 1970.

International consolidation

If TA was conceived in Berne's early studies of intuition, and born with the presentation of his 1957 paper, it came of age in 1978. By that year the membership of the ITAA had fallen back to 8,000. The number continued to decline, reaching the 5,000 mark in 1985.

The novelty value of TA as a media item has worn off, as it was bound to do. Yet the decline in mass interest is only a part of TA's current story, and perhaps a rather unimportant part. More to the point is that TA has found maturity as a discipline, and gained international acceptance as a professional approach. In this regard, it may have been no bad thing for TA to have lost the 'pop psychology' image it acquired in some people's minds during the years of rapid expansion.

Two books appeared in 1977 which in many ways symbolized this change. Both were symposium volumes, aimed principally at a professional audience. *Transactional Analysis After Eric Berne*, edited by Graham Barnes, documented the major growth and developments in TA theory and practice that had taken place since Berne's death. Muriel James was editor of *Techniques in Transactional Analysis for Psychotherapists and Counselors*, focusing principally on the current applications of TA.

TA writers have continued to add to the depth and breadth of TA thinking. Richard Erskine and Marilyn Zalcman's Racket System, for instance, was first presented in a 1979 *TA Journal* article.

Professional training and accreditation in TA conform to standards recognized worldwide. Currently they are administered by ITAA and by the European Association for Transactional Analysis (EATA). We give details at Appendix E.

Active interest in TA outside the USA had begun well before the main period of expansion. As early as 1964, a TA approach to group interaction was being taught in adult-education settings by Professor John Allaway of the University of Leicester, England.[6] Classes in this

287

format continue to the present day.

The ITAA's 1965 membership contained a handful of names from outside the U.S. As the worldwide surge of interest in TA got under way, non-U.S. numbers grew with the rest, until in 1976 there were some 2,000 members from outside the U.S. in the total of over 10,000. An interesting development has been that as the total ITAA membership has fallen back, the non-U.S. numbers have continued to increase. Thus the proportion of the membership roll represented by non-U.S. members has steadily risen. To an ever-increasing degree, ITAA is becoming truly international. In recognition of this fact, ITAA in the late 1980s embarked on a radical program of international affiliation (see Appendix D).

At the date of this book's fifth printing (March 1991), the total membership of ITAA is once again on the increase. Currently the organization has some 7,000 members from over 60 countries.

As interest in TA has grown throughout the world, a natural consequence has been the foundation of local, national and continental TA organizations. The European Association for Transactional Analysis was founded in 1974, and currently has more than 4,000 members. It held its first congress in 1975, and this was followed in 1976 by the first Pan-American congress. There are national TA associations in many countries of Europe, North and South America, Asia and Australasia (see Appendix D).

Though TA was slower at first to find acceptance in the countries of the Eastern bloc, it is gathering momentum there also. In January 1987, a group of ITAA visitors gave the first TA 101 course ever to be presented in the People's Republic of China.[7] More recently, the sweeping political changes in Eastern Europe have cleared the way for an upsurge of activity in TA. At the time of writing (March 1991), TA associations in Hungary, Poland and the Soviet Union are in dialog with EATA, enthusiastic to forge closer links with their TA colleagues in Europe and worldwide.

APPENDICES

Appendix A
BOOKS BY ERIC BERNE

For a complete bibliography of Berne's writings, see Cranmer, R., 'Eric Berne: annotated bibliography'. *Transactional Analysis Journal, 1,* 1, 1971, 23-9.
Following are the eight books by Berne listed in the ITAA's reference guide for the TA 101 Course.

Berne, E., *Intuition and ego states.* (McCormick, P., ed.). San Francisco: TA Press, 1977.
A compilation of the papers Berne published in professional journals from 1949 to 1962 on various topics connected with intuition. They include his first statements on the basic theory of TA.

Berne, E., *A layman's guide to psychiatry and psychoanalysis.* New York: Simon and Schuster, 1957; third edition published 1968. *Other editions:* New York: Grove Press, 1957; *and* Harmondsworth: Penguin, 1971.
A revision of *The mind in action,* originally published in 1947. The 1967 edition of *A layman's guide* introduced a chapter on transactional analysis, contributed by John Dusay.

Berne, E., *Transactional analysis in psychotherapy.* New York: Grove Press, 1961, 1966.
The first book to deal wholly with TA. It contains Berne's original, and still definitive, formulation of the ego-state model, together with expanded statements of the other elements of basic theory introduced in his earlier journal papers.

Berne, E., *The structure and dynamics of organizations and groups.* Philadelphia: J.B. Lippincott Co., 1963. *Other editions:* New York: Grove Press, 1966; *and* New York: Ballantine, 1973.
The book's content is described by its title. Includes some TA concepts, e.g. analysis of transactions and games.

Berne, E., *Games people play.* New York: Grove Press, 1964. *Other editions include:* Harmondsworth: Penguin, 1968.
The world-famous best-seller which presents the ideas on game analysis which Berne had developed by the early 1960s. (He revised this

theory in successive later books — see *TA Today*, Chapter 23.) Also contains a compendium of the games which had been named up to that time.

Berne, E., *Principles of group treatment.* New York: Oxford University Press, 1966. *Other editions:* New York: Grove Press, 1966.
A text on the theory and practice of group treatment in clinical settings, including the application of TA in this field.

Berne, E., *Sex in human loving.* New York: Simon and Schuster, 1970. *Other editions:* Harmondsworth: Penguin, 1973.
An exploration of sex in personal relationships, analyzed in a TA framework.

Berne, E., *What do you say after you say hello?* New York: Grove Press, 1972. *Other editions:* London: Corgi, 1975.
An extended statement of the theory of script as developed by Berne and his associates up to the late 1970s, with applications to therapy.

Appendix B
OTHER KEY BOOKS ON TA

In selecting the few 'key books' named in this Appendix, we do *not* intend any adverse comment on the quality of the many other books currently available on TA. The books we cite here have been chosen on two criteria. They are either compendium volumes, which give a broad overview of TA theory and practice; or widely-accepted statements of the position of one of the three 'TA schools'. In both these senses, they are 'keys' to further reading and study in TA.

We do not give any indication whether a book is currently in print, since this information may change at short notice with individual publishers' decisions.

Texts and compendium volumes

Barnes, G. (ed), *Transactional analysis after Eric Berne: teachings and practices of three TA schools.* New York: Harper's College Press, 1977.
Its 22 papers are centered mainly on the discussion of post-Bernian developments in theory, though practice is also well covered. Explores the nature and development of the three current 'schools' of TA.

James, M. (ed), *Techniques in transactional analysis for psychotherapists and counselors.* Reading: Addison-Wesley, 1977.
A symposium of 43 papers, with Muriel James contributing as well as editing. As the title indicates, the book is focused primarily on the techniques of modern TA, but theory is also examined, and there is a section examining the relationships between TA and other therapies.

James, M., and Jongeward, D., *Born to win: transactional analysis with gestalt experiments.* Reading: Addison-Wesley, 1971. *Other editions include:* New York: Signet, 1978.
The 1971 best-seller, still a sound introduction to TA basics. Notable for its use of gestalt exercises to aid learning and self-knowledge.

Kahler, T., *Transactional analysis revisited.* Little Rock: Human Development Publications, 1978.
A wide-ranging critique of TA theory, including a update and expansion of Kahler's own Miniscript concept.

Stern, E. (ed), *TA: the state of the art.* Dordrecht: Foris Publications, 1984.
With 23 papers, contributed mainly by European practitioners, this book gives a view of the 'cutting edge' of current theory and practice in TA.

Woollams, S., and Brown, M., *Transactional analysis.* Dexter: Huron Valley Institute, 1978. *Other editions:* (paperback edition with some revisions) *TA: the total handbook of transactional analysis.* Englewood Cliffs: Prentice-Hall, 1979.
A comprehensive text of TA theory and practice.

Classical school

Dusay, J., *Egograms.* New York: Harper and Row, 1977. *Other editions:* New York: Bantam, 1980.
A readable presentation of Dusay's egogram concept, plus the functional ego-state model and other aspects of classical TA.

Steiner, C., *Scripts people live: transactional analysis of life scripts.* New York: Grove Press, 1974.
A thorough discussion of the theory and implications of life-script.

Redecision school

Goulding, M., and Goulding, R., *Changing lives through redecision therapy.* New York: Brunner/Mazel, 1979.

Goulding, R., and Goulding, M., *The power is in the patient.* San Francisco: TA Press, 1978.
These two books by the Gouldings describe both the theory and the practice of their redecision work. The latter volume is a compilation of papers originally published by them in journals and professional volumes.

Cathexis school

Schiff, J., *et al., The Cathexis reader: transactional analysis treatment of psychosis.* New York: Harper and Row, 1975.
A full statement of Schiffian theory, incorporating material originally published in the *TA Journal.*

Appendix C *(Revised March 1996)*
WINNERS OF THE ERIC BERNE MEMORIAL AWARDS

The Eric Berne Memorial Scientific Award was established in 1971 to honor and perpetuate the memory of Eric Berne's scientific contributions. It was to be given annually to the originator of a new scientific concept in TA. Adjudication was by the Editorial Board of ITAA.

In 1990, the ITAA Board of Trustees decided to change the title and scope of the Award. It is now known as the Eric Berne Memorial Award in Transactional Analysis. The Award is given annually for published contributions to TA theory or practise, or for the integration or comparison of TA theory or practise with other therapeutic modalities. The winner(s) of the Award are chosen by a committee appointed by the ITAA Board of Trustees.

Following is a chronological list of winners of the Award for the years 1971-1994, together with references to the works for which they received their awards. (At print date, the 1995 Award is still under consideration).

Numbers in brackets in *italic type* following each reference indicate the chapter of *TA Today* in which the topic is covered.

1971: Claude Steiner, SCRIPT MATRIX. Steiner, C., 'Script and counterscript'. *Transactional Analysis Bulletin, 5, 18, 1966, 133-35. (13)*

1972: Stephen Karpman, DRAMA TRIANGLE. Karpman, S., 'Fairy tales and script drama analysis'. *TAB, 7, 26, 1968, 39-43. (23)*

1973: John Dusay, EGOGRAMS. Dusay, J., 'Egograms and the constancy hypothesis'. *Transactional Analysis Journal, 2, 3, 1972, 37-42. (3)*

1974: Aaron Schiff and Jacqui Schiff, PASSIVITY AND THE FOUR DISCOUNTS. Schiff, A., and Schiff, J., 'Passivity'. *TAJ, 1, 1, 1971, 71-8. (17)*

1975: Robert Goulding and Mary Goulding, REDECISION AND TWELVE INJUNCTIONS. Goulding, R., and Goulding, M., 'New directions in transactional analysis'. *In* Sager and Kaplan (eds.), *Progress in group and family therapy.* New York: Brunner/Mazel, 1972, 105-34; *and* 'Injunctions, decisions and redecisions'. *TAJ, 6, 1, 1976, 41-8. (14)*

1976: Pat Crossman, PROTECTION. Crossman, P., 'Permission and protection'. *TAB*, *5*, 19, 1966, 152-4. *(28)*

1977: Taibi Kahler, MINISCRIPT AND FIVE DRIVERS. Kahler, T., 'The miniscript'. *TAJ*, *4*, 1, 1974, 26-42. *(16)*

1978: Fanita English, RACKETS AND REAL FEELINGS: THE SUBSTITUTION FACTOR. English, F., 'The substitution factor: rackets and real feelings'. *TAJ*, *1*, 4, 1971, 225-30; *and* 'Rackets and real feelings, Part II'. *TAJ*, *2*, 1, 1972, 23-5. *(21)*

1979: Stephen Karpman, OPTIONS. Karpman, S., 'Options'. *TAJ*, *1*, 1, 1971, 79-87. *(7)*

1980: (joint award): Claude Steiner, THE STROKE ECONOMY. Steiner, C., 'The stroke economy'. *TAJ*, *1*, 3, 1971, 9-15. *(8)*

1980: (joint award): Ken Mellor and Eric Sigmund, DISCOUNTING AND REDEFINING. Mellor, K., and Sigmund, E., 'Discounting'. *TAJ*, *5*, 3, 1975, 295-302; *and* Mellor, K., and Sigmund, E., 'Redefining'. *TAJ*, *5*, 3, 1975, 303-11. *(17, 18, 19)*

1981: Franklin H. Ernst, Jr., THE OK CORRAL. Ernst, F., 'The OK corral: the grid for get-on-with'. *TAJ*, *1*, 4, 1971, 231-40. *(12)*

1982: Richard Erskine and Marilyn Zalcman, RACKET SYSTEM AND RACKET ANALYSIS. Erskine, R., and Zalcman, M., 'The racket system: a model for racket analysis'. *TAJ*, *9*, 1, 1979, 51-9. *(22)*

1983: Muriel James, SELF-REPARENTING. James, M., 'Self-reparenting: theory and process'. *TAJ*, *4*, 3, 1974, 32-9. *(28)*

1984: Pam Levin, DEVELOPMENTAL CYCLES. Levin, P., 'The cycle of development'. *TAJ*, *12*, 2, 1982, 129-39. *(References, 10)*

1985, 1986: Not awarded.

1987: Carlo Moiso, EGO STATES AND TRANSFERENCE. Moiso, C., 'Ego states and transference'. *TAJ*, *15*, 3, 1985, 194-201. *(—)*

1988 through 1993: Not awarded.

1994 (EBMA joint award): Sharon R. Dashiell *(area: Practise Applications)*. Dashiell, S., 'The Parent resolution process: reprogramming psychic incorporations in the Parent'. *TAJ*, *8*, 4, 1978, 289-94. *(—)*

1994 (EBMA joint award): John R. McNeel *(area: Practise Applications)*. McNeel, J., 'The Parent interview'. *TAJ*, *6*, 1, 1976, 61-8. *(—)*

1994 (EBMA joint award): Vann S. Joines *(area: Integration of TA with Other Theories and Approaches)*. Joines, V., 'Using redecision therapy with different personality adaptations'. *TAJ*, *16*, 3, 1986, 152-60; *and* 'Diagnosis and treatment planning using a transactional analysis framework'. *TAJ*, *18*, 3, 1988, 185-90.

Appendix D *(Revised March 1991)*
TA ORGANIZATIONS

At the date of this revision (March 1991), there is one TA organization with worldwide coverage: the International Transactional Analysis Association (ITAA). Another organization, the European Association for Transactional Analysis (EATA), covers the continent of Europe. As well as these two international organizations, there are national or regional TA associations in many countries of the world.

In Chapter 30, we gave a brief sketch of the historical development of ITAA and EATA. Appendix E will describe their activities in TA training and accreditation.

The International Transactional Analysis Association

The ITAA is a non-profit educational corporation in the terms of US law. Persons wishing to become ITAA members may do so in two alternative ways. They can join through their national or regional TA association, if it is affiliated with ITAA (see below); or, if there is no affiliated association in their region, they can join ITAA as a direct member.

ITAA offers four categories of direct membership. *Associate Membership* is a general-interest, non-voting membership which supports the humanistic goals of ITAA. *Regular Membership* is a support-level, voting membership for professionals who use TA but are certified through another source. This is also the membership for persons in the process of attaining competency-based certification from the Training and Certification Council of Transactional Analysts *(see Appendix E)*. A 'TA 101' course or exam and signature of a Teaching Member are required. *Certified Membership* is a professional-level, voting membership for TA practitioners. This membership is earned by passing written and oral exams administered by the Training and Certification Council, after study under a certified Instructor or Supervisor *(see Appendix E)*. Certified Members may specialize in clinical, organizational or educational areas. *Certified Teaching Membership* is for advanced professionals who effectively communicate the concepts of TA as instructors and/or effectively oversee the application of TA concepts as supervisors. As in the case of Certified Membership, this level of membership is attained by passing an examination administered by the Training and Certification Council.

During the late 1980s, in response to the rapid international growth of TA, the ITAA initiated a policy of affiliation with the aim of linking services with other TA organizations around the world. The European Association for Transactional Analysis affiliated with ITAA in 1989. This was followed in 1990 by the affiliation of the Canadian Association for Transactional Analysis and the Institute for Counseling and Transactional Analysis of Kerala, India. At the present date (March 1991) negotiations are in progress with TA organizations in Brazil, New Zealand and the USA.

Further information on the ITAA may be obtained from: ITAA, 450 Pacific Avenue, Suite 250, San Francisco, California 94133-4640, USA.

The European Association for Transactional Analysis

EATA is a non-profit association within Swiss law. In structure it is a federation of affiliated European national and regional TA associations, with a central secretariat and elected Council.

Membership in EATA is conferred automatically on all members of EATA-affiliated associations. EATA membership, in turn, confers membership in ITAA at the corresponding membership level. People who do not reside in Europe, and those who live in countries where there is as yet no EATA-affiliated association, may contact EATA regarding individual membership.

For further information, contact: Executive Secretary, EATA, Les Toits de l'Aune Bat. E, 3, rue Hugo-Ely, 13090 Aix-en-Provence, France.

National Associations

We do not give contact addresses for the world's numerous national or regional TA associations, because these addresses change at frequent intervals with changes in the elected officials of the organizations. The only exception known to us at this time is Britain's ITA, which has a permanent box-number address: BM Box 4104, London WC1 3XX. For the current contact addresses of other associations, direct enquiries to EATA (for organizations in Europe) or ITAA (worldwide).

Following is a list of the countries in each continent which, according to ITAA and EATA records, have active national or regional TA associations at March 1991. Some countries may have more than one association.

Europe: Austria, Belgium, Denmark, Finland, France, Italy, Netherlands, Norway, Portugal, Spain, Sweden, Switzerland, United Kingdom, West Germany, Yugoslavia. (In each of these countries, there is at least one association which is affiliated with EATA).

North America: Canada, USA.

Central and South America: Argentina, Brazil, Dominican Republic, Mexico, Peru, Puerto Rico, Venezuela.

Asia: India, Japan.

Australasia: Australia, New Zealand.

Africa: South Africa.

Appendix E *(Revised March 1991)*
TRAINING AND ACCREDITATION IN TA

At the present date (March 1991) there are two organizations offering internationally-recognized training and accreditation in TA. These are the International Transactional Analysis Association (ITAA) and the European Association for Transactional Analysis (EATA). The ITAA's training and certification operations are managed by the Training and Certification Council of Transactional Analysts (T & C Council) which is an independent certifying and standard-setting body founded by, and closely linked to, ITAA. Within the T & C Council, training matters are the responsibility of the Training Standards Committee (TSC), while examination and certification are handled by the Board of Certification (BOC). In EATA, corresponding duties are performed by Professional Training Standards Committee (PTSC) and the Commission of Certification (COC) respectively.

By an Agreement of Mutual Recognition between BOC and COC, signed in August 1986, both bodies recognize BOC as the world credentialing authority, while COC is recognized as the credentialing authority for Europe. The effect of this is that all credentials extended by one body are recognized by the other. The training and examination procedures laid down by both bodies are virtually identical.

The details given in the remaining sections of this Appendix are extracted from the 1989 revision of the *ITAA Training and Certification Manual*. However, they apply also to EATA arrangements with only minor modification, except where otherwise stated by notes in *italic type*.

Purposes of training and certification

The purposes of the international training and certification programs are: to ensure there will be competent, ethical practitioners of TA for individuals and organizations desiring help; to support the development, clarification, simplification, and evaluation of TA theory and methods; to promote competency-based evaluation of TA professionals; and to promote contractual application of TA in all areas of use.

Professional credentials may be obtained for the application of transactional analysis and for teaching and training others in TA in three areas of specialization at the present time: (1) Clinical; (2) Educational; and (3) Organizational. *(EATA currently offers a fourth specialization,*

Counseling.) Certified Membership is available to individuals who have received training and supervision and have been certified by certifying boards recognized by ITAA *(EATA)* as competent to practice TA in their area of specialization. Membership as a Certified Teaching Member is available to individuals who have been certified as competent to teach TA (Instructor) and to supervise others in the application of TA (Supervisor).

What is involved in TA training and certification?

The steps in the training process for persons in ITAA *(EATA)* who wish to become Certified Transactional Analysts are:

1. Taking the TA 101 Course or Written Examination;
2. Becoming a Regular Member in ITAA *(EATA)*;
3. Signing a Training Contract with a Teaching and Supervising Transactional Analyst or Provisional Teaching and Supervising Transactional Analyst in the area of specialization in which they wish to train;
4. Training and supervision to meet the eligibility requirements for examination by the BOC *(COC)*;
5. Passing the BOC *(COC)* Level I examination; and
6. Applying for and paying dues for Certified Transactional Analyst membership.

For those individuals interested in being certified as a TA trainer and becoming a Certified Teaching Member of ITAA *(EATA)*, they may choose to be certified as an Instructor (to teach TA) and/or Supervisor (to supervise others in the application of TA). The title "Provisional Teaching and/or Supervising Transactional Analyst" is used to designate persons in this phase of training. The steps in the training process are:

1. Becoming a Certified Transactional Analyst Member of ITAA *(EATA)* in the area of specialization in which they wish to train others;
2. Attending an official Training Endorsement Workshop and being approved by the TEW staff to initiate training programs;
3. Signing a Training Contract with a primary supervisor who is a Teaching and Supervising Transactional Analyst in the area of specialization in which they wish to train;
4. Training and supervision to meet the eligibility requirements for examination by the BOC *(COC)*;
5. Passing the BOC *(COC)* Level II examination; and
6. Applying and paying dues for Certified Teaching Membership.

The TA 101

The 'TA 101' is the term Eric Berne introduced to designate an introduction to the basic theory and methods of transactional analysis. The numbers, 101, are typically used in the United States for introductory university courses which provide a broad overview of a topic.

The TA 101 Course is a workshop officially recognized by ITAA *(EATA)* as an introduction to transactional analysis. The purpose of the 101 Course is to provide consistent and accurate information about TA concepts. In order to qualify as an official TA 101 Course, the following requirements must be met:

1. The instructor must be officially recognized to teach a TA 101 Course — i.e. the instructor must be a Teaching Transactional Analyst or a Provisional Teaching Transactional Analyst.

2. The course must include the content specified in the official TA 101 Outline. *(Authors' note: the 1984 version of the Outline, which is the current version to date, is given in Appendix F.)*

3. The course must be at least 12 hours in length. It may also be presented in various formats over various periods of time which may be longer than 12 hours (e.g. a weekend or several weeks) and include experiential exercises.

The TA 101 Written Examination was introduced as an alternative to taking a course or workshop in order to respond to the growing number of persons around the world who had an adequate knowledge of the basic principles of TA, but were unable to attend an official TA 101 Course. Such students may take the Written Examination and have it graded by a qualified teacher. If they pass, they will be eligible for entry to membership and training as though they had attended a TA 101 Course.

Requirements for advanced membership

The following is a summary of the requirements for training and supervision laid down for accreditation at Level I and Level II, referred to above at heading (4) in the respective lists of 'steps in the training process'.

Level I: the minimum training period is eighteen months. However, the emphasis is upon sufficiency of training for the attainment of competence, and most trainees can expect their training to last considerably longer than the minimum. In this period the trainee must fulfil the at least the following requirements: 250 hours' advanced TA training; a further 350 hours' advanced training relevant to the field of specialization, which may include training in TA or other modalities; 150 hours' supervision of the trainee's application of TA in the field of specialization; seminar participation and presentations; and 1500 hours' experience, which must include at least 500 hours' application of TA in the field of specialization. Though no minimum hours requirement is laid down for personal therapy, it is expected to be an integral part of training.

Accreditation for Level I entails passing a written and an oral examination. The written examination must be passed before the candidate can go on to the oral examination. The latter is taken before a board of Advanced Members, and focuses principally on the examination of audio- or videotaped samples of the candidate's work.

Level II: for certification as Instructor, the candidate must have taught a TA 101 course under the supervision of a Teaching Member, and must have completed: 300 hours' teaching in the field of specialization; 100 hours' continuing education; 12 hours' presentations at national or international conferences; and 50 hours' supervision of the candidate's teaching. Certification as Supervisor requires completion of: 500 hours' experience supervising in the field of specialization; 50 hours' supervision of the candidate's supervision; and 35 hours' attendance at a course approved by BOC *(COC)* in ethics, supervision and training (currently a TEW).

The oral examination for Level II is taken before a board of Teaching Members. It comprises three parts, covering: Theory, Organization and Ethics; Teaching; and (for Supervisor candidates only) Supervision.

Contact addresses

For further information on training and accreditation, contact either:

ITAA, 450 Pacific Avenue, Suite 250, San Francisco, California 94133-4640, USA.

Executive Secretary, EATA, Les Toits de l'Aune Bat. E, 3, rue Hugo-Ely, 13090 Aix-en-Provence, France.

The ITAA *T & C Council Training and Certification Manual* is available from Credentials Department, ITAA, at the address above. Price (as at March 1996) is $30.00, including shipping.

The EATA *Training and Examination Handbook* is available from EATA Handbook Orders, Old School House, Kingston-on-Soar, Nottingham NG11 0DE, England. Price (as at March 1996) is £15.00, including postage.

Appendix F
TA 101 COURSE OUTLINE

Following is the course outline for the TA 101, as issued by ITAA. It is the September 1984 revision, the current version to date (March 1991).
Numbers added in brackets and *italic type* indicate the principal chapter or chapters of *TA Today* in which each topic is covered.

I. STATEMENT OF THE PURPOSE OF THE TA 101 COURSE *(Appx. E)*

II. DEFINITION AND PHILOSOPHY OF TA AND ITS AREAS OF APPLICATION *(1, 27)*
a. Definition of transactional analysis *(1)*
b. Philosophical assumptions *(1, 27)*
c. Contractual method *(1, 26)*
d. Areas of application — differences in process *(28, 29, Appx. E)*
   1. Clinical *(28)*
   2. Educational *(29)*
   3. Organizational *(29)*
   4. Other *(1, Appx. E)*

III. BRIEF OVERVIEW OF THE DEVELOPMENT OF TA *(30)*
a. Eric Berne *(30)*
   1. Who was Eric Berne? *(30)*
   2. Development of ideas *(30)*
   3. Books written by him *(30, Appx. A)*
b. Growth of TA *(30)*
   1. San Francisco Social Psychiatry Seminar *(30)*
   2. International Transactional Analysis Association (ITAA) *(30, Appx. D, Appx. E)*
   3. Regional and national TA associations *(30, Appx. D, Appx. E)*

IV. STRUCTURAL ANALYSIS *(Part II)*
a. Definition of ego-states *(2)*
b. Recognition and diagnosis of ego-states *(5)*
c. Behavioral descriptions (i.e. Critical Parent, Nurturing Parent, Adult, Free Child, Adapted Child) *(3)*
d. Contamination and exclusion *(6)*

V. TRANSACTIONAL ANALYSIS PROPER *(Part III, Part V)*

a. Transactions *(7)*
   1. Definition of a transaction *(7)*
   2. Types of transactions *(7)*
   3. Rules of communication *(7)*

b. Strokes *(8)*
   1. Definition of strokes *(8)*
   2. Stimulus and recognition hunger *(8)*
   3. Types of strokes *(8)*

c. Discounts *(17, 18)*
   1. Definitions of discounts (behavior or internal process) *(8, 17)*
   2. Levels of discounts *(18)*
   3. Reasons for discounting *(17, 18, 19, 20)*

d. Social time structuring *(9)*
   1. Structure hunger *(9)*
   2. Six ways of structuring time *(9)*

VI. GAME ANALYSIS *(23, 24, 25)*

a. Definitions of games *(23)*
b. Reasons for playing games *(24)*
c. Advantages of games *(24)*
d. Examples of games *(23)*
e. Degrees of games *(23)*
f. Ways of diagramming games *(23, 24)*
   1. Transactional diagram *(23)*
   2. Formula G *(23)*
   3. Drama Triangle *(23)*

VII. RACKET ANALYSIS *(21, 22)*

a. Significance of internal intrapsychic processes *(22)*
b. Definitions of rackets and trading stamps *(21, 22)*
c. Relationship of rackets to transactions, games and script *(21, 22)*

VIII. SCRIPT ANALYSIS *(Part IV)*

a. Life positions *(12)*
   1. Definition of life positions *(12)*
   2. The four life positions *(12)*
   3. Relationship of life positions to games and scripts *(12, 16, 24)*

b. Script *(Part IV)*
   1. Definitions of script *(10)*
   2. Origin of script in child's experiences *(10, 12, 13, 14)*
   3. Process of script development (e.g. injunctions, counter-injunctions, early decisions, attributions) *(10, 13, 14)*

NOTES AND REFERENCES

Chapter 1: WHAT TA IS

1. This definition is on the page headed 'The ITAA' in each issue of the *Transactional Analysis Journal.*
2. On the philosophy and basic concepts of TA, see:

Berne, E., *Principles of group treatment.* New York: Oxford University Press, 1966 (*other editions:* New York: Grove Press, 1966), chapter 10.

James, M. (ed.), *Techniques in transactional analysis for psychotherapists and counselors.* Reading: Addison-Wesley, 1977, chapter 3.

James, M., and Jongeward, D., *Born to win: transactional analysis with gestalt experiments.* Reading: Addison-Wesley, 1971 (*other editions include:* New York: Signet, 1978), chapter 1.

Steiner, C., *Scripts people live: transactional analysis of life scripts.* New York: Grove Press, 1974, introduction.

Woollams, S., and Brown, M., *Transactional analysis.* Dexter: Huron Valley Institute, 1978, chapter 1.

Chapter 2: THE EGO-STATE MODEL

1. On the nature and definition of ego-states, see:

Berne, E., *Intuition and ego states.* (McCormick, P., ed.). San Francisco: TA Press, 1977, chapter 6.

Berne, E., *Transactional analysis in psychotherapy.* New York: Grove Press, 1961, 1966, chapter 2.

Berne, E., *Games people play.* New York: Grove Press, 1964 (*other editions include:* Harmondsworth: Penguin, 1968), chapter 1.

Berne, *Principles of group treatment,* chapter 10.

Berne, E., *Sex in human loving.* New York: Simon and Schuster, 1970 (*other editions:* Harmondsworth: Penguin, 1973), chapter 4.

Berne, E., *What do you say after you say hello?* New York: Grove Press, 1972 (*other editions:* London: Corgi, 1975), chapter 2.

James and Jongeward, *Born to win,* chapter 2.

2. Berne gave several different definitions of 'ego-state' at various points in his writings. This one is from *Principles of group treatment.* Berne does not use the word 'thinking' in defining ego-states, but the context makes it clear that thinking is to be regarded as part of 'experience'.

3. For a book-length exposition of the empirical study of ego-state clues and many other aspects of TA, see:

Steere, D., *Bodily expressions in psychotherapy*. New York: Brunner/Mazel, 1982.

See also the following journal articles:

Falkowski, W., Ben-Tovim, D., and Bland, J., 'The assessment of the ego-states'. *British Journal of Psychiatry, 137,* 1980, 572-3.

Gilmour, J., 'Psychophysiological evidence for the existence of ego-states'. *TAJ, 11,* 3, 1981, 207-12.

Williams, J., *et al.,* 'Construct validity of transactional analysis ego-states'. *TAJ, 13,* 1, 1983, 43-9.

4. For Berne's explanation of the difference between ego-states and the three Freudian constructs, see the chapters cited above in *Intuition and ego-states* and *Principles of group treatment*. See also:

Drye, R., 'The best of both worlds: a psychoanalyst looks at TA'. *In:* Barnes, G. (ed.), *Transactional analysis after Eric Berne: teachings and practices of three TA schools*. New York: Harper's College Press, 1977, chapter 20.

Drye, R., 'Psychoanalysis and TA'. *In:* James (ed.), *Techniques in transactional analysis...*, chapter 11.

Chapter 3: FUNCTIONAL ANALYSIS OF EGO-STATES

1. On functional analysis, see:

Abell, R., *Own your own life*. New York: David McKay Co., 1976.

Berne, E., *The structure and dynamics of organizations and groups*. Philadelphia: J.B. Lippincott Co., 1963 (*other editions:* New York: Grove Press, 1966; *and* New York: Ballantine, 1973), chapter 9.

Dusay, J., *Egograms*. New York: Harper and Row, 1977 (*other editions:* New York: Bantam, 1980), chapter 1.

Kahler, T., *Transactional analysis revisited*. Little Rock: Human Development Publications, 1978, chapter 1.

Woollams and Brown, *Transactional analysis*, chapter 2.

2. On the egogram, see: Dusay, *Egograms*, all chapters. See also: Dusay, J., 'Egograms and the constancy hypothesis'. *TAJ, 2,* 3, 1972, 37-42.

Dusay reserves the term 'egogram' for a bar-chart analysis of a person's functional ego-states which is carried out *by someone else*. If I do the same analysis on *myself*, then in Dusay's terminology the result would be a 'psychogram'. We have preferred to simplify by using the word 'egogram' for both these concepts.

Chapter 4: THE SECOND-ORDER STRUCTURAL MODEL

1. Basic versions of the second-order structural model are given in most of the references listed at note (1) for Chapter 2. See also:

Berne, *Transactional analysis in psychotherapy*, chapters 16 and 17.

Schiff, J., *et al.*, *The Cathexis reader: transactional analysis treatment of psychosis*. New York: Harper and Row, 1975, chapter 3.

Steiner, *Scripts people live*, chapter 2.

Woollams and Brown, *Transactional analysis*, chapter 2.

For more advanced treatment, see the following:

Drego, P., 'Ego-state models'. *TASI Darshan, 1*, 4, 1981.

Drego, P., *Towards the illumined child*. Bombay: Grail, 1979.

Erskine, R., 'A structural analysis of ego'. *Keynote speeches delivered at the EATA conference, July 1986*. Geneva: EATA, 1987, speech 2.

Hohmuth, A., and Gormly, A., 'Ego-state models and personality structure'. *TAJ, 12*, 2, 1982, 140-3.

Holloway, W., 'Transactional analysis: an integrative view'. *In:* Barnes (ed.), *Transactional analysis after Eric Berne*, chapter 11.

Trautmann, R., and Erskine, R., 'Ego-state analysis: a comparative view'. *TAJ, 11*, 2, 1981, 178-85.

Summerton, O., 'Advanced ego-state theory'. *TASI Darshan, 2*, 4, 1982.

2. English, F., 'What shall I do tomorrow? Reconceptualizing transactional analysis'. *In:* Barnes (ed.), *Transactional analysis after Eric Berne*, chapter 15.

3. For a lead into the general literature on child development, try: Donaldson, M., *Children's minds*. London: Fontana, 1978.

Rather than attempt the daunting task of reading Piaget in the original, you may wish to look at one of the many summarized interpretations of his theories, e.g.: Maier, H., *Three theories of child development*. New York: Harper and Row, 1969.

Erik Erikson's account of the child's emotional development is presented in: Erikson, E., *Childhood and society*. New York: W.W. Norton, 1950.

See also Mahler, M.S., *The psychological birth of the human infant*. New York: Basic Books, 1975.

For interpretations of child development within a TA framework, see the article by Fanita English cited at note (2) for this Chapter; see also:

Levin, P., *Becoming the way we are*. Berkeley: Levin, 1974.

Levin, P., 'The cycle of development'. *TAJ, 12*, 2, 1982, 129-39.

Schiff *et al.*, *Cathexis reader*, chapter 4.

Woollams and Brown, *Transactional analysis*, chapter 6.

4. Joines, V., 'Differentiating structural and functional'. *TAJ, 6,*, 4, 1976, 377-80. See also Kahler, *Transactional analysis revisited*, chapter 1.

Chapter 5: RECOGNIZING EGO-STATES

1. For the four ways of ego-state diagnosis, see:

Berne, *Transactional analysis in psychotherapy*, chapter 7.

Berne, *Structure and dynamics of organizations and groups*, chapter 9.

James (ed.), *Techniques in transactional analysis...*, chapter 4.

Woollams and Brown, *Transactional analysis*, chapter 2.

See also the book by David Steere, *Bodily expressions in psychotherapy*, cited at note (3) for Chapter 2.

2. On Berne's energy theory, see: *Transactional analysis in psychotherapy*, chapter 3; and *Principles of group treatment*, chapter 13. See also:

Kahler, *Transactional analysis revisited*, chapter 4.

Schiff *et al.*, *Cathexis reader*, chapter 3.

Chapter 6: STRUCTURAL PATHOLOGY

1. Regarding structural pathology, see:

Berne, *Transactional analysis in psychotherapy*, chapter 4.

Erskine, R., and Zalcman, M., 'The racket system: a model for racket analysis'. *TAJ, 9,* 1, 1979, 51-9.

Harris, T., *I'm OK, you're OK*. New York: Grove Press, 1967, chapter 6.

James, M., and Jongeward, D., *The people book*. Menlo Park: Addison-Wesley, 1975, chapter 8.

James and Jongeward, *Born to win*, chapter 9.

Schiff *et al.*, *Cathexis reader*, chapter 3.

2. For views on the relationship between double contamination and script, see:

Erskine and Zalcman, 'The racket system...', p.53.

Kahler, *Transactional analysis revisited*, chapter 47.

3. Berne's reference to the person with constant Adult as being 'unable to join in the fun' seems inconsistent with his own definition of the Adult. In terms of Berne's original ego-state model, the Adult is defined as that set of behaviors, thoughts and feelings that are a direct response to the here-and-now. It follows that a person *can* 'have fun' while in Adult, though the activities the person counts as 'having fun' are likely to be different according to whether he is in Adult or in Child. See also: Kahler, *Transactional analysis revisited*, chapter 2.

Chapter 7: TRANSACTIONS

1. On the analysis of transactions, see:

Berne, *Transactional analysis in psychotherapy*, chapter 9.

Berne, *Games people play*, chapter 2.

Berne, *Principles of group treatment*, chapter 10.

Berne, *What do you say...*, chapter 2.

James and Jongeward, *Born to win*, chapter 2.

Woollams and Brown, *Transactional analysis*, chapter 4.
Steiner, C., *Games alcoholics play*. New York: Grove Press, 1971, chapter 1.
2. Karpman, S., 'Options'. *TAJ, 1,* 1, 1971, 79-87.

Chapter 8: STROKES

1. On the nature and definition of strokes and hungers, see:
Berne, *Games people play*, Introduction.
Berne, *Sex in human loving*, chapter 6.
Haimowitz, M., and Haimowitz, N., *Suffering is optional*. Evanston: Haimowoods Press, 1976, chapter 2.
James and Jongeward, *Born to win*, chapter 3.
Steiner, *Scripts people live*, chapter 22.
Woollams and Brown, *Transactional analysis*, chapter 3.
2. Spitz, R., 'Hospitalism: genesis of psychiatric conditions in early childhood'. *Psychoanalytic studies of the child, 1,* 1945, 53-74.
3. Levine, S., 'Stimulation in infancy'. *Scientific American, 202,* 5, 80-6.
4. Steiner, C., 'The stroke economy'. *TAJ, 1,* 3, 1971, 9-15.
5. McKenna, J., 'Stroking profile'. *TAJ, 4,* 4, 1974, 20-4.
6. English, F., 'Strokes in the credit bank for David Kupfer'. *TAJ, 1,* 3, 1971, 27-9.
7. Pollitzer, J., 'Is love dangerous?' Workshop presentation, 1980, unpublished.
8. Kahler, *Transactional analysis revisited*, chapter 16.

Chapter 9: TIME STRUCTURING

1. On the modes of time-structuring, see:
Berne, *Games people play*, chapters 3, 4, 5.
Berne, *Principles of group treatment*, chapter 10.
Berne, *Sex in human loving*, chapter 3 and chapter 4. The latter chapter includes Berne's description of the ego-states involved in intimacy.
Berne, *What do you say...*, chapter 2.
James and Jongeward, *Born to win*, chapter 3.
Woollams and Brown, *Transactional analysis*, chapter 5.
2. Boyd, L., and Boyd, H., 'Caring and intimacy as a time structure'. *TAJ, 10,* 4, 1980, 281-3.

Chapter 10: THE NATURE AND ORIGINS OF LIFE-SCRIPT

1. Regarding the nature, origins and definition of script, see:
Berne, *Transactional analysis in psychotherapy*, chapter 11.
Berne, *Principles of group treatment*, chapters 10 and 12.
Berne, *What do you say...*, chapters 2, 3-6, 8-10.
English, F., 'What shall I do tomorrow? Reconceptualizing

transactional analysis'. *In:* Barnes (ed.), *Transactional analysis after Eric Berne*, chapter 15.

Holloway, W., 'Transactional analysis: an integrative view'. *In:* Barnes (ed.), *Transactional analysis after Eric Berne*, chapter 11.

Goulding, M., and Goulding, R., *Changing lives through redecision therapy*. New York: Brunner/Mazel, 1979, chapter 2.

James and Jongeward, *Born to win*, chapters 2, 4.

Steiner, *Scripts people live*, chapters 3, 4, 5.

Woollams and Brown, *Transactional analysis*, chapter 9.

2. Woollams, S., 'From 21 to 43'. *In:* Barnes (ed.), *Transactional analysis after Eric Berne*, chapter 16.

3. For sources on child development, refer to note (3) for Chapter 4. In her work on 'cycles of development', for which she won the Eric Berne Memorial Scientific Award, Pam Levin argues that script development does not come to an end with adolescence. Instead, the developmental stages are re-cycled throughout the individual's life.

Chapter 11: HOW THE SCRIPT IS LIVED OUT

1. On the classification of script content and the way script themes are lived out, see:

Berne, *What do you say...*, chapters 3, 11.

Steiner, *Scripts people live*, chapters 6-12.

2. Woollams, S., 'Cure!?' *TAJ, 10,* 2, 1980, 115-7.

3. Berne, *What do you say...*, chapters 14, 17. For other views on the physiological aspects of script, see also:

Cassius, J., *Body scripts*. Memphis: Cassius, 1975.

Lenhardt, V., 'Bioscripts'. *In:* Stern (ed.), *TA: the state of the art,* chapter 8.

Chapter 12: LIFE POSITIONS

1. On life positions, see:

Berne, *Principles of group treatment*, chapter 12.

Berne, *What do you say...*, chapter 5.

Berne, E., 'Classification of positions'. *Transactional Analysis Bulletin, 1,* 3, 1962, 23.

James and Jongeward, *Born to win*, chapter 2.

Steiner, *Scripts people live*, chapter 5.

2. Ernst, F., 'The OK corral: the grid for get-on-with'. *TAJ, 1,* 4, 1971, 231-40. In agreeing that we use his Corral diagram in this book, Franklin Ernst asked that we give it his revised subtitle 'Grid for What's Happening', as in Figure 12.1.

3. Ernst, F., 'The annual Eric Berne memorial scientific award acceptance speech'. *TAJ, 12,* 1, 1982, 5-8.

Chapter 13: SCRIPT MESSAGES AND THE SCRIPT MATRIX

1. For script messages and how they are communicated, see:
Berne, *What do you say...*, chapter 7.
English, F., 'What shall I do tomorrow? Reconceptualizing transactional analysis'. *In:* Barnes (ed.), *Transactional analysis after Eric Berne*, chapter 15.
Steiner, *Scripts people live*, chapter 6.
White, J., and White, T., 'Cultural scripting'. *TAJ, 5,* 1, 1975, 12-23.
Woollams, S., 'From 21 to 43'. *In:* Barnes (ed.), *Transactional analysis after Eric Berne*, chapter 16.
2. Berne, *Transactional analysis in psychotherapy*, chapter 5.
3. Steiner, C., 'Script and counterscript'. *TAB, 5,* 18, 1966, 133-35. For other versions of the script matrix, see:
Berne, *What do you say...*, chapter 15.
English, F., 'Sleepy, spunky and spooky'. *TAJ, 2,* 2, 1972, 64-7.
English, F., reference quoted at note (1) for this Chapter.
Holloway, W., 'Transactional analysis: an integrative view'. *In:* Barnes (ed.), *Transactional analysis after Eric Berne*, chapter 11.
James (ed.), *Techniques in transactional analysis...*, chapter 4.
Woollams, S., reference quoted at note (1) for this Chapter.
Woollams and Brown, *Transactional analysis*, chapter 9.

Chapter 14: INJUNCTIONS AND DECISIONS

1. Goulding, R., and Goulding, M., 'New directions in transactional analysis'. *In* Sager and Kaplan (eds.), *Progress in group and family therapy*. New York: Brunner/Mazel, 1972, 105-34. See also:
Goulding, R., and Goulding, M., 'Injunctions, decisions and redecisions'. *TAJ, 6,* 1, 1976, 41-8.
Goulding, R., and Goulding, M., *The power is in the patient.* San Francisco: TA Press, 1978. (Chapters 5 and 16 of this book are reprints of the two articles quoted above).
Gouldings, *Changing lives through redecision therapy,* chapters 2, 9.
Allen, J., and Allen, B., 'Scripts: the role of permission'. *TAJ, 2,* 2, 1972, 72-4.
2. English, F., 'Episcript and the "hot potato" game'. *TAB, 8,* 32, 1969, 77-82.
3. Berne, *What do you say...*, chapter 7.
4. For various versions of the formal script questionnaire, see:
Berne, *What do you say...*, chapter 23.
Holloway, W., *Clinical transactional analysis with use of the life script questionnaire.* Aptos: Holloway, undated.
James (ed.), *Techniques in transactional analysis...*, chapter 4.
McCormick, P., *Guide for use of a life-script questionnaire in transactional analysis.* San Francisco: Transactional Publications, 1971.

McCormick, P., 'Taking Occam's Razor to the life-script interview'. *Keynote speeches delivered at the EATA conference, July 1986.* Geneva: EATA, 1987, speech 5.

Woollams and Brown, *Transactional analysis*, chapter 9.

Chapter 15: SCRIPT PROCESS

1. Berne, *Sex in human loving*, chapter 5.

Berne, *What do you say...*, chapter 11.

2. Kahler, *Transactional analysis revisited*, chapters 60-65.

Chapter 16: DRIVERS AND THE MINISCRIPT

1. Kahler, *Transactional analysis revisited*, chapter 72. See also:

Kahler, T., and Capers, H., 'The miniscript'. *TAJ, 4,* 1, 1974, 26-42. Note that the version given in *Transactional analysis revisited* is a revision of the 1974 *TAJ* article.

2. Kahler, *Transactional analysis revisited*, chapters 60-65 and accompaning Summary.

See also: Woollams and Brown, *Transactional analysis*, chapter 11. Note that the driver-script correspondence given by Woollams and Brown is different from that given by Kahler in the above reference. Whereas Kahler gives the Be Strong driver as corresponding to the Never script and the Try Hard driver as corresponding to the Always script, Woollams and Brown reverse this correspondence.

3. Kahler and Capers, 'The miniscript', reference given in note (1) above.

Kahler, *Transactional analysis revisited*, chapters 68-71.

4. Kahler, T., workshop presentation, EATA conference, Villars, 1984, unpublished.

5. Capers, H., and Goodman, L., 'The survival process: clarification of the miniscript'. *TAJ, 13,* 1, 1983, 142-8.

6. Kahler, *Transactional analysis revisited*, chapters 73-75 and 78-83. See also: Kahler and Capers, 'The miniscript', reference given in note (1) above. Here again, the account presented in *Transactional analysis revisited* is Kahler's revised version of the material in the 1974 article. In our text, we have followed Kahler's updated version, with one exception: we have retained Kahler's original name 'stopper' for position 2 on the miniscript. Kahler himself, in *Transactional analysis revisited*, shifts the name 'stopper' to position 3, while using the term 'maladaptor' for position 2.

7. Kahler, *Transactional analysis revisited*, chapter 85.

Chapter 17: DISCOUNTING

1. Schiff *et al.*, *Cathexis reader*, chapter 2. See also:

Mellor, K., and Sigmund, E., 'Discounting'. *TAJ, 5,* 3, 1975, 295-302.

Schiff, A., and Schiff, J., 'Passivity'. *TAJ, 1,* 1, 1971, 71-8.
2. This definition of discounting was suggested by Shea Schiff at a workshop presentation (unpublished). We think it is more graphic than the definition given on page 14 of *Cathexis reader:* 'Discounting is an internal mechanism which involves people minimising or ignoring some aspect of themselves, others or the reality situation.'

Claude Steiner, in *Scripts people live,* chapter 9, defines the term 'discount' in a different way, as: 'a crossed transaction in which the discountee emits a stimulus from his Adult ego-state to another person's Adult and that person responds from his Parent or Child.' This makes it seem initially as though Steiner is using the word in a much wider sense than the Schiffs. However, his examples indicate that he also has in mind a situation in which one person (the one responding from Parent or Child) 'minimises or ignores' some aspect of the other person.

Chapter 18: THE DISCOUNT MATRIX

1. Schiff *et al., Cathexis reader,* chapter 2. See also:
Mellor, K., and Sigmund, E., 'Discounting', *TAJ, 5,* 3, 1975, 295-302.

Chapter 19: FRAME OF REFERENCE AND REDEFINING

1. Schiff *et al., Cathexis reader,* chapter 5. See also:
Mellor, K., and Sigmund, E., 'Redefining'. *TAJ, 5,* 3, 1975, 303-11.
2. This statement of the meaning of 'redefining' is an interpretation made by the present authors. We think it is clearer than the circular definition given in *Cathexis reader.*

Chapter 20: SYMBIOSIS

1. Schiff *et al., Cathexis reader,* chapter 2. We have altered the Schiffs' definition by one word, substituting 'single person' for their 'whole person'. See also: Schiff, A., and Schiff, J., 'Passivity'. *TAJ, 1,* 1, 1971, 71-8.

The diagram showing symbiosis has evolved through various forms. In their 1971 *TAJ* article, the Schiffs depict it only by using dotted-line and solid boundaries for the ego-state circles. In *Cathexis reader,* they add arrows running between the active ego-states in the two parties. The version of the diagram commonly used in current literature, with an 'envelope' drawn round the active ego-states (as in Figure 20.1), makes its first published appearance in the article by Woollams and Huige, cited in note (2) below.
2. Woollams, S., and Huige, K., 'Normal dependency and symbiosis'. *TAJ, 7,* 3, 1977, 217-20.
3. Schiff *et al., Cathexis reader,* chapter 4. See also:

Schiff, S., 'Personality development and symbiosis'. *TAJ, 7,* 4, 1977, 310-6.

Chapter 21: RACKETS AND STAMPS

1. On the nature and functions of rackets, see:
Berne, *Principles of group treatment*, chapter 13.
Berne, *What do you say...*, chapter 8.
English, F., references given at notes (2) and (3) below.
Ernst, F., 'Psychological rackets in the OK corral'. *TAJ, 3,* 2, 1973, 19-23.
Erskine, R., and Zalcman, M., 'The racket system: a model for racket analysis'. *TAJ, 9,* 1, 1979, 51-9.
Gouldings, *Changing lives through redecision therapy*, chapters 2, 6.
Joines, V., 'Similarities and differences in rackets and games'. *TAJ, 12,* 4, 1982, 280-3.
Zalcman, M., 'Game analysis and racket analysis'. *Keynote speeches delivered at the EATA conference, July 1986.* Geneva: EATA, 1987, speech 4.
2. English, F., 'The substitution factor: rackets and real feelings'. *TAJ, 1,* 4, 1971, 225-30.
English, F., 'Rackets and real feelings, Part II'. *TAJ, 2,* 1, 1972, 23-5.
3. Thomson, G., 'Fear, anger and sadness'. *TAJ, 13,* 1, 1983, 20-4.
4. English, F., 'Racketeering'. *TAJ, 6,* 1, 1976, 78-81.
English, F., 'Differentiating victims in the Drama Triangle'. *TAJ, 6,* 4, 1976, 384-6.
5. Berne, E., 'Trading stamps'. *TAB, 3,* 10, 127.
Berne, *What do you say...*, chapter 8.
James and Jongeward, *Born to win*, chapter 8.

Chapter 22: THE RACKET SYSTEM

1. Erskine, R., and Zalcman, M., 'The racket system: a model for racket analysis'. *TAJ, 9,* 1, 1979, 51-9.
2. The exercises in this chapter were devised originally by M. Zalcman (workshop presentations, unpublished). They are given here in modified versions developed by I. Stewart, A. Lee and K. Brown (workshop presentations, unpublished).

Chapter 23: GAMES AND GAME ANALYSIS

1. On the nature of games, see:
Berne, *Intuition and ego-states*, chapter 7.
Berne, *Transactional analysis in psychotherapy*, chapter 10.
Berne, *Games people play*, chapter 5.
Gouldings, *Changing lives through redecision therapy*, chapter 2.

James and Jongeward, *Born to win*, chapters 2, 8.

Woollams and Brown, *Transactional analysis*, chapter 8.

2. There is no consensus in TA literature on whether a game (in the singular) is to be defined as a sequence of moves engaged in by *one* person, or as a sequence of interlocking moves and counter-moves made by *two* (or more) people. Berne appeared to favor the latter definition by implication, but he was not consistent. In this book we follow the alternative account favored by the Gouldings, and define a game (singular) as being a sequence played out by *one* person. Thus when two people engage in game-playing, each person is playing his or her own game, and the two games interlock.

This has implications also for the meaning of the Switch. Given that you and I are each playing our own game, you cannot 'pull a Switch on me'. That is to say: it is not possible for you to pull the Switch in *my* game. Instead, you can pull the Switch in *your* game, and expect me to respond to your move by pulling the Switch in my own game.

3. Berne, *Games people play*, chapter 5.

Steiner, *Scripts people live*, chapter 1.

4. Berne, *What do you say…*, chapter 2. The version of Formula G given in this reference is Berne's final revision. See also references in note (9) for this Chapter.

5. Karpman, S., 'Fairy tales and script drama analysis'. *TAB, 7, 26,* 1968, 39-43.

6. Berne, *Transactional analysis in psychotherapy*, chapter 10.

Berne, *Games people play*, chapter 5.

7. Gouldings, *Changing lives through redecision therapy,* chapter 2 and page 79 (for diagram).

8. James, J., 'The game plan'. *TAJ, 3,* 4, 1973, 14-7. The modified version given here was developed by L. Collinson (workshop presentation, unpublished).

9. Regarding the definition of games, see:

Joines, V., 'Similarities and differences in rackets and games'. *TAJ, 12,* 4, 1982, 280-3.

Zalcman, M., 'Game analysis and racket analysis'. *Keynote speeches delivered at the EATA conference, July 1986.* Geneva: EATA, 1987, speech 4.

Chapter 24: WHY PEOPLE PLAY GAMES

1. Berne, *Games people play,* chapter 5.

Berne, *What do you say…*, chapter 8.

James and Jongeward, *Born to win*, chapter 8.

Steiner, *Scripts people live*, chapter 1.

Woollams and Brown, *Transactional analysis*, chapter 8.

2. Schiff *et al.*, *Cathexis reader*, chapter 2.

3. English, F., 'Racketeering'. *TAJ, 6,* 1, 1976, 78-81.
4. Berne, *Games people play,* chapter 5.
5. James, J., 'Positive payoffs after games'. *TAJ, 6,* 3, 1976, 259-62.

Chapter 25: HOW TO DEAL WITH GAMES

1. Berne, *Games people play,* chapters 6-12 and Index of Games.
2. We do not know of any formally-named games which have a P — R or V — R Switch. As an alternative to classifying games on the basis of their Drama Triangle shifts, they may be classified in terms of the life position they reinforce.
3. Gouldings, *Changing lives through redecision therapy,* chapter 4.
4. James, J., 'Positive payoffs after games'. *TAJ, 6,* 3, 1976, 259-62.
5. Woollams, S., 'When fewer strokes are better'. *TAJ, 6,* 3, 1976, 270-1.

Chapter 26: CONTRACTS FOR CHANGE

1. On the nature and function of contracts, see:
Berne, *Principles of group treatment,* chapter 4 and Glossary.
James (ed.), *Techniques in transactional analysis...,* chapter 5.
James and Jongeward, *Born to win,* chapter 9.
Gouldings, *Changing lives through redecision therapy,* chapter 4.
Steiner, *Scripts people live,* Introduction and chapter 20.
Woollams and Brown, *Transactional analysis,* chapter 12.
2. James, M., 'Self-reparenting'. Workshop presentation, EATA conference 1985, unpublished. The modified version given here has been developed by I. Stewart (workshop presentations, 1986, unpublished). See also:
James, M., *It's never too late to be happy.* Reading: Addison-Wesley, 1985, chapter 7.

Chapter 27: AIMS OF CHANGE IN TA

1. For views on autonomy, see:
Berne, *Games people play,* chapters 16, 17.
Berne, *Principles of group treatment,* chapter 13.
James and Jongeward, *Born to win,* chapter 10.
Steiner, *Scripts people live,* chapters 26, 27, 28.
2. Berne, *Transactional analysis in psychotherapy,* chapter 16. See also:
James (ed.), *Techniques in transactional analysis...,* chapter 4.
3. Berne, *Transactional analysis in psychotherapy,* chapter 14.
Berne, *Principles of group treatment,* chapter 12.
Berne, *What do you say...,* chapter 18.
4. *TAJ, 10,* 2, 1980.
5. Nelson, Portia, 'Autobiography in five short chapters'. *In:* Black, Claudia, *Repeat after me.* Denver: M.A.C. Printing and Publications, 1985.

Chapter 28: TA THERAPY

1. James, M., 'Self-reparenting: theory and process'. *TAJ*, *4*, 3, 1974, 32-9. See also:

James, M., *It's never too late to be happy.* Reading: Addison-Wesley, 1985.

2. Regarding the 'three schools' of TA, see:

Barnes, G., 'Introduction'. *In:* Barnes (ed.), *Transactional analysis after Eric Berne*, chapter 1.

See also the three papers which follow Barnes's in the same book. They are by leading figures in the classical, Cathexis and redecision schools respectively:

Dusay, J., 'The evolution of transactional analysis'. *In:* Barnes (ed.), *op. cit.,* chapter 2.

Schiff, J., 'One hundred children generate a lot of TA'. *In:* Barnes (ed.), *op. cit.,* chapter 3.

Goulding, R., 'No magic at Mt. Madonna: redecisions in marathon therapy'. *In:* Barnes (ed.), *op. cit.,* chapter 4.

3. Crossman, P., 'Permission and protection'. *TAB*, *5*, 19, 1966, 152-4.

Chapter 29: TA IN ORGANIZATIONS AND EDUCATION

1. For an overview of the differences between fields of application of TA, see:

Clarke, J., 'Differences between special fields and clinical groups'. *TAJ*, *11*, 2, 1981, 169-70. The term 'special fields' was at one time used by ITAA to designate 'fields of application other than clinical', but this usage has been discontinued.

2. On organizational applications of TA, see:

Barker, D., *TA and training.* London: Gower, 1980.

Blakeney, R., 'Organizational cure, or organizational effectiveness'. *TAJ*, *10*, 2, 1980, 154-7.

James, M., *The OK boss.* Reading: Addison-Wesley, 1976.

Jongeward, D., *Everybody wins: TA applied to organizations.* Reading: Addison-Wesley, 1973.

Jongeward, D., and Blakeney, R., 'Guidelines for organizational applications of transactional analysis'. *TAJ*, *9*, 3, 174-8.

3. Regarding educational applications, see:

Ernst, K., *Games students play.* Millbrae: Celestial Arts, 1972.

Hesterley, O., 'Cure in the classroom'. *TAJ*, *10*, 2, 1980, 158-9.

James, M., and Jongeward, D., *The people book: transactional analysis for students.* Reading: Addison-Wesley, 1975.

Stapledon, R., *De-gaming teaching and learning.* Statesboro: Effective Learning Publications, 1979.

Chapter 30: HOW TA HAS DEVELOPED

1. This outline of Berne's life history has been based principally on:
Cheney, W., 'Eric Berne: biographical sketch'. *TAJ, 1,* 1, 1971, 14-22. Material was also drawn from:
Dusay, J., 'The evolution of transactional analysis'. *In:* Barnes (ed.), *Transactional analysis after Eric Berne,* chapter 2.
Hostie, R., 'Eric Berne in search of ego-states'. *In:* Stern (ed.), *TA: the state of the art,* chapter 2.
James, M., 'Eric Berne, the development of TA, and the ITAA'. *In:* James (ed.), *Techniques in transactional analysis...,* chapter 2.
2. Cranmer, R., 'Eric Berne: annotated bibliography.' *TAJ, 1,* 1, 1971, 23-9.
3. Schiff, J., 'One hundred children generate a lot of TA'. *In:* Barnes (ed.), *Transactional analysis after Eric Berne,* chapter 3.
4. This sketch of the development of ITAA has been traced from the articles by Cheney, Dusay and James, cited at note (1) above.
5. Membership numbers for ITAA between 1971 and 1980 have been taken from a graph quoted by McNeel, J., 'Letter from the editor'. *TAJ, 11,* 1, 1981, 4. Numbers for later years are as quoted on the page headed 'The ITAA' in each issue of the *TAJ.*
6. Allaway, J., 'Transactional analysis in Britain: the beginnings'. *Transactions, 1,* 1, 1983, 5-10.
7. The script, May-June 1987, page 7.

BIBLIOGRAPHY

Abell, R., *Own your own life*. New York: David McKay Co., 1976.

Allen, J., and Allen, B., 'Scripts: the role of permission'. *Transactional Analysis Journal, 2,* 2, 1972, 72-4.

Allaway, J., 'Transactional analysis in Britain: the beginnings'. *Transactions, 1,* 1, 1983, 5-10.

Barker, D., *TA and training*. London: Gower, 1980.

Barnes, G. (ed), *Transactional analysis after Eric Berne: teachings and practices of three TA schools*. New York: Harper's College Press, 1977.

Barnes, G., 'Introduction'. *In:* Barnes (ed.), *Transactional analysis after Eric Berne*, chapter 1.

Blakeney, R., 'Organizational cure, or organizational effectiveness'. *TAJ, 10,* 2, 1980, 154-7.

Berne, E., *A layman's guide to psychiatry and psychoanalysis*. New York: Simon and Schuster, 1957; third edition published 1968. *Other editions:* New York: Grove Press, 1957; *and* Harmondsworth: Penguin, 1971.

Berne, E., *Transactional analysis in psychotherapy*. New York: Grove Press, 1961, 1966.

Berne, E., 'Classification of positions'. *Transactional Analysis Bulletin, 1,* 3, 1962, 23.

Berne, E., *The structure and dynamics of organizations and groups*. Philadelphia: J.B. Lippincott Co., 1963. *Other editions:* New York: Grove Press, 1966; *and* New York: Ballantine, 1973.

Berne, E., 'Trading stamps'. *TAB, 3,* 10, 1964, 127.

Berne, E., *Games people play*. New York: Grove Press, 1964. *Other editions include:* Harmondsworth: Penguin, 1968.

Berne, E., *Principles of group treatment*. New York: Oxford University Press, 1966. *Other editions:* New York: Grove Press, 1966.

Berne, E., *Sex in human loving*. New York: Simon and Schuster, 1970. *Other editions:* Harmondsworth: Penguin, 1973.

Berne, E., *What do you say after you say hello?* New York: Grove Press, 1972. *Other editions:* London: Corgi, 1975.

Berne, E., *Intuition and ego states.* (McCormick, P., ed.). San Francisco: TA Press, 1977.

Boyd, L., and Boyd, H., 'Caring and intimacy as a time structure'. *TAJ, 10,* 4, 1980, 281-3.

Capers, H., and Goodman, L., 'The survival process: clarification of the miniscript'. *TAJ, 13,* 1, 1983, 142-8.

Cassius, J., *Body scripts.* Memphis: Cassius, 1975.

Cheney, W., 'Eric Berne: biographical sketch'. *TAJ, 1,* 1, 1971, 14-22.

Cranmer, R., 'Eric Berne: annotated bibliography'. *TAJ, 1,* 1, 1971, 23-9.

Crossman, P., 'Permission and protection'. *TAB, 5,* 19, 1966, 152-4.

Donaldson, M., *Children's minds.* London: Fontana, 1978.

Drego, P., *Towards the illumined child.* Bombay: Grail, 1979.

Drego, P., 'Ego-state models'. *TASI Darshan, 1,* 4, 1981.

Drye, R., 'Psychoanalysis and TA'. *In:* James (ed.), *Techniques in transactional analysis...,* chapter 11.

Drye, R., 'The best of both worlds: a psychoanalyst looks at TA'. *In:* Barnes (ed.), *Transactional analysis after Eric Berne,* chapter 20.

Dusay, J., 'Egograms and the constancy hypothesis'. *TAJ, 2,* 3, 1972, 37-42.

Dusay, J., *Egograms.* New York: Harper and Row, 1977. *Other editions:* New York: Bantam, 1980.

Dusay, J., 'The evolution of transactional analysis'. *In:* Barnes (ed.), *Transactional analysis after Eric Berne,* chapter 2.

English, F., 'Episcript and the "hot potato" game'. *TAB, 8,* 32, 1969, 77-82.

English, F., 'Strokes in the credit bank for David Kupfer'. *TAJ, 1,* 3, 1971, 27-9.

English, F., 'The substitution factor: rackets and real feelings'. *TAJ, 1,* 4, 1971, 225-30.

English, F., 'Rackets and real feelings, Part II'. *TAJ, 2,* 1, 1972, 23-5.

English, F., 'Sleepy, spunky and spooky'. *TAJ, 2,* 2, 1972, 64-7.

English, F., 'Racketeering'. *TAJ, 6,* 1, 1976, 78-81.

English, F., 'Differentiating victims in the Drama Triangle'. *TAJ, 6,* 4, 1976, 384-6.

English, F., 'What shall I do tomorrow? Reconceptualizing transactional analysis'. *In:* Barnes (ed.), *Transactional analysis after Eric Berne,* chapter 15.

Erikson, E., *Childhood and society.* New York: W.W. Norton, 1950.

Ernst, F., 'The OK corral: the grid for get-on-with'. *TAJ, 1,* 4, 1971, 231-40.

Ernst, F., 'Psychological rackets in the OK corral'. *TAJ, 3,* 2, 1973, 19-23.

Ernst, F., 'The annual Eric Berne memorial scientific award acceptance speech'. *TAJ, 12,* 1, 1982, 5-8.

Ernst, K., *Games students play.* Millbrae: Celestial Arts, 1972.

Erskine, R., 'A structural analysis of ego'. *Keynote speeches delivered at the EATA conference, July 1986.* Geneva: EATA, 1987, speech 2.

Erskine, R., and Zalcman, M., 'The racket system: a model for racket analysis'. *TAJ, 9,* 1, 1979, 51-9.

Falkowski, W., Ben-Tovim, D., and Bland, J., 'Assessment of the ego-states'. *British Journal of Psychiatry, 137,* 1980, 572-3.

Gilmour, J., 'Psychophysiological evidence for the existence of ego-states'. *TAJ, 11,* 3, 1981, 207-12.

Goulding, M., and Goulding, R., *Changing lives through redecision therapy.* New York: Brunner/Mazel, 1979.

Goulding, R., 'No magic at Mt. Madonna: redecisions in marathon therapy'. *In:* Barnes (ed.), *Transactional analysis after Eric Berne,* chapter 4.

Goulding, R., and Goulding, M., 'New directions in transactional analysis'. *In* Sager and Kaplan (eds.), *Progress in group and family therapy.* New York: Brunner/Mazel, 1972, 105-34.

Goulding, R., and Goulding, M., 'Injunctions, decisions and redecisions'. *TAJ, 6,* 1, 1976, 41-8.

Goulding, R., and Goulding, M., *The power is in the patient.* San Francisco: TA Press, 1978.

Haimowitz, M., and Haimowitz, N., *Suffering is optional.* Evanston: Haimowoods Press, 1976.

Harris, T., *I'm OK, you're OK.* New York: Grove Press, 1967.

Hesterley, O., 'Cure in the classroom'. *TAJ, 10,* 2, 1980, 158-9.

Hohmuth, A., and Gormly, A., 'Ego-state models and personality structure'. *TAJ, 12,* 2, 1982, 140-3.

Holloway, W., 'Transactional analysis: an integrative view'. *In:* Barnes (ed.), *Transactional analysis after Eric Berne,* chapter 11.

Holloway, W., *Clinical transactional analysis with use of the life script questionnaire.* Aptos: Holloway, undated.

Hostie, R., 'Eric Berne in search of ego-states'. *In:* Stern (ed.), *TA: the state of the art,* chapter 2.

James, J., 'The game plan'. *TAJ, 3,* 4, 1973, 14-7.

James, J., 'Positive payoffs after games'. *TAJ, 6,* 3, 1976, 259-62.

James, M., 'Self-reparenting: theory and process'. *TAJ, 4,* 3, 1974, 32-9.

James, M., *The OK boss.* Reading: Addison-Wesley, 1976.

James, M. (ed), *Techniques in transactional analysis for psychotherapists and counselors.* Reading: Addison-Wesley, 1977.

James, M., 'Eric Berne, the development of TA, and the ITAA'. *In:* James (ed.), *Techniques in transactional analysis...,* chapter 2.

James, M., *It's never too late to be happy.* Reading: Addison-Wesley, 1985.

James, M., and Jongeward, D., *Born to win: transactional analysis with gestalt experiments.* Reading: Addison-Wesley, 1971. *Other editions include:* New York: Signet, 1978.

James, M., and Jongeward, D., *The people book: transactional analysis for students.* Reading: Addison-Wesley, 1975.

Joines, V., 'Differentiating structural and functional'. *TAJ, 6,,* 4, 1976, 377-80.

Joines, V., 'Similarities and differences in rackets and games'. *TAJ, 12,* 4, 1982, 280-3.

Jongeward, D., *Everybody wins: TA applied to organizations.* Reading: Addison-Wesley, 1973.

Jongeward, D., and Blakeney, R., 'Guidelines for organizational applications of transactional analysis'. *TAJ, 9,* 3, 174-8.

Kahler, T., with Capers, H., 'The miniscript'. *TAJ, 4,* 1, 1974, 26-42.

Kahler, T., *Transactional analysis revisited.* Little Rock: Human Development Publications, 1978.

Karpman, S., 'Fairy tales and script drama analysis'. *TAB, 7,* 26, 1968, 39-43.

Karpman, S., 'Options'. *TAJ, 1,* 1, 1971, 79-87.

Lenhardt, V., 'Bioscripts'. *In:* Stern (ed.), *TA: the state of the art,* chapter 8.

Levin, P., *Becoming the way we are.* Berkeley: Levin, 1974.

Levin, P., 'The cycle of development'. *TAJ, 12,* 2, 1982, 129-39.

Levine, S., 'Stimulation in infancy'. *Scientific American, 202,* 5, 1960, 80-6.

Mahler, M.S., *The psychological birth of the human infant.* New York: Basic Books, 1975.

Maier, H., *Three theories of child development.* New York: Harper and Row, 1969.

McCormick, P., *Guide for use of a life-script questionnaire in transactional analysis.* San Francisco: Transactional Publications, 1971.

McCormick, P., 'Taking Occam's Razor to the life-script interview'. *Keynote speeches delivered at the EATA conference, July 1986.* Geneva: EATA, 1987, speech 5.

McKenna, J., 'Stroking profile'. *TAJ, 4,* 4, 1974, 20-4.

Mellor, K., and Sigmund, E., 'Discounting'. *TAJ, 5,* 3, 1975, 295-302.

Mellor, K., and Sigmund, E., 'Redefining'. *TAJ, 5,* 3, 1975, 303-11.

Nelson, Portia, 'Autobiography in five short chapters'. *In:* Black, Claudia, *Repeat after me.* Denver: M.A.C. Printing and Publications, 1985.

Schiff, A., and Schiff, J., 'Passivity'. *TAJ, 1,* 1, 1971, 71-8.

Schiff, J., 'One hundred children generate a lot of TA'. *In:* Barnes (ed.), *Transactional analysis after Eric Berne,* chapter 3.

Schiff, J., et al., *The Cathexis reader: transactional analysis treatment of psychosis.* New York: Harper and Row, 1975.

Schiff, S., 'Personality development and symbiosis'. *TAJ, 7,* 4, 1977, 310-6.

Spitz, R., 'Hospitalism: genesis of psychiatric conditions in early childhood'. *Psychoanalytic studies of the child, 1,* 1945, 53-74.

Stapledon, R., *De-gaming teaching and learning.* Statesboro: Effective Learning Publications, 1979.

Steere, D., *Bodily expressions in psychotherapy*. New York: Brunner/ Mazel, 1982.

Steiner, C., 'Script and counterscript'. *TAB, 5*, 18, 1966, 133-35.

Steiner, C., 'The stroke economy'. *TAJ, 1*, 3, 1971, 9-15.

Steiner, C., *Games alcoholics play*. New York: Grove Press, 1971.

Steiner, C., *Scripts people live: transactional analysis of life scripts*. New York: Grove Press, 1974.

Stern, E. (ed), *TA: the state of the art*. Dordrecht: Foris Publications, 1984.

Summerton, O., 'Advanced ego-state theory'. *TASI Darshan, 2*, 4, 1982.

Thomson, G., 'Fear, anger and sadness'. *TAJ, 13*, 1, 1983, 20-4.

Trautmann, R., and Erskine, R., 'Ego-state analysis: a comparative view'. *TAJ, 11*, 2, 1981, 178-85.

White, J., and White, T., 'Cultural scripting'. *TAJ, 5*, 1, 1975, 12-23.

Williams, J., *et al.*, 'Construct validity of transactional analysis ego-states'. *TAJ, 13*, 1, 1983, 43-9.

Woollams, S., 'When fewer strokes are better'. *TAJ, 6*, 3, 1976, 270-1.

Woollams, S., 'From 21 to 43'. *In:* Barnes (ed.), *Transactional analysis after Eric Berne*, chapter 16.

Woollams, S., 'Cure!?' *TAJ, 10*, 2, 1980, 115-7.

Woollams, S., and Brown, M., *Transactional analysis*. Dexter: Huron Valley Institute, 1978.

Woollams, S., and Huige, K., 'Normal dependency and symbiosis'. *TAJ, 7*, 3, 1977, 217-20.

Zalcman, M., 'Game analysis and racket analysis'. *Keynote speeches delivered at the EATA conference, July 1986*. Geneva: EATA, 1987, speech 4.

GLOSSARY

A_1: *same as* Adult in the Child.

A_2: *same as* Adult ego-state.

A_3: part of the second-order structure of the Parent, representing Adult content introjected from a parent or parent-figure.

ACTIVITY: mode of time-structuring in which those concerned have the objective of achieving an overtly agreed goal, as opposed to merely talking about it.

ADAPTED CHILD: a subdivision of the Child in the functional model, indicating how the individual may use this ego-state in conforming to rules or societal demands.

ADULT EGO-STATE: a set of behaviors, thoughts and feelings which are direct responses to the here-and-now, not copied from parents or parent-figures nor replayed from the individual's own childhood.

ADULT IN THE CHILD: part of the second-order structure of the Child, representing the young child's strategies for reality-testing and problem-solving.

AFTER SCRIPT: the process script which reflects the belief: 'If something good happens today, I'll have to pay for it tomorrow.'

AGITATION: the passive behavior in which the person directs energy into repetitive, purposeless activity instead of into problem-solving.

ALLOWER: the positive converse of a driver.

ALMOST SCRIPT: the process script which reflects the belief: 'I almost make it, but not quite.'

ALWAYS SCRIPT: the process script which reflects the belief: 'I must always stay with the same unsatisfactory situation.'

ANGULAR TRANSACTION: an ulterior transaction involving three ego-states.

ANTISCRIPT: part of the script which a person has turned around to its opposite, following the opposite instead of the original message.

AREA: (of discounting) whether discounting relates to self, others or the situation.

ATTRIBUTION: a script message which entails the parents telling the child what he is.

AUTHENTIC FEELING: the original, uncensored feeling which the individual in childhood learned to cover with a racket feeling.

AUTONOMY: that quality which is manifested by the release or recovery of three capacities: awareness, spontaneity and intimacy; any behavior, thinking or feeling which is a response to here-and-now reality, rather than a response to script beliefs.

AWARENESS: the capacity to experience pure sensual impressions in the manner of a new-born infant, without interpretation.

BANAL SCRIPT: *same as* non-winning script.

BASIC POSITION: *same as* life position.

BEHAVIORAL DIAGNOSIS: judgment of which ego-state an individual is in by observation of that individual's behavior.

BLAMER: the third position on the miniscript, reflecting the life position I+U-.

BLOCKING TRANSACTION: a transaction in which the purpose of raising an issue is avoided by disagreeing about the definition of the issue.

C_1: *same as* Child in the Child.

C_2: *same as* Child ego-state.

C_3: part of the second-order structure of the Parent, representing Child content introjected from a parent or parent-figure.

CATHEXIS: (in energy theory) theoretical construct representing psychic energy, postulated by Berne to explain shifts between ego-states; (as proper name) name of institute founded by the Schiffs and of the 'school' of TA which uses their approach.

CHILD EGO-STATE: a set of behaviors, thoughts and feelings which are replayed from the individual's own childhood — i.e. an archaic ego-state.

CHILD IN THE CHILD: part of the second-order structure of the Child, representing stored memories of experiences from earlier stages of the child's own development.

COMPLEMENTARY TRANSACTION: a transaction in which the transactional vectors are parallel and the ego-state addressed is the one which responds.

CON: a transactional stimulus which on the psychological level conveys an invitation into game-playing.

CONDITIONAL STROKE: a stroke relating to what the individual does.

CONSTANCY HYPOTHESIS: (of egograms) the hypothesis that when one ego-state increases in intensity, another or others must decrease in order to compensate, the shift in psychic energy occurring so that the total amount of energy may remain constant.

CONSTANT: (of ego-states) *same as* excluding.

CONTAMINATION: part of the content of the Child or Parent ego-states which the individual mistakes for Adult content.

CONTENT: (of ego-states) the stored memories and strategies that are classified as belonging in the different ego-states, or subdivisions of ego-states, in the structural model — i.e. *what* is placed in each ego-state; (of script) the set of early decisions, unique to the individual, which specify *what* there is in the individual's script.

CONTRACT: an explicit bilateral commitment to a well-defined course of action; an Adult commitment to oneself and/or someone else to make a change.

CONTROLLING PARENT: a subdivision of the Parent in the functional model, indicating how the individual may use this ego-state to control, direct or criticize.

COUNTERFEIT STROKE: a stroke which superficially appears positive, but which contains a negative 'sting'.

COUNTERINJUNCTIONS: script messages issued from Parent by the parent and housed in Parent by the child.

COUNTERSCRIPT: the set of decisions made by the child in compliance with the counterinjunctions.

CRITICAL PARENT: *same as* Controlling Parent.

CROSSED TRANSACTION: a transaction in which the transactional vectors are not parallel, or in which the ego-state addressed is not the one which responds.

CROSSUP: moment of confusion experienced by a game-player immediately after the Switch.

DECISION: conclusion regarding self, others or the quality of life, adopted during childhood as the best available means of surviving and getting needs met within the constraints of the child's ways of feeling and reality-testing.

DECISIONAL MODEL: philosophical stance which holds that people decide their own destiny, and that these decisions can be changed.

DELUSION: *(used by Berne to mean)* contamination of Adult by Child.

DESPAIRER: the fourth position on the miniscript, reflecting the life position I-U-.

DISCOUNTING: unawarely ignoring information relevant to the solution of a problem.

DISCOUNT MATRIX: a model which analyzes discounting in terms of area, type and level.

DOING NOTHING: the passive behavior in which the person directs energy into stopping himself or herself from acting, instead of into problem-solving.

DRAMA TRIANGLE: diagram which illustrates how persons may adopt and move between any of three scripty roles (Persecutor, Rescuer, Victim).

DRIVER: one of five distinctive behavioral sequences, played out over a time-period between half-a-second and a few seconds, which are the functional manifestations of negative counterscripts.

DUPLEX TRANSACTION: an ulterior transaction involving four ego-states.

EARLY DECISION: *same as* decision.

EGOGRAM: a bar-chart diagram showing an intuitive assessment of the importance of each subdivision of the functional ego-state model in an individual's personality.

EGO-STATE: a consistent pattern of feeling and experience directly related to a corresponding consistent pattern of behavior.

EGO-STATE MODEL: a model depicting personality in terms of Parent, Adult and Child ego-states.

ELECTRODE: *(used by some writers to mean)* Parent in the Child.

EPISCRIPT: a negative script message which a parent passes to a child in the magical hope that by so doing the parent will be released from the impact of that message.

EXCLUDING: (of ego-states) the one ego-state remaining operational when the other two are excluded.

EXCLUSION: shutting out by the individual of one or more ego-states.

EXECUTIVE: (of ego-states) that ego-state which dictates behavior, in terms of having control of the muscular apparatus.

EXISTENTIAL POSITION: *same as* life position.

FIRST-DEGREE: (of games or losing scripts) having a payoff which the person is ready to discuss in his or her social circle.

FIRST-ORDER MODEL: an ego-state model in which the three ego-states are not further subdivided.

FIRST RULE OF COMMUNICATION: 'so long as transactions remain complementary, communication can continue indefinitely'.

FORMULA G: a formula showing the six stages in a game (Con, Gimmick, Response, Switch, Crossup, Payoff).

FRAME OF REFERENCE: the structure of associated responses which integrates the various ego-states in response to specific stimuli; it provides the individual with an overall perceptual, conceptual, affective and action set, which is used to define the self, other people and the world.

FREE CHILD: a subdivision of the Child in the functional model, indicating how the individual may use this ego-state in expressing feelings or wants without censoring and without reference to rules or societal demands.

FUNCTION: (of ego-states) how ego-states are used or expressed.

FUNCTIONAL MODEL: an ego-state model which divides the ego-states to show us *how* we use them (their process).

GALLOWS: a communication in which the individual smiles or laughs while making a statement about something painful.

GAME: *(Berne's final definition)* a series of transactions with a Con, a Gimmick, a Switch, and a Crossup, leading to a payoff.

GAME: *(Joines's definition)* the process of doing something with an

329

ulterior motive that (1) is outside of Adult awareness, (2) does not become explicit until the participants switch the way they are behaving, and (3) results in everyone feeling confused, misunderstood, and wanting to blame the other person.

GAME FORMULA: *same as* Formula G.

GAME PLAN: series of questions used in analyzing the stages in an individual's game.

GIMMICK: a transactional response which on the psychological level conveys that the person has accepted an invitation into game-playing.

GRANDIOSITY: an exaggeration of some feature of reality.

HAMARTIC SCRIPT: *same as* third-degree losing script.

HISTORICAL DIAGNOSIS: judgment of which ego-state an individual is in by gathering factual information about the individual's parents, parent-figures and own childhood.

INCAPACITATION: the passive behavior in which the person disables himself or herself in an attempt to force the environment to solve a problem.

INCONGRUITY: mis-match between the overt content of a communication and the behavioral signals shown by the individual who issues the communication.

INJUNCTIONS: negative, restrictive script messages issued from Child by the parent and housed in Child by the child.

INTEGRATED ADULT: Adult ego-state incorporating positive qualities of Child and of Parent.

INTIMACY: mode of time-structuring in which people express authentic feelings and wants to each other without censoring.

LEVEL: (of discounting) whether discounting relates to existence, significance, change possibilities or personal abilities.

LIFE COURSE: what actually happens in the individual's life (in contrast to life-script, which represents what the person planned to do in early childhood).

LIFE POSITION: a person's basic beliefs about self and others, which are used to justify decisions and behavior; a fundamental stance which a person takes up about the essential value he or she perceives in self and others.

LIFE-SCRIPT: an unconscious life-plan made in childhood, reinforced by the parents, 'justified' by subsequent events, and culminating in a chosen alternative.

LITTLE PROFESSOR: *same as* Adult in the Child.

LOSER: someone who does not accomplish a declared purpose.

LOSING SCRIPT: a script in which the payoff is painful or destructive, and/or entails failure to accomplish a declared purpose.

MAGICAL PARENT: *same as* Parent in the Child.

MARSHMALLOW-THROWING: giving out insincere positive strokes.

MARTIAN: interpretation of human behavior and communication which entails observation without preconceptions.

MINISCRIPT: a sequence of scripty behaviors and racket feelings, always beginning with a driver, in which the individual plays through his or her script in the short to medium term and thereby reinforces the script.

MODE: (of discounting) *same as* level.

NATURAL CHILD: *same as* Free Child.

NEGATIVE STROKE: a stroke which the receiver experiences as unpleasant.

NEVER SCRIPT: the process script which reflects the belief: 'I can never get what I most want.'

NON-WINNER: a person who makes neither big wins nor big losses.

NON-WINNING SCRIPT: a script in which the payoff entails neither big wins nor big losses.

NURTURING PARENT: a subdivision of the Parent in the functional model, indicating how the individual may use this ego-state in nurturing, caring or helping.

OGRE (PARENT): *(used by some writers to mean)* Parent in the Child.

OK CORRAL: diagram in which the four life positions are related to specific social operations.

OPEN-ENDED SCRIPT: the process script which reflects the belief: 'After a certain point in time, I won't know what to do.'

OPTIONS: technique of choosing ego-states in transacting so as to break free of familiar, unconstructive 'locked' interchanges with others.

OVERADAPTATION: the passive behavior in which the person complies with what he or she believes are the wishes of others, without checking and without reference to his or her own wishes.

P_1: *same as* Parent in the Child.

P_2: *same as* Parent ego-state.

P_3: part of the second-order structure of the Parent, representing Parent content introjected from a parent or parent-figure.

PAC MODEL: *same as* ego-state model.

PARALLEL TRANSACTION: *same as* complementary transaction.

PARENT EGO-STATE: a set of behaviors, thoughts and feelings which have been copied from parents or parent-figures — i.e. a borrowed ego-state.

PARENT IN THE CHILD: part of the second-order structure of the Child, representing the young child's fantasized and magical version of messages received from parents.

PASSIVE BEHAVIOR: one of four modes of behavior (doing nothing, overadaptation, agitation, incapacitation or violence) which indicate the presence of discounting and are used by the individual as an attempt to manipulate others or the environment into solving his or her problems.

PASSIVITY: how people don't do things, or don't do them effectively.

PASTIME: mode of time-structuring in which people talk about a subject but have no intention of taking action concerning it.

PAYOFF: (of games) the racket feeling experienced by the player at the close of the game; (of script) the closing scene towards which the script is directed.

PERMISSIONS: (in the script) positive, liberating script messages issued from Child by the parent and housed in Child by the child.

PERSECUTOR: (in Drama Triangle) person who puts others down or belittles them.

PHENOMENOLOGICAL DIAGNOSIS: judgment of which ego-state an individual is in on the evidence of that individual's re-experiencing events from his own past.

PIG PARENT: *(used by some writers to mean)* Parent in the Child.

PLASTIC STROKE: an insincere positive stroke.

POSITIVE STROKE: a stroke which the receiver experiences as pleasant.

PREJUDICE: *(used by Berne to mean)* contamination of Adult by Parent.

PRIMARY DRIVER: the driver which an individual shows most frequently, usually also shown first in response to a transactional stimulus.

PROCESS: (of ego-states) the ways in which the individual expresses the ego-states over time — i.e. *how* the ego-states are expressed; (of script) the ways in which the individual lives out the script through time — i.e. *how* the script is lived out.

PROGRAM: set of script messages issued from Adult by the parent and housed in Adult by the child.

PSYCHOLOGICAL-LEVEL MESSAGE: a covert message, usually conveyed by non-verbal clues.

RACKET: a set of scripty behaviors, intended outside awareness as a means of manipulating the environment, and entailing the person's experiencing a racket feeling.

RACKETEERING: mode of transacting in which the individual seeks strokes from others for his or her racket feelings.

RACKET FEELING: a familiar emotion, learned and encouraged in childhood, experienced in many different stress situations, and maladaptive as an adult means of problem-solving.

RACKET SYSTEM: a self-reinforcing, distorted system of feelings, thoughts and actions maintained by script-bound individuals.

REAL SELF: (of ego-states) that ego-state in which the individual experiences himself or herself to be.

REBELLIOUS CHILD: *(used by some writers to mean)* mode of expression of Adapted Child in which the individual rebels against rules instead of following them.

RECOGNITION-HUNGER: the need for recognition by others.

REDECISION: replacement of a self-limiting early decision by a new decision that takes account of the individual's full adult resources.

REDEFINING: distortion of an individual's perception of reality so that it fits his or her script.

REDEFINING TRANSACTION: a tangential or blocking transaction.

RESCUER: (in Drama Triangle) person who offers help to others from a one-up position, in the belief 'they are not good enough to help themselves'.

RESPONSE: (in an individual transaction) the communication which is a reply to the stimulus; (in a game) series of ulterior transactions which follow the Con and Gimmick and repeat their covert messages.

RITUAL: mode of time-structuring in which people exchange familiar pre-programmed strokes.

RUBBERBAND: a point of similarity between a here-and-now stress situation and a painful situation from the person's own childhood, usually not recalled in awareness, in response to which the person is likely to go into script.

SCRIPT: *same as* life-script.

SCRIPT MATRIX: diagram in which the transmission of script messages is analyzed in terms of ego-states.

SCRIPT MESSAGE: a verbal or non-verbal message from the parents on the basis of which the child forms conclusions about self, others and the world during the process of script-making.

SCRIPT SIGNAL: a bodily clue which indicates that the individual has gone into script.

SCRIPTY: (of behaviors, feelings etc.) exhibited by the individual when in script.

SECOND-DEGREE: (of games or losing scripts) having a payoff serious enough to be an unacceptable topic for conversation in the individual's social circle.

SECOND-ORDER (STRUCTURAL) MODEL: a structural model in which the ego-states are themselves subdivided to show the ego-state structure of the individual's own Child and of the figures incorporated in the Parent.

SECOND-ORDER SYMBIOSIS: a symbiosis occurring between P_1 and A_1 of one party and C_1 of the other party.

SECOND RULE OF COMMUNICATION: 'when a transaction is

crossed, a break in communication results and one or both individuals will need to shift ego-states in order for communication to be re-established'.

SOCIAL DIAGNOSIS: judgment of which ego-state an individual is in by observation of the ego-states used by others in transacting with that individual.

SOCIAL-LEVEL MESSAGE: an overt message, usually conveyed in verbal content.

SOMATIC CHILD: *same as* Child in the Child.

SPONTANEITY: ability to choose freely from a full range of options in feeling, thinking and behaving, including choice of ego-state.

STAMP: a racket feeling which the individual has stored away with the intention of cashing it in later for some negative payoff.

STIMULUS: the initial communication in an individual transaction (to which the response is a reply).

STIMULUS-HUNGER: the need for physical and mental stimulation.

STOPPER: the second position on the miniscript, reflecting the life position I-U+; an injunction which the individual hears when at that position.

STROKE: a unit of recognition.

STROKE BANK: collected memories of past strokes which the individual can re-use.

STROKE ECONOMY: set of restrictive Parental rules regarding stroking.

STROKE FILTER: an individual's pattern of rejecting and accepting strokes so as to conform with an existing self-image.

STROKE QUOTIENT: an individual's preferred mix of different types of stroke.

STROKING PROFILE: a bar-chart diagram to analyze an individual's preference for giving, taking, asking for and refusing to give strokes.

STRUCTURAL ANALYSIS: analysis of personality, or of a series of transactions, in terms of the ego-state model.

STRUCTURAL MODEL: an ego-state model showing *what* is classified as belonging in each ego-state or subdivision of an ego-state (i.e. showing content).

STRUCTURAL PATHOLOGY: contamination and/or exclusion.

STRUCTURE: (in the ego-state model) classification of an individual's behavior, feeling and experience in terms of ego-states.

SWEATSHIRT: a motto, signaled non-verbally by a person, which acts as a covert invitation into games or racketeering.

SWITCH: point in a game at which the player changes roles in order to collect his or her payoff.

SYMBIOSIS: a relationship in which two or more individuals behave as though between them they form a single person, hence not using their full complement of ego-states.

TANGENTIAL TRANSACTION: a transaction in which the stimulus and the response address different issues, or address the same issue from different perspectives.

THIRD-DEGREE: (of games or losing scripts) having a payoff which entails death, serious injury or illness, or a legal crisis.

THIRD RULE OF COMMUNICATION: 'the behavioral outcome of an ulterior transaction is determined at the psychological and not at the social level'.

TIME STRUCTURING: how people spend time when in pairs or groups.

TRADING STAMP: *same as* stamp.

TRANSACTION: a transactional stimulus plus a transactional response: the basic unit of social discourse.

TRANSACTIONAL ANALYSIS: *(ITAA definition)* a theory of personality and a systematic psychotherapy for personal growth and personal change.

TRANSACTIONAL ANALYSIS: *(Berne's definition)* (1) a system of psychotherapy based on the analysis of transactions and chains of transactions which occur during treatment sessions; (2) a theory of personality based on the study of specific ego-states; (3) a theory of social action based on the rigorous analysis of transactions into an exhaustive and finite number of classes based on the specific ego-states involved; (4) the analysis of single transactions by means of transactional diagrams (this is transactional analysis proper).

TYPE: (of discounting) whether discounting relates to stimuli, problems or options.

ULTERIOR TRANSACTION: a transaction in which an overt message and a covert message are conveyed at the same time.

UNCONDITIONAL STROKE: a stroke relating to what the individual is.

UNTIL SCRIPT: the process script which reflects the belief: 'Something good can't happen until something less good has been finished.'

VECTOR: arrow on a transactional diagram connecting the ego-state from which a communication is issued to the ego-state to which it is addressed.

VICTIM: (in Drama Triangle) person who views himself or herself as one-down, deserving to be belittled or unable to get by without help.

VIOLENCE: the passive behavior in which the person directs destructive energy outwards in an attempt to force the environment to solve a problem.

WINNER: someone who accomplishes a declared purpose.

WINNING SCRIPT: a script in which the payoff is happy or fulfilling, and/or entails success in accomplishing a declared purpose.

WITCH (PARENT): *(used by some writers to mean)* Parent in the Child.

WITHDRAWAL: mode of time-structuring in which the individual does not transact with others.

INDEX

Page numbers in *italic type* indicate a main entry for the item in question.

By the same authors...

Personality Adaptations
A New Guide to Human Understanding in Psychotherapy and Counselling

Vann Joines and Ian Stewart

This book is a practical guide to understanding personality. It presents a research-based model of six *personality adaptations.* Psychotherapists and counsellors, whether practising or in training, will find this model an invaluable aid to effectiveness in inviting personal change.

The book describes the six adaptations in detail, and provides a framework for understanding how each adaptation develops. It goes on to show how you can assess someone's personality adaptation(s) rapidly and accurately. With this knowledge, you can tap into a vast store of information that will apply to that person. For example, you will gain insight into their preferred area of personal contact (thinking, feeling or behaviour), and learn how you can use these contact areas to maintain rapport and achieve optimal results in therapy or counselling. You will learn the typical "life patterns" that the person is likely to play out over time, and the principal issues that are likely to arise for them in the process of change. The model shows how you can work most effectively with each personality type to help them achieve personal change that is quick, easy and lasting.

To convey the true "sound" and "feel" of working with this model, the book includes annotated transcripts of actual therapeutic work with each of the personality adaptations.

The model's usefulness is not confined to any one therapeutic or counselling approach. Whatever modality you use, you can apply this model and benefit from this book.

- If you would like to know more about *Personality Adaptations,* you can read the Contents list and Preface on our web site at: *www.lifespacebooks.com.*

Lifespace Publishing, Nottingham and Chapel Hill
ISBN 1-870244-01-X   Paperback   Pp. 417